Microsoft® Foundation Class Library Reference

Part 1 of 2

Microsoft Visual C++™

Development System for Windows® 95 and Windows NT™
Version 4

I0890990

Microsoft Corporation

PUBLISHED BY
Microsoft Press
A Division of Microsoft Corporation
One Microsoft Way
Redmond, Washington 98052-6399

Library of Congress Cataloging-in-Publication Data
Microsoft Visual C++ programmer's references / Microsoft Corporation.
    -- 2nd ed.
        p.   cm.
    Includes index.
    v. 1. Microsoft Visual C++ user's guide -- v. 2. Programming with
MFC -- v. 3. Microsoft foundation class library reference, part 1 --
v. 4. Microsoft foundation class library reference, part 2 -- v.
5.   Microsoft Visual C++ run-time library reference -- v.
6.   Microsoft Visual C/C++ language reference.
    ISBN 1-55615-915-3 (v. 1). -- ISBN 1-55615-921-8 (v. 2). -- ISBN
1-55615-922-6 (v. 3). -- ISBN 1-55615-923-4 (v. 4). -- ISBN
1-55615-924-2 (v. 5). -- ISBN 1-55615-925-0 (v. 6)
    1. C++ (Computer program language) 2. Microsoft Visual C++.
I. Microsoft Corporation.
QA76.73.C153M53   1995
005.13'3--dc20   95-35604
                                                                 CIP

Printed and bound in the United States of America.

1 2 3 4 5 6 7 8 9   QMQM   0 9 8 7 6 5

Distributed to the book trade in Canada by Macmillan of Canada, a division of Canada Publishing Corporation.

A CIP catalogue record for this book is available from the British Library.

Microsoft Press books are available through booksellers and distributors worldwide. For further information about international editions, contact your local Microsoft Corporation office. Or contact Microsoft Press International directly at fax (206) 936-7329.

Acquisitions Editor: Eric Stroo
Project Editor: Brenda L. Matteson

Contents

Introduction   xi

Class Library Overview   1
About the Microsoft Foundation Classes   1
Root Class: CObject   4
MFC Application Architecture Classes   4
Window, Dialog, and Control Classes   10
Drawing and Printing Classes   17
Simple Data Type Classes   18
Array, List, and Map Classes   19
File, Database, and Socket Classes   21
OLE Classes   24
Debugging and Exception Classes   29

Alphabetical Reference to the Microsoft Foundation Class Library   33
CAnimateCtrl   33
CArchive   38
CArchiveException   56
CArray   58
CAsyncSocket   68
CBitmap   102
CBitmapButton   112
CBrush   117
CButton   126
CByteArray   136
CCheckListBox   138
CClientDC   143
CCmdTarget   145
CCmdUI   155
CColorDialog   158
CComboBox   163
CCommandLineInfo   189
CCommonDialog   195

CConnectionPoint 197

CControlBar 201

CCreateContext 209

CCriticalSection 211

CCtrlView 214

CDaoDatabase 216

CDaoException 239

CDaoFieldExchange 245

CDaoQueryDef 250

CDaoRecordset 271

CDaoRecordView 339

CDaoTableDef 345

CDaoWorkspace 370

CDatabase 394

CDataExchange 408

CDBException 412

CDC 416

CDialog 549

CDialogBar 561

CDocItem 564

CDocTemplate 566

CDocument 579

CDragListBox 600

CDumpContext 604

CDWordArray 609

CEdit 611

CEditView 633

CEvent 643

CException 647

CFieldExchange 652

CFile 655

CFileDialog 673

CFileException 682

CFindReplaceDialog 687

CFont 694

CFontDialog 703

CFontHolder 709

CFormView 713

CFrameWnd 717

CGdiObject 736

CHeaderCtrl 744

CHotKeyCtrl 751

CImageList 755

CList 769

CListBox 780

CListCtrl 806

CListView 838

CLongBinary 840

CMap 842

CMapPtrToPtr 849

CMapPtrToWord 851

CMapStringToOb 853

CMapStringToPtr 861

CMapStringToString 863

CMapWordToOb 865

CMapWordToPtr 867

CMDIChildWnd 869

CMDIFrameWnd 874

CMemFile 882

CMemoryException 888

CMemoryState 889

CMenu 893

CMetaFileDC 917

CMiniFrameWnd 922

CMultiDocTemplate 924

CMultiLock 927

CMutex 931

CNotSupportedException 933

CObArray 934

CObject 944

CObList 952

COleBusyDialog 969

COleChangeIconDialog 973

COleChangeSourceDialog 977

COleClientItem 982

COleControl 1026

COleControlModule 1079

COleConvertDialog 1080

COleCurrency   1086

COleDataObject   1098

COleDataSource   1105

COleDateTime   1116

COleDateTimeSpan   1140

COleDialog   1154

COleDispatchDriver   1156

Index

Part 2

COleDispatchException   1163

COleDocument   1166

COleDropSource   1175

COleDropTarget   1179

COleException   1186

COleInsertDialog   1188

COleIPFrameWnd   1194

COleLinkingDoc   1197

COleLinksDialog   1201

COleMessageFilter   1204

COleObjectFactory   1211

COlePasteSpecialDialog   1218

COlePropertiesDialog   1225

COlePropertyPage   1230

COleResizeBar   1237

COleServerDoc   1239

COleServerItem   1256

COleStreamFile   1277

COleTemplateServer   1281

COleUpdateDialog   1284

COleVariant   1286

CPageSetupDialog   1292

CPaintDC   1301

CPalette   1303

CPen   1310

CPictureHolder   1318

CPoint   1324

CPrintDialog   1330

CPrintInfo   1339

CProgressCtrl   1346

CPropertyPage   1350

CPropertySheet   1358

CPropExchange   1369

CPtrArray   1374

CPtrList   1376

CRecordset   1378

CRecordView   1412

CRect   1418

CRectTracker   1435

CResourceException   1444

CRgn   1445

CRichEditCntrItem   1459

CRichEditCtrl   1461

CRichEditDoc   1490

CRichEditView   1493

CRuntimeClass   1514

CScrollBar   1515

CScrollView   1522

CSemaphore   1530

CSingleDocTemplate   1532

CSingleLock   1535

CSize   1538

CSliderCtrl   1542

CSocket   1554

CSocketFile   1560

CSpinButtonCtrl   1562

CSplitterWnd   1569

CStatic   1587

CStatusBar   1594

CStatusBarCtrl   1602

CStdioFile   1610

CString   1614

CStringArray   1641

CStringList   1643

CSyncObject   1645

CTabCtrl   1647

CTime   1660

CTimeSpan   1671

CToolBar   1679

CToolBarCtrl   1691

CToolTipCtrl   1719

CTreeCtrl   1727

CTreeView   1752

CTypedPtrArray   1754

CTypedPtrList   1757

CTypedPtrMap   1763

CUIntArray   1766

CUserException   1768

CView   1770

CWaitCursor   1790

CWinApp   1794

CWindowDC   1837

CWinThread   1839

CWnd   1850

CWordArray   2044

Macros and Globals   2046

Data Types   2047

Run-Time Object Model Services   2048

Diagnostic Services   2050

Exception Processing   2052

CString Formatting and Message-Box Display   2053

Message Map Macros   2054

Application Information and Management   2056

Standard Command and Window Ids   2057

Collection Class Helpers   2058

Record Field Exchange Functions   2058

Dialog Data Exchange Functions for CRecordView and CDaoRecordView   2060

Database Macros   2061

OLE Initialization   2061

Application Control   2062

Dispatch Maps   2062

Variant Parameter Type Constants   2063

Type Library Access   2064

Property Pages   2064

Event Maps   2066

Event Sink Maps   2067

Connection Maps   2067

Registering OLE Controls   2068

Class Factories and Licensing   2069

Persistence of OLE Controls   2070

Macros, Global Functions, and Global Variables   2070

ClassWizard Comment Delimiters   2202

Callback Functions, Structures, and Styles   2208

Callback Functions Used by MFC   2208

Structures Used by MFC   2210

Styles Used by MFC   2270

Index

Introduction

The Class Library Overview lists the classes in helpful categories. Use these lists to help locate a class that contains the functionality you are interested in. *Programming with MFC* explains how to use the class library to program for Microsoft Windows NT™, Microsoft Windows® 95, and other Win32® platforms. Practical examples and techniques are supplied in the tutorials in *Tutorials*.

The remainder of the *Class Library Reference* consists of an alphabetical listing of the classes and a Macros and Globals section that explains the global functions, global variables, and macros used with the class library.

The individual hierarchy charts included with each class are useful for locating base classes. The *Class Library Reference* usually does not describe inherited member functions, inherited operators, and overridden virtual member functions. For information on these functions, refer to the base classes depicted in the hierarchy diagrams.

In the alphabetical listing section, each class description includes a member summary by category, followed by alphabetical listings of member functions, overloaded operators, and data members.

Public and protected class members are documented only when they are normally used in application programs or derived classes. Occasionally, private members are listed because they override a public or protected member in the base class. See the class header files for a complete listing of class members.

Some C-language structures defined by Windows are so widely applicable that their descriptions have been reproduced completely in a section following the alphabetical reference.

Please note that the "See Also" sections refer to Win32 API functions by prefacing them with the scope resolution operator (::), for example, **::EqualRect**. More information on these functions can be found in the Win32 SDK documentation.

Class Library Overview

This overview categorizes and describes the classes in the Microsoft Foundation
Class Library (MFC) version 4.0. The classes in MFC, taken together, constitute an
"application framework"—the framework of an application written for the Windows
API. Your programming task is to fill in the code that is specific to your application.

About the Microsoft Foundation Classes

The library's classes are presented here in the following categories:

- Root Class: **CObject**
- MFC Application Architecture Classes
  - Application and Thread Support Classes
  - Command Routing Classes
  - Document Classes
  - View Classes (Architecture)
  - Frame Window Classes (Architecture)
  - Document-Template Classes
- Window, Dialog, and Control Classes
  - Frame Window Classes (Windows)
  - View Classes (Windows)
  - Dialog Box Classes
  - Control Classes
  - Control Bar Classes
- Drawing and Printing Classes
  - Output (Device Context) Classes
  - Drawing Tool Classes
- Simple Data Type Classes
- Array, List, and Map Classes
  - Template Classes for Arrays, Lists, and Maps
  - Ready-to-Use Array Classes
  - Ready-to-Use List Classes
  - Ready-to-Use Map Classes

1

- File, Database, and Socket Classes
  - File I/O Classes
  - DAO Classes
  - ODBC Classes
  - Windows Sockets Classes
- OLE Classes
  - OLE Container Classes
  - OLE Server Classes
  - OLE Drag-and-Drop and Data Transfer Classes
  - OLE Common Dialog Classes
  - OLE Automation Classes
  - OLE Control Classes
  - OLE-Related Classes
- Debugging and Exception Classes
  - Debugging Support Classes
  - Exception Classes

The section "General Class Design Philosophy" explains how the Microsoft Foundation Class Library was designed.

The framework is explained in detail in Chapters 1 though 8 of *Programming with MFC*. Some of the classes listed above are general-purpose classes that can be used outside of the framework. Chapter 8, "Using the General-Purpose Classes," of *Programming with MFC* details these classes, which provide useful abstractions such as collections, exceptions, files, and strings.

To see the inheritance of a class, use the Class Hierarchy Chart in Books Online.

In addition to the classes listed in this chapter, the Microsoft Foundation Class Library contains a number of global functions, global variables, and macros. There is an overview and detailed listing of these in the section "Macros and Globals," which follows the alphabetical reference to the MFC classes.

General Class Design Philosophy

Microsoft Windows was designed long before the C++ language became popular. Because thousands of applications use the C-language Windows application programming interface (API), that interface will be maintained for the foreseeable future. Any C++ Windows interface must therefore be built on top of the procedural C-language API. This guarantees that C++ applications will be able to coexist with C applications.

The Microsoft Foundation Class Library is an object-oriented interface to Windows that meets the following design goals:

- Significant reduction in the effort to write an application for Windows.
- Execution speed comparable to that of the C-language API.
- Minimum code size overhead.
- Ability to call any Windows C function directly.
- Easier conversion of existing C applications to C++.
- Ability to leverage from the existing base of C-language Windows programming experience.
- Easier use of the Windows API with C++ than with C.
- Easier-to-use yet powerful abstractions of complicated features such as OLE, database support, printing, toolbars, and status bars.
- True Windows API for C++ that effectively uses C++ language features.

The Application Framework

The core of the Microsoft Foundation Class Library is an encapsulation of a large portion of the Windows API in C++ form. Library classes represent windows, dialog boxes, device contexts, common GDI objects such as brushes and pens, controls, and other standard Windows items. These classes provide a convenient C++ member function interface to the structures in Windows that they encapsulate. For more information about these core classes, see "Windows of Your Own with CWnd" in Chapter 1 of *Programming with MFC*.

But the Microsoft Foundation Class Library also supplies a layer of additional application functionality built on the C++ encapsulation of the Windows API. This layer is a working application framework for Windows that provides most of the common user interface expected of programs for Windows, including toolbars, status bars, printing, print preview, database support, and OLE support. Chapter 1, "Using the Classes to Write Applications for Windows," of *Programming with MFC* explains the framework in detail, and *Tutorials* provides the Scribble tutorial, which teaches application-framework programming.

Relationship to the C-Language API

The single characteristic that sets the Microsoft Foundation Class Library apart from other class libraries for Windows is the very close mapping to the Windows API written in the C language. Further, you can generally mix calls to the class library freely with direct calls to the Windows API. This direct access does not, however, imply that the classes are a complete replacement for that API. Developers must still occasionally make direct calls to some Windows functions—**SetCursor** and

GetSystemMetrics, for example. A Windows function is wrapped by a class member function only when there is a clear advantage to doing so.

Because you sometimes need to make native Windows function calls, you should have access to the C-language Windows API documentation. This documentation is included with Microsoft Visual C++™. Two useful books are *Advanced Windows*, by Jeffrey Richter, and *Programming Windows 3.1*, third edition, by Charles Petzold. Both are published by Microsoft Press. Many of those books' examples can be easily converted to the Microsoft Foundation classes. For examples and additional information about programming with the Microsoft Foundation Class Library, see *Inside Visual C++* by David J. Kruglinski, also published by Microsoft Press.

Note For an overview of how the Microsoft Foundation Class Library framework operates, see Chapter 1, "Using the Classes to Write Applications for Windows," in *Programming with MFC*. The overview material is no longer located in the *Class Library Reference*.

Class Summary by Category

The following is a brief summary of the classes in the Microsoft Foundation Class Library, divided by category to help you locate what you need. In some cases, a class is listed in more than one category. To see the inheritance of a class, use the Class Hierarchy Chart in Books Online.

Root Class: CObject

Most of the classes in the Microsoft Foundation Class Library are derived from a single base class at the root of the class hierarchy. **CObject** provides a number of useful capabilities to all classes derived from it, with very low overhead. For more information about **CObject** and its capabilities, see the article "CObject Class" in *Programming with MFC*.

CObject   The ultimate base class of most MFC classes. Supports serializing data and obtaining run-time information about a class.

CRuntimeClass   Structure used to determine the exact class of an object at run time.

MFC Application Architecture Classes

Classes in this category contribute to the architecture of a framework application. They supply functionality common to most applications. You fill in the framework to add application-specific functionality. Typically, you do so by deriving new classes from the architecture classes, then adding new members and/or overriding existing member functions.

AppWizard generates several types of applications, all of which use the application framework in differing ways. SDI (single document interface) and MDI (multiple document interface) applications make full use of a part of the framework called document/view architecture. Other types of applications, such as dialog-based applications, form-based applications, and DLLs, use only some of document/view architecture features.

Document/view applications contain one or more sets of documents, views, and frame windows. A document-template object associates the classes for each document/view/frame set.

Although you do not have to use document/view architecture in your MFC application, there are a number of advantages to doing so. MFC's OLE container and server support is based on document/view architecture, as is support for printing and print preview.

All MFC applications have at least two objects: an application object derived from **CWinApp**, and some sort of main window object, derived (often indirectly) from **CWnd**. (Most often, the main window is derived from **CFrameWnd**, **CMDIFrameWnd**, or **CDialog**, all of which are derived from **CWnd**.)

Applications that use document/view architecture contain additional objects. The principal objects are as follows:

- An application object derived from class **CWinApp**, as mentioned before.

- One or more document objects derived from class **CDocument**. Document objects are responsible for the internal representation of the data manipulated in the view. They may be associated with a data file.

- One or more view objects derived from class **CView**, each attached to a document and associated with a window. Views display and manipulate the data contained in a document object.

Document/view applications also contain frame windows (derived from **CFrameWnd**) and document templates (derived from **CDocTemplate**).

Application and Thread Support Classes

Each application has one and only one application object; this object coordinates other objects in the running program and is derived from **CWinApp**.

The Microsoft Foundation Class Library supports multiple threads of execution within an application. All applications must have at least one thread; the thread used by your **CWinApp** object is this "primary" thread.

CWinThread encapsulates a portion of the operating system's threading capabilities. To make using multiple threads easier, MFC also provides synchronization object classes to provide a C++ interface to Win32 synchronization objects.

Application and Thread Classes

CWinApp Encapsulates the code to initialize, run, and terminate the application. You will derive your application object from this class.

CWinThread The base class for all threads. Use directly, or derive a class from **CWinThread** if your thread performs user-interface functions. **CWinApp** is derived from **CWinThread**.

Synchronization Object Classes

CSyncObject Base class of the synchronization object classes.

CCriticalSection A synchronization class that allows only one thread within a single process to access an object.

CSemaphore A synchronization class that allows between one and a specified maximum number of simultaneous accesses to an object.

CMutex A synchronization class that allows only one thread within any number of processes to access an object.

CEvent A synchronization class that notifies an application when an event has occurred.

CSingleLock Used in member functions of thread-safe classes to lock on one synchronization object.

CMultiLock Used in member functions of thread-safe classes to lock on one or more synchronization objects from an array of synchronization objects.

Related Classes

CCommandLineInfo Parses the command line with which your program was started.

CWaitCursor Puts a wait cursor on the screen. Used during lengthy operations.

Command Routing Classes

As the user interacts with the application by choosing menus or control-bar buttons with the mouse, the application sends messages from the affected user-interface object to an appropriate command-target object. Command-target classes derived from **CCmdTarget** include **CWinApp**, **CWnd**, **CDocTemplate**, **CDocument**, **CView**, and the classes derived from them. The framework supports automatic command routing so that commands can be handled by the most appropriate object currently active in the application.

An object of class **CCmdUI** is passed to your command targets' `OnUpdateCmdUI` handler functions to allow you to update the state of the user interface for a particular command (for instance, to check or remove the check from menu items). You call member functions of the **CCmdUI** object to update the state of the UI object. This process is the same whether the UI object associated with a particular command is a menu item or a button or both.

CCmdTarget   Serves as the base class for all classes of objects that can receive and respond to messages.

CCmdUI   Provides a programmatic interface for updating user-interface objects such as menu items or control-bar buttons. The command target object enables, disables, checks, and/or clears the user-interface object via this object.

Document Classes

Document objects, created by document-template objects, manage the application's data. You will derive a class for your document objects from one of these classes.

Document objects interact with view objects. View objects represent the client area of a window, display a document's data, and allow users to interact with it. Documents and views are created by a document-template object.

CDocument   The base class for application-specific documents. Derive your document class(es) from **CDocument**.

COleDocument   Used for OLE compound document implementation, as well as basic container support. Serves as a container for classes derived from **CDocItem**. This class can be used as the base class for container documents and is the base class for **COleServerDoc**.

COleLinkingDoc   A class derived from **COleDocument** that provides the infrastructure for linking. You should derive the document classes for your container applications from this class instead of from **COleDocument** if you want them to support links to embedded objects.

CRichEditDoc   Maintains the list of OLE client items that are in the rich edit control. Used with **CRichEditView** and **CRichEditCntrItem**.

COleServerDoc   Used as the base class for server-application document classes. **COleServerDoc** objects provide the bulk of server support through interactions with **COleServerItem** objects. Visual editing capability is provided using the class library's document/view architecture.

Related Classes

Document objects can be persistent—in other words, they can write their state to a storage medium and read it back. MFC provides the **CArchive** class to facilitate transferring the document's data to a storage medium.

CArchive   Cooperates with a **CFile** object to implement persistent storage for objects through serialization (see **CObject::Serialize**).

Documents can also contain OLE objects. **CDocItem** is the base class of the server and client items.

CDocItem   Abstract base class of **COleClientItem** and **COleServerItem**. Objects of classes derived from **CDocItem** represent parts of documents.

View Classes (Architecture)

CView and its derived classes are child windows that represent the client area of a frame window. Views show data and accept input for a document.

A view class is associated with a document class and a frame window class using a document-template object.

CView   The base class for application-specific views of a document's data. Views display data and accept user input to edit or select the data. Derive your view class(es) from **CView**.

CScrollView   The base class for views with scrolling capabilities. Derive your view class from **CScrollView** for automatic scrolling.

Form and Record Views

Form views are also scrolling views. They are based on a dialog box template.

Record views are derived from form views. In addition to the dialog box template, they also have a connection to a database.

CFormView   A scroll view whose layout is defined in a dialog resource. Derive classes from **CFormView** to implement user interfaces quickly based on dialog resources.

CDaoRecordView   Provides a form view directly connected to a Data Access Object (DAO) recordset object. Like all form views, a **CDaoRecordView** is based on a dialog template resource.

CRecordView   Provides a form view directly connected to an Open Database Connectivity (ODBC) recordset object. Like all form views, a **CRecordView** is based on a dialog template resource.

Control Views

Control views display a control as their view.

CCtrlView   The base class for all views associated with Windows controls. The views based on controls are described below.

CEditView   A view that contains a Windows standard edit control (see **CEdit**). Edit controls support text-editing, searching, replacing, and scrolling capabilities.

CRichEditView   A view that contains a Windows rich edit control (see **CRichEditCtrl**). In addition to the capabilities of an edit control, rich edit controls support fonts, colors, paragraph formatting, and embedded OLE objects.

CListView A view that contains a Windows list control (see **CListCtrl**). A list control displays icons and strings in a manner similar to the right-hand pane of the Windows 95 Explorer.

CTreeView A view that contains a Windows tree control (see **CTreeCtrl**). A tree control displays icons and strings arranged in a hierarchy in a manner similar to the left-hand pane of the Windows 95 Explorer.

Frame Window Classes (Architecture)

In document/view architecture, frame windows are windows that contain a view window. They also support having control bars attached to them.

In multiple document interface (MDI) applications, the main window is derived from **CMDIFrameWnd**. It indirectly contains the documents' frames, which are **CMDIChildWnd** objects. The **CMDIChildWnd** objects, in turn, contain the documents' views.

In single document interface (SDI) applications, the main window, derived from **CFrameWnd**, contains the view of the current document.

CFrameWnd The base class for an SDI application's main frame window. Also the base class for all other frame window classes.

CMDIFrameWnd The base class for an MDI application's main frame window.

CMDIChildWnd The base class for an MDI application's document frame windows.

COleIPFrameWnd Provides the frame window for a view when a server document is being edited in place.

Document-Template Classes

Document-template objects coordinate the creation of document, view, and frame window objects when a new document and/or view is created.

CDocTemplate The base class for document templates. You will never use this class directly; instead, you'll use one of the other document-template classes derived from this class.

CMultiDocTemplate A template for documents in the multiple document interface (MDI). MDI applications can have multiple documents open at a time.

CSingleDocTemplate A template for documents in the single document interface (SDI). SDI applications have only one document open at a time.

Related Class

> **CCreateContext**   A structure passed by a document template to window-creation functions to coordinate the creation of document, view, and frame-window objects.

Window, Dialog, and Control Classes

Class **CWnd** and its derived classes encapsulate an **HWND**, a handle to a Windows window. **CWnd** can be used by itself or as a base for deriving new classes. The derived classes supplied by the class library represent various kinds of windows.

CWnd   The base class for all windows. You can use one of the classes derived from **CWnd** or derive your own classes directly from it.

Frame Window Classes (Windows)

Frame windows are windows that frame an application or a part of an application. Frame windows usually contain other windows, such as views, tool bars, and status bars. In the case of **CMDIFrameWnd**, they may contain **CMDIChildWnd** objects indirectly.

CFrameWnd   The base class for an SDI application's main frame window. Also the base class for all other frame window classes.

CMDIFrameWnd   The base class for an MDI application's main frame window.

CMDIChildWnd   The base class for an MDI application's document frame windows.

CMiniFrameWnd   A half-height frame window typically seen around floating toolbars.

COleIPFrameWnd   Provides the frame window for a view when a server document is being edited in place.

Related Class

Class **CMenu** provides an interface through which to access your application's menus. It is useful for manipulating menus dynamically at run time; for example, when adding or deleting menu items according to context. Although menus are most often used with frame windows, they can also be used with dialog boxes and other nonchild windows.

CMenu   Encapsulates an **HMENU** handle to the application's menu bar and pop-up menus.

View Classes (Windows)

CView and its derived classes are child windows that represent the client area of a frame window. Views show data and accept input for a document.

A view class is associated with a document class and a frame window class using a document-template object.

CView   The base class for application-specific views of a document's data. Views display data and accept user input to edit or select the data. Derive your view class(es) from **CView**.

CScrollView   The base class for views with scrolling capabilities. Derive your view class from **CScrollView** for automatic scrolling.

Form and Record Views

Form views are also scrolling views. They are based on a dialog box template.

Record views are derived from form views. In addition to the dialog box template, they also have a connection to a database.

CFormView   A scroll view whose layout is defined in a dialog resource. Derive classes from **CFormView** to implement user interfaces quickly based on dialog resources.

CDaoRecordView   Provides a form view directly connected to a Data Access Object (DAO) recordset object. Like all form views, a **CDaoRecordView** is based on a dialog template resource.

CRecordView   Provides a form view directly connected to an Open Database Connectivity (ODBC) recordset object. Like all form views, a **CRecordView** is based on a dialog template resource.

Control Views

Control views display a control as their view.

CCtrlView   The base class for all views associated with Windows controls. The views based on controls are described below.

CEditView   A view that contains a Windows standard edit control (see **CEdit**). Edit controls support text-editing, searching, replacing, and scrolling capabilities.

CRichEditView   A view that contains a Windows rich edit control (see **CRichEditCtrl**). In addition to the capabilities of an edit control, rich edit controls support fonts, colors, paragraph formatting, and embedded OLE objects.

CListView   A view that contains a Windows list control (see **CListCtrl**). A list control displays a collection of items, each consisting of an icon and a label, in a manner similar to the right-hand pane of the Windows 95 Explorer.

CTreeView   A view that contains a Windows tree control (see **CTreeCtrl**). A tree control displays a hierarchical list of icons and labels arranged in a manner similar to the left-hand pane of the Windows 95 Explorer.

Related Classes

CSplitterWnd allows you to have multiple views within a single frame window. **CPrintDialog** and **CPrintInfo** support the print and print preview ability of views. **CRichEditDoc** and **CRichEditCntrItem** are used with **CRichEditView** to implement OLE container capabilities.

CSplitterWnd   A window that the user can split into multiple panes. These panes can be resizable by the user or fixed size.

CPrintDialog   Provides a standard dialog box for printing a file.

CPrintInfo   A structure containing information about a print or print preview job. Used by **CView**'s printing architecture.

CRichEditDoc   Maintains the list of OLE client items that are in a **CRichEditView**.

CRichEditCntrItem   Provides client-side access to an OLE item stored in a **CRichEditView**.

Dialog Box Classes

Class **CDialog** and its derived classes encapsulate dialog-box functionality. Since a dialog box is a special kind of window, **CDialog** is derived from **CWnd**. Derive your dialog classes from **CDialog** or use one of the common dialog classes for standard dialog boxes, such as opening or saving a file, printing, selecting a font or color, initiating a search-and-replace operation, or performing various OLE-related operations.

CDialog   The base class for all dialog boxes—both modal and modeless.

CDataExchange   Supplies data exchange and validation information for dialog boxes.

Common Dialogs

These dialog box classes encapsulate the Windows common dialog boxes. They provide easy-to-use implementations of complicated dialog boxes.

CCommonDialog   This is the base class for all common dialog boxes.

CFileDialog   Provides a standard dialog box for opening or saving a file.

CColorDialog   Provides a standard dialog box for selecting a color.

CFontDialog   Provides a standard dialog box for selecting a font.

CFindReplaceDialog   Provides a standard dialog box for a search-and-replace operation.

CPrintDialog   Provides a standard dialog box for printing a file.

CPageSetupDialog Encapsulates the services provided by the Windows common Page Setup dialog box with additional support for setting and modifying print margins.

OLE Common Dialogs

OLE adds several common dialog boxes to Windows. These classes encapsulate the OLE common dialog boxes.

COleDialog Used by the framework to contain common implementations for all OLE dialog boxes. All dialog box classes in the user-interface category are derived from this base class. Cannot be used directly.

COleInsertDialog Displays the Insert Object dialog box, the standard user interface for inserting new OLE linked or embedded items.

COlePasteSpecialDialog Displays the Paste Special dialog box, the standard user interface for implementing the Edit Paste Special command.

COleLinksDialog Displays the Edit Links dialog box, the standard user interface for modifying information about linked items.

COleChangeIconDialog Displays the Change Icon dialog box, the standard user interface for changing the icon associated with an OLE embedded or linked item.

COleConvertDialog Displays the Convert dialog box, the standard user interface for converting OLE items from one type to another.

COlePropertiesDialog Encapsulates the Windows common OLE Properties dialog box. Common OLE Properties dialog boxes provide an easy way to display and modify the properties of an OLE document item in a manner consistent with Windows standards.

COleUpdateDialog Displays the Update dialog box, the standard user interface for updating all links in a document. The dialog box contains a progress indicator to indicate how close the update procedure is to completion.

COleChangeSourceDialog Displays the Change Source dialog box, the standard user interface for changing the destination or source of a link.

COleBusyDialog Displays the Server Busy and Server Not Responding dialog boxes, the standard user interface for handling calls to busy applications. Usually displayed automatically by the **COleMessageFilter** implementation.

Property Sheet Classes

The property sheet classes allow your applications to use property sheets, also known as "tabbed dialogs." Property sheets are an efficient way to organize a large number of controls in a single dialog box.

CPropertyPage Provides the individual pages within a property sheet. Derive a class from **CPropertyPage** for each page to be added to your property sheet.

CPropertySheet   Provides the frame for multiple property pages. Derive your property sheet class from **CPropertySheet** to implement your property sheets quickly.

COlePropertyPage   Displays the properties of an OLE custom control in a graphical interface, similar to a dialog box.

Related Classes

These classes are not dialog boxes per se, but they use dialog box templates and have much of the behavior of dialog boxes.

CDialogBar   A control bar that is based on a dialog box template.

CFormView   A scroll view whose layout is defined in a dialog resource. Derive classes from **CFormView** to implement user interfaces quickly based on dialog resources.

CDaoRecordView   Provides a form view directly connected to a Data Access Object (DAO) recordset object. Like all form views, a **CDaoRecordView** is based on a dialog template resource.

CRecordView   Provides a form view directly connected to an Open Database Connectivity (ODBC) recordset object. Like all form views, a **CRecordView** is based on a dialog template resource.

CPrintInfo   A structure containing information about a print or print preview job. Used by **CView**'s printing architecture.

Control Classes

Control classes encapsulate a wide variety of standard Windows controls ranging from static text controls to tree controls. In addition, MFC provides some new controls, including buttons with bitmaps and control bars.

The controls whose class names end in "**Ctrl**" are new in Windows 95 and Windows NT version 3.51.

Static Display Controls

CStatic   A static-display window. Static controls are used to label, box, or separate other controls in a dialog box or window. They may also display graphical images rather than text or a box.

Text Controls

CEdit   An editable-text control window. Edit controls are used to accept textual input from the user.

CRichEditCtrl   A control in which the user can enter and edit text. Unlike the control encapsulated in **CEdit**, a rich edit control supports character and paragraph formatting and OLE objects.

Controls Which Represent Numbers

CSliderCtrl A control containing a slider, which the user moves to select a value or set of values.

CSpinButtonCtrl A pair of arrow buttons the user can click to increment or decrement a value.

CProgressCtrl Displays a rectangle that is gradually filled from left to right to indicate the progress of an operation.

CScrollBar A scroll-bar control window. The class provides the functionality of a scroll bar, for use as a control in a dialog box or window, through which the user can specify a position within a range.

Buttons

CButton A button control window. The class provides a programmatic interface for a pushbutton, check box, or radio button in a dialog box or window.

CBitmapButton A button with a bitmap rather than a text caption.

Lists

CListBox A list-box control window. A list box displays a list of items that the user can view and select.

CDragListBox Provides the functionality of a Windows list box; allows the user to move list box items, such as filenames and string literals, within the list box. List boxes with this capability are useful for an item list in an order other than alphabetical, such as include pathnames or files in a project.

CComboBox A combo-box control window. A combo box consists of an edit control plus a list box.

CCheckListBox Displays a list of items with check boxes, which the user can check or clear, next to each item.

CListCtrl Displays a collection of items, each consisting of an icon and a label, in a manner similar to the right-hand pane of the Windows 95 Explorer.

CTreeCtrl Displays a hierarchical list of icons and labels arranged in a manner similar to the left-hand pane of the Windows 95 Explorer.

Toolbars and Status Bars

CToolBarCtrl Provides the functionality of the Windows toolbar common control. Most MFC programs use **CToolBar** instead of this class.

CStatusBarCtrl A horizontal window, usually divided into panes, in which an application can display status information. Most MFC programs use **CStatusBar** instead of this class.

Miscellaneous Controls

CAnimateCtrl Displays a simple video clip.

CToolTipCtrl A small pop-up window that displays a single line of text describing the purpose of a tool in an application.

CHeaderCtrl Displays titles or labels for columns.

CTabCtrl A control with tabs on which the user can click, analogous to the dividers in a notebook.

CHotKeyCtrl Enables the user to create a "hot key" combination, which the user can press to perform an action quickly.

Related Classes

CImageList Provides the functionality of the Windows image list. Image lists are used with list controls and tree controls. They can also be used to store and archive a set of same-sized bitmaps.

CCtrlView The base class for all views associated with Windows controls. The views based on controls are described below.

CEditView A view that contains a Windows standard edit control.

CRichEditView A view that contains a Windows rich edit control.

CListView A view that contains a Windows list control.

CTreeView A view that contains a Windows tree control.

Control Bar Classes

Control bars are attached to a frame window. They contain buttons, status panes, or a dialog template. Free-floating control bars, also called tool palettes, are implemented by attaching them to a **CMiniFrameWnd** object.

Framework Control Bars

These control bars are an integral part of the MFC framework. They are easier to use and more powerful because they're integrated with the framework. Most MFC applications use these control bars rather than the Windows control bars.

CControlBar The base class for MFC control bars listed in this section. A control bar is a window aligned to the edge of a frame window. The control bar contains either **HWND**-based child controls or controls not based on an **HWND**, such as toolbar buttons.

CToolBar Toolbar control windows that contain bitmap command buttons not based on an **HWND**. Most MFC applications use this class rather than **CToolBarCtrl**.

CStatusBar The base class for status-bar control windows. Most MFC applications use this class rather than **CStatusBarCtrl**.

CDialogBar A control bar that is based on a dialog box template.

Windows Control Bars

These control bars are thin wrappers for the corresponding Windows controls. Since they're not integrated with the framework, they're harder to use than the control bars listed above. Most MFC applications use the control bars listed above.

CStatusBarCtrl   A horizontal window, usually divided into panes, in which an application can display status information.

CToolBarCtrl   Provides the functionality of the Windows toolbar common control.

Related Classes

CToolTipCtrl   A small pop-up window that displays a single line of text describing the purpose of a tool in an application.

Drawing and Printing Classes

In Windows, all graphical output is drawn on a virtual drawing area called a device context (or DC). MFC provides classes to encapsulate the various types of DCs, as well as encapsulations for Windows drawing tools such as bitmaps, brushes, palettes, and pens.

Output (Device Context) Classes

These classes encapsulate the different types of device contexts available in Windows.

Most of the following classes encapsulate a handle to a Windows device context. A device context is a Windows object that contains information about the drawing attributes of a device such as a display or a printer. All drawing calls are made through a device-context object. Additional classes derived from **CDC** encapsulate specialized device-context functionality, including support for Windows metafiles.

CDC   The base class for device contexts. Used directly for accessing the whole display and for accessing nondisplay contexts such as printers.

CPaintDC   A display context used in **OnPaint** member functions of windows. Automatically calls **BeginPaint** on construction and **EndPaint** on destruction.

CClientDC   A display context for client areas of windows. Used, for example, to draw in an immediate response to mouse events.

CWindowDC   A display context for entire windows, including both the client and nonclient areas.

CMetaFileDC   A device context for Windows metafiles. A Windows metafile contains a sequence of graphics device interface (GDI) commands that can be replayed to create an image. Calls made to the member functions of a **CMetaFileDC** are recorded in a metafile.

Related Classes

CPoint   Holds coordinate (x, y) pairs.

CSize   Holds distance, relative positions, or paired values.

CRect   Holds coordinates of rectangular areas.

CRgn   Encapsulates a GDI region for manipulating an elliptical, polygonal, or irregular area within a window. Used in conjunction with the clipping member functions in class **CDC**.

CRectTracker   Displays and handles the user interface for resizing and moving rectangular objects.

CColorDialog   Provides a standard dialog box for selecting a color.

CFontDialog   Provides a standard dialog box for selecting a font.

CPrintDialog   Provides a standard dialog box for printing a file.

Drawing Tool Classes

These classes encapsulate drawing tools that are used to draw on a device context.

CGdiObject   The base class for GDI drawing tools.

CBrush   Encapsulates a GDI brush that can be selected as the current brush in a device context. Brushes are used for filling interiors of objects being drawn.

CPen   Encapsulates a GDI pen that can be selected as the current pen in a device context. Pens are used for drawing the border lines of objects.

CFont   Encapsulates a GDI font that can be selected as the current font in a device context.

CBitmap   Encapsulates a GDI bitmap, providing an interface for manipulating bitmaps.

CPalette   Encapsulates a GDI color palette for use as an interface between the application and a color output device such as a display.

CRectTracker   Displays and handles the user interface for resizing and moving rectangular objects.

Simple Data Type Classes

The following classes encapsulate drawing coordinates, character strings, and time and date information, allowing convenient use of C++ syntax. These objects are used widely as parameters to the member functions of Windows classes in the class library. Because **CPoint**, **CSize**, and **CRect** correspond to the **POINT**, **SIZE**, and **RECT** structures, respectively, in the Win32 SDK, you can use objects of these C++ classes wherever you can use these C-language structures. The classes provide useful interfaces through their member functions. **CString** provides very flexible dynamic character strings. **CTime**, **COleDateTime**, **CTimeSpan**, and **COleTimeSpan** represent time and date values. For more information about these classes, see the article "Date and Time" in *Programming with MFC*.

The classes that begin with "**COle**" are encapsulations of data types provided by OLE. These data types can be used in Windows programs regardless of whether other OLE features are used.

CString   Holds character strings.

CTime   Holds absolute time and date values.

COleDateTime   Wrapper for the OLE automation type **DATE**. Represents date and time values.

CTimeSpan   Holds relative time and date values.

COleDateTimeSpan   Holds relative **COleDateTime** values, such as the difference between two **COleDateTime** values.

CPoint   Holds coordinate (x, y) pairs.

CSize   Holds distance, relative positions, or paired values.

CRect   Holds coordinates of rectangular areas.

CImageList   Provides the functionality of the Windows image list. Image lists are used with list controls and tree controls. They can also be used to store and archive a set of same-sized bitmaps.

COleVariant   Wrapper for the OLE automation type **VARIANT**. Data in **VARIANT**s can be stored in many formats.

COleCurrency   Wrapper for the OLE automation type **CURRENCY**, a fixed-point arithmetic type, with 15 digits before the decimal point and 4 digits after.

Array, List, and Map Classes

For handling aggregates of data, the class library provides a group of collection classes—arrays, lists, and "maps"—that can hold a variety of object and predefined types. The collections are dynamically sized. These classes can be used in any program, whether written for Windows or not. However, they are most useful for implementing the data structures that define your document classes in the application framework. You can readily derive specialized collection classes from these, or you can create them based on the template classes. For more information about these approaches, see the article "Collections" in *Programming with MFC* and "Template Classes for Arrays, Lists, and Maps" in this overview for a list of the template collection classes.

Arrays are one-dimensional data structures that are stored contiguously in memory. They support very fast random access since the memory address of any given element can be calculated by multiplying the index of the element by the size of an element and adding the result to the base address of the array. But arrays are very expensive if you have to insert elements into the array, since the entire array past the element inserted has to be moved to make room for the element to be inserted. Arrays can grow and shrink as necessary.

Lists are similar to arrays but are stored very differently. Each element in a list also includes a pointer to the previous and next elements, making it a doubly-linked list. It's very fast to add or delete items because doing so only involves changing a few pointers. However, searching a list can be expensive since all searches need to start at one of the list's ends.

Maps relate a key value to a data value. For instance, the key of a map could be a string and the data a pointer into a list. You would ask the map to give you the pointer associated with a particular string. Map lookups are fast because maps use hash tables for key lookups. Adding and deleting items is also fast. Maps are often used with other data structures as auxiliary indices. MFC uses a special kind of map called a "message map" to map Windows messages to a pointer to the handler function for that message.

Template Classes for Arrays, Lists, and Maps

These collection classes are templates whose parameters determine the types of the objects stored in the aggregates. The **CArray**, **CMap**, and **CList** classes use global helper functions that must usually be customized. For more information about these helper functions, see Collection Class Helpers in the "Macros and Globals" section. The typed pointer classes are "wrappers" for other classes in the class library. By using these wrappers, you enlist the compiler's type-checking to help you avoid errors. For more information on using these classes, see the article "Collections" in *Programming with MFC*.

These classes provide templates you can use to create arrays, lists, and maps using any type you like.

CArray   Template class for making arrays of arbitrary types.

CList   Template class for making lists of arbitrary types.

CMap   Template class for making maps with arbitrary key and value types.

CTypedPtrArray   Template class for type-safe arrays of pointers.

CTypedPtrList   Template class for type-safe lists of pointers.

CTypedPtrMap   Template class for type-safe maps with pointers.

Ready-to-Use Array Classes

CByteArray   Stores elements of type **BYTE** in an array.

CDWordArray   Stores elements of type **DWORD** in an array.

CObArray   Stores pointers to objects of class **CObject** or to objects of classes derived from **CObject** in an array.

CPtrArray   Stores pointers to **void** (generic pointers) in an array.

CUIntArray   Stores elements of type **UINT** in an array.

CWordArray   Stores elements of type **WORD** in an array.

CStringArray   Stores **CString** objects in an array.

Ready-to-Use List Classes

CObList   Stores pointers to objects of class **CObject** or to objects of classes derived from **CObject** in a linked list.

CPtrList   Stores pointers to **void** (generic pointers) in a linked list.

CStringList   Stores **CString** objects in a linked list.

Ready-to-Use Map Classes

CMapPtrToPtr   Uses **void** pointers as keys for finding other **void** pointers.

CMapPtrToWord   Uses **void** pointers as keys for finding data of type **WORD**.

CMapStringToOb   Uses **CString** objects as keys for finding **CObject** pointers.

CMapStringToPtr   Uses **CString** objects as keys for finding **void** pointers.

CMapStringToString   Uses **CString** objects as keys for finding other **CString** objects.

CMapWordToOb   Uses data of type **WORD** to find **CObject** pointers.

CMapWordToPtr   Uses data of type **WORD** to find **void** pointers.

File, Database, and Socket Classes

These classes allow you to store information to a database or a disk file or to exchange information with another computer via a Windows Socket. There are two sets of database classes—DAO and ODBC—which provide similar functionality. The DAO group is implemented using the Data Access Object, while the ODBC group is implemented using Open Database Connectivity. There are also a set of classes for manipulating standard files and OLE streams, and a set of classes for manipulating Windows Sockets.

File I/O Classes

These classes provide an interface to traditional disk files, in-memory files, OLE streams, and Windows sockets. All of the classes derived from **CFile** can be used with a **CArchive** object to perform serialization.

Use the following classes, particularly **CArchive** and **CFile**, if you write your own input/output processing. Normally you don't need to derive from these classes. If you use the application framework, the default implementations of the Open and Save commands on the File menu will handle file I/O (using class **CArchive**), as long as you override your document's **Serialize** function to supply details about how a document "serializes" its contents. For more information about the file classes and serialization, see the article "Files" and the article "Serialization (Object Persistence)" in *Programming with MFC*.

CFile   Provides a file interface to binary disk files.

CStdioFile   Provides a **CFile** interface to buffered stream disk files, usually in text mode.

CMemFile   Provides a **CFile** interface to in-memory files.

COleStreamFile   Uses the OLE **IStream** interface to provide **CFile** access to OLE compound files.

CSocketFile   Provides a **CFile** interface to a Windows Socket.

Related Classes

CArchive   Cooperates with a **CFile** object to implement persistent storage for objects through serialization (see **CObject::Serialize**).

CArchiveException   An archive exception.

CFileException   A file-oriented exception.

CFileDialog   Provides a standard dialog box for opening or saving a file.

DAO Classes

These classes work with the other application framework classes to give easy access to DAO (Data Access Object) databases, which use the same database engine as Microsoft Visual Basic® and Microsoft Access. The DAO classes can also access a wide variety of databases for which Open Database Connectivity (ODBC) drivers are available.

Programs that use DAO databases will have at least a **CDaoDatabase** object and a **CDaoRecordset** object.

CDaoWorkspace   Manages a named, password-protected database session from login to logoff. Most programs use the default workspace.

CDaoDatabase   A connection to a database through which you can operate on the data.

CDaoRecordset   Represents a set of records selected from a data source.

CDaoRecordView   A view that displays database records in controls.

CDaoQueryDef   Represents a query definition, usually one saved in a database.

CDaoTableDef   Represents the stored definition of a base table or an attached table.

CDaoException   Represents an exception condition arising from the DAO classes.

CDaoFieldExchange   Supports the DAO record field exchange (DFX) routines used by the DAO database classes. You will normally not directly use this class.

Related Classes

CLongBinary   Encapsulates a handle to storage for a binary large object (or BLOB), such as a bitmap. **CLongBinary** objects are used to manage large data objects stored in database tables.

COleCurrency   Wrapper for the OLE automation type **CURRENCY**, a fixed-point arithmetic type, with 15 digits before the decimal point and 4 digits after.

COleDateTime   Wrapper for the OLE automation type **DATE**. Represents date and time values.

COleVariant   Wrapper for the OLE automation type **VARIANT**. Data in **VARIANT**s can be stored in many formats.

ODBC Classes

These classes work with the other application framework classes to give easy access to a wide variety of databases for which Open Database Connectivity (ODBC) drivers are available.

Programs that use ODBC databases will have at least a **CDatabase** object and a **CRecordset** object.

CDatabase   Encapsulates a connection to a data source, through which you can operate on the data source.

CRecordset   Encapsulates a set of records selected from a data source. Recordsets enable scrolling from record to record, updating records (adding, editing, and deleting records), qualifying the selection with a filter, sorting the selection, and parameterizing the selection with information obtained or calculated at run time.

CRecordView Provides a form view directly connected to a recordset object. The dialog data exchange (DDX) mechanism exchanges data between the recordset and the controls of the record view. Like all form views, a record view is based on a dialog template resource. Record views also support moving from record to record in the recordset, updating records, and closing the associated recordset when the record view closes.

CDBException An exception resulting from failures in data access processing. This class serves the same purpose as other exception classes in the exception-handling mechanism of the class library.

CFieldExchange Supplies context information to support record field exchange (RFX), which exchanges data between the field data members and parameter data members of a recordset object and the corresponding table columns on the data source. Analogous to class **CDataExchange**, which is used similarly for dialog data exchange (DDX).

Related Class

CLongBinary Encapsulates a handle to storage for a binary large object (or BLOB), such as a bitmap. **CLongBinary** objects are used to manage large data objects stored in database tables.

Windows Sockets Classes

Windows Sockets provide a network protocol-independent way to communicate between two computers. These sockets can be synchronous (your program waits until the communication is done) or asynchronous (your program continues running while the communication is going on).

CAsyncSocket Encapsulates the Windows Sockets API in a thin wrapper.

CSocket Higher-level abstraction derived from **CAsyncSocket**. It operates synchronously.

CSocketFile Provides a **CFile** interface to a Windows Socket.

OLE Classes

The OLE classes work with the other application framework classes to provide easy access to the OLE API, giving your programs an easy way to provide the power of OLE to your users. Using OLE, you can:

- Create OLE documents, which allow users to create and edit documents containing data created by multiple applications, including text, graphics, spreadsheets, sound, or other types of data.
- Create OLE objects that can be embedded in OLE documents.

- Use OLE drag and drop to copy data between applications.
- Use OLE automation to control one program with another.

The following categories of classes support OLE:

- OLE Container Classes
- OLE Server Classes
- OLE Drag-and-Drop and Data Transfer Classes
- OLE Common Dialog Classes
- OLE Automation Classes
- OLE Control Classes
- OLE-Related Classes

To see the inheritance of a class, use the Class Hierarchy Chart in Books Online.

OLE Container Classes

These classes are used by container applications. Both **COleLinkingDoc** and **COleDocument** manage collections of **COleClientItem** objects. Rather than deriving your document class from **CDocument**, you'll derive it from **COleLinkingDoc** or **COleDocument**, depending on whether or not you want support for links to objects embedded in your document.

Use a **COleClientItem** object to represent each OLE item in your document that is embedded from another document or is a link to another document.

COleDocument   Used for OLE compound document implementation, as well as basic container support. Serves as a container for classes derived from **CDocItem**. This class can be used as the base class for container documents and is the base class for **COleServerDoc**.

COleLinkingDoc   A class derived from **COleDocument** that provides the infrastructure for linking. You should derive the document classes for your container applications from this class instead of from **COleDocument** if you want them to support links to embedded objects.

CRichEditDoc   Maintains the list of OLE client items that are in the rich edit control. Used with **CRichEditView** and **CRichEditCntrItem**.

CDocItem   Abstract base class of **COleClientItem** and **COleServerItem**. Objects of classes derived from **CDocItem** represent parts of documents.

COleClientItem   A client item class that represents the client's side of the connection to an embedded or linked OLE item. Derive your client items from this class.

CRichEditCntrItem Provides client-side access to an OLE item stored in a rich edit control when used with **CRichEditView** and **CRichEditDoc**.

COleException An exception resulting from a failure in OLE processing. This class is used by both containers and servers.

OLE Server Classes

These classes are used by server applications. Server documents are derived from **COleServerDoc** rather than **CDocument**. Note that since **COleServerDoc** is derived from **COleLinkingDoc**, server documents can also be containers that support linking.

The **COleServerItem** class represents a document or portion of a document that can be embedded in another document or linked to.

COleIPFrameWnd and **COleResizeBar** support in-place editing while the object is in a container, and **COleTemplateServer** supports creation of document/view pairs so OLE objects from other applications can be edited.

COleServerDoc Used as the base class for server-application document classes. **COleServerDoc** objects provide the bulk of server support through interactions with **COleServerItem** objects. Visual editing capability is provided using the class library's document/view architecture.

CDocItem Abstract base class of **COleClientItem** and **COleServerItem**. Objects of classes derived from **CDocItem** represent parts of documents.

COleServerItem Used to represent the OLE interface to **COleServerDoc** items. There is usually one **COleServerDoc** object, which represents the embedded part of a document. In servers that support links to parts of documents, there can be many **COleServerItem** objects, each of which represents a link to a portion of the document.

COleIPFrameWnd Provides the frame window for a view when a server document is being edited in place.

COleResizeBar Provides the standard user interface for in-place resizing. Objects of this class are always used in conjunction with **COleIPFrameWnd** objects.

COleTemplateServer Used to create documents using the framework's document/view architecture. A **COleTemplateServer** object delegates most of its work to an associated **CDocTemplate** object.

COleException An exception resulting from a failure in OLE processing. This class is used by both containers and servers.

OLE Drag-and-Drop and Data Transfer Classes

These classes are used in OLE data transfers. They allow data to be transferred between applications by using the Clipboard or through drag and drop.

COleDropSource Controls the drag-and-drop operation from start to finish. This class determines when the drag operation starts and when it ends. It also displays cursor feedback during the drag-and-drop operation.

COleDataSource Used when an application provides data for a data transfer. **COleDataSource** could be viewed as an object-oriented Clipboard object.

COleDropTarget Represents the target of a drag-and-drop operation. A **COleDropTarget** object corresponds to a window on screen. It determines whether to accept any data dropped onto it and implements the actual drop operation.

COleDataObject Used as the receiver side to **COleDataSource**. **COleDataObject** objects provide access to the data stored by a **COleDataSource** object.

OLE Common Dialog Classes

These classes handle common OLE tasks by implementing a number of standard OLE dialog boxes. They also provide a consistent user interface for OLE functionality.

COleDialog Used by the framework to contain common implementations for all OLE dialog boxes. All dialog box classes in the user-interface category are derived from this base class. Cannot be used directly.

COleInsertDialog Displays the Insert Object dialog box, the standard user interface for inserting new OLE linked or embedded items.

COlePasteSpecialDialog Displays the Paste Special dialog box, the standard user interface for implementing the Edit Paste Special command.

COleLinksDialog Displays the Edit Links dialog box, the standard user interface for modifying information about linked items.

COleChangeIconDialog Displays the Change Icon dialog box, the standard user interface for changing the icon associated with an OLE embedded or linked item.

COleConvertDialog Displays the Convert dialog box, the standard user interface for converting OLE items from one type to another.

COlePropertiesDialog Encapsulates the Windows common OLE Properties dialog box. Common OLE Properties dialog boxes provide an easy way to display and modify the properties of an OLE document item in a manner consistent with Windows standards.

COleUpdateDialog Displays the Update dialog box, the standard user interface for updating all links in a document. The dialog box contains a progress indicator to indicate how close the update procedure is to completion.

COleChangeSourceDialog Displays the Change Source dialog box, the standard user interface for changing the destination or source of a link.

COleBusyDialog Displays the Server Busy and Server Not Responding dialog boxes, the standard user interface for handling calls to busy applications. Usually displayed automatically by the **COleMessageFilter** implementation.

OLE Automation Classes

These classes support automation clients (applications that control other applications). Automation servers (applications that can be controlled by other applications) are supported through dispatch maps.

COleDispatchDriver Used to call automation servers from your automation client. ClassWizard uses this class to create type-safe classes for automation servers that provide a type library.

COleDispatchException An exception resulting from an error during OLE automation. OLE automation exceptions are thrown by automation servers and caught by automation clients.

OLE Control Classes

These are the primary classes you'll use when writing OLE controls. The **COleControlModule** class in an OLE control module is like the **CWinApp** class in an application. Each module implements one or more OLE controls; these controls are represented by **COleControl** objects. These controls communicate with their containers using **CConnectionPoint** objects.

The **CPictureHolder** and **CFontHolder** classes encapsulate OLE interfaces for pictures and fonts, while the **COlePropertyPage** and **CPropExchange** classes help you implement property pages and property persistence for your control.

COleControlModule Replaces the **CWinApp** class for your OLE control module. Derive from the **COleControlModule** class to develop an OLE control module object. It provides member functions for initializing your OLE control's module.

COleControl Derive from the **COleControl** class to develop an OLE control. Derived from **CWnd**, this class inherits all the functionality of a Windows window object plus additional functionality specific to OLE, such as event firing and the ability to support methods and properties.

CConnectionPoint The **CConnectionPoint** class defines a special type of interface used to communicate with other OLE objects, called a "connection point." A connection point implements an outgoing interface that is able to initiate actions on other objects, such as firing events and change notifications.

CPictureHolder Encapsulates the functionality of a Windows picture object and the **IPicture** OLE interface; is used to implement the custom Picture property of an OLE control.

CFontHolder Encapsulates the functionality of a Windows font object and the **IFont** OLE interface; is used to implement the stock Font property of an OLE control.

COlePropertyPage Displays the properties of an OLE custom control in a graphical interface, similar to a dialog box.

CPropExchange Supports the implementation of property persistence for your OLE controls. Analogous to **CDataExchange** for dialog boxes.

OLE-Related Classes

These classes provide a number of different services, ranging from exceptions to file input and output.

COleObjectFactory Used to create items when requested from other OLE containers. This class serves as the base class for more specific types of factories, including **COleTemplateServer**.

COleMessageFilter Used to manage concurrency with OLE Lightweight Remote Procedure Calls (LRPC).

COleStreamFile Uses the OLE **IStream** interface to provide **CFile** access to compound files. This class (derived from **CFile**) enables MFC serialization to use OLE structured storage.

CRectTracker Used to allow moving, resizing, and reorientation of in-place items.

Debugging and Exception Classes

These classes provide support for debugging dynamic memory allocation and for passing exception information from the function where the exception is thrown to the function where it's caught.

Use classes **CDumpContext** and **CMemoryState** during development to assist with debugging, as described in the article "Diagnostics." Use **CRuntimeClass** to determine the class of any object at run time, as described in the article "CObjectClass: Accessing Run-Time Class Information." Both articles are in *Programming with MFC*. The framework uses **CRuntimeClass** to create objects of a particular class dynamically.

Debugging Support Classes

MFC provides the following classes to help you debug dynamic memory allocation problems.

CDumpContext   Provides a destination for diagnostic dumps.

CMemoryState   Structure that provides snapshots of memory use. Also used to compare earlier and later memory snapshots.

Exception Classes

The class library provides an exception-handling mechanism based on class **CException**. The application framework uses exceptions in its code; you can also use them in yours. For more information, see the article "Exceptions" in *Programming with MFC*. You can derive your own exception types from **CException**.

MFC provides an exception class from which you can derive your own exception as well as exception classes for all of the exceptions it supports.

CException   The base class for exceptions.

CArchiveException   An archive exception.

CDaoException   An exception resulting from a failure in a DAO database operation.

CDBException   An exception resulting from a failure in ODBC database processing.

CFileException   A file-oriented exception.

CMemoryException   An out-of-memory exception.

CNotSupportedException   An exception resulting from using an unsupported feature.

COleException   An exception resulting from a failure in OLE processing. This class is used by both containers and servers.

COleDispatchException   An exception resulting from an error during OLE automation. OLE automation exceptions are thrown by automation servers and caught by automation clients.

CResourceException   An exception resulting from a failure to load a Windows resource.

CUserException   An exception used to stop a user-initiated operation. Typically the user has been notified of the problem before this exception is thrown.

CAnimateCtrl

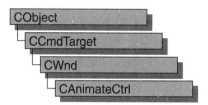

The **CAnimateCtrl** class provides the functionality of the Windows common animation control. This control (and therefore the **CAnimateCtrl** class) is available only to programs running under Windows 95 and Windows NT version 3.51 and later.

An animation control is a rectangular window that displays a clip in AVI (Audio Video Interleaved) format—the standard Windows video/audio format. An AVI clip is a series of bitmap frames, like a movie.

Animation controls can play only simple AVI clips. Specifically, the clips to be played by an animation control must meet the following requirements:

- There must be exactly one video stream and it must have at least one frame.
- There can be at most two streams in the file (typically the other stream, if present, is an audio stream, although the animation control ignores audio information).
- The clip must either be uncompressed or compressed with RLE8 compression.
- No palette changes are allowed in the video stream.

You can add the AVI clip to your application as an AVI resource, or it can accompany your application as a separate AVI file.

Since your thread continues executing while the AVI clip is displayed, one common use for an animation control is to indicate system activity during a lengthy operation. For example, the Find dialog box of the Windows 95 Explorer displays a moving magnifying glass as the system searches for a file.

If you create a **CAnimateCtrl** object within a dialog box or from a dialog resource using the dialog editor, it will be automatically destroyed when the user closes the dialog box.

If you create a **CAnimateCtrl** object within a window, you may need to destroy it. If you create the **CAnimateCtrl** object on the stack, it is destroyed automatically. If you create the **CAnimateCtrl** object on the heap by using the **new** function, you must call **delete** on the object to destroy it. If you derive a new class from **CAnimateCtrl** and allocate any memory in that class, override the **CAnimateCtrl** destructor to dispose of the allocations.

#include <afxcmn.h>

See Also "Animation Control Styles" in CAnimateCtrl::Create, **ON_CONTROL**

Construction

CAnimateCtrl	Constructs a **CAnimateCtrl** object.

Initialization

Create	Creates an animation control and attaches it to a **CAnimateCtrl** object.

Operations

Open	Opens an AVI clip from a file or resource and displays the first frame.
Play	Plays the AVI clip without sound.
Seek	Displays a selected single frame of the AVI clip.
Stop	Stops playing the AVI clip.
Close	Closes the AVI clip that was previously opened.

Member Functions

CAnimateCtrl::CAnimateCtrl

CAnimateCtrl( );

Remarks

Constructs a **CAnimateCtrl** object. You must call the **Create** member function before you can perform any other operations on the object you create.

See Also CAnimateCtrl::Create

CAnimateCtrl::Close

BOOL Close( );

Return Value

Nonzero if successful; otherwise zero.

Remarks

Use the **Close** member function to close the AVI clip that was previously opened in the animation control (if any) and remove it from memory.

See Also CAnimateCtrl::Open

CAnimateCtrl::Create

BOOL Create(DWORD *dwStyle***, const RECT&** *rect***, CWnd*** *pParentWnd***, UINT** *nID* **);**

Return Value

Nonzero if successful; otherwise zero.

Parameters

dwStyle   Specifies the animation control's style. Apply any combination of the window and animation control styles described under "Remarks" to the control.

rect   Specifies the animation control's position and size. It can be either a **CRect** object or a **RECT** structure.

pParentWnd   Specifies the animation control's parent window, usually a **CDialog**. It must not be **NULL.**

nID   Specifies the animation control's ID.

Remarks

You construct a **CAnimateCtrl** in two steps. First call the constructor, then call **Create**, which creates the animation control and attaches it to the **CAnimateCtrl** object.

Apply the following window styles to an Animation Control. (For a list of window styles, see "Window Styles" in the "Styles Used by MFC" section.

- **WS_CHILD**   Always
- **WS_VISIBLE**   Usually
- **WS_DISABLED**   Rarely

In addition to the window styles listed above, you may want to apply one or more of the following animation control styles to an animation control:

- **ACS_CENTER**   Centers the AVI clip in the animation control's window and leaves the animation control's size and position unchanged when the AVI clip is opened. If this style is not specified, the control will be resized when the AVI clip is opened to the size of the images in the AVI clip.

- **ACS_TRANSPARENT**   Causes the AVI clip to be drawn using a transparent background rather than the background color specified in the AVI clip.

- **ACS_AUTOPLAY**   Causes the AVI clip to start playing as soon as it is opened. When the clip is done playing, it will automatically be repeated.

See Also   **CAnimateCtrl::CAnimateCtrl, CAnimateCtrl::Open, CAnimateCtrl::Play, CAnimateCtrl::Seek**

CAnimateCtrl::Open

BOOL Open(LPCTSTR *lpszFileName* **);**
BOOL Open(UINT *nID* **);**

Return Value

Nonzero if successful; otherwise zero.

Parameters

lpszFileName   A **CString** object or a pointer to a null-terminated string that contains either the name of the AVI file or the name of an AVI resource. If this parameter is **NULL**, the system closes the AVI clip that was previously opened for the animation control, if any.

nID   The AVI resource identifier. If this parameter is **NULL**, the system closes the AVI clip that was previously opened for the animation control, if any.

Remarks

Call this function to open an AVI clip and display its first frame.

If the animation control has the **ACS_AUTOPLAY** style, the animation control will automatically start playing the clip immediately after it opens it. It will continue to play the clip in the background while your thread continues executing. When the clip is done playing, it will automatically be repeated.

If the animation control has the **ACS_CENTER** style, the AVI clip will be centered in the control and the size of the control will not change. If the animation control does not have the **ACS_CENTER** style, the control will be resized when the AVI clip is opened to the size of the images in the AVI clip. The position of the top left corner of the control will not change, only the size of the control.

If the animation control has the **ACS_TRANSPARENT** style, the first frame will be drawn using a transparent background rather than the background color specified in the animation clip.

See Also   **CAnimateCtrl::Close**, **CAnimateCtrl::Create**

CAnimateCtrl::Play

BOOL Play(UINT *nFrom*, **UINT** *nTo*, **UINT** *nRep* **);**

Return Value

Nonzero if successful; otherwise zero.

Parameters

nFrom   Zero-based index of the frame where playing begins. Value must be less than 65,536. A value of 0 means begin with the first frame in the AVI clip.

nTo   Zero-based index of the frame where playing ends. Value must be less than 65,536. A value of −1 means end with the last frame in the AVI clip.

nRep   Number of times to replay the AVI clip. A value of −1 means replay the file indefinitely.

Remarks

Call this function to play an AVI clip in an animation control. The animation control will play the clip in the background while your thread continues executing. If the animation control has **ACS_TRANSPARENT** style, the AVI clip will be played using a transparent background rather than the background color specified in the animation clip.

See Also   CAnimateCtrl::Open, CAnimateCtrl::Stop, CAnimateCtrl::Seek, CAnimateCtrl::Create

CAnimateCtrl::Seek

BOOL Seek(UINT *nTo*);

Return Value

Nonzero if successful; otherwise zero.

Parameters

nTo   Zero-based index of the frame to display. Value must be less than 65,536. A value of 0 means display the first frame in the AVI clip. A value of −1 means display the last frame in the AVI clip.

Remarks

Call this function to statically display a single frame of your AVI clip. If the animation control has **ACS_TRANSPARENT** style, the AVI clip will be drawn using a transparent background rather than the background color specified in the animation clip.

See Also   CAnimateCtrl::Open, CAnimateCtrl::Play, CAnimateCtrl::Create

CAnimateCtrl::Stop

BOOL Stop( );

Return Value

Nonzero if successful; otherwise zero.

Remarks

Call this function to stop playing an AVI clip in an animation control.

See Also   CAnimateCtrl::Play

CArchive

The **CArchive** class allows you to save a complex network of objects in a permanent binary form (usually disk storage) that persists after those objects are deleted. Later you can load the objects from persistent storage, reconstituting them in memory. This process of making data persistent is called "serialization."

You can think of an archive object as a kind of binary stream. Like an input/output stream, an archive is associated with a file and permits the buffered writing and reading of data to and from storage. An input/output stream processes sequences of ASCII characters, but an archive processes binary object data in an efficient, nonredundant format.

You must create a **CFile** object before you can create a **CArchive** object. In addition, you must ensure that the archive's load/store status is compatible with the file's open mode. You are limited to one active archive per file.

When you construct a **CArchive** object, you attach it to an object of class **CFile** (or a derived class) that represents an open file. You also specify whether the archive will be used for loading or storing. A **CArchive** object can process not only primitive types but also objects of **CObject**-derived classes designed for serialization. A serializable class usually has a **Serialize** member function, and it usually uses the **DECLARE_SERIAL** and **IMPLEMENT_SERIAL** macros, as described under class **CObject**.

The overloaded extraction (>>) and insertion (<<) operators are convenient archive programming interfaces that support both primitive types and **CObject**-derived classes.

CArchive also supports programming with the MFC Windows Sockets classes **CSocket** and **CSocketFile**. The **IsBufferEmpty** member function supports that usage.

For more information on **CArchive**, see "Serialization (Object Persistence)" and "Windows Sockets: Using Sockets with Archives" in *Programming with MFC*.

#include <afx.h>

See Also   CFile, CObject, CSocket, CSocketFile

Data Members

m_pDocument	Points to the **CDocument** object being serialized.

Construction

CArchive	Creates a **CArchive** object.
Close	Flushes unwritten data and disconnects from the **CFile**.

Basic Input/Output

Flush	Flushes unwritten data from the archive buffer.
operator >>	Loads objects and primitive types from the archive.
operator <<	Stores objects and primitive types to the archive.
Read	Reads raw bytes.
Write	Writes raw bytes.
WriteString	Writes a single line of text.
ReadString	Reads a single line of text.

Status

GetFile	Gets the **CFile** object pointer for this archive.
GetObjectSchema	Called from the **Serialize** function to determine the version of the object that is being deserialized.
SetObjectSchema	Sets the object schema stored in the archive object.
IsLoading	Determines whether the archive is loading.
IsStoring	Determines whether the archive is storing.
IsBufferEmpty	Determines whether the buffer has been emptied during a Windows Sockets receive process.

Object Input/Output

ReadObject	Calls an object's **Serialize** function for loading.
WriteObject	Calls an object's **Serialize** function for storing.
MapObject	Places objects in the map that are not serialized to the file, but that are available for subobjects to reference.
SetStoreParams	Sets the hash table size and the block size of the map used to identify unique objects during the serialization process.
SetLoadParams	Sets the size to which the load array grows. Must be called before any object is loaded or before **MapObject** or **ReadObject** is called.
ReadClass	Reads a class reference previously stored with **WriteClass**.
WriteClass	Writes a reference to the **CRuntimeClass** to the **CArchive**.
SerializeClass	Reads or writes the class reference to the **CArchive** object depending on the direction of the **CArchive**.

Member Functions

CArchive::CArchive

CArchive(CFile* *pFile*, UINT *nMode*, int *nBufSize* = 512, void* *lpBuf* = NULL);
    throw(CMemoryException, CArchiveException, CFileException);

Parameters

pFile   A pointer to the **CFile** object that is the ultimate source or destination of the persistent data.

nMode   A flag that specifies whether objects will be loaded from or stored to the archive. The *nMode* parameter must have one of the following values:

- **CArchive::load**   Loads data from the archive. Requires only **CFile** read permission.

- **CArchive::store**   Saves data to the archive. Requires **CFile** write permission.

- **CArchive::bNoFlushOnDelete**   Prevents the archive from automatically calling **Flush** when the archive destructor is called. If you set this flag, you are responsible for explicitly calling **Close** before the destructor is called. If you do not, your data will be corrupted.

nBufSize   An integer that specifies the size of the internal file buffer, in bytes. Note that the default buffer size is 512 bytes. If you routinely archive large objects, you will improve performance if you use a larger buffer size that is a multiple of the file buffer size.

lpBuf   An optional pointer to a user-supplied buffer of size *nBufSize*. If you do not specify this parameter, the archive allocates a buffer from the local heap and frees it when the object is destroyed. The archive does not free a user-supplied buffer.

Remarks

Constructs a **CArchive** object and specifies whether it will be used for loading or storing objects. You cannot change this specification after you have created the archive.

You may not use **CFile** operations to alter the state of the file until you have closed the archive. Any such operation will damage the integrity of the archive. You may access the position of the file pointer at any time during serialization by obtaining the archive's file object from the **GetFile** member function and then using the **CFile::GetPosition** function. You should call **CArchive::Flush** before obtaining the position of the file pointer.

Example

```
extern char* pFileName;
CFile f;
char buf[512];
if( !f.Open( pFileName, CFile::modeCreate | CFile::modeWrite ) ) {
   #ifdef _DEBUG
      afxDump << "Unable to open file" << "\n";
      exit( 1 );
   #endif
}
CArchive ar( &f, CArchive::store, 512, buf );
```

See Also   CArchive::Close, CArchive::Flush, CFile::Close

CArchive::Close

void Close( );
    throw(CArchiveException, CFileException);

Remarks

Flushes any data remaining in the buffer, closes the archive, and disconnects the archive from the file. No further operations on the archive are permitted. After you close an archive, you can create another archive for the same file or you can close the file.

The member function **Close** ensures that all data is transferred from the archive to the file, and it makes the archive unavailable. To complete the transfer from the file to the storage medium, you must first use **CFile::Close** and then destroy the **CFile** object.

See Also   **CArchive::Flush**

CArchive::Flush

void Flush( );
    throw(CFileException);

Remarks

Forces any data remaining in the archive buffer to be written to the file.

The member function **Flush** ensures that all data is transferred from the archive to the file. You must call **CFile::Close** to complete the transfer from the file to the storage medium.

See Also   **CArchive::Close**, **CFile::Flush**, **CFile::Close**

CArchive::GetFile

CFile* GetFile( ) const;

Return Value

A constant pointer to the **CFile** object in use.

Remarks

Gets the **CFile** object pointer for this archive. You must flush the archive before using **GetFile**.

Example

```
extern CArchive ar;
const CFile* fp = ar.GetFile();
```

CArchive::GetObjectSchema

UINT GetObjectSchema( );

Return Value

During deserialization, the version of the object being read.

Remarks

Call this function from the **Serialize** function to determine the version of the object that is currently being deserialized. Calling this function is only valid when the **CArchive** object is being loaded (**CArchive::IsLoading** returns nonzero). It should be the first call in the **Serialize** function and called only once. A return value of (**UINT**)–1 indicates that the version number is unknown).

A **CObject**-derived class may use **VERSIONABLE_SCHEMA** combined (using bitwise **OR**) with the schema version itself (in the **IMPLEMENT_SERIAL** macro) to create a "versionable object," that is, an object whose **Serialize** member function can read multiple versions. The default framework functionality (without **VERSIONABLE_SCHEMA**) is to throw an exception when the version is mismatched.

Example

```
IMPLEMENT_SERIAL(CMyObject, CObject, VERSIONABLE_SCHEMA|1)
    // defines version as 1 and "versionable"

CMyObject::Serialize(CArchive& ar)
{
    if ( ar.IsLoading( ) )
    {
        nVersion = GetObjectSchema( );
        switch (nVersion)
        {
            case -1:
                // read in current version
                // or report error
                break;
            case 0:
                // read in old version
                break;*
            case 1;
                // read in latest version of
                //  this object
                break;
            default:
                //report unknown version
                break;
        }
    }
```

```
    else
        // Normal storing code here
}
```

See Also **CObject::Serialize**, **CObject::IsSerializable**, **IMPLEMENT_SERIAL**, **DECLARE_SERIAL**, **CArchive::IsLoading**

CArchive::IsBufferEmpty

BOOL IsBufferEmpty( ) const;

Return Value

Nonzero if the archive's buffer is empty; otherwise 0.

Remarks

Call this member function to determine whether the archive object's internal buffer is empty. This function is supplied to support programming with the MFC Windows Sockets class **CSocketFile**. You do not need to use it for an archive associated with a **CFile** object.

The reason for using **IsBufferEmpty** with an archive associated with a **CSocketFile** object is that the archive's buffer might contain more than one message or record. After receiving one message, you should use **IsBufferEmpty** to control a loop that continues receiving data until the buffer is empty. For more information, see the **Receive** member function of class **CAsyncSocket** and the MFC Advanced Concepts sample CHATSRVR, which shows how to use **IsBufferEmpty**.

For more information, see the article "Windows Sockets: Using Sockets with Archives" in *Programming with MFC*.

See Also **CSocketFile**, **CAsyncSocket::Receive**

CArchive::IsLoading

BOOL IsLoading( ) const;

Return Value

Nonzero if the archive is currently being used for loading; otherwise 0.

Remarks

Determines whether the archive is loading data. This member function is called by the **Serialize** functions of the archived classes.

Example

```
int i;
extern CArchive ar;
if( ar.IsLoading() )
  ar >> i;
else
  ar << i;
```

See Also   **CArchive::IsStoring**

CArchive::IsStoring

BOOL IsStoring( ) const;

Return Value

Nonzero if the archive is currently being used for storing; otherwise 0.

Remarks

Determines whether the archive is storing data. This member function is called by the **Serialize** functions of the archived classes.

If the **IsStoring** status of an archive is nonzero, then its **IsLoading** status is 0, and vice versa.

Example

```
int i;
extern CArchive ar;
if( ar.IsStoring() )
  ar << i;
else
  ar >> i;
```

See Also   **CArchive::IsLoading**

CArchive::MapObject

void MapObject(const CObject* *pOb* **);**

Parameters

pOb   A constant pointer to the object being stored.

Remarks

Call this member function to place objects in the map that are not really serialized to the file, but that are available for subobjects to reference. For example, you might not serialize a document, but you would serialize the items that are part of the document. By calling **MapObject**, you allow those items, or subobjects, to reference the document. Also, serialized subitems can serialize their **m_pDoc** back pointer.

You can call **MapObject** when you store to and load from the **CArchive** object. **MapObject** adds the specified object to the internal data structures maintained by the **CArchive** object during serialization and deserialization, but unlike **ReadObject** and **WriteObject,** it does not call serialize on the object.

Example

```
class CSubItem : public CObject
{
public:
    CSubItem(CMyDocument* pDoc)
        { m_pDoc = pDoc; }

    // back pointer to owning document
    CMyDocument* m_pDoc;
    WORD m_i; // other item data
};

void CMyDocument::Serialize(CArchive& ar)
{
    //make the document pointer
    //available for subobjects...
    MapObject(this);

    //serialize the subitems in the document;
    //they will be able to serialize their m_pDoc
    //back pointer
    m_listOfSubItems.Serialize(ar);
}

void CSubItem::Serialize(CArchive& ar)
{
    if (ar.IsStoring())
    {
        // will serialize a reference
        //to the "mapped" document pointer
        ar << m_pDoc;
            ar << m_i;
    }
    else
    {
        // will load a reference to
        //the "mapped" document pointer
        ar >> m_pDoc;
            ar >> m_i;
    }
}
```

See Also   **CArchive::ReadObject**, **CArchive::WriteObject**

CArchive::Read

UINT Read(void* *lpBuf*, **UINT** *nMax* **);**
   throw(CFileException);

Return Value

An unsigned integer containing the number of bytes actually read. If the return value is less than the number requested, the end of file has been reached. No exception is thrown on the end-of-file condition.

Parameters

lpBuf   A pointer to a user-supplied buffer that is to receive the data read from the archive.

nMax   An unsigned integer specifying the number of bytes to be read from the archive.

Remarks

Reads a specified number of bytes from the archive. The archive does not interpret the bytes.

You can use the **Read** member function within your **Serialize** function for reading ordinary structures that are contained in your objects.

Example

```
extern CArchive ar;
char pb[100];
UINT nr = ar.Read( pb, 100 );
```

CArchive::ReadClass

CRuntimeClass* ReadClass(const CRuntimeClass* *pClassRefRequested* = **NULL,**
   UINT* *pSchema* = **NULL, DWORD*** *obTag* = **NULL);**
   Throw CArchiveException;
   Throw CNotSupportedException;

Return Value

A pointer to the **CRuntimeClass** structure.

Parameters

pClassRefRequested   A pointer to the **CRuntimeClass** structure that corresponds to the class reference requested. Can be **NULL**.

pSchema   A pointer to a schema of the run-time class previously stored.

obTag   A number that refers to an object's unique tag. Used internally by the implementation of **ReadObject**. Exposed for advanced programming only; *obTag* normally should be **NULL**.

Remarks

Call this member function to read a reference to a class previously stored with **WriteClass**.

If *pClassRefRequested* is not **NULL**, **ReadClass** verifies that the archived class information is compatible with your runtime class. If it is not compatible, **ReadClass** will throw a **CArchiveException**.

Your runtime class must use **DECLARE_SERIAL** and **IMPLEMENT_SERIAL**; otherwise, **ReadClass** will throw a **CNotSupportedException**.

If *pSchema* is **NULL**, the schema of the stored class can be retrieved by calling **CArchive::GetObjectSchema**; otherwise, **pSchema* will contain the schema of the run-time class that was previously stored.

You can use **SerializeClass** instead of **ReadClass**, which handles both reading and writing of the class reference.

See Also   CArchive::WriteClass, CArchive::GetObjectSchema, CArchive::SetObjectSchema, CArchiveException, CNotSupportedException, CArchive::SerializeClass

CArchive::ReadObject

CObject* ReadObject(const CRuntimeClass* *pClass* **);**
   throw(CFileException, CArchiveException, CMemoryException);

Return Value

A **CObject** pointer that must be safely cast to the correct derived class by using **CObject::IsKindOf**.

Parameters

pClass   A constant pointer to the **CRuntimeClass** structure that corresponds to the object you expect to read.

Remarks

Reads object data from the archive and constructs an object of the appropriate type.

This function is normally called by the **CArchive** extraction (**>>**) operator overloaded for a **CObject** pointer. **ReadObject**, in turn, calls the **Serialize** function of the archived class.

If you supply a nonzero *pClass* parameter, which is obtained by the **RUNTIME_CLASS** macro, then the function verifies the run-time class of the archived object. This assumes you have used the **IMPLEMENT_SERIAL** macro in the implementation of the class.

See Also   CArchive::WriteObject, CObject::IsKindOf

CArchive::ReadString

Bool ReadString(CString& *rString* **);**
LPTSTR ReadString(LPTSTR *lpsz*, **UINT** *nMax* **);**
  throw(CArchiveException);

Return Value

In the version that returns **Bool**, **TRUE** if successful; **FALSE** otherwise.

In the version that returns an **LPTSTR**, a pointer to the buffer containing the text data; **NULL** if end-of-file was reached.

Parameters

rString   A reference to a **CString** that will contain the resultant string after it is read from the file associated with the CArchive object.

lpsz   Specifies a pointer to a user-supplied buffer that will receive a null-terminated text string.

nMax   Specifies the maximum number of characters to read. Should be one less than the size of the *lpsz* buffer.

Remarks

Call this member function to read text data into a buffer from the file associated with the **CArchive** object. In the version of the member function with the *nMax* parameter, the buffer will hold up to a limit of *nMax*-1 characters. Reading is stopped by a carriage return-linefeed pair. Trailing newline characters are always removed. A null character ('\0') is appended in either case.

CArchive::Read is also available for text-mode input, but it does not terminate on a carriage return-linefeed pair.

See Also   **CArchive::Read**, **CArchive::Write**, **CArchive::WriteString**, **CArchiveException**

CArchive::SerializeClass

void SerializeClass(const CRuntimeClass* *pRuntimeClass* **);**

Parameters

pRuntimeClass   A pointer to a run-time class object for the base class.

Remarks

Call this member function when you want to store and load the version information of a base class. **SerializeClass** reads or writes the reference to a class to the **CArchive** object, depending on the direction of the **CArchive**. Use **SerializeClass** in place of **ReadClass** and **WriteClass** as a convenient way to serialize base-class objects; **SerializeClass** requires less code and fewer parameters.

Like **ReadClass**, **SerializeClass** verifies that the archived class information is compatible with your runtime class. If it is not compatible, **SerializeClass** will throw a **CArchiveException**.

Your runtime class must use **DECLARE_SERIAL** and **IMPLEMENT_SERIAL**; otherwise, **SerializeClass** will throw a **CNotSupportedException**.

Use the **RUNTIME_CLASS** macro to retrieve the value for the *pRuntimeClass* parameter. The base class must have used the **IMPLEMENT_SERIAL** macro.

Example

```
class CBaseClass : public CObject { ... };
class CDerivedClass : public CBaseClass { ... };
void CDerivedClass::Serialize(CArchive& ar)
{
    if (ar.IsStoring())
    {
        //normal code for storing contents
        //of this object
    }
    else
    {
        //normal code for reading contents
        //of this object
    }

    //allow the base class to serialize along
    //with its version information
    ar.SerializeClass(RUNTIME_CLASS(CBaseClass));
    CBaseClass::Serialize(ar);
}
```

See Also   **CArchive::ReadClass**, **CArchive::WriteClass**, **CArchive::GetObjectSchema**, **CArchive::SetObjectSchema**, **CArchiveException**, **CNotSupportedException**

CArchive::SetLoadParams

void SetLoadParams(UINT *nGrowBy* **= 1024);**

Parameters

nGrowBy   The minimum number of element slots to allocate if a size increase is necessary.

Remarks

Call **SetLoadParams** when you are going to read a large number of **CObject**-derived objects from an archive. **CArchive** uses a load array to resolve references to objects stored in the archive. **SetLoadParams** allows you to set the size to which the load array grows.

You must not call **SetLoadParams** after any object is loaded, or after **MapObject** or **ReadObject** is called.

Example

```
class CMyLargeDocument : public CDocument { ... };
void CMyLargeDocument::Serialize(CArchive& ar)
{
    if (ar.IsStoring())
        ar.SetStoreParams();  // use large defaults
    else
        ar.SetLoadParams();

    if (ar.IsStoring())
    {
        // code for storing CMyLargeDocument
    }
    else
    {
        // code for loading CMyLargeDocument
    }
}
```

See Also   **CArchive::SetStoreParams**

CArchive::SetObjectSchema

void SetObjectSchema(UINT *nSchema* **);**

Parameters

nSchema   Specifies the object's schema.

Remarks

Call this member function to set the object schema stored in the archive object to *nSchema*. The next call to **GetObjectSchema** will return the value stored in *nSchema*.

Use **SetObjectSchema** for advanced versioning; for example, when you want to force a particular version to be read in a **Serialize** function of a derived class.

See Also   **CArchive::GetObjectSchema**

CArchive::SetStoreParams

void SetStoreParams(UINT *nHashSize* **= 2053, UINT** *nBlockSize* **= 128);**

Parameters

nHashSize   The size of the hash table for interface pointer maps. Should be a prime number.

nBlockSize Specifies the memory-allocation granularity for extending the parameters. Should be a power of 2 for the best performance.

Remarks

Use **SetStoreParams** when storing a large number of **CObject**-derived objects in an archive.

SetStoreParams allows you to set the hash table size and the block size of the map used to identify unique objects during the serialization process.

You must not call **SetStoreParams** after any objects are stored, or after **MapObject** or **WriteObject** is called.

Example

```
class CMyLargeDocument : public CDocument { ... };
void CMyLargeDocument::Serialize(CArchive& ar)
{
    if (ar.IsStoring())
        ar.SetStoreParams();  // use large defaults
    else
        ar.SetLoadParams();

    if (ar.IsStoring())
    {
        // code for storing CMyLargeDocument
    }
    else
    {
        // code for loading CMyLargeDocument
    }
}
```

See Also **CArchive::SetLoadParams**

CArchive::Write

void Write(const void* *lpBuf*, **UINT** *nMax* **);**
    throw(CFileException);

Parameters

lpBuf A pointer to a user-supplied buffer that contains the data to be written to the archive.

nMax An integer that specifies the number of bytes to be written to the archive.

Remarks

Writes a specified number of bytes to the archive. The archive does not format the bytes.

You can use the **Write** member function within your **Serialize** function to write ordinary structures that are contained in your objects.

Example

```
extern CArchive ar;
char pb[100];
ar.Write( pb, 100 );
```

See Also   **CArchive::Read**

CArchive::WriteClass

void WriteClass(const CRuntimeClass* *pClassRef* **);**

Parameters

pClassRef   A pointer to the **CRuntimeClass** structure that corresponds to the class reference requested.

Remarks

Use **WriteClass** to store the version and class information of a base class during serialization of the derived class. **WriteClass** writes a reference to the **CRuntimeClass** for the base class to the **CArchive**. Use **CArchive::ReadClass** to retrieve the reference.

WriteClass verifies that the archived class information is compatible with your runtime class. If it is not compatible, **WriteClass** will throw a **CArchiveException**.

Your runtime class must use **DECLARE_SERIAL** and **IMPLEMENT_SERIAL**; otherwise, **WriteClass** will throw a **CNotSupportedException**.

You can use **SerializeClass** instead of **WriteClass**, which handles both reading and writing of the class reference.

See Also   **CArchive::ReadClass, CArchive::GetObjectSchema, CArchive::SetObjectSchema, CArchive::SerializeClass, CArchiveException, CNotSupportedException**.

CArchive::WriteObject

void WriteObject(const CObject* *pOb* **);**
   throw(CFileException, CArchiveException);

Parameters

pOb   A constant pointer to the object being stored.

Remarks

Stores the specified **CObject** to the archive.

This function is normally called by the **CArchive** insertion (<<) operator overloaded for **CObject**. **WriteObject**, in turn, calls the **Serialize** function of the archived class.

You must use the **IMPLEMENT_SERIAL** macro to enable archiving. **WriteObject** writes the ASCII class name to the archive. This class name is validated later during the load process. A special encoding scheme prevents unnecessary duplication of the class name for multiple objects of the class. This scheme also prevents redundant storage of objects that are targets of more than one pointer.

The exact object encoding method (including the presence of the ASCII class name) is an implementation detail and could change in future versions of the library.

Note Finish creating, deleting, and updating all your objects before you begin to archive them. Your archive will be corrupted if you mix archiving with object modification.

See Also **CArchive::ReadObject**

CArchive::WriteString

void WriteString(LPCTSTR *lpsz* **);**
   throw(CFileException);

Parameters

lpsz Specifies a pointer to a buffer containing a null-terminated text string.

Remarks

Use this member function to write data from a buffer to the file associated with the **CArchive** object. The terminating null character ('\0') is not written to the file; nor is a newline automatically written.

WriteString throws an exception in response to several conditions, including the disk-full condition.

Write is also available, but rather than terminating on a null character, it writes the requested number of bytes to the file.

See Also **CArchive::Write**, **CArchive::Read**, **CArchive::ReadString**, **CFileException**

Operators

CArchive::operator <<

friend CArchive& operator <<(CArchive& *ar*, **const CObject*** *pOb* **);**
   throw(CArchiveException, CFileException);
CArchive& operator <<(BYTE *by* **);**
   throw(CArchiveException, CFileException);
CArchive& operator <<(WORD *w* **);**
   throw(CArchiveException, CFileException);

```
CArchive& operator <<( LONG l );
   throw( CArchiveException, CFileException );
CArchive& operator <<( DWORD dw );
   throw( CArchiveException, CFileException );
CArchive& operator <<( float f );
   throw( CArchiveException, CFileException );
CArchive& operator <<( double d );
   throw( CArchiveException, CFileException );
```

Return Value

A **CArchive** reference that enables multiple extraction operators on a single line.

Remarks

Stores the indicated object or primitive type to the archive.

If you used the **IMPLEMENT_SERIAL** macro in your class implementation, then the insertion operator overloaded for **CObject** calls the protected **WriteObject**. This function, in turn, calls the **Serialize** function of the class.

Example

```
long l;
int i;
extern CArchive ar;
if( ar.IsStoring() )
  ar << l << i;
```

See Also   CArchive::WriteObject, CObject::Serialize

CArchive::operator >>

```
friend CArchive& operator >>( CArchive& ar, CObject *& pOb );
   throw( CArchiveException, CFileException, CMemoryException );
friend CArchive& operator >>( CArchive& ar, const CObject *& pOb );
   throw( CArchiveException, CFileException, CMemoryException );
CArchive& operator >>( BYTE& by );
   throw( CArchiveException, CFileException );
CArchive& operator >>( WORD& w );
   throw( CArchiveException, CFileException );
CArchive& operator >>( LONG& l );
   throw( CArchiveException, CFileException );
CArchive& operator >>( DWORD& dw );
   throw( CArchiveException, CFileException );
CArchive& operator >>( float& f );
   throw( CArchiveException, CFileException );
CArchive& operator >>( double& d );
   throw( CArchiveException, CFileException );
```

Return Value

A **CArchive** reference that enables multiple insertion operators on a single line.

Remarks

Loads the indicated object or primitive type from the archive.

If you used the **IMPLEMENT_SERIAL** macro in your class implementation, then the extraction operators overloaded for **CObject** call the protected **ReadObject** function (with a nonzero run-time class pointer). This function, in turn, calls the **Serialize** function of the class.

Example

```
int i;
extern CArchive ar;
if( ar.IsLoading() )
  ar >> i;
```

See Also   **CArchive::ReadObject, CObject::Serialize**

Data Members

CArchive::m_pDocument

Remarks

Set to **NULL** by default, this pointer to a **CDocument** can be set to anything the user of the **CArchive** instance wants. A common usage of this pointer is to convey additional information about the serialization process to all objects being serialized. This is achieved by initializing the pointer with the document (a **CDocument**-derived class) that is being serialized, in such a way that objects within the document can access the document if necessary. This pointer is also used by **COleClientItem** objects during serialization.

The framework sets **m_pDocument** to the document being serialized when a user issues a File Open or Save command. If you serialize an Object Linking and Embedding (OLE) container document for reasons other than File Open or Save, you must explicitly set **m_pDocument**. For example, you would do this when serializing a container document to the Clipboard.

See Also   **CDocument, COleClientItem**

CArchiveException

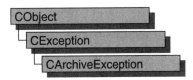

A **CArchiveException** object represents a serialization exception condition. The **CArchiveException** class includes a public data member that indicates the cause of the exception.

CArchiveException objects are constructed and thrown inside **CArchive** member functions. You can access these objects within the scope of a **CATCH** expression. The cause code is independent of the operating system. For more information about exception processing, see the article "Exceptions" in *Programming with MFC*.

#include <afx.h>

See Also **CArchive**, **AfxThrowArchiveException**

Data Members

m_cause	Indicates the exception cause.

Construction

CArchiveException	Constructs a **CArchiveException** object.

Member Functions

CArchiveException::CArchiveException

CArchiveException(int *cause* = CArchiveException::none);

Parameters

cause   An enumerated type variable that indicates the reason for the exception. For a list of the enumerators, see the **m_cause** data member.

Remarks

Constructs a **CArchiveException** object, storing the value of *cause* in the object. You can create a **CArchiveException** object on the heap and throw it yourself or let the global function **AfxThrowArchiveException** handle it for you.

Do not use this constructor directly; instead, call the global function **AfxThrowArchiveException**.

Data Members

CArchiveException::m_cause

Remarks

Specifies the cause of the exception. This data member is a public variable of type **int**. Its values are defined by a **CArchiveException** enumerated type. The enumerators and their meanings are as follows:

- **CArchiveException::none**   No error occurred.
- **CArchiveException::generic**   Unspecified error.
- **CArchiveException::readOnly**   Tried to write into an archive opened for loading.
- **CArchiveException::endOfFile**   Reached end of file while reading an object.
- **CArchiveException::writeOnly**   Tried to read from an archive opened for storing.
- **CArchiveException::badIndex**   Invalid file format.
- **CArchiveException::badClass**   Tried to read an object into an object of the wrong type.
- **CArchiveException::badSchema**   Tried to read an object with a different version of the class.

Note   These **CArchiveException** cause enumerators are distinct from the **CFileException** cause enumerators.

CArray

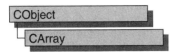

template< class *TYPE*, class *ARG_TYPE* > class CArray : public CObject

Parameters

TYPE   Template parameter specifying the type of objects stored in the array. TYPE is a parameter that is returned by **CArray**.

ARG_TYPE   Template parameter specifying the argument type used to access objects stored in the array. Often a reference to *TYPE*. ARG_TYPE is a parameter that is passed to CArray.

Remarks

The **CArray** class supports arrays that are are similar to C arrays, but can dynamically shrink and grow as necessary.

Array indexes always start at position 0. You can decide whether to fix the upper bound or allow the array to expand when you add elements past the current bound. Memory is allocated contiguously to the upper bound, even if some elements are null.

As with a C array, the access time for a **CArray** indexed element is constant and is independent of the array size.

Tip   Before using an array, use **SetSize** to establish its size and allocate memory for it. If you do not use **SetSize**, adding elements to your array causes it to be frequently reallocated and copied. Frequent reallocation and copying are inefficient and can fragment memory.

If you need a dump of individual elements in an array, you must set the depth of the **CDumpContext** object to 1 or greater.

Certain member functions of this class call global helper functions that must be customized for most uses of the **CArray** class. See the topic "Collection Class Helpers" in the "Macros and Globals" section.

When elements are removed from a **CArray** object, the helper function **DestructElements** is called. When elements are added, the helper function **ConstructElements** is called.

Array class derivation is similar to list derivation.

For more information on using **CArray**, see the article "Collections" in *Programming with MFC*.

#include <afxtempl.h>

See Also   CObArray, **DestructElements**, **ConstructElements**, "Collection Class Helpers"

Construction

CArray	Constructs an empty array.

Attributes

GetSize	Gets the number of elements in this array.
GetUpperBound	Returns the largest valid index.
SetSize	Sets the number of elements to be contained in this array.

Operations

FreeExtra	Frees all unused memory above the current upper bound.
RemoveAll	Removes all the elements from this array.

Element Access

GetAt	Returns the value at a given index.
SetAt	Sets the value for a given index; array not allowed to grow.
ElementAt	Returns a temporary reference to the element pointer within the array.
GetData	Allows access to elements in the array. Can be **NULL**.

Growing the Array

SetAtGrow	Sets the value for a given index; grows the array if necessary.
Add	Adds an element to the end of the array; grows the array if necessary.
Append	Appends another array to the array; grows the array if necessary
Copy	Copies another array to the array; grows the array if necessary.

Insertion/Removal

InsertAt	Inserts an element (or all the elements in another array) at a specified index.
RemoveAt	Removes an element at a specific index.

Operators

operator []	Sets or gets the element at the specified index.

Member Functions

CArray::Add

int Add(*ARG_TYPE newElement*);
    throw(CMemoryException);

Return Value

The index of the added element.

Parameters

ARG_TYPE   Template parameter specifying the type of arguments referencing elements in this array.

newElement   The element to be added to this array.

Remarks

Adds a new element to the end of an array, growing the array by 1. If **SetSize** has been used with an *nGrowBy* value greater than 1, then extra memory may be allocated. However, the upper bound will increase by only 1.

Example

```
// example for CArray::Add
CArray<CPoint,CPoint> ptArray;

CPoint pt(10,20);
ptArray.Add(pt);              // Element 0
ptArray.Add(CPoint(30,40));   // Element 1
```

See Also   **CArray::SetAt, CArray::SetAtGrow, CArray::InsertAt, CArray::operator []**

CArray::Append

int Append(const CArray& *src*);

Return Value

The index of the first appended element.

Parameters

src   Source of the elements to be appended to an array.

Remarks

Call this member function to add the contents of one array to the end of another. The arrays must be of the same type.

If necessary, **Append** may allocate extra memory to accommodate the elements appended to the array.

See Also   CArray::Copy

CArray::CArray

CArray( );

Remarks

Constructs an empty array. The array grows one element at a time.

See Also   CObArray::CObArray

CArray::Copy

void Copy(const CArray& *src* **);**

Parameters

src   Source of the elements to be copied to an array.

Remarks

Use this member function to copy the elements of one array to another.

Call this member function to overwrite the elements of one array with the elements of another array.

Copy does not free memory; however, if necessary, **Copy** may allocate extra memory to accommodate the elements copied to the array.

See Also   CArray::Append

CArray::ElementAt

TYPE& **ElementAt(int** *nIndex* **);**

Return Value

A reference to an array element.

Parameters

TYPE   Template parameter specifying the type of elements in the array.

nIndex   An integer index that is greater than or equal to 0 and less than or equal to the value returned by **GetUpperBound**.

Remarks

Returns a temporary reference to the specified element within the array. It is used to implement the left-side assignment operator for arrays.

See Also   **CArray::operator []**

CArray::FreeExtra

void FreeExtra( );

Remarks

Frees any extra memory that was allocated while the array was grown. This function has no effect on the size or upper bound of the array.

CArray::GetAt

TYPE **GetAt(int** *nIndex* **) const;**

Return Value

The array element currently at this index. If no element is at the index, a new object as constructed by the **ConstructElements** helper function is returned.

Parameters

TYPE   Template parameter specifying the type of the array elements.

nIndex   An integer index that is greater than or equal to 0 and less than or equal to the value returned by **GetUpperBound**.

Remarks

Returns the array element at the specified index.

See Also   **CArray::SetAt**, **CArray::operator []**, **ConstructElements**

CArray::GetData

const *TYPE** **GetData( ) const;**
TYPE* **GetData( );**

Return Value

A pointer to an array element.

Parameters

TYPE   Template parameter specifying the type of the array elements.

Remarks

Use this member function to gain direct access to the elements in an array. If no elements are available, **GetData** returns a null value.

While direct access to the elements of an array can help you work more quickly, use caution when calling **GetData**; any errors you make directly affect the elements of your array.

See Also   **CArray::GetAt**, **CArray::SetAt**, **CArray::ElementAt**

CArray::GetSize

int GetSize( ) const;

Remarks

Returns the size of the array. Since indexes are zero-based, the size is 1 greater than the largest index.

See Also   **CArray::GetUpperBound**, **CArray::SetSize**

CArray::GetUpperBound

int GetUpperBound( ) const;

Remarks

Returns the current upper bound of this array. Because array indexes are zero-based, this function returns a value 1 less than **GetSize**.

The condition **GetUpperBound( )** = −1 indicates that the array contains no elements.

See Also   **CArray::GetSize**, **CArray::SetSize**

CArray::InsertAt

void InsertAt(int *nIndex*, *ARG_TYPE newElement*, **int** *nCount* = **1**);
   throw(CMemoryException);
void InsertAt(int *nStartIndex*, **CArray*** *pNewArray*);
   throw(CMemoryException);

Parameters

nIndex   An integer index that may be greater than the value returned by **GetUpperBound**.

ARG_TYPE   Template parameter specifying the type of elements in this array.

newElement   The element to be placed in this array.

nCount   The number of times this element should be inserted (defaults to 1).

nStartIndex   An integer index that may be greater than the value returned by **GetUpperBound**.

pNewArray   Another array that contains elements to be added to this array.

Remarks

The first version of **InsertAt** inserts one element (or multiple copies of an element) at a specified index in an array. In the process, it shifts up (by incrementing the index) the existing element at this index, and it shifts up all the elements above it.

The second version inserts all the elements from another **CArray** collection, starting at the *nStartIndex* position.

The **SetAt** function, in contrast, replaces one specified array element and does not shift any elements.

Example

```
// example for CArray::InsertAt

CArray<CPoint,CPoint> ptArray;

ptArray.Add(CPoint(10,20)); // Element 0
ptArray.Add(CPoint(30,40)); // Element 1 (will become element 2)
ptArray.InsertAt(1, CPoint(50,60));  // New element 1
```

See Also   **GetUpperBound**, **CArray::SetAt**, **CArray::RemoveAt**

CArray::RemoveAll

void RemoveAll( );

Remarks

Removes all the elements from this array. If the array is already empty, the function still works.

CArray::RemoveAt

void RemoveAt(int *nIndex*, int *nCount* = 1);

Parameters

nIndex   An integer index that is greater than or equal to 0 and less than or equal to the value returned by **GetUpperBound**.

nCount   The number of elements to remove.

Remarks

Removes one or more elements starting at a specified index in an array. In the process, it shifts down all the elements above the removed element(s). It decrements the upper bound of the array but does not free memory.

If you try to remove more elements than are contained in the array above the removal point, then the Debug version of the library asserts.

See Also **CArray::SetAt**, **CArray::SetAtGrow**, **CArray::InsertAt**

CArray::SetAt

> **void SetAt(int** *nIndex***,** *ARG_TYPE newElement* **);**

Parameters

> *nIndex*   An integer index that is greater than or equal to 0 and less than or equal to the value returned by **GetUpperBound**.
>
> *ARG_TYPE*   Template parameter specifying the type of arguments used for referencing array elements.
>
> *newElement*   The new element value to be stored at the specified position.

Remarks

> Sets the array element at the specified index. **SetAt** will not cause the array to grow. Use **SetAtGrow** if you want the array to grow automatically.
>
> You must ensure that your index value represents a valid position in the array. If it is out of bounds, then the Debug version of the library asserts.
>
> **See Also** **CArray::GetAt**, **CArray::SetAtGrow**, **CArray::ElementAt**, **CArray::operator []**

CArray::SetAtGrow

> **void SetAtGrow(int** *nIndex***,** *ARG_TYPE newElement* **);**
>   **throw(CMemoryException);**

Parameters

> *nIndex*   An integer index that is greater than or equal to 0.
>
> *ARG_TYPE*   Template parameter specifying the type of elements in the array.
>
> *newElement*   The element to be added to this array. A **NULL** value is allowed.

Remarks

> Sets the array element at the specified index. The array grows automatically if necessary (that is, the upper bound is adjusted to accommodate the new element).

Example

```
// example for CArray::SetAtGrow
CArray<CPoint,CPoint> ptArray;

ptArray.Add(CPoint(10,20)); // Element 0
ptArray.Add(CPoint(30,40)); // Element 1
                            // Element 2 deliberately skipped
ptArray.SetAtGrow(3, CPoint(50,60)); // Element 3
```

See Also **CArray::GetAt**, **CArray::SetAt**, **CArray::ElementAt**, **CArray::operator []**

CArray::SetSize

void SetSize(int *nNewSize*, **int** *nGrowBy* **= –1);**
   throw(CMemoryException);

Parameters

nNewSize   The new array size (number of elements). Must be greater than or equal to 0.

nGrowBy   The minimum number of element slots to allocate if a size increase is necessary.

Remarks

Establishes the size of an empty or existing array; allocates memory if necessary.

If the new size is smaller than the old size, then the array is truncated and all unused memory is released.

Use this function to set the size of your array before you begin using the array. If you do not use **SetSize**, adding elements to your array causes it to be frequently reallocated and copied. Frequent reallocation and copying are inefficient and can fragment memory.

The *nGrowBy* parameter affects internal memory allocation while the array is growing. Its use never affects the array size as reported by **GetSize** and **GetUpperBound**. If the default value is used, MFC allocates memory in a way calculated to avoid memory fragmentation and optimize efficiency for most cases.

See Also **CArray::GetUpperBound**, **CArray::GetSize**

Operators

CArray::operator [ ]

TYPE& **operator [](int** *nIndex* **);**
TYPE **operator [](int** *nIndex* **) const;**

Parameters

TYPE   Template parameter specifying the type of elements in this array.

nIndex   Index of the element to be accessed.

Remarks

These subscript operators are a convenient substitute for the **SetAt** and **GetAt** functions.

The first operator, called for arrays that are not **const**, may be used on either the right (r-value) or the left (l-value) of an assignment statement. The second, called for **const** arrays, may be used only on the right.

The Debug version of the library asserts if the subscript (either on the left or right side of an assignment statement) is out of bounds.

See Also   **CArray::GetAt**, **CArray::SetAt**, **CArray::ElementAt**

CAsyncSocket

A **CAsyncSocket** object represents a Windows Socket — an endpoint of network communication. Class **CAsyncSocket** encapsulates the Windows Sockets API, providing an object-oriented abstraction for programmers who want to use Windows Sockets in conjunction with MFC. If you are working solely on the Windows NT platform, you can take advantage of additional socket functionality built-in to Windows NT. For more information, see "Windows Sockets for Windows NT" in the *Windows Sockets Reference*.

This class is based on the assumption that you understand network communications. You are responsible for handling blocking, byte-order differences, and conversions between Unicode and multibyte character set (MBCS) strings. If you want a more convenient interface that manages these issues for you, see class **CSocket**.

To use a **CAsyncSocket** object, call its constructor, then call the **Create** function to create the underlying socket handle (type **SOCKET**), except on accepted sockets. For a server socket call the **Listen** member function, and for a client socket call the **Connect** member function. The server socket should call the **Accept** function upon receiving a connection request. Use the remaining **CAsyncSocket** functions to carry out communications between sockets. Upon completion, destroy the **CAsyncSocket** object if it was created on the heap; the destructor automatically calls the **Close** function. The **SOCKET** data type is described in the article "Windows Sockets: Background" in *Programming with MFC*.

For more information, see "Windows Sockets: Using Class CAsyncSocket" and related articles in *Programming with MFC*, as well as "Programming with Sockets" in the Win32 SDK documentation.

#include <afxsock.h>

See Also   CSocket, CSocketFile

Construction

CAsyncSocket	Constructs a **CAsyncSocket** object.
Create	Creates a socket.

Attributes

Attach	Attaches a socket handle to a **CAsyncSocket** object.
Detach	Detaches a socket handle from a **CAsyncSocket** object.

FromHandle	Returns a pointer to a **CAsyncSocket** object, given a socket handle.
GetLastError	Gets the error status for the last operation that failed.
GetPeerName	Gets the address of the peer socket to which the socket is connected.
GetSockName	Gets the local name for a socket.
GetSockOpt	Retrieves a socket option.
SetSockOpt	Sets a socket option.

Operations

Accept	Accepts a connection on the socket.
AsyncSelect	Requests event notification for the socket.
Bind	Associates a local address with the socket.
Close	Closes the socket.
Connect	Establishes a connection to a peer socket.
IOCtl	Controls the mode of the socket.
Listen	Establishes a socket to listen for incoming connection requests.
Receive	Receives data from the socket.
ReceiveFrom	Receives a datagram and stores the source address.
Send	Sends data to a connected socket.
SendTo	Sends data to a specific destination.
ShutDown	Disables **Send** and/or **Receive** calls on the socket.

Overridable Notification Functions

OnAccept	Notifies a listening socket that it can accept pending connection requests by calling **Accept**.
OnClose	Notifies a socket that the socket connected to it has closed.
OnConnect	Notifies a connecting socket that the connection attempt is complete, whether successfully or in error.
OnOutOfBandData	Notifies a receiving socket that there is out-of-band data to be read on the socket, usually an urgent message.
OnReceive	Notifies a listening socket that there is data to be retrieved by calling **Receive**.
OnSend	Notifies a socket that it can send data by calling **Send**.

Data Members

m_hSocket	Indicates the **SOCKET** handle attached to this **CAsyncSocket** object.

Member Functions

CAsyncSocket::Accept

> **virtual BOOL Accept(CAsyncSocket&** *rConnectedSocket*, **SOCKADDR*** *lpSockAddr* = **NULL,**
> **int*** *lpSockAddrLen* = **NULL);**

Return Value

Nonzero if the function is successful; otherwise 0, and a specific error code can be retrieved by calling **GetLastError**. The following errors apply to this member function:

- **WSANOTINITIALISED** A successful **AfxSocketInit** must occur before using this API.

- **WSAENETDOWN** The Windows Sockets implementation detected that the network subsystem failed.

- **WSAEFAULT** The *lpSockAddrLen* argument is too small (less than the size of a **SOCKADDR** structure).

- **WSAEINPROGRESS** A blocking Windows Sockets call is in progress.

- **WSAEINVAL** **Listen** was not invoked prior to accept.

- **WSAEMFILE** The queue is empty upon entry to accept and there are no descriptors available.

- **WSAENOBUFS** No buffer space is available.

- **WSAENOTSOCK** The descriptor is not a socket.

- **WSAEOPNOTSUPP** The referenced socket is not a type that supports connection-oriented service.

- **WSAEWOULDBLOCK** The socket is marked as nonblocking and no connections are present to be accepted.

Parameters

rConnectedSocket A reference identifying a new socket that is available for connection.

lpSockAddr A pointer to a **SOCKADDR** structure that receives the address of the connecting socket, as known on the network. The exact format of the *lpSockAddr* argument is determined by the address family established when the socket was created. If *lpSockAddr* and/or *lpSockAddrLen* are equal to **NULL**, then no information about the remote address of the accepted socket is returned.

lpSockAddrLen A pointer to the length of the address in *lpSockAddr* in bytes. The *lpSockAddrLen* is a value-result parameter: it should initially contain the amount of space pointed to by *lpSockAddr*; on return it will contain the actual length (in bytes) of the address returned.

Remarks

Call this member function to accept a connection on a socket. This routine extracts the first connection in the queue of pending connections, creates a new socket with the same properties as this socket, and attaches it to *rConnectedSocket*. If no pending connections are present on the queue, **Accept** returns zero and **GetLastError** returns an error. The accepted socket (*rConnectedSocket*) cannot be used to accept more connections. The original socket remains open and listening.

The argument *lpSockAddr* is a result parameter that is filled in with the address of the connecting socket, as known to the communications layer. **Accept** is used with connection-based socket types such as **SOCK_STREAM**.

See Also   **CAsyncSocket::Bind**, **CAsyncSocket::Connect**, **CAsyncSocket::Listen**, **CAsyncSocket::Create**, **::WSAAsyncSelect**

CAsyncSocket::AsyncSelect

BOOL AsyncSelect(long *lEvent* **= FD_READ | FD_WRITE | FD_OOB | FD_ACCEPT | FD_CONNECT | FD_CLOSE);**

Return Value

Nonzero if the function is successful; otherwise 0, and a specific error code can be retrieved by calling **GetLastError**. The following errors apply to this member function:

- **WSANOTINITIALISED**   A successful **AfxSocketInit** must occur before using this API.

- **WSAENETDOWN**   The Windows Sockets implementation detected that the network subsystem failed.

- **WSAEINVAL**   Indicates that one of the specified parameters was invalid.

- **WSAEINPROGRESS**   A blocking Windows Sockets operation is in progress.

Parameters

lEvent   A bitmask which specifies a combination of network events in which the application is interested.

- **FD_READ**   Want to receive notification of readiness for reading.

- **FD_WRITE**   Want to receive notification when data is available to be read.

- **FD_OOB**   Want to receive notification of the arrival of out-of-band data.

- **FD_ACCEPT**   Want to receive notification of incoming connections.

- **FD_CONNECT** Want to receive notification of connection results.

- **FD_CLOSE** Want to receive notification when a socket has been closed by a peer.

Remarks

Call this member function to request event notification for a socket. This function is used to specify which MFC callback notification functions will be called for the socket. **AsyncSelect** automatically sets this socket to nonblocking mode. For more information, see the article "Windows Sockets: Socket Notifications" in *Programming with MFC* and "Programming with Sockets" in the Win32 SDK documentation.

See Also **CAsyncSocket::GetLastError, ::WSAAsyncSelect**

CAsyncSocket::Attach

BOOL Attach(SOCKET *hSocket*, **long** *lEvent* = **FD_READ | FD_WRITE | FD_OOB | FD_ACCEPT | FD_CONNECT | FD_CLOSE);**

Return Value

Nonzero if the function is successful.

Parameters

hSocket Contains a handle to a socket.

lEvent A bitmask which specifies a combination of network events in which the application is interested.

- **FD_READ** Want to receive notification of readiness for reading.

- **FD_WRITE** Want to receive notification when data is available to be read.

- **FD_OOB** Want to receive notification of the arrival of out-of-band data.

- **FD_ACCEPT** Want to receive notification of incoming connections.

- **FD_CONNECT** Want to receive notification of connection results.

- **FD_CLOSE** Want to receive notification when a socket has been closed by a peer.

Remarks

Call this member function to attach the *hSocket* handle to an **CAsyncSocket** object. The **SOCKET** handle is stored in the object's **m_hSocket** data member.

See Also **CAsyncSocket::Detach**

CAsyncSocket::Bind

BOOL Bind(UINT *nSocketPort***, LPCTSTR** *lpszSocketAddress* **= NULL);**
BOOL Bind (const SOCKADDR* *lpSockAddr***, int** *nSockAddrLen* **);**

Return Value

Nonzero if the function is successful; otherwise 0, and a specific error code can be retrieved by calling **GetLastError**. The following errors apply to this member function:

- **WSANOTINITIALISED**   A successful **AfxSocketInit** must occur before using this API.

- **WSAENETDOWN**   The Windows Sockets implementation detected that the network subsystem failed.

- **WSAEADDRINUSE**   The specified address is already in use. (See the **SO_REUSEADDR** socket option under **SetSockOpt**.)

- **WSAEFAULT**   The *nSockAddrLen* argument is too small (less than the size of a **SOCKADDR** structure).

- **WSAEINPROGRESS**   A blocking Windows Sockets call is in progress.

- **WSAEAFNOSUPPORT**   The specified address family is not supported by this port.

- **WSAEINVAL**   The socket is already bound to an address.

- **WSAENOBUFS**   Not enough buffers available, too many connections.

- **WSAENOTSOCK**   The descriptor is not a socket.

Parameters

nSocketPort   The port identifying the socket application.

lpszSocketAddress   The network address, a dotted number such as "128.56.22.8".

lpSockAddr   A pointer to a **SOCKADDR** structure that contains the address to assign to this socket.

nSockAddrLen   The length of the address in *lpSockAddr* in bytes.

Remarks

Call this member function to associate a local address with the socket. This routine is used on an unconnected datagram or stream socket, before subsequent **Connect** or **Listen** calls. Before it can accept connection requests, a listening server socket must select a port number and make it known to Windows Sockets by calling **Bind**. **Bind** establishes the local association (host address/port number) of the socket by assigning a local name to an unnamed socket.

See Also   **CAsyncSocket::Connect**, **CAsyncSocket::Listen**,
CAsyncSocket::GetSockName, **CAsyncSocket::SetSockOpt**,
CAsyncSocket::Create

CAsyncSocket::CAsyncSocket

CAsyncSocket( );

Remarks

Constructs a blank socket object. After constructing the object, you must call its **Create** member function to create the **SOCKET** data structure and bind its address. (On the server side of a Windows Sockets communication, when the listening socket creates a socket to use in the **Accept** call, you do not call **Create** for that socket.)

See Also   **CAsyncSocket::Create**

CAsyncSocket::Close

virtual void Close( );

Remarks

This function closes the socket. More precisely, it releases the socket descriptor, so that further references to it will fail with the error **WSAENOTSOCK**. If this is the last reference to the underlying socket, the associated naming information and queued data are discarded. The socket object's destructor calls **Close** for you.

For **CAsyncSocket**, but not for **CSocket**, the semantics of **Close** are affected by the socket options **SO_LINGER** and **SO_DONTLINGER**. For further information, see member function **GetSockOpt** and "Programming with Sockets" in the Win32 SDK documentation.

See Also   **CAsyncSocket::Accept, CAsyncSocket::CAsyncSocket, CAsyncSocket::IOCtl, CAsyncSocket::GetSockOpt, CAsyncSocket::SetSockOpt, CAsyncSocket::AsyncSelect**

CAsyncSocket::Connect

BOOL Connect(LPCTSTR *lpszHostAddress*, **UINT** *nHostPort* **);**
BOOL Connect(const SOCKADDR* *lpSockAddr*, **int** *nSockAddrLen* **);**

Return Value

Nonzero if the function is successful; otherwise 0, and a specific error code can be retrieved by calling **GetLastError**. If this indicates an error code of **WSAEWOULDBLOCK**, and your application is using the overridable callbacks, your application will receive an **OnConnect** message when the connect operation is complete. The following errors apply to this member function:

- **WSANOTINITIALISED**   A successful **AfxSocketInit** must occur before using this API.

- **WSAENETDOWN**   The Windows Sockets implementation detected that the network subsystem failed.

- **WSAEADDRINUSE**   The specified address is already in use.

- **WSAEINPROGRESS**   A blocking Windows Sockets call is in progress.

- **WSAEADDRNOTAVAIL**   The specified address is not available from the local machine.

- **WSAEAFNOSUPPORT**   Addresses in the specified family cannot be used with this socket.

- **WSAECONNREFUSED**   The attempt to connect was rejected.

- **WSAEDESTADDREQ**   A destination address is required.

- **WSAEFAULT**   The *nSockAddrLen* argument is incorrect.

- **WSAEINVAL**   The socket is not already bound to an address.

- **WSAEISCONN**   The socket is already connected.

- **WSAEMFILE**   No more file descriptors are available.

- **WSAENETUNREACH**   The network cannot be reached from this host at this time.

- **WSAENOBUFS**   No buffer space is available. The socket cannot be connected.

- **WSAENOTSOCK**   The descriptor is not a socket.

- **WSAETIMEDOUT**   Attempt to connect timed out without establishing a connection.

- **WSAEWOULDBLOCK**   The socket is marked as nonblocking and the connection cannot be completed immediately.

Parameters

lpszHostAddress   The network address of the socket to which this object is connected: a machine name such as "ftp.microsoft.com", or a dotted number such as "128.56.22.8".

nHostPort   The port identifying the socket application.

lpSockAddr   A pointer to a **SOCKADDR** structure that contains the address of the connected socket.

nSockAddrLen   The length of the address in *lpSockAddr* in bytes.

Remarks

Call this member function to establish a connection to an unconnected stream or datagram socket. If the socket is unbound, unique values are assigned to the local association by the system, and the socket is marked as bound. Note that if the address field of the name structure is all zeroes, **Connect** will return zero. To get extended error information, call the **GetLastError** member function.

For stream sockets (type **SOCK_STREAM**), an active connection is initiated to the foreign host. When the socket call completes successfully, the socket is ready to send/receive data.

For a datagram socket (type **SOCK_DGRAM**), a default destination is set, which will be used on subsequent **Send** and **Receive** calls.

See Also **CAsyncSocket::Accept**, **CAsyncSocket::Bind**, **CAsyncSocket::GetSockName**, **CAsyncSocket::Create**, **CAsyncSocket::AsyncSelect**

CAsyncSocket::Create

BOOL Create(UINT *nSocketPort* **= 0, int** *nSocketType* **= SOCK_STREAM, long** *lEvent* **= FD_READ I FD_WRITE I FD_OOB I FD_ACCEPT I FD_CONNECT I FD_CLOSE, LPCTSTR** *lpszSocketAddress* **= NULL);**

Return Value

Nonzero if the function is successful; otherwise 0, and a specific error code can be retrieved by calling **GetLastError**. The following errors apply to this member function:

- **WSANOTINITIALISED** A successful **AfxSocketInit** must occur before using this API.
- **WSAENETDOWN** The Windows Sockets implementation detected that the network subsystem failed.
- **WSAEAFNOSUPPORT** The specified address family is not supported.
- **WSAEINPROGRESS** A blocking Windows Sockets operation is in progress.
- **WSAEMFILE** No more file descriptors are available.
- **WSAENOBUFS** No buffer space is available. The socket cannot be created.
- **WSAEPROTONOSUPPORT** The specified port is not supported.
- **WSAEPROTOTYPE** The specified port is the wrong type for this socket.
- **WSAESOCKTNOSUPPORT** The specified socket type is not supported in this address family.

Parameters

nSocketPort A well-known port to be used with the socket, or 0 if you want Windows Sockets to select a port.

nSocketType **SOCK_STREAM** or **SOCK_DGRAM**.

lEvent A bitmask which specifies a combination of network events in which the application is interested.

- **FD_READ**   Want to receive notification of readiness for reading.

- **FD_WRITE**   Want to receive notification of readiness for writing.

- **FD_OOB**   Want to receive notification of the arrival of out-of-band data.

- **FD_ACCEPT**   Want to receive notification of incoming connections.

- **FD_CONNECT**   Want to receive notification of completed connection.

- **FD_CLOSE**   Want to receive notification of socket closure.

lpszSockAddress   A pointer to the address of a **SOCKADDR** structure that contains
the network address.

Remarks

Call the **Create** member function after constructing a socket object to create the
Windows socket and attach it. **Create** then calls **Bind** to bind the socket to the
specified address. The following socket types are supported:

- **SOCK_STREAM**   Provides sequenced, reliable, full-duplex, connection-based
byte streams. Uses the Transmission Control Protocol (TCP) for the Internet
address family.

- **SOCK_DGRAM**   Supports datagrams, which are connectionless, unreliable
packets of a fixed (typically small) maximum length. Uses the User Datagram
Protocol (UDP) for the Internet address family.

  Note   The **Accept** member function takes a reference to a new, empty **CSocket** object as
  its parameter. You must construct this object before you call **Accept**. Keep in mind that if
  this socket object goes out of scope, the connection closes. Do not call **Create** for this new
  socket object.

For more information about stream and datagram sockets, see the articles "Windows
Sockets: Background" and "Windows Sockets: Ports and Socket Addresses" in
Programming with MFC and "Programming with Sockets" in the Win32 SDK
documentation.

See Also   **CAsyncSocket::Accept, CAsyncSocket::Bind, CAsyncSocket::Connect,
CAsyncSocket::GetSockName, CAsyncSocket::IOCtl, CAsyncSocket::Listen,
CAsyncSocket::Receive, CAsyncSocket::Send, CAsyncSocket::ShutDown**

CAsyncSocket::Detach

SOCKET Detach( );

Remarks

Call this member function to detach the **SOCKET** handle in the **m_hSocket** data
member from the **CAsyncSocket** object and set **m_hSocket** to **NULL**.

See Also   **CAsyncSocket::Attach**

CAsyncSocket::FromHandle

static CAsyncSocket* PASCAL FromHandle(SOCKET *hSocket* **);**

Return Value

A pointer to an **CAsyncSocket** object, or **NULL** if there is no **CAsyncSocket** object attached to *hSocket*.

Parameters

hSocket   Contains a handle to a socket.

Remarks

Returns a pointer to a **CAsyncSocket** object. When given a **SOCKET** handle, if a **CAsyncSocket** object is not attached to the handle, the member function returns **NULL**.

See Also   **CSocket::FromHandle, CAsyncSocket::Attach, CAsyncSocket::Detach**

CAsyncSocket::GetLastError

static int GetLastError( );

Return Value

The return value indicates the error code for the last Windows Sockets API routine performed by this thread.

Remarks

Call this member function to get the error status for the last operation that failed. When a particular member function indicates that an error has occurred, **GetLastError** should be called to retrieve the appropriate error code. See the individual member function descriptions for a list of applicable error codes.

For more information about the error codes, see "Programming with Sockets" in the Win32 SDK documentation.

See Also   **::WSASetLastError**

CAsyncSocket::GetPeerName

BOOL GetPeerName(CString& *rPeerAddress*, **UINT&** *rPeerPort* **);**
BOOL GetPeerName(SOCKADDR* *lpSockAddr*, **int*** *lpSockAddrLen* **);**

Return Value

Nonzero if the function is successful; otherwise 0, and a specific error code can be retrieved by calling **GetLastError**. The following errors apply to this member function.

- **WSANOTINITIALISED** A successful **AfxSocketInit** must occur before using this API.
- **WSAENETDOWN** The Windows Sockets implementation detected that the network subsystem failed.
- **WSAEFAULT** The *lpSockAddrLen* argument is not large enough.
- **WSAEINPROGRESS** A blocking Windows Sockets call is in progress.
- **WSAENOTCONN** The socket is not connected.
- **WSAENOTSOCK** The descriptor is not a socket.

Parameters

rPeerAddress Reference to a **CString** object that receives a dotted number IP address.

rPeerPort Reference to a **UINT** that stores a port.

lpSockAddr A pointer to the **SOCKADDR** structure that receives the name of the peer socket.

lpSockAddrLen A pointer to the length of the address in *lpSockAddr* in bytes. On return, the *lpSockAddrLen* argument contains the actual size of *lpSockAddr* returned in bytes.

Remarks

Call this member function to get the address of the peer socket to which this socket is connected.

See Also **CAsyncSocket::Bind**, **CAsyncSocket::Connect**, **CAsyncSocket::Create**, **CAsyncSocket::GetSockName**

CAsyncSocket::GetSockName

BOOL GetSockName(CString& *rSocketAddress*, **UINT&** *rSocketPort* **);**
BOOL GetSockName(SOCKADDR* *lpSockAddr*, **int*** *lpSockAddrLen* **);**

Return Value

Nonzero if the function is successful; otherwise 0, and a specific error code can be retrieved by calling **GetLastError**. The following errors apply to this member function:

- **WSANOTINITIALISED** A successful **AfxSocketInit** must occur before using this API.
- **WSAENETDOWN** The Windows Sockets implementation detected that the network subsystem failed.
- **WSAEFAULT** The *lpSockAddrLen* argument is not large enough.
- **WSAEINPROGRESS** A blocking Windows Sockets operation is in progress.

- **WSAENOTSOCK**   The descriptor is not a socket.

- **WSAEINVAL**   The socket has not been bound to an address with **Bind**.

Parameters

rSocketAddress   Reference to a **CString** object that receives a dotted number IP address.

rSocketPort   Reference to a **UINT** that stores a port.

lpSockAddr   A pointer to a **SOCKADDR** structure that receives the address of the socket.

lpSockAddrLen   A pointer to the length of the address in *lpSockAddr* in bytes.

Remarks

Call this member function to get the local name for a socket. This call is especially useful when a **Connect** call has been made without doing a **Bind** first; this call provides the only means by which you can determine the local association which has been set by the system. For more information, see "Programming with Sockets" in the Win32 SDK documentation.

See Also   **CAsyncSocket::Bind**, **CAsyncSocket::Create**, **CAsyncSocket::GetPeerName**

CAsyncSocket::GetSockOpt

BOOL GetSockOpt(int *nOptionName***, void*** *lpOptionValue***, int*** *lpOptionLen***, int** *nLevel* **= SOL_SOCKET);**

Return Value

Nonzero if the function is successful; otherwise 0, and a specific error code can be retrieved by calling **GetLastError**. If an option was never set with **SetSockOpt**, then **GetSockOpt** returns the default value for the option. The following errors apply to this member function:

- **WSANOTINITIALISED**   A successful **AfxSocketInit** must occur before using this API.

- **WSAENETDOWN**   The Windows Sockets implementation detected that the network subsystem failed.

- **WSAEFAULT**   The *lpOptionLen* argument was invalid.

- **WSAEINPROGRESS**   A blocking Windows Sockets operation is in progress.

- **WSAENOPROTOOPT**   The option is unknown or unsupported. In particular, **SO_BROADCAST** is not supported on sockets of type **SOCK_STREAM**, while **SO_ACCEPTCONN, SO_DONTLINGER, SO_KEEPALIVE, SO_LINGER,** and **SO_OOBINLINE** are not supported on sockets of type **SOCK_DGRAM**.

- **WSAENOTSOCK**   The descriptor is not a socket.

Parameters

nOptionName   The socket option for which the value is to be retrieved.

lpOptionValue   A pointer to the buffer in which the value for the requested option is to be returned. The value associated with the selected option is returned in the buffer *lpOptionValue*. The integer pointed to by *lpOptionLen* should originally contain the size of this buffer in bytes; and on return, it will be set to the size of the value returned. For **SO_LINGER**, this will be the size of a **LINGER** structure; for all other options it will be the size of a **BOOL** or an **int**, depending on the option. See the list of options and their sizes in the Remarks section.

lpOptionLen   A pointer to the size of the *lpOptionValue* buffer in bytes.

nLevel   The level at which the option is defined; the only supported levels are **SOL_SOCKET** and **IPPROTO_TCP**.

Remarks

Call this member function to retrieve a socket option. **GetSockOpt** retrieves the current value for a socket option associated with a socket of any type, in any state, and stores the result in *lpOptionValue*. Options affect socket operations, such as the routing of packets, out-of-band data transfer, and so on.

The following options are supported for **GetSockOpt**. The Type identifies the type of data addressed by *lpOptionValue*. The **TCP_NODELAY** option uses level **IPPROTO_TCP**; all other options use level **SOL_SOCKET**.

Value	Type	Meaning
SO_ACCEPTCONN	**BOOL**	Socket is listening.
SO_BROADCAST	**BOOL**	Socket is configured for the transmission of broadcast messages.
SO_DEBUG	**BOOL**	Debugging is enabled.
SO_DONTLINGER	**BOOL**	If true, the **SO_LINGER** option is disabled.
SO_DONTROUTE	**BOOL**	Routing is disabled.
SO_ERROR	**int**	Retrieve error status and clear.
SO_KEEPALIVE	**BOOL**	Keep-alives are being sent.
SO_LINGER	**struct LINGER**	Returns the current linger options.
SO_OOBINLINE	**BOOL**	Out-of-band data is being received in the normal data stream.
SO_RCVBUF	**int**	Buffer size for receives.
SO_REUSEADDR	**BOOL**	The socket can be bound to an address which is already in use.
SO_SNDBUF	**int**	Buffer size for sends.

Value	Type	Meaning
SO_TYPE	int	The type of the socket (for example, SOCK_STREAM).
TCP_NODELAY	BOOL	Disables the Nagle algorithm for send coalescing.

Berkeley Software Distribution (BSD) options not supported for **GetSockOpt** are:

Value	Type	Meaning
SO_RCVLOWAT	int	Receive low water mark.
SO_RCVTIMEO	int	Receive timeout.
SO_SNDLOWAT	int	Send low water mark.
SO_SNDTIMEO	int	Send timeout.
IP_OPTIONS		Get options in IP header.
TCP_MAXSEG	int	Get TCP maximum segment size.

Calling **GetSockOpt** with an unsupported option will result in an error code of **WSAENOPROTOOPT** being returned from **GetLastError**.

See Also   **CAsyncSocket::SetSockOpt**

CAsyncSocket::IOCtl

BOOL IOCtl(long *lCommand***, DWORD*** *lpArgument* **);**

Return Value

Nonzero if the function is successful; otherwise 0, and a specific error code can be retrieved by calling **GetLastError**. The following errors apply to this member function:

- **WSANOTINITIALISED**   A successful **AfxSocketInit** must occur before using this API.

- **WSAENETDOWN**   The Windows Sockets implementation detected that the network subsystem failed.

- **WSAEINVAL**   *lCommand* is not a valid command, or *lpArgument* is not an acceptable parameter for *lCommand*, or the command is not applicable to the type of socket supplied.

- **WSAEINPROGRESS**   A blocking Windows Sockets operation is in progress.

- **WSAENOTSOCK**   The descriptor is not a socket.

Parameters

    lCommand The command to perform on the socket.

    lpArgument A pointer to a parameter for *lCommand*.

Remarks

Call this member function to control the mode of a socket. This routine can be used on any socket in any state. It is used to get or retrieve operating parameters associated with the socket, independent of the protocol and communications subsystem. The following commands are supported:

- **FIONBIO** Enable or disable nonblocking mode on the socket. The *lpArgument* parameter points at a **DWORD**, which is nonzero if nonblocking mode is to be enabled and zero if it is to be disabled. If **AsyncSelect** has been issued on a socket, then any attempt to use **IOCtl** to set the socket back to blocking mode will fail with **WSAEINVAL**. To set the socket back to blocking mode and prevent the **WSAEINVAL** error, an application must first disable **AsyncSelect** by calling **AsyncSelect** with the *lEvent* parameter equal to 0, then call **IOCtl**.

- **FIONREAD** Determine the maximum number of bytes that can be read with one **Receive** call from this socket. The *lpArgument* parameter points at a **DWORD** in which **IOCtl** stores the result. If this socket is of type **SOCK_STREAM**, **FIONREAD** returns the total amount of data which can be read in a single **Receive**; this is normally the same as the total amount of data queued on the socket. If this socket is of type **SOCK_DGRAM**, **FIONREAD** returns the size of the first datagram queued on the socket.

- **SIOCATMARK** Determine whether all out-of-band data has been read. This applies only to a socket of type **SOCK_STREAM** which has been configured for in-line reception of any out-of-band data (**SO_OOBINLINE**). If no out-of-band data is waiting to be read, the operation returns nonzero. Otherwise it returns 0, and the next **Receive** or **ReceiveFrom** performed on the socket will retrieve some or all of the data preceding the "mark"; the application should use the **SIOCATMARK** operation to determine whether any data remains. If there is any normal data preceding the "urgent" (out-of-band) data, it will be received in order. (Note that a **Receive** or **ReceiveFrom** will never mix out-of-band and normal data in the same call.) The *lpArgument* parameter points at a **DWORD** in which **IOCtl** stores the result.

This function is a subset of **ioctl()** as used in Berkeley sockets. In particular, there is no command which is equivalent to **FIOASYNC**, while **SIOCATMARK** is the only socket-level command which is supported.

See Also **CAsyncSocket::AsyncSelect**, **CAsyncSocket::Create**, **CAsyncSocket::GetSockOpt**, **CAsyncSocket::SetSockOpt**

CAsyncSocket::Listen

BOOL Listen(int *nConnectionBacklog* **= 5);**

Return Value

Nonzero if the function is successful; otherwise 0, and a specific error code can be retrieved by calling **GetLastError**. The following errors apply to this member function:

- **WSANOTINITIALISED** A successful **AfxSocketInit** must occur before using this API.

- **WSAENETDOWN** The Windows Sockets implementation detected that the network subsystem failed.

- **WSAEADDRINUSE** An attempt has been made to listen on an address in use.

- **WSAEINPROGRESS** A blocking Windows Sockets operation is in progress.

- **WSAEINVAL** The socket has not been bound with **Bind** or is already connected.

- **WSAEISCONN** The socket is already connected.

- **WSAEMFILE** No more file descriptors are available.

- **WSAENOBUFS** No buffer space is available.

- **WSAENOTSOCK** The descriptor is not a socket.

- **WSAEOPNOTSUPP** The referenced socket is not of a type that supports the **Listen** operation.

Parameters

nConnectionBacklog The maximum length to which the queue of pending connections can grow. Valid range is from 1 to 5.

Remarks

Call this member function to listen for incoming connection requests. To accept connections, the socket is first created with **Create**, a backlog for incoming connections is specified with **Listen**, and then the connections are accepted with **Accept**. **Listen** applies only to sockets that support connections, that is, those of type **SOCK_STREAM**. This socket is put into "passive" mode where incoming connections are acknowledged and queued pending acceptance by the process.

This function is typically used by servers (or any application that wants to accept connections) that could have more than one connection request at a time: if a connection request arrives with the queue full, the client will receive an error with an indication of **WSAECONNREFUSED**.

Listen attempts to continue to function rationally when there are no available ports (descriptors). It will accept connections until the queue is emptied. If ports become available, a later call to **Listen** or **Accept** will refill the queue to the current or most recent "backlog," if possible, and resume listening for incoming connections.

See Also   **CAsyncSocket::Accept**, **CAsyncSocket::Connect**, **CAsyncSocket::Create**

CAsyncSocket::OnAccept

virtual void OnAccept(int *nErrorCode* **);**

Parameters

nErrorCode   The most recent error on a socket. The following error codes applies to the **OnAccept** member function:

- **0**   The function executed successfully.

- **WSAENETDOWN**   The Windows Sockets implementation detected that the network subsystem failed.

Remarks

Called by the framework to notify a listening socket that it can accept pending connection requests by calling the **Accept** member function. For more information, see the article "Windows Sockets: Socket Notifications" in *Programming with MFC*.

See Also   **CAsyncSocket::Accept**, **CAsyncSocket::GetLastError**, **CAsyncSocket::OnClose**, **CAsyncSocket::OnConnect**, **CAsyncSocket::OnOutOfBandData**, **CAsyncSocket::OnReceive**, **CAsyncSocket::OnSend**

CAsyncSocket::OnClose

virtual void OnClose(int *nErrorCode* **);**

Parameters

nErrorCode   The most recent error on a socket. The following error codes apply to the **OnClose** member function:

- **0**   The function executed successfully.

- **WSAENETDOWN**   The Windows Sockets implementation detected that the network subsystem failed.

- **WSAECONNRESET**   The connection was reset by the remote side.

- **WSAECONNABORTED**   The connection was aborted due to timeout or other failure.

Remarks

Called by the framework to notify this socket that the connected socket is closed by its process. For more information, see the article "Windows Sockets: Socket Notifications" in *Programming with MFC*.

See Also **CAsyncSocket::Close, CAsyncSocket::GetLastError, CAsyncSocket::OnAccept, CAsyncSocket::OnConnect, CAsyncSocket::OnOutOfBandData, CAsyncSocket::OnReceive, CAsyncSocket::OnSend**

CAsyncSocket::OnConnect

virtual void OnConnect(int *nErrorCode* **);**

Parameters

nErrorCode The most recent error on a socket. The following error codes apply to the **OnConnect** member function:

- **0** The function executed successfully.

- **WSAEADDRINUSE** The specified address is already in use.

- **WSAEADDRNOTAVAIL** The specified address is not available from the local machine.

- **WSAEAFNOSUPPORT** Addresses in the specified family cannot be used with this socket.

- **WSAECONNREFUSED** The attempt to connect was forcefully rejected.

- **WSAEDESTADDRREQ** A destination address is required.

- **WSAEFAULT** The *lpSockAddrLen* argument is incorrect.

- **WSAEINVAL** The socket is already bound to an address.

- **WSAEISCONN** The socket is already connected.

- **WSAEMFILE** No more file descriptors are available.

- **WSAENETUNREACH** The network cannot be reached from this host at this time.

- **WSAENOBUFS** No buffer space is available. The socket cannot be connected.

- **WSAENOTCONN** The socket is not connected.

- **WSAENOTSOCK** The descriptor is a file, not a socket.

- **WSAETIMEDOUT** The attempt to connect timed out without establishing a connection.

Remarks

Called by the framework to notify this connecting socket that its connection attempt is completed, whether successfully or in error.

Important In **CSocket**, the **OnSend** and **OnConnect** notification functions are never called.

Note To send data, you simply call **Send**, which won't return until all the data has been sent. The use of the notification to complete this task is an MFC implementation detail for **CSocket**. For connections, you simply call **Connect**, which will return when the connection is completed (either successfully or in error). How connection notifications are handled is also an MFC implementation detail.

For more information, see the article "Windows Sockets: Socket Notifications" in *Programming with MFC*.

See Also **CAsyncSocket::Connect, CAsyncSocket::GetLastError, CAsyncSocket::OnAccept, CAsyncSocket::OnClose, CAsyncSocket::OnOutOfBandData, CAsyncSocket::OnReceive, CAsyncSocket::OnSend**

CAsyncSocket::OnOutOfBandData

virtual void OnOutOfBandData(int *nErrorCode* **);**

Parameters

nErrorCode The most recent error on a socket. The following error codes apply to the **OnOutOfBandData** member function:

- **0** The function executed successfully.

- **WSAENETDOWN** The Windows Sockets implementation detected that the network subsystem failed.

Remarks

Called by the framework to notify the receiving socket that the sending socket has out-of-band data to send. Out-of-band data is a logically independent channel that is associated with each pair of connected sockets of type **SOCK_STREAM**. The channel is generally used to send urgent data.

MFC supports out-of-band data, but users of class **CAsyncSocket** are discouraged from using it. The easier way is to create a second socket for passing such data. For more information about out-of-band data, see the article "Windows Sockets: Socket Notifications" in *Programming with MFC* and "Programming with Sockets" in the Win32 SDK documentation.

See Also **CAsyncSocket::GetLastError, CAsyncSocket::OnAccept, CAsyncSocket::OnClose, CAsyncSocket::OnConnect, CAsyncSocket::OnReceive, CAsyncSocket::OnSend**

CAsyncSocket::OnReceive

virtual void OnReceive(int *nErrorCode* **);**

Parameters

nErrorCode   The most recent error on a socket. The following error codes apply to the **OnReceive** member function:

- **0**   The function executed successfully.

- **WSAENETDOWN**   The Windows Sockets implementation detected that the network subsystem failed.

Remarks

Called by the framework to notify this socket that there is data in the buffer that can be retrieved by calling the **Receive** member function. For more information, see the article "Windows Sockets: Socket Notifications" in *Programming with MFC*.

See Also   CAsyncSocket::GetLastError, CAsyncSocket::OnAccept, CAsyncSocket::OnClose, CAsyncSocket::OnConnect, CAsyncSocket::OnOutOfBandData, CAsyncSocket::OnSend, CAsyncSocket::Receive

---

CAsyncSocket::OnSend

virtual void OnSend(int *nErrorCode* **);**

Parameters

nErrorCode   The most recent error on a socket. The following error codes apply to the **OnSend** member function:

- **0**   The function executed successfully.

- **WSAENETDOWN**   The Windows Sockets implementation detected that the network subsystem failed.

Remarks

Called by the framework to notify the socket that it can now send data by calling the **Send** member function.

Important   In **CSocket**, the **OnSend** and **OnConnect** notification functions are never called.

Note   To send data, you simply call **Send**, which won't return until all the data has been sent. The use of the notification to complete this task is an MFC implementation detail for **CSocket**. For connections, you simply call **Connect**, which will return when the connection is completed (either successfully or in error). How connection notifications are handled is also an MFC implementation detail.

For more information, see the article "Windows Sockets: Socket Notifications" in *Programming with MFC*.

See Also **CAsyncSocket::GetLastError**, **CAsyncSocket::OnAccept**, **CAsyncSocket::OnClose**, **CAsyncSocket::OnConnect**, **CAsyncSocket::OnOutOfBandData**, **CAsyncSocket::OnReceive**, **CAsyncSocket::Send**

CAsyncSocket::Receive

virtual int Receive(void* *lpBuf*, **int** *nBufLen*, **int** *nFlags* = **0**);

Return Value

If no error occurs, **Receive** returns the number of bytes received. If the connection has been closed, it returns 0. Otherwise, a value of **SOCKET_ERROR** is returned, and a specific error code can be retrieved by calling **GetLastError**. The following errors apply to this member function:

- **WSANOTINITIALISED** A successful **AfxSocketInit** must occur before using this API.

- **WSAENETDOWN** The Windows Sockets implementation detected that the network subsystem failed.

- **WSAENOTCONN** The socket is not connected.

- **WSAEINPROGRESS** A blocking Windows Sockets operation is in progress.

- **WSAENOTSOCK** The descriptor is not a socket.

- **WSAEOPNOTSUPP** **MSG_OOB** was specified, but the socket is not of type **SOCK_STREAM**.

- **WSAESHUTDOWN** The socket has been shut down; it is not possible to call **Receive** on a socket after **ShutDown** has been invoked with *nHow* set to 0 or 2.

- **WSAEWOULDBLOCK** The socket is marked as nonblocking and the **Receive** operation would block.

- **WSAEMSGSIZE** The datagram was too large to fit into the specified buffer and was truncated.

- **WSAEINVAL** The socket has not been bound with **Bind**.

- **WSAECONNABORTED** The virtual circuit was aborted due to timeout or other failure.

- **WSAECONNRESET** The virtual circuit was reset by the remote side.

Parameters

lpBuf A buffer for the incoming data.

nBufLen The length of *lpBuf* in bytes.

nFlags Specifies the way in which the call is made. The semantics of this function are determined by the socket options and the *nFlags* parameter. The latter is constructed by combining any of the following values with the C++ **OR** operator:

- **MSG_PEEK** Peek at the incoming data. The data is copied into the buffer but is not removed from the input queue.

- **MSG_OOB** Process out-of-band data (see "Programming with Sockets" in the Win32 SDK documentation for a discussion of this topic).

Remarks

Call this member function to receive data from a socket. This function is used for connected stream or datagram sockets and is used to read incoming data.

For sockets of type **SOCK_STREAM**, as much information as is currently available up to the size of the buffer supplied is returned. If the socket has been configured for in-line reception of out-of-band data (socket option **SO_OOBINLINE**) and out-of-band data is unread, only out-of-band data will be returned. The application can use the **IOCtl SIOCATMARK** option or **OnOutOfBandData** to determine whether any more out-of-band data remains to be read.

For datagram sockets, data is extracted from the first enqueued datagram, up to the size of the buffer supplied. If the datagram is larger than the buffer supplied, the buffer is filled with the first part of the datagram, the excess data is lost, and **Receive** returns a value of **SOCKET_ERROR** with the error code set to **WSAEMSGSIZE**. If no incoming data is available at the socket, a value of **SOCKET_ERROR** is returned with the error code set to **WSAEWOULDBLOCK**. The **OnReceive** callback function can be used to determine when more data arrives.

If the socket is of type **SOCK_STREAM** and the remote side has shut down the connection gracefully, a **Receive** will complete immediately with 0 bytes received. If the connection has been reset, a **Receive** will fail with the error **WSAECONNRESET**.

See Also **CAsyncSocket::AsyncSelect**, **CAsyncSocket::Create**, **CAsyncSocket::ReceiveFrom**, **CAsyncSocket::Send**

CAsyncSocket::ReceiveFrom

int ReceiveFrom(void* *lpBuf***, int** *nBufLen***, CString&** *rSocketAddress***, UINT&** *rSocketPort***, int** *nFlags* **= 0);**
int ReceiveFrom(void* *lpBuf***, int** *nBufLen***, SOCKADDR*** *lpSockAddr***, int*** *lpSockAddrLen***, int** *nFlags* **= 0);**

Return Value

If no error occurs, **ReceiveFrom** returns the number of bytes received. If the connection has been closed, it returns 0. Otherwise, a value of **SOCKET_ERROR** is returned, and a specific error code can be retrieved by calling **GetLastError**. The following errors apply to this member function:

- **WSANOTINITIALISED**   A successful **AfxSocketInit** must occur before using this API.

- **WSAENETDOWN**   The Windows Sockets implementation detected that the network subsystem failed.

- **WSAEFAULT**   The *lpSockAddrLen* argument was invalid: the *lpSockAddr* buffer was too small to accommodate the peer address.

- **WSAEINPROGRESS**   A blocking Windows Sockets operation is in progress.

- **WSAEINVAL**   The socket has not been bound with **Bind**.

- **WSAENOTCONN**   The socket is not connected (**SOCK_STREAM** only).

- **WSAENOTSOCK**   The descriptor is not a socket.

- **WSAEOPNOTSUPP**   **MSG_OOB** was specified, but the socket is not of type **SOCK_STREAM**.

- **WSAESHUTDOWN**   The socket has been shut down; it is not possible to call **ReceiveFrom** on a socket after **ShutDown** has been invoked with *nHow* set to 0 or 2.

- **WSAEWOULDBLOCK**   The socket is marked as nonblocking and the **ReceiveFrom** operation would block.

- **WSAEMSGSIZE**   The datagram was too large to fit into the specified buffer and was truncated.

- **WSAECONNABORTED**   The virtual circuit was aborted due to timeout or other failure.

- **WSAECONNRESET**   The virtual circuit was reset by the remote side.

Parameters

lpBuf   A buffer for the incoming data.

nBufLen   The length of *lpBuf* in bytes.

rSocketAddress   Reference to a **CString** object that receives a dotted number IP address.

rSocketPort   Reference to a **UINT** that stores a port.

lpSockAddr   A pointer to a **SOCKADDR** structure that holds the source address upon return.

lpSockAddrLen   A pointer to the length of the source address in *lpSockAddr* in bytes.

nFlags Specifies the way in which the call is made. The semantics of this function are determined by the socket options and the *nFlags* parameter. The latter is constructed by combining any of the following values with the C++ **OR** operator:

- **MSG_PEEK** Peek at the incoming data. The data is copied into the buffer but is not removed from the input queue.

- **MSG_OOB** Process out-of-band data (see "Programming with Sockets" in the Win32 SDK documentation for a discussion of this topic).

Remarks

Call this member function to receive a datagram and store the source address in the **SOCKADDR** structure or in *rSocketAddress*. This function is used to read incoming data on a (possibly connected) socket and capture the address from which the data was sent.

For sockets of type **SOCK_STREAM**, as much information as is currently available up to the size of the buffer supplied is returned. If the socket has been configured for in-line reception of out-of-band data (socket option **SO_OOBINLINE**) and out-of-band data is unread, only out-of-band data will be returned. The application can use the **IOCtl SIOCATMARK** option or **OnOutOfBandData** to determine whether any more out-of-band data remains to be read. The *lpSockAddr* and *lpSockAddrLen* parameters are ignored for **SOCK_STREAM** sockets.

For datagram sockets, data is extracted from the first enqueued datagram, up to the size of the buffer supplied. If the datagram is larger than the buffer supplied, the buffer is filled with the first part of the message, the excess data is lost, and **ReceiveFrom** returns a value of **SOCKET_ERROR** with the error code set to **WSAEMSGSIZE**.

If *lpSockAddr* is nonzero, and the socket is of type **SOCK_DGRAM**, the network address of the socket which sent the data is copied to the corresponding **SOCKADDR** structure. The value pointed to by *lpSockAddrLen* is initialized to the size of this structure, and is modified on return to indicate the actual size of the address stored there. If no incoming data is available at the socket, the **ReceiveFrom** call waits for data to arrive unless the socket is nonblocking. In this case, a value of **SOCKET_ERROR** is returned with the error code set to **WSAEWOULDBLOCK**. The **OnReceive** callback can be used to determine when more data arrives.

If the socket is of type **SOCK_STREAM** and the remote side has shut down the connection gracefully, a **ReceiveFrom** will complete immediately with 0 bytes received.

See Also CAsyncSocket::AsyncSelect, CAsyncSocket::Create, CAsyncSocket::Receive, CAsyncSocket::Send

CAsyncSocket::Send

virtual int Send(const void* *lpBuf*, **int** *nBufLen*, **int** *nFlags* **= 0);**

Return Value

If no error occurs, **Send** returns the total number of characters sent. (Note that this can be less than the number indicated by *nBufLen*.) Otherwise, a value of **SOCKET_ERROR** is returned, and a specific error code can be retrieved by calling **GetLastError**. The following errors apply to this member function:

- **WSANOTINITIALISED** A successful **AfxSocketInit** must occur before using this API.

- **WSAENETDOWN** The Windows Sockets implementation detected that the network subsystem failed.

- **WSAEACCES** The requested address is a broadcast address, but the appropriate flag was not set.

- **WSAEINPROGRESS** A blocking Windows Sockets operation is in progress.

- **WSAEFAULT** The *lpBuf* argument is not in a valid part of the user address space.

- **WSAENETRESET** The connection must be reset because the Windows Sockets implementation dropped it.

- **WSAENOBUFS** The Windows Sockets implementation reports a buffer deadlock.

- **WSAENOTCONN** The socket is not connected.

- **WSAENOTSOCK** The descriptor is not a socket.

- **WSAEOPNOTSUPP** **MSG_OOB** was specified, but the socket is not of type **SOCK_STREAM**.

- **WSAESHUTDOWN** The socket has been shut down; it is not possible to call **Send** on a socket after **ShutDown** has been invoked with *nHow* set to 1 or 2.

- **WSAEWOULDBLOCK** The socket is marked as nonblocking and the requested operation would block.

- **WSAEMSGSIZE** The socket is of type **SOCK_DGRAM**, and the datagram is larger than the maximum supported by the Windows Sockets implementation.

- **WSAEINVAL** The socket has not been bound with **Bind**.

- **WSAECONNABORTED** The virtual circuit was aborted due to timeout or other failure.

- **WSAECONNRESET** The virtual circuit was reset by the remote side.

Parameters

lpBuf   A buffer containing the data to be transmitted.

nBufLen   The length of the data in *lpBuf* in bytes.

nFlags   Specifies the way in which the call is made. The semantics of this function are determined by the socket options and the *nFlags* parameter. The latter is constructed by combining any of the following values with the C++ **OR** operator:

- **MSG_DONTROUTE**   Specifies that the data should not be subject to routing. A Windows Sockets supplier can choose to ignore this flag; see also the discussion of the **SO_DONTROUTE** option in "Programming with Sockets" in the Win32 SDK documentation.

- **MSG_OOB**   Send out-of-band data (**SOCK_STREAM** only; also see "Programming with Sockets" in the Win32 SDK documentation).

Remarks

Call this member function to send data on a connected socket. **Send** is used to write outgoing data on connected stream or datagram sockets. For datagram sockets, care must be taken not to exceed the maximum IP packet size of the underlying subnets, which is given by the **iMaxUdpDg** element in the **WSADATA** structure returned by **AfxSocketInit**. If the data is too long to pass atomically through the underlying protocol, the error **WSAEMSGSIZE** is returned via **GetLastError**, and no data is transmitted.

Note that for a datagram socket the successful completion of a **Send** does not indicate that the data was successfully delivered.

On **CAsyncSocket** objects of type **SOCK_STREAM**, the number of bytes written can be between 1 and the requested length, depending on buffer availability on both the local and foreign hosts.

See Also   **CAsyncSocket::Create**, **CAsyncSocket::Receive**, **CAsyncSocket::ReceiveFrom**, **CAsyncSocket::SendTo**

CAsyncSocket::SendTo

int SendTo(const void* *lpBuf***, int** *nBufLen***, UINT** *nHostPort***, LPCTSTR** *lpszHostAddress* **= NULL, int** *nFlags* **= 0);**
int SendTo(const void* *lpBuf***, int** *nBufLen***, const SOCKADDR*** *lpSockAddr***, int** *nSockAddrLen***, int** *nFlags* **= 0);**

Return Value

If no error occurs, **SendTo** returns the total number of characters sent. (Note that this can be less than the number indicated by *nBufLen*.) Otherwise, a value of **SOCKET_ERROR** is returned, and a specific error code can be retrieved by calling **GetLastError**. The following errors apply to this member function:

- **WSANOTINITIALISED** A successful **AfxSocketInit** must occur before using this API.

- **WSAENETDOWN** The Windows Sockets implementation detected that the network subsystem failed.

- **WSAEACCES** The requested address is a broadcast address, but the appropriate flag was not set.

- **WSAEINPROGRESS** A blocking Windows Sockets operation is in progress.

- **WSAEFAULT** The *lpBuf* or *lpSockAddr* parameters are not part of the user address space, or the *lpSockAddr* argument is too small (less than the size of a **SOCKADDR** structure).

- **WSAENETRESET** The connection must be reset because the Windows Sockets implementation dropped it.

- **WSAENOBUFS** The Windows Sockets implementation reports a buffer deadlock.

- **WSAENOTCONN** The socket is not connected (**SOCK_STREAM** only).

- **WSAENOTSOCK** The descriptor is not a socket.

- **WSAEOPNOTSUPP** **MSG_OOB** was specified, but the socket is not of type **SOCK_STREAM**.

- **WSAESHUTDOWN** The socket has been shut down; it is not possible to call **SendTo** on a socket after **ShutDown** has been invoked with *nHow* set to 1 or 2.

- **WSAEWOULDBLOCK** The socket is marked as nonblocking and the requested operation would block.

- **WSAEMSGSIZE** The socket is of type **SOCK_DGRAM**, and the datagram is larger than the maximum supported by the Windows Sockets implementation.

- **WSAECONNABORTED** The virtual circuit was aborted due to timeout or other failure.

- **WSAECONNRESET** The virtual circuit was reset by the remote side.

- **WSAEADDRNOTAVAIL** The specified address is not available from the local machine.

- **WSAEAFNOSUPPORT** Addresses in the specified family cannot be used with this socket.

- **WSAEDESTADDRREQ** A destination address is required.

- **WSAENETUNREACH** The network cannot be reached from this host at this time.

Parameters

lpBuf A buffer containing the data to be transmitted.

nBufLen The length of the data in *lpBuf* in bytes.

nHostPort   The port identifying the socket application.

lpszHostAddress   The network address of the socket to which this object is connected: a machine name such as "ftp.microsoft.com," or a dotted number such as "128.56.22.8".

nFlags   Specifies the way in which the call is made. The semantics of this function are determined by the socket options and the *nFlags* parameter. The latter is constructed by combining any of the following values with the C++ **OR** operator:

- **MSG_DONTROUTE**   Specifies that the data should not be subject to routing. A Windows Sockets supplier can choose to ignore this flag; see also the discussion of the **SO_DONTROUTE** option in Programming with Sockets in the Win32 SDK documentation.

- **MSG_OOB**   Send out-of-band data (**SOCK_STREAM** only).

lpSockAddr   A pointer to a **SOCKADDR** structure that contains the address of the target socket.

nSockAddrLen   The length of the address in *lpSockAddr* in bytes.

Remarks

Call this member function to send data to a specific destination. **SendTo** is used on datagram or stream sockets and is used to write outgoing data on a socket. For datagram sockets, care must be taken not to exceed the maximum IP packet size of the underlying subnets, which is given by the **iMaxUdpDg** element in the **WSADATA** structure filled out by **AfxSocketInit**. If the data is too long to pass atomically through the underlying protocol, the error **WSAEMSGSIZE** is returned, and no data is transmitted.

Note that the successful completion of a **SendTo** does not indicate that the data was successfully delivered.

SendTo is only used on a **SOCK_DGRAM** socket to send a datagram to a specific socket identified by the *lpSockAddr* parameter.

To send a broadcast (on a **SOCK_DGRAM** only), the address in the *lpSockAddr* parameter should be constructed using the special IP address **INADDR_BROADCAST** (defined in the Windows Sockets header file WINSOCK.H) together with the intended port number. Or, if the *lpszHostAddress* parameter is **NULL**, the socket is configured for broadcast. It is generally inadvisable for a broadcast datagram to exceed the size at which fragmentation can occur, which implies that the data portion of the datagram (excluding headers) should not exceed 512 bytes.

See Also   **CAsyncSocket::Create, CAsyncSocket::Receive, CAsyncSocket::ReceiveFrom, CAsyncSocket::Send**

CAsyncSocket::SetSockOpt

BOOL SetSockOpt(int *nOptionName*, **const void*** *lpOptionValue*, **int** *nOptionLen*, **int** *nLevel* = **SOL_SOCKET**);

Return Value

Nonzero if the function is successful; otherwise 0, and a specific error code can be retrieved by calling **GetLastError**. The following errors apply to this member function:

- **WSANOTINITIALISED** A successful **AfxSocketInit** must occur before using this API.

- **WSAENETDOWN** The Windows Sockets implementation detected that the network subsystem failed.

- **WSAEFAULT** *lpOptionValue* is not in a valid part of the process address space.

- **WSAEINPROGRESS** A blocking Windows Sockets operation is in progress.

- **WSAEINVAL** *nLevel* is not valid, or the information in *lpOptionValue* is not valid.

- **WSAENETRESET** Connection has timed out when **SO_KEEPALIVE** is set.

- **WSAENOPROTOOPT** The option is unknown or unsupported. In particular, **SO_BROADCAST** is not supported on sockets of type **SOCK_STREAM**, while **SO_DONTLINGER**, **SO_KEEPALIVE**, **SO_LINGER**, and **SO_OOBINLINE** are not supported on sockets of type **SOCK_DGRAM**.

- **WSAENOTCONN** Connection has been reset when **SO_KEEPALIVE** is set.

- **WSAENOTSOCK** The descriptor is not a socket.

Parameters

nOptionName The socket option for which the value is to be set.

lpOptionValue A pointer to the buffer in which the value for the requested option is supplied.

nOptionLen The size of the *lpOptionValue* buffer in bytes.

nLevel The level at which the option is defined; the only supported levels are **SOL_SOCKET** and **IPPROTO_TCP**.

Remarks

Call this member function to set a socket option. **SetSockOpt** sets the current value for a socket option associated with a socket of any type, in any state. Although options can exist at multiple protocol levels, this specification only defines options that exist at the uppermost "socket" level. Options affect socket operations, such as whether expedited data is received in the normal data stream, whether broadcast messages can be sent on the socket, and so on.

There are two types of socket options: Boolean options that enable or disable a feature or behavior, and options which require an integer value or structure. To enable a Boolean option, *lpOptionValue* points to a nonzero integer. To disable the option *lpOptionValue* points to an integer equal to zero. *nOptionLen* should be equal to **sizeof(BOOL)** for Boolean options. For other options, *lpOptionValue* points to the integer or structure that contains the desired value for the option, and *nOptionLen* is the length of the integer or structure.

SO_LINGER controls the action taken when unsent data is queued on a socket and the **Close** function is called to close the socket. For more information, see "Programming with Sockets" in the Win32 SDK documentation.

By default, a socket cannot be bound (see **Bind**) to a local address which is already in use. On occasion, however, it may be desirable to "reuse" an address in this way. Since every connection is uniquely identified by the combination of local and remote addresses, there is no problem with having two sockets bound to the same local address as long as the remote addresses are different.

To inform the Windows Sockets implementation that a **Bind** call on a socket should not be disallowed because the desired address is already in use by another socket, the application should set the **SO_REUSEADDR** socket option for the socket before issuing the **Bind** call. Note that the option is interpreted only at the time of the **Bind** call: it is therefore unnecessary (but harmless) to set the option on a socket which is not to be bound to an existing address, and setting or resetting the option after the **Bind** call has no effect on this or any other socket.

An application can request that the Windows Sockets implementation enable the use of "keep-alive" packets on Transmission Control Protocol (TCP) connections by turning on the **SO_KEEPALIVE** socket option. (For information about "keep-alive" packets, see "Programming with Sockets" in the Win32 SDK documentation.) A Windows Sockets implementation need not support the use of keep-alives: if it does, the precise semantics are implementation-specific but should conform to section 4.2.3.6 of RFC 1122: "Requirements for Internet Hosts — Communication Layers." If a connection is dropped as the result of "keep-alives" the error code **WSAENETRESET** is returned to any calls in progress on the socket, and any subsequent calls will fail with **WSAENOTCONN**.

The **TCP_NODELAY** option disables the Nagle algorithm. The Nagle algorithm is used to reduce the number of small packets sent by a host by buffering unacknowledged send data until a full-size packet can be sent. However, for some applications this algorithm can impede performance, and **TCP_NODELAY** can be used to turn it off. Application writers should not set **TCP_NODELAY** unless the impact of doing so is well-understood and desired, since setting **TCP_NODELAY** can have a significant negative impact on network performance. **TCP_NODELAY** is the only supported socket option which uses level **IPPROTO_TCP**; all other options use level **SOL_SOCKET**.

Some implementations of Windows Sockets supply output debug information if the **SO_DEBUG** option is set by an application.

The following options are supported for **SetSockOpt**. The Type identifies the type of data addressed by *lpOptionValue*.

Value	Type	Meaning
SO_BROADCAST	**BOOL**	Allow transmission of broadcast messages on the socket.
SO_DEBUG	**BOOL**	Record debugging information.
SO_DONTLINGER	**BOOL**	Don't block **Close** waiting for unsent data to be sent. Setting this option is equivalent to setting **SO_LINGER** with **l_onoff** set to zero.
SO_DONTROUTE	**BOOL**	Don't route: send directly to interface.
SO_KEEPALIVE	**BOOL**	Send keep-alives.
SO_LINGER	**struct LINGER**	Linger on **Close** if unsent data is present.
SO_OOBINLINE	**BOOL**	Receive out-of-band data in the normal data stream.
SO_RCVBUF	**int**	Specify buffer size for receives.
SO_REUSEADDR	**BOOL**	Allows the socket to be bound to an address which is already in use. (See Bind.)
SO_SNDBUF	**int**	Specify buffer size for sends.
TCP_NODELAY	**BOOL**	Disables the Nagle algorithm for send coalescing.

Berkeley Software Distribution (BSD) options not supported for **SetSockOpt** are:

Value	Type	Meaning
SO_ACCEPTCONN	**BOOL**	Socket is listening
SO_ERROR	**int**	Get error status and clear.
SO_RCVLOWAT	**int**	Receive low water mark.
SO_RCVTIMEO	**int**	Receive timeout
SO_SNDLOWAT	**int**	Send low water mark.
SO_SNDTIMEO	**int**	Send timeout.
SO_TYPE	**int**	Type of the socket.
IP_OPTIONS		Set options field in IP header.

See Also   **CAsyncSocket::AsyncSelect, CAsyncSocket::Bind, CAsyncSocket::Create, CAsyncSocket::GetSockOpt, CAsyncSocket::IOCtl**

CAsyncSocket::ShutDown

BOOL ShutDown(int *nHow* **= sends);**

Return Value

Nonzero if the function is successful; otherwise 0, and a specific error code can be retrieved by calling **GetLastError**. The following errors apply to this member function:

- **WSANOTINITIALISED** A successful **AfxSocketInit** must occur before using this API.
- **WSAENETDOWN** The Windows Sockets implementation detected that the network subsystem failed.
- **WSAEINVAL** *nHow* is not valid.
- **WSAEINPROGRESS** A blocking Windows Sockets operation is in progress.
- **WSAENOTCONN** The socket is not connected (**SOCK_STREAM** only).
- **WSAENOTSOCK** The descriptor is not a socket.

Parameters

nHow A flag that describes what types of operation will no longer be allowed, using the following enumerated values:

- **receives = 0**
- **sends = 1**
- **both = 2**

Remarks

Call this member function to disable sends and/or receives on the socket. **ShutDown** is used on all types of sockets to disable reception, transmission, or both. If *nHow* is 0, subsequent receives on the socket will be disallowed. This has no effect on the lower protocol layers.

For Transmission Control Protocol (TCP), the TCP window is not changed and incoming data will be accepted (but not acknowledged) until the window is exhausted. For User Datagram Protocol (UDP), incoming datagrams are accepted and queued. In no case will an ICMP error packet be generated. If *nHow* is 1, subsequent sends are disallowed. For TCP sockets, a FIN will be sent. Setting *nHow* to 2 disables both sends and receives as described above.

Note that **ShutDown** does not close the socket, and resources attached to the socket will not be freed until **Close** is called. An application should not rely on being able to reuse a socket after it has been shut down. In particular, a Windows Sockets implementation is not required to support the use of **Connect** on such a socket.

See Also   **CAsyncSocket::Connect**, **CAsyncSocket::Create**

Data Members

CAsyncSocket::m_hSocket

Remarks

Contains the **SOCKET** handle for the socket encapsulated by this **CAsyncSocket** object.

CBitmap

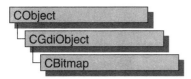

The **CBitmap** class encapsulates a Windows graphics device interface (GDI) bitmap and provides member functions to manipulate the bitmap. To use a **CBitmap** object, construct the object, attach a bitmap handle to it with one of the initialization member functions, and then call the object's member functions.

For more information on using graphic objects like **CBitmap**, see "Graphic Objects" in Chapter 1 of *Programming with MFC*.

#include <afxwin.h>

Construction

CBitmap	Constructs a **CBitmap** object.

Initialization

LoadBitmap	Initializes the object by loading a named bitmap resource from the application's executable file and attaching the bitmap to the object.
LoadOEMBitmap	Initializes the object by loading a predefined Windows bitmap and attaching the bitmap to the object.
LoadMappedBitmap	Loads a bitmap and maps colors to current system colors.
CreateBitmap	Initializes the object with a device-dependent memory bitmap that has a specified width, height, and bit pattern.
CreateBitmapIndirect	Initializes the object with a bitmap with the width, height, and bit pattern (if one is specified) given in a **BITMAP** structure.
CreateCompatibleBitmap	Initializes the object with a bitmap so that it is compatible with a specified device.
CreateDiscardableBitmap	Initializes the object with a discardable bitmap that is compatible with a specified device.

Attributes

GetBitmap	Returns a pointer to the specified **CBitmap** object.
operator HBITMAP	Returns the Windows handle attached to the **CBitmap** object.

Operations

FromHandle	Returns a pointer to a **CBitmap** object when given a handle to a Windows **HBITMAP** bitmap.
SetBitmapBits	Sets the bits of a bitmap to the specified bit values.
GetBitmapBits	Copies the bits of the specified bitmap into the specified buffer.
SetBitmapDimension	Assigns a width and height to a bitmap in 0.1-millimeter units.
GetBitmapDimension	Returns the width and height of the bitmap. The height and width are assumed to have been set previously by the **SetBitmapDimension** member function.

Member Functions

CBitmap::CBitmap

CBitmap( );

Remarks

Constructs a **CBitmap** object. The resulting object must be initialized with one of the initialization member functions.

See Also **CBitmap::LoadBitmap**, **CBitmap::LoadOEMBitmap**, **CBitmap::CreateBitmap**, **CBitmap::CreateBitmapIndirect**, **CBitmap::CreateCompatibleBitmap**, **CBitmap::CreateDiscardableBitmap**

CBitmap::CreateBitmap

BOOL CreateBitmap(int *nWidth*, **int** *nHeight*, **UINT** *nPlanes*, **UINT** *nBitcount*, **const void*** *lpBits* **);**

Return Value

Nonzero if successful; otherwise 0.

Parameters

nWidth   Specifies the width (in pixels) of the bitmap.

nHeight   Specifies the height (in pixels) of the bitmap.

nPlanes   Specifies the number of color planes in the bitmap.

nBitcount   Specifies the number of color bits per display pixel.

lpBits   Points to a short-integer array that contains the initial bitmap bit values. If it is **NULL**, the new bitmap is left uninitialized.

Remarks

Initializes a device-dependent memory bitmap that has the specified width, height, and bit pattern.

For a color bitmap, either the *nPlanes* or *nBitcount* parameter should be set to 1. If both of these parameters are set to 1, **CreateBitmap** creates a monochrome bitmap.

Although a bitmap cannot be directly selected for a display device, it can be selected as the current bitmap for a "memory device context" by using **CDC::SelectObject** and copied to any compatible device context by using the **CDC::BitBlt** function.

When you finish with the **CBitmap** object created by the **CreateBitmap** function, first select the bitmap out of the device context, then delete the **CBitmap** object.

For more information, see the description of the **bmBits** field in the **BITMAP** structure. The **BITMAP** structure is described under the **CBitmap::CreateBitmapIndirect** member function.

See Also   **CDC::SelectObject, CGdiObject::DeleteObject, CDC::BitBlt, ::CreateBitmap**

CBitmap::CreateBitmapIndirect

BOOL CreateBitmapIndirect(LPBITMAP *lpBitmap* **);**

Return Value

Nonzero if successful; otherwise 0.

Parameters

lpBitmap   Points to a **BITMAP** structure that contains information about the bitmap.

Remarks

Initializes a bitmap that has the width, height, and bit pattern (if one is specified) given in the structure pointed to by *lpBitmap*. Although a bitmap cannot be directly selected for a display device, it can be selected as the current bitmap for a memory device context by using **CDC::SelectObject** and copied to any compatible device context by using the **CDC::BitBlt** or **CDC::StretchBlt** function. (The **CDC::PatBlt** function can copy the bitmap for the current brush directly to the display device context.)

If the **BITMAP** structure pointed to by the *lpBitmap* parameter has been filled in by using the **GetObject** function, the bits of the bitmap are not specified and the bitmap is uninitialized. To initialize the bitmap, an application can use a function such as **CDC::BitBlt** or **::SetDIBits** to copy the bits from the bitmap identified by the first parameter of **CGdiObject::GetObject** to the bitmap created by **CreateBitmapIndirect**.

When you finish with the **CBitmap** object created with **CreateBitmapIndirect** function, first select the bitmap out of the device context, then delete the **CBitmap** object.

See Also　CDC::SelectObject, CDC::BitBlt, CGdiObject::DeleteObject, CGdiObject::GetObject, ::CreateBitmapIndirect

CBitmap::CreateCompatibleBitmap

BOOL CreateCompatibleBitmap(CDC* *pDC***, int** *nWidth***, int** *nHeight* **);**

Return Value

Nonzero if successful; otherwise 0.

Parameters

pDC　Specifies the device context.

nWidth　Specifies the width (in bits) of the bitmap.

nHeight　Specifies the height (in bits) of the bitmap.

Remarks

Initializes a bitmap that is compatible with the device specified by *pDC*. The bitmap has the same number of color planes or the same bits-per-pixel format as the specified device context. It can be selected as the current bitmap for any memory device that is compatible with the one specified by *pDC*.

If *pDC* is a memory device context, the bitmap returned has the same format as the currently selected bitmap in that device context. A "memory device context" is a block of memory that represents a display surface. It can be used to prepare images in memory before copying them to the actual display surface of the compatible device.

When a memory device context is created, GDI automatically selects a monochrome stock bitmap for it.

Since a color memory device context can have either color or monochrome bitmaps selected, the format of the bitmap returned by the **CreateCompatibleBitmap** function is not always the same; however, the format of a compatible bitmap for a nonmemory device context is always in the format of the device.

When you finish with the **CBitmap** object created with the **CreateCompatibleBitmap** function, first select the bitmap out of the device context, then delete the **CBitmap** object.

See Also   **::CreateCompatibleBitmap, CGdiObject::DeleteObject**

CBitmap::CreateDiscardableBitmap

BOOL CreateDiscardableBitmap(CDC* *pDC*, **int** *nWidth*, **int** *nHeight* **);**

Return Value

Nonzero if successful; otherwise 0.

Parameters

pDC   Specifies a device context.

nWidth   Specifies the width (in bits) of the bitmap.

nHeight   Specifies the height (in bits) of the bitmap.

Remarks

Initializes a discardable bitmap that is compatible with the device context identified by *pDC*. The bitmap has the same number of color planes or the same bits-per-pixel format as the specified device context. An application can select this bitmap as the current bitmap for a memory device that is compatible with the one specified by *pDC*.

Windows can discard a bitmap created by this function only if an application has not selected it into a display context. If Windows discards the bitmap when it is not selected and the application later attempts to select it, the **CDC::SelectObject** function will return **NULL**.

When you finish with the **CBitmap** object created with the **CreateDiscardableBitmap** function, first select the bitmap out of the device context, then delete the **CBitmap** object.

See Also   **::CreateDiscardableBitmap, CGdiObject::DeleteObject**

CBitmap::FromHandle

static CBitmap* PASCAL FromHandle(HBITMAP *hBitmap* **);**

Return Value

A pointer to a **CBitmap** object if successful; otherwise **NULL**.

Parameters

hBitmap   Specifies a Windows GDI bitmap.

Remarks

Returns a pointer to a **CBitmap** object when given a handle to a Windows GDI bitmap. If a **CBitmap** object is not already attached to the handle, a temporary **CBitmap** object is created and attached. This temporary **CBitmap** object is valid only until the next time the application has idle time in its event loop, at which time all temporary graphic objects are deleted. Another way of saying this is that the temporary object is only valid during the processing of one window message.

CBitmap::GetBitmap

int GetBitmap(BITMAP* *pBitMap* **);**

Return Value

Nonzero if successful; otherwise 0.

Parameters

pBitMap   Pointer to a **BITMAP** structure. Must not be **NULL**.

Remarks

Call this member function to retrieve information about a **CBitmap** object. This information is returned in the **BITMAP** structure referred to by *pBitmap*.

See Also   BITMAP

CBitmap::GetBitmapBits

DWORD GetBitmapBits(DWORD *dwCount*, **LPVOID** *lpBits* **) const;**

Return Value

The actual number of bytes in the bitmap, or 0 if there is an error.

Parameters

dwCount   Specifies the number of bytes to be copied.

lpBits   Points to the buffer that is to receive the bitmap. The bitmap is an array of bytes. The bitmap byte array conforms to a structure where horizontal scan lines are multiples of 16 bits.

Remarks

Copies the bit pattern of the **CBitmap** object into the buffer that is pointed to by *lpBits*. The *dwCount* parameter specifies the number of bytes to be copied to the buffer. Use **CGdiObject::GetObject** to determine the correct *dwCount* value for the given bitmap.

See Also   CGdiObject::GetObject, **::GetBitmapBits**

CBitmap::GetBitmapDimension

CSize GetBitmapDimension( ) const;

Return Value

The width and height of the bitmap, measured in 0.1-millimeter units. The height is in the **cy** member of the **CSize** object, and the width is in the **cx** member. If the bitmap width and height have not been set by using **SetBitmapDimension**, the return value is 0.

Remarks

Returns the width and height of the bitmap. The height and width are assumed to have been set previously by using the **SetBitmapDimension** member function.

See Also   **CBitmap::SetBitmapDimension**, **::GetBitmapDimension**

CBitmap::LoadBitmap

BOOL LoadBitmap(LPCTSTR *lpszResourceName* **);**
BOOL LoadBitmap(UINT *nIDResource* **);**

Return Value

Nonzero if successful; otherwise 0.

Parameters

lpszResourceName   Points to a null-terminated string that contains the name of the bitmap resource.

nIDResource   Specifies the resource ID number of the bitmap resource.

Remarks

Loads the bitmap resource named by *lpszResourceName* or identified by the ID number in *nIDResource* from the application's executable file. The loaded bitmap is attached to the **CBitmap** object.

If the bitmap identified by *lpszResourceName* does not exist or if there is insufficient memory to load the bitmap, the function returns 0.

An application must call the **CGdiObject::DeleteObject** function to delete any bitmap loaded by the **LoadBitmap** function.

The following bitmaps were added to Windows versions 3.1 and later:

OBM_UPARRROWI
OBM_DNARROWI
OBM_RGARROWI
OBM_LFARROWI

These bitmaps are not found in device drivers for Windows versions 3.0 and earlier. For a complete list of bitmaps and a display of their appearance, see the *Win32 Programmer's Reference*.

See Also   **CBitmap::LoadOEMBitmap**, **::LoadBitmap**, **CGdiObject::DeleteObject**

CBitmap::LoadMappedBitmap

BOOL LoadMappedBitmap(UINT *nIDBitmap***, UINT** *nFlags* **= 0, LPCOLORMAP** *lpColorMap* **= NULL, int** *nMapSize* **= 0);**

Return Value

Nonzero if successful; otherwise 0.

Parameters

nIDBitmap   The ID of the bitmap resource.

nFlags   A flag for a bitmap. Can be zero or **CMB_MASKED**.

lpColorMap   A pointer to a **COLORMAP** structure that contains the color information needed to map the bitmaps. If this parameter is **NULL**, the function uses the default color map.

nMapSize   The number of color maps pointed to by *lpColorMap*.

Remarks

Call this member function to load a bitmap and map the colors to the current system colors. By default, **LoadMappedBitmap** will map colors commonly used in button glyphs.

For information about creating a mapped bitmap, see the Windows function **::CreateMappedBitmap** and the **COLORMAP** structure in the *Win32 Programmer's Reference*.

See Also   **::LoadBitmap**, **::CreateMappedBitmap**

CBitmap::LoadOEMBitmap

BOOL LoadOEMBitmap(UINT *nIDBitmap* **);**

Return Value

Nonzero if successful; otherwise 0.

Parameters

nIDBitmap   ID number of the predefined Windows bitmap. The possible values are listed below from WINDOWS.H:

OBM_BTNCORNERS	**OBM_OLD_RESTORE**
OBM_BTSIZE	**OBM_OLD_RGARROW**
OBM_CHECK	**OBM_OLD_UPARROW**
OBM_CHECKBOXES	**OBM_OLD_ZOOM**
OBM_CLOSE	**OBM_REDUCE**
OBM_COMBO	**OBM_REDUCED**
OBM_DNARROW	**OBM_RESTORE**
OBM_DNARROWD	**OBM_RESTORED**
OBM_DNARROWI	**OBM_RGARROW**
OBM_LFARROW	**OBM_RGARROWD**
OBM_LFARROWD	**OBM_RGARROWI**
OBM_LFARROWI	**OBM_SIZE**
OBM_MNARROW	**OBM_UPARROW**
OBM_OLD_CLOSE	**OBM_UPARROWD**
OBM_OLD_DNARROW	**OBM_UPARROW**
OBM_OLD_LFARROW	**OBM_ZOOM**
OBM_OLD_REDUCE	**OBM_ZOOMD**

Remarks

Loads a predefined bitmap used by Windows.

Bitmap names that begin with **OBM_OLD** represent bitmaps used by Windows versions prior to 3.0.

Note that the constant **OEMRESOURCE** must be defined before including WINDOWS.H in order to use any of the **OBM_** constants.

See Also   **CBitmap::LoadBitmap**, **::LoadBitmap**

CBitmap::operator HBITMAP

operator HBITMAP( ) const;

Return Value

If successful, a handle to the Windows GDI object represented by the **CBitmap** object; otherwise **NULL**.

Remarks

Use this operator to get the attached Windows GDI handle of the **CBitmap** object. This operator is a casting operator, which supports direct use of an **HBITMAP** object.

For more information about using graphic objects, see "Graphic Objects" in the *Win32 Programmer's Reference*.

CBitmap::SetBitmapBits

DWORD SetBitmapBits(DWORD *dwCount*, **const void*** *lpBits* **);**

Return Value

The number of bytes used in setting the bitmap bits; 0 if the function fails.

Parameters

dwCount   Specifies the number of bytes pointed to by *lpBits*.

lpBits   Points to the **BYTE** array that contains the bit values to be copied to the **CBitmap** object.

Remarks

Sets the bits of a bitmap to the bit values given by *lpBits*.

See Also   ::SetBitmapBits

CBitmap::SetBitmapDimension

CSize SetBitmapDimension(int *nWidth*, **int** *nHeight* **);**

Return Value

The previous bitmap dimensions. Height is in the **cy** member variable of the **CSize** object, and width is in the **cx** member variable.

Parameters

nWidth   Specifies the width of the bitmap (in 0.1-millimeter units).

nHeight   Specifies the height of the bitmap (in 0.1-millimeter units).

Remarks

Assigns a width and height to a bitmap in 0.1-millimeter units. The GDI does not use these values except to return them when an application calls the **GetBitmapDimension** member function.

See Also   CBitmap::GetBitmapDimension, ::SetBitmapDimension

CBitmapButton

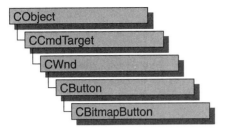

Use the **CBitmapButton** class to create pushbutton controls labeled with bitmapped images instead of text. **CBitmapButton** objects contain up to four bitmaps, which contain images for the different states a button can assume: up (or normal), down (or selected), focused, and disabled. Only the first bitmap is required; the others are optional.

Bitmap-button images include the border around the image as well as the image itself. The border typically plays a part in showing the state of the button. For example, the bitmap for the focused state usually is like the one for the up state but with a dashed rectangle inset from the border or a thick solid line at the border. The bitmap for the disabled state usually resembles the one for the up state but has lower contrast (like a dimmed or grayed menu selection).

These bitmaps can be of any size, but all are treated as if they were the same size as the bitmap for the up state.

Various applications demand different combinations of bitmap images:

Up	Down	Focused	Disabled	Application
×				Bitmap
×	×			Button without **WS_TABSTOP** style
×	×	×	×	Dialog button with all states
×	×	×		Dialog button with **WS_TABSTOP** style

When creating a bitmap-button control, set the **BS_OWNERDRAW** style to specify that the button is owner-drawn. This causes Windows to send the **WM_MEASUREITEM** and **WM_DRAWITEM** messages for the button; the framework handles these messages and manages the appearance of the button for you.

To create a bitmap-button control in a window's client area, follow these steps:

1. Create one to four bitmap images for the button.
2. Construct the **CBitmapButton** object.
3. Call the **Create** function to create the Windows button control and attach it to the **CBitmapButton** object.
4. Call the **LoadBitmaps** member function to load the bitmap resources after the bitmap button is constructed.

To include a bitmap-button control in a dialog box, follow these steps:

1. Create one to four bitmap images for the button.
2. Create a dialog template with an owner-draw button positioned where you want the bitmap button. The size of the button in the template does not matter.
3. Set the button's caption to a value such as "MYIMAGE" and define a symbol for the button such as IDC_MYIMAGE.
4. In your application's resource script, give each of the images created for the button an ID constructed by appending one of the letters "U," "D," "F," or "X" (for up, down, focused, and disabled) to the string used for the button caption in step 3. For the button caption "MYIMAGE," for example, the IDs would be "MYIMAGEU," "MYIMAGED," "MYIMAGEF," and "MYIMAGEX."
5. In your application's dialog class (derived from **CDialog**), add a **CBitmapButton** member object.
6. In the **CDialog** object's **OnInitDialog** routine, call the **CBitmapButton** object's **AutoLoad** function, using as parameters the button's control ID and the **CDialog** object's **this** pointer.

If you want to handle Windows notification messages, such as **BN_CLICKED**, sent by a bitmap-button control to its parent (usually a class derived from **CDialog**), add to the **CDialog**-derived object a message-map entry and message-handler member function for each message. The notifications sent by a **CBitmapButton** object are the same as those sent by a **CButton** object.

The class **CToolBar** takes a different approach to bitmap buttons. See **CToolBar** for more information.

For more information on **CBitmapButton**, see the article "Controls" in *Programming with MFC*.

#include <afxext.h>

See Also **CButton, CBitmapButton::AutoLoad, CToolBar**

Construction

CBitmapButton	Constructs a **CBitmapButton** object.
LoadBitmaps	Initializes the object by loading one or more named bitmap resources from the application's resource file and attaching the bitmaps to the object.
AutoLoad	Associates a button in a dialog box with an object of the **CBitmapButton** class, loads the bitmap(s) by name, and sizes the button to fit the bitmap.

Operations

SizeToContent	Sizes the button to accommodate the bitmap.

Member Functions

CBitmapButton::AutoLoad

BOOL AutoLoad(UINT *nID***, CWnd*** *pParent* **);**

Return Value

Nonzero if successful; otherwise 0.

Parameters

nID   The button's control ID.

pParent   Pointer to the object that owns the button.

Remarks

Associates a button in a dialog box with an object of the **CBitmapButton** class, loads the bitmap(s) by name, and sizes the button to fit the bitmap.

Use the **AutoLoad** function to initialize an owner-draw button in a dialog box as a bitmap button. Instructions for using this function are in the remarks for the **CBitmapButton** class.

See Also **CBitmapButton::LoadBitmaps, CBitmapButton::SizeToContent**

CBitmapButton::CBitmapButton

CBitmapButton( );

Remarks

Creates a **CBitmapButton** object.

After creating the C++ **CBitmapButton** object, call **CButton::Create** to create the Windows button control and attach it to the **CBitmapButton** object.

See Also   **CBitmapButton::LoadBitmaps**, **CBitmapButton::AutoLoad**, **CBitmapButton::SizeToContent**, **CButton::Create**

CBitmapButton::LoadBitmaps

BOOL LoadBitmaps(LPCTSTR *lpszBitmapResource*, **LPCTSTR** *lpszBitmapResourceSel* = **NULL**, **LPCTSTR** *lpszBitmapResourceFocus* = **NULL**, **LPCTSTR** *lpszBitmapResourceDisabled* = **NULL**);
BOOL LoadBitmaps(UINT *nIDBitmapResource*, **UINT** *nIDBitmapResourceSel* = **0**, **UINT** *nIDBitmapResourceFocus* = **0**, **UINT** *nIDBitmapResourceDisabled* = **0**);

Return Value

Nonzero if successful; otherwise 0.

Parameters

lpszBitmapResource   Points to the null-terminated string that contains the name of the bitmap for a bitmap button's normal or "up" state. Required.

lpszBitmapResourceSel   Points to the null-terminated string that contains the name of the bitmap for a bitmap button's selected or "down" state. May be **NULL**.

lpszBitmapResourceFocus   Points to the null-terminated string that contains the name of the bitmap for a bitmap button's focused state. May be **NULL**.

lpszBitmapResourceDisabled   Points to the null-terminated string that contains the name of the bitmap for a bitmap button's disabled state. May be **NULL**.

nIDBitmapResource   Specifies the resource ID number of the bitmap resource for a bitmap button's normal or "up" state. Required.

nIDBitmapResourceSel   Specifies the resource ID number of the bitmap resource for a bitmap button's selected or "down" state. May be 0.

nIDBitmapResourceFocus   Specifies the resource ID number of the bitmap resource for a bitmap button's focused state. May be 0.

nIDBitmapResourceDisabled   Specifies the resource ID number of the bitmap resource for a bitmap button's disabled state. May be 0.

Remarks

Use this function when you want to load bitmap images identified by their resource names or ID numbers, or when you cannot use the **AutoLoad** function because, for example, you are creating a bitmap button that is not part of a dialog box.

See Also   **CBitmapButton::AutoLoad**, **CBitmapButton::SizeToContent**, **CButton::Create**, **CBitmap::LoadBitmap**

CBitmapButton::SizeToContent

void SizeToContent( );

Remarks

Call this function to resize a bitmap button to the size of the bitmap.

See Also   CBitmapButton::LoadBitmaps, CBitmapButton::AutoLoad

CBrush

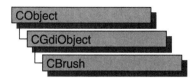

The **CBrush** class encapsulates a Windows graphics device interface (GDI) brush. To use a **CBrush** object, construct a **CBrush** object and pass it to any **CDC** member function that requires a brush.

Brushes can be solid, hatched, or patterned.

For more information on **CBrush**, see "Graphic Objects" in Chapter 1 of *Programming with MFC*.

#include <afxwin.h>

See Also   **CBitmap**, **CDC**

Construction

CBrush	Constructs a **CBrush** object.

Initialization

CreateSolidBrush	Initializes a brush with the specified solid color.
CreateHatchBrush	Initializes a brush with the specified hatched pattern and color.
CreateBrushIndirect	Initializes a brush with the style, color, and pattern specified in a **LOGBRUSH** structure.
CreatePatternBrush	Initializes a brush with a pattern specified by a bitmap.
CreateDIBPatternBrush	Initializes a brush with a pattern specified by a device-independent bitmap (DIB).
CreateSysColorBrush	Creates a brush that is the default system color.

Operations

FromHandle	Returns a pointer to a **CBrush** object when given a handle to a Windows **HBRUSH** object.

Attributes

GetLogBrush	Gets a **LOGBRUSH** structure.
operator HBRUSH	Returns the Windows handle attached to the **CBrush** object.

Member Functions

CBrush::CBrush

CBrush( );
CBrush(COLORREF *crColor* **);**
   throw(CResourceException);
CBrush(int *nIndex*, **COLORREF** *crColor* **);**
   throw(CResourceException);
CBrush(CBitmap* *pBitmap* **);**
   throw(CResourceException);

Parameters

crColor Specifies the foreground color of the brush as an RGB color. If the brush is hatched, this parameter specifies the color of the hatching.

nIndex Specifies the hatch style of the brush. It can be any one of the following values:

- **HS_BDIAGONAL** Downward hatch (left to right) at 45 degrees

- **HS_CROSS** Horizontal and vertical crosshatch

- **HS_DIAGCROSS** Crosshatch at 45 degrees

- **HS_FDIAGONAL** Upward hatch (left to right) at 45 degrees

- **HS_HORIZONTAL** Horizontal hatch

- **HS_VERTICAL** Vertical hatch

pBitmap Points to a **CBitmap** object that specifies a bitmap with which the brush paints.

Remarks

Has four overloaded constructors. The constructor with no arguments constructs an uninitialized **CBrush** object that must be initialized before it can be used.

If you use the constructor with no arguments, you must initialize the resulting **CBrush** object with **CreateSolidBrush**, **CreateHatchBrush**, **CreateBrushIndirect**, **CreatePatternBrush**, or **CreateDIBPatternBrush**. If you use one of the constructors that takes arguments, then no further initialization is necessary. The constructors with arguments can throw an exception if errors are encountered, while the constructor with no arguments will always succeed.

The constructor with a single **COLORREF** parameter constructs a solid brush with the specified color. The color specifies an RGB value and can be constructed with the **RGB** macro in WINDOWS.H.

The constructor with two parameters constructs a hatch brush. The *nIndex* parameter specifies the index of a hatched pattern. The *crColor* parameter specifies the color.

The constructor with a **CBitmap** parameter constructs a patterned brush. The parameter identifies a bitmap. The bitmap is assumed to have been created by using **CBitmap::CreateBitmap**, **CBitmap::CreateBitmapIndirect**, **CBitmap::LoadBitmap**, or **CBitmap::CreateCompatibleBitmap**. The minimum size for a bitmap to be used in a fill pattern is 8 pixels by 8 pixels.

See Also   **CBrush::CreateSolidBrush**, **CBrush::CreateHatchBrush**, **CBrush::CreateBrushIndirect**, **CBrush::CreatePatternBrush**, **CBrush::CreateDIBPatternBrush**, **CGdiObject::CreateStockObject**

CBrush::CreateBrushIndirect

BOOL CreateBrushIndirect(LPLOGBRUSH *lpLogBrush* **);**

Return Value

Nonzero if the function is successful; otherwise 0.

Parameters

lpLogBrush   Points to a **LOGBRUSH** structure that contains information about the brush.

Remarks

Initializes a brush with a style, color, and pattern specified in a **LOGBRUSH** structure. The brush can subsequently be selected as the current brush for any device context.

A brush created using a monochrome (1 plane, 1 bit per pixel) bitmap is drawn using the current text and background colors. Pixels represented by a bit set to 0 will be drawn with the current text color. Pixels represented by a bit set to 1 will be drawn with the current background color.

See Also   **CBrush::CreateDIBPatternBrush**, **CBrush::CreatePatternBrush**, **CBrush::CreateSolidBrush**, **CBrush::CreateHatchBrush**, **CGdiObject::CreateStockObject**, **CGdiObject::DeleteObject**, **::CreateBrushIndirect**

CBrush::CreateDIBPatternBrush

BOOL CreateDIBPatternBrush(HGLOBAL *hPackedDIB*, **UINT** *nUsage* **);**
BOOL CreateDIBPatternBrush(const void* *lpPackedDIB*, **UINT** *nUsage* **);**

Return Value

Nonzero if successful; otherwise 0.

Parameters

hPackedDIB   Identifies a global-memory object containing a packed device-independent bitmap (DIB).

nUsage   Specifies whether the **bmiColors[]** fields of the **BITMAPINFO** data structure (a part of the "packed DIB") contain explicit RGB values or indices into the currently realized logical palette. The parameter must be one of the following values:

- **DIB_PAL_COLORS**   The color table consists of an array of 16-bit indexes.

- **DIB_RGB_COLORS**   The color table contains literal RGB values.

The following value is available only in the second version of this member function:

- **DIB_PAL_INDICES**   No color table is provided. The bitmap itself contains indices into the logical palette of the device context into which the brush is to be selected.

lpPackedDIB   Points to a packed DIB consisting of a **BITMAPINFO** structure immediately followed by an array of bytes defining the pixels of the bitmap.

Remarks

Initializes a brush with the pattern specified by a device-independent bitmap (DIB). The brush can subsequently be selected for any device context that supports raster operations.

The two versions differ in the way you handle the DIB:

- In the first version, to obtain a handle to the DIB you call the Windows **::GlobalAlloc** function to allocate a block of global memory and then fill the memory with the packed DIB.

- In the second version, it is not necessary to call **::GlobalAlloc** to allocate memory for the packed DIB.

A packed DIB consists of a **BITMAPINFO** data structure immediately followed by the array of bytes that defines the pixels of the bitmap. Bitmaps used as fill patterns should be 8 pixels by 8 pixels. If the bitmap is larger, Windows creates a fill pattern using only the bits corresponding to the first 8 rows and 8 columns of pixels in the upper-left corner of the bitmap.

When an application selects a two-color DIB pattern brush into a monochrome device context, Windows ignores the colors specified in the DIB and instead displays the pattern brush using the current text and background colors of the device context. Pixels mapped to the first color (at offset 0 in the DIB color table) of the DIB are displayed using the text color. Pixels mapped to the second color (at offset 1 in the color table) are displayed using the background color.

For information about using the following Windows functions, see the *Win32 SDK Programmer's Reference*:

- **::CreateDIBPatternBrush** (This function is provided only for compatibility with applications written for versions of Windows earlier than 3.0; use the **::CreateDIBPatternBrushPt** function.)

- **::CreateDIBPatternBrushPt** (This function should be used for Win32-based applications.)

- **::GlobalAlloc**

See Also **CBrush::CreatePatternBrush, CBrush::CreateBrushIndirect, CBrush::CreateSolidBrush, CBrush::CreateHatchBrush, CGdiObject::CreateStockObject, CDC::SelectObject, CGdiObject::DeleteObject, CDC::GetBrushOrg, CDC::SetBrushOrg**

CBrush::CreateHatchBrush

BOOL CreateHatchBrush(int *nIndex***, COLORREF** *crColor* **);**

Return Value
Nonzero if successful; otherwise 0.

Parameters
nIndex Specifies the hatch style of the brush. It can be any one of the following values:

- **HS_BDIAGONAL** Downward hatch (left to right) at 45 degrees

- **HS_CROSS** Horizontal and vertical crosshatch

- **HS_DIAGCROSS** Crosshatch at 45 degrees

- **HS_FDIAGONAL** Upward hatch (left to right) at 45 degrees

- **HS_HORIZONTAL** Horizontal hatch

- **HS_VERTICAL** Vertical hatch

crColor Specifies the foreground color of the brush as an RGB color (the color of the hatches).

Remarks
Initializes a brush with the specified hatched pattern and color. The brush can subsequently be selected as the current brush for any device context.

See Also **CBrush::CreateBrushIndirect, CBrush::CreateDIBPatternBrush, CBrush::CreatePatternBrush, CBrush::CreateSolidBrush, CGdiObject::CreateStockObject, ::CreateHatchBrush**

CBrush::CreatePatternBrush

BOOL CreatePatternBrush(CBitmap* *pBitmap* **);**

Return Value

Nonzero if successful; otherwise 0.

Parameters

pBitmap   Identifies a bitmap.

Remarks

Initializes a brush with a pattern specified by a bitmap. The brush can subsequently be selected for any device context that supports raster operations. The bitmap identified by *pBitmap* is typically initialized by using the **CBitmap::CreateBitmap**, **CBitmap::CreateBitmapIndirect**, **CBitmap::LoadBitmap**, or **CBitmap::CreateCompatibleBitmap** function.

Bitmaps used as fill patterns should be 8 pixels by 8 pixels. If the bitmap is larger, Windows will only use the bits corresponding to the first 8 rows and columns of pixels in the upper-left corner of the bitmap.

A pattern brush can be deleted without affecting the associated bitmap. This means the bitmap can be used to create any number of pattern brushes.

A brush created using a monochrome bitmap (1 color plane, 1 bit per pixel) is drawn using the current text and background colors. Pixels represented by a bit set to 0 are drawn with the current text color. Pixels represented by a bit set to 1 are drawn with the current background color.

For information about using **::CreatePatternBrush**, a Windows function, see the *Win32 SDK Programmer's Reference*.

See Also   **CBrush::CreateBrushIndirect, CBrush::CreateDIBPatternBrush, CBrush::CreateHatchBrush, CBrush::CreateSolidBrush, CGdiObject::CreateStockObject**

CBrush::CreateSolidBrush

BOOL CreateSolidBrush(COLORREF *crColor* **);**

Return Value

Nonzero if successful; otherwise 0.

Parameters

crColor   A **COLORREF** structure that specifies the color of the brush. The color specifies an RGB value and can be constructed with the **RGB** macro in WINDOWS.H.

Remarks

Initializes a brush with a specified solid color. The brush can subsequently be selected as the current brush for any device context.

When an application has finished using the brush created by **CreateSolidBrush**, it should select the brush out of the device context.

See Also   **CBrush::CreateBrushIndirect, CBrush::CreateDIBPatternBrush, CBrush::CreateHatchBrush, CBrush::CreatePatternBrush, ::CreateSolidBrush, CGdiObject::DeleteObject**

CBrush::CreateSysColorBrush

BOOL CreateSysColorBrush(int *nIndex* **);**

Return Value

Nonzero if successful; otherwise 0.

Parameters

nIndex   Specifies the hatch style of the brush. It can be any one of the following values:

- **HS_BDIAGONAL**   Downward hatch (left to right) at 45 degrees
- **HS_CROSS**   Horizontal and vertical crosshatch
- **HS_DIAGCROSS**   Crosshatch at 45 degrees
- **HS_FDIAGONAL**   Upward hatch (left to right) at 45 degrees
- **HS_HORIZONTAL**   Horizontal hatch
- **HS_VERTICAL**   Vertical hatch

Remarks

Initializes a brush color. The brush can subsequently be selected as the current brush for any device context.

When an application has finished using the brush created by **CreateSysColorBrush**, it should select the brush out of the device context.

See Also   **CBrush::CreateBrushIndirect, CBrush::CreateDIBPatternBrush, CBrush::CreateHatchBrush, CBrush::CreatePatternBrush, ::CreateSolidBrush, CBrush::CreateSolidBrush, ::GetSysColorBrush, CGdiObject::DeleteObject**

CBrush::FromHandle

static CBrush* PASCAL FromHandle(HBRUSH *hBrush* **);**

Return Value

A pointer to a **CBrush** object if successful; otherwise **NULL**.

Parameters

hBrush   **HANDLE** to a Windows GDI brush.

Remarks

Returns a pointer to a **CBrush** object when given a handle to a Windows **HBRUSH** object. If a **CBrush** object is not already attached to the handle, a temporary **CBrush** object is created and attached. This temporary **CBrush** object is valid only until the next time the application has idle time in its event loop. At this time, all temporary graphic objects are deleted. In other words, the temporary object is valid only during the processing of one window message.

For more information about using graphic objects, see "Graphic Objects" in the *Win32 SDK Programmer's Reference*.

CBrush::GetLogBrush

int GetLogBrush(LOGBRUSH* *pLogBrush* **);**

Return Value

If the function succeeds, and *pLogBrush* is a valid pointer, the return value is the number of bytes stored into the buffer.

If the function succeeds, and *pLogBrush* is **NULL**, the return value is the number of bytes required to hold the information the function would store into the buffer.

If the function fails, the return value is 0.

Parameters

pLogBrush   Points to a **LOGBRUSH** structure that contains information about the brush.

Remarks

Call this member function to retrieve the **LOGBRUSH** structure. The **LOGBRUSH** structure defines the style, color, and pattern of a brush.

For example, call **GetLogBrush** to match the particular color or pattern of a bitmap.

Example

```
LOGBRUSH logbrush;
brushExisting.GetLogBrush( &logbrush );
CBrush brushOther( logbrush.lbColor);
```

See Also   LOGBRUSH, ::GetObject

CBrush::operator HBRUSH

operator HBRUSH( ) const;

Return Value

If successful, a handle to the Windows GDI object represented by the **CBrush** object; otherwise **NULL**.

Remarks

Use this operator to get the attached Windows GDI handle of the **CBrush** object. This operator is a casting operator, which supports direct use of an **HBRUSH** object.

For more information about using graphic objects, see "Graphic Objects" in the *Win32 SDK Programmer's Reference*.

CButton

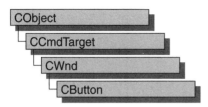

The **CButton** class provides the functionality of Windows button controls. A button control is a small, rectangular child window that can be clicked on and off. Buttons can be used alone or in groups and can either be labeled or appear without text. A button typically changes appearance when the user clicks it.

Typical buttons are the check box, radio button, and pushbutton. A **CButton** object can become any of these, according to the button style specified at its initialization by the **Create** member function. For a list of button styles, see "Button Styles" in the "Styles Used by MFC" section.

In addition, the **CBitmapButton** class derived from **CButton** supports creation of button controls labeled with bitmap images instead of text. A **CBitmapButton** can have separate bitmaps for a button's up, down, focused, and disabled states.

You can create a button control either from a dialog template or directly in your code. In both cases, first call the constructor **CButton** to construct the **CButton** object; then call the **Create** member function to create the Windows button control and attach it to the **CButton** object.

Construction can be a one-step process in a class derived from **CButton**. Write a constructor for the derived class and call **Create** from within the constructor.

If you want to handle Windows notification messages sent by a button control to its parent (usually a class derived from **CDialog**), add a message-map entry and message-handler member function to the parent class for each message.

Each message-map entry takes the following form:

ON_Notification(*id*, *memberFxn*)

where *id* specifies the child window ID of the control sending the notification and *memberFxn* is the name of the parent member function you have written to handle the notification.

The parent's function prototype is as follows:

afx_msg void *memberFxn*( );

Potential message-map entries are as follows:

Map entry	Sent to parent when...
ON_BN_CLICKED	The user clicks a button.
ON_BN_DOUBLECLICKED	The user double-clicks a button.

If you create a **CButton** object from a dialog resource, the **CButton** object is automatically destroyed when the user closes the dialog box.

If you create a **CButton** object within a window, you may need to destroy it. If you create the **CButton** object on the heap by using the **new** function, you must call **delete** on the object to destroy it when the user closes the Windows button control. If you create the **CButton** object on the stack, or it is embedded in the parent dialog object, it is destroyed automatically.

#include <afxwin.h>

See Also   **CWnd**, **CComboBox**, **CEdit**, **CListBox**, **CScrollBar**, **CStatic**, **CBitmapButton**, **CDialog**

Construction

CButton	Constructs a **CButton** object.

Initialization

Create	Creates the Windows button control and attaches it to the **CButton** object.

Operations

GetState	Retrieves the check state, highlight state, and focus state of a button control.
SetState	Sets the highlighting state of a button control.
GetCheck	Retrieves the check state of a button control.
SetCheck	Sets the check state of a button control.
GetButtonStyle	Retrieves information about the button control style.
SetButtonStyle	Changes the style of a button.
GetIcon	Retrieves the handle of the icon previously set with **SetIcon**.
SetIcon	Specifies an icon to be displayed on the button.
GetBitmap	Retrieves the handle of the bitmap previously set with **SetBitmap**.
SetBitmap	Specifies a bitmap to be displayed on the button.
GetCursor	Retrieves the handle of the cursor image previously set with **SetCursor**.
SetCursor	Specifies a cursor image to be displayed on the button.

Overridables

DrawItem	Override to draw an owner-drawn **CButton** object.

Member Functions

CButton::CButton

CButton( );

Remarks

Constructs a **CButton** object.

See Also   CButton::Create

CButton::Create

BOOL Create(LPCTSTR *lpszCaption*, **DWORD** *dwStyle*, **const RECT&** *rect*, **CWnd*** *pParentWnd*, **UINT** *nID* **);**

Return Value

Nonzero if successful; otherwise 0.

Parameters

lpszCaption   Specifies the button control's text.

dwStyle   Specifies the button control's style. Apply any combination of button styles to the button.

rect   Specifies the button control's size and position. It can be either a **CRect** object or a **RECT** structure.

pParentWnd   Specifies the button control's parent window, usually a **CDialog**. It must not be **NULL**.

nID   Specifies the button control's ID.

Remarks

You construct a **CButton** object in two steps. First call the constructor, then call **Create**, which creates the Windows button control and attaches it to the **CButton** object.

If the **WS_VISIBLE** style is given, Windows sends the button control all the messages required to activate and show the button.

Apply the following window styles to a button control: (For a list of window styles, see "Window Styles" in the "Styles Used by MFC" section.)

- **WS_CHILD**   Always
- **WS_VISIBLE**   Usually
- **WS_DISABLED**   Rarely
- **WS_GROUP**   To group controls
- **WS_TABSTOP**   To include the button in the tabbing order

See Also   **CButton::CButton**

CButton::DrawItem

virtual void DrawItem(LPDRAWITEMSTRUCT *lpDrawItemStruct* **);**

Parameters

lpDrawItemStruct   A long pointer to a **DRAWITEMSTRUCT** structure. The structure contains information about the item to be drawn and the type of drawing required.

Remarks

Called by the framework when a visual aspect of an owner-drawn button has changed. An owner-drawn button has the **BS_OWNERDRAW** style set. Override this member function to implement drawing for an owner-drawn **CButton** object. The application should restore all graphics device interface (GDI) objects selected for the display context supplied in *lpDrawItemStruct* before the member function terminates.

Also see the **BS_** style values. For a list of button styles, see "Button Styles" in the "Styles Used by MFC" section.

See Also   **CButton::SetButtonStyle**, **WM_DRAWITEM**

CButton::GetBitmap

HBITMAP GetBitmap( ) const;

Return Value

A handle to a bitmap. **NULL** if no bitmap is previously specified.

Remarks

Call this member function to get the handle of a bitmap, previously set with **SetBitmap**, that is associated with a button.

See Also   **CButton::SetBitmap**, **CBitmapButton::LoadBitmaps**

In the Win32 SDK documentation: "Bitmaps"

CButton::GetButtonStyle

UINT GetButtonStyle( ) const;

Return Value

Returns the button styles for this **CButton** object.

Remarks

This function returns only the **BS_** style values, not any of the other window styles. For a list of button styles, see "Button Styles" in the "Styles Used by MFC" section.

See Also   **CButton::SetButtonStyle**, **::GetWindowLong**

CButton::GetCheck

int GetCheck( ) const;

Return Value

The return value from a button control created with the **BS_AUTOCHECKBOX**, **BS_AUTORADIOBUTTON**, **BS_AUTO3STATE**, **BS_CHECKBOX**, **BS_RADIOBUTTON**, or **BS_3STATE** style is one of the following values:

Value	Meaning
0	Button state is unchecked.
1	Button state is checked.
2	Button state is indeterminate (applies only if the button has the **BS_3STATE** or **BS_AUTO3STATE** style).

If the button has any other style, the return value is 0.

Remarks

Retrieves the check state of a radio button or check box.

See Also   **CButton::GetState**, **CButton::SetState**, **CButton::SetCheck**, **BM_GETCHECK**

CButton::GetCursor

HCURSOR GetCursor( );

Return Value

A handle to a cursor image. **NULL** if no cursor is previously specified.

Remarks

Call this member function to get the handle of a cursor, previously set with **SetCursor**, that is associated with a button.

See Also   **CButton::SetCursor**, **CBitmapButton::LoadBitmaps**

In the Win32 SDK documentation: "Bitmaps"

CButton::GetIcon

HICON GetIcon( ) const;

Return Value

A handle to an icon. **NULL** if no icon is previously specified.

Remarks

Call this member function to get the handle of an icon, previously set with **SetIcon**, that is associated with a button.

See Also   **CButton::SetIcon**, **CBitmapButton::LoadBitmaps**

In the Win32 SDK documentation: "Bitmaps"

CButton::GetState

UINT GetState( ) const;

Return Value

Specifies the current state of the button control. You can use the following masks against the return value to extract information about the state:

Mask	Meaning
0x0003	Specifies the check state (radio buttons and check boxes only). A 0 indicates the button is unchecked. A 1 indicates the button is checked. A radio button is checked when it contains a bullet (•). A check box is checked when it contains an **X**. A 2 indicates the check state is indeterminate (three-state check boxes only). The state of a three-state check box is indeterminate when it contains a halftone pattern.
0x0004	Specifies the highlight state. A nonzero value indicates that the button is highlighted. A button is highlighted when the user clicks and holds the left mouse button. The highlighting is removed when the user releases the mouse button.
0x0008	Specifies the focus state. A nonzero value indicates that the button has the focus.

Remarks

Retrieves the state of a radio button or check box.

See Also **CButton::GetCheck**, **CButton::SetCheck**, **CButton::SetState**, **BM_GETSTATE**

CButton::SetBitmap

HBITMAP SetBitmap(HBITMAP *hBitmap* **);**

Return Value

The handle of a bitmap previously associated with the button.

Parameters

hBitmap   The handle of a bitmap.

Remarks

Call this member function to associate a new bitmap with the button.

The bitmap will be automatically placed on the face of the button, centered by default. If the bitmap is too large for the button, it will be clipped on either side. You can choose other alignment options, including the following:

- **BS_TOP**
- **BS_LEFT**
- **BS_RIGHT**
- **BS_CENTER**
- **BS_BOTTOM**
- **BS_VCENTER**

Unlike **CBitmapButton**, which uses four bitmaps per button, **SetBitmap** uses only one bitmap per the button. When the button is pressed, the bitmap appears to shift down and to the right.

See Also **CButton::GetBitmap**, **CBitmapButton**, **CBitmapButton::LoadBitmaps**

In the Win32 SDK documentation: "Bitmaps"

CButton::SetButtonStyle

void SetButtonStyle(UINT *nStyle*, **BOOL** *bRedraw* = **TRUE);**

Parameters

nStyle   Specifies the button style.

bRedraw   Specifies whether the button is to be redrawn. A nonzero value redraws the button. A 0 value does not redraw the button. The button is redrawn by default.

Remarks

Changes the style of a button.

Use the **GetButtonStyle** member function to retrieve the button style. The low-order word of the complete button style is the button-specific style.

For a list of possible button styles, see "Button Styles" in the "Styles Used by MFC" section..

See Also **CButton::GetButtonStyle, BM_SETSTYLE**

CButton::SetCheck

void SetCheck(int *nCheck* **);**

Parameters

nCheck   Specifies the check state. This parameter can be one of the following:

Value	Meaning
0	Set the button state to unchecked.
1	Set the button state to checked.
2	Set the button state to indeterminate. This value can be used only if the button has the **BS_3STATE** or **BS_AUTO3STATE** style.

Remarks

Sets or resets the check state of a radio button or check box. This member function has no effect on a pushbutton.

See Also **CButton::GetCheck, CButton::GetState, CButton::SetState, BM_SETCHECK**

CButton::SetCursor

HCURSOR SetCursor(HCURSOR *hCursor* **);**

Return Value

The handle of a cursor previously associated with the button.

Parameters

hCursor   The handle of a cursor.

Remarks

Call this member function to associate a new cursor with the button.

The cursor will be automatically placed on the face of the button, centered by default. If the cursor is too large for the button, it will be clipped on either side. You can choose other alignment options, including the following:

- **BS_TOP**
- **BS_LEFT**
- **BS_RIGHT**
- **BS_CENTER**
- **BS_BOTTOM**
- **BS_VCENTER**

Unlike **CBitmapButton**, which uses four bitmaps per button, **SetCursor** uses only one cursor per the button. When the button is pressed, the cursor appears to shift down and to the right.

See Also   **CButton::GetCursor**, **CBitmapButton::LoadBitmaps**

In the Win32 SDK documentation: "Bitmaps"

CButton::SetIcon

HICON SetIcon(HICON *hIcon* **);**

Return Value

The handle of an icon previously associated with the button.

Parameters

hIcon   The handle of an icon.

Remarks

Call this member function to associate a new icon with the button.

The icon will be automatically placed on the face of the button, centered by default. If the icon is too large for the button, it will be clipped on either side. You can choose other alignment options, including the following:

- **BS_TOP**
- **BS_LEFT**
- **BS_RIGHT**
- **BS_CENTER**
- **BS_BOTTOM**
- **BS_VCENTER**

Unlike **CBitmapButton**, which uses four bitmaps per button, **SetIcon** uses only one icon per the button. When the button is pressed, the icon appears to shift down and to the right.

See Also   **CButton::GetIcon**, **CBitmapButton::LoadBitmaps**

In the Win32 SDK documentation: "Bitmaps"

CButton::SetState

void SetState(BOOL *bHighlight* **);**

Parameters

bHighlight   Specifies whether the button is to be highlighted. A nonzero value highlights the button; a 0 value removes any highlighting.

Remarks

Sets the highlighting state of a button control.

Highlighting affects the exterior of a button control. It has no effect on the check state of a radio button or check box.

A button control is automatically highlighted when the user clicks and holds the left mouse button. The highlighting is removed when the user releases the mouse button.

See Also   **CButton::GetState**, **CButton::SetCheck**, **CButton::GetCheck**, **BM_SETSTATE**

CByteArray

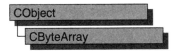

The **CByteArray** class supports dynamic arrays of bytes.

The member functions of **CByteArray** are similar to the member functions of class **CObArray**. Because of this similarity, you can use the **CObArray** reference documentation for member function specifics. Wherever you see a **CObject** pointer as a function parameter or return value, substitute a **BYTE**.

```
CObject* CObArray::GetAt( int <nIndex> ) const;
```

for example, translates to

```
BYTE CByteArray::GetAt( int <nIndex> ) const;
```

CByteArray incorporates the **IMPLEMENT_SERIAL** macro to support serialization and dumping of its elements. If an array of bytes is stored to an archive, either with the overloaded insertion (<<) operator or with the **Serialize** member function, each element is, in turn, serialized.

Note Before using an array, use **SetSize** to establish its size and allocate memory for it. If you do not use **SetSize**, adding elements to your array causes it to be frequently reallocated and copied. Frequent reallocation and copying are inefficient and can fragment memory.

If you need debug output from individual elements in the array, you must set the depth of the **CDumpContext** object to 1 or greater.

For more information on using **CByteArray**, see the article "Collections" in *Programming with MFC*.

#include <afxcoll.h>

See Also   **CObArray**

Construction

CByteArray	Constructs an empty array for bytes.

Bounds

GetSize	Gets the number of elements in this array.
GetUpperBound	Returns the largest valid index.
SetSize	Sets the number of elements to be contained in this array.

Operations

FreeExtra	Frees all unused memory above the current upper bound.
RemoveAll	Removes all the elements from this array.

Element Access

GetAt	Returns the value at a given index.
SetAt	Sets the value for a given index; array not allowed to grow.
ElementAt	Returns a temporary reference to the byte within the array.

Growing the Array

SetAtGrow	Sets the value for a given index; grows the array if necessary.
Add	Adds an element to the end of the array; grows the array if necessary.

Insertion/Removal

InsertAt	Inserts an element (or all the elements in another array) at a specified index.
RemoveAt	Removes an element at a specific index.

Operators

operator []	Sets or gets the element at the specified index.

CCheckListBox

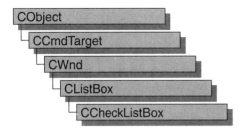

The **CCheckListBox** class provides the functionality of a Windows checklist box. A "checklist box" displays a list of items, such as filenames, that the user can view and select. A check box appears next to each item in the list; the user can check or clear the selected item's check box.

You can create a checklist box either from a dialog template or directly in your code. In both cases, call the constructor **CCheckListBox** to construct the **CCheckListBox** object, then call the **Create** member function to create the Windows checklist-box control and attach it to the **CCheckListBox** object.

Construction can be a one-step process in a class derived from **CCheckListBox**. Write a constructor for the derived class and call **Create** from within the constructor.

#include <afxwin.h>

See Also   **CListBox**

Construction

CCheckListBox	Constructs a **CCheckListBox** object.
Create	Creates the Windows checklist box and attaches it to the **CCheckListBox** object.

Attributes

SetCheckStyle	Sets the style of the control's check boxes.
GetCheckStyle	Gets the style of the control's check boxes.
SetCheck	Sets the state of an item's check box.
GetCheck	Gets the state of an item's check box.
Enable	Enables or disables a checklist box item.
IsEnabled	Determines whether an item is enabled.
OnGetCheckPosition	Called by the framework to get the position of an item's check box.

Member Functions

CCheckListBox::CCheckListBox

CCheckListBox( );

Remarks

Constructs a **CCheckListBox** object.

You construct a **CCheckListBox** object in two steps. First call the constructor **CCheckListBox**, then call **Create**, which initializes the Windows checklist box and attaches it to the **CCheckListBox**.

See Also   **CCheckListBox::Create**

CCheckListBox::Create

BOOL Create(DWORD *dwStyle***, const RECT&** *rect***, CWnd*** *pParentWnd***, UINT** *nID* **);**

Return Value

Nonzero if successful; otherwise 0.

Parameters

dwStyle   Specifies the style of the checklist box. Apply any combination of list-box styles to the box. For a list of list-box styles, see "List-Box Styles" in the "Styles" section.

rect   Specifies the checklist-box size and position. Can be either a **CRect** object or a **RECT** structure.

pParentWnd   Specifies the checklist box's parent window (usually a **CDialog** object). It must not be **NULL**.

nID   Specifies the checklist box's control ID.

Remarks

You construct a **CCheckListBox** object in two steps. First call the constructor, then call **Create**, which initializes the Windows checklist box and attaches it to the **CCheckListBox** object.

When **Create** executes, Windows sends the **WM_NCCREATE**, **WM_CREATE**, **WM_NCCALCSIZE**, and **WM_GETMINMAXINFO** messages to the checklist-box control.

These messages are handled by default by the **OnNcCreate**, **OnCreate**, **OnNcCalcSize**, and **OnGetMinMaxInfo** member functions in the **CWnd** base class. To extend the default message handling, derive a class from **CCheckListBox**, add a message map to the new class, and override the preceding message-handler member functions. Override **OnCreate**, for example, to perform needed initialization for a new class.

Apply the following window styles to a checklist-box control: (for a list of window styles, see "Window Styles" in the "Styles Used by MFC" section.)

- **WS_CHILD** Always
- **WS_VISIBLE** Usually
- **WS_DISABLED** Rarely
- **WS_VSCROLL** To add a vertical scroll bar
- **WS_HSCROLL** To add a horizontal scroll bar
- **WS_GROUP** To group controls
- **WS_TABSTOP** To allow tabbing to this control

See Also **CCheckListBox::CCheckListBox**

CCheckListBox::Enable

void Enable(int *nIndex,* **BOOL** *bEnabled* = **TRUE);**

Parameters

nIndex Index of the checklist box item to be enabled.

bEnabled Specifies whether the item is enabled or disabled.

Remarks

Call this function to enable or disable a checklist box item.

See Also **CCheckListBox::IsEnabled**

CCheckListBox::GetCheck

int GetCheck(int *nIndex* **);**

Return Value

Zero if the item is not checked, 1 if it is checked, and 2 if it is indeterminate.

Parameters

nIndex Index of the item whose check status is to be retrieved.

Remarks

Call this function to determine the check state of an item.

See Also **CCheckListBox::OnGetCheckPosition CCheckListBox::SetCheck CCheckListBox::SetCheckStyle CCheckListBox::GetCheckStyle**

CCheckListBox::GetCheckStyle

UINT GetCheckStyle( );

Return Value

The style of the control's check boxes.

Remarks

Call this function to get the checklist box's style. For information on possible styles, see **SetCheckStyle**.

See Also   **CCheckListBox::OnGetCheckPosition CCheckListBox::SetCheck CCheckListBox::SetCheckStyle CCheckListBox::GetCheck**

CCheckListBox::IsEnabled

BOOL IsEnabled(int *nIndex* **);**

Return Value

Nonzero if the item is enabled; otherwise 0.

Parameters

nIndex   Index of the item.

Remarks

Call this function to determine whether an item is enabled.

See Also   **CCheckListBox::Enable**

CCheckListBox::OnGetCheckPosition

virtual CRect OnGetCheckPosition(CRect *rectItem*, **CRect** *rectCheckBox* **);**

Return Value

The position of the check box.

Parameters

rectItem   The position of the item.

rectCheckBox   The position of the check box.

Remarks

The framework calls this function to get the position of the check box.

The default implementation only returns the position of the check box. Override this function to change the default position of the check box within the item.

See Also   **CCheckListBox::SetCheck CCheckListBox::SetCheckStyle CCheckListBox::GetCheck CCheckListBox::GetCheckStyle CCheckListBox::OnGetCheckPosition**

141

CCheckListBox::SetCheck

void SetCheck(int *nIndex***, int** *nCheck* **);**

Parameters

nIndex   Index of the item whose check box is to be set.

nCheck   State of the check box: 0 for clear, 1 for checked, and 2 for indeterminate.

Remarks

Call this function to set the check box of the item specified by *nIndex*.

See Also   **CCheckListBox::SetCheckStyle CCheckListBox::GetCheck CCheckListBox::GetCheckStyle**

CCheckListBox::SetCheckStyle

void SetCheckStyle(UINT *nStyle* **);**

Parameters

nStyle   Determines the style of check boxes in the checklist box.

Remarks

Call this function to set the style of check boxes in the checklist box. Valid styles are:

- **BS_CHECKBOX**
- **BS_AUTOCHECKBOX**
- **BS_AUTO3STATE**
- **BS_3STATE**

For information on these styles, see "Button Styles" in the "Styles" section.

See Also   **CCheckListBox::SetCheck CCheckListBox::GetCheck CCheckListBox::GetCheckStyle**

CClientDC

The **CClientDC** class is derived from **CDC** and takes care of calling the Windows functions **GetDC** at construction time and **ReleaseDC** at destruction time. This means that the device context associated with a **CClientDC** object is the client area of a window.

For more information on **CClientDC**, see "Device Contexts" in Chapter 1 of *Programming with MFC*.

#include <afxwin.h>

See Also   **CDC**

Construction

CClientDC	Constructs a **CClientDC** object connected to the **CWnd**.

Data Members

m_hWnd	The **HWND** of the window for which this **CClientDC** is valid.

Member Functions

CClientDC::CClientDC

CClientDC(CWnd* *pWnd* **);**
    throw(CResourceException);

Parameters

pWnd   The window whose client area the device context object will access.

Remarks

Constructs a **CClientDC** object that accesses the client area of the **CWnd** pointed to by *pWnd*. The constructor calls the Windows function **GetDC**.

An exception (of type **CResourceException**) is thrown if the Windows **GetDC** call fails. A device context may not be available if Windows has already allocated all of its available device contexts. Your application competes for the five common display contexts available at any given time under Windows.

Data Members

CClientDC::m_hWnd

Remarks

The **HWND** of the **CWnd** pointer used to construct the **CClientDC** object. **m_hWnd** is a protected variable.

CCmdTarget

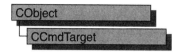

CCmdTarget is the base class for the Microsoft Foundation Class Library message-map architecture. A message map routes commands or messages to the member functions you write to handle them. (A command is a message from a menu item, command button, or accelerator key.)

Key framework classes derived from **CCmdTarget** include **CView**, **CWinApp**, **CDocument**, **CWnd**, and **CFrameWnd**. If you intend for a new class to handle messages, derive the class from one of these **CCmdTarget**-derived classes. You will rarely derive a class from **CCmdTarget** directly.

For an overview of command targets and **OnCmdMsg** routing, see the topics "Command Targets," "Command Routing," and "Message Maps" in Chapter 2 of *Programming with MFC*.

CCmdTarget includes member functions that handle the display of an hourglass cursor. Display the hourglass cursor when you expect a command to take a noticeable time interval to execute.

Dispatch maps, similar to message maps, are used to expose OLE automation **IDispatch** functionality. By exposing this interface, other applications (such as Visual Basic) can call into your application. For more information on OLE automation and **IDispatch** interfaces, see "Dispatch Interfaces," Chapter 5 of *Creating Programmable Applications*.

#include <afxwin.h>

See Also   **CCmdUI**, **CDocument**, **CDocTemplate**, **CWinApp**, **CWnd**, **CView**, **CFrameWnd**, **COleDispatchDriver**

Attributes

FromIDispatch	Returns a pointer to the **CCmdTarget** object associated with the **IDispatch** pointer.
GetIDispatch	Returns a pointer to the **IDispatch** object associated with the **CCmdTarget** object.
IsResultExpected	Returns **TRUE** if an automation function should return a value.

Operations

BeginWaitCursor	Displays the cursor as an hourglass cursor.
EnableAutomation	Allows OLE automation for the **CCmdTarget** object.
EndWaitCursor	Returns to the previous cursor.
RestoreWaitCursor	Restores the hourglass cursor.

Overridables

OnCmdMsg	Routes and dispatches command messages.
OnFinalRelease	Cleans up after the last OLE reference is released.

Member Functions

CCmdTarget::BeginWaitCursor

void BeginWaitCursor( );

Remarks

Call this function to display the cursor as an hourglass when you expect a command to take a noticeable time interval to execute. The framework calls this function to show the user that it is busy, such as when a **CDocument** object loads or saves itself to a file.

The actions of **BeginWaitCursor** are not always effective outside of a single message handler as other actions, such as **OnSetCursor** handling, could change the cursor.

Call **EndWaitCursor** to restore the previous cursor.

Example

```
// The following example illustrates the most common case
// of displaying the hourglass cursor during some lengthy
// processing of a command handler implemented in some
// CCmdTarget-derived class, such as a document or view.

void CMyView::OnSomeCommand()
{
    BeginWaitCursor(); // display the hourglass cursor

    // do some lengthy processing

    EndWaitCursor(); // remove the hourglass cursor
}

// The next example illustrates RestoreWaitCursor.
void CMyView::OnSomeCommand()
{
    BeginWaitCursor(); // display the hourglass cursor
```

```
   // do some lengthy processing

   // The dialog box will normally change the cursor to
   // the standard arrow cursor, and leave the cursor in
   // as the standard arrow cursor when the dialog box is
   // closed.
   CMyDialog dlg;
   dlg.DoModal();

   // It is necessary to call RestoreWaitCursor here in order
   // to change the cursor back to the hourglass cursor.
   RestoreWaitCursor();

   // do some more lengthy processing

   EndWaitCursor(); // remove the hourglass cursor
}

// In the above example, the dialog was clearly invoked between
// the pair of calls to BeginWaitCursor and EndWaitCursor.
// Sometimes it may not be clear whether the dialog is invoked
// in between a pair of calls to BeginWaitCursor and EndWaitCursor.
// It is permissable to call RestoreWaitCursor, even if
// BeginWaitCursor was not previously called.  This case is
// illustrated below, where CMyView::AnotherFunction does not
// need to know whether it was called in the context of an
// hourglass cursor.
void CMyView::AnotherFunction()
{
   // some processing ...

   CMyDialog dlg;
   dlg.DoModal();
   RestoreWaitCursor();

   // some more processing ...
}

// If the dialog is invoked from a member function of
// some non-CCmdTarget, then you can call CWinApp::DoWaitCursor
// with a 0 parameter value to restore the hourglass cursor.
void CMyObject::AnotherFunction()
{
   CMyDialog dlg;
   dlg.DoModal();
   AfxGetApp()->DoWaitCursor(0); // same as CCmdTarget::RestoreWaitCursor
}
```

See Also   **CWaitCursor**, **CCmdTarget::EndWaitCursor**,
CCmdTarget::RestoreWaitCursor, **CWinApp::DoWaitCursor**

CCmdTarget::EnableAutomation

void EnableAutomation( );

Remarks

Call this function to enable OLE automation for an object. This function is typically called from the constructor of your object and should only be called if a dispatch map has been declared for the class. For more information on automation see the articles "Automation Clients" and "Automation Servers" in *Programming with MFC*.

See Also **DECLARE_DISPATCH_MAP, DECLARE_OLECREATE**

CCmdTarget::EndWaitCursor

void EndWaitCursor( );

Remarks

Call this function after you have called the **BeginWaitCursor** member function to return from the hourglass cursor to the previous cursor. The framework also calls this member function after it has called the hourglass cursor.

Example

```
// The following example illustrates the most common case
// of displaying the hourglass cursor during some lengthy
// processing of a command handler implemented in some
// CCmdTarget-derived class, such as a document or view.

void CMyView::OnSomeCommand()
{
    BeginWaitCursor(); // display the hourglass cursor

    // do some lengthy processing

    EndWaitCursor(); // remove the hourglass cursor
}

// The next example illustrates RestoreWaitCursor.
void CMyView::OnSomeCommand()
{
    BeginWaitCursor(); // display the hourglass cursor

    // do some lengthy processing

    // The dialog box will normally change the cursor to
    // the standard arrow cursor, and leave the cursor in
    // as the standard arrow cursor when the dialog box is
    // closed.
    CMyDialog dlg;
    dlg.DoModal();
```

```
    // It is necessary to call RestoreWaitCursor here in order
    // to change the cursor back to the hourglass cursor.
    RestoreWaitCursor();

    // do some more lengthy processing

    EndWaitCursor(); // remove the hourglass cursor
}

// In the above example, the dialog was clearly invoked between
// the pair of calls to BeginWaitCursor and EndWaitCursor.
// Sometimes it may not be clear whether the dialog is invoked
// in between a pair of calls to BeginWaitCursor and EndWaitCursor.
// It is permissable to call RestoreWaitCursor, even if
// BeginWaitCursor was not previously called.  This case is
// illustrated below, where CMyView::AnotherFunction does not
// need to know whether it was called in the context of an
// hourglass cursor.
void CMyView::AnotherFunction()
{
    // some processing ...

    CMyDialog dlg;
    dlg.DoModal();
    RestoreWaitCursor();

    // some more processing ...
}

// If the dialog is invoked from a member function of
// some non-CCmdTarget, then you can call CWinApp::DoWaitCursor
// with a 0 parameter value to restore the hourglass cursor.
void CMyObject::AnotherFunction()
{
    CMyDialog dlg;
    dlg.DoModal();
    AfxGetApp()->DoWaitCursor(0); // same as CCmdTarget::RestoreWaitCursor
}
```

See Also   **CWaitCursor**, **CCmdTarget::BeginWaitCursor**,
CCmdTarget::RestoreWaitCursor, **CWinApp::DoWaitCursor**

CCmdTarget::FromIDispatch

static CCmdTarget* FromIDispatch(LPDISPATCH *lpDispatch* **);**

Return Value

A pointer to the **CCmdTarget** object associated with *lpDispatch*. This function
returns **NULL** if the **IDispatch** object is not recognized as a Microsoft Foundation
Class **IDispatch** object.

Parameters

    lpDispatch   A pointer to an **IDispatch** object.

Remarks

    Call this function to map an **IDispatch** pointer, received from automation member functions of a class, into the **CCmdTarget** object that implements the interfaces of the **IDispatch** object.

    The result of this function is the inverse of a call to the member function **GetIDispatch**.

    See Also   **CCmdTarget::GetIDispatch**, **COleDispatchDriver**

CCmdTarget::GetIDispatch

    LPDISPATCH GetIDispatch(BOOL *bAddRef* **);**

Return Value

    The **IDispatch** pointer associated with the object.

Parameters

    bAddRef   Specifies whether to increment the reference count for the object.

Remarks

    Call this member function to retrieve the **IDispatch** pointer from an automation method that either returns an **IDispatch** pointer or takes an **IDispatch** pointer by reference.

    For objects that call **EnableAutomation** in their constructors, making them automation enabled, this function returns a pointer to the Foundation Class implementation of **IDispatch** that is used by clients who communicate via the **IDispatch** interface. Calling this function automatically adds a reference to the pointer, so it is not necessary to make a call to **IUnknown::AddRef**.

    See Also   **CCmdTarget::EnableAutomation**, **COleDispatchDriver**

    In the OLE documentation: **IUnknown::Release**, **IUnknown::AddRef**

CCmdTarget::IsResultExpected

    BOOL IsResultExpected( );

Return Value

    Nonzero if an automation function should return a value; otherwise 0.

Remarks

    Use **IsResultExpected** to ascertain whether a client expects a return value from its call to an automation function. The OLE interface supplies information to MFC about whether the client is using or ignoring the result of a function call, and MFC in turn uses this information to determine the result of a call to **IsResultExpected**. If production of a return value is time- or resource-intensive, you can increase efficiency by calling this function before computing the return value.

This function returns 0 only once so that you will get valid return values from other automation functions if you call them from the automation function that the client has called.

IsResultExpected returns a nonzero value if called when an automation function call is not in progress.

See Also   **CCmdTarget::GetIDispatch**, **CCmdTarget::EnableAutomation**

CCmdTarget::OnCmdMsg

virtual BOOL OnCmdMsg(UINT *nID***, int** *nCode***, void*** *pExtra***,**
   AFX_CMDHANDLERINFO* *pHandlerInfo* **);**

Return Value

Nonzero if the message is handled; otherwise 0.

Parameters

nID   Contains the command ID.

nCode   Identifies the command notification code.

pExtra   Used according to the value of *nCode*.

pHandlerInfo   If not **NULL**, **OnCmdMsg** fills in the **pTarget** and **pmf** members of the *pHandlerInfo* structure instead of dispatching the command. Typically, this parameter should be **NULL**.

Remarks

Called by the framework to route and dispatch command messages and to handle the update of command user-interface objects. This is the main implementation routine of the framework command architecture.

At run time, **OnCmdMsg** dispatches a command to other objects or handles the command itself by calling the root class **CCmdTarget::OnCmdMsg**, which does the actual message-map lookup. For a complete description of the default command routing, see Chapter 2, "Working with Messages and Commands," in *Programming with MFC*.

On rare occasions, you may want to override this member function to extend the framework's standard command routing. Refer to Technical Note 21 under MFC in Books Online for advanced details of the command-routing architecture.

Example

```
// This example illustrates extending the framework's standard command
// route from the view to objects managed by the view.  This example

// is from an object-oriented drawing application, similar to the
// DRAWCLI sample application, which draws and edits "shapes".

BOOL CMyView::OnCmdMsg(UINT nID, int nCode, void* pExtra,
    AFX_CMDHANDLERINFO* pHandlerInfo)
{
   // Extend the framework's command route from the view to
   // the application-specific CMyShape that is currently selected
   // in the view. m_pActiveShape is NULL if no shape object
   // is currently selected in the view.
   if ((m_pActiveShape != NULL)
      && m_pActiveShape->OnCmdMsg(nID, nCode, pExtra, pHandlerInfo))
      return TRUE;

   // If the object(s) in the extended command route don't handle
   // the command, then let the base class OnCmdMsg handle it.
   return CView::OnCmdMsg(nID, nCode, pExtra, pHandlerInfo);
}

// The command handler for ID_SHAPE_COLOR (menu command to change
// the color of the currently selected shape) was added to
// the message map of CMyShape (note, not CMyView) using ClassWizard.

// The menu item will be automatically enabled or disabled, depending
// on whether a CMyShape is currently selected in the view, that is,
// depending on whether CMyView::m_pActiveView is NULL.  It is not
// necessary to implement an ON_UPDATE_COMMAND_UI handler to enable
// or disable the menu item.

BEGIN_MESSAGE_MAP(CMyShape, CCmdTarget)
   //{{AFX_MSG_MAP(CMyShape)
   ON_COMMAND(ID_SHAPE_COLOR, OnShapeColor)
   //}}AFX_MSG_MAP
END_MESSAGE_MAP()
```

See Also   CCmdUI

CCmdTarget::OnFinalRelease

virtual void OnFinalRelease( );

Remarks

Called by the framework when the last OLE reference to or from the object is
released. Override this function to provide special handling for this situation. The
default implementation deletes the object.

See Also   COleServerItem

CCmdTarget::RestoreWaitCursor

void RestoreWaitCursor( );

Remarks

Call this function to restore the appropriate hourglass cursor after the system cursor has changed (for example, after a message box has opened and then closed while in the middle of a lengthy operation).

Example

```
// The following example illustrates the most common case
// of displaying the hourglass cursor
 during some lengthy
// processing of a command handler implemented in some
// CCmdTarget-derived class, such as a document or view.

void CMyView::OnSomeCommand()
{
   BeginWaitCursor(); // display the hourglass cursor

   // do some lengthy processing

   EndWaitCursor(); // remove the hourglass cursor
}

// The next example illustrates RestoreWaitCursor.
void CMyView::OnSomeCommand()
{
   BeginWaitCursor(); // display the hourglass cursor

   // do some lengthy processing

   // The dialog box will normally change the cursor to
   // the standard arrow cursor, and leave the cursor in
   // as the standard arrow cursor when the dialog box is
   // closed.
   CMyDialog dlg;
   dlg.DoModal();

   // It is necessary to call RestoreWaitCursor here in order
   // to change the cursor back to the hourglass cursor.
   RestoreWaitCursor();

   // do some more lengthy processing

   EndWaitCursor(); // remove the hourglass cursor
}
```

```
// In the above example, the dialog was clearly invoked between
// the pair of calls to BeginWaitCursor and EndWaitCursor.
// Sometimes it may not be clear whether the dialog is invoked
// in between a pair of calls to BeginWaitCursor and EndWaitCursor.
// It is permissable to call RestoreWaitCursor, even if
// BeginWaitCursor was not previously called.  This case is
// illustrated below, where CMyView::AnotherFunction does not
// need to know whether it was called in the context of an
// hourglass cursor.
void CMyView::AnotherFunction()
{
    // some processing ...

    CMyDialog dlg;
    dlg.DoModal();
    RestoreWaitCursor();

    // some more processing ...
}

// If the dialog is invoked from a member function of
// some non-CCmdTarget, then you can call CWinApp::DoWaitCursor
// with a 0 parameter value to restore the hourglass cursor.
void CMyObject::AnotherFunction()
{
    CMyDialog dlg;
    dlg.DoModal();
    AfxGetApp()->DoWaitCursor(0); // same as CCmdTarget::RestoreWaitCursor
}
```

See Also   **CWaitCursor**, **CCmdTarget::EndWaitCursor**,
CCmdTarget::BeginWaitCursor, **CWinApp::DoWaitCursor**

CCmdUI

The **CCmdUI** class is used only within an **ON_UPDATE_COMMAND_UI** handler in a **CCmdTarget**-derived class.

When a user of your application pulls down a menu, each menu item needs to know whether it should be displayed as enabled or disabled. The target of a menu command provides this information by implementing an **ON_UPDATE_COMMAND_UI** handler. Use ClassWizard to browse the command user-interface objects in your application and create a message-map entry and function prototype for each handler.

When the menu is pulled down, the framework searches for and calls each **ON_UPDATE_COMMAND_UI** handler, each handler calls **CCmdUI** member functions such as **Enable** and **Check**, and the framework then appropriately displays each menu item.

A menu item can be replaced with a control-bar button or other command user-interface object without changing the code within the **ON_UPDATE_COMMAND_UI** handler.

The following table summarizes the effect **CCmdUI**'s member functions have on various command user-interface items.

User-Interface Item	Enable	SetCheck	SetRadio	SetText
Menu item	Enables or disables	Checks (×) or unchecks	Checks using dot (∙)	Sets item text
Toolbar button	Enables or disables	Selects, unselects, or indeterminate	Same as **SetCheck**	(Not applicable)
Status-bar pane	Makes text visible or invisible	Sets pop-out or normal border	Same as **SetCheck**	Sets pane text
Normal button in **CDialogBar**	Enables or disables	Checks or unchecks check box	Same as **SetCheck**	Sets button text
Normal control in **CDialogBar**	Enables or disables	(Not applicable)	(Not applicable)	Sets window text

For more on the use of this class, see Chapter 6, "Constructing the User Interface," in *Tutorials* and "How to Update User-Interface Objects" in Chapter 2 of *Programming with MFC*.

#include <afxwin.h>

See Also   CCmdTarget

Operations

Enable	Enables or disables the user-interface item for this command.
SetCheck	Sets the check state of the user-interface item for this command.
SetRadio	Like the **SetCheck** member function, but operates on radio groups.
SetText	Sets the text for the user-interface item for this command.
ContinueRouting	Tells the command-routing mechanism to continue routing the current message down the chain of handlers.

Member Functions

CCmdUI::ContinueRouting

void ContinueRouting( );

Remarks

Call this member function to tell the command-routing mechanism to continue routing the current message down the chain of handlers.

This is an advanced member function that should be used in conjunction with an **ON_COMMAND_EX** handler that returns **FALSE**. For more information, see Technical Note 21 under MFC in Books Online.

CCmdUI::Enable

virtual void Enable(BOOL *bOn* **= TRUE);**

Parameters

bOn   **TRUE** to enable the item, **FALSE** to disable it.

Remarks

Call this member function to enable or disable the user-interface item for this command.

See Also   **CCmdUI::SetCheck**

CCmdUI::SetCheck

virtual void SetCheck(int *nCheck* **= 1);**

Parameters

nCheck   Specifies the check state to set. If 0, unchecks; if 1, checks; and if 2, sets indeterminate.

Remarks

Call this member function to set the user-interface item for this command to the appropriate check state. This member function works for menu items and toolbar buttons. The indeterminate state applies only to toolbar buttons.

See Also   CCmdUI::SetRadio

CCmdUI::SetRadio

virtual void SetRadio(BOOL *bOn* **= TRUE);**

Parameters

bOn   **TRUE** to enable the item; otherwise **FALSE**.

Remarks

Call this member function to set the user-interface item for this command to the appropriate check state. This member function operates like **SetCheck**, except that it operates on user-interface items acting as part of a radio group. Unchecking the other items in the group is not automatic unless the items themselves maintain the radio-group behavior.

See Also   CCmdUI::SetCheck

CCmdUI::SetText

virtual void SetText(LPCTSTR *lpszText* **);**

Parameters

lpszText   A pointer to a text string.

Remarks

Call this member function to set the text of the user-interface item for this command.

See Also   CCmdUI::Enable

CColorDialog

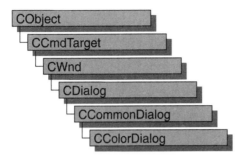

The **CColorDialog** class allows you to incorporate a color-selection dialog box into your application. A **CColorDialog** object is a dialog box with a list of colors that are defined for the display system. The user can select or create a particular color from the list, which is then reported back to the application when the dialog box exits.

To construct a **CColorDialog** object, use the provided constructor or derive a new class and use your own custom constructor.

Once the dialog box has been constructed, you can set or modify any values in the m_cc structure to initialize the values of the dialog box's controls. The **m_cc** structure is of type **CHOOSECOLOR**. For more information on this structure, see the Win32 SDK documentation.

After initializing the dialog box's controls, call the **DoModal** member function to display the dialog box and allow the user to select a color. **DoModal** returns the user's selection of either the dialog box's OK (**IDOK**) or Cancel (**IDCANCEL**) button.

If **DoModal** returns **IDOK**, you can use one of **CColorDialog**'s member functions to retrieve the information input by the user.

You can use the Windows **CommDlgExtendedError** function to determine whether an error occurred during initialization of the dialog box and to learn more about the error. For more information on this function, see the Win32 SDK documentation.

CColorDialog relies on the COMMDLG.DLL file that ships with Windows versions 3.1 and later.

To customize the dialog box, derive a class from **CColorDialog**, provide a custom dialog template, and add a message map to process the notification messages from the extended controls. Any unprocessed messages should be passed to the base class.

Customizing the hook function is not required.

Note On some installations the **CColorDialog** object will not display with a gray background if you have used the framework to make other **CDialog** objects gray.

For more information on using **CColorDialog**, see "Common Dialog Classes" in Chapter 4 of *Programming with MFC*.

#include <afxdlgs.h>

Data Members

m_cc	A structure used to customize the settings of the dialog box.

Construction

CColorDialog	Constructs a **CColorDialog** object.

Operations

DoModal	Displays a color dialog box and allows the user to make a selection.
GetColor	Returns a **COLORREF** structure containing the values of the selected color.
GetSavedCustomColors	Retrieves custom colors created by the user.
SetCurrentColor	Forces the current color selection to the specified color.

Overridables

OnColorOK	Override to validate the color entered into the dialog box.

Member Functions

CColorDialog::CColorDialog

CColorDialog(COLORREF *clrInit* **= 0, DWORD** *dwFlags* **= 0, CWnd*** *pParentWnd* **= NULL);**

Parameters

clrInit   The default color selection. If no value is specified, the default is RGB(0,0,0) (black).

dwFlags   A set of flags that customize the function and appearance of the dialog box. For more information, see the **CHOOSECOLOR** structure in the Win32 SDK documentation.

pParentWnd   A pointer to the dialog box's parent or owner window.

Remarks

Constructs a **CColorDialog** object.

See Also   **CDialog::DoModal**

CColorDialog::DoModal

virtual int DoModal( );

Return Value

IDOK or **IDCANCEL** if the function is successful; otherwise 0. **IDOK** and **IDCANCEL** are constants that indicate whether the user selected the OK or Cancel button.

If **IDCANCEL** is returned, you can call the Windows **CommDlgExtendedError** function to determine whether an error occurred.

Remarks

Call this function to display the Windows common color dialog box and allow the user to select a color.

If you want to initialize the various color dialog-box options by setting members of the **m_cc** structure, you should do this before calling **DoModal** but after the dialog-box object is constructed.

After calling **DoModal**, you can call other member functions to retrieve the settings or information input by the user into the dialog box.

See Also   **CDialog::DoModal**, **CColorDialog::CColorDialog**

CColorDialog::GetColor

COLORREF GetColor( ) const;

Return Value

A **COLORREF** value that contains the RGB information for the color selected in the color dialog box.

Remarks

Call this function after calling **DoModal** to retrieve the information about the color the user selected.

See Also   **CColorDialog::SetCurrentColor**

CColorDialog::GetSavedCustomColors

static COLORREF * GetSavedCustomColors( );

Return Value

A pointer to an array of 16 RGB color values that stores custom colors created by the user.

Remarks

CColorDialog objects permit the user, in addition to choosing colors, to define up to 16 custom colors. The **GetSavedCustomColors** member function provides access to these colors. These colors can be retrieved after **DoModal** returns **IDOK**.

Each of the 16 RGB values in the returned array is initialized to RGB(255,255,255) (white). The custom colors chosen by the user are saved only between dialog box invocations within the application. If you wish to save these colors between invocations of the application, you must save them in some other manner, such as in an initialization (.INI) file.

See Also   **CColorDialog::GetColor**

CColorDialog::OnColorOK

virtual BOOL OnColorOK( );

Return Value

Nonzero if the dialog box should not be dismissed; otherwise 0 to accept the color that was entered.

Remarks

Override this function only if you want to provide custom validation of the color entered into the dialog box. This function allows you to reject a color entered by a user into a common color dialog box for any application-specific reason. Normally, you do not need to use this function because the framework provides default validation of colors and displays a message box if an invalid color is entered.

Use the **GetColor** member function to get the RGB value of the color.

If 0 is returned, the dialog box will remain displayed in order for the user to enter another filename.

CColorDialog::SetCurrentColor

void SetCurrentColor(COLORREF *clr* **);**

Parameters

clr   An RGB color value.

Remarks

Call this function after calling **DoModal** to force the current color selection to the color value specified in *clr*. This function is called from within a message handler or **OnColorOK**. The dialog box will automatically update the user's selection based on the value of the *clr* parameter.

See Also   **CColorDialog::GetColor**, **CColorDialog::OnColorOK**

Data Members

CColorDialog::m_cc

CHOOSECOLOR m_cc;

Remarks

A structure of type **CHOOSECOLOR**, whose members store the characteristics and values of the dialog box. After constructing a **CColorDialog** object, you can use **m_cc** to set various aspects of the dialog box before calling the **DoModal** member function.

For more information on the **CHOOSECOLOR** structure, see the Win32 SDK documentation.

CComboBox

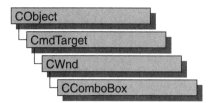

The **CComboBox** class provides the functionality of a Windows combo box.

A combo box consists of a list box combined with either a static control or edit control. The list-box portion of the control may be displayed at all times or may only drop down when the user selects the drop-down arrow next to the control.

The currently selected item (if any) in the list box is displayed in the static or edit control. In addition, if the combo box has the drop-down list style, the user can type the initial character of one of the items in the list, and the list box, if visible, will highlight the next item with that initial character.

The following table compares the three combo-box styles. (For a list of combo-box styles, see "Combo-Box Styles" in the "Styles" section.)

Style	When is list box visible?	Static or edit control?
Simple	Always	Edit
Drop-down	When dropped down	Edit
Drop-down list	When dropped down	Static

You can create a **CComboBox** object from either a dialog template or directly in your code. In both cases, first call the constructor **CComboBox** to construct the **CComboBox** object; then call the **Create** member function to create the control and attach it to the **CComboBox** object.

If you want to handle Windows notification messages sent by a combo box to its parent (usually a class derived from **CDialog**), add a message-map entry and message-handler member function to the parent class for each message.

Each message-map entry takes the following form:

ON_ Notification(*id*, *memberFxn*)

where *id* specifies the child-window ID of the combo-box control sending the notification and *memberFxn* is the name of the parent member function you have written to handle the notification.

The parent's function prototype is as follows:

afx_msg void *memberFxn*( );

The order in which certain notifications will be sent cannot be predicted. In particular, a **CBN_SELCHANGE** notification may occur either before or after a **CBN_CLOSEUP** notification.

Potential message-map entries are the following:

- **ON_CBN_CLOSEUP**   (Windows 3.1 and later.) The list box of a combo box has closed. This notification message is not sent for a combo box that has the **CBS_SIMPLE** style.

- **ON_CBN_DBLCLK**   The user double-clicks a string in the list box of a combo box. This notification message is only sent for a combo box with the **CBS_SIMPLE** style. For a combo box with the **CBS_DROPDOWN** or **CBS_DROPDOWNLIST** style, a double-click cannot occur because a single click hides the list box.

- **ON_CBN_DROPDOWN**   The list box of a combo box is about to drop down (be made visible). This notification message can occur only for a combo box with the **CBS_DROPDOWN** or **CBS_DROPDOWNLIST** style.

- **ON_CBN_EDITCHANGE**   The user has taken an action that may have altered the text in the edit-control portion of a combo box. Unlike the **CBN_EDITUPDATE** message, this message is sent after Windows updates the screen. It is not sent if the combo box has the **CBS_DROPDOWNLIST** style.

- **ON_CBN_EDITUPDATE**   The edit-control portion of a combo box is about to display altered text. This notification message is sent after the control has formatted the text but before it displays the text. It is not sent if the combo box has the **CBS_DROPDOWNLIST** style.

- **ON_CBN_ERRSPACE**   The combo box cannot allocate enough memory to meet a specific request.

- **ON_CBN_SELENDCANCEL**   (Windows 3.1 and later.) Indicates the user's selection should be canceled. The user clicks an item and then clicks another window or control to hide the list box of a combo box. This notification message is sent before the **CBN_CLOSEUP** notification message to indicate that the user's selection should be ignored. The **CBN_SELENDCANCEL** or **CBN_SELENDOK** notification message is sent even if the **CBN_CLOSEUP** notification message is not sent (as in the case of a combo box with the **CBS_SIMPLE** style).

- **ON_CBN_SELENDOK**   The user selects an item and then either presses the ENTER key or clicks the DOWN ARROW key to hide the list box of a combo box. This notification message is sent before the **CBN_CLOSEUP** message to indicate that the user's selection should be considered valid. The **CBN_SELENDCANCEL** or **CBN_SELENDOK** notification message is sent even if the **CBN_CLOSEUP** notification message is not sent (as in the case of a combo box with the **CBS_SIMPLE** style).

- **ON_CBN_KILLFOCUS**   The combo box is losing the input focus.

- **ON_CBN_SELCHANGE**   The selection in the list box of a combo box is about to be changed as a result of the user either clicking in the list box or changing the selection by using the arrow keys. When processing this message, the text in the edit control of the combo box can only be retrieved via **GetLBText** or another similar function. **GetWindowText** cannot be used.

- **ON_CBN_SETFOCUS**   The combo box receives the input focus.

If you create a **CComboBox** object within a dialog box (through a dialog resource), the **CComboBox** object is automatically destroyed when the user closes the dialog box.

If you embed a **CComboBox** object within another window object, you do not need to destroy it. If you create the **CComboBox** object on the stack, it is destroyed automatically. If you create the **CComboBox** object on the heap by using the **new** function, you must call **delete** on the object to destroy it when the Windows combo box is destroyed.

#include <afxwin.h>

See Also   CWnd, CButton, CEdit, CListBox, CScrollBar, CStatic, CDialog

Construction

CComboBox	Constructs a **CComboBox** object.

Initialization

Create	Creates the combo box and attaches it to the **CComboBox** object.
InitStorage	Preallocates blocks of memory for items and strings in the list-box portion of the combo box.

General Operations

GetCount	Retrieves the number of items in the list box of a combo box.
GetCurSel	Retrieves the index of the currently selected item, if any, in the list box of a combo box.
SetCurSel	Selects a string in the list box of a combo box.
GetEditSel	Gets the starting and ending character positions of the current selection in the edit control of a combo box.
SetEditSel	Selects characters in the edit control of a combo box.
SetItemData	Sets the 32-bit value associated with the specified item in a combo box.

SetItemDataPtr	Sets the 32-bit value associated with the specified item in a combo box to the specified pointer (**void***).
GetItemData	Retrieves the application-supplied 32-bit value associated with the specified combo-box item.
GetItemDataPtr	Retrieves the application-supplied 32-bit value associated with the specified combo-box item as a pointer (**void***).
GetTopIndex	Returns the index of the first visible item in the list-box portion of the combo box.
SetTopIndex	Tells the list-box portion of the combo box to display the item with the specified index at the top.
SetHorizontalExtent	Sets the width in pixels that the list-box portion of the combo box can be scrolled horizontally.
GetHorizontalExtent	Returns the width in pixels that the list-box portion of the combo box can be scrolled horizontally.
SetDroppedWidth	Sets the minimum allowable width for the drop-down list-box portion of a combo box.
GetDroppedWidth	Retrieves the minimum allowable width for the drop-down list-box portion of a combo box.
Clear	Deletes (clears) the current selection (if any) in the edit control.
Copy	Copies the current selection (if any) onto the Clipboard in **CF_TEXT** format.
Cut	Deletes (cuts) the current selection, if any, in the edit control and copies the deleted text onto the Clipboard in **CF_TEXT** format.
Paste	Inserts the data from the Clipboard into the edit control at the current cursor position. Data is inserted only if the Clipboard contains data in **CF_TEXT** format.
LimitText	Limits the length of the text that the user can enter into the edit control of a combo box.
SetItemHeight	Sets the height of list items in a combo box or the height of the edit-control (or static-text) portion of a combo box.
GetItemHeight	Retrieves the height of list items in a combo box.
GetLBText	Gets a string from the list box of a combo box.
GetLBTextLen	Gets the length of a string in the list box of a combo box.
ShowDropDown	Shows or hides the list box of a combo box that has the **CBS_DROPDOWN** or **CBS_DROPDOWNLIST** style.
GetDroppedControlRect	Retrieves the screen coordinates of the visible (dropped-down) list box of a drop-down combo box.

GetDroppedState	Determines whether the list box of a drop-down combo box is visible (dropped down).
SetExtendedUI	Selects either the default user interface or the extended user interface for a combo box that has the **CBS_DROPDOWN** or **CBS_DROPDOWNLIST** style.
GetExtendedUI	Determines whether a combo box has the default user interface or the extended user interface.
GetLocale	Retrieves the locale identifier for a combo box.
SetLocale	Sets the locale identifier for a combo box.

String Operations

AddString	Adds a string to the end of the list in the list box of a combo box or at the sorted position for list boxes with the **CBS_SORT** style.
DeleteString	Deletes a string from the list box of a combo box.
InsertString	Inserts a string into the list box of a combo box.
ResetContent	Removes all items from the list box and edit control of a combo box.
Dir	Adds a list of filenames to the list box of a combo box.
FindString	Finds the first string that contains the specified prefix in the list box of a combo box.
FindStringExact	Finds the first list-box string (in a combo box) that matches the specified string.
SelectString	Searches for a string in the list box of a combo box and, if the string is found, selects the string in the list box and copies the string to the edit control.

Overridables

DrawItem	Called by the framework when a visual aspect of an owner-draw combo box changes.
MeasureItem	Called by the framework to determine combo box dimensions when an owner-draw combo box is created.
CompareItem	Called by the framework to determine the relative position of a new list item in a sorted owner-draw combo box.
DeleteItem	Called by the framework when a list item is deleted from an owner-draw combo box.

Member Functions

CComboBox::AddString

int AddString(LPCTSTR *lpszString* **);**

Return Value

If the return value is greater than or equal to 0, it is the zero-based index to the string in the list box. The return value is **CB_ERR** if an error occurs; the return value is **CB_ERRSPACE** if insufficient space is available to store the new string.

Parameters

lpszString　　Points to the null-terminated string that is to be added.

Remarks

Adds a string to the list box of a combo box. If the list box was not created with the **CBS_SORT** style, the string is added to the end of the list. Otherwise, the string is inserted into the list, and the list is sorted.

To insert a string into a specific location within the list, use the **InsertString** member function.

See Also **CComboBox::InsertString**, **CComboBox::DeleteString**, **CB_ADDSTRING**

CComboBox::CComboBox

CComboBox( );

Remarks

Constructs a **CComboBox** object.

See Also **CComboBox::Create**

CComboBox::Clear

void Clear( );

Remarks

Deletes (clears) the current selection, if any, in the edit control of the combo box.

To delete the current selection and place the deleted contents onto the Clipboard, use the **Cut** member function.

See Also **CComboBox::Copy**, **CComboBox::Cut**, **CComboBox::Paste**, **WM_CLEAR**

CComboBox::CompareItem

virtual int CompareItem(LPCOMPAREITEMSTRUCT *lpCompareItemStruct* **);**

Return Value

Indicates the relative position of the two items described in the
COMPAREITEMSTRUCT structure. It can be any of the following values:

Value	Meaning
−1	Item 1 sorts before item 2.
0	Item 1 and item 2 sort the same.
1	Item 1 sorts after item 2.

See **CWnd::OnCompareItem** for a description of **COMPAREITEMSTRUCT**.

Parameters

lpCompareItemStruct   A long pointer to a **COMPAREITEMSTRUCT** structure.

Remarks

Called by the framework to determine the relative position of a new item in the list-
box portion of a sorted owner-draw combo box. By default, this member function
does nothing. If you create an owner-draw combo box with the **LBS_SORT** style,
you must override this member function to assist the framework in sorting new items
added to the list box.

See Also   **WM_COMPAREITEM, CComboBox::DrawItem,
CComboBox::MeasureItem, CComboBox::DeleteItem**

CComboBox::Copy

void Copy( );

Remarks

Copies the current selection, if any, in the edit control of the combo box onto the
Clipboard in **CF_TEXT** format.

See Also   **CComboBox::Clear, CComboBox::Cut, CComboBox::Paste,
WM_COPY**

CComboBox::Create

BOOL Create(DWORD *dwStyle*, **const RECT&** *rect*, **CWnd*** *pParentWnd*, **UINT** *nID* **);**

Return Value

Nonzero if successful; otherwise 0.

Parameters

dwStyle   Specifies the style of the combo box. Apply any combination of combo-box styles to the box. For a list of combo-box styles, see "Combo-Box Styles" in the "Styles Used by MFC" section.

rect   Points to the position and size of the combo box. Can be a **RECT** structure or a **CRect** object.

pParentWnd   Specifies the combo box's parent window (usually a **CDialog**). It must not be **NULL**.

nID   Specifies the combo box's control ID.

Remarks

You construct a **CComboBox** object in two steps. First call the constructor, then call **Create**, which creates the Windows combo box and attaches it to the **CComboBox** object.

When **Create** executes, Windows sends the **WM_NCCREATE**, **WM_CREATE**, **WM_NCCALCSIZE**, and **WM_GETMINMAXINFO** messages to the combo box.

These messages are handled by default by the **OnNcCreate**, **OnCreate**, **OnNcCalcSize**, and **OnGetMinMaxInfo** member functions in the **CWnd** base class. To extend the default message handling, derive a class from **CComboBox**, add a message map to the new class, and override the preceding message-handler member functions. Override **OnCreate**, for example, to perform needed initialization for a new class.

Apply the following window styles to a combo-box control. (For a list of window styles, see "Window Styles" in the "Styles Used by MFC" section.)

- **WS_CHILD**   Always
- **WS_VISIBLE**   Usually
- **WS_DISABLED**   Rarely
- **WS_VSCROLL**   To add vertical scrolling for the list box in the combo box
- **WS_HSCROLL**   To add horizontal scrolling for the list box in the combo box
- **WS_GROUP**   To group controls
- **WS_TABSTOP**   To include the combo box in the tabbing order

See Also   **CComboBox::CComboBox**

CComboBox::Cut

void Cut( );

Remarks

Deletes (cuts) the current selection, if any, in the combo-box edit control and copies the deleted text onto the Clipboard in **CF_TEXT** format.

To delete the current selection without placing the deleted text onto the Clipboard, call the **Clear** member function.

See Also **CComboBox::Clear**, **CComboBox::Copy**, **CComboBox::Paste**, **WM_CUT**

CComboBox::DeleteItem

virtual void DeleteItem(LPDELETEITEMSTRUCT *lpDeleteItemStruct* **);**

Parameters

lpDeleteItemStruct   A long pointer to a Windows **DELETEITEMSTRUCT** structure that contains information about the deleted item. See **CWnd::OnDeleteItem** for a description of this structure.

Remarks

Called by the framework when the user deletes an item from an owner-draw **CComboBox** object or destroys the combo box. The default implementation of this function does nothing. Override this function to redraw the combo box as needed.

See Also **CComboBox::CompareItem**, **CComboBox::DrawItem**, **CComboBox::MeasureItem**, **WM_DELETEITEM**

CComboBox::DeleteString

int DeleteString(UINT *nIndex* **);**

Return Value

If the return value is greater than or equal to 0, then it is a count of the strings remaining in the list. The return value is **CB_ERR** if *nIndex* specifies an index greater then the number of items in the list.

Parameters

nIndex   Specifies the index to the string that is to be deleted.

Remarks

Deletes a string in the list box of a combo box.

See Also **CComboBox::InsertString**, **CComboBox::AddString**, **CB_DELETESTRING**

CComboBox::Dir

int Dir(UINT *attr,* **LPCTSTR** *lpszWildCard* **);**

Return Value

If the return value is greater than or equal to 0, it is the zero-based index of the last filename added to the list. The return value is **CB_ERR** if an error occurs; the return value is **CB_ERRSPACE** if insufficient space is available to store the new strings.

Parameters

attr   Can be any combination of the **enum** values described in **CFile::GetStatus** or any combination of the following values:

- **DDL_READWRITE**   File can be read from or written to.

- **DDL_READONLY**   File can be read from but not written to.

- **DDL_HIDDEN**   File is hidden and does not appear in a directory listing.

- **DDL_SYSTEM**   File is a system file.

- **DDL_DIRECTORY**   The name specified by *lpszWildCard* specifies a directory.

- **DDL_ARCHIVE**   File has been archived.

- **DDL_DRIVES**   Include all drives that match the name specified by *lpszWildCard*.

- **DDL_EXCLUSIVE**   Exclusive flag. If the exclusive flag is set, only files of the specified type are listed. Otherwise, files of the specified type are listed in addition to "normal" files.

lpszWildCard   Points to a file-specification string. The string can contain wildcards (for example, *.*).

Remarks

Adds a list of filenames and/or drives to the list box of a combo box.

See Also   **CWnd::DlgDirList**, **CB_DIR**, **CFile::GetStatus**

CComboBox::DrawItem

virtual void DrawItem(LPDRAWITEMSTRUCT *lpDrawItemStruct* **);**

Parameters

lpDrawItemStruct   A pointer to a **DRAWITEMSTRUCT** structure that contains information about the type of drawing required.

Remarks

Called by the framework when a visual aspect of an owner-draw combo box changes. The **itemAction** member of the **DRAWITEMSTRUCT** structure defines the drawing action that is to be performed. See **CWnd::OnDrawItem** for a description of this structure.

By default, this member function does nothing. Override this member function to implement drawing for an owner-draw **CComboBox** object. Before this member function terminates, the application should restore all graphics device interface (GDI) objects selected for the display context supplied in *lpDrawItemStruct*.

See Also **CComboBox::CompareItem**, **WM_DRAWITEM**, **CComboBox::MeasureItem**, **CComboBox::DeleteItem**

CComboBox::FindString

int FindString(int *nStartAfter***, LPCTSTR** *lpszString* **) const;**

Return Value

If the return value is greater than or equal to 0, it is the zero-based index of the matching item. It is **CB_ERR** if the search was unsuccessful.

Parameters

nStartAfter Contains the zero-based index of the item before the first item to be searched. When the search reaches the bottom of the list box, it continues from the top of the list box back to the item specified by *nStartAfter*. If −1, the entire list box is searched from the beginning.

lpszString Points to the null-terminated string that contains the prefix to search for. The search is case independent, so this string can contain any combination of uppercase and lowercase letters.

Remarks

Finds, but doesn't select, the first string that contains the specified prefix in the list box of a combo box.

See Also **CComboBox::SelectString**, **CComboBox::SetCurSel**, **CB_FINDSTRING**

CComboBox::FindStringExact

int FindStringExact(int *nIndexStart***, LPCTSTR** *lpszFind* **) const;**

Return Value

The zero-based index of the matching item, or **CB_ERR** if the search was unsuccessful.

Parameters

nIndexStart   Specifies the zero-based index of the item before the first item to be searched. When the search reaches the bottom of the list box, it continues from the top of the list box back to the item specified by *nIndexStart*. If *nIndexStart* is –1, the entire list box is searched from the beginning.

lpszFind   Points to the null-terminated string to search for. This string can contain a complete filename, including the extension. The search is not case sensitive, so this string can contain any combination of uppercase and lowercase letters.

Remarks

Call the **FindStringExact** member function to find the first list-box string (in a combo box) that matches the string specified in *lpszFind*.

If the combo box was created with an owner-draw style but without the **CBS_HASSTRINGS** style, **FindStringExact** attempts to match the doubleword value against the value of *lpszFind*.

See Also   **CComboBox::FindString, CB_FINDSTRINGEXACT**

CComboBox::GetCount

int GetCount( ) const;

Return Value

The number of items. The returned count is one greater than the index value of the last item (the index is zero-based). It is **CB_ERR** if an error occurs.

Remarks

Call this member function to retrieve the number of items in the list-box portion of a combo box.

See Also   **CB_GETCOUNT**

CComboBox::GetCurSel

int GetCurSel( ) const;

Return Value

The zero-based index of the currently selected item in the list box of a combo box, or **CB_ERR** if no item is selected.

Remarks

Call this member function to determine which item in the combo box is selected. **GetCurSel** returns an index into the list.

See Also   **CComboBox::SetCurSel, CB_GETCURSEL**

CComboBox::GetDroppedControlRect

void GetDroppedControlRect(LPRECT *lprect* **) const;**

Parameters

lprect   Points to the **RECT** structure that is to receive the coordinates.

Remarks

Call the **GetDroppedControlRect** member function to retrieve the screen coordinates of the visible (dropped-down) list box of a drop-down combo box.

See Also   CB_GETDROPPEDCONTROLRECT

CComboBox::GetDroppedState

BOOL GetDroppedState( ) const;

Return Value

Nonzero if the list box is visible; otherwise 0.

Remarks

Call the **GetDroppedState** member function to determine whether the list box of a drop-down combo box is visible (dropped down).

See Also   CB_SHOWDROPDOWN, CB_GETDROPPEDSTATE

CComboBox::GetDroppedWidth

int GetDroppedWidth( ) const;

Return Value

If successful, the minimum allowable width, in pixels; otherwise, **CB_ERR**.

Remarks

Call this function to retrieve the minimum allowable width, in pixels, of the list box of a combo box. This function only applies to combo boxes with the **CBS_DROPDOWN** or **CBS_DROPDOWNLIST** style.

By default, the minimum allowable width of the drop-down list box is 0. The minimum allowable width can be set by calling **SetDroppedWidth**. When the list-box portion of the combo box is displayed, its width is the larger of the minimum allowable width or the combo box width.

See Also   CComboBox::SetDroppedWidth, CB_GETDROPPEDWIDTH

CComboBox::GetEditSel

DWORD GetEditSel( ) const;

Return Value

A 32-bit value that contains the starting position in the low-order word and the position of the first nonselected character after the end of the selection in the high-order word. If this function is used on a combo box without an edit control, **CB_ERR** is returned.

Remarks

Gets the starting and ending character positions of the current selection in the edit control of a combo box.

See Also   CComboBox::SetEditSel, CB_GETEDITSEL

CComboBox::GetExtendedUI

BOOL GetExtendedUI( ) const;

Return Value

Nonzero if the combo box has the extended user interface; otherwise 0.

Remarks

Call the **GetExtendedUI** member function to determine whether a combo box has the default user interface or the extended user interface. The extended user interface can be identified in the following ways:

- Clicking the static control displays the list box only for combo boxes with the **CBS_DROPDOWNLIST** style.
- Pressing the DOWN ARROW key displays the list box (F4 is disabled).

Scrolling in the static control is disabled when the item list is not visible (arrow keys are disabled).

See Also   CComboBox::SetExtendedUI, CB_GETEXTENDEDUI

CComboBox::GetHorizontalExtent

UINT GetHorizontalExtent( ) const;

Return Value

The scrollable width of the list-box portion of the combo box, in pixels.

Remarks

Retrieves from the combo box the width in pixels by which the list-box portion of the combo box can be scrolled horizontally. This is applicable only if the list-box portion of the combo box has a horizontal scroll bar.

See Also **CListBox::SetHorizontalExtent, CB_GETHORIZONTALEXTENT**

CComboBox::GetItemData

DWORD GetItemData(int *nIndex* **) const;**

Return Value

The 32-bit value associated with the item, or **CB_ERR** if an error occurs.

Parameters

nIndex   Contains the zero-based index of an item in the combo box's list box.

Remarks

Retrieves the application-supplied 32-bit value associated with the specified combo-box item. The 32-bit value can be set with the *dwItemData* parameter of a **SetItemData** member function call. Use the **GetItemDataPtr** member function if the 32-bit value to be retrieved is a pointer (**void***).

See Also **CComboBox::SetItemData, CComboBox::GetItemDataPtr, CComboBox::SetItemDataPtr, CB_GETITEMDATA**

CComboBox::GetItemDataPtr

void* GetItemDataPtr(int *nIndex* **) const;**

Return Value

Retrieves a pointer, or –1 if an error occurs.

Parameters

nIndex   Contains the zero-based index of an item in the combo box's list box.

Remarks

Retrieves the application-supplied 32-bit value associated with the specified combo-box item as a pointer (**void***).

See Also **CComboBox::SetItemDataPtr, CComboBox::GetItemData, CComboBox::SetItemData, CB_GETITEMDATA**

CComboBox::GetItemHeight

int GetItemHeight(int *nIndex* **) const;**

Return Value

The height, in pixels, of the specified item in a combo box. The return value is
CB_ERR if an error occurs.

Parameters

nIndex Specifies the component of the combo box whose height is to be retrieved. If
the *nIndex* parameter is –1, the height of the edit-control (or static-text) portion of
the combo box is retrieved. If the combo box has the
CBS_OWNERDRAWVARIABLE style, *nIndex* specifies the zero-based index of
the list item whose height is to be retrieved. Otherwise, *nIndex* should be set to 0.

Remarks

Call the **GetItemHeight** member function to retrieve the height of list items in a
combo box.

See Also **CComboBox::SetItemHeight**, **WM_MEASUREITEM**,
CB_GETITEMHEIGHT

CComboBox::GetLBText

int GetLBText(int *nIndex***, LPTSTR** *lpszText* **) const;**
void GetLBText(int *nIndex***, CString&** *rString* **) const;**

Return Value

The length (in bytes) of the string, excluding the terminating null character. If *nIndex*
does not specify a valid index, the return value is **CB_ERR**.

Parameters

nIndex Contains the zero-based index of the list-box string to be copied.

lpszText Points to a buffer that is to receive the string. The buffer must have
sufficient space for the string and a terminating null character.

rString A reference to a **CString**.

Remarks

Gets a string from the list box of a combo box. The second form of this member
function fills a **CString** object with the item's text.

See Also **CComboBox::GetLBTextLen**, **CB_GETLBTEXT**

CComboBox::GetLBTextLen

int GetLBTextLen(int *nIndex* **) const;**

Return Value

The length of the string in bytes, excluding the terminating null character. If *nIndex* does not specify a valid index, the return value is **CB_ERR**.

Parameters

nIndex   Contains the zero-based index of the list-box string.

Remarks

Gets the length of a string in the list box of a combo box.

See Also   **CComboBox::GetLBText, CB_GETLBTEXTLEN**

CComboBox::GetLocale

LCID GetLocale( ) const;

Return Value

The locale identifier (LCID) value for the strings in the combo box.

Remarks

Retrieves the locale used by the combo box. The locale is used, for example, to determine the sort order of the strings in a sorted combo box.

See Also   **CComboBox::SetLocale, ::GetStringTypeW, ::GetSystemDefaultLCID, ::GetUserDefaultLCID**

CComboBox::GetTopIndex

int GetTopIndex( ) const;

Return Value

The zero-based index of the first visible item in the list-box portion of the combo box if successful, **CB_ERR** otherwise.

Remarks

Retrieves the zero-based index of the first visible item in the list-box portion of the combo box. Initially, item 0 is at the top of the list box, but if the list box is scrolled, another item may be at the top.

See Also   **CComboBox::SetTopIndex, CB_GETTOPINDEX**

CComboBox::InitStorage

> **int InitStorage(int** *nItems*, **UINT** *nBytes* **);**

Return Value

If successful, the maximum number of items that the list-box portion of the combo box can store before a memory reallocation is needed, otherwise **CB_ERR**, meaning not enough memory is available.

Parameters

nItems Specifies the number of items to add.

nBytes Specifies the amount of memory, in bytes, to allocate for item strings.

Remarks

Allocates memory for storing list box items in the list-box portion of the combo box. Call this function before adding a large number of items to the list-box portion of the **CComboBox**.

Windows 95 only: The *wParam* parameter is limited to 16-bit values. This means list boxes cannot contain more than 32,767 items. Although the number of items is restricted, the total size of the items in a list box is limited only by available memory.

This function helps speed up the initialization of list boxes that have a large number of items (more than 100). It preallocates the specified amount of memory so that subsequent **AddString**, **InsertString**, and **Dir** functions take the shortest possible time. You can use estimates for the parameters. If you overestimate, some extra memory is allocated; if you underestimate, the normal allocation is used for items that exceed the preallocated amount.

See Also **CComboBox::CComboBox, CComboBox::Create, CComboBox::ResetContent, CB_INITSTORAGE**

CComboBox::InsertString

> **int InsertString(int** *nIndex*, **LPCTSTR** *lpszString* **);**

Return Value

The zero-based index of the position at which the string was inserted. The return value is **CB_ERR** if an error occurs. The return value is **CB_ERRSPACE** if insufficient space is available to store the new string.

Parameters

nIndex Contains the zero-based index to the position in the list box that will receive the string. If this parameter is –1, the string is added to the end of the list.

lpszString Points to the null-terminated string that is to be inserted.

Remarks

Inserts a string into the list box of a combo box. Unlike the **AddString** member function, the **InsertString** member function does not cause a list with the **CBS_SORT** style to be sorted.

See Also   **CComboBox::AddString**, **CComboBox::DeleteString**, **CComboBox::ResetContent**, **CB_INSERTSTRING**

CComboBox::LimitText

BOOL LimitText(int *nMaxChars* **);**

Return Value

Nonzero if successful. If called for a combo box with the style **CBS_DROPDOWNLIST** or for a combo box without an edit control, the return value is **CB_ERR**.

Parameters

nMaxChars   Specifies the length (in bytes) of the text that the user can enter. If this parameter is 0, the text length is set to 65,535 bytes.

Remarks

Limits the length in bytes of the text that the user can enter into the edit control of a combo box.

If the combo box does not have the style **CBS_AUTOHSCROLL**, setting the text limit to be larger than the size of the edit control will have no effect.

LimitText only limits the text the user can enter. It has no effect on any text already in the edit control when the message is sent, nor does it affect the length of the text copied to the edit control when a string in the list box is selected.

See Also   **CB_LIMITTEXT**

CComboBox::MeasureItem

virtual void MeasureItem(LPMEASUREITEMSTRUCT *lpMeasureItemStruct* **);**

Parameters

lpMeasureItemStruct   A long pointer to a **MEASUREITEMSTRUCT** structure.

Remarks

Called by the framework when a combo box with an owner-draw style is created.

By default, this member function does nothing. Override this member function and fill in the **MEASUREITEMSTRUCT** structure to inform Windows of the dimensions of the list box in the combo box. If the combo box is created with the **CBS_OWNERDRAWVARIABLE** style, the framework calls this member function for each item in the list box. Otherwise, this member is called only once.

Using the **CBS_OWNERDRAWFIXED** style in an owner-draw combo box created with the **SubclassDlgItem** member function of **CWnd** involves further programming considerations. See the discussion in Technical Note 14 under MFC in Books Online.

See **CWnd::OnMeasureItem** for a description of the **MEASUREITEMSTRUCT** structure.

See Also   **CComboBox::CompareItem**, **CComboBox::DrawItem**, **WM_MEASUREITEM**, **CComboBox::DeleteItem**

CComboBox::Paste

void Paste( );

Remarks

Inserts the data from the Clipboard into the edit control of the combo box at the current cursor position. Data is inserted only if the Clipboard contains data in **CF_TEXT** format.

See Also   **CComboBox::Clear**, **CComboBox::Copy**, **CComboBox::Cut**, **WM_PASTE**

CComboBox::ResetContent

void ResetContent( );

Remarks

Removes all items from the list box and edit control of a combo box.

See Also   **CB_RESETCONTENT**

CComboBox::SelectString

int SelectString(int *nStartAfter*, **LPCTSTR** *lpszString* **);**

Return Value

The zero-based index of the selected item if the string was found. If the search was unsuccessful, the return value is **CB_ERR** and the current selection is not changed.

Parameters

nStartAfter   Contains the zero-based index of the item before the first item to be searched. When the search reaches the bottom of the list box, it continues from the top of the list box back to the item specified by *nStartAfter*. If –1, the entire list box is searched from the beginning.

lpszString   Points to the null-terminated string that contains the prefix to search for. The search is case independent, so this string can contain any combination of uppercase and lowercase letters.

Remarks

Searches for a string in the list box of a combo box, and if the string is found, selects the string in the list box and copies it to the edit control.

A string is selected only if its initial characters (from the starting point) match the characters in the prefix string.

Note that the **SelectString** and **FindString** member functions both find a string, but the **SelectString** member function also selects the string.

See Also   **CComboBox::FindString**, **CB_SELECTSTRING**

CComboBox::SetCurSel

int SetCurSel(int *nSelect* **);**

Return Value

The zero-based index of the item selected if the message is successful. The return value is **CB_ERR** if *nSelect* is greater than the number of items in the list or if *nSelect* is set to –1, which clears the selection.

Parameters

nSelect   Specifies the zero-based index of the string to select. If –1, any current selection in the list box is removed and the edit control is cleared.

Remarks

Selects a string in the list box of a combo box. If necessary, the list box scrolls the string into view (if the list box is visible). The text in the edit control of the combo box is changed to reflect the new selection. Any previous selection in the list box is removed.

See Also   **CComboBox::GetCurSel**, **CB_SETCURSEL**

CComboBox::SetDroppedWidth

int SetDroppedWidth(UINT *nWidth* **);**

Return Value

If successful, the new width of the list box, otherwise **CB_ERR**.

Parameters

nWidth   The minimum allowable width of the list-box portion of the combo box, in pixels.

Remarks

Call this function to set the minimum allowable width, in pixels, of the list box of a combo box. This function only applies to combo boxes with the **CBS_DROPDOWN** or **CBS_DROPDOWNLIST** style.

By default, the minimum allowable width of the drop-down list box is 0. When the list-box portion of the combo box is displayed, its width is the larger of the minimum allowable width or the combo box width.

See Also   **CComboBox::GetDroppedWidth, CB_SETDROPPEDWIDTH**

CComboBox::SetEditSel

BOOL SetEditSel(int *nStartChar***, int** *nEndChar* **);**

Return Value

Nonzero if the member function is successful; otherwise 0. It is **CB_ERR** if **CComboBox** has the **CBS_DROPDOWNLIST** style or does not have a list box.

Parameters

nStartChar   Specifies the starting position. If the starting position is set to –1, then any existing selection is removed.

nEndChar   Specifies the ending position. If the ending position is set to –1, then all text from the starting position to the last character in the edit control is selected.

Remarks

Selects characters in the edit control of a combo box.

The positions are zero-based. To select the first character of the edit control, you specify a starting position of 0. The ending position is for the character just after the last character to select. For example, to select the first four characters of the edit control, you would use a starting position of 0 and an ending position of 4.

See Also   **CComboBox::GetEditSel, CB_SETEDITSEL**

CComboBox::SetExtendedUI

int SetExtendedUI(BOOL *bExtended* **= TRUE);**

Return Value

CB_OKAY if the operation is successful, or **CB_ERR** if an error occurs.

Parameters

bExtended   Specifies whether the combo box should use the extended user interface or the default user interface. A value of **TRUE** selects the extended user interface; a value of **FALSE** selects the standard user interface.

Remarks

Call the **SetExtendedUI** member function to select either the default user interface or the extended user interface for a combo box that has the **CBS_DROPDOWN** or **CBS_DROPDOWNLIST** style.

The extended user interface can be identified in the following ways:

- Clicking the static control displays the list box only for combo boxes with the **CBS_DROPDOWNLIST** style.

- Pressing the DOWN ARROW key displays the list box (F4 is disabled).

Scrolling in the static control is disabled when the item list is not visible (the arrow keys are disabled).

See Also   **CComboBox::GetExtendedUI, CB_SETEXTENDEDUI**

CComboBox::SetHorizontalExtent

void SetHorizontalExtent(UINT *nExtent* **);**

Parameters

nExtent   Specifies the number of pixels by which the list-box portion of the combo box can be scrolled horizontally.

Remarks

Sets the width, in pixels, by which the list-box portion of the combo box can be scrolled horizontally. If the width of the list box is smaller than this value, the horizontal scroll bar will horizontally scroll items in the list box. If the width of the list box is equal to or greater than this value, the horizontal scroll bar is hidden or, if the combo box has the **CBS_DISABLENOSCROLL** style, disabled.

See Also   **CComboBox::GetHorizontalExtent, CB_SETHORIZONTALEXTENT**

CComboBox::SetItemData

> int **SetItemData**(int *nIndex*, **DWORD** *dwItemData*);

Return Value

> **CB_ERR** if an error occurs.

Parameters

> *nIndex*   Contains a zero-based index to the item to set.
>
> *dwItemData*   Contains the new value to associate with the item.

Remarks

> Sets the 32-bit value associated with the specified item in a combo box. Use the **SetItemDataPtr** member function if the 32-bit item is to be a pointer.
>
> **See Also**   **CComboBox::GetItemData**, **CComboBox::GetItemDataPtr**, **CComboBox::SetItemDataPtr**, **CB_SETITEMDATA**, **CComboBox::AddString**, **CComboBox::InsertString**

CComboBox::SetItemDataPtr

> int **SetItemDataPtr**(int *nIndex*, **void*** *pData*);

Return Value

> **CB_ERR** if an error occurs.

Parameters

> *nIndex*   Contains a zero-based index to the item.
>
> *pData*   Contains the pointer to associate with the item.

Remarks

> Sets the 32-bit value associated with the specified item in a combo box to be the specified pointer (**void***). This pointer remains valid for the life of the combo box, even though the item's relative position within the combo box might change as items are added or removed. Hence, the item's index within the box can change, but the pointer remains reliable.
>
> **See Also**   **CComboBox::GetItemData**, **CComboBox::GetItemDataPtr**, **CComboBox::SetItemData**, **CB_SETITEMDATA**, **CComboBox::AddString**, **CComboBox::InsertString**

CComboBox::SetItemHeight

int SetItemHeight(int *nIndex***, UINT** *cyItemHeight* **);**

Return Value

CB_ERR if the index or height is invalid; otherwise 0.

Parameters

nIndex   Specifies whether the height of list items or the height of the edit-control (or static-text) portion of the combo box is set.

If the combo box has the **CBS_OWNERDRAWVARIABLE** style, *nIndex* specifies the zero-based index of the list item whose height is to be set; otherwise, *nIndex* must be 0 and the height of all list items will be set.

If *nIndex* is –1, the height of the edit-control or static-text portion of the combo box is to be set.

cyItemHeight   Specifies the height, in pixels, of the combo-box component identified by *nIndex*.

Remarks

Call the **SetItemHeight** member function to set the height of list items in a combo box or the height of the edit-control (or static-text) portion of a combo box.

The height of the edit-control (or static-text) portion of the combo box is set independently of the height of the list items. An application must ensure that the height of the edit-control (or static-text) portion is not smaller than the height of a particular list-box item.

See Also   **CComboBox::GetItemHeight, WM_MEASUREITEM, CB_SETITEMHEIGHT**

CComboBox::SetLocale

LCID SetLocale(LCID *nNewLocale* **);**

Return Value

The previous locale identifier (LCID) value for this combo box.

Parameters

nNewLocale   The new locale identifier (LCID) value to set for the combo box.

Remarks

Sets the locale identifier for this combo box. If **SetLocale** is not called, the default locale is obtained from the system. This system default locale can be modified by using Control Panel's Regional (or International) application.

See Also   **CComboBox::GetLocale**

CComboBox::SetTopIndex

int SetTopIndex(int *nIndex* **);**

Return Value

Zero if successful, or **LB_ERR** if an error occurs.

Parameters

nIndex   Specifies the zero-based index of the list-box item.

Remarks

Ensures that a particular item is visible in the list-box portion of the combo box.

The system scrolls the list box until either the item specified by *nIndex* appears at the top of the list box or the maximum scroll range has been reached.

See Also   **CComboBox::GetTopIndex**, **CB_SETTOPINDEX**

CComboBox::ShowDropDown

void ShowDropDown(BOOL *bShowIt* **= TRUE);**

Parameters

bShowIt   Specifies whether the drop-down list box is to be shown or hidden. A value of **TRUE** shows the list box. A value of **FALSE** hides the list box.

Remarks

Shows or hides the list box of a combo box that has the **CBS_DROPDOWN** or **CBS_DROPDOWNLIST** style. By default, a combo box of this style will show the list box.

This member function has no effect on a combo box created with the **CBS_SIMPLE** style.

See Also   **CB_SHOWDROPDOWN**

CCommandLineInfo

The **CCommandLineInfo** class aids in parsing the command line at application startup.

An MFC application will typically create a local instance of this class in the **InitInstance** function of its application object. This object is then passed to **CWinApp::ParseCommandLine**, which repeatedly calls **ParseParam** to fill the **CCommandLineInfo** object. The **CCommandLineInfo** object is then passed to **CWinApp::ProcessShellCommand** to handle the command-line arguments and flags.

You can use this object to encapsulate the following command-line options and parameters:

Command-line argument	Command executed
app	New file.
app filename	Open file.
app **/p** filename	Print file to default printer.
app **/pt** filename printer driver port	Print file to the specified printer.
app **/dde**	Start up and await DDE command.
app **/Automation**	Start up as an OLE automation server.
app **/Embedding**	Start up to edit an embedded OLE item.

Derive a new class from **CCommandLineInfo** to handle other flags and parameter values. Override **ParseParam** to handle the new flags.

#include <afxwin.h>

See Also   CWinApp::ParseCommandLine, CWinApp::ProcessShellCommand

Construction

CommandLineInfo	Constructs a default **CCommandLineInfo** object.

Operations

ParseParam	Override this callback to parse individual parameters.

Data Members

m_bShowSplash	Indicates if a splash screen should be shown.
m_bRunEmbedded	Indicates the command-line **/Embedding** option was found.
m_bRunAutomated	Indicates the command-line **/Automation** option was found.
m_nShellCommand	Indicates the shell command to be processed.
m_strFileName	Indicates the filename to be opened or printed; empty if the

	shell command is New or DDE.
m_strPrinterName	Indicates the printer name if the shell command is Print To; otherwise empty.
m_strDriverName	Indicates the driver name if the shell command is Print To; otherwise empty.
m_strPortName	Indicates the port name if the shell command is Print To; otherwise empty.

Member Functions

CCommandLineInfo::CCommandLineInfo

CCommandLineInfo( );

Remarks

This constructor creates a **CCommandLineInfo** object with default values. The default is to show the splash screen (**m_bShowSplash = TRUE**) and to execute the New command on the File menu (**m_nShellCommand = NewFile**).

The application framework calls **ParseParam** to fill data members of this object.

See Also   **CCommandLineInfo::ParseParam**

CCommandLineInfo::ParseParam

virtual void ParseParam(LPCTSTR *lpszParam*, **BOOL** *bFlag*, **BOOL** *bLast* **);**

Parameters

lpszParam   The parameter or flag.

bFlag   Indicates whether *lpszParam* is a parameter or a flag.

bLast   Indicates if this is the last parameter or a flag on the command line.

Remarks

The framework calls this function to parse/interpret individual parameters from the command line. **CWinApp::ParseCommandLine** calls **ParseParam** once for each parameter or flag on the command line, passing the argument to *lpszParam*. If the first character of the parameter is a '-' or a '/', then it is removed and *bFlag* is set to **TRUE**. When parsing the final parameter, *bLast* is set to **TRUE**.

The default implementation of this function recognizes the following flags: **/p**, **/pt**, **/dde**, **/Automation**, and **/Embedding**, as shown in the following table:

Command-line argument	Command executed
app	New file.
app filename	Open file.
app **/p** filename	Print file to default printer.
app **/pt** filename printer driver port	Print file to the specified printer.
app **/dde**	Start up and await DDE command.
app **/Automation**	Start up as an OLE automation server.
app **/Embedding**	Start up to edit an embedded OLE item.

This information is stored in **m_bRunAutomated**, **m_bRunEmbedded**, and **m_nShellCommand**. Flags are marked by either a forward-slash '/' or hyphen '-'.

The default implementation puts the first non-flag parameter into **m_strFileName**. In the case of the **/pt** flag, the default implementation puts the second, third, and fourth non-flag parameters into **m_strPrinterName**, **m_strDriverName**, and **m_strPortName**, respectively.

The default implementation also sets **m_bShowSplash** to **TRUE** only in the case of a new file. In the case of a new file, the user has taken action involving the application itself. In any other case, including opening existing files using the shell, the user action involves the file directly. In a document-centric standpoint, the splash screen does not need to announce the application starting up.

Override this function in your derived class to handle other flag and parameter values.

See Also **CWinApp::ParseCommandLine**

Data Members

CCommandLineInfo::m_bRunAutomated

Remarks

Indicates that the **/Automation** flag was found on the command line. If **TRUE**, this means start up as an OLE automation server.

See Also **CCommandLineInfo::ParseParam**, **CWinApp::ProcessShellCommand**

CCommandLineInfo::m_bRunEmbedded

Remarks

Indicates that the **/Embedding** flag was found on the command line. If **TRUE**, this means start up for editing an embedded OLE item.

See Also   **CCommandLineInfo::m_bShowSplash,
CWinApp::ProcessShellCommand**

CCommandLineInfo::m_bShowSplash

Remarks

Indicates that the splash screen should be displayed. If **TRUE**, this means the splash screen for this application should be displayed during startup. The default implementation of **ParseParam** sets this data member to **TRUE** if **m_nShellCommand** is equal to **CCommandLineInfo::FileNew**.

See Also   **CCommandLineInfo::m_bRunAutomated,
CCommandLineInfo::m_bRunEmbedded,
CCommandLineInfo::m_nShellCommand, CCommandLineInfo::ParseParam,
CWinApp::ProcessShellCommand**

CCommandLineInfo::m_nShellCommand

Remarks

Indicates the shell command for this instance of the application.

The type for this data member is the following enumerated type, which is defined within the **CCommandLineInfo** class.

```
enum{
    FileNew,
    FileOpen,
    FilePrint,
    FilePrintTo,
    FileDDE,
};
```

For a brief description of these values, see the following list.

- **CCommandLineInfo::FileNew**   Indicates that no filename was found on the command line.

- **CCommandLineInfo::FileOpen** Indicates that a filename was found on the command line and that none of the following flags were found on the command line: **/p**, **/pt**, **/dde**.

- **CCommandLineInfo::FilePrint** Indicates that the **/p** flag was found on the command line.

- **CCommandLineInfo::FilePrintTo** Indicates that the **/pt** flag was found on the command line.

- **CCommandLineInfo::FileDDE** Indicates that the **/dde** flag was found on the command line.

See Also **CCommandLineInfo::m_strFileName**, **CCommandLineInfo::m_strPrinterName**, **CCommandLineInfo::m_strDriverName**, **CCommandLineInfo::m_strPortName**, **CWinApp::ProcessShellCommand**

CCommandLineInfo::m_strFileName

Remarks

Stores the value of the first non-flag parameter on the command line. This parameter is typically the name of the file to open.

See Also **CCommandLineInfo::m_strPrinterName**, **CCommandLineInfo::m_strDriverName**, **CCommandLineInfo::m_strPortName**, **CWinApp::ProcessShellCommand**

CCommandLineInfo::m_strDriverName

Remarks

Stores the value of the third non-flag parameter on the command line. This parameter is typically the name of the printer driver for a Print To shell command. The default implementation of **ParseParam** sets this data member only if the **/pt** flag was found on the command line.

See Also **CCommandLineInfo::m_strFileName**, **CCommandLineInfo::m_strPrinterName**, **CCommandLineInfo::m_strPortName**, **CWinApp::ProcessShellCommand**

CCommandLineInfo::m_strPortName

Remarks

Stores the value of the fourth non-flag parameter on the command line. This parameter is typically the name of the printer port for a Print To shell command. The default implementation of **ParseParam** sets this data member only if the **/pt** flag was found on the command line.

See Also **CCommandLineInfo::m_strFileName**, **CCommandLineInfo::m_strPrinterName**, **CCommandLineInfo::m_strDriverName**, **CWinApp::ProcessShellCommand**

CCommandLineInfo::m_strPrinterName

Remarks

Stores the value of the second non-flag parameter on the command line. This parameter is typically the name of the printer for a Print To shell command. The default implementation of **ParseParam** sets this data member only if the **/pt** flag was found on the command line.

See Also **CCommandLineInfo::m_strFileName**, **CCommandLineInfo::m_strDriverName**, **CCommandLineInfo::m_strPortName**, **CWinApp::ProcessShellCommand**

CCommonDialog

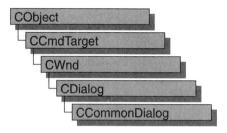

CCommonDialog is the base class for classes that encapsulate functionality of the Windows common dialogs:

- **CFileDialog**
- **CFontDialog**
- **CColorDialog**
- **CPageSetupDialog**
- **CPrintDialog**
- **CFindReplaceDialog**
- **COleDialog**

#include <afxdlgs.h>

See Also   **CFileDialog**, **CFontDialog**, **CColorDialog**, **CPageSetupDialog**, **CPrintDialog**, **CFindReplaceDialog**, **COleDialog**

Construction

CCommonDialog	Constructs a **CCommonDialog** object.

Member Functions

CCommonDialog::CCommonDialog

CCommonDialog(CWnd* *pParentWnd* **);**

Parameters

pParentWnd   Points to the parent or owner window object (of type **CWnd**) to which the dialog object belongs. If it is **NULL**, the dialog object's parent window is set to the main application window.

Remarks

Constructs a **CCommonDialog** object. See **CDialog::CDialog** for complete information.

See Also **CDialog::CDialog**

CConnectionPoint

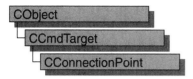

The **CConnectionPoint** class defines a special type of interface used to communicate with other OLE objects, called a "connection point." Unlike normal OLE interfaces, which are used to implement and expose the functionality of an OLE control, a connection point implements an outgoing interface that is able to initiate actions on other objects, such as firing events and change notifications.

A connection consists of two parts: the object calling the interface, called the "source," and the object implementing the interface, called the "sink." By exposing a connection point, a source allows sinks to establish connections to itself. Through the connection point mechanism, a source object obtains a pointer to the sink's implementation of a set of member functions. For example, to fire an event implemented by the sink, the source can call the appropriate method of the sink's implementation.

By default, a **COleControl**-derived class implements two connection points: one for events and one for property change notifications. These connections are used, respectively, for event firing and for notifying a sink (for example, the control's container) when a property value has changed. Support is also provided for OLE controls to implement additional connection points. For each additional connection point implemented in your control class, you must declare a "connection part" that implements the connection point. If you implement one or more connection points, you also need to declare a single "connection map" in your control class.

The following example demonstrates a simple connection map and one connection point for the Sample OLE control, consisting of two fragments of code: the first portion declares the connection map and point; the second implements this map and point. The first fragment is inserted into the declaration of the control class, under the **protected** section:

```
// Connection point for ISample interface
BEGIN_CONNECTION_PART(CSampleCtrl, SampleConnPt)
    CONNECTION_IID(IID_ISampleSink)
END_CONNECTION_PART(SampleConnPt)

DECLARE_CONNECTION_MAP()
```

The **BEGIN_CONNECTION_PART** and **END_CONNECTION_PART** macros declare an embedded class, XSampleConnPt (derived from **CConnectionPoint**) that implements this particular connection point. If you want to override any **CConnectionPoint** member functions, or add member functions of your own, declare them between these two macros. For example, the **CONNECTION_IID** macro overrides the **CConnectionPoint::GetIID** member function when placed between these two macros.

The second code fragment is inserted into the implementation file (.CPP) of your control class. This code implements the connection map, which includes the additional connection point, SampleConnPt:

```
BEGIN_CONNECTION_MAP(CSampleCtrl, COleControl)
    CONNECTION_PART(CSampleCtrl, IID_ISampleSink, SampleConnPt)
END_CONNECTION_MAP()
```

Once these code fragments have been inserted, the Sample OLE control exposes a connection point for the **ISampleSink** interface.

Typically, connection points support "multicasting"; the ability to broadcast to multiple sinks connected to the same interface. The following code fragment demonstrates how to accomplish multicasting by iterating through each sink on a connection point:

```
void CSampleCtrl::CallSinkFunc()
{
    const CPtrArray* pConnections = m_xSampleConnPt.GetConnections();
    ASSERT(pConnections != NULL);

    int cConnections = pConnections->GetSize();
    ISampleSink* pSampleSink;
    for (int i = 0; i < cConnections; i++)
    {
        pSampleSink = (ISampleSink*)(pConnections->GetAt(i));
        ASSERT(pSampleSink != NULL);
        pSampleSink->SinkFunc();
    }
}
```

This example retrieves the current set of connections on the SampleConnPt connection point with a call to CConnectionPoint::GetConnections. It then iterates through the connections and calls ISampleSink::SinkFunc on every active connection.

For more information on using **CConnectionPoint**, see the article "Connection Points" and Appendix A, "OLE Controls Architecture," in *Programming with MFC*.

#include <afxctl.h>

Operations

| **GetConnections** | Retrieves all connection points in a connection map. |

GetContainer	Retrieves the container of the control that owns the connection map.
GetIID	Retrieves the interface ID of a connection point.
GetMaxConnections	Retrieves the maximum number of connection points supported by a control.
OnAdvise	Called by the framework when establishing or breaking connections.

Member Functions

CConnectionPoint::GetConnections

const CPtrArray* GetConnections( );

Return Value

A pointer to an array of active connections (sinks). Each pointer in this array can be safely converted to a pointer to the sink interface using a cast operator.

Remarks

Call this function to retrieve all active connections for a connection point.

See Also **CConnectionPoint::GetMaxConnections**

CConnectionPoint::GetContainer

virtual LPCONNECTIONPOINTCONTAINER GetContainer( ) = 0;

Return Value

If successful, a pointer to the container; otherwise **NULL**.

Remarks

Called by the framework to retrieve the **IConnectionPointContainer** for the connection point. This function is typically implemented by the **BEGIN_CONNECTION_PART** macro.

See Also **BEGIN_CONNECTION_PART**

CConnectionPoint::GetIID

virtual REFIID GetIID( ) = 0;

Return Value

A reference to the connection point's interface ID.

Remarks

Called by the framework to retrieve the interface ID of a connection point.

Override this function to return the interface ID for this connection point.

See Also   CONNECTION_IID

CConnectionPoint::GetMaxConnections

virtual int GetMaxConnections( );

Return Value

The maximum number of connections supported by the control, or -1 if no limit.

Remarks

Called by the framework to retrieve the maximum number of connections supported by the connection point. The default implementation returns -1, indicating no limit.

Override this function if you want to limit the number of sinks that can connect to your control.

See Also   CConnectionPoint::GetConnections

CConnectionPoint::OnAdvise

virtual void OnAdvise(BOOL *bAdvise* **);**

Parameters

bAdvise   **TRUE**, if a connection is being established; otherwise **FALSE**.

Remarks

Called by the framework when a connection is being established or broken. The default implementation does nothing.

Override this function if you want notification when sinks connect to or disconnect from your connection point.

CControlBar

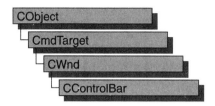

CControlBar is the base class for the control-bar classes **CStatusBar**, **CToolBar**, **CDialogBar**, and **COleResizeBar**. A control bar is a window that is usually aligned to the left or right of a frame window. It may contain child items that are either **HWND**-based controls, which are Windows windows that generate and respond to Windows messages, or non-**HWND**-based items, which are not windows and are managed by application code or framework code. List boxes and edit controls are examples of **HWND**-based controls; status-bar panes and bitmap buttons are examples of non-**HWND**-based controls.

Control-bar windows are usually child windows of a parent frame window and are usually siblings to the client view or MDI client of the frame window. A **CControlBar** object uses information about the parent window's client rectangle to position itself. It then informs the parent window as to how much space remains unallocated in the parent window's client area.

For more information on **CControlBar**, see the article "Control Bars" in *Programming with MFC* and Technical Note 31, "Control Bars," available under MFC in Books Online.

#include <afxext.h>

See Also   **CToolBar**, **CDialogBar**, **CStatusBar**

Data Members

m_bAutoDelete	If nonzero, the **CControlBar** object is deleted when the Windows control bar is destroyed.

Attributes

GetBarStyle	Retrieves the control bar style settings.
SetBarStyle	Modifies the control bar style settings.
GetCount	Returns the number of non-**HWND** elements in the control bar.
GetDockingFrame	Returns a pointer to the frame to which a control bar is docked.

IsFloating	Returns a nonzero value if the control bar in question is a floating control bar.
CalcFixedLayout	Returns the size of the control bar as a **CSize** object.
CalcDynamicLayout	Returns the size of a dynamic control bar as a **CSize** object.

Overridables

OnUpdateCmdUI	Calls the Command UI handlers.

Operations

EnableDocking	Allows a control bar to be docked or floating.

Member Functions

CControlBar::CalcDynamicLayout

virtual CSize CalcDynamicLayout(int *nLength*, **DWORD** *dwMode* **);**

Return Value

The control bar size, in pixels, of a **CSize** object.

Parameters

nLength   The requested dimension of the control bar, either horizontal or vertical, depending on *dwMode*.

dwMode   The following predefined flags are used to determine the height and width of the dynamc control bar. Use the bitwise-OR (|) operator to combine the flags.

Layout mode flags	What it means
LM_STRETCH	Indicates whether the control bar should be stretched to the size of the frame. Set if the bar is not a docking bar (not available for docking). Not set when the bar is docked or floating (available for docking). If set, **LM_STRETCH** ignores *nLength* and returns dimensions based on the **LM_HORZ** state. **LM_STRETCH** works similarly to the the *bStretch* parameter used in **CalcFixedLayout**; see that member function for more information about the relationship between stretching and orientation.
LM_HORZ	Indicates that the bar is horizontally or vertically oriented. Set if the bar is horizontally oriented, and if it is vertically oriented, it is not set. **LM_HORZ** works similarly to the the *bHorz* parameter used in **CalcFixedLayout**; see that member function for more information about the relationship between stretching and orientation.
LM_MRUWIDTH	Most Recently Used Dynamic Width. Ignores *nLength* parameter and uses the remembered most recently used width.

Layout mode flags	What it means
LM_HORZDOCK	Horizontal Docked Dimensions. Ignores *nLength* parameter and returns the dynamic size with the largest width.
LM_VERTDOCK	Vertical Docked Dimensions. Ignores *nLength* parameter and returns the dynamic size with the largest height.
LM_LENGTHY	Set if *nLength* indicates height (Y-direction) instead of width.
LM_COMMIT	Resets **LM_MRUWIDTH** to current width of floating control bar.

Remarks

The framework calls this member function to calculate the dimensions of a dynamic toolbar.

Override this member function to provide your own dynamic layout in classes you derive from **CControlBar**. MFC classes derived from **CControlBar**, such as **CToolbar**, override this member function and provide their own implementation.

See Also   **CControlBar::CalcFixedLayout**, **CToolbar**

CControlBar::CalcFixedLayout

virtual CSize CalcFixedLayout(BOOL *bStretch*, BOOL *bHorz*);

Return Value

The control bar size, in pixels, of a **CSize** object.

Parameters

bStretch   Indicates whether the bar should be stretched to the size of the frame. The *bStretch* parameter is nonzero when the bar is not a docking bar (not available for docking) and is 0 when it is docked or floating (available for docking).

bHorz   Indicates that the bar is horizontally or vertically oriented. The *bHorz* parameter is nonzero if the bar is horizontally oriented and is 0 if it is vertically oriented.

Remarks

Call this member function to calculate the horizontal size of a control bar.

Control bars such as toolbars can stretch horizontally or vertically to accommodate the buttons contained in the control bar.

If *bStretch* is **TRUE**, stretch the dimension along the orientation provided by *bHorz*. In other words, if *bHorz* is **FALSE**, the control bar is stretched vertically. If *bStretch* is **FALSE**, no stretch occurs. The following table shows the possible permutations, and resulting control-bar styles, of *bStretch* and *bHorz*.

bStretch	bHorz	Stretching	Orientation	Docking/Not docking
TRUE	TRUE	Horizontal stretching	Horizontally oriented	Not docking
TRUE	FALSE	Vertical stretching	Vertically oriented	Not docking
FALSE	TRUE	No stretching available	Horizontally oriented	Docking
FALSE	FALSE	No stretching available	Vertically oriented	Docking

See Also   **CControlBar::CalcDynamicLayout**

CControlBar::EnableDocking

void EnableDocking(DWORD *dwStyle* **);**

Parameters

dwStyle   Specifies whether the control bar supports docking and the sides of its parent window to which the control bar can be docked, if supported. Can be one or more of the following:

- **CBRS_ALIGN_TOP**   Allows docking at the top of the client area.

- **CBRS_ALIGN_BOTTOM**   Allows docking at the bottom of the client area.

- **CBRS_ALIGN_LEFT**   Allows docking on the left side of the client area.

- **CBRS_ALIGN_RIGHT**   Allows docking on the right side of the client area.

- **CBRS_ALIGN_ANY**   Allows docking on any side of the client area.

- **CBRS_FLOAT_MULTI**   Allows multiple control bars to be floated in a single mini-frame window.

If 0 (that is, indicating no flags), the control bar will not dock.

Remarks

Call this function to enable a control bar to be docked. The sides specified must match one of the sides enabled for docking in the destination frame window, or the control bar cannot be docked to that frame window.

See Also   **CFrameWnd::EnableDocking, CFrameWnd::DockControlBar, CFrameWnd::FloatControlBar, CControlBar::SetBarStyle**

CControlBar::GetBarStyle

DWORD GetBarStyle( );

Return Value

The current **CBRS_** (control bar styles) settings for the control bar. See **CControlBar::SetBarStyle** for the complete list of available styles.

Remarks

Call this function to determine which **CBRS_** (control bar styles) settings are currently set for the control bar. Does not handle **WS_** (window style) styles.

See Also   **CControlBar::SetBarStyle**

CControlBar::GetCount

int GetCount( ) const;

Return Value

The number of non-**HWND** items on the **CControlBar** object. This function returns 0 for a **CDialogBar** object.

Remarks

Returns the number of non-**HWND** items on the **CControlBar** object. The type of the item depends on the derived object: panes for **CStatusBar** objects, and buttons and separators for **CToolBar** objects.

See Also   **CToolBar::SetButtons, CStatusBar::SetIndicators, CStatusBar, CToolBar, CDialogBar**

CControlBar::GetDockingFrame

CFrameWnd* GetDockingFrame( ) const;

Return Value

A pointer to a frame window if successful; otherwise **NULL**.

Remarks

Call this member function to obtain a pointer to the current frame window to which your control bar is docked.

For more information about dockable control bars, see **CControlBar::EnableDocking** and **CFrameWnd::DockControlBar**.

See Also   **CControlBar::EnableDocking, CFrameWnd::DockControlBar**

CControlBar::IsFloating

BOOL IsFloating( ) const;

Return Value

Nonzero if the control bar is floating; otherwise 0.

Remarks

Call this member function to determine whether the control bar is floating or docked.

To change the state of a control bar from docked to floating, call
CFrameWnd::FloatControlBar.

See Also   CFrameWnd::FloatControlBar

CControlBar::OnUpdateCmdUI

virtual void OnUpdateCmdUI(CFrameWnd* *pTarget***, BOOL** *bDisableIfNoHndler* **) = 0;**

Parameters

pTarget   Points to the main frame window of the application. This pointer is used for routing update messages.

bDisableIfNoHndler   Flag that indicates whether a control that has no update handler should be automatically displayed as disabled.

Remarks

This member function is called by the framework to update the status of the toolbar or status bar.

To update an individual button or pane, use the **ON_UPDATE_COMMAND_UI** macro in your message map to set an update handler appropriately. See **ON_UPDATE_COMMAND_UI** for more information about using this macro.

OnUpdateCmdUI is called by the framework when the application is idle. The frame window to be updated must be a child window, at least indirectly, of a visible frame window. **OnUpdateCmdUI** is an advanced overridable.

See Also   ON_UPDATE_COMMAND_UI, Technical Note 31: "Control Bars"

CControlBar::SetBarStyle

void SetBarStyle(DWORD *dwStyle* **);**

Parameters

dwStyle   The desired styles for the control bar. Can be one or more of the following:

- **CBRS_ALIGN_TOP**   Allows the control bar to be docked to the top of the client area of a frame window.

- **CBRS_ALIGN_BOTTOM**   Allows the control bar to be docked to the bottom of the client area of a frame window.

- **CBRS_ALIGN_LEFT**   Allows the control bar to be docked to the left side of the client area of a frame window.

- **CBRS_ALIGN_RIGHT**   Allows the control bar to be docked to the right side of the client area of a frame window.

- **CBRS_ALIGN_ANY**   Allows the control bar to be docked to any side of the client area of a frame window.

- **CBRS_BORDER_TOP**   Causes a border to be drawn on the top edge of the control bar when it would be visible.

- **CBRS_BORDER_BOTTOM**   Causes a border to be drawn on the bottom edge of the control bar when it would be visible.

- **CBRS_BORDER_LEFT**   Causes a border to be drawn on the left edge of the control bar when it would be visible.

- **CBRS_BORDER_RIGHT**   Causes a border to be drawn on the right edge of the control bar when it would be visible.

- **CBRS_FLOAT_MULTI**   Allows multiple control bars to be floated in a single mini-frame window.

- **CBRS_TOOLTIPS**   Causes tool tips to be displayed for the control bar.

- **CBRS_FLYBY**   Causes message text to be updated at the same time as tool tips.

Remarks

Call this function to set the desired **CBRS_** styles for the control bar. Does not affect the **WS_** (window style) settings.

See Also   **CControlBar::GetBarStyle**

Data Members

CControlBar::m_bAutoDelete

Remarks

m_bAutoDelete is a public variable of type **BOOL**. If it is nonzero when the Windows control-bar object is destroyed, the **CControlBar** object is deleted.

A control-bar object is usually embedded in a frame-window object. In this case, **m_bAutoDelete** is 0 because the embedded control-bar object is destroyed when the frame window is destroyed.

Set this variable to a nonzero value if you allocate a **CControlBar** object on the heap and you do not plan to call **delete**.

See Also   CWnd::DestroyWindow

CCreateContext

The framework uses the **CCreateContext** structure when it creates the frame windows and views associated with a document. When creating a window, the values in this structure provide information used to connect the components that make up a document and the view of its data. You will only need to use **CCreateContext** if you are overriding parts of the creation process.

A **CCreateContext** structure contains pointers to the document, the frame window, the view, and the document template. It also contains a pointer to a **CRuntimeClass** that identifies the type of view to create. The run-time class information and the current document pointer are used to create a new view dynamically. The following table suggests how and when each **CCreateContext** member might be used:

Member	What it is for
m_pNewViewClass	**CRuntimeClass** of the new view to create.
m_pCurrentDoc	The existing document to be associated with the new view.
m_pNewDocTemplate	The document template associated with the creation of a new MDI frame window.
m_pLastView	The original view upon which additional views are modeled, as in the creation of a splitter window's views or the creation of a second view on a document.
m_pCurrentFrame	The frame window upon which additional frame windows are modeled, as in the creation of a second frame window on a document.

When a document template creates a document and its associated components, it validates the information stored in the **CCreateContext** structure. For example, a view should not be created for a nonexistent document.

Note All of the pointers in **CCreateContext** are optional and can be **NULL** if unspecified or unknown.

CCreateContext is used by the member functions listed under "See Also." Consult the descriptions of these functions for specific information if you plan to override them.

Here are a few general guidelines:

- When passed as an argument for window creation, as in **CWnd::Create**, **CFrameWnd::Create**, and **CFrameWnd::LoadFrame**, the create context specifies what the new window should be connected to. For most windows, the entire structure is optional and a **NULL** pointer can be passed.

- For overridable member functions, such as **CFrameWnd::OnCreateClient**, the **CCreateContext** argument is optional.

- For member functions involved in view creation, you must provide enough information to create the view. For example, for the first view in a splitter window, you must supply the view class information and the current document.

In general, if you use the framework defaults, you can ignore **CCreateContext**. If you attempt more advanced modifications, the Microsoft Foundation Class Library source code or the sample programs, such as VIEWEX, will guide you. If you do forget a required parameter, a framework assertion will tell you what you forgot.

For more information on **CCreateContext**, see the MFC sample VIEWEX.

#include <afxext.h>

See Also **CFrameWnd::Create, CFrameWnd::LoadFrame, CFrameWnd::OnCreateClient, CSplitterWnd::Create, CSplitterWnd::CreateView, CWnd::Create**

CCriticalSection

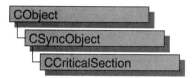

An object of class **CCriticalSection** represents a "critical section"—a synchronization object that allows one thread at a time to access a resource or section of code. Critical sections are useful when only one thread at a time can be allowed to modify data or some other controlled resource. For example, adding nodes to a linked list is a process that should only be allowed by one thread at a time. By using a **CCriticalSection** object to control the linked list, only one thread at a time can gain access to the list.

Critical sections are used instead of mutexes when speed is critical and the resource will not be used across process boundaries. For more information on using mutexes in MFC, see **CMutex**.

To use a **CCriticalSection** object, construct the **CCriticalSection** object when it is needed. You can then access the critical section when the constructor returns. Call **Unlock** when you are done accessing the critical section.

An alternative method for using **CCriticalSection** objects is to add a variable of type **CCriticalSection** as a data member to the class you wish to control. During construction of the controlled object, call the constructor of the **CCriticalSection** data member specifying if the critical section is initially owned and the desired security attributes.

To access a resource controlled by a **CCriticalSection** object in this manner, first create a variable of either type **CSingleLock** or type **CMultiLock** in your resource's access member function. Then call the lock object's **Lock** member function (for example, **CSingleLock::Lock**). At this point, your thread will either gain access to the resource, wait for the resource to be released and gain access, or wait for the resource to be released and time out, failing to gain access to the resource. In any case, your resource has been accessed in a thread-safe manner. To release the resource, use the lock object's **Unlock** member function (for example, **CSingleLock::Unlock**), or allow the lock object to fall out of scope.

Alternatively, you can create a **CCriticalSection** object stand-alone, and access it explicitly before attempting to access the controlled resource. This method, while clearer to someone reading your source code, is more prone to error as you must remember to lock and unlock the critical section before and after access.

For more information on using **CCriticalSection** objects, see the article "Multithreading: How to Use the Synchronization Classes" in *Programming with MFC*.

#include <afxmt.h>

See Also   CMutex

Construction

CCriticalSection	Constructs a **CCriticalSection** object.

Methods

Unlock	Releases the **CCriticalSection** object.
Lock	Use to gain access to the **CCriticalSection** object.

Member Functions

CCriticalSection::CCriticalSection

CCriticalSection( );

Remarks

Constructs a **CCriticalSection** object. To access or release a **CCriticalSection** object, create a **CMultiLock** or **CSingleLock** object and call its **Lock** and **Unlock** member functions. If the **CCriticalSection** object is being used stand-alone, call its **Unlock** member function to release it.

CCriticalSection::Lock

BOOL Lock( );
BOOL Lock(DWORD *dwTimeout* **);**

Return Value

Nonzero if the function was successful; otherwise 0.

Parameters

dwTimeout   Specifies the amount of time (in milliseconds) to wait for the critical section to become available. If not supplied, **Lock** will wait an infinite amount of time.

Remarks

Call this function to gain access to the critical section object. If the critical section is signaled (available), **Lock** will return successfully and the thread now owns the critical section. If the critical section is nonsignaled (unavailable), **Lock** will wait up to the number of milliseconds specified in *dwTimeout* for the critical section to become signaled. If the critical section did not become signaled in the specified amount of time, **Lock** returns failure.

See Also   **CSingleLock::Lock, CMultiLock::Lock**

CCriticalSection::Unlock

virtual BOOL Unlock( );

Return Value

Nonzero if the **CCriticalSection** object was owned by the thread and the release was successful; otherwise 0.

Remarks

Releases the **CCriticalSection** object for use by another thread. If the **CCriticalSection** is being used stand-alone, **Unlock** must be called immediately after completing use of the resource controlled by the critical section. If a **CSingleLock** or **CMultiLock** object is being used, **CCriticalSection::Unlock** will be called by the lock object's **Unlock** member function.

CCtrlView

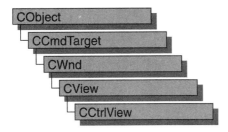

The class **CCtrlView** and its derivatives, **CEditView**, **CListView**, **CTreeView**, and **CRichEditView**, adapt the document-view architecture to the new common controls supported by Windows 95, Windows NT versions 3.51 and later, and Win32s versions 1.3 and later. For more information on the document-view architecture, see Chapter 3, "Working with Frame Windows, Documents, and Views," of *Programming with MFC*.

#include <afxwin.h>

See Also   **CTreeView**, **CListView**, **CRichEditView**

Construction

CCtrlView	Constructs a **CCtrlView** object.

Data Members

m_strClass	Contains the Windows class name for the view class.
m_dwDefaultStyle	Contains the default style for the view class.

Member Functions

CCtrlView::CCtrlView

CCtrlView(LPCTSTR *lpszClass*, **DWORD** *dwStyle* **);**

Parameters

lpszClass   Windows class name of the view class.

dwStyle   Style of the view class.

Remarks

Constructs a **CCtrlView** object. The framework calls the constructor when a new frame window is created or a window is split. Override **CView::OnInitialUpdate** to initialize the view after the document is attached. Call **CWnd::Create** or **CWnd::CreateEx** to create the Windows object.

See Also   **CWnd::PreCreateWindow**

Data Members

CCtrlView::m_dwDefaultStyle

DWORD m_dwDefaultStyle;

Remarks

Contains the default style for the view class. This style is applied when a window is created.

See Also   **CCtrlView::m_strClass**

CCtrlView::m_strClass

CString m_strClass;

Remarks

Contains the Windows class name for the view class.

See Also   **CCtrlView::m_dwDefaultStyle**

CDaoDatabase

A **CDaoDatabase** object represents a connection to a database through which you can operate on the data. For information about the database formats supported, see the **GetName** member function. You can have one or more **CDaoDatabase** objects active at a time in a given "workspace," represented by a **CDaoWorkspace** object. The workspace maintains a collection of open database objects, called the Databases collection.

Note The MFC DAO database classes are distinct from the MFC database classes based on ODBC. All DAO database class names have the "CDao" prefix. Class **CDaoDatabase** supplies an interface similar to that of the ODBC class **CDatabase**. The main difference is that **CDatabase** accesses the DBMS through Open Database Connectivity (ODBC) and an ODBC driver for that DBMS. **CDaoDatabase** accesses data through a Data Access Object (DAO) based on the Microsoft Jet database engine. In general, the MFC classes based on DAO are more capable than the MFC classes based on ODBC; the DAO-based classes can access data, including through ODBC drivers, via their own database engine. The DAO-based classes also support Data Definition Language (DDL) operations, such as adding tables via the classes, without having to call DAO directly.

Usage

You can create database objects implicitly, when you create recordset objects. But you can also create database objects explicitly. To use an existing database explicitly with **CDaoDatabase**, do either of the following:

- Construct a **CDaoDatabase** object, passing a pointer to an open **CDaoWorkspace** object.

- Or construct a **CDaoDatabase** object without specifying the workspace (MFC creates a temporary workspace object).

To create a new Microsoft Jet (.MDB) database, construct a **CDaoDatabase** object and call its **Create** member function. Do *not* call **Open** after **Create**.

To open an existing database, construct a **CDaoDatabase** object and call its **Open** member function.

Any of these techniques appends the DAO database object to the workspace's Databases collection and opens a connection to the data. When you then construct **CDaoRecordset**, **CDaoTableDef**, or **CDaoQueryDef** objects for operating on the connected database, pass the constructors for these objects a pointer to your **CDaoDatabase** object. When you finish using the connection, call the **Close** member function and destroy the **CDaoDatabase** object. **Close** closes any recordsets you have not closed previously.

Transactions

Database transaction processing is supplied at the workspace level—see the **BeginTrans**, **CommitTrans**, and **Rollback** member functions of class **CDaoWorkspace**. For more information, see the article "DAO Workspace: Managing Transactions" in *Programming with MFC*.

ODBC Connections

The recommended way to work with ODBC data sources is to attach external tables to a Microsoft Jet (.MDB) database. For more information, see the article "DAO External: Working with External Data Sources" in *Programming with MFC*.

Collections

Each database maintains its own collections of tabledef, querydef, recordset, and relation objects. Class **CDaoDatabase** supplies member functions for manipulating these objects.

Note The objects are stored in DAO, not in the MFC database object. MFC supplies classes for tabledef, querydef, and recordset objects but not for relation objects.

For more information about **CDaoDatabase**, see the article "DAO Database" in *Programming with MFC*.

#include <afxdao.h>

See Also CDaoWorkspace, CDaoRecordset, CDaoTableDef, CDaoQueryDef, CDatabase, CDaoException

Data Members

m_pWorkspace	A pointer to the **CDaoWorkspace** object that contains the database and defines its transaction space.
m_pDAODatabase	A pointer to the underlying DAO database object.

Construction

CDaoDatabase	Constructs a **CDaoDatabase** object. Call **Open** to connect the object to a database.

Attributes

CanTransact	Returns nonzero if the database supports transactions.
CanUpdate	Returns nonzero if the **CDaoDatabase** object is updatable (not read-only).

GetConnect	Returns the connect string used to connect the **CDaoDatabase** object to a database. Used for ODBC.
GetName	Returns the name of the database currently in use.
GetQueryTimeout	Returns the number of seconds after which database query operations will time out. Affects all subsequent open, add new, update, and edit operations and other operations on ODBC data sources (only) such as **Execute** calls.
GetRecordsAffected	Returns the number of records affected by the last update, edit, or add operation or by a call to **Execute**.
GetVersion	Returns the version of the database engine associated with the database.
IsOpen	Returns nonzero if the **CDaoDatabase** object is currently connected to a database.
SetQueryTimeout	Sets the number of seconds after which database query operations (on ODBC data sources only) will time out. Affects all subsequent open, add new, update, and delete operations.

Operations

Close	Closes the database connection.
Create	Creates the underlying DAO database object and initializes the **CDaoDatabase** object.
CreateRelation	Defines a new relation among the tables in the database.
DeleteQueryDef	Deletes a querydef object saved in the database's QueryDefs collection.
DeleteRelation	Deletes an existing relation between tables in the database.
DeleteTableDef	Deletes the definition of a table in the database. This deletes the actual table and all of its data.
Execute	Executes an action query. Calling **Execute** for a query that returns results throws an exception.
GetQueryDefCount	Returns the number of queries defined for the database.
GetQueryDefInfo	Returns information about a specified query defined in the database.
GetRelationCount	Returns the number of relations defined between tables in the database.
GetRelationInfo	Returns information about a specified relation defined between tables in the database.
GetTableDefCount	Returns the number of tables defined in the database.
GetTableDefInfo	Returns information about a specified table in the database.
Open	Establishes a connection to a database.

Member Functions

CDaoDatabase::CanTransact

BOOL CanTransact( );
    throw(CDaoException, CMemoryException);

Return Value

Nonzero if the database supports transactions; otherwise 0.

Remarks

Call this member function to determine whether the database allows transactions. Transactions are managed in the database's workspace. For information about transactions, see the article "DAO Workspace: Managing Transactions" in *Programming with MFC*.

See Also   **CDaoWorkspace::BeginTrans**, **CDaoWorkspace::CommitTrans**, **CDaoWorkspace::Rollback**

CDaoDatabase::CanUpdate

BOOL CanUpdate( );
    throw(CDaoException, CMemoryException);

Return Value

Nonzero if the **CDaoDatabase** object allows updates; otherwise 0, indicating either that you passed **TRUE** in *bReadOnly* when you opened the **CDaoDatabase** object or that the database itself is read-only. See the **Open** member function.

Remarks

Call this member function to determine whether the **CDaoDatabase** object allows updates. For information about database updatability, see the article "DAO Recordset: Recordset Operations" in *Programming with MFC* and see the topic "Updatable Property" in DAO Help.

CDaoDatabase::CDaoDatabase

CDaoDatabase(CDaoWorkspace* *pWorkspace* **= NULL);**

Parameters

pWorkspace   A pointer to the **CDaoWorkspace** object that will contain the new database object. If you accept the default value of **NULL**, the constructor creates a temporary **CDaoWorkspace** object that uses the default DAO workspace. You can get a pointer to the workspace object via the **m_pWorkspace** data member.

Remarks

Constructs a **CDaoDatabase** object. After constructing the object, if you are creating a new Microsoft Jet (.MDB) database, call the object's **Create** member function. If you are, instead, opening an existing database, call the object's **Open** member function.

When you finish with the object, you should call its **Close** member function and then destroy the **CDaoDatabase** object.

You might find it convenient to embed the **CDaoDatabase** object in your document class.

Note A **CDaoDatabase** object is also created implicitly if you open a **CDaoRecordset** object without passing a pointer to an existing **CDaoDatabase** object. This database object is closed when you close the recordset object.

For information about workspaces, see the article "DAO Workspace." For information about using **CDaoDatabase** objects, see the article "DAO Database." These articles are in *Programming with MFC*.

CDaoDatabase::Close

virtual void Close( );

Remarks

Call this member function to disconnect from a database and close any open recordsets, tabledefs, and querydefs associated with the database. It is good practice to close these objects yourself before you call this member function. Closing a **CDaoDatabase** object removes it from the Databases collection in the associated workspace. Because **Close** does not destroy the **CDaoDatabase** object, you can reuse the object by opening the same database or a different database.

Caution Call the **Update** member function (if there are pending edits) and the **Close** member function on all open recordset objects before you close a database. If you exit a function that declares **CDaoRecordset** or **CDaoDatabase** objects on the stack, the database is closed, any unsaved changes are lost, all pending transactions are rolled back, and any pending edits to your data are lost.

Caution If you try to close a database object while any recordset objects are open, or if you try to close a workspace object while any database objects belonging to that specific workspace are open, those recordset objects will be closed and any pending updates or edits will be rolled back. If you try to close a workspace object while any database objects belonging to it are open, the operation closes all database objects belonging to that specific workspace object, which may result in unclosed recordset objects being closed. If you do not close your database object, MFC reports an assertion failure in debug builds.

If the database object is defined outside the scope of a function, and you exit the function without closing it, the database object will remain open until explicitly closed or the module in which it is defined is out of scope.

For more information about **CDaoDatabase** objects, see the article "DAO Database" in *Programming with MFC*. For related information, see the topic "Close Method" in DAO Help.

See Also   **CDaoDatabase::Open, CDaoRecordset::Close, CDaoWorkspace::Close, CDaoQueryDef::Close, CDaoTableDef::Close**

CDaoDatabase::Create

> **virtual void Create(LPCTSTR** *lpszName*, **LPCTSTR** *lpszLocale* = **dbLangGeneral,**
> **int** *dwOptions* = **0**);
> **throw(CDaoException, CMemoryException);**

Parameters

lpszName   A string expression that is the name of the database file that you are creating. It can be the full path and filename, such as "C:\\MYDB.MDB". You must supply a name. If you do not supply a filename extension, .MDB is appended. If your network supports the uniform naming convention (UNC), you can also specify a network path, such as "\\\\MYSERVER\\MYSHARE\\MYDIR\\MYDB". Only Microsoft Jet (.MDB) database files can be created using this member function. (Double backslashes are required in string literals because "\" is the C++ escape character.)

lpszLocale   A string expression used to specify collating order for creating the database. The default value is **dbLangGeneral**. Possible values are:

- **dbLangGeneral**   English, German, French, Portuguese, Italian, and Modern Spanish

- **dbLangArabic**   Arabic

- **dbLangCyrillic**   Russian

- **dbLangCzech**   Czech

- **dbLangDutch**   Dutch

- **dbLangGreek**   Greek

- **dbLangHebrew**   Hebrew

- **dbLangHungarian**   Hungarian

- **dbLangIcelandic**   Icelandic

- **dbLangNordic**   Nordic languages (Microsoft Jet database engine version 1.0 only)

- **dbLangNorwdan**   Norwegian and Danish

- **dbLangPolish**   Polish

- **dbLangSpanish**   Traditional Spanish

- **dbLangSwedfin**   Swedish and Finnish

- **dbLangTurkish**   Turkish

dwOptions   An integer that indicates one or more options. Possible values are:

- **dbEncrypt**   Create an encrypted database.

- **dbVersion10**   Create a database with Microsoft Jet database version 1.0.

- **dbVersion11**   Create a database with Microsoft Jet database version 1.1.

- **dbVersion20**   Create a database with Microsoft Jet database version 2.0.

- **dbVersion30**   Create a database with Microsoft Jet database version 3.0.

If you omit the encryption constant, an unencrypted database is created. You can specify only one version constant. If you omit a version constant, a database that uses the Microsoft Jet database version 3.0 is created.

Caution   If a database is not encrypted, it is possible, even if you implement user/password security, to directly read the binary disk file that constitutes the database.

Remarks

To create a new Microsoft Jet (.MDB) database, call this member function after you construct a **CDaoDatabase** object. **Create** creates the database file and the underlying DAO database object and initializes the C++ object. The object is appended to the associated workspace's Databases collection. The database object is in an open state; do not call **Open** after **Create**.

Note   With **Create**, you can create only Microsoft Jet (.MDB) databases. You cannot create ISAM databases or ODBC databases.

For information about databases, see the article "DAO Database" in *Programming with MFC*. For related information, see the topic "CreateDatabase Method" in DAO Help.

See Also   **CDaoDatabase::CDaoDatabase**

CDaoDatabase::CreateRelation

void CreateRelation(LPCTSTR *lpszName*, **LPCTSTR** *lpszTable*, **LPCTSTR** *lpszForeignTable*,
    long *lAttributes*, **LPCTSTR** *lpszField*, **LPCTSTR** *lpszForeignField* **);**
    throw(CDaoException, CMemoryException);
void CreateRelation(CDaoRelationInfo& *relinfo* **);**
    throw(CDaoException, CMemoryException);

Parameters

lpszName The unique name of the relation object. The name must start with a letter
and can contain a maximum of 40 characters. It can include numbers and
underscore characters but cannot include punctuation or spaces.

lpszTable The name of the primary table in the relation. If the table does not exist,
MFC throws an exception of type **CDaoException**.

lpszForeignTable The name of the foreign table in the relation. If the table does not
exist, MFC throws an exception of type **CDaoException**.

lAttributes A long value that contains information about the relationship type. You
can use this value to enforce referential integrity, among other things. You can use
the bitwise-OR operator (|) to combine any of the following values (as long as the
combination makes sense):

- **dbRelationUnique** Relationship is one-to-one.

- **dbRelationDontEnforce** Relationship is not enforced (no referential
integrity).

- **dbRelationInherited** Relationship exists in a noncurrent database that
contains the two attached tables.

- **dbRelationUpdateCascade** Updates will cascade (for more on cascades, see
Remarks).

- **dbRelationDeleteCascade** Deletions will cascade.

lpszField A pointer to a null-terminated string containing the name of a field in the
primary table (named by *lpszTable*).

lpszForeignField A pointer to a null-terminated string containing the name of a
field in the foreign table (named by *lpszForeignTable*).

relinfo A reference to a **CDaoRelationInfo** object that contains information about
the relation you want to create.

Remarks

Call this member function to establish a relation between one or more fields in a
primary table in the database and one or more fields in a foreign table (another table
in the database). The relationship cannot involve a query or an attached table from an
external database.

Use the first version of the function when the relation involves one field in each of the two tables. Use the second version when the relation involves multiple fields. The maximum number of fields in a relation is 14.

This action creates an underlying DAO relation object, but this is an MFC implementation detail since MFC's encapsulation of relation objects is contained within class **CDaoDatabase**. MFC does not supply a class for relations.

If you set the relation object's attributes to activate cascade operations, the database engine automatically updates or deletes records in one or more other tables when changes are made to related primary key tables.

For example, suppose you establish a cascade delete relationship between a Customers table and an Orders table. When you delete records from the Customers table, records in the Orders table related to that customer are also deleted. In addition, if you establish cascade delete relationships between the Orders table and other tables, records from those tables are automatically deleted when you delete records from the Customers table.

For related information, see the topic "CreateRelation Method" in DAO Help.

See Also   CDaoDatabase::DeleteRelation

CDaoDatabase::DeleteQueryDef

void DeleteQueryDef(LPCTSTR *lpszName* **);**
   throw(CDaoException, CMemoryException);

Parameters
lpszName   The name of the saved query to delete.

Remarks
Call this member function to delete the specified querydef—saved query—from the **CDaoDatabase** object's QueryDefs collection. Afterwards, that query is no longer defined in the database.

For information about creating querydef objects, see class **CDaoQueryDef**. A querydef object becomes associated with a particular **CDaoDatabase** object when you construct the **CDaoQueryDef** object, passing it a pointer to the database object.

For information about querydefs, see the article "DAO QueryDef" in *Programming with MFC*. For related information, see the topic "Delete Method" in DAO Help.

See Also   CDaoQueryDef::Create, CDaoDatabase::CreateRelation, CDaoTableDef::Create

CDaoDatabase::DeleteRelation

void DeleteRelation(LPCTSTR *lpszName* **);**
    throw(CDaoException, CMemoryException);

Parameters

lpszName   The name of the relation to delete.

Remarks

Call this member function to delete an existing relation from the database object's Relations collection. Afterwards, the relation no longer exists.

For related information, see the topic "Delete Method" in DAO Help.

See Also   **CDaoDatabase::CreateRelation, CDaoTableDef::Create, CDaoQueryDef::Create**

CDaoDatabase::DeleteTableDef

void DeleteTableDef(LPCTSTR *lpszName* **);**
    throw(CDaoException, CMemoryException);

Parameters

lpszName   The name of the tabledef to delete.

Remarks

Call this member function to delete the specified table and all of its data from the **CDaoDatabase** object's TableDefs collection. Afterwards, that table is no longer defined in the database.

Warning Be very careful not to delete system tables.

For information about creating tabledef objects, see class **CDaoTableDef**. A tabledef object becomes associated with a particular **CDaoDatabase** object when you construct the **CDaoTableDef** object, passing it a pointer to the database object.

For information about tabledefs, see the article "DAO TableDef" in *Programming with MFC*. For related information, see the topic "Delete Method" in DAO Help.

See Also   **CDaoTableDef::Create, CDaoQueryDef::Create, CDaoDatabase::CreateRelation**

CDaoDatabase::Execute

void Execute(LPCTSTR *lpszSQL***, int** *nOptions* **= 0);**
    throw(CDaoException, CMemoryException);

Parameters

lpszSQL   Pointer to a null-terminated string containing a valid SQL command to execute.

nOptions   An integer that specifies options relating to the integrity of the query. You can use the bitwise-OR operator (|) to combine any of the following constants (provided the combination makes sense—for example, you would not combine **dbInconsistent** with **dbConsistent**):

- **dbDenyWrite**   Deny write permission to other users.

- **dbInconsistent**   (Default) Inconsistent updates.

- **dbConsistent**   Consistent updates.

- **dbSQLPassThrough**   SQL pass-through. Causes the SQL statement to be passed to an ODBC data source for processing.

- **dbFailOnError**   Roll back updates if an error occurs.

- **dbSeeChanges**   Generate a run-time error if another user is changing data you are editing.

Note   If both **dbInconsistent** and **dbConsistent** are included or if neither is included, the result is the default. For an explanation of these constants, see the topic "Execute Method" in DAO Help.

Remarks

Call this member function to run an action query or execute an SQL statement on the database. **Execute** works only for action queries or SQL pass-through queries that do not return results. It does not work for select queries, which return records.

For a definition and information about action queries, see the topics "Action Query" and "Execute Method" in DAO Help.

Tip   Given a syntactically correct SQL statement and proper permissions, the **Execute** member function will not fail even if not a single row can be modified or deleted. Therefore, always use the **dbFailOnError** option when using the **Execute** member function to run an update or delete query. This option causes MFC to throw an exception of type **CDaoException** and rolls back all successful changes if any of the records affected are locked and cannot be updated or deleted. Note that you can always call **GetRecordsAffected** to see how many records were affected.

Call the **GetRecordsAffected** member function of the database object to determine the number of records affected by the most recent **Execute** call. For example, **GetRecordsAffected** returns information about the number of records deleted, updated, or inserted when executing an action query. The count returned will not reflect changes in related tables when cascade updates or deletes are in effect.

Execute does not return a recordset. Using **Execute** on a query that selects records causes MFC to throw an exception of type **CDaoException**. (There is no **ExecuteSQL** member function analogous to **CDatabase::ExecuteSQL**.)

For more information about using the **Execute** member function, see the article "DAO Querydef: Using Querydefs" in *Programming with MFC*.

CDaoDatabase::GetConnect

CString GetConnect( );
    throw(CDaoException, CMemoryException);

Return Value

The connect string if **Open** has been called successfully on an ODBC data source; otherwise, an empty string. For a Microsoft Jet (.MDB) database, the string is always empty unless you set it for use with the **dbSQLPassThrough** option used with the **Execute** member function or used in opening a recordset.

Remarks

Call this member function to retrieve the connect string used to connect the **CDaoDatabase** object to an ODBC or ISAM database. The string provides information about the source of an open database or a database used in a pass-through query. The connect string is composed of a database type specifier and zero or more parameters separated by semicolons. For additional information about connect strings in DAO, see the topic "Connect Property" in DAO Help.

Important Using the MFC DAO classes to connect to a data source via ODBC is less efficient than connecting via an attached table. For more information, see the article "DAO External: Working with External Data Sources" in *Programming with MFC*.

Note The connect string is used to pass additional information to ODBC and certain ISAM drivers as needed. It is not used for .MDB databases. For Microsoft Jet database base tables, the connect string is an empty string ("") except when you use it for an SQL pass-through query as described under Return Value above.

See the **Open** member function for a description of how the connect string is created. Once the connect string has been set in the **Open** call, you can later use it to check the setting to determine the type, path, user ID, Password, or ODBC data source of the database.

For connect string syntax, see the topic "Connect Property" in DAO Help.

CDaoDatabase::GetName

CString GetName( );
    throw(CDaoException, CMemoryException);

Return Value

The full path and filename for the database if successful; otherwise, an empty **CString**.

Remarks

Call this member function to retrieve the name of the currently open database, which is the name of an existing database file or registered ODBC data source name. If your network supports the uniform naming convention (UNC), you can also specify a network path, such as "\\\\MYSERVER\\MYSHARE\\MYDIR\\MYDB.MDB". (Double backslashes are required in string literals because "\" is the C++ escape character.)

You might, for example, want to display this name in a heading. If an error occurs while retrieving the name, MFC throws an exception of type **CDaoException**.

Important For better performance when accessing external databases, it is recommended that you attach external database tables to a Microsoft Jet engine database (.MDB) rather than connecting directly to the data source.

The database type is indicated by the file or directory that the path points to, as follows:

Pathname points to..	Database type
.MDB file	Microsoft Jet database (Microsoft Access)
.DDF file	Btrieve® database
Directory containing .DBF file(s)	dBASE® database
Directory containing .XLS file	Microsoft Excel database
Directory containing .DBF files(s)	Microsoft FoxPro® database
Directory containing .PDX file(s)	Paradox® database
Directory containing appropriately formatted text database files	Text format database

For ODBC databases, such as Microsoft SQL Server and Oracle®, the database's connect string identifies a data source name (DSN) registered by ODBC.

For more about attaching external tables, see the article "DAO External: Attaching External Tables" in *Programming with MFC*.

See Also   **CDatabase::Open**, **CDatabase::GetConnect**

CDaoDatabase::GetQueryDefCount

> **short GetQueryDefCount( );**
>   **throw(CDaoException, CMemoryException);**

Return Value

The number of queries defined in the database.

Remarks

Call this member function to retrieve the number of queries defined in the database's QueryDefs collection. **GetQueryDefCount** is useful if you need to loop through all querydefs in the QueryDefs collection. To obtain information about a given query in the collection, see **GetQueryDefInfo**.

For information about queries and querydef objects, see the articles "DAO Queries" and "DAO QueryDef." Both articles are in *Programming with MFC*.

CDaoDatabase::GetQueryDefInfo

void GetQueryDefInfo(int *nIndex***, CDaoQueryDefInfo&** *querydefinfo***,**
   DWORD *dwInfoOptions* **= AFX_DAO_PRIMARY_INFO);**
   throw(CDaoException, CMemoryException);
void GetQueryDefInfo(LPCTSTR *lpszName***, CDaoQueryDefInfo&** *querydefinfo***,**
   DWORD *dwInfoOptions* **= AFX_DAO_PRIMARY_INFO);**
   throw(CDaoException, CMemoryException);

Parameters

nIndex The index of the predefined query in the database's QueryDefs collection, for lookup by index.

querydefinfo A reference to a **CDaoQueryDefInfo** object that returns the information requested.

dwInfoOptions Options that specify which information about the recordset to retrieve. The available options are listed here along with what they cause the function to return about the recordset:

- **AFX_DAO_PRIMARY_INFO** (Default) Name, Type

- **AFX_DAO_SECONDARY_INFO** Primary information plus: Date Created, Date of Last Update, Returns Records, Updatable

- **AFX_DAO_ALL_INFO** Primary and secondary information plus: SQL, Connect, ODBCTimeout

lpszName A string containing the name of a query defined in the database, for lookup by name.

Remarks

Call this member function to obtain various kinds of information about a query defined in the database. Two versions of the function are supplied so you can select a query either by index in the database's QueryDefs collection or by the name of the query.

For a description of the information returned in *querydefinfo*, see the **CDaoQueryDefInfo** structure. This structure has members that correspond to the items of information listed above in the description of *dwInfoOptions*. If you request one level of information, you get any prior levels of information as well.

For information about queries and querydef objects, see the articles "DAO Queries" and "DAO QueryDef." Both articles are in *Programming with MFC*.

See Also   **CDaoDatabase::GetQueryDefCount**

CDaoDatabase::GetQueryTimeout

short GetQueryTimeout( );
    throw(CDaoException, CMemoryException);

Return Value

A short integer containing the timeout value in seconds.

Remarks

Call this member function to retrieve the current number of seconds to allow before subsequent operations on the connected database are timed out. An operation might time out due to network access problems, excessive query processing time, and so on. While the setting is in effect, it affects all open, add new, update, and delete operations on any recordsets associated with this **CDaoDatabase** object. You can change the current timeout setting by calling **SetQueryTimeout**. Changing the query timeout value for a recordset after opening does not change the value for the recordset. For example, subsequent **Move** operations do not use the new value. The default value is initially set when the database engine is initialized.

The default value for query timeouts is taken from the Windows registry. If there is no registry setting, the default is 60 seconds. Not all databases support the ability to set a query timeout value. If you set a query timeout value of 0, no timeout occurs; and communication with the database may hang. This behavior may be useful during development. If the call fails, MFC throws an exception of type **CDaoException**.

For more information about database objects, see the article "DAO Database" in *Programming with MFC*. For related information, see the topic "QueryTimeout Property" in DAO Help.

See Also   **CDaoWorkspace::SetLoginTimeout**

CDaoDatabase::GetRecordsAffected

long GetRecordsAffected( );
    throw(CDaoException, CMemoryException);

Return Value

A long integer containing the number of records affected.

Remarks

Call this member function to determine the number of records affected by the most recent call of the **Execute** member function. The value returned includes the number of records deleted, updated, or inserted by an action query run with **Execute**. The count returned will not reflect changes in related tables when cascade updates or deletes are in effect.

For more information about database objects, see the article "DAO Database" in *Programming with MFC*. For related information, see the topic "RecordsAffected Property" in DAO Help.

CDaoDatabase::GetRelationCount

short GetRelationCount( );
   throw(CDaoException, CMemoryException);

Return Value

The number of relations defined between tables in the database.

Remarks

Call this member function to obtain the number of relations defined between tables in the database. **GetRelationCount** is useful if you need to loop through all defined relations in the database's Relations collection. To obtain information about a given relation in the collection, see **GetRelationInfo**.

To illustrate the concept of a relation, consider a Suppliers table and a Products table, which might have a one-to-many relationship. In this relationship, one supplier can supply more than one product. Other relations are one-to-one and many-to-many.

For more information about database objects, see the article "DAO Database" in *Programming with MFC*.

CDaoDatabase::GetRelationInfo

void GetRelationInfo(int *nIndex*, **CDaoRelationInfo&** *relinfo*,
   DWORD *dwInfoOptions* = **AFX_DAO_PRIMARY_INFO);**
   throw(CDaoException, CMemoryException);
void GetRelationInfo(LPCTSTR *lpszName*, **CDaoRelationInfo&** *relinfo*,
   DWORD *dwInfoOptions* = **AFX_DAO_PRIMARY_INFO);**
   throw(CDaoException, CMemoryException);

Parameters

nIndex The index of the relation object in the database's Relations collection, for lookup by index.

relinfo   A reference to a **CDaoRelationInfo** object that returns the information requested.

dwInfoOptions   Options that specify which information about the relation to retrieve. The available options are listed here along with what they cause the function to return about the relation:

- **AFX_DAO_PRIMARY_INFO**   (Default) Name, Table, Foreign Table

- **AFX_DAO_SECONDARY_INFO**   Attributes, Field Information

The Field Information is a **CDaoRelationFieldInfo** object containing the fields from the primary table involved in the relation.

lpszName   A string containing the name of the relation object, for lookup by name.

Remarks

Call this member function to obtain information about a specified relation in the database's Relations collection. Two versions of this function provide access either by index or by name. For a description of the information returned in *relinfo*, see the **CDaoRelationInfo** structure. This structure has members that correspond to the items of information listed above in the description of *dwInfoOptions*. If you request information at one level, you also get information at any prior levels as well.

Note If you set the relation object's attributes to activate cascade operations (**dbRelationUpdateCascades** or **dbRelationDeleteCascades**), the Microsoft Jet database engine automatically updates or deletes records in one or more other tables when changes are made to related primary key tables. For example, suppose you establish a cascade delete relationship between a Customers table and an Orders table. When you delete records from the Customers table, records in the Orders table related to that customer are also deleted. In addition, if you establish cascade delete relationships between the Orders table and other tables, records from those tables are automatically deleted when you delete records from the Customers table.

For more information about database objects, see the article "DAO Database" in *Programming with MFC*.

See Also   **CDaoDatabase::GetRelationCount**

CDaoDatabase::GetTableDefCount

short GetTableDefCount( );
    throw(CDaoException, CMemoryException);

Return Value

The number of tabledefs defined in the database.

Remarks

Call this member function to retrieve the number of tables defined in the database. **GetTableDefCount** is useful if you need to loop through all tabledefs in the database's TableDefs collection. To obtain information about a given table in the collection, see **GetTableDefInfo**.

For more information about tables and tabledef objects, see the article "DAO TableDef" in *Programming with MFC*.

CDaoDatabase::GetTableDefInfo

void GetTableDefInfo(int *nIndex***, CDaoTableDefInfo&** *tabledefinfo***,**
   DWORD *dwInfoOptions* **= AFX_DAO_PRIMARY_INFO);**
   throw(CDaoException, CMemoryException);
void GetTableDefInfo(LPCTSTR *lpszName***, CDaoTableDefInfo&** *tabledefinfo***,**
   DWORD *dwInfoOptions* **= AFX_DAO_PRIMARY_INFO);**
   throw(CDaoException, CMemoryException);

Parameters

nIndex   The index of the tabledef object in the database's TableDefs collection, for lookup by index.

tabledefinfo   A reference to a **CDaoTableDefInfo** object that returns the information requested.

dwInfoOptions   Options that specify which information about the table to retrieve. The available options are listed here along with what they cause the function to return about the relation:

- **AFX_DAO_PRIMARY_INFO**   (Default) Name, Updatable, Attributes

- **AFX_DAO_SECONDARY_INFO**   Primary information plus: Date Created, Date Last Updated, Source Table Name, Connect

- **AFX_DAO_ALL_INFO**   Primary and secondary information plus: Validation Rule, Validation Text, Record Count

lpszName   The name of the tabledef object, for lookup by name.

Remarks

Call this member function to obtain various kinds of information about a table defined in the database. Two versions of the function are supplied so you can select a table either by index in the database's TableDefs collection or by the name of the table.

For a description of the information returned in *tabledefinfo*, see the **CDaoTableDefInfo** structure. This structure has members that correspond to the items of information listed above in the description of *dwInfoOptions*. If you request information at one level, you get information for any prior levels as well.

Warning The **AFX_DAO_ALL_INFO** option provides information that can be slow to obtain. In this case, counting the records in the table could be very time consuming if there are many records.

For more information about tables and tabledef objects, see the article "DAO TableDef" in *Programming with MFC*.

See Also   **CDaoDatabase::GetTableDefCount**

CDaoDatabase::GetVersion

CString GetVersion( );
   throw(CDaoException, CMemoryException);

Return Value

A **CString** that indicates the version of the database file associated with the object.

Remarks

Call this member function to determine the version of the Microsoft Jet database file. The value returned represents the version number in the form "major.minor"; for example, "3.0". The product version number (for example, 3.0) consists of the version number (3), a period, and the release number (0). The versions to date are 1.0, 1.1, 2.0, and 3.0.

For more information about database objects, see the article "DAO Database" in *Programming with MFC*. For related information, see the topic "Version Property" in DAO Help.

CDaoDatabase::IsOpen

BOOL IsOpen( ) const;

Return Value

Nonzero if the **CDaoDatabase** object is currently open; otherwise 0.

Remarks

Call this member function to determine whether the **CDaoDatabase** object is currently open on a database.

For more information about database objects, see the article "DAO Database" in *Programming with MFC*.

See Also   **CDatabase::Open**

CDaoDatabase::Open

virtual void Open(LPCTSTR *lpszName***, BOOL** *bExclusive* **= FALSE,**
    BOOL *bReadOnly* **= FALSE, LPCTSTR** *lpszConnect* **= _T(""));**
    throw(CDaoException, CMemoryException);

Parameters

lpszName   A string expression that is the name of an existing Microsoft Jet (.MDB) database file. If the filename has an extension, it is required. If your network supports the uniform naming convention (UNC), you can also specify a network path, such as "\\\\MYSERVER\\MYSHARE\\MYDIR\\MYDB.MDB". (Double backslashes are required in string literals because "\" is the C++ escape character.)

Some considerations apply when using *lpszName*. If it:

- Refers to a database that is already open for exclusive access by another user, MFC throws an exception of type **CDaoException**. Trap that exception to let your user know that the database is unavailable.

- Is an empty string ("") and *lpszConnect* is "ODBC;", a dialog box listing all registered ODBC data source names is displayed so the user can select a database. You should avoid direct connections to ODBC data sources; use an attached table instead. For information, see the article "DAO External: Working with External Data Sources" in *Programming with MFC*.

- Otherwise does not refer to an existing database or valid ODBC data source name, MFC throws an exception of type **CDaoException**.

Note   For details about DAO error codes, see the DAOERR.H file. For related information, see the topic "Trappable Data Access Errors" in DAO Help.

bExclusive   A Boolean value that is **TRUE** if the database is to be opened for exclusive (nonshared) access and **FALSE** if the database is to be opened for shared access. If you omit this argument, the database is opened for shared access.

bReadOnly   A Boolean value that is **TRUE** if the database is to be opened for read-only access and **FALSE** if the database is to be opened for read/write access. If you omit this argument, the database is opened for read/write access. All dependent recordsets inherit this attribute.

lpszConnect   A string expression used for opening the database. This string constitutes the ODBC connect arguments. You must supply the exclusive and read-only arguments to supply a source string. For syntax, see the topic "Connect Property" in DAO Help. If the database is a Microsoft Jet database (.MDB), this string is empty (""). The syntax for the default value—_T("")—provides portability for Unicode as well as ANSI builds of your application.

Remarks

You must call this member function to initialize a newly constructed **CDaoDatabase** object that represents an existing database. **Open** associates the database with the underlying DAO object. You cannot use the database object to construct recordset, tabledef, or querydef objects until it is initialized. **Open** appends the database object to the associated workspace's Databases collection.

Use the parameters as follows:

- If you are opening a Microsoft Jet (.MDB) database, use the *lpszName* parameter and pass an empty string for the *lpszConnect* parameter or pass a password string of the form "PWD=password" if the database is password-protected (.MDB databases only).

- If you are opening an ODBC data source, pass a valid ODBC connect string in *lpszConnect* and an empty string in *lpszName*.

For related information, see the topic "OpenDatabase Method" in DAO Help.

Important   For better performance when accessing external databases, including ISAM databases and ODBC data sources, it is recommended that you attach external database tables to a Microsoft Jet engine database (.MDB) rather than connecting directly to the data source.

It is possible for a connection attempt to time out if, for example, the DBMS host is unavailable. If the connection attempt fails, **Open** throws an exception of type **CDaoException**.

The remaining remarks apply only to ODBC databases:

If the database is an ODBC database and the parameters in your **Open** call do not contain enough information to make the connection, the ODBC driver opens a dialog box to obtain the necessary information from the user. When you call **Open**, your connect string, *lpszConnect*, is stored privately and is available by calling the **GetConnect** member function.

If you wish, you can open your own dialog box before you call **Open** to get information from the user, such as a password, then add that information to the connect string you pass to **Open**. Or you might want to save the connect string you pass (perhaps in the Windows registry) so you can reuse it the next time your application calls **Open** on a **CDaoDatabase** object.

You can also use the connect string for multiple levels of login authorization (each for a different **CDaoDatabase** object) or to convey other database-specific information.

For related information about connect strings, see the topic "Connect Property" in DAO Help.

See Also   **CDatabase::CDatabase**, **CDatabase::Close**

CDaoDatabase::SetQueryTimeout

void SetQueryTimeout(short *nSeconds* **);**
 throw(CDaoException, CMemoryException);

Parameters

nSeconds The number of seconds to allow before a query attempt times out.

Remarks

Call this member function to override the default number of seconds to allow before subsequent operations on the connected database time out. An operation might time out due to network access problems, excessive query processing time, and so on. Call **SetQueryTimeout** prior to opening your recordset or prior to calling the recordset's **AddNew**, **Update**, or **Delete** member functions if you want to change the query timeout value. The setting affects all subsequent **Open**, **AddNew**, **Update**, and **Delete** calls to any recordsets associated with this **CDaoDatabase** object. Changing the query timeout value for a recordset after opening does not change the value for the recordset. For example, subsequent **Move** operations do not use the new value.

The default value for query timeouts is 60 seconds. Not all databases support the ability to set a query timeout value. If you set a query timeout value of 0, no timeout occurs; the communication with the database may hang. This behavior may be useful during development.

For related information, see the topic "QueryTimeout Property" in DAO Help.

 See Also **CDaoWorkspace::SetLoginTimeout**

Data Members

CDaoDatabase::m_pDAODatabase

Remarks

Contains a pointer to the OLE interface for the DAO database object underlying the **CDaoDatabase** object. Use this pointer if you need to access the DAO interface directly.

For more information about DAO databases, see the article "DAO Database" in *Programming with MFC*. For information about calling DAO directly, see Technical Note 54. Technical Notes are available under MFC in Books Online.

CDaoDatabase::m_pWorkspace

Remarks

Contains a pointer to the **CDaoWorkspace** object that contains the database object. Use this pointer if you need to access the workspace directly—for example, to obtain pointers to other database objects in the workspace's Databases collection.

For more information about workspaces, see the article "DAO Workspace" in *Programming with MFC*.

CDaoException

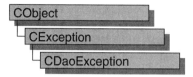

A **CDaoException** object represents an exception condition arising from the MFC database classes based on data access objects (DAO). The class includes public data members you can use to determine the cause of the exception. **CDaoException** objects are constructed and thrown by member functions of the DAO database classes.

Note The DAO database classes are distinct from the MFC database classes based on Open Database Connectivity (ODBC). All DAO database class names have the "CDao" prefix. You can still access ODBC data sources with the DAO classes. In general, the MFC classes based on DAO are more capable than the MFC classes based on ODBC; the DAO-based classes can access data, including through ODBC drivers, via their own database engine. The DAO-based classes also support Data Definition Language (DDL) operations, such as adding tables via the classes, without having to call DAO directly. For information on exceptions thrown by the ODBC classes, see **CDBException**.

You can access exception objects within the scope of a **CATCH** expression. You can also throw **CDaoException** objects from your own code with the **AfxThrowDaoException** global function.

In MFC, all DAO errors are expressed as exceptions, of type **CDaoException**. When you catch an exception of this type, you can use **CDaoException** member functions to retrieve information from any DAO error objects stored in the database engine's Errors collection. As each error occurs, one or more error objects are placed in the Errors collection. (Normally the collection contains only one error object; if you are using an ODBC data source, you are more likely to get multiple error objects.) When another DAO operation generates an error, the Errors collection is cleared, and the new error object is placed in the Errors collection. DAO operations that do not generate an error have no effect on the Errors collection.

For DAO error codes, see the file DAOERR.H. For related information, see the topic "Trappable Data Access Errors" in DAO Help.

For more information about exception handling in general, or about **CDaoException** objects, see the articles "Exceptions" and "Exceptions: Database Exceptions" in *Programming with MFC*. The second article contains example code that illustrates exception handling in DAO.

#include <afxdao.h>

See Also   **CException**

Data Members

m_scode	The **SCODE** value associated with the error.
m_nAfxDaoError	Contains an extended error code for any error in the MFC DAO classes.
m_pErrorInfo	A pointer to a **CDaoErrorInfo** object that contains information about one DAO error object.

Construction

CDaoException	Constructs a **CDaoException** object.

Operations

GetErrorCount	Returns the number of errors in the database engine's Errors collection.
GetErrorInfo	Returns error information about a particular error object in the Errors collection.

Member Functions

CDaoException::CDaoException

CDaoException( );

Remarks

Constructs a **CDaoException** object. Ordinarily, the framework creates exception objects when its code throws an exception. You seldom need to construct an exception object explicitly. If you want to throw a **CDaoException** from your own code, call the global function **AfxThrowDaoException**.

However, you might want to explicitly create an exception object if you are making direct calls to DAO via the DAO interface pointers that MFC classes encapsulate. In that case, you might need to retrieve error information from DAO. Suppose an error occurs in DAO when you call a DAO method via, say, the DAODatabases interface to a workspace's Databases collection. To retrieve the DAO error information:

1. Construct a **CDaoException** object.

2. Call the exception object's **GetErrorCount** member function to determine how many error objects are in the database engine's Errors collection. (Normally only one, unless you are using an ODBC data source.)

3. Call the exception object's **GetErrorInfo** member function to retrieve one specific error object at a time, by index in the collection, via the exception object. Think of the exception object as a proxy for one DAO error object.

4. Examine the current **CDaoErrorInfo** structure that **GetErrorInfo** returns in the **m_pErrorInfo** data member. Its members provide information on the DAO error.

5. In the case of an ODBC data source, repeat steps 3 and 4 as needed, for more error objects.

6. If you constructed the exception object on the heap, delete it with the **delete** operator when you finish.

For more information about handling errors in the MFC DAO classes, see the article "Exceptions: Database Exceptions" in *Programming with MFC*.

CDaoException::GetErrorCount

short GetErrorCount( );

Return Value

The number of DAO error objects in the database engine's Errors collection.

Remarks

Call this member function to retrieve the number of DAO error objects in the database engine's Errors collection. This information is useful for looping through the Errors collection to retrieve each of the one or more DAO error objects in the collection. To retrieve an error object by index or by DAO error number, call the **GetErrorInfo** member function.

Note Normally there is only one error object in the Errors collection. If you are working with an ODBC data source, however, there could be more than one.

CDaoException::GetErrorInfo

void GetErrorInfo(int *nIndex*);

Parameters

nIndex The index of the error information in the database engine's Errors collection, for lookup by index.

Remarks

Call this member function to obtain the following kinds of information about the exception:

- Error Code
- Source
- Description
- Help File
- Help Context

GetErrorInfo stores the information in the exception object's **m_pErrorInfo** data member. For a brief description of the information returned, see **m_pErrorInfo**. If you catch an exception of type **CDaoException** thrown by MFC, the **m_pErrorInfo** member will already be filled in. If you choose to call DAO directly, you must call the exception object's **GetErrorInfo** member function yourself to fill **m_pErrorInfo**. For a more detailed description, see the **CDaoErrorInfo** structure.

For information about DAO exceptions, and example code, see the article "Exceptions: Database Exceptions." For more about getting information from DAO object collections, see the article "DAO: Obtaining Information About DAO Objects." Both articles are in *Programming with MFC*.

See Also   **CDaoException::GetErrorCount**

Data Members

CDaoException::m_nAfxDaoError

Remarks

Contains an MFC extended error code. This code is supplied in cases where a specific component of the MFC DAO classes has erred.

Possible values are:

- **NO_AFX_DAO_ERROR**   The most recent operation did not result in an MFC extended error. However, the operation could have produced other errors from DAO or OLE, so you should check **m_pErrorInfo** and possibly **m_scode**.

- **AFX_DAO_ERROR_ENGINE_INITIALIZATION**   MFC could not initialize the Microsoft Jet database engine. OLE might have failed to initialize, or it might have been impossible to create an instance of the DAO database engine object. These problems usually suggest a bad installation of either DAO or OLE.

- **AFX_DAO_ERROR_DFX_BIND**   An address used in a DAO record field exchange (DFX) function call does not exist or is invalid (the address was not used to bind data). You might have passed a bad address in a DFX call, or the address might have become invalid between DFX operations.

- **AFX_DAO_ERROR_OBJECT_NOT_OPEN**   You attempted to open a recordset based on a querydef or a tabledef object that was not in an open state.

For more information about DFX, see the article "DAO Record Field Exchange (DFX)" in *Programming with MFC*.

See Also   CDaoException::GetErrorCount, CDaoException::GetErrorInfo

CDaoException::m_pErrorInfo

Remarks

Contains a pointer to a **CDaoErrorInfo** structure that provides information on the DAO error object that you last retrieved by calling **GetErrorInfo**. This object contains the following information:

CDaoErrorInfo member	Information	Meaning
m_lErrorCode	Error Code	The DAO error code
m_strSource	Source	The name of the object or application that originally generated the error
m_strDescription	Description	A descriptive string associated with the error
m_strHelpFile	Help File	A path to a Windows Help file in which the user can get information about the problem
m_lHelpContext	Help Context	The context ID for a topic in the DAO Help file

For full details about the information contained in the **CDaoErrorInfo** object, see the **CDaoErrorInfo** structure.

See Also   CDaoException::m_scode, CDaoException::m_nAfxDaoError

CDaoException::m_scode

Remarks

Contains a value of type **SCODE** that describes the error. This is an OLE code. You will seldom need to use this value because, in almost all cases, more specific MFC or DAO error information is available in the other **CDaoException** data members.

For information about **SCODE**, see the topic "Structure of OLE Error Codes" in the Win32 SDK, *OLE Programmer's Reference, Volume 1*. The **SCODE** data type maps to the **HRESULT** data type.

See Also   **CDaoException::m_pErrorInfo, CDaoException::m_nAfxDaoError**

CDaoFieldExchange

The **CDaoFieldExchange** class supports the DAO record field exchange (DFX) routines used by the DAO database classes. Use this class if you are writing data exchange routines for custom data types; otherwise, you will not directly use this class. DFX exchanges data between the field data members of your **CDaoRecordset** object and the corresponding fields of the current record on the data source. DFX manages the exchange in both directions, from the data source and to the data source. See Technical Note 53, available under MFC in Books Online, for information about writing custom DFX routines.

Note The DAO database classes are distinct from the MFC database classes based on Open Database Connectivity (ODBC). All DAO database class names have the "CDao" prefix. You can still access ODBC data sources with the DAO classes. In general, the MFC classes based on DAO are more capable than the MFC classes based on ODBC. The DAO-based classes can access data, including through ODBC drivers, via their own database engine. They also support Data Definition Language (DDL) operations, such as adding tables via the classes instead of having to call DAO yourself.

Note DAO record field exchange (DFX) is very similar to record field exchange (RFX) in the ODBC-based MFC database classes (**CDatabase**, **CRecordset**). If you understand RFX, you will find it easy to use DFX.

A **CDaoFieldExchange** object provides the context information needed for DAO record field exchange to take place. **CDaoFieldExchange** objects support a number of operations, including binding parameters and field data members and setting various flags on the fields of the current record. DFX operations are performed on recordset-class data members of types defined by the **enum FieldType** in **CDaoFieldExchange**. Possible **FieldType** values are:

- **CDaoFieldExchange::outputColumn** for field data members.
- **CDaoFieldExchange::param** for parameter data members.

The **IsValidOperation** member function is provided for writing your own custom DFX routines. You will use **SetFieldType** frequently in your **CDaoRecordset::DoFieldExchange** functions. For details about the DFX global functions, see "Record Field Exchange Functions" in the "Macros and Globals" section. For information about writing custom DFX routines for your own data types, see Technical Note 53, available under MFC in Books Online.

For information about DFX, see the article "DAO Record Field Exchange (DFX)" in *Programming with MFC*.

#include <afxdao.h>

See Also **CDaoRecordset**

Data Members

m_nOperation	The DFX operation being performed by the current call to the recordset's **DoFieldExchange** member function.
m_prs	A pointer to the recordset on which DFX operations are being performed.

Member Functions

IsValidOperation	Returns nonzero if the current operation is appropriate for the type of field being updated.
SetFieldType	Specifies the type of recordset data member—column or parameter—represented by all subsequent calls to DFX functions until the next call to **SetFieldType**.

Member Functions

CDaoFieldExchange::IsValidOperation

BOOL IsValidOperation( );

Return Value

Nonzero if the current operation is appropriate for the type of field being updated.

Remarks

If you write your own DFX function, call **IsValidOperation** at the beginning of your function to determine whether the current operation can be performed on a particular field data member type (a **CDaoFieldExchange::outputColumn** or a **CDaoFieldExchange::param**). Some of the operations performed by the DFX mechanism apply only to one of the possible field types. Follow the model of the existing DFX functions.

For more information about DFX, see the article "DAO Record Field Exchange (DFX)" in *Programming with MFC*. For additional information on writing custom DFX routines, see Technical Note 53, available under MFC in Books Online.

See Also **CDaoFieldExchange::SetFieldType**

CDaoFieldExchange::SetFieldType

void SetFieldType(UINT *nFieldType* **);**

Parameters

nFieldType   A value of the **enum FieldType**, declared in **CDaoFieldExchange**, which can be either of the following:

- **CDaoFieldExchange::outputColumn**

- **CDaoFieldExchange::param**

Remarks

Call **SetFieldType** in your **CDaoRecordset** class's **DoFieldExchange** override. Normally, ClassWizard writes this call for you. If you write your own function and are using the wizard to write your **DoFieldExchange** function, add calls to your own function outside the field map. If you do not use the wizard, there will be a field map. The call precedes calls to DFX functions, one for each field data member of your class, and identifies the field type as **CDaoFieldExchange::outputColumn**.

If you parameterize your recordset class, you should add DFX calls for all parameter data members (outside the field map) and precede these calls with a call to **SetFieldType**. Pass the value **CDaoFieldExchange::param**. (You can, instead, use a **CDaoQueryDef** and set its parameter values.)

In general, each group of DFX function calls associated with field data members or parameter data members must be preceded by a call to **SetFieldType**. The *nFieldType* parameter of each **SetFieldType** call identifies the type of the data members represented by the DFX function calls that follow the **SetFieldType** call.

For more information about DFX, see the article "DAO Record Field Exchange (DFX)" in *Programming with MFC*.

See Also   **CDaoFieldExchange::IsValidOperation**, **CDaoRecordset::DoFieldExchange**

Data Members

CDaoFieldExchange::m_nOperation

Remarks

Identifies the operation to be performed on the **CDaoRecordset** object associated with the field exchange object. The **CDaoFieldExchange** object supplies the context for a number of different DFX operations on the recordset.

Note The **PSEUDO NULL** value described under the MarkForAddNew and SetFieldNull operations below is a value used to mark fields Null. The DAO record field exchange mechanism (DFX) uses this value to determine which fields have been explicitly marked Null. **PSEUDO NULL** is not required for **COleDateTime** and **COleCurrency** fields.

For more information about DFX and these operations, see the article "DAO Record Field Exchange (DFX)" in *Programming with MFC*.

Possible values of **m_nOperation** are:

Operation	Description
AddToParameterList	Builds the **PARAMETERS** clause of the SQL statement.
AddToSelectList	Builds the **SELECT** clause of the SQL statement.
BindField	Binds a field in the database to a memory location in your application.
BindParam	Sets parameter values for the recordset's query.
Fixup	Sets the Null status for a field.
AllocCache	Allocates the cache used to check for "dirty" fields in the recordset.
StoreField	Saves the current record to the cache.
LoadField	Restores the cached data member variables in the recordset.
FreeCache	Frees the cache used to check for "dirty" fields in the recordset.
SetFieldNull	Sets a field's status to Null and value to **PSEUDO NULL**.
MarkForAddNew	Marks fields "dirty" if not **PSEUDO NULL**.
MarkForEdit	Marks fields "dirty" if they do not match the cache.
SetDirtyField	Sets field values marked as "dirty."
DumpField	Dumps a field's contents (debug only).
MaxDFXOperation	Used for input checking.

See Also **CDaoFieldExchange::IsValidOperation**, **CDaoFieldExchange::m_prs**, **CDaoRecordset::DoFieldExchange**

CDaoFieldExchange::m_prs

Remarks

Contains a pointer to the **CDaoRecordset** object associated with the **CDaoFieldExchange** object.

For more information about DFX, see the article "DAO Record Field Exchange (DFX)" in *Programming with MFC*.

See Also   **CDaoFieldExchange::m_nOperation**, **CDaoRecordset**

CDaoQueryDef

A **CDaoQueryDef** object represents a query definition, or "querydef," usually one saved in a database. A querydef is a data access object that contains the SQL statement that describes a query, and its properties, such as "Date Created" and "ODBC Timeout." You can also create temporary querydef objects without saving them, but it is convenient — and much more efficient — to save commonly reused queries in a database. A **CDaoDatabase** object maintains a collection, called the QueryDefs collection, that contains its saved querydefs.

Note The DAO database classes are distinct from the MFC database classes based on Open Database Connectivity (ODBC). All DAO database class names have the "CDao" prefix. You can still access ODBC data sources with the DAO classes. In general, the MFC classes based on DAO are more capable than the MFC classes based on ODBC; the DAO-based classes can access data, including through ODBC drivers, via their own database engine. The DAO-based classes also support Data Definition Language (DDL) operations, such as adding tables via the classes, without having to call DAO directly.

Usage

Use querydef objects either to work with an existing saved query or to create a new saved query or temporary query:

1. In all cases, first construct a **CDaoQueryDef** object, supplying a pointer to the **CDaoDatabase** object to which the query belongs.

2. Then do the following, depending on what you want:

   - To use an existing saved query, call the querydef object's **Open** member function, supplying the name of the saved query.

   - To create a new saved query, call the querydef object's **Create** member function, supplying the name of the query. Then call **Append** to save the query by appending it to the database's QueryDefs collection. **Create** puts the querydef into an open state, so after calling **Create** you do not call **Open**.

   - To create a temporary querydef, call **Create**. Pass an empty string for the query name. Do not call **Append**.

When you finish using a querydef object, call its **Close** member function; then destroy the querydef object.

Tip The easiest way to create saved queries is to create them and store them in your database using Microsoft Access. Then you can open and use them in your MFC code.

Purposes

You can use a querydef object for any of the following purposes:

- To create a **CDaoRecordset** object
- To call the object's **Execute** member function to directly execute an action query or an SQL pass-through query

You can use a querydef object for any type of query, including select, action, crosstab, delete, update, append, make-table, data definition, SQL pass-through, union, and bulk queries. The query's type is determined by the content of the SQL statement that you supply. For information about query types, see the **Execute** and **GetType** member functions. Recordsets are commonly used for row-returning queries, usually those using the **SELECT ... FROM** keywords. **Execute** is most commonly used for bulk operations. For more information, see **Execute** and **CDaoRecordset**.

Querydefs and Recordsets

To use a querydef object to create a **CDaoRecordset** object, you typically create or open a querydef as described above. Then construct a recordset object, passing a pointer to your querydef object when you call **CDaoRecordset::Open**. The querydef you pass must be in an open state. For more information, see class **CDaoRecordset**.

You cannot use a querydef to create a recordset (the most common use for a querydef) unless it is in an open state. Put the querydef into an open state by calling either **Open** or **Create**.

External Databases

Querydef objects are the preferred way to use the native SQL dialect of an external database engine. For example, you can create a Transact SQL query (as used on Microsoft SQL Server) and store it in a querydef object. When you need to use a SQL query not based on the Microsoft Jet database engine, you must provide a connect string that points to the external data source. Queries with valid connect strings bypass the database engine and pass the query directly to the external database server for processing.

Tip The preferred way to work with ODBC tables is to attach them to a Microsoft Jet (.MDB) database. For more information, see the article "DAO External: Working with External Data Sources" in *Programming with MFC*.

For more information about querydefs, see the article "DAO Querydef" in *Programming with MFC*. For related information, see the topics "QueryDef Object," "QueryDefs Collection," and "Accessing External Databases with DAO" in DAO Help.

#include <afxdao.h>

See Also   CDaoRecordset, CDaoDatabase, CDaoTableDef, CDaoException

Data Members

m_pDatabase	A pointer to the **CDaoDatabase** object with which the querydef is associated. The querydef might be saved in the database or not.
m_pDAOQueryDef	A pointer to the OLE interface for the underlying DAO querydef object.

Construction

CDaoQueryDef	Constructs a **CDaoQueryDef** object. Next call **Open** or **Create**, depending on your needs.
Create	Creates the underlying DAO querydef object. Use the querydef as a temporary query, or call **Append** to save it in the database.
Append	Appends the querydef to the database's QueryDefs collection as a saved query.
Open	Opens an existing querydef stored in the database's QueryDefs collection.
Close	Closes the querydef object. Destroy the C++ object when you finish with it.

Attributes

CanUpdate	Returns nonzero if the query can update the database.
GetConnect	Returns the connect string associated with the querydef. The connect string identifies the data source. (For SQL pass-through queries only; otherwise an empty string.)
GetDateCreated	Returns the date the saved query was created.
GetDateLastUpdated	Returns the date the saved query was last updated.
GetName	Returns the name of the querydef.
GetODBCTimeout	Returns the timeout value used by ODBC (for an ODBC query) when the querydef is executed. This determines how long to allow for the query's action to complete.
GetRecordsAffected	Returns the number of records affected by an action query.
GetReturnsRecords	Returns nonzero if the query defined by the querydef returns records.
GetSQL	Returns the SQL string that specifies the query defined by the querydef.
GetType	Returns the query type: delete, update, append, make-table, and so on.
IsOpen	Returns nonzero if the querydef is open and can be executed.

SetConnect	Sets the connect string for an SQL pass through query on an ODBC data source.
SetName	Sets the name of the saved query, replacing the name in use when the querydef was created.
SetODBCTimeout	Sets the timeout value used by ODBC (for an ODBC query) when the querydef is executed.
SetReturnsRecords	Specifies whether the querydef returns records. Setting this attribute to **TRUE** is only valid for SQL pass-through queries.
SetSQL	Sets the SQL string that specifies the query defined by the querydef.

Operations

Execute	Executes the query defined by the querydef object.
GetFieldCount	Returns the number of fields defined by the querydef.
GetFieldInfo	Returns information about a specified field defined in the query.
GetParameterCount	Returns the number of parameters defined for the query.
GetParameterInfo	Returns information about a specified parameter to the query.
GetParamValue	Returns the value of a specified parameter to the query.
SetParamValue	Sets the value of a specified parameter to the query.

Member Functions

CDaoQueryDef::Append

virtual void Append( );
    throw(CDaoException, CMemoryException);

Remarks

Call this member function after you call **Create** to create a new querydef object. **Append** saves the querydef in the database by appending the object to the database's QueryDefs collection. You can use the querydef as a temporary object without appending it, but if you want it to persist, you must call **Append**.

If you attempt to append a temporary querydef object, MFC throws an exception of type **CDaoException**.

For information about querydefs, see the article "DAO Querydef" in *Programming with MFC*.

CDaoQueryDef::CanUpdate

BOOL CanUpdate( );
   throw(CDaoException, CMemoryException);

Return Value

Nonzero if you are permitted to modify the querydef; otherwise 0.

Remarks

Call this member function to determine whether you can modify the
querydef — such as changing its name or SQL string. You can modify
the querydef if:

- It is not based on a database that is open read-only.

- You have update permissions for the database.

   This depends on whether you have implemented security features. MFC does not
   provide support for security; you must implement it yourself by calling DAO
   directly or by using Microsoft Access. See the topic "Permissions Property" in
   DAO Help.

For information about querydefs, see the article "DAO Querydef" in *Programming
with MFC*.

CDaoQueryDef::CDaoQueryDef

CDaoQueryDef(CDaoDatabase* *pDatabase* **);**

Parameters

pDatabase   A pointer to an open **CDaoDatabase** object.

Remarks

Constructs a **CDaoQueryDef** object. The object can represent an existing querydef
stored in the database's QueryDefs collection, a new query to be stored in the
collection, or a temporary query, not to be stored. Your next step depends on the
type of querydef:

- If the object represents an existing querydef, call the object's **Open** member
  function to initialize it.

- If the object represents a new querydef to be saved, call the object's **Create**
  member function. This adds the object to the database's QueryDefs collection.
  Then call **CDaoQueryDef** member functions to set the object's attributes. Finally,
  call **Append**.

- If the object represents a temporary querydef (not to be saved in the database), call
  Create, passing an empty string for the query's name. After calling **Create**,
  initialize the querydef by directly setting its attributes. Do not call **Append**.

To set the attributes of the querydef, you can use the **SetName**, **SetSQL**, **SetConnect**, **SetODBCTimeout**, and **SetReturnsRecords** member functions.

When you finish with the querydef object, call its **Close** member function. If you have a pointer to the querydef, use the **delete** operator to destroy the C++ object.

For information about querydefs, see the article "DAO Querydef" in *Programming with MFC*.

See Also   **CDaoQueryDef::GetConnect**, **CDaoQueryDef::GetDateCreated**, **CDaoQueryDef::GetDateLastUpdated**, **CDaoQueryDef::GetName**, **CDaoQueryDef::GetODBCTimeout**, **CDaoQueryDef::GetReturnsRecords**, **CDaoQueryDef::GetSQL**

CDaoQueryDef::Close

virtual void Close( );

Remarks

Call this member function when you finish using the querydef object. Closing the querydef releases the underlying DAO object but does not destroy the saved DAO querydef object or the C++ **CDaoQueryDef** object. This is not the same as **CDaoDatabase::DeleteQueryDef**, which deletes the querydef from the database's QueryDefs collection in DAO (if not a temporary querydef).

For information about querydefs, see the article "DAO Querydef" in *Programming with MFC*.

See Also   **CDaoQueryDef::Open**, **CDaoQueryDef::Create**, **CDaoQueryDef::CDaoQueryDef**

CDaoQueryDef::Create

virtual void Create(LPCTSTR *lpszName* **= NULL, LPCTSTR** *lpszSQL* **= NULL);**
   throw(CDaoException, CMemoryException);

Parameters

lpszName   The unique name of the query saved in the database. For details about the string, see the topic CreateQueryDef Method in DAO Help. If you accept the default value, an empty string, a temporary querydef is created. Such a query is not saved in the QueryDefs collection.

lpszSQL   The SQL string that defines the query. If you accept the default value of **NULL**, you must later call **SetSQL** to set the string. Until then, the query is undefined. You can, however, use the undefined query to open a recordset; see "Remarks" for details. The SQL statement must be defined before you can append the querydef to the QueryDefs collection.

Remarks

Call this member function to create a new saved query or a new temporary query. If you pass a name in *lpszName*, you can then call **Append** to save the querydef in the database's QueryDefs collection. Otherwise, the object is a temporary querydef and is not saved. In either case, the querydef is in an open state, and you can either use it to create a **CDaoRecordset** object or call the querydef's **Execute** member function.

If you do not supply an SQL statement in *lpszSQL*, you cannot run the query with **Execute** but you can use it to create a recordset. In that case, MFC uses the recordset's default SQL statement.

For information about querydefs, see the article "DAO Querydef" in *Programming with MFC*.

See Also   **CDaoQueryDef::Open, CDaoQueryDef::CDaoQueryDef, CDaoRecordset::GetSQL**

CDaoQueryDef::Execute

virtual void Execute(int *nOptions* **= 0);**
   throw(CDaoException, CMemoryException);

Parameters

nOptions   An integer that determines the characteristics of the query. For related information, see the topic "Execute Method" in DAO Help. You can use the bitwise-OR operator (|) to combine the following constants for this argument:

- **dbDenyWrite**   Deny write permission to other users.

- **dbInconsistent**   (Default) Inconsistent updates.

- **dbConsistent**   Consistent updates.

- **dbSQLPassThrough**   SQL pass-through. Causes the SQL statement to be passed to an ODBC database for processing.

- **dbFailOnError**   Roll back updates if an error occurs and report the error to the user.

- **dbSeeChanges**   Generate a run-time error if another user is changing data you are editing.

Note   For an explanation of the terms "inconsistent" and "consistent," see the topic "Execute Method" in DAO Help.

Remarks

Call this member function to run the query defined by the querydef object. Querydef objects used for execution in this manner can only represent one of the following query types:

- Action queries
- SQL pass-through queries

Execute does not work for queries that return records, such as select queries. **Execute** is commonly used for bulk operation queries, such as **UPDATE**, **INSERT**, or **SELECT INTO**, or for data definition language (DDL) operations.

For an explanation of action queries and SQL pass-through queries, see the article "DAO Querydef: Action Queries and SQL Pass-Through Queries" in *Programming with MFC.*

Tip The preferred way to work with ODBC data sources is to attach tables to a Microsoft Jet (.MDB) database. For more information, see the topic "Accessing External Databases with DAO" in DAO Help and the article "DAO External: Working with External Data Sources" in *Programming with MFC.*

Call the **GetRecordsAffected** member function of the querydef object to determine the number of records affected by the most recent **Execute** call. For example, **GetRecordsAffected** returns information about the number of records deleted, updated, or inserted when executing an action query. The count returned will not reflect changes in related tables when cascade updates or deletes are in effect.

If you include both **dbInconsistent** and **dbConsistent** or if you include neither, the result is the default, **dbInconsistent**.

Execute does not return a recordset. Using **Execute** on a query that selects records causes MFC to throw an exception of type **CDaoException**.

For more information about using the **Execute** member function for querydef objects, see the article "DAO Querydef: Using Querydefs" in *Programming with MFC.*

CDaoQueryDef::GetConnect

CString GetConnect( );
    throw(CDaoException, CMemoryException);

Return Value

A **CString** containing the connect string for the querydef.

Remarks

Call this member function to get the connect string associated with the querydef's data source. This function is used only with ODBC data sources and certain ISAM drivers. It is not used with Microsoft Jet (.MDB) databases; in this case, **GetConnect** returns an empty string. For more information, see **SetConnect**.

Tip The preferred way to work with ODBC tables is to attach them to an .MDB database. For more information, see the topic "Accessing External Databases with DAO" in DAO Help and the article "DAO External: Working with External Data Sources" in *Programming with MFC*.

For information about connect strings, see the topic "Connect Property" in DAO Help. For information about querydefs, see the article "DAO Querydef" in *Programming with MFC*.

CDaoQueryDef::GetDateCreated

COleDateTime GetDateCreated( );
    throw(CDaoException, CMemoryException);

Return Value

A **COleDateTime** object containing the date and time the querydef was created.

Remarks

Call this member function to get the date the querydef object was created.

For information about querydefs, see the article "DAO Querydef" in *Programming with MFC*. For related information, see the topic "DateCreated, LastUpdated Properties" in DAO Help.

See Also   **CDaoQueryDef::GetDateLastUpdated**

CDaoQueryDef::GetDateLastUpdated

COleDateTime GetDateLastUpdated( );
    throw(CDaoException, CMemoryException);

Return Value

A **COleDateTime** object containing the date and time the querydef was last updated.

Remarks

Call this member function to get the date the querydef object was last updated — when any of its properties were changed, such as its name, its SQL string, or its connect string.

For information about querydefs, see the article "DAO Querydef" in *Programming with MFC*. For related information, see the topic "DateCreated, LastUpdated Properties" in DAO Help.

See Also   **CDaoQueryDef::GetDateCreated**

CDaoQueryDef::GetFieldCount

short GetFieldCount( );
    throw(CDaoException, CMemoryException);

Return Value

The number of fields defined in the query.

Remarks

Call this member function to retrieve the number of fields in the query.
GetFieldCount is useful for looping through all fields in the querydef. For that
purpose, use **GetFieldCount** in conjunction with **GetFieldInfo**.

For information about obtaining information about querydef fields, see the article
"DAO: Obtaining Information About DAO Objects" in *Programming with MFC*.

CDaoQueryDef::GetFieldInfo

void GetFieldInfo(int *nIndex*, **CDaoFieldInfo&** *fieldinfo*,
    DWORD *dwInfoOptions* = **AFX_DAO_PRIMARY_INFO**);
    throw(CDaoException, CMemoryException);
void GetFieldInfo(LPCTSTR *lpszName*, **CDaoFieldInfo&** *fieldinfo*,
    DWORD *dwInfoOptions* = **AFX_DAO_PRIMARY_INFO**);
    throw(CDaoException, CMemoryException);

Parameters

nIndex   The zero-based index of the desired field in the querydef's Fields collection,
for lookup by index.

fieldinfo   A reference to a **CDaoFieldInfo** object that returns the information
requested.

dwInfoOptions   Options that specify which information about the field to retrieve.
The available options are listed here along with what they cause the function to
return:

- **AFX_DAO_PRIMARY_INFO**   (Default) Name, Type, Size, Attributes

- **AFX_DAO_SECONDARY_INFO**   Primary information plus: Ordinal
Position, Required, Allow Zero Length, Source Field, Foreign Name, Source
Table, Collating Order

- **AFX_DAO_ALL_INFO**   Primary and secondary information plus: Default
Value, Validation Text, Validation Rule

lpszName   A string containing the name of the desired field, for lookup by name.
You can use a **CString**.

Remarks

Call this member function to obtain various kinds of information about a field defined in the querydef. For a description of the information returned in *fieldinfo*, see the **CDaoFieldInfo** structure. This structure has members that correspond to the descriptive information under *dwInfoOptions* above. If you request one level of information, you get any prior levels of information as well.

For more information about obtaining field information, see the article "DAO: Obtaining Information About DAO Objects" in *Programming with MFC*.

See Also   CDaoQueryDef::GetFieldCount

CDaoQueryDef::GetName

CString GetName( );
   throw(CDaoException, CMemoryException);

Return Value

The name of the query.

Remarks

Call this member function to retrieve the name of the query represented by the querydef. Querydef names are unique user-defined names. For more information about querydef names, see the topic "Name Property" in DAO Help.

For information about querydefs, see the article "DAO Querydef" in *Programming with MFC*.

See Also   CDaoQueryDef::SetName, CDaoQueryDef::GetSQL, CDaoQueryDef::GetReturnsRecords, CDaoQueryDef::GetODBCTimeout

---

CDaoQueryDef::GetODBCTimeout

short GetODBCTimeout( );
   throw(CDaoException, CMemoryException);

Return Value

The number of seconds before a query times out.

Remarks

Call this member function to retrieve the current time limit before a query to an ODBC data source times out. For information about this time limit, see the topic "ODBCTimeout Property" in DAO Help.

Tip   The preferred way to work with ODBC tables is to attach them to a Microsoft Jet (.MDB) database. For more information, see the topic "Accessing External Databases with DAO" in DAO Help and the article "DAO External: Working with External Data Sources" in *Programming with MFC*.

For information about querydefs, see the article "DAO Querydef" in *Programming with MFC*.

See Also   **CDaoQueryDef::SetODBCTimeout**, **CDaoQueryDef::GetName**, **CDaoQueryDef::GetSQL**, **CDaoQueryDef::GetReturnsRecords**

CDaoQueryDef::GetParameterCount

short GetParameterCount( );
  throw(CDaoException, CMemoryException);

Return Value
The number of parameters defined in the query.

Remarks
Call this member function to retrieve the number of parameters in the saved query. **GetParameterCount** is useful for looping through all parameters in the querydef. For that purpose, use **GetParameterCount** in conjunction with **GetParameterInfo**.

For information about parameterizing queries, see the article "DAO Queries: Filtering and Parameterizing Queries" in *Programming with MFC*. For related information, see the topics "Parameter Object," "Parameters Collection," and "PARAMETERS Declaration (SQL)" in DAO Help.

See Also   **CDaoQueryDef::GetParamValue**, **CDaoQueryDef::SetParamValue**

CDaoQueryDef::GetParameterInfo

void GetParameterInfo(int *nIndex*, **CDaoParameterInfo&** *paraminfo*,
  DWORD *dwInfoOptions* = **AFX_DAO_PRIMARY_INFO**);
  throw(CDaoException, CMemoryException);
void GetParameterInfo(LPCTSTR *lpszName*, **CDaoParameterInfo&** *paraminfo*,
  DWORD *dwInfoOptions* = **AFX_DAO_PRIMARY_INFO**);
  throw(CDaoException, CMemoryException);

Parameters
nIndex   The zero-based index of the desired parameter in the querydef's Parameters collection, for lookup by index.

paraminfo   A reference to a **CDaoParameterInfo** object that returns the information requested.

dwInfoOptions   Options that specify which information about the parameter to retrieve. The available option is listed here along with what it causes the function to return:

- **AFX_DAO_PRIMARY_INFO**   (Default) Name, Type

lpszName   A string containing the name of the desired parameter, for lookup by name. You can use a **CString**.

Remarks

Call this member function to obtain information about a parameter defined in the querydef. For a description of the information returned in *paraminfo*, see the **CDaoParameterInfo** structure. This structure has members that correspond to the descriptive information under *dwInfoOptions* above.

For more information about obtaining parameter information, see the article "DAO: Obtaining Information About DAO Objects." For more information about parameterizing queries, see the article "DAO Queries: Filtering and Parameterizing Queries." Both articles are in *Programming with MFC*. For related information, see the topic "PARAMETERS Declaration (SQL)" in DAO Help.

See Also   **CDaoQueryDef::GetParameterCount**

CDaoQueryDef::GetParamValue

COleVariant GetParamValue(LPCTSTR *lpszName*);
   throw(CDaoException, CMemoryException);
COleVariant GetParamValue(int *nIndex*);
   throw(CDaoException, CMemoryException);

Return Value

An object of class **COleVariant** that contains the parameter's value.

Parameters

lpszName   The name of the parameter whose value you want, for lookup by name.

nIndex   The zero-based index of the parameter in the querydef's Parameters collection, for lookup by index. You can obtain this value with calls to **GetParameterCount** and **GetParameterInfo**.

Remarks

Call this member function to retrieve the current value of the specified parameter stored in the querydef's Parameters collection. You can access the parameter either by name or by its ordinal position in the collection.

For examples and more information about parameterizing queries, see the article "DAO Queries: Filtering and Parameterizing Queries" in *Programming with MFC*. For related information, see the topic "PARAMETERS Declaration (SQL)" in DAO Help.

See Also   **CDaoQueryDef::SetParamValue**

CDaoQueryDef::GetRecordsAffected

long GetRecordsAffected( );
    throw(CDaoException, CMemoryException);

Return Value

The number of records affected.

Remarks

Call this member function to determine how many records were affected by the last call of **Execute**. The count returned will not reflect changes in related tables when cascade updates or deletes are in effect.

For information about querydefs, see the article "DAO Querydef" in *Programming with MFC*. For related information see the topic "RecordsAffected Property" in DAO Help.

CDaoQueryDef::GetReturnsRecords

BOOL GetReturnsRecords( );
    throw(CDaoException, CMemoryException);

Return Value

Nonzero if the querydef is based on a query that returns records; otherwise 0.

Remarks

Call this member function to determine whether the querydef is based on a query that returns records. This member function is only used for SQL pass-through queries. For more information about SQL queries, see the **Execute** member function. For more information about working with SQL pass-through queries, see the **SetReturnsRecords** member function.

For information about querydefs, see the article "DAO Querydef" in *Programming with MFC*. For related information, see the topic "ReturnsRecords Property" in DAO Help.

See Also **CDaoQueryDef::GetName**, **CDaoQueryDef::GetSQL**, **CDaoQueryDef::GetODBCTimeout**

CDaoQueryDef::GetSQL

CString GetSQL( );
    throw(CDaoException, CMemoryException);

Return Value

The SQL statement that defines the query on which the querydef is based.

Remarks

Call this member function to retrieve the SQL statement that defines the query on which the querydef is based. You will then probably parse the string for keywords, table names, and so on.

For information about querydefs, see the article "DAO Querydef" in *Programming with MFC*. For related information, see the topics "SQL Property," "Comparison of Microsoft Jet Database Engine SQL and ANSI SQL," and "Querying a Database with SQL in Code" in DAO Help.

See Also   **CDaoQueryDef::SetSQL, CDaoQueryDef::GetName, CDaoQueryDef::GetReturnsRecords, CDaoQueryDef::GetODBCTimeout**

CDaoQueryDef::GetType

short GetType( );
   throw(CDaoException, CMemoryException);

Return Value

The type of the query defined by the querydef. For values, see "Remarks."

Remarks

Call this member function to determine the query type of the querydef. The query type is set by what you specify in the querydef's SQL string when you create the querydef or call an existing querydef's **SetSQL** member function. The query type returned by this function can be one of the following values:

- **dbQSelect**   Select
- **dbQAction**   Action
- **dbQCrosstab**   Crosstab
- **dbQDelete**   Delete
- **dbQUpdate**   Update
- **dbQAppend**   Append
- **dbQMakeTable**   Make-table
- **dbQDDL**   Data-definition
- **dbQSQLPassThrough**   Pass-through
- **dbQSetOperation**   Union
- **dbQSPTBulk**   Used with **dbQSQLPassThrough** to specify a query that does not return records.

Note To create an SQL pass-through query, don't set the **dbSQLPassThrough** constant. This is set automatically by the Microsoft Jet database engine when you create a querydef object and set the connect string.

For information about SQL strings, see **GetSQL**. For information about query types, see **Execute**.

CDaoQueryDef::IsOpen

BOOL IsOpen( ) const;

Return Value
Nonzero if the **CDaoQueryDef** object is currently open; otherwise 0.

Remarks
Call this member function to determine whether the **CDaoQueryDef** object is currently open. A querydef must be in an open state before you use it to call **Execute** or to create a **CDaoRecordset** object. To put a querydef into an open state call either **Create** (for a new querydef) or **Open** (for an existing querydef).

For information about querydefs, see the article "DAO Querydef" in *Programming with MFC*.

CDaoQueryDef::Open

virtual void Open(LPCTSTR *lpszName* **= NULL);**
  throw(CDaoException, CMemoryException);

Parameters
lpszName   A string that contains the name of the saved querydef to open. You can use a **CString**.

Remarks
Call this member function to open a querydef previously saved in the database's QueryDefs collection. Once the querydef is open, you can call its **Execute** member function or use the querydef to create a **CDaoRecordset** object.

For information about querydefs, see the article "DAO Querydef" in *Programming with MFC*.

See Also   **CDaoQueryDef::IsOpen**, **CDaoQueryDef::Close**, **CDaoQueryDef::SetName**, **CDaoQueryDef::Create**

CDaoQueryDef::SetConnect

void SetConnect(LPCTSTR *lpszConnect* **);**
   throw(CDaoException, CMemoryException);

Parameters

lpszConnect   A string that contains a connect string for the associated
   CDaoDatabase object.

Remarks

Call this member function to set the querydef object's connect string. The connect
string is used to pass additional information to ODBC and certain ISAM drivers as
needed. It is not used for Microsoft Jet (.MDB) databases.

Tip   The preferred way to work with ODBC tables is to attach them to an .MDB database. For
more information, see the topic "Accessing External Databases with DAO" in DAO Help and
the article "DAO External: Working with External Data Sources" in *Programming with MFC*.

Before executing a querydef that represents an SQL pass-through query to an ODBC
data source, set the connect string with **SetConnect** and call **SetReturnsRecords** to
specify whether the query returns records.

For more information about the connect string's structure and examples of connect
string components, see the topic "Connect Property" in DAO Help. For information
about querydefs, see the article "DAO Querydef" in *Programming with MFC*.

CDaoQueryDef::SetName

void SetName(LPCTSTR *lpszName* **);**
   throw(CDaoException, CMemoryException);

Parameters

lpszName   A string that contains the new name for a nontemporary query in the
   associated **CDaoDatabase** object.

Remarks

Call this member function if you want to change the name of a querydef that is not
temporary. Querydef names are unique, user-defined names. You can call **SetName**
before the querydef object is appended to the QueryDefs collection.

For information about querydefs, see the article "DAO Querydef" in *Programming
with MFC*. For more information about the querydef name, see the topic "Name
Property" in DAO Help.

See Also   **CDaoQueryDef::GetName, CDaoQueryDef::SetSQL,
CDaoQueryDef::SetConnect, CDaoQueryDef::SetODBCTimeout,
CDaoQueryDef::SetReturnsRecords**

CDaoQueryDef::SetODBCTimeout

> **void SetODBCTimeout(short** *nODBCTimeout* **);**
> **throw(CDaoException, CMemoryException);**

Parameters

nODBCTimeout   The number of seconds before a query times out.

Remarks

Call this member function to set the time limit before a query to an ODBC data source times out.

Tip The preferred way to work with ODBC tables is to attach them to a Microsoft Jet (.MDB) database. For more information, see the topic "Accessing External Databases with DAO" in DAO Help and the article "DAO External: Working with External Data Sources" in *Programming with MFC*.

This member function lets you override the default number of seconds before subsequent operations on the connected data source "time out." An operation might time out due to network access problems, excessive query processing time, and so on. Call **SetODBCTimeout** prior to executing a query with this querydef if you want to change the query timeout value. (As ODBC reuses connections, the timeout value is the same for all clients on the same connection.)

The default value for query timeouts is 60 seconds.

For information about querydefs, see the article "DAO Querydef" in *Programming with MFC*. For related information, see the topic "ODBCTimeout Property" in DAO Help.

See Also   **CDaoQueryDef::GetODBCTimeout, CDaoQueryDef::SetName, CDaoQueryDef::SetSQL, CDaoQueryDef::SetConnect, CDaoQueryDef::SetReturnsRecords**

CDaoQueryDef::SetParamValue

> **void SetParamValue(LPCTSTR** *lpszName*, **const COleVariant&** *varValue* **);**
> **throw(CDaoException, CMemoryException);**
> **void SetParamValue(int** *nOrdinal*, **const COleVariant&** *varValue* **);**
> **throw(CDaoException, CMemoryException);**

Parameters

lpszName   The name of the parameter whose value you want to set.

varValue   The value to set; see "Remarks."

nOrdinal   The ordinal position of the parameter in the querydef's Parameters collection. You can obtain this value with calls to **GetParameterCount** and **GetParameterInfo**.

Remarks

Call this member function to set the value of a parameter in the querydef at run time. The parameter must already have been established as part of the querydef's SQL string. You can access the parameter either by name or by its ordinal position in the collection.

Specify the value to set as a **COleVariant** object. For information about setting the desired value and type in your **COleVariant** object, see class **COleVariant**.

For examples and more information about parameterizing queries, see the article "DAO Queries: Filtering and Parameterizing Queries" in *Programming with MFC*. For related information, see the topic "PARAMETERS Declaration (SQL)" in DAO Help.

See Also   **CDaoQueryDef::GetParamValue**

CDaoQueryDef::SetReturnsRecords

void SetReturnsRecords(BOOL *bReturnsRecords* **);**
throw(CDaoException, CMemoryException);

Parameters

bReturnsRecords   Pass **TRUE** if the query on an external database returns records; otherwise, **FALSE**.

Remarks

Call this member function as part of the process of setting up an SQL pass-through query to an external database. In such a case, you must create the querydef and set its properties using other **CDaoQueryDef** member functions. For a description of external databases, see **SetConnect**.

For information about querydefs, see the article "DAO Querydef." For information about external data sources, see the article "DAO External: Working with External Data Sources." Both articles are in *Programming with MFC*. For related information, see the topic "ReturnsRecords Property" in DAO Help.

See Also   **CDaoQueryDef::GetReturnsRecords**, **CDaoQueryDef::SetName**, **CDaoQueryDef::SetSQL**, **CDaoQueryDef::SetConnect**, **CDaoQueryDef::SetODBCTimeout**

CDaoQueryDef::SetSQL

void SetSQL(LPCTSTR *lpszSQL* **);**
   throw(CDaoException, CMemoryException);

Parameters

   lpszSQL   A string containing a complete SQL statement, suitable for execution. The syntax of this string depends on the DBMS that your query targets. For a discussion of syntax used in the Microsoft Jet database engine, see the topic "Building SQL Statements in Code" in DAO Help.

Remarks

   Call this member function to set the SQL statement that the querydef executes. A typical use of **SetSQL** is setting up a querydef object for use in an SQL pass-through query. (For the syntax of SQL pass-through queries on your target DBMS, see the documentation for your DBMS.)

   For information about querydefs, see the article "DAO Querydef" in *Programming with MFC*. For more information about SQL, see the topics "SQL Property," "Microsoft Jet Database Engine SQL Data Types," and "Querying a Database with SQL in Code" in DAO Help.

   See Also   **CDaoQueryDef::GetSQL, CDaoQueryDef::SetName, CDaoQueryDef::SetConnect, CDaoQueryDef::SetODBCTimeout, CDaoQueryDef::SetReturnsRecords**

Data Members

CDaoQueryDef::m_pDatabase

Remarks

   Contains a pointer to the **CDaoDatabase** object associated with the querydef object. Use this pointer if you need to access the database directly — for example, to obtain pointers to other querydef or recordset objects in the database's collections.

   For information about querydefs, see the article "DAO Querydef" in *Programming with MFC*.

CDaoQueryDef::m_pDAOQueryDef

Remarks

Contains a pointer to the OLE interface for the underlying DAO querydef object. This pointer is provided for completeness and consistency with the other classes. However, because MFC rather fully encapsulates DAO querydefs, you are unlikely to need it. If you do use it, do so cautiously — in particular, do not change the value of the pointer unless you know what you are doing.

For information about querydefs, see the article "DAO Querydef" in *Programming with MFC*.

CDaoRecordset

A **CDaoRecordset** object represents a set of records selected from a data source. Known as "recordsets," **CDaoRecordset** objects are available in three forms: table-type recordsets, dynaset-type recordsets, and snapshot-type recordsets.

- Table-type recordsets represent a base table that you can use to examine, add, change, or delete records from a single database table.

- Dynaset-type recordsets are the result of a query that can have updatable records. A dynaset-type recordset is a set of records that you can use to examine, add, change, or delete records from an underlying database table or tables. A dynaset-type recordset can contain fields from one or more tables in a database.

- A snapshot-type recordsets is a static copy of a set of records that you can use to find data or generate reports. A snapshot-type recordset can contain fields from one or more tables in a database but cannot be updated.

Each form of recordset represents a set of records fixed at the time the recordset is opened. When you scroll to a record in a table-type recordset or a dynaset-type recordset, it reflects changes made to the record after the recordset is opened, either by other users or by other recordsets in your application. (A snapshot-type recordset cannot be updated.) You can use **CDaoRecordset** directly or derive an application-specific recordset class from **CDaoRecordset**. You can then:

- Scroll through the records.

- Set an index and quickly look for records using **Seek** (table-type recordsets only).

- Find records based on a string comparison: "<", "<=", "=", ">=", or ">" (dynaset-type and snapshot-type recordsets).

- Update the records and specify a locking mode (except snapshot-type recordsets).

- Filter the recordset to constrain which records it selects from those available on the data source.

- Sort the recordset.

- Parameterize the recordset to customize its selection with information not known until run time.

Class **CDaoRecordset** supplies an interface similar to that of class **CRecordset**. The main difference is that class **CDaoRecordset** accesses data through a Data Access Object (DAO) based on OLE. Class **CRecordset** accesses the DBMS through Open Database Connectivity (ODBC) and an ODBC driver for that DBMS.

Note The DAO database classes are distinct from the MFC database classes based on Open Database Connectivity (ODBC). All DAO database class names have the "CDao" prefix. You can still access ODBC data sources with the DAO classes; the DAO classes generally offer superior capabilities because they are specific to the Microsoft Jet database engine.

You can either use **CDaoRecordset** directly or derive a class from **CDaoRecordset**. To use a recordset class in either case, open a database and construct a recordset object, passing the constructor a pointer to your **CDaoDatabase** object. You can also construct a **CDaoRecordset** object and let MFC create a temporary **CDaoDatabase** object for you. Then call the recordset's **Open** member function, specifying whether the object is a table-type recordset, a dynaset-type recordset, or a snapshot-type recordset. Calling **Open** selects data from the database and retrieves the first record.

Use the object's member functions and data members to scroll through the records and operate on them. The operations available depend on whether the object is a table-type recordset, a dynaset-type recordset, or a snapshot-type recordset, and whether it is updatable or read-only—this depends on the capability of the database or Open Database Connectivity (ODBC) data source. To refresh records that may have been changed or added since the **Open** call, call the object's **Requery** member function. Call the object's **Close** member function and destroy the object when you finish with it.

CDaoRecordset uses DAO record field exchange (DFX) to support reading and updating of record fields through type-safe C++ members of your **CDaoRecordset** or **CDaoRecordset**-derived class. You can also implement dynamic binding of columns in a database without using the DFX mechanism using **GetFieldValue** and **SetFieldValue**.

For more information about recordsets, see the article "DAO: Recordset Architecture" in *Programming with MFC*. For related information, see the topic "Recordset Object" in DAO Help.

#include <afxdao.h>

See Also   **CDaoTableDef**, **CDaoWorkspace**, **CDaoDatabase**, **CDaoQueryDef**

Data Members

m_bCheckCacheForDirtyFields	Contains a flag indicating whether fields are automatically marked as changed.
m_pDAORecordset	A pointer to the DAO interface underlying the recordset object.
m_nParams	Contains the number of parameter data members in the recordset class — the number of parameters passed with the recordset's query
m_pDatabase	Source database for this result set. Contains a pointer to a **CDaoDatabase** object.
m_strFilter	Contains a string used to construct an SQL **WHERE**

| | statement. |
| **m_strSort** | Contains a string used to construct an SQL **ORDER BY** statement. |

Construction

CDaoRecordset	Constructs a **CDaoRecordset** object.
Close	Closes the recordset.
Open	Creates a new recordset from a table, dynaset, or snapshot.

Attributes

CanAppend	Returns nonzero if new records can be added to the recordset via the **AddNew** member function.
CanBookmark	Returns nonzero if the recordset supports bookmarks.
CanRestart	Returns nonzero if **Requery** can be called to run the recordset's query again.
CanScroll	Returns nonzero if you can scroll through the records.
CanTransact	Returns nonzero if the data source supports transactions.
CanUpdate	Returns nonzero if the recordset can be updated (you can add, update, or delete records).
GetCurrentIndex	Returns a **CString** containing the name of the index most recently used on an indexed, table-type **CDaoRecordset**.
GetDateCreated	Returns the date and time the base table underlying a **CDaoRecordset** object was created
GetDateLastUpdated	Returns the date and time of the most recent change made to the design of a base table underlying a **CDaoRecordset** object.
GetEditMode	Returns a value that indicates the state of editing for the current record.
GetLastModifiedBookmark	Used to determine the most recently added or updated record.
GetName	Returns a **CString** containing the name of the recordset.
GetParamValue	Retrieves the current value of the specified parameter stored in the underlying DAOParameter object.
GetRecordCount	Returns the number of records accessed in a recordset object.
GetSQL	Gets the SQL string used to select records for the recordset.
GetType	Called to determine the type of a recordset: table-type, dynaset-type, or snapshot-type.

GetValidationRule	Returns a **CString** containing the value that validates data as it is entered into a field.
GetValidationText	Retrieves the text that is displayed when a validation rule is not satisfied.
IsBOF	Returns nonzero if the recordset has been positioned before the first record. There is no current record.
IsDeleted	Returns nonzero if the recordset is positioned on a deleted record.
IsEOF	Returns nonzero if the recordset has been positioned after the last record. There is no current record.
IsFieldDirty	Returns nonzero if the specified field in the current record has been changed.
IsFieldNull	Returns nonzero if the specified field in the current record is Null (having no value).
IsFieldNullable	Returns nonzero if the specified field in the current record can be set to Null (having no value).
IsOpen	Returns nonzero if **Open** has been called previously.
SetCurrentIndex	Called to set an index on a table-type recordset.
SetParamValue	Sets the current value of the specified parameter stored in the underlying DAOParameter object
SetParamValueNull	Sets the current value of the specified parameter to Null (having no value).

Recordset Update Operations

AddNew	Prepares for adding a new record. Call **Update** to complete the addition.
CancelUpdate	Cancels any pending updates due to an **Edit** or **AddNew** operation.
Delete	Deletes the current record from the recordset. You must explicitly scroll to another record after the deletion.
Edit	Prepares for changes to the current record. Call **Update** to complete the edit.
Update	Completes an **AddNew** or **Edit** operation by saving the new or edited data on the data source.

Recordset Navigation Operations

Find	Locates the first, next, previous, or last location of a particular string in a dynaset-type recordset that satisfies the specified criteria and makes that record the current record.
FindFirst	Locates the first record in a dynaset-type or snapshot-type recordset that satisfies the specified criteria and makes that record the current record.
FindLast	Locates the last record in a dynaset-type or snapshot-type recordset that satisfies the specified criteria and makes that record the current record.
FindNext	Locates the next record in a dynaset-type or snapshot-type recordset that satisfies the specified criteria and makes that record the current record.
FindPrev	Locates the previous record in a dynaset-type or snapshot-type recordset that satisfies the specified criteria and makes that record the current record.
GetAbsolutePosition	Returns the record number of a recordset object's current record.
GetBookmark	Returns a value that represents the bookmark on a record.
GetPercentPosition	Returns the position of the current record as a percentage of the total number of records.
Move	Positions the recordset to a specified number of records from the current record in either direction.
MoveFirst	Positions the current record on the first record in the recordset.
MoveLast	Positions the current record on the last record in the recordset.
MoveNext	Positions the current record on the next record in the recordset.
MovePrev	Positions the current record on the previous record in the recordset.
Seek	Locates the record in an indexed table-type recordset object that satisfies the specified criteria for the current index and makes that record the current record.
SetAbsolutePosition	Sets the record number of a recordset object's current record.
SetBookmark	Positions the recordset on a record containing the specified bookmark.
SetPercentPosition	Sets the position of the current record to a location corresponding to a percentage of the total number of records in a recordset.

Other Recordset Operations

FillCache	Fills all or a part of a local cache for a recordset object that contains data from an ODBC data source.
GetCacheSize	Returns a value that specifies the number of records in a dynaset-type recordset containing data to be locally cached from an ODBC data source.
GetCacheStart	Returns a value that specifies the bookmark of the first record in the recordset to be cached.
GetFieldCount	Returns a value that represents the number of fields in a recordset.
GetFieldInfo	Returns specific kinds of information about the fields in the recordset.
GetFieldValue	Returns the value of a field in a recordset.
GetIndexCount	Retrieves the number of indexes in a table underlying a recordset.
GetIndexInfo	Returns various kinds of information about an index.
GetLockingMode	Returns a value that indicates the type of locking that is in effect during editing.
Requery	Runs the recordset's query again to refresh the selected records.
SetCacheSize	Sets a value that specifies the number of records in a dynaset-type recordset containing data to be locally cached from an ODBC data source.
SetCacheStart	Sets a value that specifies the bookmark of the first record in the recordset to be cached.
SetFieldDirty	Marks the specified field in the current record as changed.
SetFieldNull	Sets the value of the specified field in the current record to Null (having no value).
SetFieldValue	Sets the value of a field in a recordset.
SetFieldValueNull	Sets the value of a field in a recordset to Null (having no value).
SetLockingMode	Sets a value that indicates the type of locking to put into effect during editing.

Overridables

DoFieldExchange	Called to exchange data (in both directions) between the field data members of the recordset and the corresponding record on the data source. Implements DAO record field exchange (DFX).
GetDefaultDBName	Returns the name of the default data source.
GetDefaultSQL	Called to get the default SQL string to execute.

Member Functions

CDaoRecordset::AddNew

virtual void AddNew( );
   throw(CDaoException, CMemoryException);

Remarks

Call this member function to add a new record to a table-type or dynaset-type recordset. The record's fields are initially Null. (In database terminology, Null means "having no value" and is not the same as **NULL** in C++.) To complete the operation, you must call the **Update** member function. **Update** saves your changes to the data source.

Caution If you edit a record and then scroll to another record without calling **Update**, your changes are lost without warning.

If you add a record to a dynaset-type recordset by calling **AddNew**, the record is visible in the recordset and included in the underlying table where it becomes visible to any new **CDaoRecordset** objects.

The position of the new record depends on the type of recordset:

- In a dynaset-type recordset, records are inserted at the end of the recordset, regardless of any sorting or ordering rules that may have been in effect when the recordset was opened.

- In a table-type recordset for which an index has been specified, records are returned in their proper place in the sort order. If no index has been specified, new records are returned at the end of the recordset.

The record that was current before you used **AddNew** remains current. If you want to make the new record current and the recordset supports bookmarks, call **SetBookmark** to the bookmark identified by the LastModified property setting of the underlying DAO recordset object. Doing so is useful for determining the value for counter (auto-increment) fields in an added record. For more information, see **GetLastModifiedBookmark**.

If the database supports transactions, you can make your **AddNew** call part of a transaction. For more information about transactions, see class **CDaoWorkspace**. Note that you should call **CDaoWorkspace::BeginTrans** before calling **AddNew**.

It is illegal to call **AddNew** for a recordset whose **Open** member function has not been called. A **CDaoException** is thrown if you call **AddNew** for a recordset that cannot be appended. You can determine whether the recordset is updatable by calling **CanAppend**.

The framework marks changed field data members to ensure they will be written to the record on the data source by the DAO record field exchange (DFX) mechanism. Changing the value of a field generally sets the field dirty automatically, so you will seldom need to call **SetFieldDirty** yourself, but you might sometimes want to ensure that columns will be explicitly updated or inserted regardless of what value is in the field data member. The DFX mechanism also employs the use of **PSEUDO NULL**. For more information, see **CDaoFieldExchange::m_nOperation**.

If the double-buffering mechanism is not being used, then changing the value of the field does not automatically set the field as dirty. In this case, it will be necessary to explicity set the field dirty. The flag contained in **m_bCheckCacheForDirtyFields** controls this automatic field checking.

Note   If records are double-buffered (that is, automatic field checking is enabled), calling **CancelUpdate** will restore the member variables to the values they had before **AddNew** or **Edit** was called.

For more information about updating records, see the article "DAO Recordset: Recordset Operations" in *Programming with MFC*. For related information, see the topics "AddNew Method," "CancelUpdate Method," "LastModified Property," and "EditMode Property" in DAO Help.

See Also   **CDaoRecordset::CanUpdate**, **CDaoRecordset::CancelUpdate**, **CDaoRecordset::Delete**, **CDaoRecordset::Edit**, **CDaoRecordset::Update**, **CDaoRecordset::CanTransact**

CDaoRecordset::CanAppend

BOOL CanAppend( ) const;

Return Value

Nonzero if the recordset allows adding new records; otherwise 0. **CanAppend** will return 0 if you opened the recordset as read-only.

Remarks

Call this member function to determine whether the previously opened recordset allows you to add new records by calling the **AddNew** member function.

For more information about updating records, see the article "DAO Recordset: Recordset Operations" in *Programming with MFC*. For related information, see the topic "Append Method" in DAO Help.

See Also   **CDaoRecordset::CanBookmark**, **CDaoRecordset::CanRestart**, **CDaoRecordset::CanScroll**, **CDaoRecordset::CanTransact**, **CDaoRecordset::CanUpdate**

CDaoRecordset::CanBookmark

BOOL CanBookmark( ) const;
    throw(CDaoException, CMemoryException);

Return Value

Nonzero if the recordset supports bookmarks, otherwise 0.

Remarks

Call this member function to determine whether the previously opened recordset allows you to individually mark records using bookmarks. If you are using recordsets based entirely on Microsoft Jet database engine tables, bookmarks can be used except on snapshot-type recordsets flagged as forward-only scrolling recordsets. Other database products (external ODBC data sources) may not support bookmarks.

For more information about recordset navigation, see the article "DAO Recordset: Recordset Navigation" in *Programming with MFC*. For related information, see the topic "Bookmarkable Property" in DAO Help.

See Also **CDaoRecordset::CanAppend**, **CDaoRecordset::CanRestart**, **CDaoRecordset::CanScroll**, **CDaoRecordset::CanTransact**, **CDaoRecordset::CanUpdate**

CDaoRecordset::CancelUpdate

virtual void CancelUpdate( );
    throw(CDaoException, CMemoryException);

Remarks

The **CancelUpdate** member function cancels any pending updates due to an **Edit** or **AddNew** operation. For example, if an application calls the **Edit** or **AddNew** member function and has not called **Update**, **CancelUpdate** cancels any changes made after **Edit** or **AddNew** was called.

Note If records are double-buffered (that is, automatic field checking is enabled), calling **CancelUpdate** will restore the member variables to the values they had before **AddNew** or **Edit** was called.

If there is no **Edit** or **AddNew** operation pending, **CancelUpdate** causes MFC to throw an exception. Call the **GetEditMode** member function to determine if there is a pending operation that can be canceled.

For more information about updating data, see the article "DAO Recordset: Recordset Operations" in *Programming with MFC*. For related information, see the topic "CancelUpdate Method" in DAO Help.

See Also **CDaoRecordset::AddNew**, **CDaoRecordset::Delete**, **CDaoRecordset::Edit**, **CDaoRecordset::Update**, **CDaoRecordset::CanTransact**

CDaoRecordset::CanRestart

BOOL CanRestart( );
    throw(CDaoException, CMemoryException);

Return Value

Nonzero if **Requery** can be called to run the recordset's query again, otherwise 0.

Remarks

Call this member function to determine whether the recordset allows restarting its query (to refresh its records) by calling the **Requery** member function. Table-type recordsets do not support **Requery**.

If **Requery** is not supported, call **Close** then **Open** to refresh the data. You can call **Requery** to update a recordset object's underlying parameter query after the parameter values have been changed.

For more information about working with DAO objects, see the article "DAO: Creating, Opening, and Closing DAO Objects" in *Programming with MFC*. For related information, see the topic "Restartable Property" in DAO Help.

See Also   **CDaoRecordset::CanAppend**, **CDaoRecordset::CanBookmark**, **CDaoRecordset::CanScroll**, **CDaoRecordset::CanTransact**, **CDaoRecordset::CanUpdate**

CDaoRecordset::CanScroll

BOOL CanScroll( ) const;

Return Value

Nonzero if you can scroll through the records, otherwise 0.

Remarks

Call this member function to determine whether the recordset allows scrolling. If you call **Open** with **dbForwardOnly**, the recordset can only scroll forward.

For more information about navigating through recordsets, see the article "DAO Recordset: Recordset Navigation" in *Programming with MFC*. For related information, see the topic "Positioning the Current Record Pointer with DAO" in DAO Help.

See Also   **CDaoRecordset::CanAppend**, **CDaoRecordset::CanBookmark**, **CDaoRecordset::CanRestart**, **CDaoRecordset::CanTransact**, **CDaoRecordset::CanUpdate**, **CDaoRecordset::Open**

CDaoRecordset::CanTransact

BOOL CanTransact( ) const;
    throw(CDaoException, CMemoryException);

Return Value

Nonzero if the underlying data source supports transactions, otherwise 0.

Remarks

Call this member function to determine whether the recordset allows transactions.

For more information about updating data, see the article "DAO Recordset: Recordset Operations" in *Programming with MFC*. For related information, see the topic "Transactions Property" in DAO Help.

See Also   **CDaoRecordset::AddNew**, **CDaoRecordset::CanAppend**, **CDaoRecordset::CancelUpdate**, **CDaoRecordset::CanScroll**, **CDaoRecordset::CanRestart**, **CDaoRecordset::CanUpdate**, **CDaoRecordset::Delete**, **CDaoRecordset::Edit**, **CDaoRecordset::Update**

CDaoRecordset::CanUpdate

BOOL CanUpdate( ) const;
    throw(CDaoException, CMemoryException);

Return Value

Nonzero if the recordset can be updated (add, update, and delete records), otherwise 0.

Remarks

Call this member function to determine whether the recordset can be updated. A recordset might be read-only if the underlying data source is read-only or if you specified **dbReadOnly** for *nOptions* when you called **Open** for the recordset.

For more information about updating data, see the article "DAO Recordset: Recordset Operations" in *Programming with MFC*. For related information, see the topics "AddNew Method," "Edit Method," "Delete Method," "Update Method," and "Updatable Property" in DAO Help.

See Also   **CDaoRecordset::CanAppend**, **CDaoRecordset::CanBookmark**, **CDaoRecordset::CanScroll**, **CDaoRecordset::CanRestart**, **CDaoRecordset::CanTransact**

CDaoRecordset::CDaoRecordset

CDaoRecordset(CDaoDatabase* *pDatabase* **= NULL);**

Parameters

pDatabase Contains a pointer to a **CDaoDatabase** object or the value **NULL**. If not **NULL** and the **CDaoDatabase** object's **Open** member function has not been called to connect it to the data source, the recordset attempts to open it for you during its own **Open** call. If you pass **NULL**, a **CDaoDatabase** object is constructed and connected for you using the data source information you specified if you derived your recordset class from **CDaoRecordset**.

Remarks

Constructs a **CDaoRecordset** object. You can either use **CDaoRecordset** directly or derive an application-specific class from **CDaoRecordset**. You can use ClassWizard to derive your recordset classes.

Note If you derive a **CDaoRecordset** class, your derived class must supply its own constructor. In the constructor of your derived class, call the constructor **CDaoRecordset::CDaoRecordset**, passing the appropriate parameters along to it.

Pass **NULL** to your recordset constructor to have a **CDaoDatabase** object constructed and connected for you automatically. This is a useful shortcut that does not require you to construct and connect a **CDaoDatabase** object prior to constructing your recordset. If the **CDaoDatabase** object is not open, a **CDaoWorkspace** object will also be created for you that uses the default workspace. For more information, see **CDaoDatabase::CDaoDatabase**.

For more information about constructing recordsets, see the article "DAO: Creating, Opening, and Closing DAO Objects" in *Programming with MFC*.

See Also **CDaoRecordset::GetDefaultDBName**, **CDaoRecordset::GetDefaultSQL**, **CDaoRecordset::GetDateCreated**, **CDaoRecordset::GetDateLastUpdated**

CDaoRecordset::Close

virtual void Close( );
    throw(CDaoException);

Remarks

Closing a **CDaoRecordset** object removes it from the collection of open recordsets in the associated database. Because **Close** does not destroy the **CDaoRecordset** object, you can reuse the object by calling **Open** on the same data source or a different data source.

All pending **AddNew** or **Edit** statements are canceled, and all pending transactions are rolled back. If you want to preserve pending additions or edits, call **Update** before you call **Close** for each recordset.

You can call **Open** again after calling **Close**. This lets you reuse the recordset object. A better alternative is to call **Requery**, if possible.

For more information about working with recordsets, see the article "DAO: Creating, Opening, and Closing DAO Objects" in *Programming with MFC*. For related information, see the topic "Close Method" in DAO Help.

See Also   **CDaoRecordset::Open**, **CDaoRecordset::CDaoRecordset**

CDaoRecordset::Delete

virtual void Delete( );
throw(CDaoException, CMemoryException);

Remarks

Call this member function to delete the current record in an open dynaset-type or table-type recordset object. After a successful deletion, the recordset's field data members are set to a Null value, and you must explicitly call one of the recordset navigation member functions (**Move**, **Seek**, **SetBookmark**, and so on) in order to move off the deleted record. When you delete records from a recordset, there must be a current record in the recordset before you call **Delete**; otherwise, MFC throws an exception.

Delete removes the current record and makes it inaccessible. Although you cannot edit or use the deleted record, it remains current. Once you move to another record, however, you cannot make the deleted record current again.

Caution   The recordset must be updatable and there must be a valid record current in the recordset when you call **Delete**. For example, if you delete a record but do not scroll to a new record before you call **Delete** again, **Delete** throws a **CDaoException**.

You can undelete a record if you use transactions and you call the **CDaoWorkspace::Rollback** member function. If the base table is the primary table in a cascade delete relationship, deleting the current record may also delete one or more records in a foreign table. For more information, see the definition of cascade delete in DAO Help.

Unlike **AddNew** and **Edit**, a call to **Delete** is not followed by a call to **Update**.

For more information about updating data, see the article "DAO Recordset: Recordset Operations" in *Programming with MFC*. For related information, see the topics "AddNew Method," "Edit Method," "Delete Method," "Update Method," and "Updatable Property" in DAO Help.

See Also **CDaoRecordset::AddNew**, **CDaoRecordset::CancelUpdate**, **CDaoRecordset::Edit**, **CDaoRecordset::Update**, **CDaoRecordset::CanTransact**

CDaoRecordset::DoFieldExchange

virtual void DoFieldExchange(CDaoFieldExchange* *pFX* **);**

Parameters

pFX Contains a pointer to a **CDaoFieldExchange** object. The framework will already have set up this object to specify a context for the field exchange operation.

Remarks

The framework calls this member function to automatically exchange data between the field data members of your recordset object and the corresponding columns of the current record on the data source. It also binds your parameter data members, if any, to parameter placeholders in the SQL statement string for the recordset's selection. The exchange of field data, called DAO record field exchange (DFX), works in both directions: from the recordset object's field data members to the fields of the record on the data source, and from the record on the data source to the recordset object. If you are binding columns dynamically, you are not required to implement **DoFieldExchange**.

The only action you must normally take to implement **DoFieldExchange** for your derived recordset class is to create the class with ClassWizard and specify the names and data types of the field data members. You might also add code to what ClassWizard writes to specify parameter data members. If all fields are to be bound dynamically, this function will be inactive unless you specify parameter data members. For more information, see the article "DAO Recordset: Binding Records Dynamically" in *Programming with MFC*.

When you declare your derived recordset class with ClassWizard, the wizard writes an override of **DoFieldExchange** for you, which resembles the following example:

```
void CCustSet::DoFieldExchange(CDaoFieldExchange* pFX)
{
    //{{AFX_FIELD_MAP(CCustSet)
    pFX->SetFieldType(CFieldExchange::outputColumn);
    DFX_Text(pFX, "Name", m_strName);
    DFX_Short(pFX, "Age", m_wAge);
    //}}AFX_FIELD_MAP
}
```

For more information about record field exchange, see the article "DAO Record Field Exchange (DFX)" in *Programming with MFC*.

See Also **CDaoException**

CDaoRecordset::Edit

virtual void Edit( );
   throw(CDaoException, CMemoryException);

Remarks

Call this member function to allow changes to the current record.

Once you call the **Edit** member function, changes made to the current record's fields are copied to the copy buffer. After you make the desired changes to the record, call **Update** to save your changes. **Edit** saves the values of the recordset's data members. If you call **Edit**, make changes, then call **Edit** again, the record's values are restored to what they were before the first **Edit** call.

Caution If you edit a record and then perform any operation that moves to another record without first calling **Update**, your changes are lost without warning. In addition, if you close the recordset or the parent database, your edited record is discarded without warning.

In some cases, you may want to update a column by making it Null (containing no data). To do so, call **SetFieldNull** with a parameter of **TRUE** to mark the field Null; this also causes the column to be updated. If you want a field to be written to the data source even though its value has not changed, call **SetFieldDirty** with a parameter of **TRUE**. This works even if the field had the value Null.

The framework marks changed field data members to ensure they will be written to the record on the data source by the DAO record field exchange (DFX) mechanism. Changing the value of a field generally sets the field dirty automatically, so you will seldom need to call **SetFieldDirty** yourself, but you might sometimes want to ensure that columns will be explicitly updated or inserted regardless of what value is in the field data member. The DFX mechanism also employs the use of **PSEUDO NULL**. For more information, see **CDaoFieldExchange::m_nOperation**.

If the double-buffering mechanism is not being used, then changing the value of the field does not automatically set the field as dirty. In this case, it will be necessary to explicity set the field dirty. The flag contained in **m_bCheckCacheForDirtyFields** controls this automatic field checking.

When the recordset object is pessimistically locked in a multiuser environment, the record remains locked from the time **Edit** is used until the updating is complete. If the recordset is optimistically locked, the record is locked and compared with the pre-edited record just before it is updated in the database. If the record has changed since you called **Edit**, the **Update** operation fails and MFC throws an exception. You can change the locking mode with **SetLockingMode**.

Note Optimistic locking is always used on external database formats, such as ODBC and installable ISAM.

The current record remains current after you call **Edit**. To call **Edit**, there must be a current record. If there is no current record or if the recordset does not refer to an open table-type or dynaset-type recordset object, an exception occurs. Calling **Edit** causes a **CDaoException** to be thrown under the following conditions:

- There is no current record.
- The database or recordset is read-only.
- No fields in the record are updatable.
- The database or recordset was opened for exclusive use by another user.
- Another user has locked the page containing your record.

If the data source supports transactions, you can make the **Edit** call part of a transaction. Note that you should call **CDaoWorkspace::BeginTrans** before calling **Edit** and after the recordset has been opened. Also note that calling **CDaoWorkspace::CommitTrans** is not a substitute for calling **Update** to complete the **Edit** operation. For more information about transactions, see class **CDaoWorkspace**.

For more information about updating data, see the article "DAO Recordset: Recordset Operations" in *Programming with MFC*. For related information, see the topics "AddNew Method," "Edit Method," "Delete Method," "Update Method," and "Updatable Property" in DAO Help.

See Also   **CDaoRecordset::AddNew**, **CDaoRecordset::CancelUpdate**, **CDaoRecordset::CanTransact**, **CDaoRecordset::Delete**, **CDaoRecordset::Update**

CDaoRecordset::FillCache

void FillCache(long* *pSize* **= NULL, COleVariant*** *pBookmark* **= NULL);**
   throw(CDaoException, CMemoryException);

Parameters

pSize   Specifies the number of rows to fill in the cache. If you omit this parameter, the value is determined by the CacheSize property setting of the underlying DAO object.

pBookmark   A **COleVariant** specifying a bookmark. The cache is filled starting from the record indicated by this bookmark. If you omit this parameter, the cache is filled starting from the record indicated by the CacheStart property of the underlying DAO object.

Remarks

Call this member function to cache a specified number of records from the recordset. Caching improves the performance of an application that retrieves, or fetches, data from a remote server. A cache is space in local memory that holds the data most recently fetched from the server on the assumption that the data will probably be requested again while the application is running. When data is requested, the Microsoft Jet database engine checks the cache for the data first rather than fetching it from the server, which takes more time. Using data caching on non-ODBC data sources has no effect as the data is not saved in the cache.

Rather than waiting for the cache to be filled with records as they are fetched, you can explicitly fill the cache at any time by calling the **FillCache** member function. This is a faster way to fill the cache because **FillCache** fetches several records at once instead of one at a time. For example, while each screenful of records is being displayed, you can have your application call **FillCache** to fetch the next screenful of records.

Any ODBC database accessed with recordset objects can have a local cache. To create the cache, open a recordset object from the remote data source, and then call the **SetCacheSize** and **SetCacheStart** member functions of the recordset. If *lSize* and *lBookmark* create a range that is partly or wholly outside the range specified by **SetCacheSize** and **SetCacheStart**, the portion of the recordset outside this range is ignored and is not loaded into the cache. If **FillCache** requests more records than remain in the remote data source, only the remaining records are fetched, and no exception is thrown.

Records fetched from the cache do not reflect changes made concurrently to the source data by other users.

FillCache fetches only records not already cached. To force an update of all the cached data, call the **SetCacheSize** member function with an *lSize* parameter equal to 0, call **SetCacheSize** again with the *lSize* parameter equal to the size of the cache you originally requested, and then call **FillCache**.

For more information about caching records, see the article "DAO External: Improving Performance with External Data Sources" in *Programming with MFC*. For related information, see the topic "FillCache Method" in DAO Help.

See Also   **CDaoRecordset::GetCacheSize**, **CDaoRecordset::GetCacheStart**, **CDaoRecordset::SetCacheSize**, **CDaoRecordset::SetCacheStart**

CDaoRecordset::Find

virtual BOOL Find(long *lFindType***, LPCTSTR** *lpszFilter* **);**
    throw(CDaoException, CMemoryException);

Return Value

Nonzero if matching records are found, otherwise 0.

Parameters

lFindType A value indicating the type of Find operation desired. The possible values are:

- **AFX_DAO_NEXT** Find the next location of a matching string.

- **AFX_DAO_PREV** Find the previous location of a matching string.

- **AFX_DAO_FIRST** Find the first location of a matching string.

- **AFX_DAO_LAST** Find the last location of a matching string.

lpszFilter A string expression (like the **WHERE** clause in an SQL statement without the word **WHERE**) used to locate the record. For example:

```
Find(AFX_DAO_FIRST, "colRecID = 7"), "customer name = 'Jones'"
```

Remarks

Call this member function to locate a particular string in the recordset using a comparison operator. You can find the first, next, previous, or last instance of the string. **Find** is a virtual function, so you can override it and add your own implementation. The **FindFirst**, **FindLast**, **FindNext**, and **FindPrev** member functions call the **Find** member function, so you can use **Find** to control the behavior of all Find operations.

Tip The smaller the set of records you have, the more effective **Find** will be. In general, and especially with ODBC data, it is better to create a new query that retrieves just the records you want. With table-type recordsets, it is faster to set an index and call **Seek**.

For more information about finding records, see the article "DAO Recordset: Recordset Navigation" in *Programming with MFC*. For related information, see the topic "FindFirst, FindLast, FindNext, FindPrevious Methods" in DAO Help.

See Also **CDaoRecordset::FindFirst, CDaoRecordset::FindLast, CDaoRecordset::FindNext, CDaoRecordset::FindPrev**

CDaoRecordset::FindFirst

BOOL FindFirst(LPCTSTR *lpszFilter* **);**
    throw(CDaoException, CMemoryException);

Return Value

Nonzero if matching records are found, otherwise 0.

Parameters

lpszFilter   A string expression (like the **WHERE** clause in an SQL statement without the word **WHERE**) used to locate the record.

Remarks

Call this member function to find the first record that matches a specified condition. The **FindFirst** member function begins its search from the beginning of the recordset and searches to the end of the recordset.

If you want to include all the records in your search (not just those that meet a specific condition) use one of the Move operations to move from record to record. To locate a record in a table-type recordset, call the **Seek** member function.

If a record matching the criteria is not located, the current record pointer is undetermined, and **Find** returns zero. If the recordset contains more than one record that satisfies the criteria, **FindFirst** locates the first occurrence, **FindNext** locates the next occurrence, and so on.

Caution   If you edit the current record, be sure to save the changes by calling the **Update** member function before you move to another record. If you move to another record without updating, your changes are lost without warning.

The **Find** member functions search from the location and in the direction specified in the following table:

Find operations	Begin	Search direction
FindFirst	Beginning of recordset	End of recordset
FindLast	End of recordset	Beginning of recordset
FindNext	Current record	End of recordset
FindPrevious	Current record	Beginning of recordset

Important   When you call **FindLast**, the Microsoft Jet database engine fully populates your recordset before beginning the search, if this has not already been done. The first search may take longer than subsequent searches.

Using one of the Find operations is not the same as calling **MoveFirst** or **MoveNext**, however, which simply makes the first or next record current without specifying a condition. You can follow a Find operation with a Move operation.

Keep the following in mind when using the Find operations:

- If **Find** returns nonzero, the current record is not defined. In this case, you must position the current record pointer back to a valid record.

- You cannot use a Find operation with a forward-only scrolling snapshot-type recordset.

- You should use the U.S. date format (month-day-year) when you search for fields containing dates, even if you are not using the U.S. version of the Microsoft Jet database engine; otherwise, matching records may not be found.

- When working with ODBC databases and large dynasets, you may discover that using the the Find operations is slow, especially when working with large recordsets. You can improve performance by using SQL queries with customized **ORDER BY** or **WHERE** clauses, parameter queries, or **CDaoQuerydef** objects that retrieve specific indexed records.

For more information about finding records, see the article "DAO Recordset: Recordset Navigation" in *Programming with MFC*. For related information, see the topic "FindFirst, FindLast, FindNext, FindPrevious Methods" in DAO Help.

See Also **CDaoRecordset::Find**, **CDaoRecordset::FindLast**, **CDaoRecordset::FindNext**, **CDaoRecordset::FindPrev**

CDaoRecordset::FindLast

BOOL FindLast(LPCTSTR *lpszFilter* **);**
   throw(CDaoException, CMemoryException);

Return Value

Nonzero if matching records are found, otherwise 0.

Parameters

lpszFilter   A string expression (like the **WHERE** clause in an SQL statement without the word **WHERE**) used to locate the record.

Remarks

Call this member function to find the last record that matches a specified condition. The **FindLast** member function begins its search at the end of the recordset and searches backward towards the begining of the recordset.

If you want to include all the records in your search (not just those that meet a specific condition) use one of the Move operations to move from record to record. To locate a record in a table-type recordset, call the **Seek** member function.

If a record matching the criteria is not located, the current record pointer is undetermined, and calling the **IsNoMatch** member function returns nonzero. If the recordset contains more than one record that satisfies the criteria, **FindFirst** locates the first occurrence, **FindNext** locates the next occurrence after the first occurrence, and so on.

> **Caution** If you edit the current record, be sure you save the changes by calling the **Update** member function before you move to another record. If you move to another record without updating, your changes are lost without warning.

Using one of the Find operations is not the same as calling **MoveFirst** or **MoveNext**, however, which simply makes the first or next record current without specifying a condition. You can follow a Find operation with a Move operation.

Keep the following in mind when using the Find operations:

- If **Find** returns nonzero, the current record is not defined. In this case, you must position the current record pointer back to a valid record.

- You cannot use a Find operation with a forward-only scrolling snapshot-type recordset.

- You should use the U.S. date format (month-day-year) when you search for fields containing dates, even if you are not using the U.S. version of the Microsoft Jet database engine; otherwise, matching records may not be found.

- When working with ODBC databases and large dynasets, you may discover that using the the Find operations is slow, especially when working with large recordsets. You can improve performance by using SQL queries with customized **ORDER BY** or **WHERE** clauses, parameter queries, or **CDaoQuerydef** objects that retrieve specific indexed records.

For more information about finding records, see the article "DAO Recordset: Recordset Navigation" in *Programming with MFC*. For related information, see the topic "FindFirst, FindLast, FindNext, FindPrevious Methods" in DAO Help.

See Also **CDaoRecordset::Find**, **CDaoRecordset::FindFirst**, **CDaoRecordset::FindNext**, **CDaoRecordset::FindPrev**

CDaoRecordset::FindNext

BOOL FindNext(LPCTSTR *lpszFilter* **);**
    throw(CDaoException, CMemoryException);

Return Value

Nonzero if matching records are found, otherwise 0.

Parameters

lpszFilter A string expression (like the **WHERE** clause in an SQL statement without the word **WHERE**) used to locate the record.

Remarks

Call this member function to find the next record that matches a specified condition. The **FindNext** member function begins its search at the current record and searches to the end of the recordset.

If you want to include all the records in your search (not just those that meet a specific condition) use one of the Move operations to move from record to record. To locate a record in a table-type recordset, call the **Seek** member function.

If a record matching the criteria is not located, the current record pointer is undetermined, and calling the **IsNoMatch** member function returns nonzero. If the recordset contains more than one record that satisfies the criteria, **FindFirst** locates the first occurrence, **FindNext** locates the next occurrence, and so on.

Caution   If you edit the current record, be sure you save the changes by calling the **Update** member function before you move to another record. If you move to another record without updating, your changes are lost without warning.

Using one of the Find operations is not the same as calling **MoveFirst** or **MoveNext**, however, which simply makes the first or next record current without specifying a condition. You can follow a Find operation with a Move operation.

Keep the following in mind when using the Find operations:

- If **Find** returns nonzero, the current record is not defined. In this case, you must position the current record pointer back to a valid record.

- You cannot use a Find operation with a forward-only scrolling snapshot-type recordset.

- You should use the U.S. date format (month-day-year) when you search for fields containing dates, even if you are not using the U.S. version of the Microsoft Jet database engine; otherwise, matching records may not be found.

- When working with ODBC databases and large dynasets, you may discover that using the the Find operations is slow, especially when working with large recordsets. You can improve performance by using SQL queries with customized **ORDER BY** or **WHERE** clauses, parameter queries, or **CDaoQuerydef** objects that retrieve specific indexed records.

For more information about finding records, see the article "DAO Recordset: Recordset Navigation" in *Programming with MFC*. For related information, see the topic "FindFirst, FindLast, FindNext, FindPrevious Methods" in DAO Help.

See Also   **CDaoRecordset::Find**, **CDaoRecordset::FindFirst**, **CDaoRecordset::FindLast**, **CDaoRecordset::FindPrev**

CDaoRecordset::FindPrev

BOOL FindPrev(LPCTSTR *lpszFilter* **);**
    throw(CDaoException, CMemoryException);

Return Value

Nonzero if matching records are found, otherwise 0.

Parameters

   lpszFilter   A string expression (like the **WHERE** clause in an SQL statement without the word **WHERE**) used to locate the record.

Remarks

Call this member function to find the previous record that matches a specified condition. The **FindPrev** member function begins its search at the current record and searches backward towards the beginning of the recordset.

If you want to include all the records in your search (not just those that meet a specific condition) use one of the Move operations to move from record to record. To locate a record in a table-type recordset, call the **Seek** member function.

If a record matching the criteria is not located, the current record pointer is undetermined, and calling the **IsNoMatch** member function returns nonzero. If the recordset contains more than one record that satisfies the criteria, **FindFirst** locates the first occurrence, **FindNext** locates the next occurrence, and so on.

Caution   If you edit the current record, be sure you save the changes by calling the **Update** member function before you move to another record. If you move to another record without updating, your changes are lost without warning.

Using one of the Find operations is not the same as calling **MoveFirst** or **MoveNext**, however, which simply makes the first or next record current without specifying a condition. You can follow a Find operation with a Move operation.

Keep the following in mind when using the Find operations:

- If **Find** returns nonzero, the current record is not defined. In this case, you must position the current record pointer back to a valid record.

- You cannot use a Find operation with a forward-only scrolling snapshot-type recordset.

- You should use the U.S. date format (month-day-year) when you search for fields containing dates, even if you are not using the U.S. version of the Microsoft Jet database engine; otherwise, matching records may not be found.

- When working with ODBC databases and large dynasets, you may discover that using the the Find operations is slow, especially when working with large recordsets. You can improve performance by using SQL queries with customized **ORDER BY** or **WHERE** clauses, parameter queries, or **CDaoQuerydef** objects that retrieve specific indexed records.

For more information about finding records, see the article "DAO Recordset: Recordset Navigation" in *Programming with MFC*. For related information, see the topic "FindFirst, FindLast, FindNext, FindPrevious Methods" in DAO Help.

See Also   **CDaoRecordset::Find**, **CDaoRecordset::FindFirst**, **CDaoRecordset::FindLast**, **CDaoRecordset::FindNext**

CDaoRecordset::GetAbsolutePosition

long GetAbsolutePosition( );
    throw(CDaoException, CMemoryException);

Return Value

An integer from 0 to the number of records in the recordset. Corresponds to the ordinal position of the current record in the recordset.

Remarks

Returns the record number of a recordset object's current record. The AbsolutePosition property value of the underlying DAO object is zero-based; a setting of 0 refers to the first record in the recordset. You can determine the number of populated records in the recordset by calling **GetRecordCount**. Calling **GetRecordCount** may take some time because it must access all records to determine the count.

If there is no current record, as when there are no records in the recordset, −1 is returned. If the current record is deleted, the AbsolutePosition property value is not defined, and MFC throws an exception if it is referenced. For dynaset-type recordsets, new records are added to the end of the sequence.

Note This property is not intended to be used as a surrogate record number. Bookmarks are still the recommended way of retaining and returning to a given position and are the only way to position the current record across all types of recordset objects. In particular, the position of a given record changes when record(s) preceding it are deleted. There is also no assurance that a given record will have the same absolute position if the recordset is re-created again because the order of individual records within a recordset is not guaranteed unless it is created with an SQL statement using an **ORDER BY** clause.

Note This member function is valid only for dynaset-type and snapshot-type recordsets.

For more information about finding records, see the article "DAO Recordset: Recordset Navigation" in *Programming with MFC*. For related information, see the topic "AbsolutePosition Property" in DAO Help.

See Also **CDaoRecordset::SetAbsolutePosition**

CDaoRecordset::GetBookmark

COleVariant GetBookmark( );
    throw(CDaoException, CMemoryException);

Return Value

Returns a value representing the bookmark on the current record.

Remarks

Call this member function to obtain the bookmark value in a particular record. When a recordset object is created or opened, each of its records already has a unique bookmark if it supports them. Call **CanBookmark** to determine whether a recordset supports bookmarks.

You can save the bookmark for the current record by assigning the value of the bookmark to a **COleVariant** object. To quickly return to that record at any time after moving to a different record, call **SetBookmark** with a parameter corresponding to the value of that **COleVariant** object.

For more information about finding records, see the article "DAO Recordset: Recordset Navigation" in *Programming with MFC*. For related information, see the topic "Bookmark Property" in DAO Help.

See Also   CDaoRecordset::SetBookmark, CDaoRecordset::CanBookmark

---

CDaoRecordset::GetCacheSize

long GetCacheSize( );
    throw(CDaoException, CMemoryException);

Return Value

A value that specifies the number of records in a dynaset-type recordset containing data to be locally cached from an ODBC data source.

Remarks

Call this member function to obtain the number of records cached. Data caching improves the performance of an application that retrieves data from a remote server through dynaset-type recordset objects. A cache is a space in local memory that holds the data most recently retrieved from the server in the event that the data will be requested again while the application is running. When data is requested, the Microsoft Jet database engine checks the cache for the requested data first rather than retrieving it from the server, which takes more time. Data that does not come from an ODBC data source is not saved in the cache.

Any ODBC data source, such as an attached table, can have a local cache.

For more information about caching records, see the article "DAO External: Improving Performance with External Data Sources" in *Programming with MFC*. For related information, see the topic "CacheSize, CacheStart Properties" in DAO Help.

See Also   CDaoRecordset::FillCache, CDaoRecordset::GetCacheStart, CDaoRecordset::SetCacheSize, CDaoRecordset::SetCacheStart

CDaoRecordset::GetCacheStart

COleVariant GetCacheStart( );
    throw(CDaoException, CMemoryException);

Return Value

A **COleVariant** that specifies the bookmark of the first record in the recordset to be cached.

Remarks

Call this member function to obtain the bookmark value of the first record in the recordset to be cached. The Microsoft Jet database engine requests records within the cache range from the cache, and it requests records outside the cache range from the server.

Note Records retrieved from the cache do not reflect changes made concurrently to the source data by other users.

For more information about caching records, see the article "DAO External: Improving Performance with External Data Sources" in *Programming with MFC*. For related information, see the topic "CacheSize, CacheStart Properties" in DAO Help.

See Also **CDaoRecordset::FillCache**, **CDaoRecordset::GetCacheSize**, **CDaoRecordset::SetCacheSize**, **CDaoRecordset::SetCacheStart**

CDaoRecordset::GetCurrentIndex

CString GetCurrentIndex( );
    throw(CDaoException, CMemoryException);

Return Value

A **CString** containing the name of the index currently in use with a table-type recordset. Returns an empty string if no index has been set.

Remarks

Call this member function to determine the index currently in use in an indexed table-type **CDaoRecordset** object. This index is the basis for ordering records in a table-type recordset, and is used by the **Seek** member function to locate records.

A **CDaoRecordset** object can have more than one index but can use only one index at a time (although a **CDaoTableDef** object may have several indexes defined on it).

For more information about finding records, see the article "DAO Recordset: Recordset Navigation" in *Programming with MFC*. For related information, see the topic "Index Object" and the definition of current index in DAO Help.

See Also **CDaoRecordset::SetCurrentIndex**

CDaoRecordset::GetDateCreated

COleDateTime GetDateCreated( );
    throw(CDaoException, CMemoryException);

Return Value

A **COleDateTime** object containing the date and time the base table was created.

Remarks

Call this member function to retrieve the date and time a base table was created. Date and time settings are derived from the computer on which the base table was created.

For more information about creating recordsets, see the article "DAO: Creating, Opening, and Closing DAO Objects" in *Programming with MFC*. For related information, see the topic "DateCreated, LastUpdated Properties" in DAO Help.

See Also **CDaoRecordset::GetDateLastUpdated**

CDaoRecordset::GetDateLastUpdated

COleDateTime GetDateLastUpdated( );
    throw(CDaoException, CMemoryException);

Return Value

A **COleDateTime** object containing the date and time the base table structure (schema) was last updated.

Remarks

Call this member function to retrieve the date and time the schema was last updated. Date and time settings are derived from the computer on which the base table structure (schema) was last updated.

For more information about creating recordsets, see the article "DAO: Creating, Opening, and Closing DAO Objects" in *Programming with MFC*. For related information, see the topic "DateCreated, LastUpdated Properties" in DAO Help.

See Also **CDaoRecordset::GetDateCreated**

CDaoRecordset::GetDefaultDBName

virtual CString GetDefaultDBName( );

Return Value

A **CString** that contains the path and name of the database from which this recordset is derived.

Remarks

Call this member function to determine the name of the database for this recordset. If a recordset is created without a pointer to a **CDaoDatabase**, then this path is used by the recordset to open the default database. By default, this function returns an empty string. When ClassWizard derives a new recordset from **CDaoRecordset**, it will create this function for you.

The following example illustrates the use of the double backslash (\\) in the string, as is required for the string to be interpreted correctly.

```
CString CMyRecordset::GetDefaultDBName
{
    return _T("c:\\mydir\\datasrc.mdb");
}
```

For more information about connecting to databases, see the article "DAO: Creating, Opening, and Closing DAO Objects" in *Programming with MFC*.

See Also   **CDaoRecordset::GetDefaultSQL**, **CDaoRecordset::GetName**, **CDaoRecordset::GetSQL**, **CDaoRecordset::GetType**

CDaoRecordset::GetDefaultSQL

virtual CString GetDefaultSQL( );

Return Value

A **CString** that contains the default SQL statement.

Remarks

The framework calls this member function to get the default SQL statement on which the recordset is based. This might be a table name or an SQL **SELECT** statement.

You indirectly define the default SQL statement by declaring your recordset class with ClassWizard, and ClassWizard performs this task for you.

If you pass a null SQL string to **Open**, then this function is called to determine the table name or SQL for your recordset.

For more information about connecting to databases, see the article "DAO: Creating, Opening, and Closing DAO Objects" in *Programming with MFC*.

See Also   **CDaoRecordset::GetDefaultDBName**, **CDaoRecordset::GetName**, **CDaoRecordset::GetSQL**, **CDaoRecordset::GetType**

CDaoRecordset::GetEditMode

short GetEditMode( );
  throw(CDaoException, CMemoryException);

Return Value

Returns a value that indicates the state of editing for the current record.

Remarks

Call this member function to determine the state of editing, which is one of the following values:

Value	Description
dbEditNone	No editing operation is in progress.
dbEditInProgress	**Edit** has been called.
dbEditAdd	**AddNew** has been called.

For more information about updating data, see the article "DAO Recordset: Recordset Operations" in *Programming with MFC*. For related information, see the topic "EditMode Property" in DAO Help.

CDaoRecordset::GetFieldCount

short GetFieldCount( );
  throw(CDaoException, CMemoryException);

Return Value

The number of fields in the recordset.

Remarks

Call this member function to retrieve the number of fields (columns) defined in the recordset.

For more information about creating recordsets, see the article "DAO Recordset: Creating Recordsets" in *Programming with MFC*. For related information, see the topic "Count Property" in DAO Help.

See Also **CDaoRecordset::GetFieldInfo**, **CDaoRecordset::GetFieldValue**, **CDaoRecordset::GetIndexCount**, **CDaoRecordset::GetIndexInfo**

CDaoRecordset::GetFieldInfo

void GetFieldInfo(int *nIndex***, CDaoFieldInfo&** *fieldinfo***,**
   DWORD *dwInfoOptions* **= AFX_DAO_PRIMARY_INFO);**
   throw(CDaoException, CMemoryException);
void GetFieldInfo(LPCTSTR *lpszName***, CDaoFieldInfo&** *fieldinfo***,**
   DWORD *dwInfoOptions* **= AFX_DAO_PRIMARY_INFO);**
   throw(CDaoException, CMemoryException);

Parameters

nIndex   The zero-based index of the predefined field in the recordset's Fields collection, for lookup by index.

fieldinfo   A reference to a **CDaoFieldInfo** structure.

dwInfoOptions   Options that specify which information about the recordset to retrieve. The available options are listed here along with what they cause the function to return. For best performance, retrieve only the level of information you need:

- **AFX_DAO_PRIMARY_INFO**   (Default) Name, Type, Size, Attributes

- **AFX_DAO_SECONDARY_INFO**   Primary information, plus: Ordinal Position, Required, Allow Zero Length, Collating Order, Foreign Name, Source Field, Source Table

- **AFX_DAO_ALL_INFO**   Primary and secondary information, plus: Default Value, Validation Rule, Validation Text

lpszName   The name of the field.

Remarks

Call this member function to obtain information about the fields in a recordset. One version of the function lets you look up a field by index. The other version lets you look up a field by name.

For a description of the information returned, see the **CDaoFieldInfo** structure. This structure has members that correspond to the items of information listed above in the description of *dwInfoOptions*. When you request information at one level, you get information for any prior levels as well.

For more information about creating recordsets, see the article "DAO Recordset: Creating Recordsets" in *Programming with MFC*. For related information, see the topic "Attributes Property" in DAO Help.

See Also   **CDaoRecordset::GetFieldCount, CDaoRecordset::GetFieldValue, CDaoRecordset::GetIndexCount, CDaoRecordset::GetIndexInfo**

CDaoRecordset::GetFieldValue

virtual COleVariant GetFieldValue (LPCTSTR *lpszName* **);**
 throw(CDaoException, CMemoryException);
virtual COleVariant GetFieldValue(int *nIndex* **);**
 throw(CDaoException, CMemoryException);

Return Value

A **COleVariant** object that contains the value of a field.

Parameters

lpszName   A pointer to a string that contains the name of a field.

nIndex   A zero-based index of the field in the recordset's Fields collection, for lookup by index.

Remarks

Call this member function to retrieve data in a recordset. One version of the function lets you look up a field by ordinal position. The other version lets you look up a field by name.

Use **GetFieldValue** and **SetFieldValue** to dynamically bind fields at run time rather than statically binding columns using the **DoFieldExchange** mechanism.

GetFieldValue and the **DoFieldExchange** mechanism can be combined to improve performance. For example, use **GetFieldValue** to retrieve a value that you need only on demand, and assign that call to a "More Information" button in the interface.

For more information about binding fields dynamically, see the article "DAO Recordset: Binding Records Dynamically" in *Programming with MFC*. For related information, see the topics "Field Object" and "Value Property" in DAO Help.

See Also   **CDaoRecordset::SetFieldValue**

CDaoRecordset::GetIndexCount

short GetIndexCount( );
 throw(CDaoException, CMemoryException);

Return Value

The number of indexes in the table-type recordset.

Remarks

Call this member function to determine the number of indexes available on the table-type recordset. **GetIndexCount** is useful for looping through all indexes in the recordset. For that purpose, use **GetIndexCount** in conjunction with **GetIndexInfo**. If you call this member function on dynaset-type or snapshot-type recordsets, MFC throws an exception.

For more information about creating recordsets, see the article "DAO Recordset: Creating Recordsets" in *Programming with MFC*. For related information, see the topic "Attributes Property" in DAO Help.

See Also   **CDaoRecordset::GetFieldCount**, **CDaoRecordset::GetFieldInfo**, **CDaoRecordset::GetIndexInfo**

CDaoRecordset::GetIndexInfo

void GetIndexInfo(int *nIndex***, CDaoIndexInfo&** *indexinfo***,**
   DWORD *dwInfoOptions* **= AFX_DAO_PRIMARY_INFO);**
   throw(CDaoException, CMemoryException);
void GetIndexInfo(LPCTSTR *lpszName***, CDaoIndexInfo&** *indexinfo***,**
   DWORD *dwInfoOptions* **= AFX_DAO_PRIMARY_INFO);**
   throw(CDaoException, CMemoryException);

Parameters

nIndex   The zero-based index in the table's Indexes collection, for lookup by numerical position.

indexinfo   A reference to a **CDaoIndexInfo** structure.

dwInfoOptions   Options that specify which information about the index to retrieve. The available options are listed here along with what they cause the function to return. For best performance, retrieve only the level of information you need:

- **AFX_DAO_PRIMARY_INFO**   (Default) Name, Field Info, Fields

- **AFX_DAO_SECONDARY_INFO**   Primary information, plus: Primary, Unique, Clustered, IgnoreNulls, Required, Foreign

- **AFX_DAO_ALL_INFO**   Primary and secondary information, plus: Distinct Count

lpszName   A pointer to the name of the index object, for lookup by name.

Remarks

Call this member function to obtain various kinds of information about an index defined in the base table underlying a recordset. One version of the function lets you look up a index by its position in the collection. The other version lets you look up an index by name.

For a description of the information returned, see the **CDaoIndexInfo** structure. This structure has members that correspond to the items of information listed above in the description of *dwInfoOptions*. When you request information at one level, you get information for any prior levels as well.

For more information about creating recordsets, see the article "DAO Recordset: Creating Recordsets" in *Programming with MFC*. For related information, see the topic "Attributes Property" in DAO Help.

See Also **CDaoRecordset::GetFieldCount**, **CDaoRecordset::GetFieldInfo**, **CDaoRecordset::GetIndexCount**, **CDaoRecordset::GetLastModifiedBookmark**

CDaoRecordset::GetLastModifiedBookmark

COleVariant GetLastModifiedBookmark( );
 throw(CDaoException, CMemoryException);

Return Value

A **COleVariant** containing a bookmark that indicates the most recently added or changed record.

Remarks

Call this member function to retrieve the bookmark of the most recently added or updated record. When a recordset object is created or opened, each of its records already has a unique bookmark if it supports them. Call **GetBookmark** to determine if the recordset supports bookmarks. If the recordset does not support bookmarks, a **CDaoException** is thrown.

When you add a record, it appears at the end of the recordset, and is not the current record. To make the new record current, call **GetLastModifiedBookmark** and then call **SetBookmark** to return to the newly added record.

For more information about navigating in recordsets, see the article "DAO Recordset: Recordset Navigation" in *Programming with MFC*. For related information, see the topic "LastModified Property" in DAO Help.

See Also **CDaoRecordset::GetBookmark**, **CDaoRecordset::SetBookmark**

CDaoRecordset::GetLockingMode

BOOL GetLockingMode( );
 throw(CDaoException, CMemoryException);

Return Value

Nonzero if the type of locking is pessimistic, otherwise 0 for optimistic record locking.

Remarks

Call this member function to determine the type of locking in effect for the recordset. When pessimistic locking is in effect, the data page containing the record you are editing is locked as soon as you call the **Edit** member function. The page is unlocked when you call the **Update** or **Close** member function or any of the Move or Find operations.

When optimistic locking is in effect, the data page containing the record is locked only while the record is being updated with the **Update** member function.

When working with ODBC data sources, the locking mode is always optimistic.

For more information about updating data, see the article "DAO Recordset: Recordset Operations" in *Programming with MFC*. For related information, see the topics "LockEdits Property" and "Locking Behavior in Multiuser Applications" in DAO Help.

See Also   **CDaoRecordset::SetLockingMode**

CDaoRecordset::GetName

CString GetName( );
    throw(CDaoException, CMemoryException);

Return Value

A **CString** containing the name of the recordset.

Remarks

Call this member function to retrieve the name of the recordset. The name of the recordset must start with a letter and can contain a maximum of 40 characters. It can include numbers and underscore characters but can't include punctuation or spaces.

For more information about creating recordsets, see the article "DAO Recordset: Creating Recordsets" in *Programming with MFC*. For related information, see the topic "Name Property" in DAO Help.

See Also   **CDaoRecordset::GetDefaultDBName, CDaoRecordset::GetDefaultSQL, CDaoRecordset::GetSQL, CDaoRecordset::GetType**

CDaoRecordset::GetParamValue

virtual COleVariant GetParamValue(int *nIndex* **);**
    throw(CDaoException, CMemoryException);
virtual COleVariant GetParamValue(LPCTSTR *lpszName* **);**
    throw(CDaoException, CMemoryException);

Return Value

An object of class **COleVariant** that contains the parameter's value.

Parameters

nIndex   The numerical position of the parameter in the underlying DAOParameter object.

lpszName   The name of the parameter whose value you want.

Remarks

Call this member function to retrieve the current value of the specified parameter stored in the underlying DAOParameter object. You can access the parameter either by name or by its numerical position in the collection.

For more information about parameters, see the article "DAO Queries: Filtering and Parameterizing Queries" in *Programming with MFC*. For related information, see the topic "Parameter Object" in DAO Help.

See Also   **CDaoRecordset::SetParamValue**, **CDaoRecordset::m_nParams**

CDaoRecordset::GetPercentPosition

float GetPercentPosition( );
   throw(CDaoException, CMemoryException);

Return Value

A number between 0 and 100 that indicates the approximate location of the current record in the recordset object based on a percentage of the records in the recordset.

Remarks

When working with a dynaset-type or snapshot-type recordset, if you call **GetPercentPosition** before fully populating the recordset, the amount of movement is relative to the number of records accessed as indicated by calling **GetRecordCount**. You can move to the last record by calling **MoveLast** to complete the population of all recordsets, but this may take a significant amount of time.

You can call **GetPercentPosition** on all three types of recordset objects, including tables without indexes. However, you cannot call **GetPercentPosition** on forward-only scrolling snapshots, or on a recordset opened from a pass-through query against an external database. If there is no current record, or the current record has been deleted, a **CDaoException** is thrown.

For more information about navigating in recordsets, see the article "DAO Recordset: Recordset Navigation" in *Programming with MFC*. For related information, see the topic "PercentPosition Property" in DAO Help.

See Also   **CDaoRecordset::SetPercentPosition**

CDaoRecordset::GetRecordCount

long GetRecordCount( );
    throw(CDaoException, CMemoryException);

Return Value

Returns the number of records in a recordset.

Remarks

Call this member function to find out how many records in a recordset have been accessed. **GetRecordCount** does not indicate how many records are contained in a dynaset-type or snapshot-type recordset until all records have been accessed. This member function call may take a significant amount of time to complete.

Once the last record has been accessed, the return value indicates the total number of undeleted records in the recordset. To force the last record to be accessed, call the **MoveLast** or **FindLast** member function for the recordset. You can also use a SQL Count to determine the approximate number of records your query will return.

As your application deletes records in a dynaset-type recordset, the return value of **GetRecordCount** decreases. However, records deleted by other users are not reflected by **GetRecordCount** until the current record is positioned to a deleted record. If you execute a transaction that affects the record count and subsequently roll back the transaction, **GetRecordCount** will not reflect the actual number of remaining records.

The value of **GetRecordCount** from a snapshot-type recordset is not affected by changes in the underlying tables.

The value of **GetRecordCount** from a table-type recordset reflects the approximate number of records in the table and is affected immediately as table records are added and deleted.

A recordset with no records returns a value of 0. When working with attached tables or ODBC databases, **GetRecordCount** always returns -1. Calling the **Requery** member function on a recordset resets the value of **GetRecordCount** just as if the query were re-executed.

For more information about navigating in recordsets, see the article "DAO Recordset: Recordset Navigation" in *Programming with MFC*. For related information, see the topic "RecordCount Property" in DAO Help.

See Also   **CDaoRecordset::GetFieldCount, CDaoRecordset::GetFieldInfo, CDaoRecordset::GetIndexCount, CDaoRecordset::GetIndexInfo**

CDaoRecordset::GetSQL

CString GetSQL( ) const;

Return Value

A **CString** that contains the SQL statement.

Remarks

Call this member function to get the SQL statement that was used to select the recordset's records when it was opened. This will generally be an SQL **SELECT** statement.

The string returned by **GetSQL** is typically different from any string you may have passed to the recordset in the *lpszSQL* parameter to the **Open** member function. This is because the recordset constructs a full SQL statement based on what you passed to **Open**, what you specified with ClassWizard, and what you may have specified in the **m_strFilter** and **m_strSort** data members.

Important   Call this member function only after calling **Open**.

For more information about creating recordsets, see the article "DAO Recordset: Creating Recordsets" in *Programming with MFC*. For related information, see the topic "SQL Property" in DAO Help.

See Also   **CDaoRecordset::GetDefaultSQL**, **CDaoRecordset::GetDefaultDBName**, **CDaoRecordset::GetName**, **CDaoRecordset::GetType**

CDaoRecordset::GetType

short GetType( );
   throw(CDaoException, CMemoryException);

Return Value

One of the following values that indicates the type of a recordset:

- **dbOpenTable**   Table-type recordset
- **dbOpenDynaset**   Dynaset-type recordset
- **dbOpenSnapshot**   Snapshot-type recordset

Remarks

Call this member function after opening the recordset to determine the type of the recordset object.

For more information about creating recordsets, see the article "DAO Recordset: Creating Recordsets" in *Programming with MFC*. For related information, see the topic "Type Property" in DAO Help.

See Also   **CDaoRecordset::GetDefaultDBName, CDaoRecordset::GetDefaultSQL, CDaoRecordset::GetName, CDaoRecordset::GetSQL**

CDaoRecordset::GetValidationRule

CString GetValidationRule( );
    throw(CDaoException, CMemoryException);

Return Value

A **CString** object containing a value that validates the data in a record as it is changed or added to a table.

Remarks

Call this member function to determine the rule used to validate data. This rule is text-based, and is applied each time the underlying table is changed. If the data is not legal, MFC throws an exception. The returned error message is the text of the ValidationText property of the underlying field object, if specified, or the text of the expression specified by the ValidationRule property of the underlying field object. You can call **GetValidationText** to obtain the text of the error message.

For example, a field in a record that requires the day of the month might have a validation rule such as "DAY BETWEEN 1 AND 31."

For more information about creating recordsets, see the article "DAO Recordset: Creating Recordsets" in *Programming with MFC*. For related information, see the topic "ValidationRule Property" in DAO Help.

See Also   **CDaoRecordset::GetValidationText**

CDaoRecordset::GetValidationText

CString GetValidationText( );
    throw(CDaoException, CMemoryException);

Return Value

A **CString** object containing the text of the message that is displayed if the value of a field does not satisfy the validation rule of the underlying field object.

Remarks

Call this member function to retrieve the text of the ValidationText property of the underlying field object.

For more information about creating recordsets, see the article "DAO Recordset: Creating Recordsets" in *Programming with MFC*. For related information, see the topic "ValidationText Property" in DAO Help.

See Also **CDaoRecordset::GetValidationRule**

CDaoRecordset::IsBOF

BOOL IsBOF( ) const;
    throw(CDaoException, CMemoryException);

Return Value

Nonzero if the recordset contains no records or if you have scrolled backward before the first record; otherwise 0.

Remarks

Call this member function before you scroll from record to record to learn whether you have gone before the first record of the recordset. You can also call **IsBOF** along with **IsEOF** to determine whether the recordset contains any records or is empty. Immediately after you call **Open**, if the recordset contains no records, **IsBOF** returns nonzero. When you open a recordset that has at least one record, the first record is the current record and **IsBOF** returns 0.

If the first record is the current record and you call **MovePrev**, **IsBOF** will subsequently return nonzero. If **IsBOF** returns nonzero and you call **MovePrev**, an exception is thrown. If **IsBOF** returns nonzero, the current record is undefined, and any action that requires a current record will result in an exception.

Effect of specific methods on **IsBOF** and **IsEOF** settings:

- Calling **Open** internally makes the first record in the recordset the current record by calling **MoveFirst**. Therefore, calling **Open** on an empty set of records causes **IsBOF** and **IsEOF** to return nonzero. (See the following table for the behavior of a failed **MoveFirst** or **MoveLast** call.)

- All Move operations that successfully locate a record cause both **IsBOF** and **IsEOF** to return 0.

- An **AddNew** call followed by an **Update** call that successfully inserts a new record will cause **IsBOF** to return 0, but only if **IsEOF** is already nonzero. The state of **IsEOF** will always remain unchanged. As defined by the Microsoft Jet database engine, the current record pointer of an empty recordset is at the end of a file, so any new record is inserted after the current record.

- Any **Delete** call, even if it removes the only remaining record from a recordset, will not change the value of **IsBOF** or **IsEOF**.

This table shows which Move operations are allowed with different combinations of **IsBOF/IsEOF**.

	MoveFirst, MoveLast	MovePrev, Move < 0	Move 0	MoveNext, Move > 0
IsBOF=nonzero, **IsEOF**=0	Allowed	Exception	Exception	Allowed
IsBOF=0, **IsEOF**=nonzero	Allowed	Allowed	Exception	Exception
Both nonzero	Exception	Exception	Exception	Exception
Both 0	Allowed	Allowed	Allowed	Allowed

Allowing a Move operation does not mean that the operation will successfully locate a record. It merely indicates that an attempt to perform the specified Move operation is allowed and will not generate an exception. The value of the **IsBOF** and **IsEOF** member functions may change as a result of the attempted move.

The effect of Move operations that do not locate a record on the value of **IsBOF** and **IsEOF** settings is shown in the following table.

	IsBOF	IsEOF
MoveFirst, **MoveLast**	Nonzero	Nonzero
Move 0	No change	No change
MovePrev, **Move** < 0	Nonzero	No change
MoveNext, **Move** > 0	No change	Nonzero

For more information about navigating in recordsets, see the article "DAO Recordset: Recordset Navigation" in *Programming with MFC*. For related information, see the topic "BOF, EOF Properties" in DAO Help.

See Also   **CDaoRecordset::IsEOF**

CDaoRecordset::IsDeleted

BOOL IsDeleted( ) const;

Return Value

Nonzero if the recordset is positioned on a deleted record; otherwise 0.

Remarks

Call this member function to determine whether the current record has been deleted. If it has, you must scroll to another record before you can perform any other recordset operations. **IsDeleted** returns nonzero only if you deleted a record and did not scroll off that record.

For more information about navigating in recordsets, see the article "DAO Recordset: Recordset Navigation" in *Programming with MFC*. For related information, see the topics "Delete Method," "LastModified Property," and "EditMode Property" in DAO Help.

See Also   **CDaoRecordset::IsBOF**, **CDaoRecordset::IsEOF**

CDaoRecordset::IsEOF

BOOL IsEOF( ) const;
    throw(CDaoException, CMemoryException);

Return Value

Nonzero if the recordset contains no records or if you have scrolled beyond the last record; otherwise 0.

Remarks

Call this member function as you scroll from record to record to learn whether you have gone beyond the last record of the recordset. You can also call **IsEOF** to determine whether the recordset contains any records or is empty. Immediately after you call **Open**, if the recordset contains no records, **IsEOF** returns nonzero. When you open a recordset that has at least one record, the first record is the current record and **IsEOF** returns 0.

If the last record is the current record when you call **MoveNext**, **IsEOF** will subsequently return nonzero. If **IsEOF** returns nonzero and you call **MoveNext**, an exception is thrown. If **IsEOF** returns nonzero, the current record is undefined, and any action that requires a current record will result in an exception.

Effect of specific methods on **IsBOF** and **IsEOF** settings:

- Calling **Open** internally makes the first record in the recordset the current record by calling **MoveFirst**. Therefore, calling **Open** on an empty set of records causes **IsBOF** and **IsEOF** to return nonzero. (See the following table for the behavior of a failed **MoveFirst** call.)

- All Move operations that successfully locate a record cause both **IsBOF** and **IsEOF** to return 0.

- An **AddNew** call followed by an **Update** call that successfully inserts a new record will cause **IsBOF** to return 0, but only if **IsEOF** is already nonzero. The state of **IsEOF** will always remain unchanged. As defined by the Microsoft Jet database engine, the current record pointer of an empty recordset is at the end of a file, so any new record is inserted after the current record.

- Any **Delete** call, even if it removes the only remaining record from a recordset, will not change the value of **IsBOF** or **IsEOF**.

This table shows which Move operations are allowed with different combinations of **IsBOF/IsEOF**.

	MoveFirst, MoveLast	MovePrev, Move < 0	Move 0	MoveNext, Move > 0
IsBOF=nonzero, **IsEOF**=0	Allowed	Exception	Exception	Allowed
IsBOF=0, **IsEOF**=nonzero	Allowed	Allowed	Exception	Exception
Both nonzero	Exception	Exception	Exception	Exception
Both 0	Allowed	Allowed	Allowed	Allowed

Allowing a Move operation does not mean that the operation will successfully locate a record. It merely indicates that an attempt to perform the specified Move operation is allowed and will not generate an exception. The value of the **IsBOF** and **IsEOF** member functions may change as a result of the attempted Move.

The effect of Move operations that do not locate a record on the value of **IsBOF** and **IsEOF** settings is shown in the following table.

	IsBOF	IsEOF
MoveFirst, **MoveLast**	Nonzero	Nonzero
Move 0	No change	No change
MovePrev, **Move** < 0	Nonzero	No change
MoveNext, **Move** > 0	No change	Nonzero

For more information about navigating in recordsets, see the article "DAO Recordset: Recordset Navigation" in *Programming with MFC*. For related information, see the topic "BOF, EOF Properties" in DAO Help.

See Also   **CDaoRecordset::IsBOF**

CDaoRecordset::IsFieldDirty

BOOL IsFieldDirty(void* *pv* **) const;**
    throw(CDaoException, CMemoryException);

Return Value

Nonzero if the specified field data member is flagged as dirty; otherwise 0.

Parameters

pv   A pointer to the field data member whose status you want to check, or **NULL** to determine if any of the fields are dirty.

Remarks

Call this member function to determine whether the specified field data member of a dynaset has been flagged as "dirty" (changed). The data in all dirty field data members will be transferred to the record on the data source when the current record is updated by a call to the **Update** member function of **CDaoRecordset** (following a call to **Edit** or **AddNew**). With this knowledge, you can take further steps, such as unflagging the field data member to mark the column so it will not be written to the data source. For more information on the dirty flag, see the article "DAO Recordset: Caching Multiple Records" in *Programming with MFC*.

IsFieldDirty is implemented through **DoFieldExchange**.

For more information about record field exchange, see the article "DAO Record Field Exchange (DFX)" in *Programming with MFC*.

See Also   **CDaoRecordset::IsFieldNull**, **CDaoRecordset::IsFieldNullable**

CDaoRecordset::IsFieldNull

BOOL IsFieldNull(void* *pv* **);**
   throw(CDaoException, CMemoryException);
BOOL IsFieldNull(short *nIndex* **);**
   throw(CDaoException, CMemoryException);
BOOL IsFieldNull(LPCTSTR *lpszName* **);**
   throw(CDaoException, CMemoryException);

Return Value

Nonzero if the specified field data member is flagged as Null; otherwise 0.

Parameters

pv   A pointer to the field data member whose status you want to check, or **NULL** to determine if any of the fields are Null.

nIndex   The index of the field in the recordset, for lookup by zero-based index.

lpszName   The name of the field in the recordset, for lookup by name.

Remarks

Call this member function to determine whether the specified field data member of a recordset has been flagged as Null. (In database terminology, Null means "having no value" and is not the same as **NULL** in C++.) If a field data member is flagged as Null, it is interpreted as a column of the current record for which there is no value.

The first version of **IsFieldNull** is used for fields bound in the **DoFieldExchange** mechanism. If you choose to bind your fields dynamically, you must use either the second or third version of this member function. You can mix the calls as necessary.

For more information about record field exchange, see the article "DAO Record Field Exchange (DFX)" in *Programming with MFC*.

See Also **CDaoRecordset::IsFieldDirty**, **CDaoRecordset::IsFieldNullable**

CDaoRecordset::IsFieldNullable

BOOL IsFieldNullable(void* *pv* **);**
   throw(CDaoException, CMemoryException);
BOOL IsFieldNullable(short *nIndex* **);**
   throw(CDaoException, CMemoryException);
BOOL IsFieldNullable(LPCTSTR *lpszName* **);**
   throw(CDaoException, CMemoryException);

Return Value

Nonzero if the specified field data member can be made Null; otherwise 0.

Parameters

pv A pointer to the field data member whose status you want to check, or **NULL** to determine if any of the fields are Null.

nIndex The index of the field in the recordset, for lookup by zero-based index.

lpszName The name of the field in the recordset, for lookup by name.

Remarks

Call this member function to to determine whether the specified field data member is "nullable" (can be set to a Null value; C++ **NULL** is not the same as Null, which, in database terminology, means "having no value").

A field that cannot be Null must have a value. If you attempt to set such a field to Null when adding or updating a record, the data source rejects the addition or update, and **Update** will throw an exception. The exception occurs when you call **Update**, not when you call **SetFieldNull**.

The first version of **IsFieldNullable** is used for fields bound in the **DoFieldExchange** mechanism. If you choose to bind your fields dynamically, you must use either the second or third version of this member function. You can mix the calls as necessary.

For more information about record field exchange, see the article "DAO Record Field Exchange (DFX)" in *Programming with MFC*.

See Also **CDaoRecordset::IsFieldDirty**, **CDaoRecordset::IsFieldNull**

CDaoRecordset::IsOpen

BOOL IsOpen( ) const;

Return Value

Nonzero if the recordset object's **Open** or **Requery** member function has previously been called and the recordset has not been closed; otherwise 0.

Remarks

Call this member function to determine if the recordset is open.

For more information about creating recordsets, see the article "DAO Recordset: Creating Recordsets" in *Programming with MFC*.

See Also **CDaoRecordset::Open**, **CDaoRecordset::Close**

CDaoRecordset::Move

virtual void Move(long *lRows*);
    throw(CDaoException, CMemoryException);

Parameters

lRows The number of records to move forward or backward. Positive values move forward, toward the end of the recordset. Negative values move backward, toward the beginning.

Remarks

Call this member function to position the recordset *lRows* records from the current record. You can move forward or backward. Move(1) is equivalent to **MoveNext**, and Move(-1) is equivalent to **MovePrev**.

Caution Calling any of the **Move** functions throws an exception if the recordset has no records. In general, call both **IsBOF** and **IsEOF** before a Move operation to determine whether the recordset has any records. After you call **Open** or **Requery**, call either **IsBOF** or **IsEOF**.

If you have scrolled past the beginning or end of the recordset (**IsBOF** or **IsEOF** returns nonzero), a call to **Move** throws a **CDaoException**.

If you call any of the **Move** functions while the current record is being updated or added, the updates are lost without warning.

When you call **Move** on a forward-only scrolling snapshot, the *lRows* parameter must be a positive integer and bookmarks are not allowed, so you can move forward only.

To make the first, last, next, or previous record in a recordset the current record, call the **MoveFirst**, **MoveLast**, **MoveNext**, or **MovePrev** member function.

For more information about finding records, see the article "DAO Recordset: Recordset Navigation" in *Programming with MFC*. For related information, see the topics "Move Method" and "MoveFirst, MoveLast, MoveNext, MovePrevious Methods" in DAO Help.

See Also **CDaoRecordset::MoveFirst, CDaoRecordset::MoveLast, CDaoRecordset::MoveNext, CDaoRecordset::MovePrev**

CDaoRecordset::MoveFirst

void MoveFirst( );
   throw(CDaoException, CMemoryException);

Remarks

Call this member function to make the first record in the recordset (if any) the current record. You do not have to call **MoveFirst** immediately after you open the recordset. At that time, the first record (if any) is automatically the current record.

Caution   Calling any of the **Move** functions throws an exception if the recordset has no records. In general, call both **IsBOF** and **IsEOF** before a Move operation to determine whether the recordset has any records. After you call **Open** or **Requery**, call either **IsBOF** or **IsEOF**.

If you call any of the **Move** functions while the current record is being updated or added, the updates are lost without warning.

Use the **Move** functions to move from record to record without applying a condition. Use the Find operations to locate records in a dynaset-type or snapshot-type recordset object that satisfy a certain condition. To locate a record in a table-type recordset object, call **Seek**.

If the recordset refers to a table-type recordset, movement follows the table's current index. You can set the current index by using the Index property of the underlying DAO object. If you do not set the current index, the order of returned records is undefined.

If you call **MoveLast** on a recordset object based on an SQL query or querydef, the query is forced to completion and the recordset object is fully populated.

You cannot call the **MoveFirst** or **MovePrev** member function with a forward-only scrolling snapshot.

To move the position of the current record in a recordset object a specific number of records forward or backward, call **Move**.

For more information about finding records, see the article "DAO Recordset: Recordset Navigation" in *Programming with MFC*. For related information, see the topics "Move Method" and "MoveFirst, MoveLast, MoveNext, MovePrevious Methods" in DAO Help.

See Also   **CDaoRecordset::Move, CDaoRecordset::MoveLast, CDaoRecordset::MoveNext, CDaoRecordset::MovePrev**

CDaoRecordset::MoveLast

void MoveLast( );
  throw(CDaoException, CMemoryException);

Remarks

Call this member function to make the last record (if any) in the recordset the current record.

Caution   Calling any of the **Move** functions throws an exception if the recordset has no records. In general, call both **IsBOF** and **IsEOF** before a Move operation to determine whether the recordset has any records. After you call **Open** or **Requery**, call either **IsBOF** or **IsEOF**.

If you call any of the **Move** functions while the current record is being updated or added, the updates are lost without warning.

Use the **Move** functions to move from record to record without applying a condition. Use the Find operations to locate records in a dynaset-type or snapshot-type recordset object that satisfy a certain condition. To locate a record in a table-type recordset object, call **Seek**.

If the recordset refers to a table-type recordset, movement follows the table's current index. You can set the current index by using the Index property of the underlying DAO object. If you do not set the current index, the order of returned records is undefined.

If you call **MoveLast** on a recordset object based on an SQL query or querydef, the query is forced to completion and the recordset object is fully populated.

To move the position of the current record in a recordset object a specific number of records forward or backward, call **Move**.

For more information about finding records, see the article "DAO Recordset: Recordset Navigation" in *Programming with MFC*. For related information, see the topics "Move Method" and "MoveFirst, MoveLast, MoveNext, MovePrevious Methods" in DAO Help.

See Also   **CDaoRecordset::Move, CDaoRecordset::MoveFirst, CDaoRecordset::MoveNext, CDaoRecordset::MovePrev**

CDaoRecordset::MoveNext

void MoveNext( );
    throw(CDaoException, CMemoryException);

Remarks

Call this member function to make the next record in the recordset the current record. It is recommended that you call **IsBOF** before you attempt to move to the previous record. A call to **MovePrev** will throw a **CDaoException** if **IsBOF** returns nonzero, indicating either that you have already scrolled before the first record or that no records were selected by the recordset.

Caution   Calling any of the **Move** functions throws an exception if the recordset has no records. In general, call both **IsBOF** and **IsEOF** before a Move operation to determine whether the recordset has any records. After you call **Open** or **Requery**, call either **IsBOF** or **IsEOF**.

If you call any of the **Move** functions while the current record is being updated or added, the updates are lost without warning.

Use the **Move** functions to move from record to record without applying a condition. Use the Find operations to locate records in a dynaset-type or snapshot-type recordset object that satisfy a certain condition. To locate a record in a table-type recordset object, call **Seek**.

If the recordset refers to a table-type recordset, movement follows the table's current index. You can set the current index by using the Index property of the underlying DAO object. If you do not set the current index, the order of returned records is undefined.

To move the position of the current record in a recordset object a specific number of records forward or backward, call **Move**.

For more information about finding records, see the article "DAO Recordset: Recordset Navigation" in *Programming with MFC*. For related information, see the topics "Move Method" and "MoveFirst, MoveLast, MoveNext, MovePrevious Methods" in DAO Help.

See Also   **CDaoRecordset::Move, CDaoRecordset::MoveFirst, CDaoRecordset::MoveLast, CDaoRecordset::MovePrev**

CDaoRecordset::MovePrev

void MovePrev( );
    throw(CDaoException, CMemoryException);

Remarks

Call this member function to make the previous record in the recordset the current record.

It is recommended that you call **IsBOF** before you attempt to move to the previous record. A call to **MovePrev** will throw a **CDaoException** if **IsBOF** returns nonzero, indicating either that you have already scrolled before the first record or that no records were selected by the recordset.

Caution Calling any of the **Move** functions throws an exception if the recordset has no records. In general, call both **IsBOF** and **IsEOF** before a Move operation to determine whether the recordset has any records. After you call **Open** or **Requery**, call either **IsBOF** or **IsEOF**.

If you call any of the **Move** functions while the current record is being updated or added, the updates are lost without warning.

Use the **Move** functions to move from record to record without applying a condition. Use the Find operations to locate records in a dynaset-type or snapshot-type recordset object that satisfy a certain condition. To locate a record in a table-type recordset object, call **Seek**.

If the recordset refers to a table-type recordset, movement follows the table's current index. You can set the current index by using the Index property of the underlying DAO object. If you do not set the current index, the order of returned records is undefined.

You cannot call the **MoveFirst** or **MovePrev** member function with a forward-only scrolling snapshot.

To move the position of the current record in a recordset object a specific number of records forward or backward, call **Move**.

For more information about finding records, see the article "DAO Recordset: Recordset Navigation" in *Programming with MFC*. For related information, see the topics "Move Method" and "MoveFirst, MoveLast, MoveNext, MovePrevious Methods" in DAO Help.

See Also **CDaoRecordset::Move, CDaoRecordset::MoveFirst, CDaoRecordset::MoveLast, CDaoRecordset::MoveNext**

CDaoRecordset::Open

virtual void Open(int *nOpenType* **= AFX_DAO_USE_DEFAULT_TYPE,**
   LPCTSTR *lpszSQL* **= NULL, int** *nOptions* **= 0);**
   throw(CDaoException, CMemoryException);
virtual void Open(CDaoTableDef* *pTableDef*, **int** *nOpenType* **= dbOpenTable, int** *nOptions* **= 0);**
   throw(CDaoException, CMemoryException);
virtual void Open(CDaoQueryDef* *pQueryDef*,
   int *nOpenType* **= dbOpenDynaset, int** *nOptions* **= 0);**
   throw(CDaoException, CMemoryException);

Parameters

nOpenType   One of the following values:

- **dbOpenDynaset**   A dynaset-type recordset with bidirectional scrolling. This is the default.

- **dbOpenTable**   A table-type recordset with bidirectional scrolling.

- **dbOpenSnapshot**   A snapshot-type recordset with bidirectional scrolling.

lpszSQL   A string pointer containing one of the following:

- A **NULL** pointer.

- The name of one or more tabledefs and/or querydefs (comma-separated).

- An SQL **SELECT** statement (optionally with an SQL **WHERE** or **ORDER BY** clause).

- A pass-through query.

nOptions   One or more of the options listed below. The default value is 0. Possible values are as follows:

- **dbAppendOnly**   You can only append new records (dynaset-type recordset only). This option means literally that records may only be appended. The MFC ODBC database classes have an append-only option that allows records to be retrieved and appended.

- **dbForwardOnly**   The recordset is a forward-only scrolling snapshot.

- **dbSeeChanges**   Generate an exception if another user is changing data you are editing.

- **dbDenyWrite**   Other users cannot modify or add records.

- **dbDenyRead**   Other users cannot view records (table-type recordset only).

- **dbReadOnly**   You can only view records; other users can modify them.

- **dbInconsistent**   Inconsistent updates are allowed (dynaset-type recordset only).

- **dbConsistent**   Only consistent updates are allowed (dynaset-type recordset only).

  Note The constants **dbConsistent** and **dbInconsistent** are mutually exclusive. You can use one or the other, but not both in a given instance of **Open**.

pTableDef   A pointer to a **CDaoTableDef** object. This version is valid only for table-type recordsets. When using this option, the **CDaoDatabase** pointer used to construct the **CDaoRecordset** is not used; rather, the database in which the tabledef resides is used.

pQueryDef   A pointer to a **CDaoQueryDef** object. This version is valid only for dynaset-type and snapshot-type recordsets. When using this option, the **CDaoDatabase** pointer used to construct the **CDaoRecordset** is not used; rather, the database in which the querydef resides is used.

Remarks

You must call this member function to retrieve the records for the recordset. Before calling **Open**, you must construct the recordset object. There are several ways to do this:

- When you construct the recordset object, pass a pointer to a **CDaoDatabase** object that is already open.

- When you construct the recordset object, pass a pointer to a **CDaoDatabase** object that is not open. The recordset opens a **CDaoDatabase** object, but will not close it when the recordset object closes.

- When you construct the recordset object, pass a **NULL** pointer. The recordset object calls **GetDefaultDBName** to get the name of the Microsoft Access .MDB file to open. The recordset then opens a **CDaoDatabase** object and keeps it open as long as the recordset is open. When you call **Close** on the recordset, the **CDaoDatabase** object is also closed.

  Note When the recordset opens the **CDaoDatabase** object, it opens the data source with nonexclusive access.

For the version of **Open** that uses the *lpszSQL* parameter, once the recordset is open you can retrieve records in one of several ways. The first option is to have DFX functions in your **DoFieldExchange**. The second option is to use dynamic binding by calling the **GetFieldValue** member function. These options can be implemented separately or in combination. If they are combined, you will have to pass in the SQL statement yourself on the call to **Open**. For more information about dynamic binding, see the article "DAO Recordset: Binding Records Dynamically" in *Programming with MFC*.

When you use the second version of **Open** where you pass in a **CDaoTableDef** object, the resulting columns will be available for you to bind via **DoFieldExchange** and the DFX mechanism, and/or bind dynamically via **GetFieldValue**.

Note   You can only call **Open** using a **CDaoTableDef** object for table-type recordsets.

When you use the third version of **Open** where you pass in a **CDaoQueryDef** object, that query will be executed, and the resulting columns will be available for you to bind via **DoFieldExchange** and the DFX mechanism, and/or bind dynamically via **GetFieldValue**.

Note   You can only call **Open** using a **CDaoQueryDef** object for dynaset-type and snapshot-type recordsets.

For the first version of **Open** that uses the *lpszSQL* parameter, records are selected based on criteria shown in the following table.

Value of the *lpszSQL* parameter	Records selected are determined by	Example
NULL	The string returned by **GetDefaultSQL**.	
A comma-separated list of one or more tabledefs and/or querydef names.	All columns represented in the **DoFieldExchange**.	`"Customer"`
SELECT column-list **FROM** table-list	The specified columns from the specified tabledef(s) and/or querydef(s).	`"SELECT CustId, CustName FROM Customer"`

The usual procedure is to pass **NULL** to **Open**; in that case, **Open** calls **GetDefaultSQL**, an overridable member function that ClassWizard generates when creating a **CDaoRecordset**-derived class. This value gives the tabledef(s) and/or querydef name(s) you specified in ClassWizard. You can instead specify other information in the *lpszSQL* parameter.

Whatever you pass, **Open** constructs a final SQL string for the query (the string may have SQL **WHERE** and **ORDER BY** clauses appended to the *lpszSQL* string you passed) and then executes the query. You can examine the constructed string by calling **GetSQL** after calling **Open**.

The field data members of your recordset class are bound to the columns of the data selected. If any records are returned, the first record becomes the current record.

If you want to set options for the recordset, such as a filter or sort, set **m_strSort** or **m_strFilter** after you construct the recordset object but before you call **Open**. If you want to refresh the records in the recordset after the recordset is already open, call **Requery**.

If you call **Open** on a dynaset-type or snapshot-type recordset, or if the data source refers to an SQL statement or a tabledef that represents an attached table, you cannot use **dbOpenTable** for the type argument; if you do, MFC throws an exception. To determine whether a tabledef object represents an attached table, create a **CDaoTableDef** object and call its **GetConnect** member function.

Use the **dbSeeChanges** flag if you wish to trap changes made by another user or another program on your machine when you are editing or deleting the same record. For example, if two users start editing the same record, the first user to call the **Update** member function succeeds. When **Update** is called by the second user, a **CDaoException** is thrown. Similarly, if the second user tries to call **Delete** to delete the record, and it has already been changed by the first user, a **CDaoException** occurs.

Typically, if the user gets this **CDaoException** while updating, your code should refresh the contents of the fields and retrieve the newly modified values. If the exception occurs in the process of deleting, your code could display the new record data to the user and a message indicating that the data has recently changed. At this point, your code can request a confirmation that the user still wants to delete the record.

Tip Use the forward-only scrolling option (**dbForwardOnly**) to improve performance when your application makes a single pass through a recordset opened from an ODBC data source.

For more information about opening recordsets, see the articles "DAO Recordset: Creating Recordsets" and "DAO: Creating, Opening, and Closing DAO Objects" in *Programming with MFC*. For related information, see the topic "OpenRecordset Method" in DAO Help.

See Also   **CDaoRecordset::Close, CDaoRecordset::CDaoRecordset**

CDaoRecordset::Requery

virtual void Requery( );
  throw(CDaoException, CMemoryException);

Remarks

Call this member function to rebuild (refresh) a recordset. If any records are returned, the first record becomes the current record.

In order for the recordset to reflect the additions and deletions that you or other users are making to the data source, you must rebuild the recordset by calling **Requery**. If the recordset is a dynaset, it automatically reflects updates that you or other users make to its existing records (but not additions). If the recordset is a snapshot, you must call **Requery** to reflect edits by other users as well as additions and deletions.

For either a dynaset or a snapshot, call **Requery** any time you want to rebuild the recordset using parameter values. Set the new filter or sort by setting **m_strFilter** and **m_strSort** before calling **Requery**. Set new parameters by assigning new values to parameter data members before calling **Requery**.

If the attempt to rebuild the recordset fails, the recordset is closed. Before you call **Requery**, you can determine whether the recordset can be requeried by calling the **CanRestart** member function. **CanRestart** does not guarantee that **Requery** will succeed.

Caution Call **Requery** only after you have called **Open**.

You can't call **Requery** on a dynaset-type or snapshot-type recordset if calling **CanRestart** returns 0, nor can you use it on a table-type recordset.

If both **IsBOF** and **IsEOF** return nonzero after you call **Requery**, the query didn't return any records and the recordset will contain no data.

For more information about updating data, see the article "DAO Recordset: Recordset Operations" in *Programming with MFC*. For related information, see the topic "Requery Method" in DAO Help.

See Also **CDaoRecordset::CanRestart**

CDaoRecordset::Seek

BOOL Seek(LPCTSTR *lpszComparison*, **COleVariant*** *pKey1*,
  COleVariant* *pKey2* = **NULL**, **COleVariant*** *pKey3* = **NULL**);
  throw(CDaoException, CMemoryException);
BOOL Seek (LPCTSTR *lpszComparison*, **COleVariant*** *pKeyArray*, **WORD** *nKeys*);
  throw(CDaoException, CMemoryException);

Return Value

Nonzero if matching records are found, otherwise 0.

Parameters

lpszComparison One of the following string expressions: "<", "<=", "=", ">=", or ">".

pKey1 A pointer to a **COleVariant** whose value corresponds to the first field in the index. Required.

pKey2 A pointer to a **COleVariant** whose value corresponds to the second field in the index, if any. Defaults to **NULL**.

pKey3 A pointer to a **COleVariant** whose value corresponds to the third field in the index, if any. Defaults to **NULL**.

pKeyArray A pointer to an array of variants. The array size corresponds to the number of fields in the index.

nKeys An integer corresponding to the size of the array, which is the number of fields in the index.

Remarks

Call this member function to locate the record in an indexed table-type recordset object that satisfies the specified criteria for the current index and make that record the current record. Use the second (array) version of **Seek** to handle indexes of four fields or more.

Seek enables high-performance index searching on table-type recordsets. You must set the current index by calling **SetCurrentIndex** before calling **Seek**. If the index identifies a nonunique key field or fields, **Seek** locates the first record that satisfies the criteria. If you do not set an index, an exception is thrown.

When you call **Seek**, you pass one or more key values and a comparison operator ("<", "<=", "=", ">=", or ">"). **Seek** searches through the specified key fields and locates the first record that satisfies the criteria specified by *lpszComparison* and *pKey1*. Once found, **Seek** returns nonzero, and makes that record current. If **Seek** fails to locate a match, **Seek** returns nonzero, and the current record is undefined. When using DAO directly, you must explicitly check the NoMatch property.

If *lpszComparison* is "=", ">=", or ">", **Seek** starts at the beginning of the index. If *lpszComparison* is "<" or "<=", **Seek** starts at the end of the index and searches backward unless there are duplicate index entries at the end. In this case, **Seek** starts at an arbitrary entry among the duplicate index entries at the end of the index.

There does not have to be a current record when you use **Seek**.

To locate a record in a dynaset-type or snapshot-type recordset that satisfies a specific condition, use the Find operations. To include all records, not just those that satisfy a specific condition, use the Move operations to move from record to record.

You cannot call **Seek** on an attached table of any type because attached tables must be opened as dynaset-type or snapshot-type recordsets. However, if you call **CDaoDatabase::Open** to directly open an installable ISAM database, you can call **Seek** on tables in that database, although the performance may be slow.

For more information about finding records, see the article "DAO Recordset: Recordset Navigation" in *Programming with MFC*. For related information, see the topic "Seek Method" in DAO Help.

See Also   CDaoRecordset::FindFirst, CDaoRecordset::FindLast, CDaoRecordset::FindNext, CDaoRecordset::FindPrev, CDaoRecordset::Move, CDaoRecordset::MoveFirst, CDaoRecordset::MoveLast, CDaoRecordset::MoveNext, CDaoRecordset::MovePrev

CDaoRecordset::SetAbsolutePosition

void SetAbsolutePosition(long *lPosition* **);**
   throw(CDaoException, CMemoryException);

Parameters

   lPosition   Corresponds to the ordinal position of the current record in the recordset.

Remarks

   Sets the relative record number of a recordset object's current record. Calling **SetAbsolutePosition** enables you to position the current record pointer to a specific record based on its ordinal position in a dynaset-type or snapshot-type recordset. You can also determine the current record number by calling **GetAbsolutePosition**.

   Note   This member function is valid only for dynaset-type and snapshot-type recordsets.

   The AbsolutePosition property value of the underlying DAO object is zero-based; a setting of 0 refers to the first record in the recordset. Setting a value greater than the number of populated records causes MFC to throw an exception. You can determine the number of populated records in the recordset by calling the **GetRecordCount** member function.

   If there is no current record, as when there are no records in the recordset, −1 is returned. If the current record is deleted, the AbsolutePosition property value is not defined, and MFC throws an exception if it is referenced. New records are added to the end of the sequence.

   Note   This property is not intended to be used as a surrogate record number. Bookmarks are still the recommended way of retaining and returning to a given position and are the only way to position the current record across all types of recordset objects that support bookmarks. In particular, the position of a given record changes when record(s) preceding it are deleted. There is also no assurance that a given record will have the same absolute position if the recordset is re-created again because the order of individual records within a recordset is not guaranteed unless it is created with an SQL statement using an **ORDER BY** clause.

   For more information about finding records, see the article "DAO Recordset: Recordset Navigation" in *Programming with MFC*. For related information, see the topic "AbsolutePosition Property" in DAO Help.

   See Also   **CDaoRecordset::GetAbsolutePosition**

CDaoRecordset::SetBookmark

   void SetBookmark(COleVariant *varBookmark* **);**
      throw(CDaoException, CMemoryException);

Parameters

   varBookmark   A **COleVariant** object containing the bookmark value for a specific record.

Remarks

Call this member function to position the recordset on the record containing the specified bookmark. When a recordset object is created or opened, each of its records already has a unique bookmark. You can retrieve the bookmark for the current record by calling **GetBookmark** and saving the value to a **COleVariant** object. You can later return to that record by calling **SetBookmark** using the saved bookmark value.

For more information about finding records, see the article "DAO Recordset: Recordset Navigation" in *Programming with MFC*. For related information, see the topics "Bookmark Property" and "Bookmarkable Property" in DAO Help.

See Also   **CDaoRecordset::GetBookmark**

CDaoRecordset::SetCacheSize

void SetCacheSize(long *lSize* **);**
   throw(CDaoException, CMemoryException);

Parameters

lSize   Specifies the number of records. A typical value is 100. A setting of 0 turns off caching. The setting must be between 5 and 1200 records. The cache may use a considerable amount of memory.

Remarks

Call this member function to set the number of records to be cached. A cache is a space in local memory that holds the data most recently retrieved from the server in the event that the data will be requested again while the application is running. Data caching improves the performance of an application that retrieves data from a remote server through dynaset-type recordset objects. When data is requested, the Microsoft Jet database engine checks the cache for the requested data first rather than retrieving it from the server, which takes more time. Data that does not come from an ODBC data source is not saved in the cache.

Any ODBC data source, such as an attached table, can have a local cache. To create the cache, open a recordset object from the remote data source, call the **SetCacheSize** and **SetCacheStart** member functions, and then call the **FillCache** member function or step through the records by using one of the Move operations. The *lSize* parameter of the **SetCacheSize** member function can be based on the number of records your application can work with at one time. For example, if you are using a recordset as the source of the data to be displayed on screen, you could pass the **SetCacheSize** *lSize* parameter as 20 to display 20 records at one time.

For more information about finding records, see the article "DAO Recordset: Recordset Navigation" in *Programming with MFC*. For related information, see the topic "CacheSize, CacheStart Properties" in DAO Help.

See Also   **CDaoRecordset::FillCache, CDaoRecordset::GetCacheSize, CDaoRecordset::GetCacheStart, CDaoRecordset::SetCacheStart**

CDaoRecordset::SetCacheStart

void SetCacheStart(COleVariant *varBookmark* **);**
   throw(CDaoException, CMemoryException);

Parameters

varBookmark   A **COleVariant** that specifies the bookmark of the first record in the recordset to be cached.

Remarks

Call this member function to specify the bookmark of the first record in the recordset to be cached. You can use the bookmark value of any record for the *varBookmark* parameter of the **SetCacheStart** member function. Make the record you want to start the cache with the current record, establish a bookmark for that record using **SetBookmark**, and pass the bookmark value as the parameter for the **SetCacheStart** member function.

The Microsoft Jet database engine requests records within the cache range from the cache, and it requests records outside the cache range from the server.

Records retrieved from the cache do not reflect changes made concurrently to the source data by other users.

To force an update of all the cached data, pass the *lSize* parameter of **SetCacheSize** as 0, call **SetCacheSize** again with the size of the cache you originally requested, and then call the **FillCache** member function.

For more information about finding records, see the article "DAO Recordset: Recordset Navigation" in *Programming with MFC*. For related information, see the topic "CacheSize, CacheStart Properties" in DAO Help.

See Also   **CDaoRecordset::FillCache, CDaoRecordset::GetCacheSize, CDaoRecordset::GetCacheStart, CDaoRecordset::SetCacheSize**

CDaoRecordset::SetCurrentIndex

void SetCurrentIndex(LPCTSTR *lpszIndex* **);**
   throw(CDaoException, CMemoryException);

Parameters

lpszIndex   A pointer containing the name of the index to be set.

Remarks

Call this member function to set an index on a table-type recordset. Records in base tables are not stored in any particular order. Setting an index changes the order of records returned from the database, but it does not affect the order in which the records are stored. The specified index must already be defined. If you try to use an index object that does not exist, or if the index is not set when you call **Seek**, MFC throws an exception.

You can create a new index for the table by calling **CDaoTableDef::CreateIndex** and appending the new index to the Indexes collection of the underlying tabledef by calling **CDaoTableDef::Append**, and then reopening the recordset.

Records returned from a table-type recordset can be ordered only by the indexes defined for the underlying tabledef. To sort records in some other order, you can open a dynaset-type or snapshot-type recordset using an SQL **ORDER BY** clause stored in **CDaoRecordset::m_strSort**.

For more information about finding records, see the article "DAO Recordset: Recordset Navigation" in *Programming with MFC*. For related information, see the topic "Index Object" and the definition of current index in DAO Help.

See Also   CDaoRecordset::GetCurrentIndex

CDaoRecordset::SetFieldDirty

void SetFieldDirty(void* *pv*, **BOOL** *bDirty* = **TRUE**);
   throw(CDaoException, CMemoryException);

Parameters

pv Contains the address of a field data member in the recordset or **NULL**. If **NULL**, all field data members in the recordset are flagged. (C++ **NULL** is not the same as Null in database terminology, which means "having no value.")

bDirty **TRUE** if the field data member is to be flagged as "dirty" (changed). Otherwise **FALSE** if the field data member is to be flagged as "clean" (unchanged).

Remarks

Call this member function to flag a field data member of the recordset as changed or as unchanged. Marking fields as unchanged ensures the field is not updated.

The framework marks changed field data members to ensure they will be written to the record on the data source by the DAO record field exchange (DFX) mechanism. Changing the value of a field generally sets the field dirty automatically, so you will seldom need to call **SetFieldDirty** yourself, but you might sometimes want to ensure that columns will be explicitly updated or inserted regardless of what value is in the field data member. The DFX mechanism also employs the use of **PSEUDO NULL**. For more information, see **CDaoFieldExchange::m_nOperation**.

If the double-buffering mechanism is not being used, then changing the value of the field does not automatically set the field as dirty. In this case, it will be necessary to explicity set the field as dirty. The flag contained in **m_bCheckCacheForDirtyFields** controls this automatic field checking.

Important   Call this member function only after you have called **Edit** or **AddNew**.

Using **NULL** for the first argument of the function will apply the function to all **outputColumns**, not **params** in **CDaoFieldExchange**. For instance, the call

```
SetFieldDirty( NULL );
```

will set only **outputColumns** to **NULL**. The value of **param** will be unaffected.

To work on a **param**, you must supply the actual address of the individual **param** you want to work on, such as:

```
SetFieldDirty( &m_strParam );
```

This means you cannot set all **params NULL**, as you can with **outputColumns**.

SetFieldDirty is implemented through **DoFieldExchange**.

For more information about record field exchange, see the articles "DAO Record Field Exchange (DFX)" and "DAO Recordset: Binding Records Dynamically" in *Programming with MFC*.

See Also   **CDaoRecordset::SetFieldNull**, **CDaoRecordset::SetFieldValue**

CDaoRecordset::SetFieldNull

void SetFieldNull(void* *pv*, **BOOL** *bNull* = **TRUE**);
 throw(CDaoException, CMemoryException);

Parameters

pv   Contains the address of a field data member in the recordset or **NULL**. If **NULL**, all field data members in the recordset are flagged. (C++ **NULL** is not the same as Null in database terminology, which means "having no value.")

bNull   Nonzero if the field data member is to be flagged as having no value (Null). Otherwise 0 if the field data member is to be flagged as non-Null.

Remarks

Call this member function to flag a field data member of the recordset as Null (specifically having no value) or as non-Null. The first version of **SetFieldNull** is used for fields bound in the **DoFieldExchange** mechanism. If you choose to bind your fields dynamically, you must use either the second or third version of this member function. You can mix the calls as necessary.

When you add a new record to a recordset, all field data members are initially set to a Null value and flagged as "dirty" (changed). When you retrieve a record from a data source, its columns either already have values or are Null. If it is not appropriate to make a field Null, a **CDaoException** is thrown.

If you are using the double-buffering mechanism, for example, if you specifically wish to designate a field of the current record as not having a value, call **SetFieldNull** with *bNull* set to **TRUE** to flag it as Null. If a field was previously marked Null and you now want to give it a value, simply set its new value. You do not have to remove the Null flag with **SetFieldNull**. To determine whether the field is allowed to be Null, call **IsFieldNullable**.

If you are not using the double-buffering mechanism, then changing the value of the field does not automatically set the field as dirty and non-Null. You must specifically set the fields dirty and non-Null. The flag contained in **m_bCheckCacheForDirtyFields** controls this automatic field checking.

The DFX mechanism employs the use of **PSEUDO NULL**. For more information, see **CDaoFieldExchange::m_nOperation**.

Important Call this member function only after you have called **Edit** or **AddNew**.

Using **NULL** for the first argument of the function will apply the function only to **outputColumns**, not **params** in **CDaoFieldExchange**. For instance, the call

```
SetFieldNull( NULL );
```

will set only **outputColumns** to **NULL**. The value of **param** will be unaffected.

For more information about record field exchange, see the articles "DAO Record Field Exchange (DFX)" and "DAO Recordset: Binding Records Dynamically" in *Programming with MFC*.

See Also CDaoRecordset::SetParamValue

CDaoRecordset::SetFieldValue

void SetFieldValue(LPCTSTR *lpszName*, **const COleVariant&** *varValue* **);**
   throw(CDaoException, CMemoryException);
void SetFieldValue(int *nOrdinal*, **const COleVariant&** *varValue* **);**
   throw(CDaoException, CMemoryException);

Parameters

lpszName   A pointer to a string containing the name of a field.

varValue   A reference to a **COleVariant** object containing the value of the field's contents.

nOrdinal   An integer that represents the ordinal position of the field in the recordset's Fields collection (zero-based).

Remarks

Call this member function to set the value of a field, either by ordinal position or by changing the value of the string. Use **SetFieldValue** and **GetFieldValue** to dynamically bind fields at run time rather than statically binding columns using the **DoFieldExchange** mechanism.

For more information about record field exchange, see the articles "DAO Record Field Exchange (DFX)" and "DAO Recordset: Binding Records Dynamically" in *Programming with MFC*. For related information, see the topics "Field Object" and "Value Property" in DAO Help.

See Also **CDaoRecordset::GetFieldValue**, **CDaoRecordset::m_nParams**, **CDaoRecordset::SetFieldValueNull**

CDaoRecordSet::SetFieldValueNull

> **void SetFieldValueNull(short** *nIndex* **);**
>   **throw(CDaoException, CMemoryException);**
> **void SetFieldValueNull(LPCTSTR** *lpszName* **);**
>   **throw(CDaoException, CMemoryException);**

Parameters

nIndex   The index of the field in the recordset, for lookup by zero-based index.

lpszName   The name of the field in the recordset, for lookup by name.

Remarks

Call this member function to set the field to a Null value. C++ **NULL** is not the same as Null, which, in database terminology, means "having no value."

For more information about record field exchange, see the articles "DAO Record Field Exchange (DFX)" and "DAO Recordset: Binding Records Dynamically" in *Programming with MFC*. For related information, see the topics "Field Object" and "Value Property" in DAO Help.

See Also **CDaoRecordset::SetFieldValue**

CDaoRecordset::SetLockingMode

> **void SetLockingMode(BOOL** *bPessimistic* **);**
>   **throw(CDaoException, CMemoryException);**

Parameters

bPessimistic   A flag that indicates the type of locking.

Remarks

Call this member function to set the type of locking for the recordset. When pessimistic locking is in effect, the 2K page containing the record you are editing is locked as soon as you call the **Edit** member function. The page is unlocked when you call the **Update** or **Close** member function or any of the Move or Find operations.

When optimistic locking is in effect, the 2K page containing the record is locked only while the record is being updated with the **Update** member function.

If a page is locked, no other user can edit records on the same page. If you call **SetLockingMode** and pass a nonzero value and another user already has the page locked, an exception is thrown when you call **Edit**. Other users can read data from locked pages.

If you call **SetLockingMode** with a zero value and later call **Update** while the page is locked by another user, an exception occurs. To see the changes made to your record by another user (and lose your changes), call the **SetBookmark** member function with the bookmark value of the current record.

When working with ODBC data sources, the locking mode is always optimistic.

For more information about updating data, see the article "DAO Recordset: Recordset Operations" in *Programming with MFC*. For related information, see the topics "LockEdits Property," "EditMode Property," and "Locking Behavior in Multiuser Applications" in DAO Help.

See Also   **CDaoRecordset::GetLockingMode**

CDaoRecordset::SetParamValue

virtual void SetParamValue(int *nIndex*, **const COleVariant&** *var* **);**
   throw(CDaoException, CMemoryException);
virtual void SetParamValue(LPCTSTR *lpszName*, **const COleVariant&** *var* **);**
   throw(CDaoException, CMemoryException);

Parameters

nIndex   The numerical position of the parameter in the querydef's Parameters collection.

var   The value to set; see "Remarks."

lpszName   The name of the parameter whose value you want to set.

Remarks

Call this member function to set the value of a parameter in the recordset at run time. The parameter must already have been established as part of the recordset's SQL string. You can access the parameter either by name or by its index position in the collection.

Specify the value to set as a **COleVariant** object. For information about setting the desired value and type in your **COleVariant** object, see class **COleVariant**.

For more information about updating data, see the article "DAO Recordset: Recordset Operations" in *Programming with MFC*. For related information, see the topic "Parameter Object" in DAO Help.

See Also   **CDaoRecordset::GetParamValue, CDaoRecordset::m_nParams, CDaoRecordset::SetParamValueNull**

CDaoRecordSet::SetParamValueNull

> **void SetParamValueNull(short** *nIndex* **);**
>   **throw(CDaoException, CMemoryException);**
> **void SetParamValueNull(LPCTSTR** *lpszName* **);**
>   **throw(CDaoException, CMemoryException);**

Parameters

nIndex   The index of the field in the recordset, for lookup by zero-based index.

lpszName   The name of the field in the recordset, for lookup by name.

Remarks

Call this member function to set the parameter to a Null value. C++ **NULL** is not the same as Null, which, in database terminology, means "having no value."

For more information about updating data, see the article "DAO Recordset: Recordset Operations" in *Programming with MFC*. For related information, see the topic "Parameter Object" in DAO Help.

CDaoRecordset::SetPercentPosition

> **void SetPercentPosition(float** *fPosition* **);**
>   **throw(CDaoException, CMemoryException);**

Parameters

fPosition   A number between 0 and 100.

Remarks

Call this member function to set a value that changes the approximate location of the current record in the recordset object based on a percentage of the records in the recordset.

When working with a dynaset-type or snapshot-type recordset, first populate the recordset by moving to the last record before you call **SetPercentPosition**. If you call **SetPercentPosition** before fully populating the recordset, the amount of movement is relative to the number of records accessed as indicated by the value of **GetRecordCount**. You can move to the last record by calling **MoveLast**.

Once you call **SetPercentPosition**, the record at the approximate position corresponding to that value becomes current.

Note Calling **SetPercentPosition** to move the current record to a specific record in a recordset is not recommended. Call the **SetBookmark** member function instead.

For more information about navigating in recordsets, see the article "DAO Recordset: Recordset Navigation" in *Programming with MFC*. For related information, see the topic "PercentPosition Property" in DAO Help.

See Also   **CDaoRecordset::GetPercentPosition**

CDaoRecordset::Update

virtual void Update( );
    throw(CDaoException, CMemoryException);

Remarks

Call this member function after a call to the **AddNew** or **Edit** member function. This call is required to complete the **AddNew** or **Edit** operation.

Both **AddNew** and **Edit** prepare an edit buffer in which the added or edited data is placed for saving to the data source. **Update** saves the data. Only those fields marked or detected as changed are updated.

If the data source supports transactions, you can make the **Update** call (and its corresponding **AddNew** or **Edit** call) part of a transaction. For more information about transactions, see the article "DAO Workspace: Managing Transactions" in *Programming with MFC*.

Caution   If you call **Update** without first calling either **AddNew** or **Edit**, **Update** throws a **CDaoException**. If you call **AddNew** or **Edit**, you must call **Update** before you call **MoveNext** or close either the recordset or the data source connection. Otherwise, your changes are lost without notification.

When the recordset object is pessimistically locked in a multiuser environment, the record remains locked from the time **Edit** is used until the updating is complete. If the recordset is optimistically locked, the record is locked and compared with the pre-edited record just before it is updated in the database. If the record has changed since you called **Edit**, the **Update** operation fails and MFC throws an exception. You can change the locking mode with **SetLockingMode**.

Note Optimistic locking is always used on external database formats, such as ODBC and installable ISAM.

For more information about updating data, see the article "DAO Recordset: Recordset Operations" in *Programming with MFC*. For related information, see the topics "AddNew Method," "CancelUpdate Method," "Delete Method," "LastModified Property," "Update Method," and "EditMode Property" in DAO Help.

See Also **CDaoRecordset::AddNew**, **CDaoRecordset::CancelUpdate**, **CDaoRecordset::Delete**, **CDaoRecordset::Edit**, **CDaoRecordset::CanTransact**

Data Members

CDaoRecordset::m_bCheckCacheForDirtyFields

Remarks

Contains a flag indicating whether cached fields are automatically marked as dirty (changed) and Null. The flag defaults to **TRUE**. The setting in this data member controls the entire double-buffering mechanism. If you set the flag to **TRUE**, you can turn off the caching on a field-by-field basis using the DFX mechanism. If you set the flag to **FALSE**, you must call **SetFieldDirty** and **SetFieldNull** yourself.

Set this data member before calling **Open**. This mechanism is primarily for ease-of-use. Performance may be slower because of the double-buffering of fields as changes are made.

For more information about binding records dynamically, see the article "DAO Recordset: Binding Records Dynamically" in *Programming with MFC*.

See Also **CDaoRecordset::SetFieldNull**, **CDaoRecordset::IsFieldNull**, **CDaoRecordset::IsFieldDirty**, **CDaoRecordset::SetFieldDirty**

CDaoRecordset::m_nParams

Remarks

Contains the number of parameter data members in the recordset class — the number of parameters passed with the recordset's query. If your recordset class has any parameter data members, the constructor for the class must initialize **m_nParams** with the correct number. The value of **m_nParams** defaults to 0. If you add parameter data members — which you must do manually — you must also manually add an initialization in the class constructor to reflect the number of parameters (which must be at least as large as the number of '?' placeholders in your **m_strFilter** or **m_strSort** string).

The framework uses this number when it parameterizes the recordset's query.

Important This number must correspond to the number of "params" registered in **DoFieldExchange** after a call to **SetFieldType** with the parameter **CFieldExchange::param**.

For more information about selecting records, see the article "DAO Queries: Filtering and Parameterizing Queries" in *Programming with MFC*. For related information, see the topic "Parameter Object" in DAO Help.

CDaoRecordset::m_pDAORecordset

Remarks

Contains a pointer to the OLE interface for the DAO recordset object underlying the **CDaoRecordset** object. Use this pointer if you need to access the DAO interface directly.

For more information about accessing underlying DAO objects, see the article "DAO: Obtaining Information About DAO Objects" in *Programming with MFC*. For related information, see the topic "Recordset Object" in DAO Help.

See Also   **CDaoRecordset::m_pDatabase**

CDaoRecordset::m_pDatabase

Remarks

Contains a pointer to the **CDaoDatabase** object through which the recordset is connected to a data source. This variable is set in two ways. Typically, you pass a pointer to an already open **CDaoDatabase** object when you construct the recordset object. If you pass **NULL** instead, **CDaoRecordset** creates a **CDaoDatabase** object for you and opens it. In either case, **CDaoRecordset** stores the pointer in this variable.

Normally you will not directly need to use the pointer stored in **m_pDatabase**. If you write your own extensions to **CDaoRecordset**, however, you might need to use the pointer. For example, you might need the pointer if you throw your own **CDaoException**(s).

For more information about accessing underlying DAO objects, see the article "DAO: Obtaining Information About DAO Objects" in *Programming with MFC*. For related information, see the topic "Database Object" in DAO Help.

See Also   **CDaoRecordset::m_pDAORecordset**

CDaoRecordset::m_strFilter

Remarks

Contains a string that is used to construct the **WHERE** clause of an SQL statement. It does not include the reserved word **WHERE** to filter the recordset. The use of this data member is not applicable to table-type recordsets. The use of **m_strFilter** has no effect when opening a recordset using a **CDaoQueryDef** pointer.

Use the U.S. date format (month-day-year) when you filter fields containing dates, even if you are not using the U.S. version of the Microsoft Jet database engine; otherwise, the data may not be filtered as you expect.

For more information about selecting records, see the article "DAO Queries: Filtering and Parameterizing Queries" in *Programming with MFC*. For related information, see the topic "Filter Property" in DAO Help.

See Also   **CDaoRecordset::m_strSort**

CDaoRecordset::m_strSort

Remarks

Contains a string containing the **ORDER BY** clause of an SQL statement without the reserved words **ORDER BY**. You can sort on dynaset- and snapshot-type recordset objects.

You cannot sort table-type recordset objects. To determine the sort order of a table-type recordset, call **SetCurrentIndex**.

The use of **m_strSort** has no effect when opening a recordset using a **CDaoQueryDef** pointer.

For more information about selecting records, see the article "DAO Queries: Filtering and Parameterizing Queries" in *Programming with MFC*. For related information, see the topic "Sort Property" in DAO Help.

See Also   **CDaoRecordset::m_strFilter**

CDaoRecordView

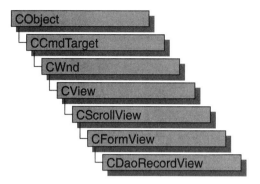

A **CDaoRecordView** object is a view that displays database records in controls. The view is a form view directly connected to a **CDaoRecordset** object. The view is created from a dialog template resource and displays the fields of the **CDaoRecordset** object in the dialog template's controls. The **CDaoRecordView** object uses dialog data exchange (DDX) and DAO record field exchange (DFX) to automate the movement of data between the controls on the form and the fields of the recordset. **CDaoRecordView** also supplies a default implementation for moving to the first, next, previous, or last record and an interface for updating the record currently in view.

Note The DAO database classes are distinct from the MFC database classes based on Open Database Connectivity (ODBC). All DAO database class names have the "CDao" prefix. You can still access ODBC data sources with the DAO classes; the DAO classes generally offer superior capabilities because they use the Microsoft Jet database engine.

The most common way to create your record view is with AppWizard. AppWizard creates both the record view class and its associated recordset class as part of your skeleton starter application.

If you simply need a single form, the AppWizard approach is easier. ClassWizard lets you decide to use a record view later in the development process. If you don't create the record view class with AppWizard, you can create it later with ClassWizard. Using ClassWizard to create a record view and a recordset separately and then connect them is the most flexible approach because it gives you more control in naming the recordset class and its .H/.CPP files. This approach also lets you have multiple record views on the same recordset class.

To make it easy for end-users to move from record to record in the record view, AppWizard creates menu (and optionally toolbar) resources for moving to the first, next, previous, or last record. If you create a record view class with ClassWizard, you need to create these resources yourself with the menu and bitmap editors. For more information about these resources, see the articles "AppWizard: Database Support" and "ClassWizard: Creating a Database Form."

For information about the default implementation for moving from record to record, see **IsOnFirstRecord** and **IsOnLastRecord** and the article "Record Views: Using a Record View," which appplies to both **CRecordView** and **CDaoRecordView**.

CDaoRecordView keeps track of the user's position in the recordset so that the record view can update the user interface. When the user moves to either end of the recordset, the record view disables user interface objects — such as menu items or toolbar buttons— for moving further in the same direction.

For more information about declaring and using your record view and recordset classes, see the article "Designing and Creating a Record View." For more information about how record views work and how to use them, see the articles "Forms," "Record Views," and "Record Views: Using a Record View." All the articles mentioned above apply to both **CRecordView** and **CDaoRecordView**, and are found in *Programming with MFC*.

#include <afxdao.h>

See Also   **CDaoRecordset**, **CDaoTableDef**, **CDaoQueryDef**, **CDaoDatabase**, **CDaoWorkspace**, **CFormView**

Construction

CDaoRecordView	Constructs a **CDaoRecordView** object.

Attributes

OnGetRecordset	Returns a pointer to an object of a class derived from **CDaoRecordset**. ClassWizard overrides this function for you and creates the recordset if necessary.
IsOnLastRecord	Returns nonzero if the current record is the last record in the associated recordset.
IsOnFirstRecord	Returns nonzero if the current record is the first record in the associated recordset.

Operations

OnMove	If the current record has changed, updates it on the data source, then moves to the specified record (next, previous, first, or last).

Member Functions

CDaoRecordView::CDaoRecordView

CDaoRecordView(**LPCSTR** *lpszTemplateName*);
CDaoRecordView(**UINT** *nIDTemplate*);

Parameters

lpszTemplateName   Contains a null-terminated string that is the name of a dialog template resource.

nIDTemplate   Contains the ID number of a dialog template resource.

Remarks

When you create an object of a type derived from **CDaoRecordView**, call either form of the constructor to initialize the view object and identify the dialog resource on which the view is based. You can either identify the resource by name (pass a string as the argument to the constructor) or by its ID (pass an unsigned integer as the argument). Using a resource ID is recommended.

Note   Your derived class must supply its own constructor. In the constructor of your derived class, call the constructor **CDaoRecordView::CDaoRecordView** with the resource name or ID as an argument.

CDaoRecordView::OnInitialUpdate calls **CWnd::UpdateData**, which calls **CWnd::DoDataExchange**. This initial call to **DoDataExchange** connects **CDaoRecordView** controls (indirectly) to **CDaoRecordset** field data members created by ClassWizard. These data members cannot be used until after you call the base class **CFormView::OnInitialUpdate** member function.

Note   If you use ClassWizard, the wizard defines an **enum** value CDaoRecordView::IDD and specifies it in the member initialization list for the constructor where you see IDD_MYFORM.

```
CMyRecordView::CMyRecordView()

    : CDaoRecordView( IDD_MYFORM )
{
    //{{AFX_DATA_INIT( CMyRecordView )
        // NOTE: the ClassWizard will add member initialization here
    //}}AFX_DATA_INIT
    // Other construction code, such as data initialization
}
```

See Also   **CWnd::UpdateData**, **CWnd::DoDataExchange**

CDaoRecordView::IsOnFirstRecord

BOOL IsOnFirstRecord( );

Return Value

Nonzero if the current record is the first record in the recordset; otherwise 0.

Remarks

Call this member function to determine whether the current record is the first record in the recordset object associated with this record view. This function is useful for writing your own implementations of the default command update handlers written by ClassWizard.

If the user moves to the first record, the framework disables any user interface objects (for example, menu items or toolbar buttons) you have for moving to the first or the previous record.

See Also **CDaoRecordView::IsOnLastRecord**

CDaoRecordView::IsOnLastRecord

BOOL IsOnLastRecord( );

Return Value

Nonzero if the current record is the last record in the recordset; otherwise 0.

Remarks

Call this member function to determine whether the current record is the last record in the recordset object associated with this record view. This function is useful for writing your own implementations of the default command update handlers that ClassWizard writes to support a user interface for moving from record to record.

Caution   The result of this function is reliable except that the view may not be able to detect the end of the recordset until the user has moved past it. The user might have to move beyond the last record before the record view can tell that it must disable any user interface objects for moving to the next or last record. If the user moves past the last record and then moves back to the last record (or before it), the record view can track the user's position in the recordset and disable user interface objects correctly.

See Also **CDaoRecordView::IsOnFirstRecord**

CDaoRecordView::OnGetRecordset

virtual CDaoRecordset* OnGetRecordset( ) = 0;

Return Value

A pointer to a **CDaoRecordset**-derived object if the object was successfully created; otherwise a **NULL** pointer.

Remarks

Returns a pointer to the **CDaoRecordset**-derived object associated with the record view. You must override this member function to construct or obtain a recordset object and return a pointer to it. If you declare your record view class with ClassWizard, the wizard writes a default override for you. ClassWizard's default implementation returns the recordset pointer stored in the record view if one exists. If not, it constructs a recordset object of the type you specified with ClassWizard and calls its **Open** member function to open the table or run the query, and then returns a pointer to the object.

For more information and examples, see the article "Record Views: Using a Record View" in *Programming with MFC*.

See Also   **CDaoRecordset**, **CDaoRecordset::Open**

CDaoRecordView::OnMove

virtual BOOL OnMove(UINT *nIDMoveCommand* **);**

Return Value

Nonzero if the move was successful; otherwise 0 if the move request was denied.

Parameters

nIDMoveCommand   One of the following standard command ID values:

- **ID_RECORD_FIRST**   Move to the first record in the recordset.
- **ID_RECORD_LAST**   Move to the last record in the recordset.
- **ID_RECORD_NEXT**   Move to the next record in the recordset.
- **ID_RECORD_PREV**   Move to the previous record in the recordset.

Remarks

Call this member function to move to a different record in the recordset and display its fields in the controls of the record view. The default implementation calls the appropriate Move member function of the **CDaoRecordset** object associated with the record view.

By default, **OnMove** updates the current record on the data source if the user has changed it in the record view.

AppWizard creates a menu resource with First Record, Last Record, Next Record, and Previous Record menu items. If you select the Initial Toolbar option, AppWizard also creates a toolbar with buttons corresponding to these commands.

If you move past the last record in the recordset, the record view continues to display the last record. If you move backward past the first record, the record view continues to display the first record.

Caution Calling **OnMove** throws an exception if the recordset has no records. Call the appropriate user interface update handler function — **OnUpdateRecordFirst**, **OnUpdateRecordLast**, **OnUpdateRecordNext**, or **OnUpdateRecordPrev** — before the corresponding move operation to determine whether the recordset has any records. For information about the update handlers, see the article "AppWizard: Database Support" in *Programming with MFC*.

See Also **CDaoRecordset::Move**

CDaoTableDef

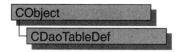

A **CDaoTableDef** object represents the stored definition of a base table or an attached table. Each DAO database object maintains a collection, called TableDefs, that contains all saved DAO tabledef objects.

You manipulate a table definition using a **CDaoTableDef** object. For example, you can:

- Examine the field and index structure of any local, attached, or external table in a database.

- Call the **SetConnect** and **SetSourceTableName** member functions for attached tables, and use the **RefreshLink** member function to update connections to attached tables.

- Call the **CanUpdate** member function to determine if you can edit field definitions in the table.

- Get or set validation conditions using the **GetValidationRule** and **SetValidationRule**, and the **GetValidationText** and **SetValidationText** member functions.

- Use the **Open** member function to create a table-, dynaset-, or snapshot-type **CDaoRecordset** object.

Note The DAO database classes are distinct from the MFC database classes based on Open Database Connectivity (ODBC). All DAO database class names have the "CDao" prefix. You can still access ODBC data sources with the DAO classes; the DAO classes generally offer superior capabilities because they are specific to the Microsoft Jet database engine.

Use tabledef objects either to work with an existing table or to create a new table:

1. In all cases, first construct a **CDaoTableDef** object, supplying the a pointer to a **CDaoDatabase** object to which the table belongs.

2. Then do the following, depending on what you want:
   - To use an existing saved table, call the tabledef object's **Open** member function, supplying the name of the saved table.

- To create a new table, call the tabledef object's **Create** member function, supplying the name of the table. Call **CreateField** and **CreateIndex** to add fields and indexes to the table.

- Call **Append** to save the table by appending it to the database's TableDefs collection. **Create** puts the tabledef into an open state, so after calling **Create** you do not call **Open**.

Tip The easiest way to create saved tables is to create them and store them in your database using Microsoft Access. Then you can open and use them in your MFC code.

To use the tabledef object you have opened or created, create and open a **CDaoRecordset** object, specifying the name of the tabledef with a **dbOpenTable** value in the *nOpenType* parameter.

To use a tabledef object to create a **CDaoRecordset** object, you typically create or open a tabledef as described above, then construct a recordset object, passing a pointer to your tabledef object when you call **CDaoRecordset::Open**. The tabledef you pass must be in an open state. For more information, see class **CDaoRecordset**.

When you finish using a tabledef object, call its **Close** member function; then destroy the tabledef object.

For more information on tabledefs, see the articles "DAO Tabledef" and "DAO Tabledef: Using Tabledefs" in *Programming with MFC*.

#include <afxdao.h>

See Also   CDaoDatabase, CDaoRecordset

Data Members

m_pDatabase	Source database for this table.
m_pDAOTableDef	A pointer to the DAO interface underlying the tabledef object.

Construction

Append	Adds a new table to the database.
CDaoTableDef	Constructs a **CDaoTableDef** object.
Close	Closes an open tabledef.
Create	Creates a table which can be added to the database using **Append**.
Open	Opens an existing tabledef stored in the database's TableDef's collection.

Attributes

CanUpdate	Returns nonzero if the table can be updated (you can modify the definition of fields or the table properties).
GetAttributes	Returns a value that indicates one or more characteristics of a **CDaoTableDef** object.
GetConnect	Returns a value that provides information about the source of a table.
GetDateCreated	Returns the date and time the base table underlying a **CDaoTableDef** object was created.
GetDateLastUpdated	Returns the date and time of the most recent change made to the design of the base table.
GetFieldCount	Returns a value that represents the number of fields in the table.
GetFieldInfo	Returns specific kinds of information about the fields in the table.
GetIndexCount	Returns the number of indexes for the table.
GetIndexInfo	Returns specific kinds of information about the indexes for the table.
GetName	Returns the user-defined name of the table.
GetRecordCount	Returns the number of records in the table.
GetSourceTableName	Returns a value that specifies the name of the attached table in the source database.
GetValidationRule	Returns a value that validates the data in a field as it is changed or added to a table.
GetValidationText	Returns a value that specifies the text of the message that your application displays if the value of a Field object does not satisfy the specified validation rule.
IsOpen	Returns nonzero if the table is open.
SetAttributes	Sets a value that indicates one or more characteristics of a **CDaoTableDef** object.
SetConnect	Sets a value that provides information about the source of a table.
SetName	Sets the name of the table.
SetSourceTableName	Sets a value that specifies the name of an attached table in the source database.
SetValidationRule	Sets a value that validates the data in a field as it is changed or added to a table.
SetValidationText	Sets a value that specifies the text of the message that your application displays if the value of a Field object does not satisfy the specified validation rule.

Operations	
CreateField	Called to create a field for a table.
CreateIndex	Called to create an index for a table.
DeleteField	Called to delete a field from a table.
DeleteIndex	Called to delete an index from a table.
RefreshLink	Updates the connection information for an attached table.

Member Functions

CDaoTableDef::Append

virtual void Append( );
    throw(CDaoException, CMemoryException);

Remarks

Call this member function after you call **Create** to create a new tabledef object to save the tabledef in the database. The function appends the object to the database's TableDefs collection. You can use the tabledef as a temporary object while defining it by not appending it, but if you want to save and use it, you must call **Append**.

Note If you attempt to append an unnamed tabledef (containing a null or empty string), MFC throws an exception.

For more information on tabledefs, see the articles "DAO Tabledef" and "DAO Tabledef: Using Tabledefs" in *Programming with MFC*. For related information, see the topic "Append Method" in DAO Help.

See Also **CDaoTableDef::Create**

CDaoTableDef::CanUpdate

BOOL CanUpdate( );
    throw(CDaoException, CMemoryException);

Return Value

Nonzero if the table structure (schema) can be modified (add or delete fields and indexes), otherwise 0.

Remarks

Call this member function to determine whether the definition of the table underlying a **CDaoTableDef** object can be changed.

By default, a newly created table underlying a **CDaoTableDef** object can be updated, and an attached table underlying a **CDaoTableDef** object cannot be updated. A **CDaoTableDef** object may be updatable, even if the resulting recordset is not updatable.

For more information on tabledefs, see the articles "DAO Tabledef" and "DAO Tabledef: Using Tabledefs" in *Programming with MFC*. For related information, see the topic "Updatable Property" in DAO Help.

See Also **CDaoTableDef::GetDateLastUpdated**

CDaoTableDef::CDaoTableDef

CDaoTableDef(CDaoDatabase* *pDatabase* **);**

Parameters
pDatabase   A pointer to a **CDaoDatabase** object.

Remarks
Constructs a **CDaoTableDef** object. After constructing the object, you must call the **Create** or **Open** member function. When you finish with the object, you must call its **Close** member function and destroy the **CDaoTableDef** object.

For more information on tabledefs, see the articles "DAO Tabledef" and "DAO Tabledef: Using Tabledefs" in *Programming with MFC*.

See Also   **CDaoTableDef::Open**, **CDaoTableDef::Close**, **CDaoTableDef::Create**, **CDaoDatabase**

CDaoTableDef::Close

virtual void Close( );
    throw(CDaoException, CMemoryException);

Remarks
Call this member function to close and release the tabledef object. Usually after calling **Close**, you delete the tabledef object if it was allocated with **new**.

You can call **Open** again after calling **Close**. This lets you reuse the tabledef object.

For more information on tabledefs, see the articles "DAO Tabledef" and "DAO Tabledef: Using Tabledefs" in *Programming with MFC*. For related information, see the topic "Close Method" in DAO Help.

See Also   **CDaoTableDef::Open**, **CDaoTableDef::Create**

CDaoTableDef::Create

virtual void Create(LPCTSTR *lpszName***, long** *lAttributes* **= 0, LPCTSTR** *lpszSrcTable* **= NULL,**
LPCTSTR *lpszConnect* **= NULL);**
throw(CDaoException, CMemoryException);

Parameters

lpszName   A pointer to a string containing the name of the table.

lAttributes   A value corresponding to characteristics of the table represented by the
tabledef object. You can use the bitwise-OR to combine any of the following
constants:

Constant	Description
dbAttachExclusive	For databases that use the Microsoft Jet database engine, indicates the table is an attached table opened for exclusive use.
dbAttachSavePWD	For databases that use the Microsoft Jet database engine, indicates that the user ID and password for the attached table are saved with the connection information.
dbSystemObject	Indicates the table is a system table provided by the Microsoft Jet database engine.
dbHiddenObject	Indicates the table is a hidden table provided by the Microsoft Jet database engine.
dbAttachedTable	Indicates the table is an attached table from a non-ODBC database, such as a Paradox database.
dbAttachedODBC	Indicates the table is an attached table from an ODBC database, such as Microsoft SQL Server.

lpszSrcTable   A pointer to a string containing the source table name. By default this
value is initialized as **NULL**.

lpszConnect   A pointer to a string containing the default connect string. By default
this value is initialized as **NULL**.

Remarks

Call this member function to create a new saved table. Once you have named the
tabledef, you can then call **Append** to save the tabledef in the database's TableDefs
collection. After calling **Append**, the tabledef is in an open state, and you can use it
to create a **CDaoRecordset** object.

For more information on tabledefs, see the articles "DAO Tabledef" and "DAO
Tabledef: Using Tabledefs" in *Programming with MFC*. For related information, see
the topic "CreateTableDef Method" in DAO Help.

See Also   **CDaoTableDef::Open**, **CDaoTableDef::Close**, **CDaoRecordset**

CDaoTableDef::CreateField

void CreateField(LPCTSTR *lpszName***, short** *nType,* **long** *lSize***, long** *lAttributes* **= 0);**
    throw(CDaoException, CMemoryException);
void CreateField(CDaoFieldInfo& *fieldinfo* **);**
    throw(CDaoException, CMemoryException);

Parameters

lpszName A pointer to a string expression specifying the name of this field.

nType A value indicating the data type of the field. The setting can be one of these values:

Type	Size (bytes)	Description
dbBoolean	1 byte	BOOL
dbByte	1	BYTE
dbInteger	2	int
dbLong	4	long
dbCurrency	8	Currency (**COleCurrency**)
dbSingle	4	float
dbDouble	8	double
dbDate	8	Date/Time (**COleDateTime**)
dbText	1–255	Text (**CString**)
dbLongBinary	0	Long Binary (OLE Object), **CLongBinary** or **CByteArray**
dbMemo	0	Memo (**CString**)

lSize A value that indicates the maximum size, in bytes, of a field that contains text, or the fixed size of a field that contains text or numeric values. The *lSize* parameter is ignored for all but text fields.

lAttributes A value corresponding to characteristics of the field and that can be combined using a bitwise-OR.

Constant	Description
dbFixedField	The field size is fixed (default for Numeric fields).
dbVariableField	The field size is variable (Text fields only).
dbAutoIncrField	The field value for new records is automatically incremented to a unique long integer that cannot be changed. Only supported for Microsoft Jet database tables.

Constant	Description
dbUpdatableField	The field value can be changes.
dbDescending	The field is sorted in descending (Z–A or 100–0) order (applies only to a Field object in a Fields collection of an Index object). If you omit this constant, the field is sorted in ascending (A–Z or 0–100) order (default).

fieldinfo A reference to a **CDaoFieldInfo** structure.

Remarks

Call this member function to add a field to the table. A **DAOField** (OLE) object is created and appended to the Fields collection of the **DAOTableDef** (OLE) object. Besides its use for examining object properties, you can also use **CDaoFieldInfo** to construct an input parameter for creating new fields in a tabledef. The first version of **CreateField** is simpler to use, but if you want finer control, you can use the second version of **CreateField**, which takes a **CDaoFieldInfo** parameter.

If you use the version of **CreateField** that takes a **CDaoFieldInfo** parameter, you must carefully set each of the following members of the **CDaoFieldInfo** structure:

- **m_strName**
- **m_nType**
- **m_lSize**
- **m_lAttributes**
- **m_bAllowZeroLength**

The remaining members of **CDaoFieldInfo** should be set to **0**, **FALSE**, or an empty string, as appropriate for the member, or a **CDaoException** may occur.

For more information on tabledefs, see the articles "DAO Tabledef" and "DAO Tabledef: Using Tabledefs" in *Programming with MFC*. For related information, see the topic "CreateField Method" in DAO Help.

See Also   **CDaoTableDef::DeleteField, CDaoTableDef::CreateIndex, CDaoTableDef::DeleteIndex**

CDaoTableDef::CreateIndex

void CreateIndex(CDaoIndexInfo& *indexinfo* **);**
   throw(CDaoException, CMemoryException);

Parameters

indexinfo A reference to a **CDaoIndexInfo** structure.

Remarks

Call this function to add an index to a table. Indexes specify the order of records accessed from database tables and whether or not duplicate records are accepted. Indexes also provide efficient access to data.

You do not have to create indexes for tables, but in large, unindexed tables, accessing a specific record or creating a recordset can take a long time. On the other hand, creating too many indexes slows down update, append, and delete operations as all indexes are automatically updated. Consider these factors as you decide which indexes to create.

The following members of the **CDaoIndexInfo** structure must be set:

- **m_strName**   A name must be supplied.

- **m_pFieldInfos**   Must point to an array of **CDaoIndexFieldInfo** structures.

- **m_nFields**   Must specify the number of fields in the array of **CDaoFieldInfo** structures.

The remaining members will be ignored if set to **FALSE**. In addition, the **m_lDistinctCount** member is ignored during creation of the index.

For more information on tabledefs, see the articles "DAO Tabledef" and "DAO Tabledef: Using Tabledefs" in *Programming with MFC*. For related information, see the topic "CreateIndex Method" in DAO Help.

See Also   **CDaoTableDef::DeleteIndex**, **CDaoTableDef::CreateField**, **CDaoTableDef::DeleteField**, **CDaoIndexInfo**

CDaoTableDef::DeleteField

void DeleteField(LPCTSTR *lpszName* **);**
 throw(CDaoException, CMemoryException);
void DeleteField(int *nIndex* **);**
 throw(CDaoException, CMemoryException);

Parameters

lpszName   A pointer to a string expression that is the name of an existing field.

nIndex   The index of the field in the table's zero-based Fields collection, for lookup by index.

Remarks

Call this member function to remove a field and make it inaccessible. You can use this member function on a new object that has not been appended to the database or when **CanUpdate** returns nonzero.

For more information on tabledefs, see the articles "DAO Tabledef" and "DAO Tabledef: Using Tabledefs" in *Programming with MFC*. For related information, see the topic "Delete Method" in DAO Help.

See Also   **CDaoTableDef::CreateField, CDaoTableDef::CreateIndex, CDaoTableDef::DeleteIndex**

CDaoTableDef::DeleteIndex

void DeleteIndex(LPCTSTR *lpszName* **);**
   throw(CDaoException, CMemoryException);
void DeleteIndex(int *nIndex* **);**
   throw(CDaoException, CMemoryException);

Parameters

lpszName   A pointer to a string expression that is the name of an existing index.

nIndex   The array index of the predefined index object in the database's zero-based TableDefs collection, for lookup by index.

Remarks

Call this member function to delete an index in an underlying table. You can use this member function on a new object that hasn't been appended to the database or when **CanUpdate** returns nonzero.

For more information on tabledefs, see the articles "DAO Tabledef" and "DAO Tabledef: Using Tabledefs" in *Programming with MFC*. For related information, see the topic "Delete Method" in DAO Help.

See Also   **CDaoTableDef::CreateIndex, CDaoTableDef::CreateField, CDaoTableDef::DeleteField**

CDaoTableDef::GetAttributes

long GetAttributes( );
   throw(CDaoException, CMemoryException);

Return Value

Returns a value that indicates one or more characteristics of a **CDaoTableDef** object.

Remarks

For a **CDaoTableDef** object, the return value specifies characteristics of the table represented by the **CDaoTableDef** object and can be a sum of these constants:

Constant	Description
dbAttachExclusive	For databases that use the Microsoft Jet database engine, indicates the table is an attached table opened for exclusive use.
dbAttachSavePWD	For databases that use the Microsoft Jet database engine, indicates that the user ID and password for the attached table are saved with the connection information.
dbSystemObject	Indicates the table is a system table provided by the Microsoft Jet database engine.
dbHiddenObject	Indicates the table is a hidden table provided by the Microsoft Jet database engine.
dbAttachedTable	Indicates the table is an attached table from a non-ODBC database, such as a Paradox database.
dbAttachedODBC	Indicates the table is an attached table from an ODBC database, such as Microsoft SQL Server.

A system table is a table created by the Microsoft Jet database engine to contain various internal information.

A hidden table is a table created for temporary use by the Microsoft Jet database engine.

For more information on tabledefs, see the articles "DAO Tabledef" and "DAO Tabledef: Using Tabledefs" in *Programming with MFC*. For related information, see the topic "Attributes Property" in DAO Help.

See Also   **CDaoTableDef::SetAttributes**

CDaoTableDef::GetConnect

CString GetConnect( );
throw(CDaoException, CMemoryException);

Return Value

A **CString** object containing the path and database type for the table.

Remarks

Call this member function to obtain the connect string for a data source. For a **CDaoTableDef** object that represents an attached table, the **CString** object consists of one or two parts (a database type specifier and a path to the database).

The path as shown in the table below is the full path for the directory containing the database files and must be preceded by the identifier "DATABASE=". In some cases (as with Microsoft Jet, Btrieve, and Microsoft Excel databases), a specific filename is included in the database path argument.

The following table shows possible database types and their corresponding database specifiers and paths:

Database type	Specifier	Path
Database using the Jet database engine	";"	"drive:\path\filename.MDB"
dBASE III	"dBASE III;"	"drive:\path"
dBASE IV	"dBASE IV;"	"drive:\path"
Paradox 3.x	"Paradox 3.x;"	"drive:\path"
Paradox 4.x	"Paradox 4.x;"	"drive:\path"
Btrieve	"Btrieve;"	"drive:\path\filename.DDF"
FoxPro 2.0	"FoxPro 2.0;"	"drive:\path"
FoxPro 2.5	"FoxPro 2.5;"	"drive:\path"
FoxPro 2.6	"FoxPro 2.6;"	"drive:\path"
Excel 3.0	"Excel 3.0;"	"drive:\path\filename.XLS"
Excel 4.0	"Excel 4.0;"	"drive:\path\filename.XLS"
Excel 5.0	"Excel 5.0;"	"drive:\path\filename.XLS"
Text	"Text;"	"drive:\path"
ODBC	"ODBC; DATABASE=*defaultdatabase*; UID=*user*;PWD=*password*; DSN=*datasourcename;* LOGINTIMEOUT=*seconds*" (This may not be a complete connection string for all servers; it is just an example. It is very important not to have spaces between the parameters.)	None

For Microsoft Jet database base tables, the specifier is a empty string ("").

If a password is required but not provided, the ODBC driver displays a login dialog box the first time a table is accessed and again if the connection is closed and reopened. If an attached table has the **dbAttachSavePWD** attribute, the login prompt will not appear when the table is reopened.

For more information on tabledefs, see the articles "DAO Tabledef" and "DAO Tabledef: Using Tabledefs" in *Programming with MFC*. For related information, see the topic "Connect Property" in DAO Help.

See Also   **CDaoTableDef::SetConnect**

CDaoTableDef::GetDateCreated

COleDateTime GetDateCreated( );
   throw(CDaoException, CMemoryException);

Return Value

A value containing the date and time of the creation of the table underlying the **CDaoTableDef** object.

Remarks

Call this function to determine the date and time the table underlying the **CDaoTableDef** object was created.

The date and time settings are derived from the computer on which the base table was created or last updated. In a multiuser environment, users should get these settings directly from the file server to avoid discrepancies; that is, all clients should use a "standard" time source — perhaps from one server.

For more information on tabledefs, see the articles "DAO Tabledef" and "DAO Tabledef: Using Tabledefs" in *Programming with MFC*. For related information, see the topic "DateCreated, LastUpdated Properties" in DAO Help.

See Also   **CDaoTableDef::GetLastDateUpdated**

CDaoTableDef::GetDateLastUpdated

COleDateTime GetDateLastUpdated( );
   throw(CDaoException, CMemoryException);

Return Value

A value that contains the date and time the table underlying the **CDaoTableDef** object was last updated.

Remarks

Call this function to determine the date and time the table underlying the **CDaoTableDef** object was last updated.

The date and time settings are derived from the computer on which the base table was created or last updated. In a multiuser environment, users should get these settings directly from the file server to avoid discrepancies; that is, all clients should use a "standard" time source — perhaps from one server.

For more information on tabledefs, see the articles "DAO Tabledef" and "DAO Tabledef: Using Tabledefs" in *Programming with MFC*. For related information, see the topic "DateCreated, LastUpdated Properties" in DAO Help.

See Also   **CDaoTableDef::GetDateCreated**

CDaoTableDef::GetFieldCount

short GetFieldCount( );
   throw(CDaoException, CMemoryException);

Return Value

The number of fields in the table.

Remarks

Call this member function to retrieve the number of fields defined in the table. If its value is 0, there are no objects in the collection.

For more information on tabledefs, see the articles "DAO Tabledef" and "DAO Tabledef: Using Tabledefs" in *Programming with MFC*. For related information, see the topic "Count Property" in DAO Help.

See Also   **CDaoTableDef::GetFieldInfo**, **CDaoTableDef::GetIndexInfo**, **CDaoTableDef::GetIndexCount**

CDaoTableDef::GetFieldInfo

void GetFieldInfo(int *nIndex*, **CDaoFieldInfo&** *fieldinfo*,
   DWORD *dwInfoOptions* **= AFX_DAO_PRIMARY_INFO);**
   throw(CDaoException, CMemoryException);
void GetFieldInfo(LPCTSTR *lpszName*, **CDaoFieldInfo&** *fieldinfo*,
   DWORD *dwInfoOptions* **= AFX_DAO_PRIMARY_INFO);**
   throw(CDaoException, CMemoryException);

Parameters

nIndex   The index of the field object in the table's zero-based Fields collection, for lookup by index.

fieldinfo   A reference to a **CDaoFieldInfo** structure.

dwInfoOptions   Options that specify which information about the field to retrieve. The available options are listed here along with what they cause the function to return:

- **AFX_DAO_PRIMARY_INFO**   (Default) Name, Type, Size, Attributes. Use this option for fastest performance.

- **AFX_DAO_SECONDARY_INFO**   Primary information, plus: Ordinal Position, Required, Allow Zero Length, Collating Order, Foreign Name, Source Field, Source Table

- **AFX_DAO_ALL_INFO**   Primary and secondary information, plus: Validation Rule, Validation Text, Default Value

lpszName   A pointer to the name of the field object, for lookup by name. The name is a string with up to 14 characters that uniquely names the field.

Remarks

Call this member function to obtain various kinds of information about a field defined in the tabledef. One version of the function lets you look up a field by index. The other version lets you look up a field by name.

For a description of the information returned, see the **CDaoFieldInfo** structure. This structure has members that correspond to the items of information listed above in the description of *dwInfoOptions*. When you request information at one level, you get information for any prior levels as well.

For more information on tabledefs, see the articles "DAO Tabledef" and "DAO Tabledef: Using Tabledefs" in *Programming with MFC*. For related information, see the topic "Attributes Property" in DAO Help.

See Also   **CDaoTableDef::GetIndexInfo**, **CDaoTableDef::GetIndexCount**, **CDaoTableDef::GetFieldCount**

CDaoTableDef::GetIndexCount

short GetIndexCount( );
    throw(CDaoException, CMemoryException);

Return Value

The number of indexes for the table.

Remarks

Call this member function to obtain the number of indexes for a table. If its value is 0, there are no indexes in the collection.

For more information on tabledefs, see the articles "DAO Tabledef" and "DAO Tabledef: Using Tabledefs" in *Programming with MFC*. For related information, see the topic "Count Property" in DAO Help.

See Also   **CDaoTableDef::GetIndexInfo**, **CDaoTableDef::GetFieldInfo**, **CDaoTableDef::GetFieldCount**

CDaoTableDef::GetIndexInfo

void GetIndexInfo(int *nIndex***, CDaoIndexInfo&** *indexinfo***,**
    DWORD *dwInfoOptions* **= AFX_DAO_PRIMARY_INFO);**
    throw(CDaoException, CMemoryException);
void GetIndexInfo(LPCTSTR *lpszName***, CDaoIndexInfo&** *indexinfo***,**
    DWORD *dwInfoOptions* **= AFX_DAO_PRIMARY_INFO);**
    throw(CDaoException, CMemoryException);

Parameters

nIndex   The numeric index of the Index object in the table's zero-based Indexes collection, for lookup by its position in the collection.

indexinfo   A reference to a **CDaoIndexInfo** structure.

dwInfoOptions   Options that specify which information about the index to retrieve. The available options are listed here along with what they cause the function to return:

- **AFX_DAO_PRIMARY_INFO**   Name, Field Info, Fields. Use this option for fastest performance.

- **AFX_DAO_SECONDARY_INFO**   Primary information, plus: Primary, Unique, Clustered, Ignore Nulls, Required, Foreign

- **AFX_DAO_ALL_INFO**   Primary and secondary information, plus: Distinct Count

lpszName   A pointer to the name of the index object, for lookup by name.

Remarks

Call this member function to obtain various kinds of information about an index defined in the tabledef. One version of the function lets you look up an index by its position in the collection. The other version lets you look up an index by name.

For a description of the information returned, see the **CDaoIndexInfo** structure. This structure has members that correspond to the items of information listed above in the description of *dwInfoOptions*. When you request information at one level, you get information for any prior levels as well.

For more information on tabledefs, see the articles "DAO Tabledef" and "DAO Tabledef: Using Tabledefs" in *Programming with MFC*. For related information, see the topic "Attributes Property" in DAO Help.

See Also   **CDaoTableDef::GetFieldInfo, CDaoTableDef::GetIndexCount, CDaoTableDef::GetFieldCount**

CDaoTableDef::GetName

CString GetName( );
   throw(CDaoException, CMemoryException);

Return Value

A user-defined name for a table.

Remarks

Call this member function to obtain the user-defined name of the underlying table. This name starts with a letter and can contain a maximum of 64 characters. It can include numbers and underscore characters but cannot include punctuation or spaces.

For more information on tabledefs, see the articles "DAO Tabledef" and "DAO Tabledef: Using Tabledefs" in *Programming with MFC*. For related information, see the topic "Name Property" in DAO Help.

See Also   **CDaoTableDef::SetName**, **CDaoTableDef::GetConnect**, **CDaoTableDef::SetConnect**

CDaoTableDef::GetRecordCount

long GetRecordCount( );
   throw(CDaoException, CMemoryException);

Return Value

The number of records accessed in a tabledef object.

Remarks

Call this member function to find out how many records are in a **CDaoTableDef** object.

Calling **GetRecordCount** for a table-type **CDaoTableDef** object reflects the approximate number of records in the table and is affected immediately as table records are added and deleted. Rolled back transactions will appear as part of the record count until you call **CDaoWorkSpace::CompactDatabase**. A **CDaoTableDef** object with no records has a record count property setting of 0. When working with attached tables or ODBC databases, **GetRecordCount** always returns –1.

For more information on tabledefs, see the articles "DAO Tabledef" and "DAO Tabledef: Using Tabledefs" in *Programming with MFC*. For related information, see the topic "RecordCount Property" in DAO Help.

See Also   **CDaoTableDef::GetSourceTableName**, **CDaoTableDef::SetSourceTableName**

CDaoTableDef::GetSourceTableName

CString GetSourceTableName( );
   throw(CDaoException, CMemoryException);

Return Value

A **CString** object that specifies the source name of an attached table, or an empty string if a native data table.

Remarks

Call this member function to retrieve the name of an attached table in a source database. An attached table is a table in another database linked to a Microsoft Jet database. Data for attached tables remains in the external database, where it can be manipulated by other applications.

For more information on tabledefs, see the articles "DAO Tabledef" and "DAO Tabledef: Using Tabledefs" in *Programming with MFC*. For related information, see the topic "SourceTableName Property" in DAO Help.

See Also   **CDaoTableDef::GetRecordCount**, **CDaoTableDef::SetSourceTableName**

CDaoTableDef::GetValidationRule

CString GetValidationRule( );
   throw(CDaoException, CMemoryException);

Return Value
A **CString** object that validates the data in a field as it is changed or added to a table.

Remarks
Call this member function to retrieve the validation rule for a tabledef. Validation rules are used in connection with update operations. If a tabledef contains a validation rule, updates to that tabledef must match predetermined criteria before the data is changed. If the change does not match the criteria, an exception containing the value of **GetValidationText** is thrown. For a **CDaoTableDef** object, this **CString** is read-only for an attached table and read/write for a base table.

For more information on tabledefs, see the articles "DAO Tabledef" and "DAO Tabledef: Using Tabledefs" in *Programming with MFC*. For related information, see the topic "ValidationRule Property" in DAO Help.

See Also   **CDaoTableDef::SetValidationRule**, **CDaoTableDef::GetValidationText**, **CDaoTableDef::SetValidationText**

CDaoTableDef::GetValidationText

CString GetValidationText( );
   throw(CDaoException, CMemoryException);

Return Value
A **CString** object that specifies the text displayed if the user enters data that does not match the validation rule.

Remarks
Call this function to retrieve the string to display when a user enters data that does not match the validation rule. For a **CDaoTableDef** object, this **CString** is read-only for an attached table and read/write for a base table.

For more information on tabledefs, see the articles "DAO Tabledef" and "DAO Tabledef: Using Tabledefs" in *Programming with MFC*. For related information, see the topic "ValidationText Property" in DAO Help.

See Also   **CDaoTableDef::SetValidationRule**, **CDaoTableDef::SetValidationText**, **CDaoTableDef::GetValidationRule**

CDaoTableDef::IsOpen

BOOL IsOpen( ) const;
   throw(CDaoException, CMemoryException);

Return Value

Nonzero if the **CDaoTableDef** object is open; otherwise 0.

Remarks

Call this member function to determine whether the **CDaoTableDef** object is currently open.

For more information on tabledefs, see the articles "DAO Tabledef" and "DAO Tabledef: Using Tabledefs" in *Programming with MFC*.

See Also   **CDaoTableDef::Open**

CDaoTableDef::Open

virtual void Open(LPCTSTR *lpszName*);
   throw(CDaoException, CMemoryException);

Parameters

lpszName   A pointer to a string that specifies a table name.

Remarks

Call this member function to open a tabledef previously saved in the database's TableDef's collection.

For more information on tabledefs, see the articles "DAO Tabledef" and "DAO Tabledef: Using Tabledefs" in *Programming with MFC*.

See Also   **CDaoTableDef::IsOpen**, **CDaoTableDef::Create**, **CDaoTableDef::Close**

CDaoTableDef::RefreshLink

void RefreshLink( );
   throw(CDaoException, CMemoryException);

Remarks

Call this member function to update the connection information for an attached table. You change the connection information for an attached table by calling **SetConnect** on the corresponding **CDaoTableDef** object and then using the **RefreshLink** member function to update the information. When you call **RefreshLink**, the attached table's properties are not changed.

To force the modified connect information to take effect, all open **CDaoRecordset** objects based on this tabledef must be closed.

For more information on tabledefs, see the articles "DAO Tabledef" and "DAO Tabledef: Using Tabledefs" in *Programming with MFC*. For related information, see the topic "RefreshLink Method" in DAO Help.

See Also   **CDaoTableDef::SetConnect**

CDaoTableDef::SetAttributes

void SetAttributes(long *lAttributes* **);**
   throw(CDaoException, CMemoryException);

Parameters

lAttributes   Characteristics of the table represented by the **CDaoTableDef** object and can be a sum of these constants:

Constant	Description
dbAttachExclusive	For databases that use the Microsoft Jet database engine, indicates the table is an attached table opened for exclusive use.
dbAttachSavePWD	For databases that use the Microsoft Jet database engine, indicates that the user ID and password for the attached table are saved with the connection information.
dbSystemObject	Indicates the table is a system table provided by the Microsoft Jet database engine.
dbHiddenObject	Indicates the table is a hidden table provided by the Microsoft Jet database engine.
dbAttachedTable	Indicates the table is an attached table from a non-ODBC database, such as a Paradox database.
dbAttachedODBC	Indicates the table is an attached table from an ODBC database, such as Microsoft SQL Server.

Remarks

When setting multiple attributes, you can combine them by summing the appropriate constants using the bitwise-OR operator. Setting **dbAttachExclusive** on a nonattached table produces an exception. Combining the following values also produce an exception:

- **dbAttachExclusive | dbAttachedODBC**
- **dbAttachSavePWD | dbAttachedTable**

For more information on tabledefs, see the articles "DAO Tabledef" and "DAO Tabledef: Using Tabledefs" in *Programming with MFC*. For related information, see the topic "Attributes Property" in DAO Help.

See Also   **CDaoTableDef::SetConnect**

CDaoTableDef::SetConnect

void SetConnect(LPCTSTR *lpszConnect* **);**
    throw(CDaoException, CMemoryException);

Parameters

lpszConnect   A pointer to a string expression that specifies additional parameters to pass to ODBC or installable ISAM drivers.

Remarks

For a **CDaoTableDef** object that represents an attached table, the string object consists of one or two parts (a database type specifier and a path to the database).

The path as shown in the table below is the full path for the directory containing the database files and must be preceded by the identifier "DATABASE=". In some cases (as with Microsoft Jet, Btrieve, and Microsoft Excel databases), a specific filename is included in the database path argument.

The following table shows possible database types and their corresponding database specifiers and paths:

Database type	Specifier	Path
Database using the Jet database engine	";"	"drive:\\path\\filename.MDB"
dBASE III	"dBASE III;"	"drive:\\path"
dBASE IV	"dBASE IV;"	"drive:\\path"
Paradox 3.x	"Paradox 3.x;"	"drive:\\path"
Paradox 4.x	"Paradox 4.x;"	"drive:\\path"
Btrieve	"Btrieve;"	"drive:\\path\\filename.DDF"
FoxPro 2.0	"FoxPro 2.0;"	"drive:\\path"
FoxPro 2.5	"FoxPro 2.5;"	"drive:\\path"

Database type	Specifier	Path
FoxPro 2.6	"FoxPro 2.6;"	"drive:\\path"
Excel 3.0	"Excel 3.0;"	"drive:\\path\\filename.XLS"
Excel 4.0	"Excel 4.0;"	"drive:\\path\\filename.XLS"
Excel 5.0	"Excel 5.0;"	"drive:\\path\\filename.XLS"
Text	"Text;"	"drive:\\path"
ODBC	"ODBC; DATABASE=*defaultdatabase*; UID=*user*;PWD=*password*; DSN=*datasourcename;* LOGINTIMEOUT=*seconds*" (This may not be a complete connection string for all servers; it is just an example. It is very important not to have spaces between the parameters.)	None

For Microsoft Jet database base tables, the specifier is an empty string ("").

You must use a double backslash (\\) in the connect strings. After setting the connect string, you must then call **RefreshLink**.

If a password is required but not provided, the ODBC driver displays a login dialog box the first time a table is accessed and again if the connection is closed and reopened.

You can set the connect string for a **CDaoTableDef** object by providing a source argument to the **Create** member function. You can check the setting to determine the type, path, user ID, password, or ODBC data source of the database. For more information, see the documentation for the specific driver.

For more information on tabledefs, see the articles "DAO Tabledef" and "DAO Tabledef: Using Tabledefs" in *Programming with MFC*. For related information, see the topic "Connect Property" in DAO Help.

See Also   **CDaoTableDef::RefreshLink, CDaoTableDef::SetAttributes**

CDaoTableDef::SetName

void SetName(LPCTSTR *lpszName* **);**
    throw(CDaoException, CMemoryException);

Parameters

lpszName   A pointer to a string expression that specifies a name for a table.

Remarks

Call this member function to set a user-defined name for a table. The name must start with a letter and can contain a maximum of 64 characters. It can include numbers and underscore characters but cannot include punctuation or spaces.

For more information on tabledefs, see the articles "DAO Tabledef" and "DAO Tabledef: Using Tabledefs" in *Programming with MFC*. For related information, see the topic "Name Property" in DAO Help.

See Also   **CDaoTableDef::RefreshLink**, **CDaoTableDef::SetConnect**

CDaoTableDef::SetSourceTableName

void SetSourceTableName(LPCTSTR *lpszSrcTableName* **);**
    throw(CDaoException, CMemoryException);

Parameters

lpszSrcTableName   A pointer to a string expression that specifies a table name in the external database. For a base table, the setting is an empty string ("").

Remarks

Call this member function to specify the name of an attached table or the name of the base table on which the **CDaoTableDef** object is based, as it exists in the original source of the data. You must then call **RefreshLink**. This property setting is empty for a base table and read/write for an attached table or an object not appended to a collection.

For more information on tabledefs, see the articles "DAO Tabledef" and "DAO Tabledef: Using Tabledefs" in *Programming with MFC*. For related information, see the topic "SourceTableName Property" in DAO Help.

See Also   **CDaoTableDef::RefreshLink**, **CDaoTableDef::GetSourceTableName**

CDaoTableDef::SetValidationRule

void SetValidationRule(LPCTSTR *lpszValidationRule* **);**
    throw(CDaoException, CMemoryException);

Parameters

lpszValidationRule   A pointer to a string expression that validates an operation.

Remarks

Call this member function to set a validation rule for a tabledef. Validation rules are used in connection with update operations. If a tabledef contains a validation rule, updates to that tabledef must match predetermined criteria before the data is changed. If the change does not match the criteria, an exception containing the text of **GetValidationText** is displayed.

Validation is supported only for databases that use the Microsoft Jet database engine. The expression cannot refer to user-defined functions, domain aggregate functions, SQL aggregate functions, or queries. A validation rule for a **CDaoTableDef** object can refer to multiple fields in that object.

For example, for fields named `hire_date` and `termination_date`, a validation rule might be:

```
CString strRule = _T("termination_date>hire_date");
MyRs.SetValidationRule(strRule);
```

For more information on tabledefs, see the articles "DAO Tabledef" and "DAO Tabledef: Using Tabledefs" in *Programming with MFC*. For related information, see the topic "ValidationRule Property" in DAO Help.

See Also   **CDaoTableDef::GetValidationText**, **CDaoTableDef::SetValidationText**, **CDaoTableDef::GetValidationRule**

CDaoTableDef::SetValidationText

void SetValidationText(LPCTSTR *lpszValidationText* **);**
   throw(CDaoException, CMemoryException);

Parameters

lpszValidationText   A pointer to a string expression that specifies the text displayed if entered data is invalid.

Remarks

Call this member function to set the exception text of a validation rule for a **CDaoTableDef** object with an underlying base table supported by the Microsoft Jet database engine. You cannot set the validation text of an attached table.

For more information on tabledefs, see the articles "DAO Tabledef" and "DAO Tabledef: Using Tabledefs" in *Programming with MFC*. For related information, see the topic "ValidationText Property" in DAO Help.

See Also   **CDaoTableDef::SetValidationRule**, **CDaoTableDef::GetValidationText**, **CDaoTableDef::GetValidationRule**

Data Members

CDaoTableDef::m_pDatabase

Remarks

Contains a pointer to the **CDaoDatabase** object for this table.

For more information on accessing underlying DAO objects, see the article "DAO Collections: Obtaining Information About DAO Objects" in *Programming with MFC*.

See Also **CDaoTableDef::m_pDAOTableDef**

CDaoTableDef::m_pDAOTableDef

Remarks

Contains a pointer to the OLE interface for the DAO tabledef object underlying the **CDaoTableDef** object. Use this pointer if you need to access the DAO interface directly.

For more information on accessing underlying DAO objects, see the article "DAO Collections: Obtaining Information About DAO Objects" in *Programming with MFC*.

See Also **CDaoTableDef::m_pDatabase**

CDaoWorkspace

A **CDaoWorkspace** object manages a named, password-protected database session from login to logoff, by a single user. In most cases, you will not need multiple workspaces, and you will not need to create explicit workspace objects; when you open database and recordset objects, they use DAO's default workspace. However, if needed, you can run multiple sessions at a time by creating additional workspace objects. Each workspace object can contain multiple open database objects in its own Databases collection. In MFC, a workspace is primarily a transaction manager, specifying a set of open databases all in the same "transaction space."

Note The DAO database classes are distinct from the MFC database classes based on Open Database Connectivity (ODBC). All DAO database class names have a "CDao" prefix. In general, the MFC classes based on DAO are more capable than the MFC classes based on ODBC. The DAO-based classes access data through the Microsoft Jet database engine, including ODBC drivers. They also support Data Definition Language (DDL) operations, such as creating databases and adding tables and fields via the classes, without having to call DAO directly.

Capabilities

Class **CDaoWorkspace** provides the following:

- Explicit access, if needed, to a default workspace, created by initializing the database engine. Usually you use DAO's default workspace implicitly by creating database and recordset objects.

- A transaction space in which transactions apply to all databases open in the workspace. You can create additional workspaces to manage separate transaction spaces.

- An interface to many properties of the underlying Microsoft Jet database engine (see the static member functions). Opening or creating a workspace, or calling a static member function before open or create, initializes the database engine.

- Access to the database engine's Workspaces collection, which stores all active workspaces that have been appended to it. You can also create and work with workspaces without appending them to the collection.

Security

MFC does not implement the Users and Groups collections in DAO, which are used for security control. If you need those aspects of DAO, you must program them yourself via direct calls to DAO interfaces. For information, see Technical Note 54 under MFC in Books Online.

Usage

You can use class **CDaoWorkspace** to:

- Explicitly open the default workspace.

  Usually your use of the default workspace is implicit—when you open new **CDaoDatabase** or **CDaoRecordset** objects. But you might need to access it explicitly—for example, to access database engine properties or the Workspaces collection. See "Implicit Use of the Default Workspace" below.

- Create new workspaces. Call **Append** if you want to add them to the Workspaces collection.

- Open an existing workspace in the Workspaces collection.

Creating a new workspace that does not already exist in the Workspaces collection is described under the **Create** member function. Workspace objects do not persist in any way between datababase engine sessions. If your application links MFC statically, ending the application uninitializes the database engine. If your application links with MFC dynamically, the database engine is uninitialized when the MFC DLL is unloaded.

Explicitly opening the default workspace, or opening an existing workspace in the Workspaces collection, is described under the **Open** member function.

End a workspace session by closing the workspace with the **Close** member function. **Close** closes any databases you have not closed previously, rolling back any uncommitted transactions.

Transactions

DAO manages transactions at the workspace level; hence, transactions on a workspace with multiple open databases apply to all of the databases. For example, if two databases have uncommitted updates and you call **CommitTrans**, all of the updates are committed. If you want to limit transactions to a single database, you need a separate workspace object for it.

Implicit Use of the Default Workspace

MFC uses DAO's default workspace implicitly under the following circumstances described on the following page.

- If you create a new **CDaoDatabase** object but do not do so through an existing **CDaoWorkspace** object, MFC creates a temporary workspace object for you, which corresponds to DAO's default workspace. If you do so for multiple databases, all of the database objects are associated with the default workspace. You can access a database's workspace through a **CDaoDatabase** data member.

- Similarly, if you create a **CDaoRecordset** object without supplying a pointer to a **CDaoDatabase** object, MFC creates a temporary database object and, by extension, a temporary workspace object. You can access a recordset's database, and indirectly its workspace, through a **CDaoRecordset** data member.

Other Operations

Other database operations are also provided, such as repairing a corrupted database or compacting a database.

For more about **CDaoWorkspace**, see the article "DAO Workspace." For information about calling DAO directly and about DAO security, see Technical Note 54 under MFC in Books Online. For more about working with ODBC data sources through DAO, see the article "DAO External: Working with External Data Sources." For information about the database engine, see the article "DAO Workspace: The Database Engine." All articles are in *Programming with MFC*. The MFC Database sample DAOVIEW illustrates using **CDaoWorkspace**. Information about samples is available under MFC Samples, under MFC in Books Online.

#include <afxdao.h>

See Also   CDaoDatabase, CDaoRecordset, CDaoTableDef, CDaoQueryDef, CDaoException

Data Members

m_pDAOWorkspace	Points to the underlying DAO workspace object.

Construction

CDaoWorkspace	Constructs a workspace object. Afterwards, call **Create** or **Open**.

Attributes

GetIsolateODBCTrans	Returns a value that indicates whether multiple transactions that involve the same ODBC data source are isolated via forced multiple connections to the data source.
GetName	Returns the user-defined name for the workspace object.
GetUserName	Returns the user name specified when the workspace was created. This is the name of the workspace owner.
IsOpen	Returns nonzero if the workspace is open.
SetIsolateODBCTrans	Specifies whether multiple transactions that involve the same ODBC data source are isolated by forcing multiple connections to the data source.

Operations

Append	Appends a newly created workspace to the database engine's Workspaces collection.
BeginTrans	Begins a new transaction, which applies to all databases open in the workspace.
Close	Closes the workspace and all of the objects it contains. Pending transactions are rolled back.
CommitTrans	Completes the current transaction and saves the changes.
CompactDatabase	Compacts (or duplicates) a database.
Create	Creates a new DAO workspace object.
GetDatabaseCount	Returns the number of DAO database objects in the workspace's Databases collection.
GetDatabaseInfo	Returns information about a specified DAO database defined in the workspace's Databases collection.
GetWorkspaceCount	Returns the number of DAO workspace objects in the database engine's Workspaces collection.
GetWorkspaceInfo	Returns information about a specified DAO workspace defined in the database engine's Workspaces collection.
Open	Explicitly opens a workspace object associated with DAO's default workspace.
RepairDatabase	Attempts to repair a damaged database.
Rollback	Ends the current transaction and does not save the changes.
Idle	Allows the database engine to perform background tasks.

Database Engine Properties

GetVersion	Returns a string that contains the version of the database engine associated with the workspace.
GetIniPath	Returns the location of the Microsoft Jet database engine's initialization settings in the Windows registry.
GetLoginTimeout	Returns the number of seconds before an error occurs when the user attempts to log in to an ODBC database.
SetDefaultPassword	Sets the password that the database engine uses when a workspace object is created without a specific password.
SetDefaultUser	Sets the user name that the database engine uses when a workspace object is created without a specific user name.
SetIniPath	Sets the location of the Microsoft Jet database engine's initialization settings in the Windows registry.
SetLoginTimeout	Sets the number of seconds before an error occurs when the user attempts to log in to an ODBC data source.

Member Functions

CDaoWorkspace::Append

void Append( );
   throw(CDaoException, CMemoryException);

Remarks

Call this member function after you call **Create**. **Append** appends a newly created workspace object to the database engine's Workspaces collection. Workspaces do not persist between database engine sessions; they are stored only in memory, not on disk. You do not have to append a workspace; if you do not, you can still use it.

An appended workspace remains in the Workspaces collection, in an active, open state, until you call its **Close** member function.

For more information about workspaces, see the article "DAO Workspace." For more information about the database engine, see the article "DAO Workspace: The Database Engine." Both articles are in *Programming with MFC*. For related information, see the topic "Append Method" in DAO Help.

CDaoWorkspace::BeginTrans

void BeginTrans( );
   throw(CDaoException, CMemoryException);

Remarks

Call this member function to initiate a transaction. After you call **BeginTrans**, updates you make to your data or database structure take effect when you commit the transaction. Because the workspace defines a single transaction space, the transaction applies to all open databases in the workspace. There are two ways to complete the transaction:

- Call the **CommitTrans** member function to commit the transaction and save changes to the data source.

- Or call the **Rollback** member function to cancel the transaction.

Closing the workspace object or a database object while a transaction is pending rolls back all pending transactions.

If you need to isolate transactions on one ODBC data source from those on another ODBC data source, see the **SetIsolateODBCTrans** member function.

For information about transactions, see the article "DAO Workspace: Managing Transactions." For more information about workspaces, see the article "DAO Workspace." Both articles are in *Programming with MFC*.

See Also   **CDaoWorkspace::GetIsolateODBCTrans**, **CDaoWorkspace::CommitTrans**, **CDaoWorkspace::Rollback**

CDaoWorkspace::CDaoWorkspace

CDaoWorkspace( );

Remarks

Constructs a **CDaoWorkspace** object. After constructing the C++ object, you have two options:

- Call the object's **Open** member function to open the default workspace or to open an existing object in the Workspaces collection.

- Or call the object's **Create** member function to create a new DAO workspace object. This explicitly starts a new workspace session, which you can refer to via the **CDaoWorkspace** object. After calling **Create**, you can call **Append** if you want to add the workspace to the database engine's Workspaces collection.

See the class overview for **CDaoWorkspace** for information about when you need to explicitly create a **CDaoWorkspace** object. Usually, you use workspaces created implicitly when you open a **CDaoDatabase** object without specifying a workspace or when you open a **CDaoRecordset** object without specifying a database object. MFC DAO objects created in this way use DAO's default workspace, which is created once and reused.

To release a workspace and its contained objects, call the workspace object's **Close** member function.

For more information about workspaces, see the article "DAO Workspace." For more information about implicit workspace creation, see the article "DAO: Accessing Implicit MFC DAO Objects." Both articles are in *Programming with MFC*.

CDaoWorkspace::Close

virtual void Close( );
    throw(CDaoException, CMemoryException);

Remarks

Call this member function to close the workspace object. Closing an open workspace object releases the underlying DAO object and, if the workspace is a member of the Workspaces collection, removes it from the collection. Calling **Close** is good programming practice.

> **Caution** Closing a workspace object closes any open databases in the workspace. This results in any recordsets open in the databases being closed as well, and any pending edits or updates are rolled back. For related information, see the **CDaoDatabase::Close**, **CDaoRecordset::Close**, **CDaoTableDef::Close**, and **CDaoQueryDef::Close** member functions.

Workspace objects are not permanent; they only exist while references to them exist. This means that when the database engine session ends, the workspace and its Databases collection do not persist. You must re-create them for the next session by opening your workspace and database(s) again.

For more information about workspaces, see the article "DAO Workspace" in *Programming with MFC*. For related information, see the topic "Close Method" in DAO Help.

See Also **CDaoWorkspace::Open**

CDaoWorkspace::CommitTrans

void CommitTrans( );
    throw(CDaoException, CMemoryException);

Remarks

Call this member function to commit a transaction—save a group of edits and updates to one or more databases in the workspace. A transaction consists of a series of changes to the database's data or its structure, beginning with a call to **BeginTrans**. When you complete the transaction, either commit it or roll it back (cancel the changes) with **Rollback**. By default, without transactions, updates to records are committed immediately. Calling **BeginTrans** causes commitment of updates to be delayed until you call **CommitTrans**.

> **Caution** Within one workspace, transactions are always global to the workspace and are not limited to only one database or recordset. If you perform operations on more than one database or recordset within a workspace transaction, **CommitTrans** commits all pending updates, and **Rollback** restores all operations on those databases and recordsets.

When you close a database or workspace with pending transactions, the transactions are all rolled back.

> **Note** This is not a two-phase commit mechanism. If one update fails to commit, others still will commit.

For more information about workspaces, see the article "DAO Workspace." For more about transactions, including information about separate transaction spaces, see the article "DAO Workspace: Managing Transactions." Both articles are in *Programming with MFC*.

CDaoWorkspace::CompactDatabase

static void PASCAL CompactDatabase(LPCTSTR *lpszSrcName*, **LPCTSTR** *lpszDestName*,
    LPCTSTR *lpszLocale* = **dbLangGeneral, int** *nOptions* = **0**);
    throw(CDaoException, CMemoryException);
static void PASCAL CompactDatabase(LPCTSTR *lpszSrcName*, **LPCTSTR** *lpszDestName*,
    LPCTSTR *lpszLocale*, **int** *nOptions*, **LPCTSTR** *lpszPassword*);
    throw(CDaoException, CMemoryException);

Parameters

lpszSrcName   The name of an existing, closed database. It can be a full path
    and filename, such as "C:\\MYDB.MDB". If the filename has an extension,
    you must specify it. If your network supports the uniform naming convention
    (UNC), you can also specify a network path, such as
    "\\\\MYSERVER\\MYSHARE\\MYDIR\\MYDB.MDB". (Double backslashes
    are required in the path strings because "\" is the C++ escape character.)

lpszDestName   The full path of the compacted database that you are creating. You
    can also specify a network path as with *lpszSrcName*. You cannot use the
    lpszDestName argument to specify the same database file as *lpszSrcName*.

lpszPassword   A password, used when you want to compact a password-protected
    database. Note that if you use the version of **CompactDatabase** that takes a
    password, you must supply all parameters.

lpszLocale   A string expression used to specify collating order for creating
    lpszDestName. If you omit this argument by accepting the default value of
    dbLangGeneral (see below), the locale of the new database is the same as that of
    the old database. Possible values are:

- **dbLangGeneral**   English, German, French, Portuguese, Italian, and Modern
    Spanish

- **dbLangArabic**   Arabic

- **dbLangCyrillic**   Russian

- **dbLangCzech**   Czech

- **dbLangDutch**   Dutch

- **dbLangGreek**   Greek

- **dbLangHebrew**   Hebrew

- **dbLangHungarian**   Hungarian

- **dbLangIcelandic**   Icelandic

- **dbLangNordic**   Nordic languages (Microsoft Jet database engine version 1.0 only)

- **dbLangNorwdan**   Norwegian and Danish

- **dbLangPolish**   Polish

- **dbLangSpanish**   Traditional Spanish

- **dbLangSwedfin**   Swedish and Finnish

- **dbLangTurkish**   Turkish

nOptions   Indicates one or more options for the target database, *lpszDestName*. If you omit this argument by accepting the default value, the *lpszDestName* will have the same encryption and the same version as *lpszSrcName*. You can combine the **dbEncrypt** or **dbDecrypt** option with one of the version options using the bitwise-OR operator. Possible values, which specify a database format, not a database engine version, are:

- **dbEncrypt**   Encrypt the database while compacting.

- **dbDecrypt**   Decrypt the database while compacting.

- **dbVersion10**   Create a database that uses the Microsoft Jet database engine version 1.0 while compacting.

- **dbVersion11**   Create a database that uses the Microsoft Jet database engine version 1.1 while compacting.

- **dbVersion20**   Create a database that uses the Microsoft Jet database engine version 2.0 while compacting.

- **dbVersion30**   Create a database that uses the Microsoft Jet database engine version 3.0 while compacting.

You can use **dbEncrypt** or **dbDecrypt** in the options argument to specify whether to encrypt or to decrypt the database as it is compacted. If you omit an encryption constant or if you include both **dbDecrypt** and **dbEncrypt**, *lpszDestName* will have the same encryption as *lpszSrcName*. You can use one of the version constants in the options argument to specify the version of the data format for the compacted database. This constant affects only the version of the data format of *lpszDestName*. You can specify only one version constant. If you omit a version constant, *lpszDestName* will have the same version as *lpszSrcName*. You can compact *lpszDestName* only to a version that is the same or later than that of *lpszSrcName*.

Caution   If a database is not encrypted, it is possible, even if you implement user/password security, to directly read the binary disk file that constitutes the database.

Remarks

Call this member function to compact a specified Microsoft Jet (.MDB) database. As you change data in a database, the database file can become fragmented and use more disk space than necessary. Periodically, you should compact your database to defragment the database file. The compacted database is usually smaller. You can also choose to change the collating order, the encryption, or the version of the data format while you copy and compact the database.

 Warning The **CompactDatabase** member function will not correctly convert a complete Microsoft Access database from one version to another. Only the data format is converted. Microsoft Access-defined objects, such as forms and reports, are not converted. However, the data is correctly converted.

Tip You can also use **CompactDatabase** to copy a database file.

For more information about workspaces, see the article "DAO Workspace" in *Programming with MFC*. For more information about compacting databases, see the topic "CompactDatabase Method" in DAO Help.

See Also **CDaoWorkspace::RepairDatabase**

CDaoWorkspace::Create

virtual void Create(LPCTSTR *lpszName***, LPCTSTR** *lpszUserName***, LPCTSTR** *lpszPassword* **);**
    throw(CDaoException, CMemoryException);

Parameters

lpszName   A string with up to 14 characters that uniquely names the new workspace object. You must supply a name. For related information, see the topic "Name Property" in DAO Help.

lpszUserName   The user name of the workspace's owner. For requirements, see the *lpszDefaultUser* parameter to the **SetDefaultUser** member function. For related information, see the topic "UserName Property" in DAO Help.

lpszPassword   The password for the new workspace object. A password can be up to 14 characters long and can contain any character except ASCII 0 (null). Passwords are case-sensitive. For related information, see the topic "Password Property" in DAO Help.

Remarks

Call this member function to create a new DAO workspace object and associate it with the MFC **CDaoWorkspace** object. The overall creation process is:

1. Construct a **CDaoWorkspace** object.

2. Call the object's **Create** member function to create the underlying DAO workspace. You must specify a workspace name.

3. Optionally call **Append** if you want to add the workspace to the database engine's Workspaces collection. You can work with the workspace without appending it.

After the **Create** call, the workspace object is in an open state, ready for use. You do not call **Open** after **Create**. You do not call **Create** if the workspace already exists in the Workspaces collection. **Create** initializes the database engine if it has not already been initialized for your application.

For more information about workspaces, see the article "DAO Workspace" in *Programming with MFC*.

See Also **CDaoWorkspace::CDaoWorkspace**, **CDaoWorkspace::Close**, **CDaoWorkspace::Open**

CDaoWorkspace::GetDatabaseCount

> **short GetDatabaseCount( );**
>   **throw(CDaoException, CMemoryException);**

Return Value

The number of open databases in the workspace.

Remarks

Call this member function to retrieve the number of DAO database objects in the workspace's Databases collection—the number of open databases in the workspace. **GetDatabaseCount** is useful if you need to loop through all defined databases in the workspace's Databases collection. To obtain information about a given database in the collection, see **GetDatabaseInfo**. Typical usage is to call **GetDatabaseCount** for the number of open databases, then use that number as a loop index for repeated calls to **GetDatabaseInfo**.

For more information about obtaining database information, see the article "DAO: Obtaining Information About DAO Objects" in *Programming with MFC*.

CDaoWorkspace::GetDatabaseInfo

> **void GetDatabaseInfo(int** *nIndex*, **CDaoDatabaseInfo&** *dbinfo*,
>   **DWORD** *dwInfoOptions* = **AFX_DAO_PRIMARY_INFO);**
>   **throw(CDaoException, CMemoryException);**
> **void GetDatabaseInfo(LPCTSTR** *lpszName*, **CDaoDatabaseInfo&** *dbinfo*,
>   **DWORD** *dwInfoOptions* = **AFX_DAO_PRIMARY_INFO);**
>   **throw(CDaoException, CMemoryException);**

Parameters

nIndex   The zero-based index of the database object in the workspace's Databases collection, for lookup by index.

dbinfo   A reference to a **CDaoDatabaseInfo** object that returns the information requested.

dwInfoOptions   Options that specify which information about the database to retrieve. The available options are listed here along with what they cause the function to return:

- **AFX_DAO_PRIMARY_INFO**   (Default) Name, Updatable, Transactions

- **AFX_DAO_SECONDARY_INFO**   Primary information plus: Version, Collating Order, Query Timeout

- **AFX_DAO_ALL_INFO**   Primary and secondary information plus: Connect

lpszName   The name of the database object, for lookup by name. The name is a string with up to 14 characters that uniquely names the new workspace object.

Remarks

Call this member function to obtain various kinds of information about a database open in the workspace. One version of the function lets you look up a database by index. The other version lets you look up a database by name.

For a description of the information returned in *dbinfo*, see the **CDaoDatabaseInfo** structure. This structure has members that correspond to the items of information listed above in the description of *dwInfoOptions*. When you request information at one level, you get information for any prior levels as well.

For more information about obtaining database information, see the article "DAO: Obtaining Information About DAO Objects" in *Programming with MFC*.

See Also   **CDaoWorkspace::GetDatabaseCount**

CDaoWorkspace::GetIniPath

static CString PASCAL GetIniPath( );
    throw(CDaoException, CMemoryException);

Return Value

A **CString** containing the registry location.

Remarks

Call this member function to obtain the location of the Microsoft Jet database engine's initialization settings in the Windows registry. You can use the location to obtain information about settings for the database engine. The information returned is actually the name of a registry subkey.

For more information about the database engine, see the article "DAO Workspace: The Database Engine" in *Programming with MFC*. For related information, see the topics "IniPath Property" and "Customizing Windows Registry Settings for Data Access" in DAO Help.

See Also   **CDaoWorkspace::SetIniPath**, **CDaoWorkspace::GetVersion**

CDaoWorkspace::GetIsolateODBCTrans

BOOL GetIsolateODBCTrans( );
   throw(CDaoException, CMemoryException);

Return Value

Nonzero if ODBC transactions are isolated; otherwise 0.

Remarks

Call this member function to get the current value of the DAO IsolateODBCTrans property for the workspace. In some situations, you might need to have multiple simultaneous transactions pending on the same ODBC database. To do this, you need to open a separate workspace for each transaction. Keep in mind that although each workspace can have its own ODBC connection to the database, this slows system performance. Because transaction isolation is not normally required, ODBC connections from multiple workspace objects opened by the same user are shared by default.

Some ODBC servers, such as Microsoft SQL Server, do not allow simultaneous transactions on a single connection. If you need to have more than one transaction at a time pending against such a database, set the IsolateODBCTrans property to **TRUE** on each workspace as soon as you open it. This forces a separate ODBC connection for each workspace.

For more information about workspaces, see the article "DAO Workspace." For more information about working with ODBC data sources through DAO, see the article "DAO External: Working with External Data Sources." Both articles are in *Programming with MFC*. For related information, see the topic "IsolateODBCTrans Property" in DAO Help.

See Also   **CDaoWorkspace::SetIsolateODBCTrans**

CDaoWorkspace::GetLoginTimeout

static short PASCAL GetLoginTimeout( );
   throw(CDaoException, CMemoryException);

Return Value

The number of seconds before an error occurs when you attempt to log in to an ODBC database.

Remarks

Call this member function to get the current value of the DAO LoginTimeout property for the workspace. This value represents the number of seconds before an error occurs when you attempt to log in to an ODBC database. The default LoginTimeout setting is 20 seconds. When LoginTimeout is set to 0, no timeout occurs and the communication with the data source might hang.

When you are attempting to log in to an ODBC database, such as Microsoft SQL Server, the connection may fail as a result of network errors or because the server is not running. Rather than waiting for the default 20 seconds to connect, you can specify how long the database engine waits before it produces an error. Logging in to the server happens implicitly as part of a number of different events, such as running a query on an external server database.

For more information about workspaces, see the article "DAO Workspace." For more information about working with ODBC data sources through DAO, see the article "DAO External: Working with External Data Sources." Both articles are in *Programming with MFC*. For related information, see the topic "LoginTimeout Property" in DAO Help.

See Also   **CDaoWorkspace::SetLoginTimeout**

CDaoWorkspace::GetName

CString GetName( );
   throw(CDaoException, CMemoryException);

Return Value

A **CString** containing the user-defined name of the DAO workspace object.

Remarks

Call this member function to get the user-defined name of the DAO workspace object underlying the **CDaoWorkspace** object. The name is useful for accessing the DAO workspace object in the database engine's Workspaces collection by name.

For more information about workspaces, see the article "DAO Workspace" in *Programming with MFC*. For related information, see the topic "Name Property" in DAO Help.

CDaoWorkspace::GetUserName

CString GetUserName( );
   throw(CDaoException, CMemoryException);

Return Value

A **CString** that represents the owner of the workspace object.

Remarks

Call this member function to obtain the name of the owner of the workspace.

To get or set the permissions for the workspace owner, call DAO directly to check the Permissions property setting; this determines what permissions that user has. To work with permissions, you need a SYSTEM.MDA file.

For more information about workspaces, see the article DAO Workspace. For information about calling DAO directly, see Technical Note 54 under MFC in Books Online. For related information, see the topic "UserName Property" in DAO Help.

See Also   **CDaoWorkspace::SetDefaultUser**

CDaoWorkspace::GetVersion

static CString PASCAL GetVersion( );
    throw(CDaoException, CMemoryException);

Return Value

A **CString** that indicates the version of the database engine associated with the object.

Remarks

Call this member function to determine the version of the Microsoft Jet database engine in use. The value returned represents the version number in the form "major.minor"; for example, "3.0". The product version number (for example, 3.0) consists of the version number (3), a period, and the release number (0).

For more information about obtaining workspace information, see the article "DAO: Obtaining Information About DAO Objects" in *Programming with MFC*. For related information, see the topic "Version Property" in DAO Help.

See Also   **CDaoDatabase::GetVersion**

CDaoWorkspace::GetWorkspaceCount

short GetWorkspaceCount( );
    throw(CDaoException, CMemoryException);

Return Value

The number of open workspaces in the Workspaces collection.

Remarks

Call this member function to retrieve the number of DAO workspace objects in the database engine's Workspaces collection. This count does not include any open workspaces not appended to the collection. **GetWorkspaceCount** is useful if you need to loop through all defined workspaces in the Workspaces collection. To obtain information about a given workspace in the collection, see **GetWorkspaceInfo**.

Typical usage is to call **GetWorkspaceCount** for the number of open workspaces, then use that number as a loop index for repeated calls to **GetWorkspaceInfo**.

For more information about obtaining workspace information, see the article "DAO: Obtaining Information About DAO Objects" in *Programming with MFC*.

CDaoWorkspace::GetWorkspaceInfo

void GetWorkspaceInfo(int *nIndex***, CDaoWorkspaceInfo&** *wkspcinfo***,**
    DWORD *dwInfoOptions* **= AFX_DAO_PRIMARY_INFO);**
    throw(CDaoException, CMemoryException);
void GetWorkspaceInfo(LPCTSTR *lpszName***, CDaoWorkspaceInfo&** *wkspcinfo***,**
    DWORD *dwInfoOptions* **= AFX_DAO_PRIMARY_INFO);**
    throw(CDaoException, CMemoryException);

Parameters

nIndex   The zero-based index of the database object in the Workspaces collection, for lookup by index.

wkspcinfo   A reference to a **CDaoWorkspaceInfo** object that returns the information requested.

dwInfoOptions   Options that specify which information about the workspace to retrieve. The available options are listed here along with what they cause the function to return:

- **AFX_DAO_PRIMARY_INFO** (Default) Name

- **AFX_DAO_SECONDARY_INFO** Primary information plus: User Name

- **AFX_DAO_ALL_INFO** Primary and secondary information plus: Isolate ODBCTrans

lpszName   The name of the workspace object, for lookup by name. The name is a string with up to 14 characters that uniquely names the new workspace object.

Remarks

Call this member function to obtain various kinds of information about a workspace open in the session. For a description of the information returned in *wkspcinfo*, see the **CDaoWorkspaceInfo** structure. This structure has members that correspond to the items of information listed above in the description of *dwInfoOptions*. When you request information at one level, you get information for prior levels as well.

For more information about obtaining workspace information, see the article "DAO: Obtaining Information About DAO Objects" in *Programming with MFC*.

See Also   **CDaoWorkspace::GetWorkspaceCount**

CDaoWorkspace::Idle

static void PASCAL Idle(int *nAction* **= dbFreeLocks);**
 throw(CDaoException, CMemoryException);

Parameters

nAction   An action to take during the idle processing. Currently the only valid action
is **dbFreeLocks**.

Remarks

Call **Idle** to provide the database engine with the opportunity to perform background
tasks that may not be up-to-date because of intense data processing. This is often true
in multiuser, multitasking environments in which there is not enough background
processing time to keep all records in a recordset current.

Important   Calling **Idle** is not necessary with databases created with version 3.0 of the
Microsoft Jet database engine. Use **Idle** only for databases created with earlier versions.

Usually, read locks are removed and data in local dynaset-type recordset objects is
updated only when no other actions (including mouse movements) are occurring. If
you periodically call **Idle**, you provide the database engine with time to catch up on
background processing tasks by releasing unneeded read locks. Specifying the
dbFreeLocks constant as an argument delays processing until all read locks are
released.

This member function is not needed in single-user environments unless multiple
instances of an application are running. The **Idle** member function may increase
performance in a multiuser environment because it forces the database engine to flush
data to disk, releasing locks on memory. You can also release read locks by making
operations part of a transaction.

For more information about workspaces, see the article "DAO Workspace" in
Programming with MFC. For related information, see the topic "Idle Method" in
DAO Help.

CDaoWorkspace::IsOpen

BOOL IsOpen( ) const;

Return Value

Nonzero if the workspace object is open; otherwise 0.

Remarks

Call this member function to determine whether the **CDaoWorkspace** object is open—that is, whether the MFC object has been initialized by a call to **Open** or a call to **Create**. You can call any of the member functions of a workspace that is in an open state.

For more information about workspaces, see the article "DAO Workspace" in *Programming with MFC*.

CDaoWorkspace::Open

virtual void Open(LPCTSTR *lpszName* **= NULL);**
   throw(CDaoException, CMemoryException);

Parameters

lpszName   The name of the DAO workspace object to open—a string with up to 14 characters that uniquely names the workspace. Accept the default value **NULL** to explicitly open the default workspace. For naming requirements, see the *lpszName* parameter for **Create**. For related information, see the topic "Name Property" in DAO Help.

Remarks

After constructing a **CDaoWorkspace** object, call this member function to do one of the following:

- Explicitly open the default workspace. Pass **NULL** for *lpszName*.

- Open an existing **CDaoWorkspace** object, a member of the Workspaces collection, by name. Pass a valid name for an existing workspace object.

Open puts the workspace object into an open state and also initializes the database engine if it has not already been initialized for your application.

Although many **CDaoWorkspace** member functions can only be called after the workspace has been opened, the following member functions, which operate on the database engine, are available after construction of the C++ object but before a call to **Open**:

Create	**GetVersion**	**SetDefaultUser**
GetIniPath	**Idle**	**SetIniPath**
GetLoginTimeout	**SetDefaultPassword**	**SetLoginTimeout**

For more information about workspaces, see the article "DAO Workspace" in *Programming with MFC*.

See Also   **CDaoWorkspace::IsOpen**, **CDaoWorkspace::CDaoWorkspace**, **CDaoWorkspace::Create**, **CDaoWorkspace::Close**

CDaoWorkspace::RepairDatabase

> **static void PASCAL RepairDatabase(LPCTSTR** *lpszName* **);**
> **throw(CDaoException, CMemoryException);**

Parameters

lpszName   The path and filename for an existing Microsoft Jet engine database file. If you omit the path, only the current directory is searched. If your system supports the uniform naming convention (UNC), you can also specify a network path, such as: "\\\\MYSERVER\\MYSHARE\\MYDIR\\MYDB.MDB". (Double backslashes are required in the path string because "\\" is the C++ escape character.)

Remarks

Call this member function if you need to attempt to repair a corrupted database that accesses the Microsoft Jet database engine. You must close the database specified by *lpszName* before you repair it. In a multiuser environment, other users cannot have *lpszName* open while you are repairing it. If *lpszName* is not closed or is not available for exclusive use, an error occurs.

This member function attempts to repair a database that was marked as possibly corrupt by an incomplete write operation. This can occur if an application using the Microsoft Jet database engine is closed unexpectedly because of a power outage or computer hardware problem. If you complete the operation and call the **Close** member function or you quit the application in a usual way, the database will not be marked as possibly corrupt.

Note   After repairing a database, it is also a good idea to compact it using the **CompactDatabase** member function to defragment the file and to recover disk space.

For more information about workspaces, see the article "DAO Workspace" in *Programming with MFC*. For more information about repairing databases, see the topic "RepairDatabase Method" in DAO Help.

CDaoWorkspace::Rollback

> **void Rollback( );**
> **throw(CDaoException, CMemoryException);**

Remarks

Call this member function to end the current transaction and restore all databases in the workspace to their condition before the transaction was begun.

Caution Within one workspace object, transactions are always global to the workspace and are not limited to only one database or recordset. If you perform operations on more than one database or recordset within a workspace transaction, **Rollback** restores all operations on all of those databases and recordsets.

If you close a workspace object without saving or rolling back any pending transactions, the transactions are automatically rolled back. If you call **CommitTrans** or **Rollback** without first calling **BeginTrans**, an error occurs.

Note When you begin a transaction, the database engine records its operations in a file kept in the directory specified by the TEMP environment variable on the workstation. If the transaction log file exhausts the available storage on your TEMP drive, the database engine will cause MFC to throw a **CDaoException** (DAO error 2004). At this point, if you call **CommitTrans**, an indeterminate number of operations are committed but the remaining uncompleted operations are lost, and the operation has to be restarted. Calling **Rollback** releases the transaction log and rolls back all operations in the transaction.

For more information about workspaces, see the article "DAO Workspace." For more about transactions, see the article "DAO Workspace: Managing Transactions." Both articles are in *Programming with MFC*.

See Also **CDaoRecordset**

CDaoWorkspace::SetDefaultPassword

static void PASCAL SetDefaultPassword(LPCTSTR *lpszPassword* **);**
    throw(CDaoException, CMemoryException);

Parameters

lpszPassword The default password. A password can be up to 14 characters long and can contain any character except ASCII 0 (null). Passwords are case-sensitive.

Remarks

Call this member function to set the default password that the database engine uses when a workspace object is created without a specific password. The default password that you set applies to new workspaces you create after the call. When you create subsequent workspaces, you do not need to specify a password in the **Create** call.

To use this member function:

1. Construct a **CDaoWorkspace** object but do not call **Create**.

2. Call **SetDefaultPassword** and, if you like, **SetDefaultUser**.

3. Call **Create** for this workspace object or subsequent ones, without specifying a password.

By default, the DefaultUser property is set to "admin" and the DefaultPassword property is set to an empty string ("").

For more information about workspaces, see the article "DAO Workspace" in *Programming with MFC*. For more about security, see the topic "Permissions Property" in DAO Help. For related information, see the topics "DefaultPassword Property" and "DefaultUser Property" in DAO Help.

CDaoWorkspace::SetDefaultUser

static void PASCAL SetDefaultUser(LPCTSTR *lpszDefaultUser* **);**
    throw(CDaoException, CMemoryException);

Parameters

lpszDefaultUser   The default user name. A user name can be 1–20 characters long and include alphabetic characters, accented characters, numbers, spaces, and symbols except for: " (quotation marks), / (forward slash), \ (backslash), [ ] (brackets), : (colon), | (pipe), < (less-than sign), > (greater-than sign), + (plus sign), = (equal sign), ; (semicolon), , (comma), ? (question mark), * (asterisk), leading spaces, and control characters (ASCII 00 to ASCII 31). For related information, see the topic "UserName Property" in DAO Help.

Remarks

Call this member function to set the default user name that the database engine uses when a workspace object is created without a specific user name. The default user name that you set applies to new workspaces you create after the call. When you create subsequent workspaces, you do not need to specify a user name in the **Create** call.

To use this member function:

1. Construct a **CDaoWorkspace** object but do not call **Create**.

2. Call **SetDefaultUser** and, if you like, **SetDefaultPassword**.

3. Call **Create** for this workspace object or subsequent ones, without specifying a user name.

By default, the DefaultUser property is set to "admin" and the DefaultPassword property is set to an empty string ("").

For more information about workspaces, see the article "DAO Workspace" in *Programming with MFC*. For related information, see the topics "DefaultUser Property" and "DefaultPassword Property" in DAO Help.

CDaoWorkspace::SetIniPath

static void PASCAL SetIniPath(LPCTSTR *lpszRegistrySubkey* **);**
   throw(CDaoException, CMemoryException);

Parameters

lpszRegistrySubkey   A string containing the name of a Windows registry subkey for
   the location of Microsoft Jet database engine settings or parameters needed for
   installable ISAM databases.

Remarks

Call this member function to specify the location of Windows registry settings for the
Microsoft Jet database engine. Call **SetIniPath** only if you need to specify special
settings. For more information, see the topic "IniPath Property" in DAO Help.

Important   Call **SetIniPath** during application installation, not when the application runs.
SetIniPath must be called before you open any workspaces, databases, or recordsets;
otherwise, MFC throws an exception.

You can use this mechanism to configure the database engine with user-provided
registry settings. The scope of this attribute is limited to your application and cannot
be changed without restarting your application.

For more information about workspaces, see the article "DAO Workspace" in
Programming with MFC.

CDaoWorkspace::SetIsolateODBCTrans

void SetIsolateODBCTrans(BOOL *bIsolateODBCTrans* **);**
   throw(CDaoException, CMemoryException);

Parameters

bIsolateODBCTrans   Pass **TRUE** if you want to begin isolating ODBC transactions.
   Pass **FALSE** if you want to stop isolating ODBC transactions.

Remarks

Call this member function to set the value of the DAO IsolateODBCTrans property
for the workspace. In some situations, you might need to have multiple simultaneous
transactions pending on the same ODBC database. To do this, you need to open a
separate workspace for each transaction. Although each workspace can have its own
ODBC connection to the database, this slows system performance. Because
transaction isolation is not normally required, ODBC connections from multiple
workspace objects opened by the same user are shared by default.

Some ODBC servers, such as Microsoft SQL Server, do not allow simultaneous transactions on a single connection. If you need to have more than one transaction at a time pending against such a database, set the IsolateODBCTrans property to **TRUE** on each workspace as soon as you open it. This forces a separate ODBC connection for each workspace.

For more information about workspaces, see the article "DAO Workspace." For more about transactions, see the article "DAO Workspace: Managing Transactions." For more about working with ODBC data sources through DAO, see the article "DAO External: Working with External Data Sources." All articles are in *Programming with MFC*.

See Also   **CDaoWorkspace::GetIsolateODBCTrans**

CDaoWorkspace::SetLoginTimeout

static void PASCAL SetLoginTimeout(short *nSeconds*);
    throw(CDaoException, CMemoryException);

Parameters

nSeconds   The number of seconds before an error occurs when you attempt to log in to an ODBC database.

Remarks

Call this member function to set the value of the DAO LoginTimeout property for the workspace. This value represents the number of seconds before an error occurs when you attempt to log in to an ODBC database. The default LoginTimeout setting is 20 seconds. When LoginTimeout is set to 0, no timeout occurs and the communication with the data source might hang.

When you are attempting to log in to an ODBC database, such as Microsoft SQL Server, the connection may fail as a result of network errors or because the server is not running. Rather than waiting for the default 20 seconds to connect, you can specify how long the database engine waits before it produces an error. Logging on to the server happens implicitly as part of a number of different events, such as running a query on an external server database. The timeout value is determined by the current setting of the LoginTimeout property.

For more information about workspaces, see the article "DAO Workspace." For more information about working with ODBC data sources through DAO, see the article "DAO External: Working with External Data Sources." Both articles are in *Programming with MFC*. For related information, see the topic "LoginTimeout Property" in DAO Help.

See Also   **CDaoWorkspace::GetLoginTimeout**

Data Members

CDaoWorkspace::m_pDAOWorkspace

Remarks

A pointer to the underlying DAO workspace object. Use this data member if you need direct access to the underlying DAO object. You can call the DAO object's interfaces through this pointer.

For information about accessing DAO objects directly, see Technical Note 54 under MFC in Books Online.

CDatabase

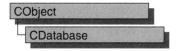

CObject

CDatabase

A **CDatabase** object represents a connection to a data source, through which you can operate on the data source. A data source is a specific instance of data hosted by some database management system (DBMS). Examples include Microsoft SQL Server, Microsoft Access, Borland® dBASE®, and xBASE. You can have one or more **CDatabase** objects active at a time in your application.

Note If you are working with the Data Access Objects (DAO) classes rather than the Open Database Connectivity (ODBC) classes, use class **CDaoDatabase** instead. For more information, see the articles "Database Overview" and "DAO and MFC." Both articles are in *Programming with MFC*.

To use **CDatabase**, construct a **CDatabase** object and call its **Open** member function. This opens a connection. When you then construct **CRecordset** objects for operating on the connected data source, pass the recordset constructor a pointer to your **CDatabase** object. When you finish using the connection, call the **Close** member function and destroy the **CDatabase** object. **Close** closes any recordsets you have not closed previously.

For more information about **CDatabase**, see the articles "Data Source (ODBC)" and "Database Overview" in *Programming with MFC*.

#include <afxdb.h>

See Also   **CRecordset**

Data Members

m_hdbc	Open Database Connectivity (ODBC) connection handle to a data source. Type **HDBC**.

Construction

CDatabase	Constructs a **CDatabase** object. You must initialize the object by calling **Open**.
Open	Establishes a connection to a data source (through an ODBC driver).
Close	Closes the data source connection.

Database Attributes

GetConnect	Returns the ODBC connect string used to connect the **CDatabase** object to a data source.
IsOpen	Returns nonzero if the **CDatabase** object is currently connected to a data source.
GetDatabaseName	Returns the name of the database currently in use.
CanUpdate	Returns nonzero if the **CDatabase** object is updatable (not read-only).
CanTransact	Returns nonzero if the data source supports transactions.
InWaitForDataSource	Returns nonzero if the **CDatabase** object is currently waiting for the server to respond.
SetLoginTimeout	Sets the number of seconds after which a data source connection attempt will time out.
SetQueryTimeout	Sets the number of seconds after which database query operations will time out. Affects all subsequent **Open**, **AddNew**, **Edit**, and **Delete** calls.
SetSynchronousMode	Enables or disables synchronous processing for all recordsets and SQL statements associated with the **CDatabase** object. Asynchronous processing is the default.

Database Operations

BeginTrans	Starts a "transaction"—a series of reversible calls to the **AddNew**, **Edit**, **Delete**, and **Update** member functions of class **CRecordset**—on the connected data source. The data source must support transactions for **BeginTrans** to have any effect.
CommitTrans	Completes a transaction begun by **BeginTrans**. Commands in the transaction that alter the data source are carried out.
Rollback	Reverses changes made during the current transaction. The data source returns to its previous state, as defined at the **BeginTrans** call, unaltered.
Cancel	Cancels an asynchronous operation.
ExecuteSQL	Executes an SQL statement. No data records are returned.

Database Overridables

OnSetOptions	Called by the framework to set standard connection options. The default implementation sets the query timeout value and the processing mode (asynchronous or synchronous). You can establish these options ahead of time by calling **SetQueryTimeout** and **SetSynchronousMode**.
OnWaitForDataSource	Called by the framework to yield processing time to other applications during a lengthy operation.

Member Functions

CDatabase::BeginTrans

> **BOOL BeginTrans( );**

Return Value

Nonzero if the call was successful and changes are committed only manually; otherwise 0.

Remarks

Call this member function to begin a transaction with the connected data source. A transaction consists of one or more calls to the **AddNew**, **Edit**, **Delete**, and **Update** **CDatabase** object. Before beginning a transaction, the **CDatabase** object must already have been connected to the data source by calling its **Open** member function. To end the transaction, call **CommitTrans** to accept all changes to the data source (and carry them out) or call **Rollback** to abort the entire transaction. Call **BeginTrans** after you open any recordsets involved in the transaction and as close to the actual update operations as possible.

Warning If you call **BeginTrans** before opening recordsets, you may have problems when you call **Rollback**. Your recordsets will be unsafe because the ODBC "cursors" the database classes use to implement your recordsets did not exist when you called **BeginTrans**. For more information about the timing of your **BeginTrans** call, see Technical Note 47 (available under MFC in Books Online).

BeginTrans may also lock data records on the server, depending on the requested concurrency and the capabilities of the data source. For information about locking data, see the article "Recordset: Locking Records (ODBC)" in *Programming with MFC*.

User-defined transactions are explained in the article "Transaction (ODBC)" in *Programming with MFC*.

BeginTrans establishes the state to which the sequence of transactions can be rolled back (reversed). To establish a new state for rollbacks, commit any current transaction, then call **BeginTrans** again.

Warning Calling **BeginTrans** again without calling **CommitTrans** or **Rollback** is an error.

Your data source may or may not sufficiently support transactions for the database classes to use them. To determine the transaction behavior of your driver, call **CanTransact**. If the data source does not sufficiently support transactions, **CDatabase** ignores transaction calls. For more information about transactions and how to tell whether they are supported, see the article "Transaction (ODBC)" in *Programming with MFC*.

Example
See the article "Transaction: Performing a Transaction in a Recordset (ODBC)" in *Programming with MFC*.

See Also   **CDatabase::CommitTrans**, **CDatabase::Rollback**, **CRecordset::CanTransact**

CDatabase::Cancel

void Cancel( );

Remarks
Call this member function to cancel an asynchronous operation in progress. This requests that the data source abort the current operation. The **OnWaitForDataSource** member function will continue to call the ODBC function until it no longer returns **SQL_STILL_EXECUTING**.

See Also   **CDatabase::SetSynchronousMode**, **CDatabase::InWaitForDataSource**, **CDatabase::OnWaitForDataSource**

CDatabase::CanTransact

BOOL CanTransact( ) const;

Return Value
Nonzero if recordsets using this **CDatabase** object allow transactions; otherwise 0.

Remarks

Call this member function to determine whether the database allows transactions. For information about transactions, see the article "Transaction (ODBC)" in *Programming with MFC*.

See Also   **CDatabase::BeginTrans**, **CDatabase::CommitTrans**, **CDatabase::Rollback**

CDatabase::CanUpdate

BOOL CanUpdate( ) const;

Return Value

Nonzero if the **CDatabase** object allows updates; otherwise 0, indicating either that you passed **TRUE** in *bReadOnly* when you opened the **CDatabase** object or that the data source itself is read-only. The data source is read-only if a call to the ODBC API function **::SQLGetInfo** for **SQL_DATASOURCE_READ_ONLY** returns "y".

Remarks

Call this member function to determine whether the **CDatabase** object allows updates. Not all drivers support updates.

CDatabase::CDatabase

CDatabase( );

Remarks

Constructs a **CDatabase** object. After constructing the object, you must call its **Open** member function to establish a connection to a specified data source.

You may find it convenient to embed the **CDatabase** object in your document class.

Example

```
//This example illustrates using CDatabase in a CDocument-derived class.

class CMyDocument : public CDocument
{
public:
    // Declare a CDatabase embedded in the document
    CDatabase m_dbCust;
    // ...
};
// ...
// Initialize when needed
CDatabase* CMyDocument::GetDatabase( )
```

```
{
    // Connect the object to a data source
    if( !m_dbCust.IsOpen( ) && !m_dbCust.Open( NULL ) )
        return NULL;
    return &m_dbCust;
}
```

See Also **CDatabase::Open**

CDatabase::Close

virtual void Close( );

Remarks

Call this member function if you want to disconnect from a data source. You must close any recordsets associated with the **CDatabase** object before you call this member function. Because **Close** does not destroy the **CDatabase** object, you can reuse the object by opening a new connection to the same data source or a different data source.

All pending **AddNew** or **Edit** statements of recordsets using the database are canceled, and all pending transactions are rolled back. Any recordsets dependent on the **CDatabase** object are left in an undefined state.

Example

```
// Close the current connection
m_dbCust.Close( );
// Perhaps connect the object to a different data source
m_dbCust.Open("MYDATASOURCE",
                        FALSE, FALSE,  "ODBC;UID=JOES");
// ...
```

See Also **CDatabase::Open**

CDatabase::CommitTrans

BOOL CommitTrans( );

Return Value

Nonzero if the updates were successfully committed; otherwise 0. If **Commit** fails, the state of the data source is undefined. You must check the data to determine its state.

Remarks

Call this member function upon completing transactions. A transaction consists of a series of calls to the **AddNew**, **Edit**, **Delete**, and **Update** member functions of a **CRecordset** object that began with a call to **BeginTrans**. **CommitTrans** commits the transaction. By default, updates are committed immediately; calling **BeginTrans** causes commitment of updates to be delayed until **CommitTrans** is called.

Until you call **CommitTrans** to end a transaction, you can call the **Rollback** member function to abort the transaction and leave the data source in its original state. To begin a new transaction, call **BeginTrans** again.

For more information about transactions, see the article "Transaction (ODBC)" in *Programming with MFC*.

Example

See the article Transaction: "Performing a Transaction in a Recordset (ODBC)" in *Programming with MFC*.

See Also   **CDatabase::BeginTrans, CDatabase::Rollback**

CDatabase::ExecuteSQL

void ExecuteSQL(LPCSTR *lpszSQL* **);**
   throw(CDBException);

Parameters

lpszSQL   Pointer to a null-terminated string containing a valid SQL command to execute. You can pass a **CString**.

Remarks

Call this member function when you need to execute an SQL command directly. Create the command as a null-terminated string. **ExecuteSQL** does not return data records. If you want to operate on records, use a recordset object instead.

Most of your commands for a data source are issued through recordset objects, which support commands for selecting data, inserting new records, deleting records, and editing records. However, not all ODBC functionality is directly supported by the database classes, so you may at times need to make a direct SQL call with **ExecuteSQL**.

Example

```
CString strCmd = "UPDATE Taxes SET Federal = 36%";
TRY
{
    m_dbCust.ExecuteSQL( strCmd );
}
CATCH(CDBException, e)
{
    // The error code is in e->m_nRetCode
}
END_CATCH
```

See Also   **CDatabase::SetSynchronousMode, CDatabase::SetLoginTimeout, CRecordset**

CDatabase::GetConnect

const CString& GetConnect( ) const;

Return Value

A **const** reference to a **CString** containing the connect string if **Open** has been called; otherwise, an empty string.

Remarks

Call this member function to retrieve the connect string used during the call to **Connect** that connected the **CDatabase** object to a data source.

See **CDatabase::Open** for a description of how the connect string is created.

See Also   **CDatabase::Open**

CDatabase::GetDatabaseName

CString GetDatabaseName( ) const;

Return Value

A **CString** containing the database name if successful; otherwise, an empty **CString**.

Remarks

Call this member function to retrieve the name of the currently connected database (provided that the data source defines a named object called "database"). This is not the same as the data source name (DSN) specified in the **Open** call. What **GetDatabaseName** returns depends on ODBC. In general, a database is a collection of tables. If this entity has a name, **GetDatabaseName** returns it.

You might, for example, want to display this name in a heading. If an error occurs while retrieving the name from ODBC, **GetDatabaseName** returns an empty **CString**.

See Also   **CDatabase::Open, CDatabase::GetConnect**

CDatabase::InWaitForDataSource

static BOOL PASCAL InWaitForDataSource( );

Return Value

Nonzero if the application is still waiting for a server to complete an operation; otherwise 0.

Remarks

Call this function from your main window's **OnCommand** or **OnCmdMsg** member function to disable user commands until a data source responds.

CDatabase::IsOpen

BOOL IsOpen( ) const;

Return Value

Nonzero if the **CDatabase** object is currently connected; otherwise 0.

Remarks

Call this member function to determine whether the **CDatabase** object is currently connected to a data source.

See Also **CDatabase::Open**

CDatabase::OnSetOptions

virtual void OnSetOptions(HSTMT *hstmt* **);**

Parameters

hstmt The ODBC statement handle for which options are being set.

Remarks

The framework calls this member function when directly executing an SQL statement with the **ExecuteSQL** member function. **CRecordset::OnSetOptions** also calls this member function. **OnSetOptions** sets options for synchronous or asynchronous processing and the login timeout value. If there have been previous calls to the **SetQueryTimeout** and **SetSynchronousMode** member functions, **OnSetOptions** reflects the current values; otherwise, it sets default values.

You do not need to override **OnSetOptions** to change the timeout and synchronous mode options. Instead, to customize the query timeout value, call **SetQueryTimeout** before creating a recordset; **OnSetOptions** will use the new value. To change the default processing mode from asynchronous to synchronous, call **SetSynchronousMode** before creating a recordset; **OnSetOptions** sets the mode to asynchronous unless you have changed it to synchronous. The values set apply to subsequent operations on all recordsets or direct SQL calls.

Override **OnSetOptions** if you want to set additional options. Your override should call the base class **OnSetOptions** either before or after you call the ODBC API function **::SQLSetStmtOption**. Follow the method illustrated in the framework's default implementation of **OnSetOptions**.

See Also **CDatabase::ExecuteSQL, CDatabase::SetQueryTimeout, CDatabase::SetSynchronousMode, CRecordset::OnSetOptions**

CDatabase::OnWaitForDataSource

virtual void OnWaitForDataSource(BOOL *bStillExecuting* **);**

Parameters

bStillExecuting   **TRUE** if this is the first time the function is called before an
asynchronous operation. Data access operations are asynchronous by default.

Remarks

The framework calls this member function to yield processing time to other
applications. You can also override it to give the user a chance to cancel a long
operation.

Override **OnWaitForDataSource** if you want to fine-tune the behavior of the default
version. For example, you may also want to detect the ESC key in your override and, if
you detect it, call the **Cancel** member function to break out of the wait loop.

CDatabase::Open

virtual BOOL Open(LPCSTR *lpszDSN*, **BOOL** *bExclusive* = **FALSE**,
BOOL *bReadOnly* = **FALSE**, **LPCSTR** *lpszConnect* = "ODBC;",
BOOL *bUseCursorLib* = **TRUE**);
throw(CDBException, CMemoryException);

Return Value

Nonzero if the connection is successfully made; otherwise 0 if the user chooses
Cancel when presented a dialog box asking for more connection information. In all
other cases, the framework throws an exception.

Parameters

lpszDSN   Specifies a data source name—a name registered with ODBC through the
ODBC Administrator program. If a DSN value is specified in *lpszConnect* (in the
form "DSN=<data-source>"), it must not be specified again in *lpszDSN*. In this
case, *lpszDSN* should be **NULL**. Otherwise, you can pass **NULL** if you want to
present the user with a Data Source dialog box in which the user can select a data
source. For further information, see "Remarks."

bExclusive   Not supported in this version of the class library. Currently, an assertion
fails if this parameter is **TRUE**. The data source is always opened as shared (not
exclusive).

bReadOnly   **TRUE** if you intend the connection to be read-only and to prohibit
updates to the data source. All dependent recordsets inherit this attribute.

lpszConnect   Specifies a connect string. The connect string concatenates
information, possibly including a data source name, a user ID valid on the data
source, a user authentication string (password, if the data source requires one),
and other information. The whole connect string must be prefixed by the string

"ODBC;" (uppercase or lowercase). The "ODBC;" string is used to indicate that the connection is to an ODBC data source; this is for upward compatibility when future versions of the class library might support non-ODBC data sources. If you do not supply *lpszConnect*, its value defaults to "ODBC;". For further information, see "Remarks."

bUseCursorLib   **TRUE** if you want the ODBC Cursor Library DLL to be loaded. The Cursor Library masks some functionality of the underlying ODBC driver, effectively preventing the use of dynasets (if the driver supports them). The only cursors supported if the Cursor Library is loaded are static snapshots and "forwardOnly" cursors. The default value is **TRUE**.

Remarks

You must call this member function to initialize a newly constructed **CDatabase** object. You cannot use the database object to construct recordset objects until it is initialized.

If the parameters in your **Open** call do not contain enough information to make the connection, the ODBC driver opens a dialog box to obtain the necessary information from the user. When you call **Open**, your connect string, *lpszConnect*, is stored privately in the **CDatabase** object and is available by calling the **GetConnect** member function.

If you wish, you can open your own dialog box before you call **Open** to get information from the user, such as a password, then add that information to the connect string you pass to **Open**. Or you might want to save the connect string you pass (perhaps in an INI file) so you can reuse it the next time your application calls **Open** on a **CDatabase** object.

You can also use the connect string for multiple levels of login authorization (each for a different **CDatabase** object) or to convey other data source-specific information. For more information about connect strings, see Chapter 5 in the ODBC *Programmer's Reference*.

It is possible for a connection attempt to time out if, for example, the DBMS host is unavailable. If the connection attempt fails, **Open** throws a **CDBException**.

Example

```
// Embed the CDatabase object in your document class
CDatabase m_dbCust( );
// ...
// Connect the object to a data source (no password)
// Instead of hard-coded values, you might use user-supplied values
m_dbCust.Open( "MYDATASOURCE", FALSE, FALSE,
                              "ODBC;UID=JOES" );
// Or query the user for all connection information
m_dbCust.Open( NULL );
```

See Also   **CDatabase::CDatabase, CDatabase::Close, CDBException, CRecordset::Open**

CDatabase::Rollback

BOOL Rollback( );

Return Value

Nonzero if the transaction was successfully reversed; otherwise 0. If a **Rollback** call fails, the data source and transaction states are undefined. If **Rollback** returns 0, you must check the data source to determine its state.

Remarks

Call this member function to reverse the changes made during a transaction. All **CRecordset AddNew**, **Edit**, **Delete**, and **Update** calls executed since the last **BeginTrans** are rolled back to the state that existed at the time of that call.

After a call to **Rollback**, the transaction is over, and you must call **BeginTrans** again for another transaction. The record that was current before you called **BeginTrans** becomes the current record again after **Rollback**.

After a rollback, the record that was current before the rollback remains current. For details about the state of the recordset and the data source after a rollback, see the article "Transaction (ODBC)" in *Programming with MFC*.

Example

See the article "Transaction: Performing a Transaction in a Recordset (ODBC)" in *Programming with MFC*.

See Also   **CDatabase::BeginTrans**, **CDatabase::CommitTrans**

CDatabase::SetSynchronousMode

void SetSynchronousMode(BOOL *bSynchronous* **);**

Parameters

bSynchronous   **TRUE** to enable synchronous processing; **FALSE** to disable.

Remarks

Call this member function to enable or disable synchronous processing of database transactions. This state applies to all subsequently opened recordsets or direct SQL calls on the **CDatabase** connection.

By default, functions are processed asynchronously. The driver returns control to an application before a function call completes; the application can continue non-database processing while the driver completes the function in progress.

Not all data sources support the ability to specify asynchronous processing.

See Also   **CDatabase::OnSetOptions**, **CDatabase::InWaitForDataSource**

CDatabase::SetLoginTimeout

void SetLoginTimeout(DWORD *dwSeconds* **);**

Parameters

dwSeconds   The number of seconds to allow before a connection attempt times out.

Remarks

Call this member function—before you call **Open**—to override the default number of seconds allowed before an attempted data source connection times out. A connection attempt might time out if, for example, the DBMS is not available. Call **SetLoginTimeout** after you construct the uninitialized **CDatabase** object but before you call **Open**.

The default value for login timeouts is 15 seconds. Not all data sources support the ability to specify a login timeout value. If the data source does not support timeout, you get trace output but not an exception. A value of 0 means "infinite."

See Also   **CDatabase::OnSetOptions**, **CDatabase::SetQueryTimeout**

CDatabase::SetQueryTimeout

void SetQueryTimeout(DWORD *dwSeconds* **);**

Parameters

dwSeconds   The number of seconds to allow before a query attempt times out.

Remarks

Call this member function to override the default number of seconds to allow before subsequent operations on the connected data source time out. An operation might time out due to network access problems, excessive query processing time, and so on. Call **SetQueryTimeout** prior to opening your recordset or prior to calling the recordset's **AddNew**, **Update** or **Delete** member functions if you want to change the query timeout value. The setting affects all subsequent **Open**, **AddNew**, **Update**, and **Delete** calls to any recordsets associated with this **CDatabase** object. Changing the query timeout value for a recordset after opening does not change the value for the recordset. For example, subsequent **Move** operations do not use the new value.

The default value for query timeouts is 15 seconds. Not all data sources support the ability to set a query timeout value. If you set a query timeout value of 0, no timeout occurs; the communication with the data source may hang. This behavior may be useful during development. If the data source does not support timeout, you get trace output but not an exception.

See Also   **CDatabase::SetLoginTimeout**

Data Members

CDatabase::m_hdbc

Remarks

Contains a public handle to an ODBC data source connection—a "connection handle." Normally, you will have no need to access this member variable directly. Instead, the framework allocates the handle when you call **Open**. The framework deallocates the handle when you call the **delete** operator on the **CDatabase** object. Note that the **Close** member function does not deallocate the handle.

Under some circumstances, however, you may need to use the handle directly. For example, if you need to call ODBC API functions directly rather than through class **CDatabase**, you may need a connection handle to pass as a parameter. See the code example below.

Example

```
// Using m_hdbc for a direct ODBC API call
// m_db is the CDatabase object; m_hdbc is its HDBC member variable
nRetcode = ::SQLGetInfo(m_db.m_hdbc, SQL_ODBC_SQL_CONFORMANCE,
                        &nValue, sizeof(nValue), &cbValue);
```

See Also   **CDatabase::Open**, **CDatabase::Close**

CDataExchange

The **CDataExchange** class supports the dialog data exchange (DDX) and dialog data validation (DDV) routines used by the Microsoft Foundation classes. Use this class if you are writing data exchange routines for custom data types or controls, or if you are writing your own data validation routines. For more information on writing your own DDX and DDV routines, see Technical Note 26 under MFC in Books Online. For an overview of DDX and DDV, see "Dialog Data Exchange and Validation" and "Dialog Boxes" in Chapter 4 of *Programming with MFC*.

A **CDataExchange** object provides the context information needed for DDX and DDV to take place. The flag **m_bSaveAndValidate** is **FALSE** when DDX is used to fill the initial values of dialog controls from data members. The flag **m_bSaveAndValidate** is **TRUE** when DDX is used to set the current values of dialog controls into data members and when DDV is used to validate the data values. If the DDV validation fails, the DDV procedure will display a message box explaining the input error. The DDV procedure will then call **Fail** to reset the focus to the offending control and throw an exception to stop the validation process.

#include <afxwin.h>

See Also **CWnd::DoDataExchange**, **CWnd::UpdateData**

Data Members

m_bSaveAndValidate	Flag for the direction of DDX and DDV.
m_pDlgWnd	The dialog box or window where the data exchange takes place.

Operations

PrepareCtrl	Prepares the specified control for data exchange or validation. Use for nonedit controls.
PrepareEditCtrl	Prepares the specified edit control for data exchange or validation.
Fail	Called when validation fails. Resets focus to the previous control and throws an exception.

Member Functions

CDataExchange::Fail

void Fail( );
throw(CUserException);

Remarks

The framework calls this member function when a dialog data validation (DDV) operation fails. **Fail** restores the focus and selection to the control whose validation failed (if there is a control to restore). **Fail** then throws an exception of type **CUserException** to stop the validation process. The exception causes a message box explaining the error to be displayed. After DDV validation fails, the user can reenter data in the offending control.

Implementors of custom DDV routines can call **Fail** from their routines when a validation fails.

For more information on writing your own DDX and DDV routines, see Technical Note 26 under MFC in Books Online. For an overview of DDX and DDV, see "Dialog Data Exchange and Validation" and "Dialog Boxes" in Chapter 4 of *Programming with MFC*.

See Also CDataExchange::PrepareCtrl, CDataExchange::PrepareEditCtrl

---

CDataExchange::PrepareCtrl

HWND PrepareCtrl(int *nIDC* **);**
    throw(CNotSupportedException);

Return Value

The **HWND** of the control being prepared for DDX or DDV.

Parameters

nIDC   The ID of the control to be prepared for DDX or DDV.

Remarks

The framework calls this member function to prepare the specified control for dialog data exchange (DDX) and validation (DDV). Use **PrepareEditCtrl** instead for edit controls; use this member function for all other controls.

Preparation consists of storing the control's **HWND** in the **CDataExchange** class. The framework uses this handle to restore the focus to the previously focused control in the event of a DDX or DDV failure.

Implementors of custom DDX or DDV routines should call **PrepareCtrl** for all non-edit controls for which they are exchanging data via DDX or validating data via DDV.

For more information on writing your own DDX and DDV routines, see Technical Note 26 under MFC in Books Online. For an overview of DDX and DDV, see "Dialog Data Exchange and Validation" and "Dialog Boxes" in Chapter 4 of *Programming with MFC*.

See Also CDataExchange::Fail

CDataExchange::PrepareEditCtrl

HWND PrepareEditCtrl(int *nIDC* **);**
    throw(CNotSupportedException);

Return Value

The **HWND** of the edit control being prepared for DDX or DDV.

Parameters

nIDC   The ID of the edit control to be prepared for DDX or DDV.

Remarks

The framework calls this member function to prepare the specified edit control for dialog data exchange (DDX) and validation (DDV). Use **PrepareCtrl** instead for all non-edit controls.

Preparation consists of two things. First, **PrepareEditCtrl** stores the control's **HWND** in the **CDataExchange** class. The framework uses this handle to restore the focus to the previously focused control in the event of a DDX or DDV failure. Second, **PrepareEditCtrl** sets a flag in the **CDataExchange** class to indicate that the control whose data is being exchanged or validated is an edit control.

Implementors of custom DDX or DDV routines should call **PrepareEditCtrl** for all edit controls for which they are exchanging data via DDX or validating data via DDV.

For more information on writing your own DDX and DDV routines, see Technical Note 26 under MFC in Books Online. For an overview of DDX and DDV, see "Dialog Data Exchange and Validation" and "Dialog Boxes" in Chapter 4 of *Programming with MFC*.

See Also   **CDataExchange::Fail**

Data Members

CDataExchange::m_bSaveAndValidate

Remarks

This flag indicates the direction of a dialog data exchange (DDX) operation. The flag is nonzero if the **CDataExchange** object is being used to move data from the dialog controls to dialog-class data members after the user edits the controls. The flag is zero if the object is being used to initialize dialog controls from dialog-class data members.

The flag is also nonzero during dialog data validation (DDV).

For more information on writing your own DDX and DDV routines, see Technical Note 26 under MFC in Books Online. For an overview of DDX and DDV, see "Dialog Data Exchange and Validation" and "Dialog Boxes" in Chapter 4 of *Programming with MFC*.

CDataExchange::m_pDlgWnd

Remarks

Contains a pointer to the **CWnd** object for which dialog data exchange (DDX) or validation (DDV) is taking place. This object is usually a **CDialog** object. Implementors of custom DDX or DDV routines can use this pointer to obtain access to the dialog window that contains the controls they are operating on.

For more information on writing your own DDX and DDV routines, see Technical Note 26 under MFC in Books Online. For an overview of DDX and DDV, see "Dialog Data Exchange and Validation" and "Dialog Boxes" in Chapter 4 of *Programming with MFC*.

CDBException

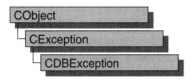

A **CDBException** object represents an exception condition arising from the database classes. The class includes two public data members you can use to determine the cause of the exception or to display a text message describing the exception. **CDBException** objects are constructed and thrown by member functions of the database classes.

Note This class is one of MFC's Open Database Connectivity (ODBC) classes. If you are instead using the newer Data Access Objects (DAO) classes, use **CDaoException** instead. All DAO class names have "CDao" as a prefix. For more information, see the articles "Database Overview" and "DAO and MFC" in *Programming with MFC*.

Exceptions are cases of abnormal execution involving conditions outside the program's control, such as data source or network I/O errors. Errors that you might expect to see in the normal course of executing your program are usually not considered exceptions.

You can access these objects within the scope of a **CATCH** expression. You can also throw **CDBException** objects from your own code with the **AfxThrowDBException** global function.

For more information about exception handling in general, or about **CDBException** objects, see the articles "Exceptions" and "Exceptions: Database Exceptions" in *Programming with MFC*.

#include <afxdb.h>

See Also   **CDatabase**, **CRecordset**, **CFieldExchange**, **AfxThrowDBException**, **CRecordset::Update**, **CRecordset::Delete**, **CException**

Data Members

m_nRetCode	Contains an Open Database Connectivity (ODBC) return code, of type **RETCODE**.
m_strError	Contains a string that describes the error in alphanumeric terms.
m_strStateNativeOrigin	Contains a string describing the error in terms of the error codes returned by ODBC.

Data Members

CDBException::m_nRetCode

Remarks

Contains an ODBC error code of type **RETCODE** returned by an ODBC application programming interface (API) function. This type includes SQL-prefixed codes defined by ODBC and AFX_SQL-prefixed codes defined by the database classes. For a **CDBException**, this member will contain one of the following values:

- **AFX_SQL_ERROR_API_CONFORMANCE** The driver for a **CDatabase::Open** call does not conform to required ODBC API Conformance level 1 (**SQL_OAC_LEVEL1**).

- **AFX_SQL_ERROR_CONNECT_FAIL** Connection to the data source failed. You passed a **NULL CDatabase** pointer to your recordset constructor and the subsequent attempt to create a connection based on **GetDefaultConnect** failed.

- **AFX_SQL_ERROR_DATA_TRUNCATED** You requested more data than you have provided storage for. For information on increasing the provided data storage for **CString** or **CByteArray** data types, see the *nMaxLength* argument for **RFX_Text** and **RFX_Binary** under "Macros and Globals."

- **AFX_SQL_ERROR_DYNASET_NOT_SUPPORTED** A call to **CRecordset::Open** requesting a dynaset failed. Dynasets are not supported by the driver.

- **AFX_SQL_ERROR_EMPTY_COLUMN_LIST** You attempted to open a table (or what you gave could not be identified as a procedure call or **SELECT** statement) but there are no columns identified in record field exchange (RFX) function calls in your **DoFieldExchange** override.

- **AFX_SQL_ERROR_FIELD_SCHEMA_MISMATCH** The type of an RFX function in your **DoFieldExchange** override is not compatible with the column data type in the recordset.

- **AFX_SQL_ERROR_ILLEGAL_MODE** You called **CRecordset::Update** without previously calling **CRecordset::AddNew** or **CRecordset::Edit**.

- **AFX_SQL_ERROR_LOCK_MODE_NOT_SUPPORTED** Your request to lock records for update could not be fulfilled because your ODBC driver does not support locking.

- **AFX_SQL_ERROR_MULTIPLE_ROWS_AFFECTED** You called **CRecordset::Update** or **Delete** for a table with no unique key and changed multiple records.

- **AFX_SQL_ERROR_NO_CURRENT_RECORD**   You attempted to edit or delete a previously deleted record. You must scroll to a new current record after a deletion.

- **AFX_SQL_ERROR_NO_POSITIONED_UPDATES**   Your request for a dynaset could not be fulfilled because your ODBC driver does not support positioned updates.

- **AFX_SQL_ERROR_NO_ROWS_AFFECTED**   You called **CRecordset::Update** or **Delete**, but when the operation began the record could no longer be found.

- **AFX_SQL_ERROR_ODBC_LOAD_FAILED**   An attempt to load the ODBC.DLL failed; Windows could not find or could not load this DLL. This error is fatal.

- **AFX_SQL_ERROR_ODBC_V2_REQUIRED**   Your request for a dynaset could not be fulfilled because a Level 2-compliant ODBC driver is required.

- **AFX_SQL_ERROR_RECORDSET_FORWARD_ONLY**   An attempt to scroll did not succeed because the data source does not support backward scrolling.

- **AFX_SQL_ERROR_SNAPSHOT_NOT_SUPPORTED**   A call to **CRecordset::Open** requesting a snapshot failed. Snapshots are not supported by the driver. (This should only occur when the ODBC cursor library— ODBCCURS.DLL—is not present.)

- **AFX_SQL_ERROR_SQL_CONFORMANCE**   The driver for a **CDatabase::Open** call does not conform to the required ODBC SQL Conformance level of "Minimum" (**SQL_OSC_MINIMUM**).

- **AFX_SQL_ERROR_SQL_NO_TOTAL**   The ODBC driver was unable to specify the total size of a **CLongBinary** data value. The operation probably failed because a global memory block could not be preallocated.

- **AFX_SQL_ERROR_RECORDSET_READONLY**   You attempted to update a read-only recordset, or the data source is read-only. No update operations can be performed with the recordset or the **CDatabase** object it is associated with.

- **SQL_ERROR**   Function failed. The error message returned by **::SQLError** is stored in the **m_strError** data member.

- **SQL_INVALID_HANDLE**   Function failed due to an invalid environment handle, connection handle, or statement handle. This indicates a programming error. No additional information is available from **::SQLError**.

The SQL-prefixed codes are defined by ODBC. The AFX-prefixed codes are defined in AFXDB.H, found in MFC\INCLUDE.

See Also   **CDatabase, CLongBinary, CRecordset**

CDBException::m_strError

Remarks

Contains a string describing the error that caused the exception. The string describes the error in alphanumeric terms. For more detailed information and an example, see **m_strStateNativeOrigin**.

See Also **CDBException::m_strStateNativeOrigin**

CDBException::m_strStateNativeOrigin

Remarks

Contains a string describing the error that caused the exception. The string is of the form "State:%s,Native:%ld,Origin:%s", where the format codes, in order, are replaced by values that describe:

- The **SQLSTATE**, a null-terminated string containing a five-character error code returned in the *szSqlState* parameter of the **::SQLError** function. **SQLSTATE** values are listed in Appendix A, "ODBC Error Codes," in the ODBC SDK *Programmer's Reference*. Example: "S0022".

- The native error code, specific to the data source, returned in the *pfNativeError* parameter of the **::SQLError** function. Example: 207.

- The error message text returned in the *szErrorMsg* parameter of the **::SQLError** function. This message consists of several bracketed names. As an error is passed from its source to the user, each ODBC component (data source, driver, Driver Manager) appends its own name. This information helps to pinpoint the origin of the error. Example: [Microsoft][ODBC SQL Server Driver][SQL Server]

The framework interprets the error string and puts its components into **m_strStateNativeOrigin**; if **m_strStateNativeOrigin** contains information for more than one error, the errors are separated by newlines. The framework puts the alphanumeric error text into **m_strError**.

For additional information about the codes used to make up this string, see the **::SQLError** function in the *ODBC SDK Programmer's Reference*.

Example

From ODBC: "State:S0022,Native:207,Origin:[Microsoft][ODBC SQL Server Driver][SQL Server] Invalid column name 'ColName'"

In **m_strStateNativeOrigin**: "State:S0022,Native:207,Origin:[Microsoft][ODBC SQL Server Driver][SQL Server]"

In **m_strError**: "Invalid column name 'ColName'"

See Also **CDBException::m_strError**

CDC

The **CDC** class defines a class of device-context objects. The **CDC** object provides member functions for working with a device context, such as a display or printer, as well as members for working with a display context associated with the client area of a window.

Do all drawing through the member functions of a **CDC** object. The class provides member functions for device-context operations, working with drawing tools, type-safe graphics device interface (GDI) object selection, and working with colors and palettes. It also provides member functions for getting and setting drawing attributes, mapping, working with the viewport, working with the window extent, converting coordinates, working with regions, clipping, drawing lines, and drawing simple shapes, ellipses, and polygons. Member functions are also provided for drawing text, working with fonts, using printer escapes, scrolling, and playing metafiles.

To use a **CDC** object, construct it, and then call its member functions that parallel Windows functions that use device contexts.

For specific uses, the Microsoft Foundation Class Library provides several classes derived from **CDC**. **CPaintDC** encapsulates calls to **BeginPaint** and **EndPaint**. **CClientDC** manages a display context associated with a window's client area. **CWindowDC** manages a display context associated with an entire window, including its frame and controls. **CMetaFileDC** associates a device context with a metafile.

CDC contains two device contexts, **m_hDC** and **m_hAttribDC**, which, on creation of a **CDC** object, refer to the same device. **CDC** directs all output GDI calls to **m_hDC** and most attribute GDI calls to **m_hAttribDC**. (An example of an attribute call is **GetTextColor**, while **SetTextColor** is an output call.)

For example, the framework uses these two device contexts to implement a **CMetaFileDC** object that will send output to a metafile while reading attributes from a physical device. Print preview is implemented in the framework in a similar fashion. You can also use the two device contexts in a similar way in your application-specific code.

There are times when you may need text-metric information from both the **m_hDC** and **m_hAttribDC** device contexts. The following pairs of functions provide this capability:

Uses m_hAttribDC	Uses m_hDC
GetTextExtent	**GetOutputTextExtent**
GetTabbedTextExtent	**GetOutputTabbedTextExtent**
GetTextMetrics	**GetOutputTextMetrics**
GetCharWidth	**GetOutputCharWidth**

For more information on **CDC**, see "Device Contexts" in Chapter 1 of *Programming with MFC*.

#include <afxwin.h>

See Also **CPaintDC**, **CWindowDC**, **CClientDC**, **CMetaFileDC**

Data Members

m_hDC	The output-device context used by this **CDC** object.
m_hAttribDC	The attribute-device context used by this **CDC** object.

Construction

CDC	Constructs a **CDC** object.

Initialization

CreateDC	Creates a device context for a specific device.
CreateIC	Creates an information context for a specific device. This provides a fast way to get information about the device without creating a device context.
CreateCompatibleDC	Creates a memory-device context that is compatible with another device context. You can use it to prepare images in memory.
DeleteDC	Deletes the Windows device context associated with this **CDC** object.
FromHandle	Returns a pointer to a **CDC** object when given a handle to a device context. If a **CDC** object is not attached to the handle, a temporary **CDC** object is created and attached.
DeleteTempMap	Called by the **CWinApp** idle-time handler to delete any temporary **CDC** object created by **FromHandle**. Also detaches the device context.
Attach	Attaches a Windows device context to this **CDC** object.
Detach	Detaches the Windows device context from this **CDC** object.
SetAttribDC	Sets **m_hAttribDC**, the attribute device context.

SetOutputDC	Sets **m_hDC**, the output device context.
ReleaseAttribDC	Releases **m_hAttribDC**, the attribute device context.
ReleaseOutputDC	Releases **m_hDC**, the output device context.
GetCurrentBitmap	Returns a pointer to the currently selected **CBitmap** object.
GetCurrentBrush	Returns a pointer to the currently selected **CBrush** object.
GetCurrentFont	Returns a pointer to the currently selected **CFont** object.
GetCurrentPalette	Returns a pointer to the currently selected **CPalette** object.
GetCurrentPen	Returns a pointer to the currently selected **CPen** object.
GetWindow	Returns the window associated with the display device context.

Device-Context Functions

GetSafeHdc	Returns **m_hDC**, the output device context.
SaveDC	Saves the current state of the device context.
RestoreDC	Restores the device context to a previous state saved with **SaveDC**.
ResetDC	Updates the **m_hAttribDC** device context.
GetDeviceCaps	Retrieves a specified kind of device-specific information about a given display device's capabilities.
IsPrinting	Determines whether the device context is being used for printing.

Drawing-Tool Functions

GetBrushOrg	Retrieves the origin of the current brush.
SetBrushOrg	Specifies the origin for the next brush selected into a device context.
EnumObjects	Enumerates the pens and brushes available in a device context.

Type-Safe Selection Helpers

| SelectObject | Selects a GDI drawing object such as a pen. |
| SelectStockObject | Selects one of the predefined stock pens, brushes, or fonts provided by Windows. |

Color and Color Palette Functions

| GetNearestColor | Retrieves the closest logical color to a specified logical color that the given device can represent. |
| SelectPalette | Selects the logical palette. |

RealizePalette	Maps palette entries in the current logical palette to the system palette.
UpdateColors	Updates the client area of the device context by matching the current colors in the client area to the system palette on a pixel-by-pixel basis.
GetHalftoneBrush	Retrieves a halftone brush.

Drawing-Attribute Functions

GetBkColor	Retrieves the current background color.
SetBkColor	Sets the current background color.
GetBkMode	Retrieves the background mode.
SetBkMode	Sets the background mode.
GetPolyFillMode	Retrieves the current polygon-filling mode.
SetPolyFillMode	Sets the polygon-filling mode.
GetROP2	Retrieves the current drawing mode.
SetROP2	Sets the current drawing mode.
GetStretchBltMode	Retrieves the current bitmap-stretching mode.
SetStretchBltMode	Sets the bitmap-stretching mode.
GetTextColor	Retrieves the current text color.
SetTextColor	Sets the text color.
GetColorAdjustment	Retrieves the color adjustment values for the device context.
SetColorAdjustment	Sets the color adjustment values for the device context using the specified values.

Mapping Functions

GetMapMode	Retrieves the current mapping mode.
SetMapMode	Sets the current mapping mode.
GetViewportOrg	Retrieves the x- and y-coordinates of the viewport origin.
SetViewportOrg	Sets the viewport origin.
OffsetViewportOrg	Modifies the viewport origin relative to the coordinates of the current viewport origin.
GetViewportExt	Retrieves the x- and y-extents of the viewport.
SetViewportExt	Sets the x- and y-extents of the viewport.
ScaleViewportExt	Modifies the viewport extent relative to the current values.
GetWindowOrg	Retrieves the x- and y-coordinates of the origin of the associated window.
SetWindowOrg	Sets the window origin of the device context.
OffsetWindowOrg	Modifies the window origin relative to the coordinates of the current window origin.

GetWindowExt	Retrieves the x- and y-extents of the associated window.
SetWindowExt	Sets the x- and y-extents of the associated window.
ScaleWindowExt	Modifies the window extents relative to the current values.

Coordinate Functions

DPtoHIMETRIC	Converts device units into **HIMETRIC** units.
DPtoLP	Converts device units into logical units.
HIMETRICtoDP	Converts **HIMETRIC** units into device units.
HIMETRICtoLP	Converts **HIMETRIC** units into logical units.
LPtoDP	Converts logical units into device units.
LPtoHIMETRIC	Converts logical units into **HIMETRIC** units.

Region Functions

FillRgn	Fills a specific region with the specified brush.
FrameRgn	Draws a border around a specific region using a brush.
InvertRgn	Inverts the colors in a region.
PaintRgn	Fills a region with the selected brush.

Clipping Functions

SetBoundsRect	Controls the accumulation of bounding-rectangle information for the specified device context.
GetBoundsRect	Returns the current accumulated bounding rectangle for the specified device context.
GetClipBox	Retrieves the dimensions of the tightest bounding rectangle around the current clipping boundary.
SelectClipRgn	Combines the given region with the current clipping region by using the specified mode.
ExcludeClipRect	Creates a new clipping region that consists of the existing clipping region minus the specified rectangle.
ExcludeUpdateRgn	Prevents drawing within invalid areas of a window by excluding an updated region in the window from a clipping region.
IntersectClipRect	Creates a new clipping region by forming the intersection of the current region and a rectangle.
OffsetClipRgn	Moves the clipping region of the given device.
PtVisible	Specifies whether the given point is within the clipping region.
RectVisible	Determines whether any part of the given rectangle lies within the clipping region.

Line-Output Functions

GetCurrentPosition	Retrieves the current position of the pen (in logical coordinates).
MoveTo	Moves the current position.
LineTo	Draws a line from the current position up to, but not including, a point.
Arc	Draws an elliptical arc.
ArcTo	Draws an elliptical arc. This function is similar to **Arc**, except that the current position is updated.
AngleArc	Draws a line segment and an arc, and moves the current position to the ending point of the arc.
GetArcDirection	Returns the current arc direction for the device context.
SetArcDirection	Sets the drawing direction to be used for arc and rectangle functions.
PolyDraw	Draws a set of line segments and Bézier splines. This function updates the current position.
Polyline	Draws a set of line segments connecting the specified points.
PolyPolyline	Draws multiple series of connected line segments. The current position is neither used nor updated by this function.
PolylineTo	Draws one or more straight lines and moves the current position to the ending point of the last line.
PolyBezier	Draws one or more Bézier splines. The current position is neither used nor updated.
PolyBezierTo	Draws one or more Bézier splines, and moves the current position to the ending point of the last Bézier spline.

Simple-Drawing Functions

FillRect	Fills a given rectangle by using a specific brush.
FrameRect	Draws a border around a rectangle.
InvertRect	Inverts the contents of a rectangle.
DrawIcon	Draws an icon.
DrawDragRect	Erases and redraws a rectangle as it is dragged.
FillSolidRect	Fills a rectangle with a solid color.
Draw3dRect	Draws a three-dimensional rectangle.
DrawEdge	Draws the edges of a rectangle.
DrawFrameControl	Draw a frame control.
DrawState	Displays an image and applies a visual effect to indicate a state.

Ellipse and Polygon Functions

Chord	Draws a chord (a closed figure bounded by the intersection of an ellipse and a line segment).
DrawFocusRect	Draws a rectangle in the style used to indicate focus.
Ellipse	Draws an ellipse.
Pie	Draws a pie-shaped wedge.
Polygon	Draws a polygon consisting of two or more points (vertices) connected by lines.
PolyPolygon	Creates two or more polygons that are filled using the current polygon-filling mode. The polygons may be disjoint or they may overlap.
Polyline	Draws a polygon consisting of a set of line segments connecting specified points.
Rectangle	Draws a rectangle using the current pen and fills it using the current brush.
RoundRect	Draws a rectangle with rounded corners using the current pen and filled using the current brush.

Bitmap Functions

PatBlt	Creates a bit pattern.
BitBlt	Copies a bitmap from a specified device context.
StretchBlt	Moves a bitmap from a source rectangle and device into a destination rectangle, stretching or compressing the bitmap if necessary to fit the dimensions of the destination rectangle.
GetPixel	Retrieves the RGB color value of the pixel at the specified point.
SetPixel	Sets the pixel at the specified point to the closest approximation of the specified color.
SetPixelV	Sets the pixel at the specified coordinates to the closest approximation of the specified color. **SetPixelV** is faster than **SetPixel** because it does not need to return the color value of the point actually painted.
FloodFill	Fills an area with the current brush.
ExtFloodFill	Fills an area with the current brush. Provides more flexibility than the **FloodFill** member function.
MaskBlt	Combines the color data for the source and destination bitmaps using the given mask and raster operation.
PlgBlt	Performs a bit-block transfer of the bits of color data from the specified rectangle in the source device context to the specified parallelogram in the given device context.

Text Functions

TextOut	Writes a character string at a specified location using the currently selected font.
ExtTextOut	Writes a character string within a rectangular region using the currently selected font.
TabbedTextOut	Writes a character string at a specified location, expanding tabs to the values specified in an array of tab-stop positions.
DrawText	Draws formatted text in the specified rectangle.
GetTextExtent	Computes the width and height of a line of text on the attribute device context using the current font to determine the dimensions.
GetOutputTextExtent	Computes the width and height of a line of text on the output device context using the current font to determine the dimensions.
GetTabbedTextExtent	Computes the width and height of a character string on the attribute device context.
GetOutputTabbedTextExtent	Computes the width and height of a character string on the output device context.
GrayString	Draws dimmed (grayed) text at the given location.
GetTextAlign	Retrieves the text-alignment flags.
SetTextAlign	Sets the text-alignment flags.
GetTextFace	Copies the typeface name of the current font into a buffer as a null-terminated string.
GetTextMetrics	Retrieves the metrics for the current font from the attribute device context.
GetOutputTextMetrics	Retrieves the metrics for the current font from the output device context.
SetTextJustification	Adds space to the break characters in a string.
GetTextCharacterExtra	Retrieves the current setting for the amount of intercharacter spacing.
SetTextCharacterExtra	Sets the amount of intercharacter spacing.

Font Functions

GetFontData	Retrieves font metric information from a scalable font file. The information to retrieve is identified by specifying an offset into the font file and the length of the information to return.
GetKerningPairs	Retrieves the character kerning pairs for the font that is currently selected in the specified device context.
GetOutlineTextMetrics	Retrieves font metric information for TrueType fonts.

GetGlyphOutline	Retrieves the outline curve or bitmap for an outline character in the current font.
GetCharABCWidths	Retrieves the widths, in logical units, of consecutive characters in a given range from the current font.
GetCharWidth	Retrieves the fractional widths of consecutive characters in a given range from the current font.
GetOutputCharWidth	Retrieves the widths of individual characters in a consecutive group of characters from the current font using the output device context.
SetMapperFlags	Alters the algorithm that the font mapper uses when it maps logical fonts to physical fonts.
GetAspectRatioFilter	Retrieves the setting for the current aspect-ratio filter.

Printer Escape Functions

QueryAbort	Calls the **AbortProc** callback function for a printing application and queries whether the printing should be terminated.
Escape	Allows applications to access facilities that are not directly available from a particular device through GDI. Also allows access to Windows escape functions. Escape calls made by an application are translated and sent to the device driver.
DrawEscape	Accesses drawing capabilities of a video display that are not directly available through the graphics device interface (GDI).
StartDoc	Informs the device driver that a new print job is starting.
StartPage	Informs the device driver that a new page is starting.
EndPage	Informs the device driver that a page is ending.
SetAbortProc	Sets a programmer-supplied callback function that Windows calls if a print job must be aborted.
AbortDoc	Terminates the current print job, erasing everything the application has written to the device since the last call of the **StartDoc** member function.
EndDoc	Ends a print job started by the **StartDoc** member function.

Scrolling Functions

ScrollDC	Scrolls a rectangle of bits horizontally and vertically.

Metafile Functions

PlayMetaFile	Plays the contents of the specified metafile on the given device. The enhanced version of **PlayMetaFile** displays the picture stored in the given enhanced-format metafile. The metafile can be played any number of times.

AddMetaFileComment	Copies the comment from a buffer into a specified enhanced-format metafile.

Path Functions

AbortPath	Closes and discards any paths in the device context.
BeginPath	Opens a path bracket in the device context.
CloseFigure	Closes an open figure in a path.
EndPath	Closes a path bracket and selects the path defined by the bracket into the device context.
FillPath	Closes any open figures in the current path and fills the path's interior by using the current brush and polygon-filling mode.
FlattenPath	Transforms any curves in the path selected into the current device context, and turns each curve into a sequence of lines.
GetMiterLimit	Returns the miter limit for the device context.
GetPath	Retrieves the coordinates defining the endpoints of lines and the control points of curves found in the path that is selected into the device context.
SelectClipPath	Selects the current path as a clipping region for the device context, combining the new region with any existing clipping region by using the specified mode.
SetMiterLimit	Sets the limit for the length of miter joins for the device context.
StrokeAndFillPath	Closes any open figures in a path, strikes the outline of the path by using the current pen, and fills its interior by using the current brush.
StrokePath	Renders the specified path by using the current pen.
WidenPath	Redefines the current path as the area that would be painted if the path were stroked using the pen currently selected into the device context.

Member Functions

CDC::AbortDoc

int AbortDoc( );

Return Value

A value greater than or equal to 0 if successful, or a negative value if an error has occurred. The following list shows common error values and their meanings:

- **SP_ERROR**   General error.

- **SP_OUTOFDISK**   Not enough disk space is currently available for spooling, and no more space will become available.
- **SP_OUTOFMEMORY**   Not enough memory is available for spooling.
- **SP_USERABORT**   User terminated the job through the Print Manager.

Remarks

Terminates the current print job and erases everything the application has written to the device since the last call to the **StartDoc** member function.

This member function replaces the **ABORTDOC** printer escape.

AbortDoc should be used to terminate the following:

- Printing operations that do not specify an abort function using **SetAbortProc**.
- Printing operations that have not yet reached their first **NEWFRAME** or **NEXTBAND** escape call.

If an application encounters a printing error or a canceled print operation, it must not attempt to terminate the operation by using either the **EndDoc** or **AbortDoc** member functions of class **CDC**. GDI automatically terminates the operation before returning the error value.

If the application displays a dialog box to allow the user to cancel the print operation, it must call **AbortDoc** before destroying the dialog box.

If Print Manager was used to start the print job, calling **AbortDoc** erases the entire spool job—the printer receives nothing. If Print Manager was not used to start the print job, the data may have been sent to the printer before **AbortDoc** was called. In this case, the printer driver would have reset the printer (when possible) and closed the print job.

See Also   **CDC::StartDoc**, **CDC::EndDoc**, **CDC::SetAbortProc**

CDC::AbortPath

BOOL AbortPath( )

Return Value

Nonzero if the function is successful; otherwise 0.

Remarks

Closes and discards any paths in the device context. If there is an open path bracket in the device context, the path bracket is closed and the path is discarded. If there is a closed path in the device context, the path is discarded.

See Also   **CDC::BeginPath**, **CDC::EndPath**

CDC::AddMetaFileComment

BOOL AddMetaFileComment(UINT *nDataSize*, **const BYTE*** *pCommentData* **);**

Return Value

Nonzero if the function is successful; otherwise 0.

Parameters

nDataSize   Specifies the length of the comment buffer, in bytes.

pCommentData   Points to the buffer that contains the comment.

Remarks

Copies the comment from a buffer into a specified enhanced-format metafile. A comment may include any private information—for example, the source of the picture and the date it was created. A comment should begin with an application signature, followed by the data. Comments should not contain position-specific data. Position-specific data specifies the location of a record, and it should not be included because one metafile may be embedded within another metafile. This function can only be used with enhanced metafiles.

See Also   CMetaFileDC::CreateEnhanced, ::GdiComment

CDC::AngleArc

BOOL AngleArc(int *x*, **int** *y*, **int** *nRadius*, **float** *fStartAngle*, **float** *fSweepAngle* **);**

Return Value

Nonzero if successful; otherwise 0.

Parameters

x   Specifies the logical x-coordinate of the center of the circle.

y   Specifies the logical y-coordinate of the center of the circle.

nRadius   Specifies the radius of the circle in logical units. This value must be positive.

fStartAngle   Specifies the starting angle in degrees relative to the x-axis.

fSweepAngle   Specifies the sweep angle in degrees relative to the starting angle.

Remarks

Draws a line segment and an arc. The line segment is drawn from the current position to the beginning of the arc. The arc is drawn along the perimeter of a circle with the given radius and center. The length of the arc is defined by the given start and sweep angles.

AngleArc moves the current position to the ending point of the arc. The arc drawn by this function may appear to be elliptical, depending on the current transformation and mapping mode. Before drawing the arc, this function draws the line segment from the current position to the beginning of the arc. The arc is drawn by constructing an imaginary circle with the specified radius around the specified center point. The starting point of the arc is determined by measuring counterclockwise from the x-axis of the circle by the number of degrees in the start angle. The ending point is similarly located by measuring counterclockwise from the starting point by the number of degrees in the sweep angle.

If the sweep angle is greater than 360 degrees the arc is swept multiple times. This function draws lines by using the current pen. The figure is not filled.

See Also   **CDC::Arc**, **CDC::ArcTo**, **CDC::MoveTo**, **::AngleArc**

CDC::Arc

BOOL Arc(int *x1*, **int** *y1*, **int** *x2*, **int** *y2*, **int** *x3*, **int** *y3*, **int** *x4*, **int** *y4* **);**
BOOL Arc(LPCRECT *lpRect*, **POINT** *ptStart*, **POINT** *ptEnd* **);**

Return Value

Nonzero if the function is successful; otherwise 0.

Parameters

x1   Specifies the x-coordinate of the upper-left corner of the bounding rectangle (in logical units).

y1   Specifies the y-coordinate of the upper-left corner of the bounding rectangle (in logical units).

x2   Specifies the x-coordinate of the lower-right corner of the bounding rectangle (in logical units).

y2   Specifies the y-coordinate of the lower-right corner of the bounding rectangle (in logical units).

x3   Specifies the x-coordinate of the point that defines the arc's starting point (in logical units). This point does not have to lie exactly on the arc.

y3   Specifies the y-coordinate of the point that defines the arc's starting point (in logical units). This point does not have to lie exactly on the arc.

x4   Specifies the x-coordinate of the point that defines the arc's endpoint (in logical units). This point does not have to lie exactly on the arc.

y4   Specifies the y-coordinate of the point that defines the arc's endpoint (in logical units). This point does not have to lie exactly on the arc.

lpRect   Specifies the bounding rectangle (in logical units). You can pass either an **LPRECT** or a **CRect** object for this parameter.

ptStart   Specifies the x- and y-coordinates of the point that defines the arc's starting point (in logical units). This point does not have to lie exactly on the arc. You can pass either a **POINT** structure or a **CPoint** object for this parameter.

ptEnd   Specifies the x- and y-coordinates of the point that defines the arc's ending point (in logical units). This point does not have to lie exactly on the arc. You can pass either a **POINT** structure or a **CPoint** object for this parameter.

Remarks

Draws an elliptical arc. The arc drawn by using the function is a segment of the ellipse defined by the specified bounding rectangle.

The actual starting point of the arc is the point at which a ray drawn from the center of the bounding rectangle through the specified starting point intersects the ellipse. The actual ending point of the arc is the point at which a ray drawn from the center of the bounding rectangle through the specified ending point intersects the ellipse. The arc is drawn in a counterclockwise direction. Since an arc is not a closed figure, it is not filled. Both the width and height of the rectangle must be greater than 2 units and less than 32,767 units.

See Also   **CDC::Chord**, **::Arc**, **POINT**, **RECT**

CDC::ArcTo

BOOL ArcTo(int *x1*, **int** *y1*, **int** *x2*, **int** *y2*, **int** *x3*, **int** *y3*, **int** *x4*, **int** *y4* **);**
BOOL ArcTo(LPCRECT *lpRect*, **POINT** *ptStart*, **POINT** *ptEnd* **);**

Return Value

Nonzero if the function is successful; otherwise 0.

Parameters

x1   Specifies the x-coordinate of the upper-left corner of the bounding rectangle (in logical units).

y1   Specifies the y-coordinate of the upper-left corner of the bounding rectangle (in logical units).

x2   Specifies the x-coordinate of the lower-right corner of the bounding rectangle (in logical units).

y2   Specifies the y-coordinate of the lower-right corner of the bounding rectangle (in logical units).

x3   Specifies the x-coordinate of the point that defines the arc's starting point (in logical units). This point does not have to lie exactly on the arc.

y3   Specifies the y-coordinate of the point that defines the arc's starting point (in logical units). This point does not have to lie exactly on the arc.

x4   Specifies the x-coordinate of the point that defines the arc's endpoint (in logical units). This point does not have to lie exactly on the arc.

y4   Specifies the y-coordinate of the point that defines the arc's endpoint (in logical units). This point does not have to lie exactly on the arc.

lpRect   Specifies the bounding rectangle (in logical units). You can pass either a pointer to a **RECT** data structure or a **CRect** object for this parameter.

ptStart   Specifies the x- and y-coordinates of the point that defines the arc's starting point (in logical units). This point does not have to lie exactly on the arc. You can pass either a **POINT** data structure or a **CPoint** object for this parameter.

ptEnd   Specifies the x- and y-coordinates of the point that defines the arc's ending point (in logical units). This point does not have to lie exactly on the arc. You can pass either a **POINT** data structure or a **CPoint** object for this parameter.

Remarks

Draws an elliptical arc. This function is similar to **CDC::Arc**, except that the current position is updated. The points $(x1,y1)$ and $(x2,y2)$ specify the bounding rectangle. An ellipse formed by the given bounding rectangle defines the curve of the arc. The arc extends counterclockwise (the default arc direction) from the point where it intersects the radial line from the center of the bounding rectangle to $(x3,y3)$. The arc ends where it intersects the radial line from the center of the bounding rectangle to $(x4,y4)$. If the starting point and ending point are the same, a complete ellipse is drawn.

A line is drawn from the current position to the starting point of the arc. If no error occurs, the current position is set to the ending point of the arc. The arc is drawn using the current pen; it is not filled.

See Also   **CDC::AngleArc**, **CDC::Arc**, **CDC::SetArcDirection**, **::ArcTo**

CDC::Attach

BOOL Attach(HDC *hDC* **);**

Return Value

Nonzero if the function is successful; otherwise 0.

Parameters

hDC   A Windows device context.

Remarks

Use this member function to attach an *hDC* to the **CDC** object. The *hDC* is stored in both **m_hDC**, the output device context, and in **m_hAttribDC**, the attribute device context.

See Also   **CDC::Detach**, **CDC::m_hDC**, **CDC::m_hAttribDC**

CDC::BeginPath

BOOL BeginPath( );

Return Value

Nonzero if the function is successful; otherwise 0.

Remarks

Opens a path bracket in the device context. After a path bracket is open, an application can begin calling GDI drawing functions to define the points that lie in the path. An application can close an open path bracket by calling the **EndPath** member function. When an application calls **BeginPath**, any previous paths are discarded.

The following drawing functions define points in a path:

AngleArc	**PolyBezierTo**
Arc	**PolyDraw**
ArcTo	**Polygon**
Chord	**Polyline**
CloseFigure	**PolylineTo**
Ellipse	**PolyPolygon**
ExtTextOut	**PolyPolyline**
LineTo	**Rectangle**
MoveToEx	**RoundRec**
Pie	**TextOut**
PolyBezier	

See Also   **CDC::EndPath, CDC::FillPath, CRgn::CreateFromPath, CDC::SelectClipPath, CDC::StrokeAndFillPath, CDC::StrokePath, CDC::WidenPath, ::BeginPath**

CDC::BitBlt

BOOL BitBlt(int *x*, **int** *y*, **int** *nWidth*, **int** *nHeight*, **CDC*** *pSrcDC*, **int** *xSrc*, **int** *ySrc*, **DWORD** *dwRop* **);**

Return Value

Nonzero if the function is successful; otherwise 0.

Parameters

x Specifies the logical x-coordinate of the upper-left corner of the destination rectangle.

y Specifies the logical y-coordinate of the upper-left corner of the destination rectangle.

nWidth Specifies the width (in logical units) of the destination rectangle and source bitmap.

nHeight Specifies the height (in logical units) of the destination rectangle and source bitmap.

pSrcDC Pointer to a **CDC** object that identifies the device context from which the bitmap will be copied. It must be **NULL** if *dwRop* specifies a raster operation that does not include a source.

xSrc Specifies the logical x-coordinate of the upper-left corner of the source bitmap.

ySrc Specifies the logical y-coordinate of the upper-left corner of the source bitmap.

dwRop Specifies the raster operation to be performed. Raster-operation codes define how the GDI combines colors in output operations that involve a current brush, a possible source bitmap, and a destination bitmap. The following lists raster-operation codes for *dwRop* and their descriptions:

- **BLACKNESS** Turns all output black.

- **DSTINVERT** Inverts the destination bitmap.

- **MERGECOPY** Combines the pattern and the source bitmap using the Boolean AND operator.

- **MERGEPAINT** Combines the inverted source bitmap with the destination bitmap using the Boolean OR operator.

- **NOTSRCCOPY** Copies the inverted source bitmap to the destination.

- **NOTSRCERASE** Inverts the result of combining the destination and source bitmaps using the Boolean OR operator.

- **PATCOPY** Copies the pattern to the destination bitmap.

- **PATINVERT** Combines the destination bitmap with the pattern using the Boolean XOR operator.

- **PATPAINT** Combines the inverted source bitmap with the pattern using the Boolean OR operator. Combines the result of this operation with the destination bitmap using the Boolean OR operator.

- **SRCAND** Combines pixels of the destination and source bitmaps using the Boolean AND operator.

- **SRCCOPY** Copies the source bitmap to the destination bitmap.

- **SRCERASE**   Inverts the desination bitmap and combines the result with the source bitmap using the Boolean AND operator.

- **SRCINVERT**   Combines pixels of the destination and source bitmaps using the Boolean XOR operator.

- **SRCPAINT**   Combines pixels of the destination and source bitmaps using the Boolean OR operator.

- **WHITENESS**   Turns all output white.

For a complete list of raster-operation codes, see "About Raster Operation Codes" in the "Appendices" section of the *Win32 SDK Programmer's Reference*.

Remarks

Copies a bitmap from the source device context to this current device context.

The application can align the windows or client areas on byte boundaries to ensure that the **BitBlt** operations occur on byte-aligned rectangles. (Set the **CS_BYTEALIGNWINDOW** or **CS_BYTEALIGNCLIENT** flags when you register the window classes.)

BitBlt operations on byte-aligned rectangles are considerably faster than **BitBlt** operations on rectangles that are not byte aligned. If you want to specify class styles such as byte-alignment for your own device context, you will have to register a window class rather than relying on the Microsoft Foundation classes to do it for you. Use the global function **AfxRegisterWndClass**.

GDI transforms *nWidth* and *nHeight*, once by using the destination device context, and once by using the source device context. If the resulting extents do not match, GDI uses the Windows **StretchBlt** function to compress or stretch the source bitmap as necessary.

If destination, source, and pattern bitmaps do not have the same color format, the **BitBlt** function converts the source and pattern bitmaps to match the destination. The foreground and background colors of the destination bitmap are used in the conversion.

When the **BitBlt** function converts a monochrome bitmap to color, it sets white bits (1) to the background color and black bits (0) to the foreground color. The foreground and background colors of the destination device context are used. To convert color to monochrome, **BitBlt** sets pixels that match the background color to white and sets all other pixels to black. **BitBlt** uses the foreground and background colors of the color device context to convert from color to monochrome.

Note that not all device contexts support **BitBlt**. To check whether a given device context does support **BitBlt**, use the **GetDeviceCaps** member function and specify the **RASTERCAPS** index.

See Also   **CDC::GetDeviceCaps**, **CDC::PatBlt**, **CDC::SetTextColor**, **CDC::StretchBlt**, **::StretchDIBits**, **::BitBlt**

CDC::CDC

CDC( );

Remarks

Constructs a **CDC** object.

See Also **CDC::CreateDC**, **CDC::CreateIC**, **CDC::CreateCompatibleDC**

CDC::Chord

BOOL Chord(int *x1*, **int** *y1*, **int** *x2*, **int** *y2*, **int** *x3*, **int** *y3*, **int** *x4*, **int** *y4* **);**
BOOL Chord(LPCRECT *lpRect*, **POINT** *ptStart*, **POINT** *ptEnd* **);**

Return Value

Nonzero if the function is successful; otherwise 0.

Parameters

x1 Specifies the x-coordinate of the upper-left corner of the chord's bounding rectangle (in logical units).

y1 Specifies the y-coordinate of the upper-left corner of the chord's bounding rectangle (in logical units).

x2 Specifies the x-coordinate of the lower-right corner of the chord's bounding rectangle (in logical units).

y2 Specifies the y-coordinate of the lower-right corner of the chord's bounding rectangle (in logical units).

x3 Specifies the x-coordinate of the point that defines the chord's starting point (in logical units).

y3 Specifies the y-coordinate of the point that defines the chord's starting point (in logical units).

x4 Specifies the x-coordinate of the point that defines the chord's endpoint (in logical units).

y4 Specifies the y-coordinate of the point that defines the chord's endpoint (in logical units).

lpRect Specifies the bounding rectangle (in logical units). You can pass either a **LPRECT** or a **CRect** object for this parameter.

ptStart Specifies the x- and y-coordinates of the point that defines the chord's starting point (in logical units). This point does not have to lie exactly on the chord. You can pass either a **POINT** structure or a **CPoint** object for this parameter.

ptEnd   Specifies the x- and y-coordinates of the point that defines the chord's ending point (in logical units). This point does not have to lie exactly on the chord. You can pass either a **POINT** structure or a **CPoint** object for this parameter.

Remarks

Draws a chord (a closed figure bounded by the intersection of an ellipse and a line segment). The (*x1*, *y1*) and (*x2*, *y2*) parameters specify the upper-left and lower-right corners, respectively, of a rectangle bounding the ellipse that is part of the chord. The (*x3*, *y3*) and (*x4*, *y4*) parameters specify the endpoints of a line that intersects the ellipse. The chord is drawn by using the selected pen and filled by using the selected brush.

The figure drawn by the **Chord** function extends up to, but does not include the right and bottom coordinates. This means that the height of the figure is *y2 – y1* and the width of the figure is *x2 – x1*.

See Also   CDC::Arc, ::Chord, POINT

CDC::CloseFigure

BOOL CloseFigure( );

Return Value

Nonzero if the function is successful; otherwise 0.

Remarks

Closes an open figure in a path. The function closes the figure by drawing a line from the current position to the first point of the figure (usually, the point specified by the most recent call to the **MoveTo** member function) and connects the lines by using the line join style. If a figure is closed by using the **LineTo** member function instead of **CloseFigure**, end caps are used to create the corner instead of a join. **CloseFigure** should only be called if there is an open path bracket in the device context.

A figure in a path is open unless it is explicitly closed by using this function. (A figure can be open even if the current point and the starting point of the figure are the same.) Any line or curve added to the path after **CloseFigure** starts a new figure.

See Also   CDC::BeginPath, CDC::EndPath, CDC::MoveTo, ::CloseFigure

CDC::CreateCompatibleDC

virtual BOOL CreateCompatibleDC(CDC* *pDC*);

Return Value

Nonzero if the function is successful; otherwise 0.

Parameters

pDC   A pointer to a device context. If *pDC* is **NULL**, the function creates a memory device context that is compatible with the system display.

Remarks

Creates a memory device context that is compatible with the device specified by *pDC*. A memory device context is a block of memory that represents a display surface. It can be used to prepare images in memory before copying them to the actual device surface of the compatible device.

When a memory device context is created, GDI automatically selects a 1-by-1 monochrome stock bitmap for it. GDI output functions can be used with a memory device context only if a bitmap has been created and selected into that context.

This function can only be used to create compatible device contexts for devices that support raster operations. See the **CDC::BitBlt** member function for information regarding bit-block transfers between device contexts. To determine whether a device context supports raster operations, see the **RC_BITBLT** raster capability in the member function **CDC::GetDeviceCaps**.

See Also   **CDC::CDC**, **CDC::GetDeviceCaps**, **::CreateCompatibleDC**, **CDC::BitBlt**, **CDC::CreateDC**, **CDC::CreateIC**, **CDC::DeleteDC**

CDC::CreateDC

virtual BOOL CreateDC(LPCTSTR *lpszDriverName*, **LPCTSTR** *lpszDeviceName*, **LPCTSTR** *lpszOutput*, **const void*** *lpInitData* **);**

Return Value

Nonzero if the function is successful; otherwise 0.

Parameters

lpszDriverName   Points to a null-terminated string that specifies the filename (without extension) of the device driver (for example, "EPSON"). You can also pass a **CString** object for this parameter.

lpszDeviceName   Points to a null-terminated string that specifies the name of the specific device to be supported (for example, "EPSON FX-80"). The *lpszDeviceName* parameter is used if the module supports more than one device. You can also pass a **CString** object for this parameter.

lpszOutput   Points to a null-terminated string that specifies the file or device name for the physical output medium (file or output port). You can also pass a **CString** object for this parameter.

lpInitData   Points to a **DEVMODE** structure containing device-specific initialization data for the device driver. The Windows **DocumentProperties** function retrieves this structure filled in for a given device. The *lpInitData* parameter must be **NULL** if the device driver is to use the default initialization (if any) specified by the user through the Control Panel.

Remarks

Creates a device context for the specified device.

The PRINT.H header file is required if the **DEVMODE** structure is used.

Device names follow these conventions: an ending colon (:) is recommended, but optional. Windows strips the terminating colon so that a device name ending with a colon is mapped to the same port as the same name without a colon. The driver and port names must not contain leading or trailing spaces. GDI output functions cannot be used with information contexts.

See Also   ::**DocumentProperties**, ::**CreateDC**, **CDC::DeleteDC**, **CDC::CreateIC**

CDC::CreateIC

virtual BOOL CreateIC(LPCTSTR *lpszDriverName*, **LPCTSTR** *lpszDeviceName*, **LPCTSTR** *lpszOutput*, **const void*** *lpInitData*);

Return Value

Nonzero if successful; otherwise 0.

Parameters

lpszDriverName   Points to a null-terminated string that specifies the filename (without extension) of the device driver (for example, "EPSON"). You can pass a **CString** object for this parameter.

lpszDeviceName   Points to a null-terminated string that specifies the name of the specific device to be supported (for example, "EPSON FX-80"). The *lpszDeviceName* parameter is used if the module supports more than one device. You can pass a **CString** object for this parameter.

lpszOutput   Points to a null-terminated string that specifies the file or device name for the physical output medium (file or port). You can pass a **CString** object for this parameter.

lpInitData   Points to device-specific initialization data for the device driver. The *lpInitData* parameter must be **NULL** if the device driver is to use the default initialization (if any) specified by the user through the Control Panel. See **CreateDC** for the data format for device-specific initialization.

Remarks

Creates an information context for the specified device. The information context provides a fast way to get information about the device without creating a device context.

Device names follow these conventions: an ending colon (:) is recommended, but optional. Windows strips the terminating colon so that a device name ending with a colon is mapped to the same port as the same name without a colon. The driver and port names must not contain leading or trailing spaces. GDI output functions cannot be used with information contexts.

See Also   **CDC::CreateDC**, **::CreateIC**, **CDC::DeleteDC**

CDC::DeleteDC

virtual BOOL DeleteDC( );

Return Value

Nonzero if the function completed successfully; otherwise 0.

Remarks

In general, do not call this function; the destructor will do it for you. The **DeleteDC** member function deletes the Windows device contexts that are associated with **m_hDC** in the current **CDC** object. If this **CDC** object is the last active device context for a given device, the device is notified and all storage and system resources used by the device are released.

An application should not call **DeleteDC** if objects have been selected into the device context. Objects must first be selected out of the device context before it it is deleted.

An application must not delete a device context whose handle was obtained by calling **CWnd::GetDC**. Instead, it must call **CWnd::ReleaseDC** to free the device context. The **CClientDC** and **CWindowDC** classes are provided to wrap this functionality.

The **DeleteDC** function is generally used to delete device contexts created with **CreateDC**, **CreateIC**, or **CreateCompatibleDC**.

See Also   **CDC::CDC**, **::DeleteDC**, **CDC::CreateDC**, **CDC::CreateIC**, **CDC::CreateCompatibleDC**, **CWnd::GetDC**, **CWnd::ReleaseDC**

CDC::DeleteTempMap

static void PASCAL DeleteTempMap( );

Remarks

> Called automatically by the **CWinApp** idle-time handler, **DeleteTempMap** deletes any temporary **CDC** objects created by **FromHandle**, but does not destroy the device context handles (**hDCs**) temporarily associated with the **CDC** objects.
>
> **See Also**   **CDC::Detach**, **CDC::FromHandle**, **CWinApp::OnIdle**

CDC::Detach

> **HDC Detach( );**

Return Value

> A Windows device context.

Remarks

> Call this function to detach **m_hDC** (the output device context) from the **CDC** object and set both **m_hDC** and **m_hAttribDC** to **NULL**.
>
> **See Also**   **CDC::Attach**, **CDC::m_hDC**, **CDC::m_hAttribDC**

CDC::DPtoHIMETRIC

> **void DPtoHIMETRIC(LPSIZE** *lpSize* **) const;**

Parameters

> *lpSize*   Points to a **SIZE** structure or **CSize** object.

Remarks

> Use this function when you give **HIMETRIC** sizes to OLE, converting pixels to **HIMETRIC**.
>
> If the mapping mode of the device context object is **MM_LOENGLISH**, **MM_HIENGLISH**, **MM_LOMETRIC**, or **MM_HIMETRIC**, then the conversion is based on the number of pixels in the physical inch. If the mapping mode is one of the other non-constrained modes (e.g., **MM_TEXT**), then the conversion is based on the number of pixels in the logical inch.
>
> **See Also**   **CDC::DPtoLP**, **CDC::LPtoDP**, **CDC::HIMETRICtoLP**, **CDC::HIMETRICtoDP**, **CDC::LPtoHIMETRIC**

CDC::DPtoLP

> **void DPtoLP(LPPOINT** *lpPoints*, **int** *nCount* = **1) const;**
> **void DPtoLP(LPRECT** *lpRect* **) const;**
> **void DPtoLP(LPSIZE** *lpSize* **) const;**

Parameters

lpPoints   Points to an array of **POINT** structures or **CPoint** objects.

nCount   The number of points in the array.

lpRect   Points to a **RECT** structure or **CRect** object. This parameter is used for the simple case of converting one rectangle from device points to logical points.

lpSize   Points to a **SIZE** structure or **CSize** object.

Remarks

Converts device units into logical units. The function maps the coordinates of each point, or dimension of a size, from the device coordinate system into GDI's logical coordinate system. The conversion depends on the current mapping mode and the settings of the origins and extents for the device's window and viewport.

See Also   CDC::LPtoDP, CDC::HIMETRICtoDP, ::DPtoLP, POINT, RECT, CDC::GetWindowExt, CDC::GetWindowOrg

CDC::Draw3dRect

void Draw3dRect(LPCRECT *lpRect,* **COLORREF** *clrTopLeft,* **COLORREF** *clrBottomRight* **);**
void Draw3dRect(int *x,* **int** *y,* **int** *cx,* **int** *cy,* **COLORREF** *clrTopLeft,*
   COLORREF *clrBottomRight* **);**

Parameters

lpRect   Specifies the bounding rectangle (in logical units). You can pass either a pointer to a **RECT** structure or a **CRect** object for this parameter.

clrTopLeft   Specifies the color of the top and left sides of the three-dimensional rectangle.

clrBottomRight   Specifies the color of the bottom and right sides of the three-dimensional rectangle.

x   Specifies the logical x-coordinate of the upper-left corner of the three-dimensional rectangle.

y   Specifies the logical y-coordinate of the upper-left corner of the three-dimensional rectangle.

cx   Specifies the width of the three-dimensional rectangle.

cy   Specifies the height of the three-dimensional rectangle.

Remarks

Call this member function to draw a three-dimensional rectangle. The rectangle will be drawn with the top and left sides in the color specified by *clrTopLeft* and the bottom and right sides in the color specified by *clrBottomRight*.

See Also   RECT, CRect

CDC::DrawDragRect

void DrawDragRect(LPCRECT *lpRect*, **SIZE** *size*, **LPCRECT** *lpRectLast*, **SIZE** *sizeLast*,
CBrush* *pBrush* = **NULL, CBrush*** *pBrushLast* = **NULL**);

Parameters

lpRect   Points to a **RECT** structure or a **CRect** object that specifies the logical
coordinates of a rectangle—in this case, the end position of the rectangle being
redrawn.

size   Specifies the displacement from the top-left corner of the outer border to the
top-left corner of the inner border (that is, the thickness of the border) of a
rectangle.

lpRectLast   Points to a **RECT** structure or a **CRect** object that specifies the logical
coordinates of the position of a rectangle—in this case, the original position of the
rectangle being redrawn.

sizeLast   Specifies the displacement from the top-left corner of the outer border to
the top-left corner of the inner border (that is, the thickness of the border) of the
original rectangle being redrawn.

pBrush   Pointer to a brush object. Set to **NULL** to use the default halftone brush.

pBrushLast   Pointer to the last brush object used. Set to **NULL** to use the default
halftone brush.

Remarks

Call this member function repeatedly to redraw a drag rectangle. Call it in a
loop as you sample mouse position, in order to give visual feedback. When you
call **DrawDragRect**, the previous rectangle is erased and a new one is drawn.
For example, as the user drags a rectangle across the screen, **DrawDragRect** will
erase the original rectangle and redraw a new one in its new position. By default,
DrawDragRect draws the rectangle by using a halftone brush to eliminate flicker
and to create the appearance of a smoothly moving rectangle.

The first time you call **DrawDragRect**, the *lpRectLast* parameter should be **NULL**.

See Also   RECT, CRect, CDC::GetHalftoneBrush

CDC::DrawEdge

BOOL DrawEdge(LPRECT *lpRect*, **UINT** *nEdge*, **UINT** *nFlags*);

Return Value

Nonzero if successful; otherwise 0.

Parameters

lpRect   A pointer to a **RECT** structure that contains the logical coordinates of the
rectangle.

nEdge Specifies the type of inner and outer edge to draw. This parameter must be a combination of one inner-border flag and one outer-border flag. See the "Remarks" section for a table of the parameter's types.

nFlags The flags that specify the type of border to be drawn. See the "Remarks" section for a table of the parameter's values:

Remarks

Call this member function to draw the edges of a rectangle of the specified type and style.

The inner and outer border flags are as follows:

- Inner-border flags
  - **BDR_RAISEDINNER** Raised inner edge.
  - **BDR_SUNKENINNER** Sunken inner edge.
- Outer-border flags
  - **BDR_RAISEDOUTER** Raised outer edge.
  - **BDR_SUNKENOUTER** Sunken outer edge.

The *nEdge* parameter must be a combination of one inner and one outer border flag. The *nEdge* parameter can specify one of the following flags:

- **EDGE_BUMP** Combination of **BDR_RAISEDOUTER** and **BDR_SUNKENINNER**.
- **EDGE_ETCHED** Combination of **BDR_SUNKENOUTER** and **BDR_RAISEDINNER**.
- **EDGE_RAISED** Combination of **BDR_RAISEDOUTER** and **BDR_RAISEDINNER**.
- **EDGE_SUNKEN** Combination of **BDR_SUNKENOUTER** and **BDR_SUNKENINNER**.

The *nFlags* parameter types are as follows:

- **BF_RECT** Entire border rectangle.
- **BF_LEFT** Left side of border rectangle.
- **BF_BOTTOM** Bottom of border rectangle.
- **BF_RIGHT** Right side of border rectangle.
- **BF_TOP** Top of border rectangle.
- **BF_TOPLEFT** Top and left side of border rectangle.
- **BF_TOPRIGHT** Top and right side of border rectangle.
- **BF_BOTTOMLEFT** Bottom and left side of border rectangle.
- **BF_BOTTOMRIGHT** Bottom and right side of border rectangle.

For diagonal lines, the **BF_RECT** flags specify the end point of the vector bounded by the rectangle parameter.

- **BF_DIAGONAL_ENDBOTTOMLEFT**   Diagonal border. The end point is the bottom-left corner of the rectangle; the origin is top-right corner.

- **BF_DIAGONAL_ENDBOTTOMRIGHT**   Diagonal border. The end point is the bottom-right corner of the rectangle; the origin is top-left corner.

- **BF_DIAGONAL_ENDTOPLEFT**   Diagonal border. The end point is the top-left corner of the rectangle; the origin is bottom-right corner.

- **BF_DIAGONAL_ENDTOPRIGHT**   Diagonal border. The end point is the top-right corner of the rectangle; the origin is bottom-left corner.

For more information about the Windows API **DrawEdge**, see **::DrawEdge** in the *Win32 SDK Programmer's Reference*.

See Also   **::DrawEdge**

CDC::DrawEscape

int DrawEscape(int *nEscape*, **int** *nInputSize*, **LPCSTR** *lpszInputData* **);**

Return Value

Specifies the outcome of the function. Greater than zero if successful, except for the **QUERYESCSUPPORT** draw escape, which checks for implementation only; or zero if the escape is not implemented; or less than zero if an error occurred.

Parameters

nEscape   Specifies the escape function to be performed.

nInputSize   Specifies the number of bytes of data pointed to by the *lpszInputData* parameter.

lpszInputData   Points to the input structure required for the specified escape.

Remarks

Accesses drawing capabilities of a video display that are not directly available through the graphics device interface (GDI). When an application calls **DrawEscape**, the data identified by *nInputSize* and *lpszInputData* is passed directly to the specified display driver.

See Also   **CDC::Escape**, **::DrawEscape**

CDC::DrawFocusRect

void DrawFocusRect(LPCRECT *lpRect* **);**

Parameters

lpRect   Points to a **RECT** structure or a **CRect** object that specifies the logical
coordinates of the rectangle to be drawn.

Remarks

Draws a rectangle in the style used to indicate that the rectangle has the focus.

Since this is a Boolean XOR function, calling this function a second time with the
same rectangle removes the rectangle from the display. The rectangle drawn by this
function cannot be scrolled. To scroll an area containing a rectangle drawn by this
function, first call **DrawFocusRect** to remove the rectangle from the display, then
scroll the area, and then call **DrawFocusRect** again to draw the rectangle in the new
position.

See Also   **CDC::FrameRect, ::DrawFocusRect, RECT**

CDC::DrawFrameControl

BOOL DrawFrameControl(LPRECT *lpRect***, UINT** *nType***, UINT** *nState* **);**

Return Value

Nonzero if successful; otherwise 0.

Parameters

lpRect   A pointer to a **RECT** structure that contains the logical coordinates of the
rectangle.

nType   Specifies the type of frame control to draw. This parameter can be one of the
following values:

- **DFC_BUTTON**   Standard button
- **DFC_CAPTION**   Title bar
- **DFC_MENU**   Menu
- **DFC_SCROLL**   Scroll bar

nState   Specifies the initial state of the frame control. See the "Remarks" section for
a table of the parameter's values:

Remarks

Call this member function to draw a frame control of the specified type and style.

Use the *nState* value **DFCS_ADJUSTRECT** to adjust the bounding rectangle to exclude the surrounding edge of the push button. One or more of the following values can be used to set the state of the control to be drawn:

- **DFCS_CHECKED** Button is checked.
- **DFCS_FLAT** Button has a flat border.
- **DFCS_INACTIVE** Button is inactive (grayed).
- **DFCS_MONO** Button has a monochrome border.
- **DFCS_PUSHED** Button is pushed.

In several cases, *nState* depends on the *nType* parameter. The following list shows the relationship between the four *nType* values and *nState*:

- **DFC_BUTTON**
  - **DFCS_BUTTON3STATE** Three-state button
  - **DFCS_BUTTONCHECK** Check box
  - **DFCS_BUTTONPUSH** Push button
  - **DFCS_BUTTONRADIO** Radio button
  - **DFCS_BUTTONRADIOIMAGE** Image for radio button (nonsquare needs image)
  - **DFCS_BUTTONRADIOMASK** Mask for radio button (nonsquare needs mask)
- **DFC_CAPTION**
  - **DFCS_CAPTIONCLOSE** Close button
  - **DFCS_CAPTIONHELP** Help button
  - **DFCS_CAPTIONMAX** Maximize button
  - **DFCS_CAPTIONMIN** Minimize button
  - **DFCS_CAPTIONRESTORE** Restore button
- **DFC_MENU**
  - **DFCS_MENUARROW** Submenu arrow
  - **DFCS_MENUBULLET** Bullet
  - **DFCS_MENUCHECK** Check mark
- **DFC_SCROLL**
  - **DFCS_SCROLLCOMBOBOX** Combo box scroll bar
  - **DFCS_SCROLLDOWN** Down arrow of scroll bar
  - **DFCS_SCROLLLEFT** Left arrow of scroll bar
  - **DFCS_SCROLLRIGHT** Right arrow of scroll bar

- **DFCS_SCROLLSIZEGRIP** Size grip in bottom-right corner of window
- **DFCS_SCROLLUP** Up arrow of scroll bar

For more information about the Windows API **DrawFrameControl**, see
::DrawFrameControl in the *Win32 SDK Programmer's Reference*.

See Also **::DrawFrameControl**

CDC::DrawIcon

BOOL DrawIcon(int *x*, **int** *y*, **HICON** *hIcon* **);**
BOOL DrawIcon(POINT *point*, **HICON** *hIcon* **);**

Return Value
Nonzero if the function completed successfully; otherwise 0.

Parameters
x Specifies the logical x-coordinate of the upper-left corner of the icon.

y Specifies the logical y-coordinate of the upper-left corner of the icon.

hIcon Identifies the handle of the icon to be drawn.

point Specifies the logical x- and y-coordinates of the upper-left corner of the icon.
You can pass a **POINT** structure or a **CPoint** object for this parameter.

Remarks
Draws an icon on the device represented by the current **CDC** object. The function
places the icon's upper-left corner at the location specified by *x* and *y*. The location is
subject to the current mapping mode of the device context.

The icon resource must have been previously loaded by using the functions
CWinApp::LoadIcon, **CWinApp::LoadStandardIcon**, or
CWinApp::LoadOEMIcon. The **MM_TEXT** mapping mode must be selected prior
to using this function.

See Also **CWinApp::LoadIcon**, **CWinApp::LoadStandardIcon**,
CWinApp::LoadOEMIcon, **CDC::GetMapMode**, **CDC::SetMapMode**,
::DrawIcon, **POINT**

CDC::DrawState

BOOL DrawState(CPoint *pt*, **CSize** *size*, **HBITMAP** *hBitmap*, **UINT** *nFlags*,
HBRUSH *hBrush* = **NULL** **);**
BOOL DrawState(CPoint *pt*, **CSize** *size*, **CBitmap*** *pBitmap*, **UINT** *nFlags*,
CBrush* *pBrush* = **NULL** **);**
BOOL DrawState(CPoint *pt*, **CSize** *size*, **HICON** *hIcon*, **UINT** *nFlags*,
HBRUSH *hBrush* = **NULL** **);**

BOOL DrawState(CPoint *pt*, **CSize** *size*, **HICON** *hIcon*, **UINT** *nFlags*,
    CBrush* *pBrush* **= NULL);**

BOOL DrawState(CPoint *pt*, **CSize** *size*, **LPCTSTR** *lpszText*, **UINT** *nFlags*,
    BOOL *bPrefixText* **= TRUE, int** *nTextLen* **= 0, HBRUSH** *hBrush* **= NULL);**

BOOL DrawState(CPoint *pt*, **CSize** *size*, **LPCTSTR** *lpszText*, **UINT** *nFlags*,
    BOOL *bPrefixText* **= TRUE, int** *nTextLen* **= 0, CBrush*** *pBrush* **= NULL);**

BOOL DrawState(CPoint *pt*, **CSize** *size*, **DRAWSTATEPROC** *lpDrawProc*,
    LPARAM *lData*, **UINT** *nFlags*, **HBRUSH** *hBrush* **= NULL);**

BOOL DrawState(CPoint *pt*, **CSize** *size*, **DRAWSTATEPROC** *lpDrawProc*,
    LPARAM *lData*, **UINT** *nFlags*, **CBrush*** *pBrush* **= NULL);**

Return Value

Nonzero if successful; otherwise 0.

Parameters

pt   Specifies the location of the image.

size   Specifies the size of the image.

hBitmap   A handle to a bitmap.

nFlags   Flags that specify the image type and state. See the "Remarks" section for
the possible *nFlags* types and states.

hBrush   A handle to a brush.

pBitmap   A pointer to a Cbitmap object.

pBrush   A pointer to a Cbrush object.

hIcon   A handle to an icon.

lpszText   A pointer to text.

bPrefixText   Text that may contain an accelerator mnemonic. The *lData* parameter
specifies the address of the string, and the *nTextLen* parameter specifies the length.
If *nTextLen* is 0, the string is assumed to be null-terminated.

nTextLen   Length of the text string pointed to by *lpszText*. If *nTextLen* is 0, the string
is assumed to be null-terminated.

lpDrawProc   A pointer to a callback function used to render an image. This
parameter is required if the image type in *nFlags* is **DST_COMPLEX**. It is
optional and can be **NULL** if the image type is **DST_TEXT**. For all other image
types, this parameter is ignored. For more information about the callback function,
see the **::DrawStateProc** function in the *Win32 SDK Programmer's Reference*.

lData   Specifies information about the image. The meaning of this parameter
depends on the image type.

Remarks

Call this member function to display an image and apply a visual effect to indicate a
state, such as a disabled or default state.

The parameter *nFlag* type can be set to one of the following values:

- **DST_BITMAP**   The image is a bitmap. The low-order word of the *lData* parameter is the bitmap handle.
- **DST_COMPLEX**   The image is application defined. To render the image, **DrawState** calls the callback function specified by the *lpDrawProc* parameter.
- **DST_ICON**   The image is an icon. The low-order word of *lData* is the icon handle.
- **DST_PREFIXTEXT**   The image is text that may contain an accelerator mnemonic. **DrawState** interprets the ampersand (&) prefix character as a directive to underscore the character that follows. The *lData* parameter specifies the address of the string.
- **DST_TEXT**   The image is text. The *lData* parameter specifies the address of the string.

The parameter *nFlag* state can be one of following values:

- **DSS_NORMAL**   Draws the image without any modification.
- **DSS_UNION**   Dithers the image.
- **DSS_DISABLED**   Embosses the image.
- **DSS_DEFAULT**   Makes the image bold.
- **DSS_MONO**   Draws the image using the brush specified by the *hBrush* or *pBrush* parameter.

Note   For all *nFlag* states except **DSS_NORMAL**, the image is converted to monochrome before the visual effect is applied.

For more information about the Windows API **DrawState**, see **::DrawState** in the *Win32 SDK Programmer's Reference*.

See Also   **::DrawState**, **::DrawStateProc**

CDC::DrawText

virtual int DrawText(LPCTSTR *lpszString*, **int** *nCount*, **LPRECT** *lpRect*, **UINT** *nFormat* **);**
int DrawText(const CString& *str*, **LPRECT** *lpRect*, **UINT** *nFormat* **);**

Return Value

The height of the text if the function is successful.

Parameters

lpszString   Points to the string to be drawn. If *nCount* is –1, the string must be null-terminated.

nCount   Specifies the number of chars in the string. If *nCount* is –1, then *lpszString* is assumed to be a long pointer to a null-terminated string and **DrawText** computes the character count automatically.

lpRect   Points to a **RECT** structure or **CRect** object that contains the rectangle (in logical coordinates) in which the text is to be formatted.

str   A **CString** object that contains the specified characters to be drawn.

nFormat   Specifies the method of formatting the text. It can be any combination of the following values (combine using the bitwise OR operator):

- **DT_BOTTOM**   Specifies bottom-justified text. This value must be combined with **DT_SINGLELINE**.

- **DT_CALCRECT**   Determines the width and height of the rectangle. If there are multiple lines of text, **DrawText** will use the width of the rectangle pointed to by *lpRect* and extend the base of the rectangle to bound the last line of text. If there is only one line of text, **DrawText** will modify the right side of the rectangle so that it bounds the last character in the line. In either case, **DrawText** returns the height of the formatted text, but does not draw the text.

- **DT_CENTER**   Centers text horizontally.

- **DT_EXPANDTABS**   Expands tab characters. The default number of characters per tab is eight.

- **DT_EXTERNALLEADING**   Includes the font's external leading in the line height. Normally, external leading is not included in the height of a line of text.

- **DT_LEFT**   Aligns text flush-left.

- **DT_NOCLIP**   Draws without clipping. **DrawText** is somewhat faster when **DT_NOCLIP** is used.

- **DT_NOPREFIX**   Turns off processing of prefix characters. Normally, **DrawText** interprets the ampersand (**&**) mnemonic-prefix character as a directive to underscore the character that follows, and the two-ampersand (**&&**) mnemonic-prefix characters as a directive to print a single ampersand. By specifying **DT_NOPREFIX**, this processing is turned off.

- **DT_RIGHT**   Aligns text flush-right.

- **DT_SINGLELINE**   Specifies single line only. Carriage returns and linefeeds do not break the line.

- **DT_TABSTOP**   Sets tab stops. The high-order byte of *nFormat* is the number of characters for each tab. The default number of characters per tab is eight.

- **DT_TOP**   Specifies top-justified text (single line only).

- **DT_VCENTER** Specifies vertically centered text (single line only).

- **DT_WORDBREAK** Specifies word-breaking. Lines are automatically broken between words if a word would extend past the edge of the rectangle specified by *lpRect*. A carriage return–linefeed sequence will also break the line.

Note The values **DT_CALCRECT**, **DT_EXTERNALLEADING**, **DT_INTERNAL**, **DT_NOCLIP**, and **DT_NOPREFIX** cannot be used with the **DT_TABSTOP** value.

Remarks

Call this member function to format text in the given rectangle. It formats text by expanding tabs into appropriate spaces, aligning text to the left, right, or center of the given rectangle, and breaking text into lines that fit within the given rectangle. The type of formatting is specified by *nFormat*.

This member function uses the device context's selected font, text color, and background color to draw the text. Unless the **DT_NOCLIP** format is used, **DrawText** clips the text so that the text does not appear outside the given rectangle. All formatting is assumed to have multiple lines unless the **DT_SINGLELINE** format is given.

If the selected font is too large for the specified rectangle, the **DrawText** member function does not attempt to substitute a smaller font.

If the **DT_CALCRECT** flag is specified, the rectangle specified by *lpRect* will be updated to reflect the width and height needed to draw the text.

If the **TA_UPDATECP** text-alignment flag has been set (see **CDC::SetTextAlign**), **DrawText** will display text starting at the current position, rather than at the left of the given rectangle. **DrawText** will not wrap text when the **TA_UPDATECP** flag has been set (that is, the **DT_WORDBREAK** flag will have no effect).

The text color may be set by **CDC::SetTextColor**.

See Also   **CDC::SetTextColor**, **CDC::ExtTextOut**, **CDC::TabbedTextOut**, **CDC::TextOut**, **::DrawText**, **RECT**, **CDC::SetTextAlign**

CDC::Ellipse

BOOL Ellipse(int *x1***, int** *y1***, int** *x2***, int** *y2* **);**
BOOL Ellipse(LPCRECT *lpRect* **);**

Return Value

Nonzero if the function is successful; otherwise 0.

Parameters

x1 Specifies the logical x-coordinate of the upper-left corner of the ellipse's bounding rectangle.

y1 Specifies the logical y-coordinate of the upper-left corner of the ellipse's bounding rectangle.

x2 Specifies the logical x-coordinate of the lower-right corner of the ellipse's bounding rectangle.

y2 Specifies the logical y-coordinate of the lower-right corner of the ellipse's bounding rectangle.

lpRect Specifies the ellipse's bounding rectangle. You can also pass a **CRect** object for this parameter.

Remarks

Draws an ellipse. The center of the ellipse is the center of the bounding rectangle specified by *x1*, *y1*, *x2*, and *y2*, or *lpRect*. The ellipse is drawn with the current pen, and its interior is filled with the current brush.

The figure drawn by this function extends up to, but does not include, the right and bottom coordinates. This means that the height of the figure is $y2 - y1$ and the width of the figure is $x2 - x1$.

If either the width or the height of the bounding rectangle is 0, no ellipse is drawn.

See Also **CDC::Arc**, **CDC::Chord**, **::Ellipse**

CDC::EndDoc

int EndDoc( );

Return Value

Greater than or equal to 0 if the function is successful, or a negative value if an error occurred. The following list shows common error values:

- **SP_ERROR** General error.
- **SP_OUTOFDISK** Not enough disk space is currently available for spooling, and no more space will become available.
- **SP_OUTOFMEMORY** Not enough memory is available for spooling.
- **SP_USERABORT** User ended the job through the Print Manager.

Remarks

Ends a print job started by a call to the **StartDoc** member function. This member function replaces the **ENDDOC** printer escape, and should be called immediately after finishing a successful print job.

If an application encounters a printing error or a canceled print operation, it must not attempt to terminate the operation by using either **EndDoc** or **AbortDoc**. GDI automatically terminates the operation before returning the error value.

This function should not be used inside metafiles.

See Also   **CDC::AbortDoc**, **CDC::Escape**, **CDC::StartDoc**

CDC::EndPage

int EndPage( );

Return Value

Greater than or equal to 0 if successful; otherwise it is an error value, which can be one of the following:

- **SP_ERROR**   General error.
- **SP_APPABORT**   Job was ended because the application's abort function returned 0.
- **SP_USERABORT**   User ended the job through Print Manager.
- **SP_OUTOFDISK**   Not enough disk space is currently available for spooling, and no more space will become available.
- **SP_OUTOFMEMORY**   Not enough memory is available for spooling.

Remarks

Informs the device that the application has finished writing to a page. This member function is typically used to direct the device driver to advance to a new page.

This member function replaces the **NEWFRAME** printer escape. Unlike **NEWFRAME**, this function is always called after printing a page.

See Also   **CDC::StartPage**, **CDC::StartDoc**, **CDC::Escape**

CDC::EndPath

BOOL EndPath( );

Return Value

Nonzero if the function is successful; otherwise 0.

Remarks

Closes a path bracket and selects the path defined by the bracket into the device context.

See Also   **CDC::BeginPath**

CDC::EnumObjects

int EnumObjects(int *nObjectType***, int (CALLBACK EXPORT*** *lpfn* **)(LPVOID, LPARAM), LPARAM** *lpData* **);**

Return Value

Specifies the last value returned by the callback function. Its meaning is user-defined. For more information about the callback function, see "Callback Functions for CDC::EnumObjects" in the "Callback Functions Used by MFC" section.

Parameters

nObjectType Specifies the object type. It can have the values **OBJ_BRUSH** or **OBJ_PEN**.

lpfn Is the procedure-instance address of the application-supplied callback function. See the "Remarks" section below.

lpData Points to the application-supplied data. The data is passed to the callback function along with the object information.

Remarks

Enumerates the pens and brushes available in a device context. For each object of a given type, the callback function that you pass is called with the information for that object. The system calls the callback function until there are no more objects or the callback function returns 0.

Note that new features of Microsoft Visual C++ let you use an ordinary function as the function passed to **EnumObjects**. The address passed to **EnumObjects** is a pointer to a function exported with **EXPORT** and with the Pascal calling convention. In protect-mode applications, you do not have to create this function with the Windows **MakeProcInstance** function or free the function after use with the **FreeProcInstance** Windows function.

You also do not have to export the function name in an **EXPORTS** statement in your application's module-definition file. You can instead use the **EXPORT** function modifier, as in

int CALLBACK EXPORT AFunction(**LPSTR, LPSTR**);

to cause the compiler to emit the proper export record for export by name without aliasing. This works for most needs. For some special cases, such as exporting a function by ordinal or aliasing the export, you still need to use an **EXPORTS** statement in a module-definition file.

For compiling Microsoft Foundation programs, you will normally use the /GA and /GEs compiler options. The /Gw compiler option is not used with the Microsoft Foundation classes. (If you do use the Windows function **MakeProcInstance**, you will need to explicitly cast the returned function pointer from **FARPROC** to the type needed in this API.) Callback registration interfaces are now type-safe (you must pass in a function pointer that points to the right kind of function for the specific callback).

Also note that all callback functions must trap Microsoft Foundation exceptions before returning to Windows, since exceptions cannot be thrown across callback boundaries. For more information about exceptions, see the article "Exceptions" in *Programming with the Microsoft Foundation Class Library*.

See Also **::EnumObjects**

CDC::Escape

virtual int Escape(int *nEscape,* **int** *nCount,* **LPCSTR** *lpszInData,* **LPVOID** *lpOutData* **);**
    int ExtEscape(int *nEscape,* **int** *nInputSize,* **LPCSTR** *lpszInputData,*
    int *nOutputSize,* **LPSTR** *lpszOutputData* **);**

Return Value

Positive if the function is successful, except for the **QUERYESCSUPPORT** escape, which only checks for implementation. Zero is returned if the escape is not implemented, and a negative value is returned if an error occurred. The following are common error values:

- **SP_ERROR** General error.
- **SP_OUTOFDISK** Not enough disk space is currently available for spooling, and no more space will become available.
- **SP_OUTOFMEMORY** Not enough memory is available for spooling.
- **SP_USERABORT** User ended the job through the Print Manager.

Parameters

nEscape Specifies the escape function to be performed.

For a complete list of escape functions, see the information on printer escapes in the Windows Software Development Kit documentation.

nCount Specifies the number of bytes of data pointed to by *lpszInData.*

lpszInData Points to the input data structure required for this escape.

lpOutData Points to the structure that is to receive output from this escape. The *lpOutData* parameter is **NULL** if no data is returned.

nInputSize Specifies the number of bytes of data pointed to by the *lpszInputData* parameter.

lpszInputData Points to the input structure required for the specified escape.

nOutputSize Specifies the number of bytes of data pointed to by the *lpszOutputData* parameter.

lpszOutputData Points to the structure that receives output from this escape. This parameter should be **NULL** if no data is returned.

Remarks

Allows applications to access facilities of a particular device that are not directly available through GDI. Use the first version of **Escape** to pass a driver-defined escape value to a device. Use the second version of **Escape** to pass one of the escape values defined by Windows to a device. Escape calls made by an application are translated and sent to the device driver.

The *nEscape* parameter specifies the escape function to be performed. For possible values, see the information on printer escapes in the Windows SDK documentation.

See Also   **CDC::StartDoc**, **CDC::StartPage**, **CDC::EndPage**, **CDC::SetAbortProc**, **CDC::AbortDoc**, **CDC::EndDoc**, **CDC::GetDeviceCaps**, **::ExtEscape**, **::Escape**

CDC::ExcludeClipRect

virtual int ExcludeClipRect(int *x1*, **int** *y1*, **int** *x2*, **int** *y2* **);**
virtual int ExcludeClipRect(LPCRECT *lpRect* **);**

Return Value

Specifies the new clipping region's type. It can be any of the following values:

- **COMPLEXREGION**   The region has overlapping borders.
- **ERROR**   No region was created.
- **NULLREGION**   The region is empty.
- **SIMPLEREGION**   The region has no overlapping borders.

Parameters

x1   Specifies the logical x-coordinate of the upper-left corner of the rectangle.

y1   Specifies the logical y-coordinate of the upper-left corner of the rectangle.

x2   Specifies the logical x-coordinate of the lower-right corner of the rectangle.

y2   Specifies the logical y-coordinate of the lower-right corner of the rectangle.

lpRect   Specifies the rectangle. Can also be a **CRect** object.

Remarks

Creates a new clipping region that consists of the existing clipping region minus the specified rectangle.

The width of the rectangle, specified by the absolute value of $x2 - x1$, must not exceed 32,767 units. This limit applies to the height of the rectangle as well.

See Also   **CDC::ExcludeUpdateRgn**, **::ExcludeClipRect**

CDC::ExcludeUpdateRgn

int ExcludeUpdateRgn(CWnd* *pWnd* **);**

Return Value

The type of excluded region. It can be any one of the following values:

- **COMPLEXREGION** The region has overlapping borders.
- **ERROR** No region was created.
- **NULLREGION** The region is empty.
- **SIMPLEREGION** The region has no overlapping borders.

Parameters

pWnd Points to the window object whose window is being updated.

Remarks

Prevents drawing within invalid areas of a window by excluding an updated region in the window from the clipping region associated with the **CDC** object.

See Also **CDC::ExcludeClipRect**, **::ExcludeUpdateRgn**

CDC::ExtFloodFill

BOOL ExtFloodFill(int *x*, **int** *y*, **COLORREF** *crColor*, **UINT** *nFillType* **);**

Return Value

Nonzero if the function is successful; otherwise 0 if the filling could not be completed, if the given point has the boundary color specified by *crColor* (if **FLOODFILLBORDER** was requested), if the given point does not have the color specified by *crColor* (if **FLOODFILLSURFACE** was requested), or if the point is outside the clipping region.

Parameters

x Specifies the logical x-coordinate of the point where filling begins.

y Specifies the logical y-coordinate of the point where filling begins.

crColor Specifies the color of the boundary or of the area to be filled. The interpretation of *crColor* depends on the value of *nFillType*.

nFillType Specifies the type of flood fill to be performed. It must be either of the following values:

- **FLOODFILLBORDER** The fill area is bounded by the color specified by *crColor*. This style is identical to the filling performed by **FloodFill**.
- **FLOODFILLSURFACE** The fill area is defined by the color specified by *crColor*. Filling continues outward in all directions as long as the color is encountered. This style is useful for filling areas with multicolored boundaries.

Remarks

Fills an area of the display surface with the current brush. This member function offers more flexibility than **FloodFill** because you can specify a fill type in *nFillType*.

If *nFillType* is set to **FLOODFILLBORDER**, the area is assumed to be completely bounded by the color specified by *crColor*. The function begins at the point specified by *x* and *y* and fills in all directions to the color boundary.

If *nFillType* is set to **FLOODFILLSURFACE**, the function begins at the point specified by *x* and *y* and continues in all directions, filling all adjacent areas containing the color specified by *crColor*.

Only memory-device contexts and devices that support raster-display technology support **ExtFloodFill**. For more information, see the **GetDeviceCaps** member function.

See Also   **CDC::FloodFill**, **CDC::GetDeviceCaps**, **::ExtFloodFill**

CDC::ExtTextOut

virtual BOOL ExtTextOut(int *x*, **int** *y*, **UINT** *nOptions*, **LPCRECT** *lpRect*, **LPCTSTR** *lpszString*, **UINT** *nCount*, **LPINT** *lpDxWidths* **);**
BOOL ExtTextOut(int *x*, **int** *y*, **UINT** *nOptions*, **LPCRECT** *lpRect*, **const CString&** *str*, **LPINT** *lpDxWidths* **);**

Return Value

Nonzero if the function is successful; otherwise 0.

Parameters

x   Specifies the logical x-coordinate of the character cell for the first character in the specified string.

y   Specifies the logical y-coordinate of the top of the character cell for the first character in the specified string.

nOptions   Specifies the rectangle type. This parameter can be one, both, or neither of the following values:

- **ETO_CLIPPED**   Specifies that text is clipped to the rectangle.

- **ETO_OPAQUE**   Specifies that the current background color fills the rectangle. (You can set and query the current background color with the **SetBkColor** and **GetBkColor** member functions.)

lpRect   Points to a **RECT** structure that determines the dimensions of the rectangle. This parameter can be **NULL**. You can also pass a **CRect** object for this parameter.

lpszString   Points to the specified character string to be drawn. You can also pass a **CString** object for this parameter.

nCount   Specifies the number of characters in the string. If -1, the length will be calculated.

lpDxWidths   Points to an array of values that indicate the distance between origins of adjacent character cells. For instance, *lpDxWidths*[*i*] logical units will separate the origins of character cell *i* and character cell *i* + 1. If *lpDxWidths* is **NULL**, **ExtTextOut** uses the default spacing between characters.

str   A **CString** object that contains the specified characters to be drawn.

Remarks

Call this member function to write a character string within a rectangular region using the currently selected font. The rectangular region can be opaque (filled with the current background color), and it can be a clipping region.

If *nOptions* is 0 and *lpRect* is **NULL**, the function writes text to the device context without using a rectangular region. By default, the current position is not used or updated by the function. If an application needs to update the current position when it calls **ExtTextOut**, the application can call the **CDC** member function **SetTextAlign** with *nFlags* set to **TA_UPDATECP**. When this flag is set, Windows ignores *x* and *y* on subsequent calls to **ExtTextOut** and uses the current position instead. When an application uses **TA_UPDATECP** to update the current position, **ExtTextOut** sets the current position either to the end of the previous line of text or to the position specified by the last element of the array pointed to by *lpDxWidths*, whichever is greater.

See Also   **CDC::SetTextAlign, CDC::TabbedTextOut, CDC::TextOut, CDC::GetBkColor, CDC::SetBkColor, CDC::SetTextColor, ::ExtTextOut, RECT**

CDC::FillPath

BOOL FillPath( );

Return Value

Nonzero if the function is successful; otherwise 0.

Remarks

Closes any open figures in the current path and fills the path's interior by using the current brush and polygon-filling mode. After its interior is filled, the path is discarded from the device context.

See Also   **CDC::BeginPath, CDC::SetPolyFillMode, CDC::StrokeAndFillPath, CDC::StrokePath, ::FillPath**

CDC::FillRect

void FillRect(LPCRECT *lpRect,* **CBrush*** *pBrush* **);**

Parameters

lpRect   Points to a **RECT** structure that contains the logical coordinates of the rectangle to be filled. You can also pass a **CRect** object for this parameter.

pBrush   Identifies the brush used to fill the rectangle.

Remarks

Call this member function to fill a given rectangle using the specified brush. The function fills the complete rectangle, including the left and top borders, but it does not fill the right and bottom borders.

The brush needs to either be created using the **CBrush** member functions **CreateHatchBrush**, **CreatePatternBrush**, and **CreateSolidBrush**, or retrieved by the **::GetStockObject** Windows function.

When filling the specified rectangle, **FillRect** does not include the rectangle's right and bottom sides. GDI fills a rectangle up to, but does not include, the right column and bottom row, regardless of the current mapping mode. **FillRect** compares the values of the **top**, **bottom**, **left**, and **right** members of the specified rectangle. If **bottom** is less than or equal to **top**, or if **right** is less than or equal to **left**, the rectangle is not drawn.

FillRect is similar to **CDC::FillSolidRect**; however, **FillRect** takes a brush and therefore can be used to fill a rectangle with a solid color, a dithered color, hatched brushes, or a pattern. **FillSolidRect** uses only solid colors (indicated by a **COLORREF** parameter). **FillRect** usually is slower than **FillSolidRect**.

See Also   **CBrush::CreateHatchBrush, CBrush::CreatePatternBrush, CBrush::CreateSolidBrush, ::FillRect, ::GetStockObject, RECT, CBrush, CDC::FillSolidRect**

CDC::FillRgn

BOOL FillRgn(CRgn* *pRgn,* **CBrush*** *pBrush* **);**

Return Value

Nonzero if the function is successful; otherwise 0.

Parameters

pRgn   A pointer to the region to be filled. The coordinates for the given region are specified in device units.

pBrush   Identifies the brush to be used to fill the region.

Remarks

Fills the region specified by *pRgn* with the brush specified by *pBrush*.

The brush must either be created using the **CBrush** member functions **CreateHatchBrush**, **CreatePatternBrush**, **CreateSolidBrush**, or be retrieved by **GetStockObject**.

See Also   **CDC::PaintRgn**, **CDC::FillRect**, **CBrush**, **CRgn**, **::FillRgn**

CDC::FillSolidRect

void FillSolidRect(LPCRECT *lpRect*, **COLORREF** *clr* **);**
void FillSolidRect(int *x*, **int** *y*, **int** *cx*, **int** *cy*, **COLORREF** *clr* **);**

Parameters

lpRect   Specifies the bounding rectangle (in logical units). You can pass either a pointer to a **RECT** data structure or a **CRect** object for this parameter.

clr   Specifies the color to to be used to fill the rectangle.

x   Specifies the logical x-coordinate of the upper-left corner of the rectangle.

y   Specifies the logical y-coordinate of the upper-left corner of the destination rectangle.

cx   Specifies the width of the rectangle.

cy   Specifies the height of the rectangle.

Remarks

Call this member function to fill the given rectangle with the specified solid color.

FillSolidRect is very similar to **CDC::FillRect**; however, **FillSolidRect** uses only solid colors (indicated by the **COLORREF** parameter), while **FillRect** takes a brush and therefore can be used to fill a rectangle with a solid color, a dithered color, hatched brushes, or a pattern. **FillSolidRect** usually is faster than **FillRect**.

Note   When you call **FillSolidRect**, the background color, which was previously set using **SetBkColor**, is set to the color indicated by *clr*.

See Also   **RECT**, **CRect**, **CDC::FillRect**

CDC::FlattenPath

BOOL FlattenPath( );

Return Value

Nonzero if the function is successful; otherwise 0.

Remarks

Transforms any curves in the path selected into the current device context, and turns each curve into a sequence of lines.

See Also   **CDC::WidenPath**

CDC::FloodFill

BOOL FloodFill(int *x*, **int** *y*, **COLORREF** *crColor* **);**

Return Value

Nonzero if the function is successful; otherwise 0 is returned if the filling could not be completed, the given point has the boundary color specified by *crColor*, or the point is outside the clipping region.

Parameters

x   Specifies the logical x-coordinate of the point where filling begins.

y   Specifies the logical y-coordinate of the point where filling begins.

crColor   Specifies the color of the boundary.

Remarks

Fills an area of the display surface with the current brush. The area is assumed to be bounded as specified by *crColor*. The **FloodFill** function begins at the point specified by *x* and *y* and continues in all directions to the color boundary.

Only memory-device contexts and devices that support raster-display technology support the **FloodFill** member function. For information about **RC_BITBLT** capability, see the **GetDeviceCaps** member function.

The **ExtFloodFill** function provides similar capability but greater flexibility.

See Also   **CDC::ExtFloodFill**, **CDC::GetDeviceCaps**, **::FloodFill**

CDC::FrameRect

void FrameRect(LPCRECT *lpRect*, **CBrush*** *pBrush* **);**

Parameters

lpRect   Points to a **RECT** structure or **CRect** object that contains the logical coordinates of the upper-left and lower-right corners of the rectangle. You can also pass a **CRect** object for this parameter.

pBrush   Identifies the brush to be used for framing the rectangle.

Remarks

Draws a border around the rectangle specified by *lpRect*. The function uses the given brush to draw the border. The width and height of the border is always 1 logical unit.

If the rectangle's **bottom** coordinate is less than or equal to **top**, or if **right** is less than or equal to **left**, the rectangle is not drawn.

The border drawn by **FrameRect** is in the same position as a border drawn by the **Rectangle** member function using the same coordinates (if **Rectangle** uses a pen that is 1 logical unit wide). The interior of the rectangle is not filled by **FrameRect**.

See Also   CBrush, ::FrameRect, CDC::Rectangle, CDC::FrameRgn, RECT

CDC::FrameRgn

BOOL FrameRgn(CRgn* *pRgn*, **CBrush*** *pBrush*, **int** *nWidth*, **int** *nHeight* **)**;

Return Value

Nonzero if the function is successful; otherwise 0.

Parameters

pRgn   Points to the **CRgn** object that identifies the region to be enclosed in a border. The coordinates for the given region are specified in device units.

pBrush   Points to the **CBrush** object that identifies the brush to be used to draw the border.

nWidth   Specifies the width of the border in vertical brush strokes in device units.

nHeight   Specifies the height of the border in horizontal brush strokes in device units.

Remarks

Draws a border around the region specified by *pRgn* using the brush specified by *pBrush*.

See Also   CDC::Rectangle, CDC::FrameRect, CBrush, CRgn, ::FrameRgn

CDC::FromHandle

static CDC* PASCAL FromHandle(HDC *hDC* **)**;

Return Value

The pointer may be temporary and should not be stored beyond immediate use.

Parameters

hDC   Contains a handle to a Windows device context.

Remarks

Returns a pointer to a **CDC** object when given a handle to a device context. If a **CDC** object is not attached to the handle, a temporary **CDC** object is created and attached.

See Also   CDC::DeleteTempMap

CDC::GetArcDirection

int GetArcDirection( ) const;

Return Value

Specifies the current arc direction, if successful. Following are the valid return values:

- **AD_COUNTERCLOCKWISE** Arcs and rectangles drawn counterclockwise.
- **AD_CLOCKWISE** Arcs and rectangles drawn clockwise.

If an error occurs, the return value is zero.

Remarks

Returns the current arc direction for the device context. Arc and rectangle functions use the arc direction.

See Also **CDC::SetArcDirection**, **::GetArcDirection**

CDC::GetAspectRatioFilter

CSize GetAspectRatioFilter( ) const;

Return Value

A **CSize** object representing the aspect ratio used by the current aspect ratio filter.

Remarks

Retrieves the setting for the current aspect-ratio filter. The aspect ratio is the ratio formed by a device's pixel width and height. Information about a device's aspect ratio is used in the creation, selection, and display of fonts. Windows provides a special filter, the aspect-ratio filter, to select fonts designed for a particular aspect ratio from all of the available fonts. The filter uses the aspect ratio specified by the **SetMapperFlags** member function.

See Also **CDC::SetMapperFlags**, **::GetAspectRatioFilter**, **CSize**

CDC::GetBkColor

COLORREF GetBkColor( ) const;

Return Value

An RGB color value.

Remarks

Returns the current background color. If the background mode is **OPAQUE**, the system uses the background color to fill the gaps in styled lines, the gaps between hatched lines in brushes, and the background in character cells. The system also uses the background color when converting bitmaps between color and monochrome device contexts.

See Also **CDC::GetBkMode**, **CDC::SetBkColor**, **CDC::SetBkMode**, **::GetBkColor**

CDC::GetBkMode

int GetBkMode( ) const;

Return Value

The current background mode, which can be **OPAQUE**, **TRANSPARENT**, or **TRANSPARENT1**.

Remarks

Returns the background mode. The background mode defines whether the system removes existing background colors on the drawing surface before drawing text, hatched brushes, or any pen style that is not a solid line.

See Also **CDC::GetBkColor**, **CDC::SetBkColor**, **CDC::SetBkMode**, **::GetBkMode**

CDC::GetBoundsRect

UINT GetBoundsRect(LPRECT *lpRectBounds*, **UINT** *flags* **);**

Return Value

Specifies the current state of the bounding rectangle if the function is successful. It can be a combination of the following values:

- **DCB_ACCUMULATE** Bounding rectangle accumulation is occurring.
- **DCB_RESET** Bounding rectangle is empty.
- **DCB_SET** Bounding rectangle is not empty.
- **DCB_ENABLE** Bounding accumulation is on.
- **DCB_DISABLE** Bounding accumulation is off.

Parameters

lpRectBounds Points to a buffer that will receive the current bounding rectangle. The rectangle is returned in logical coordinates.

flags   Specifies whether the bounding rectangle is to be cleared after it is returned. This parameter can be either of the following values:

- **DCB_RESET**   Forces the bounding rectangle to be cleared after it is returned.

- **DCB_WINDOWMGR**   Queries the Windows bounding rectangle instead of the application's.

Remarks

Returns the current accumulated bounding rectangle for the specified device context.

See Also   **CDC::SetBoundsRect, ::GetBoundsRect**

CDC::GetBrushOrg

CPoint GetBrushOrg( ) const;

Return Value

The current origin of the brush (in device units) as a **CPoint** object.

Remarks

Retrieves the origin (in device units) of the brush currently selected for the device context.

The initial brush origin is at (0,0) of the client area. The return value specifies this point in device units relative to the origin of the desktop window.

See Also   **CDC::SetBrushOrg, ::GetBrushOrg, CPoint**

CDC::GetCharABCWidths

BOOL GetCharABCWidths(UINT *nFirstChar*, **UINT** *nLastChar*, **LPABC** *lpabc* **) const;**
BOOL GetCharABCWidths(UINT *nFirstChar*, **UINT** *nLastChar*, **LPABCFLOAT** *lpABCF* **) const;**

Return Value

Nonzero if the function is successful; otherwise 0.

Parameters

nFirstChar   Specifies the first character in the range of characters from the current font for which character widths are returned.

nLastChar   Specifies the last character in the range of characters from the current font for which character widths are returned.

lpabc   Points to an array of **ABC** structures that receive the character widths when the function returns. This array must contain at least as many **ABC** structures as there are characters in the range specified by the *nFirstChar* and *nLastChar* parameters.

lpABCF   Points to an application-supplied buffer with an array of **ABCFLOAT** structures to receive the character widths when the function returns. The widths returned by this function are in the IEEE floating-point format.

Remarks

Retrieves the widths of consecutive characters in a specified range from the current TrueType font. The widths are returned in logical units. This function succeeds only with TrueType fonts.

The TrueType rasterizer provides "ABC" character spacing after a specific point size has been selected. "A" spacing is the distance that is added to the current position before placing the glyph. "B" spacing is the width of the black part of the glyph. "C" spacing is added to the current position to account for the white space to the right of the glyph. The total advanced width is given by A + B + C.

When the **GetCharABCWidths** member function retrieves negative "A" or "C" widths for a character, that character includes underhangs or overhangs.

To convert the ABC widths to font design units, an application should create a font whose height (as specified in the **lfHeight** member of the **LOGFONT** structure) is equal to the value stored in the **ntmSizeEM** member of the **NEWTEXTMETRIC** structure. (The value of the **ntmSizeEM** member can be retrieved by calling the **EnumFontFamilies** Windows function.)

The ABC widths of the default character are used for characters that are outside the range of the currently selected font.

To retrieve the widths of characters in non-TrueType fonts, applications should use the **GetCharWidth** member function.

See Also   **::EnumFontFamilies, CDC::GetCharWidth, ::GetCharABCWidths, ::GetCharABCWidthsFloat, ::GetCharWidthFloat, ::EnumFontFamilies, ::GetCharABCWidths**

CDC::GetCharWidth

BOOL GetCharWidth(UINT *nFirstChar*, **UINT** *nLastChar*, **LPINT** *lpBuffer*) **const;**
BOOL GetCharWidth(UINT *nFirstChar*, **UINT** *nLastChar*, **float*** *lpFloatBuffer*) **const;**

Return Value

Nonzero if the function is successful; otherwise 0.

Parameters

nFirstChar   Specifies the first character in a consecutive group of characters in the current font.

nLastChar   Specifies the last character in a consecutive group of characters in the current font.

lpBuffer Points to a buffer that will receive the width values for a consecutive group of characters in the current font.

lpFloatBuffer Points to a buffer to receive the character widths. The returned widths are in the 32-bit IEEE floating-point format. (The widths are measured along the base line of the characters.)

Remarks

Retrieves the widths of individual characters in a consecutive group of characters from the current font, using **m_hAttribDC**, the input device context. For example, if *nFirstChar* identifies the letter 'a' and *nLastChar* identifies the letter 'z', the function retrieves the widths of all lowercase characters.

The function stores the values in the buffer pointed to by *lpBuffer*. This buffer must be large enough to hold all of the widths. That is, there must be at least 26 entries in the example given.

If a character in the consecutive group of characters does not exist in a particular font, it will be assigned the width value of the default character.

See Also   **CDC::GetOutputCharWidth, CDC::m_hAttribDC, CDC::m_hDC, CDC::GetCharABCWidths, ::GetCharWidth, ::GetCharABCWidths, ::GetCharABCWidthsFloat, ::GetCharWidthFloat**

CDC::GetClipBox

virtual int GetClipBox(LPRECT *lpRect* **) const;**

Return Value

The clipping region's type. It can be any of the following values:

- **COMPLEXREGION** Clipping region has overlapping borders.
- **ERROR** Device context is not valid.
- **NULLREGION** Clipping region is empty.
- **SIMPLEREGION** Clipping region has no overlapping borders.

Parameters

lpRect Points to the **RECT** structure or **CRect** object that is to receive the rectangle dimensions.

Remarks

Retrieves the dimensions of the tightest bounding rectangle around the current clipping boundary. The dimensions are copied to the buffer pointed to by *lpRect*.

See Also   **CDC::SelectClipRgn, ::GetClipBox, RECT**

CDC::GetColorAdjustment

BOOL GetColorAdjustment(LPCOLORADJUSTMENT *lpColorAdjust* **) const;**

Return Value

Nonzero if the function is successful; otherwise 0.

Parameters

lpColorAdjust   Points to a **COLORADJUSTMENT** data structure to receive the color adjustment values.

Remarks

Retrieves the color adjustment values for the device context.

See Also   CDC::SetColorAdjustment

CDC::GetCurrentBitmap

CBitmap* GetCurrentBitmap( ) const;

Return Value

Pointer to a **CBitmap** object, if successful; otherwise **NULL**.

Remarks

Returns a pointer to the currently selected **CBitmap** object. This member function may return temporary objects.

See Also   CDC::SelectObject, ::GetCurrentObject

CDC::GetCurrentBrush

CBrush* GetCurrentBrush( ) const;

Return Value

Pointer to a **CBrush** object, if successful; otherwise **NULL**.

Remarks

Returns a pointer to the currently selected **CBrush** object. This member function may return temporary objects.

See Also   CDC::SelectObject, ::GetCurrentObject

CDC::GetCurrentFont

CFont* GetCurrentFont( ) const;

Return Value

Pointer to a **CFont** object, if successful; otherwise **NULL**.

Remarks

Returns a pointer to the currently selected **CFont** object. This member function may return temporary objects.

See Also   **CDC::SelectObject, ::GetCurrentObject**

CDC::GetCurrentPalette

CPalette* GetCurrentPalette( ) const;

Return Value

Pointer to a **CPalette** object, if successful; otherwise **NULL**.

Remarks

Returns a pointer to the currently selected **CPalette** object. This member function may return temporary objects.

See Also   **CDC::SelectObject, ::GetCurrentObject**

CDC::GetCurrentPen

CPen* GetCurrentPen( ) const;

Return Value

Pointer to a **CPen** object, if successful; otherwise **NULL**.

Remarks

Returns a pointer to the currently selected **CPen** object. This member function may return temporary objects.

See Also   **CDC::SelectObject, ::GetCurrentObject**

CDC::GetCurrentPosition

CPoint GetCurrentPosition( ) const;

Return Value

The current position as a **CPoint** object.

Remarks

Retrieves the current position (in logical coordinates). The current position can be set with the **MoveTo** member function.

See Also   **CDC::MoveTo, CPoint, ::GetCurrentPosition**

CDC::GetDeviceCaps

int GetDeviceCaps(int *nIndex* **) const;**

Return Value

The value of the requested capability if the function is successful.

Parameters

nIndex   Specifies the type of information to return. It can be any one of the following values:

- **DRIVERVERSION**   Version number; for example, 0x100 for 1.0.
- **TECHNOLOGY**   Device technology. It can be any one of the following:

Value	Meaning
DT_PLOTTER	Vector plotter
DT_RASDISPLAY	Raster display
DT_RASPRINTER	Raster printer
DT_RASCAMERA	Raster camera
DT_CHARSTREAM	Character stream
DT_METAFILE	Metafile
DT_DISPFILE	Display file

- **HORZSIZE**   Width of the physical display (in millimeters).
- **VERTSIZE**   Height of the physical display (in millimeters).
- **HORZRES**   Width of the display (in pixels).
- **VERTRES**   Height of the display (in raster lines).
- **LOGPIXELSX**   Number of pixels per logical inch along the display width.
- **LOGPIXELSY**   Number of pixels per logical inch along the display height.
- **BITSPIXEL**   Number of adjacent color bits for each pixel.
- **PLANES**   Number of color planes.
- **NUMBRUSHES**   Number of device-specific brushes.
- **NUMPENS**   Number of device-specific pens.
- **NUMFONTS**   Number of device-specific fonts.
- **NUMCOLORS**   Number of entries in the device's color table.
- **ASPECTX**   Relative width of a device pixel as used for line drawing.
- **ASPECTY**   Relative height of a device pixel as used for line drawing.
- **ASPECTXY**   Diagonal width of the device pixel as used for line drawing.
- **PDEVICESIZE**   Size of the **PDEVICE** internal data structure.

- **CLIPCAPS** Clipping capabilities of the device. It can be one of the following:

Value	Meaning
CP_NONE	Output is not clipped.
CP_RECTANGLE	Output is clipped to rectangles.
CP_REGION	Output is clipped to regions.

- **SIZEPALETTE** Number of entries in the system palette. This index is valid only if the device driver sets the **RC_PALETTE** bit in the **RASTERCAPS** index.

- **NUMRESERVED** Number of reserved entries in the system palette. This index is valid only if the device driver sets the **RC_PALETTE** bit in the **RASTERCAPS** index.

- **COLORRES** Actual color resolution of the device in bits per pixel. This index is valid only if the device driver sets the **RC_PALETTE** bit in the **RASTERCAPS** index.

- **RASTERCAPS** Value that indicates the raster capabilities of the device. It can be a combination of the following:

Value	Meaning
RC_BANDING	Requires banding support.
RC_BIGFONT	Supports fonts larger than 64K.
RC_BITBLT	Capable of transferring bitmaps.
RC_BITMAP64	Supports bitmaps larger than 64K.
RC_DEVBITS	Supports device bitmaps.
RC_DI_BITMAP	Capable of supporting the **SetDIBits** and **GetDIBits** Windows functions.
RC_DIBTODEV	Capable of supporting the **SetDIBitsToDevice** Windows function.
RC_FLOODFILL	Capable of performing flood fills.
RC_GDI20_OUTPUT	Capable of supporting Windows version 2.0 features.
RC_GDI20_STATE	Includes a state block in the device context.
RC_NONE	Supports no raster operations.
RC_OP_DX_OUTPUT	Supports dev opaque and DX array.
RC_PALETTE	Specifies a palette-based device.
RC_SAVEBITMAP	Capable of saving bitmaps locally.
RC_SCALING	Capable of scaling.
RC_STRETCHBLT	Capable of performing the **StretchBlt** member function.
RC_STRETCHDIB	Capable of performing the **StretchDIBits** Windows function.

- **CURVECAPS** The curve capabilities of the device. It can be a combination of the following:

Value	Meaning
CC_NONE	Supports curves.
CC_CIRCLES	Supports circles.
CC_PIE	Supports pie wedges.
CC_CHORD	Supports chords.
CC_ELLIPSES	Supports ellipses.
CC_WIDE	Supports wide borders.
CC_STYLED	Supports styled borders.
CC_WIDESTYLED	Supports wide, styled borders.
CC_INTERIORS	Supports interiors.
CC_ROUNDRECT	Supports rectangles with rounded corners.

- **LINECAPS** Line capabilities the device supports. It can be a combination of the following:

Value	Meaning
LC_NONE	Supports no lines.
LC_POLYLINE	Supports polylines.
LC_MARKER	Supports markers.
LC_POLYMARKER	Supports polymarkers.
LC_WIDE	Supports wide lines.
LC_STYLED	Supports styled lines.
LC_WIDESTYLED	Supports wide, styled lines.
LC_INTERIORS	Supports interiors.

- **POLYGONALCAPS** Polygonal capabilities the device supports. It can be a combination of the following:

Value	Meaning
PC_NONE	Supports no polygons.
PC_POLYGON	Supports alternate fill polygons.
PC_RECTANGLE	Supports rectangles.
PC_WINDPOLYGON	Supports winding number fill polygons.
PC_SCANLINE	Supports scan lines.
PC_WIDE	Supports wide borders.
PC_STYLED	Supports styled borders.
PC_WIDESTYLED	Supports wide, styled borders.
PC_INTERIORS	Supports interiors.

- **TEXTCAPS**   Text capabilities the device supports. It can be a combination of the following:

Value	Meaning
TC_OP_CHARACTER	Supports character output precision, which indicates the device can place device fonts at any pixel location. This is required for any device with device fonts.
TC_OP_STROKE	Supports stroke output precision, which indicates the device can omit any stroke of a device font.
TC_CP_STROKE	Supports stroke clip precision, which indicates the device can clip device fonts to a pixel boundary.
TC_CR_90	Supports 90-degree character rotation, which indicates the device can rotate characters only 90 degrees at a time.
TC_CR_ANY	Supports character rotation at any degree, which indicates the device can rotate device fonts through any angle.
TC_SF_X_YINDEP	Supports scaling independent of x and y directions, which indicates the device can scale device fonts separately in x and y directions.
TC_SA_DOUBLE	Supports doubled characters for scaling, which indicates the device can double the size of device fonts.
TC_SA_INTEGER	Supports integer multiples for scaling, which indicates the device can scale the size of device fonts in any integer multiple.
TC_SA_CONTIN	Supports any multiples for exact scaling, which indicates the device can scale device fonts by any amount but still preserve the x and y ratios.
TC_EA_DOUBLE	Supports double-weight characters, which indicates the device can make device fonts bold. If this bit is not set for printer drivers, GDI attempts to create bold device fonts by printing them twice.
TC_IA_ABLE	Supports italics, which indicates the device can make device fonts italic. If this bit is not set, GDI assumes italics are not available.
TC_UA_ABLE	Supports underlining, which indicates the device can underline device fonts. If this bit is not set, GDI creates underlines for device fonts.
TC_SO_ABLE	Supports strikeouts, which indicates the device can strikeout device fonts. If this bit is not set, GDI creates strikeouts for device fonts.

Value	Meaning
TC_RA_ABLE	Supports raster fonts, which indicates that GDI should enumerate any raster or TrueType fonts available for this device in response to a call to the **EnumFonts** or **EnumFontFamilies** Windows functions. If this bit is not set, GDI-supplied raster or TrueType fonts are not enumerated when these functions are called.
TC_VA_ABLE	Supports vector fonts, which indicates that GDI should enumerate any vector fonts available for this device in response to a call to the **EnumFonts** or **EnumFontFamilies** Windows functions. This is significant for vector devices only (that is, for plotters). Display drivers (which must be able to use raster fonts) and raster printer drivers always enumerate vector fonts, because GDI rasterizes vector fonts before sending them to the driver.
TC_RESERVED	Reserved; must be 0.

Remarks

Retrieves a wide range of device-specific information about the display device.

See Also   **::GetDeviceCaps**

CDC::GetFontData

DWORD GetFontData(DWORD *dwTable***, DWORD** *dwOffset***, LPVOID** *lpData***, DWORD** *cbData* **) const;**

Return Value

Specifies the number of bytes returned in the buffer pointed to by *lpData* if the function is successful; otherwise –1.

Parameters

dwTable   Specifies the name of the metric table to be returned. This parameter can be one of the metric tables documented in the TrueType Font Files specification published by Microsoft Corporation. If this parameter is 0, the information is retrieved starting at the beginning of the font file.

dwOffset   Specifies the offset from the beginning of the table at which to begin retrieving information. If this parameter is 0, the information is retrieved starting at the beginning of the table specified by the *dwTable* parameter. If this value is greater than or equal to the size of the table, **GetFontData** returns 0.

lpData   Points to a buffer that will receive the font information. If this value is **NULL**, the function returns the size of the buffer required for the font data specified in the *dwTable* parameter.

    cbData   Specifies the length, in bytes, of the information to be retrieved. If this parameter is 0, **GetFontData** returns the size of the data specified in the *dwTable* parameter.

Remarks

Retrieves font-metric information from a scalable font file. The information to retrieve is identified by specifying an offset into the font file and the length of the information to return.

An application can sometimes use the **GetFontData** member function to save a TrueType font with a document. To do this, the application determines whether the font can be embedded and then retrieves the entire font file, specifying 0 for the *dwTable*, *dwOffset*, and *cbData* parameters.

Applications can determine whether a font can be embedded by checking the **otmfsType** member of the **OUTLINETEXTMETRIC** structure. If bit 1 of **otmfsType** is set, embedding is not permitted for the font. If bit 1 is clear, the font can be embedded. If bit 2 is set, the embedding is read only.

If an application attempts to use this function to retrieve information for a non-TrueType font, the **GetFontData** member function returns −1.

See Also   **CDC::GetOutlineTextMetrics**, **::GetFontData**, **OUTLINETEXTMETRIC**

CDC::GetGlyphOutline

    DWORD GetGlyphOutline(UINT *nChar*, **UINT** *nFormat*, **LPGLYPHMETRICS** *lpgm*, **DWORD** *cbBuffer*, **LPVOID** *lpBuffer*, **const MAT2 FAR*** *lpmat2* **) const;**

Return Value

The size, in bytes, of the buffer required for the retrieved information if *cbBuffer* is 0 or *lpBuffer* is **NULL**. Otherwise, it is a positive value if the function is successful, or −1 if there is an error.

Parameters

    nChar   Specifies the character for which information is to be returned.

    nFormat   Specifies the format in which the function is to return information. It can be one of the following values, or 0.

Value	Meaning
GGO_BITMAP	Returns the glyph bitmap. When the function returns, the buffer pointed to by *lpBuffer* contains a 1-bit-per-pixel bitmap whose rows start on doubleword boundaries.
GGO_NATIVE	Returns the curve data points in the rasterizer's native format, using device units. When this value is specified, any transformation specified in *lpmat2* is ignored.

When the value of *nFormat* is 0, the function fills in a **GLYPHMETRICS** structure but does not return glyph-outline data.

lpgm Points to a **GLYPHMETRICS** structure that describes the placement of the glyph in the character cell.

cbBuffer Specifies the size of the buffer into which the function copies information about the outline character. If this value is 0 and the *nFormat* parameter is either the **GGO_BITMAP** or **GGO_NATIVE** values, the function returns the required size of the buffer.

lpBuffer Points to a buffer into which the function copies information about the outline character. If *nFormat* specifies the **GGO_NATIVE** value, the information is copied in the form of **TTPOLYGONHEADER** and **TTPOLYCURVE** structures. If this value is **NULL** and *nFormat* is either the **GGO_BITMAP** or **GGO_NATIVE** value, the function returns the required size of the buffer.

lpmat2 Points to a **MAT2** structure that contains a transformation matrix for the character. This parameter cannot be **NULL**, even when the **GGO_NATIVE** value is specified for *nFormat*.

Remarks

Retrieves the outline curve or bitmap for an outline character in the current font.

An application can rotate characters retrieved in bitmap format by specifying a 2-by-2 transformation matrix in the structure pointed to by *lpmat2*.

A glyph outline is returned as a series of contours. Each contour is defined by a **TTPOLYGONHEADER** structure followed by as many **TTPOLYCURVE** structures as are required to describe it. All points are returned as **POINTFX** structures and represent absolute positions, not relative moves. The starting point given by the **pfxStart** member of the **TTPOLYGONHEADER** structure is the point at which the outline for a contour begins. The **TTPOLYCURVE** structures that follow can be either polyline records or spline records. Polyline records are a series of points; lines drawn between the points describe the outline of the character. Spline records represent the quadratic curves used by TrueType (that is, quadratic b-splines).

See Also   **CDC::GetOutlineTextMetrics**, **::GetGlyphOutline**, **GLYPHMETRICS**, **TTPOLYGONHEADER**, **TTPOLYCURVE**

CDC::GetHalftoneBrush

static CBrush* PASCAL GetHalftoneBrush( );

Return Value

A pointer to a **CBrush** object if successful; otherwise **NULL**.

Remarks

Call this member function to retrieve a halftone brush. A halftone brush shows pixels that are alternately foreground and background colors to create a dithered pattern. The following is an example of a dithered pattern created by a halftone brush.

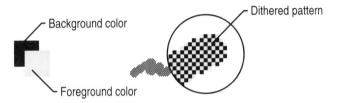

See Also   CBrush

CDC::GetKerningPairs

int GetKerningPairs(int *nPairs*, **LPKERNINGPAIR** *lpkrnpair*) **const;**

Return Value

Specifies the number of kerning pairs retrieved or the total number of kerning pairs in the font, if the function is successful. Zero is returned if the function fails or there are no kerning pairs for the font.

Parameters

nPairs   Specifies the number of **KERNINGPAIR** structures pointed to by *lpkrnpair*. The function will not copy more kerning pairs than specified by *nPairs*.

lpkrnpair   Points to an array of **KERNINGPAIR** structures that receive the kerning pairs when the function returns. This array must contain at least as many structures as specified by *nPairs*. If this parameter is **NULL**, the function returns the total number of kerning pairs for the font.

Remarks

Retrieves the character kerning pairs for the font that is currently selected in the specified device context.

See Also   ::GetKerningPairs, KERNINGPAIR

CDC::GetMapMode

int GetMapMode( ) const;

Return Value

The mapping mode.

Remarks

Retrieves the current mapping mode.

See the **SetMapMode** member function for a description of the mapping modes.

See Also **CDC::SetMapMode, ::GetMapMode**

CDC::GetMiterLimit

float GetMiterLimit( ) const;

Return Value

Nonzero if the function is successful; otherwise 0.

Remarks

Returns the miter limit for the device context. The miter limit is used when drawing geometric lines that have miter joins.

See Also **CDC::SetMiterLimit, ::GetMiterLimit**

CDC::GetNearestColor

COLORREF GetNearestColor(COLORREF *crColor* **) const;**

Return Value

An RGB (red, green, blue) color value that defines the solid color closest to the *crColor* value that the device can represent.

Parameters

crColor Specifies the color to be matched.

Remarks

Returns the solid color that best matches a specified logical color. The given device must be able to represent this color.

See Also **::GetNearestColor, CPalette::GetNearestPaletteIndex**

CDC::GetOutlineTextMetrics

UINT CDC::GetOutlineTextMetrics(UINT *cbData*, **LPOUTLINETEXTMETRIC** *lpotm* **) const**

Return Value

Nonzero if the function is successful; otherwise 0.

Parameters

lpotm   Points to an array of **OUTLINETEXTMETRIC** structures. If this parameter is **NULL**, the function returns the size of the buffer required for the retrieved metric data.

cbData   Specifies the size, in bytes, of the buffer to which information is returned.

lpotm   Points to an **OUTLINETEXTMETRIC** structure. If this parameter is **NULL**, the function returns the size of the buffer required for the retrieved metric information.

Remarks

Retrieves metric information for TrueType fonts.

The **OUTLINETEXTMETRIC** structure contains most of the font metric information provided with the TrueType format, including a **TEXTMETRIC** structure. The last four members of the **OUTLINETEXTMETRIC** structure are pointers to strings. Applications should allocate space for these strings in addition to the space required for the other members. Because there is no system-imposed limit to the size of the strings, the simplest method for allocating memory is to retrieve the required size by specifying **NULL** for *lpotm* in the first call to the **GetOutlineTextMetrics** function.

See Also   **::GetTextMetrics, ::GetOutlineTextMetrics, CDC::GetTextMetrics**

CDC::GetOutputCharWidth

BOOL GetOutputCharWidth(UINT *nFirstChar*, **UINT** *nLastChar*, **LPINT** *lpBuffer* **) const;**

Return Value

Nonzero if the function is successful; otherwise 0.

Parameters

nFirstChar   Specifies the first character in a consecutive group of characters in the current font.

nLastChar   Specifies the last character in a consecutive group of characters in the current font.

lpBuffer   Points to a buffer that will receive the width values for a consecutive group of characters in the current font.

Remarks

Uses the output device context, **m_hDC**, and retrieves the widths of individual characters in a consecutive group of characters from the current font. For example, if *nFirstChar* identifies the letter 'a' and *nLastChar* identifies the letter 'z', the function retrieves the widths of all lowercase characters.

The function stores the values in the buffer pointed to by *lpBuffer*. This buffer must be large enough to hold all of the widths; that is, there must be at least 26 entries in the example given.

If a character in the consecutive group of characters does not exist in a particular font, it will be assigned the width value of the default character.

See Also   **CDC::GetCharWidth**, **CDC::m_hAttribDC**, **CDC::m_hDC**, **::GetCharWidth**

CDC::GetOutputTabbedTextExtent

CSize GetOutputTabbedTextExtent(LPCTSTR *lpszString*, **int** *nCount*, **int** *nTabPositions*, **LPINT** *lpnTabStopPositions*) **const;**

CSize GetOutputTabbedTextExtent(const CString& *str*, **int** *nTabPositions*, **LPINT** *lpnTabStopPositions*) **const;**

Return Value

The dimensions of the string (in logical units) in a **CSize** object.

Parameters

lpszString   Points to a character string to be measured. You can also pass a **CString** object for this parameter.

nCount   Specifies the number of characters in the string. If *nCount* is –1, the length is calculated.

nTabPositions   Specifies the number of tab-stop positions in the array pointed to by *lpnTabStopPositions*.

lpnTabStopPositions   Points to an array of integers containing the tab-stop positions in logical units. The tab stops must be sorted in increasing order; the smallest x-value should be the first item in the array. Back tabs are not allowed.

str   A **CString** object that contains the specified characters to be measured.

Remarks

Call this member function to compute the width and height of a character string using **m_hDC**, the output device context. If the string contains one or more tab characters, the width of the string is based upon the tab stops specified by *lpnTabStopPositions*. The function uses the currently selected font to compute the dimensions of the string.

The current clipping region does not offset the width and height returned by the **GetOutputTabbedTextExtent** function.

Since some devices do not place characters in regular cell arrays (that is, they kern the characters), the sum of the extents of the characters in a string may not be equal to the extent of the string.

If *nTabPositions* is 0 and *lpnTabStopPositions* is **NULL**, tabs are expanded to eight average character widths. If *nTabPositions* is 1, the tab stops will be separated by the distance specified by the first value in the array to which *lpnTabStopPositions* points. If *lpnTabStopPositions* points to more than a single value, a tab stop is set for each value in the array, up to the number specified by *nTabPositions*.

See Also **CDC::GetTextExtent, CDC::m_hAttribDC, CDC::m_hDC, CDC::GetTabbedTextExtent, CDC::GetOutputTextExtent, CDC::TabbedTextOut, ::GetTabbedTextExtent, CSize**

CDC::GetOutputTextExtent

CSize GetOutputTextExtent(LPCTSTR *lpszString*, **int** *nCount* **) const;**
CSize GetOutputTextExtent(const CString& *str* **) const;**

Return Value

The dimensions of the string (in logical units) returned in a **CSize** object.

Parameters

lpszString Points to a string of characters. You can also pass a **CString** object for this parameter.

nCount Specifies the number of characters in the string. If *nCount* is –1, the length is calculated.

str A **CString** object that contains the specified characters to be measured.

Remarks

Call this member function to use the output device context, **m_hDC**, and compute the width and height of a line of text, using the current font.

The current clipping region does not affect the width and height returned by **GetOutputTextExtent**.

Since some devices do not place characters in regular cell arrays (that is, they carry out kerning), the sum of the extents of the characters in a string may not be equal to the extent of the string.

See Also **CDC::GetTabbedTextExtent, CDC::GetOutputTabbedTextExtent, CDC::m_hAttribDC, CDC::m_hDC, CDC::GetTextExtent, ::GetTextExtent, CDC::SetTextJustification, CSize**

CDC::GetOutputTextMetrics

BOOL GetOutputTextMetrics(LPTEXTMETRIC *lpMetrics* **) const;**

Return Value

Nonzero if the function is successful; otherwise 0.

Parameters

lpMetrics   Points to the **TEXTMETRIC** structure that receives the metrics.

Remarks

Retrieves the metrics for the current font using **m_hDC**, the output device context.

See Also   **CDC::GetTextAlign, CDC::m_hAttribDC, CDC::m_hDC, CDC::GetTextMetrics, CDC::GetTextExtent, CDC::GetTextFace, CDC::SetTextJustification, ::GetTextMetrics**

CDC::GetPath

int GetPath(LPPOINT *lpPoints***, LPBYTE** *lpTypes***, int** *nCount* **) const;**

Return Value

If the *nCount* parameter is nonzero, the number of points enumerated. If *nCount* is 0, the total number of points in the path (and **GetPath** writes nothing to the buffers). If *nCount* is nonzero and is less than the number of points in the path, the return value is -1.

Parameters

lpPoints   Points to an array of **POINT** data structures or **CPoint** objects where the line endpoints and curve control points are placed.

lpTypes   Points to an array of bytes where the vertex types are placed. Values are one of the following:

- **PT_MOVETO**   Specifies that the corresponding point in *lpPoints* starts a disjoint figure.

- **PT_LINETO**   Specifies that the previous point and the corresponding point in *lpPoints* are the endpoints of a line.

- **PT_BEZIERTO**   Specifies that the corresponding point in *lpPoints* is a control point or ending point for a Bézier curve.

  PT_BEZIERTO types always occur in sets of three. The point in the path immediately preceding them defines the starting point for the Bézier curve. The first two **PT_BEZIERTO** points are the control points, and the third **PT_BEZIERTO** point is the end point (if hard-coded).

A **PT_LINETO** or **PT_BEZIERTO** type may be combined with the following flag (by using the bitwise operator **OR**) to indicate that the corresponding point is the last point in a figure and that the figure should be closed:

- **PT_CLOSEFIGURE**   Specifies that the figure is automatically closed after the corresponding line or curve is drawn. The figure is closed by drawing a line from the line or curve endpoint to the point corresponding to the last **PT_MOVETO**.

nCount   Specifies the total number of **POINT** data structures that may be placed in the *lpPoints* array. This value must be the same as the number of bytes that may be placed in the *lpTypes* array.

Remarks

Retrieves the coordinates defining the endpoints of lines and the control points of curves found in the path that is selected into the device context. The device context must contain a closed path. The points of the path are returned in logical coordinates. Points are stored in the path in device coordinates, so **GetPath** changes the points from device coordinates to logical coordinates by using the inverse of the current transformation. The **FlattenPath** member function may be called before **GetPath**, to convert all curves in the path into line segments.

See Also   **CDC::FlattenPath, CDC::PolyDraw, CDC::WidenPath**

CDC::GetPixel

COLORREF GetPixel(int *x*, **int** *y* **) const;**
COLORREF GetPixel(POINT *point* **) const;**

Return Value

For either version of the function, an RGB color value for the color of the given point. It is -1 if the coordinates do not specify a point in the clipping region.

Parameters

x   Specifies the logical x-coordinate of the point to be examined.

y   Specifies the logical y-coordinate of the point to be examined.

point   Specifies the logical x- and y-coordinates of the point to be examined.

Remarks

Retrieves the RGB color value of the pixel at the point specified by *x* and *y*. The point must be in the clipping region. If the point is not in the clipping region, the function has no effect and returns -1.

Not all devices support the **GetPixel** function. For more information, see the **RC_BITBLT** raster capability under the **GetDeviceCaps** member function.

The **GetPixel** member function has two forms. The first takes two coordinate values; the second takes either a **POINT** structure or a **CPoint** object.

See Also   **CDC::GetDeviceCaps, CDC::SetPixel, ::GetPixel, POINT, CPoint**

CDC::GetPolyFillMode

int GetPolyFillMode( ) const;

Return Value

The current polygon-filled mode, **ALTERNATE** or **WINDING**, if the function is successful.

Remarks

Retrieves the current polygon-filling mode.

See the **SetPolyFillMode** member function for a description of the polygon-filling modes.

See Also   **CDC::SetPolyFillMode, ::GetPolyFillMode**

CDC::GetROP2

int GetROP2( ) const;

Return Value

The drawing mode. For a list of the drawing mode values, see the **SetROP2** member function.

Remarks

Retrieves the current drawing mode. The drawing mode specifies how the colors of the pen and the interior of filled objects are combined with the color already on the display surface.

See Also   **CDC::GetDeviceCaps, CDC::SetROP2, ::GetROP2**

CDC::GetSafeHdc

HDC GetSafeHdc( ) const;

Return Value

A device context handle.

Remarks

Call this member function to get **m_hDC**, the output device context. This member function also works with null pointers.

CDC::GetStretchBltMode

int GetStretchBltMode( ) const;

Return Value

The return value specifies the current bitmap-stretching mode—
STRETCH_ANDSCANS, **STRETCH_DELETESCANS**, or
STRETCH_ORSCANS—if the function is successful.

Remarks

Retrieves the current bitmap-stretching mode. The bitmap-stretching mode defines
how information is removed from bitmaps that are stretched or compressed by the
StretchBlt member function.

The **STRETCH_ANDSCANS** and **STRETCH_ORSCANS** modes are
typically used to preserve foreground pixels in monochrome bitmaps. The
STRETCH_DELETESCANS mode is typically used to preserve color in
color bitmaps.

See Also   **CDC::StretchBlt**, **CDC::SetStretchBltMode**, **::GetStretchBltMode**

CDC::GetTabbedTextExtent

CSize GetTabbedTextExtent(LPCTSTR *lpszString*, **int** *nCount*, **int** *nTabPositions*,
  LPINT *lpnTabStopPositions* **) const;**
CSize GetTabbedTextExtent(const CString& *str*, **int** *nTabPositions*, **LPINT** *lpnTabStopPositions* **)**
  const;

Return Value

The dimensions of the string (in logical units) in a **CSize** object.

Parameters

lpszString   Points to a character string. You can also pass a **CString** object for this
  parameter.

nCount   Specifies the number of characters in the string. If *nCount* is –1, the length
  is calculated.

nTabPositions   Specifies the number of tab-stop positions in the array pointed to by
  lpnTabStopPositions.

lpnTabStopPositions   Points to an array of integers containing the tab-stop positions
  in logical units. The tab stops must be sorted in increasing order; the smallest x-
  value should be the first item in the array. Back tabs are not allowed.

str   A **CString** object that contains the specified characters to be drawn.

Remarks

Call this member function to compute the width and height of a character string
using **m_hAttribDC**, the attribute device context. If the string contains one or more

485

tab characters, the width of the string is based upon the tab stops specified by *lpnTabStopPositions*. The function uses the currently selected font to compute the dimensions of the string.

The current clipping region does not offset the width and height returned by the **GetTabbedTextExtent** function.

Since some devices do not place characters in regular cell arrays (that is, they kern the characters), the sum of the extents of the characters in a string may not be equal to the extent of the string.

If *nTabPositions* is 0 and *lpnTabStopPositions* is **NULL**, tabs are expanded to eight times the average character width. If *nTabPositions* is 1, the tab stops will be separated by the distance specified by the first value in the array to which *lpnTabStopPositions* points. If *lpnTabStopPositions* points to more than a single value, a tab stop is set for each value in the array, up to the number specified by *nTabPositions*.

See Also   **CDC::GetTextExtent, CDC::GetOutputTabbedTextExtent, CDC::GetOutputTextExtent, CDC::TabbedTextOut, ::GetTabbedTextExtent, CSize**

CDC::GetTextAlign

UINT GetTextAlign( ) const;

Return Value

The status of the text-alignment flags. The return value is one or more of the following values:

- **TA_BASELINE** Specifies alignment of the x-axis and the baseline of the chosen font within the bounding rectangle.
- **TA_BOTTOM** Specifies alignment of the x-axis and the bottom of the bounding rectangle.
- **TA_CENTER** Specifies alignment of the y-axis and the center of the bounding rectangle.
- **TA_LEFT** Specifies alignment of the y-axis and the left side of the bounding rectangle.
- **TA_NOUPDATECP** Specifies that the current position is not updated.
- **TA_RIGHT** Specifies alignment of the y-axis and the right side of the bounding rectangle.
- **TA_TOP** Specifies alignment of the x-axis and the top of the bounding rectangle.
- **TA_UPDATECP** Specifies that the current position is updated.

Remarks

Retrieves the status of the text-alignment flags for the device context.

The text-alignment flags determine how the **TextOut** and **ExtTextOut** member functions align a string of text in relation to the string's starting point. The text-alignment flags are not necessarily single-bit flags and may be equal to 0. To test whether a flag is set, an application should follow these steps:

1. Apply the bitwise OR operator to the flag and its related flags, grouped as follows:

   - **TA_LEFT**, **TA_CENTER**, and **TA_RIGHT**
   - **TA_BASELINE**, **TA_BOTTOM**, and **TA_TOP**
   - **TA_NOUPDATECP** and **TA_UPDATECP**

2. Apply the bitwise-AND operator to the result and the return value of **GetTextAlign**.

3. Test for the equality of this result and the flag.

See Also   **CDC::ExtTextOut**, **CDC::SetTextAlign**, **CDC::TextOut**, **::GetTextAlign**

CDC::GetTextCharacterExtra

int GetTextCharacterExtra( ) const;

Return Value

The amount of the intercharacter spacing.

Remarks

Retrieves the current setting for the amount of intercharacter spacing. GDI adds this spacing to each character, including break characters, when it writes a line of text to the device context.

The default value for the amount of intercharacter spacing is 0.

See Also   **CDC::SetTextCharacterExtra**, **::GetTextCharacterExtra**

CDC::GetTextColor

COLORREF GetTextColor( ) const;

Return Value

The current text color as an RGB color value.

Remarks

Retrieves the current text color. The text color is the foreground color of characters drawn by using the GDI text-output member functions **TextOut**, **ExtTextOut**, and **TabbedTextOut**.

See Also **CDC::GetBkColor**, **CDC::GetBkMode**, **CDC::SetBkMode**, **CDC::SetTextColor**, **::GetTextColor**

CDC::GetTextExtent

CSize GetTextExtent(LPCTSTR *lpszString*, **int** *nCount* **) const;**
CSize GetTextExtent(const CString& *str* **) const;**

Return Value

The dimensions of the string (in logical units) in a **CSize** object.

Parameters

lpszString   Points to a string of characters. You can also pass a **CString** object for this parameter.

nCount   Specifies the number of characters in the string. If *nCount* is –1, the length is calculated.

str   A **CString** object that contains the specified characters.

Remarks

Call this member function to compute the width and height of a line of text using the current font to determine the dimensions. The information is retrieved from **m_hAttribDC**, the attribute device context.

The current clipping region does not affect the width and height returned by **GetTextExtent**.

Since some devices do not place characters in regular cell arrays (that is, they carry out kerning), the sum of the extents of the characters in a string may not be equal to the extent of the string.

See Also **CDC::GetTabbedTextExtent**, **CDC::m_hAttribDC**, **CDC::m_hDC**, **CDC::GetOutputTextExtent**, **::GetTextExtent**, **CDC::SetTextJustification**, **CSize**

CDC::GetTextFace

int GetTextFace(int *nCount*, **LPTSTR** *lpszFacename* **) const;**
int GetTextFace(CString& *rString* **) const;**

Return Value

The number of bytes copied to the buffer, not including the terminating null character. It is 0 if an error occurs.

Parameters

nCount   Specifies the size of the buffer (in bytes). If the typeface name is longer than the number of bytes specified by this parameter, the name is truncated.

lpszFacename   Points to the buffer for the typeface name.

rString   A reference to a **CString** object.

Remarks

Call this member function to copy the typeface name of the current font into a buffer. The typeface name is copied as a null-terminated string.

See Also   **CDC::GetTextMetrics**, **CDC::SetTextAlign**, **CDC::TextOut**, **::GetTextFace**

CDC::GetTextMetrics

BOOL GetTextMetrics(LPTEXTMETRIC *lpMetrics* **) const;**

Return Value

Nonzero if the function is successful; otherwise 0.

Parameters

lpMetrics   Points to the **TEXTMETRIC** structure that receives the metrics.

Remarks

Retrieves the metrics for the current font using the attribute device context.

See Also   **CDC::GetTextAlign**, **CDC::m_hAttribDC**, **CDC::m_hDC**, **CDC::GetOutputTextMetrics**, **CDC::GetTextExtent**, **CDC::GetTextFace**, **CDC::SetTextJustification**, **::GetTextMetrics**

CDC::GetViewportExt

CSize GetViewportExt( ) const;

Return Value

The x- and y-extents (in device units) as a **CSize** object.

Remarks

Retrieves the x- and y-extents of the device context's viewport.

See Also   **CDC::SetViewportExt**, **CSize**, **::GetViewportExt**, **CDC::SetWindowExt**

489

CDC::GetViewportOrg

CPoint GetViewportOrg( ) const;

Return Value

The origin of the viewport (in device coordinates) as a **CPoint** object.

Remarks

Retrieves the x- and y-coordinates of the origin of the viewport associated with the device context.

See Also **CDC::GetWindowOrg, CPoint, ::GetViewportOrg, CDC::SetViewportOrg**

CDC::GetWindow

CWnd* GetWindow( ) const;

Return Value

Pointer to a **CWnd** object if successful; otherwise **NULL**.

Remarks

Returns the window associated with the display device context. This is an advanced function. For example, this member function may not return the view window when printing or in print preview. It always returns the window associated with output. Output functions that use the given DC draw into this window.

See Also **CWnd::GetDC, CWnd::GetWindowDC, ::GetWindow**

CDC::GetWindowExt

CSize GetWindowExt( ) const;

Return Value

The x- and y-extents (in logical units) as a **CSize** object.

Remarks

Retrieves the x- and y-extents of the window associated with the device context.

See Also **CDC::SetWindowExt, CSize, ::GetWindowExt, CDC::GetViewportExt**

CDC::GetWindowOrg

CPoint GetWindowOrg( ) const;

Return Value

The origin of the window (in logical coordinates) as a **CPoint** object.

Remarks

Retrieves the x- and y-coordinates of the origin of the window associated with the device context.

See Also   **CDC::GetViewportOrg**, **CDC::SetWindowOrg**, **CPoint**, **::GetWindowOrg**

CDC::GrayString

virtual BOOL GrayString(CBrush* *pBrush***, BOOL (CALLBACK EXPORT*** *lpfnOutput* **)**
   (HDC, LPARAM, int), LPARAM *lpData***, int** *nCount***, int** *x***, int** *y***, int** *nWidth***, int** *nHeight* **);**

Return Value

Nonzero if the string is drawn, or 0 if either the **TextOut** function or the application-supplied output function returned 0, or if there was insufficient memory to create a memory bitmap for dimming.

Parameters

pBrush   Identifies the brush to be used for dimming (graying).

lpfnOutput   Specifies the procedure-instance address of the application-supplied callback function that will draw the string. For more information, see the description of the Windows **OutputFunc** callback function in "Callback Function for CDC::Gray String" in the "Callback Functions Used by MFC" section. If this parameter is **NULL**, the system uses the Windows **TextOut** function to draw the string, and *lpData* is assumed to be a long pointer to the character string to be output.

lpData   Specifies a far pointer to data to be passed to the output function. If *lpfnOutput* is **NULL**, *lpData* must be a long pointer to the string to be output.

nCount   Specifies the number of characters to be output. If this parameter is 0, **GrayString** calculates the length of the string (assuming that *lpData* is a pointer to the string). If *nCount* is –1 and the function pointed to by *lpfnOutput* returns 0, the image is shown but not dimmed.

x   Specifies the logical x-coordinate of the starting position of the rectangle that encloses the string.

y   Specifies the logical y-coordinate of the starting position of the rectangle that encloses the string.

nWidth   Specifies the width (in logical units) of the rectangle that encloses the string. If *nWidth* is 0, **GrayString** calculates the width of the area, assuming *lpData* is a pointer to the string.

nHeight   Specifies the height (in logical units) of the rectangle that encloses the string. If *nHeight* is 0, **GrayString** calculates the height of the area, assuming *lpData* is a pointer to the string.

Remarks

Draws dimmed (gray) text at the given location by writing the text in a memory bitmap, dimming the bitmap, and then copying the bitmap to the display. The function dims the text regardless of the selected brush and background. The **GrayString** member function uses the currently selected font. The **MM_TEXT** mapping mode must be selected before using this function.

An application can draw dimmed (grayed) strings on devices that support a solid gray color without calling the **GrayString** member function. The system color **COLOR_GRAYTEXT** is the solid-gray system color used to draw disabled text. The application can call the **GetSysColor** Windows function to retrieve the color value of **COLOR_GRAYTEXT**. If the color is other than 0 (black), the application can call the **SetTextColor** member function to set the text color to the color value and then draw the string directly. If the retrieved color is black, the application must call **GrayString** to dim (gray) the text.

If *lpfnOutput* is **NULL**, GDI uses the Windows **TextOut** function, and *lpData* is assumed to be a far pointer to the character to be output. If the characters to be output cannot be handled by the **TextOut** member function (for example, the string is stored as a bitmap), the application must supply its own output function.

Also note that all callback functions must trap Microsoft Foundation exceptions before returning to Windows, since exceptions cannot be thrown across callback boundaries. For more information about exceptions, see the article "Exceptions" in *Programming with MFC*.

The callback function passed to **GrayString** must use the Pascal calling convention, must be exported with **__export**, and must be declared **FAR**.

When the framework is in preview mode, a call to the **GrayString** member function is translated to a **TextOut** call, and the callback function is not called.

See Also   ::GetSysColor, **CDC::SetTextColor**, **CDC::TextOut**, **::GrayString**

CDC::HIMETRICtoDP

void HIMETRICtoDP(LPSIZE *lpSize* **) const;**

Parameters

lpSize   Points to a **SIZE** structure or **CSize** object.

Remarks

Use this function when you convert **HIMETRIC** sizes from OLE to pixels.

If the mapping mode of the device context object is **MM_LOENGLISH**, **MM_HIENGLISH**, **MM_LOMETRIC** or **MM_HIMETRIC**, then the conversion is based on the number of pixels in the physical inch. If the mapping mode is one of the other non-constrained modes (e.g., **MM_TEXT**), then the conversion is based on the number of pixels in the logical inch.

See Also   **CDC::LPtoDP**, **CDC::HIMETRICtoLP**

CDC::HIMETRICtoLP

> **void HIMETRICtoLP(LPSIZE** *lpSize* **) const;**

Parameters

> *lpSize*   Points to a **SIZE** structure or **CSize** object.

Remarks

> Call this function to convert **HIMETRIC** units into logical units. Use this function when you get **HIMETRIC** sizes from OLE and wish to convert them to your application's natural mapping mode.
>
> The conversion is accomplished by first converting the **HIMETRIC** units into pixels and then converting these units into logical units using the device context's current mapping units. Note that the extents of the device's window and viewport will affect the result.
>
> **See Also**   **CDC::HIMETRICtoDP**, **CDC::DPtoLP**

CDC::IntersectClipRect

> **virtual int IntersectClipRect(int** *x1*, **int** *y1*, **int** *x2*, **int** *y2* **);**
> **virtual int IntersectClipRect(LPCRECT** *lpRect* **);**

Return Value

> The new clipping region's type. It can be any one of the following values:
>
> - **COMPLEXREGION**   New clipping region has overlapping borders.
> - **ERROR**   Device context is not valid.
> - **NULLREGION**   New clipping region is empty.
> - **SIMPLEREGION**   New clipping region has no overlapping borders.

Parameters

> *x1*   Specifies the logical x-coordinate of the upper-left corner of the rectangle.
>
> *y1*   Specifies the logical y-coordinate of the upper-left corner of the rectangle.
>
> *x2*   Specifies the logical x-coordinate of the lower-right corner of the rectangle.
>
> *y2*   Specifies the logical y-coordinate of the lower-right corner of the rectangle.
>
> *lpRect*   Specifies the rectangle. You can pass either a **CRect** object or a pointer to a **RECT** structure for this parameter.

Remarks

Creates a new clipping region by forming the intersection of the current region and the rectangle specified by *x1*, *y1*, *x2*, and *y2*. GDI clips all subsequent output to fit within the new boundary. The width and height must not exceed 32,767.

See Also   ::**IntersectClipRect**, **CRect**, **RECT**

CDC::InvertRect

void InvertRect(LPCRECT *lpRect* **);**

Parameters

lpRect   Points to a **RECT** that contains the logical coordinates of the rectangle to be inverted. You can also pass a **CRect** object for this parameter.

Remarks

Inverts the contents of the given rectangle. Inversion is a logical NOT operation and flips the bits of each pixel. On monochrome displays, the function makes white pixels black and black pixels white. On color displays, the inversion depends on how colors are generated for the display. Calling **InvertRect** twice with the same rectangle restores the display to its previous colors.

If the rectangle is empty, nothing is drawn.

See Also   **CDC::FillRect**, **::InvertRect**, **CRect**, **RECT**

CDC::InvertRgn

BOOL InvertRgn(CRgn* *pRgn* **);**

Return Value

Nonzero if the function is successful; otherwise 0.

Parameters

pRgn   Identifies the region to be inverted. The coordinates for the region are specified in device units.

Remarks

Inverts the colors in the region specified by *pRgn*. On monochrome displays, the function makes white pixels black and black pixels white. On color displays, the inversion depends on how the colors are generated for the display.

See Also   **CDC::FillRgn**, **CDC::PaintRgn**, **CRgn**, **::InvertRgn**

CDC::IsPrinting

BOOL IsPrinting( ) const;

Return Value

Nonzero if the **CDC** object is a printer DC; otherwise 0.

CDC::LineTo

BOOL LineTo(int *x***, int** *y* **);**
BOOL LineTo(POINT *point* **);**

Return Value

Nonzero if the line is drawn; otherwise 0.

Parameters

x   Specifies the logical x-coordinate of the endpoint for the line.

y   Specifies the logical y-coordinate of the endpoint for the line.

point   Specifies the endpoint for the line. You can pass either a **POINT** structure or a
CPoint object for this parameter.

Remarks

Draws a line from the current position up to, but not including, the point specified by
x and *y* (or *point*). The line is drawn with the selected pen. The current position is set
to *x,y* or to *point*.

See Also   **CDC::MoveTo, CDC::GetCurrentPosition, ::LineTo, CPoint, POINT**

CDC::LPtoDP

void LPtoDP(LPPOINT *lpPoints***, int** *nCount* **= 1) const;**
void LPtoDP(LPRECT *lpRect* **) const;**
void LPtoDP(LPSIZE *lpSize* **) const;**

Parameters

lpPoints   Points to an array of points. Each point in the array is a **POINT** structure
or a **CPoint** object.

nCount   The number of points in the array.

lpRect   Points to a **RECT** structure or a **CRect** object. This parameter is used for the
common case of mapping a rectangle from logical to device units.

lpSize   Points to a **SIZE** structure or a **CSize** object.

Remarks

Converts logical units into device units. The function maps the coordinates of each point, or dimensions of a size, from GDI's logical coordinate system into a device coordinate system. The conversion depends on the current mapping mode and the settings of the origins and extents of the device's window and viewport.

The x- and y-coordinates of points are 2-byte signed integers in the range –32,768 through 32,767. In cases where the mapping mode would result in values larger than these limits, the system sets the values to –32,768 and 32,767, respectively.

See Also CDC::DPtoLP, CDC::HIMETRICtoLP, ::LPtoDP, CDC::GetWindowOrg, CDC::GetWindowExt

CDC::LPtoHIMETRIC

void LPToHIMETRIC(LPSIZE *lpSize* **) const;**

Parameters

lpSize Points to a **SIZE** structure or a **CSize** object.

Remarks

Call this function to convert logical units into **HIMETRIC** units. Use this function when you give **HIMETRIC** sizes to OLE, converting from your application's natural mapping mode. Note that the extents of the device's window and viewport will affect the result.

The conversion is accomplished by first converting the logical units into pixels using the device context's current mapping units and then converting these units into **HIMETRIC** units.

See Also CDC::HIMETRICtoLP, CDC::LPtoDP, CDC::DPtoHIMETRIC

CDC::MaskBlt

BOOL MaskBlt(int *x*, **int** *y*, **int** *nWidth*, **int** *nHeight*, **CDC*** *pSrcDC*, **int** *xSrc*, **int** *ySrc*, **CBitmap&** *maskBitmap*, **int** *xMask*, **int** *yMask*, **DWORD** *dwRop* **);**

Return Value

Nonzero if the function is successful; otherwise 0.

Parameters

x Specifies the logical x-coordinate of the upper-left corner of the destination rectangle.

y Specifies the logical y-coordinate of the upper-left corner of the destination rectangle.

nWidth   Specifies the width, in logical units, of the destination rectangle and source bitmap.

nHeight   Specifies the height, in logical units, of the destination rectangle and source bitmap.

pSrcDC   Identifies the device context from which the bitmap is to be copied. It must be zero if the *dwRop* parameter specifies a raster operation that does not include a source.

xSrc   Specifies the logical x-coordinate of the upper-left corner of the source bitmap.

ySrc   Specifies the logical y-coordinate of the upper-left corner of the source bitmap.

maskBitmap   Identifies the monochrome mask bitmap combined with the color bitmap in the source device context.

xMask   Specifies the horizontal pixel offset for the mask bitmap specified by the *maskBitmap* parameter.

yMask   Specifies the vertical pixel offset for the mask bitmap specified by the *maskBitmap* parameter.

dwRop   Specifies both foreground and background ternary raster operation codes, which the function uses to control the combination of source and destination data. The background raster operation code is stored in the high byte of the high word of this value; the foreground raster operation code is stored in the low byte of the high word of this value; the low word of this value is ignored, and should be zero. The macro **MAKEROP4** creates such combinations of foreground and background raster operation codes. See the "Remarks" section for a discussion of foreground and background in the context of this function. See the **BitBlt** member function for a list of common raster operation codes.

Remarks

Combines the color data for the source and destination bitmaps using the given mask and raster operation. A value of 1 in the mask specified by *maskBitmap* indicates that the foreground raster operation code specified by *dwRop* should be applied at that location. A value of 0 in the mask indicates that the background raster operation code specified by *dwRop* should be applied at that location. If the raster operations require a source, the mask rectangle must cover the source rectangle. If it does not, the function will fail. If the raster operations do not require a source, the mask rectangle must cover the destination rectangle. If it does not, the function will fail.

If a rotation or shear transformation is in effect for the source device context when this function is called, an error occurs. However, other types of transformations are allowed.

If the color formats of the source, pattern, and destination bitmaps differ, this function converts the pattern or source format, or both, to match the destination format. If the mask bitmap is not a monochrome bitmap, an error occurs. When an enhanced metafile is being recorded, an error occurs (and the function returns 0) if the source device context identifies an enhanced-metafile device context. Not all devices support **MaskBlt**. An application should call **GetDeviceCaps** to determine whether a device supports this function. If no mask bitmap is supplied, this function behaves exactly like **BitBlt**, using the foreground raster operation code. The pixel offsets in the mask bitmap map to the point (0,0) in the source device context's bitmap. This is useful for cases in which a mask bitmap contains a set of masks; an application can easily apply any one of them to a mask-blitting task by adjusting the pixel offsets and rectangle sizes sent to **MaskBlt**.

See Also   **CDC::BitBlt, CDC::GetDeviceCaps, CDC::PlgBlt, CDC::StretchBlt, ::MaskBlt**

CDC::MoveTo

CPoint MoveTo(int *x***, int** *y* **);**
CPoint MoveTo(POINT *point* **);**

Return Value

The x- and y-coordinates of the previous position as a **CPoint** object.

Parameters

x   Specifies the logical x-coordinate of the new position.

y   Specifies the logical y-coordinate of the new position.

point   Specifies the new position. You can pass either a **POINT** structure or a **CPoint** object for this parameter.

Remarks

Moves the current position to the point specified by *x* and *y* (or by *point*).

See Also   **CDC::GetCurrentPosition, CDC::LineTo, ::MoveTo, CPoint, POINT**

CDC::OffsetClipRgn

virtual int OffsetClipRgn(int *x***, int** *y* **);**
virtual int OffsetClipRgn(SIZE *size* **);**

Return Value

The new region's type. It can be any one of the following values:

- **COMPLEXREGION**   Clipping region has overlapping borders.
- **ERROR**   Device context is not valid.
- **NULLREGION**   Clipping region is empty.
- **SIMPLEREGION**   Clipping region has no overlapping borders.

Parameters

> *x* Specifies the number of logical units to move left or right.
>
> *y* Specifies the number of logical units to move up or down.
>
> *size* Specifies the amount to offset.

Remarks

> Moves the clipping region of the device context by the specified offsets. The function moves the region *x* units along the x-axis and *y* units along the y-axis.
>
> **See Also** **CDC::SelectClipRgn**, **::OffsetClipRgn**

CDC::OffsetViewportOrg

> **virtual CPoint OffsetViewportOrg(int** *nWidth*, **int** *nHeight* **);**

Return Value

> The previous viewport origin (in device coordinates) as a **CPoint** object.

Parameters

> *nWidth* Specifies the number of device units to add to the current origin's x-coordinate.
>
> *nHeight* Specifies the number of device units to add to the current origin's y-coordinate.

Remarks

> Modifies the coordinates of the viewport origin relative to the coordinates of the current viewport origin.
>
> **See Also** **CDC::GetViewportOrg**, **CDC::OffsetWindowOrg**, **CDC::SetViewportOrg**, **::OffsetViewportOrg**, **CPoint**

CDC::OffsetWindowOrg

> **CPoint OffsetWindowOrg(int** *nWidth*, **int** *nHeight* **);**

Return Value

> The previous window origin (in logical coordinates) as a **CPoint** object.

Parameters

> *nWidth* Specifies the number of logical units to add to the current origin's x-coordinate.
>
> *nHeight* Specifies the number of logical units to add to the current origin's y-coordinate.

Remarks

Modifies the coordinates of the window origin relative to the coordinates of the current window origin.

See Also   **CDC::GetWindowOrg, CDC::OffsetViewportOrg, CDC::SetWindowOrg, ::OffsetWindowOrg, CPoint**

CDC::PaintRgn

BOOL PaintRgn(CRgn* *pRgn* **);**

Return Value

Nonzero if the function is successful; otherwise 0.

Parameters

pRgn   Identifies the region to be filled. The coordinates for the given region are specified in device units.

Remarks

Fills the region specified by *pRgn* using the current brush.

See Also   **CBrush, CDC::SelectObject, CDC::FillRgn, ::PaintRgn, CRgn**

CDC::PatBlt

BOOL PatBlt(int *x***, int** *y***, int** *nWidth***, int** *nHeight***, DWORD** *dwRop* **);**

Return Value

Nonzero if the function is successful; otherwise 0.

Parameters

x   Specifies the logical x-coordinate of the upper-left corner of the rectangle that is to receive the pattern.

y   Specifies the logical y-coordinate of the upper-left corner of the rectangle that is to receive the pattern.

nWidth   Specifies the width (in logical units) of the rectangle that is to receive the pattern.

nHeight   Specifies the height (in logical units) of the rectangle that is to receive the pattern.

dwRop   Specifies the raster-operation code. Raster-operation codes (ROPs) define how GDI combines colors in output operations that involve a current brush, a possible source bitmap, and a destination bitmap. This parameter can be one of the following values:

- **PATCOPY**   Copies pattern to destination bitmap.

- **PATINVERT**   Combines destination bitmap with pattern using the Boolean XOR operator.

- **DSTINVERT**   Inverts the destination bitmap.

- **BLACKNESS**   Turns all output black.

- **WHITENESS**   Turns all output white.

- **PATPAINT**   Paints the destination bitmap.

Remarks

Creates a bit pattern on the device. The pattern is a combination of the selected brush and the pattern already on the device. The raster-operation code specified by *dwRop* defines how the patterns are to be combined. The raster operations listed for this function are a limited subset of the full 256 ternary raster-operation codes; in particular, a raster-operation code that refers to a source cannot be used.

Not all device contexts support the **PatBlt** function. To determine whether a device context supports **PatBlt**, call the **GetDeviceCaps** member function with the **RASTERCAPS** index and check the return value for the **RC_BITBLT** flag.

See Also   **CDC::GetDeviceCaps**, **::PatBlt**

CDC::Pie

BOOL Pie(int *x1*, **int** *y1*, **int** *x2*, **int** *y2*, **int** *x3*, **int** *y3*, **int** *x4*, **int** *y4* **);**
BOOL Pie(LPCRECT *lpRect*, **POINT** *ptStart*, **POINT** *ptEnd* **);**

Return Value

Nonzero if the function is successful; otherwise 0.

Parameters

x1   Specifies the x-coordinate of the upper-left corner of the bounding rectangle (in logical units).

y1   Specifies the y-coordinate of the upper-left corner of the bounding rectangle (in logical units).

x2   Specifies the x-coordinate of the lower-right corner of the bounding rectangle (in logical units).

y2   Specifies the y-coordinate of the lower-right corner of the bounding rectangle (in logical units).

x3   Specifies the x-coordinate of the arc's starting point (in logical units). This point does not have to lie exactly on the arc.

y3 Specifies the y-coordinate of the arc's starting point (in logical units). This point does not have to lie exactly on the arc.

x4 Specifies the x-coordinate of the arc's endpoint (in logical units). This point does not have to lie exactly on the arc.

y4 Specifies the y-coordinate of the arc's endpoint (in logical units). This point does not have to lie exactly on the arc.

lpRect Specifies the bounding rectangle. You can pass either a **CRect** object or a pointer to a **RECT** structure for this parameter.

ptStart Specifies the starting point of the arc. This point does not have to lie exactly on the arc. You can pass either a **POINT** structure or a **CPoint** object for this parameter.

ptEnd Specifies the endpoint of the arc. This point does not have to lie exactly on the arc. You can pass either a **POINT** structure or a **CPoint** object for this parameter.

Remarks

Draws a pie-shaped wedge by drawing an elliptical arc whose center and two endpoints are joined by lines. The center of the arc is the center of the bounding rectangle specified by *x1*, *y1*, *x2*, and *y2* (or by *lpRect*). The starting and ending points of the arc are specified by *x3*, *y3*, *x4*, and *y4* (or by *ptStart* and *ptEnd*).

The arc is drawn with the selected pen, moving in a counterclockwise direction. Two additional lines are drawn from each endpoint to the arc's center. The pie-shaped area is filled with the current brush. If *x3* equals *x4* and *y3* equals *y4*, the result is an ellipse with a single line from the center of the ellipse to the point (*x3*, *y3*) or (*x4*, *y4*).

The figure drawn by this function extends up to but does not include the right and bottom coordinates. This means that the height of the figure is *y2* – *y1* and the width of the figure is *x2* – *x1*. Both the width and the height of the bounding rectangle must be greater than 2 units and less than 32,767 units.

See Also **CDC::Chord**, **::Pie**, **RECT**, **POINT**, **CRect**, **CPoint**

CDC::PlayMetaFile

BOOL PlayMetaFile(HMETAFILE *hMF* **);**
BOOL PlayMetaFile(HENHMETAFILE *hEnhMetaFile*, **LPCRECT** *lpBounds* **);**

Return Value

Nonzero if the function is successful; otherwise 0.

Parameters

hMF   Identifies the metafile to be played.

hEnhMetaFile   Identifies the enhanced metafile.

lpBounds   Points to a **RECT** structure or a **CRect** object that contains the coordinates of the bounding rectangle used to display the picture. The coordinates are specified in logical units.

Remarks

Plays the contents of the specified metafile on the device context. The metafile can be played any number of times.

The second version of **PlayMetaFile** displays the picture stored in the given enhanced-format metafile. When an application calls the second version of **PlayMetaFile**, Windows uses the picture frame in the enhanced-metafile header to map the picture onto the rectangle pointed to by the *lpBounds* parameter. (This picture may be sheared or rotated by setting the world transform in the output device before calling **PlayMetaFile**.) Points along the edges of the rectangle are included in the picture. An enhanced-metafile picture can be clipped by defining the clipping region in the output device before playing the enhanced metafile.

If an enhanced metafile contains an optional palette, an application can achieve consistent colors by setting up a color palette on the output device before calling the second version of **PlayMetaFile**. To retrieve the optional palette, use the **::GetEnhMetaFilePaletteEntries** function. An enhanced metafile can be embedded in a newly created enhanced metafile by calling the second version of **PlayMetaFile** and playing the source enhanced metafile into the device context for the new enhanced metafile.

The states of the output device context are preserved by this function. Any object created but not deleted in the enhanced metafile is deleted by this function. To stop this function, an application can call the **::CancelDC** function from another thread to terminate the operation. In this case, the function returns zero.

See Also   **::CancelDC**, **::GetEnhMetaFileHeader**, **::GetEnhMetaFilePaletteEntries**, **::SetWorldTransform**, **::PlayMetaFile**, **::PlayEnhMetaFile**, **::PlayMetaFile**

CDC::PlgBlt

BOOL PlgBlt(POINT *lpPoint*, **CDC*** *pSrcDC*, **int** *xSrc*, **int** *ySrc*, **int** *nWidth*, **int** *nHeight*, **CBitmap&** *maskBitmap*, **int** *xMask*, **int** *yMask* **);**

Return Value

Nonzero if the function is successful; otherwise 0.

Parameters

lpPoint Points to an array of three points in logical space that identifies three corners of the destination parallelogram. The upper-left corner of the source rectangle is mapped to the first point in this array, the upper-right corner to the second point in this array, and the lower-left corner to the third point. The lower-right corner of the source rectangle is mapped to the implicit fourth point in the parallelogram.

pSrcDC Identifies the source device context.

xSrc Specifies the x-coordinate, in logical units, of the upper-left corner of the source rectangle.

ySrc Specifies the y-coordinate, in logical units, of the upper-left corner of the source rectangle.

nWidth Specifies the width, in logical units, of the source rectangle.

nHeight Specifies the height, in logical units, of the source rectangle.

maskBitmap Identifies an optional monochrome bitmap that is used to mask the colors of the source rectangle.

xMask Specifies the x-coordinate of the upper-left corner of the monochrome bitmap.

yMask Specifies the y-coordinate of the upper-left corner of the monochrome bitmap.

Remarks

Performs a bit-block transfer of the bits of color data from the specified rectangle in the source device context to the specified parallelogram in the given device context. If the given bitmask handle identifies a valid monochrome bitmap, the function uses this bitmap to mask the bits of color data from the source rectangle.

The fourth vertex of the parallelogram (D) is defined by treating the first three points (A, B, and C) as vectors and computing $D = B + C - A$.

If the bitmask exists, a value of 1 in the mask indicates that the source pixel color should be copied to the destination. A value of 0 in the mask indicates that the destination pixel color is not to be changed.

If the mask rectangle is smaller than the source and destination rectangles, the function replicates the mask pattern.

Scaling, translation, and reflection transformations are allowed in the source device context; however, rotation and shear transformations are not. If the mask bitmap is not a monochrome bitmap, an error occurs. The stretching mode for the destination device context is used to determine how to stretch or compress the pixels, if that is necessary. When an enhanced metafile is being recorded, an error occurs if the source device context identifies an enhanced-metafile device context.

The destination coordinates are transformed according to the destination device context; the source coordinates are transformed according to the source device context. If the source transformation has a rotation or shear, an error is returned. If the destination and source rectangles do not have the same color format, **PlgBlt** converts the source rectangle to match the destination rectangle. Not all devices support **PlgBlt**. For more information, see the description of the **RC_BITBLT** raster capability in the **CDC::GetDeviceCaps** member function.

If the source and destination device contexts represent incompatible devices, **PlgBlt** returns an error.

See Also **CDC::BitBlt**, **CDC::GetDeviceCaps**, **CDC::MaskBlt**, **CDC::StretchBlt**, **::SetStretchBltMode** , **::PlgBlt**

CDC::PolyBezier

BOOL PolyBezier(const POINT* *lpPoints***, int** *nCount* **);**

Return Value

Nonzero if the function is successful; otherwise 0.

Parameters

lpPoints   Points to an array of **POINT** data structures that contain the endpoints and control points of the spline(s).

nCount   Specifies the number of points in the *lpPoints* array. This value must be one more than three times the number of splines to be drawn, because each Bézier spline requires two control points and an endpoint, and the initial spline requires an additional starting point.

Remarks

Draws one or more Bézier splines. This function draws cubic Bézier splines by using the endpoints and control points specified by the *lpPoints* parameter. The first spline is drawn from the first point to the fourth point by using the second and third points as control points. Each subsequent spline in the sequence needs exactly three more points: the end point of the previous spline is used as the starting point, the next two points in the sequence are control points, and the third is the end point.

The current position is neither used nor updated by the **PolyBezier** function. The figure is not filled. This function draws lines by using the current pen.

See Also **CDC::PolyBezierTo**, **::PolyBezier**

CDC::PolyBezierTo

BOOL PolyBezierTo(const POINT* *lpPoints***, int** *nCount* **);**

Return Value

Nonzero if the function is successful; otherwise 0.

Parameters

lpPoints   Points to an array of **POINT** data structures that contains the endpoints and control points.

nCount   Specifies the number of points in the *lpPoints* array. This value must be three times the number of splines to be drawn, because each Bézier spline requires two control points and an end point.

Remarks

Draws one or more Bézier splines. This function draws cubic Bézier splines by using the control points specified by the *lpPoints* parameter. The first spline is drawn from the current position to the third point by using the first two points as control points. For each subsequent spline, the function needs exactly three more points, and uses the end point of the previous spline as the starting point for the next. **PolyBezierTo** moves the current position to the end point of the last Bézier spline. The figure is not filled. This function draws lines by using the current pen.

See Also   **CDC::MoveTo, CDC::PolyBezier, ::PolyBezierTo**

CDC::PolyDraw

BOOL PolyDraw(const POINT* *lpPoints***, const BYTE*** *lpTypes***, int** *nCount* **);**

Return Value

Nonzero if the function is successful; otherwise 0.

Parameters

lpPoints   Points to an array of **POINT** data structures that contains the endpoints for each line segment and the endpoints and control points for each Bézier spline.

lpTypes   Points to an array that specifies how each point in the *lpPoints* array is used. Values can be one of the following:

- **PT_MOVETO**   Specifies that this point starts a disjoint figure. This point becomes the new current position.

- **PT_LINETO**   Specifies that a line is to be drawn from the current position to this point, which then becomes the new current position.

- **PT_BEZIERTO**   Specifies that this point is a control point or ending point for a Bézier spline.

PT_BEZIERTO types always occur in sets of three. The current position defines the starting point for the Bézier spline. The first two **PT_BEZIERTO** points are the control points, and the third **PT_BEZIERTO** point is the ending point. The ending point becomes the new current position. If there are not three consecutive **PT_BEZIERTO** points, an error results.

A **PT_LINETO** or **PT_BEZIERTO** type can be combined with the following constant by using the bitwise operator OR to indicate that the corresponding point is the last point in a figure and the figure is closed:

• **PT_CLOSEFIGURE**   Specifies that the figure is automatically closed after the **PT_LINETO** or **PT_BEZIERTO** type for this point is done. A line is drawn from this point to the most recent **PT_MOVETO** or **MoveTo** point.

This flag is combined with the **PT_LINETO** type for a line, or with the **PT_BEZIERTO** type of ending point for a Bézier spline, by using the bitwise **OR** operator. The current position is set to the ending point of the closing line.

nCount   Specifies the total number of points in the *lpPoints* array, the same as the number of bytes in the *lpTypes* array.

Remarks

Draws a set of line segments and Bézier splines. This function can be used to draw disjoint figures in place of consecutive calls to **CDC::MoveTo**, **CDC::LineTo**, and **CDC::PolyBezierTo** member functions. The lines and splines are drawn using the current pen, and figures are not filled. If there is an active path started by calling the **CDC::BeginPath** member function, **PolyDraw** adds to the path. The points contained in the *lpPoints* array and in *lpTypes* indicate whether each point is part of a **CDC::MoveTo**, a **CDC::LineTo**, or a **CDC::BezierTo** operation. It is also possible to close figures. This function updates the current position.

See Also   **CDC::BeginPath**, **CDC::EndPath**, **CDC::LineTo**, **CDC::MoveTo**, **CDC::PolyBezierTo**, **CDC::PolyLine**, **::PolyDraw**

CDC::Polygon

BOOL Polygon(LPPOINT *lpPoints***, int** *nCount* **);**

Return Value

Nonzero if the function is successful; otherwise 0.

Parameters

lpPoints   Points to an array of points that specifies the vertices of the polygon. Each point in the array is a **POINT** structure or a **CPoint** object.

nCount   Specifies the number of vertices in the array.

Remarks

Draws a polygon consisting of two or more points (vertices) connected by lines, using the current pen. The system closes the polygon automatically, if necessary, by drawing a line from the last vertex to the first.

The current polygon-filling mode can be retrieved or set by using the **GetPolyFillMode** and **SetPolyFillMode** member functions.

See Also   CDC::GetPolyFillMode, CDC::Polyline, CDC::PolyPolygon, CDC::SetPolyFillMode, CPoint, ::Polygon

CDC::Polyline

BOOL Polyline(LPPOINT *lpPoints***, int** *nCount* **);**

Return Value

Nonzero if the function is successful; otherwise 0.

Parameters

lpPoints   Points to an array of **POINT** structures or **CPoint** objects to be connected.

nCount   Specifies the number of points in the array. This value must be at least 2.

Remarks

Draws a set of line segments connecting the points specified by *lpPoints*. The lines are drawn from the first point through subsequent points using the current pen. Unlike the **LineTo** member function, the **Polyline** function neither uses nor updates the current position.

For more information, see **::PolyLine** in the *Win32 Programmer's Reference*.

See Also   CDC::LineTo, CDC::Polygon, POINT, CPoint

CDC::PolylineTo

BOOL PolylineTo(const POINT* *lpPoints***, int** *nCount* **);**

Return Value

Nonzero if the function is successful; otherwise 0.

Parameters

lpPoints   Points to an array of **POINT** data structures that contains the vertices of the line.

nCount   Specifies the number of points in the array.

Remarks

Draws one or more straight lines. A line is drawn from the current position to the first point specified by the *lpPoints* parameter by using the current pen. For each additional line, the function draws from the ending point of the previous line to the next point specified by *lpPoints*. **PolylineTo** moves the current position to the ending point of the last line. If the line segments drawn by this function form a closed figure, the figure is not filled.

See Also   **CDC::LineTo**, **CDC::Polyline**, **CDC::MoveTo**, **::PolylineTo**

CDC::PolyPolygon

BOOL PolyPolygon(LPPOINT *lpPoints***, LPINT** *lpPolyCounts***, int** *nCount* **);**

Return Value

Nonzero if the function is successful; otherwise 0.

Parameters

lpPoints   Points to an array of **POINT** structures or **CPoint** objects that define the vertices of the polygons.

lpPolyCounts   Points to an array of integers, each of which specifies the number of points in one of the polygons in the *lpPoints* array.

nCount   The number of entries in the *lpPolyCounts* array. This number specifies the number of polygons to be drawn. This value must be at least 2.

Remarks

Creates two or more polygons that are filled using the current polygon-filling mode. The polygons may be disjoint or overlapping.

Each polygon specified in a call to the **PolyPolygon** function must be closed. Unlike polygons created by the **Polygon** member function, the polygons created by **PolyPolygon** are not closed automatically.

The function creates two or more polygons. To create a single polygon, an application should use the **Polygon** member function.

The current polygon-filling mode can be retrieved or set by using the **GetPolyFillMode** and **SetPolyFillMode** member functions.

See Also   **CDC::GetPolyFillMode**, **CDC::Polygon**, **CDC::Polyline**, **CDC::SetPolyFillMode**, **::PolyPolygon**, **POINT**, **CPoint**

CDC::PolyPolyline

BOOL PolyPolyline(const POINT* *lpPoints***, const DWORD*** *lpPolyPoints***, int** *nCount* **);**

Return Value

Nonzero if the function is successful; otherwise 0.

Parameters

lpPoints   Points to an array of structures that contains the vertices of the polylines. The polylines are specified consecutively.

lpPolyPoints   Points to an array of variables specifying the number of points in the *lpPoints* array for the corresponding polygon. Each entry must be greater than or equal to 2.

nCount   Specifies the total number of counts in the *lpPolyPoints* array.

Remarks

Draws multiple series of connected line segments. The line segments are drawn by using the current pen. The figures formed by the segments are not filled. The current position is neither used nor updated by this function.

See Also   **CDC::Polyline**, **CDC::PolylineTo**, **::PolyPolyline**

CDC::PtVisible

virtual BOOL PtVisible(int *x***, int** *y* **) const;**
virtual BOOL PtVisible(POINT *point* **) const;**

Return Value

Nonzero if the specified point is within the clipping region; otherwise 0.

Parameters

x   Specifies the logical x-coordinate of the point.

y   Specifies the logical y-coordinate of the point.

point   Specifies the point to check in logical coordinates. You can pass either a **POINT** structure or a **CPoint** object for this parameter.

Remarks

Determines whether the given point is within the clipping region of the device context.

See Also   **CDC::RectVisible**, **CDC::SelectClipRgn**, **CPoint**, **::PtVisible**, **POINT**

CDC::QueryAbort

BOOL QueryAbort( ) const;

Return Value

The return value is nonzero if printing should continue or if there is no abort procedure. It is 0 if the print job should be terminated. The return value is supplied by the abort function.

Remarks

Calls the abort function installed by the **SetAbortProc** member function for a printing application and queries whether the printing should be terminated.

See Also   CDC::SetAbortProc

CDC::RealizePalette

UINT RealizePalette( );

Return Value

Indicates how many entries in the logical palette were mapped to different entries in the system palette. This represents the number of entries that this function remapped to accommodate changes in the system palette since the logical palette was last realized.

Remarks

Maps entries from the current logical palette to the system palette.

A logical color palette acts as a buffer between color-intensive applications and the system, allowing an application to use as many colors as needed without interfering with its own displayed colors or with colors displayed by other windows.

When a window has the input focus and calls **RealizePalette**, Windows ensures that the window will display all the requested colors, up to the maximum number simultaneously available on the screen. Windows also displays colors not found in the window's palette by matching them to available colors.

In addition, Windows matches the colors requested by inactive windows that call the function as closely as possible to the available colors. This significantly reduces undesirable changes in the colors displayed in inactive windows.

See Also   CDC::SelectPalette, CPalette, ::RealizePalette

CDC::Rectangle

BOOL Rectangle(int *x1*, **int** *y1*, **int** *x2*, **int** *y2* **);**
BOOL Rectangle(LPCRECT *lpRect* **);**

Return Value

Nonzero if the function is successful; otherwise 0.

Parameters

x1 Specifies the x-coordinate of the upper-left corner of the rectangle (in logical units).

y1 Specifies the y-coordinate of the upper-left corner of the rectangle (in logical units).

x2 Specifies the x-coordinate of the lower-right corner of the rectangle (in logical units).

y2 Specifies the y-coordinate of the lower-right corner of the rectangle (in logical units).

lpRect Specifies the rectangle in logical units. You can pass either a **CRect** object or a pointer to a **RECT** structure for this parameter.

Remarks

Draws a rectangle using the current pen. The interior of the rectangle is filled using the current brush.

The rectangle extends up to, but does not include, the right and bottom coordinates. This means that the height of the rectangle is $y2 - y1$ and the width of the rectangle is $x2 - x1$. Both the width and the height of a rectangle must be greater than 2 units and less than 32,767 units.

See Also **::Rectangle**, **CDC::PolyLine**, **CDC::RoundRect**, **RECT**, **CRect**

CDC::RectVisible

virtual BOOL RectVisible(LPCRECT *lpRect* **) const;**

Return Value

Nonzero if any portion of the given rectangle lies within the clipping region; otherwise 0.

Parameters

lpRect Points to a **RECT** structure or a **CRect** object that contains the logical coordinates of the specified rectangle.

Remarks

Determines whether any part of the given rectangle lies within the clipping region of the display context.

See Also **CDC::PtVisible**, **CDC::SelectClipRgn**, **CRect**, **::RectVisible**, **RECT**

CDC::ReleaseAttribDC

virtual void ReleaseAttribDC( );

Remarks

Call this member function to set **m_hAttribDC** to **NULL**. This does not cause a **Detach** to occur. Only the output device context is attached to the **CDC** object, and only it can be detached.

See Also **CDC::SetOutputDC**, **CDC::SetAttribDC**, **CDC::ReleaseOutputDC**, **CDC::m_hAttribDC**

CDC::ReleaseOutputDC

virtual void ReleaseOutputDC( );

Remarks

Call this member function to set the **m_hDC** member to **NULL**. This member function cannot be called when the output device context is attached to the **CDC** object. Use the **Detach** member function to detach the output device context.

See Also **CDC::SetAttribDC**, **CDC::SetOutputDC**, **CDC::ReleaseAttribDC**, **CDC::m_hDC**

CDC::ResetDC

BOOL ResetDC(const DEVMODE* *lpDevMode* **);**

Return Value

Nonzero if the function is successful; otherwise 0.

Parameters

lpDevMode A pointer to a Windows **DEVMODE** structure.

Remarks

Call this member function to update the device context wrapped by the **CDC** object. The device context is updated from the information specified in the Windows **DEVMODE** structure. This member function only resets the attribute device context.

An application will typically use the **ResetDC** member function when a window processes a **WM_DEVMODECHANGE** message. You can also use this member function to change the paper orientation or paper bins while printing a document.

You cannot use this member function to change the driver name, device name, or output port. When the user changes the port connection or device name, you must delete the original device context and create a new device context with the new information.

Before you call this member function, you must ensure that all objects (other than stock objects) that had been selected into the device context have been selected out.

See Also   **CDC::m_hAttribDC**, **::ResetDC**, **WM_DEVMODECHANGE**, **DEVMODE**

CDC::RestoreDC

virtual BOOL RestoreDC(int *nSavedDC* **);**

Return Value

Nonzero if the specified context was restored; otherwise 0.

Parameters

nSavedDC   Specifies the device context to be restored. It can be a value returned by a previous **SaveDC** function call. If *nSavedDC* is –1, the most recently saved device context is restored.

Remarks

Restores the device context to the previous state identified by *nSavedDC*. **RestoreDC** restores the device context by popping state information off a stack created by earlier calls to the **SaveDC** member function.

The stack can contain the state information for several device contexts. If the context specified by *nSavedDC* is not at the top of the stack, **RestoreDC** deletes all state information between the device context specified by *nSavedDC* and the top of the stack. The deleted information is lost.

See Also   **CDC::SaveDC**, **::RestoreDC**

CDC::RoundRect

BOOL RoundRect(int *x1*, **int** *y1*, **int** *x2*, **int** *y2*, **int** *x3*, **int** *y3* **)**
BOOL RoundRect(LPCRECT *lpRect*, **POINT** *point* **);**

Return Value

Nonzero if the function is successful; otherwise 0.

Parameters

x1 Specifies the x-coordinate of the upper-left corner of the rectangle (in logical units).

y1 Specifies the y-coordinate of the upper-left corner of the rectangle (in logical units).

x2 Specifies the x-coordinate of the lower-right corner of the rectangle (in logical units).

y2 Specifies the y-coordinate of the lower-right corner of the rectangle (in logical units).

x3 Specifies the width of the ellipse used to draw the rounded corners (in logical units).

y3 Specifies the height of the ellipse used to draw the rounded corners (in logical units).

lpRect Specifies the bounding rectangle in logical units. You can pass either a **CRect** object or a pointer to a **RECT** structure for this parameter.

point The x-coordinate of *point* specifies the width of the ellipse to draw the rounded corners (in logical units). The y-coordinate of *point* specifies the height of the ellipse to draw the rounded corners (in logical units). You can pass either a **POINT** structure or a **CPoint** object for this parameter.

Remarks

Draws a rectangle with rounded corners using the current pen. The interior of the rectangle is filled using the current brush.

The figure this function draws extends up to but does not include the right and bottom coordinates. This means that the height of the figure is $y2 - y1$ and the width of the figure is $x2 - x1$. Both the height and the width of the bounding rectangle must be greater than 2 units and less than 32,767 units.

See Also   **CDC::Rectangle**, **::RoundRect**, **CRect**, **RECT**, **POINT**, **CPoint**

CDC::SaveDC

virtual int SaveDC( );

Return Value

An integer identifying the saved device context. It is 0 if an error occurs. This return value can be used to restore the device context by calling **RestoreDC**.

Remarks

Saves the current state of the device context by copying state information (such as clipping region, selected objects, and mapping mode) to a context stack maintained by Windows. The saved device context can later be restored by using **RestoreDC**.

SaveDC can be used any number of times to save any number of device-context states.

See Also **CDC::RestoreDC**, **::SaveDC**

CDC::ScaleViewportExt

virtual CSize ScaleViewportExt(int *xNum*, **int** *xDenom*, **int** *yNum*, **int** *yDenom* **);**

Return Value

The previous viewport extents (in device units) as a **CSize** object.

Parameters

xNum   Specifies the amount by which to multiply the current x-extent.

xDenom   Specifies the amount by which to divide the result of multiplying the current x-extent by the value of the *xNum* parameter.

yNum   Specifies the amount by which to multiply the current y-extent.

yDenom   Specifies the amount by which to divide the result of multiplying the current y-extent by the value of the *yNum* parameter.

Remarks

Modifies the viewport extents relative to the current values. The formulas are written as follows:

```
xNewVE = ( xOldVE * xNum ) / xDenom
yNewVE = ( yOldVE * yNum ) / yDenom
```

The new viewport extents are calculated by multiplying the current extents by the given numerator and then dividing by the given denominator.

See Also **CDC::GetViewportExt**, **::ScaleViewportExt**, **CSize**

CDC::ScaleWindowExt

virtual CSize ScaleWindowExt(int *xNum*, **int** *xDenom*, **int** *yNum*,
   int *yDenom* **);**

Return Value

The previous window extents (in logical units) as a **CSize** object.

Parameters

xNum   Specifies the amount by which to multiply the current x-extent.

xDenom   Specifies the amount by which to divide the result of multiplying the current x-extent by the value of the *xNum* parameter.

yNum   Specifies the amount by which to multiply the current y-extent.

yDenom   Specifies the amount by which to divide the result of multiplying the current y-extent by the value of the *yNum* parameter.

Remarks

Modifies the window extents relative to the current values. The formulas are written as follows:

```
xNewWE = ( xOldWE * xNum ) / xDenom
yNewWE = ( yOldWE * yNum ) / yDenom
```

The new window extents are calculated by multiplying the current extents by the given numerator and then dividing by the given denominator.

See Also   **CDC::GetWindowExt**, **::ScaleWindowExt**, **CSize**

CDC::ScrollDC

BOOL ScrollDC(int *dx*, **int** *dy*, **LPCRECT** *lpRectScroll*, **LPCRECT** *lpRectClip*, **CRgn*** *pRgnUpdate*, **LPRECT** *lpRectUpdate* **);**

Return Value

Nonzero if scrolling is executed; otherwise 0.

Parameters

dx   Specifies the number of horizontal scroll units.

dy   Specifies the number of vertical scroll units.

lpRectScroll   Points to the **RECT** structure or **CRect** object that contains the coordinates of the scrolling rectangle.

lpRectClip   Points to the **RECT** structure or **CRect** object that contains the coordinates of the clipping rectangle. When this rectangle is smaller than the original one pointed to by *lpRectScroll*, scrolling occurs only in the smaller rectangle.

pRgnUpdate   Identifies the region uncovered by the scrolling process. The **ScrollDC** function defines this region; it is not necessarily a rectangle.

lpRectUpdate   Points to the **RECT** structure or **CRect** object that receives the coordinates of the rectangle that bounds the scrolling update region. This is the largest rectangular area that requires repainting. The values in the structure or object when the function returns are in client coordinates, regardless of the mapping mode for the given device context.

Remarks

Scrolls a rectangle of bits horizontally and vertically.

If *lpRectUpdate* is **NULL**, Windows does not compute the update rectangle. If both *pRgnUpdate* and *lpRectUpdate* are **NULL**, Windows does not compute the update region. If *pRgnUpdate* is not **NULL**, Windows assumes that it contains a valid pointer to the region uncovered by the scrolling process (defined by the **ScrollDC** member function). The update region returned in *lpRectUpdate* can be passed to **CWnd::InvalidateRgn** if required.

An application should use the **ScrollWindow** member function of class **CWnd** when it is necessary to scroll the entire client area of a window. Otherwise, it should use **ScrollDC**.

See Also   **CWnd::InvalidateRgn**, **CWnd::ScrollWindow**, **::ScrollDC**, **CRgn**, **RECT**, **CRect**

CDC::SelectClipPath

BOOL SelectClipPath(int *nMode* **);**

Return Value

Nonzero if the function is successful; otherwise 0.

Parameters

nMode   Specifies the way to use the path. The following values are allowed:

- **RGN_AND**   The new clipping region includes the intersection (overlapping areas) of the current clipping region and the current path.

- **RGN_COPY**   The new clipping region is the current path.

- **RGN_DIFF**   The new clipping region includes the areas of the current clipping region, and those of the current path are excluded.

- **RGN_OR**   The new clipping region includes the union (combined areas) of the current clipping region and the current path.

- **RGN_XOR**   The new clipping region includes the union of the current clipping region and the current path, but without the overlapping areas.

Remarks

Selects the current path as a clipping region for the device context, combining the new region with any existing clipping region by using the specified mode. The device context identified must contain a closed path.

See Also   **CDC::BeginPath**, **CDC::EndPath**

CDC::SelectClipRgn

virtual int SelectClipRgn(CRgn* *pRgn* **);**
int SelectClipRgn(CRgn* *pRgn*, **int** *nMode* **);**

Return Value

The region's type. It can be any of the following values:

- **COMPLEXREGION**   New clipping region has overlapping borders.

- **ERROR**   Device context or region is not valid.

- **NULLREGION**   New clipping region is empty.

- **SIMPLEREGION**   New clipping region has no overlapping borders.

Parameters

pRgn   Identifies the region to be selected.

- For the first version of this function, if this value is **NULL**, the entire client area is selected and output is still clipped to the window.

- For the second version of this function, this handle can be **NULL** only when the **RGN_COPY** mode is specified.

nMode   Specifies the operation to be performed. It must be one of the following values:

- **RGN_AND**   The new clipping region combines the overlapping areas of the current clipping region and the region identified by *pRgn*.

- **RGN_COPY**   The new clipping region is a copy of the region identified by *pRgn*. This is functionality is identical to the first version of **SelectClipRgn**.

- If the region identified by *pRgn* is **NULL**, the new clipping region becomes the default clipping region (a null region).

- **RGN_DIFF**   The new clipping region combines the areas of the current clipping region with those areas excluded from the region identified by *pRgn*.

- **RGN_OR**   The new clipping region combines the current clipping region and the region identified by *pRgn*.

- **RGN_XOR**   The new clipping region combines the current clipping region and the region identified by *pRgn* but excludes any overlapping areas.

Remarks

Selects the given region as the current clipping region for the device context. Only a copy of the selected region is used. The region itself can be selected for any number of other device contexts, or it can be deleted.

The function assumes that the coordinates for the given region are specified in device units. Some printer devices support text output at a higher resolution than graphics output in order to retain the precision needed to express text metrics. These devices report device units at the higher resolution, that is, in text units. These devices then scale coordinates for graphics so that several reported device units map to only 1 graphic unit. You should always call the **SelectClipRgn** function using text units.

Applications that must take the scaling of graphics objects in the GDI can use the **GETSCALINGFACTOR** printer escape to determine the scaling factor. This scaling factor affects clipping. If a region is used to clip graphics, GDI divides the coordinates by the scaling factor. If the region is used to clip text, GDI makes no scaling adjustment. A scaling factor of 1 causes the coordinates to be divided by 2; a scaling factor of 2 causes the coordinates to be divided by 4; and so on.

See Also CDC::GetClipBox, CDC::Escape, CRgn ::SelectClipRgn

CDC::SelectObject

CPen* SelectObject(CPen* *pPen* **);**
CBrush* SelectObject(CBrush* *pBrush* **);**
virtual CFont* SelectObject(CFont* *pFont* **);**
CBitmap* SelectObject(CBitmap* *pBitmap* **);**
int SelectObject(CRgn* *pRgn* **);**

Return Value

A pointer to the object being replaced. This is a pointer to an object of one of the classes derived from **CGdiObject**, such as **CPen**, depending on which version of the function is used. The return value is **NULL** if there is an error. This function may return a pointer to a temporary object. This temporary object is only valid during the processing of one Windows message. For more information, see **CGdiObject::FromHandle**.

The version of the member function that takes a region parameter performs the same task as the **SelectClipRgn** member function. Its return value can be any of the following:

- **COMPLEXREGION** New clipping region has overlapping borders.
- **ERROR** Device context or region is not valid.
- **NULLREGION** New clipping region is empty.
- **SIMPLEREGION** New clipping region has no overlapping borders.

Parameters

pPen A pointer to a **CPen** object to be selected.

pBrush A pointer to a **CBrush** object to be selected.

pFont A pointer to a **CFont** object to be selected.

pBitmap   A pointer to a **CBitmap** object to be selected.

pRgn   A pointer to a **CRgn** object to be selected.

Remarks

Selects an object into the device context. Class **CDC** provides five versions specialized for particular kinds of GDI objects, including pens, brushes, fonts, bitmaps, and regions. The newly selected object replaces the previous object of the same type. For example, if *pObject* of the general version of **SelectObject** points to a **CPen** object, the function replaces the current pen with the pen specified by *pObject*.

An application can select a bitmap into memory device contexts only and into only one memory device context at a time. The format of the bitmap must either be monochrome or compatible with the device context; if it is not, **SelectObject** returns an error.

For Windows 3.1 and later, the **SelectObject** function returns the same value whether it is used in a metafile or not. Under previous versions of Windows, **SelectObject** returned a nonzero value for success and 0 for failure when it was used in a metafile.

See Also   CGdiObject::DeleteObject, CGdiObject::FromHandle, CDC::SelectClipRgn, CDC::SelectPalette, ::SelectObject

CDC::SelectPalette

CPalette* SelectPalette(CPalette* *pPalette*, **BOOL** *bForceBackground* **);**

Return Value

A pointer to a **CPalette** object identifying the logical palette replaced by the palette specified by *pPalette*. It is **NULL** if there is an error.

Parameters

pPalette   Identifies the logical palette to be selected. This palette must already have been created with the **CPalette** member function **CreatePalette**.

bForceBackground   Specifies whether the logical palette is forced to be a background palette. If *bForceBackground* is nonzero, the selected palette is always a background palette, regardless of whether the window has the input focus. If *bForceBackground* is 0 and the device context is attached to a window, the logical palette is a foreground palette when the window has the input focus.

Remarks

Selects the logical palette that is specified by *pPalette* as the selected palette object of the device context. The new palette becomes the palette object used by GDI to control colors displayed in the device context and replaces the previous palette.

An application can select a logical palette into more than one device context. However, changes to a logical palette will affect all device contexts for which it is selected. If an application selects a palette into more than one device context, the device contexts must all belong to the same physical device.

See Also **CDC::RealizePalette**, **CPalette**, **::SelectPalette**

CDC::SelectStockObject

virtual CGdiObject* SelectStockObject(int *nIndex* **);**

Return Value

A pointer to the **CGdiObject** object that was replaced if the function is successful. The actual object pointed to is a **CPen**, **CBrush**, or **CFont** object. If the call is unsuccessful, the return value is **NULL**.

Parameters

nIndex Specifies the kind of stock object desired. It can be one of the following values:

- **BLACK_BRUSH** Black brush.
- **DKGRAY_BRUSH** Dark gray brush.
- **GRAY_BRUSH** Gray brush.
- **HOLLOW_BRUSH** Hollow brush.
- **LTGRAY_BRUSH** Light gray brush.
- **NULL_BRUSH** Null brush.
- **WHITE_BRUSH** White brush.
- **BLACK_PEN** Black pen.
- **NULL_PEN** Null pen.
- **WHITE_PEN** White pen.
- **ANSI_FIXED_FONT** ANSI fixed system font.
- **ANSI_VAR_FONT** ANSI variable system font.
- **DEVICE_DEFAULT_FONT** Device-dependent font.
- **OEM_FIXED_FONT** OEM-dependent fixed font.
- **SYSTEM_FONT** The system font. By default, Windows uses the system font to draw menus, dialog-box controls, and other text. In Windows versions 3.0 and later, the system font is proportional width; earlier versions of Windows use a fixed-width system font.

- **SYSTEM_FIXED_FONT** The fixed-width system font used in Windows prior to version 3.0. This object is available for compatibility with earlier versions of Windows.

- **DEFAULT_PALETTE** Default color palette. This palette consists of the 20 static colors in the system palette.

Remarks

Selects a **CGdiObject** object that corresponds to one of the predefined stock pens, brushes, or fonts.

See Also **CGdiObject::GetObject**

CDC::SetAbortProc

int SetAbortProc(BOOL (CALLBACK EXPORT* *lpfn* **)(HDC, int));**

Return Value

Specifies the outcome of the **SetAbortProc** function. Some of the following values are more probable than others, but all are possible.

- **SP_ERROR** General error.

- **SP_OUTOFDISK** Not enough disk space is currently available for spooling, and no more space will become available.

- **SP_OUTOFMEMORY** Not enough memory is available for spooling.

- **SP_USERABORT** User ended the job through the Print Manager.

Parameters

lpfn A pointer to the abort function to install as the abort procedure. For more about the callback function, see "Callback Function for CDC::SetAbortProc" in the "Callback Functions Used by MFC" section.

Remarks

Installs the abort procedure for the print job.

If an application is to allow the print job to be canceled during spooling, it must set the abort function before the print job is started with the **StartDoc** member function. The Print Manager calls the abort function during spooling to allow the application to cancel the print job or to process out-of-disk-space conditions. If no abort function is set, the print job will fail if there is not enough disk space for spooling.

Note that the features of Microsoft Visual C++ simplify the creation of the callback function passed to **SetAbortProc**. The address passed to the **EnumObjects** member function is a pointer to a function exported with **__export** and with the Pascal calling convention. In protect-mode applications, you do not have to create this function with the Windows **MakeProcInstance** function or free the function after use with the Windows function **FreeProcInstance**.

You also do not have to export the function name in an **EXPORTS** statement in your application's module-definition file. You can instead use the **EXPORT** function modifier, as in

BOOL CALLBACK EXPORT AFunction(**HDC**, **int**);

to cause the compiler to emit the proper export record for export by name without aliasing. This works for most needs. For some special cases, such as exporting a function by ordinal or aliasing the export, you still need to use an **EXPORTS** statement in a module-definition file.

For compiling Microsoft Foundation programs, you'll normally use the /GA and /GEs compiler options. The /Gw compiler option is not used with the Microsoft Foundation classes. (If you do use the Windows function **MakeProcInstance**, you will need to explicitly cast the returned function pointer from **FARPROC** to the type needed by this member function.) Callback registration interfaces are now type-safe (you must pass in a function pointer that points to the right kind of function for the specific callback).

Also note that all callback functions must trap Microsoft Foundation exceptions before returning to Windows, since exceptions cannot be thrown across callback boundaries. For more information about exceptions, see the article "Exceptions" in *Programming with MFC*.

CDC::SetArcDirection

int SetArcDirection(int *nArcDirection* **);**

Return Value

Specifies the old arc direction, if successful; otherwise 0.

Parameters

nArcDirection   Specifies the new arc direction. This parameter can be either of the following values:

- **AD_COUNTERCLOCKWISE**   Figures drawn counterclockwise.

- **AD_CLOCKWISE**   Figures drawn clockwise.

Remarks

Sets the drawing direction to be used for arc and rectangle functions. The default direction is counterclockwise. The **SetArcDirection** function specifies the direction in which the following functions draw:

Arc	**Pie**
ArcTo	**Rectangle**
Chord	**RoundRect**
Ellipse	

See Also   **CDC::GetArcDirection, ::SetArcDirection**

CDC::SetAttribDC

virtual void SetAttribDC(HDC *hDC* **);**

Parameters

hDC   A Windows device context.

Remarks

Call this function to set the attribute device context, **m_hAttribDC**. This member function does not attach the device context to the **CDC** object. Only the output device context is attached to a **CDC** object.

See Also   **CDC::SetOutputDC, CDC::ReleaseAttribDC, CDC::ReleaseOutputDC**

CDC::SetBkColor

virtual COLORREF SetBkColor(COLORREF *crColor* **);**

Return Value

The previous background color as an RGB color value. If an error occurs, the return value is 0x80000000.

Parameters

crColor   Specifies the new background color.

Remarks

Sets the current background color to the specified color. If the background mode is **OPAQUE**, the system uses the background color to fill the gaps in styled lines, the gaps between hatched lines in brushes, and the background in character cells. The system also uses the background color when converting bitmaps between color and monochrome device contexts.

If the device cannot display the specified color, the system sets the background color to the nearest physical color.

See Also   **CDC::BitBlt**, **CDC::GetBkColor**, **CDC::GetBkMode**, **CDC::SetBkMode**, **CDC::StretchBlt**, **::SetBkColor**

CDC::SetBkMode

int SetBkMode(int *nBkMode* **);**

Return Value

The previous background mode.

Parameters

nBkMode   Specifies the mode to be set. This parameter can be either of the following values:

- **OPAQUE**   Background is filled with the current background color before the text, hatched brush, or pen is drawn. This is the default background mode.

- **TRANSPARENT**   Background is not changed before drawing.

Remarks

Sets the background mode. The background mode defines whether the system removes existing background colors on the drawing surface before drawing text, hatched brushes, or any pen style that is not a solid line.

See Also   **CDC::GetBkColor**, **CDC::GetBkMode**, **CDC::SetBkColor**, **::SetBkMode**

CDC::SetBoundsRect

UINT SetBoundsRect(LPCRECT *lpRectBounds*, **UINT** *flags* **);**

Return Value

The current state of the bounding rectangle, if the function is successful. Like *flags*, the return value can be a combination of **DCB_** values:

- **DCB_ACCUMULATE**   The bounding rectangle is not empty. This value will always be set.

- **DCB_DISABLE**   Bounds accumulation is off.

- **DCB_ENABLE**   Bounds accumulation is on.

Parameters

lpRectBounds   Points to a **RECT** structure or **CRect** object that is used to set the bounding rectangle. Rectangle dimensions are given in logical coordinates. This parameter can be **NULL**.

flags   Specifies how the new rectangle will be combined with the accumulated rectangle. This parameter can be a combination of the following values:

- **DCB_ACCUMULATE**   Add the rectangle specified by *lpRectBounds* to the bounding rectangle (using a rectangle-union operation).

- **DCB_DISABLE**   Turn off bounds accumulation.

- **DCB_ENABLE**   Turn on bounds accumulation. (The default setting for bounds accumulation is disabled.)

Remarks

Controls the accumulation of bounding-rectangle information for the specified device context.

Windows can maintain a bounding rectangle for all drawing operations. This rectangle can be queried and reset by the application. The drawing bounds are useful for invalidating bitmap caches.

See Also   **CDC::GetBoundsRect**, **::SetBoundsRect**, **RECT**, **CRect**

CDC::SetBrushOrg

CPoint SetBrushOrg(int *x*, int *y*);
CPoint SetBrushOrg(POINT *point*);

Return Value

The previous origin of the brush in device units.

Parameters

x   Specifies the x-coordinate (in device units) of the new origin. This value must be in the range 0–7.

y   Specifies the y-coordinate (in device units) of the new origin. This value must be in the range 0–7.

point   Specifies the x- and y-coordinates of the new origin. Each value must be in the range 0–7. You can pass either a **POINT** structure or a **CPoint** object for this parameter.

Remarks

Specifies the origin that GDI will assign to the next brush that the application selects into the device context.

The default coordinates for the brush origin are (0, 0). To alter the origin of a brush, call the **UnrealizeObject** function for the **CBrush** object, call **SetBrushOrg**, and then call the **SelectObject** member function to select the brush into the device context.

Do not use **SetBrushOrg** with stock **CBrush** objects.

See Also   **CBrush**, **CDC::GetBrushOrg**, **CDC::SelectObject**,
CGdiObject::UnrealizeObject, **::SetBrushOrg**, **POINT**, **CPoint**

CDC::SetColorAdjustment

BOOL SetColorAdjustment(const COLORADJUSTMENT* *lpColorAdjust* **);**

Return Value

Nonzero if successful; otherwise 0.

Parameters

lpColorAdjust   Points to a **COLORADJUSTMENT** data structure containing the
color adjustment values.

Remarks

Sets the color adjustment values for the device context using the specified values. The
color adjustment values are used to adjust the input color of the source bitmap for
calls to the **CDC::StretchBlt** member function when **HALFTONE** mode is set.

See Also   **CDC::SetStretchBltMode**, **CDC::StretchBlt**, **::StretchDIBits**

CDC::SetMapMode

virtual int SetMapMode(int *nMapMode* **);**

Return Value

The previous mapping mode.

Parameters

nMapMode   Specifies the new mapping mode. It can be any one of the following
values:

MM_ANISOTROPIC   Logical units are converted to arbitrary units with arbitrarily
scaled axes. Setting the mapping mode to **MM_ANISOTROPIC** does not change
the current window or viewport settings. To change the units, orientation, and
scaling, call the **SetWindowExt** and **SetViewportExt** member functions.

- **MM_HIENGLISH**   Each logical unit is converted to 0.001 inch. Positive x is
to the right; positive y is up.

- **MM_HIMETRIC**   Each logical unit is converted to 0.01 millimeter. Positive
x is to the right; positive y is up.

- **MM_ISOTROPIC** Logical units are converted to arbitrary units with equally scaled axes; that is, 1 unit along the x-axis is equal to 1 unit along the y-axis. Use the **SetWindowExt** and **SetViewportExt** member functions to specify the desired units and the orientation of the axes. GDI makes adjustments as necessary to ensure that the x and y units remain the same size.

- **MM_LOENGLISH** Each logical unit is converted to 0.01 inch. Positive x is to the right; positive y is up.

- **MM_LOMETRIC** Each logical unit is converted to 0.1 millimeter. Positive x is to the right; positive y is up.

- **MM_TEXT** Each logical unit is converted to 1 device pixel. Positive x is to the right; positive y is down.

- **MM_TWIPS** Each logical unit is converted to 1/20 of a point. (Because a point is 1/72 inch, a twip is 1/1440 inch.) Positive x is to the right; positive y is up.

Remarks

Sets the mapping mode. The mapping mode defines the unit of measure used to convert logical units to device units; it also defines the orientation of the device's x- and y-axes. GDI uses the mapping mode to convert logical coordinates into the appropriate device coordinates. The **MM_TEXT** mode allows applications to work in device pixels, where 1 unit is equal to 1 pixel. The physical size of a pixel varies from device to device.

The **MM_HIENGLISH**, **MM_HIMETRIC**, **MM_LOENGLISH**, **MM_LOMETRIC**, and **MM_TWIPS** modes are useful for applications that must draw in physically meaningful units (such as inches or millimeters). The **MM_ISOTROPIC** mode ensures a 1:1 aspect ratio, which is useful when it is important to preserve the exact shape of an image. The **MM_ANISOTROPIC** mode allows the x- and y-coordinates to be adjusted independently.

See Also **CDC::SetViewportExt**, **CDC::SetWindowExt**, **::SetMapMode**

CDC::SetMapperFlags

DWORD SetMapperFlags(DWORD *dwFlag* **);**

Return Value

The previous value of the font-mapper flag.

Parameters

dwFlag   Specifies whether the font mapper attempts to match a font's aspect height and width to the device. When this value is **ASPECT_FILTERING**, the mapper selects only fonts whose x-aspect and y-aspect exactly match those of the specified device.

Remarks

Changes the method used by the font mapper when it converts a logical font to a physical font. An application can use **SetMapperFlags** to cause the font mapper to attempt to choose only a physical font that exactly matches the aspect ratio of the specified device.

An application that uses only raster fonts can use the **SetMapperFlags** function to ensure that the font selected by the font mapper is attractive and readable on the specified device. Applications that use scalable (TrueType) fonts typically do not use **SetMapperFlags**.

If no physical font has an aspect ratio that matches the specification in the logical font, GDI chooses a new aspect ratio and selects a font that matches this new aspect ratio.

See Also   **::SetMapperFlags**

CDC::SetMiterLimit

BOOL SetMiterLimit(float *fMiterLimit* **);**

Return Value

Nonzero if the function is successful; otherwise 0.

Parameters

fMiterLimit   Specifies the new miter limit for the device context.

Remarks

Sets the limit for the length of miter joins for the device context. The miter length is defined as the distance from the intersection of the line walls on the inside of the join to the intersection of the line walls on the outside of the join. The miter limit is the maximum allowed ratio of the miter length to the line width. The default miter limit is 10.0.

See Also   **CDC::GetMiterLimit**, **::SetMiterLimit**

CDC::SetOutputDC

virtual void SetOutputDC(HDC *hDC* **);**

Parameters

hDC   A Windows device context.

Remarks

Call this member function to set the output device context, **m_hDC**. This member function can only be called when a device context has not been attached to the **CDC** object. This member function sets **m_hDC** but does not attach the device context to the **CDC** object.

See Also   **CDC::SetAttribDC**, **CDC::ReleaseAttribDC**, **CDC::ReleaseOutputDC**, **CDC::m_hDC**

CDC::SetPixel

COLORREF SetPixel(int *x*, **int** *y*, **COLORREF** *crColor* **);**
COLORREF SetPixel(POINT *point*, **COLORREF** *crColor* **);**

Return Value

An RGB value for the color that the point is actually painted. This value can be different from that specified by *crColor* if an approximation of that color is used. If the function fails (if the point is outside the clipping region), the return value is –1.

Parameters

x   Specifies the logical x-coordinate of the point to be set.

y   Specifies the logical y-coordinate of the point to be set.

crColor   Specifies the color used to paint the point.

point   Specifies the logical x- and y-coordinates of the point to be set. You can pass either a **POINT** structure or a **CPoint** object for this parameter.

Remarks

Sets the pixel at the point specified to the closest approximation of the color specified by *crColor*. The point must be in the clipping region. If the point is not in the clipping region, the function does nothing.

Not all devices support the **SetPixel** function. To determine whether a device supports **SetPixel**, call the **GetDeviceCaps** member function with the **RASTERCAPS** index and check the return value for the **RC_BITBLT** flag.

See Also   **CDC::GetDeviceCaps**, **CDC::GetPixel**, **::SetPixel**, **POINT**, **CPoint**

CDC::SetPixelV

BOOL SetPixelV(int *x*, **int** *y*, **COLORREF** *crColor*);
BOOL SetPixelV(POINT *point*, **COLORREF** *crColor* **);**

Return Value

Nonzero if the function is successful; otherwise 0.

Parameters

x Specifies the x-coordinate, in logical units, of the point to be set.

y Specifies the y-coordinate, in logical units, of the point to be set.

crColor Specifies the color to be used to paint the point.

point Specifies the logical x- and y-coordinates of the point to be set. You can pass either a **POINT** data structure or a **CPoint** object for this parameter.

Remarks

Sets the pixel at the specified coordinates to the closest approximation of the specified color. The point must be in both the clipping region and the visible part of the device surface. Not all devices support the member function. For more information, see the **RC_BITBLT** capability in the **CDC::GetDeviceCaps** member function. **SetPixelV** is faster than **SetPixel** because it does not need to return the color value of the point actually painted.

See Also **CDC::GetDeviceCaps**, **CDC::SetPixel**, **::SetPixelV**

CDC::SetPolyFillMode

> **int SetPolyFillMode(int** *nPolyFillMode* **);**

Return Value

The previous filling mode, if successful; otherwise 0.

Parameters

nPolyFillMode Specifies the new filling mode. This value may be either **ALTERNATE** or **WINDING**. The default mode set in Windows is **ALTERNATE**.

Remarks

Sets the polygon-filling mode.

When the polygon-filling mode is **ALTERNATE**, the system fills the area between odd-numbered and even-numbered polygon sides on each scan line. That is, the system fills the area between the first and second side, between the third and fourth side, and so on. This mode is the default.

When the polygon-filling mode is **WINDING**, the system uses the direction in which a figure was drawn to determine whether to fill an area. Each line segment in a polygon is drawn in either a clockwise or a counterclockwise direction. Whenever an imaginary line drawn from an enclosed area to the outside of a figure passes through a clockwise line segment, a count is incremented. When the line passes through a counterclockwise line segment, the count is decremented. The area is filled if the count is nonzero when the line reaches the outside of the figure.

See Also **CDC::GetPolyFillMode**, **CDC::PolyPolygon**, **::SetPolyFillMode**

CDC::SetROP2

int SetROP2(int *nDrawMode* **);**

Return Value

The previous drawing mode.

It can be any of the values given in the Windows SDK documentation.

Parameters

nDrawMode   Specifies the new drawing mode. It can be any of the following values:

- **R2_BLACK**   Pixel is always black.

- **R2_WHITE**   Pixel is always white.

- **R2_NOP**   Pixel remains unchanged.

- **R2_NOT**   Pixel is the inverse of the screen color.

- **R2_COPYPEN**   Pixel is the pen color.

- **R2_NOTCOPYPEN**   Pixel is the inverse of the pen color.

- **R2_MERGEPENNOT**   Pixel is a combination of the pen color and the inverse of the screen color (final pixel = (NOT screen pixel) OR pen).

- **R2_MASKPENNOT**   Pixel is a combination of the colors common to both the pen and the inverse of the screen (final pixel = (NOT screen pixel) AND pen).

- **R2_MERGENOTPEN**   Pixel is a combination of the screen color and the inverse of the pen color (final pixel = (NOT pen) OR screen pixel).

- **R2_MASKNOTPEN**   Pixel is a combination of the colors common to both the screen and the inverse of the pen (final pixel = (NOT pen) AND screen pixel).

- **R2_MERGEPEN**   Pixel is a combination of the pen color and the screen color (final pixel = pen OR screen pixel).

- **R2_NOTMERGEPEN**   Pixel is the inverse of the **R2_MERGEPEN** color (final pixel = NOT(pen OR screen pixel)).

- **R2_MASKPEN**   Pixel is a combination of the colors common to both the pen and the screen (final pixel = pen AND screen pixel).

- **R2_NOTMASKPEN**   Pixel is the inverse of the **R2_MASKPEN** color (final pixel = NOT(pen AND screen pixel)).

- **R2_XORPEN**   Pixel is a combination of the colors that are in the pen or in the screen, but not in both (final pixel = pen XOR screen pixel).

- **R2_NOTXORPEN**   Pixel is the inverse of the **R2_XORPEN** color (final pixel = NOT(pen XOR screen pixel)).

Remarks

Sets the current drawing mode. The drawing mode specifies how the colors of the pen and the interior of filled objects are combined with the color already on the display surface.

The drawing mode is for raster devices only; it does not apply to vector devices. Drawing modes are binary raster-operation codes representing all possible Boolean combinations of two variables, using the binary operators AND, OR, and XOR (exclusive OR), and the unary operation NOT.

See Also   **CDC::GetDeviceCaps**, **CDC::GetROP2**, **::SetROP2**

CDC::SetStretchBltMode

int **SetStretchBltMode**(int *nStretchMode*);

Return Value

The previous stretching mode. It can be **STRETCH_ANDSCANS**, **STRETCH_DELETESCANS**, or **STRETCH_ORSCANS**.

Parameters

nStretchMode   Specifies the stretching mode. It can be any of the following values:

Value	Description
BLACKONWHITE	Performs a Boolean AND operation using the color values for the eliminated and existing pixels. If the bitmap is a monochrome bitmap, this mode preserves black pixels at the expense of white pixels.
COLORONCOLOR	Deletes the pixels. This mode deletes all eliminated lines of pixels without trying to preserve their information.
HALFTONE	Maps pixels from the source rectangle into blocks of pixels in the destination rectangle. The average color over the destination block of pixels approximates the color of the source pixels.
	After setting the **HALFTONE** stretching mode, an application must call the Win32 function **::SetBrushOrgEx** to set the brush origin. If it fails to do so, brush misalignment occurs.
STRETCH_ANDSCANS	**Windows 95**: Same as **BLACKONWHITE**

Value	Description
STRETCH_DELETESCANS	**Windows 95**: Same as **COLORONCOLOR**
STRETCH_HALFTONE	**Windows 95**: Same as **HALFTONE**
STRETCH_ORSCANS	**Windows 95**: Same as **WHITEONBLACK**
WHITEONBLACK	Performs a Boolean OR operation using the color values for the eliminated and existing pixels. If the bitmap is a monochrome bitmap, this mode preserves white pixels at the expense of black pixels.

Remarks

Sets the bitmap-stretching mode for the **StretchBlt** member function. The bitmap-stretching mode defines how information is removed from bitmaps that are compressed by using the function.

The **BLACKONWHITE** (**STRETCH_ANDSCANS**) and **WHITEONBLACK** (**STRETCH_ORSCANS**) modes are typically used to preserve foreground pixels in monochrome bitmaps. The **COLORONCOLOR** (**STRETCH_DELETESCANS**) mode is typically used to preserve color in color bitmaps.

The **HALFTONE** mode requires more processing of the source image than the other three modes; it is slower than the others, but produces higher quality images. Also note that **SetBrushOrgEx** must be called after setting the **HALFTONE** mode to avoid brush misalignment.

Additional stretching modes might also be available depending on the capabilities of the device driver.

See Also   **CDC::GetStretchBltMode**, **CDC::StretchBlt**, **SetStretchBltMode**

CDC::SetTextAlign

UINT SetTextAlign(UINT *nFlags* **);**

Return Value

The previous text-alignment setting, if successful. The low-order byte contains the horizontal setting and the high-order byte contains the vertical setting; otherwise 0.

Parameters

nFlags   Specifies text-alignment flags. The flags specify the relationship between a point and a rectangle that bounds the text. The point can be either the current position or coordinates specified by a text-output function. The rectangle that bounds the text is defined by the adjacent character cells in the text string. The *nFlags* parameter can be one or more flags from the following three categories. Choose only one flag from each category. The first category affects text alignment in the x-direction:

- **TA_CENTER**   Aligns the point with the horizontal center of the bounding rectangle.

- **TA_LEFT**   Aligns the point with the left side of the bounding rectangle. This is the default setting.

- **TA_RIGHT**   Aligns the point with the right side of the bounding rectangle.

The second category affects text alignment in the y-direction:

- **TA_BASELINE**   Aligns the point with the base line of the chosen font.

- **TA_BOTTOM**   Aligns the point with the bottom of the bounding rectangle.

- **TA_TOP**   Aligns the point with the top of the bounding rectangle. This is the default setting.

The third category determines whether the current position is updated when text is written:

- **TA_NOUPDATECP**   Does not update the current position after each call to a text-output function. This is the default setting.

- **TA_UPDATECP**   Updates the current x-position after each call to a text-output function. The new position is at the right side of the bounding rectangle for the text. When this flag is set, the coordinates specified in calls to the **TextOut** member function are ignored.

Remarks

Sets the text-alignment flags.

The **TextOut** and **ExtTextOut** member functions use these flags when positioning a string of text on a display or device. The flags specify the relationship between a specific point and a rectangle that bounds the text. The coordinates of this point are passed as parameters to the **TextOut** member function. The rectangle that bounds the text is formed by the adjacent character cells in the text string.

See Also   CDC::ExtTextOut, CDC::GetTextAlign, CDC::TabbedTextOut, CDC::TextOut, ::SetTextAlign

---

CDC::SetTextCharacterExtra

int SetTextCharacterExtra(int *nCharExtra* **);**

Return Value

The amount of the previous intercharacter spacing.

Parameters

nCharExtra Specifies the amount of extra space (in logical units) to be added to each character. If the current mapping mode is not **MM_TEXT**, *nCharExtra* is transformed and rounded to the nearest pixel.

Remarks

Sets the amount of intercharacter spacing. GDI adds this spacing to each character, including break characters, when it writes a line of text to the device context. The default value for the amount of intercharacter spacing is 0.

See Also   CDC::GetTextCharacterExtra, ::SetTextCharacterExtra

CDC::SetTextColor

virtual COLORREF SetTextColor(COLORREF *crColor* **);**

Return Value

An RGB value for the previous text color.

Parameters

crColor Specifies the color of the text as an RGB color value.

Remarks

Sets the text color to the specified color. The system will use this text color when writing text to this device context and also when converting bitmaps between color and monochrome device contexts.

If the device cannot represent the specified color, the system sets the text color to the nearest physical color. The background color for a character is specified by the **SetBkColor** and **SetBkMode** member functions.

See Also   CDC::GetTextColor, CDC::BitBlt, CDC::SetBkColor, CDC::SetBkMode, ::SetTextColor

CDC::SetTextJustification

int SetTextJustification(int *nBreakExtra***, int** *nBreakCount* **);**

Return Value

One if the function is successful; otherwise 0.

Parameters

nBreakExtra Specifies the total extra space to be added to the line of text (in logical units). If the current mapping mode is not **MM_TEXT**, the value given by this parameter is converted to the current mapping mode and rounded to the nearest device unit.

nBreakCount Specifies the number of break characters in the line.

Remarks

Adds space to the break characters in a string. An application can use the **GetTextMetrics** member functions to retrieve a font's break character.

After the **SetTextJustification** member function is called, a call to a text-output function (such as **TextOut**) distributes the specified extra space evenly among the specified number of break characters. The break character is usually the space character (ASCII 32), but may be defined by a font as some other character.

The member function **GetTextExtent** is typically used with **SetTextJustification**. **GetTextExtent** computes the width of a given line before alignment. An application can determine how much space to specify in the *nBreakExtra* parameter by subtracting the value returned by **GetTextExtent** from the width of the string after alignment.

The **SetTextJustification** function can be used to align a line that contains multiple runs in different fonts. In this case, the line must be created piecemeal by aligning and writing each run separately.

Because rounding errors can occur during alignment, the system keeps a running error term that defines the current error. When aligning a line that contains multiple runs, **GetTextExtent** automatically uses this error term when it computes the extent of the next run. This allows the text-output function to blend the error into the new run.

After each line has been aligned, this error term must be cleared to prevent it from being incorporated into the next line. The term can be cleared by calling **SetTextJustification** with *nBreakExtra* set to 0.

See Also   **CDC::GetMapMode**, **CDC::GetTextExtent**, **CDC::GetTextMetrics**, **CDC::SetMapMode**, **CDC::TextOut**, **::SetTextJustification**

CDC::SetViewportExt

virtual CSize SetViewportExt(int *cx***, int** *cy* **);**
virtual CSize SetViewportExt(SIZE *size* **);**

Return Value

The previous extents of the viewport as a **CSize** object. When an error occurs, the x- and y-coordinates of the returned **CSize** object are both set to 0.

Parameters

cx   Specifies the x-extent of the viewport (in device units).

cy   Specifies the y-extent of the viewport (in device units).

size   Specifies the x- and y-extents of the viewport (in device units).

Remarks

Sets the x- and y-extents of the viewport of the device context. The viewport, along with the device-context window, defines how GDI maps points in the logical coordinate system to points in the coordinate system of the actual device. In other words, they define how GDI converts logical coordinates into device coordinates.

When the following mapping modes are set, calls to **SetWindowExt** and **SetViewportExt** are ignored:

MM_HIENGLISH	**MM_LOMETRIC**
MM_HIMETRIC	**MM_TEXT**
MM_LOENGLISH	**MM_TWIPS**

When **MM_ISOTROPIC** mode is set, an application must call the **SetWindowExt** member function before it calls **SetViewportExt**.

See Also   CDC::SetWindowExt, ::SetViewportExt, CSize, CDC::GetViewportExt

CDC::SetViewportOrg

virtual CPoint SetViewportOrg(int *x***, int** *y* **);**
virtual CPoint SetViewportOrg(POINT *point* **);**

Return Value

The previous origin of the viewport (in device coordinates) as a **CPoint** object.

Parameters

x   Specifies the x-coordinate (in device units) of the origin of the viewport. The value must be within the range of the device coordinate system.

y   Specifies the y-coordinate (in device units) of the origin of the viewport. The value must be within the range of the device coordinate system.

point   Specifies the origin of the viewport. The values must be within the range of the device coordinate system. You can pass either a **POINT** structure or a **CPoint** object for this parameter.

Remarks

Sets the viewport origin of the device context. The viewport, along with the device-context window, defines how GDI maps points in the logical coordinate system to points in the coordinate system of the actual device. In other words, they define how GDI converts logical coordinates into device coordinates.

The viewport origin marks the point in the device coordinate system to which GDI maps the window origin, a point in the logical coordinate system specified by the **SetWindowOrg** member function. GDI maps all other points by following the same process required to map the window origin to the viewport origin. For example, all points in a circle around the point at the window origin will be in a circle around the point at the viewport origin. Similarly, all points in a line that passes through the window origin will be in a line that passes through the viewport origin.

See Also   **CDC::SetWindowOrg**, **::SetViewportOrg**, **CPoint**, **POINT**, **CDC::GetViewportOrg**

CDC::SetWindowExt

virtual CSize SetWindowExt(int *cx*, **int** *cy* **);**
virtual CSize SetWindowExt(SIZE *size* **);**

Return Value

The previous extents of the window (in logical units) as a **CSize** object. If an error occurs, the x- and y-coordinates of the returned **CSize** object are both set to 0.

Parameters

cx   Specifies the x-extent (in logical units) of the window.

cy   Specifies the y-extent (in logical units) of the window.

size   Specifies the x- and y-extents (in logical units) of the window.

Remarks

Sets the x- and y-extents of the window associated with the device context. The window, along with the device-context viewport, defines how GDI maps points in the logical coordinate system to points in the device coordinate system.

When the following mapping modes are set, calls to **SetWindowExt** and **SetViewportExt** functions are ignored:

- **MM_HIENGLISH**
- **MM_HIMETRIC**
- **MM_LOENGLISH**
- **MM_LOMETRIC**
- **MM_TEXT**
- **MM_TWIPS**

When **MM_ISOTROPIC** mode is set, an application must call the **SetWindowExt** member function before calling **SetViewportExt**.

See Also   **CDC::GetWindowExt**, **CDC::SetViewportExt**, **::SetWindowExt**, **CSize**

CDC::SetWindowOrg

CPoint SetWindowOrg(int *x*, **int** *y* **);**
CPoint SetWindowOrg(POINT *point* **);**

Return Value

The previous origin of the window as a **CPoint** object.

Parameters

x   Specifies the logical x-coordinate of the new origin of the window.

y   Specifies the logical y-coordinate of the new origin of the window.

point   Specifies the logical coordinates of the new origin of the window. You can pass either a **POINT** structure or a **CPoint** object for this parameter.

Remarks

Sets the window origin of the device context. The window, along with the device-context viewport, defines how GDI maps points in the logical coordinate system to points in the device coordinate system.

The window origin marks the point in the logical coordinate system from which GDI maps the viewport origin, a point in the device coordinate system specified by the **SetWindowOrg** function. GDI maps all other points by following the same process required to map the window origin to the viewport origin. For example, all points in a circle around the point at the window origin will be in a circle around the point at the viewport origin. Similarly, all points in a line that passes through the window origin will be in a line that passes through the viewport origin.

See Also   **::SetWindowOrg**, **::SetViewportOrg**, **CPoint**, **POINT**, **CDC::GetWindowOrg**

CDC::StartDoc

int StartDoc(LPDOCINFO *lpDocInfo* **);**

Return Value

The value –1 if there is an error such as insufficient memory or an invalid port specification occurs; otherwise a positive value.

Parameters

lpDocInfo   Points to a **DOCINFO** structure containing the name of the document file and the name of the output file.

Remarks

Informs the device driver that a new print job is starting and that all subsequent **StartPage** and **EndPage** calls should be spooled under the same job until an **EndDoc** call occurs. This ensures that documents longer than one page will not be interspersed with other jobs.

For Windows versions 3.1 and later, this function replaces the **STARTDOC** printer escape. Using this function ensures that documents containing more than one page are not interspersed with other print jobs.

StartDoc should not be used inside metafiles.

See Also   **CDC::Escape**, **CDC::EndDoc**, **CDC::AbortDoc**

CDC::StartPage

int StartPage( );

Remarks

Call this member function to prepare the printer driver to receive data. **StartPage** supersedes the **NEWFRAME** and **BANDINFO** escapes.

For an overview of the sequence of printing calls, see the **StartDoc** member function.

The system disables the **ResetDC** member function between calls to **StartPage** and **EndPage**.

See Also   **CDC::Escape**, **CDC::EndPage**

CDC::StretchBlt

BOOL StretchBlt(int *x*, **int** *y*, **int** *nWidth*, **int** *nHeight*, **CDC*** *pSrcDC*, **int** *xSrc*, **int** *ySrc*, **int** *nSrcWidth*, **int** *nSrcHeight*, **DWORD** *dwRop* **);**

Return Value

Nonzero if the bitmap is drawn; otherwise 0.

Parameters

x   Specifies the x-coordinate (in logical units) of the upper-left corner of the destination rectangle.

y   Specifies the y-coordinate (in logical units) of the upper-left corner of the destination rectangle.

nWidth   Specifies the width (in logical units) of the destination rectangle.

nHeight   Specifies the height (in logical units) of the destination rectangle.

pSrcDC   Specifies the source device context.

xSrc   Specifies the x-coordinate (in logical units) of the upper-left corner of the source rectangle.

ySrc   Specifies the x-coordinate (in logical units) of the upper-left corner of the source rectangle.

nSrcWidth   Specifies the width (in logical units) of the source rectangle.

nSrcHeight   Specifies the height (in logical units) of the source rectangle.

dwRop   Specifies the raster operation to be performed. Raster operation codes define how GDI combines colors in output operations that involve a current brush, a possible source bitmap, and a destination bitmap. This parameter may be one of the following values:

- **BLACKNESS**   Turns all output black.

- **DSTINVERT**   Inverts the destination bitmap.

- **MERGECOPY**   Combines the pattern and the source bitmap using the Boolean AND operator.

- **MERGEPAINT**   Combines the inverted source bitmap with the destination bitmap using the Boolean OR operator.

- **NOTSRCCOPY**   Copies the inverted source bitmap to the destination.

- **NOTSRCERASE**   Inverts the result of combining the destination and source bitmaps using the Boolean OR operator.

- **PATCOPY**   Copies the pattern to the destination bitmap.

- **PATINVERT**   Combines the destination bitmap with the pattern using the Boolean XOR operator.

- **PATPAINT**   Combines the inverted source bitmap with the pattern using the Boolean OR operator. Combines the result of this operation with the destination bitmap using the Boolean OR operator.

- **SRCAND**   Combines pixels of the destination and source bitmaps using the Boolean AND operator.

- **SRCCOPY**   Copies the source bitmap to the destination bitmap.

- **SRCERASE**   Inverts the destination bitmap and combines the result with the source bitmap using the Boolean AND operator.

- **SRCINVERT**   Combines pixels of the destination and source bitmaps using the Boolean XOR operator.

- **SRCPAINT**   Combines pixels of the destination and source bitmaps using the Boolean OR operator.

- **WHITENESS**   Turns all output white.

Remarks

Copies a bitmap from a source rectangle into a destination rectangle, stretching or compressing the bitmap if necessary to fit the dimensions of the destination rectangle. The function uses the stretching mode of the destination device context (set by **SetStretchBltMode**) to determine how to stretch or compress the bitmap.

The **StretchBlt** function moves the bitmap from the source device given by *pSrcDC* to the destination device represented by the device-context object whose member function is being called. The *xSrc*, *ySrc*, *nSrcWidth*, and *nSrcHeight* parameters define the upper-left corner and dimensions of the source rectangle. The *x*, *y*, *nWidth*, and *nHeight* parameters give the upper-left corner and dimensions of the destination rectangle. The raster operation specified by *dwRop* defines how the source bitmap and the bits already on the destination device are combined.

The **StretchBlt** function creates a mirror image of a bitmap if the signs of the *nSrcWidth* and *nWidth* or *nSrcHeight* and *nHeight* parameters differ. If *nSrcWidth* and *nWidth* have different signs, the function creates a mirror image of the bitmap along the x-axis. If *nSrcHeight* and *nHeight* have different signs, the function creates a mirror image of the bitmap along the y-axis.

The **StretchBlt** function stretches or compresses the source bitmap in memory and then copies the result to the destination. If a pattern is to be merged with the result, it is not merged until the stretched source bitmap is copied to the destination. If a brush is used, it is the selected brush in the destination device context. The destination coordinates are transformed according to the destination device context; the source coordinates are transformed according to the source device context.

If the destination, source, and pattern bitmaps do not have the same color format, **StretchBlt** converts the source and pattern bitmaps to match the destination bitmaps. The foreground and background colors of the destination device context are used in the conversion.

If **StretchBlt** must convert a monochrome bitmap to color, it sets white bits (1) to the background color and black bits (0) to the foreground color. To convert color to monochrome, it sets pixels that match the background color to white (1) and sets all other pixels to black (0). The foreground and background colors of the device context with color are used.

Not all devices support the **StretchBlt** function. To determine whether a device supports **StretchBlt**, call the **GetDeviceCaps** member function with the **RASTERCAPS** index and check the return value for the **RC_STRETCHBLT** flag.

See Also   **CDC::BitBlt, CDC::GetDeviceCaps, CDC::SetStretchBltMode, ::StretchBlt**

CDC::StrokeAndFillPath

BOOL StrokeAndFillPath( );

Return Value

Nonzero if the function is successful; otherwise 0.

Remarks

Closes any open figures in a path, strokes the outline of the path by using the current pen, and fills its interior by using the current brush. The device context must contain a closed path. The **StrokeAndFillPath** member function has the same effect as closing all the open figures in the path, and stroking and filling the path separately, except that the filled region will not overlap the stroked region even if the pen is wide.

See Also **CDC::BeginPath**, **CDC::FillPath**, **CDC::SetPolyFillMode**, **CDC::StrokePath**, **::StrokeAndFillPath**

CDC::StrokePath

BOOL StrokePath( );

Return Value

Nonzero if the function is successful; otherwise 0.

Remarks

Renders the specified path by using the current pen. The device context must contain a closed path.

See Also **CDC::BeginPath**, **CDC::EndPath**, **::StrokePath**

CDC::TabbedTextOut

virtual CSize TabbedTextOut(int *x*, **int** *y*, **LPCTSTR** *lpszString*, **int** *nCount*, **int** *nTabPositions*,
  LPINT *lpnTabStopPositions*, **int** *nTabOrigin*);
CSize TabbedTextOut(int *x*, **int** *y*, **const CString&** *str*, **int** *nTabPositions*,
  LPINT *lpnTabStopPositions*, **int** *nTabOrigin*);

Return Value

The dimensions of the string (in logical units) as a **CSize** object.

Parameters

x Specifies the logical x-coordinate of the starting point of the string.

y Specifies the logical y-coordinate of the starting point of the string.

lpszString Points to the character string to draw. You can pass either a pointer to an array of characters or a **CString** object for this parameter.

nCount Specifies the number of characters in the string. If *nCount* is –1, the length is calculated.

nTabPositions Specifies the number of values in the array of tab-stop positions.

lpnTabStopPositions Points to an array containing the tab-stop positions (in logical units). The tab stops must be sorted in increasing order; the smallest x-value should be the first item in the array.

    nTabOrigin   Specifies the x-coordinate of the starting position from which tabs are expanded (in logical units).

    str   A **CString** object that contains the specified characters.

Remarks

Call this member function to write a character string at the specified location, expanding tabs to the values specified in the array of tab-stop positions. Text is written in the currently selected font. If *nTabPositions* is 0 and *lpnTabStopPositions* is **NULL**, tabs are expanded to eight times the average character width.

If *nTabPositions* is 1, the tab stops are separated by the distance specified by the first value in the *lpnTabStopPositions* array. If the *lpnTabStopPositions* array contains more than one value, a tab stop is set for each value in the array, up to the number specified by *nTabPositions*. The *nTabOrigin* parameter allows an application to call the **TabbedTextOut** function several times for a single line. If the application calls the function more than once with the *nTabOrigin* set to the same value each time, the function expands all tabs relative to the position specified by *nTabOrigin*.

By default, the current position is not used or updated by the function. If an application needs to update the current position when it calls the function, the application can call the **SetTextAlign** member function with *nFlags* set to **TA_UPDATECP**. When this flag is set, Windows ignores the *x* and *y* parameters on subsequent calls to **TabbedTextOut**, using the current position instead.

See Also   **CDC::GetTabbedTextExtent**, **CDC::SetTextAlign**, **CDC::TextOut**, **CDC::SetTextColor**, **::TabbedTextOut**, **CSize**

CDC::TextOut

    virtual BOOL TextOut(int *x*, **int** *y*, **LPCTSTR** *lpszString*, **int** *nCount* **);**
    BOOL TextOut(int *x*, **int** *y*, **const CString&** *str* **);**

Return Value

Nonzero if the function is successful; otherwise 0.

Parameters

    x   Specifies the logical x-coordinate of the starting point of the text.

    y   Specifies the logical y-coordinate of the starting point of the text.

    lpszString   Points to the character string to be drawn.

    nCount   Specifies the number of bytes in the string.

    str   A **CString** object that contains the characters to be drawn.

Remarks

Writes a character string at the specified location using the currently selected font.

Character origins are at the upper-left corner of the character cell. By default, the current position is not used or updated by the function.

If an application needs to update the current position when it calls **TextOut**, the application can call the **SetTextAlign** member function with *nFlags* set to **TA_UPDATECP**. When this flag is set, Windows ignores the *x* and *y* parameters on subsequent calls to **TextOut**, using the current position instead.

See Also   **CDC::ExtTextOut, CDC::GetTextExtent, CDC::SetTextAlign, CDC::SetTextColor, CDC::TabbedTextOut, ::TextOut**

CDC::UpdateColors

void UpdateColors( );

Remarks

Updates the client area of the device context by matching the current colors in the client area to the system palette on a pixel-by-pixel basis. An inactive window with a realized logical palette may call **UpdateColors** as an alternative to redrawing its client area when the system palette changes.

For more information about using color palettes, see **::UpdateColors** in the *Win32 SDK Programmer's Reference*.

The **UpdateColors** member function typically updates a client area faster than redrawing the area. However, because the function performs the color translation based on the color of each pixel before the system palette changed, each call to this function results in the loss of some color accuracy.

See Also   **CDC::RealizePalette, CPalette, ::UpdateColors**

CDC::WidenPath

BOOL WidenPath( );

Return Value

Nonzero if the function is successful; otherwise 0.

Remarks

> Redefines the current path as the area that would be painted if the path were stroked using the pen currently selected into the device context. This function is successful only if the current pen is a geometric pen created by the second version of **CreatePen** member function, or if the pen is created with the first version of **CreatePen** and has a width, in device units, of greater than 1. The device context must contain a closed path. Any Bézier curves in the path are converted to sequences of straight lines approximating the widened curves. As such, no Bézier curves remain in the path after **WidenPath** is called.
>
> **See Also**   **CDC::BeginPath**, **CDC::EndPath**, **CDC::SetMiterLimit**, **::WidenPath**

CDC::m_hAttribDC

Remarks

> The attribute device context for this **CDC** object. By default, this device context is equal to **m_hDC**. In general, **CDC** GDI calls that request information from the device context are directed to **m_hAttribDC**. See the **CDC** class description for more on the use of these two device contexts.
>
> **See Also**   **CDC::m_hDC**, **CDC::SetAttribDC**, **CDC::ReleaseAttribDC**

CDC::m_hDC

Remarks

> The output device context for this **CDC** object. By default, **m_hDC** is equal to **m_hAttribDC**, the other device context wrapped by **CDC**. In general, **CDC** GDI calls that create output go to the **m_hDC** device context. You can initialize **m_hDC** and **m_hAttribDC** to point to different devices. See the **CDC** class description for more on the use of these two device contexts.
>
> **See Also**   **CDC::m_hAttribDC**, **CDC::SetOutputDC**, **CDC::ReleaseOutputDC**

CDialog

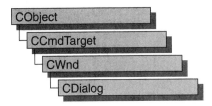

The **CDialog** class is the base class used for displaying dialog boxes on the screen. Dialog boxes are of two types: modal and modeless. A modal dialog box must be closed by the user before the application continues. A modeless dialog box allows the user to display the dialog box and return to another task without canceling or removing the dialog box.

A **CDialog** object is a combination of a dialog template and a **CDialog**-derived class. Use the dialog editor to create the dialog template and store it in a resource, then use ClassWizard to create a class derived from **CDialog**.

A dialog box, like any other window, receives messages from Windows. In a dialog box, you are particularly interested in handling notification messages from the dialog box's controls since that is how the user interacts with your dialog box. ClassWizard browses through the potential messages generated by each control in your dialog box, and you can select which messages you wish to handle. ClassWizard then adds the appropriate message-map entries and message-handler member functions to the new class for you. You only need to write application-specific code in the handler member functions.

If you prefer, you can always write message-map entries and member functions yourself instead of using ClassWizard.

In all but the most trivial dialog box, you add member variables to your derived dialog class to store data entered in the dialog box's controls by the user or to display data for the user. ClassWizard browses through those controls in your dialog box that can be mapped to data and prompts you to create a member variable for each control. At the same time, you choose a variable type and permissible range of values for each variable. ClassWizard adds the member variables to your derived dialog class.

ClassWizard then writes a data map to automatically handle the exchange of data between the member variables and the dialog box's controls. The data map provides functions that initialize the controls in the dialog box with the proper values, retrieve the data, and validate the data.

To create a modal dialog box, construct an object on the stack using the constructor for your derived dialog class and then call **DoModal** to create the dialog window and its controls. If you wish to create a modeless dialog, call **Create** in the constructor of your dialog class.

You can also create a template in memory by using a **DLGTEMPLATE** data structure as described in the Win32 SDK documentation. After you construct a **CDialog** object, call **CreateIndirect** to create a modeless dialog box, or call **InitModalIndirect** and **DoModal** to create a modal dialog box.

ClassWizard writes the exchange and validation data map in an override of **CWnd::DoDataExchange** that ClassWizard adds to your new dialog class. See the **DoDataExchange** member function in **CWnd** for more on the exchange and validation functionality.

Both the programmer and the framework call **DoDataExchange** indirectly through a call to **CWnd::UpdateData**.

The framework calls **UpdateData** when the user clicks the OK button to close a modal dialog box. (The data is not retrieved if the Cancel button is clicked.) The default implementation of **OnInitDialog** also calls **UpdateData** to set the initial values of the controls. You typically override **OnInitDialog** to further initialize controls. **OnInitDialog** is called after all the dialog controls are created and just before the dialog box is displayed.

You can call **CWnd::UpdateData** at any time during the execution of a modal or modeless dialog box.

If you develop a dialog box by hand, you add the necessary member variables to the derived dialog-box class yourself, and you add member functions to set or get these values.

For more on ClassWizard, see Chapter 14, "Working with Classes," in the *Visual C++ User's Guide*.

Call **CWinApp::SetDialogBkColor** to set the background color for dialog boxes in your application.

A modal dialog box closes automatically when the user presses the OK or Cancel buttons or when your code calls the **EndDialog** member function.

When you implement a modeless dialog box, always override the **OnCancel** member function and call **DestroyWindow** from within it. Don't call the base class **CDialog::OnCancel**, because it calls **EndDialog**, which will make the dialog box invisible but will not destroy it. You should also override **PostNcDestroy** for modeless dialog boxes in order to delete **this**, since modeless dialog boxes are usually allocated with **new**. Modal dialog boxes are usually constructed on the frame and do not need **PostNcDestroy** cleanup.

For more information on **CDialog**, see the article "Dialog Boxes" in *Programming with MFC*.

#include <afxwin.h>

Construction

CDialog	Constructs a **CDialog** object.

Initialization

Create	Initializes the **CDialog** object. Creates a modeless dialog box and attaches it to the **CDialog** object.
CreateIndirect	Creates a modeless dialog box from a dialog-box template in memory (not resource-based).
InitModalIndirect	Creates a modal dialog box from a dialog-box template in memory (not resource-based). The parameters are stored until the function **DoModal** is called.

Operations

DoModal	Calls a modal dialog box and returns when done.
MapDialogRect	Converts the dialog-box units of a rectangle to screen units.
NextDlgCtrl	Moves the focus to the next dialog-box control in the dialog box.
PrevDlgCtrl	Moves the focus to the previous dialog-box control in the dialog box.
GotoDlgCtrl	Moves the focus to a specified dialog-box control in the dialog box.
SetDefID	Changes the default pushbutton control for a dialog box to a specified pushbutton.
GetDefID	Gets the ID of the default pushbutton control for a dialog box.
SetHelpID	Sets a context-sensitive help ID for the dialog box.
EndDialog	Closes a modal dialog box.

Overridables

OnInitDialog	Override to augment dialog-box initialization.
OnSetFont	Override to specify the font that a dialog-box control is to use when it draws text.
OnOK	Override to perform the OK button action in a modal dialog box. The default closes the dialog box and **DoModal** returns **IDOK**.
OnCancel	Override to perform the Cancel button or ESC key action. The default closes the dialog box and **DoModal** returns **IDCANCEL**.

Member Functions
CDialog::CDialog

CDialog(LPCTSTR *lpszTemplateName,* **CWnd*** *pParentWnd* = **NULL**);
CDialog(UINT *nIDTemplate,* **CWnd*** *pParentWnd* = **NULL**);
CDialog( );

Parameters

lpszTemplateName   Contains a null-terminated string that is the name of a dialog-box template resource.

nIDTemplate   Contains the ID number of a dialog-box template resource.

pParentWnd   Points to the parent or owner window object (of type **CWnd**) to which the dialog object belongs. If it is **NULL**, the dialog object's parent window is set to the main application window.

Remarks

To construct a resource-based modal dialog box, call either public form of the constructor. One form of the constructor provides access to the dialog resource by template name. The other constructor provides access by template ID number, usually with an **IDD_** prefix (for example, IDD_DIALOG1).

To construct a modal dialog box from a template in memory, first invoke the parameterless, protected constructor and then call **InitModalIndirect**.

After you construct a modal dialog box with one of the above methods, call **DoModal**.

To construct a modeless dialog box, use the protected form of the **CDialog** constructor. The constructor is protected because you must derive your own dialog-box class to implement a modeless dialog box. Construction of a modeless dialog box is a two-step process. First call the constructor; then call the **Create** member function to create a resource-based dialog box, or call **CreateIndirect** to create the dialog box from a template in memory.

See Also   **CDialog::Create, CWnd::DestroyWindow, CDialog::InitModalIndirect, CDialog::DoModal, ::CreateDialog**

CDialog::Create

BOOL Create(LPCTSTR *lpszTemplateName,* **CWnd*** *pParentWnd* = **NULL**);
BOOL Create(UINT *nIDTemplate,* **CWnd*** *pParentWnd* = **NULL**);

Return Value

Both forms return nonzero if dialog-box creation and initialization were successful; otherwise 0.

Parameters

lpszTemplateName   Contains a null-terminated string that is the name of a dialog-box template resource.

pParentWnd   Points to the parent window object (of type **CWnd**) to which the dialog object belongs. If it is **NULL**, the dialog object's parent window is set to the main application window.

nIDTemplate   Contains the ID number of a dialog-box template resource.

Remarks

Call **Create** to create a modeless dialog box using a dialog-box template from a resource. You can put the call to **Create** inside the constructor or call it after the constructor is invoked.

Two forms of the **Create** member function are provided for access to the dialog-box template resource by either template name or template ID number (for example, IDD_DIALOG1).

For either form, pass a pointer to the parent window object. If *pParentWnd* is **NULL**, the dialog box will be created with its parent or owner window set to the main application window.

The **Create** member function returns immediately after it creates the dialog box.

Use the **WS_VISIBLE** style in the dialog-box template if the dialog box should appear when the parent window is created. Otherwise, you must call **ShowWindow**. For further dialog-box styles and their application, see the **DLGTEMPLATE** structure in the Win32 SDK documentation and "Window Styles" in the *Class Library Reference*.

Use the **CWnd::DestroyWindow** function to destroy a dialog box created by the **Create** function.

See Also   CDialog::CDialog, CWnd::DestroyWindow, CDialog::InitModalIndirect, CDialog::DoModal, ::CreateDialog

---

CDialog::CreateIndirect

BOOL CreateIndirect(LPCDLGTEMPLATE *lpDialogTemplate*, **CWnd*** *pParentWnd* = **NULL**);
BOOL CreateIndirect(HGLOBAL *hDialogTemplate*, **CWnd*** *pParentWnd* = **NULL**);

Return Value

Nonzero if the dialog box was created and initialized successfully; otherwise 0.

Parameters

lpDialogTemplate   Points to memory that contains a dialog-box template used to create the dialog box. This template is in the form of a **DLGTEMPLATE** structure and control information. For more information on this structure, see the Win32 SDK documentation.

pParentWnd   Points to the dialog object's parent window object (of type **CWnd**). If it is **NULL**, the dialog object's parent window is set to the main application window.

hDialogTemplate   Contains a handle to global memory containing a dialog-box template. This template is in the form of a **DLGTEMPLATE** structure and data for each control in the dialog box.

Remarks

Call this member function to create a modeless dialog box from a dialog-box template in memory.

The **CreateIndirect** member function returns immediately after it creates the dialog box.

Use the **WS_VISIBLE** style in the dialog-box template if the dialog box should appear when the parent window is created. Otherwise, you must call **ShowWindow** to cause it to appear. For more information on how you can specify other dialog-box styles in the template, see the **DLGTEMPLATE** structure in the Win32 SDK documentation.

Use the **CWnd::DestroyWindow** function to destroy a dialog box created by the **CreateIndirect** function.

See Also   **CDialog::CDialog**, **CWnd::DestroyWindow**, **CDialog::Create**, **::CreateDialogIndirect**

CDialog::DoModal

virtual int DoModal( );

Return Value

An **int** value that specifies the value of the *nResult* parameter that was passed to the **CDialog::EndDialog** member function, which is used to close the dialog box. The return value is –1 if the function could not create the dialog box, or **IDABORT** if some other error occurred.

Remarks

Call this member function to invoke the modal dialog box and return the dialog-box result when done. This member function handles all interaction with the user while the dialog box is active. This is what makes the dialog box modal; that is, the user cannot interact with other windows until the dialog box is closed.

If the user clicks one of the pushbuttons in the dialog box, such as OK or Cancel, a message-handler member function, such as **OnOK** or **OnCancel**, is called to attempt to close the dialog box. The default **OnOK** member function will validate and update the dialog-box data and close the dialog box with result **IDOK**, and the default **OnCancel** member function will close the dialog box with result **IDCANCEL** without validating or updating the dialog-box data. You can override these message-handler functions to alter their behavior.

Note **PreTranslateMessage** is now called for modal dialog box message processing.

See Also **::DialogBox**, **CWnd::IsDialogMessage**

CDialog::EndDialog

> **void EndDialog(int** *nResult* **);**

Parameters

> *nResult* Contains the value to be returned from the dialog box to the caller of **DoModal**.

Remarks

> Call this member function to terminate a modal dialog box. This member function returns *nResult* as the return value of **DoModal**. You must use the **EndDialog** function to complete processing whenever a modal dialog box is created.
>
> You can call **EndDialog** at any time, even in **OnInitDialog**, in which case you should close the dialog box before it is shown or before the input focus is set.
>
> **EndDialog** does not close the dialog box immediately. Instead, it sets a flag that directs the dialog box to close as soon as the current message handler returns.
>
> **See Also** **CDialog::DoModal**, **CDialog::OnOK**, **CDialog::OnCancel**

CDialog::GetDefID

> **DWORD GetDefID( ) const;**

Return Value

> A 32-bit value (**DWORD**). If the default pushbutton has an ID value, the high-order word contains **DC_HASDEFID** and the low-order word contains the ID value. If the default pushbutton does not have an ID value, the return value is 0.

Remarks

> Call the **GetDefID** member function to get the ID of the default pushbutton control for a dialog box. This is usually an OK button.
>
> **See Also** **CDialog::SetDefID**, **DM_GETDEFID**

CDialog::GotoDlgCtrl

void GotoDlgCtrl(CWnd* *pWndCtrl* **);**

Parameters

pWndCtrl   Identifies the window (control) that is to receive the focus.

Remarks

Moves the focus to the specified control in the dialog box.

To get a pointer to the control (child window) to pass as *pWndCtrl*, call the **CWnd::GetDlgItem** member function, which returns a pointer to a **CWnd** object.

See Also   **CWnd::GetDlgItem**, **CDialog::PrevDlgCtrl**, **CDialog::NextDlgCtrl**

CDialog::InitModalIndirect

BOOL InitModalIndirect(LPCDLGTEMPLATE *lpDialogTemplate*,
    CWnd* *pParentWnd* **= NULL);**
BOOL InitModalIndirect(HGLOBAL *hDialogTemplate*, **CWnd*** *pParentWnd* **= NULL);**

Return Value

Nonzero if the dialog object was created and initialized successfully; otherwise 0.

Parameters

lpDialogTemplate   Points to memory that contains a dialog-box template used to create the dialog box. This template is in the form of a **DLGTEMPLATE** structure and control information. For more information on this structure, see the Win32 SDK documentation.

hDialogTemplate   Contains a handle to global memory containing a dialog-box template. This template is in the form of a **DLGTEMPLATE** structure and data for each control in the dialog box.

pParentWnd   Points to the parent or owner window object (of type **CWnd**) to which the dialog object belongs. If it is **NULL**, the dialog object's parent window is set to the main application window.

Remarks

Call this member function to initialize a modal dialog object using a dialog-box template that you construct in memory.

To create a modal dialog box indirectly, first allocate a global block of memory and fill it with the dialog box template. Then call the empty **CDialog** constructor to construct the dialog-box object. Next, call **InitModalIndirect** to store your handle to the in-memory dialog-box template. The Windows dialog box is created and displayed later, when the **DoModal** member function is called.

See Also **::DialogBoxIndirect**, **CDialog::DoModal**, **CWnd::DestroyWindow**, **CDialog::CDialog**

CDialog::MapDialogRect

void MapDialogRect(LPRECT *lpRect* **) const;**

Parameters

lpRect   Points to a **RECT** structure or **CRect** object that contains the dialog-box coordinates to be converted.

Remarks

Call to convert the dialog-box units of a rectangle to screen units. Dialog-box units are stated in terms of the current dialog-box base unit derived from the average width and height of characters in the font used for dialog-box text. One horizontal unit is one-fourth of the dialog-box base-width unit, and one vertical unit is one-eighth of the dialog-box base height unit.

The **GetDialogBaseUnits** Windows function returns size information for the system font, but you can specify a different font for each dialog box if you use the **DS_SETFONT** style in the resource-definition file. The **MapDialogRect** Windows function uses the appropriate font for this dialog box.

The **MapDialogRect** member function replaces the dialog-box units in *lpRect* with screen units (pixels) so that the rectangle can be used to create a dialog box or position a control within a box.

See Also **::GetDialogBaseUnits**, **::MapDialogRect**, **WM_SETFONT**

CDialog::NextDlgCtrl

void NextDlgCtrl( ) const;

Remarks

Moves the focus to the next control in the dialog box. If the focus is at the last control in the dialog box, it moves to the first control.

See Also **CDialog::PrevDlgCtrl**, **CDialog::GotoDlgCtrl**

CDialog::OnCancel

virtual void OnCancel( );

Remarks

The framework calls this member function when the user clicks the Cancel button or presses the ESC key in a modal or modeless dialog box.

Override this member function to perform Cancel button action. The default simply terminates a modal dialog box by calling **EndDialog** and causing **DoModal** to return **IDCANCEL**.

If you implement the Cancel button in a modeless dialog box, you must override the **OnCancel** member function and call **DestroyWindow** from within it. Don't call the base-class member function, because it calls **EndDialog**, which will make the dialog box invisible but not destroy it.

See Also   **CDialog::OnOK**, **CDialog::EndDialog**

CDialog::OnInitDialog

virtual BOOL OnInitDialog( );

Return Value

Specifies whether the application has set the input focus to one of the controls in the dialog box. If **OnInitDialog** returns nonzero, Windows sets the input focus to the first control in the dialog box. The application can return 0 only if it has explicitly set the input focus to one of the controls in the dialog box.

Remarks

This member function is called in response to the **WM_INITDIALOG** message. This message is sent to the dialog box during the **Create**, **CreateIndirect**, or **DoModal** calls, which occur immediately before the dialog box is displayed.

Override this member function if you need to perform special processing when the dialog box is initialized. In the overridden version, first call the base class **OnInitDialog** but disregard its return value. You will normally return **TRUE** from your overridden member function.

Windows calls the **OnInitDialog** function via the standard global dialog-box procedure common to all Microsoft Foundation Class Library dialog boxes, rather than through your message map, so you do not need a message-map entry for this member function.

See Also   **CDialog::Create**, **CDialog::CreateIndirect**, **WM_INITDIALOG**

CDialog::OnOK

virtual void OnOK( );

Remarks

Called when the user clicks the OK button (the button with an ID of **IDOK**).

Override this member function to perform the OK button action. If the dialog box includes automatic data validation and exchange, the default implementation of this member function validates the dialog-box data and updates the appropriate variables in your application.

If you implement the OK button in a modeless dialog box, you must override the **OnOK** member function and call **DestroyWindow** from within it. Don't call the base-class member function, because it calls **EndDialog**, which makes the dialog box invisible but does not destroy it.

See Also   **CDialog::OnCancel**, **CDialog::EndDialog**

CDialog::OnSetFont

virtual void OnSetFont(CFont* *pFont* **);**

Parameters

pFont   Specifies a pointer to the font. Used as the default font for all controls in this dialog box.

Remarks

Specifies the font a dialog-box control will use when drawing text. The dialog-box control will use the specified font as the default for all dialog-box controls.

The dialog editor typically sets the dialog-box font as part of the dialog-box template resource.

See Also   **WM_SETFONT**, **CWnd::SetFont**

CDialog::PrevDlgCtrl

void PrevDlgCtrl( ) const;

Remarks

Sets the focus to the previous control in the dialog box. If the focus is at the first control in the dialog box, it moves to the last control in the box.

See Also   **CDialog::NextDlgCtrl**, **CDialog::GotoDlgCtrl**

CDialog::SetDefID

void SetDefID(UINT *nID* **);**

Parameters

nID   Specifies the ID of the pushbutton control that will become the default.

Remarks

Changes the default pushbutton control for a dialog box.

See Also   CDialog::GetDefID

CDialog::SetHelpID

void SetHelpID(UINT *nIDR* **);**

Parameters

nIDR   Specifies the context-sensitive help ID.

Remarks

Sets a context-sensitive help ID for the dialog box.

CDialogBar

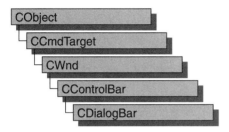

The **CDialogBar** class provides the functionality of a Windows modeless dialog box in a control bar. A dialog bar resembles a dialog box in that it contains standard Windows controls that the user can tab between. Another similarity is that you create a dialog template to represent the dialog bar.

Creating and using a dialog bar is similar to creating and using a **CFormView** object. First, use the dialog editor to define a dialog template with the style **WS_CHILD** and no other style (see the *Visual C++ User's Guide*, Chapter 6, "Using the Dialog Editor"). The template must not have the style **WS_VISIBLE**. In your application code, call
the constructor to construct the **CDialogBar** object, then call **Create** to create the dialog-bar window and attach it to the **CDialogBar** object.

For more information on **CDialogBar**, see the article "Dialog Bars" in *Programming with MFC* and Technical Note 31, "Control Bars," available under MFC in Books Online.

#include <afxext.h>

See Also **CFormView**, **CControlBar**

Construction

CDialogBar	Constructs a **CDialogBar** object.
Create	Creates a Windows dialog bar and attaches it to the **CDialogBar** object.

Member Functions

CDialogBar::CDialogBar

CDialogBar( );

Remarks

Constructs a **CDialogBar** object.

See Also   **CControlBar**

CDialogBar::Create

BOOL Create(CWnd* *pParentWnd*, **LPCTSTR** *lpszTemplateName*, **UINT** *nStyle*, **UINT** *nID* **);**
BOOL Create(CWnd* *pParentWnd*, **UINT** *nIDTemplate*, **UINT** *nStyle*, **UINT** *nID* **);**

Return Value

Nonzero if successful; otherwise 0.

Parameters

pParentWnd   A pointer to the parent **CWnd** object.

lpszTemplateName   A pointer to the name of the **CDialogBar** object's dialog-box resource template.

nStyle   The alignment style of the dialog bar. The following styles are supported:

- **CBRS_TOP**   Control bar is at the top of the frame window.

- **CBRS_BOTTOM**   Control bar is at the bottom of the frame window.

- **CBRS_NOALIGN**   Control bar is not repositioned when the parent is resized.

- **CBRS_LEFT**   Control bar is at the left of the frame window.

- **CBRS_RIGHT**   Control bar is at the right of the frame window.

nID   The control ID of the dialog bar.

nIDTemplate   The resource ID of the **CDialogBar** object's dialog-box template.

Remarks

Loads the dialog-box resource template specified by *lpszTemplateName* or *nIDTemplate*, creates the dialog-bar window, sets its style, and associates it with the **CDialogBar** object.

If you specify the **CBRS_TOP** or **CBRS_BOTTOM** alignment style, the dialog bar's width is that of the frame window and its height is that of the resource specified by *nIDTemplate*. If you specify the **CBRS_LEFT** or **CBRS_RIGHT** alignment style, the dialog bar's height is that of the frame window and its width is that of the resource specified by *nIDTemplate*.

See Also   **CDialogBar::CDialogBar**

CDocItem

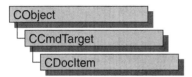

CDocItem is the base class for document items, which are components of a document's data. **CDocItem** objects are used to represent OLE items in both client and server documents.

For more information, see the article "Containers: Implementing a Container" in *Programming with MFC*.

#include <afxole.h>

See Also **COleDocument**, **COleServerItem**, **COleClientItem**

Operations

GetDocument	Returns the document that contains the item.

Overridables

IsBlank	Determines whether the item contains any information.

Member Functions

CDocItem::IsBlank

virtual BOOL IsBlank( ) const;

Return Value

Nonzero if the item contains no information; otherwise 0.

Remarks

Called by the framework when default serialization occurs.

By default, **CDocItem** objects are not blank. **COleClientItem** objects are sometimes blank because they derive directly from **CDocItem**. However, **COleServerItem** objects are always blank. By default, OLE applications containing **COleClientItem** objects that have no x or y extent are serialized. This is done by returning **TRUE** from an override of **IsBlank** when the item has no x or y extent.

Override this function if you want to implement other actions during serialization.

See Also **CObject::Serialize**

CDocItem::GetDocument

CDocument* GetDocument( ) const;

Return Value

A pointer to the document that contains the item; **NULL**, if the item is not part of a document.

Remarks

Call this function to get the document that contains the item.

This function is overridden in the derived classes **COleClientItem** and **COleServerItem**, returning a pointer to either a **COleDocument**, a **COleLinkingDoc**, or a **COleServerDoc** object.

See Also **COleDocument**, **COleLinkingDoc**, **COleServerDoc**, **COleClientItem**, **COleServerItem**

CDocTemplate

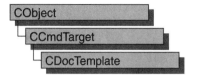

CDocTemplate is an abstract base class that defines the basic functionality for document templates. You usually create one or more document templates in the implementation of your application's **InitInstance** function. A document template defines the relationships among three types of classes:

- A document class, which you derive from **CDocument**.

- A view class, which displays data from the document class listed above. You can derive this class from **CView**, **CScrollView**, **CFormView**, or **CEditView**. (You can also use **CEditView** directly.)

- A frame window class, which contains the view. For a single document interface (SDI) application, you derive this class from **CFrameWnd**. For a multiple document interface (MDI) application, you derive this class from **CMDIChildWnd**. If you don't need to customize the behavior of the frame window, you can use **CFrameWnd** or **CMDIChildWnd** directly without deriving your own class.

Your application has one document template for each type of document that it supports. For example, if your application supports both spreadsheets and text documents, the application has two document template objects. Each document template is responsible for creating and managing all the documents of its type.

The document template stores pointers to the **CRuntimeClass** objects for the document, view, and frame window classes. These **CRuntimeClass** objects are specified when constructing a document template.

The document template contains the ID of the resources used with the document type (such as menu, icon, or accelerator table resources). The document template also has strings containing additional information about its document type. These include the name of the document type (for example, "Worksheet") and the file extension (for example, ".xls"). Optionally, it can contain other strings used by the application's user interface, the Windows File Manager, and Object Linking and Embedding (OLE) support.

If your application is an OLE container and/or server, the document template also defines the ID of the menu used during in-place activation. If your application is an OLE server, the document template defines the ID of the toolbar and menu used during in-place activation. You specify these additional OLE resources by calling **SetContainerInfo** and **SetServerInfo**.

Because **CDocTemplate** is an abstract class, you cannot use the class directly. A typical application uses one of the two **CDocTemplate**-derived classes provided by the Microsoft Foundation Class Library: **CSingleDocTemplate**, which implements SDI, and **CMultiDocTemplate**, which implements MDI. See those classes for more information on using document templates.

If your application requires a user-interface paradigm that is fundamentally different from SDI or MDI, you can derive your own class from **CDocTemplate**.

For more information on **CDocTemplate**, see "Document Templates" in Chapter 2 of *Programming with MFC*.

include# <afxwin.h>

See Also   **CSingleDocTemplate**, **CMultiDocTemplate**, **CDocument**, **CView**, **CScrollView**, **CEditView**, **CFormView**, **CFrameWnd**, **CMDIChildWnd**

Constructors

CDocTemplate	Constructs a **CDocTemplate** object.

Attributes

SetContainerInfo	Determines the resources for OLE containers when editing an in-place OLE item.
SetServerInfo	Determines the resources and classes when the server document is embedded or edited in-place.
GetFirstDocPosition	Retrieves the position of the first document associated with this template.
GetNextDoc	Retrieves a document and the position of the next one.
LoadTemplate	Loads the resources for a given **CDocTemplate** or derived class.

Operations

AddDocument	Adds a document to a template.
RemoveDocument	Removes a document from a template.
GetDocString	Retrieves a string associated with the document type.
CreateOleFrame	Creates an OLE-enabled frame window.

Overridables

MatchDocType	Determines the degree of confidence in the match between a document type and this template.
CreateNewDocument	Creates a new document.
CreateNewFrame	Creates a new frame window containing a document and view.
InitialUpdateFrame	Initializes the frame window, and optionally makes it visible.
SaveAllModified	Saves all documents associated with this template which have been modified.
CloseAllDocuments	Closes all documents associated with this template.
OpenDocumentFile	Opens a file specified by a pathname.
SetDefaultTitle	Displays the default title in the document window's title bar.

Member Functions

CDocTemplate::AddDocument

virtual void AddDocument(CDocument* *pDoc* **);**

Parameters

pDoc   A pointer to the document to be added.

Remarks

Use this function to add a document to a template. The derived classes **CMultiDocTemplate** and **CSingleDocTemplate** override this function. If you derive your own document-template class from **CDocTemplate**, your derived class must override this function.

See Also   **CDocTemplate::RemoveDocument**, **CMultiDocTemplate**, **CSingleDocTemplate**

CDocTemplate::CDocTemplate

CDocTemplate (UINT *nIDResource*, **CRuntimeClass*** *pDocClass*, **CRuntimeClass*** *pFrameClass*, **CRuntimeClass*** *pViewClass* **);**

Parameters

nIDResource   Specifies the ID of the resources used with the document type. This may include menu, icon, accelerator table, and string resources.

The string resource consists of up to seven substrings separated by the '\n' character (the '\n' character is needed as a place holder if a substring is not included; however, trailing '\n' characters are not necessary); these substrings describe the document type. For information on the substrings, see **GetDocString**. This string resource is found in the application's resource file. For example:

```
// MYCALC.RC
STRINGTABLE PRELOAD DISCARDABLE
BEGIN
    IDR_SHEETTYPE "\nSheet\nWorksheet\nWorksheets (*.myc)\n.myc\n
MyCalcSheet\nMyCalc Worksheet"
END
```

Note that the string begins with a '\n' character; this is because the first substring is not used for MDI applications and so is not included. You can edit this string using the string editor; the entire string appears as a single entry in the String Editor, not as seven separate entries.

For more information about these resource types, see the *Visual C++ User's Guide*.

pDocClass   Points to the **CRuntimeClass** object of the document class. This class is a **CDocument**-derived class you define to represent your documents.

pFrameClass   Points to the **CRuntimeClass** object of the frame window class. This class can be a **CFrameWnd**-derived class, or it can be **CFrameWnd** itself if you want default behavior for your main frame window.

pViewClass   Points to the **CRuntimeClass** object of the view class. This class is a **CView**-derived class you define to display your documents.

Remarks

Use this member function to construct a **CDocTemplate** object. Dynamically allocate a **CDocTemplate** object and pass it to **CWinApp::AddDocTemplate** from the InitInstance member function of your application class.

See Also   CDocTemplate::GetDocString, CWinApp::AddDocTemplate, CWinApp::InitInstance, CRuntimeClass

CDocTemplate::CloseAllDocuments

virtual void CloseAllDocuments(BOOL *bEndSession* **);**

Parameters

bEndSession   Specifies whether or not the session is being ended. It is **TRUE** if the session is being ended; otherwise **FALSE**.

Remarks

Call this member function to close all open documents. This member function is typically used as part of the File Exit command. The default implementation of this function calls the **CDocument::DeleteContents** member function to delete the document's data and then closes the frame windows for all the views attached to the document.

Override this function if you want to require the user to perform special cleanup processing before the document is closed. For example, if the document represents a record in a database, you may want to override this function to close the database.

See Also   **CDocTemplate::OpenDocumentFile**, **CDocTemplate::SaveAllModified**

CDocTemplate::CreateNewDocument

virtual CDocument* CreateNewDocument( );

Return Value

A pointer to the newly created document, or **NULL** if an error occurs.

Remarks

Call this member function to create a new document of the type associated with this document template.

See Also   **CDocTemplate::CreateNewFrame**

CDocTemplate::CreateNewFrame

virtual CFrameWnd* CreateNewFrame(CDocument* *pDoc***, CFrameWnd*** *pOther* **);**

Return Value

A pointer to the newly created frame window, or **NULL** if an error occurs.

Parameters

pDoc   The document to which the new frame window should refer. Can be **NULL**.

pOther   The frame window on which the new frame window is to be based. Can be **NULL**.

Remarks

CreateNewFrame uses the **CRuntimeClass** objects passed to the constructor to create a new frame window with a view and document attached. If the *pDoc* parameter is **NULL**, the framework outputs a TRACE message.

The *pOther* parameter is used to implement the Window New command. It provides a frame window on which to model the new frame window. The new frame window is usually created invisible. Call this function to create frame windows outside the standard framework implementation of File New and File Open.

See Also   **CCreateContext**, **CFrameWnd::LoadFrame**, **CDocTemplate::InitialUpdateFrame**

CDocTemplate::CreateOleFrame

CFrameWnd* CreateOleFrame(CWnd* *pParentWnd*, **CDocument*** *pDoc*, **BOOL** *bCreateView* **);**

Return Value

A pointer to a frame window if successful; otherwise **NULL**.

Parameters

pParentWnd   A pointer to the frame's parent window.

pDoc   A pointer to the document to which the new OLE frame window should refer.

bCreateView   Determines whether a view is created along with the frame.

Remarks

Creates an OLE frame window. If *bCreateView* is zero, an empty frame is created.

See Also   CDocTemplate::CreateNewFrame, COleDocument, COleIPFrameWnd

---

CDocTemplate::GetDocString

virtual BOOL GetDocString(CString& *rString*, **enum DocStringIndex** *index* **) const;**

Return Value

Nonzero if the specified substring was found; otherwise 0.

Parameters

rString   A reference to a **CString** object that will contain the string when the function returns.

index   An index of the substring being retrieved from the string that describes the document type. This parameter can have one of the following values:

- **CDocTemplate::windowTitle**   Name that appears in the application window's title bar (for example, "Microsoft Excel"). Present only in the document template for SDI applications.

- **CDocTemplate::docName**   Root for the default document name (for example, "Sheet"). This root, plus a number, is used for the default name of a new document of this type whenever the user chooses the New command from the File menu (for example, "Sheet1" or "Sheet2"). If not specified, "Untitled" is used as the default.

- **CDocTemplate::fileNewName**   Name of this document type. If the application supports more than one type of document, this string is displayed in the File New dialog box (for example, "Worksheet"). If not specified, the document type is inaccessible using the File New command.

- **CDocTemplate::filterName** Description of the document type and a wildcard filter matching documents of this type. This string is displayed in the List Files Of Type drop-down list in the File Open dialog box (for example, "Worksheets (*.xls)"). If not specified, the document type is inaccessible using the File Open command.

- **CDocTemplate::filterExt** Extension for documents of this type (for example, ".xls"). If not specified, the document type is inaccessible using the File Open command.

- **CDocTemplate::regFileTypeId** Identifier for the document type to be stored in the registration database maintained by Windows. This string is for internal use only (for example, "ExcelWorksheet"). If not specified, the document type cannot be registered with the Windows File Manager.

- **CDocTemplate::regFileTypeName** Name of the document type to be stored in the registration database. This string may be displayed in dialog boxes of applications that access the registration database (for example, "Microsoft Excel Worksheet").

Remarks

Call this function to retrieve a specific substring describing the document type. The string containing these substrings is stored in the document template and is derived from a string in the resource file for the application. The framework calls this function to get the strings it needs for the application's user interface. If you have specified a filename extension for your application's documents, the framework also calls this function when adding an entry to the Windows registration database; this allows documents to be opened from the Windows File Manager.

Call this function only if you are deriving your own class from **CDocTemplate**.

See Also   **CMultiDocTemplate::CMultiDocTemplate**, **CSingleDocTemplate::CSingleDocTemplate**, **CWinApp::RegisterShellFileTypes**

CDocTemplate::GetFirstDocPosition

virtual POSITION GetFirstDocPosition( ) const = 0;

Return Value

A **POSITION** value that can be used to iterate through the list of documents associated with this document template; or **NULL** if the list is empty.

Remarks

Use this function to get the position of the first document in the list of documents associated with this template. Use the **POSITION** value as an argument to **CDocTemplate::GetNextDoc** to iterate through the list of documents associated with the template.

CSingleDocTemplate and CMultiDocTemplate both override this pure virtual function. Any class you derive from CDocTemplate must also override this function.

See Also   CDocTemplate::GetNextDoc, CSingleDocTemplate, CMultiDocTemplate

CDocTemplate::GetNextDoc

virtual CDocument* GetNextDoc(POSITION& *rPos*) const = 0;

Return Value

A pointer to the next document in the list of documents associated with this template.

Parameters

rPos   A reference to a **POSITION** value returned by a previous call to **GetFirstDocPosition** or **GetNextDoc**.

Remarks

Retrieves the list element identified by *rPos*, then sets r*rPos* to the **POSITION** value of the next entry in the list. If the retrieved element is the last in the list, then the new value of *rPos* is set to **NULL**.

You can use **GetNextDoc** in a forward iteration loop if you establish the initial position with a call to **GetFirstDocPosition**.

You must ensure that your **POSITION** value represents a valid position in the list. If it is invalid, then the Debug version of the Microsoft Foundation Class Library asserts.

See Also   CDocTemplate::GetFirstDocPosition

CDocTemplate::InitialUpdateFrame

virtual void InitialUpdateFrame(CFrameWnd* *pFrame*, CDocument* *pDoc*, BOOL *bMakeVisible* = TRUE);

Parameters

pFrame   The frame window that needs the initial update.

pDoc   The document to which the frame is associated. Can be **NULL**.

bMakeVisible   Indicates whether the frame should become visible and active.

Remarks

Call **IntitialUpdateFrame** after creating a new frame with **CreateNewFrame**. Calling this function causes the views in that frame window to receive their **OnInitialUpdate** calls. Also, if there was not previously an active view, the primary view of the frame window is made active; the primary view is a view with a child ID of **AFX_IDW_PANE_FIRST**. Finally, the frame window is made visible if *bMakeVisible* is non-zero. If *bMakeVisible* is zero, the current focus and visible state of the frame window will remain unchanged.

It is not necessary to call this function when using the framework's implementation of File New and File Open.

See Also   **CView::OnInititalUpdate**, **CFrameWnd::SetActiveView**, **CDocTemplate::CreateNewFrame**

CDocTempate::LoadTemplate

virtual void LoadTemplate( );

Remarks

This member function is called by the framework to load the resources for a given **CDocTemplate** or derived class. Normally it is called during construction, except when the template is being constructed globally. In that case, the call to **LoadTemplate** is delayed until **CWinApp::AddDocTemplate** is called.

See Also   **CWinApp::AddDocTemplate**

CDocTemplate::MatchDocType

virtual Confidence MatchDocType(LPCTSTR *lpszPathName*, **CDocument*&** *rpDocMatch* **);**
virtual Confidence MatchDocType(LPCTSTR *lpszPathName*, **DWORD** *dwFileType*, **CDocument*&** *rpDocMatch* **);**

Return Value

A value from the **Confidence** enumeration, which is defined as follows:

```
enum Confidence
{
        noAttempt,
        maybeAttemptForeign,
        maybeAttemptNative,
        yesAttemptForeign,
        yesAttemptNative,
        yesAlreadyOpen
};
```

Parameters

lpszPathName   Pathname of the file whose type is to be determined.

rpDocMatch   Pointer to a document that is assigned the matching document, if the file specified by *lpszPathName* is already open.

dwFileType   The type of the document (Macintosh® only).

Remarks

Use this function to determine the type of document template to use for opening a file. If your application supports multiple file types, for example, you can use this function to determine which of the available document templates is appropriate for a given file by calling **MatchDocType** for each template in turn, and choosing a template according to the confidence value returned.

If the file specified by *lpszPathName* is already open, this function returns **CDocTemplate::yesAlreadyOpen** and copies the file's **Cdocument** object into the object at *rpDocMatch*.

If the file is not open but the extension in *lpszPathName* matches the extension specified by **CDocTemplate::filterExt** (or the Macintosh file type matches), this function returns **CDocTemplate::yesAttemptNative** and sets *rpDocMatch* to **NULL**. For more information on **CDocTemplate::filterExt**, see **CDocTemplate::GetDocString**.

If neither case is true, the function returns **CDocTemplate::yesAttemptForeign**.

The default implementation does not return **CDocTemplate::maybeAttemptForeign** or **CDocTemplate::maybeAttemptNative**. Override this function to implement type-matching logic appropriate to your application, perhaps using these two values from the **Confidence** enumeration.

See Also   CDocTemplate::GetDocString

CDocTemplate::OpenDocumentFile

virtual CDocument* OpenDocumentFile(LPCTSTR *lpszPathName*,
BOOL *bMakeVisible* **= TRUE) = 0;**

Return Value

A pointer to the document whose file is named by *lpszPathName*; **NULL** if unsuccessful.

Parameters

lpszPathName   Pointer to the pathname of the file containing the document to be opned.

bMakeVisible   Determines whether the window containing the document is to be made visible.

Remarks

Opens the file whose pathname is specified by *lpzsPathName*. If *lpszPathName* is **NULL**, a new file, containing a document of the type associated with this template, is created.

See Also   CDocTemplate::CloseAllDocuments

CDocTemplate::RemoveDocument

virtual void RemoveDocument(CDocument* *pDoc* **);**

Parameters

pDoc   Pointer to the document to be removed.

Remarks

Removes the document pointed to by *pDoc* from the list of documents associated with this template. The derived classes **CMultiDocTemplate** and **CSingleDocTemplate** override this function. If you derive your own document-template class from **CDocTemplate**, your derived class must override this function.

See Also   CDocTemplate::AddDocument, CMultiDocTemplate, CSingleDocTemplate

---

CDocTemplate::SaveAllModified

virtual BOOL SaveAllModified( );

Return Value

Non-zero if successful; otherwise 0.

Remarks

Saves all documents that have been modified.

See Also   CDocTemplate::OpenDocumentFile, CDocTemplate::CloseAllDocuments

---

CDocTemplate::SetContainerInfo

void SetContainerInfo(UINT *nIDOleInPlaceContainer* **);**

Parameters

nIDOleInPlaceContainer   The ID of the resources used when an embedded object is activated.

Remarks

Call this function to set the resources to be used when an OLE 2 object is in-place activated. These resources may include menus and accelerator tables. This function is usually called in the **CWinApp::InitInstance** function of your application.

The menu associated with *nIDOleInPlaceContainer* contains separators that allow the menu of the activated in-place item to merge with the menu of the container application. For more information about merging server and container menus, see the article "Menus and Resources" in *Programming with MFC*.

See Also   **CDocTemplate::SetServerInfo, CWinApp::InitInstance, CMultiDocTemplate::CMultiDocTemplate**

CDocTemplate::SetDefaultTitle

virtual void SetDefaultTitle(CDocument* *pDocument* **) = 0;**

Parameters

pDocument   Pointer to the document whose title is to be set.

Remarks

Call this function to load the document's default title and display it in the document's title bar. For information on the default title, see the description of **CDocTemplate::docName** in **CDocTemplate::GetDocString**.

See Also   **CDocTemplate::GetDocString**

CDocTemplate::SetServerInfo

void SetServerInfo(UINT *nIDOleEmbedding*, **UINT** *nIDOleInPlaceServer* = 0, **CRuntimeClass*** *pOleFrameClass* = **NULL, CRuntimeClass*** *pOleViewClass* = **NULL);**

Parameters

nIDOleEmbedding   The ID of the resources used when an embedded object is opened in a separate window.

nIDOleInPlaceServer   The ID of the resources used when an embedded object is activated in-place.

pOleFrameClass   Pointer to a **CRuntimeClass** structure containing class information for the frame window object created when in-place activation occurs.

pOleViewClass   Pointer to a **CRuntimeClass** structure containing class information for the view object created when in-place activation occurs.

Remarks

Call this member function to identify resources that will be used by the server application when the user requests activation of an embedded object. These resources consist of menus and accelerator tables. This function is usually called in the **InitInstance** of your application.

The menu associated with *nIDOleInPlaceServer* contains separators that allow the server menu to merge with the menu of the container. For more information about merging server and container menus, see the article "Menus and Resources" in *Programming with MFC*.

See Also **CMultiDocTemplate::CMultiDocTemplate**, **CDocTemplate::SetContainerInfo**, **CWinApp::InitInstance**

CDocument

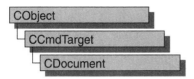

The **CDocument** class provides the basic functionality for user-defined document classes. A document represents the unit of data that the user typically opens with the File Open command and saves with the File Save command.

CDocument supports standard operations such as creating a document, loading it, and saving it. The framework manipulates documents using the interface defined by **CDocument**.

An application can support more than one type of document; for example, an application might support both spreadsheets and text documents. Each type of document has an associated document template; the document template specifies what resources (for example, menu, icon, or accelerator table) are used for that type of document. Each document contains a pointer to its associated **CDocTemplate** object.

Users interact with a document through the **CView** object(s) associated with it. A view renders an image of the document in a frame window and interprets user input as operations on the document. A document can have multiple views associated with it. When the user opens a window on a document, the framework creates a view and attaches it to the document. The document template specifies what type of view and frame window are used to display each type of document.

Documents are part of the framework's standard command routing and consequently receive commands from standard user-interface components (such as the File Save menu item). A document receives commands forwarded by the active view. If the document doesn't handle a given command, it forwards the command to the document template that manages it.

When a document's data is modified, each of its views must reflect those modifications. **CDocument** provides the **UpdateAllViews** member function for you to notify the views of such changes, so the views can repaint themselves as necessary. The framework also prompts the user to save a modified file before closing it.

To implement documents in a typical application, you must do the following:

- Derive a class from **CDocument** for each type of document.

- Add member variables to store each document's data.

- Implement member functions for reading and modifying the document's data. The document's views are the most important users of these member functions.

- Override the **CObject::Serialize** member function in your document class to write and read the document's data to and from disk.

CDocument supports sending your document via mail if mail support (MAPI) is present. See the articles "MAPI" and "MAPI Support in MFC" in Part 2 of *Programming with MFC*.

For more information on **CDocument**, see the article "Serialization (Object Persistence), Documents and Views" in Chapter 3, and "Document/View Creation" in Chapter 1 of *Programming with MFC*.

#include <afxwin.h>

See Also   **CCmdTarget**, **CView**, **CDocTemplate**

Construction

CDocument	Constructs a **CDocument** object.

Operations

AddView	Attaches a view to the document.
GetDocTemplate	Returns a pointer to the document template that describes the type of the document.
GetFirstViewPosition	Returns the position of the first in the list of views; used to begin iteration.
GetNextView	Iterates through the list of views associated with the document.
GetPathName	Returns the path of the document's data file.
GetTitle	Returns the document's title.
IsModified	Indicates whether the document has been modified since it was last saved.
RemoveView	Detaches a view from the document.
SetModifiedFlag	Sets a flag indicating that you have modified the document since it was last saved.
SetPathName	Sets the path of the data file used by the document.
SetTitle	Sets the document's title.
UpdateAllViews	Notifies all views that document has been modified.

Overridables

CanCloseFrame	Advanced overridable; called before closing a frame window viewing this document.
DeleteContents	Called to perform cleanup of the document.
OnChangedViewList	Called after a view is added to or removed from the document.

OnCloseDocument	Called to close the document.
OnNewDocument	Called to create a new document.
OnOpenDocument	Called to open an existing document.
OnSaveDocument	Called to save the document to disk.
ReportSaveLoadException	Advanced overridable; called when an open or save operation cannot be completed because of an exception.
GetFile	Returns a pointer to the desired **CFile** object.
ReleaseFile	Releases a file to make it available for use by other applications.
SaveModified	Advanced overridable; called to ask the user whether the document should be saved.
PreCloseFrame	Called before the frame window is closed.

Mail Functions

OnFileSendMail	Sends a mail message with the document attached.
OnUpdateFileSendMail	Enables the Send Mail command if mail support is present.

Member Functions

CDocument::AddView

> **void AddView(CView*** *pView* **);**

Parameters

pView   Points to the view being added.

Remarks

Call this function to attach a view to the document. This function adds the specified view to the list of views associated with the document; the function also sets the view's document pointer to this document. The framework calls this function when attaching a newly created view object to a document; this occurs in response to a File New, File Open, or New Window command or when a splitter window is split.

Call this function only if you are manually creating and attaching a view. Typically you will let the framework connect documents and views by defining a **CDocTemplate** object to associate a document class, view class, and frame window class.

Example

```
// The following example toggles two views in an SDI (single document
// interface) frame window.  A design decision must be made as to

// whether to leave the inactive view connected to the document,
// such that the inactive view continues to receive OnUpdate
// notifications from the document.  It is usually desirable to
// keep the inactive view continuously in sync with the document, even
// though it is inactive.  However, doing so incurs a performance cost,
// as well as the programming cost of implementing OnUpdate hints.
// It may be less expensive, in terms of performance and/or programming,
// to re-sync the inactive view with the document only with it is
// reactivated.  This example illustrates this latter approach, by
// reconnecting the newly active view and disconnecting the newly
// inactive view, via calls to CDocument::AddView and RemoveView.

BOOL CMainFrame::OnViewChange(UINT nCmdID)
{
   CView* pViewAdd;
   CView* pViewRemove;
   CDocument* pDoc = GetActiveDocument();
   if (nCmdID == ID_VIEW_VIEW2)
   {
      if (m_pView2 == NULL)
      {
         m_pView1 = GetActiveView();
         m_pView2 = new CMyView2;
         m_pView2->Create(NULL, NULL, AFX_WS_DEFAULT_VIEW,
            rectDefault, this, AFX_IDW_PANE_FIRST + 1, NULL);
      }
      pViewAdd = m_pView2;
      pViewRemove = m_pView1;
   }
   else
   {
      pViewAdd = m_pView1;
      pViewRemove = m_pView2;
   }

   // Set the child i.d. of the active view to AFX_IDW_PANE_FIRST,
   // so that CFrameWnd::RecalcLayout will allocate to this
   // "first pane" that portion of  the frame window's client area
   // not allocated to control  bars.  Set the child i.d. of the
   // other view to anything other than AFX_IDW_PANE_FIRST; this
   // examples switches the child id's of the two views.
```

```
    int nSwitchChildID = pViewAdd->GetDlgCtrlID();
    pViewAdd->SetDlgCtrlID(AFX_IDW_PANE_FIRST);
    pViewRemove->SetDlgCtrlID(nSwitchID);
        // Show the newly active view and hide the inactive view.
    pViewAdd->ShowWindow(SW_SHOW);
    pViewRemove->ShowWindow(SW_HIDE);

    // Connect the newly active view to the document, and
    // disconnect the inactive view.
    pDoc->AddView(pViewAdd);
    pDoc->RemoveView(pViewRemove);

    // Inform the frame window which view is now active;
    // and reallocate the frame window's client area to the
    // new view. Implement logic to resync the view to the
    // document in an override of CView::OnActivateView,
    // which is called from CFrameWnd::SetActiveView.
    SetActiveView(pViewAdd);
    RecalcLayout();

    return TRUE;
}
```

See Also   **CDocTemplate, CDocument::GetFirstViewPosition,
CDocument::GetNextView, CDocument::RemoveView, CView::GetDocument**

CDocument::CanCloseFrame

virtual BOOL CanCloseFrame(CFrameWnd* *pFrame* **);**

Return Value

Nonzero if it is safe to close the frame window; otherwise 0.

Parameters

pFrame   Points to the frame window of a view attached to the document.

Remarks

Called by the framework before a frame window displaying the document is closed.
The default implementation checks if there are other frame windows displaying the
document. If the specified frame window is the last one that displays the document,
the function prompts the user to save the document if it has been modified. Override
this function if you want to perform special processing when a frame window is
closed. This is an advanced overridable.

See Also   **CDocument::SaveModified**

CDocument::CDocument

CDocument( );

Remarks

Constructs a **CDocument** object. The framework handles document creation for you. Override the **OnNewDocument** member function to perform initialization on a per-document basis; this is particularly important in single document interface (SDI) applications.

See Also **CDocument::OnNewDocument, CDocument::OnOpenDocument**

CDocument::DeleteContents

virtual void DeleteContents( );

Remarks

Called by the framework to delete the document's data without destroying the document object itself. It is called just before the document is to be destroyed. It is also called to ensure that a document is empty before it is reused. This is particularly important for an SDI application, which uses only one document object; the document object is reused whenever the user creates or opens another document. Call this function to implement an "Edit Clear All" or similar command that deletes all of the document's data. The default implementation of this function does nothing. Override this function to delete the data in your document.

Example

```
// This example is the handler for an Edit Clear All command.

void CMyDoc::OnEditClearAll()
{
   DeleteContents();
   UpdateAllViews(NULL);
}

void CMyDoc::DeleteContents()
{
   // Re-initialize document data here.

}
```

See Also **CDocument::OnCloseDocument, CDocument::OnNewDocument, CDocument::OnOpenDocument**

CDocument::GetDocTemplate

CDocTemplate* GetDocTemplate( ) const;

Return Value

A pointer to the document template for this document type, or **NULL** if the document is not managed by a document template.

Remarks

Call this function to get a pointer to the document template for this document type.

Example

```
// This example accesses the doc template object to construct
// a default document name such as SHEET.XLS, where "sheet"
// is the base document name and ".xls" is the file extension
// for the document type.
CString strDefaultDocName, strBaseName, strExt;
CDocTemplate* pDocTemplate = GetDocTemplate();
if (!pDocTemplate->GetDocString(strBaseName, CDocTemplate::docName)
   || !pDocTemplate->GetDocString(strExt, CDocTemplate::filterExt))
{
   AfxThrowUserException(); // These doc template strings will
      // be available if you created the application using AppWizard
      // and specified the file extension as an option for
      // the document class produced by AppWizard.
}
strDefaultDocName = strBaseName + strExt;
```

See Also   CDocTemplate

CDocument::GetFile

virtual CFile* GetFile(LPCTSTR *lpszFileName*, **UINT** *nOpenFlags*, **CFileException*** *pError* **);**

Return Value

A pointer to a **CFile** object.

Parameters

lpszFileName   A string that is the path to the desired file. The path may be relative or absolute.

pError   A pointer to an existing file-exception object that indicates the completion status of the operation.

nOpenFlags   Sharing and access mode. Specifies the action to take when opening the file. You can combine options listed in the CFile constructor **CFile::CFile** by using the bitwise OR (I) operator. One access permission and one share option are required; the **modeCreate** and **modeNoInherit** modes are optional.

Remarks

Call this member function to get a pointer to a **CFile** object.

See Also **CDocTemplate**

CDocument::GetFirstViewPosition

virtual POSITION GetFirstViewPosition( ) const;

Return Value

A **POSITION** value that can be used for iteration with the **GetNextView** member function.

Remarks

Call this function to get the position of the first view in the list of views associated with the document.

Example

```
//To get the first view in the list of views:

POSITION pos = GetFirstViewPosition();
CView* pFirstView = GetNextView( pos );
// This example uses CDocument::GetFirstViewPosition
// and GetNextView to repaint each view.
void CMyDoc::OnRepaintAllViews()
{
    POSITION pos = GetFirstViewPosition();
    while (pos != NULL)
    {
        CView* pView = GetNextView(pos);
        pView->UpdateWindow();
    }
}

// An easier way to accomplish the same result is to call
// UpdateAllViews(NULL);
```

See Also **CDocument::GetNextView**

CDocument::GetNextView

virtual CView* GetNextView(POSITION& *rPosition* **) const;**

Return Value

A pointer to the view identified by *rPosition*.

Parameters

rPosition A reference to a **POSITION** value returned by a previous call to the **GetNextView** or **GetFirstViewPosition** member functions. This value must not be **NULL**.

Remarks

Call this function to iterate through all of the document's views. The function returns the view identified by *rPosition* and then sets *rPosition* to the **POSITION** value of the next view in the list. If the retrieved view is the last in the list, then *rPosition* is set to **NULL**.

Example

```
// This example uses CDocument::GetFirstViewPosition
// and GetNextView to repaint each view.
void CMyDoc::OnRepaintAllViews()
{
    POSITION pos = GetFirstViewPosition();
    while (pos != NULL)
    {
        CView* pView = GetNextView(pos);
        pView->UpdateWindow();
    }
}

// An easier way to accomplish the same result is to call
// UpdateAllViews(NULL);
```

See Also **CDocument::AddView, CDocument::GetFirstViewPosition, CDocument::RemoveView, CDocument::UpdateAllViews**

CDocument::GetPathName

const CString& GetPathName( ) const;

Return Value

The document's fully qualified path. This string is empty if the document has not been saved or does not have a disk file associated with it.

Remarks

Call this function to get the fully qualified path of the document's disk file.

See Also **CDocument::SetPathName**

CDocument::GetTitle

const CString& GetTitle( ) const;

Return Value

The document's title.

Remarks

Call this function to get the document's title, which is usually derived from the document's filename.

See Also   **CDocument::SetTitle**

CDocument::IsModified

BOOL IsModified( );

Return Value

Nonzero if the document has been modified since it was last saved; otherwise 0.

Remarks

Call this function to determine whether the document has been modified since it was last saved.

See Also   **CDocument::SetModifiedFlag**, **CDocument::SaveModified**

CDocument::OnChangedViewList

virtual void OnChangedViewList( );

Remarks

Called by the framework after a view is added to or removed from the document. The default implementation of this function checks whether the last view is being removed and, if so, deletes the document. Override this function if you want to perform special processing when the framework adds or removes a view. For example, if you want a document to remain open even when there are no views attached to it, override this function.

See Also   **CDocument::AddView**, **CDocument::RemoveView**

CDocument::OnCloseDocument

virtual void OnCloseDocument( );

Remarks

Called by the framework when the document is closed, typically as part of the File Close command. The default implementation of this function calls the **DeleteContents** member function to delete the document's data and then closes the frame windows for all the views attached to the document.

Override this function if you want to perform special cleanup processing when the framework closes a document. For example, if the document represents a record in a database, you may want to override this function to close the database. You should call the base class version of this function from your override.

See Also   **CDocument::DeleteContents**, **CDocument::OnNewDocument**,
CDocument::OnOpenDocument

CDocument::OnFileSendMail

void OnFileSendMail( );

Remarks

Sends a message via the resident mail host (if any) with the document as an
attachment. **OnFileSendMail** calls **OnSaveDocument** to serialize (save) untitled and
modified documents to a temporary file, which is then sent via electronic mail. If the
document has not been modified, a temporary file is not needed; the original is sent.
OnFileSendMail loads MAPI32.DLL if it has not already been loaded.

A special implementation of **OnFileSendMail** for **COleDocument** handles
compound files correctly.

CDocument supports sending your document via mail if mail support (MAPI) is
present. See the articles "MAPI" and "MAPI Support in MFC" in Part 2 of
Programming with MFC.

See Also   **CDocument::OnUpdateFileSendMail**,
COleDocument::OnFileSendMail, **CDocument::OnSaveDocument**.
In the *Client Developer's Guide*: **::MAPISendMail**

CDocument::OnNewDocument

virtual BOOL OnNewDocument( );

Return Value

Nonzero if the document was successfully initialized; otherwise 0.

Remarks

Called by the framework as part of the File New command. The default
implementation of this function calls the **DeleteContents** member function to ensure
that the document is empty and then marks the new document as clean. Override this
function to initialize the data structure for a new document. You should call the base
class version of this function from your override.

If the user chooses the File New command in an SDI application, the framework uses
this function to reinitialize the existing document object, rather than creating a new
one. If the user chooses File New in a multiple document interface (MDI) application,
the framework creates a new document object each time and then calls this function
to initialize it. You must place your initialization code in this function instead of in
the constructor for the File New command to be effective in SDI applications.

Example

```
// The follow examples illustrate alternative methods of
// initializing a document object.

// Method 1: In an MDI application, the simplest place to do
// initialization is in the document constructor.  The framework
// always creates a new document object for File New or File Open.

CMyDoc::CMyDoc()
{
   // Do initialization of MDI document here.
   // ...
}

// Method 2: In an SDI or MDI application, do all initialization
// in an override of OnNewDocument, if you are certain that
// the initialization is effectively saved upon File Save
// and fully restored upon File Open, via serialization.

BOOL CMyDoc::OnNewDocument()
{
   if (!CDocument::OnNewDocument())
      return FALSE;

   // Do initialization of new document here.

   return TRUE;
}

// Method 3: If the initialization of your document is not
// effectively saved and restored by serialization (during File Save
// and File Open), then implement the initialization in single
// function (named InitMyDocument in this example).  Call the
// shared initialization function from overrides of both
// OnNewDocument and OnOpenDocument.

BOOL CMyDoc::OnNewDocument()
{
   if (!CDocument::OnNewDocument())
      return FALSE;

   InitMyDocument(); // call your shared initialization function

   // If your new document object requires additional initialization
   // not necessary when the document is deserialized via File Open,
   // then perform that additional initialization here.

   return TRUE;
}
```

```
BOOL CMyDoc::OnOpenDocument(LPCTSTR lpszPathName)
{
    if (!CDocument::OnOpenDocument(lpszPathName))
        return FALSE;

    InitMyDocument();

    return TRUE;
}
```

See Also   **CDocument::CDocument, CDocument::DeleteContents,
CDocument::OnCloseDocument, CDocument::OnOpenDocument,
CDocument::OnSaveDocument**

CDocument::OnOpenDocument

virtual BOOL OnOpenDocument(LPCTSTR *lpszPathName* **);**

Return Value
Nonzero if the document was successfully loaded; otherwise 0.

Parameters
lpszPathName   Points to the path of the document to be opened.

Remarks
Called by the framework as part of the File Open command. The default
implementation of this function opens the specified file, calls the **DeleteContents**
member function to ensure that the document is empty, calls **CObject::Serialize** to
read the file's contents, and then marks the document as clean. Override this function
if you want to use something other than the archive mechanism or the file
mechanism. For example, you might write an application where documents represent
records in a database rather than separate files.

If the user chooses the File Open command in an SDI application, the framework
uses this function to reinitialize the existing document object, rather than creating a
new one. If the user chooses File Open in an MDI application, the framework
constructs a new document object each time and then calls this function to initialize
it. You must place your initialization code in this function instead of in the
constructor for the File Open command to be effective in SDI applications.

Example
```
// The follow examples illustrate alternative methods of
// initializing a document object.

// Method 1: In an MDI application, the simplest place to do
// initialization is in the document constructor.  The framework
// always creates a new document object for File New or File Open.

CMyDoc::CMyDoc()
```

```
{
   // Do initialization of MDI document here.
   // ...
}

// Method 2: In an SDI or MDI application, do all initialization
// in an override of OnNewDocument, if you are certain that
// the initialization is effectively saved upon File Save
// and fully restored upon File Open, via serialization.

BOOL CMyDoc::OnNewDocument()
{
   if (!CDocument::OnNewDocument())
      return FALSE;

   // Do initialization of new document here.

   return TRUE;
}

// Method 3: If the initialization of your document is not
// effectively saved and restored by serialization (during File Save
// and File Open), then implement the initialization in single
// function (named InitMyDocument in this example).  Call the
// shared initialization function from overrides of both
// OnNewDocument and OnOpenDocument.

BOOL CMyDoc::OnNewDocument()
{
   if (!CDocument::OnNewDocument())
      return FALSE;

   InitMyDocument(); // call your shared initialization function

   // If your new document object requires additional initialization
   // not necessary when the document is deserialized via File Open,
   // then perform that additional initialization here.

   return TRUE;
}

BOOL CMyDoc::OnOpenDocument(LPCTSTR lpszPathName)
{
   if (!CDocument::OnOpenDocument(lpszPathName))
      return FALSE;

   InitMyDocument();

   return TRUE;
}
```

See Also   **CDocument::DeleteContents, CDocument::OnCloseDocument, CDocument::OnNewDocument, CDocument::OnSaveDocument, CDocument::ReportSaveLoadException, CObject::Serialize**

CDocument::OnSaveDocument

virtual BOOL OnSaveDocument(LPCTSTR *lpszPathName* **);**

Return Value

Nonzero if the document was successfully saved; otherwise 0.

Parameters

lpszPathName   Points to the fully qualified path to which the file should be saved.

Remarks

Called by the framework as part of the File Save or File Save As command. The default implementation of this function opens the specified file, calls **CObject::Serialize** to write the document's data to the file, and then marks the document as clean. Override this function if you want to perform special processing when the framework saves a document. For example, you might write an application where documents represent records in a database rather than separate files.

See Also   **CDocument::OnCloseDocument, CDocument::OnNewDocument, CDocument::OnOpenDocument, CDocument::ReportSaveLoadException, CObject::Serialize**

CDocument::OnUpdateFileSendMail

void OnUpdateFileSendMail(CCmdUI* *pCmdUI* **);**

Parameters

pCmdUI   A pointer to the **CCmdUI** object associated with the **ID_FILE_SEND_MAIL** command.

Remarks

Enables the **ID_FILE_SEND_MAIL** command if mail support (MAPI) is present. Otherwise the function removes the **ID_FILE_SEND_MAIL** command from the menu, including separators above or below the menu item as appropriate. MAPI is enabled if MAPI32.DLL is present in the path and, in the [Mail] section of the WIN.INI file, MAPI=1. Most applications put this command on the File menu.

CDocument supports sending your document via mail if mail support (MAPI) is present. See the articles "MAPI" and "MAPI Support in MFC" in Part 2 of *Programming with MFC*.

See Also   **CDocument::OnFileSendMail**

CDocument::PreCloseFrame

virtual void PreCloseFrame(CFrameWnd* *pFrame* **);**

Parameters

pFrame   Pointer to the **CFrameWnd** that holds the associated **CDocument** object.

Remarks

This member function is called by the framework before the frame window is destroyed. It can be overridden to provide custom cleanup, but be sure to call the base class as well.

The default of **PreCloseFrame** does nothing in **CDocument**. The **CDocument**-derived classes **COleDocument** and **CRichEditDoc** use this member function.

CDocument::ReleaseFile

virtual void ReleaseFile(CFile* *pFile***, BOOL** *bAbort* **);**

Parameters

pFile   A pointer to the CFile object to be released.

bAbort   Specifies whether the file is to be released by using either **CFile::Close** or **CFile::Abort**. **FALSE** if the file is to be released using **CFile::Close**; **TRUE** if the file is to be released using **CFile::Abort**.

Remarks

This member function is called by the framework to release a file, making it available for use by other applications. If *bAbort* is **TRUE**, **ReleaseFile** calls **CFile::Abort**, and the file is released. **CFile::Abort** will not throw an exception.

If *bAbort* is **FALSE**, **ReleaseFile** calls **CFile::Close** and the file is released.

Override this member function to require an action by the user before the file is released.

See Also   **CDocTemplate, CFile::Close, CFile::Abort**

CDocument::RemoveView

void RemoveView(CView* *pView* **);**

Parameters

pView   Points to the view being removed.

Remarks

Call this function to detach a view from a document. This function removes the specified view from the list of views associated with the document; it also sets the view's document pointer to **NULL**. This function is called by the framework when a frame window is closed or a pane of a splitter window is closed.

Call this function only if you are manually detaching a view. Typically you will let the framework detach documents and views by defining a **CDocTemplate** object to associate a document class, view class, and frame window class.

Example

```
// The following example toggles two views in an SDI (single document
// interface) frame window.  A design decision must be made as to
// whether to leave the inactive view connected to the document,
// such that the inactive view continues to receive OnUpdate
// notifications from the document.  It is usually desirable to
// keep the inactive view continuously in sync with the document, even
// though it is inactive.  However, doing so incurs a performance cost,
// as well as the programming cost of implementing OnUpdate hints.
// It may be less expensive, in terms of performance and/or programming,
// to re-sync the inactive view with the document only with it is
// reactivated.  This example illustrates this latter approach, by
// reconnecting the newly active view and disconnecting the newly
// inactive view, via calls to CDocument::AddView and RemoveView.

BOOL CMainFrame::OnViewChange(UINT nCmdID)
{
    CView* pViewAdd;
    CView* pViewRemove;
    CDocument* pDoc = GetActiveDocument();
    if (nCmdID == ID_VIEW_VIEW2)
    {
        if (m_pView2 == NULL)
        {
            m_pView1 = GetActiveView();
            m_pView2 = new CMyView2;
            m_pView2->Create(NULL, NULL, AFX_WS_DEFAULT_VIEW,
                rectDefault, this, AFX_IDW_PANE_FIRST + 1, NULL);
        }
        pViewAdd = m_pView2;
        pViewRemove = m_pView1;
    }
    else
    {
        pViewAdd = m_pView1;
        pViewRemove = m_pView2;
    }

    // Set the child i.d. of the active view to AFX_IDW_PANE_FIRST,
    // so that CFrameWnd::RecalcLayout will allocate to this
    // "first pane" that portion of   the frame window's client area
    // not allocated to control   bars.  Set the child i.d. of the
    // other view to anything other than AFX_IDW_PANE_FIRST; this
    // examples switches the child id's of the two views.
```

```
     int nSwitchChildID = pViewAdd->GetDlgCtrlID();
     pViewAdd->SetDlgCtrlID(AFX_IDW_PANE_FIRST);
     pViewRemove->SetDlgCtrlID(nSwitchID);
        // Show the newly active view and hide the inactive view.
     pViewAdd->ShowWindow(SW_SHOW);
     pViewRemove->ShowWindow(SW_HIDE);

     // Connect the newly active view to the document, and
     // disconnect the inactive view.
     pDoc->AddView(pViewAdd);
     pDoc->RemoveView(pViewRemove);

     // Inform the frame window which view is now active;
     // and reallocate the frame window's client area to the
     // new view. Implement logic to resync the view to the
     // document in an override of CView::OnActivateView,
     // which is called from CFrameWnd::SetActiveView.
     SetActiveView(pViewAdd);
     RecalcLayout();

     return TRUE;
   }
```

See Also   **CDocument::AddView**, **CDocument::GetFirstViewPosition**,
CDocument::GetNextView

CDocument::ReportSaveLoadException

virtual void ReportSaveLoadException(LPCTSTR *lpszPathName***, CException*** *e***, BOOL** *bSaving***,
UINT** *nIDPDefault* **);**

Parameters

lpszPathName   Points to name of document that was being saved or loaded.

e   Points to the exception that was thrown. May be **NULL**.

bSaving   Flag indicating what operation was in progress; nonzero if the document
was being saved, 0 if the document was being loaded.

nIDPDefault   Identifier of the error message to be displayed if the function does not
specify a more specific one.

Remarks

Called if an exception is thrown (typically a **CFileException** or **CArchiveException**)
while saving or loading the document. The default implementation examines the
exception object and looks for an error message that specifically describes the cause.

If a specific message is not found or if *e* is **NULL**, the general message specified by the *nIDPDefault* parameter is used. The function then displays a message box containing the error message. Override this function if you want to provide additional, customized failure messages. This is an advanced overridable.

See Also   **CDocument::OnOpenDocument**, **CDocument::OnSaveDocument**, **CFileException**, **CArchiveException**

CDocument::SaveModified

virtual BOOL SaveModified( );

Return Value

Nonzero if it is safe to continue and close the document; 0 if the document should not be closed.

Remarks

Called by the framework before a modified document is to be closed. The default implementation of this function displays a message box asking the user whether to save the changes to the document, if any have been made. Override this function if your program requires a different prompting procedure. This is an advanced overridable.

See Also   **CDocument::CanCloseFrame**, **CDocument::IsModified**, **CDocument::OnNewDocument**, **CDocument::OnOpenDocument**, **CDocument::OnSaveDocument**

CDocument::SetModifiedFlag

void SetModifiedFlag(BOOL *bModified* **= TRUE);**

Parameters

bModified   Flag indicating whether the document has been modified.

Remarks

Call this function after you have made any modifications to the document. By calling this function consistently, you ensure that the framework prompts the user to save changes before closing a document. Typically you should use the default value of **TRUE** for the *bModified* parameter. To mark a document as clean (unmodified), call this function with a value of **FALSE**.

See Also   **CDocument::IsModified**, **CDocument::SaveModified**

CDocument::SetPathName

virtual void SetPathName(LPCTSTR *lpszPathName*, **BOOL** *bAddToMRU* **= TRUE);**

Parameters

lpszPathName   Points to the string to be used as the path for the document.

bAddToMRU   Determines whether the filename is added to the most recently used (MRU) file list. If **TRUE,** the filename is added; if **FALSE**, it is not added.

Remarks

Call this function to specify the fully qualified path of the document's disk file. Depending on the value of *bAddToMRU* the path is added, or not added, to the MRU list maintained by the application. Note that some documents are not associated with a disk file. Call this function only if you are overriding the default implementation for opening and saving files used by the framework.

See Also   CDocument::GetPathName, CWinApp::AddToRecentFileList

---

CDocument::SetTitle

virtual void SetTitle(LPCTSTR *lpszTitle* **);**

Parameters

lpszTitle   Points to the string to be used as the document's title.

Remarks

Call this function to specify the document's title (the string displayed in the title bar of a frame window). Calling this function updates the titles of all frame windows that display the document.

See Also   CDocument::GetTitle

CDocument::UpdateAllViews

void UpdateAllViews(CView* *pSender*, **LPARAM** *lHint* **= 0L, CObject*** *pHint* **= NULL);**

Parameters

pSender   Points to the view that modified the document, or **NULL** if all views are to be updated.

lHint   Contains information about the modification.

pHint   Points to an object storing information about the modification.

Remarks

Call this function after the document has been modified. You should call this function after you call the **SetModifiedFlag** member function. This function informs each view attached to the document, except for the view specified by *pSender*, that the document has been modified. You typically call this function from your view class after the user has changed the document through a view.

This function calls the **CView::OnUpdate** member function for each of the document's views except the sending view, passing *pHint* and *lHint*. Use these parameters to pass information to the views about the modifications made to the document. You can encode information using *lHint* and/or you can define a **CObject**-derived class to store information about the modifications and pass an object of that class using *pHint*. Override the **CView::OnUpdate** member function in your **CView**-derived class to optimize the updating of the view's display based on the information passed.

See Also **CDocument::SetModifiedFlag**, **CDocument::GetFirstViewPosition**, **CDocument::GetNextView**, **CView::OnUpdate**

CDragListBox

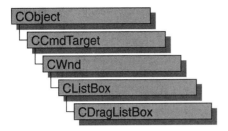

In addition to providing the functionality of a Windows list box, the **CDragListBox** class allows the user to move list box items, such as filenames and string literals, within the list box. List boxes with this capability are useful for an item list in an order other than alphabetic, such as include pathnames or files in a project. By default, the list box will move the item, along with the data, to the new location. However, **CDragListBox** objects can be customized to copy items instead of moving them.

To use a drag list box in an existing dialog box of your application, add a list box control to your dialog template using the dialog editor and then assign a member variable (of Category `Control` and Variable Type `CDragListBox`) corresponding to the list box control in your dialog template.

For more information on assigning controls to member variables, see "Shortcut for Defining Member Variables for Dialog Controls" in Chapter 14 of the *Visual C++ User's Guide*.

#include <afxcmn.h>

See Also **CListBox**

Attributes

ItemFromPt	Returns the coordinates of the item being dragged.

Construction

CDragListBox	Constructs a **CDragListBox** object.

Operations

DrawInsert	Draws the insertion guide of the drag list box.

Overridables

BeginDrag	Called by the framework when a drag operation starts.
CancelDrag	Called by the framework when a drag operation has been canceled.
Dragging	Called by the framework during a drag operation.
Dropped	Called by the framework after the item has been dropped.

Member Functions

CDragListBox::BeginDrag

virtual BOOL BeginDrag(CPoint *pt* **);**

Return Value

Nonzero if dragging is allowed, otherwise 0.

Parameters

pt   A **CPoint** object that contains the coordinates of the item being dragged.

Remarks

Called by the framework when an event occurs that could begin a drag operation, such as pressing the left mouse button. Override this function if you want to control what happens when a drag operation begins. The default implementation captures the mouse and stays in drag mode until the user clicks the left or right mouse button or presses ESC, at which time the drag operation is canceled.

See Also   **CDragListBox::CancelDrag**, **CDragListBox::Dragging**

CDragListBox::CancelDrag

virtual void CancelDrag(CPoint *pt* **);**

Parameters

pt   A **CPoint** object that contains the coordinates of the item being dragged.

Remarks

Called by the framework when a drag operation has been canceled. Override this function to handle any special processing for your list box control.

See Also   **CDragListBox::BeginDrag**, **CDragListBox::Dragging**

CDragListBox::CDragListBox

CDragListBox( );

Remarks

Constructs a **CDragListBox** object.

See Also   **CListBox::Create**

CDragListBox::Dragging

virtual UINT Dragging(CPoint *pt* **);**

Return Value

The resource ID of the cursor to be displayed. The following values are possible:

- **DL_COPYCURSOR**   Indicates that the item will be copied.
- **DL_MOVECURSOR**   Indicates that the item will be moved.
- **DL_STOPCURSOR**   Indicates that the current drop target is not acceptable.

Parameters

pt   A **CPoint** object that contains the x and y screen coordinates of the cursor.

Remarks

Called by the framework when a list box item is being dragged within the **CDragListBox** object. The default behavior returns **DL_MOVECURSOR**. Override this function if you want to provide additional functionality.

See Also   **CDragListBox::BeginDrag**, **CDragListBox::CancelDrag**

CDragListBox::DrawInsert

virtual void DrawInsert(int *nItem* **);**

Parameters

nItem   Zero-based index of the insertion point.

Remarks

Called by the framework to draw the insertion guide before the item with the indicated index. A value of -1 clears the insertion guide. Override this function to modify the appearance or behavior of the insertion guide.

CDragListBox::Dropped

virtual void Dropped(int *nSrcIndex***, CPoint** *pt* **);**

Parameters

nSrcIndex   Specifies the zero-based index of the dropped string.

pt   A **CPoint** object that contains the coordinates of the drop site.

Remarks

Called by the framework when an item is dropped within a **CDragListBox** object. The default behavior copies the list box item and its data to the new location and then deletes the original item. Override this function to customize the default behavior, such as enabling copies of list box items to be dragged to other locations within the list.

See Also   **CDragListBox::BeginDrag**

CDragListBox::ItemFromPt

int ItemFromPt(CPoint *pt***, BOOL** *bAutoScroll* **= TRUE);**

Return Value

Zero-based index of the drag list box item.

Parameters

pt   A **CPoint** object containing the coordinates of a point within the list box.

bAutoScroll   Nonzero if scrolling is allowed, otherwise 0.

Remarks

Call this function to retrieve the zero-based index of the list box item located at *pt*.

CDumpContext

The **CDumpContext** class supports stream-oriented diagnostic output in the form of human-readable text. You can use **afxDump**, a predeclared **CDumpContext** object, for most of your dumping. The **afxDump** object is available only in the Debug version of the Microsoft Foundation Class Library.

Several of the memory diagnostic functions use **afxDump** for their output.

Under the Windows environment, the output from the predefined **afxDump** object, conceptually similar to the **cerr** stream, is routed to the debugger via the Windows function **OutputDebugString**.

The **CDumpContext** class has an overloaded insertion (**<<**) operator for **CObject** pointers that dumps the object's data. If you need a custom dump format for a derived object, override **CObject::Dump**. Most Microsoft Foundation classes implement an overridden **Dump** member function.

Classes that are not derived from **CObject**, such as **CString**, **CTime**, and **CTimeSpan**, have their own overloaded **CDumpContext** insertion operators, as do often-used structures such as **CFileStatus**, **CPoint**, and **CRect**.

If you use the **IMPLEMENT_DYNAMIC** or **IMPLEMENT_SERIAL** macro in the implementation of your class, then **CObject::Dump** will print the name of your **CObject**-derived class. Otherwise, it will print `CObject`.

The **CDumpContext** class is available with both the Debug and Release versions of the library, but the **Dump** member function is defined only in the Debug version. Use **#ifdef _DEBUG / #endif** statements to bracket your diagnostic code, including your custom **Dump** member functions.

Before you create your own **CDumpContext** object, you must create a **CFile** object that serves as the dump destination.

For more information on **CDumpContext**, see the articles "Diagnostics: Dumping Object Contents" and "Diagnostics: Dumping All Objects" in *Programming with MFC*.

#define _DEBUG

#include <afx.h>

See Also   CFile, CObject

Construction

CDumpContext	Constructs a **CDumpContext** object.

Basic Input/Output

Flush	Flushes any data in the dump context buffer.
operator <<	Inserts variables and objects into the dump context.
HexDump	Dumps bytes in hexadecimal format.

Status

GetDepth	Gets an integer corresponding to the depth of the dump.
SetDepth	Sets the depth of the dump.

Member Functions

CDumpContext::CDumpContext

CDumpContext(CFile* *pFile* **);**
    throw(CMemoryException, CFileException);

Parameters

pFile   A pointer to the **CFile** object that is the dump destination.

Remarks

Constructs an object of class **CDumpContext**. The **afxDump** object is constructed automatically.

Do not write to the underlying **CFile** while the dump context is active; otherwise, you will interfere with the dump. Under the Windows environment, the output is routed to the debugger via the Windows function **OutputDebugString**.

Example

```
//example for CDumpContext::CDumpContext
CFile f;
if( !f.Open( "dump.txt", CFile::modeCreate | CFile::modeWrite ) ) {
   afxDump << "Unable to open file" << "\n";
   exit( 1 );
}
CDumpContext dc( &f );
```

CDumpContext::Flush

void Flush( );
    throw(CFileException);

Remarks

Forces any data remaining in buffers to be written to the file attached to the dump context.

Example

```
//example for CDumpContext::Flush
afxDump.Flush();
```

CDumpContext::GetDepth

int GetDepth( ) const;

Return Value

The depth of the dump as set by **SetDepth**.

Remarks

Determines whether a deep or shallow dump is in process.

Example

See the example for **SetDepth**.

See Also   CDumpContext::SetDepth

CDumpContext::HexDump

void HexDump(LPCTSTR *lpszLine*, **BYTE*** *pby*, **int** *nBytes*, **int** *nWidth* **);**
   throw(CFileException);

Parameters

lpszLine   A string to output at the start of a new line.

pby   A pointer to a buffer containing the bytes to dump.

nBytes   The number of bytes to dump.

nWidth   Maximum number of bytes dumped per line (not the width of the output line).

Remarks

Dumps an array of bytes formatted as hexadecimal numbers.

Example

```
//example for CDumpContext::HexDump
char test[] = "This is a test of CDumpContext::HexDump\n";
afxDump.HexDump( ".", (BYTE*) test, sizeof test, 20 );
```

The output from this program is:

```
. 54 68 69 73 20 69 73 20 61 20 74 65 73 74 20 6F 66 20 43 44
. 75 6D 70 43 6F 6E 74 65 78 74 3A 3A 48 65 78 44 75 6D 70 0A
. 00
```

CDumpContext::SetDepth

void SetDepth(int *nNewDepth* **);**

Parameters

nNewDepth   The new depth value.

Remarks

Sets the depth for the dump. If you are dumping a primitive type or simple **CObject** that contains no pointers to other objects, then a value of 0 is sufficient. A value greater than 0 specifies a deep dump where all objects are dumped recursively. For example, a deep dump of a collection will dump all elements of the collection. You may use other specific depth values in your derived classes.

Note   Circular references are not detected in deep dumps and can result in infinite loops.

Example

```
//example for CDumpContext::SetDepth
afxDump.SetDepth( 1 );  // Specifies deep dump
ASSERT( afxDump.GetDepth() == 1 );
```

See Also   **CObject::Dump**

Operators

CDumpContext::operator <<

CDumpContext& operator <<(const CObject* *pOb* **);**
   throw(CFileException);
CDumpContext& operator <<(const CObject& *ob* **);**
   throw(CFileException);
CDumpContext& operator <<(LPCTSTR *lpsz* **);**
   throw(CFileException);
CDumpContext& operator <<(const void* *lp* **);**
   throw(CFileException);
CDumpContext& operator <<(BYTE *by* **);**
   throw(CFileException);
CDumpContext& operator <<(WORD *w* **);**
   throw(CFileException);
CDumpContext& operator <<(DWORD *dw* **);**
   throw(CFileException);
CDumpContext& operator <<(int *n* **);**
   throw(CFileException);
CDumpContext& operator <<(double *d* **);**
   throw(CFileException);

CDumpContext& operator <<(float *f* **);**
   throw(CFileException);
CDumpContext& operator <<(LONG *l* **);**
   throw(CFileException);
CDumpContext& operator <<(UINT *u* **);**
   throw(CFileException);
CDumpContext& operator <<(LPCWSTR *lpsz* **);**
   throw(CFileException);
CDumpContext& operator <<(LPCSTR *lpsz* **);**
   throw(CFileException);

Return Value

A **CDumpContext** reference. Using the return value, you can write multiple insertions on a single line of source code.

Remarks

Outputs the specified data to the dump context.

The insertion operator is overloaded for **CObject** pointers as well as for most primitive types. A pointer to character results in a dump of string contents; a pointer to **void** results in a hexadecimal dump of the address only.

If you use the **IMPLEMENT_DYNAMIC** or **IMPLEMENT_SERIAL** macro in the implementation of your class, then the insertion operator, through **CObject::Dump**, will print the name of your **CObject**-derived class. Otherwise, it will print CObject. If you override the **Dump** function of the class, then you can provide a more meaningful output of the object's contents instead of a hexadecimal dump.

Example

```
//example for CDumpContext::operator <<
extern CObList li;
CString s = "test";
int i = 7;
long lo = 1000000000L;
afxDump << "list=" << &li << "string="
        << s << "int=" << i << "long=" << lo << "\n";
```

CDWordArray

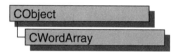

The **CDWordArray** class supports arrays of 32-bit doublewords.

The member functions of **CDWordArray** are similar to the member functions of class **CObArray**. Because of this similarity, you can use the **CObArray** reference documentation for member function specifics. Wherever you see a **CObject** pointer as a function parameter or return value, substitute a **DWORD**.

```
CObject* CObArray::GetAt( int <nIndex> ) const;
```

for example, translates to

```
DWORD CDWordArray::GetAt( int <nIndex> ) const;
```

CDWordArray incorporates the **IMPLEMENT_SERIAL** macro to support serialization and dumping of its elements. If an array of doublewords is stored to an archive, either with the overloaded insertion (<<) operator or with the **Serialize** member function, each element is, in turn, serialized.

Note Before using an array, use **SetSize** to establish its size and allocate memory for it. If you do not use **SetSize**, adding elements to your array causes it to be frequently reallocated and copied. Frequent reallocation and copying are inefficient and can fragment memory.

If you need debug output from individual elements in the array, you must set the depth of the **CDumpContext** object to 1 or greater.

For more information on using **CDWordArray**, see the article "Collections" in *Programming with MFC*.

#include <afxcoll.h>

See Also **CObArray**

Construction

CDWordArray	Constructs an empty array for doublewords.

Bounds

GetSize	Gets the number of elements in this array.
GetUpperBound	Returns the largest valid index.
SetSize	Sets the number of elements to be contained in this array.

Operations

FreeExtra	Frees all unused memory above the current upper bound.
RemoveAll	Removes all the elements from this array.

Element Access

GetAt	Returns the value at a given index.
SetAt	Sets the value for a given index; array not allowed to grow.
ElementAt	Returns a temporary reference to the doubleword within the array.

Growing the Array

SetAtGrow	Sets the value for a given index; grows the array if necessary.
Add	Adds an element to the end of the array; grows the array if necessary.

Insertion/Removal

InsertAt	Inserts an element (or all the elements in another array) at a specified index.
RemoveAt	Removes an element at a specific index.

Operators

operator []	Sets or gets the element at the specified index.

CEdit

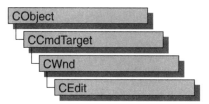

The **CEdit** class provides the functionality of a Windows edit control. An edit control is a rectangular child window in which the user can enter text.

You can create an edit control either from a dialog template or directly in your code. In both cases, first call the constructor **CEdit** to construct the **CEdit** object, then call the **Create** member function to create the Windows edit control and attach it to the **CEdit** object.

Construction can be a one-step process in a class derived from **CEdit**. Write a constructor for the derived class and call **Create** from within the constructor.

CEdit inherits significant functionality from **CWnd**. To set and retrieve text from a **CEdit** object, use the **CWnd** member functions **SetWindowText** and **GetWindowText**, which set or get the entire contents of an edit control, even if it is a multiline control. Also, if an edit control is multiline, get and set part of the control's text by calling the **CEdit** member functions **GetLine**, **SetSel**, **GetSel**, and **ReplaceSel**.

If you want to handle Windows notification messages sent by an edit control to its parent (usually a class derived from **CDialog**), add a message-map entry and message-handler member function to the parent class for each message.

Each message-map entry takes the following form:

ON_Notification(*id, memberFxn*)

where *id* specifies the child window ID of the edit control sending the notification, and *memberFxn* is the name of the parent member function you have written to handle the notification.

The parent's function prototype is as follows:

afx_msg void memberFxn( );

Following is a list of potential message-map entries and a description of the cases in which they would be sent to the parent:

- **ON_EN_CHANGE**   The user has taken an action that may have altered text in an edit control. Unlike the **EN_UPDATE** notification message, this notification message is sent after Windows updates the display.

- **ON_EN_ERRSPACE**   The edit control cannot allocate enough memory to meet a specific request.

- **ON_EN_HSCROLL**   The user clicks an edit control's horizontal scroll bar. The parent window is notified before the screen is updated.

- **ON_EN_KILLFOCUS**   The edit control loses the input focus.

- **ON_EN_MAXTEXT**   The current insertion has exceeded the specified number of characters for the edit control and has been truncated. Also sent when an edit control does not have the **ES_AUTOHSCROLL** style and the number of characters to be inserted would exceed the width of the edit control. Also sent when an edit control does not have the **ES_AUTOVSCROLL** style and the total number of lines resulting from a text insertion would exceed the height of the edit control.

- **ON_EN_SETFOCUS**   Sent when an edit control receives the input focus.

- **ON_EN_UPDATE**   The edit control is about to display altered text. Sent after the control has formatted the text but before it screens the text so that the window size can be altered, if necessary.

- **ON_EN_VSCROLL**   The user clicks an edit control's vertical scroll bar. The parent window is notified before the screen is updated.

If you create a **CEdit** object within a dialog box, the **CEdit** object is automatically destroyed when the user closes the dialog box.

If you create a **CEdit** object from a dialog resource using the dialog editor, the **CEdit** object is automatically destroyed when the user closes the dialog box.

If you create a **CEdit** object within a window, you may also need to destroy it. If you create the **CEdit** object on the stack, it is destroyed automatically. If you create the **CEdit** object on the heap by using the **new** function, you must call **delete** on the object to destroy it when the user terminates the Windows edit control. If you allocate any memory in the **CEdit** object, override the **CEdit** destructor to dispose of the allocations.

For more information on **CEdit**, see the article "Controls" in *Programming with MFC*.

#include <afxwin.h>

See Also   CWnd, CButton, CComboBox, CListBox, CScrollBar, CStatic, CDialog

Construction

CEdit	Constructs a **CEdit** control object.
Create	Creates the Windows edit control and attaches it to the **CEdit** object.

General Operations

GetSel	Gets the starting and ending character positions of the current selection in an edit control.
ReplaceSel	Replaces the current selection in an edit control with the specified text.
SetSel	Selects a range of characters in an edit control.
Clear	Deletes (clears) the current selection (if any) in the edit control.
Copy	Copies the current selection (if any) in the edit control to the Clipboard in **CF_TEXT** format.
Cut	Deletes (cuts) the current selection (if any) in the edit control and copies the deleted text to the Clipboard in **CF_TEXT** format.
Paste	Inserts the data from the Clipboard into the edit control at the current cursor position. Data is inserted only if the Clipboard contains data in **CF_TEXT** format.
Undo	Reverses the last edit-control operation.
CanUndo	Determines whether an edit-control operation can be undone.
EmptyUndoBuffer	Resets (clears) the undo flag of an edit control.
GetModify	Determines whether the contents of an edit control have been modified.
SetModify	Sets or clears the modification flag for an edit control.
SetReadOnly	Sets the read-only state of an edit control.
GetPasswordChar	Retrieves the password character displayed in an edit control when the user enters text.
SetPasswordChar	Sets or removes a password character displayed in an edit control when the user enters text.
GetFirstVisibleLine	Determines the topmost visible line in an edit control.
LineLength	Retrieves the length of a line in an edit control.
LineScroll	Scrolls the text of a multiple-line edit control.
LineFromChar	Retrieves the line number of the line that contains the specified character index.
GetRect	Gets the formatting rectangle of an edit control.
LimitText	Limits the length of the text that the user may enter into an edit control.

Multiple-Line Operations

GetLineCount	Retrieves the number of lines in a multiple-line edit control.
GetLine	Retrieves a line of text from an edit control.
LineIndex	Retrieves the character index of a line within a multiple-line edit control.
FmtLines	Sets the inclusion of soft line-break characters on or off within a multiple-line edit control.
SetTabStops	Sets the tab stops in a multiple-line edit control.
SetRect	Sets the formatting rectangle of a multiple-line edit control and updates the control.
SetRectNP	Sets the formatting rectangle of a multiple-line edit control without redrawing the control window.
GetHandle	Retrieves a handle to the memory currently allocated for a multiple-line edit control.
SetHandle	Sets the handle to the local memory that will be used by a multiple-line edit control.

Windows 95 Operations

GetMargins	Gets the left and right margins for this **CEdit**.
SetMargins	Sets the left and right margins for this **CEdit**.
GetLimitText	Gets the maximum amount of text this **CEdit** can contain.
SetLimitText	Sets the maximum amount of text this **CEdit** can contain.
CharFromPos	Retrieves the line and character indices for the character closest to a specified position.
PosFromChar	Retrieves the coordinates of the upper-left corner of a specified character index.

Member Functions

CEdit::CanUndo

BOOL CanUndo( ) const;

Return Value

Nonzero if the last edit operation can be undone by a call to the **Undo** member function; 0 if it cannot be undone.

Remarks

Call this function to determine if the last edit operation can be undone.

For more information, see **EM_CANUNDO** in the Win32 documentation.

See Also   **CEdit::Undo**, **CEdit::EmptyUndoBuffer**

CEdit::CEdit

CEdit( );

Remarks

Constructs a **CEdit** object. Use **Create** to construct the Windows edit control.

See Also   **CEdit::Create**

CEdit::CharFromPos

int CharFromPos(CPoint *pt* **) const;**

Return Value

The character index in the low-order **WORD**, and the line index in the high-order **WORD**.

Parameters

pt   The coordinates of a point in the client area of this **CEdit** object.

Remarks

Call this function to retrieve the zero-based line and character indices of the character nearest the specified point in this **CEdit** control

Note   This member function is available only in Windows 95.

For more information, see **EM_CHARFROMPOS** in the Win32 documentation.

See Also   **CEdit::PosFromChar**

CEdit::Clear

void Clear( );

Remarks

Call this function to delete (clear) the current selection (if any) in the edit control.

The deletion performed by **Clear** can be undone by calling the **Undo** member function.

To delete the current selection and place the deleted contents into the Clipboard, call the **Cut** member function.

For more information, see **WM_CLEAR** in the Win32 documentation.

See Also   **CEdit::Undo**, **CEdit::Copy**, **CEdit::Cut**, **CEdit::Paste**

CEdit::Copy

void Copy( );

Remarks

Call this function to coy the current selection (if any) in the edit control to the Clipboard in **CF_TEXT** format.

For more information, see **WM_COPY** in the Win32 documentation.

See Also   **CEdit::Clear**, **CEdit::Cut**, **CEdit::Paste**

CEdit::Create

BOOL Create(DWORD *dwStyle*, **const RECT&** *rect*, **CWnd*** *pParentWnd*, **UINT** *nID* **);**

Return Value

Nonzero if initialization is successful; otherwise 0.

Parameters

dwStyle   Specifies the edit control's style. Apply any combination of edit styles to the control. For a list of edit styles, see "Edit Styles" in the "Styles Used by MFC" section.

rect   Specifies the edit control's size and position. Can be a **CRect** object or **RECT** structure.

pParentWnd   Specifies the edit control's parent window (usually a **CDialog**). It must not be **NULL**.

nID   Specifies the edit control's ID.

Remarks

You construct a **CEdit** object in two steps. First, call the **CEdit** constructor, then call **Create**, which creates the Windows edit control and attaches it to the **CEdit** object.

When **Create** executes, Windows sends the **WM_NCCREATE**, **WM_NCCALCSIZE**, **WM_CREATE**, and **WM_GETMINMAXINFO** messages to the edit control.

These messages are handled by default by the **OnNcCreate**, **OnNcCalcSize**, **OnCreate**, and **OnGetMinMaxInfo** member functions in the **CWnd** base class. To extend the default message handling, derive a class from **CEdit**, add a message map to the new class, and override the above message-handler member functions. Override **OnCreate**, for example, to perform needed initialization for the new class.

Apply the following window styles to an edit control. For a list of window styles, see "Window Styles" in the "Styles Used by MFC" section.

- **WS_CHILD** Always
- **WS_VISIBLE** Usually
- **WS_DISABLED** Rarely
- **WS_GROUP** To group controls
- **WS_TABSTOP** To include edit control in the tabbing order

See Also **CEdit::CEdit**

CEdit::Cut

void Cut( );

Remarks

Call this function to delete (cut) the current selection (if any) in the edit control and copy the deleted text to the Clipboard in **CF_TEXT** format.

The deletion performed by **Cut** can be undone by calling the **Undo** member function.

To delete the current selection without placing the deleted text into the Clipboard, call the **Clear** member function.

For more information, see **WM_CUT** in the Win32 documentation.

See Also **CEdit::Undo**, **CEdit::Clear**, **CEdit::Copy**, **CEdit::Paste**

CEdit::EmptyUndoBuffer

void EmptyUndoBuffer( );

Remarks

Call this function to reset (clear) the undo flag of an edit control. The edit control will now be unable to undo the last operation. The undo flag is set whenever an operation within the edit control can be undone.

The undo flag is automatically cleared whenever the **SetWindowText** or **SetHandle CWnd** member functions are called.

For more information, see **EM_EMPTYUNDOBUFFER** in the Win32 documentation.

See Also **CEdit::CanUndo**, **CEdit::SetHandle**, **CEdit::Undo**, **CWnd::SetWindowText**

CEdit::FmtLines

BOOL FmtLines(BOOL *bAddEOL* **);**

Return Value

Nonzero if any formatting occurs; otherwise 0.

Parameters

bAddEOL   Specifies whether soft line-break characters are to be inserted. A value of **TRUE** inserts the characters; a value of **FALSE** removes them.

Remarks

Call this function to set the inclusion of soft line-break characters on or off within a multiple-line edit control. A soft line break consists of two carriage returns and a linefeed inserted at the end of a line that is broken because of word wrapping. A hard line break consists of one carriage return and a linefeed. Lines that end with a hard line break are not affected by **FmtLines**.

Windows will only respond if the **CEdit** object is a multiple-line edit control.

FmtLines only affects the buffer returned by **GetHandle** and the text returned by **WM_GETTEXT**. It has no impact on the display of the text within the edit control.

For more information, see **EM_FMTLINES** in the Win32 documentation.

See Also   **CEdit::GetHandle**, **CWnd::GetWindowText**

CEdit::GetFirstVisibleLine

int GetFirstVisibleLine( ) const;

Return Value

The zero-based index of the topmost visible line. For single-line edit controls, the return value is 0.

Remarks

Call this function to determine the topmost visible line in an edit control.

For more information, see **EM_GETFIRSTVISIBLELINE** in the Win32 documentation.

See Also   **CEdit::GetLine**

CEdit::GetHandle

HLOCAL GetHandle( ) const;

Return Value

A local memory handle that identifies the buffer holding the contents of the edit control. If an error occurs, such as sending the message to a single-line edit control, the return value is 0.

Remarks

Call this function to retrieve a handle to the memory currently allocated for a multiple-line edit control. The handle is a local memory handle and may be used by any of the **Local** Windows memory functions that take a local memory handle as a parameter.

GetHandle is processed only by multiple-line edit controls.

Call **GetHandle** for a multiple-line edit control in a dialog box only if the dialog box was created with the **DS_LOCALEDIT** style flag set. If the **DS_LOCALEDIT** style is not set, you will still get a nonzero return value, but you will not be able to use the returned value.

For more information, see **EM_GETHANDLE** in the Win32 documentation.

See Also　**CEdit::SetHandle**

CEdit::GetLimitText

UINT GetLimitText( ) const;

Return Value

The current text limit, in bytes, for this **CEdit** object.

Remarks

Call this member function to get the text limit for this **CEdit** object. The text limit is the maximum amount of text, in bytes, that the edit control can accept.

Note　This member function is available only in Windows 95.

For more information, see **EM_GETLIMITTEXT** in the Win32 documentation.

See Also　**CEdit::SetLimitText**, **CEdit::LimitText**

CEdit::GetLine

int GetLine(int *nIndex***, LPTSTR** *lpszBuffer* **) const;**
int GetLine(int *nIndex***, LPTSTR** *lpszBuffer***, int** *nMaxLength* **) const;**

Return Value

The number of bytes actually copied. The return value is 0 if the line number specified by *nIndex* is greater then the number of lines in the edit control.

Parameters

nIndex   Specifies the line number to retrieve from a multiple-line edit control. Line numbers are zero-based; a value of 0 specifies the first line. This parameter is ignored by a single-line edit control.

lpszBuffer   Points to the buffer that receives a copy of the line. The first word of the buffer must specify the maximum number of bytes that can be copied to the buffer.

nMaxLength   Specifies the maximum number of bytes that can be copied to the buffer. **GetLine** places this value in the first word of *lpszBuffer* before making the call to Windows.

Remarks

Call this function to retrieve a line of text from an edit control and places it in *lpszBuffer*. This call is not processed for a single-line edit control.

The copied line does not contain a null-termination character.

For more information, see **EM_GETLINE** in the Win32 documentation.

See Also   **CEdit::LineLength**, **CWnd::GetWindowText**

CEdit::GetLineCount

int GetLineCount( ) const;

Return Value

An integer containing the number of lines in the multiple-line edit control. If no text has been entered into the edit control, the return value is 1.

Remarks

Call this function to retrieve the number of lines in a multiple-line edit control.

GetLineCount is only processed by multiple-line edit controls.

For more information, see **EM_GETLINECOUNT** in the Win32 documentation.

CEdit::GetMargins

DWORD GetMargins( ) const;

Return Value

The width of the left margin in the low-order **WORD** and the width of the right margin in the high-order **WORD**.

Remarks

Call this member function to retrieve the left and right margins of this edit control. Margins are measured in pixels.

Note This member function is available only in Windows 95.

For more information, see **EM_GETMARGINS** in the Win32 documentation.

See Also **CEdit::SetMargins**

CEdit::GetModify

BOOL GetModify( ) const;

Return Value

Nonzero if the edit-control contents have been modified; 0 if they have remained unchanged.

Remarks

Call this function to determine whether the contents of an edit control have been modified.

Windows maintains an internal flag indicating whether the contents of the edit control have been changed. This flag is cleared when the edit control is first created and may also be cleared by calling the **SetModify** member function.

For more information, see **EM_GETMODIFY** in the Win32 documentation.

See Also **CEdit::SetModify**

CEdit::GetPasswordChar

TCHAR GetPasswordChar( ) const;

Return Value

Specifies the character to be displayed in place of the character typed by the user. The return value is **NULL** if no password character exists.

Remarks

Call this function to retrieve the password character displayed in an edit control when the user enters text.

If the edit control is created with the **ES_PASSWORD** style, the default password character is set to an asterisk (*).

For more information, see **EM_GETPASSWORDCHAR** in the Win32 documentation.

See Also   **CEdit::SetPasswordChar**

CEdit::GetRect

void GetRect(LPRECT *lpRect* **) const;**

Parameters

lpRect   Points to the **RECT** structure that receives the formatting rectangle.

Remarks

Call this function to get the formatting rectangle of an edit control. The formatting rectangle is the limiting rectangle of the text, which is independent of the size of the edit-control window.

The formatting rectangle of a multiple-line edit control can be modified by the **SetRect** and **SetRectNP** member functions.

For more information, see **EM_GETRECT** in the Win32 documentation.

See Also   **CEdit::SetRect**, **CEdit::SetRectNP**

CEdit::GetSel

DWORD GetSel( ) const;
void GetSel(int& *nStartChar*, **int&** *nEndChar* **) const;**

Return Value

The version that returns a **DWORD** returns a value that contains the starting position in the low-order word and the position of the first nonselected character after the end of the selection in the high-order word.

Parameters

nStartChar   Reference to an integer that will receive the position of the first character in the current selection.

nEndChar   Reference to an integer that will receive the position of the first nonselected character past the end of the current selection.

Remarks

Call this function to get the starting and ending character positions of the current selection (if any) in an edit control, using either the return value or the parameters.

For more information, see **EM_GETSEL** in the Win32 documentation.

See Also   **CEdit::SetSel**

CEdit::LimitText

void LimitText(int *nChars* **= 0);**

Parameters

nChars   Specifies the length (in bytes) of the text that the user can enter. If this parameter is 0, the text length is set to **UINT_MAX** bytes. This is the default behavior.

Remarks

Call this function to limit the length of the text that the user may enter into an edit control.

Changing the text limit restricts only the text the user can enter. It has no effect on any text already in the edit control, nor does it affect the length of the text copied to the edit control by the **SetWindowText** member function in **CWnd**. If an application uses the **SetWindowText** function to place more text into an edit control than is specified in the call to **LimitText**, the user can delete any of the text within the edit control. However, the text limit will prevent the user from replacing the existing text with new text, unless deleting the current selection causes the text to fall below the text limit.

Note   In Win32 (Windows NT and Windows 95), **SetLimitText** replaces this function.

For more information, see **EM_LIMITTEXT** in the Win32 documentation.

See Also   **CWnd::SetWindowText**, **CEdit::GetLimitText**, **CEdit::SetLimitText**

CEdit::LineFromChar

int LineFromChar(int *nIndex* **= –1) const;**

Return Value

The zero-based line number of the line containing the character index specified by *nIndex*. If *nIndex* is –1, the number of the line that contains the first character of the selection is returned. If there is no selection, the current line number is returned.

Parameters

nIndex   Contains the zero-based index value for the desired character in the text of the edit control, or contains –1. If *nIndex* is –1, it specifies the current line, that is, the line that contains the caret.

Remarks

Call this function to retrieve the line number of the line that contains the specified character index. A character index is the number of characters from the beginning of the edit control.

This member function is only used by multiple-line edit controls.

For more information, see **EM_LINEFROMCHAR** in the Win32 documentation.

See Also **CEdit::LineIndex**

CEdit::LineIndex

int LineIndex(int *nLine* = –1) const;

Return Value

The character index of the line specified in *nLine* or –1 if the specified line number is greater then the number of lines in the edit control.

Parameters

nLine   Contains the index value for the desired line in the text of the edit control, or contains –1. If *nLine* is –1, it specifies the current line, that is, the line that contains the caret.

Remarks

Call this function to retrieve the character index of a line within a multiple-line edit control. The character index is the number of characters from the beginning of the edit control to the specified line.

This member function is only processed by multiple-line edit controls.

For more information, see **EM_LINEINDEX** in the Win32 documentation.

See Also **CEdit::LineFromChar**

CEdit::LineLength

int LineLength(int *nLine* = –1) const;

Return Value

When **LineLength** is called for a multiple-line edit control, the return value is the length (in bytes) of the line specified by *nLine*. When **LineLength** is called for a single-line edit control, the return value is the length (in bytes) of the text in the edit control.

Parameters

nLine Specifies the character index of a character in the line whose length is to be retrieved. If this parameter is –1, the length of the current line (the line that contains the caret) is returned, not including the length of any selected text within the line. When **LineLength** is called for a single-line edit control, this parameter is ignored.

Remarks

Call this function to retrieve the length of a line in an edit control.

Use the **LineIndex** member function to retrieve a character index for a given line number within a multiple-line edit control.

For more information, see **EM_LINELENGTH** in the Win32 documentation.

See Also   **CEdit::LineIndex**

CEdit::LineScroll

void LineScroll(int *nLines*, **int** *nChars* **= 0);**

Parameters

nLines   Specifies the number of lines to scroll vertically.

nChars   Specifies the number of character positions to scroll horizontally. This value is ignored if the edit control has either the **ES_RIGHT** or **ES_CENTER** style.

Remarks

Call this function to scroll the text of a multiple-line edit control.

This member function is processed only by multiple-line edit controls.

The edit control does not scroll vertically past the last line of text in the edit control. If the current line plus the number of lines specified by *nLines* exceeds the total number of lines in the edit control, the value is adjusted so that the last line of the edit control is scrolled to the top of the edit-control window.

LineScroll can be used to scroll horizontally past the last character of any line.

For more information, see **EM_LINESCROLL** in the Win32 documentation.

See Also   **CEdit::LineIndex**

CEdit::Paste

void Paste( );

Remarks

Call this function to insert the data from the Clipboard into the **CEdit** at the insertion point. Data is inserted only if the Clipboard contains data in **CF_TEXT** format.

For more information, see **WM_PASTE** in the Win32 documentation.

See Also   **CEdit::Clear**, **CEdit::Copy**, **CEdit::Cut**

CEdit::PosFromChar

CPoint PosFromChar(UINT *nChar* **) const;**

Return Value

The coordinates of the top-left corner of the character specified by *nChar*.

Parameters

nChar   The zero-based index of the specified character.

Remarks

Call this function to get the position (top-left corner) of a given character within this **CEdit** object. The character is specified by giving its zero-based index value. If *nChar* is greater than the index of the last character in this **CEdit** object, the return value specifies the coordinates of the character position just past the last character in this **CEdit** object.

Note   This member function is available only in Windows 95.

For more information, see **EM_POSFROMCHAR** in the Win32 documentation.

See Also   **CEdit::CharFromPos**

CEdit::ReplaceSel

void ReplaceSel(LPCTSTR *lpszNewText* **);**

Parameters

lpszNewText   Points to a null-terminated string containing the replacement text.

Remarks

Call this function to replace the current selection in an edit control with the text specified by *lpszNewText*.

Replaces only a portion of the text in an edit control. If you want to replace all of the text, use the **CWnd::SetWindowText** member function.

If there is no current selection, the replacement text is inserted at the current cursor location.

For more information, see **EM_REPLACESEL** in the Win32 documentation.

See Also   **CWnd::SetWindowText**

CEdit::SetHandle

void SetHandle(HLOCAL *hBuffer* **);**

Parameters

hBuffer   Contains a handle to the local memory. This handle must have been created by a previous call to the **LocalAlloc** Windows function using the **LMEM_MOVEABLE** flag. The memory is assumed to contain a null-terminated string. If this is not the case, the first byte of the allocated memory should be set to 0.

Remarks

Call this function to set the handle to the local memory that will be used by a multiple-line edit control. The edit control will then use this buffer to store the currently displayed text instead of allocating its own buffer.

This member function is processed only by multiple-line edit controls.

Before an application sets a new memory handle, it should use the **GetHandle** member function to get the handle to the current memory buffer and free that memory using the **LocalFree** Windows function.

SetHandle clears the undo buffer (the **CanUndo** member function then returns 0) and the internal modification flag (the **GetModify** member function then returns 0). The edit-control window is redrawn.

You can use this member function in a multiple-line edit control in a dialog box only if you have created the dialog box with the **DS_LOCALEDIT** style flag set.

For more information, see **EM_SETHANDLE**, **LocalAlloc**, and **LocalFree** in the Win32 documentation.

See Also   **CEdit::CanUndo**, **CEdit::GetHandle**, **CEdit::GetModify**

CEdit::SetLimitText

void SetLimitText(UINT *nMax* **);**

Parameters

nMax   The new text limit, in bytes.

Remarks

Call this member function to set the text limit for this **CEdit** object. The text limit is the maximum amount of text, in bytes, that the edit control can accept.

Changing the text limit restricts only the text the user can enter. It has no effect on any text already in the edit control, nor does it affect the length of the text copied to the edit control by the **SetWindowText** member function in **CWnd**. If an application uses the **SetWindowText** function to place more text into an edit control than is specified in the call to **LimitText**, the user can delete any of the text within the edit control. However, the text limit will prevent the user from replacing the existing text with new text, unless deleting the current selection causes the text to fall below the text limit.

This function replaces **LimitText** in Win32.

Note This member function is not available in Win32s. Use **LimitText** in Win32s.

For more information, see **EM_SETLIMITTEXT** in the Win32 documentation.

See Also **CEdit::GetLimitText**, **CEdit::LimitText**

CEdit::SetMargins

void SetMargins(UINT *nLeft*, **UINT** *nRight* **);**

Parameters

nLeft The width of the new left margin, in pixels.

nRight The width of the new right margin, in pixels.

Remarks

Call this member function to set the left and right margins of this edit control.

Note This member function is available only in Windows 95.

For more information, see **EM_SETMARGINS** in the Win32 documentation.

See Also **CEdit::GetMargins**

CEdit::SetModify

void SetModify(BOOL *bModified* = **TRUE);**

Parameters

bModified A value of **TRUE** indicates that the text has been modified, and a value of **FALSE** indicates it is unmodified. By default, the modified flag is set.

Remarks

Call this function to set or clear the modified flag for an edit control. The modified flag indicates whether or not the text within the edit control has been modified. It is automatically set whenever the user changes the text. Its value may be retrieved with the **GetModify** member function.

For more information, see **EM_SETMODIFY** in the Win32 documentation.

See Also **CEdit::GetModify**

CEdit::SetPasswordChar

void SetPasswordChar(TCHAR *ch* **);**

Parameters

ch   Specifies the character to be displayed in place of the character typed by the user. If *ch* is 0, the actual characters typed by the user are displayed.

Remarks

Call this function to set or remove a password character displayed in an edit control when the user types text. When a password character is set, that character is displayed for each character the user types.

This member function has no effect on a multiple-line edit control.

When the **SetPasswordChar** member function is called, **CEdit** will redraw all visible characters using the character specified by *ch*.

If the edit control is created with the **ES_PASSWORD** style, the default password character is set to an asterisk (*). This style is removed if **SetPasswordChar** is called with *ch* set to 0.

For more information, see **EM_SETPASSWORDCHAR** in the Win32 documentation.

See Also   **CEdit::GetPasswordChar**

CEdit::SetReadOnly

BOOL SetReadOnly(BOOL *bReadOnly* **= TRUE);**

Return Value

Nonzero if the operation is successful, or 0 if an error occurs.

Parameters

bReadOnly   Specifies whether to set or remove the read-only state of the edit control. A value of **TRUE** sets the state to read-only; a value of **FALSE** sets the state to read/write.

Remarks

Calls this function to set the read-only state of an edit control.

The current setting can be found by testing the **ES_READONLY** flag in the return value of **CWnd::GetStyle**.

For more information, see **EM_SETREADONLY** in the Win32 documentation.

See Also   **CWnd::GetStyle**

CEdit::SetRect

void SetRect(LPCRECT *lpRect* **);**

Parameters

lpRect   Points to the **RECT** structure or **CRect** object that specifies the new
dimensions of the formatting rectangle.

Remarks

Call this function to set the dimensions of a rectangle using the specified coordinates.
This member is processed only by multiple-line edit controls.

Use **SetRect** to set the formatting rectangle of a multiple-line edit control. The
formatting rectangle is the limiting rectangle of the text, which is independent of the
size of the edit-control window. When the edit control is first created, the formatting
rectangle is the same as the client area of the edit-control window. By using the
SetRect member function, an application can make the formatting rectangle larger or
smaller than the edit-control window.

If the edit control has no scroll bar, text will be clipped, not wrapped, if the
formatting rectangle is made larger than the window. If the edit control contains a
border, the formatting rectangle is reduced by the size of the border. If you adjust the
rectangle returned by the **GetRect** member function, you must remove the size of the
border before you pass the rectangle to **SetRect**.

When **SetRect** is called, the edit control's text is also reformatted and redisplayed.

For more information, see **EM_SETRECT** in the Win32 documentation.

See Also   **CRect::CRect**, **CRect::CopyRect**, **CRect::operator =**,
CRect::SetRectEmpty, **CEdit::GetRect**, **CEdit::SetRectNP**

CEdit::SetRectNP

void SetRectNP(LPCRECT *lpRect* **);**

Parameters

lpRect   Points to a **RECT** structure or **CRect** object that specifies the new
dimensions of the rectangle.

Remarks

Call this function to set the formatting rectangle of a multiple-line edit control. The
formatting rectangle is the limiting rectangle of the text, which is independent of the
size of the edit-control window.

SetRectNP is identical to the **SetRect** member function except that the edit-control
window is not redrawn.

When the edit control is first created, the formatting rectangle is the same as the client area of the edit-control window. By calling the **SetRectNP** member function, an application can make the formatting rectangle larger or smaller than the edit-control window.

If the edit control has no scroll bar, text will be clipped, not wrapped, if the formatting rectangle is made larger than the window.

This member is processed only by multiple-line edit controls.

For more information, see **EM_SETRECTNP** in the Win32 documentation.

See Also   **CRect::CRect**, **CRect::CopyRect**, **CRect::operator =**, **CRect::SetRectEmpty**, **CEdit::GetRect**, **CEdit::SetRect**

CEdit::SetSel

void SetSel(DWORD *dwSelection*, **BOOL** *bNoScroll* = **FALSE**);
void SetSel(int *nStartChar*, **int** *nEndChar*, **BOOL** *bNoScroll* = **FALSE**);

Parameters

dwSelection   Specifies the starting position in the low-order word and the ending position in the high-order word. If the low-order word is 0 and the high-order word is −1, all the text in the edit control is selected. If the low-order word is −1, any current selection is removed.

bNoScroll   Indicates whether the caret should be scrolled into view. If **FALSE**, the caret is scrolled into view. If **TRUE**, the caret is not scrolled into view.

nStartChar   Specifies the starting position. If *nStartChar* is 0 and *nEndChar* is −1, all the text in the edit control is selected. If *nStartChar* is −1, any current selection is removed.

nEndChar   Specifies the ending position.

Remarks

Call this function to select a range of characters in an edit control.

For more information, see **EM_SETSEL** in the Win32 documentation.

See Also   **CEdit::GetSel**, **CEdit::ReplaceSel**

CEdit::SetTabStops

void SetTabStops( );
BOOL SetTabStops(const int& *cxEachStop*);
BOOL SetTabStops(int *nTabStops*, **LPINT** *rgTabStops*);

Return Value

Nonzero if the tabs were set; otherwise 0.

Parameters

cxEachStop   Specifies that tab stops are to be set at every *cxEachStop* dialog units.

nTabStops   Specifies the number of tab stops contained in *rgTabStops*. This number must be greater than 1.

rgTabStops   Points to an array of unsigned integers specifying the tab stops in dialog units. A dialog unit is a horizontal or vertical distance. One horizontal unit is equal to one-fourth of the current base width unit, and 1 vertical unit is equal to one-eighth of the current base height unit. The base units are computed based on the height and width of the current system font. The **GetDialogBaseUnits** Windows function returns the current dialog base units in pixels.

Remarks

Call this function to set the tab stops in a multiple-line edit control. When text is copied to a multiple-line edit control, any tab character in the text will cause space to be generated up to the next tab stop.

To set tab to the default size of 32 dialog units, call the parameterless version of this function. To set tab stops to a size other than 32, call the version with the *cxEachStop* parameter. To set tab stops to an array of sizes, use the version with two parameters. .

SetTabStops does not automatically redraw the edit window. If you change the tab stops for text already in the edit control, call **CWnd::InvalidateRect** to redraw the edit window.

For more information, see **EM_SETTABSTOPS** and **GetDialogBaseUnits** in the Win32 documentation.

See Also   **CWnd::InvalidateRect**

CEdit::Undo

BOOL Undo( );

Return Value

For a single-line edit control, the return value is always nonzero. For a multiple-line edit control, the return value is nonzero if the undo operation is successful, or 0 if the undo operation fails.

Remarks

Call this function to undo the last edit-control operation.

An undo operation can also be undone. For example, you can restore deleted text with the first call to **Undo**. As long as there is no intervening edit operation, you can remove the text again with a second call to **Undo**.

For more information, see **EM_UNDO** in the Win32 documentation.

See Also   **CEdit::CanUndo**

CEditView

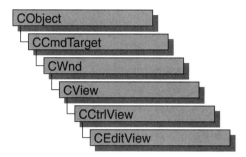

A **CEditView** object is a view that, like the **CEdit** class, provides the functionality of a Windows edit control and can be used to implement simple text-editor functionality. The **CEditView** class provides the following additional functions:

- Printing
- Find and replace

Because class **CEditView** is a derivative of class **CView**, objects of class **CEditView** can be used with documents and document templates.

Each **CEditView** control's text is kept in its own global memory object. Your application can have any number of **CEditView** objects.

Create objects of type **CEditView** if you want an edit window with the added functionality listed above, or if you want simple text-editor functionality. A **CEditView** object can occupy the entire client area of a window. Derive your own classes from **CEditView** to add or modify the basic functionality, or to declare classes that can be added to a document template.

The default implementation of class **CEditView** handles the following commands: **ID_EDIT_SELECT_ALL**, **ID_EDIT_FIND**, **ID_EDIT_REPLACE**, **ID_EDIT_REPEAT**, and **ID_FILE_PRINT**.

Objects of type **CEditView** (or of types derived from **CEditView**) have the following limitations:

- **CEditView** does not implement true WYSIWYG (what you see is what you get) editing. Where there is a choice between readability on the screen and matching printed output, **CEditView** opts for screen readability.
- **CEditView** can display text in only a single font. No special character formatting is supported. See class **CRichEditView** for greater capabilities.
- The amount of text a **CEditView** can contain is limited. The limits are the same as for the **CEdit** control.

For more information on **CEditView**, see "Special View Classes" in Chapter 1 of
Programming with MFC.

#include <afxext.h>

See Also   **CEdit**, **CDocument**, **CDocTemplate**, **CCtrlView**, **CRichEditView**

Data Members

dwStyleDefault	Default style for objects of type **CEditView.**

Construction

CEditView	Constructs an object of type **CEditView**.

Attributes

GetEditCtrl	Provides access to the **CEdit** portion of a **CEditView** object (the Windows edit control).
GetPrinterFont	Retrieves the current printer font.
GetSelectedText	Retrieves the current text selection.
LockBuffer	Locks the buffer.
UnlockBuffer	Unlocks the buffer.
GetBufferLength	Obtains the length of the character buffer.
SetPrinterFont	Sets a new printer font.
SetTabStops	Sets tab stops for both screen display and printing.

Operations

FindText	Searches for a string within the text.
PrintInsideRect	Renders text inside a given rectangle.
SerializeRaw	Serializes a **CEditView** object to disk as raw text.

Overridables

OnFindNext	Finds next occurrence of a text string.
OnReplaceAll	Replaces all occurrences of a given string with a new string.
OnReplaceSel	Replaces current selection.
OnTextNotFound	Called when a find operation fails to match any further text.

Member Functions

CEditView::CEditView

CEditView( );

Remarks

Constructs an object of type **CEditView**. After constructing the object, you must call the **CWnd::Create** function before the edit control is used. If you derive a class from **CEditView** and add it to the template using **CWinApp::AddDocTemplate**, the framework calls both this constructor and the **Create** function.

See Also CWnd::Create, CWinApp::AddDocTemplate

CEditView::FindText

BOOL FindText(LPCTSTR *lpszFind***, BOOL** *bNext* **= TRUE, BOOL** *bCase* **= TRUE);**

Return Value

Nonzero if the search text is found; otherwise 0.

Parameters

lpszFind   The text to be found.

bNext   Specifies the direction of the search. If **TRUE**, the search direction is toward the end of the buffer. If **FALSE**, the search direction is toward the beginning of the buffer.

bCase   Specifies whether the search is case sensitive. If **TRUE**, the search is case sensitive. If **FALSE**, the search is not case sensitive.

Remarks

Call the **FindText** function to search the **CEditView** object's text buffer. This function searches the text in the buffer for the text specified by *lpszFind*, starting at the current selection, in the direction specified by *bNext*, and with case sensitivity specified by *bCase*. If the text is found, it sets the selection to the found text and returns a nonzero value. If the text is not found, the function returns 0.

You normally do not need to call the **FindText** function unless you override **OnFindNext**, which calls **FindText**.

See Also CEditView::OnFindNext, CEditView::OnReplaceAll, CEditView::OnReplaceSel, CEditView::OnTextNotFound

CEditView::GetBufferLength

UINT GetBufferLength( ) const;

Return Value

The length of the string in the buffer.

Remarks

Call this member function to obtain the number of characters currently in the edit control's buffer, not including the null terminator.

See Also   **CEditView::LockBuffer**, **CEditView::UnlockBuffer**

CEditView::GetEditCtrl

CEdit& GetEditCtrl( ) const;

Return Value

A reference to a **CEdit** object.

Remarks

Call **GetEditCtrl** to get a reference to the edit control used by the edit view. This control is of type **CEdit**, so you can manipulate the Windows edit control directly using the **CEdit** member functions.

Warning   Using the **CEdit** object can change the state of the underlying Windows edit control. For example, you should not change the tab settings using the **CEdit::SetTabStops** function because **CEditView** caches these settings for use both in the edit control and in printing. Instead, use **CEditView::SetTabStops**.

See Also   **CEdit**, **CEditView::SetTabStops**

CEditView::GetPrinterFont

CFont* GetPrinterFont( ) const;

Return Value

A pointer to a **CFont** object that specifies the current printer font; **NULL** if the printer font has not been set. The pointer may be temporary and should not be stored for later use.

Remarks

Call **GetPrinterFont** to get a pointer to a **CFont** object that describes the current printer font. If the printer font has not been set, the default printing behavior of the **CEditView** class is to print using the same font used for display.

Use this function to determine the current printer font. If it is not the desired printer font, use **CEditView::SetPrinterFont** to change it.

See Also **CEditView::SetPrinterFont**

CEditView::GetSelectedText

void GetSelectedText(CString& *strResult* **) const;**

Parameters

strResult A reference to the **CString** object that is to receive the selected text.

Remarks

Call **GetSelectedText** to copy the selected text into a **CString** object, up to the end of the selection or the character preceding the first carriage-return character in the selection.

See Also **CEditView::OnReplaceSel**

CEditView::LockBuffer

LPCTSTR LockBuffer( ) const;

Return Value

A pointer to the edit control's buffer.

Remarks

Call this member function to obtain a pointer to the buffer. The buffer should not be modified.

See Also **CEditView::UnlockBuffer, CEditView::GetBufferLength**

CEditView::OnFindNext

virtual void OnFindNext(LPCTSRT *lpszFind***, BOOL** *bNext***, BOOL** *bCase* **);**

Parameters

lpszFind The text to be found.

bNext Specifies the direction of the search. If **TRUE**, the search direction is toward the end of the buffer. If **FALSE**, the search direction is toward the beginning of the buffer.

bCase Specifies whether the search is case sensitive. If **TRUE**, the search is case sensitive. If **FALSE**, the search is not case sensitive.

Remarks

Searches the text in the buffer for the text specified by *lpszFind*, in the direction specified by *bNext*, with case sensitivity specified by *bCase*. The search starts at the beginning of the current selection and is accomplished through a call to **FindText**. In the default implementation, **OnFindNext** calls **OnTextNotFound** if the text is not found.

Override **OnFindNext** to change the way a **CEditView**-derived object searches text. **CEditView** calls **OnFindNext** when the user chooses the Find Next button in the standard Find dialog box.

See Also   CEditView::OnTextNotFound, CEditView::FindText, CEditView::OnReplaceAll, CEditView::OnReplaceSel

CEditView::OnReplaceAll

virtual void OnReplaceAll(LPCTSTR *lpszFind*, **LPCTSTR** *lpszReplace*, **BOOL** *bCase*);

Parameters

lpszFind   The text to be found.

lpszReplace   The text to replace the search text.

bCase   Specifies whether search is case sensitive. If **TRUE**, the search is case sensitive. If **FALSE**, the search is not case sensitive.

Remarks

CEditView calls **OnReplaceAll** when the user selects the Replace All button in the standard Replace dialog box. **OnReplaceAll** searches the text in the buffer for the text specified by *lpszFind*, with case sensitivity specified by *bCase*. The search starts at the beginning of the current selection. Each time the search text is found, this function replaces that occurrence of the text with the text specified by *lpszReplace*. The search is accomplished through a call to **FindText**. In the default implementation, **OnTextNotFound** is called if the text is not found.

If the current selection does not match *lpszFind*, the selection is updated to the first occurrence of the text specified by *lpszFind* and a replace is not performed. This allows the user to confirm that this is what they want to do when the selection does not match the text to be replaced.

Override **OnReplaceAll** to change the way a **CEditView**-derived object replaces text.

See Also   CEditView::OnFindNext, CEditView::OnTextNotFound, CEditView::FindText, CEditView::OnReplaceSel

CEditView::OnReplaceSel

virtual void OnReplaceSel(LPCTSTR *lpszFind*, **BOOL** *bNext*, **BOOL** *bCase*,
LPCTSTR *lpszReplace*);

Parameters

lpszFind   The text to be found.

bNext   Specifies the direction of the search. If **TRUE**, the search direction is toward
the end of the buffer. If **FALSE**, the search direction is toward the beginning of
the buffer.

bCase   Specifies whether the search is case sensitive. If **TRUE**, the search is case
sensitive. If **FALSE**, the search is not case sensitive.

lpszReplace   The text to replace the found text.

Remarks

CEditView calls **OnReplaceSel** when the user selects the Replace button in the
standard Replace dialog box.

After replacing the selection, this function searches the text in the buffer for the next
occurrence of the text specified by *lpszFind*, in the direction specified by *bNext*, with
case sensitivity specified by *bCase*. The search is accomplished through a call to
FindText. If the text is not found, **OnTextNotFound** is called.

Override **OnReplaceSel** to change the way a **CEditView**-derived object replaces the
selected text.

See Also   **CEditView::OnFindNext, CEditView::OnTextNotFound,
CEditView::FindText, CEditView::OnReplaceAll**

CEditView::OnTextNotFound

virtual void OnTextNotFound(LPCTSTR *lpszFind*);

Parameters

lpszFind   The text to be found.

Remarks

Override this function to change the default implementation, which calls the
Windows function **MessageBeep**.

See Also   **CEditView::FindText, CEditView::OnFindNext,
CEditView::OnReplaceAll, CEditView::OnReplaceSel**

CEditView::PrintInsideRect

UINT PrintInsideRect(CDC **pDC*, **RECT&** *rectLayout*, **UINT** *nIndexStart*, **UINT** *nIndexStop* **);**

Return Value

The index of the next character to be printed (that is, the character following the last character rendered).

Parameters

pDC   Pointer to the printer device context.

rectLayout   Reference to a **CRect** object or **RECT** structure specifying the rectangle in which the text is to be rendered.

nIndexStart   Index within the buffer of the first character to be rendered.

nIndexStop   Index within the buffer of the character following the last character to be rendered.

Remarks

Call **PrintInsideRect** to print text in the rectangle specified by *rectLayout*.

If the **CEditView** control does not have the style **ES_AUTOHSCROLL**, text is wrapped within the rendering rectangle. If the control does have the style **ES_AUTOHSCROLL**, the text is clipped at the right edge of the rectangle.

The **rect.bottom** element of the *rectLayout* object is changed so that the rectangle's dimensions define the part of the original rectangle that is occupied by the text.

See Also   **CEditView::SetPrinterFont**, **CEditView::GetPrinterFont**

CEditView::SerializeRaw

void SerializeRaw(CArchive& *ar* **);**

Parameters

ar   Reference to the **CArchive** object that stores the serialized text.

Remarks

Call **SerializeRaw** to have a **CArchive** object read or write the text in the **CEditView** object to a text file. **SerializeRaw** differs from **CEditView**'s internal implementation of **Serialize** in that it reads and writes only the text, without preceding object-description data.

See Also   **CArchive**, **CObject::Serialize**

CEditView::SetPrinterFont

void SetPrinterFont(CFont* *pFont* **);**

Parameters

pFont   A pointer to an object of type **CFont**. If **NULL**, the font used for printing is based on the display font.

Remarks

Call **SetPrinterFont** to set the printer font to the font specified by *pFont*.

If you want your view to always use a particular font for printing, include a call to **SetPrinterFont** in your class's **OnPreparePrinting** function. This virtual function is called before printing occurs, so the font change takes place before the view's contents are printed.

See Also   CWnd::SetFont, CFont, CView::OnPreparePrinting

CEditView::SetTabStops

void SetTabStops(int *nTabStops* **);**

Parameters

nTabStops   Width of each tab stop, in dialog units.

Remarks

Call this function to set the tab stops used for display and printing. Only a single tab-stop width is supported. (**CEdit** objects support multiple tab widths.) Widths are in dialog units, which equal one-fourth of the average character width (based on uppercase and lowercase alphabetic characters only) of the font used at the time of printing or displaying. You should not use **CEdit::SetTabStops** because **CEditView** must cache the tab-stop value.

This function modifies only the tabs of the object for which it is called. To change the tab stops for each **CEditView** object in your application, call each object's **SetTabStops** function.

See Also   CWnd::SetFont, CEditView::SetPrinterFont

CEditView::UnlockBuffer

void UnlockBuffer( ) const;

Remarks

Call this member function to unlock the buffer. Call **UnlockBuffer** after you have finished using the pointer returned by **LockBuffer**.

See Also   CEditView::LockBuffer, CEditView::GetBufferLength

Data Members

CEditView::dwStyleDefault

Remarks

Pass this static member as the *dwStyle* parameter of the **Create** function to obtain the default style for the **CEditView** object. **dwStyleDefault** is a public member of type **DWORD**.

CEvent

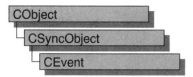

An object of class **CEvent** represents an "event"—a synchronization object that allows one thread to notify another that an event has occurred. Events are useful when a thread needs to know when to perform its task. For example, a thread that copies data to a data archive would need to be notified when new data is available. By using a **CEvent** object to notify the copy thread when new data is available, the thread can perform its task as soon as possible.

CEvent objects have two types: manual and automatic. A manual **CEvent** object stays in the state set by **SetEvent** or **ResetEvent** until the other function is called. An automatic **CEvent** object automatically returns to a nonsignaled (unavailable) state after at least one thread is released.

To use a **CEvent** object, construct the **CEvent** object when it is needed. Specify the name of the event you wish to wait on, and that your application should initially own it. You can then access the event when the constructor returns. Call **SetEvent** to signal (make available) the event object and then call **Unlock** when you are done accessing the controlled resource.

An alternative method for using **CEvent** objects is to add a variable of type **CEvent** as a data member to the class you wish to control. During construction of the controlled object, call the constructor of the **CEvent** data member specifying if the event is initially signaled, the type of event object you want, the name of the event (if it will be used across process boundaries), and desired security attributes.

To access a resource controlled by a **CEvent** object in this manner, first create a variable of either type **CSingleLock** or type **CMultiLock** in your resource's access member function. Then call the lock object's **Lock** member function (for example, **CMultiLock::Lock**). At this point, your thread will either gain access to the resource, wait for the resource to be released and gain access, or wait for the resource to be released and time out, failing to gain access to the resource. In any case, your resource has been accessed in a thread-safe manner. To release the resource, call **SetEvent** to signal the event object, and then use the lock object's **Unlock** member function (for example, **CMultiLock::Unlock**), or allow the lock object to fall out of scope.

For more information on using **CEvent** objects, see the article "Multithreading: How to Use the Synchronization Classes" in *Programming with MFC*.

#include <afxmt.h>

Construction

CEvent	Constructs a **CEvent** object.

Methods

SetEvent	Sets the event to available (signaled) and releases any waiting threads.
PulseEvent	Sets the event to available (signaled), releases waiting threads, and sets the event to unavailable (nonsignaled).
ResetEvent	Sets the event to unavailable (nonsignaled).
Unlock	Releases the event object.

Member Functions

CEvent::CEvent

CEvent(BOOL *bInitiallyOwn* **= FALSE, BOOL** *bManualReset* **= FALSE, LPCTSTR** *lpszName* **= NULL, LPSECURITY_ATTRIBUTES** *lpsaAttribute* **= NULL);**

Parameters

bInitiallyOwn   If **TRUE**, specifies that the event object is initially owned, and all threads wanting to access the resource must wait; otherwise the event object is not initially owned.

bManualReset   If **TRUE**, specifies that the event object is a manual event, otherwise the event object is an automatic event.

lpszName   Name of the **CEvent** object. Must be supplied if the object will be used across process boundaries. If the name matches an existing event, the constructor builds a new **CEvent** object which references the event of that name. If the name matches an existing synchronization object that is not an event, the construction will fail. If **NULL**, the name will be null.

lpsaAttribute   Security attributes for the event object. For a full description of this structure, see **SECURITY_ATTRIBUTES** in the *Win32 SDK Programmer's Reference*.

Remarks

Constructs a named or unnamed **CEvent** object. To access or release a **CEvent** object, create a **CMultiLock** or **CSingleLock** object and call its **Lock** and **Unlock** member functions.

To change the state of a **CEvent** object to signaled (threads do not have to wait), call **SetEvent** or **PulseEvent**. To set the state of a **CEvent** object to nonsignaled (threads must wait), call **ResetEvent**.

CEvent::PulseEvent

BOOL PulseEvent( );

Return Value

Nonzero if the function was successful; otherwise 0.

Remarks

Sets the state of the event to signaled (available), releases any waiting threads, and resets it to nonsignaled (unavailable) automatically. If the event is manual, all waiting threads are released, the event is set to nonsignaled, and **PulseEvent** returns. If the event is automatic, a single thread is released, the event is set to nonsignaled, and **PulseEvent** returns.

If no threads are waiting, or no threads can be released immediately, **PulseEvent** sets the state of the event to nonsignaled and returns.

CEvent::ResetEvent

BOOL ResetEvent( );

Return Value

Nonzero if the function was successful; otherwise 0.

Remarks

Sets the state of the event to nonsignaled until explicitly set to signaled by the **SetEvent** member function. This causes all threads wishing to access this event to wait.

This member function is not used by automatic events.

CEvent::SetEvent

BOOL SetEvent( );

Return Value

Nonzero if the function was successful, otherwise 0.

Remarks

Sets the state of the event to signaled, releasing any waiting threads. If the event is manual, the event will remain signaled until **ResetEvent** is called. More than one thread can be released in this case. If the event is automatic, the event will remain signaled until a single thread is released. The system will then set the state of the event to nonsignaled. If no threads are waiting, the state remains signaled until one thread is released.

CEvent::Unlock

virtual BOOL Unlock( );

Return Value

Nonzero if the thread owned the event object and the event is an automatic event; otherwise 0.

Remarks

Releases the event object. This member function is called by threads that currently own an automatic event to release it after they are done, if their lock object is to be reused. If the lock object is not to be reused, this function will be called by the lock object's destructor.

CException

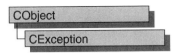

CException is the base class for all exceptions in the Microsoft Foundation Class Library. The derived classes and their descriptions are listed below:

CMemoryException	Out-of-memory exception
CNotSupportedException	Request for an unsupported operation
CArchiveException	Archive-specific exception
CFileException	File-specific exception
CResourceException	Windows resource not found or not createable
COleException	OLE exception
CDBException	Database exception (that is, exception conditions arising for MFC database classes based on Open Database Connectivity)
COleDispatchException	OLE dispatch (automation) exception
CUserException	Exception that indicates that a resource could not be found
CDaoException	Data access object exception (that is, exception conditions arising for for DAO classes)

These exceptions are intended to be used with the **THROW**, **THROW_LAST**, **TRY**, **CATCH**, **AND_CATCH**, and **END_CATCH** macros. For more information on exceptions, see Exception Processing, or see the article "Exceptions" in *Programming with MFC*.

To catch a specific exception, use the appropriate derived class. To catch all types of exceptions, use **CException**, and then use **CObject::IsKindOf** to differentiate among **CException**-derived classes. Note that **CObject::IsKindOf** works only for classes declared with the **IMPLEMENT_DYNAMIC** macro, in order to take advantage of dynamic type checking. Any **CException**-derived class that you create should use the **IMPLEMENT_DYNAMIC** macro, too.

You can report details about exceptions to the user by calling **GetErrorMessage** or **ReportError**, two member functions that work with any of **CException**'s derived classes.

If an exception is caught by one of the macros, the **CException** object is deleted automatically; do not delete it yourself. If an exception is caught by using a **catch** keyword, it is not automatically deleted. See the article "Exceptions" in *Programming with MFC* for more information about when to delete an exeption object.

CException is an abstract base class. You cannot create **CException** objects; you must create objects of derived classes. If you need to create your own **CException** type, use one of the derived classes listed above as a model. Make sure that your derived class also uses **IMPLEMENT_DYNAMIC**.

#include <afx.h>

See Also Exception Processing

Operations

GetErrorMessage	Retrieves the message describing an exception.
ReportError	Reports an error message in a message box to the user.

Member Functions

CException::GetErrorMessage

virtual BOOL GetErrorMessage(LPTSTR *lpszError*, **UINT** *nMaxError*, **PUINT** *pnHelpContext* = **NULL**);

Return Value

Nonzero if the function is successful; otherwise 0 if no error message text is available.

Parameters

lpszError   A pointer to a buffer that will receive an error message.

nMaxError   The maximum number of characters the buffer can hold, including the **NULL** terminator.

pnHelpContext   The address of a **UINT** that will receive the help context ID. If **NULL**, no ID will be returned.

Remarks

Call this member function to provide text about an error that has occurred. For example, call **GetErrorMessage** to retrieve a string describing the error which caused MFC to throw a **CFileException** when writing to a **CFile** object.

Note GetErrorMessage will not copy more than *nMaxError -1* characters to the buffer, and it will always add a trailing null to end the string. If the buffer is too small, the error message may be truncated.

Example

Here is an example of the use of **CException::GetErrorMessage**.

```
CFile fileInput;
CFileException ex;

// try to open a file for reading.
// The file will certainly not
// exist because there are too many explicit
// directories in the name.

// if the call to Open() fails, ex will be
// initialized with exception
// information.  the call to ex.GetErrorString()
// will retrieve an appropriate message describing
// the error, and we'll add our own text
// to make sure the user is perfectly sure what
// went wrong.

if (!fileInput.Open("\\Too\\Many\\Bad\\Dirs.DAT", CFile::modeRead, &ex))
{
    TCHAR    szCause[255];
    CString strFormatted;

    ex.GetErrorMessage(szCause, 255);

    // (in real life, it's probably more
    // appropriate to read this from
    //  a string resource so it would be easy to
    // localize)

    strFormatted = _T("The data file could not be opened because of this error: ");
    strFormatted += szCause;

    AfxMessageBox(strFormatted);
}
else
{
    // the file was opened, so do whatever work
    // with fileInput
    // we were planning...
    // :

    fileInput.Close();
}
```

See Also   **CException::ReportError**

CException::ReportError

virtual int ReportError(UINT *nType* **= MB_OK, UINT** *nMessageID* **= 0);**

Return Value

An **AfxMessageBox** value; otherwise 0 if there is not enough memory to display the message box. See **AfxMessageBox** for the possible return values.

Parameters

nType   Specifies the style of the message box. Apply any combination of the message-box styles to the box. If you don't specify this parameter, the default is **MB_OK**.

nMessageID   Specifies the resource ID (string table entry) of a message to display if the exception object does not have an error message. If 0, the message "No error message is available" is displayed.

Remarks

Call this member function to report error text in a message box to the user.

Example

Here is an example of the use of **CException::ReportError**.

```
CFile fileInput;
CFileException ex;

// try to open a file for reading.
// The file will certainly not
// exist because there are too many explicit
// directories in the name.

// if the call to Open() fails, ex will be
// initialized with exception
// information.  the call to ex.ReportError() will
// display an appropriate
// error message to the user, such as
// "\Too\Many\Bad\Dirs.DAT contains an
// invalid path."  The error message text will be
// appropriate for the
// file name and error condition.

if (!fileInput.Open("\\Too\\Many\\Bad\\Dirs.DAT", CFile::modeRead, &ex))
{
    ex.ReportError();
}
else
```

```
{
    // the file was opened, so do whatever work
    // with fileInput we were planning...
    // :
    fileInput.Close();
}
```

See Also **AfxMessageBox**, **CException::GetErrorMessage**

CFieldExchange

The **CFieldExchange** class supports the record field exchange (RFX) routines used by the database classes. Use this class if you are writing data exchange routines for custom data types; otherwise, you will not directly use this class. RFX exchanges data between the field data members of your recordset object and the corresponding fields of the current record on the data source. RFX manages the exchange in both directions, from the data source and to the data source.

Note If you are working with the Data Access Objects (DAO) classes rather than the Open Database Connectivity (ODBC) classes, use class **CDaoFieldExchange** instead. For more information, see the articles "Database Overview" and "DAO and MFC" in *Programming with MFC*.

A **CFieldExchange** object provides the context information needed for record field exchange to take place. **CFieldExchange** objects support a number of operations, including binding parameters and field data members and setting various flags on the fields of the current record. RFX operations are performed on recordset-class data members of types defined by the **enum FieldType** in **CFieldExchange**. Possible **FieldType** values are:

- **CFieldExchange::outputColumn** for field data members.
- **CFieldExchange::param** for parameter data members.

Most of the class's member functions and data members are provided for writing your own custom RFX routines. You will use **SetFieldType** frequently. For more information about RFX and the use of **CFieldExchange** objects, see the articles "Record Field Exchange (RFX)" and "Recordset (ODBC)" in *Programming with MFC*. For details about the RFX global functions, see "Record Field Exchange Functions" in the "Macros and Globals" section in this manual.

#include <afxdb.h>

See Also   CRecordset

Operations

IsFieldType	Returns nonzero if the current operation is appropriate for the type of field being updated.
SetFieldType	Specifies the type of recordset data member—column or parameter—represented by all following calls to RFX functions until the next call to **SetFieldType**.

Member Functions

CFieldExchange::IsFieldType

BOOL IsFieldType(UINT* *pnField* **);**

Return Value

Nonzero if the current operation can be performed on the current field type.

Parameters

pnField   The sequential number of the field data member is returned in this parameter. This number corresponds to the field's order in the **CRecordset::DoFieldExchange** function.

Remarks

If you write your own RFX function, call **IsFieldType** at the beginning of your function to determine whether the current operation can be performed on a particular field data member type (a **CFieldExchange::outputColumn** or a **CFieldExchange::param**). Follow the model of the existing RFX functions.

CFieldExchange::SetFieldType

void SetFieldType(UINT *nFieldType* **);**

Parameters

nFieldType   A value of the **enum FieldType**, declared in **CFieldExchange**, which can be either of the following:

- **CFieldExchange::outputColumn**
- **CFieldExchange::param**

Remarks

You need a call to **SetFieldType** in the field map section of your recordset class's **DoFieldExchange** override. ClassWizard places the **SetFieldType** call for you. The call precedes calls to RFX functions, one for each field data member of your class, and identifies the field type as **CFieldExchange::outputColumn**.

If you parameterize your recordset class, you must add RFX calls for all parameter data members (outside the field map) and precede these calls with a call to **SetFieldType**. Pass the value **CFieldExchange::param**.

In general, each group of RFX function calls associated with field data members or parameter data members must be preceded by a call to **SetFieldType**. The *nFieldType* parameter of each **SetFieldType** call identifies the type of the data members represented by the RFX function calls that follow the **SetFieldType** call.

Example

This example shows several calls to RFX functions with accompanying calls to **SetFieldType**. ClassWizard normally writes the first call to **SetFieldType**, and its associated RFX calls. You must write the second, and its RFX call. Note that **SetFieldType** is called through the *pFX* pointer to a **CFieldExchange** object.

```
void CSections::DoFieldExchange(CFieldExchange* pFX)
{
    //{{AFX_FIELD_MAP(CSections)
    pFX->SetFieldType(pFX, CFieldExchange::outputColumn);
    RFX_Text(pFX, 1, "CourseID", m_strCourseID);
    RFX_Text(pFX, 2, "InstructorID", m_strInstructorID);
    RFX_Text(pFX, 3, "RoomNo", m_strRoomNo);
    RFX_Text(pFX, 4, "Schedule", m_strSchedule);
    RFX_Text(pFX, 5, "SectionNo", m_strSectionNo);
    //}}AFX_FIELD_MAP
    pFX->SetFieldType(pFX, CFieldExchange::param);
    RFX_Text(pFX, "Name," m_strNameParam);
}
```

See Also   **CRecordset::DoFieldExchange**, "Record Field Exchange Functions" in the "Macros and Globals" section

CFile

CFile is the base class for Microsoft Foundation file classes. It directly provides unbuffered, binary disk input/output services, and it indirectly supports text files and memory files through its derived classes. **CFile** works in conjunction with the **CArchive** class to support serialization of Microsoft Foundation Class objects.

The hierarchical relationship between this class and its derived classes allows your program to operate on all file objects through the polymorphic **CFile** interface. A memory file, for example, behaves like a disk file.

Use **CFile** and its derived classes for general-purpose disk I/O. Use **ofstream** or other Microsoft iostream classes for formatted text sent to a disk file.

Normally, a disk file is opened automatically on **CFile** construction and closed on destruction. Static member functions permit you to interrogate a file's status without opening the file.

For more information on using **CFile**, see the article "Files" in *Programming with MFC* and "File Handling" in the *Run-Time Library Reference*.

#include <afx.h>

See Also   **CStdioFile**, **CMemFile**

Data Members

m_hFile	Usually contains the operating-system file handle.

Construction

CFile	Constructs a **CFile** object from a path or file handle.
Abort	Closes a file ignoring all warnings and errors.
Duplicate	Constructs a duplicate object based on this file.
Open	Safely opens a file with an error-testing option.
Close	Closes a file and deletes the object.

Input/Output

Read	Reads (unbuffered) data from a file at the current file position.
ReadHuge	Can read more than 64K of (unbuffered) data from a file at the current file position. Obsolete in 32-bit programming. See **Read**.
Write	Writes (unbuffered) data in a file to the current file position.
WriteHuge	Can write more than 64K of (unbuffered) data in a file to the current file position. Obsolete in 32-bit programming. See **Write**.
Flush	Flushes any data yet to be written.

Position

Seek	Positions the current file pointer.
SeekToBegin	Positions the current file pointer at the beginning of the file.
SeekToEnd	Positions the current file pointer at the end of the file.
GetLength	Retrieves the length of the file.
SetLength	Changes the length of the file.

Locking

LockRange	Locks a range of bytes in a file.
UnlockRange	Unlocks a range of bytes in a file.

Status

GetPosition	Retrieves the current file pointer.
GetStatus	Retrieves the status of this open file.
GetFileName	Retrieves the filename of the selected file.
GetFileTitle	Retrieves the title of the selected file.
GetFilePath	Retrieves the full file path of the selected file.
SetFilePath	Sets the full file path of the selected file.

Static

Rename	Renames the specified file (static function).
Remove	Deletes the specified file (static function).
GetStatus	Retrieves the status of the specified file (static, virtual function).
SetStatus	Sets the status of the specified file (static, virtual function).

Member Functions

CFile::Abort

virtual void Abort( );

Remarks

Closes the file associated with this object and makes the file unavailable for reading or writing. If you have not closed the file before destroying the object, the destructor closes it for you.

When handling exceptions, **CFile::Abort** differs from **CFile::Close** in two important ways. First, the **Abort** function will not throw an exception on failures because failures are ignored by **Abort**. Second, **Abort** will not **ASSERT** if the file has not been opened or was closed previously.

If you used **new** to allocate the **CFile** object on the heap, then you must delete it after closing the file. **Abort** sets **m_hFile** to **CFile::hFileNull**.

Example

```
//example for CFile::Abort
CStdioFile fileTest;
char* pFileName = "test.dat";
TRY
{
    // do stuff that may throw exceptions
    fileTest.Open( pFileName, CFile::modeWrite );
}
CATCH_ALL( e )
{
    fileTest.Abort();    // close file safely and quietly
    THROW_LAST();
}
END_CATCH_ALL
```

See Also   **CFile::Close, CFile::Open**

CFile::CFile

CFile( );
CFile(int *hFile* **);**
CFile(LPCTSTR *lpszFileName***, UINT** *nOpenFlags* **);**
   throw(CFileException);

Parameters

hFile   The handle of a file that is already open.

lpszFileName   A string that is the path to the desired file. The path can be relative or absolute.

nOpenFlags   Sharing and access mode. Specifies the action to take when opening the file. You can combine options listed below by using the bitwise-OR (l) operator. One access permission and one share option are required; the **modeCreate** and **modeNoInherit** modes are optional. The values are as follows:

- **CFile::modeCreate**   Directs the constructor to create a new file. If the file exists already, it is truncated to 0 length.

- **CFile::modeNoTruncate**   Combine this value with **modeCreate**. If the file being created already exists, it is not truncated to 0 length. Thus the file is guaranteed to open, either as a newly created file or as an existing file. This might be useful, for example, when opening a settings file that may or may not exist already. This option applies to **CStdioFile** as well.

- **CFile::modeRead**   Opens the file for reading only.

- **CFile::modeReadWrite**   Opens the file for reading and writing.

- **CFile::modeWrite**   Opens the file for writing only.

- **CFile::modeNoInherit**   Prevents the file from being inherited by child processes.

- **CFile::shareDenyNone**   Opens the file without denying other processes read or write access to the file. **Create** fails if the file has been opened in compatibility mode by any other process.

- **CFile::shareDenyRead**   Opens the file and denies other processes read access to the file. **Create** fails if the file has been opened in compatibility mode or for read access by any other process.

- **CFile::shareDenyWrite**   Opens the file and denies other processes write access to the file. **Create** fails if the file has been opened in compatibility mode or for write access by any other process.

- **CFile::shareExclusive**   Opens the file with exclusive mode, denying other processes both read and write access to the file. Construction fails if the file has been opened in any other mode for read or write access, even by the current process.

- **CFile::shareCompat**   Opens the file with compatibility mode, allowing any process on a given machine to open the file any number of times. Construction fails if the file has been opened with any of the other sharing modes.

- **CFile::typeText**   Sets text mode with special processing for carriage return–linefeed pairs (used in derived classes only).

- **CFile::typeBinary**   Sets binary mode (used in derived classes only).

Remarks

The default constructor does not open a file but rather sets **m_hFile** to **CFile::hFileNull**. Because this constructor does not throw an exception, it does not make sense to use **TRY/CATCH** logic. Use the **Open** member function, then test directly for exception conditions. For a discussion of exception-processing strategy, see the article "Exceptions" in *Programming with MFC*.

The constructor with one argument creates a **CFile** object that corresponds to an existing operating-system file identified by *hFile*. No check is made on the access mode or file type. When the **CFile** object is destroyed, the operating-system file will not be closed. You must close the file yourself.

The constructor with two arguments creates a **CFile** object and opens the corresponding operating-system file with the given path. This constructor combines the functions of the first constructor and the **Open** member function. It throws an exception if there is an error while opening the file. Generally, this means that the error is unrecoverable and that the user should be alerted.

Example

```
//example for CFile::CFile
char* pFileName = "test.dat";
TRY
{
    CFile f( pFileName, CFile::modeCreate | CFile::modeWrite );
}
CATCH( CFileException, e )
{
    #ifdef _DEBUG
        afxDump << "File could not be opened " << e->m_cause << "\n";
    #endif
}
END_CATCH
```

CFile::Close

virtual void Close( );
    throw(CFileException);

Remarks

Closes the file associated with this object and makes the file unavailable for reading or writing. If you have not closed the file before destroying the object, the destructor closes it for you.

If you used **new** to allocate the **CFile** object on the heap, then you must delete it after closing the file. **Close** sets **m_hFile** to **CFile::hFileNull**.

See Also **CFile::Open**

CFile::Duplicate

> **virtual CFile* Duplicate( ) const;**
> **throw(CFileException);**

Return Value

A pointer to a duplicate **CFile** object.

Remarks

Constructs a duplicate **CFile** object for a given file. This is equivalent to the C run-time function **_dup**.

CFile::Flush

> **virtual void Flush( );**
> **throw(CFileException);**

Remarks

Forces any data remaining in the file buffer to be written to the file.

The use of **Flush** does not guarantee flushing of **CArchive** buffers. If you are using an archive, call **CArchive::Flush** first.

CFile::GetFileName

> **virtual CString GetFileName( ) const;**

Return Value

The name of the file.

Remarks

Call this member function to retrieve the name of a specified file. For example, when you call **GetFileName** to generate a message to the user about the file c:\windows\write\myfile.wri, the filename, myfile.wri, is returned. To return the entire path of the file, including the name, call **GetFilePath**. To return the title of the file (in this example, myfile), call **GetFileTitle**.

See Also   **CFile::GetFilePath**, **CFile::GetFileTitle**

CFile::GetFilePath

> **virtual CString GetFilePath( ) const;**

Return Value

The full path of the specified file.

Remarks

Call this member function to retrieve the full path of a specified file. For example, when you call **GetFilePath** to generate a message to the user about the file c:\windows\write\myfile.wri, the file path, c:\windows\write\myfile.wri, is returned. To return just the name of the file (myfile.wri), call **GetFileName**. To return the title of the file (myfile), call **GetFileTitle**.

See Also   **CFile::SetFilePath**, **CFile::GetFileTitle**, **CFile::GetFileName**

CFile::GetFileTitle

virtual CString GetFileTitle( ) const;

Return Value

The title of the specified file.

Remarks

Call this member function to retrieve the file title for a specified file. For example, when you call **GetFileTitle** to generate a message to the user about the file c:\windows\write\myfile.wri, the file title (myfile) is returned. The file title typically does not include the extention.

See Also   **CFile::GetFileName**, **CFile::GetFilePath**

CFile::GetLength

virtual DWORD GetLength( ) const;
   throw(CFileException);

Return Value

The length of the file.

Remarks

Obtains the current logical length of the file in bytes, not the amount.

See Also   **CFile::SetLength**

CFile::GetPosition

virtual DWORD GetPosition( ) const;
   throw(CFileException);

Return Value

The file pointer as a 32-bit doubleword.

Remarks

Obtains the current value of the file pointer, which can be used in subsequent calls to **Seek**.

Example

```
//example for CFile::GetPosition
extern CFile cfile;
DWORD dwPosition = cfile.GetPosition();
```

CFile::GetStatus

BOOL GetStatus(CFileStatus& *rStatus* **) const;**
static BOOL PASCAL GetStatus(LPCTSTR *lpszFileName*, **CFileStatus&** *rStatus* **);**

Return Value

Nonzero if no error, in which case *rStatus* is valid; otherwise 0. A value of 0 indicates that the file does not exist.

Parameters

rStatus   A reference to a user-supplied **CFileStatus** structure that will receive the status information. The **CFileStatus** structure has the following fields:

- **CTime m_ctime**   The date and time the file was created.

- **CTime m_mtime**   The date and time the file was last modified.

- **CTime m_atime**   The date and time the file was last accessed for reading.

- **LONG m_size**   The logical size of the file in bytes, as reported by the DIR command.

- **BYTE m_attribute**   The attribute byte of the file.

- **char m_szFullName[_MAX_PATH]**   The absolute filename in the Windows character set.

lpszFileName   A string in the Windows character set that is the path to the desired file. The path can be relative or absolute, but cannot contain a network name.

Remarks

The virtual version of **GetStatus** retrieves the status of the open file associated with this **CFile** object. It does not insert a value into the **m_szFullName** structure member.

The static version gets the status of the named file and copies the filename to **m_szFullName**. This function obtains the file status from the directory entry without actually opening the file. It is useful for testing the existence and access rights of a file.

The **m_attribute** is the file attribute. The Microsoft Foundation classes provide an **enum** type attribute so that you can specify attributes symbolically:

```
enum Attribute {
   normal =    0x00,
   readOnly =  0x01,
   hidden =    0x02,
   system =    0x04,
   volume =    0x08,
   directory = 0x10,
   archive =   0x20
   };
```

Example

```
//example for CFile::GetStatus
CFileStatus status;
extern CFile cfile;
if( cfile.GetStatus( status ) )    // virtual member function
   {
        #ifdef _DEBUG
            afxDump << "File size = " << status.m_size << "\n";
        #endif
   }
char* pFileName = "test.dat";
if( CFile::GetStatus( pFileName, status ) )   // static function
   {
        #ifdef _DEBUG
            afxDump << "Full file name = " << status.m_szFullName << "\n";
        #endif
   }
```

See Also   **CFile::SetStatus, CTime**

CFile::LockRange

virtual void LockRange(DWORD *dwPos*, **DWORD** *dwCount* **);**
   throw(CFileException);

Parameters

dwPos   The byte offset of the start of the byte range to lock.

dwCount   The number of bytes in the range to lock.

Remarks

Locks a range of bytes in an open file, throwing an exception if the file is already locked. Locking bytes in a file prevents access to those bytes by other processes. You can lock more than one region of a file, but no overlapping regions are allowed.

When you unlock the region, using the **UnlockRange** member function, the byte range must correspond exactly to the region that was previously locked. The **LockRange** function does not merge adjacent regions; if two locked regions are adjacent, you must unlock each region separately.

Note   This function is not available for the **CMemFile**-derived class.

Example

```
//example for CFile::LockRange
extern DWORD dwPos;
extern DWORD dwCount;
extern CFile cfile;
cfile.LockRange( dwPos, dwCount );
```

See Also   **CFile::UnlockRange**

CFile::Open

virtual BOOL Open(LPCTSTR *lpszFileName***, UINT** *nOpenFlags***,
    CFileException*** *pError* = **NULL**);

Return Value

Nonzero if the open was successful; otherwise 0. The *pError* parameter is meaningful only if 0 is returned.

Parameters

lpszFileName   A string that is the path to the desired file. The path can be relative or absolute but cannot contain a network name.

nOpenFlags   A **UINT** that defines the file's sharing and access mode. It specifies the action to take when opening the file. You can combine options by using the bitwise-OR (|) operator. One access permission and one share option are required; the **modeCreate** and **modeNoInherit** modes are optional. See the **CFile** constructor for a list of mode options.

pError   A pointer to an existing file-exception object that will receive the status of a failed operation.

Remarks

Open is designed for use with the default **CFile** constructor. The two functions form a "safe" method for opening a file where a failure is a normal, expected condition.

While the **CFile** constructor will throw an exception in an error condition, **Open** will return **FALSE** for error conditions. **Open** can still initialize a **CFileException** object to describe the error, however. If you don't supply the *pError* parameter, or if you pass **NULL** for *pError*, **Open** will return **FALSE** and not throw a **CFileException**. If you pass a pointer to an existing **CFileException**, and **Open** encounters an error, the function will fill it with information describing that error. In neither case will **Open** throw an exception.

The following table describes the possible results of **Open**.

pError	Error encountered?	Return value	CFileException content
NULL	No	**TRUE**	n/a
ptr to **CFileException**	No	**TRUE**	unchanged
NULL	Yes	**FALSE**	n/a
ptr to **CFileException**	Yes	**FALSE**	initialized to describe error

Example

```
//example for CFile::Open
CFile f;
CFileException e;
char* pFileName = "test.dat";
if( !f.Open( pFileName, CFile::modeCreate | CFile::modeWrite, &e ) )
    {
#ifdef _DEBUG
    afxDump << "File could not be opened " << e.m_cause << "\n";
#endif
    }
```

See Also   **CFile::CFile**, **CFile::Close**

CFile::Read

> **virtual UINT Read(void*** *lpBuf*, **UINT** *nCount* **);**
> **throw(CFileException);**

Return Value

The number of bytes transferred to the buffer. Note that for all **CFile** classes, the return value may be less than *nCount* if the end of file was reached.

Parameters

lpBuf   Pointer to the user-supplied buffer that is to receive the data read from the file.

nCount   The maximum number of bytes to be read from the file. For text-mode files, carriage return–linefeed pairs are counted as single characters.

Remarks

Reads data into a buffer from the file associated with the **CFile** object.

Example

```
//example for CFile::Read
extern CFile cfile;
char pbuf[100];
UINT nBytesRead = cfile.Read( pbuf, 100 );
```

CFile::ReadHuge

DWORD ReadHuge(void* *lpBuffer*, **DWORD** *dwCount* **);**
   throw(CFileException);

Return Value

The number of bytes transferred to the buffer. Note that for all **CFile** objects, the return value can be less than *dwCount* if the end of file was reached.

Parameters

lpBuf   Pointer to the user-supplied buffer that is to receive the data read from the file.

dwCount   The maximum number of bytes to be read from the file. For text-mode files, carriage return–linefeed pairs are counted as single characters.

Remarks

Reads data into a buffer from the file associated with the **CFile** object.

This function differs from **Read** in that more than 64K–1 bytes of data can be read by **ReadHuge**. This function can be used by any object derived from **CFile**.

Note   ReadHuge is provided only for backward compatiblity. **ReadHuge** and **Read** have the same semantics under Win32.

See Also   CFile::Write, CFile::WriteHuge, CFile::Read

CFile::Remove

static void PASCAL Remove(LPCTSTR *lpszFileName* **);**
   throw(CFileException);

Parameters

lpszFileName   A string that is the path to the desired file. The path can be relative or absolute but cannot contain a network name.

Remarks

This static function deletes the file specified by the path. It will not remove a directory.

The **Remove** member function throws an exception if the connected file is open or if the file cannot be removed. This is equivalent to the DEL command.

Example

```
//example for CFile::Remove
char* pFileName = "test.dat";
TRY
{
    CFile::Remove( pFileName );
}
CATCH( CFileException, e )
```

```
{
#ifdef _DEBUG
    afxDump << "File " << pFileName << " cannot be removed\n";
#endif
}
END_CATCH
```

CFile::Rename

static void PASCAL Rename(LPCTSTR *lpszOldName***, LPCTSTR** *lpszNewName* **);**
   throw(CFileException);

Parameters

lpszOldName   The old path.

lpszNewName   The new path.

Remarks

This static function renames the specified file. Directories cannot be renamed. This is equivalent to the REN command.

Example

```
//example for CFile::Rename
extern char* pOldName;
extern char* pNewName;
TRY
{
    CFile::Rename( pOldName, pNewName );
}
CATCH( CFileException, e )
{
#ifdef _DEBUG
    afxDump << "File " << pOldName << " not found, cause = "
        << e->m_cause << "\n";
#endif
}
END_CATCH
```

CFile::Seek

virtual LONG Seek(LONG *lOff***, UINT** *nFrom* **);**
   throw(CFileException);

Return Value

If the requested position is legal, **Seek** returns the new byte offset from the beginning of the file. Otherwise, the return value is undefined and a **CFileException** object is thrown.

Parameters

lOff   Number of bytes to move the pointer.

nFrom Pointer movement mode. Must be one of the following values:

- **CFile::begin** Move the file pointer *lOff* bytes forward from the beginning of the file.

- **CFile::current** Move the file pointer *lOff* bytes from the current position in the file.

- **CFile::end** Move the file pointer *lOff* bytes from the end of the file. Note that *lOff* must be negative to seek into the existing file; positive values will seek past the end of the file.

Remarks

Repositions the pointer in a previously opened file. The **Seek** function permits random access to a file's contents by moving the pointer a specified amount, absolutely or relatively. No data is actually read during the seek.

When a file is opened, the file pointer is positioned at offset 0, the beginning of the file.

Example

```
//example for CFile::Seek
extern CFile cfile;
LONG lOffset = 1000, lActual;
lActual = cfile.Seek( lOffset, CFile::begin );
```

CFile::SeekToBegin

void SeekToBegin( );
    throw(CFileException);

Remarks

Sets the value of the file pointer to the beginning of the file. `SeekToBegin()` is equivalent to `Seek( 0L, CFile::begin )`.

Example

```
//example for CFile::SeekToBegin
extern CFile cfile;
cfile.SeekToBegin();
```

CFile::SeekToEnd

DWORD SeekToEnd( );
    throw(CFileException);

Return Value

The length of the file in bytes.

Remarks

Sets the value of the file pointer to the logical end of the file. `SeekToEnd()` is equivalent to `CFile::Seek( 0L, CFile::end )`.

Example

```
//example for CFile::SeekToEnd
extern CFile cfile;
DWORD dwActual = cfile.SeekToEnd();
```

See Also   **CFile::GetLength**, **CFile::Seek**, **CFile::SeekToBegin**

CFile::SetFilePath

virtual void SetFilePath(LPCTSTR *lpszNewName* **);**

Parameters

lpszNewName   Pointer to a string specifying the new path.

Remarks

Call this function to specify the path of the file; for example, if the path of a file is not available when a **CFile** object is constructed, call **SetFilePath** to provide it.

Note   **SetFilePath** does not open the file or create the file; it simply associates the **CFile** object with a path name, which can then be used.

See Also   **CFile::GetFilePath**, **CFile::CFile**

CFile::SetLength

virtual void SetLength(DWORD *dwNewLen* **);**
    throw(CFileException);

Parameters

dwNewLen   Desired length of the file in bytes. This value can be larger or smaller than the current length of the file. The file will be extended or truncated as appropriate.

Remarks

Call this function to change the length of the file.

Note   With **CMemFile**, this function could throw a **CMemoryException** object.

Example

```
//example for CFile::SetLength
extern CFile cfile;
DWORD dwNewLength = 10000;
cfile.SetLength( dwNewLength );
```

CFile::SetStatus

static void SetStatus(LPCTSTR *lpszFileName*, **const CFileStatus&** *status* **);**
   throw(CFileException);

Parameters

lpszFileName A string that is the path to the desired file. The path can be relative or absolute but cannot contain a network name.

status The buffer containing the new status information. Call the **GetStatus** member function to prefill the **CFileStatus** structure with current values, then make changes as required. If a value is 0, then the corresponding status item is not updated. See the **GetStatus** member function for a description of the **CFileStatus** structure.

Remarks

Sets the status of the file associated with this file location.

To set the time, modify the **m_mtime** field of *status*.

Please note that when you make a call to **SetStatus** in an attempt to change only the attributes of the file, and the **m_mtime** member of the file status structure is nonzero, the attributes may also be affected (changing the time stamp may have side effects on the attributes). If you want to only change the attributes of the file, first set the **m_mtime** member of the file status structure to zero and then make a call to **SetStatus**.

Example

```
//example for CFile::SetStatus
char* pFileName = "test.dat";
extern BYTE newAttribute;
CFileStatus status;
CFile::GetStatus( pFileName, status );
status.m_attribute = newAttribute;
CFile::SetStatus( pFileName, status );
```

See Also **CFile::GetStatus**

CFile::UnlockRange

virtual void UnlockRange(DWORD *dwPos*, **DWORD** *dwCount* **);**
   throw(CFileException);

Parameters

dwPos The byte offset of the start of the byte range to unlock.

dwCount The number of bytes in the range to unlock.

Remarks

Unlocks a range of bytes in an open file. See the description of the **LockRange** member function for details.

Note This function is not available for the **CMemFile**-derived class.

Example

```
//example for CFile::UnlockRange
extern DWORD dwPos;
extern DWORD dwCount;
extern CFile cfile;
cfile.UnlockRange( dwPos, dwCount );
```

See Also **CFile::LockRange**

CFile::Write

virtual void Write(const void* *lpBuf*, **UINT** *nCount* **);**
   throw(CFileException);

Parameters

lpBuf   A pointer to the user-supplied buffer that contains the data to be written to the file.

nCount   The number of bytes to be transferred from the buffer. For text-mode files, carriage return–linefeed pairs are counted as single characters.

Remarks

Writes data from a buffer to the file associated with the **CFile** object.

Write throws an exception in response to several conditions, including the disk-full condition.

Example

```
//example for CFile::Write
extern CFile cfile;
char pbuf[100];
cfile.Write( pbuf, 100 );
```

See Also **CFile::Read**, **CStdioFile::WriteString**

CFile::WriteHuge

void WriteHuge(const void* *lpBuf*, **DWORD** *dwCount* **);**
   throw(CFileException);

Parameters

lpBuf   A pointer to the user-supplied buffer that contains the data to be written to the file.

> *dwCount* The number of bytes to be transferred from the buffer. For text-mode files, carriage return–linefeed pairs are counted as single characters.

Remarks

Writes data from a buffer to the file associated with the **CFile** object. **WriteHuge** throws an exception in response to several conditions, including the disk-full condition.

This function differs from **Write** in that more than 64K–1 bytes of data can be written by **WriteHuge**. This function can be used by any object derived from **CFile**.

Note **WriteHuge** is provided only for backward compatiblity. **WriteHuge** and **Write** have the same semantics under Win32.

See Also **CFile::Read**, **CFile::ReadHuge**, **CFile::Write**, **CStdioFile::WriteString**

Data Members

CFile::m_hFile

Remarks

Contains the operating-system file handle for an open file. **m_hFile** is a public variable of type **UINT**. It contains **CFile::hFileNull** (an operating-system-independent empty file indicator) if the handle has not been assigned.

Use of **m_hFile** is not recommended because the member's meaning depends on the derived class. **m_hFile** is made a public member for convenience in supporting nonpolymorphic use of the class.

CFileDialog

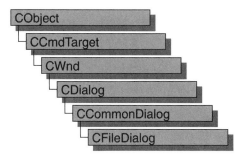

CObject
CCmdTarget
CWnd
CDialog
CCommonDialog
CFileDialog

The **CFileDialog** class encapsulates the Windows common file dialog box. Common file dialog boxes provide an easy way to implement File Open and File Save As dialog boxes (as well as other file-selection dialog boxes) in a manner consistent with Windows standards.

You can use **CFileDialog** "as is" with the constructor provided, or you can derive your own dialog class from **CFileDialog** and write a constructor to suit your needs. In either case, these dialog boxes will behave like standard Microsoft Foundation class dialog boxes because they are derived from the **CCommonDialog** class.

To use a **CFileDialog** object, first create the object using the **CFileDialog** constructor. After the dialog box has been constructed, you can set or modify any values in the **m_ofn** structure to initialize the values or states of the dialog box's controls. The **m_ofn** structure is of type **OPENFILENAME**. For more information, see the **OPENFILENAME** structure in the Win32 SDK documentation.

After initializing the dialog box's controls, call the **DoModal** member function to display the dialog box and allow the user to enter the path and file. **DoModal** returns whether the user selected the OK (**IDOK**) or the Cancel (**IDCANCEL**) button.

If **DoModal** returns **IDOK**, you can use one of **CFileDialog**'s public member functions to retrieve the information input by the user.

CFileDialog includes several protected members that enable you to do custom handling of share violations, filename validation, and list-box change notification. These protected members are callback functions that most applications do not need to use, since default handling is done automatically. Message-map entries for these functions are not necessary because they are standard virtual functions.

You can use the Windows **CommDlgExtendedError** function to determine whether an error occurred during initialization of the dialog box and to learn more about the error.

The destruction of **CFileDialog** objects is handled automatically. It is not necessary to call **CDialog::EndDialog**.

To allow the user to select multiple files, set the **OFN_ALLOWMULTISELECT** flag before calling **DoModal**. You need to supply your own filename buffer to accommodate the returned list of multiple filenames. Do this by replacing **m_ofn.lpstrFile** with a pointer to a buffer you have allocated, after constructing the **CFileDialog**, but before calling **DoModal**.

CFileDialog relies on the COMMDLG.DLL file that ships with Windows versions 3.1 and later.

If you derive a new class from **CFileDialog**, you can use a message map to handle any messages. To extend the default message handling, derive a class from **CWnd**, add a message map to the new class, and provide member functions for the new messages. You do not need to provide a hook function to customize the dialog box.

To customize the dialog box, derive a class from **CFileDialog**, provide a custom dialog template, and add a message map to process the notification messages from the extended controls. Any unprocessed messages should be passed to the base class.

Customizing the hook function is not required.

For more information on using **CFileDialog**, see "Common Dialog Classes" in Chapter 4 of *Programming with MFC*.

#include <afxdlgs.h>

Data Members

m_ofn	The Windows **OPENFILENAME** structure. Provides access to basic file dialog box parameters.

Construction

CFileDialog	Constructs a **CFileDialog** object.

Operations

DoModal	Displays the dialog box and allows the user to make a selection.
GetPathName	Returns the full path of the selected file.
GetFileName	Returns the filename of the selected file.
GetFileExt	Returns the file extension of the selected file.
GetFileTitle	Returns the title of the selected file.
GetNextPathName	Returns the full path of the next selected file.
GetReadOnlyPref	Returns the read-only status of the selected file.
GetStartPosition	Returns the position of the first element of the filename list.

Overridables

OnShareViolation	Called when a share violation occurs.
OnFileNameOK	Called to validate the filename entered in the dialog box.
OnLBSelChangedNotify	Called when the list box selection changes.

Member Functions

CFileDialog::CFileDialog

CFileDialog(BOOL *bOpenFileDialog*, **LPCTSTR** *lpszDefExt* = **NULL, LPCTSTR** *lpszFileName* = **NULL, DWORD** *dwFlags* = **OFN_HIDEREADONLY | OFN_OVERWRITEPROMPT, LPCTSTR** *lpszFilter* = **NULL, CWnd*** *pParentWnd* = **NULL);**

Parameters

bOpenFileDialog   Set to **TRUE** to construct a File Open dialog box or **FALSE** to construct a File Save As dialog box.

lpszDefExt   The default filename extension. If the user does not include an extension in the Filename edit box, the extension specified by *lpszDefExt* is automatically appended to the filename. If this parameter is **NULL**, no file extension is appended.

lpszFileName   The initial filename that appears in the filename edit box. If **NULL**, no filename initially appears.

dwFlags   A combination of one or more flags that allow you to customize the dialog box. For a description of these flags, see the **OPENFILENAME** structure in the Win32 SDK documentation. If you modify the **m_ofn.Flags** structure member, use a bitwise-OR operator in your changes to keep the default behavior intact.

lpszFilter   A series of string pairs that specify filters you can apply to the file. If you specify file filters, only selected files will appear in the Files list box. See the "Remarks" section for more information on how to work with file filters.

pParentWnd   A pointer to the file dialog-box object's parent or owner window.

Remarks

Call this function to construct a standard Windows file dialog box-object. Either a File Open or File Save As dialog box is constructed, depending on the value of *bOpenFileDialog*.

The *lpszFilter* parameter is used to determine the type of filename a file must have to be displayed in the file list box. The first string in the string pair describes the filter; the second string indicates the file extension to use. Multiple extensions may be specified using ';' as the delimiter. The string ends with two 'I' characters, followed by a **NULL** character. You can also use a **CString** object for this parameter.

For example, Microsoft Excel permits users to open files with extensions .XLC (chart) or .XLS (worksheet), among others. The filter for Excel could be written as:

```
static char BASED_CODE szFilter[] = "Chart Files (*.xlc) | *.xlc | Worksheet Files
(*.xls) | *.xls | Data Files (*.xlc;*.xls) | *.xlc; *.xls | All Files (*.*) | *.* ||"
```

See Also   **CFileDialog::DoModal, ::GetOpenFileName, ::GetSaveFileName**

CFileDialog::DoModal

virtual int DoModal( );

Return Value

IDOK or **IDCANCEL** if the function is successful; otherwise 0. **IDOK** and **IDCANCEL** are constants that indicate whether the user selected the OK or Cancel button.

If **IDCANCEL** is returned, you can call the Windows **CommDlgExtendedError** function to determine whether an error occurred.

Remarks

Call this function to display the Windows common file dialog box and allow the user to browse files and directories and enter a filename.

If you want to initialize the various file dialog-box options by setting members of the **m_ofn** structure, you should do this before calling **DoModal**, but after the dialog object is constructed.

When the user clicks the dialog box's OK or Cancel buttons, or selects the Close option from the dialog box's control menu, control is returned to your application. You can then call other member functions to retrieve the settings or information the user inputs into the dialog box.

DoModal is a virtual function overridden from class **CDialog**.

See Also   **CDialog::DoModal, CFileDialog::CFileDialog**

CFileDialog::GetFileExt

CString GetFileExt( ) const;

Return Value

The extension of the filename.

Remarks

Call this function to retrieve the extension of the filename entered into the dialog box. For example, if the name of the file entered is DATA.TXT, **GetFileExt** returns "TXT".

If **m_ofn.Flags** has the **OFN_ALLOWMULTISELECT** flag set, this string contains a sequence of null-terminated strings, with the first string being the directory path of the file group selected, followed by the names of all files selected by the user. To retrieve file pathnames, use the **GetStartPosition** and **GetNextPathName** member functions.

See Also   **CFileDialog::GetPathName**, **CFileDialog::GetFileName**, **CFileDialog::GetFileTitle**

CFileDialog::GetFileName

    CString GetFileName( ) const;

Return Value

The name of the file.

Remarks

Call this function to retrieve the name of the file entered in the dialog box. The name of the file includes only its prefix, without the path or the extension. For example, **GetFileName** will return "TEXT" for the file C:\FILES\TEXT.DAT.

If **m_ofn.Flags** has the **OFN_ALLOWMULTISELECT** flag set, you should call **GetNextPathName** to retrieve a file pathname.

See Also   **CFileDialog::GetPathName**, **GetStartPosition**, **CFileDialog::GetFileTitle**

CFileDialog::GetFileTitle

    CString GetFileTitle( ) const;

Return Value

The title of the file.

Remarks

Call this function to retrieve the title of the filename entered in the dialog box. The title of the filename includes both the name and the extension. For example, **GetFileTitle** will return "TEXT.DAT" for the file C:\FILES\TEXT.DAT.

If **m_ofn.Flags** has the **OFN_ALLOWMULTISELECT** flag set, this string contains a sequence of null-teminated strings, with the first string being the directory path of the file group selected, followed by the names of all files selected by the user. For this reason, use the **GetStartPosition** and **GetNextPathName** member functions to retrieve the next file name in the list.

See Also   **CFileDialog::GetPathName**, **CFileDialog::GetFileName**, **CFileDialog::GetFileExt**, **::GetFileTitle**

CFileDialog::GetNextPathName

CString GetNextPathName(POSITION& *pos* **) const;**

Parameters

pos   A reference to a **POSITION** value returned by a previous **GetNextPathName** or **GetStartPosition** function call. **NULL** if the end of the list has been reached.

Return Value

The full path of the file.

Remarks

Call this function to retrieve the next filename from the group selected in the dialog box. The path of the filename includes the file's title plus the entire directory path. For example, **GetNextPathName** will return "C:\FILES\TEXT.DAT" for the file C:\FILES\TEXT.DAT. You can use **GetNextPathName** in a forward iteration loop if you establish the initial position with a call to **GetStartPosition**.

If the selection consists of only one file, that file name will be returned.

See Also   **CFileDialog::GetFileName, CFileDialog::GetStartPosition**

CFileDialog::GetPathName

CString GetPathName( ) const;

Return Value

The full path of the file.

Remarks

Call this function to retrieve the full path of the file entered in the dialog box. The path of the filename includes the file's title plus the entire directory path. For example, **GetPathName** will return "C:\FILES\TEXT.DAT" for the file C:\FILES\TEXT.DAT.

If **m_ofn.Flags** has the **OFN_ALLOWMULTISELECT** flag set, this string contains a sequence of null-teminated strings, with the first string being the directory path of the file group selected, followed by the names of all files selected by the user. For this reason, use the **GetStartPosition** and **GetNextPathName** member functions to retrieve the next file name in the list.

See Also   **CFileDialog::GetFileName, CFileDialog::GetFileExt, CFileDialog::GetFileTitle**

CFileDialog::GetReadOnlyPref

BOOL GetReadOnlyPref( ) const;

Return Value

Non-zero if the Read Only check box in the dialog box is selected; otherwise 0.

Remarks

Call this function to determine whether the Read Only check box has been selected in the Windows standard File Open and File Save As dialog boxes. The Read Only check box can be hidden by setting the **OFN_HIDEREADONLY** style in the **CFileDialog** constructor.

See Also **CFileDialog::CFileDialog, CFileDialog::GetPathName, CFileDialog::GetFileExt**

CFileDialog::GetStartPosition

POSITION GetStartPosition( ) const;

Return Value

A **POSITION** value that can be used for iteration; **NULL** if the list is empty.

Remarks

Call this function to retrieve the position of the first file path name in the list, if **m_ofn.Flags** has the **OFN_ALLOWMULTISELECT** flag set.

If the selection consists of only one file, that filename will be returned.

See Also **CFileDialog::GetFileName, CFileDialog::GetNextPathName, CFileDialog::GetStartPosition**

CFileDialog::OnFileNameOK

virtual BOOL OnFileNameOK( );

Return Value

Nonzero if the filename is not a valid filename; otherwise 0.

Remarks

Override this function only if you want to provide custom validation of filenames that are entered into a common file dialog box. This function allows you to reject a filename for any application-specific reason. Normally, you do not need to use this function because the framework provides default validation of filenames and displays a message box if an invalid filename is entered.

If a nonzero value is returned, the dialog box will remain displayed for the user to enter another filename.

See Also **OPENFILENAME**

CFileDialog::OnLBSelChangedNotify

virtual void OnLBSelChangedNotify(UINT *nIDBox***, UINT** *iCurSel***, UINT** *nCode***);**

Parameters

nIDBox   The ID of the list box or combo box in which the selection occurred.

iCurSel   The index of the current selection.

nCode   The control notification code. This parameter must have one of the following values:

- **CD_LBSELCHANGE**   Specifies *iCurSel* is the selected item in a single-selection list box.

- **CD_LBSELSUB**   Specifies that *iCurSel* is no longer selected in a multiselection list box.

- **CD_LBSELADD**   Specifies that *iCurSel* is selected in a multiselection list box.

- **CD_LBSELNOITEMS**   Specifies that no selection exists in a multiselection list box.

For more information, see "About Common Dialog Boxes" in the Win32 SDK documentation.

Remarks

This function is called whenever the current selection in a list box is about to change. Override this function to provide custom handling of selection changes in the list box. For example, you can use this function to display the access rights or date-last-modified of each file the user selects.

CFileDialog::OnShareViolation

virtual UINT OnShareViolation(LPCTSTR *lpszPathName* **);**

Return Value

One of the following values:

- **OFN_SHAREFALLTHROUGH**   The filename is returned from the dialog box.

- **OFN_SHARENOWARN**   No further action needs to be taken.

- **OFN_SHAREWARN**   The user receives the standard warning message for this error.

Parameters

lpszPathName   The path of the file on which the share violation occurred.

Remarks

Override this function to provide custom handling of share violations. Normally, you do not need to use this function because the framework provides default checking of share violations and displays a message box if a share violation occurs.

If you want to disable share violation checking, use the bitwise OR operator to combine the flag **OFN_SHAREAWARE** with **m_ofn.Flags**.

See Also   **CFileDialog::OnFileNameOK**

Data Members

CFileDialog::m_ofn

Remarks

m_ofn is a structure of type **OPENFILENAME**. Use this structure to initialize the appearance of a File Open or File Save As dialog box after it is constructed but before it is displayed with the **DoModal** member function. For example, you can set the **lpszTitle** member of **m_ofn** to the caption you want the dialog box to have.

For more information, see the **OPENFILENAME** structure in the Win32 SDK documentation.

CFileException

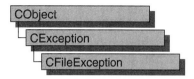

A **CFileException** object represents a file-related exception condition. The **CFileException** class includes public data members that hold the portable cause code and the operating-system-specific error number. The class also provides static member functions for throwing file exceptions and for returning cause codes for both operating-system errors and C run-time errors.

CFileException objects are constructed and thrown in **CFile** member functions and in member functions of derived classes. You can access these objects within the scope of a **CATCH** expression. For portability, use only the cause code to get the reason for an exception. For more information about exceptions, see the article "Exceptions" in *Programming with MFC*.

#include <afx.h>

See Also   "Exception Processing"

Data Members

m_cause	Contains portable code corresponding to the exception cause.
m_lOsError	Contains the related operating-system error number.

Construction

CFileException	Constructs a **CFileException** object.

Code Conversion

OsErrorToException	Returns a cause code corresponding to an operating system error code.
ErrnoToException	Returns cause code corresponding to a run-time error number.

Helper Functions

ThrowOsError	Throws a file exception based on an operating-system error number.
ThrowErrno	Throws a file exception based on a run-time error number.

Member Functions

CFileException::CFileException

> **CFileException(int** *cause* **= CFileException::none, LONG** *lOsError* **= –1);**

Parameters

> *cause*   An enumerated type variable that indicates the reason for the exception.
> See **CFileException::m_cause** for a list of the possible values.

> *lOsError*   An operating-system-specific reason for the exception, if available.
> The *lOsError* parameter provides more information than *cause* does.

Remarks

> Constructs a **CFileException** object that stores the cause code and the operating-system code in the object.

> Do not use this constructor directly, but rather call the global function
> **AfxThrowFileException**.

> **Note**   The variable *lOsError* applies only to **CFile** and **CStdioFile** objects. The **CMemFile** class does not handle this error code.

> **See Also**   **AfxThrowFileException**

CFileException::ErrnoToException

> **static int PASCAL ErrnoToException(int** *nErrno* **);**

Return Value

> Enumerated value that corresponds to a given run-time library error value.

Parameters

> *nErrno*   An integer error code as defined in the run-time include file ERRNO.H.

Remarks

> Converts a given run-time library error value to a **CFileException** enumerated error value. See **CFileException::m_cause** for a list of the possible enumerated values.

Example

```
//example for CFileException::ErrnoToException
#include <errno.h>
ASSERT( CFileException::ErrnoToException( EACCES ) ==
                 CFileException::accessDenied );
```

> **See Also**   **CFileException::OsErrorToException**

CFileException::OsErrorToException

static int PASCAL OsErrorToException(LONG *lOsError* **);**

Return Value

Enumerated value that corresponds to a given operating-system error value.

Parameters

lOsError   An operating-system-specific error code.

Remarks

Returns an enumerator that corresponds to a given *lOsError* value. If the error code is unknown, then the function returns **CFileException::generic**.

Example

```
//example for CFileException::OsErrorToException
ASSERT( CFileException::OsErrorToException( 5 ) ==
                CFileException::accessDenied );
```

See Also   **CFileException::ErrnoToException**

CFileException::ThrowErrno

static void PASCAL ThrowErrno(int *nErrno* **);**

Parameters

nErrno   An integer error code as defined in the run-time include file ERRNO.H.

Remarks

Constructs a **CFileException** object corresponding to a given *nErrno* value, then throws the exception.

Example

```
//example for CFileException::ThrowErrno
#include <errno.h>
CFileException::ThrowErrno( EACCES );  // "access denied"
```

See Also   **CFileException::ThrowOsError**

CFileException::ThrowOsError

static void PASCAL ThrowOsError(LONG *lOsError* **);**

Parameters

lOsError   An operating-system-specific error code.

Remarks

Throws a **CFileException** corresponding to a given *lOsError* value. If the error code is unknown, then the function throws an exception coded as **CFileException::generic**.

Example

```
//example for CFileException::ThrowOsError
FileException::ThrowOsError( 5 );  // "access denied"
```

See Also **CFileException::ThrowErrno**

Data Members

CFileException::m_cause

Remarks

Contains values defined by a **CFileException** enumerated type. This data member is a public variable of type **int**. The enumerators and their meanings are as follows:

- **CFileException::none**   No error occurred.
- **CFileException::generic**   An unspecified error occurred.
- **CFileException::fileNotFound**   The file could not be located.
- **CFileException::badPath**   All or part of the path is invalid.
- **CFileException::tooManyOpenFiles**   The permitted number of open files was exceeded.
- **CFileException::accessDenied**   The file could not be accessed.
- **CFileException::invalidFile**   There was an attempt to use an invalid file handle.
- **CFileException::removeCurrentDir**   The current working directory cannot be removed.
- **CFileException::directoryFull**   There are no more directory entries.
- **CFileException::badSeek**   There was an error trying to set the file pointer.
- **CFileException::hardIO**   There was a hardware error.
- **CFileException::sharingViolation**   SHARE.EXE was not loaded, or a shared region was locked.
- **CFileException::lockViolation**   There was an attempt to lock a region that was already locked.
- **CFileException::diskFull**   The disk is full.
- **CFileException::endOfFile**   The end of file was reached.

Note   These **CFileException** cause enumerators are distinct from the **CArchiveException** cause enumerators.

Example

```
//example for CFileException::m_cause
extern char* pFileName;
TRY
{
    CFile f( pFileName, CFile::modeCreate | CFile::modeWrite );
}
CATCH( CFileException, e)
{
    if( e->m_cause == CFileException::fileNotFound )
        printf( "ERROR: File not found\n");
}
```

CFileException::m_lOsError

Remarks

Contains the operating-system error code for this exception. See your operating-system technical manual for a listing of error codes. This data member is a public variable of type **LONG**.

CFindReplaceDialog

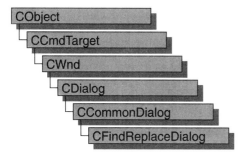

The **CFindReplaceDialog** class allows you to implement standard string Find/Replace dialog boxes in your application. Unlike the other Windows common dialog boxes, **CFindReplaceDialog** objects are modeless, allowing users to interact with other windows while they are on screen. There are two kinds of **CFindReplaceDialog** objects: Find dialog boxes and Find/Replace dialog boxes. Although the dialog boxes allow the user to input search and search/replace strings, they do not perform any of the searching or replacing functions. You must add these to the application.

To construct a **CFindReplaceDialog** object, use the provided constructor (which has no arguments). Since this is a modeless dialog box, allocate the object on the heap using the **new** operator, rather than on the stack.

Once a **CFindReplaceDialog** object has been constructed, you must call the **Create** member function to create and display the dialog box.

Use the **m_fr** structure to initialize the dialog box before calling **Create**. The **m_fr** structure is of type **FINDREPLACE**. For more information on this structure, see the Win32 SDK documentation.

In order for the parent window to be notified of find/replace requests, you must use the Windows **RegisterMessage** function and use the **ON_REGISTERED_MESSAGE** message-map macro in your frame window that handles this registered message. You can call any of the member functions listed in the "Operations" section in the table below from the frame window's callback function.

You can determine whether the user has decided to terminate the dialog box with the **IsTerminating** member function.

CFindReplaceDialog relies on the COMMDLG.DLL file that ships with Windows versions 3.1 and later.

To customize the dialog box, derive a class from **CFindReplaceDialog**, provide a custom dialog template, and add a message map to process the notification messages from the extended controls. Any unprocessed messages should be passed to the base class.

Customizing the hook function is not required.

For more information on using **CFindReplaceDialog**, see "Common Dialog Classes" in Chapter 4 of *Programming with MFC*.

#include <afxdlgs.h>

Data Members

m_fr	A structure used to customize a **CFindReplaceDialog** object.

Construction

CFindReplaceDialog	Call this function to construct a **CFindReplaceDialog** object.
Create	Creates and displays a **CFindReplaceDialog** dialog box.

Operations

FindNext	Call this function to determine whether the user wants to find the next occurrence of the find string.
GetNotifier	Call this function to retrieve the **FINDREPLACE** structure in your registered message handler.
GetFindString	Call this function to retrieve the current find string.
GetReplaceString	Call this function to retrieve the current replace string.
IsTerminating	Call this function to determine whether the dialog box is terminating.
MatchCase	Call this function to determine whether the user wants to match the case of the find string exactly.
MatchWholeWord	Call this function to determine whether the user wants to match entire words only.
ReplaceAll	Call this function to determine whether the user wants all occurrences of the string to be replaced.
ReplaceCurrent	Call this function to determine whether the user wants the current word to be replaced.
SearchDown	Call this function to determine whether the user wants the search to proceed in a downward direction.

Member Functions

CFindReplaceDialog::CFindReplaceDialog

CFindReplaceDialog( );

Remarks

Constructs a **CFindReplaceDialog** object. **CFindReplaceDialog** objects are constructed on the heap with the **new** operator. For more information on the construction of **CFindReplaceDialog** objects, see the **CFindReplaceDialog** overview. Use the **Create** member function to display the dialog box.

See Also   CFindReplaceDialog::Create

CFindReplaceDialog::Create

BOOL Create(BOOL *bFindDialogOnly*, **LPCTSTR** *lpszFindWhat*, **LPCTSTR** *lpszReplaceWith* = **NULL, DWORD** *dwFlags* = **FR_DOWN, CWnd*** *pParentWnd* = **NULL);**

Return Value

Nonzero if the dialog box object was successfully created; otherwise 0.

Parameters

bFindDialogOnly   Set this parameter to **TRUE** to display the standard Windows Find dialog box. Set it to **FALSE** to display the Windows Find/Replace dialog box.

lpszFindWhat   Specifies the string for which to search.

lpszReplaceWith   Specifies the default string with which to replace found strings.

dwFlags   One or more flags you can use to customize the settings of the dialog box, combined using the bitwise OR operator. The default value is **FR_DOWN**, which specifies that the search is to proceed in a downward direction. See the **FINDREPLACE** structure in the Win32 SDK documentation for more information on these flags.

pParentWnd   A pointer to the dialog box's parent or owner window. This is the window that will receive the special message indicating that a find/replace action is requested. If **NULL**, the application's main window is used.

Remarks

Creates and displays either a Find or Find/Replace dialog box object, depending on the value of *bFindDialogOnly*.

In order for the parent window to be notified of find/replace requests, you must use the Windows **RegisterMessage** function whose return value is a message number unique to the application's instance. Your frame window should have a message map entry that declares the callback function (**OnFindReplace** in the example that follows) that handles this registered message. The following code fragment is an example of how to do this for a frame window class named CMyFrameWnd:

```
class CMyFrameWnd : public CFrameWnd
{
protected:
    afx_msg LONG LRESULT OnFindReplace(WPARAM wParam, LPARAM lParam);

    DECLARE_MESSAGE_MAP()
};
static UINT WM_FINREPLACE = ::RegisterMessage(FINDMSGSTRING);

BEGIN_MESSAGE_MAP( CMyFrameWnd, CFrameWnd )
    //Normal message map entries here.
    ON_REGISTERED_MESSAGE( WM_FINDREPLACE, OnFindReplace )
END_MESSAGE_MAP
```

Within your **OnFindReplace** function, you interpret the intentions of the user and create the code for the find/replace operations.

See Also **CFindReplaceDialog::CFindReplaceDialog**

CFindReplaceDialog::FindNext

BOOL FindNext( ) const;

Return Value

Nonzero if the user wants to find the next occurrence of the search string; otherwise 0.

Remarks

Call this function from your callback function to determine whether the user wants to find the next occurrence of the search string.

See Also **CFindReplaceDialog::GetFindString**, **CFindReplaceDialog::SearchDown**

CFindReplaceDialog::GetFindString

CString GetFindString( ) const;

Return Value

The default string to find.

Remarks

Call this function from your callback function to retrieve the default string to find.

See Also **CFindReplaceDialog::FindNext**, **CFindReplaceDialog::GetReplaceString**

CFindReplaceDialog::GetNotifier

static CFindReplaceDialog* PASCAL GetNotifier(LPARAM *lParam* **);**

Return Value

A pointer to the current dialog box.

Parameters

lParam   The **lparam** value passed to the frame window's **OnFindReplace** member function.

Remarks

Call this function to retrieve a pointer to the current Find Replace dialog box. It should be used within your callback function to access the current dialog box, call its member functions, and access the **m_fr** structure.

CFindReplaceDialog::GetReplaceString

CString GetReplaceString( ) const;

Return Value

The default string with which to replace found strings.

Remarks

Call this function to retrieve the current replace string.

See Also   **CFindReplaceDialog::GetFindString**

CFindReplaceDialog::IsTerminating

BOOL IsTerminating( ) const;

Return Value

Nonzero if the user has decided to terminate the dialog box; otherwise 0.

Remarks

Call this function within your callback function to determine whether the user has decided to terminate the dialog box. If this function returns nonzero, you should call the **DestroyWindow** member function of the current dialog box and set any dialog box pointer variable to **NULL**. Optionally, you can also store the find/replace text last entered and use it to initialize the next find/replace dialog box.

CFindReplaceDialog::MatchCase

BOOL MatchCase( ) const;

Return Value

Nonzero if the user wants to find occurrences of the search string that exactly match the case of the search string; otherwise 0.

Remarks

Call this function to determine whether the user wants to match the case of the find string exactly.

See Also   **CFindReplaceDialog::MatchWholeWord**

CFindReplaceDialog::MatchWholeWord

BOOL MatchWholeWord( ) const;

Return Value

Nonzero if the user wants to match only the entire words of the search string; otherwise 0.

Remarks

Call this function to determine whether the user wants to match entire words only.

See Also   **CFindReplaceDialog::MatchCase**

CFindReplaceDialog::ReplaceAll

BOOL ReplaceAll( ) const;

Return Value

Nonzero if the user has requested that all strings matching the replace string be replaced; otherwise 0.

Remarks

Call this function to determine whether the user wants all occurrences of the string to be replaced.

See Also   **CFindReplaceDialog::ReplaceCurrent**

CFindReplaceDialog::ReplaceCurrent

BOOL ReplaceCurrent( ) const;

Return Value

Nonzero if the user has requested that the currently selected string be replaced with the replace string; otherwise 0.

Remarks

Call this function to determine whether the user wants the current word to be replaced.

See Also   **CFindReplaceDialog::ReplaceAll**

CFindReplaceDialog::SearchDown

BOOL SearchDown( ) const;

Return Value

Nonzero if the user wants the search to proceed in a downward direction; 0 if the user wants the search to proceed in an upward direction.

Remarks

Call this function to determine whether the user wants the search to proceed in a downward direction.

Data Members

CFindReplaceDialog::m_fr

Remarks

m_fr is a structure of type **FINDREPLACE**. Its members store the characteristics of the dialog-box object. After constructing a **CFindReplaceDialog** object, you can use **m_fr** to modify various values in the dialog box.

For more information on this structure, see the **FINDREPLACE** structure in the Win32 SDK documentation.

CFont

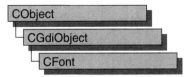

The **CFont** class encapsulates a Windows graphics device interface (GDI) font and provides member functions for manipulating the font. To use a **CFont** object, construct a **CFont** object and attach a Windows font to it with **CreateFont**, **CreateFontIndirect**, **CreatePointFont**, or **CreatePointFontIndirect**, and then use the object's member functions to manipulate the font.

The **CreatePointFont** and **CreatePointFontIndirect** functions are often easier to use than **CreateFont** or **CreateFontIndirect** since they do the conversion for the height of the font from a point size to logical units automatically.

For more information on **CFont**, see "Graphic Objects" in Chapter 1 of *Programming with MFC*.

#include <afxwin.h>

Construction

CFont	Constructs a **CFont** object.

Initialization

CreateFontIndirect	Initializes a **CFont** object with the characteristics given in a **LOGFONT** structure.
CreateFont	Initializes a **CFont** with the specified characteristics.
CreatePointFont	Initializes a **CFont** with the specified height, measured in tenths of a point, and typeface.
CreatePointFontIndirect	Same as **CreateFontIndirect** except that the font height is measured in tenths of a point rather than logical units.

Operations

FromHandle	Returns a pointer to a **CFont** object when given a Windows **HFONT**.

Attributes

operator HFONT	Returns the Windows GDI font handle attached to the **CFont** object.
GetLogFont	Fills a **LOGFONT** with information about the logical font attached to the **CFont** object.

Member Functions

CFont::CFont

CFont( );

Remarks

Constructs a **CFont** object. The resulting object must be initialized with **CreateFont**, **CreateFontIndirect**, **CreatePointFont**, or **CreatePointFontIndirect** before it can be used.

See Also   CFont::CreateFontIndirect, CFont::CreateFont, CFont::CreatePointFont, CFont::CreatePointFontIndirect, ::EnumFonts

---

CFont::CreateFont

BOOL CreateFont(int *nHeight,* **int** *nWidth,* **int** *nEscapement,* **int** *nOrientation,* **int** *nWeight,* **BYTE** *bItalic,* **BYTE** *bUnderline,* **BYTE** *cStrikeOut,* **BYTE** *nCharSet,* **BYTE** *nOutPrecision,* **BYTE** *nClipPrecision,* **BYTE** *nQuality,* **BYTE** *nPitchAndFamily,* **LPCTSTR** *lpszFacename* **);**

Return Value

Nonzero if successful; otherwise 0.

Parameters

nHeight   Specifies the desired height (in logical units) of the font. The font height can be specified in the following ways:

- Greater than 0, in which case the height is transformed into device units and matched against the cell height of the available fonts.

- Equal to 0, in which case a reasonable default size is used.

- Less than 0, in which case the height is transformed into device units and the absolute value is matched against the character height of the available fonts.

The absolute value of *nHeight* must not exceed 16,384 device units after it is converted. For all height comparisons, the font mapper looks for the largest font that does not exceed the requested size or the smallest font if all the fonts exceed the requested size.

nWidth   Specifies the average width (in logical units) of characters in the font. If *nWidth* is 0, the aspect ratio of the device will be matched against the digitization aspect ratio of the available fonts to find the closest match, which is determined by the absolute value of the difference.

nEscapement   Specifies the angle (in 0.1-degree units) between the escapement vector and the x-axis of the display surface. The escapement vector is the line through the origins of the first and last characters on a line. The angle is measured counterclockwise from the x-axis.

nOrientation   Specifies the angle (in 0.1-degree units) between the baseline of a character and the x-axis. The angle is measured counterclockwise from the x-axis for coordinate systems in which the y-direction is down and clockwise from the x-axis for coordinate systems in which the y-direction is up.

nWeight   Specifies the font weight (in inked pixels per 1000). Although *nWeight* can be any integer value from 0 to 1000, the common constants and values are as follows:

Constant	Value
FW_DONTCARE	0
FW_THIN	100
FW_EXTRALIGHT	200
FW_ULTRALIGHT	200
FW_LIGHT	300
FW_NORMAL	400
FW_REGULAR	400
FW_MEDIUM	500
FW_SEMIBOLD	600
FW_DEMIBOLD	600
FW_BOLD	700
FW_EXTRABOLD	800
FW_ULTRABOLD	800
FW_BLACK	900
FW_HEAVY	900

These values are approximate; the actual appearance depends on the typeface. Some fonts have only **FW_NORMAL**, **FW_REGULAR**, and **FW_BOLD** weights. If **FW_DONTCARE** is specified, a default weight is used.

bItalic   Specifies whether the font is italic.

bUnderline   Specifies whether the font is underlined.

cStrikeOut   Specifies whether characters in the font are struck out. Specifies a strikeout font if set to a nonzero value.

nCharSet   Specifies the font's character set. The following constants and values are predefined:

Constant	Value
ANSI_CHARSET	0
DEFAULT_CHARSET	1
SYMBOL_CHARSET	2
SHIFTJIS_CHARSET	128
OEM_CHARSET	255

The OEM character set is system-dependent.

Fonts with other character sets may exist in the system. An application that uses a font with an unknown character set must not attempt to translate or interpret strings that are to be rendered with that font. Instead, the strings should be passed directly to the output device driver.

The font mapper does not use the **DEFAULT_CHARSET** value. An application can use this value to allow the name and size of a font to fully describe the logical font. If a font with the specified name does not exist, a font from any character set can be substituted for the specified font. To avoid unexpected results, applications should use the **DEFAULT_CHARSET** value sparingly.

nOutPrecision   Specifies the desired output precision. The output precision defines how closely the output must match the requested font's height, width, character orientation, escapement, and pitch. It can be any one of the following values:

OUT_CHARACTER_PRECIS	**OUT_STRING_PRECIS**
OUT_DEFAULT_PRECIS	**OUT_STROKE_PRECIS**
OUT_DEVICE_PRECIS	**OUT_TT_PRECIS**
OUT_RASTER_PRECIS	

Applications can use the **OUT_DEVICE_PRECIS**, **OUT_RASTER_PRECIS**, and **OUT_TT_PRECIS** values to control how the font mapper chooses a font when the system contains more than one font with a given name. For example, if a system contains a font named Symbol in raster and TrueType form, specifying **OUT_TT_PRECIS** forces the font mapper to choose the TrueType version. (Specifying **OUT_TT_PRECIS** forces the font mapper to choose a TrueType font whenever the specified font name matches a device or raster font, even when there is no TrueType font of the same name.)

nClipPrecision   Specifies the desired clipping precision. The clipping precision defines how to clip characters that are partially outside the clipping region. It can be any one of the following values:

CLIP_CHARACTER_PRECIS	CLIP_MASK
CLIP_DEFAULT_PRECIS	CLIP_STROKE_PRECIS
CLIP_ENCAPSULATE	CLIP_TT_ALWAYS
CLIP_LH_ANGLES	

To use an embedded read-only font, an application must specify **CLIP_ENCAPSULATE**.

To achieve consistent rotation of device, TrueType, and vector fonts, an application can use the OR operator to combine the **CLIP_LH_ANGLES** value with any of the other *nClipPrecision* values. If the **CLIP_LH_ANGLES** bit is set, the rotation for all fonts depends on whether the orientation of the coordinate system is left-handed or right-handed. (For more information about the orientation of coordinate systems, see the description of the nOrientation parameter.) If **CLIP_LH_ANGLES** is not set, device fonts always rotate counterclockwise, but the rotation of other fonts is dependent on the orientation of the coordinate system.

nQuality Specifies the font's output quality, which defines how carefully the GDI must attempt to match the logical-font attributes to those of an actual physical font. It can be one of the following values:

- **DEFAULT_QUALITY** Appearance of the font does not matter.

- **DRAFT_QUALITY** Appearance of the font is less important than when **PROOF_QUALITY** is used. For GDI raster fonts, scaling is enabled. Bold, italic, underline, and strikeout fonts are synthesized if necessary.

- **PROOF_QUALITY** Character quality of the font is more important than exact matching of the logical-font attributes. For GDI raster fonts, scaling is disabled and the font closest in size is chosen. Bold, italic, underline, and strikeout fonts are synthesized if necessary.

nPitchAndFamily Specifies the pitch and family of the font. The two low-order bits specify the pitch of the font and can be any one of the following values:

DEFAULT_PITCH VARIABLE_PITCH
FIXED_PITCH

Applications can add **TMPF_TRUETYPE** to the *nPitchAndFamily* parameter to choose a TrueType font. The four high-order bits of the parameter specify the font family and can be any one of the following values:

- **FF_DECORATIVE** Novelty fonts: Old English, for example.

- **FF_DONTCARE** Don't care or don't know.

- **FF_MODERN** Fonts with constant stroke width (fixed-pitch), with or without serifs. Fixed-pitch fonts are usually modern faces. Pica, Elite, and Courier New are examples.

- **FF_ROMAN** Fonts with variable stroke width (proportionally spaced) and with serifs. Times New Roman and Century Schoolbook are examples.

- **FF_SCRIPT** Fonts designed to look like handwriting. Script and Cursive are examples.

- **FF_SWISS** Fonts with variable stroke width (proportionally spaced) and without serifs. MS Sans Serif is an example.

An application can specify a value for *nPitchAndFamily* by using the Boolean OR operator to join a pitch constant with a family constant.

Font families describe the look of a font in a general way. They are intended for specifying fonts when the exact typeface desired is not available.

lpszFacename A **CString** or pointer to a null-terminated string that specifies the typeface name of the font. The length of this string must not exceed 30 characters. The Windows **EnumFontFamilies** function can be used to enumerate all currently available fonts. If *lpszFacename* is **NULL**, the GDI uses a device-independent typeface.

Remarks

Initializes a **CFont** object with the specified characteristics. The font can subsequently be selected as the font for any device context.

The **CreateFont** function does not create a new Windows GDI font. It merely selects the closest match from the fonts available in the GDI's pool of physical fonts.

Applications can use the default settings for most of these parameters when creating a logical font. The parameters that should always be given specific values are *nHeight* and *lpszFacename*. If *nHeight* and *lpszFacename* are not set by the application, the logical font that is created is device-dependent.

When you finish with the **CFont** object created by the **CreateFont** function, first select the font out of the device context, then delete the **CFont** object.

See Also **CFont::CreateFontIndirect**, **CFont::CreatePointFont**, **::CreateFont**, **::EnumFontFamilies**, **::EnumFonts**

CFont::CreateFontIndirect

BOOL CreateFontIndirect(const LOGFONT* *lpLogFont* **);**

Return Value

Nonzero if successful; otherwise 0.

Parameters

lpLogFont Points to a **LOGFONT** structure that defines the characteristics of the logical font.

Remarks

Initializes a **CFont** object with the characteristics given in a **LOGFONT** structure pointed to by *lpLogFont*. The font can subsequently be selected as the current font for any device.

This font has the characteristics specified in the **LOGFONT** structure. When the font is selected by using the **CDC::SelectObject** member function, the GDI's font mapper attempts to match the logical font with an existing physical font. If it fails to find an exact match for the logical font, it provides an alternative whose characteristics match as many of the requested characteristics as possible.

When you finish with the **CFont** object created by the **CreateFontIndirect** function, first select the font out of the device context, then delete the **CFont** object.

See Also   **CFont::CreateFont**, **CFont::CreatePointFontIndirect**, **CDC::SelectObject**, **CGdiObject::DeleteObject**, **::CreateFontIndirect**

CFont::CreatePointFont

BOOL CreatePointFont(int *nPointSize*, **LPCTSTR** *lpszFaceName*, **CDC*** *pDC* **= NULL);**

Return Value

Nonzero if successful, otherwise 0.

Parameters

nPointSize   Requested font height in tenths of a point. (For instance, pass 120 to request a 12-point font.)

lpszFaceName   A **CString** or pointer to a null-terminated string that specifies the typeface name of the font. The length of this string must not exceed 30 characters. The Windows **EnumFontFamilies** function can be used to enumerate all currently available fonts. If *lpszFaceName* is **NULL**, the GDI uses a device-independent typeface.

pDC   Pointer to the **CDC** object to be used to convert the height in *nPointSize* to logical units. If **NULL**, a screen device context is used for the conversion.

Remarks

This function provides a simple way to create a font of a specified typeface and point size. It automatically converts the height in *nPointSize* to logical units using the **CDC** object pointed to by *pDC*.

When you finish with the **CFont** object created by the **CreatePointFont** function, first select the font out of the device context, then delete the **CFont** object.

See Also   **CFont::CreatePointFontIndirect**, **CFont::CreateFont**

CFont::CreatePointFontIndirect

BOOL CreatePointFontIndirect(const LOGFONT* *lpLogFont***, CDC*** *pDC* **= NULL);**

Return Value

Nonzero if successful, otherwise 0.

Parameters

lpLogFont   Points to a **LOGFONT** structure that defines the characteristics of the logical font. The *lfHeight* member of the **LOGFONT** structure is measured in tenths of a point rather than logical units. (For instance, set *lfHeight* to 120 to request a 12 point font.)

pDC   pointer to the **CDC** object to be used to convert the height in *nPointSize* to logical units. If **NULL**, a screen device context is used for the conversion.

Remarks

This function is the same as **CreateFontIndirect** except that the *lfHeight* member of the **LOGFONT** is interpreted in tenths of a point rather than device units. This function automatically converts the height in *lfHeight* to logical units using the **CDC** object pointed to by *pDC* before passing the **LOGFONT** structure on to Windows.

When you finish with the **CFont** object created by the **CreatePointFontIndirect** function, first select the font out of the device context, then delete the **CFont** object.

See Also   **CFont::CreatePointFont**, **CFont::CreateFontIndirect**

CFont::FromHandle

static CFont* PASCAL FromHandle(HFONT *hFont* **);**

Return Value

A pointer to a **CFont** object if successful; otherwise **NULL**.

Parameters

hFont   An **HFONT** handle to a Windows font.

Remarks

Returns a pointer to a **CFont** object when given an **HFONT** handle to a Windows GDI font object. If a **CFont** object is not already attached to the handle, a temporary **CFont** object is created and attached. This temporary **CFont** object is valid only until the next time the application has idle time in its event loop, at which time all temporary graphic objects are deleted. Another way of saying this is that the temporary object is valid only during the processing of one window message.

CFont::GetLogFont

int GetLogFont(LOGFONT * *pLogFont*);

Return Value

Nonzero if the function succeeds, otherwise 0.

Parameters

pLogFont   Pointer to the **LOGFONT** structure to receive the font information.

Remarks

Call this function to retrieve a copy of the **LOGFONT** structure for **CFont**.

See Also   LOGFONT, ::GetObject

CFont::operator HFONT

operator HFONT( ) const;

Return Value

The handle of the Windows GDI font object attached to **CFont** if successful; otherwise **NULL**.

Remarks

Use this operator to get the Windows GDI handle of the font attached to the **CFont** object.

Since this operator is automatically used for conversions from **CFont** to **Fonts and Text**, you can pass **CFont** objects to functions that expect **HFONT**s.

For more information about using graphic objects, see "Graphic Objects" in the Win32 SDK documentation.

CFontDialog

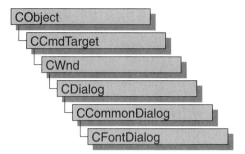

The **CFontDialog** class allows you to incorporate a font-selection dialog box into your application. A **CFontDialog** object is a dialog box with a list of fonts that are currently installed in the system. The user can select a particular font from the list, and this selection is then reported back to the application.

To construct a **CFontDialog** object, use the provided constructor or derive a new subclass and use your own custom constructor.

Once a **CFontDialog** object has been constructed, you can use the **m_cf** structure to initialize the values or states of controls in the dialog box. The **m_cf** structure is of type **CHOOSEFONT**. For more information on this structure, see the Win32 SDK documentation.

After initializing the dialog object's controls, call the **DoModal** member function to display the dialog box and allow the user to select a font. **DoModal** returns whether the user selected the OK (**IDOK**) or Cancel (**IDCANCEL**) button.

If **DoModal** returns **IDOK**, you can use one of **CFontDialog**'s member functions to retrieve the information input by the user.

You can use the Windows **CommDlgExtendedError** function to determine whether an error occurred during initialization of the dialog box and to learn more about the error. For more information on this function, see the Win32 SDK documentation.

CFontDialog relies on the COMMDLG.DLL file that ships with Windows versions 3.1 and later.

To customize the dialog box, derive a class from **CFontDialog**, provide a custom dialog template, and add a message-map to process the notification messages from the extended controls. Any unprocessed messages should be passed to the base class.

Customizing the hook function is not required.

For more information on using **CFontDialog**, see "Common Dialog Classes" in Chapter 4 of *Programming with MFC*.

#include <afxdlgs.h>

Data Members

m_cf	A structure used to customize a **CFontDialog** object.

Construction

CFontDialog	Constructs a **CFontDialog** object.

Operations

DoModal	Displays the dialog and allows the user to make a selection.
GetCurrentFont	Retrieves the name of the currently selected font.
GetFaceName	Returns the face name of the selected font.
GetStyleName	Returns the style name of the selected font.
GetSize	Returns the point size of the selected font.
GetColor	Returns the color of the selected font.
GetWeight	Returns the weight of the selected font.
IsStrikeOut	Determines whether the font is displayed with strikeout.
IsUnderline	Determines whether the font is underlined.
IsBold	Determines whether the font is bold.
IsItalic	Determines whether the font is italic.

Member Functions

CFontDialog::CFontDialog

CFontDialog(LPLOGFONT *lplfInitial* **= NULL, DWORD** *dwFlags* **= CF_EFFECTS | CF_SCREENFONTS, CDC*** *pdcPrinter* **= NULL, CWnd*** *pParentWnd* **= NULL);**

Parameters

lplfInitial   A pointer to a **LOGFONT** data structure that allows you to set some of the font's characteristics.

dwFlags   Specifies one or more choose-font flags. One or more preset values can be combined using the bitwise OR operator. If you modify the **m_cf.Flags** structure member, be sure to use a bitwise OR operator in your changes to keep the default behavior intact. For details on each of these flags, see the description of the **CHOOSEFONT** structure in the Win32 SDK documentation.

pdcPrinter   A pointer to a printer-device context. If supplied, this parameter points to a printer-device context for the printer on which the fonts are to be selected.

pParentWnd   A pointer to the font dialog box's parent or owner window.

Remarks

Constructs a **CFontDialog** object. Note that the constructor automatically fills in the members of the **CHOOSEFONT** structure. You should only change these if you want a font dialog different than the default.

See Also   **CFontDialog::DoModal**

CFontDialog::DoModal

virtual int DoModal( );

Return Value

IDOK or **IDCANCEL** if the function is successful; otherwise 0. **IDOK** and **IDCANCEL** are constants that indicate whether the user selected the OK or Cancel button.

If **IDCANCEL** is returned, you can call the Windows **CommDlgExtendedError** function to determine whether an error occurred.

Remarks

Call this function to display the Windows common font dialog box and allow the user to choose a font.

If you want to initialize the various font dialog controls by setting members of the **m_cf** structure, you should do this before calling **DoModal**, but after the dialog object is constructed.

If **DoModal** returns **IDOK**, you can call other member functions to retrieve the settings or information input by the user into the dialog box.

See Also   **CDialog::DoModal**, **CFontDialog::CFontDialog**

CFontDialog::GetColor

COLORREF GetColor( ) const;

Return Value

The color of the selected font.

Remarks

Call this function to retrieve the selected font color.

See Also   **CFontDialog::GetCurrentFont**

CFontDialog::GetCurrentFont

void GetCurrentFont(LPLOGFONT *lplf* **);**

Parameters

lplf   A pointer to a **LOGFONT** structure.

Remarks

Call this function to assign the characteristics of the currently selected font to the members of a **LOGFONT** structure. Other **CFontDialog** member functions are provided to access individual characteristics of the current font.

If this function is called during a call to **DoModal**, it returns the current selection at the time (what the user sees or has changed in the dialog). If this function is called after a call to **DoModal** (only if **DoModal** returns **IDOK**), it returns what the user actually selected.

See Also   **CFontDialog::GetFaceName, CFontDialog::GetStyleName**

CFontDialog::GetFaceName

CString GetFaceName( ) const;

Return Value

The face name of the font selected in the **CFontDialog** dialog box.

Remarks

Call this function to retrieve the face name of the selected font.

See Also   **CFontDialog::GetCurrentFont, CFontDialog::GetStyleName**

CFontDialog::GetSize

int GetSize( ) const;

Return Value

The font's size, in tenths of a point.

Remarks

Call this function to retrieve the size of the selected font.

See Also   **CFontDialog::GetWeight, CFontDialog::GetCurrentFont**

CFontDialog::GetStyleName

CString GetStyleName( ) const;

Return Value

The style name of the font.

Remarks

Call this function to retrieve the style name of the selected font.

See Also **CFontDialog::GetFaceName**, **CFontDialog::GetCurrentFont**

CFontDialog::GetWeight

int GetWeight( ) const;

Return Value

The weight of the selected font.

Remarks

Call this function to retrieve the weight of the selected font. For more information on the weight of a font, see **CFont::CreateFont**.

See Also **CFontDialog::GetCurrentFont**, **CFontDialog::IsBold**

CFontDialog::IsBold

BOOL IsBold( ) const;

Return Value

Nonzero if the selected font has the Bold characteristic enabled; otherwise 0.

Remarks

Call this function to determine if the selected font is bold.

See Also **CFontDialog::GetCurrentFont**

CFontDialog::IsItalic

BOOL IsItalic( ) const;

Return Value

Nonzero if the selected font has the Italic characteristic enabled; otherwise 0.

Remarks

Call this function to determine if the selected font is italic.

See Also **CFontDialog::GetCurrentFont**

CFontDialog::IsStrikeOut

BOOL IsStrikeOut( ) const;

Return Value

Nonzero if the selected font has the Strikeout characteristic enabled; otherwise 0.

Remarks

Call this function to determine if the selected font is displayed with strikeout.

See Also   CFontDialog::GetCurrentFont

CFontDialog::IsUnderline

BOOL IsUnderline( ) const;

Return Value

Nonzero if the selected font has the Underline characteristic enabled; otherwise 0.

Remarks

Call this function to determine if the selected font is underlined.

See Also   CFontDialog::GetCurrentFont

Data Members

CFontDialog::m_cf

Remarks

A structure whose members store the characteristics of the dialog object. After constructing a **CFontDialog** object, you can use **m_cf** to modify various aspects of the dialog box before calling the **DoModal** member function. For more information on this structure, see **CHOOSEFONT** in the Win32 SDK documentation.

CFontHolder

The **CFontHolder** class, which encapsulates the functionality of a Windows font object and the **IFont** interface, is used to implement the stock Font property.

Use this class to implement custom font properties for your control. For information on creating such properties, see the article "OLE Controls: Using Fonts in an OLE Control" in *Programming with MFC*.

#include <afxctl.h>

See Also CPropExchange

Data Members

m_pFont	A pointer to the **CFontHolder** object's **IFont** interface.

Construction/Destruction

CFontHolder	Constructs a **CFontHolder** object.

Operations

GetFontDispatch	Returns the font's **IDispatch** interface.
GetDisplayString	Retrieves the string displayed in a container's property browser.
GetFontHandle	Returns a handle to a Windows font.
InitializeFont	Initializes a **CFontHolder** object.
ReleaseFont	Disconnects the **CFontHolder** object from the **IFont** and **IFontNotification** interfaces.
Select	Selects a font resource into a device context.
SetFont	Connects the **CFontHolder** object to an **IFont** interface.

Member Functions

CFontHolder::CFontHolder

CFontHolder(LPPROPERTYNOTIFYSINK *pNotify* **);**

Parameters

pNotify Pointer to the font's **IPropertyNotifySink** interface.

Remarks

Constructs a **CFontHolder** object. You must call **InitializeFont** to initialize the resulting object before using it.

See Also CFontHolder::InitializeFont

CFontHolder::GetDisplayString

BOOL GetDisplayString(CString& *strValue* **);**

Return Value

Nonzero if the string is successfully retrieved; otherwise 0.

Parameters

strValue   Reference to the **CString** that is to hold the display string.

Remarks

Retrieves a string that can be displayed in a container's property browser.

CFontHolder::GetFontDispatch

LPFONTDISP GetFontDispatch( );

Return Value

A pointer to the **CFontHolder** object's **IFontDisp** interface. Note that the function that calls **GetFontDispatch** must call **IUnknown::Release** on this interface pointer when done with it.

Remarks

Call this function to retrieve a pointer to the font's dispatch interface. Call **InitializeFont** before calling **GetFontDispatch**.

See Also   **CFontHolder::InitializeFont**

CFontHolder::GetFontHandle

HFONT GetFontHandle( );
HFONT GetFontHandle(long *cyLogical*, **long** *cyHimetric* **);**

Return Value

A handle to the Font object; otherwise **NULL**.

Parameters

cyLogical   Height, in logical units, of the rectangle in which the control is drawn.

cyHimetric   Height, in **MM_HIMETRIC** units, of the control.

Remarks

Call this function to get a handle to a Windows font.

The ratio of *cyLogical* and *cyHimetric* is used to calculate the proper display size, in logical units, for the font's point size expressed in **MM_HIMETRIC** units:

Display size = (*cyLogical* / *cyHimetric*) X font size

The version with no parameters returns a handle to a font sized correctly for the screen.

CFontHolder::InitializeFont

void InitializeFont(const FONTDESC FAR* *pFontDesc* **= NULL,**
   LPDISPATCH *pFontDispAmbient* **= NULL);**

Parameters

pFontDesc   Pointer to a font description structure that specifies the font's characteristics. For more information on this structure, see "Standard Font Type" in Appendix A of *Programming with MFC*.

pFontDispAmbient   Pointer to the container's ambient Font property.

Remarks

Initializes a **CFontHolder** object.

If *pFontDispAmbient* is not **NULL**, the **CFontHolder** object is connected to a clone of the **IFont** interface used by the container's ambient Font property.

If *pFontDispAmbient* is **NULL**, a new Font object is created either from the font description pointed to by *pFontDesc* or, if *pFontDesc* is **NULL**, from a default description.

Call this function after constructing a **CFontHolder** object.

See Also   **CFontHolder::CFontHolder**

CFontHolder::ReleaseFont

void ReleaseFont( );

Remarks

This function disconnects the **CFontHolder** object from its **IFont** interface.

See Also   **CFontHolder::SetFont**

CFontHolder::Select

CFont* Select(CDC* *pDC,* **long** *cyLogical,* **long** *cyHimetric* **);**

Return Value

A pointer to the font that is being replaced.

Parameters

pDC   Device context into which the font is selected.

cyLogical   Height, in logical units, of the rectangle in which the control is drawn.

cyHimetric   Height, in **MM_HIMETRIC** units, of the control.

Remarks

Call this function to select your control's font into the specified device context.

See **GetFontHandle** for a discussion of the *cyLogical* and *cyHimetric* parameters.

CFontHolder::SetFont

void SetFont(LPFONT *pNewFont* **);**

Parameters

pNewFont   Pointer to the new **IFont** interface.

Remarks

Releases any existing font and connects the **CFontHolder** object to an **IFont** interface.

See Also   CFontHolder::ReleaseFont

Data Members

CFontHolder::m_pFont

Remarks

A pointer to the **CFontHolder** object's **IFont** interface.

See Also   CFontHolder::SetFont

CFormView

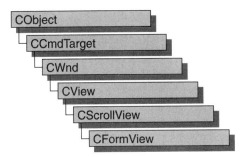

The **CFormView** class is the base class used for views containing controls. These controls are laid out based on a dialog-template resource. Use **CFormView** if you want form-based documents in your application. These views support scrolling, as needed, using the **CScrollView** functionality.

Creating a view based on **CFormView** is similar to creating a dialog box.

To use **CFormView**, take the following steps:

1. Design a dialog template.

   Use the dialog editor to design the dialog box. Then, in the Styles property page, set the following properties:

   - In the Style box, select Child (**WS_CHILD** on).
   - In the Border box, select None (**WS_BORDER** off).
   - Clear the Visible check box (**WS_VISIBLE** off).
   - Clear the Titlebar check box (**WS_CAPTION** off).

   These steps are necessary because a form view is not a true dialog box. For more information about creating a dialog-box resource, see "Creating a Form View Dialog Box" in Chapter 6 of the *Visual C++ User's Guide*.

2. Create a view class.

   With your dialog template open, run ClassWizard and choose **CFormView** as the class type when you are filling in the Add Class dialog box. ClassWizard creates a **CFormView**-derived class and connects it to the dialog template you just designed. This connection is established in the constructor for your class; ClassWizard generates a call to the base-class constructor, **CFormView::CFormView**, and passes the resource ID of your dialog template. For example:

```
CMyFormView::CMyFormView()
    : CFormView( CMyFormView::IDD )
{
    //{{AFX_DATA_INIT( CMyFormView )
    // NOTE: the ClassWizard will add member
    // initialization here
    //}}AFX_DATA_INIT

    // Other construction code, such as data initialization
}
```

Note   If you choose not to use ClassWizard, you must define the appropriate ID you supply to the **CFormView** constructor (that is, `CMyFormView::IDD` is not predefined). ClassWizard declares `IDD` as an **enum** value in the class it creates for you.

If you want to define member variables in your view class that correspond to the controls in your form view, use the Edit Variables button in the ClassWizard dialog box. This allows you to use the dialog data exchange (DDX) mechanism. If you want to define message handlers for control-notification messages, use the Add Function button in the ClassWizard dialog box. For more information on using ClassWizard, see Chapter 14, "Working with Classes," in the *Visual C++ User's Guide*.

3. Override the **OnUpdate** member function.

   The **OnUpdate** member function is defined by **CView** and is called to update the form view's appearance. Override this function to update the member variables in your view class with the appropriate values from the current document. Then, if you are using DDX, use the **UpdateData** member function (defined by **CWnd**) with an argument of **FALSE** to update the controls in your form view.

   The **OnInitialUpdate** member function (also defined by **CView**) is called to perform one-time initialization of the view. **CFormView** overrides this function to use DDX to set the initial values of the controls you have mapped using ClassWizard. Override **OnInitialUpdate** if you want to perform custom initialization.

4. Implement a member function to move data from your view to your document.

   This member function is typically a message handler for a control-notification message or for a menu command. If you are using DDX, call the **UpdateData** member function to update the member variables in your view class. Then move their values to the document associated with the form view.

5. Override the **OnPrint** member function (optional).

   The **OnPrint** member function is defined by **CView** and prints the view. By default, printing and print preview are not supported by the **CFormView** class. To add printing support, override the **OnPrint** function in your derived class. See the MFC General sample VIEWEX for more information about how to add printing capabilities to a view derived from **CFormView**.

6. Associate your view class with a document class and a frame-window class using a document template.

Unlike ordinary views, form views do not require you to override the **OnDraw** member function defined by **CView**. This is because controls are able to paint themselves. Only if you want to customize the display of your form view (for example, to provide a background for your view) should you override **OnDraw**. If you do so, be careful that your updating does not conflict with the updating done by the controls.

If your view contains controls that are derived from (or instances of) **CSliderCtrl** or **CSpinButtonCtrl** and you have message handlers for **WM_HSCROLL** and **WM_VSCROLL**, you should write code that calls the proper routines. The code example below calls **CWnd::OnHScroll** if a **WM_HSCROLL** message is sent by either a spin button or slider control.

```
void CMyFormView::OnHScroll( UINT nSBCode, UINT nPos, CScrollBar* pScrollBar )
{
if ( pScrollbar->IsKindOf( RUNTIME_CLASS( CScrollBar ) ))
{
    CFormView::OnHScroll( nSBCode, nPos, pScrollBar );
}
else if ( pScrollbar->IsKindOf( RUNTIME_CLASS( CSliderCtrl ) ))
{
    CWnd::OnHScroll( nSBCode, nPos, pScrollBar );
}
else if ( pScrollbar->IsKindOf( RUNTIME_CLASS( CSpinButtonCtrl ) ))
{
    CWnd::OnHScroll( nSBCode, nPos, pScrollBar );
}
}
```

If the view becomes smaller than the dialog template, scroll bars appear automatically. Views derived from **CFormView** support only the **MM_TEXT** mapping mode.

If you are not using DDX, use the **CWnd** dialog functions to move data between the member variables in your view class and the controls in your form view.

For more information about DDX, see "Defining Member Variables" in Chapter 14 of the *Visual C++ User's Guide*. For more information on **CFormView**, see "Special View Classes" in Chapter 1 and "Documents and Views" in Chapter 3 of *Programming with MFC*.

#include <afxext.h>

See Also   CDialog, CScrollView, CView::OnUpdate, CView::OnInitialUpdate, CView::OnPrint, CWnd::UpdateData, CScrollView::ResizeParentToFit

Construction

CFormView   Constructs a **CFormView** object.

Member Functions

CFormView::CFormView

CFormView(LPCTSTR *lpszTemplateName* **);**
CFormView(UINT *nIDTemplate* **);**

Parameters

lpszTemplateName   Contains a null-terminated string that is the name of a dialog-template resource.

nIDTemplate   Contains the ID number of a dialog-template resource.

Remarks

When you create an object of a type derived from **CFormView**, invoke one of the constructors to create the view object and identify the dialog resource on which the view is based. You can identify the resource either by name (pass a string as the argument to the constructor) or by its ID (pass an unsigned integer as the argument).

The form-view window and child controls are not created until **CWnd::Create** is called. **CWnd::Create** is called by the framework as part of the document and view creation process, which is driven by the document template.

Note   Your derived class *must* supply its own constructor. In the constructor, invoke the constructor, **CFormView::CFormView**, with the resource name or ID as an argument as shown in the preceding class overview.

See Also   **CWnd::Create**

CFrameWnd

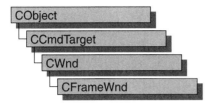

The **CFrameWnd** class provides the functionality of a Windows single document interface (SDI) overlapped or pop-up frame window, along with members for managing the window.

To create a useful frame window for your application, derive a class from **CFrameWnd**. Add member variables to the derived class to store data specific to your application. Implement message-handler member functions and a message map in the derived class to specify what happens when messages are directed to the window.

There are three ways to construct a frame window:

- Directly construct it using **Create**.
- Directly construct it using **LoadFrame**.
- Indirectly construct it using a document template.

Before you call either **Create** or **LoadFrame**, you must construct the frame-window object on the heap using the C++ **new** operator. Before calling **Create**, you can also register a window class with the **AfxRegisterWndClass** global function to set the icon and class styles for the frame.

Use the **Create** member function to pass the frame's creation parameters as immediate arguments.

LoadFrame requires fewer arguments than **Create**, and instead retrieves most of its default values from resources, including the frame's caption, icon, accelerator table, and menu. To be accessible by **LoadFrame**, all these resources must have the same resource ID (for example, **IDR_MAINFRAME**).

When a **CFrameWnd** object contains views and documents, they are created indirectly by the framework instead of directly by the programmer. The **CDocTemplate** object orchestrates the creation of the frame, the creation of the containing views, and the connection of the views to the appropriate document. The parameters of the **CDocTemplate** constructor specify the **CRuntimeClass** of the three classes involved (document, frame, and view). A **CRuntimeClass** object is used by the framework to dynamically create new frames when specified by the user (for example, by using the File New command or the multiple document interface (MDI) Window New command).

A frame-window class derived from **CFrameWnd** must be declared with **DECLARE_DYNCREATE** in order for the above **RUNTIME_CLASS** mechanism to work correctly.

A **CFrameWnd** contains default implementations to perform the following functions of a main window in a typical application for Windows:

- A **CFrameWnd** frame window keeps track of a currently active view that is independent of the Windows active window or the current input focus. When the frame is reactivated, the active view is notified by calling **CView::OnActivateView**.

- Command messages and many common frame-notification messages, including those handled by the **OnSetFocus**, **OnHScroll**, and **OnVScroll** functions of **CWnd**, are delegated by a **CFrameWnd** frame window to the currently active view.

- The currently active view (or currently active MDI child frame window in the case of an MDI frame) can determine the caption of the frame window. This feature can be disabled by turning off the **FWS_ADDTOTITLE** style bit of the frame window.

- A **CFrameWnd** frame window manages the positioning of the control bars, views, and other child windows inside the frame window's client area. A frame window also does idle-time updating of toolbar and other control-bar buttons. A **CFrameWnd** frame window also has default implementations of commands for toggling on and off the toolbar and status bar.

- A **CFrameWnd** frame window manages the main menu bar. When a pop-up menu is displayed, the frame window uses the **UPDATE_COMMAND_UI** mechanism to determine which menu items should be enabled, disabled, or checked. When the user selects a menu item, the frame window updates the status bar with the message string for that command.

- A **CFrameWnd** frame window has an optional accelerator table that automatically translates keyboard accelerators.

- A **CFrameWnd** frame window has an optional help ID set with **LoadFrame** that is used for context-sensitive help. A frame window is the main orchestrator of semimodal states such as context-sensitive help (SHIFT+F1) and print-preview modes.

- A **CFrameWnd** frame window will open a file dragged from the File Manager and dropped on the frame window. If a file extension is registered and associated with the application, the frame window responds to the dynamic data exchange (DDE) open request that occurs when the user opens a data file in the File Manager or when the **ShellExecute** Windows function is called.

- If the frame window is the main application window (that is, **CWinThread::m_pMainWnd**), when the user closes the application, the frame window prompts the user to save any modified documents (for **OnClose** and **OnQueryEndSession**).

- If the frame window is the main application window, the frame window is the context for running WinHelp. Closing the frame window will shut down WINHELP.EXE if it was launched for help for this application.

Do not use the C++ **delete** operator to destroy a frame window. Use **CWnd::DestroyWindow** instead. The **CFrameWnd** implementation of **PostNcDestroy** will delete the C++ object when the window is destroyed. When the user closes the frame window, the default **OnClose** handler will call **DestroyWindow**.

For more information on **CFrameWnd**, see "Frame Windows" in Chapter 3 of *Programming with MFC*.

#include <afxwin.h>

See Also   CWnd, CMDIFrameWnd, CMDIChildWnd, CView, CDocTemplate, **CRuntimeClass**

Data Members

m_bAutoMenuEnable	Controls automatic enable and disable functionality for menu items.
rectDefault	Pass this static **CRect** as a parameter when creating a **CFrameWnd** object to allow Windows to choose the window's initial size and position.

Construction

CFrameWnd	Constructs a **CFrameWnd** object.

Initialization

Create	Call to create and initialize the Windows frame window associated with the **CFrameWnd** object.
LoadFrame	Call to dynamically create a frame window from resource information.
LoadAccelTable	Call to load an accelerator table.
LoadBarState	Call to restore control bar settings.
SaveBarState	Call to save control bar settings.
ShowControlBar	Call to show the control bar.
SetDockState	Call to dock the frame window in the main window.
GetDockState	Retrieves the dock state of a frame window.

Operations

ActivateFrame	Makes the frame visible and available to the user.
InitialUpdateFrame	Causes the **OnInitialUpdate** member function belonging to all views in the frame window to be called.
GetActiveFrame	Returns the active **CFrameWnd** object.
SetActiveView	Sets the active **CView** object.
GetActiveView	Returns the active **CView** object.
CreateView	Creates a view within a frame that is not derived from **CView**.
GetActiveDocument	Returns the active **CDocument** object.
GetControlBar	Retrieves the control bar.
GetMessageString	Retrieves message corresponding to a command ID.
IsTracking	Determines if splitter bar is currently being moved.
SetMessageText	Sets the text of a standard status bar.
EnableDocking	Allows a control bar to be docked.
DockControlBar	Docks a control bar.
FloatControlBar	Floats a control bar.
BeginModalState	Sets the frame window to modal.
EndModalState	Ends the frame window's modal state. Enables all of the windows disabled by **BeginModalState**.
InModalState	Returns a value indicating whether or not a frame window is in a modal state.
ShowOwnedWindows	Shows all windows that are descendants of the **CFrameWnd** object.
RecalcLayout	Repositions the control bars of the **CFrameWnd** object.

Overridables

OnCreateClient	Creates a client window for the frame.
OnSetPreviewMode	Sets the application's main frame window into and out of print-preview mode.
GetMessageBar	Returns a pointer to the status bar belonging to the frame window.
NegotiateBorderSpace	Negotiates border space in the frame window.

Command Handlers

OnContextHelp	Handles SHIFT+F1 Help for in-place items.

Member Functions

CFrameWnd::ActivateFrame

virtual void ActivateFrame(int *nCmdShow* **= – 1);**

Parameters

nCmdShow   Specifies the parameter to pass to **CWnd::ShowWindow**. By default, the frame is shown and correctly restored.

Remarks

Call this member function to activate and restore the frame window so that it is visible and available to the user. This member function is usually called after a non-user interface event such as a DDE, OLE, or other event that may show the frame window or its contents to the user.

The default implementation activates the frame and brings it to the top of the Z-order and, if necessary, carries out the same steps for the application's main frame window.

Override this member function to change how a frame is activated. For example, you can force MDI child windows to be maximized. Add the appropriate functionality, then call the base class version with an explicit *nCmdShow*.

CFrameWnd::BeginModalState

virtual void BeginModalState( );

Remarks

Call this member function to make a frame window modal.

CFrameWnd::CFrameWnd

CFrameWnd( );

Remarks

Constructs a **CFrameWnd** object, but does not create the visible frame window. Call **Create** to create the visible window.

See Also   **CFrameWnd::Create**, **CFrameWnd::LoadFrame**

CFrameWnd::Create

BOOL Create(LPCTSTR *lpszClassName*, **LPCTSTR** *lpszWindowName*,
   DWORD *dwStyle* = **WS_OVERLAPPEDWINDOW, const RECT&** *rect* = **rectDefault,**
   CWnd* *pParentWnd* = **NULL, LPCTSTR** *lpszMenuName* = **NULL, DWORD** *dwExStyle* = **0,**
   CCreateContext* *pContext* = **NULL);**

Return Value

Nonzero if initialization is successful; otherwise 0.

Parameters

lpszClassName   Points to a null-terminated character string that names the Windows
class. The class name can be any name registered with the **AfxRegisterWndClass**
global function or the **RegisterClass** Windows function. If **NULL**, uses the
predefined default **CFrameWnd** attributes.

lpszWindowName   Points to a null-terminated character string that represents the
window name. Used as text for the title bar.

dwStyle   Specifies the window style attributes. Include the **FWS_ADDTOTITLE**
style if you want the title bar to automatically display the name of the document
represented in the window. For a list of window styles, see "Window Styles" in the
"Styles Used by MFC" section.

rect   Specifies the size and position of the window. The **rectDefault** value allows
Windows to specify the size and position of the new window.

pParentWnd   Specifies the parent window of this frame window. This parameter
should be **NULL** for top-level frame windows.

lpszMenuName   Identifies the name of the menu resource to be used with the
window. Use **MAKEINTRESOURCE** if the menu has an integer ID instead of a
string. This parameter can be **NULL**.

dwExStyle   Specifies the window extended style attributes. For a list of extended
window styles, see "Extended Window Styles" in the "Styles Used by MFC"
section.

pContext   Specifies a pointer to a **CCreateContext** structure. This parameter can
be **NULL**.

Remarks

Construct a **CFrameWnd** object in two steps. First invoke the constructor, which
constructs the **CFrameWnd** object, then call **Create**, which creates the Windows
frame window and attaches it to the **CFrameWnd** object. **Create** initializes the
window's class name and window name and registers default values for its style,
parent, and associated menu.

Use **LoadFrame** rather than **Create** to load the frame window from a resource instead of specifying its arguments.

See Also **CFrameWnd::CFrameWnd**, **CFrameWnd::LoadFrame**, **CCreateContext**, **CWnd::Create**, **CWnd::PreCreateWindow**

CFrameWnd::CreateView

CWnd* CreateView(CCreateContext* *pContext*, **UINT** *nID* = **AFX_IDW_PANE_FIRST**);

Return Value

Pointer to a **CWnd** object if successful; otherwise **NULL**.

Parameters

pContext   Specifies the type of view and document.

nID   The ID number of a view.

Remarks

Call **CreateView** to create a view within a frame. Use this member function to create "views" that are not **CView**-derived within a frame. After calling **CreateView**, you must manually set the view to active and set it to be visible; these tasks are not automatically performed by **CreateView**.

Note The MFC Advanced Concepts sample COLLECT uses **CreateView** to get correct 3D effects in Windows 95.

CFrameWnd::DockControlBar

void DockControlBar(CControlBar * *pBar*, **UINT** *nDockBarID* = 0, **LPCRECT** *lpRect* = NULL);

Parameters

pBar   Points to the control bar to be docked.

nDockBarID   Determines which sides of the frame window to consider for docking. It can be 0, or one or more of the following:

- **AFX_IDW_DOCKBAR_TOP**   Dock to the top side of the window.

- **AFX_IDW_DOCKBAR_BOTTOM**   Dock to the bottom side of the window.

- **AFX_IDW_DOCKBAR_LEFT**   Dock to the left side of the window.

- **AFX_IDW_DOCKBAR_RIGHT**   Dock to the right side of the window.

If 0, the control bar can be docked to any side enabled for docking in the destination frame window.

lpRect   Determines, in screen coordinates, where the control bar will be docked in the nonclient area of the destination frame window.

Remarks

Causes a control bar to be docked to the frame window. The control bar will be docked to one of the sides of the frame window specified in the calls to both **CControlBar::EnableDocking** and **CFrameWnd::EnableDocking**. The side chosen is determined by *nDockBarID*.

See Also **CFrameWnd::FloatControlBar**

CFrameWnd::EnableDocking

void EnableDocking(DWORD *dwDockStyle* **);**

Parameters

dwDockStyle Specifies which sides of the frame window can serve as docking sites for control bars. It can be one or more of the following:

- **CBRS_ALIGN_TOP** Allows docking at the top of the client area.
- **CBRS_ALIGN_BOTTOM** Allows docking at the bottom of the client area.
- **CBRS_ALIGN_LEFT** Allows docking on the left side of the client area.
- **CBRS_ALIGN_RIGHT** Allows docking on the right side of the client area.
- **CBRS_ALIGN_ANY** Allows docking on any side of the client area.

Remarks

Call this function to enable dockable control bars in a frame window. By default, control bars will be docked to a side of the frame window in the following order: top, bottom, left, right.

See Also **CControlBar::EnableDocking**, **CFrameWnd::DockControlBar**, **CFrameWnd::FloatControlBar**

CFrameWnd::EndModalState

virtual void EndModalState( );

Remarks

Call this member function to change a frame window from modal to modeless. **EndModalState** enables all of the windows disabled by **BeginModalState**.

CFrameWnd::FloatControlBar

CFrameWnd* FloatControlBar(CControlBar * *pBar***, CPoint** *point***, DWORD** *dwStyle* **= CBRS_ALIGN_TOP);**

Return Value

Pointer to the current frame window.

Parameters

pBar   Points to the control bar to be floated.

point   The location, in screen coordinates, where the top left corner of the control bar will be placed.

dwStyle   Specifies whether to align the control bar horizontally or vertically within its new frame window. It can be any one of the following:

- **CBRS_ALIGN_TOP**   Orients the control bar vertically.

- **CBRS_ALIGN_BOTTOM**   Orients the control bar vertically.

- **CBRS_ALIGN_LEFT**   Orients the control bar horizontally.

- **CBRS_ALIGN_RIGHT**   Orients the control bar horizontally.

If styles are passed specifying both horizontal and vertical orientation, the toolbar will be oriented horizontally.

Remarks

Call this function to cause a control bar to not be docked to the frame window. Typically, this is done at application startup when the program is restoring settings from the previous execution.

This function is called by the framework when the user causes a drop operation by releasing the left mouse button while dragging the control bar over a location that is not available for docking.

See Also   **CFrameWnd::DockControlBar**

CFrameWnd::GetActiveDocument

virtual CDocument* GetActiveDocument( );

Return Value

A pointer to the current **CDocument**. If there is no current document, returns **NULL**.

Remarks

Call this member function to obtain a pointer to the current **CDocument** attached to the current active view.

See Also   **CFrameWnd::GetActiveView**

CFrameWnd::GetActiveFrame

virtual CFrameWnd* GetActiveFrame( );

Return Value

A pointer to the active MDI child window. If the application is an SDI application, or the MDI frame window has no active document, the implicit **this** pointer will be returned.

Remarks

Call this member function to obtain a pointer to the active multiple document interface (MDI) child window of an MDI frame window.

If there is no active MDI child or the application is a single document interface (SDI), the implicit **this** pointer is returned.

See Also **CFrameWnd::GetActiveView**, **CFrameWnd::GetActiveDocument**, **CMDIFrameWnd**

CFrameWnd::GetActiveView

CView* GetActiveView( ) const;

Return Value

A pointer to the current **CView**. If there is no current view, returns **NULL**.

Remarks

Call this member function to obtain a pointer to the active view.

See Also **CFrameWnd::SetActiveView**, **CFrameWnd::GetActiveDocument**

CFrameWnd::GetControlBar

CControlBar* GetControlBar(UINT *nID*);

Return Value

A pointer to the control bar that is associated with the ID.

Parameters

nID   The ID number of a control bar.

Remarks

Call **GetControlBar** to gain access to the control bar that is associated with the ID. **GetControlBar** will return the control bar even if it is floating and thus is not currently a child window of the frame.

CFrameWnd::GetDockState

void GetDockState(CDockState& *state* **) const;**

Parameters

state   Contains the current state of the frame window upon return.

Remarks

Call this member function to specify the current dock state of the frame window.

CFrameWnd::GetMessageBar

virtual CWnd* GetMessageBar( );

Return Value

Pointer to the status-bar window.

Remarks

Call this member function to get a pointer to the status bar.

CFrameWnd::GetMessageString

virtual void GetMessageString(UINT *nID*, **CString&** *rMessage* **) const;**

Parameters

nID   Resource ID of the desired message.

rMessage   **CString** object into which to place the message.

Remarks

Override this function to provide custom strings for command IDs. The default implementation simply loads the string specified by *nID* from the resource file. This function is called by the framework when the message string in the status bar needs updating.

See Also   **CFrameWnd::SetMessageText**

CFrameWnd::InitialUpdateFrame

void InitialUpdateFrame(CDocument* *pDoc*, **BOOL** *bMakeVisible* **);**

Parameters

pDoc   Points to the document to which the frame window is associated. Can be **NULL**.

bMakeVisible   If **TRUE**, indicates that the frame should become visible and active. If **FALSE**, no descendants are made visible.

Remarks

Call **IntitialUpdateFrame** after creating a new frame with **Create**. This causes all views in that frame window to receive their **OnInitialUpdate** calls.

Also, if there was not previously an active view, the primary view of the frame window is made active. The primary view is a view with a child ID of **AFX_IDW_PANE_FIRST**. Finally, the frame window is made visible if *bMakeVisible* is nonzero. If *bMakeVisible* is 0, the current focus and visible state of the frame window will remain unchanged. It is not necessary to call this function when using the framework's implementation of File New and File Open.

See Also   **CView::OnInitialUpdate**, **CFrameWnd::SetActiveView**, **CDocTemplate::CreateNewFrame**

CFrameWnd::InModalState

BOOL InModalState( ) const;

Return Value

Nonzero if yes; otherwise 0.

Remarks

Call this member function to check if a frame window is modal or modeless.

CFrameWnd::IsTracking

BOOL IsTracking( ) const;

Return Value

Nonzero if a splitter operation is in progress; otherwise 0.

Remarks

Call this member function to determine if the splitter bar in the window is currently being moved.

CFrameWnd::LoadAccelTable

BOOL LoadAccelTable(LPCTSTR *lpszResourceName* **);**

Return Value

Nonzero if the accelerator table was successfully loaded; otherwise 0.

Parameters

lpszResourceName   Identifies the name of the accelerator resource. Use **MAKEINTRESOURCE** if the resource is identified with an integer ID.

Remarks

Call to load the specified accelerator table. Only one table can be loaded at a time.

Accelerator tables loaded from resources are freed automatically when the application terminates.

If you call **LoadFrame** to create the frame window, the framework loads an accelerator table along with the menu and icon resources, and a subsequent call to this member function is then unnecessary.

See Also   **CFrameWnd::LoadFrame**, **::LoadAccelerators**

CFrameWnd::LoadBarState

void LoadBarState(LPCTSTR *lpszProfileName* **);**

Parameters

lpszProfileName   Name of a section in the initialization file or a key in the Windows registry where state information is stored.

Remarks

Call this function to restore the settings of each control bar owned by the frame window. This information is written to the initialization file using **SaveBarState**. Information restored includes visibility, horizontal/vertical orientation, docking state, and control-bar position.

See Also   **CFrameWnd::SaveBarState**, **CWinApp::SetRegistryKey**, **CWinApp::m_pszProfileName**

CFrameWnd::LoadFrame

virtual BOOL LoadFrame(UINT *nIDResource*,
    DWORD *dwDefaultStyle* = **WS_OVERLAPPEDWINDOW | FWS_ADDTOTITLE**,
    CWnd* *pParentWnd* = **NULL, CCreateContext*** *pContext* = **NULL**);

Parameters

nIDResource   The ID of shared resources associated with the frame window.

dwDefaultStyle   The frame's style. Include the **FWS_ADDTOTITLE** style if you want the title bar to automatically display the name of the document represented in the window. For a list of window styles, see "Window Styles" in the "Styles Used by MFC" section.

pParentWnd   A pointer to the frame's parent.

pContext   A pointer to a **CCreateContext** structure. This parameter can be **NULL**.

Remarks

Construct a **CFrameWnd** object in two steps. First invoke the constructor, which constructs the **CFrameWnd** object, then call **LoadFrame**, which loads the Windows frame window and associated resources and attaches the frame window to the **CFrameWnd** object. The *nIDResource* parameter specifies the menu, the accelerator table, the icon, and the string resource of the title for the frame window.

Use the **Create** member function rather than **LoadFrame** when you want to specify all of the frame window's creation parameters.

The framework calls **LoadFrame** when it creates a frame window using a document template object.

The framework uses the *pContext* argument to specify the objects to be connected to the frame window, including any contained view objects. You can set the *pContext* argument to **NULL** when you call **LoadFrame**.

See Also   **CDocTemplate**, **CFrameWnd::Create**, **CFrameWnd::CFrameWnd**, **CWnd::PreCreateWindow**

CFrameWnd::NegotiateBorderSpace

virtual BOOL NegotiateBorderSpace(UINT *nBorderCmd*, **LPRECT** *lpRectBorder* **);**

Return Value

Nonzero if successful; otherwise 0.

Parameters

nBorderCmd   Contains one of the following values from the **enum BorderCmd**:

- **borderGet** = 1
- **borderRequest** = 2
- **borderSet** = 3

lpRectBorder   Pointer to a **RECT** structure or a **CRect** object that specifies the coordinates of the border.

Remarks

Call this member function to negotiate border space in a frame window during OLE inplace activation. This member function is the **CFrameWnd** implementation of OLE border space negotiation.

See Also   In the OLE documentation: **IOleInPlaceUIWindow**

CFrameWnd::OnContextHelp

afx_msg void OnContextHelp( );

Remarks

To enable context-sensitive help, you must add an

```
ON_COMMAND( ID_CONTEXT_HELP, OnContextHelp )
```

statement to your **CFrameWnd** class message map and also add an accelerator-table entry, typically SHIFT+F1, to enable this member function.

If your application is an OLE Container, **OnContextHelp** puts all in-place items contained within the frame window object into Help mode. The cursor changes to an arrow and a question mark, and the user can then move the mouse pointer and press the left mouse button to select a dialog box, window, menu, or command button. This member function calls the Windows function **WinHelp** with the Help context of the object under the cursor.

See Also **CWinApp::OnHelp**, **CWinApp::WinHelp**

CFrameWnd::OnCreateClient

virtual BOOL OnCreateClient(LPCREATESTRUCT *lpcs***, CCreateContext*** *pContext* **);**

Parameters

lpcs   A pointer to a Windows **CREATESTRUCT** structure.

pContext   A pointer to a **CCreateContext** structure.

Remarks

Called by the framework during the execution of **OnCreate**. Never call this function.

The default implementation of this function creates a **CView** object from the information provided in *pContext*, if possible.

Override this function to override values passed in the **CCreateContext** object or to change the way controls in the main client area of the frame window are created. The **CCreateContext** members you can override are described in the **CCreateContext** class.

Note Do not replace values passed in the **CREATESTRUCT** structure. They are for informational use only. If you want to override the initial window rectangle, for example, override the **CWnd** member function **PreCreateWindow**.

CFrameWnd::OnSetPreviewMode

virtual void OnSetPreviewMode(BOOL *bPreview*, **CPrintPreviewState*** *pModeStuff* **);**

Parameters

bPreview   Specifies whether or not to place the application in print-preview mode. Set to **TRUE** to place in print preview, **FALSE** to cancel preview mode.

pModeStuff   A pointer to a **CPrintPreviewState** structure.

Remarks

Call this member function to set the application's main frame window into and out of print-preview mode.

The default implementation disables all standard toolbars and hides the main menu and the main client window. This turns MDI frame windows into temporary SDI frame windows.

Override this member function to customize the hiding and showing of control bars and other frame window parts during print preview. Call the base class implementation from within the overridden version.

CFrameWnd::RecalcLayout

virtual void RecalcLayout(BOOL *bNotify* = **TRUE** **);**

Parameters

bNotify   Determines whether the active in-place item for the frame window receives notification of the layout change. If **TRUE**, the item is notified; otherwise **FALSE**.

Remarks

Called by the framework when the standard control bars are toggled on or off or when the frame window is resized. The default implementation of this member function calls the **CWnd** member function **RepositionBars** to reposition all the control bars in the frame as well as in the main client window (usually a **CView** or **MDICLIENT**).

Override this member function to control the appearance and behavior of control bars after the layout of the frame window has changed. For example, call it when you turn control bars on or off or add another control bar.

See Also   **CWnd::RepositionBars**

CFrameWnd::SaveBarState

void SaveBarState(LPCTSTR *lpszProfileName* **) const;**

Parameters

lpszProfileName   Name of a section in the initialization file or a key in the Windows registry where state information is stored.

Remarks

Call this function to store information about each control bar owned by the frame window. This information can be read from the initialization file using **LoadBarState**. Information stored includes visibility, horizontal/vertical orientation, docking state, and control bar position.

See Also   **CFrameWnd::LoadBarState**, **CWinApp::SetRegistryKey**, **CWinApp::m_pszProfileName**

CFrameWnd::SetActiveView

void SetActiveView(CView* *pViewNew***, BOOL** *bNotify* **= TRUE);**

Parameters

pViewNew   Specifies a pointer to a **CView** object, or **NULL** for no active view.

bNotify   Specifies whether the view is to be notified of activation. If **TRUE**, **OnActivateView** is called for the new view; if **FALSE**, it is not.

Remarks

Call this member function to set the active view. The framework will call this function automatically as the user changes the focus to a view within the frame window. You can explicitly call **SetActiveView** to change the focus to the specified view.

See Also   **CFrameWnd::GetActiveView**, **CView::OnActivateView**, **CFrameWnd::GetActiveDocument**

CFrameWnd::SetDockState

void SetDockState(const CDockState& *state* **);**

Parameters

state   Specifies the state of the frame window.

Remarks

Call this member function to set the dock state of the frame window.

CFrameWnd::SetMessageText

void SetMessageText(LPCTSTR *lpszText* **);**
void SetMessageText(UINT *nID* **);**

Parameters

lpszText   Points to the string to be placed on the status bar.

nID   String resource ID of the string to be placed on the status bar.

Remarks

Call this function to place a string in the status-bar pane that has an ID of 0. This is typically the leftmost, and longest, pane of the status bar.

See Also   CStatusBar

CFrameWnd::ShowControlBar

void ShowControlBar(CControlBar* *pBar*, **BOOL** *bShow*, **BOOL** *bDelay* **);**

Parameters

pBar   Pointer to the control bar to be shown or hidden.

bShow   If **TRUE**, specifies that the control bar is to be shown. If **FALSE**, specifies that the control bar is to be hidden.

bDelay   If **TRUE**, delay showing the control bar. If **FALSE**, show the control bar immediately.

Remarks

Call this member function to show or hide the control bar.

CFrameWnd::ShowOwnedWindows

void ShowOwnedWindows(BOOL *bShow* **);**

Parameters

bShow   Specifies whether the owned windows are to be shown or hidden.

Remarks

Call this member function to show all windows that are descendants of the **CFrameWnd** object.

Data Members

CFrameWnd::m_bAutoMenuEnable

Remarks

When this data member is enabled (which is the default), menu items that do not have **ON_UPDATE_COMMAND_UI** or **ON_COMMAND** handlers will be automatically disabled when the user pulls down a menu.

Menu items that have an **ON_COMMAND** handler but no **ON_UPDATE_COMMAND_UI** handler will be automatically enabled.

When this data member is set, menu items are automatically enabled in the same way that toolbar buttons are enabled.

This data member simplifies the implementation of optional commands based on the current selection and reduces the need for an application to write **ON_UPDATE_COMMAND_UI** handlers for enabling and disabling menu items.

See Also   **CCmdUI**, **CCmdTarget**

CFrameWnd::rectDefault

Remarks

Pass this static **CRect** as a parameter when creating a window to allow Windows to choose the window's initial size and position.

CGdiObject

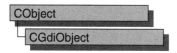

The **CGdiObject** class provides a base class for various kinds of Windows graphics device interface (GDI) objects such as bitmaps, regions, brushes, pens, palettes, and fonts. You never create a **CGdiObject** directly. Rather, you create an object from one of its derived classes, such as **CPen** or **CBrush**.

For more information on **CGdiObject**, see "Graphic Objects" in Chapter 1 of *Programming with MFC*.

#include <afxwin.h>

See Also   **CBitmap**, **CBrush**, **CFont**, **CPalette**, **CPen**, **CRgn**

Data Members

m_hObject	A **HANDLE** containing the **HBITMAP**, **HPALETTE**, **HRGN**, **HBRUSH**, **HPEN**, or **HFONT** attached to this object.

Construction

CGdiObject	Constructs a **CGdiObject** object.

Operations

GetSafeHandle	Returns **m_hObject** unless **this** is **NULL**, in which case **NULL** is returned.
FromHandle	Returns a pointer to a **CGdiObject** object given a handle to a Windows GDI object.
Attach	Attaches a Windows GDI object to a **CGdiObject** object.
Detach	Detaches a Windows GDI object from a **CGdiObject** object and returns a handle to the Windows GDI object.
DeleteObject	Deletes the Windows GDI object attached to the **CGdiObject** object from memory by freeing all system storage associated with the object.
DeleteTempMap	Deletes any temporary **CGdiObject** objects created by **FromHandle**.
GetObject	Fills a buffer with data that describes the Windows GDI object attached to the **CGdiObject** object.

CreateStockObject	Retrieves a handle to one of the Windows predefined stock pens, brushes, or fonts.
UnrealizeObject	Resets the origin of a brush or resets a logical palette.
GetObjectType	Retrieves the type of the GDI object.

Member Functions

CGdiObject::Attach

BOOL Attach(HGDIOBJ *hObject* **);**

Return Value

Nonzero if attachment is successful; otherwise 0.

Parameters

hObject   A **HANDLE** to a Windows GDI object (for example, **HPEN** or **HBRUSH**).

Remarks

Attaches a Windows GDI object to a **CGdiObject** object.

See Also   **CGdiObject::Detach**

CGdiObject::CGdiObject

CGdiObject( );

Remarks

Constructs a **CGdiObject** object. You never create a **CGdiObject** directly. Rather, you create an object from one of its derived classes, such as **CPen** or **CBrush**.

See Also   **CPen**, **CBrush**, **CFont**, **CBitmap**, **CRgn**, **CPalette**

CGdiObject::CreateStockObject

BOOL CreateStockObject(int *nIndex* **);**

Return Value

Nonzero if the function is successful; otherwise 0.

Parameters

nIndex   A constant specifying the type of stock object desired. It can be one of the following values:

- **BLACK_BRUSH**   Black brush.

- **DKGRAY_BRUSH**   Dark gray brush.

- **GRAY_BRUSH**   Gray brush.

- **HOLLOW_BRUSH**   Hollow brush.

- **LTGRAY_BRUSH**   Light gray brush.

- **NULL_BRUSH**   Null brush.

- **WHITE_BRUSH**   White brush.

- **BLACK_PEN**   Black pen.

- **NULL_PEN**   Null pen.

- **WHITE_PEN**   White pen.

- **ANSI_FIXED_FONT**   ANSI fixed system font.

- **ANSI_VAR_FONT**   ANSI variable system font.

- **DEVICE_DEFAULT_FONT**   Device-dependent font.

- **OEM_FIXED_FONT**   OEM-dependent fixed font.

- **SYSTEM_FONT**   The system font. By default, Windows uses the system font to draw menus, dialog-box controls, and other text. In Windows versions 3.0 and later, the system font is proportional width; earlier versions of Windows use a fixed-width system font.

- **SYSTEM_FIXED_FONT**   The fixed-width system font used in Windows prior to version 3.0. This object is available for compatibility with earlier versions of Windows.

- **DEFAULT_PALETTE**   Default color palette. This palette consists of the 20 static colors in the system palette.

Remarks

Retrieves a handle to one of the predefined stock Windows GDI pens, brushes, or fonts, and attaches the GDI object to the **CGdiObject** object. Call this function with one of the derived classes that corresponds to the Windows GDI object type, such as **CPen** for a stock pen.

See Also   **CPen::CPen**, **CBrush::CBrush**, **CFont::CFont**, **CPalette::CPalette**

CGdiObject::DeleteObject

BOOL DeleteObject( );

Return Value

Nonzero if the GDI object was successfully deleted; otherwise 0.

Remarks

Deletes the attached Windows GDI object from memory by freeing all system storage associated with the Windows GDI object. The storage associated with the **CGdiObject** object is not affected by this call. An application should not call **DeleteObject** on a **CGdiObject** object that is currently selected into a device context.

When a pattern brush is deleted, the bitmap associated with the brush is not deleted. The bitmap must be deleted independently.

See Also   **CGdiObject::Detach**

CGdiObject::DeleteTempMap

static void PASCAL DeleteTempMap( );

Remarks

Called automatically by the **CWinApp** idle-time handler, **DeleteTempMap** deletes any temporary **CGdiObject** objects created by **FromHandle**. **DeleteTempMap** detaches the Windows GDI object attached to a temporary **CGdiObject** object before deleting the **CGdiObject** object.

See Also   **CGdiObject::Detach**, **CGdiObject::FromHandle**

CGdiObject::Detach

HGDIOBJ Detach( );

Return Value

A **HANDLE** to the Windows GDI object detached; otherwise **NULL** if no GDI object is attached.

Remarks

Detaches a Windows GDI object from a **CGdiObject** object and returns a handle to the Windows GDI object.

See Also   **CGdiObject::Attach**

CGdiObject::FromHandle

static CGdiObject* PASCAL FromHandle(HGDIOBJ *hObject* **);**

Return Value

A pointer to a **CGdiObject** that may be temporary or permanent.

Parameters

hObject   A **HANDLE** to a Windows GDI object.

Remarks

Returns a pointer to a **CGdiObject** object given a handle to a Windows GDI object. If a **CGdiObject** object is not already attached to the Windows GDI object, a temporary **CGdiObject** object is created and attached.

This temporary **CGdiObject** object is only valid until the next time the application has idle time in its event loop, at which time all temporary graphic objects are deleted. Another way of saying this is that the temporary object is only valid during the processing of one window message.

See Also   **CGdiObject::DeleteTempMap**

CGdiObject::GetObject

int GetObject(int *nCount*, **LPVOID** *lpObject* **) const;**

Return Value

The number of bytes retrieved; otherwise 0 if an error occurs.

Parameters

nCount   Specifies the number of bytes to copy into the *lpObject* buffer.

lpObject   Points to a user-supplied buffer that is to receive the information.

Remarks

Fills a buffer with data that defines a specified object. The function retrieves a data structure whose type depends on the type of graphic object, as shown by the following list:

Object	Buffer type
CPen	**LOGPEN**
CBrush	**LOGBRUSH**
CFont	**LOGFONT**
CBitmap	**BITMAP**
CPalette	**int**
CRgn	Not supported

If the object is a **CBitmap** object, **GetObject** returns only the width, height, and color format information of the bitmap. The actual bits can be retrieved by using **CBitmap::GetBitmapBits**.

If the object is a **CPalette** object, **GetObject** retrieves an integer that specifies the number of entries in the palette. The function does not retrieve the **LOGPALETTE** structure that defines the palette. An application can get information on palette entries by calling **CPalette::GetPaletteEntries**.

See Also   **CBitmap::GetBitmapBits**, **CPalette::GetPaletteEntries**

CGdiObject::GetObjectType

UINT GetObjectType( ) const;

Return Value

The type of the object, if successful; otherwise 0. The value can be one of the following:

- **OBJ_BITMAP**   Bitmap
- **OBJ_BRUSH**   Brush
- **OBJ_FONT**   Font
- **OBJ_PAL**   Palette
- **OBJ_PEN**   Pen
- **OBJ_EXTPEN**   Extended pen
- **OBJ_REGION**   Region
- **OBJ_DC**   Device context
- **OBJ_MEMDC**   Memory device context
- **OBJ_METAFILE**   Metafile
- **OBJ_METADC**   Metafile device context
- **OBJ_ENHMETAFILE**   Enhanced metafile
- **OBJ_ENHMETADC**   Enhanced-metafile device context

Remarks

Retrieves the type of the GDI object.

See Also   **CGdiObject::GetObject**, **CDC::SelectObject**

CGdiObject::GetSafeHandle

HGDIOBJ GetSafeHandle( ) const;

Return Value

A **HANDLE** to the attached Windows GDI object; otherwise **NULL** if no object is attached.

Remarks

Returns **m_hObject** unless **this** is **NULL**, in which case **NULL** is returned. This is part of the general handle interface paradigm and is useful when **NULL** is a valid or special value for a handle.

CGdiObject::UnrealizeObject

BOOL UnrealizeObject( );

Return Value

Nonzero if successful; otherwise 0.

Remarks

Resets the origin of a brush or resets a logical palette. While **UnrealizeObject** is a member function of the **CGdiObject** class, it should be invoked only on **CBrush** or **CPalette** objects.

For **CBrush** objects, **UnrealizeObject** directs the system to reset the origin of the given brush the next time it is selected into a device context. If the object is a **CPalette** object, **UnrealizeObject** directs the system to realize the palette as though it had not previously been realized. The next time the application calls the **CDC::RealizePalette** function for the specified palette, the system completely remaps the logical palette to the system palette.

The **UnrealizeObject** function should not be used with stock objects. The **UnrealizeObject** function must be called whenever a new brush origin is set (by means of the **CDC::SetBrushOrg** function). The **UnrealizeObject** function must not be called for the currently selected brush or currently selected palette of any display context.

See Also **CDC::RealizePalette, CDC::SetBrushOrg**

Data Members

CGdiObject::m_hObject

Remarks

A **HANDLE** containing the **HBITMAP**, **HRGN**, **HBRUSH**, **HPEN**, **HPALETTE**, or **HFONT** attached to this object.

CHeaderCtrl

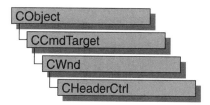

A "header control" is a window usually positioned above columns of text or numbers. It contains a title for each column, and it can be divided into parts. The user can drag the dividers that separate the parts to set the width of each column.

The **CHeaderCtrl** class provides the functionality of the Windows common header control. This control (and therefore the **CHeaderCtrl** class) is available only to programs running under Windows 95 and Windows NT version 3.51 and later.

#include <afxcmn.h>

See Also   **CTabCtrl**, **CListCtrl**

Construction

CHeaderCtrl	Constructs a **CHeaderCtrl** object.
Create	Creates a header control and attaches it to a **CHeaderCtrl** object.

Attributes

GetItemCount	Retrieves a count of the items in a header control.
GetItem	Retrieves information about an item in a header control.
SetItem	Sets the attributes of the specified item in a header control.

Operations

InsertItem	Inserts a new item into a header control.
DeleteItem	Deletes an item from a header control.
Layout	Retrieves the size and position of a header control within a given rectangle.

Overridables

DrawItem	Draws the specified item of a header control.

Member Functions

CHeaderCtrl::CHeaderCtrl

CHeaderCtrl( );

Remarks

Creates a **CHeaderCtrl** object.

See Also   **CHeaderCtrl::Create**

CHeaderCtrl::Create

BOOL Create(DWORD *dwStyle*, **const RECT&** *rect*, **CWnd*** *pParentWnd*, **UINT** *nID* **);**

Return Value

Nonzero if initialization was successful; otherwise zero.

Parameters

dwStyle   Specifies the header control's style. Apply any combination of header control styles needed to the control.

rect   Specifies the header control's size and position. It can be either a **CRect** object or a **RECT** structure.

pParentWnd   Specifies the header control's parent window, usually a **CDialog**. It must not be **NULL**.

nID   Specifies the header control's ID.

Remarks

You construct a **CHeaderCtrl** object in two steps. First call the contructor, then call **Create**, which creates the header control and attaches it to the **CHeaderCtrl** object.

The following styles can be applied to a header control:

- **HDS_BUTTONS**   Header items behave like buttons.
- **HDS_HORZ**   The header control is horizontal.
- **HDS_DIVIDERTRACK**   The header control allows the user to set the width by dragging the item's divider.
- **HDS_VERT**   The header control is vertical (this style is not currently implemented).
- **HDS_HIDDEN**   The header control is not visible in details mode.

745

In addition, you can use the following common control styles to determine how the header control positions and resizes itself:

- **CCS_BOTTOM**   Causes the control to position itself at the bottom of the parent window's client area and sets the width to be the same as the parent window's width.

- **CCS_NODIVIDER**   Prevents a two-pixel highlight from being drawn at the top of the control.

- **CCS_NOHILITE**   Prevents a one-pixel highlight from being drawn at the top of the control.

- **CCS_NOMOVEY**   Causes the control to resize and move itself horizontally, but not vertically, in response to a **WM_SIZE** message. If the **CCS_NORESIZE** style is used, this style does not apply. Header controls have this style by default.

- **CCS_NOPARENTALIGN**   Prevents the control from automatically moving to the top or bottom of the parent window. Instead, the control keeps its position within the parent window despite changes to the size of the parent window. If the **CCS_TOP** or **CCS_BOTTOM** style is also used, the height is adjusted to the default, but the position and width remain unchanged.

- **CCS_NORESIZE**   Prevents the control from using the default width and height when setting its initial size or a new size. Instead, the control uses the width and height specified in the request for creation or sizing.

- **CCS_TOP**   Causes the control to position itself at the top of the parent window's client area and sets the width to be the same as the parent window's width.

You can also apply the following window styles to a header control:

- **WS_CHILD**   Creates a child window. Cannot be used with the **WS_POPUP** style.

- **WS_VISIBLE**   Creates a window that is initially visible.

- **WS_DISABLED**   Creates a window that is initially disabled.

- **WS_GROUP**   Specifies the first control of a group of controls in which the user can move from one control to the next with the arrow keys. All controls defined with the **WS_GROUP** style after the first control belong to the same group. The next control with the **WS_GROUP** style ends the style group and starts the next group (that is, one group ends where the next begins).

- **WS_TABSTOP**   Specifies one of any number of controls through which the user can move by using the TAB key. The TAB key moves the user to the next control specified by the **WS_TABSTOP** style.

See Also   **CHeaderCtrl::CHeaderCtrl**

CHeaderCtrl::DeleteItem

BOOL DeleteItem(int *nPos* **);**

Return Value
Nonzero if successful; otherwise 0.

Parameters
nPos   Specifies the zero-based index of the item to delete.

Remarks
Deletes an item from a header control.

See Also   CHeaderCtrl::InsertItem

CHeaderCtrl::DrawItem

void DrawItem(LPDRAWITEMSTRUCT *lpDrawItemStruct* **);**

Parameters
lpDrawItemStruct   A pointer to a **DRAWITEMSTRUCT** structure describing the item to be painted.

Remarks
Called by the framework when a visual aspect of an owner-draw header control changes. The **itemAction** member of the **DRAWITEMSTRUCT** structure defines the drawing action that is to be performed.

By default, this member function does nothing. Override this member function to implement drawing for an owner-draw **CHeaderCtrl** object.

The application should restore all graphics device interface (GDI) objects selected for the display context supplied in *lpDrawItemStruct* before this member function terminates.

See Also   CWnd::OnDrawItem

CHeaderCtrl::GetItem

BOOL GetItem(int *nPos*, **HD_ITEM*** *pHeaderItem* **) const;**

Return Value
Nonzero if successful; otherwise 0.

Parameters
nPos Specifies the zero-based index of the item to retrieve.

pHeaderItem   Pointer to an **HD_ITEM** structure that receives the new item. This structure is used with the **InsertItem** and **SetItem** member functions. You should set the flags in the mask element before calling to request the other elements get filled in. If **mask** is zero, no data will be returned.

Remarks

Retrieves information about a header control item.

The **HD_ITEM** structure is defined as follows:

```
typedef struct _HD_ITEM
{
    UINT    mask;
    int     cxy;          // width or height of item
    LPSTR   pszText;      // address of item string
    HBITMAP hbm;          // handle of item bitmap
    int     cchTextMax;   // length of item string, in characters
    int     fmt;
    LPARAM  lParam;       // application-defined item data
} HD_ITEM;
```

mask   Mask flags that indicate which of the other structure members contain valid data. Can be a combination of these flags:

- **HDI_BITMAP**   The **hbm** member is valid.

- **HDI_FORMAT**   The **fmt** member is valid.

- **HDI_HEIGHT**   The **cxy** member is valid and specifies the height of the item.

- **HDI_LPARAM**   The **lParam** member is valid.

- **HDI_TEXT**   The **pszText** and **cchTextMax** members are valid.

- **HDI_WIDTH**   The **cxy** member is valid and specifies the width of the item.

fmt   Format flags. Can be a combination of the following values:

- **HDF_CENTER**   Center contents of item.

- **HDF_LEFT**   Left justify contents of item.

- **HDF_RIGHT**   Right justify contents of item.

- **HDF_BITMAP**   The item displays a bitmap.

- **HDF_OWNERDRAW**   The owner window of the header control draws the item.

- **HDF_STRING**   The item displays a string.

See Also   **CHeaderCtrl::SetItem**

CHeaderCtrl::GetItemCount

int GetItemCount( ) const;

Return Value

Number of header control items if successful; otherwise −1.

Remarks

Retrieves a count of the items in a header control.

See Also   **CHeaderCtrl::GetItem, CHeaderCtrl::SetItem**

CHeaderCtrl::InsertItem

int InsertItem(int *nPos*, **HD_ITEM*** *phdi* **);**

Return Value

Index of the new item if successful; otherwise −1.

Parameters

nPos   The zero-based index of the item to be inserted. If the value is zero, the item is inserted at the beginning of the header control. If the value is greater than the maximum value, the item is inserted at the end of the header control.

phdi   Pointer to an **HD_ITEM** structure that contains information about the item to be inserted. For more information on this structure, see **CHeaderCtrl::GetItem**.

Remarks

Inserts a new item into a header control at the specified index.

See Also   **CHeaderCtrl::DeleteItem, CHeaderCtrl::GetItem**

CHeaderCtrl::Layout

BOOL Layout(HD_LAYOUT* *pHeaderLayout* **);**

Return Value

Nonzero if successful; otherwise 0.

Parameters

pHeaderLayout   Pointer to an **HD_LAYOUT** structure, which contains information used to set the size and position of a header control.

Remarks

Retrieves the size and position of a header control within a given rectangle. This function is used to determine the appropriate dimensions for a new header control that is to occupy the given rectangle.

The **HD_LAYOUT** structure is defined as follows:

```
typedef struct _HD_LAYOUT {  // hdl
    RECT FAR* prc;           // see below
    WINDOWPOS FAR* pwpos; // see below
} HD_LAYOUT;
```

prc   Pointer to a **RECT** structure that contains the coordinates of the rectangle in which a header control is to be drawn.

pwpos   Pointer to a **WINDOWPOS** structure that receives information about the appropriate size and position of the header control.

CHeaderCtrl::SetItem

BOOL SetItem(int *nPos***, HD_ITEM*** *pHeaderItem* **);**

Return Value

Nonzero if successful; otherwise 0.

Parameters

nPos   The zero-based index of the item to be manipulated.

pHeaderItem   Pointer to an **HD_ITEM** structure that contains information about the new item. For more information on this structure, see **CHeaderCtrl::GetItem**.

Remarks

Sets the attributes of the specified item in a header control.

See Also   **CHeaderCtrl::GetItem**,**CHeaderCtrl::GetItemCount**

CHotKeyCtrl

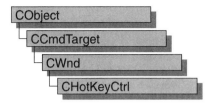

A "hot key control" is a window that enables the user to create a hot key. A "hot key" is a key combination that the user can press to perform an action quickly. (For example, a user can create a hot key that activates a given window and brings it to the top of the Z order.) The hot key control displays the user's choices and ensures that the user selects a valid key combination.

The **CHotKeyCtrl** class provides the functionality of the Windows common hot key control. This control (and therefore the **CHotKeyCtrl** class) is available only to programs running under Windows 95 and Windows NT version 3.51 and later.

When the user has chosen a key combination, the application can retrieve the specified key combination from the control and use the **WM_SETHOTKEY** message to set up the hot key in the system. Whenever the user presses the hot key thereafter, from any part of the system, the window specified in the **WM_SETHOTKEY** message receives a **WM_SYSCOMMAND** message specifying **SC_HOTKEY**. This message activates the window that receives it. The hot key remains valid until the application that called **WM_SETHOTKEY** exits.

This mechanism is different from the hot key support that depends on the **WM_HOTKEY** message and the Windows **RegisterHotKey** and **UnregisterHotKey** functions.

#include <afxcmn.h>

Construction

CHotKeyCtrl	Constructs a **CHotKeyCtrl** object.
Create	Creates a hot key control and attaches it to a **CHotKeyCtrl** object.

Attributes

SetHotKey	Sets the hot key combination for a hot key control.
GetHotKey	Retrieves the virtual-key code and modifier flags of a hot key from a hot key control.

Operations

SetRules	Defines the invalid combinations and the default modifier combination for a hot key control.

Member Functions

CHotKeyCtrl::CHotKeyCtrl

CHotKeyCtrl( );

Remarks

Constructs a **CHotKeyCtrl** object.

See Also   CHotKeyCtrl::Create

CHotKeyCtrl::Create

BOOL Create(DWORD *dwStyle*, **const RECT&** *rect*, **CWnd*** *pParentWnd*, **UINT** *nID* **);**

Return Value

Nonzero, if initialization was successful; otherwise 0.

Parameters

dwStyle   Specifies the hot key control's style. Apply any combination of control styles.

rect   Specifies the hot key control's size and position. It can be either a **CRect** object or a **RECT** structure.

pParentWnd   Specifies the hot key control's parent window, usually a **CDialog**. It must not be **NULL**.

nID   Specifies the hot key control's ID.

Remarks

You construct a **CHotKeyCtrl** object in two steps. First call the constructor, then call **Create**, which creates the hot key control and attaches it to the **CHotKeyCtrl** object.

See Also   CHotKeyCtrl::CHotKeyCtrl

CHotKeyCtrl::GetHotKey

DWORD GetHotKey( ) const;
void GetHotKey(WORD &*wVirtualKeyCode***, WORD &***wModifiers* **) const;**

Return Value

The virtual-key code and modifier flags. The virtual-key code is in the low-order byte, and the modifier flags are in the high-order byte. The modifier flags can be a combination of the following values:

- **HOTKEYF_ALT**   ALT key
- **HOTKEYF_CONTROL**   CTRL key
- **HOTKEYF_EXT**   Extended key
- **HOTKEYF_SHIFT**   SHIFT key

The 16-bit value returned by this member function can be used as the parameter in the **SetHotKey** member function.

Parameters

wVirtualKeyCode   Virtual-key code of the hot key.

wModifiers   Modifier flags indicating the keys that, when used in combination with *wVirtualKeyCode*, define a hot key combination.

Remarks

Call this function to retrieve the virtual-key code and modifier flags of a hot key from a hot key control.

See Also   **CHotKeyCtrl::SetHotKey**

CHotKeyCtrl::SetHotKey

void SetHotKey(WORD *wVirtualKeyCode***, WORD** *wModifiers* **);**

Parameters

wVirtualKeyCode   Virtual-key code of the hot key.

wModifiers   Modifier flags indicating the keys that, when used in combination with *wVirtualKeyCode*, define a hot key combination. For more information on the modifier flags, see **GetHotKey**.

Remarks

Call this function to set the hot key combination for a hot key control.

See Also   **CHotKeyCtrl::GetHotKey**

CHotKeyCtrl::SetRules

void SetRules(WORD *wInvalidComb***, WORD** *wModifiers* **);**

Parameters

wInvalidComb   Array of flags that specifies invalid key combinations. It can be a combination of the following values:

- **HKCOMB_A**   ALT

- **HKCOMB_C**   CTRL

- **HKCOMB_CA**   CTRL+ALT

- **HKCOMB_NONE**   Unmodified keys

- **HKCOMB_S**   SHIFT

- **HKCOMB_SA**   SHIFT+ALT

- **HKCOMB_SC**   SHIFT+CTRL

- **HKCOMB_SCA**   SHIFT+CTRL+ALT

wModifiers   Array of flags that specifies the key combination to use when the user enters an invalid combination. For more information on the modifier flags, see **GetHotKey**.

Remarks

Call this function to define the invalid combinations and the default modifier combination for a hot key control. When a user enters an invalid key combination, as defined by flags specified in *wInvalidComb*, the system uses the OR operator to combine the keys entered by the user with the flags specified in *wModifiers*. The resulting key combination is converted into a string and then displayed in the hot key control.

See Also   **CHotKeyCtrl::GetHotKey**, **CHotKeyCtrl::SetHotKey**

CImageList

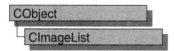

An "image list" is a collection of same-sized images, each of which can be referred to by its zero-based index. Image lists are used to efficiently manage large sets of icons or bitmaps. All images in an image list are contained in a single, wide bitmap in screen device format. An image list may also include a monochrome bitmap that contains masks used to draw images transparently (icon style). The Microsoft Win32 application programming interface (API) provides image list functions that enable you to draw images, create and destroy image lists, add and remove images, replace images, merge images, and drag images.

The **CImageList** class provides the functionality of the Windows common image list control. This control (and therefore the **CImageList** class) is available only to programs running under Windows 95 and Windows NT version 3.51 and later.

#include <afxcmn.h>

See Also **CListCtrl**, **CTabCtrl**

Data Members

m_hImageList	A handle containing the image list attached to this object.

Construction

CImageList	Constructs a **CImageList** object.
Create	Initializes an image list and attaches it to a **CImageList** object.

Attributes

GetSafeHandle	Retrieves **m_hImageList**.
GetImageCount	Retrieves the number of images in an image list.
SetBkColor	Sets the background color for an image list.
GetBkColor	Retrieves the current background color for an image list.
GetImageInfo	Retrieves information about an image.

Operations

Attach	Attaches an image list to a **CImageList** object.
Detach	Detaches an image list object from a **CImageList** object and returns a handle to an image list.

DeleteImageList	Deletes an image list.
Add	Adds an image or images to an image list.
Remove	Removes an image from an image list.
Replace	Replaces an image in an image list with a new image.
ExtractIcon	Creates an icon based on an image and mask in an image list.
Draw	Draws the image that is being dragged during a drag-and-drop operation.
SetOverlayImage	Adds the zero-based index of an image to the list of images to be used as overlay masks.
SetDragCursorImage	Creates a new drag image.
GetDragImage	Gets the temporary image list that is used for dragging.
Read	Reads an image list from an archive.
Write	Writes an image list to an archive.
BeginDrag	Begins dragging an image.
DragEnter	Locks updates during a drag operation and displays the drag image at a specified position.
EndDrag	Ends a drag operation.
DragLeave	Unlocks the window and hides the drag image so that the window can be updated.
DragMove	Moves the image that is being dragged during a drag-and-drop operation.
DragShowNolock	Shows or hides the drag image during a drag operation, without locking the window.

Member Functions

CImageList::Add

> **int Add(CBitmap*** *pbmImage*, **CBitmap*** *pbmMask* **);**
> **int Add(CBitmap*** *pbmImage*, **COLORREF** *crMask* **);**
> **int Add(HICON** *hIcon* **);**

Return Value

Zero-based index of the first new image if successful; otherwise −1.

Parameters

pbmImage   Pointer to the bitmap containing the image or images. The number of images is inferred from the width of the bitmap.

pbmMask   Pointer to the bitmap containing the mask. If no mask is used with the image list, this parameter is ignored.

crMask   Color used to generate the mask. Each pixel of this color in the given bitmap is changed to black and the corresponding bit in the mask is set to one.

hIcon   Handle of the icon that contains the bitmap and mask for the new image.

Remarks

Call this function to add one or more images or an icon to an image list.

See Also   **CImageList::Remove**, **CImageList::Replace**, **COLORREF** in the Win32 Programmer's Reference

---

CImageList::Attach

BOOL Attach(HIMAGELIST *hImageList* **);**

Return Value

Nonzero if the attachment was successful; otherwise 0.

Parameters

hImageList   A handle to an image list object.

Remarks

Call this function to attach an image list to a **CImageList** object.

See Also   **CImageList::Detach**, **CImageList::GetSafeHandle**

CImageList::BeginDrag

BOOL BeginDrag(int *nImage*, **CPoint** *ptHotSpot* **);**

Return Value

Nonzero if successful; otherwise 0.

Parameters

nImage   Zero-based index of the image to drag.

ptHotSpot   Coordinates of the starting drag position (typically, the cursor position). The coordinates are relative to the upper left corner of the image.

Remarks

Call this function to begin dragging an image. This function creates a temporary image list that is used for dragging. The image combines the specified image and its mask with the current cursor. In response to subsequent **WM_MOUSEMOVE** messages, you can move the drag image by using the **DragMove** member function. To end the drag operation, you can use the **EndDrag** member function.

See Also   **CImageList::Draw**, **CImageList::EndDrag**, **CImageList::DragMove**

CImageList::CImageList

CImageList( );

Remarks

Constructs a **CImageList** object.

See Also **CImageList::Create**

CImageList::Create

BOOL Create(int *cx***, int** *cy***, BOOL** *bMask***, int** *nInitial***, int** *nGrow* **);**
BOOL Create(UINT *nBitmapID***, int** *cx***, int** *nGrow***, COLORREF** *crMask* **);**
BOOL Create(LPCTSTR *lpszBitmapID***, int** *cx***, int** *nGrow***, COLORREF** *crMask* **);**
BOOL Create(CImageList& *imagelist1***, int** *nImage1***, CImageList&** *imagelist2***,**
    int *nImage2***, int** *dx***, int** *dy* **);**

Return Value

Nonzero if successful; otherwise 0.

Parameters

cx Dimensions of each image, in pixels.

cy Dimensions of each image, in pixels.

bMask **TRUE** if the image contains a mask; otherwise **FALSE**.

nInitial Number of images that the image list initially contains.

nGrow Number of images by which the image list can grow when the system needs to resize the list to make room for new images. This parameter represents the number of new images the resized image list can contain.

nBitmapID Resource IDs of the bitmap to be associated with the image list.

crMask Color used to generate a mask. Each pixel of this color in the specified bitmap is changed to black, and the corresponding bit in the mask is set to one.

lpszBitmapID A string containing the resource IDs of the images.

imagelist1 A pointer to a **CImageList** object.

nImage1 Number of images contained in *imagelist1*.

imagelist2 A pointer to a **CImageList** object.

nImage2 Number of images contained in *imagelist2*.

dx Dimensions of each image, in pixels.

dy Dimensions of each image, in pixels.

Remarks

You construct a **CImageList** in two steps. First call the constructor, then call **Create**, which creates the image list and attaches it to the **CImageList** object.

See Also **CImageList::CImageList**, **COLORREF** in the Win32 Programmer's Reference

CImageList::DeleteImageList

BOOL DeleteImageList( );

Return Value

Nonzero if successful; otherwise 0.

Remarks

Call this function to delete an image list.

See Also **CImageList::Detach**

CImageList::Detach

HIMAGELIST Detach( );

Return Value

A handle to an image list object.

Remarks

Call this function to detach an image list object from a **CImageList** object. This function returns a handle to the image list object.

See Also **CImageList::Attach**, **CImageList::DeleteImageList**

CImageList::DragEnter

static BOOL DragEnter(CWnd* *pWndLock*, **CPoint** *point* **);**

Return Value

Nonzero if successful; otherwise 0.

Parameters

pWndLock Pointer to the window that owns the drag image.

point Position at which to display the drag image. Coordinates are relative to the upper left corner of the window (not the client area).

Remarks

During a drag operation, locks updates to the window specified by *pWndLock* and displays the drag image at the position specified by *point*.

The coordinates are relative to the window's upper left corner, so you must compensate for the widths of window elements, such as the border, title bar, and menu bar, when specifying the coordinates.

If *pWndLock* is **NULL**, this function draws the image in the display context associated with the desktop window, and coordinates are relative to the upper left corner of the screen.

This function locks all other updates to the given window during the drag operation. If you need to do any drawing during a drag operation, such as highlighting the target of a drag-and-drop operation, you can temporarily hide the dragged image by using the **CImageList::DragLeave** function.

See Also   **CImageList::BeginDrag**, **CImageList::EndDrag**, **CImageList::DragMove**, **CImageList::DragLeave**

CImageList::DragLeave

static BOOL DragLeave(CWnd* *pWndLock* **);**

Return Value

Nonzero if successful; otherwise 0.

Parameters

pWndLock   Pointer to the window that owns the drag image.

Remarks

Unlocks the window specified by *pWndLock* and hides the drag image, allowing the window to be updated.

See Also   **CImageList::BeginDrag**, **CImageList::EndDrag**, **CImageList::DragMove**, **CImageList::DragEnter**

CImageList::DragMove

static BOOL DragMove(CPoint *pt* **);**

Return Value

Nonzero if successful; otherwise 0.

Parameters

pt   New drag position.

Remarks

Call this function to move the image that is being dragged during a drag-and-drop operation. This function is typically called in response to a **WM_MOUSEMOVE** message. To begin a drag operation, use the **BeginDrag** member function.

See Also **CImageList::BeginDrag**, **CImageList::EndDrag**, **CImageList::Draw**

CImageList::DragShowNolock

static BOOL DragShowNolock(BOOL *bShow* **);**

Return Value

Nonzero if successful; otherwise 0.

Parameters

bShow   Specifies whether the drag image is to be shown.

Remarks

Shows or hides the drag image during a drag operation, without locking the window.

The **CImageList::DragEnter** function locks all updates to the window during a drag operation. This function, however, does not lock the window.

See Also **CImageList::BeginDrag**, **CImageList::EndDrag**, **CImageList::DragEnter**, **CImageList::DragLeave**, **CImageList::Draw**

CImageList::Draw

BOOL Draw(CDC* *pdc***, int** *nImage***, POINT** *pt***, UINT** *nStyle* **);**

Return Value

Nonzero if successful; otherwise 0.

Parameters

pdc   Pointer to the destination device context.

nImage   Zero-based index of the image to draw.

pt   Location at which to draw within the specified device context.

nStyle   Flag specifying the drawing style. It can be one or more of these values:

- **ILD_NORMAL**   Draws the image using the background color for the image list. If the background color is **CLR_NONE**, the image is drawn transparently using the mask.

- **ILD_TRANSPARENT**   Draws the image transparently using the mask, regardless of the background color. This value has no effect if the image list does not contain a mask.

- **ILD_BLEND50** Draws the image dithered with the highlight color to indicate that it is selected. This value has no effect if the image list does not contain a mask.

- **ILD_BLEND25** Draws the image striped with the highlight color to indicate that it has the focus.

- **ILD_OVERLAYMASK** Draws the image and overlays it with an overlay mask. The zero-based index of the overlay mask must be combined with this style. The zero-based index must also be specified by using the **INDEXTOOVERLAYMASK** macro.

Remarks

Call this function to draw the image that is being dragged during a drag-and-drop operation.

See Also   **CImageList::BeginDrag, CImageList::EndDrag, CImageList::DragMove**

CImageList::EndDrag

static void EndDrag( );

Remarks

Call this function to end a drag operation. To begin a drag operation, use the **BeginDrag** member function.

See Also   **CImageList::BeginDrag, CImageList::Draw, CImageList::DragMove**

CImageList::ExtractIcon

HICON ExtractIcon(int *nImage* **);**

Return Value

Handle of the icon if successful; otherwise **NULL**.

Parameters

nImage   Zero-based index of the image.

Remarks

Call this function to create an icon based on an image and its related mask in an image list.

See Also   **CImageList::Replace**

CImageList::GetBkColor

COLORREF GetBkColor( ) const;

Return Value

The RGB color value of the **CImageList** object background color.

Remarks

Call this function to retrieve the current background color for an image list.

See Also **CImageList::SetBkColor**, **COLORREF** in the Win32 Programmer's Reference

---

CImageList::GetDragImage

static CImageList* GetDragImage(LPPOINT *lpPoint*, **LPPOINT** *lpPointHotSpot* **);**

Return Value

If successful, a pointer to the temporary image list that is used for dragging; otherwise, **NULL**.

Parameters

lpPoint Address of a **POINT** structure that receives the current drag position.

lpPointHotSpot Address of a **POINT** structure that receives the offset of the drag image relative to the drag position.

Remarks

Gets the temporary image list that is used for dragging.

See Also **CImageList::SetDragCursorImage**

CImageList::GetImageCount

int GetImageCount( ) const;

Return Value

The number of images.

Remarks

Call this function to retrieve the number of images in an image list.

See Also **CImageList::GetImageInfo**

CImageList::GetImageInfo

BOOL GetImageInfo(int *nImage*, **IMAGEINFO*** *pImageInfo* **) const;**

Return Value

Nonzero if successful; otherwise 0.

Parameters

nImage   Zero-based index of the image.

pImageInfo   Pointer to an **IMAGEINFO** structure that receives information about the image. The information in this structure can be used to directly manipulate the bitmaps for the image.

Remarks

Call this function to retrieve information about an image.

The **IMAGEINFO** structure contains information about an image in an image list:

```
typedef struct _IMAGEINFO {
    HBITMAP hbmImage;       // bitmap containing the images
    HBITMAP hbmMask;
    int     cPlanes;        // number of color planes in hbmImage
    int     cBitsPerPixel;  // bits per pixel in hbmImage
    RECT    rcImage;
} IMAGEINFO;
```

hbmMask   Handle of a monochrome bitmap containing the masks for the images. If the image list does not contain a mask, this member is **NULL**.

rcImage   Bounding rectangle of the image within the bitmap specified by **hbmImage**.

See Also   **CImageList::GetImageCount**

CImageList::GetSafeHandle

HIMAGELIST GetSafeHandle( ) const;

Return Value

A handle to the attached image list; otherwise **NULL** if no object is attached.

Remarks

Call this function to retrieve the **m_hImageList** data member.

See Also   **CImageList::Attach, CImageList::Detach, CImageList::m_hImageList**

CImageList::Read

BOOL Read(CArchive* *pArchive* **);**

Return Value

Nonzero if successful; otherwise 0.

Parameters

pArchive   A pointer to a **CArchive** object from which the image list is to be read.

Remarks

Call this function to read an image list from an archive.

See Also   CImageList::Write

CImageList::Remove

BOOL Remove(int *nImage* **);**

Return Value

Nonzero if successful; otherwise 0.

Parameters

nImage   Zero-based index of the image to remove.

Remarks

Call this function to remove an image from an image list object.

See Also   CImageList::DeleteImageList

CImageList::Replace

BOOL Replace(int *nImage*, **CBitmap*** *pbmImage*, **CBitmap*** *pbmMask* **);**
int Replace(int *nImage*, **HICON** *hIcon* **);**

Return Value

The version returning **BOOL** returns nonzero if successful; otherwise 0.

The version returning **int** returns the zero-based index of the image if successful; otherwise −1.

Parameters

nImage   Zero-based index of the image to replace.

pbmImage   A pointer to the bitmap containing the image.

pbmMask   A pointer to the bitmap containing the mask. If no mask is used with the image list, this parameter is ignored.

hIcon   A handle to the icon that contains the bitmap and mask for the new image.

Remarks

Call this function to replace an image in an image list with a new image.

See Also **CImageList::Remove**

CImageList::SetBkColor

COLORREF SetBkColor(COLORREF *cr* **);**

Return Value

The previous background color if successful; otherwise **CLR_NONE**.

Parameters

cr   Background color to set. It can be **CLR_NONE**. In that case, images are drawn transparently using the mask.

Remarks

Call this function to set the background color for an image list.

See Also **CImageList::GetBkColor**, **COLORREF** in the Win32 Programmer's Reference

---

CImageList::SetDragCursorImage

BOOL SetDragCursorImage(int *nDrag*, **CPoint** *ptHotSpot* **);**

Return Value

Nonzero if successful; otherwise 0.

Parameters

nDrag   Index of the new image to be combined with the drag image.

ptHotSpot   Position of the hot spot within the new image.

Remarks

Creates a new drag image by combining the given image (typically a mouse cursor image) with the current drag image.

Because the dragging functions use the new image during a drag operation, you should use the Windows **ShowCursor** function to hide the actual mouse cursor after calling **CImageList::SetDragCursorImage**. Otherwise, the system may appear to have two mouse cursors for the duration of the drag operation.

See Also   CImageList::BeginDrag, CImageList::EndDrag,
CImageList::GetDragImage

CImageList::SetOverlayImage

BOOL SetOverlayImage(int *nImage***, int** *nOverlay* **);**

Return Value

Nonzero if successful; otherwise 0.

Parameters

nImage   Zero-based index of the image to use as an overlay mask.

nOverlay   One-based index of the overlay mask.

Remarks

Call this function to add the zero-based index of an image to the list of images to be
used as overlay masks. Up to four indices can be added to the list.

An overlay mask is an image drawn transparently over another image. You draw an
overlay mask over an image by using the **CImageList::Draw** member function with
the **ILD_OVERLAYMASK** style combined with the one-based index of the overlay
mask. The one-based index must be specified by using the
INDEXTOOVERLAYMASK macro.

See Also   CImageList::Add

CImageList::Write

BOOL Write(CArchive* *pArchive* **);**

Return Value

Nonzero if successful; otherwise 0.

Parameters

pArchive   A pointer to a **CArchive** object in which the image list is to be stored.

Remarks

Call this function to write an image list object to an archive.

See Also   CImageList::Read

Data Members

CImageList::m_hImageList

HIMAGELIST m_hImageList;

Remarks

A handle of the image list attached to this object. The **m_hImageList** data member is a public variable of type **HIMAGELIST**.

See Also **CImageList::Attach**, **CImageList::Detach**, **CImageList::Attach**

CList

template< class *TYPE*, **class** *ARG_TYPE* >
class CList : public CObject

Parameters

TYPE   Type of object stored in the list.

ARG_TYPE   Type used to reference objects stored in the list. Can be a reference.

Remarks

The **CList** class supports ordered lists of nonunique objects accessible sequentially or by value. **CList** lists behave like doubly-linked lists.

A variable of type **POSITION** is a key for the list. You can use a **POSITION** variable as an iterator to traverse a list sequentially and as a bookmark to hold a place. A position is not the same as an index, however.

Element insertion is very fast at the list head, at the tail, and at a known **POSITION**. A sequential search is necessary to look up an element by value or index. This search can be slow if the list is long.

If you need a dump of individual elements in the list, you must set the depth of the dump context to 1 or greater.

Certain member functions of this class call global helper functions that must be customized for most uses of the **CList** class. See "Collection Class Helpers" in the "Macros and Globals" section.

For more information on using **CList**, see the article "Collections" in *Programming with MFC.*

#include <afxtempl.h>

See Also   **CMap**, **CArray**, Collection Class Helpers

Head/Tail Access

GetHead	Returns the head element of the list (cannot be empty).
GetTail	Returns the tail element of the list (cannot be empty).

Operations

RemoveHead	Removes the element from the head of the list.
RemoveTail	Removes the element from the tail of the list.

AddHead	Adds an element (or all the elements in another list) to the head of the list (makes a new head).
AddTail	Adds an element (or all the elements in another list) to the tail of the list (makes a new tail).
RemoveAll	Removes all the elements from this list.

Iteration

GetHeadPosition	Returns the position of the head element of the list.
GetTailPosition	Returns the position of the tail element of the list.
GetNext	Gets the next element for iterating.
GetPrev	Gets the previous element for iterating.

Retrieval/Modification

GetAt	Gets the element at a given position.
SetAt	Sets the element at a given position.
RemoveAt	Removes an element from this list, specified by position.

Insertion

InsertBefore	Inserts a new element before a given position.
InsertAfter	Inserts a new element after a given position.

Searching

Find	Gets the position of an element specified by pointer value.
FindIndex	Gets the position of an element specified by a zero-based index.

Status

GetCount	Returns the number of elements in this list.
IsEmpty	Tests for the empty list condition (no elements).

Member Functions

CList::AddHead

POSITION AddHead(*ARG_TYPE newElement* **);**
void AddHead(CList* *pNewList* **);**

Return Value

The first version returns the **POSITION** value of the newly inserted element.

Parameters

ARG_TYPE   Template parameter specifying the type of the list element (can be a reference).

newElement   The new element.

pNewList   A pointer to another **CList** list. The elements in *pNewList* will be added to this list.

Remarks

Adds a new element or list of elements to the head of this list. The list can be empty before the operation.

See Also   **CList::GetHead**, **CList::RemoveHead**

CList::AddTail

POSITION AddTail(*ARG_TYPE newElement* **);**
void AddTail(CList* *pNewList* **);**

Return Value

The first version returns the **POSITION** value of the newly inserted element.

Parameters

ARG_TYPE   Template parameter specifying the type of the list element (can be a reference).

newElement   The element to be added to this list.

pNewList   A pointer to another **CList** list. The elements in *pNewList* will be added to this list.

Remarks

Adds a new element or list of elements to the tail of this list. The list can be empty before the operation.

See Also   **CObList::GetTail**, **CObList::RemoveTail**

CList::Find

POSITION Find(*ARG_TYPE searchValue*, **POSITION** *startAfter* = **NULL) const;**

Return Value

A **POSITION** value that can be used for iteration or object pointer retrieval; **NULL** if the object is not found.

Parameters

ARG_TYPE   Template parameter specifying the type of the list element (can be a reference).

searchValue   The value to be found in the list.

startAfter   The start position for the search.

Remarks

Searches the list sequentially to find the first element matching the specified *searchValue*. Note that the pointer values are compared, not the contents of the objects.

See Also   **CList::GetNext**, **CList::GetPrev**

CList::FindIndex

POSITION FindIndex(int *nIndex* **) const;**

Return Value

A **POSITION** value that can be used for iteration or object pointer retrieval; **NULL** if *nIndex* is negative or too large.

Parameters

nIndex   The zero-based index of the list element to be found.

Remarks

Uses the value of *nIndex* as an index into the list. It starts a sequential scan from the head of the list, stopping on the *n*th element.

See Also   **CObList::Find**, **CObList::GetNext**, **CObList::GetPrev**

CList::GetAt

*TYPE***& GetAt(POSITION** *position* **);**
TYPE **GetAt(POSITION** *position* **) const;**

Return Value

See the return value description for **GetHead**.

Parameters

TYPE   Template parameter specifying the type of object in the list.

position   A **POSITION** value returned by a previous **GetHeadPosition** or **Find** member function call.

Remarks

A variable of type **POSITION** is a key for the list. It is not the same as an index, and you cannot operate on a **POSITION** value yourself. **GetAt** returns the element (or a reference to the element) associated with a given position.

You must ensure that your **POSITION** value represents a valid position in the list. If it is invalid, then the Debug version of the Microsoft Foundation Class Library asserts.

See Also   **CList::Find**, **CList::SetAt**, **CList::GetNext**, **CList::GetPrev**, **CList::GetHead**

CList::GetCount

int GetCount() const;

Return Value

An integer value containing the element count.

Remarks

Gets the number of elements in this list.

See Also **CList::IsEmpty**

CList::GetHead

*TYPE***& GetHead( );**
TYPE **GetHead( ) const;**

Return Value

If the list is **const**, **GetHead** returns a copy of the element at the head of the list. This allows the function to be used only on the right side of an assignment statement and protects the list from modification.

If the list is not **const**, **GetHead** returns a reference to an element of the list. This allows the function to be used on either side of an assignment statement and thus allows the list entries to be modified.

Parameters

TYPE   Template parameter specifying the type of object in the list.

Remarks

Gets the head element (or a reference to the head element) of this list.

You must ensure that the list is not empty before calling **GetHead**. If the list is empty, then the Debug version of the Microsoft Foundation Class Library asserts. Use **IsEmpty** to verify that the list contains elements.

See Also **CList::GetTail, CList::GetTailPosition, CList::AddHead, CList::RemoveHead**

CList::GetHeadPosition

POSITION GetHeadPosition( ) const;

Return Value

A **POSITION** value that can be used for iteration or object pointer retrieval; **NULL** if the list is empty.

Remarks

Gets the position of the head element of this list.

See Also **CList::GetTailPosition**

CList::GetNext

TYPE& **GetNext(POSITION&** *rPosition* **);**
TYPE **GetNext(POSITION&** *rPosition* **) const;**

Return Value

If the list is **const**, **GetNext** returns a copy of the element at the head of the list. This allows the function to be used only on the right side of an assignment statement and protects the list from modification.

If the list is not **const**, **GetNext** returns a reference to an element of the list. This allows the function to be used on either side of an assignment statement and thus allows the list entries to be modified.

Parameters

TYPE   Template parameter specifying the type of the elements in the list.

rPosition   A reference to a **POSITION** value returned by a previous **GetNext**, **GetHeadPosition**, or other member function call.

Remarks

Gets the list element identified by *rPosition*, then sets *rPosition* to the **POSITION** value of the next entry in the list. You can use **GetNext** in a forward iteration loop if you establish the initial position with a call to **GetHeadPosition** or **Find**.

You must ensure that your **POSITION** value represents a valid position in the list. If it is invalid, then the Debug version of the Microsoft Foundation Class Library asserts.

If the retrieved element is the last in the list, then the new value of *rPosition* is set to **NULL**.

See Also **CList::Find**, **CList::GetHeadPosition**, **CList::GetTailPosition**, **CList::GetPrev**, **CList::GetHead**

CList::GetPrev

TYPE& **GetPrev(POSITION&** *rPosition* **);**
TYPE **GetPrev(POSITION&** *rPosition* **) const;**

Return Value

If the list is **const**, **GetPrev** returns a copy of the element at the head of the list. This allows the function to be used only on the right side of an assignment statement and protects the list from modification.

If the list is not **const**, **GetPrev** returns a reference to an element of the list. This allows the function to be used on either side of an assignment statement and thus allows the list entries to be modified.

Parameters

TYPE   Template parameter specifying the type of the elements in the list.

rPosition   A reference to a **POSITION** value returned by a previous **GetPrev** or other member function call.

Remarks

Gets the list element identified by *rPosition*, then sets *rPosition* to the **POSITION** value of the previous entry in the list. You can use **GetPrev** in a reverse iteration loop if you establish the initial position with a call to **GetTailPosition** or **Find**.

You must ensure that your **POSITION** value represents a valid position in the list. If it is invalid, then the Debug version of the Microsoft Foundation Class Library asserts.

If the retrieved element is the first in the list, then the new value of *rPosition* is set to **NULL**.

See Also   **CList::Find**, **CList::GetTailPosition**, **CList::GetHeadPosition**, **CList::GetNext**, **CList::GetHead**

CList::GetTail

TYPE& **GetTail( );**
TYPE **GetTail() const;**

Return Value

See the return value description for **GetHead**.

Parameters

TYPE   Template parameter specifying the type of elements in the list.

Remarks

Gets the **CObject** pointer that represents the tail element of this list.

You must ensure that the list is not empty before calling **GetTail**. If the list is empty, then the Debug version of the Microsoft Foundation Class Library asserts. Use **IsEmpty** to verify that the list contains elements.

See Also   **CList::AddTail**, **CList::AddHead**, **CList::RemoveHead**, **CList::GetHead**

CList::GetTailPosition

POSITION GetTailPosition( ) const;

Return Value

A **POSITION** value that can be used for iteration or object pointer retrieval; **NULL** if the list is empty.

Remarks

Gets the position of the tail element of this list; **NULL** if the list is empty.

See Also   **CList::GetHeadPosition**, **CList::GetTail**

CList::InsertAfter

POSITION InsertAfter(POSITION *position*, *ARG_TYPE newElement* **);**

Return Value

A **POSITION** value that can be used for iteration or list element retrieval.

Parameters

position   A **POSITION** value returned by a previous **GetNext**, **GetPrev**, or **Find** member function call.

ARG_TYPE   Template parameter specifying the type of the list element.

newElement   The element to be added to this list.

Remarks

Adds an element to this list after the element at the specified position.

See Also   **CList::Find**, **CList::InsertBefore**

CList::InsertBefore

POSITION InsertBefore(POSITION *position*, *ARG_TYPE newElement* **);**

Return Value

A **POSITION** value that can be used for iteration or list element retrieval; **NULL** if the list is empty.

Parameters

position   A **POSITION** value returned by a previous **GetNext**, **GetPrev**, or **Find** member function call.

ARG_TYPE   Template parameter specifying the type of the list element (can be a reference).

newElement   The element to be added to this list.

Remarks

Adds an element to this list before the element at the specified position.

See Also   **CList::Find, CList::InsertAfter**

CList::IsEmpty

BOOL IsEmpty( ) const;

Return Value

Nonzero if this list is empty; otherwise 0.

Remarks

Indicates whether this list contains no elements.

See Also   **CList::GetCount**

CList::RemoveAll

void RemoveAll( );

Remarks

Removes all the elements from this list and frees the associated memory. No error is generated if the list is already empty.

See Also   **CList::RemoveAt**

CList::RemoveAt

void RemoveAt(POSITION *position* **);**

Parameters

position   The position of the element to be removed from the list.

Remarks

Removes the specified element from this list.

You must ensure that your **POSITION** value represents a valid position in the list. If it is invalid, then the Debug version of the Microsoft Foundation Class Library asserts.

See Also   **CList::RemoveAll**

CList::RemoveHead

TYPE **RemoveHead( );**

Return Value

The element previously at the head of the list.

Parameters

TYPE   Template parameter specifying the type of elements in the list.

Remarks

Removes the element from the head of the list and returns a pointer to it.

You must ensure that the list is not empty before calling **RemoveHead**. If the list is empty, then the Debug version of the Microsoft Foundation Class Library asserts. Use **IsEmpty** to verify that the list contains elements.

See Also   **CList::GetHead, CList::AddHead**

CList::RemoveTail

TYPE **RemoveTail( );**

Return Value

The element that was at the tail of the list.

Parameters

TYPE   Template parameter specifying the type of elements in the list.

Remarks

Removes the element from the tail of the list and returns a pointer to it.

You must ensure that the list is not empty before calling **RemoveTail**. If the list is empty, then the Debug version of the Microsoft Foundation Class Library asserts. Use **IsEmpty** to verify that the list contains elements.

See Also   **CList::GetTail, CList::AddTail**

CList::SetAt

void SetAt(POSITION *pos*, *ARG_TYPE newElement* **);**

Parameters

pos   The **POSITION** of the element to be set.

ARG_TYPE   Template parameter specifying the type of the list element (can be a reference).

newElement   The element to be added to the list.

Remarks

A variable of type **POSITION** is a key for the list. It is not the same as an index, and you cannot operate on a **POSITION** value yourself. **SetAt** writes the element to the specified position in the list.

You must ensure that your **POSITION** value represents a valid position in the list. If it is invalid, then the Debug version of the Microsoft Foundation Class Library asserts.

See Also   **CList::Find**, **CList::GetAt**, **CList::GetNext**, **CList::GetPrev**

CListBox

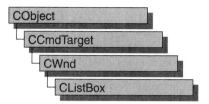

The **CListBox** class provides the functionality of a Windows list box. A list box displays a list of items, such as filenames, that the user can view and select.

In a single-selection list box, the user can select only one item. In a multiple-selection list box, a range of items can be selected. When the user selects an item, it is highlighted and the list box sends a notification message to the parent window.

You can create a list box either from a dialog template or directly in your code. To create it directly, construct the **CListBox** object, then call the **Create** member function to create the Windows list-box control and attach it to the **CListBox** object. To use a list box in a dialog template, declare a list-box variable in your dialog box class, then use **DDX_Control** in your dialog box class's **DoDataExchange** function to connect the member variable to the control. (ClassWizard does this for you automatically when you add a control variable to your dialog box class.)

Construction can be a one-step process in a class derived from **CListBox**. Write a constructor for the derived class and call **Create** from within the constructor.

If you want to handle Windows notification messages sent by a list box to its parent (usually a class derived from **CDialog**), add a message-map entry and message-handler member function to the parent class for each message.

Each message-map entry takes the following form:

ON_Notification(*id***,** *memberFxn*)

where *id* specifies the child window ID of the list-box control sending the notification and *memberFxn* is the name of the parent member function you have written to handle the notification.

The parent's function prototype is as follows:

afx_msg void *memberFxn*( );

Following is a list of potential message-map entries and a description of the cases in which they would be sent to the parent:

- **ON_LBN_DBLCLK**   The user double-clicks a string in a list box. Only a list box that has the **LBS_NOTIFY** style will send this notification message. For a list of list-box styles, see "List-Box Styles"in the "Styles Used by MFC" section.

- **ON_LBN_ERRSPACE**   The list box cannot allocate enough memory to meet the request.

- **ON_LBN_KILLFOCUS**   The list box is losing the input focus.

- **ON_LBN_SELCANCEL**   The current list-box selection is canceled. This message is only sent when a list box has the **LBS_NOTIFY** style.

- **ON_LBN_SELCHANGE**   The selection in the list box is about to change. This notification is not sent if the selection is changed by the **CListBox::SetCurSel** member function. This notification applies only to a list box that has the **LBS_NOTIFY** style. The **LBN_SELCHANGE** notification message is sent for a multiple-selection list box whenever the user presses an arrow key, even if the selection does not change.

- **ON_LBN_SETFOCUS**   The list box is receiving the input focus.

- **ON_WM_CHARTOITEM**   An owner-draw list box that has no strings receives a **WM_CHAR** message.

- **ON_WM_VKEYTOITEM**   A list box with the **LBS_WANTKEYBOARDINPUT** style receives a **WM_KEYDOWN** message.

If you create a **CListBox** object within a dialog box (through a dialog resource), the **CListBox** object is automatically destroyed when the user closes the dialog box.

If you create a **CListBox** object within a window, you may need to destroy the **CListBox** object. If you create the **CListBox** object on the stack, it is destroyed automatically. If you create the **CListBox** object on the heap by using the **new** function, you must call **delete** on the object to destroy it when the user closes the parent window.

If you allocate any memory in the **CListBox** object, override the **CListBox** destructor to dispose of the allocation.

#include <afxwin.h>

See Also   CWnd, CButton, CComboBox, CEdit, CScrollBar, CStatic, CDialog

Construction

CListBox	Constructs a **CListBox** object.

Initialization

Create	Creates the Windows list box and attaches it to the **CListBox** object.
InitStorage	Preallocates blocks of memory for list box items and strings.

General Operations

GetCount	Returns the number of strings in a list box.
GetHorizontalExtent	Returns the width in pixels that a list box can be scrolled horizontally.
SetHorizontalExtent	Sets the width in pixels that a list box can be scrolled horizontally.
GetTopIndex	Returns the index of the first visible string in a list box.
SetTopIndex	Sets the zero-based index of the first visible string in a list box.
GetItemData	Returns the 32-bit value associated with the list-box item.
GetItemDataPtr	Returns a pointer to a list-box item.
SetItemData	Sets the 32-bit value associated with the list-box item.
SetItemDataPtr	Sets a pointer to the list-box item.
GetItemRect	Returns the bounding rectangle of the list-box item as it is currently displayed.
ItemFromPoint	Returns the index of the list-box item nearest a point.
SetItemHeight	Sets the height of items in a list box.
GetItemHeight	Determines the height of items in a list box.
GetSel	Returns the selection state of a list-box item.
GetText	Copies a list-box item into a buffer.
GetTextLen	Returns the length in bytes of a list-box item.
SetColumnWidth	Sets the column width of a multicolumn list box.
SetTabStops	Sets the tab-stop positions in a list box.
GetLocale	Retrieves the locale identifier for a list box.
SetLocale	Sets the locale identifier for a list box.

Single-Selection Operations

GetCurSel	Returns the zero-based index of the currently selected string in a list box.
SetCurSel	Selects a list-box string.

Multiple-Selection Operations

SetSel	Selects or deselects a list-box item in a multiple-selection list box.
GetCaretIndex	Determines the index of the item that has the focus rectangle in a multiple-selection list box.
SetCaretIndex	Sets the focus rectangle to the item at the specified index in a multiple-selection list box.
GetSelCount	Returns the number of strings currently selected in a multiple-selection list box.
GetSelItems	Returns the indices of the strings currently selected in a list box.
SelItemRange	Selects or deselects a range of strings in a multiple-selection list box.
SetAnchorIndex	Sets the anchor in a multiple-selection list box to begin an extended selection.
GetAnchorIndex	Retrieves the zero-based index of the current anchor item in a list box.

String Operations

AddString	Adds a string to a list box.
DeleteString	Deletes a string from a list box.
InsertString	Inserts a string at a specific location in a list box.
ResetContent	Clears all the entries from a list box.
Dir	Adds filenames from the current directory to a list box.
FindString	Searches for a string in a list box.
FindStringExact	Finds the first list-box string that matches a specified string.
SelectString	Searches for and selects a string in a single-selection list box.

Overridables

DrawItem	Called by the framework when a visual aspect of an owner-draw list box changes.
MeasureItem	Called by the framework when an owner-draw list box is created to determine list-box dimensions.
CompareItem	Called by the framework to determine the position of a new item in a sorted owner-draw list box.
DeleteItem	Called by the framework when the user deletes an item from an owner-draw list box.
VKeyToItem	Override to provide custom **WM_KEYDOWN** handling for list boxes with the **LBS_WANTKEYBOARDINPUT** style set.
CharToItem	Override to provide custom **WM_CHAR** handling for owner-draw list boxes which don't have strings.

Member Functions

CListBox::AddString

int AddString(LPCTSTR *lpszItem* **);**

Return Value

The zero-based index to the string in the list box. The return value is **LB_ERR** if an error occurs; the return value is **LB_ERRSPACE** if insufficient space is available to store the new string.

Parameters

lpszItem   Points to the null-terminated string that is to be added.

Remarks

Call this member function to add a string to a list box. If the list box was not created with the **LBS_SORT** style, the string is added to the end of the list. Otherwise, the string is inserted into the list, and the list is sorted. If the list box was created with the **LBS_SORT** style but not the **LBS_HASSTRINGS** style, the framework sorts the list by one or more calls to the **CompareItem** member function. For a list of list-box styles, see "List-Box Styles" in the "Styles Used by MFC" section.

Use **InsertString** to insert a string into a specific location within the list box.

See Also   **CListBox::InsertString**, **CListBox::CompareItem**, **LB_ADDSTRING**

CListBox::CharToItem

virtual int CharToItem(UINT *nKey***, UINT** *nIndex* **);**

Return Value

Returns −1 or −2 for no further action or a nonnegative number to specify an index of a list-box item on which to perform the default action for the keystroke. The default implementation returns −1.

Parameters

nKey   The ANSI code of the character the user typed.

nIndex   The current position of the list-box caret.

Remarks

This function is called by the framework when the list box's parent window receives a **WM_CHARTOITEM** message from the list box. The **WM_CHARTOITEM** message is sent by the list box when it receives a **WM_CHAR** message, but only if the list box meets all of these criteria:

- Is an owner-draw list box.

- Does not have the **LBS_HASSTRINGS** style set.

- Has at least one item.

You should never call this function yourself. Override this function to provide your own custom handling of keyboard messages.

In your override, you must return a value to tell the framework what action you performed. A return value of −1 or −2 indicates that you handled all aspects of selecting the item and requires no further action by the list box. Before returning −1 or −2, you could set the selection or move the caret or both. To set the selection, use **SetCurSel** or **SetSel**. To move the caret, use **SetCaretIndex**.

A return value of 0 or greater specifies the index of an item in the list box and indicates that the list box should perform the default action for the keystroke on the given item.

See Also   **CListBox::VKeyToItem, CListBox::SetCurSel, CListBox::SetSel, CListBox::SetCaretIndex, WM_CHARTOITEM**

CListBox::CListBox

CListBox( );

Remarks

You construct a **CListBox** object in two steps. First call the constructor **CListBox**, then call **Create**, which initializes the Windows list box and attaches it to the **CListBox**.

See Also   **CListBox::Create**

CListBox::CompareItem

virtual int CompareItem(LPCOMPAREITEMSTRUCT *lpCompareItemStruct* **);**

Return Value

Indicates the relative position of the two items described in the **COMPAREITEMSTRUCT** structure. It may be any of the following values:

Value	Meaning
−1	Item 1 sorts before item 2.
0	Item 1 and item 2 sort the same.
1	Item 1 sorts after item 2.

See **CWnd::OnCompareItem** for a description of the **COMPAREITEMSTRUCT** structure.

Parameters

lpCompareItemStruct   A long pointer to a **COMPAREITEMSTRUCT** structure.

Remarks

Called by the framework to determine the relative position of a new item in a sorted owner-draw list box. By default, this member function does nothing. If you create an owner-draw list box with the **LBS_SORT** style, you must override this member function to assist the framework in sorting new items added to the list box.

See Also   **WM_COMPAREITEM**, **CWnd::OnCompareItem**, **CListBox::DrawItem**, **CListBox::MeasureItem**, **CListBox::DeleteItem**

CListBox::Create

BOOL Create(DWORD *dwStyle***, const RECT&** *rect***, CWnd*** *pParentWnd***, UINT** *nID* **);**

Return Value

Nonzero if successful; otherwise 0.

Parameters

dwStyle   Specifies the style of the list box. Apply any combination of list-box styles to the box. For a list of list-box styles, see "List-Box Styles" in the "Styles Used by MFC" section.

rect   Specifies the list-box size and position. Can be either a **CRect** object or a **RECT** structure.

pParentWnd   Specifies the list box's parent window (usually a **CDialog** object). It must not be **NULL**.

nID   Specifies the list box's control ID.

Remarks

You construct a **CListBox** object in two steps. First call the constructor, then call **Create**, which initializes the Windows list box and attaches it to the **CListBox** object.

When **Create** executes, Windows sends the **WM_NCCREATE**, **WM_CREATE**, **WM_NCCALCSIZE**, and **WM_GETMINMAXINFO** messages to the list-box control.

These messages are handled by default by the **OnNcCreate**, **OnCreate**, **OnNcCalcSize**, and **OnGetMinMaxInfo** member functions in the **CWnd** base class. To extend the default message handling, derive a class from **CListBox**, add a message map to the new class, and override the preceding message-handler member functions. Override **OnCreate**, for example, to perform needed initialization for a new class.

Apply the following window styles to a list-box control. For a list of window styles, see "Window Styles" in the "Styles Used by MFC" section.

- **WS_CHILD** Always
- **WS_VISIBLE** Usually
- **WS_DISABLED** Rarely
- **WS_VSCROLL** To add a vertical scroll bar
- **WS_HSCROLL** To add a horizontal scroll bar
- **WS_GROUP** To group controls
- **WS_TABSTOP** To allow tabbing to this control

See Also   **CListBox::CListBox**

CListBox::DeleteItem

virtual void DeleteItem(LPDELETEITEMSTRUCT *lpDeleteItemStruct* **);**

Parameters

lpDeleteItemStruct   A long pointer to a Windows **DELETEITEMSTRUCT** structure that contains information about the deleted item.

Remarks

Called by the framework when the user deletes an item from an owner-draw **CListBox** object or destroys the list box. The default implementation of this function does nothing. Override this function to redraw an owner-draw list box as needed.

See **CWnd::OnDeleteItem** for a description of the **DELETEITEMSTRUCT** structure.

See Also   **CListBox::CompareItem, CWnd::OnDeleteItem, CListBox::DrawItem, CListBox::MeasureItem, ::DeleteItem**

CListBox::DeleteString

int DeleteString(UINT *nIndex* **);**

Return Value

A count of the strings remaining in the list. The return value is **LB_ERR** if *nIndex* specifies an index greater than the number of items in the list.

Parameters

nIndex   Specifies the zero-based index of the string to be deleted.

Remarks

Deletes an item in a list box.

See Also   LB_DELETESTRING, CListBox::AddString, CListBox::InsertString

CListBox::Dir

int Dir(UINT *attr*, **LPCTSTR** *lpszWildCard* **);**

Return Value

The zero-based index of the last filename added to the list. The return value is
LB_ERR if an error occurs; the return value is **LB_ERRSPACE** if insufficient space
is available to store the new strings.

Parameters

attr   Can be any combination of the **enum** values described in **CFile::GetStatus**, or
any combination of the following values:

Value	Meaning
0x0000	File can be read from or written to.
0x0001	File can be read from but not written to.
0x0002	File is hidden and does not appear in a directory listing.
0x0004	File is a system file.
0x0010	The name specified by *lpszWildCard* specifies a directory.
0x0020	File has been archived.
0x4000	Include all drives that match the name specified by *lpszWildCard*.
0x8000	Exclusive flag. If the exclusive flag is set, only files of the specified type are listed. Otherwise, files of the specified type are listed in addition to "normal" files.

lpszWildCard   Points to a file-specification string. The string can contain wildcards
(for example, *.*).

Remarks

Adds a list of filenames and/or drives to a list box.

See Also   CWnd::DlgDirList, LB_DIR, CFile::GetStatus

CListBox::DrawItem

virtual void DrawItem(LPDRAWITEMSTRUCT *lpDrawItemStruct* **);**

Parameters

lpDrawItemStruct   A long pointer to a **DRAWITEMSTRUCT** structure that
contains information about the type of drawing required.

Remarks

Called by the framework when a visual aspect of an owner-draw list box changes. The **itemAction** and **itemState** members of the **DRAWITEMSTRUCT** structure define the drawing action that is to be performed.

By default, this member function does nothing. Override this member function to implement drawing for an owner-draw **CListBox** object. The application should restore all graphics device interface (GDI) objects selected for the display context supplied in *lpDrawItemStruct* before this member function terminates.

See **CWnd::OnDrawItem** for a description of the **DRAWITEMSTRUCT** structure.

See Also **CListBox::CompareItem**, **CWnd::OnDrawItem**, **WM_DRAWITEM**, **CListBox::MeasureItem**, **CListBox::DeleteItem**

CListBox::FindString

int FindString(int *nStartAfter*, **LPCTSTR** *lpszItem* **) const;**

Return Value

The zero-based index of the matching item, or **LB_ERR** if the search was unsuccessful.

Parameters

nStartAfter   Contains the zero-based index of the item before the first item to be searched. When the search reaches the bottom of the list box, it continues from the top of the list box back to the item specified by *nStartAfter*. If *nStartAfter* is −1, the entire list box is searched from the beginning.

lpszItem   Points to the null-terminated string that contains the prefix to search for. The search is case independent, so this string may contain any combination of uppercase and lowercase letters.

Remarks

Finds the first string in a list box that contains the specified prefix without changing the list-box selection. Use the **SelectString** member function to both find and select a string.

See Also **CListBox::SelectString**, **CListBox::AddString**, **CListBox::InsertString**, **LB_FINDSTRING**

CListBox::FindStringExact

int FindStringExact(int *nIndexStart*, **LPCTSTR** *lpszFind* **) const;**

Return Value

The index of the matching item, or **LB_ERR** if the search was unsuccessful.

Parameters

> *nIndexStart*   Specifies the zero-based index of the item before the first item to be
> searched. When the search reaches the bottom of the list box, it continues from the
> top of the list box back to the item specified by *nIndexStart*. If *nIndexStart* is –1,
> the entire list box is searched from the beginning.

> *lpszFind*   Points to the null-terminated string to search for. This string can contain a
> complete filename, including the extension. The search is not case sensitive, so the
> string can contain any combination of uppercase and lowercase letters.

Remarks

> An application calls the **FindStringExact** member function to find the first list-box
> string that matches the string specified in *lpszFind*. If the list box was created with an
> owner-draw style but without the **LBS_HASSTRINGS** style, the **FindStringExact**
> member function attempts to match the doubleword value against the value of
> *lpszFind*.

> **See Also**   **CListBox::FindString, LB_FINDSTRING, LB_FINDSTRINGEXACT**

CListBox::GetAnchorIndex

> **int GetAnchorIndex( ) const;**

Return Value

> The index of the current anchor item, if successful; otherwise **LB_ERR**.

Remarks

> Retrieves the zero-based index of the current anchor item in the list box. In a
> multiple-selection list box, the anchor item is the first or last item in a block of
> contiguous selected items.

> **See Also**   **CListBox::SetAnchorIndex**

CListBox::GetCaretIndex

> **int GetCaretIndex( ) const;**

Return Value

> The zero-based index of the item that has the focus rectangle in a list box. If the list
> box is a single-selection list box, the return value is the index of the item that is
> selected, if any.

Remarks

> An application calls the **GetCaretIndex** member function to determine the index of
> the item that has the focus rectangle in a multiple-selection list box. The item may or
> may not be selected.

> **See Also**   **CListBox::SetCaretIndex, LB_GETCARETINDEX**

CListBox::GetCount

int GetCount( ) const;

Return Value

The number of items in the list box, or **LB_ERR** if an error occurs.

Remarks

Retrieves the number of items in a list box.

The returned count is one greater than the index value of the last item (the index is zero-based).

See Also **LB_GETCOUNT**

CListBox::GetCurSel

int GetCurSel( ) const;

Return Value

The zero-based index of the currently selected item. It is **LB_ERR** if no item is currently selected or if the list box is a multiple-selection list box.

Remarks

Retrieves the zero-based index of the currently selected item, if any, in a single-selection list box.

GetCurSel should not be called for a multiple-selection list box.

See Also **LB_GETCURSEL, CListBox::SetCurSel**

CListBox::GetHorizontalExtent

int GetHorizontalExtent( ) const;

Return Value

The scrollable width of the list box, in pixels.

Remarks

Retrieves from the list box the width in pixels by which it can be scrolled horizontally. This is applicable only if the list box has a horizontal scroll bar.

See Also **CListBox::SetHorizontalExtent, LB_GETHORIZONTALEXTENT**

CListBox::GetItemData

DWORD GetItemData(int *nIndex* **) const;**

Return Value

The 32-bit value associated with the item, or **LB_ERR** if an error occurs.

Parameters

nIndex   Specifies the zero-based index of the item in the list box.

Remarks

Retrieves the application-supplied doubleword value associated with the specified list-box item.

The doubleword value was the *dwItemData* parameter of a **SetItemData** call.

See Also   **CListBox::AddString, CListBox::GetItemDataPtr, CListBox::SetItemDataPtr, CListBox::InsertString, CListBox::SetItemData, LB_GETITEMDATA**

CListBox::GetItemDataPtr

void* GetItemDataPtr(int *nIndex* **) const;**

Return Value

Retrieves a pointer, or −1 if an error occurs.

Parameters

nIndex   Specifies the zero-based index of the item in the list box.

Remarks

Retrieves the application-supplied 32-bit value associated with the specified list-box item as a pointer (**void***).

See Also   **CListBox::AddString, CListBox::GetItemData, CListBox::InsertString, CListBox::SetItemData, LB_GETITEMDATA**

CListBox::GetItemHeight

int GetItemHeight(int *nIndex* **) const;**

Return Value

The height, in pixels, of the items in the list box. If the list box has the **LBS_OWNERDRAWVARIABLE** style, the return value is the height of the item specified by *nIndex*. If an error occurs, the return value is **LB_ERR**.

Parameters

    nIndex   Specifies the zero-based index of the item in the list box. This parameter is used only if the list box has the **LBS_OWNERDRAWVARIABLE** style; otherwise, it should be set to 0.

Remarks

    An application calls the **GetItemHeight** member function to determine the height of items in a list box.

    See Also   **LB_GETITEMHEIGHT**, **CListBox::SetItemHeight**

CListBox::GetItemRect

    int GetItemRect(int *nIndex***, LPRECT** *lpRect* **) const;**

Return Value

    LB_ERR if an error occurs.

Parameters

    nIndex   Specifies the zero-based index of the item.

    lpRect   Specifies a long pointer to a **RECT** tructure that receives the list-box client coordinates of the item.

Remarks

    Retrieves the dimensions of the rectangle that bounds a list-box item as it is currently displayed in the list-box window.

    See Also   **LB_GETITEMRECT**

CListBox::GetLocale

    LCID GetLocale( ) const;

Return Value

    The locale identifier (LCID) value for the strings in the list box.

Remarks

    Retrieves the locale used by the list box. The locale is used, for example, to determine the sort order of the strings in a sorted list box.

    See Also   **CListBox::SetLocale**, **::GetStringTypeW**, **::GetSystemDefaultLCID**, **::GetUserDefaultLCID**

CListBox::GetSel

int GetSel(int *nIndex* **) const;**

Return Value

A positive number if the specified item is selected; otherwise, it is 0. The return value is **LB_ERR** if an error occurs.

Parameters

nIndex   Specifies the zero-based index of the item.

Remarks

Retrieves the selection state of an item. This member function works with both single- and multiple-selection list boxes.

See Also   **LB_GETSEL**, **CListBox::SetSel**

CListBox::GetSelCount

int GetSelCount( ) const;

Return Value

The count of selected items in a list box. If the list box is a single-selection list box, the return value is **LB_ERR**.

Remarks

Retrieves the total number of selected items in a multiple-selection list box.

See Also   **CListBox::SetSel**, **LB_GETSELCOUNT**

CListBox::GetSelItems

int GetSelItems(int *nMaxItems***, LPINT** *rgIndex* **) const;**

Return Value

The actual number of items placed in the buffer. If the list box is a single-selection list box, the return value is **LB_ERR**.

Parameters

nMaxItems   Specifies the maximum number of selected items whose item numbers are to be placed in the buffer.

rgIndex   Specifies a long pointer to a buffer large enough for the number of integers specified by *nMaxItems*.

Remarks

Fills a buffer with an array of integers that specifies the item numbers of selected items in a multiple-selection list box.

See Also   LB_GETSELITEMS

CListBox::GetText

int GetText(int *nIndex***, LPTSTR** *lpszBuffer* **) const;**
void GetText(int *nIndex***, CString&** *rString* **) const;**

Return Value

The length (in bytes) of the string, excluding the terminating null character. If *nIndex* does not specify a valid index, the return value is **LB_ERR**.

Parameters

nIndex   Specifies the zero-based index of the string to be retrieved.

lpszBuffer   Points to the buffer that receives the string. The buffer must have sufficient space for the string and a terminating null character. The size of the string can be determined ahead of time by calling the **GetTextLen** member function.

rString   A reference to a **CString** object.

Remarks

Gets a string from a list box. The second form of this member function fills a **CString** object with the string text.

See Also   **CListBox::GetTextLen**, **LB_GETTEXT**

CListBox::GetTextLen

int GetTextLen(int *nIndex* **) const;**

Return Value

The length of the string in bytes, excluding the terminating null character. If *nIndex* does not specify a valid index, the return value is **LB_ERR**.

Parameters

nIndex   Specifies the zero-based index of the string.

Remarks

Gets the length of a string in a list-box item.

See Also   **CListBox::GetText**, **LB_GETTEXTLEN**

CListBox::GetTopIndex

int GetTopIndex( ) const;

Return Value

The zero-based index of the first visible item in a list box if successful, **CB_ERR** otherwise.

Remarks

Retrieves the zero-based index of the first visible item in a list box. Initially, item 0 is at the top of the list box, but if the list box is scrolled, another item may be at the top.

See Also **CListBox::SetTopIndex**, **LB_GETTOPINDEX**

CListBox::InitStorage

int InitStorage(int *nItems*, UINT *nBytes*);

Return Value

If successful, the maximum number of items that the list box can store before a memory reallocation is needed, otherwise **LB_ERRSPACE**, meaning not enough memory is available.

Parameters

nItems Specifies the number of items to add.

nBytes Specifies the amount of memory, in bytes, to allocate for item strings.

Remarks

Allocates memory for storing list-box items. Call this function before adding a large number of items to a **CListBox**.

This function helps speed up the initialization of list boxes that have a large number of items (more than 100). It preallocates the specified amount of memory so that subsequent **AddString**, **InsertString**, and **Dir** functions take the shortest possible time. You can use estimates for the parameters. If you overestimate, some extra memory is allocated; if you underestimate, the normal allocation is used for items that exceed the preallocated amount.

Windows 95 only: The *nItems* parameter is limited to 16-bit values. This means list boxes cannot contain more than 32,767 items. Although the number of items is restricted, the total size of the items in a list box is limited only by available memory.

See Also **CListBox::CListBox**, **CListBox::Create**, **CListBox::ResetContent**, **LB_INITSTORAGE**

CListBox::InsertString

int InsertString(int *nIndex*, **LPCTSTR** *lpszItem* **);**

Return Value

The zero-based index of the position at which the string was inserted. The return value is **LB_ERR** if an error occurs; the return value is **LB_ERRSPACE** if insufficient space is available to store the new string.

Parameters

nIndex   Specifies the zero-based index of the position to insert the string. If this parameter is –1, the string is added to the end of the list.

lpszItem   Points to the null-terminated string that is to be inserted.

Remarks

Inserts a string into the list box. Unlike the **AddString** member function, **InsertString** does not cause a list with the **LBS_SORT** style to be sorted.

See Also   CListBox::AddString, LB_INSERTSTRING

CListBox::ItemFromPoint

UINT ItemFromPoint(CPoint *pt*, **BOOL&** *bOutside* **) const;**

Return Value

The index of the nearest item to the point specified in *pt*.

Parameters

pt   Point for which to find the nearest item, specified relative to the upper-left corner of the client area of the list box.

bOutside   Reference to a **BOOL** variable which will be set to **TRUE** if *pt* is outside the client area of the list box, **FALSE** if *pt* is inside the client area of the list box.

Remarks

Call this function to determine the list-box item nearest the point specified in *pt*. You could use this function to determine which list-box item the mouse cursor moves over.

See Also   CListBox::GetItemRect, LB_ITEMFROMPOINT

CListBox::MeasureItem

virtual void MeasureItem(LPMEASUREITEMSTRUCT *lpMeasureItemStruct* **);**

Parameters

lpMeasureItemStruct   A long pointer to a **MEASUREITEMSTRUCT** structure.

Remarks

Called by the framework when a list box with an owner-draw style is created.

By default, this member function does nothing. Override this member function and fill in the **MEASUREITEMSTRUCT** structure to inform Windows of the list-box dimensions. If the list box is created with the **LBS_OWNERDRAWVARIABLE** style, the framework calls this member function for each item in the list box. Otherwise, this member is called only once.

For further information about using the **LBS_OWNERDRAWFIXED** style in an owner-draw list box created with the **SubclassDlgItem** member function of **CWnd**, see the discussion in Technical Note 14 under MFC in Books Online.

See **CWnd::OnMeasureItem** for a description of the **MEASUREITEMSTRUCT** structure.

See Also   **CListBox::CompareItem**, **CWnd::OnMeasureItem**, **CListBox::DrawItem**, **CListBox::DeleteItem**

CListBox::ResetContent

void ResetContent( );

Remarks

Removes all items from a list box.

See Also   **LB_RESETCONTENT**

CListBox::SelectString

int SelectString(int *nStartAfter*, **LPCTSTR** *lpszItem* **);**

Return Value

The index of the selected item if the search was successful. If the search was unsuccessful, the return value is **LB_ERR** and the current selection is not changed.

Parameters

nStartAfter   Contains the zero-based index of the item before the first item to be searched. When the search reaches the bottom of the list box, it continues from the top of the list box back to the item specified by *nStartAfter*. If *nStartAfter* is –1, the entire list box is searched from the beginning.

lpszItem   Points to the null-terminated string that contains the prefix to search for. The search is case independent, so this string may contain any combination of uppercase and lowercase letters.

Remarks

Searches for a list-box item that matches the specified string, and if a matching item is found, it selects the item.

The list box is scrolled, if necessary, to bring the selected item into view.

This member function cannot be used with a list box that has the **LBS_MULTIPLESEL** style. For a list of list-box styles, see "List-Box Styles" in the "Styles Used by MFC" section.

An item is selected only if its initial characters (from the starting point) match the characters in the string specified by *lpszItem*.

Use the **FindString** member function to find a string without selecting the item.

See Also   **CListBox::FindString**, **LB_SELECTSTRING**

CListBox::SelItemRange

int SelItemRange(BOOL *bSelect*, **int** *nFirstItem*, **int** *nLastItem* **);**

Return Value

LB_ERR if an error occurs.

Parameters

bSelect   Specifies how to set the selection. If *bSelect* is **TRUE**, the string is selected and highlighted; if **FALSE**, the highlight is removed and the string is no longer selected.

nFirstItem   Specifies the zero-based index of the first item to set.

nLastItem   Specifies the zero-based index of the last item to set.

Remarks

Selects multiple consecutive items in a multiple-selection list box.

Use this member function only with multiple-selection list boxes. If you need to select only one item in a multiple-selection list box—that is, if *nFirstItem* is equal to *nLastItem*—call the **SetSel** member function instead.

See Also   **LB_SELITEMRANGE**, **CListBox::GetSelItems**

CListBox::SetAnchorIndex

void SetAnchorIndex(int *nIndex* **);**

Parameters

nIndex   Specifies the zero-based index of the list-box item that will be the anchor.

Remarks

Sets the anchor in a multiple-selection list box to begin an extended selection. In a multiple-selection list box, the anchor item is the first or last item in a block of contiguous selected items.

See Also   CListBox::GetAnchorIndex

CListBox::SetCaretIndex

int SetCaretIndex(int *nIndex***, BOOL** *bScroll* **= TRUE);**

Return Value

LB_ERR if an error occurs.

Parameters

nIndex   Specifies the zero-based index of the item to receive the focus rectangle in the list box.

bScroll   If this value is 0, the item is scrolled until it is fully visible. If this value is not 0, the item is scrolled until it is at least partially visible.

Remarks

An application calls the **SetCaretIndex** member function to set the focus rectangle to the item at the specified index in a multiple-selection list box. If the item is not visible, it is scrolled into view.

See Also   CListBox::GetCaretIndex, LB_SETCARETINDEX

CListBox::SetColumnWidth

void SetColumnWidth(int *cxWidth* **);**

Parameters

cxWidth   Specifies the width in pixels of all columns.

Remarks

Sets the width in pixels of all columns in a multicolumn list box (created with the **LBS_MULTICOLUMN** style). For more information on list-box styles, see "List-Box Styles" in the "Styles Used by MFC" section.

See Also   LB_SETCOLUMNWIDTH

CListBox::SetCurSel

int SetCurSel(int *nSelect* **);**

Return Value

LB_ERR if an error occurs.

Parameters

> *nSelect*   Specifies the zero-based index of the string to be selected. If *nSelect* is –1, the list box is set to have no selection.

Remarks

> Selects a string and scrolls it into view, if necessary. When the new string is selected, the list box removes the highlight from the previously selected string.

> Use this member function only with single-selection list boxes. It cannot be used to set or remove a selection in a multiple-selection list box.

> **See Also**   **LB_SETCURSEL**, **CListBox::GetCurSel**

CListBox::SetHorizontalExtent

> **void SetHorizontalExtent(int** *cxExtent* **);**

Parameters

> *cxExtent*   Specifies the number of pixels by which the list box can be scrolled horizontally.

Remarks

> Sets the width, in pixels, by which a list box can be scrolled horizontally. If the size of the list box is smaller than this value, the horizontal scroll bar will horizontally scroll items in the list box. If the list box is as large or larger than this value, the horizontal scroll bar is hidden.

> To respond to a call to **SetHorizontalExtent**, the list box must have been defined with the **WS_HSCROLL** style. For a list of window styles, see "Window Styles" in the "Styles Used by MFC" section.

> This member function is not useful for multicolumn list boxes. For multicolumn list boxes, call the **SetColumnWidth** member function.

> **See Also**   **CListBox::GetHorizontalExtent**, **CListBox::SetColumnWidth**, **LB_SETHORIZONTALEXTENT**

CListBox::SetItemData

> **int SetItemData(int** *nIndex***, DWORD** *dwItemData* **);**

Return Value

> **LB_ERR** if an error occurs.

Parameters

> *nIndex*   Specifies the zero-based index of the item.

> *dwItemData*   Specifies the value to be associated with the item.

Remarks

Sets a 32-bit value associated with the specified item in a list box.

See Also **CListBox::SetItemDataPtr, CListBox::GetItemData,
LB_SETITEMDATA**

CListBox::SetItemDataPtr

int SetItemDataPtr(int *nIndex***, void*** *pData* **);**

Return Value

LB_ERR if an error occurs.

Parameters

nIndex   Specifies the zero-based index of the item.

pData   Specifies the pointer to be associated with the item.

Remarks

Sets the 32-bit value associated with the specified item in a list box to be the specified
pointer (**void***). This pointer remains valid for the life of the list box, even though the
item's relative position within the list box might change as items are added or
removed. Hence, the item's index within the box can change, but the pointer remains
reliable.

See Also **CListBox::SetItemData, CListBox::GetItemData,
CListBox::GetItemDataPtr, LB_SETITEMDATA**

CListBox::SetItemHeight

int SetItemHeight(int *nIndex***, UINT** *cyItemHeight* **);**

Return Value

LB_ERR if the index or height is invalid.

Parameters

nIndex   Specifies the zero-based index of the item in the list box. This parameter is
used only if the list box has the **LBS_OWNERDRAWVARIABLE** style;
otherwise, it should be set to 0.

cyItemHeight   Specifies the height, in pixels, of the item.

Remarks

An application calls the **SetItemHeight** member function to set the height of items in
a list box. If the list box has the **LBS_OWNERDRAWVARIABLE** style, this
function sets the height of the item specified by *nIndex*. Otherwise, this function sets
the height of all items in the list box.

See Also **CListBox::GetItemHeight, LB_SETITEMHEIGHT**

CListBox::SetLocale

LCID SetLocale(LCID *nNewLocale* **);**

Return Value

The previous locale identifier (LCID) value for this list box.

Parameters

nNewLocale   The new locale identifier (LCID) value to set for the list box.

Remarks

Sets the locale identifier for this list box. If **SetLocale** is not called, the default locale is obtained from the system. This system default locale can be modified by using Control Panel's Regional (or International) application.

See Also   **CListBox::GetLocale**

CListBox::SetSel

int SetSel(int *nIndex*, **BOOL** *bSelect* = **TRUE** **);**

Return Value

LB_ERR if an error occurs.

Parameters

nIndex   Contains the zero-based index of the string to be set. If −1, the selection is added to or removed from all strings, depending on the value of *bSelect*.

bSelect   Specifies how to set the selection. If *bSelect* is **TRUE**, the string is selected and highlighted; if **FALSE**, the highlight is removed and the string is no longer selected. The specified string is selected and highlighted by default.

Remarks

Selects a string in a multiple-selection list box.

Use this member function only with multiple-selection list boxes.

See Also   **CListBox::GetSel, LB_SETSEL**

CListBox::SetTabStops

void SetTabStops( );
BOOL SetTabStops(const int& *cxEachStop* **);**
BOOL SetTabStops(int *nTabStops*, **LPINT** *rgTabStops* **);**

Return Value

Nonzero if all the tabs were set; otherwise 0.

Parameters

cxEachStop   Tab stops are set at every *cxEachStop* dialog units. See *rgTabStops* for a description of a dialog unit.

nTabStops   Specifies the number of tab stops to have in the list box.

rgTabStops   Points to the first member of an array of integers containing the tab-stop positions in dialog units. A dialog unit is a horizontal or vertical distance. One horizontal dialog unit is equal to one-fourth of the current dialog base width unit, and one vertical dialog unit is equal to one-eighth of the current dialog base height unit. The dialog base units are computed based on the height and width of the current system font. The **GetDialogBaseUnits** Windows function returns the current dialog base units in pixels. The tab stops must be sorted in increasing order; back tabs are not allowed.

Remarks

Sets the tab-stop positions in a list box.

To set tab stops to the default size of 2 dialog units, call the parameterless version of this member function. To set tab stops to a size other than 2, call the version with the *cxEachStop* argument.

To set tab stops to an array of sizes, use the version with the *rgTabStops* and *nTabStops* arguments. A tab stop will be set for each value in *rgTabStops*, up to the number specified by *nTabStops*.

To respond to a call to the **SetTabStops** member function, the list box must have been created with the **LBS_USETABSTOPS** style.

See Also   LB_SETTABSTOPS, **::GetDialogBaseUnits**

CListBox::SetTopIndex

int SetTopIndex(int *nIndex* **);**

Return Value

Zero if successful, or **LB_ERR** if an error occurs.

Parameters

nIndex   Specifies the zero-based index of the list-box item.

Remarks

Ensures that a particular list-box item is visible.

The system scrolls the list box until either the item specified by *nIndex* appears at the top of the list box or the maximum scroll range has been reached.

See Also   CListBox::GetTopIndex, **LB_SETTOPINDEX**

CListBox::VKeyToItem

virtual int VKeyToItem(UINT *nKey*, **UINT** *nIndex* **);**

Return Value

Returns −2 for no further action, −1 for default action, or a nonnegative number to specify an index of a list box item on which to perform the default action for the keystroke.

Parameters

nKey   The virtual-key code of the key the user pressed.

nIndex   The current position of the list-box caret.

Remarks

This function is called by the framework when the list box's parent window receives a **WM_VKEYTOITEM** message from the list box. The **WM_VKEYTOITEM** message is sent by the list box when it receives a **WM_KEYDOWN** message, but only if the list box meets both of the following:

- Has the **LBS_WANTKEYBOARDINPUT** style set.

- Has at least one item.

You should never call this function yourself. Override this function to provide your own custom handling of keyboard messages.

You must return a value to tell the framework what action your override performed. A return value of −2 indicates that the application handled all aspects of selecting the item and requires no further action by the list box. Before returning −2, you could set the selection or move the caret or both. To set the selection, use **SetCurSel** or **SetSel**. To move the caret, use **SetCaretIndex**.

A return value of −1 indicates that the list box should perform the default action in response to the keystroke.The default implementation returns −1.

A return value of 0 or greater specifies the index of an item in the list box and indicates that the list box should perform the default action for the keystroke on the given item.

See Also   **CListBox::CharToItem**, **CListBox::SetCurSel**, **CListBox::SetSel**, **CListBox::SetCaretIndex**

CListCtrl

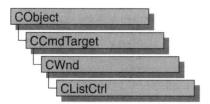

The **CListCtrl** class encapsulates the functionality of a "list view control," which displays a collection of items each consisting of an icon and a label. List views provide several ways of arranging items and displaying individual items. For example, additional information about each item can be displayed in colums to the right of the icon and label.

The **CListCtrl** class provides the functionality of the Windows common list view control. This control (and therefore the **CListCtrl** class) is available only to programs running under Windows 95, Windows NT version 3.51 and later, and Win32s® version 1.3.

Views

List view controls can display their contents in four different ways, called "views." The current view is specified by the control's window style. Additional window styles specify the alignment of items and control-specific aspects of the list view control's functionality. Information about the four views follows.

View	Description
Icon view	Specified by the **LVS_ICON** window style.
	Each item appears as a full-sized icon with a label below it. The user can drag the items to any location in the list view window.
Small icon view	Specified by the **LVS_SMALLICON** window style.
	Each item appears as a small icon with the label to the right of it. The user can drag the items to any location.
List view	Specified by the **LVS_LIST** window style.
	Each item appears as a small icon with a label to the right of it. Items are arranged in columns and cannot be dragged to any arbitrary location by the user.
Report view	Specified by the **LVS_REPORT** window style.
	Each item appears on its own line with information arranged in columns. The leftmost column contains the small icon and label, and subsequent columns contain subitems as specified by the application. Unless the **LVS_NOCOLUMNHEADER** window style is also specified, each column has a header.

To change the view and alignment style after creating the control, use the Windows functions **GetWindowLong** and **SetWindowLong**.

You can control the way items are arranged in icon or small icon view by specifying a window style of **LVS_ALIGNTOP** (the default style) or **LVS_ALIGNLEFT**. You can change the alignment after a list view control is created. To isolate the window styles that specify the alignment of items, use the **LVS_ALIGNMASK** value.

Additional window styles control other options—for example, whether a user can edit labels in place, whether more than one item can be selected at a time, and so on.

Image Lists

The icons for list view items are contained in image lists, which you create and assign to the list view control. One image list contains the full-sized icons used in icon view, and a separate image list contains smaller versions of the same icons for use in other views. You can also specify a third image list that contains state images, which are displayed next to an item's icon to indicate an application-defined state.

You assign an image list to a list view control by using the **CListCtrl::SetImageList** function, specifying whether the image list contains large icons, small icons, or state images. You can retrieve the handle of an image list currently assigned to a list view control by using the **CListCtrl::GetImageList** function.

The large and small icon image lists typically contain icons for each type of list view item. You need not create both of these image lists if only one is used—for example, if a list view control is never in icon view. If you create both image lists, they must contain the same images in the same order because a single value is used to identify a list view item's icon in both image lists.

The large and small icon image lists can also contain overlay images, which are designed to be superimposed on item icons. A nonzero value in bits 8 through 11 of a list view item's state specifies the one-based index of an overlay image (zero indicates no overlay image). Because a 4-bit, one-based index is used, overlay images must be among the first 15 images in the image lists.

If a state image list is specified, a list view control reserves space to the left of each item's icon for a state image. An application can use state images, such as checked and cleared check boxes, to indicate application-defined item states. A nonzero value in bits 12 through 15 specifies the one-based index of a state image (zero indicates no state image). State images are typically not used in icon view.

By default, a list view control destroys the image lists assigned to it when it is destroyed. If a list view control has the **LVS_SHAREIMAGELISTS** window style, however, the application is responsible for destroying the image lists when they are no longer in use. You should specify this style if you assign the same image lists to multiple list view controls; otherwise, more than one control might try to destroy the same image list.

Items and Subitems

Each item in a list view control consists of an icon, a label, a current state, and an application-defined value. One or more subitems can also be associated with each item. A "subitem" is a string that, in report view, can be displayed in a column to the right of an item's icon and label. All items in a list view control have the same number of subitems. By using list view messages, you can add, modify, retrieve information about, and delete items. You can also find items with specific attributes.

The **LV_ITEM** structure defines a list view item or subitem. The **iItem** member is the zero-based index of the item. The **iSubItem** member is the one-based index of a subitem, or zero if the structure contains information about an item. Additional members specify the item's text, icon, state, and item data. "Item data" is an application-defined value associated with a list view item. For more information about the **LV_ITEM** structure, see **CListCtrl::GetItem**.

Callback Items

A "callback item" is a list view item for which the application—rather than the control—stores the text, icon, or both. Although a list view control can store these attributes for you, you may want to use callback items if your application already maintains some of this information. The callback mask specifies which item state bits are maintained by the application, and it applies to the whole control rather than to a specific item. The callback mask is zero by default, meaning that the control tracks all item states. If an application uses callback items or specifies a nonzero callback mask, it must be able to supply list view item attributes on demand.

You can define a callback item by specifying appropriate values for the **pszText** and **iImage** members of the **LV_ITEM** structure (see **CListCtrl::GetItem**). If the application maintains the item's or subitem's text, specify the **LPSTR_TEXTCALLBACK** value for the **pszText** member. If the application keeps track of the icon for the item, specify the **I_IMAGECALLBACK** value for the **iImage** member.

#include <afxcmn.h>

See Also   CImageList

Construction

ListCtrl	Constructs a **CListCtrl** object.
Create	Creates a list control and attaches it to a **CListCtrl** object.

Attributes

GetBkColor	Retrieves the background color of a list view control.
SetBkColor	Sets the background color of the list view control.
GetImageList	Retrieves the handle of an image list used for drawing list view items.
SetImageList	Assigns an image list to a list view control.

GetItemCount	Retrieves the number of items in a list view control.
GetItem	Retrieves a list view item's attributes.
GetItemData	Retrieves the application-specific value associated with an item.
SetItem	Sets some or all of a list view item's attributes.
SetItemData	Sets the item's application-specific value.
GetCallbackMask	Retrieves the callback mask for a list view control.
SetCallbackMask	Sets the callback mask for a list view control.
GetNextItem	Searches for a list view item with specified properties and with specified relationship to a given item.
GetItemRect	Retrieves the bounding rectangle for an item.
SetItemPosition	Moves an item to a specified position in a list view control.
GetItemPosition	Retrieves the position of a list view item.
GetStringWidth	Determines the minimum column width necessary to display all of a given string.
GetEditControl	Retrieves the handle of the edit control used to edit an item's text.
GetColumn	Retrieves the attributes of a control's column.
SetColumn	Sets the attributes of a list view column.
GetColumnWidth	Retrieves the width of a column in report view or list view.
SetColumnWidth	Changes the width of a column in report view or list view.
GetViewRect	Retrieves the bounding rectangle of all items in the list view control.
GetTextColor	Retrieves the text color of a list view control.
SetTextColor	Sets the text color of a list view control.
GetTextBkColor	Retrieves the text background color of a list view control.
SetTextBkColor	Sets the background color of text in a list view control.
GetTopIndex	Retrieves the index of the topmost visible item.
GetCountPerPage	Calculates the number of items that can fit vertically in a list view control.
GetOrigin	Retrieves the current view origin for a list view control.
SetItemState	Changes the state of an item in a list view control.
GetItemState	Retrieves the state of a list view item.
GetItemText	Retrieves the text of a list view item or subitem.
SetItemText	Changes the text of a list view item or subitem.
SetItemCount	Prepares a list view control for adding a large number of items.
GetSelectedCount	Retrieves the number of selected items in the list view control.

Operations

InsertItem	Inserts a new item in a list view control.
DeleteItem	Deletes an item from the control.
DeleteAllItems	Deletes all items from the control.
FindItem	Searches for a list view item having specified characteristics.
SortItems	Sorts list view items using an application-defined comparison function.
HitTest	Determines which list view item is at a specified position.
EnsureVisible	Ensures that an item is visible.
Scroll	Scrolls the content of a list view control.
RedrawItems	Forces a list view control to repaint a range of items.
Update	Forces the control to repaint a specified item.
Arrange	Aligns items on a grid.
EditLabel	Begins in-place editing of an item's text.
InsertColumn	Inserts a new column in a list view control.
DeleteColumn	Deletes a column from the list view control.
CreateDragImage	Creates a drag image list for a specified item.

Overridables

DrawItem	Called when a visual aspect of an owner-draw control changes.

Member Functions

CListCtrl::Arrange

BOOL Arrange(UINT *nCode* **);**

Return Value

Nonzero if successful; otherwise zero.

Parameters

nCode   Specifies the alignment style for the items. It can be one of the following values:

- **LVA_ALIGNLEFT**   Aligns items along the left edge of the window.

- **LVA_ALIGNTOP**   Aligns items along the top edge of the window.

- **LVA_DEFAULT** Aligns items according to the list view's current alignment styles (the default value).

- **LVA_SNAPTOGRID** Snaps all icons to the nearest grid position.

The alignment code can be combined with an optional sort flag:

- **LVA_SORTASCENDING** Sorts items in ascending order.

- **LVA_SORTDESCENDING** Sorts items in descending order.

Remarks

Call this function to reposition items in an icon view so that they align on a grid. The *nCode* parameter specifies the alignment style and an optional sort order. If no sort flag is included with *nCode*, this function does not change the items' indexes.

See Also **CListCtrl::EnsureVisible**

CListCtrl::CListCtrl

CListCtrl( );

Remarks

Constructs a **CListCtrl** object.

See Also **CListCtrl::Create**

CListCtrl::Create

BOOL Create(DWORD *dwStyle*, **const RECT&** *rect*, **CWnd*** *pParentWnd*, **UINT** *nID* **);**

Return Value

Nonzero if successful; otherwise zero.

Parameters

dwStyle Specifies the list control's style. Apply any combination of list control styles to the control. See the "Remarks" section for a list of possible styles.

rect Specifies the list control's size and position. It can be either a **CRect** object or a **RECT** structure.

pParentWnd Specifies the list control's parent window, usually a **CDialog**. It must not be **NULL**.

nID Specifies the list control's ID.

Remarks

You construct a **CListCtrl** in two steps. First call the constructor, then call **Create**, which creates the list view control and attaches it to the **CListCtrl** object.

The *dwStyle* parameter can be a combination of the following values:

- **LVS_ALIGNLEFT**   Specifies that items are left-aligned in icon and small icon view.

- **LVS_ALIGNTOP**   Specifies that items are aligned with the top of the control in icon and small icon view.

- **LVS_AUTOARRANGE**   Specifies that icons are automatically kept arranged in icon view and small icon view.

- **LVS_BUTTON**   Specifies that item icons look like buttons in large icon view.

- **LVS_EDITLABELS**   Allows item text to be edited in place. The parent window must process the **LVN_ENDLABELEDIT** notification message.

- **LVS_ICON**   Specifies icon view.

- **LVS_LIST**   Specifies list view.

- **LVS_NOCOLUMNHEADER**   Specifies that a column header is not displayed in report view. By default, columns have headers in report view.

- **LVS_NOITEMDATA**   Allocates only enough space to store the state of each item, not the label, icon, subitem strings, or application-defined data. The parent window must process the **LVN_GETDISPINFO** notification message to provide this information to the list view control on demand.

- **LVS_NOLABELWRAP**   Displays item text on a single line in icon view. By default, item text can wrap in icon view.

- **LVS_NOSCROLL**   Disables scrolling. All items must be within the client area.

- **LVS_NOSORTHEADER**   Specifies that column headers do not work like buttons. This style is useful if clicking a column header in report view does not carry out an action, such as sorting.

- **LVS_OWNERDRAWFIXED**   Enables the owner window to paint items in report view. The list view control sends a **WM_DRAWITEM** message to paint each item; it does not send separate messages for each subitem. The **itemData** member of the **DRAWITEMSTRUCT** structure contains the item data for the specified list
view item.

- **LVS_REPORT**   Specifies report view.

- **LVS_SHAREIMAGELISTS**   Specifies that the control does not take ownership of the image lists assigned to it (that is, it does not destroy the image lists when it is destroyed). This style enables the same image lists to be used with multiple list view controls.

- **LVS_SINGLESEL**   Allows only one item at a time to be selected. By default, multiple items can be selected.

- **LVS_SMALLICON**   Specifies small icon view.

- **LVS_SORTASCENDING**   Sorts items based on item text in ascending order.
- **LVS_SORTDESCENDING**   Sorts items based on item text in descending order.

See Also   **CListCtrl::CListCtrl**

CListCtrl::CreateDragImage

CImagelist* CreateDragImage(int *nItem***, LPPOINT** *lpPoint* **);**

Return Value

A pointer to the drag image list if successful; otherwise **NULL**.

Parameters

nItem   Index of the item whose drag image list is to be created.

lpPoint   Address of a **POINT** structure that receives the initial location of the upper-left corner of the image, in view coordinates.

Remarks

Call this function to create a drag image list for the item specified by *nItem*.

See Also   **CImageList**, **CListCtrl::GetImageList**, **CListCtrl::SetImageList**

CListCtrl::DeleteAllItems

BOOL DeleteAllItems( );

Return Value

Nonzero if successful; otherwise zero.

Remarks

Call this function to delete all items from the list view control.

See Also   **CListCtrl::InsertItem**, **CListCtrl::DeleteItem**

CListCtrl::DeleteColumn

BOOL DeleteColumn(int *nCol* **);**

Return Value

Nonzero if successful; otherwise zero.

Parameters

nCol   Index of the column to be deleted.

Remarks

Call this function to delete a column from the list view control.

See Also   **CListCtrl::InsertColumn, CListCtrl::DeleteAllItems**

CListCtrl::DeleteItem

BOOL DeleteItem(int *nItem* **);**

Return Value

Nonzero if successful; otherwise zero.

Parameters

nItem   Specifies the index of the item to be deleted.

Remarks

Call this function to delete an item from a list view control.

See Also   **CListCtrl::InsertItem, CListCtrl::DeleteAllItems**

CListCtrl::DrawItem

virtual void DrawItem(LPDRAWITEMSTRUCT *lpDrawItemStruct* **);**

Parameters

lpDrawItemStruct   A long pointer to a **DRAWITEMSTRUCT** structure that contains information about the type of drawing required.

Remarks

Called by the framework when a visual aspect of an owner-draw list view control changes. The **itemAction** member of the **DRAWITEMSTRUCT** structure defines the drawing action that is to be performed.

By default, this member function does nothing. Override this member function to implement drawing for an owner-draw **CListViewCtrl** object.

The application should restore all graphics device interface (GDI) objects selected for the display context supplied in *lpDrawItemStruct* before this member function terminates.

See Also   **CWnd::OnDrawItem**

CListCtrl::EditLabel

CEdit* EditLabel(int *nItem* **);**

Return Value

If successful, a pointer to the **CEdit** object that is used to edit the item text; otherwise **NULL**.

Parameters

nItem   Index of the list view item that is to be edited.

Remarks

A list view control that has the **LVS_EDITLABELS** window style enables a user to edit item labels in place. The user begins editing by clicking the label of an item that has the focus.

Use this function to begin in-place editing of the specified list view item's text.

See Also   **CListCtrl::GetEditControl**

CListCtrl::EnsureVisible

BOOL EnsureVisible(int *nItem*, **BOOL** *bPartialOK* **);**

Return Value

Nonzero if successful; otherwise zero.

Parameters

nItem   Index of the list view item that is to be visible.

bPartialOK   Specifies whether partial visibility is acceptable.

Remarks

Call this function to ensure that a list view item is at least partially visible. The list view control is scrolled if necessary. If the *bPartialOK* parameter is nonzero, no scrolling occurs if the item is partially visible.

See Also   **CListCtrl::Scroll**

CListCtrl::FindItem

int FindItem(LV_FINDINFO* *pFindInfo*, **int** *nStart* = –1 **) const;**

Return Value

The index of the item if successful or –1 otherwise.

Parameters

pFindInfo   A pointer to a **LV_FINDINFO** structure containing information about the item to be searched for.

> *nStart*   Index of the item to begin the search with, or –1 to start from the beginning. The item at *nStart* is excluded from the search if *nStart* is not equal to –1.

Remarks

Use this function to search for a list view item having specified characteristics.

The *pFindInfo* parameter points to an **LV_FINDINFO** structure, which contains information used to search for a list view item:

```
typedef struct _LV_FINDINFO {
    UINT flags;     //see below
    LPCSTR psz;     //see below
    LPARAM lParam;  //see below
} LV_FINDINFO;
```

The members are as follows:

flags   Type of search to perform. It can be one or more of these values:

- **LVFI_PARAM**   Searches based on the **lParam** member. The **lParam** member of the matching item's **LV_ITEM** structure must match the **lParam** member of this structure. (For information on the **LV_ITEM** structure, see **CListCtrl::GetItem**.) If this value is specified, all other values are ignored.

- **LVFI_PARTIAL**   Matches if the item text begins with the string pointed to by the **psz** member. This value implies use of the **LVFI_STRING** value.

- **LVFI_STRING**   Searches based on item text. Unless additional values are specified, the item text of the matching item must exactly match the string pointed to by the **psz** member.

- **LVFI_WRAP**   Continues the search at the beginning if no match is found.

- **LVFI_NEARESTXY**   Finds the item nearest the specified position in the specified direction.

psz   Address of a null-terminated string to compare with item text if the **flags** member specifies the **LVFI_STRING** or **LVFI_PARTIAL** value.

lParam   Value to compare with the **lParam** member of a list view item's **LV_ITEM** structure if the **flags** member specifies the **LVFI_PARAM** value.

See Also   **CListCtrl::SortItems**

CListCtrl::GetBkColor

COLORREF GetBkColor( ) const;

Return Value

A 32-bit value used to specify an RGB color.

Remarks

Retrieves the background color of a list view control.

See Also   **CListCtrl::SetBkColor**

In the Win32 Programmer's Reference: **COLORREF**

CListCtrl::GetCallbackMask

UINT GetCallbackMask( ) const;

Return Value

The list view control's callback mask.

Remarks

Retrieves the callback mask for a list view control.

A "callback item" is a list view item for which the application—rather than the control—stores the text, icon, or both. Although a list view control can store these attributes for you, you may want to use callback items if your application already maintains some of this information. The callback mask specifies which item state bits are maintained by the application, and it applies to the whole control rather than to a specific item. The callback mask is zero by default, meaning that the control tracks all item states. If an application uses callback items or specifies a nonzero callback mask, it must be able to supply list view item attributes on demand.

See Also   **CListCtrl::SetCallbackMask**

CListCtrl::GetColumn

BOOL GetColumn(int *nCol***, LV_COLUMN*** *pColumn* **) const;**

Return Value

Nonzero if successful; otherwise zero.

Parameters

nCol   Index of the column whose attributes are to be retrieved.

pColumn   Address of an **LV_COLUMN** structure that specifies the information to retrieve and receives information about the column. The **mask** member specifies which column attributes to retrieve. If the **mask** member specifies the **LVCF_TEXT** value, the **pszText** member must contain the address of the buffer that receives the item text and the **cchTextMax** member must specify the size of the buffer.

Remarks

Retrieves the attributes of a list view control's column.

The **LV_COLUMN** structure contains information about a column in report view:

```
typedef struct _LV_COLUMN {
    UINT mask;          // see below
    int fmt;            // see below
    int cx;             // width of the column, in pixels
    LPSTR pszText;      // see below
    int cchTextMax;     // see below
    int iSubItem;       // index of subitem associated with column
} LV_COLUMN;
```

The members are as follows:

mask   Variable specifying which members contain valid information. It can be zero or one or more of these values (combine values with the bitwise-OR operator):

- **LVCF_FMT**   The **fmt** member is valid.

- **LVCF_SUBITEM**   The **iSubItem** member is valid.

- **LVCF_TEXT**   The **pszText** member is valid.

- **LVCF_WIDTH**   The **cx** member is valid.

fmt   Alignment of the column. It can be one of these values: **LVCFMT_LEFT**, **LVCFMT_RIGHT**, or **LVCFMT_CENTER**.

pszText   Address of a null-terminated string containing the column heading if the structure contains information about a column. If the structure is receiving information about a column, this member specifies the address of the buffer that receives the column heading.

cchTextMax   Size of the buffer pointed to by the **pszText** member. If the structure is not receiving information about a column, this member is ignored.

See Also   **CListCtrl::SetColumn, CListCtrl::GetColumnWidth**

CListCtrl::GetColumnWidth

int GetColumnWidth(int *nCol* **) const;**

Return Value

The width, in pixels, of the column specified by *nCol*.

Parameters

nCol   Specifies the index of the column whose width is to be retrieved.

Remarks

Retrieves the width of a column in report view or list view.

See Also   **CListCtrl::SetColumnWidth, CListCtrl::GetColumn**

CListCtrl::GetCountPerPage

int GetCountPerPage( ) const;

Return Value

The number of items that can fit vertically in the visible area of a list view control when in list view or report view.

Remarks

Calculates the number of items that can fit vertically in the visible area of a list view control when in list view or report view.

See Also　**CListCtrl::GetTopIndex**

CListCtrl::GetEditControl

CEdit* GetEditControl( ) const;

Return Value

If successful, a pointer to the **CEdit** object that is used to edit the item text; otherwise **NULL**.

Remarks

Retrieves the handle of the edit control used to edit a list view item's text.

See Also　**CListCtrl::EditLabel**

CListCtrl::GetImageList

CImageList* GetImageList(int *nImageList*) const;

Return Value

A pointer to the image list used for drawing list view items.

Parameters

nImageList　Value specifying which image list to retrieve. It can be one of these values:

- **LVSIL_NORMAL**　Image list with large icons.
- **LVSIL_SMALL**　Image list with small icons.
- **LVSIL_STATE**　Image list with state images.

Remarks

Retrieves the handle of an image list used for drawing list view items.

See Also　**CImageList, CListCtrl::SetImageList**

CListCtrl::GetItem

BOOL GetItem(LV_ITEM* *pItem*) const;

Return Value

Nonzero if successful; otherwise zero.

Parameters

pItem   Pointer to an **LV_ITEM** structure that receives the item's attributes.

Remarks

Retrieves some or all of a list view item's attributes.

The **LV_ITEM** structure specifies or receives the attributes of a list view item:

```
typedef struct _LV_ITEM {
    UINT    mask;           // see below
    int     iItem;          // see below
    int     iSubItem;       // see below
    UINT    state;          // see below
    UINT    stateMask;      // see below
    LPSTR   pszText;        // see below
    int     cchTextMax;     // see below
    int     iImage;         // see below
    LPARAM  lParam;         // 32-bit value to associate with item
} LV_ITEM;
```

Members are as follows:

mask   Variable specifying which members contain valid data or which members are to be filled in. It can be one or more of these values:

- **LVIF_TEXT**   The **pszText** member is valid.
- **LVIF_IMAGE**   The **iImage** member is valid
- **LVIF_PARAM**   The **lParam** member is valid.
- **LVIF_STATE**   The **state** member is valid.

item   Index of the item this structure refers to.

iSubItem   A "subitem" is a string that, in report view, can be displayed in a column to the right of an item's icon and label. All items in a list view have the same number of subitems. This member is the one-based index of a subitem, or zero if the structure contains information about an item.

state and **stateMask**   Current state of the item, and the valid states of the item. These members can be any valid combination of the following state flags:

- **LVIS_CUT**   The item is marked for a cut and paste operation.
- **LVIS_DROPHILITED**   The item is highlighted as a drag and drop target.

- **LVIS_FOCUSED** The item has the focus, so it is surrounded by a standard focus rectangle. Although more than one item may be selected, only one item can have the focus.
- **LVIS_SELECTED** The item is selected. The appearance of a selected item depends on whether it has the focus and on the system colors used for selection.

pszText Address of a null-terminated string containing the item text if the structure specifies item attributes. If this member is the **LPSTR_TEXTCALLBACK** value, the item is a callback item. If the structure is receiving item attributes, this member is the address of the buffer that receives the item text.

cchTextMax Size of the buffer pointed to by the **pszText** member if the structure is receiving item attributes. If the structure specifies item attributes, this member is ignored.

iImage Index of the list view item's icon in the large icon and small icon image lists. If this member is the **I_IMAGECALLBACK** value, the item is a callback item.

See Also **CListCtrl::SetItem**

CListCtrl::GetItemCount

int GetItemCount( );

Return Value

The number of items in the list view control.

Remarks

Retrieves the number of items in a list view control.

See Also **CListCtrl::SetItemCount, CListCtrl::GetSelectedCount**

CListCtrl::GetItemData

DWORD GetItemData(int *nItem*) const;

Return Value

A 32-bit application-specific value associated with the specified item.

Parameters

nItem Index of the list item whose data is to be retrieved.

Remarks

This function retrieves the 32-bit application-specific value associated with the item specified by *nItem*. This value is the **lParam** member of the **LV_ITEM** structure; for more information on this structure, see **GetItem**.

See Also   **CListCtrl::SetItemData**

CListCtrl::GetItemPosition

BOOL GetItemPosition(int *nItem***, LPPOINT** *lpPoint* **) const;**

Return Value

Nonzero if successful; otherwise zero.

Parameters

nItem   The index of the item whose position is to be retrieved.

lpPoint   Address of a **POINT** structure that receives the position of the item's upper-left corner, in view coordinates.

Remarks

Retrieves the position of a list view item.

See Also   **CListCtrl::SetItemPosition, CListCtrl::GetOrigin**

CListCtrl::GetItemRect

BOOL GetItemRect(int *nItem***, LPRECT** *lpRect***, UINT** *nCode* **) const;**

Return Value

Nonzero if successful; otherwise zero.

Parameters

nItem   The index of the item whose position is to be retrieved.

lpRect   Address of a **RECT** structure that receives the bounding rectangle.

nCode   Portion of the list view item for which to retrieve the bounding rectangle. It can be one of these values:

- **LVIR_BOUNDS**   Returns the bounding rectangle of the entire item, including the icon and label.

- **LVIR_ICON**   Returns the bounding rectangle of the icon or small icon.

- **LVIR_LABEL**   Returns the bounding rectangle of the item text.

Remarks

Retrieves the bounding rectangle for all or part of an item in the current view.

See Also   **CListCtrl::GetItemPosition**, **CListCtrl::SetItemPosition**,
CListCtrl::GetOrigin

CListCtrl::GetItemState

UINT GetItemState(int *nItem*, **UINT** *nMask* **) const;**

Return Value

The state flags for the specified list view item.

Parameters

nItem   The index of the item whose position is to be retrieved.

nMask   Mask specifying which of the item's state flags to return.

Remarks

Retrieves the state of a list view item.

An item's state is specified by the **state** member of the **LV_ITEM** structure. When
you specify or change an item's state, the **stateMask** member specifies which state
bits you want to change. For more information on the **LV_ITEM** structure, see
CListCtrl::GetItem.

See Also   **CListCtrl::SetItemState**, **CListCtrl::GetItem**

CListCtrl::GetItemText

int GetItemText(int *nItem*, **int** *nSubItem*, **LPTSTR** *lpszText*, **int** *nLen* **) const;**
CString GetItemText(int *nItem*, **int** *nSubItem* **) const;**

Return Value

The version returning **int** returns the length of the retrieved string.

The version returning a **CString** returns the item text.

Parameters

nItem   The index of the item whose text is to be retrieved.

nSubItem   Specifies the subitem whose text is to be retrieved.

lpszText   Pointer to a string that is to receive the item text.

nLen   Length of the buffer pointed to by *lpszText*.

Remarks

Retrieves the text of a list view item or subitem. If *nSubItem* is zero, this function retrieves the item label; if *nSubItem* is nonzero, it retrieves the text of the subitem. For more information on the subitem argument, see the discussion of the **LV_ITEM** structure in **CListCtrl::GetItem**.

See Also   **CListCtrl::GetItem**

CListCtrl::GetNextItem

int GetNextItem(int *nItem*, **int** *nFlags* **) const;**

Return Value

The index of the next item if successful, or −1 otherwise.

Parameters

nItem   Index of the item to begin the searching with, or −1 to find the first item that matches the specified flags. The specified item itself is excluded from the search.

nFlags   Geometric relation of the requested item to the specified item, and the state of the requested item. The geometric relation can be one of these values:

- **LVNI_ABOVE**   Searches for an item that is above the specified item.
- **LVNI_ALL**   Searches for a subsequent item by index (the default value).
- **LVNI_BELOW**   Searches for an item that is below the specified item.
- **LVNI_TOLEFT**   Searches for an item to the left of the specified item.
- **LVNI_TORIGHT**   Searches for an item to the right of the specified item.

The state can be zero, or it can be one or more of these values:

- **LVNI_DROPHILITED**   The item has the **LVIS_DROPHILITED** state flag set.
- **LVNI_FOCUSED**   The item has the **LVIS_FOCUSED** state flag set.
- **LVNI_HIDDEN**   The item has the **LVIS_HIDDEN** state flag set.
- **LVNI_MARKED**   The item has the **LVIS_MARKED** state flag set.
- **LVNI_SELECTED**   The item has the **LVIS_SELECTED** state flag set.

If an item does not have all of the specified state flags set, the search continues with the next item.

Remarks

Searches for a list view item that has the specified properties and that bears the specified relationship to a given item.

See Also   **CListCtrl::GetItem**

CListCtrl::GetOrigin

BOOL GetOrigin(LPPOINT *lpPoint* **) const;**

Return Value

Nonzero if successful; otherwise zero.

Parameters

lpPoint   Address of a **POINT** structure that receives the view origin.

Remarks

Retrieves the current view origin for a list view control.

See Also   **CListCtrl::GetItemPosition, CListCtrl::SetItemPosition**

CListCtrl::GetSelectedCount

UINT GetSelectedCount( ) const;

Return Value

The number of selected items in the list view control.

Remarks

Retrieves the number of selected items in the list view control.

See Also   **CListCtrl::SetItemCount, CListCtrl::GetItemCount**

CListCtrl::GetStringWidth

int GetStringWidth(LPCTSTR *lpsz* **) const;**

Return Value

The width, in pixels, of the string pointed to by *lpsz*.

Parameters

lpsz   Address of a null-terminated string whose width is to be determined.

Remarks

Determines the minimum column width necessary to display all of a given string.

The returned width takes into account the control's current font and column margins, but not the width of a small icon.

See Also   **CListCtrl::GetColumnWidth, CListCtrl::SetColumnWidth**

CListCtrl::GetTextBkColor

COLORREF GetTextBkColor( ) const;

Return Value

A 32-bit value used to specify an RGB color.

Remarks

Retrieves the text background color of a list view control.

See Also   CListCtrl::SetTextBkColor, CListCtrl::GetTextColor

In the *Win32 Programmer's Reference*: **COLORREF**

CListCtrl::GetTextColor

COLORREF GetTextColor( ) const;

Return Value

A 32-bit value used to specify an RGB color.

Remarks

Retrieves the text color of a list view control.

See Also   CListCtrl::SetTextColor, CListCtrl::GetTextBkColor

In the *Win32 Programmer's Reference*: **COLORREF**

CListCtrl::GetTopIndex

int GetTopIndex( ) const;

Return Value

The index of the topmost visible item.

Remarks

Retrieves the index of the topmost visible item when in list view or report view.

See Also   CListCtrl::GetCountPerPage

CListCtrl::GetViewRect

BOOL GetViewRect(LPRECT *lpRect* **) const;**

Return Value

Nonzero if successful; otherwise zero.

Parameters

lpRect   Address of a **RECT** structure.

Remarks

Retrieves the bounding rectangle of all items in the list view control. The list view must be in icon view or small icon view.

See Also **CListCtrl::GetTopIndex**

CListCtrl::HitTest

int HitTest(LV_HITTESTINFO* *pHitTestInfo* **) const;**
int HitTest(CPoint *pt*, **UINT*** *pFlags* **= NULL) const;**

Return Value

The index of the item at the position specified by *pHitTestInfo*, if any, or –1 otherwise.

Parameters

pHitTestInfo Address of a **LV_HITTESTINFO** structure that contains the position to hit test and that receives information about the results of the hit test.

pt Point to be tested.

pFlags Pointer to an integer that receives information about the results of the test. See the explanation of the **flags** member of the **LV_HITTESTINFO** structure under Remarks.

Remarks

Determines which list view item, if any, is at a specified position.

The **LV_HITTESTINFO** structure contains information about a hit test:

```
typedef struct _LV_HITTESTINFO {
    POINT pt;     // position to hit test, in client coordinates
    UINT flags;   // see below
    int iItem;    // receives the index of the matching item
} LV_HITTESTINFO;
```

Its members are as follows:

flags Variable that receives information about the results of a hit test. It can be one or more of these values:

- **LVHT_ABOVE** The position is above the client area of the control.
- **LVHT_BELOW** The position is below the client area of the control.
- **LVHT_NOWHERE** The position is inside the list view control's client window but is not over a list item.
- **LVHT_ONITEMICON** The position is over a list view item's icon.
- **LVHT_ONITEMLABEL** The position is over a list view item's text.

- **LVHT_ONITEMSTATEICON**   The position is over the state image of a list view item.

- **LVHT_TOLEFT**   The position is to the left of the list view control's client area.

- **LVHT_TORIGHT**   The position is to the right of the list view control's client area.

You can use the **LVHT_ABOVE**, **LVHT_BELOW**, **LVHT_TOLEFT**, and **LVHT_TORIGHT** values to determine whether to scroll the contents of a list view control. Two of these flags can be combined, for example, if the position is above and to the left of the client area.

You can test for the **LVHT_ONITEM** value to determine whether a given position is over a list view item. This value is a bitwise-OR operation on the **LVHT_ONITEMICON**, **LVHT_ONITEMLABEL**, and **LVHT_ONITEMSTATEICON** values.

See Also   **CListCtrl::SetItemPosition**, **CListCtrl::GetItemPosition**

CListCtrl::InsertColumn

int InsertColumn(int *nCol*, **const LV_COLUMN*** *pColumn* **);**
int InsertColumn(int *nCol*, **LPCTSTR** *lpszColumnHeading*, **int** *nFormat* = **LVCFMT_LEFT,**
   int *nWidth* = **–1, int** *nSubItem* = **–1);**

Return Value

The index of the new column if successful or –1 otherwise.

Parameters

nCol   The index of the new column.

pColumn   Address of an **LV_COLUMN** structure that contains the attributes of the new column.

lpszColumnHeading   Address of a string containing the column's heading.

nFormat   Integer specifying the alignment of the column. It can be one of these values: **LVCFMT_LEFT**, **LVCFMT_RIGHT**, or **LVCFMT_CENTER**.

nWidth   Width of the column, in pixels. If this parameter is –1, the column width is not set.

nSubItem   Index of the subitem associated with the column. If this parameter is –1, no subitem is associatied with the column.

Remarks

Inserts a new column in a list view control.

The **LV_COLUMN** structure contains the attributes of a column in report view. It is also used to receive information about a column. For more information on the **LV_COLUMN** structure, see **CListCtrl::GetColumn**.

See Also   **CListCtrl::DeleteColumn**

CListCtrl::InsertItem

int InsertItem(const LV_ITEM* *pItem* **);**
int InsertItem(int *nItem*, **LPCTSTR** *lpszItem* **);**
int InsertItem(int *nItem*, **LPCTSTR** *lpszItem*, **int** *nImage* **);**
int InsertItem(UINT *nMask*, **int** *nItem*, **LPCTSTR** *lpszItem*, **UINT** *nState*, **UINT** *nStateMask*, **int** *nImage*, **LPARAM** *lParam* **);**

Return Value

The index of the new item if successful or –1 otherwise.

Parameters

pItem   Pointer to an **LV_ITEM** structure that specifies the item's attributes. For information on the **LV_ITEM** structure, see **CListCtrl::GetItem**.

nItem   Index of the item to be inserted.

lpszItem   Address of a string containing the item's label, or **LPSTR_TEXTCALLBACK** if the item is a callback item. For information on callback items, see **CListCtrl::GetCallbackMask**.

nImage   Index of the item's image, or **I_IMAGECALLBACK** if the item is a callback item. For information on callback items, see **CListCtrl::GetCallbackMask**.

nMask   Specifies which attributes are valid (see the Remarks).

nState   Specifies values for states to be changed (see the Remarks).

nStateMask   Specifies which states are valid (see the Remarks).

nImage   Index of the item's image within the image list.

lParam   A 32-bit application-specific value associated with the item.

Remarks

Inserts an item into the list view control.

The *nMask* parameter specifies which item attributes are valid. It can have one of two values:

- **LVIF_TEXT**   The *lpszItem* parameter is the address of a null-terminated string.

- **LVIF_STATE**   The *nStateMask* parameter specifies which item states are valid and the *nState* parameter contains the values for those states.

See Also   **CListCtrl::DeleteItem**, **CListCtrl::DeleteAllItems**

CListCtrl::RedrawItems

BOOL RedrawItems(int *nFirst***, int** *nLast* **);**

Return Value
Nonzero if successful; otherwise zero.

Parameters
nFirst   Index of the first item to be repainted.

nLast   Index of the last item to be repainted.

Remarks
Forces a list view control to repaint a range of items.

The specified items are not actually repainted until the list view window receives a **WM_PAINT** message. To repaint immediately, call the Windows **UpdateWindow** function after using this function.

See Also   **CListCtrl::DrawItem**

CListCtrl::Scroll

BOOL Scroll(CSize *size* **);**

Return Value
Nonzero if successful; otherwise zero.

Parameters
size   A **CSize** object specifying the amount of horizontal and vertical scrolling, in pixels. The **y** member of *size* is divided by the height, in pixels, of the list view control's line, and the control is scrolled by the resulting number of lines.

Remarks
Scrolls the content of a list view control.

See Also   **CListCtrl::EnsureVisible**

CListCtrl::SetBkColor

BOOL SetBkColor(COLORREF *cr* **);**

Return Value
Nonzero if successful; otherwise zero.

Parameters

cr   Background color to set, or the **CLR_NONE** value for no background color. List view controls with background colors redraw themselves significantly faster than those without background colors. For information, see **COLORREF** in the Win32 Programmer's Reference.

Remarks

Sets the background color of the list view control.

See Also   **CListCtrl::GetBkColor**

CListCtrl::SetCallbackMask

BOOL SetCallbackMask(UINT *nMask* **);**

Return Value

Nonzero if successful; otherwise zero.

Parameters

nMask   New value of the callback mask.

Remarks

Sets the callback mask for a list view control.

See Also   **CListCtrl::GetCallbackMask**

CListCtrl::SetColumn

BOOL SetColumn(int *nCol***, const LV_COLUMN*** *pColumn* **);**

Return Value

Nonzero if successful; otherwise zero.

Parameters

nCol   Index of the column whose attributes are to be set.

pColumn   Address of an **LV_COLUMN** structure that contains the new column attributes. The **mask** member specifies which column attributes to set. If the **mask** member specifies the **LVCF_TEXT** value, the **pszText** member is the address of a null-terminated string and the **cchTextMax** member is ignored. For more information on the **LV_COLUMN** structure, see **CListCtrl::GetColumn**.

Remarks

Sets the attributes of a list view column.

See Also   **CListCtrl::GetColumn**

CListCtrl::SetColumnWidth

BOOL SetColumnWidth(int *nCol***, int** *cx* **);**

Return Value

Nonzero if successful; otherwise zero.

Parameters

nCol   Index of the column whose width is to be set. In list view, this parameter
must be –1.

cx   The new width of the column.

Remarks

Changes the width of a column in report view or list view.

See Also   **CListCtrl::GetColumnWidth**, **CListCtrl::GetStringWidth**

CListCtrl::SetImageList

CImageList* SetImageList(CImageList* *pImageList***, int** *nImageList* **);**

Return Value

A pointer to the previous image list.

Parameters

pImageList   Pointer to the image list to assign.

nImageList   Type of image list. It can be one of these values:

- **LVSIL_NORMAL**   Image list with large icons.
- **LVSIL_SMALL**   Image list with small icons.
- **LVSIL_STATE**   Image list with state images.

Remarks

Assigns an image list to a list view control.

See Also   **CImageList**, **CListCtrl::GetImageList**

CListCtrl::SetItem

BOOL SetItem(const LV_ITEM* *pItem* **);**
BOOL SetItem(int *nItem***, int** *nSubItem***, UINT** *nMask***, LPCTSTR** *lpszItem***, int** *nImage***,**
UINT *nState***, UINT** *nStateMask***, LPARAM** *lParam* **);**

Return Value

Nonzero if successful; otherwise zero.

Parameters

pItem   Address of an **LV_ITEM** structure that contains the new item attributes. The **iItem** and **iSubItem** members identify the item or subitem, and the **mask** member specifies which attributes to set. For more information on the **mask** member, see the Remarks. For more information on the **LV_ITEM** structure, see **CListCtrl::GetItem**.

nItem   Index of the item whose attributes are to be set.

nSubItem   Index of the subitem whose attributes are to be set.

nMask   Specifies which attributes are to be set (see the Remarks).

lpszItem   Address of a null-terminated string specifying the item's label.

nImage   Index of the item's image within the image list.

nState   Specifies values for states to be changed (see the Remarks).

nStateMask   Specifies which states are to be changed (see the Remarks).

lParam   A 32-bit application-specific value to be associated with the item.

Remarks

Sets some or all of a list view item's attributes.

The **iItem** and **iSubItem** members of the **LV_ITEM** structure and the *nItem* and *nSubItem* parameters identify the item and subitem whose attributes are to be set.

The **mask** member of the **LV_ITEM** structure and the *nMask* parameter specify which item attributes are to be set:

- **LVIF_TEXT**   The **pszText** member or the *lpszItem* parameter is the address of a null-terminated string; the **cchTextMax** member is ignored.

- **LVIF_STATE**   The **stateMask** member or *nStateMask* parameter specifies which item states to change and the **state** member or *nState* parameter contains the values for those states.

See Also   **CListCtrl::GetItem**

CListCtrl::SetItemCount

void SetItemCount(int *nItems*);

Parameters

nItems   Number of items that the control will ultimately contain.

Remarks

Prepares a list view control for adding a large number of items.

By calling this function before adding a large number of items, you enable a list view control to reallocate its internal data structures only once rather than every time you add an item.

See Also **CListCtrl::GetItemCount, CListCtrl::GetSelectedCount**

CListCtrl::SetItemData

BOOL SetItemData(int *nItem*, **DWORD** *dwData* **);**

Return Value

Nonzero if successful; otherwise 0.

Parameters

nItem   Index of the list item whose data is to be set.

dwData   A 32-bit value to be associated with the item.

Remarks

This function sets the 32-bit application-specific value associated with the item specified by *nItem*. This value is the **lParam** member of the **LV_ITEM** structure; for more information on this structure, see **GetItem**.

See Also **CListCtrl::GetItemData**

CListCtrl::SetItemPosition

BOOL SetItemPosition(int *nItem*, **POINT** *pt* **);**

Return Value

Nonzero if successful; otherwise zero.

Parameters

nItem   Index of the item whose position is to be set.

pt   A **POINT** structure specifying the new position, in view coordinates, of the item's upper-left corner.

Remarks

Moves an item to a specified position in a list view control. The control must be in icon or small icon view.

If the list view control has the **LVS_AUTOARRANGE** style, the list view is arranged after the position of the item is set. This function cannot be used for list views that have the **LVS_NOITEMDATA** style.

See Also **CListCtrl::GetItemPosition, CListCtrl::GetOrigin**

CListCtrl::SetItemState

BOOL SetItemState(int *nItem*, **LV_ITEM*** *pItem* **);**
BOOL SetItemState(int *nItem*, **UINT** *nState*, **UINT** *nMask* **);**

Return Value

Nonzero if successful; otherwise zero.

Parameters

nItem   Index of the item whose state is to be set.

pItem   Address of an **LV_ITEM** structure. The **stateMask** member specifies which state bits to change, and the **state** member contains the new values for those bits. The other members are ignored. For more information on the **LV_ITEM** structure, see **CListCtrl::GetItem**.

nState   New values for the state bits.

nMask   Mask specifying which state bits to change.

Remarks

Changes the state of an item in a list view control.

An item's "state" is a value that specifies the item's availability, indicates user actions, or otherwise reflects the item's status. A list view control changes some state bits, such as when the user selects an item. An application might change other state bits to disable or hide the item, or to specify an overlay image or state image.

See Also   **CListCtrl::GetItemState**

CListCtrl::SetItemText

BOOL SetItemText(int *nItem*, **int** *nSubItem*, **LPTSTR** *lpszText* **);**

Return Value

Nonzero if successful; otherwise zero.

Parameters

nItem   Index of the item whose text is to be set.

nSubItem   Index of the subitem, or zero to set the item label.

lpszText   Pointer to a string that contains the new item text.

Remarks

Changes the text of a list view item or subitem.

See Also   **CListCtrl::GetItemText**

CListCtrl::SetTextBkColor

BOOL SetTextBkColor(COLORREF *cr* **);**

Return Value

Nonzero if successful; otherwise zero.

Parameters

cr   A **COLORREF** specifying the new text background color. For information, see **COLORREF** in the Win32 Programmer's Reference.

Remarks

Sets the background color of text in a list view control.

See Also   **CListCtrl::GetTextBkColor**

CListCtrl::SetTextColor

BOOL SetTextColor(COLORREF *cr* **);**

Return Value

Nonzero if successful; otherwise zero.

Parameters

cr   A **COLORREF** specifying the new text color. For information, see **COLORREF** in the Win32 Programmer's Reference.

Remarks

Sets the text color of a list view control.

See Also   **CListCtrl::SetTextBkColor**

CListCtrl::SortItems

BOOL SortItems(PFNLVCOMPARE *pfnCompare*, **DWORD** *dwData* **);**

Return Value

Nonzero if successful; otherwise zero.

Parameters

pfnCompare   Address of the application-defined comparison function. The comparison function is called during the sort operation each time the relative order of two list items needs to be compared.

dwData   Application-defined value that is passed to the comparison function.

Remarks

Sorts list view items using an application-defined comparison function. The index of each item changes to reflect the new sequence.

The comparison function has the following form:

```
int CALLBACK CompareFunc(LPARAM lParam1, LPARAM lParam2,
    LPARAM lParamSort);
```

The comparison function must return a negative value if the first item should precede the second, a positive value if the first item should follow the second, or zero if the two items are equivalent.

The *lParam1* and *lParam2* parameters specify the item data for the two items being compared. The *lParamSort* parameter is the same as the *dwData* value.

See Also   **CListCtrl::FindItem**

CListCtrl::Update

BOOL Update(int *nItem* **);**

Return Value
Nonzero if successful; otherwise zero.

Parameters
nItem   Index of the item to be updated.

Remarks
Call this function to force the list view control to repaint the item specified by *nItem*. This function also arranges the list view control if it has the **LVS_AUTOARRANGE** style.

See Also   **CListCtrl::DrawItem**

CListView

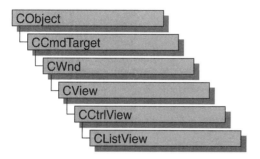

The **CListView** class simplifies use of the list control and of **CListCtrl**, the class that encapsulates list-control functionality, with MFC's document-view architecture. For more information on this architecture, see the overview for the **CView** class and the cross-references cited there.

#include <afxcview.h>

See Also   **CView, CCtrlView, CListCtrl**

Construction
___

CListView	Constructs a **CListView** object.

Attributes
___

GetListCtrl	Returns the list control associated with the view.

Member Functions

CListView::CListView

CListView( );

Remarks

Constructs a **CListView** object. The framework calls the constructor when a new frame window is created or a window is split. Override **CView::OnInitialUpdate** to initialize the view after the document is attached. Call **CWnd::Create** or **CWnd::CreateEx** to create the Windows object.

CListView::GetListCtrl

CListCtrl& GetListCtrl( ) const;

Return Value

A reference to the list control associated with the view.

Remarks

Call this member function to get a reference to the list control associated with
the view.

See Also   CListCtrl

CLongBinary

Class **CLongBinary** simplifies working with very large binary data objects (often called BLOBs, or "binary large objects") in a database. For example, a record field in an SQL table might contain a bitmap representing a picture. A **CLongBinary** object stores such an object and keeps track of its size.

Note In general, it is better practice now to use **CByteArray** in conjunction with the **DFX_Binary** function. You can still use **CLongBinary**, but in general **CByteArray** provides more functionality under Win32, since there is no longer the size limitation encountered with 16-bit **CByteArray**. This advice applies to programming with Data Access Objects (DAO) as well as Open Database Connectivity (ODBC).

To use a **CLongBinary** object, declare a field data member of type **CLongBinary** in your recordset class. This member will be an embedded member of the recordset class and will be constructed when the recordset is constructed. After the **CLongBinary** object is constructed, the record field exchange (RFX) mechanism loads the data object from a field in the current record on the data source and stores it back to the record when the record is updated. RFX queries the data source for the size of the binary large object, allocates storage for it (via the **CLongBinary** object's **m_hData** data member), and stores an **HGLOBAL** handle to the data in **m_hData**. RFX also stores the actual size of the data object in the **m_dwDataLength** data member. Work with the data in the object through **m_hData**, using the same techniques you would normally use to manipulate the data stored in a Windows **HGLOBAL** handle.

When you destroy your recordset, the embedded **CLongBinary** object is also destroyed, and its destructor deallocates the **HGLOBAL** data handle.

For more information about large objects and the use of **CLongBinary**, see the articles "Recordset (ODBC)" and "Recordset: Working with Large Data Items (ODBC)" in *Programming with MFC*.

#include <afxdb.h>

See Also crecordset

Data Members

m_dwDataLength	Contains the actual size in bytes of the data object whose handle is stored in **m_hData**.
m_hData	Contains a Windows **HGLOBAL** handle to the actual image object.

Construction

CLongBinary	Constructs a **CLongBinary** object.

Member Functions

CLongBinary::CLongBinary

    CLongBinary( );

Remarks

Constructs a **CLongBinary** object.

Data Members

CLongBinary::m_dwDataLength

Remarks

Stores the actual size in bytes of the data stored in the **HGLOBAL** handle in **m_hData**. This size may be smaller than the size of the memory block allocated for the data. Call **::GlobalSize** to get the allocated size.

CLongBinary::m_hData

Remarks

Stores a Windows **HGLOBAL** handle to the actual binary large object data.

CMap

> **template< class** *KEY*, **class** *ARG_KEY*, **class** *VALUE*,
> **class** *ARG_VALUE* >**class CMap : public CObject**

Parameters

KEY   Class of the object used as the key to the map.

ARG_KEY   Data type used for *KEY* arguments; usually a reference to *KEY*.

VALUE   Class of the object stored in the map.

ARG_VALUE   Data type used for *VALUE* arguments; usually a reference to *VALUE*.

Remarks

CMap is a dictionary collection class that maps unique keys to values. Once you have inserted a key-value pair (element) into the map, you can efficiently retrieve or delete the pair using the key to access it. You can also iterate over all the elements in the map.

A variable of type **POSITION** is used for alternate access to entries. You can use a **POSITION** to "remember" an entry and to iterate through the map. You might think that this iteration is sequential by key value; it is not. The sequence of retrieved elements is indeterminate.

Certain member functions of this class call global helper functions that must be customized for most uses of the **CMap** class. See "Collection Class Helpers" in the "Macros and Globals" section of the *MFC Reference*.

CMap incorporates the **IMPLEMENT_SERIAL** macro to support serialization and dumping of its elements. Each element is serialized in turn if a map is stored to an archive, either with the overloaded insertion (<<) operator or with the **Serialize** member function.

If you need a diagnostic dump of the individual elements in the map (the keys and the values), you must set the depth of the dump context to 1 or greater.

When a **CMap** object is deleted, or when its elements are removed, the keys and values both are removed.

Map class derivation is similar to list derivation. See the article "Collections" in *Programming with MFC* for an illustration of the derivation of a special-purpose list class.

#include <afxtempl.h>

See Also "Collection Class Helpers"

Construction

CMap	Constructs a collection that maps keys to values.

Operations

Lookup	Looks up the value mapped to a given key.
SetAt	Inserts an element into the map; replaces an existing element if a matching key is found.
operator []	Inserts an element into the map—operator substitution for **SetAt**.
RemoveKey	Removes an element specified by a key.
RemoveAll	Removes all the elements from this map.
GetStartPosition	Returns the position of the first element.
GetNextAssoc	Gets the next element for iterating.
GetHashTableSize	Returns the size (number of elements) of the hash table.
InitHashTable	Initializes the hash table and specifies its size.

Status

GetCount	Returns the number of elements in this map.
IsEmpty	Tests for the empty-map condition (no elements).

Member Functions

CMap::CMap

CMap(int *nBlockSize* **= 10);**

Parameters

nBlockSize   Specifies the memory-allocation granularity for extending the map.

Remarks

Constructs an empty map. As the map grows, memory is allocated in units of *nBlockSize* entries.

CMap::GetCount

int GetCount( ) const;

Return Value

The number of elements.

Remarks

Call this member function to retrieve the number of elements in the map.

See Also   CMap::IsEmpty

CMap::GetHashTableSize

UINT GetHashTableSize( ) const;

Return Value

The number of elements in the hash table.

Remarks

Call this member function to determine the number of elements in the hash table for the map.

See Also   CMap::InitHashTable

CMap::GetNextAssoc

void GetNextAssoc(POSITION& *rNextPosition***, KEY&** *rKey***, VALUE&** *rValue* **) const;**

Parameters

rNextPosition   Specifies a reference to a **POSITION** value returned by a previous **GetNextAssoc** or **GetStartPosition** call.

KEY   Template parameter specifying the type of the map's key.

rKey   Specifies the returned key of the retrieved element (a string).

VALUE   Template parameter specifying the type of the map's value.

rValue   Specifies the returned value of the retrieved element (a **CObject** pointer).

Remarks

Retrieves the map element at *rNextPosition*, then updates *rNextPosition* to refer to the next element in the map. This function is most useful for iterating through all the elements in the map. Note that the position sequence is not necessarily the same as the key value sequence.

If the retrieved element is the last in the map, then the new value of *rNextPosition* is set to **NULL**.

See Also   CMap::GetStartPosition

CMap::GetStartPosition

POSITION GetStartPosition( ) const;

Return Value

A **POSITION** value that indicates a starting position for iterating the map; or **NULL** if the map is empty.

Remarks

Starts a map iteration by returning a **POSITION** value that can be passed to a **GetNextAssoc** call. The iteration sequence is not predictable; therefore, the "first element in the map" has no special significance.

See Also **CMap::GetNextAssoc**

CMap::InitHashTable

void InitHashTable(UINT *hashSize* **);**

Parameters

hashSize   Number of entries in the hash table.

Remarks

Initializes the hash table. For best performance, the hash table size should be a prime number. To minimize collisions the size should be roughly 20 percent larger than the largest anticipated data set.

See Also **CMap::GetHashTableSize**

CMap::IsEmpty

BOOL IsEmpty( ) const;

Return Value

Nonzero if this map contains no elements; otherwise 0.

Remarks

Call this member function to determine whether the map is empty.

Example

See the example for **CMapStringToOB::RemoveAll**.

See Also **CMap::GetCount**

CMap::Lookup

BOOL Lookup(*ARG_KEY key*, *VALUE*& *rValue*) **const;**

Return Value

Nonzero if the element was found; otherwise 0.

Parameters

ARG_KEY   Template parameter specifying the type of the *key* value.

key   Specifies the string key that identifies the element to be looked up.

VALUE   Specifies the type of the value to be looked up.

rValue   Receives the looked-up value.

Remarks

Lookup uses a hashing algorithm to quickly find the map element with a key that exactly matches the given key.

See Also   CMap::operator []

CMap::RemoveAll

void RemoveAll( );

Remarks

Removes all the values from this map by calling the global helper function **DestructElements**.

The function works correctly if the map is already empty.

See Also   CMap::RemoveKey, DestructElements

CMap::RemoveKey

BOOL RemoveKey(*ARG_KEY key* **);**

Return Value

Nonzero if the entry was found and successfully removed; otherwise 0.

Parameters

ARG_KEY   Template parameter specifying the type of the key.

key   Key for the element to be removed.

Remarks

Looks up the map entry corresponding to the supplied key; then, if the key is found, removes the entry.

The **DestructElements** helper function is used to remove the entry.

See Also   **CMap::RemoveAll**

CMap::SetAt

void SetAt(*ARG_KEY key*, *ARG_VALUE newValue*);

Parameters

ARG_KEY   Template parameter specifying the type of the *key* parameter.

key   Specifies the string that is the key of the new element.

ARG_VALUE   Template parameter specifying the type of the *newValue* parameter.

newValue   Specifies the value of the new element.

Remarks

The primary means to insert an element in a map. First, the key is looked up. If the key is found, then the corresponding value is changed; otherwise a new key-value pair is created.

See Also   **CMap::Lookup**, **CMap::operator []**

Operators

CMap::operator [ ]

VALUE& **operator[]**(*ARG_KEY key*);

Parameters

VALUE   Template parameter specifying the type of the map value.

ARG_KEY   Template parameter specifying the type of the key value.

key   The key used to retrieve the value from the map.

Remarks

This operator is a convenient substitute for the **SetAt** member function. Thus it can be used only on the left side of an assignment statement (an l-value). If there is no map element with the specified key, then a new element is created.

There is no "right side" (r-value) equivalent to this operator because there is a possibility that a key may not be found in the map. Use the **Lookup** member function for element retrieval.

See Also   **CMap::SetAt**, **CMap::Lookup**

CMapPtrToPtr

The **CMapPtrToPtr** class supports maps of void pointers keyed by void pointers.

The member functions of **CMapPtrToPtr** are similar to the member functions of class **CMapStringToOb**. Because of this similarity, you can use the **CMapStringToOb** reference documentation for member function specifics. Wherever you see a **CObject** pointer as a function parameter or return value, substitute a pointer to **void**. Wherever you see a **CString** or a **const** pointer to **char** as a function parameter or return value, substitute a pointer to **void**.

```
BOOL CMapStringToOb::Lookup( const char* <key>,
                             CObject*& <rValue> ) const;
```

for example, translates to

```
BOOL CMapPtrToPtr::Lookup( void* <key>, void*& <rValue> ) const;
```

CMapPtrToPtr incorporates the **IMPLEMENT_DYNAMIC** macro to support runtime type access and dumping to a **CDumpContext** object. If you need a dump of individual map elements (pointer values), you must set the depth of the dump context to 1 or greater.

Pointer-to-pointer maps may not be serialized.

When a **CMapPtrToPtr** object is deleted, or when its elements are removed, only the pointers are removed, not the entities they reference.

For more information on **CMapPtrToPtr**, see the article "Collections" in *Programming with MFC*.

#include <afxcoll.h>

See Also   CMapStringToOb

Construction

CMapPtrToPtr	Constructs a collection that maps void pointers to void pointers.

Operations

Lookup	Looks up a void pointer based on the void pointer key. The pointer value, not the entity it points to, is used for the key comparison.
SetAt	Inserts an element into the map; replaces an existing element if a matching key is found.
operator [ ]	Inserts an element into the map—operator substitution for **SetAt**.
RemoveKey	Removes an element specified by a key.
RemoveAll	Removes all the elements from this map.
GetStartPosition	Returns the position of the first element.
GetNextAssoc	Gets the next element for iterating.

Status

GetCount	Returns the number of elements in this map.
IsEmpty	Tests for the empty-map condition (no elements).

CMapPtrToWord

The **CMapPtrToWord** class supports maps of 16-bit words keyed by void pointers.

The member functions of **CMapPtrToWord** are similar to the member functions of class **CMapStringToOb**. Because of this similarity, you can use the **CMapStringToOb** reference documentation for member function specifics. Wherever you see a **CObject** pointer as a function parameter or return value, substitute **WORD**. Wherever you see a **CString** or a **const** pointer to **char** as a function parameter or return value, substitute a pointer to **void**.

```
BOOL CMapStringToOb::Lookup( const char* <key>,
                            CObject*& <rValue> ) const;
```

for example, translates to

```
BOOL CMapPtrToWord::Lookup( const void* <key>, WORD& <rValue> ) const;
```

CMapWordToPtr incorporates the **IMPLEMENT_DYNAMIC** macro to support run-time type access and dumping to a **CDumpContext** object. If you need a dump of individual map elements, you must set the depth of the dump context to 1 or greater.

Pointer-to-word maps may not be serialized.

When a **CMapPtrToWord** object is deleted, or when its elements are removed, the pointers and the words are removed. The entities referenced by the key pointers are not removed.

For more information on **CMapPtrToWord**, see the article "Collections" in *Programming with MFC*.

#include <afxcoll.h>

See Also   **CMapStringToOb**

Construction

CMapPtrToWord	Constructs a collection that maps void pointers to 16-bit words.

Operations

Lookup	Returns a **WORD** using a void pointer as a key. The pointer value, not the entity it points to, is used for the key comparison.
SetAt	Inserts an element into the map; replaces an existing element if a matching key is found.
operator []	Inserts an element into the map—operator substitution for **SetAt**.
RemoveKey	Removes an element specified by a key.
RemoveAll	Removes all the elements from this map.
GetStartPosition	Returns the position of the first element.
GetNextAssoc	Gets the next element for iterating.

Status

GetCount	Returns the number of elements in this map.
IsEmpty	Tests for the empty-map condition (no elements).

CMapStringToOb

CMapStringToOb is a dictionary collection class that maps unique **CString** objects to **CObject** pointers. Once you have inserted a **CString**-**CObject*** pair (element) into the map, you can efficiently retrieve or delete the pair using a string or a **CString** value as a key. You can also iterate over all the elements in the map.

A variable of type **POSITION** is used for alternate entry access in all map variations. You can use a **POSITION** to "remember" an entry and to iterate through the map. You might think that this iteration is sequential by key value; it is not. The sequence of retrieved elements is indeterminate.

CMapStringToOb incorporates the **IMPLEMENT_SERIAL** macro to support serialization and dumping of its elements. Each element is serialized in turn if a map is stored to an archive, either with the overloaded insertion (**<<**) operator or with the **Serialize** member function.

If you need a diagnostic dump of the individual elements in the map (the **CString** value and the **CObject** contents), you must set the depth of the dump context to 1 or greater.

When a **CMapStringToOb** object is deleted, or when its elements are removed, the **CString** objects and the **CObject** pointers are removed. The objects referenced by the **CObject** pointers are not destroyed.

Map class derivation is similar to list derivation. See the article "Collections" in *Programming with MFC* for an illustration of the derivation of a special-purpose list class.

#include <afxcoll.h>

See Also   **CMapPtrToPtr, CMapPtrToWord, CMapStringToPtr, CMapStringToString, CMapWordToOb, CMapWordToPtr**

Construction

CMapStringToOb	Constructs a collection that maps **CString** values to **CObject** pointers.

Operations	
Lookup	Returns a **CObject** pointer based on a **CString** value.
SetAt	Inserts an element into the map; replaces an existing element if a matching key is found.
operator []	Inserts an element into the map—operator substitution for **SetAt**.
RemoveKey	Removes an element specified by a key.
RemoveAll	Removes all the elements from this map.
GetStartPosition	Returns the position of the first element.
GetNextAssoc	Gets the next element for iterating.

Status	
GetCount	Returns the number of elements in this map.
IsEmpty	Tests for the empty-map condition (no elements).

Member Functions

CMapStringToOb::CMapStringToOb

CMapStringToOb(int *nBlockSize* **= 10);**

Parameters

nBlockSize   Specifies the memory-allocation granularity for extending the map.

Remarks

Constructs an empty **CString**-to-**CObject*** map. As the map grows, memory is allocated in units of *nBlockSize* entries.

Example

```
// example for CMapStringToOb::CMapStringToOb
```

See **CObList::CObList** for a listing of the CAge class used in all collection examples.

```
CMapStringToOb map(20);  // Map on the stack with blocksize of 20

CMapStringToOb* pm = new CMapStringToOb;  // Map on the heap
                                          // with default blocksize
```

CMapStringToOb::GetCount

int GetCount( ) const;

Return Value

The number of elements in this map.

Remarks

Call this member function to determine how many elements are in the map.

Example

```
// example for CMapStringToOb::GetCount
CMapStringToOb map;

map.SetAt( "Bart", new CAge( 13 ) );
map.SetAt( "Homer", new CAge( 36 ) );
ASSERT( map.GetCount() == 2 );
```

See Also **CMapStringToOb::IsEmpty**

CMapStringToOb::GetNextAssoc

void GetNextAssoc(POSITION& *rNextPosition*, **CString&** *rKey*, **CObject*&** *rValue* **) const;**

Parameters

rNextPosition   Specifies a reference to a **POSITION** value returned by a previous **GetNextAssoc** or **GetStartPosition** call.

rKey   Specifies the returned key of the retrieved element (a string).

rValue   Specifies the returned value of the retrieved element (a **CObject** pointer). See "Remarks" for more about this parameter.

Remarks

Retrieves the map element at *rNextPosition*, then updates *rNextPosition* to refer to the next element in the map. This function is most useful for iterating through all the elements in the map. Note that the position sequence is not necessarily the same as the key value sequence.

If the retrieved element is the last in the map, then the new value of *rNextPosition* is set to **NULL**.

For the *rValue* parameter, be sure to cast your object type to **CObject*&**, which is what the compiler requires, as shown in the following example:

```
CMyObject* ob;
map.GetNextAssoc(pos, key, (CObject*&)ob);
```

This is not true of **GetNextAssoc** for maps based on templates.

Example

```
// example for CMapStringToOb::GetNextAssoc and CMapStringToOb::GetStartPosition
   CMapStringToOb map;
   POSITION pos;
   CString key;
   CAge* pa;

   map.SetAt( "Bart", new CAge( 13 ) );
   map.SetAt( "Lisa", new CAge( 11 ) );
   map.SetAt( "Homer", new CAge( 36 ) );
```

```
        map.SetAt( "Marge", new CAge( 35 ) );
        // Iterate through the entire map, dumping both name and age.
        for( pos = map.GetStartPosition(); pos != NULL; )
        {
        map.GetNextAssoc( pos, key, (CObject*&)pa );
#ifdef _DEBUG
            afxDump << key << " : " << pa << "\n";
#endif
        }
```

The results from this program are as follows:

```
Lisa : a CAge at $4724 11
Marge : a CAge at $47A8 35
Homer : a CAge at $4766 36
Bart : a CAge at $45D4 13
```

See Also   **CMapStringToOb::GetStartPosition**

CMapStringToOb::GetStartPosition

POSITION GetStartPosition( ) const;

Return Value

A **POSITION** value that indicates a starting position for iterating the map; or **NULL** if the map is empty.

Remarks

Starts a map iteration by returning a **POSITION** value that can be passed to a **GetNextAssoc** call. The iteration sequence is not predictable; therefore, the "first element in the map" has no special significance.

CMapStringToOb::IsEmpty

BOOL IsEmpty( ) const;

Return Value

Nonzero if this map contains no elements; otherwise 0.

Remarks

Call this member function to determine whether the map is empty.

Example

See the example for **RemoveAll**.

CMapStringToOb::Lookup

BOOL Lookup(LPCTSTR *key*, **CObject*&** *rValue*) **const;**

Return Value

Nonzero if the element was found; otherwise 0.

Parameters

key   Specifies the string key that identifies the element to be looked up.

rValue   Specifies the returned value from the looked-up element.

Remarks

Lookup uses a hashing algorithm to quickly find the map element with a key that matches exactly (**CString** value).

Example

```
// example for CMapStringToOb::LookUp
CMapStringToOb map;
CAge* pa;

map.SetAt( "Bart", new CAge( 13 ) );
map.SetAt( "Lisa", new CAge( 11 ) );
map.SetAt( "Homer", new CAge( 36 ) );
map.SetAt( "Marge", new CAge( 35 ) );
ASSERT( map.Lookup( "Lisa", ( CObject*& ) pa ) ); // Is "Lisa" in the map?
ASSERT( *pa == CAge( 11 ) ); // Is she 11?
```

See Also   CMapStringToOb::operator []

CMapStringToOb::RemoveAll

void RemoveAll( );

Remarks

Removes all the elements from this map and destroys the **CString** key objects. The **CObject** objects referenced by each key are not destroyed. The **RemoveAll** function can cause memory leaks if you do not ensure that the referenced **CObject** objects are destroyed.

The function works correctly if the map is already empty.

Example

```
// example for CMapStringToOb::RemoveAll
{
    CMapStringToOb map;

    CAge age1( 13 ); // Two objects on the stack
    CAge age2( 36 );
    map.SetAt( "Bart", &age1 );
    map.SetAt( "Homer", &age2 );
```

```
    ASSERT( map.GetCount() == 2 );
    map.RemoveAll(); // CObject pointers removed; objects not removed.
    ASSERT( map.GetCount() == 0 );
    ASSERT( map.IsEmpty() );
} // The two CAge objects are deleted when they go out of scope.
```

See Also   CMapStringToOb::RemoveKey

CMapStringToOb::RemoveKey

BOOL RemoveKey(LPCTSTR *key* **);**

Return Value

Nonzero if the entry was found and successfully removed; otherwise 0.

Parameters

key   Specifies the string used for map lookup.

Remarks

Looks up the map entry corresponding to the supplied key; then, if the key is found, removes the entry. This can cause memory leaks if the **CObject** object is not deleted elsewhere.

Example

```
// example for CMapStringToOb::RemoveKey
    CMapStringToOb map;

    map.SetAt( "Bart", new CAge( 13 ) );
    map.SetAt( "Lisa", new CAge( 11 ) );
    map.SetAt( "Homer", new CAge( 36 ) );
    map.SetAt( "Marge", new CAge( 35 ) );
    map.RemoveKey( "Lisa" ); // Memory leak: CAge object not
                             // deleted.
#ifdef _DEBUG
    afxDump.SetDepth( 1 );
    afxDump << "RemoveKey example: " << &map << "\n";
#endif
```

The results from this program are as follows:

```
RemoveKey example: A CMapStringToOb with 3 elements
    [Marge] = a CAge at $49A0 35
    [Homer] = a CAge at $495E 36
    [Bart] = a CAge at $4634 13
```

See Also   CMapStringToOb::RemoveAll

CMapStringToOb::SetAt

void SetAt(LPCTSTR *key***, CObject*** *newValue* **);**
    throw(CMemoryException);

Parameters

key   Specifies the string that is the key of the new element.

newValue   Specifies the **CObject** pointer that is the value of the new element.

Remarks

The primary means to insert an element in a map. First, the key is looked up. If the key is found, then the corresponding value is changed; otherwise a new key-value element is created.

Example

```
// example for CMapStringToOb::SetAt
    CMapStringToOb map;
    CAge* pa;

    map.SetAt( "Bart", new CAge( 13 ) );
    map.SetAt( "Lisa", new CAge( 11 ) ); // Map contains 2
                                         // elements.
#ifdef _DEBUG
    afxDump.SetDepth( 1 );
    afxDump << "before Lisa's birthday: " << &map << "\n";
#endif
    if( map.Lookup( "Lisa", pa ) )
    { // CAge 12 pointer replaces CAge 11 pointer.
        map.SetAt( "Lisa", new CAge( 12 ) );
        delete pa;  // Must delete CAge 11 to avoid memory leak.
    }
#ifdef _DEBUG
    afxDump << "after Lisa's birthday: " << &map << "\n";
#endif
```

The results from this program are as follows:

```
before Lisa's birthday: A CMapStringToOb with 2 elements
    [Lisa] = a CAge at $493C 11
    [Bart] = a CAge at $4654 13
after Lisa's birthday: A CMapStringToOb with 2 elements
    [Lisa] = a CAge at $49C0 12
    [Bart] = a CAge at $4654 13
```

See Also   **CMapStringToOb::Lookup, CMapStringToOb::operator []**

Operators

CMapStringToOb::operator [ ]

CObject*& operator [ ](LPCTSTR *key* **);**

Return Value

A reference to a pointer to a **CObject** object; or **NULL** if the map is empty or *key* is out of range.

Remarks

This operator is a convenient substitute for the **SetAt** member function. Thus it can be used only on the left side of an assignment statement (an l-value). If there is no map element with the specified key, then a new element is created.

There is no "right side" (r-value) equivalent to this operator because there is a possibility that a key may not be found in the map. Use the **Lookup** member function for element retrieval.

Example

```
// example for CMapStringToOb::operator[]
    CMapStringToOb map;

    map["Bart"] = new CAge( 13 );
    map["Lisa"] = new CAge( 11 );
#ifdef _DEBUG
    afxDump.SetDepth( 1 );
    afxDump << "Operator [] example: " << &map << "\n";
#endif
```

The results from this program are as follows:

```
Operator [] example: A CMapStringToOb with 2 elements
    [Lisa] = a CAge at $4A02 11
    [Bart] = a CAge at $497E 13
```

See Also **CMapStringToOb::SetAt, CMapStringToOb::Lookup**

CMapStringToPtr

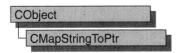

The **CMapStringToPtr** class supports maps of void pointers keyed by **CString** objects.

The member functions of **CMapStringToPtr** are similar to the member functions of class **CMapStringToOb**. Because of this similarity, you can use the **CMapStringToOb** reference documentation for member function specifics. Wherever you see a **CObject** pointer as a function parameter or return value, substitute a pointer to **void**.

```
BOOL CMapStringToOb::Lookup( const char* <key>,
                             CObject*& <rValue> ) const;
```

for example, translates to

```
BOOL CMapStringToPtr::Lookup( LPCTSTR <key>, void*& <rValue> )
                             const;
```

CMapStringToPtr incorporates the **IMPLEMENT_DYNAMIC** macro to support run-time type access and dumping to a **CDumpContext** object. If you need a dump of individual map elements, you must set the depth of the dump context to 1 or greater.

String-to-pointer maps may not be serialized.

When a **CMapStringToPtr** object is deleted, or when its elements are removed, the **CString** key objects and the words are removed.

#include <afxcoll.h>

See Also   **CMapStringToOb**

Construction

CMapStringToPtr	Constructs a collection that maps **CString** objects to void pointers.

Operations

Lookup	Returns a void pointer based on a **CString** value.
SetAt	Inserts an element into the map; replaces an existing element if a matching key is found.
operator []	Inserts an element into the map—operator substitution for **SetAt**.
RemoveKey	Removes an element specified by a key.
RemoveAll	Removes all the elements from this map.
GetStartPosition	Returns the position of the first element.
GetNextAssoc	Gets the next element for iterating.

Status

GetCount	Returns the number of elements in this map.
IsEmpty	Tests for the empty-map condition (no elements).

CMapStringToString

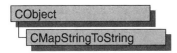

The **CMapStringToString** class supports maps of **CString** objects keyed by **CString** objects.

The member functions of **CMapStringToString** are similar to the member functions of class **CMapStringToOb**. Because of this similarity, you can use the **CMapStringToOb** reference documentation for member function specifics. Wherever you see a **CObject** pointer as a return value or "output" function parameter, substitute a pointer to **char**. Wherever you see a **CObject** pointer as an "input" function parameter, substitute a pointer to **char**.

```
BOOL CMapStringToOb::Lookup( const char* <key>,
                             CObject*& <rValue> ) const;
```

for example, translates to

```
BOOL CMapStringToString::Lookup( LPCTSTR <key>,
                                 CString& <rValue> ) const;
```

CMapStringToString incorporates the **IMPLEMENT_SERIAL** macro to support serialization and dumping of its elements. Each element is serialized in turn if a map is stored to an archive, either with the overloaded insertion (<<) operator or with the **Serialize** member function.

If you need a dump of individual **CString**-**CString** elements, you must set the depth of the dump context to 1 or greater.

When a **CMapStringToString** object is deleted, or when its elements are removed, the **CString** objects are removed as appropriate.

For more information on **CMapStringToString**, see the article "Collections" in *Programming with MFC*.

#include <afxcoll.h>

See Also   CMapStringToOb

Construction

CMapStringToString	Constructs a collection that maps **CString** objects to **CString** objects.

Operations

Lookup	Returns a **CString** using a **CString** value as a key.
SetAt	Inserts an element into the map; replaces an existing element if a matching key is found.
operator []	Inserts an element into the map—operator substitution for **SetAt**.
RemoveKey	Removes an element specified by a key.
RemoveAll	Removes all the elements from this map.
GetStartPosition	Returns the position of the first element.
GetNextAssoc	Gets the next element for iterating.

Status

GetCount	Returns the number of elements in this map.
IsEmpty	Tests for the empty-map condition (no elements).

CMapWordToOb

The **CMapWordToOb** class supports maps of **CObject** pointers keyed by 16-bit words.

The member functions of **CMapWordToOb** are similar to the member functions of class **CMapStringToOb**. Because of this similarity, you can use the **CMapStringToOb** reference documentation for member function specifics. Wherever you see a **CString** or a **const** pointer to **char** as a function parameter or return value, substitute **WORD**.

```
BOOL CMapStringToOb::Lookup( const char* <key>,
                            CObject*& <rValue> ) const;
```

for example, translates to

```
BOOL CMapWordToOb::Lookup( WORD <key>, CObject*& <rValue> ) const;
```

CMapWordToOb incorporates the **IMPLEMENT_SERIAL** macro to support serialization and dumping of its elements. Each element is serialized in turn if a map is stored to an archive, either with the overloaded insertion (**<<**) operator or with the **Serialize** member function.

If you need a dump of individual **WORD-CObject** elements, you must set the depth of the dump context to 1 or greater.

When a **CMapWordToOb** object is deleted, or when its elements are removed, the **CObject** objects are deleted as appropriate.

For more information on **CMapWordToOb**, see the article "Collections" in *Programming with MFC*.

#include <afxcoll.h>

See Also   **CMapStringToOb**

Construction

CMapWordToOb	Constructs a collection that maps words to **CObject** pointers.

Operations

Lookup	Returns a **CObject** pointer using a word value as a key.
SetAt	Inserts an element into the map; replaces an existing element if a matching key is found.
operator []	Inserts an element into the map—operator substitution for **SetAt**.
RemoveKey	Removes an element specified by a key.
RemoveAll	Removes all the elements from this map.
GetStartPosition	Returns the position of the first element.
GetNextAssoc	Gets the next element for iterating.

Status

GetCount	Returns the number of elements in this map.
IsEmpty	Tests for the empty-map condition (no elements).

CMapWordToPtr

The **CMapWordToPtr** class supports maps of void pointers keyed by 16-bit words.

The member functions of **CMapWordToPtr** are similar to the member functions of class **CMapStringToOb**. Because of this similarity, you can use the **CMapStringToOb** reference documentation for member function specifics. Wherever you see a **CObject** pointer as a function parameter or return value, substitute a pointer to **void**. Wherever you see a **CString** or a **const** pointer to **char** as a function parameter or return value, substitute **WORD**.

```
BOOL CMapStringToOb::Lookup( const char* <key>,
                            CObject*& <rValue> ) const;
```

for example, translates to

```
BOOL CMapWordToPtr::Lookup( WORD <key>, void*& <rValue> ) const;
```

CMapWordToPtr incorporates the **IMPLEMENT_DYNAMIC** macro to support run-time type access and dumping to a **CDumpContext** object. If you need a dump of individual map elements, you must set the depth of the dump context to 1 or greater.

Word-to-pointer maps may not be serialized.

When a **CMapWordToPtr** object is deleted, or when its elements are removed, the words and the pointers are removed. The entities referenced by the pointers are not removed.

For more information on **CMapWordToPtr**, see the article "Collections" in *Programming with MFC*.

#include <afxcoll.h>

See Also   **CMapStringToOb**

Construction

CMapWordToPtr	Constructs a collection that maps words to void pointers.

Operations

Lookup	Returns a void pointer using a word value as a key.
SetAt	Inserts an element into the map; replaces an existing element if a matching key is found.
operator []	Inserts an element into the map—operator substitution for **SetAt**.
RemoveKey	Removes an element specified by a key.
RemoveAll	Removes all the elements from this map.
GetStartPosition	Returns the position of the first element.
GetNextAssoc	Gets the next element for iterating.

Status

GetCount	Returns the number of elements in this map.
IsEmpty	Tests for the empty-map condition (no elements).

CMDIChildWnd

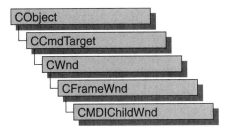

The **CMDIChildWnd** class provides the functionality of a Windows multiple document interface (MDI) child window, along with members for managing the window.

An MDI child window looks much like a typical frame window, except that the MDI child window appears inside an MDI frame window rather than on the desktop. An MDI child window does not have a menu bar of its own, but instead shares the menu of the MDI frame window. The framework automatically changes the MDI frame menu to represent the currently active MDI child window.

To create a useful MDI child window for your application, derive a class from **CMDIChildWnd**. Add member variables to the derived class to store data specific to your application. Implement message-handler member functions and a message map in the derived class to specify what happens when messages are directed to the window.

There are three ways to construct an MDI child window:

- Directly construct it using **Create**.
- Directly construct it using **LoadFrame**.
- Indirectly construct it through a document template.

Before you call **Create** or **LoadFrame**, you must construct the frame-window object on the heap using the C++ **new** operator. Before calling **Create** you can also register a window class with the **AfxRegisterWndClass** global function to set the icon and class styles for the frame.

Use the **Create** member function to pass the frame's creation parameters as immediate arguments.

LoadFrame requires fewer arguments than **Create**, and instead retrieves most of its default values from resources, including the frame's caption, icon, accelerator table, and menu. To be accessible by **LoadFrame**, all these resources must have the same resource ID (for example, **IDR_MAINFRAME**).

When a **CMDIChildWnd** object contains views and documents, they are created indirectly by the framework instead of directly by the programmer. The **CDocTemplate** object orchestrates the creation of the frame, the creation of the containing views, and the connection of the views to the appropriate document. The parameters of the **CDocTemplate** constructor specify the **CRuntimeClass** of the three classes involved (document, frame, and view). A **CRuntimeClass** object is used by the framework to dynamically create new frames when specified by the user (for example, by using the File New command or the MDI Window New command).

A frame-window class derived from **CMDIChildWnd** must be declared with **DECLARE_DYNCREATE** in order for the above **RUNTIME_CLASS** mechanism to work correctly.

The **CMDIChildWnd** class inherits much of its default implementation from **CFrameWnd**. For a detailed list of these features, please refer to the **CFrameWnd** class description. The **CMDIChildWnd** class has the following additional features:

- In conjunction with the **CMultiDocTemplate** class, multiple **CMDIChildWnd** objects from the same document template share the same menu, saving Windows system resources.

- The currently active MDI child window menu entirely replaces the MDI frame window's menu, and the caption of the currently active MDI child window is added to the MDI frame window's caption. For further examples of MDI child window functions that are implemented in conjunction with an MDI frame window, see the **CMDIFrameWnd** class description.

Do not use the C++ **delete** operator to destroy a frame window. Use **CWnd::DestroyWindow** instead. The **CFrameWnd** implementation of **PostNcDestroy** will delete the C++ object when the window is destroyed. When the user closes the frame window, the default **OnClose** handler will call **DestroyWindow**.

For more information on **CMDIChildWnd**, see "Frame Windows" in Chapter 3 of *Programming with MFC*.

#include <afxwin.h>

See Also CWnd, CFrameWnd, CMDIFrameWnd

Construction

CMDIChildWnd	Constructs a **CMDIChildWnd** object.

Initialization

Create	Creates the Windows MDI child window associated with the **CMDIChildWnd** object.

Operations

MDIDestroy	Destroys this MDI child window.
MDIActivate	Activates this MDI child window.
MDIMaximize	Maximizes this MDI child window.
MDIRestore	Restores this MDI child window from maximized or minimized size.
GetMDIFrame	Returns the parent MDI frame of the MDI client window.

Member Functions

CMDIChildWnd::CMDIChildWnd

CMDIChildWnd( );

Remarks

Call to construct a **CMDIChildWnd** object. Call **Create** to create the visible window.

See Also   **CMDIChildWnd::Create**

CMDIChildWnd::Create

BOOL Create(LPCTSTR *lpszClassName***, LPCTSTR** *lpszWindowName***, DWORD** *dwStyle* **= WS_CHILD | WS_VISIBLE | WS_OVERLAPPEDWINDOW, const RECT&** *rect* **= rectDefault, CMDIFrameWnd*** *pParentWnd* **= NULL, CCreateContext*** *pContext* **= NULL);**

Return Value

Nonzero if successful; otherwise 0.

Parameters

lpszClassName   Points to a null-terminated character string that names the Windows class (a **WNDCLASS** structure). The class name can be any name registered with the **AfxRegisterWndClass** global function. Should be **NULL** for a standard **CMDIChildWnd**.

lpszWindowName   Points to a null-terminated character string that represents the window name. Used as text for the title bar.

dwStyle   Specifies the window style attributes. The **WS_CHILD** style is required. For a list of window styles, see "Window Styles" in the "Styles Used by MFC" section.

rect   Contains the size and position of the window. The **rectDefault** value allows Windows to specify the size and position of the new **CMDIChildWnd**.

pParentWnd   Specifies the window's parent. If **NULL**, the main application window is used.

pContext   Specifies a **CCreateContext** structure. This parameter can be **NULL**.

Remarks

Call this member function to create a Windows MDI child window and attach it to the **CMDIChildWnd** object.

The currently active MDI child frame window can determine the caption of the parent frame window. This feature is disabled by turning off the **FWS_ADDTOTITLE** style bit of the child frame window.

The framework calls this member function in response to a user command to create a child window, and the framework uses the *pContext* parameter to properly connect the child window to the application. When you call **Create**, *pContext* can be **NULL**.

See Also   **CMDIChildWnd::CMDIChildWnd**, **CWnd::PreCreateWindow**

CMDIChildWnd::GetMDIFrame

CMDIFrameWnd* GetMDIFrame( );

Return Value

A pointer to the MDI parent frame window.

Remarks

Call this function to return the MDI parent frame. The frame returned is two parents removed from the **CMDIChildWnd** and is the parent of the window of type **MDICLIENT** that manages the **CMDIChildWnd** object. Call the **GetParent** member function to return the **CMDIChildWnd** object's immediate **MDICLIENT** parent as a temporary **CWnd** pointer.

See Also   **CWnd::GetParent**

CMDIChildWnd::MDIActivate

void MDIActivate( );

Remarks

Call this member function to activate an MDI child window independently of the MDI frame window. When the frame becomes active, the child window that was last activated will be activated as well.

See Also   **CMDIFrameWnd::MDIGetActive**, **CWnd::OnNcActivate**, **CMDIFrameWnd::MDINext**, **WM_MDIACTIVATE**

CMDIChildWnd::MDIDestroy

void MDIDestroy( );

Remarks

Call this member function to destroy an MDI child window.

The member function removes the title of the child window from the frame window and deactivates the child window.

See Also   **WM_MDIDESTROY, CMDIChildWnd::Create**

CMDIChildWnd::MDIMaximize

void MDIMaximize( );

Remarks

Call this member function to maximize an MDI child window. When a child window is maximized, Windows resizes it to make its client area fill the client area of the frame window. Windows places the child window's Control menu in the frame's menu bar so that the user can restore or close the child window and adds the title of the child window to the frame-window title.

See Also   **WM_MDIMAXIMIZE, CMDIChildWnd::MDIRestore**

CMDIChildWnd::MDIRestore

void MDIRestore( );

Remarks

Call this member function to restore an MDI child window from maximized or minimized size.

See Also   **CMDIChildWnd::MDIMaximize, WM_MDIRESTORE**

CMDIFrameWnd

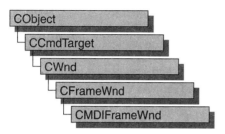

The **CMDIFrameWnd** class provides the functionality of a Windows multiple document interface (MDI) frame window, along with members for managing the window.

To create a useful MDI frame window for your application, derive a class from **CMDIFrameWnd**. Add member variables to the derived class to store data specific to your application. Implement message-handler member functions and a message map in the derived class to specify what happens when messages are directed to the window.

You can construct an MDI frame window by calling the **Create** or **LoadFrame** member function of **CFrameWnd**.

Before you call **Create** or **LoadFrame**, you must construct the frame window object on the heap using the C++ **new** operator. Before calling **Create** you can also register a window class with the **AfxRegisterWndClass** global function to set the icon and class styles for the frame.

Use the **Create** member function to pass the frame's creation parameters as immediate arguments.

LoadFrame requires fewer arguments than **Create**, and instead retrieves most of its default values from resources, including the frame's caption, icon, accelerator table, and menu. To be accessed by **LoadFrame**, all these resources must have the same resource ID (for example, **IDR_MAINFRAME**).

Though **MDIFrameWnd** is derived from **CFrameWnd**, a frame window class derived from **CMDIFrameWnd** need not be declared with **DECLARE_DYNCREATE**.

The **CMDIFrameWnd** class inherits much of its default implementation from **CFrameWnd**. For a detailed list of these features, refer to the **CFrameWnd** class description. The **CMDIFrameWnd** class has the following additional features:

- An MDI frame window manages the **MDICLIENT** window, repositioning it in conjunction with control bars. The MDI client window is the direct parent of MDI child frame windows. The **WS_HSCROLL** and **WS_VSCROLL** window styles specified on a **CMDIFrameWnd** apply to the MDI client window rather than the main frame window so the user can scroll the MDI client area (as in the Windows Program Manager, for example).

- An MDI frame window owns a default menu that is used as the menu bar when there is no active MDI child window. When there is an active MDI child, the MDI frame window's menu bar is automatically replaced by the MDI child window menu.

- An MDI frame window works in conjunction with the current MDI child window, if there is one. For instance, command messages are delegated to the currently active MDI child before the MDI frame window.

- An MDI frame window has default handlers for the following standard Window menu commands:

  - **ID_WINDOW_TILE_VERT**
  - **ID_WINDOW_TILE_HORZ**
  - **ID_WINDOW_CASCADE**
  - **ID_WINDOW_ARRANGE**

- An MDI frame window also has an implementation of **ID_WINDOW_NEW**, which creates a new frame and view on the current document. An application can override these default command implementations to customize MDI window handling.

Do not use the C++ **delete** operator to destroy a frame window. Use **CWnd::DestroyWindow** instead. The **CFrameWnd** implementation of **PostNcDestroy** will delete the C++ object when the window is destroyed. When the user closes the frame window, the default **OnClose** handler will call **DestroyWindow**.

For more information on **CMDIFrameWnd**, see "Frame Windows" in Chapter 3 of *Programming with MFC*.

#include <afxwin.h>

See Also   CWnd, CFrameWnd, CMDIChildWnd

Construction

CMDIFrameWnd	Constructs a **CMDIFrameWnd**.

Operations

MDIActivate	Activates a different MDI child window.
MDIGetActive	Retrieves the currently active MDI child window, along with a flag indicating whether or not the child is maximized.

MDIIconArrange	Arranges all minimized document child windows.
MDIMaximize	Maximizes an MDI child window.
MDINext	Activates the child window immediately behind the currently active child window and places the currently active child window behind all other child windows.
MDIRestore	Restores an MDI child window from maximized or minimized size.
MDISetMenu	Replaces the menu of an MDI frame window, the Window pop-up menu, or both.
MDITile	Arranges all child windows in a tiled format.
MDICascade	Arranges all child windows in a cascaded format.

Overridables

CreateClient	Creates a Windows **MDICLIENT** window for this **CMDIFrameWnd**. Called by the **OnCreate** member function of **CWnd**.
GetWindowMenuPopup	Returns the Window pop-up menu.

Member Functions

CMDIFrameWnd::CMDIFrameWnd

CMDIFrameWnd( );

Remarks

Call this member function to construct a **CMDIFrameWnd** object. Call the **Create** or **LoadFrame** member function to create the visible MDI frame window.

See Also   **CFrameWnd::Create**, **CFrameWnd::LoadFrame**

CMDIFrameWnd::CreateClient

virtual BOOL CreateClient(LPCREATESTRUCT *lpCreateStruct*, **CMenu*** *pWindowMenu* **);**

Return Value

Nonzero if successful; otherwise 0.

Parameters

lpCreateStruct   A long pointer to a **CREATESTRUCT** structure.

pWindowMenu   A pointer to the Window pop-up menu.

Remarks

Creates the MDI client window that manages the **CMDIChildWnd** objects.

This member function should be called if you override the **OnCreate** member function directly.

See Also   **CMDIFrameWnd::CMDIFrameWnd**

CMDIFrameWnd::GetWindowMenuPopup

virtual HMENU GetWindowMenuPopup(HMENU *hMenuBar* **);**

Return Value

The Window pop-up menu if one exists; otherwise **NULL**.

Parameters

hMenuBar   The current menu bar.

Remarks

Call this member function to obtain a handle to the current pop-up menu named "Window" (the pop-up menu with menu items for MDI window management).

The default implementation looks for a pop-up menu containing standard Window menu commands such as **ID_WINDOW_NEW** and **ID_WINDOW_TILE_HORZ**.

Override this member function if you have a Window menu that does not use the standard menu command IDs.

See Also   **CMDIFrameWnd::MDIGetActive**

CMDIFrameWnd::MDIActivate

void MDIActivate(CWnd* *pWndActivate* **);**

Parameters

pWndActivate   Points to the MDI child window to be activated.

Remarks

Call this member function to activate a different MDI child window. This member function sends the **WM_MDIACTIVATE** message to both the child window being activated and the child window being deactivated.

This is the same message that is sent if the user changes the focus to an MDI child window by using the mouse or keyboard.

Note An MDI child window is activated independently of the MDI frame window. When the frame becomes active, the child window that was last activated is sent a **WM_NCACTIVATE** message to draw an active window frame and caption bar, but it does not receive another **WM_MDIACTIVATE** message.

See Also **CMDIFrameWnd::MDIGetActive, CMDIFrameWnd::MDINext, WM_ACTIVATE, WM_NCACTIVATE**

CMDIFrameWnd::MDICascade

void MDICascade( );
void MDICascade(int *nType* **);**

Parameters

nType Specifies a cascade flag. Only the following flag can be specified: **MDITILE_SKIPDISABLED**, which prevents disabled MDI child windows from being cascaded.

Remarks

Call this member function to arrange all the MDI child windows in a cascade format.

The first version of **MDICascade**, with no parameters, cascades all MDI child windows, including disabled ones. The second version optionally does not cascade disabled MDI child windows if you specify **MDITILE_SKIPDISABLED** for the *nType* parameter.

See Also **CMDIFrameWnd::MDIIconArrange, CMDIFrameWnd::MDITile, WM_MDICASCADE**

CMDIFrameWnd::MDIGetActive

CMDIChildWnd* MDIGetActive(BOOL* *pbMaximized* **= NULL) const;**

Return Value

A pointer to the active MDI child window.

Parameters

pbMaximized A pointer to a **BOOL** return value. Set to **TRUE** on return if the window is maximized; otherwise **FALSE**.

Remarks

Retrieves the current active MDI child window, along with a flag indicating whether the child window is maximized.

See Also **CMDIFrameWnd::MDIActivate, WM_MDIGETACTIVE**

CMDIFrameWnd::MDIIconArrange

void MDIIconArrange( );

Remarks

Arranges all minimized document child windows. It does not affect child windows that are not minimized.

See Also **CMDIFrameWnd::MDICascade**, **CMDIFrameWnd::MDITile**, **WM_MDIICONARRANGE**

CMDIFrameWnd::MDIMaximize

void MDIMaximize(CWnd* *pWnd* **);**

Parameters

pWnd Points to the window to maximize.

Remarks

Call this member function to maximize the specified MDI child window. When a child window is maximized, Windows resizes it to make its client area fill the client window. Windows places the child window's Control menu in the frame's menu bar so the user can restore or close the child window. It also adds the title of the child window to the frame-window title.

If another MDI child window is activated when the currently active MDI child window is maximized, Windows restores the currently active child and maximizes the newly activated child window.

See Also **WM_MDIMAXIMIZE**, **CMDIFrameWnd::MDIRestore**

CMDIFrameWnd::MDINext

void MDINext( );

Remarks

Activates the child window immediately behind the currently active child window and places the currently active child window behind all other child windows.

If the currently active MDI child window is maximized, the member function restores the currently active child and maximizes the newly activated child.

See Also **CMDIFrameWnd::MDIActivate**, **CMDIFrameWnd::MDIGetActive**, **WM_MDINEXT**

CMDIFrameWnd::MDIRestore

void MDIRestore(CWnd* *pWnd* **);**

Parameters

pWnd   Points to the window to restore.

Remarks

Restores an MDI child window from maximized or minimized size.

See Also   **CMDIFrameWnd::MDIMaximize**, **WM_MDIRESTORE**

CMDIFrameWnd::MDISetMenu

CMenu* MDISetMenu(CMenu* *pFrameMenu*, **CMenu*** *pWindowMenu* **);**

Return Value

A pointer to the frame-window menu replaced by this message. The pointer may be temporary and should not be stored for later use.

Parameters

pFrameMenu   Specifies the menu of the new frame-window menu. If **NULL**, the menu is not changed.

pWindowMenu   Specifies the menu of the new Window pop-up menu. If **NULL**, the menu is not changed.

Remarks

Call this member function to replace the menu of an MDI frame window, the Window pop-up menu, or both.

After calling **MDISetMenu**, an application must call the **DrawMenuBar** member function of **CWnd** to update the menu bar.

If this call replaces the Window pop-up menu, MDI child-window menu items are removed from the previous Window menu and added to the new Window pop-up menu.

If an MDI child window is maximized and this call replaces the MDI frame-window menu, the Control menu and restore controls are removed from the previous frame-window menu and added to the new menu.

Do not call this member function if you use the framework to manage your MDI child windows.

See Also   **CWnd::DrawMenuBar**, **WM_MDISETMENU**

CMDIFrameWnd::MDITile

void MDITile( );
void MDITile(int *nType* **);**

Parameters

nType   Specifies a tiling flag. This parameter can be any one of the following flags:

- **MDITILE_HORIZONTAL**   Tiles MDI child windows so that one window appears above another.

- **MDITILE_SKIPDISABLED**   Prevents disabled MDI child windows from being tiled.

- **MDITILE_VERTICAL**   Tiles MDI child windows so that one window appears beside another.

Remarks

Call this member function to arrange all child windows in a tiled format.

The first version of **MDITile**, without parameters, tiles the windows vertically under Windows versions 3.1 and later. The second version tiles windows vertically or horizontally, depending on the value of the *nType* parameter.

See Also   **CMDIFrameWnd::MDICascade**,
CMDIFrameWnd::MDIIconArrange, **WM_MDITILE**

CMemFile

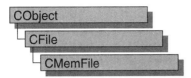

CMemFile is the **CFile**-derived class that supports memory files. These memory files behave like disk files except that the file is stored in RAM rather than on disk. A memory file is useful for fast temporary storage or for transferring raw bytes or serialized objects between independent processes.

CMemFile objects can automatically allocate their own memory or you can attach your own memory block to the **CMemFile** object by calling **Attach**. In either case, memory for growing the memory file automatically is allocated in *nGrowBytes*-sized increments if *nGrowBytes* is not zero.

The memory block will automatically be deleted upon destruction of the **CMemFile** object if the memory was originally allocated by the **CMemFile** object; otherwise, you are responsible for deallocating the memory you attached to the object.

You can access the memory block through the pointer supplied when you detach it from the **CMemFile** object by calling **Detach**.

The most common use of **CMemFile** is to create a **CMemFile** object and use it by calling **CFile** member functions. Note that creating a **CMemFile** automatically opens it: you do not call **CFile::Open**, which is only used for disk files. Because **CMemFile** doesn't use a disk file, the data member **CFile::m_hFile** is not used and has no meaning.

The **CFile** member functions **Duplicate**, **LockRange**, and **UnlockRange** are not implemented for **CMemFile**. If you call these functions on a **CMemFile** object, you will get a **CNotSupportedException**.

CMemFile uses the run-time library functions **malloc**, **realloc**, and **free** to allocate, reallocate, and deallocate memory; and the intrinsic **memcpy** to block copy memory when reading and writing. If you'd like to change this behavior or the behavior when **CMemFile** grows a file, derive your own class from **CMemFile** and override the appropriate functions.

For more information on **CMemFile**, see the article "Files" in *Programming with MFC* and "File Handling" in the *Run-Time Library Reference*.

#include <afx.h>

See Also   CFile, CMemFile::CMemFile, CMemFile::Attach, CMemFile::Detach

Construction	
CMemFile	Constructs a memory file object.

Operations	
Attach	Attaches a block of memory to **CMemFile**.
Detach	Detaches the block of memory from **CMemFile** and returns a pointer to the block of memory detached.

Advanced Overridables	
Alloc	Override to modify memory allocation behavior.
Free	Override to modify memory deallocation behavior.
Realloc	Override to modify memory reallocation behavior.
Memcpy	Override to modify memory copy behavior when reading and writing files.
GrowFile	Override to modify behavior when growing a file.

Member Functions

CMemFile::Alloc

BYTE * Alloc(DWORD *nBytes* **);**

Return Value

A pointer to the memory block that was allocated, or **NULL** if the allocation failed.

Parameters

nBytes   Number of bytes of memory to be allocated.

Remarks

This function is called by **CMemFile** member functions. Override this function to implement custom memory allocation. If you override this function, you'll probably want to override **Free** and **Realloc** as well.

The default implementation uses the run-time library function **malloc** to allocate memory.

See Also   **CMemFile::Free**, **CMemFile::Realloc**, **malloc**

CMemFile::Attach

void Attach(BYTE* *lpBuffer*, **UINT** *nBufferSize*, **UINT** *nGrowBytes* = **0**);

Parameters

lpBuffer   Pointer to the buffer to be attached to **CMemFile**.

nBufferSize   An integer that specifies the size of the buffer in bytes.

nGrowBytes   The memory allocation increment in bytes.

Remarks

Call this function to attach a block of memory to **CMemFile**. This causes **CMemFile** to use the block of memory as the memory file.

If *nGrowBytes* is 0, **CMemFile** will set the file length to *nBufferSize*. This means that the data in the memory block before it was attached to **CMemFile** will be used as the file. Memory files created in this manner cannot be grown.

Since the file cannot be grown, be careful not to cause **CMemFile** to attempt to grow the file. For example, don't call the **CMemFile** overrides of **CFile:Write** to write past the end or don't call **CFile:SetLength** with a length longer than *nBufferSize*.

If *nGrowBytes* is greater than 0, **CMemFile** will ignore the contents of the memory block you've attached. You'll have to write the contents of the memory file from scratch using the **CMemFile** override of **CFile::Write**. If you attempt to write past the end of the file or grow the file by calling the **CMemFile** override of **CFile::SetLength**, **CMemFile** will grow the memory allocation in increments of *nGrowBytes*. Growing the memory allocation will fail if the memory block you pass to **Attach** wasn't allocated with a method compatible with **Alloc**. To be compatible with the default implementation of **Alloc**, you must allocate the memory with the run-time library function **malloc** or **calloc**.

See Also   **CMemFile::CMemFile**, **CMemFile::Detach**, **CMemFile::Alloc**, **CFile::Write**, **CFile::SetLength**

CMemFile::CMemFile

CMemFile(UINT *nGrowBytes* **= 1024);**
CMemFile(BYTE* *lpBuffer*, **UINT** *nBufferSize*, **UINT** *nGrowBytes* **= 0);**

Parameters

nGrowBytes   The memory allocation increment in bytes.

lpBuffer   Pointer to a buffer that receives information of the size *nBufferSize*.

nBufferSize   An integer that specifies the size of the file buffer, in bytes.

Remarks

The first overload opens an empty memory file. Note that the file is opened by the constructor and that you should not call **CFile::Open**.

The second overload acts the same as if you used the first constructor and immediately called **Attach** with the same parameters. See **Attach** for details.

Example

```
// example for CMemFile::CMemFile
CMemFile f; // Ready to use - no Open necessary.

BYTE * pBuf = (BYTE *)new char [1024];
CMemFile g( pBuf, 1024, 256 );
// same as CMemFile g; g.Attach( pBuf, 1024, 256 );
```

See Also   **CMemFile::Attach**

CMemFile::Detach

BYTE * Detach( );

Return Value

A pointer to the memory block that contains the contents of the memory file.

Remarks

Call this function to get a pointer to the memory block being used by **CMemFile**.

Calling this function also closes the **CMemFile**. You can reattach the memory block to **CMemFile** by calling **Attach**. If you want to reattach the file and use the data in it, you should call **CFile::GetLength** to get the length of the file before calling **Detach**. Note that if you attach a memory block to **CMemFile** so that you can use its data (*nGrowBytes* == 0), then you won't be able to grow the memory file.

See Also   **CMemFile::Attach**, **CFile::GetLength**

CMemFile::Free

void Free(BYTE * *lpMem*);

Parameters

lpMem   Pointer to the memory to be deallocated.

Remarks

This function is called by **CMemFile** member functions. Override this function to implement custom memory deallocation. If you override this function, you'll probably want to override **Alloc** and **Realloc** as well.

See Also   **CMemFile::Alloc**, **CMemFile::Realloc**

CMemFile::GrowFile

void GrowFile(DWORD *dwNewLen*);

Parameters

dwNewLen   New size of the memory file.

Remarks

This function is called by several of the **CMemFile** member functions. You can override it if you want to change how **CMemFile** grows its file. The default implementation calls **Realloc** to grow an existing block (or **Alloc** to create a memory block), allocating memory in multiples of the *nGrowBytes* value specified in the constructor or **Attach** call.

See Also   **CMemFile::Alloc, CMemFile::Realloc, CMemFile::CMemFile, CMemFile::Attach**

CMemFile::Memcpy

BYTE * Memcpy(BYTE* *lpMemTarget*, **BYTE*** *lpMemSource*, **UINT** *nBytes* **);**

Return Value

A copy of *lpMemTarget*.

Parameters

lpMemTarget   Pointer to the memory block into which the source memory will be copied.

lpMemSource   Pointer to the source memory block.

nBytes   Number of bytes to be copied.

Remarks

This function is called by the **CMemFile** overrides of **CFile::Read** and **CFile::Write** to transfer data to and from the memory file. Override this function if you want to change the way that **CMemFile** does these memory copies.

See Also   **CFile::Read**, **CFile::Write**

CMemFile::Realloc

BYTE * Realloc(BYTE* *lpMem*, **DWORD** *nBytes* **);**

Return Value

A pointer to the memory block that was reallocated (and possibly moved), or **NULL** if the reallocation failed.

Parameters

lpMem   A pointer to the memory block to be reallocated.

nBytes   New size for the memory block.

Remarks

This function is called by **CMemFile** member functions. Override this function to implement custom memory reallocation. If you override this function, you'll probably want to override **Alloc** and **Free** as well.

See Also   **CMemFile::Alloc**, **CMemFile::Free**

CMemoryException

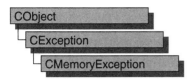

A **CMemoryException** object represents an out-of-memory exception condition. No further qualification is necessary or possible. Memory exceptions are thrown automatically by **new**. If you write your own memory functions, using **malloc**, for example, then you are responsible for throwing memory exceptions.

For more information on **CMemoryException**, see the article "Exceptions" in *Programming with MFC*.

#include <afx.h>

See Also

Construction

CMemoryException	Constructs a **CMemoryException** object.

Member Functions

CMemoryException::CMemoryException

CMemoryException( );

Remarks

Constructs a **CMemoryException** object. Do not use this constructor directly, but rather call the global function **AfxThrowMemoryException**. This global function can succeed in an out-of-memory situation because it constructs the exception object in previously allocated memory. For more information about exception processing, see the article "Exceptions" in *Programming with MFC*.

See Also   **AfxThrowMemoryException**, Exception Processing

CMemoryState

CMemoryState provides a convenient way to detect memory leaks in your program. A "memory leak" occurs when memory for an object is allocated on the heap but not deallocated when it is no longer required. Such memory leaks can eventually lead to out-of-memory errors. There are several ways to allocate and deallocate memory in your program:

- Using the **malloc/free** family of functions from the run-time library.

- Using the Windows API memory management functions, **LocalAlloc/LocalFree** and **GlobalAlloc/GlobalFree**.

- Using the C++ **new** and **delete** operators.

The **CMemoryState** diagnostics only help detect memory leaks caused when memory allocated using the **new** operator is not deallocated using **delete**. The other two groups of memory-management functions are for non-C++ programs, and mixing them with **new** and **delete** in the same program is not recommended. An additional macro, **DEBUG_NEW**, is provided to replace the **new** operator when you need file and line-number tracking of memory allocations. **DEBUG_NEW** is used whenever you would normally use the **new** operator.

As with other diagnostics, the **CMemoryState** diagnostics are only available in debug versions of your program. A debug version must have the **_DEBUG** constant defined.

If you suspect your program has a memory leak, you can use the **Checkpoint**, **Difference**, and **DumpStatistics** functions to discover the difference between the memory state (objects allocated) at two different points in program execution. This information can be useful in determining whether a function is cleaning up all the objects it allocates.

If simply knowing where the imbalance in allocation and deallocation occurs does not provide enough information, you can use the **DumpAllObjectsSince** function to dump all objects allocated since the previous call to **Checkpoint**. This dump shows the order of allocation, the source file and line where the object was allocated (if you are using **DEBUG_NEW** for allocation), and the derivation of the object, its address, and its size. **DumpAllObjectsSince** also calls each object's **Dump** function to provide information about its current state.

For more information about how to use **CMemoryState** and other diagnostics, see the article "Diagnostics: Detecting Memory Leaks" in *Programming with MFC*.

Note Declarations of objects of type **CMemoryState** and calls to member functions should be bracketed by `#if defined(_DEBUG)/#endif` directives. This causes memory diagnostics to be included only in debugging builds of your program.

Construction	
CMemoryState	Constructs a class-like structure that controls memory checkpoints.
Checkpoint	Obtains a snapshot or "checkpoint" of the current memory state.

Operations	
Difference	Computes the difference between two objects of type **CMemoryState**.
DumpAllObjectsSince	Dumps a summary of all currently allocated objects since a previous checkpoint.
DumpStatistics	Prints memory allocation statistics for a **CMemoryState** object.

Member Functions

CMemoryState::Checkpoint

void Checkpoint( );

Remarks

Takes a snapshot summary of memory and stores it in this **CMemoryState** object. The **CMemoryState** member functions **Difference** and **DumpAllObjectsSince** use this snapshot data.

Example

See the example for the **CMemoryState** constructor.

CMemoryState::CMemoryState

CMemoryState( );

Remarks

Constructs an empty **CMemoryState** object that must be filled in by the **Checkpoint** or **Difference** member function.

Example

```
// example for CMemoryState::CMemoryState
// Includes all CMemoryState functions
CMemoryState msOld, msNew, msDif;
msOld.Checkpoint();
CAge* page1 = new CAge( 21 );
CAge* page2 = new CAge( 22 );
msOld.DumpAllObjectsSince();
```

```
msNew.Checkpoint();
msDif.Difference( msOld, msNew );
msDif.DumpStatistics();
```

The results from this program are as follows:

```
// The results of this program are as follows:
Dumping objects ->
{2} a CObject at $190A
{1} a CObject at $18EA
Object dump complete.
0 bytes in 0 Free Blocks
8 bytes in 2 Object Blocks
0 bytes in 0 Non-Object Blocks
Largest number used: 8 bytes
Total allocations: 8 bytes
```

CMemoryState::Difference

BOOL Difference(const CMemoryState& *oldState***, const CMemoryState&** *newState* **);**

Return Value

Nonzero if the two memory states are different; otherwise 0.

Parameters

oldState   The initial memory state as defined by a **CMemoryState** checkpoint.

newState   The new memory state as defined by a **CMemoryState** checkpoint.

Remarks

Compares two **CMemoryState** objects, then stores the difference into this **CMemoryState** object. **Checkpoint** must have been called for each of the two memory-state parameters.

Example

See the example for the **CMemoryState** constructor.

CMemoryState::DumpAllObjectsSince

void DumpAllObjectsSince( ) const;

Remarks

Calls the **Dump** function for all objects of a type derived from class **CObject** that were allocated (and are still allocated) since the last **Checkpoint** call for this **CMemoryState** object.

Calling **DumpAllObjectsSince** with an uninitialized **CMemoryState** object will dump out all objects currently in memory.

Example

See the example for the **CMemoryState** constructor.

CMemoryState::DumpStatistics

void DumpStatistics( ) const;

Remarks

Prints a concise memory statistics report from a **CMemoryState** object that is filled by the **Difference** member function. The report, which is printed on the **afxDump** device, shows the following:

- Number of "object" blocks (blocks of memory allocated using **CObject::operator new**) still allocated on the heap.

- Number of nonobject blocks still allocated on the heap.

- The maximum memory used by the program at any one time (in bytes).

- The total memory currently used by the program (in bytes).

A sample report looks like this:

```
0 bytes in 0 Free Blocks
8 bytes in 2 Object Blocks
0 bytes in 0 Non-Object Blocks
Largest number used: 8 bytes
Total allocations: 8 bytes
```

- The first line describes the number of blocks whose deallocation was delayed if **afxMemDF** was set to **delayFreeMemDF**. For more information, see **afxMemDF**, in the "Macros and Globals" section.

- The second line describes how many object blocks still remain allocated on the heap.

- The third line describes how many nonobject blocks (arrays or structures allocated with new) were allocated on the heap and not deallocated.

- The fourth line gives the maximum memory used by your program at any one time.

- The last line lists the total amount of memory used by your program.

Example

See the example for the **CMemoryState** constructor.

CMenu

The **CMenu** class is an encapsulation of the Windows **HMENU**. It provides member functions for creating, tracking, updating, and destroying a menu.

Create a **CMenu** object on the stack frame as a local, then call **CMenu**'s member functions to manipulate the new menu as needed. Next, call **CWnd::SetMenu** to set the menu to a window, followed immediately by a call to the **CMenu** object's **Detach** member function. The **CWnd::SetMenu** member function sets the window's menu to the new menu, causes the window to be redrawn to reflect the menu change, and also passes ownership of the menu to the window. The call to **Detach** detaches the **HMENU** from the **CMenu** object, so that when the local **CMenu** variable passes out of scope, the **CMenu** object destructor does not attempt to destroy a menu it no longer owns. The menu itself is automatically destroyed when the window is destroyed.

You can use the **LoadMenuIndirect** member function to create a menu from a template in memory, but a menu created from a resource by a call to **LoadMenu** is more easily maintained, and the menu resource itself can be created and modified by the menu editor.

#include <afxwin.h>

See Also   CObject

Data Members

m_hMenu	Specifies the handle to the Windows menu attached to the **CMenu** object.

Construction

CMenu	Constructs a **CMenu** object.

Initialization

Attach	Attaches a Windows menu handle to a **CMenu** object.
Detach	Detaches a Windows menu handle from a **CMenu** object and returns the handle.
FromHandle	Returns a pointer to a **CMenu** object given a Windows menu handle.
GetSafeHmenu	Returns the **m_hMenu** wrapped by this **CMenu** object.
DeleteTempMap	Deletes any temporary **CMenu** objects created by the **FromHandle** member function.

CreateMenu	Creates an empty menu and attaches it to a **CMenu** object.
CreatePopupMenu	Creates an empty pop-up menu and attaches it to a **CMenu** object.
LoadMenu	Loads a menu resource from the executable file and attaches it to a **CMenu** object.
LoadMenuIndirect	Loads a menu from a menu template in memory and attaches it to a **CMenu** object.
DestroyMenu	Destroys the menu attached to a **CMenu** object and frees any memory that the menu occupied.

Menu Operations

| DeleteMenu | Deletes a specified item from the menu. If the menu item has an associated pop-up menu, destroys the handle to the pop-up menu and frees the memory used by it. |
| TrackPopupMenu | Displays a floating pop-up menu at the specified location and tracks the selection of items on the pop-up menu. |

Menu Item Operations

AppendMenu	Appends a new item to the end of this menu.
CheckMenuItem	Places a check mark next to or removes a check mark from a menu item in the pop-up menu.
CheckMenuRadioItem	Places a radio button next to a menu item and removes the radio button from all of the other menu items in the group.
EnableMenuItem	Enables, disables, or dims (grays) a menu item.
GetMenuItemCount	Determines the number of items in a pop-up or top-level menu.
GetMenuItemID	Obtains the menu-item identifier for a menu item located at the specified position.
GetMenuState	Returns the status of the specified menu item or the number of items in a pop-up menu.
GetMenuString	Retrieves the label of the specified menu item.
GetSubMenu	Retrieves a pointer to a pop-up menu.
InsertMenu	Inserts a new menu item at the specified position, moving other items down the menu.
ModifyMenu	Changes an existing menu item at the specified position.
RemoveMenu	Deletes a menu item with an associated pop-up menu from the specified menu.

Overridables

DrawItem	Called by the framework when a visual aspect of an owner-drawn menu changes.
MeasureItem	Called by the framework to determine menu dimensions when an owner-drawn menu is created.

Member Functions

CMenu::AppendMenu

BOOL AppendMenu(UINT *nFlags*, **UINT** *nIDNewItem* = **0, LPCTSTR** *lpszNewItem* = **NULL);**
BOOL AppendMenu(UINT *nFlags*, **UINT** *nIDNewItem*, **const CBitmap*** *pBmp* **);**

Return Value

Nonzero if the function is successful; otherwise 0.

Parameters

nFlags   Specifies information about the state of the new menu item when it is added to the menu. It consists of one or more of the values listed in the Remarks section in Books Online.

nIDNewItem   Specifies either the command ID of the new menu item or, if *nFlags* is set to **MF_POPUP**, the menu handle (**HMENU**) of a pop-up menu. The *nIDNewItem* parameter is ignored (not needed) if *nFlags* is set to **MF_SEPARATOR**.

lpszNewItem   Specifies the content of the new menu item. The *nFlags* parameter is used to interpret *lpszNewItem* in the following way:

nFlags	Interpretation of lpszNewItem
MF_OWNERDRAW	Contains an application-supplied 32-bit value that the application can use to maintain additional data associated with the menu item. This 32-bit value is available to the application when it processes **WM_MEASUREITEM** and **WM_DRAWITEM** messages. The value is stored in the **itemData** member of the structure supplied with those messages.
MF_STRING	Contains a pointer to a null-terminated string. This is the default interpretation.
MF_SEPARATOR	The *lpszNewItem* parameter is ignored (not needed).

pBmp   Points to a **CBitmap** object that will be used as the menu item.

Remarks

Appends a new item to the end of a menu. The application can specify the state of the menu item by setting values in *nFlags*. When *nIDNewItem* specifies a pop-up menu, it becomes part of the menu to which it is appended. If that menu is destroyed, the appended menu will also be destroyed. An appended menu should be detached from a **CMenu** object to avoid conflict. Note that **MF_STRING** and **MF_OWNERDRAW** are not valid for the bitmap version of **AppendMenu**.

The following list describes the flags that may be set in *nFlags*.

- **MF_CHECKED** Acts as a toggle with **MF_UNCHECKED** to place the default check mark next to the item. When the application supplies check-mark bitmaps (see the **SetMenuItemBitmaps** member function), the "check mark on" bitmap is displayed.

- **MF_UNCHECKED** Acts as a toggle with **MF_CHECKED** to remove a check mark next to the item. When the application supplies check-mark bitmaps (see the **SetMenuItemBitmaps** member function), the "check mark off" bitmap is displayed.

- **MF_DISABLED** Disables the menu item so that it cannot be selected but does not dim it.

- **MF_ENABLED** Enables the menu item so that it can be selected and restores it from its dimmed state.

- **MF_GRAYED** Disables the menu item so that it cannot be selected and dims it.

- **MF_MENUBARBREAK** Places the item on a new line in static menus or in a new column in pop-up menus. The new pop-up menu column will be separated from the old column by a vertical dividing line.

- **MF_MENUBREAK** Places the item on a new line in static menus or in a new column in pop-up menus. No dividing line is placed between the columns.

- **MF_OWNERDRAW** Specifies that the item is an owner-draw item. When the menu is displayed for the first time, the window that owns the menu receives a **WM_MEASUREITEM** message, which retrieves the height and width of the menu item. The **WM_DRAWITEM** message is the one sent whenever the owner must update the visual appearance of the menu item. This option is not valid for a top-level menu item.

- **MF_POPUP** Specifies that the menu item has a pop-up menu associated with it. The ID parameter specifies a handle to a pop-up menu that is to be associated with the item. This is used for adding either a top-level pop-up menu or a hierarchical pop-up menu to a pop-up menu item.

- **MF_SEPARATOR** Draws a horizontal dividing line. Can only be used in a pop-up menu. This line cannot be dimmed, disabled, or highlighted. Other parameters are ignored.

- **MF_STRING** Specifies that the menu item is a character string.

Each of the following groups lists flags that are mutually exclusive and cannot be used together:

- **MF_DISABLED**, **MF_ENABLED**, and **MF_GRAYED**
- **MF_STRING**, **MF_OWNERDRAW**, **MF_SEPARATOR**, and the bitmap version
- **MF_MENUBARBREAK** and **MF_MENUBREAK**
- **MF_CHECKED** and **MF_UNCHECKED**

Whenever a menu that resides in a window is changed (whether or not the window is displayed), the application should call **CWnd::DrawMenuBar**.

See Also CWnd::DrawMenuBar, CMenu::InsertMenu, CMenu::RemoveMenu, CMenu::SetMenuItemBitmaps, CMenu::Detach, ::AppendMenu

CMenu::Attach

BOOL Attach(HMENU *hMenu* **);**

Return Value
Nonzero if the operation was successful; otherwise 0.

Parameters
hMenu   Specifies a handle to a Windows menu.

Remarks
Attaches an existing Windows menu to a **CMenu** object. This function should not be called if a menu is already attached to the **CMenu** object. The menu handle is stored in the **m_hMenu** data member.

If the menu you want to manipulate is already associated with a window, you can use the **CWnd::GetMenu** function to get a handle to the menu.

Example
```
CMenu mnu;
HMENU hmnu = pWnd->GetMenu( );
mnu.Attach( hmnu );
// Now you can manipulate the window's menu as a CMenu
// object...
```

See Also CMenu::Detach, CMenu::CMenu, CWnd::GetMenu

CMenu::CheckMenuItem

UINT CheckMenuItem(UINT *nIDCheckItem***, UINT** *nCheck* **);**

Return Value

The previous state of the item: **MF_CHECKED** or **MF_UNCHECKED**, or –1 if the menu item did not exist.

Parameters

nIDCheckItem   Specifies the menu item to be checked, as determined by *nCheck*.

nCheck   Specifies how to check the menu item and how to determine the item's position in the menu. The *nCheck* parameter can be a combination of **MF_CHECKED** or **MF_UNCHECKED** with **MF_BYPOSITION** or **MF_BYCOMMAND** flags. These flags can be combined by using the bitwise OR operator. They have the following meanings:

- **MF_BYCOMMAND**   Specifies that the parameter gives the command ID of the existing menu item. This is the default.

- **MF_BYPOSITION**   Specifies that the parameter gives the position of the existing menu item. The first item is at position 0.

- **MF_CHECKED**   Acts as a toggle with **MF_UNCHECKED** to place the default check mark next to the item.

- **MF_UNCHECKED**   Acts as a toggle with **MF_CHECKED** to remove a check mark next to the item.

Remarks

Adds check marks to or removes check marks from menu items in the pop-up menu. The *nIDCheckItem* parameter specifies the item to be modified.

The *nIDCheckItem* parameter may identify a pop-up menu item as well as a menu item. No special steps are required to check a pop-up menu item. Top-level menu items cannot be checked. A pop-up menu item must be checked by position since it does not have a menu-item identifier associated with it.

See Also   **CMenu::GetMenuState**, **::CheckMenuItem**, **CMenu::CheckMenuRadioItem**

CMenu::CheckMenuRadioItem

BOOL CheckMenuRadioItem(UINT *nIDFirst***, UINT** *nIDLast***, UINT** *nIDItem***, UINT** *nFlags* **);**

Return Value

Nonzero if successful; otherwise 0

Parameters

nIDFirst   Specifies (as an ID or offset, depending on the value of *nFlags*) the first menu item in the radio button group.

nIDLast   Specifies (as an ID or offset, depending on the value of *nFlags*) the last menu item in the radio button group.

nIDItem   Specifies (as an ID or offset, depending on the value of *nFlags*) the item in the group which will be checked with a radio button.

nFlags   Specifies interpretation of *nIDFirst*, *nIDLast*, and *nIDItem* in the following way:

nFlags	Interpretation
MF_BYCOMMAND	Specifies that the parameter gives the command ID of the existing menu item. This is the default if neither **MF_BYCOMMAND** nor **MF_BYPOSITION** is set.
MF_BYPOSITION	Specifies that the parameter gives the position of the existing menu item. The first item is at position 0.

Remarks

Checks a specified menu item and makes it a radio item. At the same time, the function unchecks all other menu items in the associated group and clears the radio-item type flag for those items. The checked item is displayed using a radio button (or bullet) bitmap instead of a check mark bitmap.

See Also   CMenu::CheckMenuItem, CMenu::GetMenuState, ::CheckMenuRadioItem

CMenu::CMenu

CMenu( );

Remarks

The menu is not created until you call one of the create or load member functions of **CMenu**, as listed in "See Also."

See Also   CMenu::CreateMenu, CMenu::CreatePopupMenu, CMenu::LoadMenu, CMenu::LoadMenuIndirect, CMenu::Attach

CMenu::CreateMenu

BOOL CreateMenu( );

Return Value

Nonzero if the menu was created successfully; otherwise 0.

Remarks

Creates a menu and attaches it to the **CMenu** object.

The menu is initially empty. Menu items can be added by using the **AppendMenu** or **InsertMenu** member function.

If the menu is assigned to a window, it is automatically destroyed when the window is destroyed.

Before exiting, an application must free system resources associated with a menu if the menu is not assigned to a window. An application frees a menu by calling the **DestroyMenu** member function.

See Also   **CMenu::CMenu**, **CMenu::DestroyMenu**, **CMenu::InsertMenu**, **CWnd::SetMenu**, **::CreateMenu**, **CMenu::AppendMenu**

CMenu::CreatePopupMenu

> **BOOL CreatePopupMenu( );**

Return Value

Nonzero if the pop-up menu was successfully created; otherwise 0.

Remarks

Creates a pop-up menu and attaches it to the **CMenu** object.

The menu is initially empty. Menu items can be added by using the **AppendMenu** or **InsertMenu** member function. The application can add the pop-up menu to an existing menu or pop-up menu. The **TrackPopupMenu** member function may be used to display this menu as a floating pop-up menu and to track selections on the pop-up menu.

If the menu is assigned to a window, it is automatically destroyed when the window is destroyed. If the menu is added to an existing menu, it is automatically destroyed when that menu is destroyed.

Before exiting, an application must free system resources associated with a pop-up menu if the menu is not assigned to a window. An application frees a menu by calling the **DestroyMenu** member function.

See Also   **CMenu::CreateMenu**, **CMenu::InsertMenu**, **CWnd::SetMenu**, **CMenu::TrackPopupMenu**, **::CreatePopupMenu**, **CMenu::AppendMenu**

CMenu::DeleteMenu

> **BOOL DeleteMenu(UINT** *nPosition***, UINT** *nFlags* **);**

Return Value

Nonzero if the function is successful; otherwise 0.

Parameters

nPosition Specifies the menu item that is to be deleted, as determined by *nFlags*.

nFlags Is used to interpret *nPosition* in the following way:

nFlags	Interpretation of nPosition
MF_BYCOMMAND	Specifies that the parameter gives the command ID of the existing menu item. This is the default if neither **MF_BYCOMMAND** nor **MF_BYPOSITION** is set.
MF_BYPOSITION	Specifies that the parameter gives the position of the existing menu item. The first item is at position 0.

Remarks

Deletes an item from the menu. If the menu item has an associated pop-up menu, **DeleteMenu** destroys the handle to the pop-up menu and frees the memory used by the pop-up menu.

Whenever a menu that resides in a window is changed (whether or not the window is displayed), the application must call **CWnd::DrawMenuBar**.

See Also CWnd::DrawMenuBar, ::DeleteMenu

CMenu::DeleteTempMap

static void PASCAL DeleteTempMap( );

Remarks

Called automatically by the **CWinApp** idle-time handler, **DeleteTempMap** deletes any temporary **CMenu** objects created by the **FromHandle** member function. **DeleteTempMap** detaches the Windows menu object attached to a temporary **CMenu** object before deleting the **CMenu** object.

CMenu::DestroyMenu

BOOL DestroyMenu( );

Return Value

Nonzero if the menu is destroyed; otherwise 0.

Remarks

Destroys the menu and any Windows resources that were used. The menu is detached from the **CMenu** object before it is destroyed. The Windows **DestroyMenu** function is automatically called in the **CMenu** destructor.

See Also ::DestroyMenu

CMenu::Detach

HMENU Detach( );

Return Value

The handle, of type **HMENU**, to a Windows menu, if successful; otherwise **NULL**.

Remarks

Detaches a Windows menu from a **CMenu** object and returns the handle. The **m_hMenu** data member is set to **NULL**.

See Also   CMenu::Attach

CMenu::DrawItem

virtual void DrawItem(LPDRAWITEMSTRUCT *lpDrawItemStruct* **);**

Parameters

lpDrawItemStruct   A pointer to a **DRAWITEMSTRUCT** structure that contains information about the type of drawing required.

Remarks

Called by the framework when a visual aspect of an owner-drawn menu changes. The *itemAction* member of the **DRAWITEMSTRUCT** structure defines the drawing action that is to be performed. Override this member function to implement drawing for an owner-draw **CMenu** object. The application should restore all graphics device interface (GDI) objects selected for the display context supplied in *lpDrawItemStruct* before the termination of this member function.

See **CWnd::OnDrawItem** for a description of the **DRAWITEMSTRUCT** structure.

CMenu::EnableMenuItem

UINT EnableMenuItem(UINT *nIDEnableItem*, **UINT** *nEnable* **);**

Return Value

Previous state (**MF_DISABLED**, **MF_ENABLED**, or **MF_GRAYED**) or –1 if not valid.

Parameters

nIDEnableItem   Specifies the menu item to be enabled, as determined by *nEnable*. This parameter can specify pop-up menu items as well as standard menu items.

nEnable   Specifies the action to take. It can be a combination of **MF_DISABLED**, **MF_ENABLED**, or **MF_GRAYED**, with **MF_BYCOMMAND** or **MF_BYPOSITION**. These values can be combined by using the bitwise OR operator. These values have the following meanings:

- **MF_BYCOMMAND**   Specifies that the parameter gives the command ID of the existing menu item. This is the default.

- **MF_BYPOSITION**   Specifies that the parameter gives the position of the existing menu item. The first item is at position 0.

- **MF_DISABLED**   Disables the menu item so that it cannot be selected but does not dim it.

- **MF_ENABLED**   Enables the menu item so that it can be selected and restores it from its dimmed state.

- **MF_GRAYED**   Disables the menu item so that it cannot be selected and dims it.

Remarks

Enables, disables, or dims a menu item. The **CreateMenu**, **InsertMenu**, **ModifyMenu**, and **LoadMenuIndirect** member functions can also set the state (enabled, disabled, or dimmed) of a menu item.

Using the **MF_BYPOSITION** value requires an application to use the correct **CMenu**. If the **CMenu** of the menu bar is used, a top-level menu item (an item in the menu bar) is affected. To set the state of an item in a pop-up or nested pop-up menu by position, an application must specify the **CMenu** of the pop-up menu.

When an application specifies the **MF_BYCOMMAND** flag, Windows checks all pop-up menu items that are subordinate to the **CMenu**; therefore, unless duplicate menu items are present, using the **CMenu** of the menu bar is sufficient.

See Also   **CMenu::GetMenuState**, **::EnableMenuItem**

CMenu::FromHandle

static CMenu* PASCAL FromHandle(HMENU *hMenu* **);**

Return Value

A pointer to a **CMenu** that may be temporary or permanent.

Parameters

hMenu   A Windows handle to a menu.

Remarks

Returns a pointer to a **CMenu** object given a Windows handle to a menu. If a **CMenu** object is not already attached to the Windows menu object, a temporary **CMenu** object is created and attached.

This temporary **CMenu** object is only valid until the next time the application has idle time in its event loop, at which time all temporary objects are deleted.

CMenu::GetMenuContextHelpId

DWORD GetMenuContextHelpId( ) const;

Return Value

The context help ID currently associated with **CMenu** if it has one; zero otherwise.

Remarks

Call this function to retrieve the context help ID associated with **CMenu**.

See Also   **CMenu::SetMenuContextHelpID**, **::GetMenuContextHelpId**

CMenu::GetMenuItemCount

UINT GetMenuItemCount( ) const;

Return Value

The number of items in the menu if the function is successful; otherwise –1.

Remarks

Determines the number of items in a pop-up or top-level menu.

See Also   **CWnd::GetMenu**, **CMenu::GetMenuItemID**, **CMenu::GetSubMenu**, **::GetMenuItemCount**

CMenu::GetMenuItemID

UINT GetMenuItemID(int *nPos* **) const;**

Return Value

The item ID for the specified item in a pop-up menu if the function is successful. If the specified item is a pop-up menu (as opposed to an item within the pop-up menu), the return value is –1. If *nPos* corresponds to a **SEPARATOR** menu item, the return value is 0.

Parameters

nPos   Specifies the position (zero-based) of the menu item whose ID is being retrieved.

Remarks

Obtains the menu-item identifier for a menu item located at the position defined by *nPos*.

See Also   **CWnd::GetMenu**, **CMenu::GetMenuItemCount**, **CMenu::GetSubMenu**, **::GetMenuItemID**

CMenu::GetMenuState

UINT GetMenuState(UINT *nID*, **UINT** *nFlags* **) const;**

Return Value

The value –1 if the specified item does not exist. If *nId* identifies a pop-up menu, the high-order byte contains the number of items in the pop-up menu and the low-order byte contains the menu flags associated with the pop-up menu. Otherwise the return value is a mask (Boolean OR) of the values from the following list (this mask describes the status of the menu item that *nId* identifies):

- **MF_CHECKED** Acts as a toggle with **MF_UNCHECKED** to place the default check mark next to the item. When the application supplies check-mark bitmaps (see the **SetMenuItemBitmaps** member function), the "check mark on" bitmap is displayed.

- **MF_DISABLED** Disables the menu item so that it cannot be selected but does not dim it.

- **MF_ENABLED** Enables the menu item so that it can be selected and restores it from its dimmed state. Note that the value of this constant is 0; an application should not test against 0 for failure when using this value.

- **MF_GRAYED** Disables the menu item so that it cannot be selected and dims it.

- **MF_MENUBARBREAK** Places the item on a new line in static menus or in a new column in pop-up menus. The new pop-up menu column will be separated from the old column by a vertical dividing line.

- **MF_MENUBREAK** Places the item on a new line in static menus or in a new column in pop-up menus. No dividing line is placed between the columns.

- **MF_SEPARATOR** Draws a horizontal dividing line. Can only be used in a pop-up menu. This line cannot be dimmed, disabled, or highlighted. Other parameters are ignored.

- **MF_UNCHECKED** Acts as a toggle with **MF_CHECKED** to remove a check mark next to the item. When the application supplies check-mark bitmaps (see the **SetMenuItemBitmaps** member function), the "check mark off" bitmap is displayed. Note that the value of this constant is 0; an application should not test against 0 for failure when using this value.

Parameters

nID   Specifies the menu item ID, as determined by *nFlags*.

nFlags   Specifies the nature of *nID*. It can be one of the following values:

- **MF_BYCOMMAND**   Specifies that the parameter gives the command ID of the existing menu item. This is the default.

- **MF_BYPOSITION**   Specifies that the parameter gives the position of the existing menu item. The first item is at position 0.

Remarks

Returns the status of the specified menu item or the number of items in a pop-up menu.

See Also   ::GetMenuState, **CMenu::CheckMenuItem**, **CMenu::EnableMenuItem**

CMenu::GetMenuString

> **int GetMenuString(UINT** *nIDItem***, LPTSTR** *lpString***, int** *nMaxCount***, UINT** *nFlags* **) const;**
> **int GetMenuString(UINT** *nIDItem***, CString&** *rString***, UINT** *nFlags* **) const;**

Return Value

Specifies the actual number of bytes copied to the buffer, not including the null terminator.

Parameters

nIDItem   Specifies the integer identifier of the menu item or the offset of the menu item in the menu, depending on the value of *nFlags*.

lpString   Points to the buffer that is to receive the label.

rString   A reference to a **CString** object that is to receive the copied menu string.

nMaxCount   Specifies the maximum length (in bytes) of the label to be copied. If the label is longer than the maximum specified in *nMaxCount*, the extra characters are truncated.

nFlags   Specifies the interpretation of the *nIDItem* parameter. It can be one of the following values:

nFlags	Interpretation of nIDItem
MF_BYCOMMAND	Specifies that the parameter gives the command ID of the existing menu item. This is the default if neither **MF_BYCOMMAND** nor **MF_BYPOSITION** is set.
MF_BYPOSITION	Specifies that the parameter gives the position of the existing menu item. The first item is at position 0.

Remarks

Copies the label of the specified menu item to the specified buffer.

The *nMaxCount* parameter should be one larger than the number of characters in the label to accommodate the null character that terminates a string.

See Also **CMenu::GetMenuState, CMenu::ModifyMenu, ::GetMenuString**

CMenu::GetSubMenu

CMenu* GetSubMenu(int *nPos* **) const;**

Return Value

A pointer to a **CMenu** object whose **m_hMenu** member contains a handle to the pop-up menu if a pop-up menu exists at the given position; otherwise **NULL**. If a **CMenu** object does not exist, then a temporary one is created. The **CMenu** pointer returned should not be stored.

Parameters

nPos Specifies the position of the pop-up menu contained in the menu. Position values start at 0 for the first menu item. The pop-up menu's identifier cannot be used in this function.

Remarks

Retrieves the **CMenu** object of a pop-up menu.

See Also **CWnd::GetMenu, CMenu::GetMenuItemID, ::GetMenuString**

CMenu::GetSafeHmenu

HMENU GetSafeHmenu( ) const;

Remarks

Returns the **HMENU** wrapped by this **CMenu** object, or a **NULL CMenu** pointer.

See Also **::GetSubMenu**

CMenu::InsertMenu

BOOL InsertMenu(UINT *nPosition***, UINT** *nFlags***, UINT** *nIDNewItem* **= 0,**
  LPCTSTR *lpszNewItem* **= NULL);**
BOOL InsertMenu(UINT *nPosition***, UINT** *nFlags***, UINT** *nIDNewItem***, const CBitmap*** *pBmp* **);**

Return Value

Nonzero if the function is successful; otherwise 0.

Parameters

nPosition Specifies the menu item before which the new menu item is to be inserted. The *nFlags* parameter can be used to interpret *nPosition* in the following ways:

nFlags	Interpretation of nPosition
MF_BYCOMMAND	Specifies that the parameter gives the command ID of the existing menu item. This is the default if neither **MF_BYCOMMAND** nor **MF_BYPOSITION** is set.
MF_BYPOSITION	Specifies that the parameter gives the position of the existing menu item. The first item is at position 0. If *nPosition* is −1, the new menu item is appended to the end of the menu.

nFlags Specifies how *nPosition* is interpreted and specifies information about the state of the new menu item when it is added to the menu. For a list of the flags that may be set, see the **AppendMenu** member function. To specify more than one value, use the bitwise OR operator to combine them with the **MF_BYCOMMAND** or **MF_BYPOSITION** flag.

nIDNewItem Specifies either the command ID of the new menu item or, if *nFlags* is set to **MF_POPUP**, the menu handle (**HMENU**) of the pop-up menu. The *nIDNewItem* parameter is ignored (not needed) if *nFlags* is set to **MF_SEPARATOR**.

lpszNewItem Specifies the content of the new menu item. *nFlags* can be used to interpret *lpszNewItem* in the following ways:

nFlags	Interpretation of lpszNewItem
MF_OWNERDRAW	Contains an application-supplied 32-bit value that the application can use to maintain additional data associated with the menu item. This 32-bit value is available to the application in the **itemData** member of the structure supplied by the **WM_MEASUREITEM** and **WM_DRAWITEM** messages. These messages are sent when the menu item is initially displayed or is changed.
MF_STRING	Contains a long pointer to a null-terminated string. This is the default interpretation.
MF_SEPARATOR	The *lpszNewItem* parameter is ignored (not needed).

pBmp Points to a **CBitmap** object that will be used as the menu item.

Remarks

Inserts a new menu item at the position specified by *nPosition* and moves other items down the menu. The application can specify the state of the menu item by setting values in *nFlags*.

Whenever a menu that resides in a window is changed (whether or not the window is displayed), the application should call **CWnd::DrawMenuBar**.

When *nIDNewItem* specifies a pop-up menu, it becomes part of the menu in which it is inserted. If that menu is destroyed, the inserted menu will also be destroyed. An inserted menu should be detached from a **CMenu** object to avoid conflict.

If the active multiple document interface (MDI) child window is maximized and an application inserts a pop-up menu into the MDI application's menu by calling this function and specifying the **MF_BYPOSITION** flag, the menu is inserted one position farther left than expected. This happens because the Control menu of the active MDI child window is inserted into the first position of the MDI frame window's menu bar. To position the menu properly, the application must add 1 to the position value that would otherwise be used. An application can use the **WM_MDIGETACTIVE** message to determine whether the currently active child window is maximized.

See Also **CMenu::AppendMenu**, **CWnd::DrawMenuBar**, **CMenu::SetMenuItemBitmaps**, **CMenu::Detach**, **::InsertMenu**

CMenu::LoadMenu

BOOL LoadMenu(LPCTSTR *lpszResourceName* **);**
BOOL LoadMenu(UINT *nIDResource* **);**

Return Value

Nonzero if the menu resource was loaded successfully; otherwise 0.

Parameters

lpszResourceName   Points to a null-terminated string that contains the name of the menu resource to load.

nIDResource   Specifies the menu ID of the menu resource to load.

Remarks

Loads a menu resource from the application's executable file and attaches it to the **CMenu** object.

Before exiting, an application must free system resources associated with a menu if the menu is not assigned to a window. An application frees a menu by calling the **DestroyMenu** member function.

See Also **CMenu::AppendMenu**, **CMenu::DestroyMenu**, **CMenu::LoadMenuIndirect**, **::LoadMenu**

CMenu::LoadMenuIndirect

BOOL LoadMenuIndirect(const void* *lpMenuTemplate* **);**

Return Value

Nonzero if the menu resource was loaded successfully; otherwise 0.

Parameters

lpMenuTemplate   Points to a menu template (which is a single **MENUITEMTEMPLATEHEADER** structure and a collection of one or more **MENUITEMTEMPLATE** structures).

The **MENUITEMTEMPLATEHEADER** structure has the following generic form:

```
typedef struct {
    UINT    versionNumber;
    UINT    offset;
} MENUITEMTEMPLATEHEADER;
```

The **MENUITEMTEMPLATE** structure has the following generic form:

```
typedef struct {
    UINT mtOption;
    UINT mtID;
    char mtString[1];
} MENUITEMTEMPLATE;
```

For more information on the above two structures, see the Windows Software Development Kit (SDK).

Remarks

Loads a resource from a menu template in memory and attaches it to the **CMenu** object. A menu template is a header followed by a collection of one or more **MENUITEMTEMPLATE** structures, each of which may contain one or more menu items and pop-up menus.

The version number should be 0.

The **mtOption** flags should include **MF_END** for the last item in a pop-up list and for the last item in the main list. See the **AppendMenu** member function for other flags. The **mtId** member must be omitted from the **MENUITEMTEMPLATE** structure when **MF_POPUP** is specified in **mtOption**.

The space allocated for the **MENUITEMTEMPLATE** structure must be large enough for **mtString** to contain the name of the menu item as a null-terminated string.

Before exiting, an application must free system resources associated with a menu if the menu is not assigned to a window. An application frees a menu by calling the **DestroyMenu** member function.

See Also   **CMenu::DestroyMenu**, **CMenu::LoadMenu**, **::LoadMenuIndirect**, **CMenu::AppendMenu**

CMenu::MeasureItem

virtual void MeasureItem(LPMEASUREITEMSTRUCT *lpMeasureItemStruct* **);**

Parameters

lpMeasureItemStruct   A pointer to a **MEASUREITEMSTRUCT** structure.

Remarks

Called by the framework when a menu with the owner-draw style is created. By default, this member function does nothing. Override this member function and fill in the **MEASUREITEMSTRUCT** structure to inform Windows of the menu's dimensions.

See **CWnd::OnMeasureItem** for a description of the **MEASUREITEMSTRUCT** structure.

CMenu::ModifyMenu

BOOL ModifyMenu(UINT *nPosition*, **UINT** *nFlags*, **UINT** *nIDNewItem* = 0,
  LPCTSTR *lpszNewItem* = NULL **);**
BOOL ModifyMenu(UINT *nPosition*, **UINT** *nFlags*, **UINT** *nIDNewItem*, **const CBitmap*** *pBmp* **);**

Return Value

Nonzero if the function is successful; otherwise 0.

Parameters

nPosition   Specifies the menu item to be changed. The *nFlags* parameter can be used to interpret *nPosition* in the following ways:

nFlags	Interpretation of nPosition
MF_BYCOMMAND	Specifies that the parameter gives the command ID of the existing menu item. This is the default if neither **MF_BYCOMMAND** nor **MF_BYPOSITION** is set.
MF_BYPOSITION	Specifies that the parameter gives the position of the existing menu item. The first item is at position 0.

nFlags   Specifies how *nPosition* is interpreted and gives information about the changes to be made to the menu item. For a list of flags that may be set, see the **AppendMenu** member function.

nIDNewItem   Specifies either the command ID of the modified menu item or, if *nFlags* is set to **MF_POPUP**, the menu handle (**HMENU**) of a pop-up menu. The *nIDNewItem* parameter is ignored (not needed) if *nFlags* is set to **MF_SEPARATOR**.

lpszNewItem   Specifies the content of the new menu item. The *nFlags* parameter can be used to interpret *lpszNewItem* in the following ways:

nFlags	Interpretation of lpszNewItem
MF_OWNERDRAW	Contains an application-supplied 32-bit value that the application can use to maintain additional data associated with the menu item. This 32-bit value is available to the application when it processes **MF_MEASUREITEM** and **MF_DRAWITEM**.
MF_STRING	Contains a long pointer to a null-terminated string or to a **CString**.
MF_SEPARATOR	The *lpszNewItem* parameter is ignored (not needed).

pBmp   Points to a **CBitmap** object that will be used as the menu item.

Remarks

Changes an existing menu item at the position specified by *nPosition*. The application specifies the new state of the menu item by setting values in *nFlags*. If this function replaces a pop-up menu associated with the menu item, it destroys the old pop-up menu and frees the memory used by the pop-up menu.

When *nIDNewItem* specifies a pop-up menu, it becomes part of the menu in which it is inserted. If that menu is destroyed, the inserted menu will also be destroyed. An inserted menu should be detached from a **CMenu** object to avoid conflict.

Whenever a menu that resides in a window is changed (whether or not the window is displayed), the application should call **CWnd::DrawMenuBar**. To change the attributes of existing menu items, it is much faster to use the **CheckMenuItem** and **EnableMenuItem** member functions.

See Also   CMenu::AppendMenu, CMenu::InsertMenu, **CMenu::CheckMenuItem**, **CWnd::DrawMenuBar**, **CMenu::EnableMenuItem**, **CMenu::SetMenuItemBitmaps**, **CMenu::Detach**, **::ModifyMenu**

CMenu::RemoveMenu

BOOL RemoveMenu(UINT *nPosition*, **UINT** *nFlags* **);**

Return Value

Nonzero if the function is successful; otherwise 0.

Parameters

nPosition   Specifies the menu item to be removed. The *nFlags* parameter can be used to interpret *nPosition* in the following ways:

nFlags	Interpretation of nPosition
MF_BYCOMMAND	Specifies that the parameter gives the command ID of the existing menu item. This is the default if neither **MF_BYCOMMAND** nor **MF_BYPOSITION** is set.
MF_BYPOSITION	Specifies that the parameter gives the position of the existing menu item. The first item is at position 0.

nFlags   Specifies how *nPosition* is interpreted.

Remarks

Deletes a menu item with an associated pop-up menu from the menu. It does not destroy the handle for a pop-up menu, so the menu can be reused. Before calling this function, the application may call the **GetSubMenu** member function to retrieve the pop-up **CMenu** object for reuse.

Whenever a menu that resides in a window is changed (whether or not the window is displayed), the application must call **CWnd::DrawMenuBar**.

See Also   **CWnd::DrawMenuBar**, **CMenu::GetSubMenu**, **::RemoveMenu**

CMenu::SetMenuContextHelpId

BOOL SetMenuContextHelpId(DWORD *dwContextHelpId* **);**

Return Value

Nonzero if successful; otherwise 0

Parameters

dwContextHelpId   Context help ID to associate with **CMenu**.

Remarks

Call this function to associate a context help ID with **CMenu**. All items in the menu share this identifier—it is not possible to attach a help context identifier to the individual menu items.

See Also   **CMenu::GetMenuContextHelpID**, **::SetMenuContextHelpId**

CMenu::SetMenuItemBitmaps

BOOL SetMenuItemBitmaps(UINT *nPosition*, **UINT** *nFlags*, **const CBitmap*** *pBmpUnchecked*, **const CBitmap*** *pBmpChecked* **);**

Return Value

Nonzero if the function is successful; otherwise 0.

Parameters

nPosition   Specifies the menu item to be changed. The *nFlags* parameter can be used to interpret *nPosition* in the following ways:

nFlags	Interpretation of nPosition
MF_BYCOMMAND	Specifies that the parameter gives the command ID of the existing menu item. This is the default if neither **MF_BYCOMMAND** nor **MF_BYPOSITION** is set.
MF_BYPOSITION	Specifies that the parameter gives the position of the existing menu item. The first item is at position 0.

nFlags   Specifies how *nPosition* is interpreted.

pBmpUnchecked   Specifies the bitmap to use for menu items that are not checked.

pBmpChecked   Specifies the bitmap to use for menu items that are checked.

Remarks

Associates the specified bitmaps with a menu item. Whether the menu item is checked or unchecked, Windows displays the appropriate bitmap next to the menu item.

If either *pBmpUnchecked* or *pBmpChecked* is **NULL**, then Windows displays nothing next to the menu item for the corresponding attribute. If both parameters are **NULL**, Windows uses the default check mark when the item is checked and removes the check mark when the item is unchecked.

When the menu is destroyed, these bitmaps are not destroyed; the application must destroy them.

The Windows **GetMenuCheckMarkDimensions** function retrieves the dimensions of the default check mark used for menu items. The application uses these values to determine the appropriate size for the bitmaps supplied with this function. Get the size, create your bitmaps, then set them.

See Also   **::GetMenuCheckMarkDimensions**, **::SetMenuItemBitmaps**

CMenu::TrackPopupMenu

BOOL TrackPopupMenu(UINT *nFlags***, int** *x***, int** *y***, CWnd*** *pWnd***, LPCRECT** *lpRect* **= 0);**

Return Value

Nonzero if the function is successful; otherwise 0.

Parameters

nFlags   Specifies a screen-position flag and a mouse-button flag. The screen-position flag can be one of the following:

- **TPM_CENTERALIGN**   Centers the pop-up menu horizontally relative to the coordinate specified by *x*.

- **TPM_LEFTALIGN**   Positions the pop-up menu so that its left side is aligned with the coordinate specified by *x*.

- **TPM_RIGHTALIGN**   Positions the pop-up menu so that its right side is aligned with the coordinate specified by *x*.

The mouse-button flag can be either of the following:

- **TPM_LEFTBUTTON**   Causes the pop-up menu to track the left mouse button.

- **TPM_RIGHTBUTTON**   Causes the pop-up menu to track the right mouse button.

x   Specifies the horizontal position in screen coordinates of the pop-up menu. Depending on the value of the *nFlags* parameter, the menu can be left-aligned, right-aligned, or centered relative to this position.

y   Specifies the vertical position in screen coordinates of the top of the menu on the screen.

pWnd   Identifies the window that owns the pop-up menu. This window receives all **WM_COMMAND** messages from the menu. In Windows versions 3.1 and later, the window does not receive **WM_COMMAND** messages until **TrackPopupMenu** returns. In Windows 3.0, the window receives **WM_COMMAND** messages before **TrackPopupMenu** returns.

lpRect   Points to a **RECT** structure or **CRect** object that contains the screen coordinates of a rectangle within which the user can click without dismissing the pop-up menu. If this parameter is **NULL**, the pop-up menu is dismissed if the user clicks outside the pop-up menu. This must be **NULL** for Windows 3.0.

For Windows 3.1 and later, you can use the following constants:

- **TPM_CENTERALIGN**
- **TPM_LEFTALIGN**
- **TPM_RIGHTALIGN**
- **TPM_RIGHTBUTTON**

Remarks

Displays a floating pop-up menu at the specified location and tracks the selection of items on the pop-up menu. A floating pop-up menu can appear anywhere on the screen.

See Also   **CMenu::CreatePopupMenu**, **CMenu::GetSubMenu**, **::TrackPopupMenu**

Data Members

CMenu::m_hMenu

Remarks

Specifies the **HMENU** handle of the Windows menu attached to the **CMenu** object.

CMetaFileDC

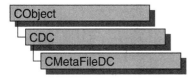

A Windows metafile contains a sequence of graphics device interface (GDI) commands that you can replay to create a desired image or text.

To implement a Windows metafile, first create a **CMetaFileDC** object. Invoke the **CMetaFileDC** constructor, then call the **Create** member function, which creates a Windows metafile device context and attaches it to the **CMetaFileDC** object.

Next send the **CMetaFileDC** object the sequence of **CDC** GDI commands that you intend for it to replay. Only those GDI commands that create output, such as **MoveTo** and **LineTo**, can be used.

After you have sent the desired commands to the metafile, call the **Close** member function, which closes the metafile device contexts and returns a metafile handle. Then dispose of the **CMetaFileDC** object.

CDC::PlayMetaFile can then use the metafile handle to play the metafile repeatedly. The metafile can also be manipulated by Windows functions such as **CopyMetaFile**, which copies a metafile to disk.

When the metafile is no longer needed, delete it from memory with the **DeleteMetaFile** Windows function.

You can also implement the **CMetaFileDC** object so that it can handle both output calls and attribute GDI calls such as **GetTextExtent**. Such a metafile is more flexible and can more easily reuse general GDI code, which often consists of a mix of output and attribute calls. The **CMetaFileDC** class inherits two device contexts, **m_hDC** and **m_hAttribDC**, from **CDC**. The **m_hDC** device context handles all **CDC** GDI output calls and the **m_hAttribDC** device context handles all **CDC** GDI attribute calls. Normally, these two device contexts refer to the same device. In the case of **CMetaFileDC**, the attribute DC is set to **NULL** by default.

Create a second device context that points to the screen, a printer, or device other than a metafile, then call the **SetAttribDC** member function to associate the new device context with **m_hAttribDC**. GDI calls for information will now be directed to the new **m_hAttribDC**. Output GDI calls will go to **m_hDC**, which represents the metafile.

For more information on **CMetaFileDC**, see "Device Contexts" in Chapter 1 of *Programming with MFC*.

#include <afxext.h>

See Also   CDC

Construction

CMetaFileDC	Constructs a **CMetaFileDC** object.

Initialization

Create	Creates the Windows metafile device context and attaches it to the **CMetaFileDC** object.
CreateEnhanced	Creates a metafile device context for an enhanced-format metafile.

Operations

Close	Closes the device context and creates a metafile handle.
CloseEnhanced	Closes an enhanced-metafile device context and creates an enhanced-metafile handle.

Member Functions

CMetaFileDC::Close

HMETAFILE Close( );

Return Value

A valid **HMETAFILE** if the function is successful; otherwise **NULL**.

Remarks

Closes the metafile device context and creates a Windows metafile handle that can be used to play the metafile by using the **CDC::PlayMetaFile** member function. The Windows metafile handle can also be used to manipulate the metafile with Windows functions such as **CopyMetaFile**.

Delete the metafile after use by calling the Windows **DeleteMetaFile** function.

See Also   CDC::PlayMetaFile, ::CloseMetaFile, ::GetMetaFileBits, ::CopyMetaFile, ::DeleteMetaFile

CMetaFileDC::CloseEnhanced

HENHMETAFILE CloseEnhanced( );

Return Value

A handle of an enhanced metafile, if successful; otherwise **NULL**.

Remarks

Closes an enhanced-metafile device context and returns a handle that identifies an enhanced-format metafile. An application can use the enhanced-metafile handle returned by this function to perform the following tasks:

- Display a picture stored in an enhanced metafile
- Create copies of the enhanced metafile
- Enumerate, edit, or copy individual records in the enhanced metafile
- Retrieve an optional description of the metafile contents from the enhanced-metafile header
- Retrieve a copy of the enhanced-metafile header
- Retrieve a binary copy of the enhanced metafile
- Enumerate the colors in the optional palette
- Convert an enhanced-format metafile into a Windows-format metafile

When the application no longer needs the enhanced metafile handle, it should release the handle by calling the **::DeleteEnhMetaFile** function.

See Also   CDC::PlayMetaFile, CMetaFileDC::CreateEnhanced, ::DeleteEnhMetaFile

---

CMetaFileDC::CMetaFileDC

CMetaFileDC( );

Remarks

Construct a **CMetaFileDC** object in two steps. First, call **CMetaFileDC**, then call **Create**, which creates the Windows metafile device context and attaches it to the **CMetaFileDC** object.

See Also   CMetaFileDC::Create

CMetaFileDC::Create

BOOL Create(LPCTSTR *lpszFilename* = **NULL**);

Return Value

Nonzero if the function is successful; otherwise 0.

Parameters

lpszFilename   Points to a null-terminated character string. Specifies the filename of the metafile to create. If *lpszFilename* is **NULL**, a new in-memory metafile is created.

Remarks

Construct a **CMetaFileDC** object in two steps. First, call the constructor **CMetaFileDC**, then call **Create**, which creates the Windows metafile device context and attaches it to the **CMetaFileDC** object.

See Also   **CMetaFileDC::CMetaFileDC**, **CDC::SetAttribDC**, **::CreateMetaFile**

CMetaFileDC::CreateEnhanced

BOOL CreateEnhanced(CDC* *pDCRef*, **LPCTSTR** *lpszFileName*, **LPCRECT** *lpBounds*, **LPCTSTR** *lpszDescription*);

Return Value

A handle of the device context for the enhanced metafile, if successful; otherwise **NULL**.

Parameters

pDCRef   Identifies a reference device for the enhanced metafile.

lpszFileName   Points to a null-terminated character string. Specifies the filename for the enhanced metafile to be created. If this parameter is **NULL**, the enhanced metafile is memory based and its contents lost when the object is destroyed or when the **::DeleteEnhMetaFile** function is called.

lpBounds   Points to a **RECT** data structure or a **CRect** object that specifies the dimensions in **HIMETRIC** units (in .01-millimeter increments) of the picture to be stored in the enhanced metafile.

lpszDescription   Points to a zero-terminated string that specifies the name of the application that created the picture, as well as the picture's title.

Remarks

Creates a device context for an enhanced-format metafile. This DC can be used to store a device-independent picture.

Windows uses the reference device identified by the *pDCRef* parameter to record the resolution and units of the device on which a picture originally appeared. If the *pDCRef* parameter is **NULL**, it uses the current display device for reference.

The left and top members of the **RECT** data structure pointed to by the *lpBounds* parameter must be smaller than the right and bottom members, respectively. Points along the edges of the rectangle are included in the picture. If *lpBounds* is **NULL**, the graphics device interface (GDI) computes the dimensions of the smallest rectangle that can enclose the picture drawn by the application. The *lpBounds* parameter should be supplied where possible.

The string pointed to by the *lpszDescription* parameter must contain a null character between the application name and the picture name and must terminate with two null characters —for example, "XYZ Graphics Editor\0Bald Eagle\0\0," where \0 represents the null character. If *lpszDescription* is **NULL**, there is no corresponding entry in the enhanced-metafile header.

Applications use the DC created by this function to store a graphics picture in an enhanced metafile. The handle identifying this DC can be passed to any GDI function.

After an application stores a picture in an enhanced metafile, it can display the picture on any output device by calling the **CDC::PlayMetaFile** function. When displaying the picture, Windows uses the rectangle pointed to by the *lpBounds* parameter and the resolution data from the reference device to position and scale the picture. The device context returned by this function contains the same default attributes associated with any new DC.

Applications must use the **::GetWinMetaFileBits** function to convert an enhanced metafile to the older Windows metafile format.

The filename for the enhanced metafile should use the .EMF extension.

See Also **CMetaFileDC::CloseEnhanced**, **CDC::PlayMetaFile**, **::CloseEnhMetaFile**, **::DeleteEnhMetaFile**, **::GetEnhMetaFileDescription**, **::GetEnhMetaFileHeader**, **::GetWinMetaFileBits**, **::PlayEnhMetaFile**

CMiniFrameWnd

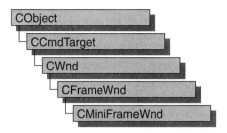

A **CMiniFrameWnd** object represents a half-height frame window typically seen around floating toolbars. These mini-frame windows behave like normal frame windows, except that they do not have minimize/maximize buttons or menus and you only have to single-click on the system menu to dismiss them.

To use a **CMiniFrameWnd** object, first define the object. Then call the **Create** member function to display the mini-frame window.

For more information on how to use **CMiniFrameWnd** objects, see the article "Toolbars: Docking and Floating" in *Programming with MFC*.

#include <afxwin.h>

See Also   **CFrameWnd**

Construction

CMiniFrameWnd	Constructs a **CMiniFrameWnd** object.
Create	Creates a **CMiniFrameWnd** object after construction.

Member Functions

CMiniFrameWnd::CMiniFrameWnd

CMiniFrameWnd( );

Remarks

Constructs a **CMiniFrameWnd** object, but does not create the window. To create the window, call **CMiniFrameWnd::Create**.

See Also   **CFrameWnd**

CMiniFrameWnd::Create

BOOL Create(LPCTSTR *lpClassName*, **LPCTSTR** *lpWindowName*, **DWORD** *dwStyle*, **const RECT&** *rect*, **CWnd*** *pParentWnd* = **NULL, UINT** *nID* = **0);**

Return Value

Nonzero if successful; otherwise 0.

Parameters

lpClassName   Points to a null-terminated character string that names the Windows class. The class name can be any name registered with the global **AfxRegisterWndClass** function. If **NULL**, the window class will be registered for you by the framework.

lpWindowName   Points to a null-terminated character string that contains the window name.

dwStyle   Specifies the window style attributes. These can include standard window styles and one or more of the following special styles:

- **MFS_MOVEFRAME**   Allows the mini-frame window to be moved by clicking on any edge of the window, not just the caption.

- **MFS_4THICKFRAME**   Disables resizing of the mini-frame window.

- **MFS_SYNCACTIVE**   Synchronizes the activation of the mini-frame window to the activation of its parent window.

- **MFS_THICKFRAME**   Allows the mini-frame window to be sized as small as the contents of the client area allow.

  See **CWnd::Create** for a description of possible window style values. The typical combination used for mini-frame windows is **WS_POPUP|WS_CAPTION|WS_SYSMENU**.

rect   A **RECT** structure specifying the desired dimensions of the window.

pParentWnd   Points to the parent window. Use **NULL** for top-level windows.

nID   If the mini-frame window is created as a child window, this is the identifier of the child control; otherwise 0.

Remarks

Creates the Windows mini-frame window and attaches it to the **CMiniFrameWnd** object. **Create** initializes the window's class name and window name and registers default values for its style and parent.

See Also   **CFrameWnd::Create**, **CWnd::Create**, **CWnd::CreateEx**, **CFrameWnd**

CMultiDocTemplate

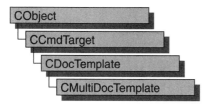

The **CMultiDocTemplate** class defines a document template that implements the multiple document interface (MDI). An MDI application uses the main frame window as a workspace in which the user can open zero or more document frame windows, each of which displays a document. For a more detailed description of the MDI, see *The Windows Interface: An Application Design Guide*.

A document template defines the relationships among three types of classes:

- A document class, which you derive from **CDocument**.

- A view class, which displays data from the document class listed above. You can derive this class from **CView**, **CScrollView**, **CFormView**, or **CEditView**. (You can also use **CEditView** directly.)

- A frame window class, which contains the view. For an MDI document template, you can derive this class from **CMDIChildWnd**, or, if you don't need to customize the behavior of the document frame windows, you can use **CMDIChildWnd** directly without deriving your own class.

An MDI application can support more than one type of document, and documents of different types can be open at the same time. Your application has one document template for each document type that it supports. For example, if your MDI application supports both spreadsheets and text documents, the application has two **CMultiDocTemplate** objects.

The application uses the document template(s) when the user creates a new document. If the application supports more than one type of document, then the framework gets the names of the supported document types from the document templates and displays them in a list in the File New dialog box. Once the user has selected a document type, the application creates a document object, a frame window object, and a view object and attaches them to each other.

You do not need to call any member functions of **CMultiDocTemplate** except the constructor. The framework handles **CMultiDocTemplate** objects internally.

For more information on **CMultiDocTemplate**, see "Document Templates" in Chapter 1 of *Programming with MFC*.

include# <afxwin.h>

See Also   **CDocTemplate, CDocument, CMDIChildWnd, CSingleDocTemplate, CView, CWinApp**

Construction

CMultiDocTemplate   Constructs a **CMultiDocTemplate** object.

Member Functions

CMultiDocTemplate::CMultiDocTemplate

CMultiDocTemplate(UINT *nIDResource*, **CRuntimeClass*** *pDocClass*, **CRuntimeClass*** *pFrameClass*, **CRuntimeClass*** *pViewClass* **);**

Parameters

nIDResource   Specifies the ID of the resources used with the document type. This may include menu, icon, accelerator table, and string resources.

The string resource consists of up to seven substrings separated by the '\n' character (the '\n' character is needed as a place holder if a substring is not included; however, trailing '\n' characters are not necessary); these substrings describe the document type. For information on the substrings, see **CDocTemplate::GetDocString**. This string resource is found in the application's resource file. For example:

```
// MYCALC.RC
STRINGTABLE PRELOAD DISCARDABLE
BEGIN
    IDR_SHEETTYPE "\nSheet\nWorksheet\nWorksheets (*.myc)\n.myc\n
MyCalcSheet\nMyCalc Worksheet"
END
```

Note that the string begins with a '\n' character; this is because the first substring is not used for MDI applications and so is not included. You can edit this string using the string editor; the entire string appears as a single entry in the String Editor, not as seven separate entries.

For more information about these resource types, see the *Visual C++ User's Guide*, Chapter 5, "Working with Resources."

pDocClass   Points to the **CRuntimeClass** object of the document class. This class is a **CDocument**-derived class you define to represent your documents.

pFrameClass   Points to the **CRuntimeClass** object of the frame-window class. This
class can be a **CMDIChildWnd**-derived class, or it can be **CMDIChildWnd** itself
if you want default behavior for your document frame windows.

pViewClass   Points to the **CRuntimeClass** object of the view class. This class is a
CView-derived class you define to display your documents.

Remarks

Constructs a **CMultiDocTemplate** object. Dynamically allocate one
CMultiDocTemplate object for each document type that your application supports
and pass each one to **CWinApp::AddDocTemplate** from the `InitInstance` member
function of your application class.

Example

```
//example for CMultiDocTemplate
BOOL CMyApp::InitInstance()
{
        // ...
        // Establish all of the document types
        // supported by the application

        AddDocTemplate( new CMultiDocTemplate( IDR_SHEETTYPE,
                             RUNTIME_CLASS( CSheetDoc ),
                             RUNTIME_CLASS( CMDIChildWnd ),
                             RUNTIME_CLASS( CSheetView ) ) );

        AddDocTemplate( new CMultiDocTemplate( IDR_NOTETYPE,
                             RUNTIME_CLASS( CNoteDoc ),
                             RUNTIME_CLASS( CMDIChildWnd ),
                             RUNTIME_CLASS( CNoteView ) ) );
        // ...
}
```

See Also   **CDocTemplate::GetDocString**, **CWinApp::AddDocTemplate**,
CWinApp::InitInstance, **CRuntimeClass**

CMultiLock

A object of class **CMultiLock** represents the access-control mechanism used in controlling access to resources in a multithreaded program. To use the synchronization classes **CSemaphore**, **CMutex**, **CCriticalSection**, and **CEvent**, you can create either a **CMultiLock** or **CSingleLock** object to wait on and release the synchronization object. Use **CMultiLock** when there are multiple objects that you could use at a particular time. Use **CSingleLock** when you only need to wait on one object at a time.

To use a **CMultiLock** object, first create an array of the synchronization objects that you wish to wait on. Next, call the **CMultiLock** object's constructor inside a member function in the controlled resource's class. Then call the **Lock** member function to determine if a resource is available (signaled). If one is, continue with the remainder of the member function. If no resource is available, either wait for a specified amount of time for a resource to be released, or return failure. After use of a resource is complete, either call the **Unlock** function if the **CMultiLock** object is to be used again, or allow the **CMultiLock** object to be destroyed.

CMultiLock objects are most useful when a thread has a large number of **CEvent** objects it can respond to. Create an array containing all the **CEvent** pointers, and call **Lock**. This will cause the thread to wait until one of the events is signaled.

For more information on how to use **CMultiLock** objects, see the article "Multithreading: How to Use the Synchronization Classes" in *Programming with MFC*.

#include <afxmt.h>

Construction

CMultiLock	Constructs a **CMultiLock** object.

Methods

IsLocked	Determines if a specific synchronization object in the array is locked.
Lock	Waits on the array of synchronization objects.
Unlock	Releases any owned synchronization objects.

Member Functions

CMultiLock::CMultiLock

CMultiLock(CSyncObject* *ppObjects*[ ], **DWORD** *dwCount*, **BOOL** *bInitialLock* = **FALSE**);

Parameters

ppObjects   Array of pointers to the synchronization objects to be waited on. Cannot be **NULL**.

dwCount   Number of objects in *ppObjects*. Must be greater than 0.

bInitialLock   Specifies whether to initially attempt to access any of the supplied objects.

Remarks

Constructs a **CMultiLock** object. This function is called after creating the array of synchronization objects to be waited on. It is usually called from within the thread that must wait for one of the synchronization objects to become available.

CMultiLock::IsLocked

BOOL IsLocked(DWORD *dwObject*);

Return Value

Nonzero if the specified object is locked; otherwise 0.

Parameters

dwObject   The index in the array of objects corresponding to the object whose state is being queried.

Remarks

Determines if the specified object is nonsignaled (unavailable).

CMultiLock::Lock

DWORD Lock(DWORD *dwTimeOut* = **INFINITE, BOOL** *bWaitForAll* = **TRUE,**
   DWORD *dwWakeMask* = **0**);

Return Value

If **Lock** fails, it returns −1. If successful, it returns one of the following values:

- Between **WAIT_OBJECT_0** and **WAIT_OBJECT_0** + (number of objects − 1)

  If *bWaitForAll* is **TRUE**, all objects are signaled (available). If *bWaitForAll* is **FALSE**, the return value − **WAIT_OBJECT_0** is the index in the array of objects of the object that is signaled (available).

- **WAIT_OBJECT_0** + (number of objects)

  An event specified in *dwWakeMask* is available in the thread's input queue.

- Between **WAIT_ABANDONED_0** and **WAIT_ABANDONED_0** + (number of objects − 1)

  If *bWaitForAll* is **TRUE**, all objects are signaled, and at least one of the objects is an abandoned mutex object. If *bWaitForAll* is **FALSE**, the return value − **WAIT_ABANDONED_0** is the index in the array of objects of the abandoned mutex object that satisfied the wait.

- **WAIT_TIMEOUT**

  The timeout interval specified in *dwTimeOut* expired without the wait succeeding.

Parameters

dwTimeOut   Specifies the amount of time to wait for the synchronization object to be available (signaled). If **INFINITE**, **Lock** will wait until the object is signaled before returning.

bWaitForAll   Specifies whether all objects waited on must become signaled at the same time before returning. If **FALSE**, **Lock** will return when any one of the objects waited on is signaled.

dwWakeMask   Specifies other conditions that are allowed to abort the wait. For a full list of the available options for this parameter, see **MsgWaitForMultipleObjects** in the *Win32 Programmer's Reference*.

Remarks

Call this function to gain access to one or more of the resources controlled by the synchronization objects supplied to the **CMultiLock** constructor. If *bWaitForAll* is **TRUE**, **Lock** will return successfully as soon as all the synchronization objects become signaled simultaneously. If *bWaitForAll* is **FALSE**, **Lock** will return as soon as one or more of the synchronization objects becomes signaled.

If **Lock** is not able to return immediately, it will wait for no more than the number of milliseconds specified in the *dwTimeOut* parameter before returning. If *dwTimeOut* is **INFINITE**, **Lock** will not return until access to an object is gained or a condition specified in *dwWakeMask* was met. Otherwise, if **Lock** was able to acquire a synchronization object, it will return successfully; if not, it will return failure.

CMultiLock::Unlock

BOOL Unlock( );
BOOL Unlock(LONG *lCount*, **LPLONG** *lPrevCount* = **NULL);**

Return Value

Nonzero if the function was successful; otherwise 0.

Parameters

lCount   Number of reference counts to release. Must be greater than 0. If the specified amount would cause the object's count to exceed its maximum, the count is not changed and the function returns **FALSE**.

lPrevCount   Points to a variable to receive the previous count for the synchronization object. If **NULL**, the previous count is not returned.

Remarks

Releases the synchronization object owned by **CMultiLock**. This function is called by **CMultiLock**'s destructor.

CMutex

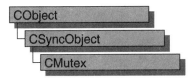

An object of class **CMutex** represents a "mutex"—a synchronization object that allows one thread mutually exclusive access to a resource. Mutexes are useful when only one thread at a time can be allowed to modify data or some other controlled resource. For example, adding nodes to a linked list is a process that should only be allowed by one thread at a time. By using a **CMutex** object to control the linked list, only one thread at a time can gain access to the list.

To use a **CMutex** object, construct the **CMutex** object when it is needed. Specify the name of the mutex you wish to wait on, and that your application should initially own it. You can then access the mutex when the constructor returns. Call **CSyncObject::Unlock** when you are done accessing the controlled resource.

An alternative method for using **CMutex** objects is to add a variable of type **CMutex** as a data member to the class you wish to control. During construction of the controlled object, call the constructor of the **CMutex** data member specifying if the mutex is initially owned, the name of the mutex (if it will be used across process boundaries), and desired security attributes.

To access resources controlled by **CMutex** objects in this manner, first create a variable of either type **CSingleLock** or type **CMultiLock** in your resource's access member function. Then call the lock object's **Lock** member function (for example, **CSingleLock::Lock**). At this point, your thread will either gain access to the resource, wait for the resource to be released and gain access, or wait for the resource to be released and time out, failing to gain access to the resource. In any case, your resource has been accessed in a thread-safe manner. To release the resource, use the lock object's **Unlock** member function (for example, **CSingleLock::Unlock**), or allow the lock object to fall out of scope.

For more information on using **CMutex** objects, see the article "Multithreading: How to Use the Synchronization Classes" in *Programming with MFC*.

#include <afxmt.h>

Construction

CMutex	Constructs a **CMutex** object.

Member Functions

CMutex::CMutex

CMutex(BOOL *bInitiallyOwn* **= FALSE, LPCTSTR** *lpszName* **= NULL,
LPSECURITY_ATTRIBUTES** *lpsaAttribute* **= NULL);**

Parameters

bInitiallyOwn   Specifies if the thread creating the **CMutex** object initially has access
to the resource controlled by the mutex.

lpszName   Name of the **CMutex** object. If another mutex with the same name exists,
lpszName must be supplied if the object will be used across process boundaries. If
NULL, the mutex will be unnamed. If the name matches an existing mutex, the
constructor builds a new **CMutex** object which references the mutex of that name.
If the name matches an existing synchronization object that is not a mutex, the
construction will fail.

lpsaAttribute   Security attributes for the mutex object. For a full description of this
structure, see **SECURITY_ATTRIBUTES** in the *Win32 Programmer's
Reference*.

Remarks

Constructs a named or unnamed **CMutex** object. To access or release a **CMutex**
object, create a **CMultiLock** or **CSingleLock** object and call its **Lock** and **Unlock**
member functions. If the **CMutex** object is being used stand-alone, call its **Unlock**
member function to release it.

CNotSupportedException

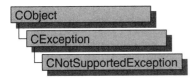

A **CNotSupportedException** object represents an exception that is the result of a request for an unsupported feature. No further qualification is necessary or possible.

For more information on using **CNotSupportedException**, see the article "Exceptions" in *Programming with MFC*.

#include <afx.h>

Construction

CNotSupportedException	Constructs a **CNotSupportedException** object.

Member Functions

CNotSupportedException::CNotSupportedException

CNotSupportedException( );

Remarks

Constructs a **CNotSupportedException** object.

Do not use this constructor directly, but rather call the global function **AfxThrowNotSupportedException**. For more information about exception processing, see the article "Exceptions" in *Programming with MFC*.

See Also   **AfxThrowNotSupportedException**

CObArray

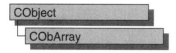

The **CObArray** class supports arrays of **CObject** pointers. These object arrays are similar to C arrays, but they can dynamically shrink and grow as necessary.

Array indexes always start at position 0. You can decide whether to fix the upper bound or allow the array to expand when you add elements past the current bound. Memory is allocated contiguously to the upper bound, even if some elements are null.

Under Win32, the size of a **CObArray** object is limited only to available memory.

As with a C array, the access time for a **CObArray** indexed element is constant and is independent of the array size.

CObArray incorporates the **IMPLEMENT_SERIAL** macro to support serialization and dumping of its elements. If an array of **CObject** pointers is stored to an archive, either with the overloaded insertion operator or with the **Serialize** member function, each **CObject** element is, in turn, serialized along with its array index.

If you need a dump of individual **CObject** elements in an array, you must set the depth of the **CDumpContext** object to 1 or greater.

When a **CObArray** object is deleted, or when its elements are removed, only the **CObject** pointers are removed, not the objects they reference.

Note Before using an array, use **SetSize** to establish its size and allocate memory for it. If you do not use **SetSize**, adding elements to your array causes it to be frequently reallocated and copied. Frequent reallocation and copying are inefficient and can fragment memory.

Array class derivation is similar to list derivation. For details on the derivation of a special-purpose list class, see the article "Collections" in *Programming with MFC*.

Note You must use the **IMPLEMENT_SERIAL** macro in the implementation of your derived class if you intend to serialize the array.

#include <afxcoll.h>

See Also   CStringArray, CPtrArray, CByteArray, CWordArray, CDWordArray

Construction	
CObArray	Constructs an empty array for **CObject** pointers.

Bounds	
GetSize	Gets the number of elements in this array.
GetUpperBound	Returns the largest valid index.
SetSize	Sets the number of elements to be contained in this array.

Operations	
FreeExtra	Frees all unused memory above the current upper bound.
RemoveAll	Removes all the elements from this array.

Element Access	
GetAt	Returns the value at a given index.
SetAt	Sets the value for a given index; array not allowed to grow.
ElementAt	Returns a temporary reference to the element pointer within the array.

Growing the Array	
SetAtGrow	Sets the value for a given index; grows the array if necessary.
Add	Adds an element to the end of the array; grows the array if necessary.

Insertion/Removal	
InsertAt	Inserts an element (or all the elements in another array) at a specified index.
RemoveAt	Removes an element at a specific index.

Operators	
operator []	Sets or gets the element at the specified index.

Member Functions

CObArray::Add

> **int Add(CObject*** *newElement* **);**
> **throw(CMemoryException);**

Return Value

The index of the added element.

Parameters

newElement   The **CObject** pointer to be added to this array.

Remarks

Adds a new element to the end of an array, growing the array by 1. If **SetSize** has been used with an *nGrowBy* value greater than 1, then extra memory may be allocated. However, the upper bound will increase by only 1.

Example

```
// example for CObArray::Add
    CObArray array;

    array.Add( new CAge( 21 ) ); // Element 0
    array.Add( new CAge( 40 ) ); // Element 1
#ifdef _DEBUG
    afxDump.SetDepth( 1 );
    afxDump << "Add example: " << &array << "\n";
#endif
```

The results from this program are as follows:

```
Add example: A CObArray with 2 elements
    [0] = a CAge at $442A 21
    [1] = a CAge at $4468 40
```

See Also   **CObArray::SetAt**, **CObArray::SetAtGrow**, **CObArray::InsertAt**, **CObArray::operator []**

CObArray::CObArray

CObArray( );

Remarks

Constructs an empty **CObject** pointer array. The array grows one element at a time.

Example

```
CObArray array(20); //Array on the stack with blocksize = 20
CObArray* pArray = new CObArray; //Array on the heap with default blocksize
```

See Also   **CObList::CObList**

CObArray::ElementAt

CObject*& ElementAt(int *nIndex*);

Return Value

A reference to a **CObject** pointer.

Parameters

nIndex An integer index that is greater than or equal to 0 and less than or equal to the value returned by **GetUpperBound**.

Remarks

Returns a temporary reference to the element pointer within the array. It is used to implement the left-side assignment operator for arrays. Note that this is an advanced function that should be used only to implement special array operators.

See Also **CObArray::operator []**

CObArray::FreeExtra

void FreeExtra( );

Remarks

Frees any extra memory that was allocated while the array was grown. This function has no effect on the size or upper bound of the array.

CObArray::GetAt

CObject* GetAt(int *nIndex* **) const;**

Return Value

The **CObject** pointer element currently at this index; **NULL** if no element is stored at the index.

Parameters

nIndex An integer index that is greater than or equal to 0 and less than or equal to the value returned by **GetUpperBound**.

Remarks

Returns the array element at the specified index.

Example

```
// example for CObArray::GetAt
CObArray array;

array.Add( new CAge( 21 ) ); // Element 0
array.Add( new CAge( 40 ) ); // Element 1
ASSERT( *(CAge*) array.GetAt( 0 ) == CAge( 21 ) );
```

See Also **CObArray::SetAt**, **CObArray::operator []**

CObArray::GetSize

int GetSize( ) const;

Remarks

Returns the size of the array. Since indexes are zero-based, the size is 1 greater than the largest index.

See Also **CObArray::GetUpperBound**, **CObArray::SetSize**

CObArray::GetUpperBound

int GetUpperBound( ) const;

Return Value

The index of the upper bound (zero-based).

Remarks

Returns the current upper bound of this array. Because array indexes are zero-based, this function returns a value 1 less than **GetSize**.

The condition **GetUpperBound( )** = –1 indicates that the array contains no elements.

Example

```
// example for CObArray::GetUpperBound
CObArray array;

array.Add( new CAge( 21 ) ); // Element 0
array.Add( new CAge( 40 ) ); // Element 1
ASSERT( array.GetUpperBound() == 1 ); // Largest index
```

See Also **CObArray::GetSize**, **CObArray::SetSize**

CObArray::InsertAt

void InsertAt(int *nIndex*, **CObject*** *newElement*, **int** *nCount* = **1**);
throw(CMemoryException);
void InsertAt(int *nStartIndex*, **CObArray*** *pNewArray*);
throw(CMemoryException);

Parameters

nIndex   An integer index that may be greater than the value returned by **GetUpperBound**.

newElement   The **CObject** pointer to be placed in this array. A *newElement* of value **NULL** is allowed.

nCount   The number of times this element should be inserted (defaults to 1).

nStartIndex   An integer index that may be greater than the value returned by **GetUpperBound**.

pNewArray   Another array that contains elements to be added to this array.

Remarks

The first version of **InsertAt** inserts one element (or multiple copies of an element) at a specified index in an array. In the process, it shifts up (by incrementing the index) the existing element at this index, and it shifts up all the elements above it.

The second version inserts all the elements from another **CObArray** collection, starting at the *nStartIndex* position.

The **SetAt** function, in contrast, replaces one specified array element and does not shift any elements.

Example

```
// example for CObArray::InsertAt
    CObArray array;

    array.Add( new CAge( 21 ) ); // Element 0
    array.Add( new CAge( 40 ) ); // Element 1 (will become 2).
    array.InsertAt( 1, new CAge( 30 ) );  // New element 1
#ifdef _DEBUG
    afxDump.SetDepth( 1 );
    afxDump << "InsertAt example: " << &array << "\n";
#endif
```

The results from this program are as follows:

```
InsertAt example: A CObArray with 3 elements
    [0] = a CAge at $45C8 21
    [1] = a CAge at $4646 30
    [2] = a CAge at $4606 40
```

See Also   **CObArray::SetAt**, **CObArray::RemoveAt**

CObArray::RemoveAll

void RemoveAll( );

Remarks

Removes all the pointers from this array but does not actually delete the **CObject** objects. If the array is already empty, the function still works.

The **RemoveAll** function frees all memory used for pointer storage.

Example

```
// example for CObArray::RemoveAll
CObArray array;
CAge* pa1;
CAge* pa2;

array.Add( pa1 = new CAge( 21 ) ); // Element 0
array.Add( pa2 = new CAge( 40 ) ); // Element 1
ASSERT( array.GetSize() == 2 );
array.RemoveAll(); // Pointers removed but objects not deleted.
ASSERT( array.GetSize() == 0 );
delete pa1;
delete pa2;  // Cleans up memory.
```

CObArray::RemoveAt

void RemoveAt(int *nIndex,* **int** *nCount* **= 1);**

Parameters

nIndex   An integer index that is greater than or equal to 0 and less than or equal to the value returned by **GetUpperBound**.

nCount   The number of elements to remove.

Remarks

Removes one or more elements starting at a specified index in an array. In the process, it shifts down all the elements above the removed element(s). It decrements the upper bound of the array but does not free memory.

If you try to remove more elements than are contained in the array above the removal point, then the Debug version of the library asserts.

The **RemoveAt** function removes the **CObject** pointer from the array, but it does not delete the object itself.

Example

```
// example for CObArray::RemoveAt
   CObArray array;
   CObject* pa;

   array.Add( new CAge( 21 ) ); // Element 0
   array.Add( new CAge( 40 ) ); // Element 1
   if( ( pa = array.GetAt( 0 ) ) != NULL )
   {
       array.RemoveAt( 0 );  // Element 1 moves to 0.
       delete pa; // Delete the original element at 0.
   }
#ifdef _DEBUG
   afxDump.SetDepth( 1 );
   afxDump << "RemoveAt example: " << &array << "\n";
#endif
```

The results from this program are as follows:

```
RemoveAt example: A CObArray with 1 elements
    [0] = a CAge at $4606 40
```

See Also **CObArray::SetAt, CObArray::SetAtGrow, CObArray::InsertAt**

CObArray::SetAt

void SetAt(int *nIndex*, **CObject*** *newElement* **);**

Parameters

nIndex   An integer index that is greater than or equal to 0 and less than or equal to the value returned by **GetUpperBound**.

newElement   The object pointer to be inserted in this array. A **NULL** value is allowed.

Remarks

Sets the array element at the specified index. **SetAt** will not cause the array to grow. Use **SetAtGrow** if you want the array to grow automatically.

You must ensure that your index value represents a valid position in the array. If it is out of bounds, then the Debug version of the library asserts.

Example

```
// example for CObArray::SetAt
    CObArray array;
    CObject* pa;

    array.Add( new CAge( 21 ) ); // Element 0
    array.Add( new CAge( 40 ) ); // Element 1
    if( ( pa = array.GetAt( 0 ) ) != NULL )
    {
        array.SetAt( 0, new CAge( 30 ) );  // Replace element 0.
        delete pa; // Delete the original element at 0.
    }
#ifdef _DEBUG
    afxDump.SetDepth( 1 );
    afxDump << "SetAt example: " << &array << "\n";
#endif
```

The results from this program are as follows:

```
SetAt example: A CObArray with 2 elements
    [0] = a CAge at $47E0 30
    [1] = a CAge at $47A0 40
```

See Also **CObArray::GetAt, CObArray::SetAtGrow, CObArray::ElementAt, CObArray::operator []**

CObArray::SetAtGrow

void SetAtGrow(int *nIndex*, **CObject*** *newElement* **);**
   throw(CMemoryException);

Parameters

nIndex   An integer index that is greater than or equal to 0.

newElement   The object pointer to be added to this array. A **NULL** value is allowed.

Remarks

Sets the array element at the specified index. The array grows automatically if necessary (that is, the upper bound is adjusted to accommodate the new element).

Example

```
// example for CObArray::SetAtGrow
   CObArray array;

   array.Add( new CAge( 21 ) ); // Element 0
   array.Add( new CAge( 40 ) ); // Element 1
   array.SetAtGrow( 3, new CAge( 65 ) ); // Element 2 deliberately
                                          // skipped.
#ifdef _DEBUG
   afxDump.SetDepth( 1 );
   afxDump << "SetAtGrow example: " << &array << "\n";
#endif
```

The results from this program are as follows:

```
SetAtGrow example: A CObArray with 4 elements
    [0] = a CAge at $47C0 21
    [1] = a CAge at $4800 40
    [2] = NULL
    [3] = a CAge at $4840 65
```

See Also   CObArray::GetAt, CObArray::SetAt, CObArray::ElementAt, CObArray::operator []

CObArray::SetSize

void SetSize(int *nNewSize*, **int** *nGrowBy* = **–1);**
   throw(CMemoryException);

Parameters

nNewSize   The new array size (number of elements). Must be greater than or equal to 0.

nGrowBy   The minimum number of element slots to allocate if a size increase is necessary.

Remarks

Establishes the size of an empty or existing array; allocates memory if necessary. If the new size is smaller than the old size, then the array is truncated and all unused memory is released. For efficiency, call **SetSize** to set the size of the array before using it. This prevents the need to reallocate and copy the array each time an item is added.

The *nGrowBy* parameter affects internal memory allocation while the array is growing. Its use never affects the array size as reported by **GetSize** and **GetUpperBound**.

Operators

CObArray::operator [ ]

CObject*& operator [ ](int *nIndex* **);**
CObject* operator [ ](int *nIndex* **) const;**

Remarks

These subscript operators are a convenient substitute for the **SetAt** and **GetAt** functions.

The first operator, called for arrays that are not **const**, may be used on either the right (r-value) or the left (l-value) of an assignment statement. The second, called for **const** arrays, may be used only on the right.

The Debug version of the library asserts if the subscript (either on the left or right side of an assignment statement) is out of bounds.

Example

```
// example for CObArray::operator []
CObArray array;
CAge* pa;

array.Add( new CAge( 21 ) ); // Element 0
array.Add( new CAge( 40 ) ); // Element 1
pa = (CAge*)array[0]; // Get element 0
ASSERT( *pa == CAge( 21 ) ); // Get element 0
array[0] = new CAge( 30 ); // Replace element 0
delete pa;
ASSERT( *(CAge*) array[0] == CAge( 30 ) ); // Get new element 0
```

See Also **CObArray::GetAt**, **CObArray::SetAt**

CObject

CObject is the principal base class for the Microsoft Foundation Class Library. It serves as the root not only for library classes such as **CFile** and **CObList**, but also for the classes that you write. **CObject** provides basic services, including

- Serialization support
- Run-time class information
- Object diagnostic output
- Compatibility with collection classes

Note that **CObject** does not support multiple inheritance. Your derived classes can have only one **CObject** base class, and that **CObject** must be leftmost in the hierarchy. It is permissible, however, to have structures and non-**CObject**-derived classes in right-hand multiple-inheritance branches.

You will realize major benefits from **CObject** derivation if you use some of the optional macros in your class implementation and declarations.

The first-level macros, **DECLARE_DYNAMIC** and **IMPLEMENT_DYNAMIC**, permit run-time access to the class name and its position in the hierarchy. This, in turn, allows meaningful diagnostic dumping.

The second-level macros, **DECLARE_SERIAL** and **IMPLEMENT_SERIAL**, include all the functionality of the first-level macros, and they enable an object to be "serialized" to and from an "archive."

For information about deriving Microsoft Foundation classes and C++ classes in general and using **CObject**, see the articles "CObject Class" and "Serialization (Object Persistence)" in *Programming with MFC*.

#include <afx.h>

Construction

CObject	Default constructor.
CObject	Copy constructor.
operator new	Special **new** operator.
operator delete	Special **delete** operator.
operator =	Assignment operator.

Diagnostics

AssertValid	Validates this object's integrity.
Dump	Produces a diagnostic dump of this object.

Serialization	
IsSerializable	Tests to see whether this object can be serialized.
Serialize	Loads or stores an object from/to an archive.

Miscellaneous	
GetRuntimeClass	Returns the **CRuntimeClass** structure corresponding to this object's class.
IsKindOf	Tests this object's relationship to a given class.

Member Functions

CObject::AssertValid

virtual void AssertValid( ) const;

Remarks

AssertValid performs a validity check on this object by checking its internal state. In the Debug version of the library, **AssertValid** may assert and thus terminate the program with a message that lists the line number and filename where the assertion failed.

When you write your own class, you should override the **AssertValid** function to provide diagnostic services for yourself and other users of your class. The overridden **AssertValid** usually calls the **AssertValid** function of its base class before checking data members unique to the derived class.

Because **AssertValid** is a **const** function, you are not permitted to change the object state during the test. Your own derived class **AssertValid** functions should not throw exceptions but rather should assert whether they detect invalid object data.

The definition of "validity" depends on the object's class. As a rule, the function should perform a "shallow check." That is, if an object contains pointers to other objects, it should check to see whether the pointers are not null, but it should not perform validity testing on the objects referred to by the pointers.

Example

```
// example for CObject::AssertValid
```

See **CObList::CObList** for a listing of the CAge class used in all **CObject** examples.

```
void CAge::AssertValid() const
{
    CObject::AssertValid();
    ASSERT( m_years > 0 );
    ASSERT( m_years < 105 );
}
```

CObject::CObject

CObject( );
CObject(constCObject& *objectSrc* **);**

Parameters

objectSrc   A reference to another **CObject**

Remarks

These functions are the standard **CObject** constructors. The default version is automatically called by the constructor of your derived class.

If your class is serializable (it incorporates the **IMPLEMENT_SERIAL** macro), then you must have a default constructor (a constructor with no arguments) in your class declaration. If you do not need a default constructor, declare a private or protected "empty" constructor. For more information, see the article "CObject Class" in *Programming with MFC*.

The standard C++ default class copy constructor does a member-by-member copy. The presence of the private **CObject** copy constructor guarantees a compiler error message if the copy constructor of your class is needed but not available. You must therefore provide a copy constructor if your class requires this capability.

CObject::Dump

virtual void Dump(CDumpContext& *dc* **) const;**

Parameters

dc   The diagnostic dump context for dumping, usually **afxDump**.

Remarks

Dumps the contents of your object to a **CDumpContext** object.

When you write your own class, you should override the **Dump** function to provide diagnostic services for yourself and other users of your class. The overridden **Dump** usually calls the **Dump** function of its base class before printing data members unique to the derived class. **CObject::Dump** prints the class name if your class uses the **IMPLEMENT_DYNAMIC** or **IMPLEMENT_SERIAL** macro.

Note   Your **Dump** function should not print a newline character at the end of its output.

Dump calls make sense only in the Debug version of the Microsoft Foundation Class Library. You should bracket calls, function declarations, and function implementations with **#ifdef _DEBUG/#endif** statements for conditional compilation.

Since **Dump** is a **const** function, you are not permitted to change the object state during the dump.

The **CDumpContext insertion (<<) operator** calls **Dump** when a **CObject** pointer is inserted.

Dump permits only "acyclic" dumping of objects. You can dump a list of objects, for example, but if one of the objects is the list itself, you will eventually overflow the stack.

Example
```
// example for CObject::Dump
void CAge::Dump( CDumpContext &dc ) const
 {
 CObject::Dump( dc );
 dc << "Age = " << m_years;
 }
```

CObject::GetRuntimeClass

virtual CRuntimeClass* GetRuntimeClass( ) const;

Return Value

A pointer to the **CRuntimeClass** structure corresponding to this object's class; never **NULL**.

Remarks

There is one **CRuntimeClass** structure for each **CObject**-derived class. The structure members are as follows:

- **const char* m_pszClassName**   A null-terminated string containing the ASCII class name.
- **int m_nObjectSize**   The actual size of the object. If the object has data members that point to allocated memory, the size of that memory is not included.
- **WORD m_wSchema**   The schema number (–1 for nonserializable classes). See the **IMPLEMENT_SERIAL** macro for a description of schema number.
- **void (*m_pfnConstruct)(void* p)**   A pointer to the default constructor of your class (valid only if the class is serializable).
- **CRuntimeClass* m_pBaseClass**   A pointer to the **CRuntimeClass** structure that corresponds to the base class.

This function requires use of the **IMPLEMENT_DYNAMIC** or **IMPLEMENT_SERIAL** macro in the class implementation. You will get incorrect results otherwise.

Example

```
// example for CObject::GetRuntimeClass
CAge a(21);
CRuntimeClass* prt = a.GetRuntimeClass();
ASSERT( strcmp( prt->m_pszClassName, "CAge" )  == 0 );
```

See Also   **CObject::IsKindOf**, **RUNTIME_CLASS Macro**

CObject::IsKindOf

BOOL IsKindOf(const CRuntimeClass* *pClass* **) const;**

Return Value

Nonzero if the object corresponds to the class; otherwise 0.

Parameters

pClass   A pointer to a **CRuntimeClass** structure associated with your
   CObject-derived class.

Remarks

Tests *pClass* to see if (1) it is an object of the specified class or (2) it is an object of a
class derived from the specified class. This function works only for classes declared
with the **DECLARE_DYNAMIC** or **DECLARE_SERIAL** macro.

Do not use this function extensively because it defeats the C++ polymorphism
feature. Use virtual functions instead.

Example

```
// example for CObject::IsKindOf
CAge a(21); // Must use IMPLEMENT_DYNAMIC or IMPLEMENT_SERIAL
ASSERT( a.IsKindOf( RUNTIME_CLASS( CAge ) ) );
ASSERT( a.IsKindOf( RUNTIME_CLASS( CObject ) ) );
```

See Also   **CObject::GetRuntimeClass**, **RUNTIME_CLASS**

CObject::IsSerializable

BOOL IsSerializable( ) const;

Return Value

Nonzero if this object can be serialized; otherwise 0.

Remarks

Tests whether this object is eligible for serialization. For a class to be serializable, its
declaration must contain the **DECLARE_SERIAL** macro, and the implementation
must contain the **IMPLEMENT_SERIAL** macro.

Note   Do not override this function.

Example

```
// example for CObject::IsSerializable
CAge a(21);
ASSERT( a.IsSerializable() );
```

See Also **CObject::Serialize**

CObject::Serialize

virtual void Serialize(CArchive& *ar* **);**
   throw(CMemoryException);
   throw(CArchiveException);
   throw(CFileException);

Parameters

ar A **CArchive** object to serialize to or from.

Remarks

Reads or writes this object from or to an archive.

You must override **Serialize** for each class that you intend to serialize. The overridden **Serialize** must first call the **Serialize** function of its base class.

You must also use the **DECLARE_SERIAL** macro in your class declaration, and you must use the **IMPLEMENT_SERIAL** macro in the implementation.

Use **CArchive::IsLoading** or **CArchive::IsStoring** to determine whether the archive is loading or storing.

Serialize is called by **CArchive::ReadObject** and **CArchive::WriteObject**. These functions are associated with the **CArchive** insertion operator (**<<**) and extraction operator (**>>**).

For serialization examples, see the article "Serialization (Object Persistence)" in *Programming with MFC*.

Example

```
// example for CObject::Serialize
void CAge::Serialize( CArchive& ar )
 {
 CObject::Serialize( ar );
    if( ar.IsStoring() )
    ar << m_years;
    else
    ar >> m_years;
 }
```

Operators

CObject::operator =

void operator =(const CObject& *src* **);**

Remarks

The standard C++ default class assignment behavior is a member-by-member copy. The presence of this private assignment operator guarantees a compiler error message if you assign without the overridden operator. You must therefore provide an assignment operator in your derived class if you intend to assign objects of your derived class.

CObject::operator delete

void operator delete(void* *p* **);**

Remarks

For the Release version of the library, operator **delete** simply frees the memory allocated by operator **new**. In the Debug version, operator **delete** participates in an allocation-monitoring scheme designed to detect memory leaks. If you override operators **new** and **delete**, you forfeit the diagnostic capability.

See Also **CObject::operator new**

CObject::operator new

void* operator new(size_t *nSize* **);**
    throw(CMemoryException);
void* operator new(size_t *nSize*, **LPCSTR** *lpszFileName*, **int** *nLine* **);**
    throw(CMemoryException);

Remarks

For the Release version of the library, operator **new** performs an optimal memory allocation in a manner similar to **malloc**. In the Debug version, operator **new** participates in an allocation-monitoring scheme designed to detect memory leaks.

If you use the code line

```
#define new DEBUG_NEW
```

before any of your implementations in a .CPP file, then the second version of **new** will be used, storing the filename and line number in the allocated block for later reporting. You do not have to worry about supplying the extra parameters; a macro takes care of that for you.

Even if you do not use **DEBUG_NEW** in Debug mode, you still get leak detection, but without the source-file line-number reporting described above.

Note If you override this operator, you must also override **delete**. Do not use the standard library **_new_handler** function.

See Also **CObject::operator delete**

CObList

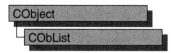

The **CObList** class supports ordered lists of nonunique **CObject** pointers accessible sequentially or by pointer value. **CObList** lists behave like doubly-linked lists.

A variable of type **POSITION** is a key for the list. You can use a **POSITION** variable both as an iterator to traverse a list sequentially and as a bookmark to hold a place. A position is not the same as an index, however.

Element insertion is very fast at the list head, at the tail, and at a known **POSITION**. A sequential search is necessary to look up an element by value or index. This search can be slow if the list is long.

CObList incorporates the **IMPLEMENT_SERIAL** macro to support serialization and dumping of its elements. If a list of **CObject** pointers is stored to an archive, either with an overloaded insertion operator or with the **Serialize** member function, each **CObject** element is serialized in turn.

If you need a dump of individual **CObject** elements in the list, you must set the depth of the dump context to 1 or greater.

When a **CObList** object is deleted, or when its elements are removed, only the **CObject** pointers are removed, not the objects they reference.

You can derive your own classes from **CObList**. Your new list class, designed to hold pointers to objects derived from **CObject**, adds new data members and new member functions. Note that the resulting list is not strictly type safe, because it allows insertion of any **CObject** pointer.

Note   You must use the **IMPLEMENT_SERIAL** macro in the implementation of your derived class if you intend to serialize the list.

For more information on using **CObList**, see the article "Collections" in *Programming with MFC*.

#include <afxcoll.h>

See Also   **CStringList**, **CPtrList**

Construction

CObList	Constructs an empty list for **CObject** pointers.

Head/Tail Access

GetHead	Returns the head element of the list (cannot be empty).
GetTail	Returns the tail element of the list (cannot be empty).

Operations

RemoveHead	Removes the element from the head of the list.
RemoveTail	Removes the element from the tail of the list.
AddHead	Adds an element (or all the elements in another list) to the head of the list (makes a new head).
AddTail	Adds an element (or all the elements in another list) to the tail of the list (makes a new tail).
RemoveAll	Removes all the elements from this list.

Iteration

GetHeadPosition	Returns the position of the head element of the list.
GetTailPosition	Returns the position of the tail element of the list.
GetNext	Gets the next element for iterating.
GetPrev	Gets the previous element for iterating.

Retrieval/Modification

GetAt	Gets the element at a given position.
SetAt	Sets the element at a given position.
RemoveAt	Removes an element from this list, specified by position.

Insertion

InsertBefore	Inserts a new element before a given position.
InsertAfter	Inserts a new element after a given position.

Searching

Find	Gets the position of an element specified by pointer value.
FindIndex	Gets the position of an element specified by a zero-based index.

Status

GetCount	Returns the number of elements in this list.
IsEmpty	Tests for the empty list condition (no elements).

Member Functions

CObList::AddHead

> **POSITION AddHead(CObject*** *newElement* **);**
>   **throw(CMemoryException);**
> **void AddHead(CObList*** *pNewList* **);**
>   **throw(CMemoryException);**

Return Value

The first version returns the **POSITION** value of the newly inserted element.

Parameters

newElement   The **CObject** pointer to be added to this list.

pNewList   A pointer to another **CObList** list. The elements in *pNewList* will be added to this list.

Remarks

Adds a new element or list of elements to the head of this list. The list can be empty before the operation.

Example

```
    CObList list;
    list.AddHead( new CAge( 21 ) ); // 21 is now at head.
    list.AddHead( new CAge( 40 ) ); // 40 replaces 21 at head.
#ifdef _DEBUG
    afxDump.SetDepth( 1 );
    afxDump << "AddHead example: " << &list << "\n";
#endif
```

The results from this program are as follows:

```
AddHead example: A CObList with 2 elements
    a CAge at $44A8 40
    a CAge at $442A 21
```

See Also   **CObList::GetHead**, **CObList::RemoveHead**

CObList::AddTail

> **POSITION AddTail(CObject*** *newElement* **);**
>   **throw(CMemoryException);**
> **void AddTail(CObList*** *pNewList* **);**
>   **throw(CMemoryException);**

Return Value

The first version returns the **POSITION** value of the newly inserted element.

Parameters

newElement   The **CObject** pointer to be added to this list.

pNewList   A pointer to another **CObList** list. The elements in *pNewList* will be added to this list.

Remarks

Adds a new element or list of elements to the tail of this list. The list can be empty before the operation.

Example

```
    CObList list;
    list.AddTail( new CAge( 21 ) );
    list.AddTail( new CAge( 40 ) ); // List now contains (21, 40).
#ifdef _DEBUG
    afxDump.SetDepth( 1 );
    afxDump << "AddTail example: " << &list << "\n";
#endif
```

The results from this program are as follows:

```
AddTail example: A CObList with 2 elements
    a CAge at $444A 21
    a CAge at $4526 40
```

See Also   **CObList::GetTail**, **CObList::RemoveTail**

CObList::CObList

CObList(int *nBlockSize* **= 10);**

Parameters

nBlockSize   The memory-allocation granularity for extending the list.

Remarks

Constructs an empty **CObject** pointer list. As the list grows, memory is allocated in units of *nBlockSize* entries. If a memory allocation fails, a **CMemoryException** is thrown.

Example

Below is a listing of the **CObject**-derived class CAge used in all the collection examples:

```
// Simple CObject-derived class for CObList examples
class CAge : public CObject
{
    DECLARE_SERIAL( CAge )
private:
    int m_years;
public:
    CAge() { m_years = 0; }
    CAge( int age ) { m_years = age; }
```

```
        CAge( const CAge& a ) { m_years = a.m_years; } // Copy constructor
        void Serialize( CArchive& ar );
        void AssertValid() const;
        const CAge& operator=( const CAge& a )
        {
            m_years = a.m_years; return *this;
        }
        BOOL operator==(CAge a)
        {
            return m_years == a.m_years;
        }
    #ifdef _DEBUG
        void Dump( CDumpContext& dc ) const
        {
            CObject::Dump( dc );
            dc << m_years;
        }
    #endif
    };
```

Below is an example of **CObList** constructor usage:

```
CObList list( 20 );  // List on the stack with blocksize = 20.

CObList* plist = new CObList; // List on the heap with default
                             // blocksize.
```

CObList::Find

POSITION Find(CObject* *searchValue***, POSITION** *startAfter* **= NULL) const;**

Return Value

A **POSITION** value that can be used for iteration or object pointer retrieval; **NULL** if the object is not found.

Parameters

searchValue   The object pointer to be found in this list.

startAfter   The start position for the search.

Remarks

Searches the list sequentially to find the first **CObject** pointer matching the specified **CObject** pointer. Note that the pointer values are compared, not the contents of the objects.

Example

```
CObList list;
CAge* pa1;
CAge* pa2;
POSITION pos;
list.AddHead( pa1 = new CAge( 21 ) );
list.AddHead( pa2 = new CAge( 40 ) );    // List now contains (40, 21).
```

```
if( ( pos = list.Find( pal ) ) != NULL ) // Hunt for pal
{                                          // starting at head by default.
    ASSERT( *(CAge*) list.GetAt( pos ) == CAge( 21 ) );
}
```

See Also   **CObList::GetNext**, **CObList::GetPrev**

CObList::FindIndex

POSITION FindIndex(int *nIndex*) const;

Return Value

A **POSITION** value that can be used for iteration or object pointer retrieval; **NULL** if *nIndex* is too large. (The framework generates an assertion if *nIndex* is negative.)

Parameters

nIndex   The zero-based index of the list element to be found.

Remarks

Uses the value of *nIndex* as an index into the list. It starts a sequential scan from the head of the list, stopping on the *n*th element.

Example

```
CObList list;
POSITION pos;

list.AddHead( new CAge( 21 ) );
list.AddHead( new CAge( 40 ) ); // List now contains (40, 21).
if( ( pos = list.FindIndex( 0 )) != NULL )
{
    ASSERT( *(CAge*) list.GetAt( pos ) == CAge( 40 ) );
}
```

See Also   **CObList::Find**, **CObList::GetNext**, **CObList::GetPrev**

CObList::GetAt

CObject*& GetAt(POSITION *position*);
CObject* GetAt(POSITION *position*) const;

Return Value

See the return value description for **GetHead**.

Parameters

position   A **POSITION** value returned by a previous **GetHeadPosition** or **Find** member function call.

Remarks

A variable of type **POSITION** is a key for the list. It is not the same as an index, and you cannot operate on a **POSITION** value yourself. **GetAt** retrieves the **CObject** pointer associated with a given position.

You must ensure that your **POSITION** value represents a valid position in the list. If it is invalid, then the Debug version of the Microsoft Foundation Class Library asserts.

Example

See the example for **FindIndex**.

See Also   **CObList::Find**, **CObList::SetAt**, **CObList::GetNext**, **CObList::GetPrev**, **CObList::GetHead**

CObList::GetCount

int GetCount( ) const;

Return Value

An integer value containing the element count.

Remarks

Gets the number of elements in this list.

Example

```
CObList list;

list.AddHead( new CAge( 21 ) );
list.AddHead( new CAge( 40 ) ); // List now contains (40, 21).
ASSERT( list.GetCount() == 2 );
```

See Also   **CObList::IsEmpty**

CObList::GetHead

CObject*& GetHead( );
CObject* GetHead( ) const;

Return Value

If the list is accessed through a pointer to a **const CObList**, then **GetHead** returns a **CObject** pointer. This allows the function to be used only on the right side of an assignment statement and thus protects the list from modification.

If the list is accessed directly or through a pointer to a **CObList**, then **GetHead** returns a reference to a **CObject** pointer. This allows the function to be used on either side of an assignment statement and thus allows the list entries to be modified.

Remarks

Gets the **CObject** pointer that represents the head element of this list.

You must ensure that the list is not empty before calling **GetHead**. If the list is empty, then the Debug version of the Microsoft Foundation Class Library asserts. Use **IsEmpty** to verify that the list contains elements.

Example

The following example illustrates the use of **GetHead** on the left side of an assignment statement.

```
const CObList* cplist;

CObList* plist = new CObList;
CAge* page1 = new CAge( 21 );
CAge* page2 = new CAge( 30 );
CAge* page3 = new CAge( 40 );
plist->AddHead( page1 );
plist->AddHead( page2 );  // List now contains (30, 21).
// The following statement REPLACES the head element.
plist->GetHead() = page3; // List now contains (40, 21).
ASSERT( *(CAge*) plist->GetHead() == CAge( 40 ) );
cplist = plist;  // cplist is a pointer to a const list.
// cplist->GetHead() = page3; // Does not compile!
ASSERT( *(CAge*) plist->GetHead() == CAge( 40 ) ); // OK

delete page1;
delete page2;
delete page3;
delete plist; // Cleans up memory.
```

See Also **CObList::GetTail**, **CObList::GetTailPosition**, **CObList::AddHead**, **CObList::RemoveHead**

CObList::GetHeadPosition

POSITION GetHeadPosition( ) const;

Return Value

A **POSITION** value that can be used for iteration or object pointer retrieval; **NULL** if the list is empty.

Remarks

Gets the position of the head element of this list.

Example

```
CObList list;
POSITION pos;

list.AddHead( new CAge( 21 ) );
list.AddHead( new CAge( 40 ) ); // List now contains (40, 21).
if( ( pos = list.GetHeadPosition() ) != NULL )
{
    ASSERT( *(CAge*) list.GetAt( pos ) == CAge( 40 ) );
}
```

See Also **CObList::GetTailPosition**

CObList::GetNext

CObject*& GetNext(POSITION& *rPosition* **);**
CObject* GetNext(POSITION& *rPosition* **) const;**

Return Value

See the return value description for **GetHead**.

Parameters

rPosition   A reference to a **POSITION** value returned by a previous **GetNext**, **GetHeadPosition**, or other member function call.

Remarks

Gets the list element identified by *rPosition*, then sets *rPosition* to the **POSITION** value of the next entry in the list. You can use **GetNext** in a forward iteration loop if you establish the initial position with a call to **GetHeadPosition** or **Find**.

You must ensure that your **POSITION** value represents a valid position in the list. If it is invalid, then the Debug version of the Microsoft Foundation Class Library asserts.

If the retrieved element is the last in the list, then the new value of *rPosition* is set to **NULL**.

It is possible to remove an element during an iteration. See the example for **RemoveAt**.

Example

```
CObList list;
POSITION pos;
list.AddHead( new CAge( 21 ) );
list.AddHead( new CAge( 40 ) ); // List now contains (40, 21).
// Iterate through the list in head-to-tail order.
#ifdef _DEBUG
    for( pos = list.GetHeadPosition(); pos != NULL; )
```

```
    {
    afxDump << list.GetNext( pos ) << "\n";
    }
#endif
```

The results from this program are as follows:

```
a CAge at $479C 40
a CAge at $46C0 21
```

See Also   **CObList::Find**, **CObList::GetHeadPosition**, **CObList::GetTailPosition**,
CObList::GetPrev, **CObList::GetHead**

CObList::GetPrev

CObject*& GetPrev(POSITION& *rPosition* **);**
CObject* GetPrev(POSITION& *rPosition* **) const;**

Return Value

See the return value description for **GetHead**.

Parameters

rPosition   A reference to a **POSITION** value returned by a previous **GetPrev** or
other member function call.

Remarks

Gets the list element identified by *rPosition*, then sets *rPosition* to the **POSITION**
value of the previous entry in the list. You can use **GetPrev** in a reverse iteration loop
if you establish the initial position with a call to **GetTailPosition** or **Find**.

You must ensure that your **POSITION** value represents a valid position in the list. If
it is invalid, then the Debug version of the Microsoft Foundation Class Library
asserts.

If the retrieved element is the first in the list, then the new value of *rPosition* is set
to **NULL**.

Example

```
    CObList list;
    POSITION pos;

    list.AddHead( new CAge(21) );
    list.AddHead( new CAge(40) ); // List now contains (40, 21).
    // Iterate through the list in tail-to-head order.
    for( pos = list.GetTailPosition(); pos != NULL; )
    {
#ifdef _DEBUG
    afxDump << list.GetPrev( pos ) << "\n";
#endif
    }
```

The results from this program are as follows:

```
a CAge at $421C 21
a CAge at $421C 40
```

See Also   **CObList::Find**, **CObList::GetTailPosition**, **CObList::GetHeadPosition**, **CObList::GetNext**, **CObList::GetHead**

CObList::GetTail

CObject*& GetTail( );
CObject* GetTail( ) const;

Return Value

See the return value description for **GetHead**.

Remarks

Gets the **CObject** pointer that represents the tail element of this list.

You must ensure that the list is not empty before calling **GetTail**. If the list is empty, then the Debug version of the Microsoft Foundation Class Library asserts. Use **IsEmpty** to verify that the list contains elements.

Example

```
CObList list;

list.AddHead( new CAge( 21 ) );
list.AddHead( new CAge( 40 ) ); // List now contains (40, 21).
ASSERT( *(CAge*) list.GetTail() == CAge( 21 ) );
```

See Also   **CObList::AddTail**, **CObList::AddHead**, **CObList::RemoveHead**, **CObList::GetHead**

CObList::GetTailPosition

POSITION GetTailPosition( ) const;

Return Value

A **POSITION** value that can be used for iteration or object pointer retrieval; **NULL** if the list is empty.

Remarks

Gets the position of the tail element of this list; **NULL** if the list is empty.

Example

```
CObList list;
POSITION pos;

list.AddHead( new CAge( 21 ) );
list.AddHead( new CAge( 40 ) ); // List now contains (40, 21).
if( ( pos = list.GetTailPosition() ) != NULL )
{
    ASSERT( *(CAge*) list.GetAt( pos ) == CAge( 21 ) );
}
```

See Also   **CObList::GetHeadPosition**, **CObList::GetTail**

CObList::InsertAfter

POSITION InsertAfter(POSITION *position*, **CObject*** *newElement* **);**
   throw (CMemoryException);

Parameters

position   A **POSITION** value returned by a previous **GetNext**, **GetPrev**, or **Find** member function call.

newElement   The object pointer to be added to this list.

Remarks

Adds an element to this list after the element at the specified position.

Example

```
CObList list;
POSITION pos1, pos2;
list.AddHead( new CAge( 21 ) );
list.AddHead( new CAge( 40 ) ); // List now contains (40, 21).
if( ( pos1 = list.GetHeadPosition() ) != NULL )
{
    pos2 = list.InsertAfter( pos1, new CAge( 65 ) );
}
#ifdef _DEBUG
    afxDump.SetDepth( 1 );
    afxDump << "InsertAfter example: " << &list << "\n";
#endif
```

The results from this program are as follows:

```
InsertAfter example: A CObList with 3 elements
    a CAge at $4A44 40
    a CAge at $4A64 65
    a CAge at $4968 21
```

See Also   **CObList::Find**, **CObList::InsertBefore**

CObList::InsertBefore

POSITION InsertBefore(POSITION *position***, CObject*** *newElement* **);**
    throw (CMemoryException);

Return Value

A **POSITION** value that can be used for iteration or object pointer retrieval; **NULL** if the list is empty.

Parameters

position   A **POSITION** value returned by a previous **GetNext**, **GetPrev**, or **Find** member function call.

newElement   The object pointer to be added to this list.

Remarks

Adds an element to this list before the element at the specified position.

Example

```
CObList list;
POSITION pos1, pos2;
list.AddHead( new CAge( 21 ) );
list.AddHead( new CAge( 40 ) ); // List now contains (40, 21).
if( ( pos1 = list.GetTailPosition() ) != NULL )
{
    pos2 = list.InsertBefore( pos1, new CAge( 65 ) );
}
#ifdef _DEBUG
afxDump.SetDepth( 1 );
afxDump << "InsertBefore example: " << &list << "\n";
#endif
```

The results from this program are as follows:

```
InsertBefore example: A CObList with 3 elements
    a CAge at $4AE2 40
    a CAge at $4B02 65
    a CAge at $49E6 21
```

See Also   **CObList::Find**, **CObList::InsertAfter**

CObList::IsEmpty

BOOL IsEmpty( ) const;

Return Value

Nonzero if this list is empty; otherwise 0.

Remarks

Indicates whether this list contains no elements.

Example

See the example for **RemoveAll**.

See Also   **CObList::GetCount**

CObList::RemoveAll

void RemoveAll( );

Remarks

Removes all the elements from this list and frees the associated **CObList** memory. No error is generated if the list is already empty.

When you remove elements from a **CObList**, you remove the object pointers from the list. It is your responsibility to delete the objects themselves.

Example

```
CObList list;
CAge* pa1;
CAge* pa2;
ASSERT( list.IsEmpty()); // Yes it is.
list.AddHead( pa1 = new CAge( 21 ) );
list.AddHead( pa2 = new CAge( 40 ) ); // List now contains (40, 21).
ASSERT( !list.IsEmpty()); // No it isn't.
list.RemoveAll(); // CAge's aren't destroyed.
ASSERT( list.IsEmpty()); // Yes it is.
delete pa1;     // Now delete the CAge objects.
delete pa2;
```

CObList::RemoveAt

void RemoveAt(POSITION *position* **);**

Parameters

position   The position of the element to be removed from the list.

Remarks

Removes the specified element from this list.

When you remove an element from a **CObList**, you remove the object pointer from the list. It is your responsibility to delete the objects themselves.

You must ensure that your **POSITION** value represents a valid position in the list. If it is invalid, then the Debug version of the Microsoft Foundation Class Library asserts.

Example

Be careful when removing an element during a list iteration. The following example shows a removal technique that guarantees a valid **POSITION** value for **GetNext**.

```
CObList list;
POSITION pos1, pos2;
CObject* pa;

list.AddHead( new CAge( 21 ) );
list.AddHead( new CAge( 40 ) );
list.AddHead( new CAge( 65 ) ); // List now contains (65 40, 21).
for( pos1 = list.GetHeadPosition(); ( pos2 = pos1 ) != NULL; )
{
    if( *(CAge*) list.GetNext( pos1 ) == CAge( 40 ) )
    {
        pa = list.GetAt( pos2 ); // Save the old pointer for
                                 //deletion.
        list.RemoveAt( pos2 );
        delete pa; // Deletion avoids memory leak.
    }
}
#ifdef _DEBUG
    afxDump.SetDepth( 1 );
    afxDump << "RemoveAt example: " << &list << "\n";
#endif
```

The results from this program are as follows:

```
RemoveAt example: A CObList with 2 elements
    a CAge at $4C1E 65
    a CAge at $4B22 21
```

CObList::RemoveHead

CObject* RemoveHead( );

Return Value

The **CObject** pointer previously at the head of the list.

Remarks

Removes the element from the head of the list and returns a pointer to it.

You must ensure that the list is not empty before calling **RemoveHead**. If the list is empty, then the Debug version of the Microsoft Foundation Class Library asserts. Use **IsEmpty** to verify that the list contains elements.

Example

```
CObList list;
CAge* pa1;
CAge* pa2;

list.AddHead( pa1 = new CAge( 21 ) );
list.AddHead( pa2 = new CAge( 40 ) ); // List now contains (40, 21).
ASSERT( *(CAge*) list.RemoveHead() == CAge( 40 ) );  // Old head
ASSERT( *(CAge*) list.GetHead() == CAge( 21 ) );  // New head
delete pa1;
delete pa2;
```

See Also   **CObList::GetHead, CObList::AddHead**

CObList::RemoveTail

CObject* RemoveTail( );

Return Value

A pointer to the object that was at the tail of the list.

Remarks

Removes the element from the tail of the list and returns a pointer to it.

You must ensure that the list is not empty before calling **RemoveTail**. If the list is empty, then the Debug version of the Microsoft Foundation Class Library asserts. Use **IsEmpty** to verify that the list contains elements.

Example

```
CObList list;
CAge* pa1;
CAge* pa2;

list.AddHead( pa1 = new CAge( 21 ) );
list.AddHead( pa2 = new CAge( 40 ) ); // List now contains (40, 21).
ASSERT( *(CAge*) list.RemoveTail() == CAge( 21 ) );  // Old tail
ASSERT( *(CAge*) list.GetTail() == CAge( 40 ) );  // New tail
delete pa1;
delete pa2; // Clean up memory.
```

See Also   **CObList::GetTail, CObList::AddTail**

CObList::SetAt

void SetAt(POSITION *pos*, **CObject*** *newElement* **);**

Parameters

pos   The **POSITION** of the element to be set.

newElement   The **CObject** pointer to be written to the list.

Remarks

A variable of type **POSITION** is a key for the list. It is not the same as an index, and you cannot operate on a **POSITION** value yourself. **SetAt** writes the **CObject** pointer to the specified position in the list.

You must ensure that your **POSITION** value represents a valid position in the list. If it is invalid, then the Debug version of the Microsoft Foundation Class Library asserts.

Example

```
CObList list;
CObject* pa;
POSITION pos;

list.AddHead( new CAge( 21 ) );
list.AddHead( new CAge( 40 ) ); // List now contains (40, 21).
if( ( pos = list.GetTailPosition()) != NULL )
{
    pa = list.GetAt( pos ); // Save the old pointer for
                            //deletion.
    list.SetAt( pos, new CAge( 65 ) );  // Replace the tail
                                        //element.
    delete pa;  // Deletion avoids memory leak.
}
#ifdef _DEBUG
    afxDump.SetDepth( 1 );
    afxDump << "SetAt example: " << &list << "\n";
#endif
```

The results from this program are as follows:

```
SetAt example: A CObList with 2 elements
    a CAge at $4D98 40
    a CAge at $4DB8 65
```

See Also   **CObList::Find**, **CObList::GetAt**, **CObList::GetNext**,
CObList::GetPrev

COleBusyDialog

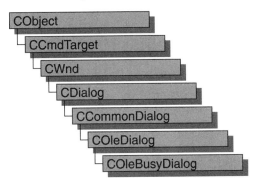

The **COleBusyDialog** class is used for the OLE Server Not Responding or Server Busy dialog boxes. Create an object of class **COleBusyDialog** when you want to call these dialog boxes. After a **COleBusyDialog** object has been constructed, you can use the **m_bz** structure to initialize the values or states of controls in the dialog box. The **m_bz** structure is of type **OLEUIBUSY**. For more information about using this dialog class, see the **DoModal** member function.

Note AppWizard-generated container code uses this class.

For more information, see the **OLEUIBUSY** structure in the *OLE 2.01 User Interface Library*.

For more information on OLE-specific dialog boxes, see the article "Dialog Boxes in OLE" in *Programming with MFC*.

#include <afxodlgs.h>

See Also   COleDialog

Data Members

m_bz	Structure of type **OLEUIBUSY** that controls the behavior of the dialog box.

Construction

COleBusyDialog	Constructs a **COleBusyDialog** object.

Operations

DoModal	Displays the OLE Server Busy dialog box.
GetSelectionType	Determines the choice made in the dialog box.

Member Functions

COleBusyDialog::COleBusyDialog

COleBusyDialog(HTASK *htaskBusy*, **BOOL** *bNotResponding* = **FALSE, DWORD** *dwFlags* = **0,**
CWnd* *pParentWnd* = **NULL**);

Parameters

htaskBusy   Handle to the server task that is busy.

bNotResponding   If **TRUE**, call the Not Responding dialog box instead of the Server
Busy dialog box. The wording in the Not Responding dialog box is slightly
different than the wording in the Server Busy dialog box, and the Cancel button is
disabled.

dwFlags   Creation flag. Can contain zero or more of the following values combined
with the bitwise-OR operator:

- **BZ_DISABLECANCELBUTTON**   Disable the Cancel button when calling
  the dialog box.

- **BZ_DISABLESWITCHTOBUTTON**   Disable the Switch To button when
  calling the dialog box.

- **BZ_DISABLERETRYBUTTON**   Disable the Retry button when calling the
  dialog box.

pParentWnd   Points to the parent or owner window object (of type **CWnd**) to which
the dialog object belongs. If it is **NULL**, the parent window of the dialog object is
set to the main application window.

Remarks

This function only constructs a **COleBusyDialog** object. To display the dialog box,
call **DoModal**.

For more information, see the **OLEUIBUSY** structure in the *OLE 2.01 User
Interface Library*.

See Also   **COleBusyDialog::DoModal**

COleBusyDialog::DoModal

virtual int DoModal( ) const;

Return Value

Completion status for the dialog box. One of the following values:

- **IDOK** if the dialog box was successfully displayed.

- **IDCANCEL** if the user canceled the dialog box.

- **IDABORT** if an error occurred. If **IDABORT** is returned, call the **COleDialog::GetLastError** member function to get more information about the type of error that occurred. For a listing of possible errors, see the **OleUIBusy** function in the *OLE 2.01 User Interface Library*.

Remarks

Call this function to display the OLE Server Busy or Server Not Responding dialog box.

If you want to initialize the various dialog box controls by setting members of the **m_bz** structure, you should do this before calling **DoModal**, but after the dialog object is constructed.

If **DoModal** returns **IDOK**, you can call other member functions to retrieve the settings or information that was input by the user into the dialog box.

See Also   **COleDialog::GetLastError**, **CDialog::DoModal**, **COleBusyDialog::GetSelectionType**, **COleBusyDialog::m_bz**

COleBusyDialog::GetSelectionType

UINT GetSelectionType( );

Return Value

Type of selection made.

Remarks

Call this function to get the selection type chosen by the user in the Server Busy dialog box.

The return type values are specified by the **Selection** enumeration type declared in the **COleBusyDialog** class.

```
enum Selection
{
    switchTo,
    retry,
    callUnblocked
};
```

Brief descriptions of these values follow:

- **COleBusyDialog::switchTo**   Switch To button was pressed.

- **COleBusyDialog::retry**   Retry button was pressed.

- **COleBusyDialog::callUnblocked**   Call to activate the server is now unblocked.

See Also   **COleBusyDialog::DoModal**

Data Members

COleBusyDialog::m_bz

Remarks

Structure of type **OLEUIBUSY** used to control the behavior of the Server Busy dialog box. Members of this structure can be modified directly or through member functions.

For more information, see the **OLEUIBUSY** structure in the *OLE 2.01 User Interface Library*.

See Also **COleBusyDialog::COleBusyDialog**, **COleBusyDialog::DoModal**

COleChangeIconDialog

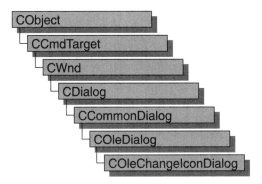

The **COleChangeIconDialog** class is used for the OLE Change Icon dialog box. Create an object of class **COleChangeIconDialog** when you want to call this dialog box. After a **COleChangeIconDialog** object has been constructed, you can use the **m_ci** structure to initialize the values or states of controls in the dialog box. The **m_ci** structure is of type **OLEUICHANGEICON**. For more information about using this dialog class, see the **DoModal** member function.

For more information, see the **OLEUICHANGEICON** structure in the *OLE 2.01 User Interface Library*.

For more information about OLE-specific dialog boxes, see the article "Dialog Boxes in OLE" in *Programming with MFC*.

#include <afxodlgs.h>

See Also   COleDialog

Data Members

m_ci	A structure that controls the behavior of the dialog box.

Construction

COleChangeIconDialog	Constructs a **COleChangeIconDialog** object.

Operations and Attributes

DoModal	Displays the OLE 2 Change Icon dialog box.
DoChangeIcon	Performs the change specified in the dialog box.
GetIconicMetafile	Gets a handle to the metafile associated with the iconic form of this item.

Member Functions

COleChangeIconDialog::COleChangeIconDialog

COleChangeIconDialog (COleClientItem* *pItem*, **DWORD** *dwFlags* = **CIF_SELECTCURRENT**,
CWnd* *pParentWnd* = **NULL**);

Parameters

pItem Points to the item to be converted.

dwFlags Creation flag, which contains any number of the following values
combined using the bitwise-or operator:

- **CIF_SELECTCURRENT** Specifies that the Current radio button will be
  selected initially when the dialog box is called. This is the default.

- **CIF_SELECTDEFAULT** Specifies that the Default radio button will be
  selected initially when the dialog box is called.

- **CIF_SELECTFROMFILE** Specifies that the From File radio button will be
  selected initially when the dialog box is called.

- **CIF_SHOWHELP** Specifies that the Help button will be displayed when the
  dialog box is called.

- **CIF_USEICONEXE** Specifies that the icon should be extracted from the
  executable specified in the **szIconExe** field of **m_ci** instead of retrieved from
  the type. This is useful for embedding or linking to non-OLE files.

pParentWnd Points to the parent or owner window object (of type **CWnd**) to which
the dialog object belongs. If it is **NULL**, the parent window of the dialog box will
be set to the main application window.

Remarks

This function constructs only a **COleChangeIconDialog** object. To display the dialog
box, call the **DoModal** function.

For more information, see the **OLEUICHANGEICON** structure in the *OLE 2.01
User Interface Library*.

See Also **COleClientItem**, **COleChangeIconDialog::DoModal**

COleChangeIconDialog::DoChangeIcon

BOOL DoChangeIcon(COleClientItem* *pItem*);

Return Value

Nonzero if change is successful; otherwise 0.

Parameters

pItem   Points to the item whose icon is changing.

Remarks

Call this function to change the icon representing the item to the one selected in the dialog box after **DoModal** returns **IDOK**.

See Also   **COleChangeIconDialog::DoModal**

COleChangeIconDialog::DoModal

virtual int DoModal( );

Return Value

Completion status for the dialog box. One of the following values:

- **IDOK** if the dialog box was successfully displayed.
- **IDCANCEL** if the user canceled the dialog box.
- **IDABORT** if an error occurred. If **IDABORT** is returned, call the **COleDialog::GetLastError** member function to get more information about the type of error that occurred. For a listing of possible errors, see the **OleUIChangeIcon** function in the *OLE 2.01 User Interface Library*.

Remarks

Call this function to display the OLE Change Icon dialog box.

If you want to initialize the various dialog box controls by setting members of the **m_ci** structure, you should do this before calling **DoModal**, but after the dialog object is constructed.

If **DoModal** returns **IDOK**, you can call other member functions to retrieve the settings or information that was input by the user into the dialog box.

See Also   **COleDialog::GetLastError**, **CDialog::DoModal**, **COleChangeIconDialog::m_ci**, **COleChangeIconDialog::DoChangeIcon**, **COleChangeIconDialog::GetIconicMetafile**

COleChangeIconDialog::GetIconicMetafile

HGLOBAL GetIconicMetafile( ) const;

Return Value

The handle to the metafile containing the iconic aspect of the new icon, if the dialog box was dismissed by choosing **OK**; otherwise, the icon as it was before the dialog was displayed.

Remarks

> Call this function to get a handle to the metafile that contains the iconic aspect of the selected item.
>
> **See Also** **COleChangeIconDialog::DoModal**,
> **COleChangeIconDialog::COleChangeIconDialog**,
> **COleChangeIconDialog::DoChangeIcon**

Data Members

COleChangeIconDialog::m_ci

Remarks

> Structure of type **OLEUICHANGEICON** used to control the behavior of the Change Icon dialog box. Members of this structure can be modified either directly or through member functions.
>
> For more information, see the **OLEUICHANGEICON** structure in the *OLE 2.01 User Interface Library*.
>
> **See Also** **COleChangeIconDialog::COleChangeIconDialog**

COleChangeSourceDialog

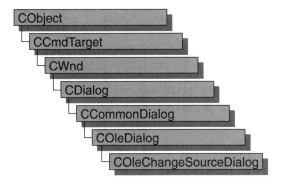

The **COleChangeSourceDialog** class is used for the OLE Change Source dialog box. Create an object of class **COleChangeSourceDialog** when you want to call this dialog box. After a **COleChangeSourceDialog** object has been constructed, you can use the **m_cs** structure to initialize the values or states of controls in the dialog box. The **m_cs** structure is of type **OLEUICHANGESOURCE**. For more information about using this dialog class, see the **DoModal** member function.

For more information, see the **OLEUICHANGESOURCE** structure in the *OLE 2.01 User Interface Library*.

For more information about OLE-specific dialog boxes, see the article "Dialog Boxes in OLE" in *Programming with MFC*.

#include <afxodlgs.h>

See Also   **COleDialog**

Constructor

COleChangeSourceDialog	Constructs a **COleChangeSourceDialog** object.

Operations

DoModal	Displays the OLE Change Source dialog box.

Attributes

IsValidSource	Indicates if the source is valid.
GetFileName	Gets the filename from the source name.
GetDisplayName	Gets the complete source display name.
GetItemName	Gets the item name from the source name.
GetFromPrefix	Gets the prefix of the previous source.
GetToPrefix	Gets the prefix of the new source

Data Member

m_cs	A structure that controls the behavior of the dialog box.

Member Functions

COleChangeSourceDialog::COleChangeSourceDialog

COleChangeSourceDialog(COleClientItem* *pItem*, CWnd* *pParentWnd* = NULL);

Parameters

pItem   Pointer to the linked **COleClientItem** whose source is to be updated.

pParentWnd   Points to the parent or owner window object (of type **CWnd**) to which the dialog object belongs. If it is **NULL**, the parent window of the dialog box will be set to the main application window.

Remarks

This function constructs a **COleChangeSourceDialog** object. To display the dialog box, call the **DoModal** function.

For more information, see the **OLEUICHANGESOURCE** structure and **OleUIChangeSource** function in the *OLE 2.01 User Interface Library*.

COleChangeSourceDialog::DoModal

virtual int DoModal( );

Return Value

Completion status for the dialog box. One of the following values:

- **IDOK** if the dialog box was successfully displayed.
- **IDCANCEL** if the user canceled the dialog box.
- **IDABORT** if an error occurred. If **IDABORT** is returned, call the **COleDialog::GetLastError** member function to get more information about the type of error that occurred. For a listing of possible errors, see the **OleUIChangeSource** function in the *OLE 2.01 User Interface Library*.

Remarks

Call this function to display the OLE Change Source dialog box.

If you want to initialize the various dialog box controls by setting members of the **m_cs** structure, you should do this before calling **DoModal**, but after the dialog object is constructed.

If **DoModal** returns **IDOK**, you can call member functions to retrieve user-entered settings or information from the dialog box. The following list names typical query functions:

- **GetFileName**
- **GetDisplayName**
- **GetItemName**

See Also   **COleChangeSourceDialog::COleChangeSourceDialog**

COleChangeSourceDialog::GetDisplayName

CString GetDisplayName( );

Return Value

The complete source display name (moniker) for the **COleClientItem** specified in the constructor.

Remarks

Call this function to retrieve the complete display name for the linked client item.

See Also   **COleChangeSourceDialog::GetFileName**, **COleChangeSourceDialog::GetItemName**

COleChangeSourceDialog::GetFileName

CString GetFileName( );

Return Value

The file moniker portion of the source display name for the **COleClientItem** specified in the constructor.

Remarks

Call this function to retrieve the file moniker portion of the display name for the linked client item. The file moniker together with the item moniker gives the complete display name.

See Also   **COleChangeSourceDialog::GetDisplayName**, **COleChangeSourceDialog::GetItemName**

COleChangeSourceDialog::GetFromPrefix

CString GetFromPrefix( );

Return Value

The previous prefix string of the source.

Remarks

Call this function to get the previous prefix string for the source. Call this function only after **DoModal** returns **IDOK**.

This value comes directly from the **lpszFrom** member of the **OLEUICHANGESOURCE** structure.

For more information, see the **OLEUICHANGESOURCE** structure in the *OLE 2.01 User Interface Library*.

See Also   **COleChangeSourceDialog::GetToPrefix**

COleChangeSourceDialog::GetItemName

CString GetItemName( );

Return Value

The item moniker portion of the source display name for the **COleClientItem** specified in the constructor.

Remarks

Call this function to retrieve the item moniker portion of the display name for the linked client item. The file moniker together with the item moniker gives the complete display name.

See Also   **COleChangeSourceDialog::GetFileName**, **COleChangeSourceDialog::GetDisplayName**

COleChangeSourceDialog::GetToPrefix

CString GetToPrefix( );

Return Value

The new prefix string of the source.

Remarks

Call this function to get the new prefix string for the source. Call this function only after **DoModal** returns **IDOK**.

This value comes directly from the **lpszTo** member of the **OLEUICHANGESOURCE** structure.

For more information, see the **OLEUICHANGESOURCE** structure in the *OLE 2.01 User Interface Library*.

See Also   **COleChangeSourceDialog::GetFromPrefix**

COleChangeSourceDialog::IsValidSource

BOOL IsValidSource( );

Return Value

Nonzero if the new source is valid, otherwise 0.

Remarks

Call this function to determine if the new source is valid. Call this function only after **DoModal** returns **IDOK**.

For more information, see the **OLEUICHANGESOURCE** structure in the *OLE 2.01 User Interface Library*.

See Also   COleChangeSourceDialog::DoModal

Data Members

COleChangeSourceDialog::m_cs

Remarks

This data member is a structure of type **OLEUICHANGESOURCE**. **OLEUICHANGESOURCE** is used to control the behavior of the OLE Change Source dialog box. Members of this structure can be modified directly.

For more information, see the **OLEUICHANGESOURCE** structure the in *OLE 2.01 User Interface Library*.

See Also   COleChangeSourceDialog::COleChangeSourceDialog

COleClientItem

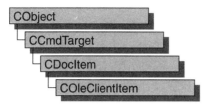

The **COleClientItem** class defines the container interface to OLE items. An OLE item represents data, created and maintained by a server application, which can be "seamlessly" incorporated into a document so that it appears to the user to be a single document. The result is a "compound document" made up of the OLE item and a containing document.

An OLE item can be either embedded or linked. If it is embedded, its data is stored as part of the compound document. If it is linked, its data is stored as part of a separate file created by the server application, and only a link to that file is stored in the compound document. All OLE items contain information specifying the server application that should be called to edit them.

COleClientItem defines several overridable functions that are called in response to requests from the server application; these overridables usually act as notifications. This allows the server application to inform the container of changes the user makes when editing the OLE item, or to retrieve information needed during editing.

COleClientItem can be used with either the **COleDocument**, **COleLinkingDoc**, or **COleServerDoc** class. To use **COleClientItem**, derive a class from it and implement the **OnChange** member function, which defines how the container responds to changes made to the item. To support in-place activation, override the **OnGetItemPosition** member function. This function provides information about the displayed position of the OLE item.

For more information about using the container interface, see the articles "Containers: Implementing a Container" and "Activation" in *Programming with MFC*.

Note The OLE documentation refers to embedded and linked items as "objects" and refers to types of items as "classes." This reference uses the term "item" to distinguish the OLE entity from the corresponding C++ object and the term "type" to distinguish the OLE category from the C++ class.

#include <afxole.h>

See Also   **COleDocument, COleLinkingDoc, COleServerItem**

Construction

COleClientItem	Constructs a **COleClientItem** object.

Creation

CreateFromClipboard	Creates an embedded item from the Clipboard.
CreateFromData	Creates an embedded item from a data object.
CanCreateFromData	Indicates whether a container application can create an embedded object.
CreateFromFile	Creates an embedded item from a file.
CreateStaticFromClipboard	Creates a static item from the Clipboard.
CreateStaticFromData	Creates a static item from a data object.
CreateLinkFromClipboard	Creates a linked item from the Clipboard.
CreateLinkFromData	Creates a linked item from a data object.
CanCreateLinkFromData	Indicates whether a container application can create a linked object.
CreateLinkFromFile	Creates a linked item from a file.
CreateNewItem	Creates a new embedded item by launching the server application.
CreateCloneFrom	Creates a duplicate of an existing item.

Status

GetLastStatus	Returns the status of the last OLE operation.
GetType	Returns the type (embedded, linked, or static) of the OLE item.
GetExtent	Returns the bounds of the OLE item's rectangle.
GetCachedExtent	Returns the bounds of the OLE item's rectangle.
GetClassID	Gets the present item's class ID.
GetUserType	Gets a string describing the item's type.
GetIconicMetafile	Gets the metafile used for drawing the item's icon.
SetIconicMetafile	Caches the metafile used for drawing the item's icon.
GetDrawAspect	Gets the item's current view for rendering.
SetDrawAspect	Sets the item's current view for rendering.
GetItemState	Gets the item's current state.
GetActiveView	Gets the view on which the item is activated in place.
IsModified	Returns **TRUE** if the item has been modified since it was last saved.
IsRunning	Returns **TRUE** if the item's server application is running.

IsInPlaceActive	Returns **TRUE** if the item is in-place active.
IsOpen	Returns **TRUE** if the item is currently open in the server application.

Data Access

GetDocument	Returns the **COleDocument** object that contains the present item.
AttachDataObject	Accesses the data in the OLE object.

Object Conversion

ConvertTo	Converts the item to another type.
ActivateAs	Activates the item as another type.
Reload	Reloads the item after a call to **ActivateAs**.

Clipboard Operations

CanPaste	Indicates whether the Clipboard contains an embeddable or static OLE item.
CanPasteLink	Indicates whether the Clipboard contains a linkable OLE item.
DoDragDrop	Performs a drag-and-drop operation.
CopyToClipboard	Copies the OLE item to the Clipboard.
GetClipboardData	Gets the data that would be placed on the Clipboard by calling the **CopyToClipboard** member function.

General Operations

Close	Closes a link to a server but does not destroy the OLE item.
Release	Releases the connection to an OLE linked item and closes it if it was open. Does not destroy the client item.
Delete	Deletes or closes the OLE item if it was a linked item.
Draw	Draws the OLE item.
Run	Runs the application associated with the item.
SetPrintDevice	Sets the print-target device for this client item.

Activation

Activate	Opens the OLE item for an operation and then executes the specified verb.
DoVerb	Executes the specified verb.
Deactivate	Deactivates the item.

DeactivateUI	Restores the container application's user interface to its original state.
ReactivateAndUndo	Reactivates the item and undoes the last in-place editing operation.
SetItemRects	Sets the item's bounding rectangle.
GetInPlaceWindow	Returns a pointer to the item's in-place editing window.

Embedded Object Operations

| **SetHostNames** | Sets the names the server displays when editing the OLE item. |
| **SetExtent** | Sets the bounding rectangle of the OLE item. |

Linked Object Operations and Status

GetLinkUpdateOptions	Returns the update mode for a linked item (advanced feature).
SetLinkUpdateOptions	Sets the update mode for a linked item (advanced feature).
UpdateLink	Updates the presentation cache of an item.
IsLinkUpToDate	Returns **TRUE** if a linked item is up to date with its source document.

Overridables

OnChange	Called when the server changes the OLE item. Implementation required.
OnGetClipboardData	Called by the framework to get the data to be copied to the Clipboard.
OnInsertMenus	Called by the framework to create a composite menu.
OnSetMenu	Called by the framework to install and remove a composite menu.
OnRemoveMenus	Called by the framework to remove the container's menus from a composite menu.
OnUpdateFrameTitle	Called by the framework to update the frame window's title bar.
OnShowControlBars	Called by the framework to show and hide control bars.
OnGetItemPosition	Called by the framework to get the item's position relative to the view.
OnScrollBy	Called by the framework to scroll the item into view.
OnDeactivateUI	Called by the framework when the server has removed its in-place user interface.

OnDiscardUndoState	Called by the framework to discard the item's undo state information.
OnDeactivateAndUndo	Called by the framework to undo after activation.
OnShowItem	Called by the framework to display the OLE item.
OnGetClipRect	Called by the framework to get the item's clipping-rectangle coordinates.
CanActivate	Called by the framework to determine whether in-place activation is allowed.
OnActivate	Called by the framework to notify the item that it is activated.
OnActivateUI	Called by the framework to notify the item that it is activated and should show its user interface.
OnGetWindowContext	Called by the framework when an item is activated in place.
OnDeactivate	Called by the framework when an item is deactivated.
OnChangeItemPosition	Called by the framework when an item's position changes.

Member Functions

COleClientItem::Activate

void Activate(LONG *nVerb*, **CView*** *pView*, **LPMSG** *lpMsg* = **NULL**);

Parameters

nVerb   Specifies the verb to execute. It can be one of the following:

Value	Meaning	Symbol
0	Primary verb	**OLEIVERB_PRIMARY**
1	Secondary verb	(None)
−1	Display item for editing	**OLEIVERB_SHOW**
−2	Edit item in separate window	**OLEIVERB_OPEN**
−3	Hide item	**OLEIVERB_HIDE**

The −1 value is typically an alias for another verb. If open editing is not supported, −2 has the same effect as −1. For additional values, see **IOleObject::DoVerb** in the OLE documentation.

pView   Pointer to the container view window that contains the OLE item; this is used by the server application for in-place activation. This parameter should be **NULL** if the container does not support in-place activation.

lpMsg   Pointer to the message that caused the item to be activated.

Remarks

Call this function to execute the specified verb instead of **DoVerb** so that you can do your own processing when an exception is thrown.

If the server application was written using the Microsoft Foundation Class Library, this function causes the **OnDoVerb** member function of the corresponding **COleServerItem** object to be executed.

If the primary verb is Edit and zero is specified in the *nVerb* parameter, the server application is launched to allow the OLE item to be edited. If the container application supports in-place activation, editing can be done in place. If the container does not support in-place activation (or if the Open verb is specified), the server is launched in a separate window and editing can be done there. Typically, when the user of the container application double-clicks the OLE item, the value for the primary verb in the *nVerb* parameter determines which action the user can take. However, if the server supports only one action, it takes that action, no matter which value is specified in the *nVerb* parameter.

For more information, see **IOleObject::DoVerb** in the OLE documentation.

See Also   **COleClientItem::DoVerb, COleServerItem::OnDoVerb**

COleClientItem::ActivateAs

BOOL ActivateAs(LPCTSTR *lpszUserType*, **REFCLSID** *clsidOld*, **REFCLSID** *clsidNew* **);**

Return Value

Nonzero if successful; otherwise 0.

Parameters

lpszUserType   Pointer to a string representing the target user type, such as "Word Document."

clsidOld   A reference to the item's current class ID. The class ID should represent the type of the actual object, as stored, unless it is a link. In that case, it should be the CLSID of the item to which the link refers. The **COleConvertDialog** automatically provides the correct class ID for the item.

clsidNew   A reference to the target class ID.

Remarks

Uses OLE's object conversion facilities to activate the item as though it were an item of the type specified by *clsidNew*. This is called automatically by **COleConvertDialog::DoConvert**. It is not usually called directly.

See Also   **COleConvertDialog, COleClientItem::ConvertTo, COleClientItem::Reload**

COleClientItem::AttachDataObject

void AttachDataObject(COleDataObject& *rDataObject* **) const;**

Parameters

rDataObject   Reference to a **COleDataObject** object that will be initialized to allow access to the data in the OLE item.

Remarks

Call this function to initialize a **COleDataObject** for accessing the data in the OLE item.

See Also   **COleDataObject**

COleClientItem::CanActivate

virtual BOOL CanActivate( );

Return Value

Nonzero if in-place activation is allowed; otherwise 0.

Remarks

Called by the framework when the user requests in-place activation of the OLE item; this function's return value determines whether in-place activation is allowed. The default implementation allows in-place activation if the container has a valid window. Override this function to implement special logic for accepting or refusing the activation request. For example, an activation request can be refused if the OLE item is too small or not currently visible.

For more information, see **IOleInPlaceSite::CanInPlaceActivate** in the OLE documentation.

COleClientItem::CanCreateFromData

static BOOL PASCAL CanCreateFromData(const COleDataObject* *pDataObject* **);**

Return Value

Nonzero if the container can create an embedded object from the **COleDataObject** object; otherwise 0.

Parameters

pDataObject   Pointer to the **COleDataObject** object from which the OLE item is to be created.

Remarks

Checks whether a container application can create an embedded object from the given **COleDataObject** object. The **COleDataObject** class is used in data transfers for retrieving data in various formats from the Clipboard, through drag and drop, or from an embedded OLE item.

Containers can use this function to decide to enable or disable their Edit Paste and Edit Paste Special commands.

For more information, see the article "Data Objects and Data Sources (OLE)" in *Programming with MFC*.

See Also **COleDataObject**

COleClientItem::CanCreateLinkFromData

static BOOL PASCAL CanCreateLinkFromData(const COleDataObject* *pDataObject* **);**

Return Value

Nonzero if the container can create a linked object from the **COleDataObject** object.

Parameters

pDataObject   Pointer to the **COleDataObject** object from which the OLE item is to be created.

Remarks

Checks whether a container application can create a linked object from the given **COleDataObject** object. The **COleDataObject** class is used in data transfers for retrieving data in various formats from the Clipboard, through drag and drop, or from an embedded OLE item.

Containers can use this function to decide to enable or disable their Edit Paste Special and Edit Paste Link commands.

For more information, see the article "Data Objects and Data Sources (OLE)" in *Programming with MFC*.

See Also **COleDataObject**

COleClientItem::CanPaste

static BOOL PASCAL CanPaste( );

Return Value

Nonzero if an embedded OLE item can be pasted from the Clipboard; otherwise 0.

Remarks

Call this function to see whether an embedded OLE item can be pasted from the Clipboard.

For more information, see **OleGetClipboard** and **OleQueryCreateFromData** in the OLE documentation.

See Also **COleClientItem::CanPasteLink**,
COleClientItem::CreateFromClipboard,
COleClientItem::CreateStaticFromClipboard, **COleDocument**

COleClientItem::CanPasteLink

> **static BOOL PASCAL CanPasteLink( );**

Return Value

Nonzero if a linked OLE item can be pasted from the Clipboard; otherwise 0.

Remarks

Call this function to see whether a linked OLE item can be pasted from the Clipboard.

For more information, see **OleGetClipboard** and **OleQueryLinkFromData** in the OLE documentation.

See Also **COleClientItem::CanPaste**,
COleClientItem::CreateLinkFromClipboard

COleClientItem::Close

> **void Close(OLECLOSE** *dwCloseOption* **= OLECLOSE_SAVEIFDIRTY);**

Parameters

dwCloseOption Flag specifying under what circumstances the OLE item is saved when it returns to the loaded state. It can have one of the following values:

- **OLECLOSE_SAVEIFDIRTY** Save the OLE item.

- **OLECLOSE_NOSAVE** Do not save the OLE item.

- **OLECLOSE_PROMPTSAVE** Prompt the user on whether to save the OLE item.

Remarks

Call this function to change the state of an OLE item from the running state to the loaded state, that is, loaded with its handler in memory but with the server not running. This function has no effect when the OLE item is not running.

For more information, see **IOleObject::Close** in the OLE documentation.

See Also **COleClientItem::UpdateLink**

COleClientItem::COleClientItem

COleClientItem(COleDocument* *pContainerDoc* = **NULL**);

Parameters

pContainerDoc   Pointer to the container document that will contain this item. This can be any **COleDocument** derivative.

Remarks

Constructs a **COleClientItem** object and adds it to the container document's collection of document items, which constructs only the C++ object and does not perform any OLE initialization. If you pass a **NULL** pointer, no addition is made to the container document. You must explicitly call **COleDocument::AddItem**.

You must call one of the following creation member functions before you use the OLE item:

- **CreateFromClipboard**
- **CreateFromData**
- **CreateFromFile**
- **CreateStaticFromClipboard**
- **CreateStaticFromData**
- **CreateLinkFromClipboard**
- **CreateLinkFromData**
- **CreateLinkFromFile**
- **CreateNewItem**
- **CreateCloneFrom**

See Also   **COleDocument, COleDocument::AddItem**

COleClientItem::ConvertTo

BOOL ConvertTo(REFCLSID *clsidNew*);

Return Value

Nonzero if successful; otherwise 0.

Parameters

clsidNew   The class ID of the target type.

Remarks

Call this member function to convert the item to the type specified by *clsidNew*. This is called automatically by **COleConvertDialog**. It is not necessary to call it directly.

See Also   **COleClientItem::ActivateAs, COleConvertDialog**

COleClientItem::CopyToClipboard

void CopyToClipboard(BOOL *bIncludeLink* = **FALSE);**

Parameters

bIncludeLink   **TRUE** if link information should be copied to the Clipboard, allowing a linked item to be pasted; otherwise **FALSE**.

Remarks

Call this function to copy the OLE item to the Clipboard. Typically, you call this function when writing message handlers for the Copy or Cut commands from the Edit menu. You must implement item selection in your container application if you want to implement the Copy or Cut commands.

For more information, see **OleSetClipboard** in the OLE documentation.

COleClientItem::CreateCloneFrom

BOOL CreateCloneFrom(const COleClientItem* *pSrcItem* **);**

Return Value

Nonzero if successful; otherwise 0.

Parameters

pSrcItem   Pointer to the OLE item to be duplicated.

Remarks

Call this function to create a copy of the specified OLE item. The copy is identical to the source item. You can use this function to support undo operations.

See Also   **COleClientItem::CreateNewItem**

COleClientItem::CreateFromClipboard

BOOL CreateFromClipboard(OLERENDER *render* = **OLERENDER_DRAW,**
CLIPFORMAT *cfFormat* = **0, LPFORMATETC** *lpFormatEtc* = **NULL);**

Return Value

Nonzero if successful; otherwise 0.

Parameters

render   Flag specifying how the server will render the OLE item. For the possible values, see **OLERENDER** in the OLE documentation.

cfFormat   Specifies the Clipboard data format to be cached when creating the OLE item.

lpFormatEtc   Pointer to a **FORMATETC** structure used if *render* is
OLERENDER_FORMAT or **OLERENDER_DRAW**. Provide a value for this
parameter only if you want to specify additional format information beyond the
Clipboard format specified by *cfFormat*. If you omit this parameter, default values
are used for the other fields in the **FORMATETC** structure.

Remarks

Call this function to create an embedded item from the contents of the Clipboard. You
typically call this function from the message handler for the Paste command on the
Edit menu. (The Paste command is enabled by the framework if the **CanPaste**
member function returns nonzero.)

For more information, see **OLERENDER** and **FORMATETC** in the OLE
documentation.

See Also   **COleDataObject::AttachClipboard**,
COleClientItem::CreateFromData, **COleClientItem::CanPaste**

COleClientItem::CreateFromData

BOOL CreateFromData(COleDataObject* *pDataObject***,**
OLERENDER *render* **= OLERENDER_DRAW, CLIPFORMAT** *cfFormat* **= 0,**
LPFORMATETC *lpFormatEtc* **= NULL);**

Return Value

Nonzero if successful; otherwise 0.

Parameters

pDataObject   Pointer to the **COleDataObject** object from which the OLE item is to
be created.

render   Flag specifying how the server will render the OLE item. For the possible
values, see **OLERENDER** in the OLE documentation.

cfFormat   Specifies the Clipboard data format to be cached when creating the
OLE item.

lpFormatEtc   Pointer to a **FORMATETC** structure used if *render* is
OLERENDER_FORMAT or **OLERENDER_DRAW**. Provide a value for this
parameter only if you want to specify additional format information beyond the
Clipboard format specified by *cfFormat*. If you omit this parameter, default values
are used for the other fields in the **FORMATETC** structure.

Remarks

Call this function to create an embedded item from a **COleDataObject** object. Data
transfer operations, such as pasting from the Clipboard or drag-and-drop operations,
provide **COleDataObject** objects containing the information offered by a server
application. It is usually used in your override of **CView:OnDrop**.

For more information, see **OleCreateFromData**, **OLERENDER**, and **FORMATETC** in the OLE documentation.

See Also **COleDataObject::AttachClipboard**, **COleClientItem::CreateFromClipboard**, **COleDataObject**

COleClientItem::CreateFromFile

BOOL CreateFromFile(LPCTSTR *lpszFileName***, REFCLSID** *clsid* **= CLSID_NULL, OLERENDER** *render* **= OLERENDER_DRAW, CLIPFORMAT** *cfFormat* **= 0, LPFORMATETC** *lpFormatEtc* **= NULL);**

Return Value

Nonzero if successful; otherwise 0.

Parameters

lpszFileName   Pointer to the name of the file from which the OLE item is to be created.

clsid   Reserved for future use.

render   Flag specifying how the server will render the OLE item. For the possible values, see **OLERENDER** in the OLE documentation.

cfFormat   Specifies the Clipboard data format to be cached when creating the OLE item.

lpFormatEtc   Pointer to a **FORMATETC** structure used if *render* is **OLERENDER_FORMAT** or **OLERENDER_DRAW**. Provide a value for this parameter only if you want to specify additional format information beyond the Clipboard format specified by *cfFormat*. If you omit this parameter, default values are used for the other fields in the **FORMATETC** structure.

Remarks

Call this function to create an embedded OLE item from a file. The framework calls this function from **COleInsertDialog::CreateItem** if the user chooses OK from the Insert Object dialog box when the Create from File button is selected.

For more information, see **OleCreateFromFile**, **OLERENDER**, and **FORMATETC** in the OLE documentation.

See Also **COleInsertDialog::CreateItem**

COleClientItem::CreateLinkFromClipboard

BOOL CreateLinkFromClipboard(OLERENDER *render* **= OLERENDER_DRAW, CLIPFORMAT** *cfFormat* **= 0, LPFORMATETC** *lpFormatEtc* **= NULL);**

Return Value

Nonzero if successful; otherwise 0.

Parameters

render   Flag specifying how the server will render the OLE item. For the possible values, see **OLERENDER** in the OLE documentation.

cfFormat   Specifies the Clipboard data format to be cached when creating the OLE item.

lpFormatEtc   Pointer to a **FORMATETC** structure used if *render* is **OLERENDER_FORMAT** or **OLERENDER_DRAW**. Provide a value for this parameter only if you want to specify additional format information beyond the Clipboard format specified by *cfFormat*. If you omit this parameter, default values are used for the other fields in the **FORMATETC** structure.

Remarks

Call this function to create a linked item from the contents of the Clipboard. You typically call this function from the message handler for the Paste Link command on the Edit menu. (The Paste Link command is enabled in the default implementation of **COleDocument** if the Clipboard contains an OLE item that can be linked to.)

For more information, see **OLERENDER** and **FORMATETC** in the OLE documentation.

See Also   **COleClientItem::CanPasteLink**, **COleClientItem::CreateLinkFromData**, **COleDataObject::AttachClipboard**

COleClientItem::CreateLinkFromData

BOOL CreateLinkFromData(COleDataObject* *pDataObject*, **OLERENDER** *render* **= OLERENDER_DRAW, CLIPFORMAT** *cfFormat* **= 0, LPFORMATETC** *lpFormatEtc* **= NULL);**

Return Value

Nonzero if successful; otherwise 0.

Parameters

pDataObject   Pointer to the **COleDataObject** object from which the OLE item is to be created.

render   Flag specifying how the server will render the OLE item. For the possible values, see **OLERENDER** in the OLE documentation.

cfFormat   Specifies the Clipboard data format to be cached when creating the OLE item.

lpFormatEtc   Pointer to a **FORMATETC** structure used if *render* is **OLERENDER_FORMAT** or **OLERENDER_DRAW**. Provide a value for this parameter only if you want to specify additional format information beyond the Clipboard format specified by *cfFormat*. If you omit this parameter, default values are used for the other fields in the **FORMATETC** structure.

Remarks

Call this function to create a linked item from a **COleDataObject** object. Call this during a drop operation when the user indicates a link should be created. It can also be used to handle the Edit Paste command. It is called by the framework in **COleClientItem::CreateLinkFromClipboard** and in **COlePasteSpecialDialog::CreateItem** when the Link option has been selected.

For more information, see **OleCreateLinkFromData**, **OLERENDER**, and **FORMATETC** in the OLE documentation.

See Also   **COleDataObject::AttachClipboard, COleDataObject, COleClientItem::CreateLinkFromClipboard**

COleClientItem::CreateLinkFromFile

BOOL CreateLinkFromFile(LPCTSTR *lpszFileName,* **OLERENDER** *render* = **OLERENDER_DRAW, CLIPFORMAT** *cfFormat* = **0, LPFORMATETC** *lpFormatEtc* = **NULL);**

Return Value

Nonzero if successful; otherwise 0.

Parameters

lpszFileName   Pointer to the name of the file from which the OLE item is to be created.

render   Flag specifying how the server will render the OLE item. For the possible values, see **OLERENDER** in the OLE documentation.

cfFormat   Specifies the Clipboard data format to be cached when creating the OLE item.

lpFormatEtc   Pointer to a **FORMATETC** structure used if *render* is **OLERENDER_FORMAT** or **OLERENDER_DRAW**. Provide a value for this parameter only if you want to specify additional format information beyond the Clipboard format specified by *cfFormat*. If you omit this parameter, default values are used for the other fields in the **FORMATETC** structure.

Remarks

Call this function to create a linked OLE item from a file. The framework calls this function if the user chooses OK from the Insert Object dialog box when the Create from File button is selected and the Link check box is checked. It is called from **COleInsertDialog::CreateItem**.

For more information, see **OleCreateLinkToFile**, **OLERENDER**, and **FORMATETC** in the OLE documentation.

See Also   **COleInsertDialog::CreateItem**

COleClientItem::CreateNewItem

BOOL CreateNewItem(REFCLSID *clsid*, **OLERENDER** *render* = **OLERENDER_DRAW**, **CLIPFORMAT** *cfFormat* = **0**, **LPFORMATETC** *lpFormatEtc* = **NULL**);

Return Value

Nonzero if successful; otherwise 0.

Parameters

clsid   ID that uniquely identifies the type of OLE item to create.

render   Flag specifying how the server will render the OLE item. For the possible values, see **OLERENDER** in the OLE documentation.

cfFormat   Specifies the Clipboard data format to be cached when creating the OLE item.

lpFormatEtc   Pointer to a **FORMATETC** structure used if *render* is **OLERENDER_FORMAT** or **OLERENDER_DRAW**. Provide a value for this parameter only if you want to specify additional format information beyond the Clipboard format specified by *cfFormat*. If you omit this parameter, default values are used for the other fields in the **FORMATETC** structure.

Remarks

Call this function to create an embedded item; this function launches the server application that allows the user to create the OLE item. The framework calls this function if the user chooses OK from the Insert Object dialog box when the Create New button is selected.

For more information, see **OleCreate**, **OLERENDER**, and **FORMATETC** in the OLE documentation.

See Also   **COleInsertDialog::CreateItem**

COleClientItem::CreateStaticFromClipboard

BOOL CreateStaticFromClipboard(OLERENDER *render* **= OLERENDER_DRAW, CLIPFORMAT** *cfFormat* **= 0, LPFORMATETC** *lpFormatEtc* **= NULL);**

Return Value

Nonzero if successful; otherwise 0.

Parameters

render   Flag specifying how the server will render the OLE item. For the possible values, see **OLERENDER** in the OLE documentation.

cfFormat   Specifies the Clipboard data format to be cached when creating the OLE item.

lpFormatEtc   Pointer to a **FORMATETC** structure used if *render* is **OLERENDER_FORMAT** or **OLERENDER_DRAW**. Provide a value for this parameter only if you want to specify additional format information beyond the Clipboard format specified by *cfFormat*. If you omit this parameter, default values are used for the other fields in the **FORMATETC** structure.

Remarks

Call this function to create a static item from the contents of the Clipboard. A static item contains the presentation data but not the native data; consequently it cannot be edited. You typically call this function if the **CreateFromClipboard** member function fails.

For more information, see **OLERENDER** and **FORMATETC** in the OLE documentation.

See Also   **COleDataObject::AttachClipboard, COleClientItem::CanPaste, COleClientItem::CreateStaticFromData**

COleClientItem::CreateStaticFromData

BOOL CreateStaticFromData(COleDataObject* *pDataObject*, **OLERENDER** *render* **= OLERENDER_DRAW, CLIPFORMAT** *cfFormat* **= 0, LPFORMATETC** *lpFormatEtc* **= NULL);**

Return Value

Nonzero if successful; otherwise 0.

Parameters

pDataObject   Pointer to the **COleDataObject** object from which the OLE item is to be created.

render   Flag specifying how the server will render the OLE item. For the possible values, see **OLERENDER** in the OLE documentation.

cfFormat Specifies the Clipboard data format to be cached when creating the OLE item.

lpFormatEtc Pointer to a **FORMATETC** structure used if *render* is **OLERENDER_FORMAT** or **OLERENDER_DRAW**. Provide a value for this parameter only if you want to specify additional format information beyond the Clipboard format specified by *cfFormat*. If you omit this parameter, default values are used for the other fields in the **FORMATETC** structure.

Remarks

Call this function to create a static item from a **COleDataObject** object. A static item contains the presentation data but not the native data; consequently, it cannot be edited. This is essentially the same as **CreateStaticFromClipboard** except that a static item can be created from an arbitrary **COleDataObject**, not just from the Clipboard.

Used in **COlePasteSpecialDialog::CreateItem** when Static is selected.

For more information, see **OleCreateStaticFromData**, **OLERENDER**, and **FORMATETC** in the OLE documentation.

See Also **COleDataObject::AttachClipboard**, **COleDataObject**

COleClientItem::Deactivate

void Deactivate( );

Remarks

Call this function to deactivate the OLE item and free any associated resources. You typically deactivate an in-place active OLE item when the user clicks the mouse on the client area outside the bounds of the item. Note that deactivating the OLE item will discard its undo state, making it impossible to call the **ReactivateAndUndo** member function.

If your application supports undo, do not call **Deactivate**; instead, call **DeactivateUI**.

For more information, see **IOleInPlaceObject::InPlaceDeactivate** in the OLE documentation.

See Also **COleClientItem::ReactivateAndUndo**, **COleClientItem::DeactivateUI**

COleClientItem::DeactivateUI

void DeactivateUI( );

Remarks

Call this function when the user deactivates an item that was activated in place. This function restores the container application's user interface to its original state, hiding any menus and other controls that were created for in-place activation.

This function does not flush the undo state information for the item. That information is retained so that **ReactivateAndUndo** can later be used to execute an undo command in the server application, in case the container's undo command is chosen immediately after deactivating the item.

For more information, see **IOleInPlaceObject::InPlaceDeactivate** in the OLE documentation.

See Also **COleClientItem::ReactivateAndUndo, COleClientItem::Activate**

COleClientItem::Delete

void Delete(BOOL *bAutoDelete* = **TRUE);**

Parameters

bAutoDelete Specifies whether the item is to be removed from the document.

Remarks

Call this function to delete the OLE item from the container document. This function calls the **Release** member function, which in turn deletes the C++ object for the item, permanently removing the OLE item from the document. If the OLE item is embedded, the native data for the item is deleted. It always closes a running server; therefore, if the item is an open link, this function closes it.

See Also **COleClientItem::Release**

COleClientItem::DoDragDrop

DROPEFFECT DoDragDrop(LPCRECT *lpItemRect*, **CPoint** *ptOffset*,
    BOOL *bIncludeLink* = **FALSE,**
    DWORD *dwEffects* = **DROPEFFECT_COPY I DROPEFFECT_MOVE,**
    LPCRECT *lpRectStartDrag* = **NULL);**

Return Value

A **DROPEFFECT** value. If it is **DROPEFFECT_MOVE**, the original data should be removed.

Parameters

lpItemRect   The item's rectangle on screen in client coordinates (pixels).

ptOffset   The offset from *lpItemRect* where the mouse position was at the time of the drag.

bIncludeLink   Set this to **TRUE** if the link data should be copied to the Clipboard. Set it to **FALSE** if your server application does not support links.

dwEffects   Determines the effects that the drag source will allow in the drag operation.

lpRectStartDrag   Pointer to the rectangle that defines where the drag actually starts. For more information, see the following "Remarks" section.

Remarks

Call the **DoDragDrop** member function to perform a drag-and-drop operation. The drag-and-drop operation does not start immediately. It waits until the mouse cursor leaves the rectangle specified by *lpRectStartDrag* or until a specified number of milliseconds have passed. If *lpRectStartDrag* is **NULL**, the size of the rectangle is one pixel. The delay time is specified by the **DragDelay** value in the [Windows] section of WIN.INI. If this value is not in WIN.INI, the default value of 200 milliseconds is used.

See Also   **COleDataSource::DoDragDrop**, **COleClientItem::CopyToClipboard**

COleClientItem::DoVerb

virtual BOOL DoVerb(LONG *nVerb*, **CView*** *pView*, **LPMSG** *lpMsg* **= NULL);**

Return Value

Nonzero if the verb was successfully executed; otherwise 0.

Parameters

nVerb   Specifies the verb to execute. It can include one of the following:

Value	Meaning	Symbol
0	Primary verb	**OLEIVERB_PRIMARY**
1	Secondary verb	(None)
−1	Display item for editing	**OLEIVERB_SHOW**
−2	Edit item in separate window	**OLEIVERB_OPEN**
−3	Hide item	**OLEIVERB_HIDE**

The −1 value is typically an alias for another verb. If open editing is not supported, −2 has the same effect as −1. For additional values, see **IOleObject::DoVerb** in the OLE documentation.

pView Pointer to the view window; this is used by the server for in-place activation. This parameter should be **NULL** if the container application does not allow in-place activation.

lpMsg Pointer to the message that caused the item to be activated.

Remarks

Call **DoVerb** to execute the specified verb. This function calls the **Activate** member function to execute the verb. It also catches exceptions and displays a message box to the user if one is thrown.

If the primary verb is Edit and zero is specified in the *nVerb* parameter, the server application is launched to allow the OLE item to be edited. If the container application supports in-place activation, editing can be done in place. If the container does not support in-place activation (or if the Open verb is specified), the server is launched in a separate window and editing can be done there. Typically, when the user of the container application double-clicks the OLE item, the value for the primary verb in the *nVerb* parameter determines which action the user can take. However, if the server supports only one action, it takes that action, no matter which value is specified in the *nVerb* parameter.

See Also **COleClientItem::Activate**

COleClientItem::Draw

BOOL Draw(CDC* *pDC***, LPCRECT** *lpBounds***, DVASPECT** *nDrawAspect* = **(DVASPECT)-1);**

Return Value

Nonzero if successful; otherwise 0.

Parameters

pDC Pointer to a **CDC** object used for drawing the OLE item.

lpBounds Pointer to a **CRect** object or **RECT** structure that defines the bounding rectangle in which to draw the OLE item (in logical units determined by the device context).

nDrawAspect Specifies the aspect of the OLE item, that is, how it should be displayed. If *nDrawAspect* is –1, the last aspect set by using **SetDrawAspect** is used. For more information about possible values for this flag, see **SetDrawAspect**.

Remarks

Call this function to draw the OLE item into the specified bounding rectangle using the specified device context. The function may use the metafile representation of the OLE item created by the **OnDraw** member function of **COleServerItem**.

Typically you use **Draw** for screen display, passing the screen device context as *pDC*. In this case, you need to specify only the first two parameters.

The *lpBounds* parameter identifies the rectangle in the target device context (relative to its current mapping mode). Rendering may involve scaling the picture and can be used by container applications to impose a view that scales between the displayed view and the final printed image.

For more information, see **IViewObject::Draw** in the OLE documentation.

See Also   **COleClientItem::SetExtent**, **COleServerItem::OnDraw**

COleClientItem::GetActiveView

CView* GetActiveView( ) const;

Return Value

A pointer to the view; otherwise **NULL** if the item is not in-place activated.

Remarks

Returns the view on which the item is in-place activated.

See Also   **COleClientItem::IsInPlaceActive**, **COleClientItem::GetDocument**

COleClientItem::GetCachedExtent

BOOL GetCachedExtent(LPSIZE *lpSize*, **DVASPECT** *nDrawAspect* = **(DVASPECT)-1**);

Return Value

Nonzero if successful; 0 if the OLE item is blank.

Parameters

lpSize   Pointer to a **SIZE** structure or a **CSize** object that will receive the size information.

nDrawAspect   Specifies the aspect of the OLE item whose bounds are to be retrieved. For possible values, see **SetDrawAspect**.

Remarks

Call this function to retrieve the OLE item's size. This function provides the same information as **GetExtent**. However, you can call **GetCachedExtent** to get extent information during the processing of other OLE handlers, such as **OnChange**. The dimensions are in **MM_HIMETRIC** units.

This is possible because **GetCachedExtent** uses the **IViewObject2** interface rather than use the **IOleObject** interface to get the extent of this item. The **IViewObject2** COM object caches the extent information used in the previous call to **IViewObject::Draw**.

For more information, see **IViewObject2::GetExtent** in the OLE documentation.

See Also **COleClientItem::GetExtent**, **COleClientItem::SetExtent**, **COleServerItem::OnGetExtent**

COleClientItem::GetClassID

void GetClassID(CLSID* *pClassID* **) const;**

Parameters

pClassID   Pointer to a structure of type **CLSID** to retrieve the class ID. For information on the **CLSID** structure, see the OLE documentation.

Remarks

Returns the class ID of the item into the memory pointed to by *pClassID*. The class ID is a 128-bit number that uniquely identifies the application that edits the item.

For more information, see **IPersist::GetClassID** in the OLE documentation.

COleClientItem::GetClipboardData

void GetClipboardData(COleDataSource* *pDataSource*, **BOOL** *bIncludeLink* = **FALSE**, **LPPOINT** *lpOffset* = **NULL**, **LPSIZE** *lpSize* = **NULL**);

Parameters

pDataSource   Pointer to a **COleDataSource** object that will receive the data contained in the OLE item.

bIncludeLink   **TRUE** if link data should be included; otherwise **FALSE**.

lpOffset   The offset of the mouse cursor from the origin of the object in pixels.

lpSize   The size of the object in pixels.

Remarks

Call this function to get a **COleDataSource** object containing all the data that would be placed on the Clipboard by a call to the **CopyToClipboard** member function.

Override **GetClipboardData** only if you want to offer data formats in addition to those offered by **CopyToClipboard**. Place those formats in the **COleDataSource** object before or after calling **CopyToClipboard**, and then pass the **COleDataSource** object to the **COleDataSource::SetClipboard** function. For example, if you want the OLE item's position in its container document to accompany it on the Clipboard, you would define your own format for passing that information and place it in the **COleDataSource** before calling **CopyToClipboard**.

See Also **COleDataSource**, **COleClientItem::CopyToClipboard**, **COleDataSource::SetClipboard**

COleClientItem::GetDocument

COleDocument* GetDocument( ) const;

Return Value

A pointer to the document that contains the OLE item. **NULL** if the item is not part of a document.

Remarks

Call this function to get a pointer to the document that contains the OLE item. This pointer allows access to the document object that you passed as an argument to the **COleClientItem** constructor.

See Also **COleClientItem::COleClientItem, COleDocument, COleLinkingDoc**

COleClientItem::GetDrawAspect

DVASPECT GetDrawAspect( ) const;

Return Value

A value from the **DVASPECT** enumeration, whose values are listed in the reference for **SetDrawAspect**.

Remarks

Call the **GetDrawAspect** member function to determine the current "aspect," or view, of the item. The aspect specifies how the item is to be rendered.

See Also **COleClientItem::SetDrawAspect, COleClientItem::Draw**

COleClientItem::GetExtent

BOOL GetExtent(LPSIZE *lpSize***, DVASPECT** *nDrawAspect* = **(DVASPECT)-1);**

Return Value

Nonzero if successful; 0 if the OLE item is blank.

Parameters

lpSize   Pointer to a **SIZE** structure or a **CSize** object that will receive the size information.

nDrawAspect   Specifies the aspect of the OLE item whose bounds are to be retrieved. For possible values, see **SetDrawAspect**.

Remarks

Call this function to retrieve the OLE item's size.

If the server application was written using the Microsoft Foundation Class Library, this function causes the **OnGetExtent** member function of the corresponding **COleServerItem** object to be called. Note that the retrieved size may differ from the size last set by the **SetExtent** member function; the size specified by **SetExtent** is treated as a suggestion. The dimensions are in **MM_HIMETRIC** units.

Note Do not call **GetExtent** during the processing of an OLE handler, such as **OnChange**. Call **GetCachedExtent** instead.

For more information, see **IOleObject::GetExtent** in the OLE documentation.

See Also **COleClientItem::SetExtent, COleClientItem::GetCachedExtent, COleServerItem::OnGetExtent**

COleClientItem::GetIconicMetafile

HGLOBAL GetIconicMetafile( );

Return Value

A handle to the metafile if successful; otherwise **NULL**.

Remarks

Retrieves the metafile used for drawing the item's icon. If there is no current icon, a default icon is returned. This is called automatically by the MFC/OLE dialogs and is usually not called directly.

This function also calls **SetIconicMetafile** to cache the metafile for later use.

See Also **COleClientItem::SetIconicMetafile**

COleClientItem::GetInPlaceWindow

CWnd* GetInPlaceWindow( );

Return Value

A pointer to the item's in-place editing window; **NULL** if the item is not active or if its server is unavailable.

Remarks

Call the **GetInPlaceWindow** member function to get a pointer to the window in which the item has been opened for in-place editing. This function should be called only for items that are in-place active.

See Also **COleClientItem::Activate, COleClientItem::Deactivate, COleClientItem::SetItemRects**

COleClientItem::GetItemState

UINT GetItemState( ) const;

Return Value

A **COleClientItem::ItemState** enumerated value, which can be one of the following: **emptyState**, **loadedState**, **openState**, **activeState**, **activeUIState**. For information about these states, see the article "Containers: Client-Item States" in *Programming with MFC*.

Remarks

Call this function to get the OLE item's current state. To be notified when the OLE item's state changes, use the **OnChange** member function.

For more information, see the article "Containers: Client-Item States" in *Programming with MFC*.

See Also   COleClientItem::OnChange

COleClientItem::GetLastStatus

SCODE GetLastStatus( ) const;

Return Value

An **SCODE** value.

Remarks

Returns the status code of the last OLE operation. For member functions that return a **BOOL** value of **FALSE**, or other member functions that return **NULL**, **GetLastStatus** returns more detailed failure information. Be aware that most OLE member functions throw exceptions for more serious errors. The specific information on the interpretation of the **SCODE** depends on the underlying OLE call that last returned an **SCODE** value.

For more information on **SCODE**, see "Structure of OLE Error Codes" in the OLE documentation.

COleClientItem::GetLinkUpdateOptions

OLEUPDATE GetLinkUpdateOptions( );

Return Value

One of the following values:

- **OLEUPDATE_ALWAYS** Update the linked item whenever possible. This option supports the Automatic link-update radio button in the Links dialog box.

- **OLEUPDATE_ONCALL** Update the linked item only on request from the container application (when the **UpdateLink** member function is called). This option supports the Manual link-update radio button in the Links dialog box.

Remarks

Call this function to get the current value of the link-update option for the OLE item. This is an advanced operation.

This function is called automatically by the **COleLinksDialog** class.

For more information, see **IOleLink::GetUpdateOptions** in the OLE documentation.

See Also **COleClientItem::SetLinkUpdateOptions**, **COleLinksDialog**

COleClientItem::GetType

OLE_OBJTYPE GetType( ) const;

Return Value

An unsigned integer with one of the following values:

- **OT_LINK** The OLE item is a link.
- **OT_EMBEDDED** The OLE item is embedded.
- **OT_STATIC** The OLE item is static, that is, it contains only presentation data, not native data, and thus cannot be edited.

Remarks

Call this function to determine whether the OLE item is embedded or linked, or static.

See Also **COleClientItem::GetUserType**

COleClientItem::GetUserType

void GetUserType(USERCLASSTYPE *nUserClassType*, **CString&** *rString* **);**

Parameters

nUserClassType A value indicating the desired variant of the string describing the OLE item's type. This can have one of the following values:

- **USERCLASSTYPE_FULL** The full type name displayed to the user.
- **USERCLASSTYPE_SHORT** A short name (15 characters maximum) for use in pop-up menus and the Edit Links dialog box.
- **USERCLASSTYPE_APPNAME** Name of the application servicing the class.

rString   A reference to a **CString** object to which the string describing the OLE item's type is to be returned.

Remarks

Call this function to get the user-visible string describing the OLE item's type, such as "Word document." This is often the entry in the system registration database.

If the full type name is requested but not available, the short name is used instead. If no entry for the type of OLE item is found in the registration database, or if there are no user types registered for the type of OLE item, then the user type currently stored in the OLE item is used. If that user type name is an empty string, "Unknown Object" is used.

For more information, see **IOleObject::GetUserType** in the OLE documentation.

See Also   **COleClientItem::GetType**

COleClientItem::IsInPlaceActive

BOOL IsInPlaceActive( ) const;

Return Value

Nonzero if the OLE item is in-place active; otherwise 0.

Remarks

Call this function to see whether the OLE item is in-place active. It is common to execute different logic depending on whether the item is being edited in place. The function checks whether the current item state is equal to either the **activeState** or the **activeUIState**.

See Also   **COleClientItem::GetItemState**

COleClientItem::IsLinkUpToDate

BOOL IsLinkUpToDate( ) const;

Return Value

Nonzero if the OLE item is up to date; otherwise 0.

Remarks

Call this function to see whether the OLE item is up to date. A linked item can be out of date if its source document has been updated. An embedded item that contains links within it can similarly become out of date. The function does a recursive check of the OLE item. Note that determining whether an OLE item is out of date can be as expensive as actually performing an update.

This is called automatically by the **COleLinksDialog** implementation.

For more information, see **IOleObject::IsUpToDate** in the OLE documentation.

COleClientItem::IsModified

BOOL IsModified( ) const;

Return Value

Nonzero if the OLE item is dirty; otherwise 0.

Remarks

Call this function to see whether the OLE item is dirty (modified since it was last saved).

For more information, see **IPersistStorage::IsDirty** in the OLE documentation.

COleClientItem::IsOpen

BOOL IsOpen( ) const;

Return Value

Nonzero if the OLE item is open; otherwise 0.

Remarks

Call this function to see whether the OLE item is open; that is, opened in an instance of the server application running in a separate window. It is used to determine when to draw the object with a hatching pattern. An open object should have a hatch pattern drawn on top of the object. You can use a **CRectTracker** object to accomplish this.

See Also   **COleClientItem::GetItemState**, **CRectTracker**

COleClientItem::IsRunning

BOOL IsRunning( ) const;

Return Value

Nonzero if the OLE item is running; otherwise 0.

Remarks

Call this function to see whether the OLE item is running; that is, whether the item is loaded and running in the server application.

For more information, see **OleIsRunning** in the OLE documentation.

COleClientItem::OnActivate

virtual void OnActivate( );

Remarks

Called by the framework to notify the item that it has just been activated in place. Note that this function is called to indicate that the server is running, not to indicate that its user interface has been installed in the container application. At this point, the object does not have an active user interface (is not **activeUIState**). It has not installed its menus or toolbar. The **OnActivateUI** member function is called when that happens.

The default implementation calls the **OnChange** member function with **OLE_CHANGEDSTATE** as a parameter. Override this function to perform custom processing when an item becomes in-place active.

See Also **COleClientItem::OnDeactivate**, **COleClientItem::OnDeactivateUI**, **COleClientItem::OnActivateUI**, **COleClientItem::CanActivate**

COleClientItem::OnActivateUI

virtual void OnActivateUI( );

Remarks

The framework calls **OnActivateUI** when the object has entered the active UI state. The object has now installed its tool bar and menus.

The default implementation remembers the server's **HWND** for later **GetServerWindow** calls.

See Also **COleClientItem::OnDeactivate**, **COleClientItem::OnDeactivateUI**, **COleClientItem::OnActivate**, **COleClientItem::CanActivate**

COleClientItem::OnChange

virtual void OnChange(OLE_NOTIFICATION *nCode*, **DWORD** *dwParam* **);**

Parameters

nCode The reason the server changed this item. It can have one of the following values:

- **OLE_CHANGED** The OLE item's appearance has changed.
- **OLE_SAVED** The OLE item has been saved.
- **OLE_CLOSED** The OLE item has been closed.
- **OLE_CHANGED_STATE** The OLE item has changed from one state to another.

dwParam   If *nCode* is **OLE_SAVED** or **OLE_CLOSED**, this parameter is not used. If *nCode* is **OLE_CHANGED**, this parameter specifies the aspect of the OLE item that has changed. For possible values, see the *dwParam* parameter of **COleClientItem::Draw**. If *nCode* is **OLE_CHANGED_STATE**, this parameter is a **COleClientItem::ItemState** enumerated value and describes the state being entered. It can have one of the following values: **emptyState**, **loadedState**, **openState**, **activeState**, or **activeUIState**.

Remarks

Called by the framework when the user modifies, saves, or closes the OLE item. (If the server application is written using the Microsoft Foundation Class Library, this function is called in response to the **Notify** member functions of **COleServerDoc** or **COleServerItem**.) The default implementation marks the container document as modified if *nCode* is **OLE_CHANGED** or **OLE_SAVED**.

For **OLE_CHANGED_STATE**, the current state returned from **GetItemState** will still be the old state, meaning the state that was current prior to this state change.

Override this function to respond to changes in the OLE item's state. Typically you update the item's appearance by invalidating the area in which the item is displayed. Call the base class implementation at the beginning of your override.

See Also   **COleClientItem::GetItemState**, **COleServerItem::NotifyChanged**, **COleServerDoc::NotifyChanged**, **COleServerDoc::NotifyClosed**, **COleServerDoc::NotifySaved**

COleClientItem::OnChangeItemPosition

virtual BOOL OnChangeItemPosition(const CRect& *rectPos* **);**

Return Value

Nonzero if the item's position is successfully changed; otherwise 0.

Parameters

rectPos   Indicates the item's position relative to the container application's client area.

Remarks

Called by the framework to notify the container that the OLE item's extent has changed during in-place activation. The default implementation determines the new visible rectangle of the OLE item and calls **SetItemRects** with the new values. The default implementation calculates the visible rectangle for the item and passes that information to the server.

Override this function to apply special rules to the resize/move operation. If the application is written in MFC, this call results because the server called **COleServerDoc::RequestPositionChange**.

See Also **COleServerDoc::RequestPositionChange**

COleClientItem::OnDeactivate

virtual void OnDeactivate( );

Remarks

Called by the framework when the OLE item transitions from the in-place active state (**activeState**) to the loaded state, meaning that it is deactivated after an in-place activation. Note that this function is called to indicate that the OLE item is closed, not that its user interface has been removed from the container application. When that happens, the **OnDeactivateUI** member function is called.

The default implementation calls the **OnChange** member function with **OLE_CHANGEDSTATE** as a parameter. Override this function to perform custom processing when an in-place active item is deactivated. For example, if you support the undo command in your container application, you can override this function to discard the undo state, indicating that the last operation performed on the OLE item cannot be undone once the item is deactivated.

See Also **COleClientItem::OnGetWindowContext**, **COleClientItem::OnDeactivateUI**, **COleClientItem::OnActivateUI**, **COleClientItem::OnActivate**, **COleClientItem::CanActivate**, **CDocTemplate::SetContainerInfo**

COleClientItem::OnDeactivateAndUndo

virtual void OnDeactivateAndUndo( );

Remarks

Called by the framework when the user invokes the undo command after activating the OLE item in place. The default implementation calls **DeactivateUI** to deactivate the server's user interface. Override this function if you are implementing the undo command in your container application. In your override, call the base class version of the function and then undo the last command executed in your application.

For more information, see **IOleInPlaceSite::DeactivateAndUndo** in the OLE documentation.

See Also **COleClientItem::DeactivateUI**

COleClientItem::OnDeactivateUI

>virtual void **OnDeactivateUI**(**BOOL** *bUndoable*);

Parameters

>*bUndoable*   Specifies whether the editing changes are undoable.

Remarks

>Called when the user deactivates an item that was activated in place. This function restores the container application's user interface to its original state, hiding any menus and other controls that were created for in-place activation.

>If *bUndoable* is **FALSE**, the container should disable the undo command, in effect discarding the undo state of the container, because it indicates that the last operation performed by the server is not undoable.

>**See Also**   **COleClientItem::OnActivateUI**, **COleClientItem::OnDeactivateAndUndo**, **COleClientItem::OnDeactivate**

COleClientItem::OnDiscardUndoState

>virtual void **OnDiscardUndoState**( );

Remarks

>Called by the framework when the user performs an action that discards the undo state while editing the OLE item. The default implementation does nothing. Override this function if you are implementing the undo command in your container application. In your override, discard the container application's undo state.

>If the server was written with the Microsoft Foundation Class Library, the server can cause this function to be called by calling **COleServerDoc::DiscardUndoState**.

>For more information, see **IOleInPlaceSite::DiscardUndoState** in the OLE documentation.

>**See Also**   **COleServerDoc::DiscardUndoState**

COleClientItem::OnGetClipboardData

>virtual **COleDataSource* OnGetClipboardData**(**BOOL** *bIncludeLink*, **LPPOINT** *lpOffset*, **LPSIZE** *lpSize*);

Return Value

>A pointer to a **COleDataSource** object containing the Clipboard data.

Parameters

>*bIncludeLink*   Set this to **TRUE** if link data should be copied to the Clipboard. Set this to **FALSE** if your server application does not support links.

lpOffset   Pointer to the offset of the mouse cursor from the origin of the object in pixels.

lpSize   Pointer to the size of the object in pixels.

Remarks

Called by the framework to get a **COleDataSource** object containing all the data that would be placed on the Clipboard by a call to either the **CopyToClipboard** or the **DoDragDrop** member function. The default implementation of this function calls **GetClipboardData**.

See Also   **COleDataSource, COleClientItem::CopyToClipboard, COleClientItem::GetClipboardData, COleDataSource::SetClipboard**

COleClientItem::OnGetClipRect

virtual void OnGetClipRect(CRect& *rClipRect* **);**

Parameters

rClipRect   Pointer to an object of class **CRect** that will hold the clipping-rectangle coordinates of the item.

Remarks

The framework calls the **OnGetClipRect** member function to get the clipping-rectangle coordinates of the item that is being edited in place. Coordinates are in pixels relative to the container application window's client area.

The default implementation simply returns the client rectangle of the view on which the item is in-place active.

See Also   **COleClientItem::OnActivate**

COleClientItem::OnGetItemPosition

virtual void OnGetItemPosition(CRect& *rPosition* **);**

Parameters

rPosition   Reference to the **CRect** object that will contain the item's position coordinates.

Remarks

The framework calls the **OnGetItemPosition** member function to get the coordinates of the item that is being edited in place. Coordinates are in pixels relative to the container application window's client area.

The default implementation of this function does nothing. Applications that support in-place editing require its implementation.

See Also   **COleClientItem::OnActivate, COleClientItem::OnActivateUI**

COleClientItem::OnGetWindowContext

virtual BOOL OnGetWindowContext(CFrameWnd** *ppMainFrame*,
CFrameWnd** *ppDocFrame*, **LPOLEINPLACEFRAMEINFO** *lpFrameInfo* **);**

Return Value

Nonzero if successful; otherwise 0.

Parameters

ppMainFrame   Pointer to a pointer to the main frame window.

ppDocFrame   Pointer to a pointer to the document frame window.

lpFrameInfo   Pointer to an **OLEINPLACEFRAMEINFO** structure that will receive
frame window information.

Remarks

Called by the framework when an item is activated in place. This function is used to
retrieve information about the OLE item's parent window.

If the container is an MDI application, the default implementation returns a pointer
to the **CMDIFrameWnd** object in *ppMainFrame* and a pointer to the active
CMDIChildWnd object in *ppDocFrame*. If the container is an SDI application, the
default implementation returns a pointer to the **CFrameWnd** object in *ppMainFrame*
and returns **NULL** in *ppDocFrame*. The default implementation also fills in the
members of *lpFrameInfo*.

Override this function only if the default implementation does not suit your
application; for example, if your application has a user-interface paradigm that differs
from SDI or MDI. This is an advanced overridable.

For more information, see **IOleInPlaceSite::GetWindowContext** and the
OLEINPLACEFRAMEINFO structure in the OLE documentation.

COleClientItem::OnInsertMenus

virtual void OnInsertMenus(CMenu* *pMenuShared*,
LPOLEMENUGROUPWIDTHS *lpMenuWidths* **);**

Parameters

pMenuShared   Points to an empty menu.

lpMenuWidths   Points to an array of six **LONG** values indicating how many menus
are in each of the following menu groups: File, Edit, Container, Object, Window,
Help. The container application is responsible for the File, Container, and Window
menu groups, corresponding to elements 0, 2, and 4 of this array.

Remarks

Called by the framework during in-place activation to insert the container application's menus into an empty menu. This menu is then passed to the server, which inserts its own menus, creating a composite menu. This function can be called repeatedly to build several composite menus.

The default implementation inserts into *pMenuShared* the in-place container menus; that is, the File, Container, and Window menu groups.
CDocTemplate::SetContainerInfo is used to set this menu resource. The default implementation also assigns the appropriate values to elements 0, 2, and 4 in *lpMenuWidths*, depending on the menu resource. Override this function if the default implementation is not appropriate for your application; for example, if your application does not use document templates for associating resources with document types. If you override this function, you should also override **OnSetMenu** and **OnRemoveMenus**. This is an advanced overridable.

For more information, see **IOleInPlaceFrame::InsertMenus** in the OLE documentation.

See Also   **COleClientItem::OnRemoveMenus**, **COleClientItem::OnSetMenu**

COleClientItem::OnRemoveMenus

virtual void OnRemoveMenus(CMenu* *pMenuShared* **);**

Parameters

pMenuShared   Points to the composite menu constructed by calls to the **OnInsertMenus** member function.

Remarks

Called by the framework to remove the container's menus from the specified composite menu when in-place activation ends.

The default implementation removes from *pMenuShared* the in-place container menus, that is, the File, Container, and Window menu groups. Override this function if the default implementation is not appropriate for your application; for example, if your application does not use document templates for associating resources with document types. If you override this function, you should probably override **OnInsertMenus** and **OnSetMenu** as well. This is an advanced overridable.

The submenus on *pMenuShared* may be shared by more than one composite menu if the server has repeatedly called **OnInsertMenus**. Therefore you should not delete any submenus in your override of **OnRemoveMenus**; you should only detach them.

For more information, see **IOleInPlaceFrame::RemoveMenus** in the OLE documentation.

See Also   **COleClientItem::OnInsertMenus**, **COleClientItem::OnSetMenu**

COleClientItem::OnScrollBy

virtual BOOL OnScrollBy(CSize *sizeExtent* **);**

Return Value

Nonzero if the item was scrolled; 0 if the item could not be scrolled.

Parameters

sizeExtent   Specifies the distances, in pixels, to scroll in the x and y directions.

Remarks

Called by the framework to scroll the OLE item in response to requests from the server. For example, if the OLE item is partially visible and the user moves outside the visible region while performing in-place editing, this function is called to keep the cursor visible. The default implementation does nothing. Override this function to scroll the item by the specified amount. Note that as a result of scrolling, the visible portion of the OLE item can change. Call **SetItemRects** to update the item's visible rectangle.

For more information, see **IOleInPlaceSite::Scroll** in the OLE documentation.

See Also   **COleClientItem::SetItemRects**

COleClientItem::OnSetMenu

virtual void OnSetMenu(CMenu* *pMenuShared*, **HOLEMENU** *holemenu*,
HWND *hwndActiveObject* **);**

Parameters

pMenuShared   Pointer to the composite menu constructed by calls to the **OnInsertMenus** member function and the **::InsertMenu** function.

holemenu   Handle to the menu descriptor returned by the **::OleCreateMenuDescriptor** function, or **NULL** if the dispatching code is to be removed.

hwndActiveObject   Handle to the editing window for the OLE item. This is the window that will receive editing commands from OLE.

Remarks

Called by the framework two times when in-place activation begins and ends; the first time to install the composite menu and the second time (with *holemenu* equal to **NULL**) to remove it. The default implementation installs or removes the composite menu and then calls the **OleSetMenuDescriptor** function to install or remove the dispatching code. Override this function if the default implementation is not appropriate for your application. If you override this function, you should probably override **OnInsertMenus** and **OnRemoveMenus** as well. This is an advanced overridable.

For more information, see **OleCreateMenuDescriptor**, **OleSetMenuDescriptor**, and **IOleInPlaceFrame::SetMenu** in the OLE documentation.

See Also **COleClientItem::OnInsertMenus**, **COleClientItem::OnRemoveMenus**

COleClientItem::OnShowControlBars

virtual BOOL OnShowControlBars(CFrameWnd* *pFrameWnd***, BOOL** *bShow* **);**

Return Value

Nonzero if the function call causes a change in the control bars' state; 0 if the call causes no change, or if *pFrameWnd* does not point to the container's frame window.

Parameters

pFrameWnd   Pointer to the container application's frame window. This can be either a main frame window or an MDI child window.

bShow   Specifies whether control bars are to be shown or hidden.

Remarks

Called by the framework to show and hide the container application's control bars. This function returns 0 if the control bars are already in the state specified by *bShow*. This would occur, for example, if the control bars are hidden and *bShow* is **FALSE**.

The default implementation removes the toolbar from the top-level frame window.

See Also **COleClientItem::OnInsertMenus**, **COleClientItem::OnSetMenu**, **COleClientItem::OnRemoveMenus**, **COleClientItem::OnUpdateFrameTitle**

COleClientItem::OnShowItem

virtual void OnShowItem( );

Remarks

Called by the framework to display the OLE item, making it totally visible during editing. It is used when your container application supports links to embedded items (that is, if you have derived your document class from **COleLinkingDoc**). This function is called during in-place activation or when the OLE item is a link source and the user wants to edit it. The default implementation activates the first view on the container document. Override this function to scroll the document so that the OLE item is visible.

See Also **COleLinkingDoc**

COleClientItem::OnUpdateFrameTitle

virtual BOOL OnUpdateFrameTitle( );

Return Value

Nonzero if this function successfully updated the frame title, otherwise zero.

Remarks

Called by the framework during in-place activation to update the frame window's title bar. The default implementation does not change the frame window title. Override this function if you want a different frame title for your application, for example "*server app - item* in *docname*" (as in, "Microsoft Excel - spreadsheet in REPORT.DOC"). This is an advanced overridable.

COleClientItem::ReactivateAndUndo

BOOL ReactivateAndUndo( );

Return Value

Nonzero if successful; otherwise 0.

Remarks

Call this function to reactivate the OLE item and undo the last operation performed by the user during in-place editing. If your container application supports the undo command, call this function if the user chooses the undo command immediately after deactivating the OLE item.

If the server application is written with the Microsoft Foundation Class Libraries, this function causes the server to call **COleServerDoc::OnReactivateAndUndo**.

For more information, see **IOleInPlaceObject::ReactivateAndUndo** in the OLE documentation.

See Also **COleServerDoc::OnReactivateAndUndo**, **COleClientItem::OnDeactivateAndUndo**

COleClientItem::Release

virtual void Release(OLECLOSE *dwCloseOption* **= OLECLOSE_NOSAVE);**

Parameters

dwCloseOption   Flag specifying under what circumstances the OLE item is saved when it returns to the loaded state. For a list of possible values, see **COleClientItem::Close**.

Remarks

Call this function to clean up resources used by the OLE item. **Release** is called by the **COleClientItem** destructor.

For more information, see **IUnknown::Release** in the OLE documentation.

See Also **COleClientItem::Close, COleClientItem::Delete**

COleClientItem::Reload

BOOL Reload( );

Return Value

Nonzero if successful; otherwise 0.

Remarks

Closes and reloads the item. Call the **Reload** function after activating the item as an item of another type by a call to **ActivateAs**.

See Also **COleClientItem::ActivateAs**

COleClientItem::Run

void Run( );

Remarks

Runs the application associated with this item.

Call the **Run** member function to launch the server application before activating the item. This is done automatically by **Activate** and **DoVerb**, so it is usually not necessary to call this function. Call this function if it is necessary to run the server in order to set an item attribute, such as **SetExtent**, before executing **DoVerb**.

See Also **COleClientItem::IsRunning**

COleClientItem::SetDrawAspect

void SetDrawAspect(DVASPECT *nDrawAspect* **);**

Parameters

nDrawAspect A value from the **DVASPECT** enumeration. This parameter can have one of the following values:

- **DVASPECT_CONTENT** Item is represented in such a way that it can be displayed as an embedded object inside its container.

- **DVASPECT_THUMBNAIL** Item is rendered in a "thumbnail" representation so that it can be displayed in a browsing tool.

- **DVASPECT_ICON** Item is represented by an icon.

- **DVASPECT_DOCPRINT** Item is represented as if it were printed using the Print command from the File menu.

Remarks

Call the **SetDrawAspect** member function to set the "aspect," or view, of the item. The aspect specifies how the item is to be rendered by **Draw** when the default value for that function's *nDrawAspect* argument is used.

This function is called automatically by the Change Icon (and other dialogs that call the Change Icon dialog directly) to enable the iconic display aspect when requested by the user.

See Also **COleClientItem::GetDrawAspect**, **COleClientItem::Draw**

COleClientItem::SetExtent

void SetExtent(const CSize& *size***, DVASPECT** *nDrawAspect* **= DVASPECT_CONTENT);**

Parameters

size A **CSize** object that contains the size information.

nDrawAspect Specifies the aspect of the OLE item whose bounds are to be set. For possible values, see **SetDrawAspect**.

Remarks

Call this function to specify how much space is available to the OLE item. If the server application was written using the Microsoft Foundation Class Library, this causes the **OnSetExtent** member function of the corresponding **COleServerItem** object to be called. The OLE item can then adjust its display accordingly. The dimensions must be in **MM_HIMETRIC** units. Call this function when the user resizes the OLE item or if you support some form of layout negotiation.

For more information, see **IOleObject::SetExtent** in the OLE documentation.

See Also **COleClientItem::GetExtent**, **COleClientItem::GetCachedExtent**, **COleServerItem::OnSetExtent**

COleClientItem::SetHostNames

void SetHostNames(LPCTSTR *lpszHost***, LPCTSTR** *lpszHostObj* **);**

Parameters

lpszHost Pointer to the user-visible name of the container application.

lpszHostObj Pointer to an identifying string of the container that contains the OLE item.

Remarks

Call this function to specify the name of the container application and the container's name for an embedded OLE item. If the server application was written using the Microsoft Foundation Class Library, this function calls the **OnSetHostNames** member function of the **COleServerDoc** document that contains the OLE item. This information is used in window titles when the OLE item is being edited. Each time a container document is loaded, the framework calls this function for all the OLE items in the document. **SetHostNames** is applicable only to embedded items. It is not necessary to call this function each time an embedded OLE item is activated for editing.

This is also called automatically with the application name and document name when an object is loaded or when a file is saved under a different name. Accordingly, it is not usually necessary to call this function directly.

For more information, see **IOleObject::SetHostNames** in the OLE documentation.

See Also **COleServerDoc::OnSetHostNames**

COleClientItem::SetIconicMetafile

BOOL SetIconicMetafile(HGLOBAL *hMetaPict* **);**

Return Value

Nonzero if successful; otherwise 0.

Parameters

hMetaPict A handle to the metafile used for drawing the item's icon.

Remarks

Caches the metafile used for drawing the item's icon. Use **GetIconicMetafile** to retrieve the metafile.

The *hMetaPict* parameter is copied into the item; therefore, *hMetaPict* must be freed by the caller.

See Also **COleClientItem::GetIconicMetafile**

COleClientItem::SetItemRects

BOOL SetItemRects(LPCRECT *lpPosRect* **= NULL, LPCRECT** *lpClipRect* **= NULL);**

Return Value

Nonzero if successful; otherwise, 0.

Parameters

lprcPosRect Pointer to the rectangle containing the bounds of the OLE item relative to its parent window, in client coordinates.

lprcClipRect   Pointer to the rectangle containing the bounds of the visible portion of the OLE item relative to its parent window, in client coordinates.

Remarks

Call this function to set the bounding rectangle or the visible rectangle of the OLE item. This function is called by the default implementation of the **OnChangeItemPosition** member function. You should call this function whenever the position or visible portion of the OLE item changes. Usually this means that you call it from your view's **OnSize** and **OnScrollBy** member functions.

For more information, see **IOleInPlaceObject::SetObjectRects** in the OLE documentation.

See Also   **COleClientItem::OnChangeItemPosition**, **COleClientItem::OnGetItemPosition**

COleClientItem::SetLinkUpdateOptions

void SetLinkUpdateOptions(OLEUPDATE *dwUpdateOpt* **);**

Parameters

dwUpdateOpt   The value of the link-update option for this item. This value must be one of the following:

- **OLEUPDATE_ALWAYS**   Update the linked item whenever possible. This option supports the Automatic link-update radio button in the Links dialog box.

- **OLEUPDATE_ONCALL**   Update the linked item only on request from the container application (when the **UpdateLink** member function is called). This option supports the Manual link-update radio button in the Links dialog box.

Remarks

Call this function to set the link-update option for the presentation of the specified linked item. Typically, you should not change the update options chosen by the user in the Links dialog box.

For more information, see **IOleLink::SetUpdateOptions** in the OLE documentation.

See Also   **COleClientItem::GetLinkUpdateOptions**, **COleLinksDialog**

COleClientItem::SetPrintDevice

BOOL SetPrintDevice(const DVTARGETDEVICE* *ptd* **);**
BOOL SetPrintDevice(const PRINTDLG* *ppd* **);**

Return Value

Nonzero if the function was successful; otherwise 0.

Parameters

ptd Pointer to a **DVTARGETDEVICE** data structure, which contains information about the new print-target device. Can be **NULL**.

ppd Pointer to a **PRINTDLG** data structure, which contains information about the new print-target device. Can be **NULL**.

Remarks

Call this function to change the print-target device for this item. This function updates the print-target device for the item but does not refresh the presentation cache. To update the presentation cache for an item, call **UpdateLink**.

The arguments to this function contain information that the OLE system uses to identify the target device. The **PRINTDLG** structure contains information that Windows uses to initialize the common Print dialog box. After the user closes the dialog box, Windows returns information about the user's selections in this structure. The **m_pd** member of a **CPrintDialog** object is a **PRINTDLG** structure.

For more information about this structure, see **PRINTDLG** in the Win32 documentation.

For more information, see **DVTARGETDEVICE** in the OLE documentation.

See Also   **COleClientItem::UpdateLink**, **CPrintDialog**

COleClientItem::UpdateLink

BOOL UpdateLink( );

Return Value

Nonzero on success; otherwise 0.

Remarks

Call this function to update the presentation data of the OLE item immediately. For linked items, the function finds the link source to obtain a new presentation for the OLE item. This process may involve running one or more server applications, which could be time-consuming. For embedded items, the function operates recursively, checking whether the embedded item contains links that might be out of date and updating them. The user can also manually update individual links using the Links dialog box.

For more information, see **IOleLink::Update** in the OLE documentation.

See Also   **COleLinksDialog**

COleControl

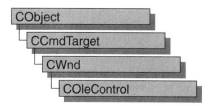

The **COleControl** class is a powerful base class for developing OLE controls. Derived from **CWnd**, this class inherits all the functionality of a Windows window object plus additional functionality specific to OLE, such as event firing and the ability to support methods and properties.

OLE controls can be inserted into OLE container applications and communicate with the container by using a two-way system of event firing and exposing methods and properties to the container. Note that standard OLE containers only support the basic functionality of an OLE control. They are unable to support extended features of an OLE control. Event firing occurs when events are sent to the container as a result of certain actions taking place in the control. In turn, the container communicates with the control by using an exposed set of methods and properties analogous to the member functions and data members of a C++ class. This approach allows the developer to control the appearance of the control and notify the container when certain actions occur.

For more information on developing an OLE control framework, see the articles "Developing OLE Controls," "OLE Controls," and "OLE ControlWizard" in *Programming with MFC*. For more information on adding functionality beyond the basic framework, see the Circle Sample Tutorial in *Tutorials*.

#include <afxctl.h>

See Also   **COlePropertyPage**, **CFontHolder**, **CPictureHolder**

Construction/Destruction

COleControl	Creates a **COleControl** object.
RecreateControlWindow	Destroys and re-creates the control's window.

Initialization

InitializeIIDs	Informs the base class of the IIDs the control will use.
SetInitialSize	Sets the size of an OLE control when first displayed in a container.

Control Modification Functions

IsModified	Determines if the control state has changed.
SetModifiedFlag	Changes the modified state of a control.

Persistence

ExchangeExtent	Serializes the control's width and height.
ExchangeStockProps	Serializes the control's stock properties.
ExchangeVersion	Serializes the control's version number.
IsConvertingVBX	Allows specialized loading of an OLE control.
SetModifiedFlag	Changes the modified state of a control.
WillAmbientsBeValidDuring Load	Determines whether ambient properties will be available the next time the control is loaded.

Update/Painting Functions

DoSuperclassPaint	Redraws an OLE control that has been subclassed from a Windows control.
InvalidateControl	Invalidates an area of the displayed control, causing it to be redrawn.
SelectFontObject	Selects a custom Font property into a device context.
SelectStockFont	Selects the stock Font property into a device context.
TranslateColor	Converts an **OLE_COLOR** value to a **COLORREF** value.

Dispatch Exceptions

GetNotSupported	Prevents access to a control's property value by the user.
SetNotPermitted	Indicates that an edit request has failed.
SetNotSupported	Prevents modification to a control's property value by the user.
ThrowError	Signals that an error has occurred in an OLE control.

Ambient Property Functions

AmbientBackColor	Returns the value of the ambient BackColor property.
AmbientDisplayName	Returns the name of the control as specified by the container.
AmbientForeColor	Returns the value of the ambient ForeColor property.
AmbientFont	Returns the value of the ambient Font property.
AmbientLocaleID	Returns the container's locale ID.
AmbientScaleUnits	Returns the type of units used by the container.
AmbientShowGrabHandles	Determines if grab handles should be displayed.
AmbientShowHatching	Determines if hatching should be displayed.

Ambient Property Functions

AmbientTextAlign	Returns the type of text alignment specified by the container.
AmbientUIDead	Determines if the control should respond to user-interface actions.
AmbientUserMode	Determines the mode of the container.
GetAmbientProperty	Returns the value of the specified ambient property.

Event Firing Functions

FireClick	Fires the stock Click event.
FireDblClick	Fires the stock DblClick event.
FireError	Fires the stock Error event.
FireEvent	Fires a custom event.
FireKeyDown	Fires the stock KeyDown event.
FireKeyPress	Fires the stock KeyPress event.
FireKeyUp	Fires the stock KeyUp event.
FireMouseDown	Fires the stock MouseDown event.
FireMouseMove	Fires the stock MouseMove event.
FireMouseUp	Fires the stock MouseUp event.

Stock Methods/Properties

DoClick	Implementation of the stock DoClick method.
Refresh	Forces a repaint of a control's appearance.
GetBackColor	Returns the value of the stock BackColor property.
SetBackColor	Sets the value of the stock BackColor property.
GetBorderStyle	Returns the value of the stock BorderStyle property.
SetBorderStyle	Sets the value of the stock BorderStyle property.
GetEnabled	Returns the value of the stock Enabled property.
SetEnabled	Sets the value of the stock Enabled property.
GetForeColor	Returns the value of the stock ForeColor property.
SetForeColor	Sets the value of the stock ForeColor property.
GetFont	Returns the value of the stock Font property.
GetFontTextMetrics	Returns the metrics of a **CFontHolder** object.
GetStockTextMetrics	Returns the metrics of the stock Font property.
InternalGetFont	Returns a **CFontHolder** object for the stock Font property.
SetFont	Sets the value of the stock Font property.
SelectStockFont	Selects the control's stock Font property into a device context.

Stock Methods/Properties

GetHwnd	Returns the value of the stock hWnd property.
GetText	Returns the value of the stock Text or Caption property.
InternalGetText	Retrieves the stock Caption or Text property.
SetText	Sets the value of the stock Text or Caption property.

OLE Control Sizing Functions

GetControlSize	Returns the position and size of the OLE control.
SetControlSize	Sets the position and size of the OLE control.
GetRectInContainer	Returns the control's rectangle relative to its container.
SetRectInContainer	Sets the control's rectangle relative to its container.

OLE Data Binding Functions

BoundPropertyChanged	Notifies the container that a bound property has been changed.
BoundPropertyRequestEdit	Requests permission to edit the property value.

Simple Frame Functions

EnableSimpleFrame	Enables simple frame support for a control.

OLE Control Site Functions

ControlInfoChanged	Call this function after the set of mnemonics handled by the control has changed.
GetExtendedControl	Retrieves a pointer to an extended control object belonging to the container.
LockInPlaceActive	Determines if your control can be deactivated by the container.
TransformCoords	Transforms coordinate values between a container and the control.

Modal Dialog Functions

PreModalDialog	Notifies the container that a modal dialog box is about to be displayed.
PostModalDialog	Notifies the container that a modal dialog box has been closed.

Overridables

DisplayError	Displays stock Error events to the control's user.
DoPropExchange	Serializes the properties of a **COleControl** object.
GetClassID	Retrieves the OLE class ID of the control.
GetMessageString	Provides status bar text for a menu item.

Overridables

IsSubclassedControl	Called to determine if the control subclasses a Windows control.
OnClick	Called to fire the stock Click event.
OnDoVerb	Called after a control verb has been executed.
OnDraw	Called when a control is requested to redraw itself.
OnDrawMetafile	Called by the container when a control is requested to redraw itself using a metafile device context.
OnEdit	Called by the container to UI Activate an OLE control.
OnEnumVerbs	Called by the container to enumerate a control's verbs.
OnEventAdvise	Called when event handlers are connected or disconnected from a control.
OnGetColorSet	Notifies the control that **IOleObject::GetColorSet** has been called.
OnKeyDownEvent	Called after the stock KeyDown event has been fired.
OnKeyPressEvent	Called after the stock KeyPress event has been fired.
OnKeyUpEvent	Called after the stock KeyUp event has been fired.
OnProperties	Called when the control's "Properties" verb has been invoked.
OnResetState	Resets a control's properties to the default values.

Change Notification Functions

OnBackColorChanged	Called when the stock BackColor property is changed.
OnBorderStyleChanged	Called when the stock BorderStyle property is changed.
OnEnabledChanged	Called when the stock Enabled property is changed.
OnFontChanged	Called when the stock Font property is changed.
OnForeColorChanged	Called when the stock ForeColor property is changed.
OnTextChanged	Called when the stock Text or Caption property is changed.

OLE Interface Notification Functions

OnAmbientPropertyChange	Called when an ambient property is changed.
OnFreezeEvents	Called when a control's events are frozen or unfrozen.
OnGetControlInfo	Provides mnemonic information to the container.
OnMnemonic	Called when a mnemonic key of the control has been pressed.
OnRenderData	Called by the framework to retrieve data in the specified format.

OLE Interface Notification Functions

OnRenderFileData	Called by the framework to retrieve data from a file in the specified format.
OnRenderGlobalData	Called by the framework to retrieve data from global memory in the specified format.
OnSetClientSite	Notifies the control that **IOleControl::SetClientSite** has been called.
OnSetData	Replaces the control's data with another value.
OnSetExtent	Called after the control's extent has changed.
OnSetObjectRects	Called after the control's dimensions have been changed.

In-Place Activation Functions

OnGetInPlaceMenu	Requests the handle of the control's menu that will be merged with the container menu.
OnHideToolBars	Called by the container when the control is UI deactivated.
OnShowToolBars	Called when the control has been UI activated.

Property Browsing Functions

OnGetDisplayString	Called to obtain a string to represent a property value.
OnGetPredefinedStrings	Returns strings representing possible values for a property.
OnGetPredefinedValue	Returns the value corresponding to a predefined string.
OnMapPropertyToPage	Indicates which property page to use for editing a property.

Member Functions

COleControl::AmbientBackColor

OLE_COLOR AmbientBackColor( );

Return Value

The current value of the container's ambient BackColor property, if any. If the property is not supported, this function returns the system-defined Windows background color.

Remarks

The ambient BackColor property is available to all controls and is defined by the container. Note that the container is not required to support this property.

See Also   **COleControl::TranslateColor, COleControl::GetBackColor, COleControl::AmbientForeColor**

COleControl::AmbientDisplayName

CString AmbientDisplayName( );

Return Value

The name of the OLE control. The default is a zero-length string.

Remarks

The name the container has assigned to the control can be used in error messages displayed to the user. Note that the container is not required to support this property.

COleControl::AmbientFont

LPFONTDISP AmbientFont( );

Return Value

A pointer to the container's ambient Font dispatch interface. The default value is **NULL**. If the return is not equal to **NULL**, you are responsible for releasing the font by calling its **IUnknown::Release** member function.

Remarks

The ambient Font property is available to all controls and is defined by the container. Note that the container is not required to support this property.

See Also   **COleControl::GetFont, COleControl::SetFont**

COleControl::AmbientForeColor

OLE_COLOR AmbientForeColor( );

Return Value

The current value of the container's ambient ForeColor property, if any. If not supported, this function returns the system-defined Windows text color.

Remarks

The ambient ForeColor property is available to all controls and is defined by the container. Note that the container is not required to support this property.

See Also   **COleControl::AmbientBackColor, COleControl::GetForeColor, COleControl::TranslateColor**

COleControl::AmbientLocaleID

LCID AmbientLocaleID( );

Return Value

The value of the container's LocaleID property, if any. If this property is not supported, this function returns 0.

Remarks

The control can use the LocaleID to adapt its user interface for specific locales. Note that the container is not required to support this property.

COleControl::AmbientScaleUnits

CString AmbientScaleUnits( );

Return Value

A string containing the ambient ScaleUnits of the container. If this property is not supported, this function returns a zero-length string.

Remarks

The container's ambient ScaleUnits property can be used to display positions or dimensions, labeled with the chosen unit, such as twips or centimeters. Note that the container is not required to support this property.

See Also   COleControl::TransformCoords

COleControl::AmbientShowGrabHandles

BOOL AmbientShowGrabHandles( );

Return Value

Nonzero if grab handles should be displayed; otherwise 0. If this property is not supported, this function returns nonzero.

Remarks

Call this function to determine whether the container allows the control to display grab handles for itself when active. Note that the container is not required to support this property.

See Also   COleControl::AmbientShowHatching

COleControl::AmbientShowHatching

BOOL AmbientShowHatching( );

Return Value

Nonzero if the hatched pattern should be shown; otherwise 0. If this property is not supported, this function returns nonzero.

Remarks

Call this function to determine whether the container allows the control to display itself with a hatched pattern when UI active. Note that the container is not required to support this property.

See Also   COleControl::AmbientShowGrabHandles

COleControl::AmbientTextAlign

short AmbientTextAlign( );

Return Value

The status of the container's ambient TextAlign property. If this property is not supported, this function returns 0.

The following is a list of valid return values:

Return Value	Meaning
0	General alignment (numbers to the right, text to the left).
1	Left justify
2	Center
3	Right justify

Remarks

Call this function to determine the ambient text alignment preferred by the control container. This property is available to all embedded controls and is defined by the container. Note that the container is not required to support this property.

COleControl::AmbientUIDead

BOOL AmbientUIDead( );

Return Value

Nonzero if the control should respond to user-interface actions; otherwise 0. If this property is not supported, this function returns 0.

Remarks

Call this function to determine if the container wants the control to respond to user-interface actions. For example, a container might set this to **TRUE** in design mode.

See Also   **COleControl::AmbientUserMode**

COleControl::AmbientUserMode

BOOL AmbientUserMode( );

Return Value

Nonzero if the container is in user mode; otherwise 0 (in design mode). If this property is not supported, this function returns 0.

Remarks

Call this function to determine if the container is in design mode or user mode. For example, a container might set this to **FALSE** in design mode.

See Also   **COleControl::AmbientUIDead**

COleControl::BoundPropertyChanged

void BoundPropertyChanged(DISPID *dispid* **);**

Parameters

dispid   The dispatch ID of a bound property of the control.

Remarks

Call this function to signal that the bound property value has changed. This must be called every time the value of the property changes, even in cases where the change was not made through the property Set method. Be particularly aware of bound properties that are mapped to member variables. Any time such a member variable changes, **BoundPropertyChanged** must be called.

See Also   **COleControl::BoundPropertyRequestEdit**

COleControl::BoundPropertyRequestEdit

BOOL BoundPropertyRequestEdit(DISPID *dispid* **);**

Return Value

Nonzero if the change is permitted; otherwise 0. The default value is nonzero.

Parameters

dispid   The dispatch ID of a bound property of the control.

Remarks

Call this function to request permission from the **IPropChangeNotify** interface to change a bound property value provided by the control. If permission is denied, the control must not let the value of the property change. This can be done by ignoring or failing the action that attempted to change the property value.

See Also **COleControl::BoundPropertyChanged**

COleControl::COleControl

COleControl( );

Remarks

Constructs a **COleControl** object. This function is normally not called directly. Instead the OLE control is usually created by its class factory.

COleControl::ControlInfoChanged

void ControlInfoChanged( );

Remarks

Call this function when the set of mnemonics supported by the control has changed. Upon receiving this notification, the control's container obtains the new set of mnemonics by making a call to **IOleControl::GetControlInfo**. Note that the container is not required to respond to this notification. For more information on **IOleControl::GetControlInfo,** see "IOleControl and IOleControlSite," in Appendix A of *Programming with MFC*.

COleControl::DisplayError

virtual void DisplayError(SCODE *scode*, **LPCTSTR** *lpszDescription*, **LPCTSTR** *lpszSource*, **LPCTSTR** *lpszHelpFile*, **UINT** *nHelpID* **);**

Parameters

scode   The status code value to be reported. For a complete list of possible codes, see the article "OLE Controls: Advanced Topics" in *Programming with MFC*.

lpszDescription   The description of the error being reported.

lpszSource   The name of the module generating the error (typically, the name of the OLE control module).

lpszHelpFile   The name of the help file containing a description of the error.

nHelpID   The Help Context ID of the error being reported.

Remarks

Called by the framework after the stock Error event has been handled (unless the event handler has suppressed the display of the error). The default behavior displays a message box containing the description of the error, contained in *lpszDescription*.

Override this function to customize how errors are displayed.

See Also   **COleControl::FireError**

COleControl::DoClick

void DoClick( );

Remarks

Call this function to simulate a mouse click action on the control. The overridable **COleControl::OnClick** member function will be called, and a stock Click event will be fired, if supported by the control.

This function is supported by the **COleControl** base class as a stock method, called DoClick. For more information, see the article "Methods" in *Programming with MFC*.

See Also   **COleControl::OnClick**

COleControl::DoPropExchange

virtual void DoPropExchange(CPropExchange* *pPX* **);**

Parameters

pPX   A pointer to a **CPropExchange** object. The framework supplies this object to establish the context of the property exchange, including its direction.

Remarks

Called by the framework when loading or storing a control from a persistent storage representation, such as a stream or property set. This function normally makes calls to the **PX_** family of functions to load or store specific user-defined properties of an OLE control.

If Control Wizard has been used to create the OLE control project, the overridden version of this function will serialize the stock properties supported by **COleControl** with a call to the base class function, **COleControl::DoPropExchange**. As you add user-defined properties to your OLE control you will need to modify this function to serialize your new properties. For more information on serialization, see the article "OLE Controls: Serializing" in *Programming with MFC*.

See Also   **PX_Bool, PX_Short**

COleControl::DoSuperclassPaint

void DoSuperclassPaint(CDC* *pDC*, **const CRect&** *rcBounds* **);**

Parameters

pDC   A pointer to the device context of the control container.

rcBounds   A pointer to the area in which the control is to be drawn.

Remarks

Call this function to properly handle the painting of a nonactive OLE control. This function should only be used if the OLE control subclasses a Windows control and should be called in the OnDraw function of your control.

For more information on this function and subclassing a Windows control, see the article "OLE Controls: Subclassing a Windows Control" in *Programming with MFC*.

See Also   **COleControl::OnDraw**

COleControl::DrawContent

void DrawContent(CDC* *pDC*, **CRect&** *rc* **);**

Parameters

pDC   Pointer to the device context.

rc   Rectangular area to be drawn in.

Remarks

Called by the framework when the control's appearance needs to be updated. This function directly calls the overridable **OnDraw** function.

See Also   **COleControl::OnDraw**, **COleControl::DrawMetafile**, **COleControl::OnDrawMetafile**

COleControl::DrawMetafile

void DrawMetafile(CDC* *pDC*, **CRect&** *rc***);**

Parameters

pDC   Pointer to the metafile device context.

rc   Rectangular area to be drawn in.

Remarks

Called by the framework when the metafile device context is being used.

See Also   **COleControl::OnDraw**, **COleControl::DrawContent**, **COleControl::OnDrawMetafile**

COleControl::EnableSimpleFrame

void EnableSimpleFrame( );

Remarks

Call this function to enable the simple frame characteristic for an OLE control. This characteristic allows a control to support visual containment of other controls, but not true OLE containment. An example would be a group box with several controls inside. These controls are not OLE contained, but they are in the same group box.

COleControl::ExchangeExtent

BOOL ExchangeExtent(CPropExchange* *pPX* **);**

Return Value

Nonzero if the function succeeded; 0 otherwise.

Parameters

pPX   A pointer to a **CPropExchange** object. The framework supplies this object to establish the context of the property exchange, including its direction.

Remarks

Call this function to serialize or initialize the state of the control's extent (its dimensions in **HIMETRIC** units). This function is normally called by the default implementation of **COleControl::DoPropExchange**.

See Also   **COleControl::DoPropExchange**

COleControl::ExchangeStockProps

void ExchangeStockProps(CPropExchange* *pPX* **);**

Parameters

pPX   A pointer to a **CPropExchange** object. The framework supplies this object to establish the context of the property exchange, including its direction.

Remarks

Call this function to serialize or initialize the state of the control's stock properties. This function is normally called by the default implementation of **COleControl::DoPropExchange**.

See Also   **COleControl::DoPropExchange**

COleControl::ExchangeVersion

BOOL ExchangeVersion(CPropExchange* *pPX***, DWORD** *dwVersionDefault***,**
   BOOL *bConvert* **= TRUE);**

Return Value

Nonzero of the function succeeded; 0 otherwise.

Parameters

pPX   A pointer to a **CPropExchange** object. The framework supplies this object to
   establish the context of the property exchange, including its direction.

dwVersionDefault   The current version number of the control.

bConvert   Indicates whether persistent data should be converted to the latest format
   when saved, or maintained in the same format that was loaded.

Remarks

Call this function to serialize or initialize the state of a control's version information.
Typically, this will be the first function called by a control's override of
COleControl::DoPropExchange. When loading, this function reads the version
number of the persistent data, and sets the version attribute of the **CPropExchange**
object accordingly. When saving, this function writes the version number of the
persistent data.

For more information on persistence and versioning, see the article "OLE Controls:
Serializing" in *Programming with MFC*.

See Also   **COleControl::DoPropExchange**

COleControl::FireClick

void FireClick( );

Remarks

Called by the framework when the mouse is clicked over an active control. If this
event is defined as a custom event, you determine when the event is fired.

For automatic firing of a Click event to occur, the control's Event map must have a
stock Click event defined.

See Also   **COleControl::FireDblClick, COleControl::FireMouseDown,
COleControl::FireMouseUp**

COleControl::FireDblClick

void FireDblClick( );

Remarks

Called by the framework when the mouse is double-clicked over an active control. If this event is defined as a custom event, you determine when the event is fired.

For automatic firing of a DblClick event to occur, the control's Event map must have a stock DblClick event defined.

See Also **COleControl::FireClick, COleControl::FireMouseDown, COleControl::FireMouseUp**

COleControl::FireError

void FireError(SCODE *scode***, LPCTSTR** *lpszDescription***, UINT** *nHelpID* **= 0);**

Parameters

scode   The status code value to be reported. For a complete list of possible codes, see the article "OLE Controls: Advanced Topics" in *Programming with MFC*.

lpszDescription   The description of the error being reported.

nHelpID   The Help ID of the error being reported.

Remarks

Call this function to fire the stock Error event. This event provides a way of signalling, at appropriate places in your code, that an error has occurred within your control. Unlike other stock events, such as Click or MouseMove, Error is never fired by the framework.

To report an error that occurs during a property get function, property set function, or automation method, call **COleControl::ThrowError**.

See Also **COleControl::DisplayError**

COleControl::FireEvent

void FireEvent(DISPID *dispid***, BYTE FAR*** *pbParams***, ...);**

Parameters

dispid   The dispatch ID of the event to be fired.

pbParams   A descriptor for the event's parameter types.

Remarks

Call this function, with any number of optional arguments, to fire a user-defined event from your control. Usually this function should not be called directly. Instead you will call the event-firing functions generated by ClassWizard in the event map section of your control's class declaration.

The *pbParams* argument is a space-separated list of **VTS_**. One or more of these values, separated by spaces (not commas), specifies the function's parameter list. Possible values are as follows:

Symbol	Parameter Type
VTS_COLOR	**OLE_COLOR**
VTS_FONT	**IFontDisp***
VTS_HANDLE	**HWND**
VTS_PICTURE	**IPictureDisp***
VTS_OPTEXCLUSIVE	**OLE_OPTEXCLUSIVE***
VTS_TRISTATE	**OLE_TRISTATE**
VTS_XPOS_HIMETRIC	**OLE_XPOS_HIMETRIC**
VTS_YPOS_HIMETRIC	**OLE_YPOS_HIMETRIC**
VTS_XPOS_PIXELS	**OLE_XPOS_PIXELS**
VTS_YPOS_PIXELS	**OLE_YPOS_PIXELS**
VTS_XSIZE_PIXELS	**OLE_XSIZE_PIXELS**
VTS_YSIZE_PIXELS	**OLE_XSIZE_PIXELS**
VTS_XSIZE_HIMETRIC	**OLE_XSIZE_HIMETRIC**
VTS_YSIZE_HIMETRIC	**OLE_XSIZE_HIMETRIC**

Note Additional variant constants have been defined for all variant types, with the exception of **VTS_FONT** and **VTS_PICTURE**, that provide a pointer to the variant data constant. These constants are named using the **VTS_P***constantname* convention. For example, **VTS_PCOLOR** is a pointer to a **VTS_COLOR** constant.

COleControl::FireKeyDown

void FireKeyDown(USHORT* *pnChar*, **short** *nShiftState* **);**

Parameters

pnChar Pointer to the virtual-key code value of the pressed key.

nShiftState Contains a combination of the following flags:

- **SHIFT_MASK** The SHIFT key was pressed during the action.

- **CTRL_MASK** The CTRL key was pressed during the action.

- **ALT_MASK** The ALT key was pressed during the action.

Remarks

Called by the framework when a key is pressed while the control is UI active. If this event is defined as a custom event, you determine when the event is fired.

For automatic firing of a KeyDown event to occur, the control's Event map must have a stock KeyDown event defined.

See Also **COleControl::FireKeyUp**, **COleControl::FireKeyPress**, **COleControl::OnKeyPressEvent**

COleControl::FireKeyPress

void FireKeyPress(USHORT* *pnChar* **);**

Parameters

pnChar A pointer to the character value of the key pressed.

Remarks

Called by the framework when a key is pressed and released while the custom control is UI Active within the container. If this event is defined as a custom event, you determine when the event is fired.

The recipient of the event may modify *pnChar*, for example, convert all lowercase characters to uppercase. If you want to examine the modified character, override **OnKeyPressEvent**.

For automatic firing of a KeyPress event to occur, the control's Event map must have a stock KeyPress event defined.

See Also **COleControl::OnKeyPressEvent**, **COleControl::FireKeyDown**, **COleControl::FireKeyUp**

COleControl::FireKeyUp

void FireKeyUp(USHORT* *pnChar***, short** *nShiftState* **);**

Parameters

pnChar Pointer to the virtual-key code value of the released key.

nShiftState Contains a combination of the following flags:

- **SHIFT_MASK** The SHIFT key was pressed during the action.

- **CTRL_MASK** The CTRL key was pressed during the action.

- **ALT_MASK** The ALT key was pressed during the action.

Remarks

Called by the framework when a key is released while the custom control is UI Active within the container. If this event is defined as a custom event, you determine when the event is fired.

For automatic firing of a KeyUp event to occur, the control's Event map must have a stock KeyUp event defined.

See Also   **COleControl::FireKeyDown, COleControl::FireKeyPress, COleControl::OnKeyUpEvent**

COleControl::FireMouseDown

void FireMouseDown(short *nButton***, short** *nShiftState***, OLE_XPOS_PIXELS** *x***, OLE_YPOS_PIXEL** *y* **);**

Parameters

nButton   The numeric value of the mouse button pressed. It can contain one of the following values:

- **LEFT_BUTTON**   The left mouse button was pressed down.
- **MIDDLE_BUTTON**   The middle mouse button was pressed down.
- **RIGHT_BUTTON**   The right mouse button was pressed down.

nShiftState   Contains a combination of the following flags:

- **SHIFT_MASK**   The SHIFT key was pressed during the action.
- **CTRL_MASK**   The CTRL key was pressed during the action.
- **ALT_MASK**   The ALT key was pressed during the action.

x   The x-coordinate of the cursor when a mouse button was pressed down. The coordinate is relative to the upper-left corner of the control window.

y   The y-coordinate of the cursor when a mouse button was pressed down. The coordinate is relative to the upper-left corner of the control window.

Remarks

Called by the framework when a mouse button is pressed over an active custom control. If this event is defined as a custom event, you determine when the event is fired.

For automatic firing of a MouseDown event to occur, the control's Event map must have a stock MouseDown event defined.

See Also   **COleControl::FireMouseUp, COleControl::FireMouseMove, COleControl::FireClick**

COleControl::FireMouseMove

void FireMouseMove(short *nButton*, **short** *nShiftState*, **OLE_XPOS_PIXELS** *x*, **OLE_YPOS_PIXELS** *y* **);**

Parameters

nButton   The numeric value of the mouse buttons pressed. Contains a combination of the following values:

- **LEFT_BUTTON**   The left mouse button was pressed down during the action.
- **MIDDLE_BUTTON**   The middle mouse button was pressed down during the action.
- **RIGHT_BUTTON**   The right mouse button was pressed down during the action.

nShiftState   Contains a combination of the following flags:

- **SHIFT_MASK**   The SHIFT key was pressed during the action.
- **CTRL_MASK**   The CTRL key was pressed during the action.
- **ALT_MASK**   The ALT key was pressed during the action.

x   The x-coordinate of the cursor. The coordinate is relative to the upper-left corner of the control window.

y   The y-coordinate of the cursor. The coordinate is relative to the upper-left corner of the control window.

Remarks

Called by the framework when the cursor is moved over an active custom control. If this event is defined as a custom event, you determine when the event is fired.

For automatic firing of a MouseMove event to occur, the control's Event map must have a stock MouseMove event defined.

COleControl::FireMouseUp

void FireMouseUp(short *nButton*, **short** *nShiftState*, **OLE_XPOS_PIXELS** *x*, **OLE_YPOS_PIXELS** *y* **);**

Parameters

nButton   The numeric value of the mouse button released. It can have one of the following values:

- **LEFT_BUTTON**   The left mouse button was released.
- **MIDDLE_BUTTON**   The middle mouse button was released.
- **RIGHT_BUTTON**   The right mouse button was released.

nShiftState   Contains a combination of the following flags:

- **SHIFT_MASK**   The SHIFT key was pressed during the action.

- **CTRL_MASK**   The CTRL key was pressed during the action.

- **ALT_MASK**   The ALT key was pressed during the action.

x   The x-coordinate of the cursor when a mouse button was released. The coordinate is relative to the upper-left corner of the control window.

y   The y-coordinate of a cursor when a mouse button was released. The coordinate is relative to the upper-left corner of the control window.

Remarks

Called by the framework when a mouse button is released over an active custom control. If this event is defined as a custom event, you determine when the event is fired.

For automatic firing of a MouseUp event to occur, the control's Event map must have a stock MouseUp event defined.

See Also   **COleControl::FireMouseDown**, **COleControl::FireClick**, **COleControl::FireDblClick**

COleControl::GetAmbientProperty

BOOL GetAmbientProperty(DISPID *dwDispid***, VARTYPE** *vtProp***, void*** *pvProp* **);**

Return Value

Nonzero if the ambient property is supported; otherwise 0.

Parameters

dwDispid   The dispatch ID of the desired ambient property.

vtProp   A variant type tag that specifies the type of the value to be returned in *pvProp*.

pvProp   A pointer to the address of the variable that will receive the property value or return value. The actual type of this pointer must match the type specified by *vtProp*.

vtProp	Type of pvProp
VT_BOOL	**BOOL***
VT_BSTR	**CString***
VT_I2	**short***
VT_I4	**long***
VT_R4	**float***
VT_R8	**double***

vtProp	Type of pvProp
VT_CY	CY*
VT_COLOR	OLE_COLOR*
VT_DISPATCH	LPDISPATCH*
VT_FONT	LPFONTDISP*

Remarks

Call this function to get the value of an ambient property of the container. If you use **GetAmbientProperty** to retrieve the ambient DisplayName and ScaleUnits properties, set *vtProp* to **VT_BSTR** and *pvProp* to **CString***. If you are retrieving the ambient Font property, set *vtProp* to **VT_FONT** and *pvProp* to **LPFONTDISP***.

Note that functions have already been provided for common ambient properties, such as **AmbientBackColor** and **AmbientFont**.

See Also   **COleControl::AmbientForeColor**, **COleControl::AmbientScaleUnits**, **COleControl::AmbientShowGrabHandles**

COleControl::GetBackColor

OLE_COLOR GetBackColor( );

Return Value

The return value specifies the current background color as a **OLE_COLOR** value, if successful. This value can be translated to a **COLORREF** value with a call to **TranslateColor**.

Remarks

This function implements the Get function of your control's stock BackColor property.

See Also   **COleControl::AmbientBackColor**, **COleControl::TranslateColor**, **COleControl::SetBackColor**, **COleControl::GetForeColor**

COleControl::GetBorderStyle

short GetBorderStyle( );

Return Value

1 if the control has a normal border; 0 if the control has no border.

Remarks

This function implements the Get function of your control's stock BorderStyle property.

See Also   **COleControl::SetBorderStyle**, **COleControl::OnBorderStyleChanged**

COleControl::GetClassID

virtual HRESULT GetClassID(LPCLSID *pclsid* **) = 0;**

Return Value

Nonzero if the call was not successful; otherwise 0.

Parameters

pclsid   Pointer to the location of the class ID.

Remarks

Called by the framework to retrieve the OLE class ID of the control. Usually implemented by the **IMPLEMENT_OLECREATE_EX** macro.

COleControl::GetControlSize

void GetControlSize(int* *pcx*, **int*** *pcy* **);**

Parameters

pcx   Specifies the width of the control in pixels.

pcy   Specifies the height of the control in pixels.

Remarks

Call this function to retrieve the size of the OLE control window.

Note that all coordinates for control windows are relative to the upper-left corner of the control.

See Also   **COleControl::GetRectInContainer**, **COleControl::SetControlSize**

COleControl::GetEnabled

BOOL GetEnabled( );

Return Value

Nonzero if the control is enabled; otherwise 0.

Remarks

This function implements the Get function of your control's stock Enabled property.

See Also   **COleControl::SetEnabled**, **COleControl::OnEnabledChanged**

COleControl::GetExtendedControl

LPDISPATCH GetExtendedControl( );

Return Value

A pointer to the container's extended control object. If there is no object available, the value is **NULL**.

This object may be manipulated through its **IDispatch** interface. You can also use **QueryInterface** to obtain other available interfaces provided by the object. However, the object is not required to support a specific set of interfaces. Note that relying on the specific features of a container's extended control object limits the portability of your control to other arbitrary containers.

Remarks

Call this function to obtain a pointer to an object maintained by the container that represents the control with an extended set of properties. The function that calls this function is responsible for releasing the pointer when finished with the object. Note that the container is not required to support this object.

COleControl::GetFont

LPFONTDISP GetFont( );

Return Value

A pointer to the font dispatch interface of the control's stock Font property.

Remarks

This function implements the Get function of the stock Font property. Note that the caller must release the object when finished. Within the implementation of the control, use **InternalGetFont** to access the control's stock Font object. For more information on using fonts in your control, see the article "OLE Controls: Using Fonts in Your Control" in *Programming with MFC*.

See Also   **COleControl::SetFont**, **COleControl::AmbientFont**, **COleControl::InternalGetFont**

COleControl::GetFontTextMetrics

void GetFontTextMetrics(LPTEXTMETRIC *lptm*, **CFontHolder&** *fontHolder* **);**

Parameters

lptm   Pointer to a **TEXTMETRIC** structure.

fontHolder   Reference to a **CFontHolder** object.

Remarks

Call this function to measure the text metrics for any **CFontHolder** object owned by the control. Such a font can be selected with the **COleControl::SelectFontObject** function. **GetFontTextMetrics** will initialize the **TEXTMETRIC** structure pointed to by *lptm* with valid metrics information about *fontHolder*'s font if successful, or fill the structure with zeros if not successful. You should use this function instead of **::GetTextMetrics** when painting your control because controls, like any embedded OLE object, may be required to render themselves into a metafile.

The **TEXTMETRIC** structure for the default font is refreshed when the **SelectFontObject** function is called. You should call **GetFontTextMetrics** only after selecting the stock Font property to assure the information it provides is valid.

COleControl::GetForeColor

OLE_COLOR GetForeColor( );

Return Value

The return value specifies the current foreground color as a **OLE_COLOR** value, if successful. This value can be translated to a **COLORREF** value with a call to **TranslateColor**. For more information on the **OLE_COLOR** data type, see "Standard Color Type," in Appendix A of *Programming with MFC*.

Remarks

This function implements the Get function of the stock ForeColor property.

See Also   **COleControl::AmbientForeColor**, **COleControl::TranslateColor**, **COleControl::GetBackColor**, **COleControl::SetForeColor**

COleControl::GetHwnd

OLE_HANDLE GetHwnd( );

Return Value

The OLE control's window handle, if any; otherwise **NULL**.

Remarks

This function implements the Get function of the stock hWnd property.

COleControl::GetMessageString

virtual void GetMessageString(UINT *nID*, CString& *rMessage*) const;

Parameters

nID   A menu item ID.

rMessage   A reference to a **CString** object through which a string will be returned.

Remarks

Called by the framework to obtain a short string that describes the purpose of the menu item identified by *nID*. This can be used to obtain a message for display in a status bar while the menu item is highlighted. The default implementation attempts to load a string resource identified by *nID*.

COleControl::GetNotSupported

void GetNotSupported( );

Remarks

Call this function in place of the Get function of any property where retrieval of the property by the control's user is not supported. One example would be a property that is write-only.

See Also   **COleControl::SetNotSupported**

COleControl::GetRectInContainer

BOOL GetRectInContainer(LPRECT *lpRect* **);**

Return Value

Nonzero if the control is in-place active; otherwise 0.

Parameters

lpRect   A pointer to the rectangle structure into which the control's coordinates will be copied.

Remarks

Call this function to obtain the coordinates of the control's rectangle relative to the container, expressed in device units. The rectangle is only valid if the control is in-place active.

See Also   **COleControl::SetRectInContainer**, **COleControl::GetControlSize**

COleControl::GetStockTextMetrics

void GetStockTextMetrics(LPTEXTMETRIC *lptm* **);**

Parameters

lptm   A pointer to a **TEXTMETRIC** structure.

Remarks

Call this function to measure the text metrics for the control's stock Font property, which can be selected with the **SelectStockFont** function. The **GetStockTextMetrics** function will initialize the **TEXTMETRIC** structure pointed to by *lptm* with valid metrics information if successful, or fill the structure with zeros if not successful. Use this function instead of **::GetTextMetrics** when painting your control because controls, like any embedded OLE object, may be required to render themselves into a metafile.

The **TEXTMETRIC** structure for the default font is refreshed when the **SelectStockFont** function is called. You should call this function only after selecting the stock font to assure the information it provides is valid.

COleControl::GetText

BSTR GetText( );

Return Value

The current value of the control text string or a zero-length string if no string is present.

Note For more information on the **BSTR** data type, see "Data Types" in the "Macros and Globals" section.

Remarks

This function implements the Get function of the stock Text or Caption property. Note that the caller of this function must call **SysFreeString** on the string returned in order to free the resource. Within the implementation of the control, use **InternalGetText** to access the control's stock Text or Caption property.

See Also **COleControl::InternalGetText, COleControl::SetText**

COleControl::InitializeIIDs

void InitializeIIDs(const IID* *piidPrimary*, **const IID*** *piidEvents* **);**

Parameters

piidPrimary   Pointer to the interface ID of the control's primary dispatch interface.

piidEvents   Pointer to the interface ID of the control's event interface.

Remarks

Call this function in the control's constructor to inform the base class of the interface IDs your control will be using.

COleControl::InternalGetFont

CFontHolder& InternalGetFont( );

Return Value

A reference to a **CFontHolder** object that contains the stock Font object.

Remarks

Call this function to access the stock Font property of your control

See Also   **COleControl::GetFont**, **COleControl::SetFont**

COleControl::InternalGetText

const CString& InternalGetText( );

Return Value

A reference to the control text string.

Remarks

Call this function to access the stock Text or Caption property of your control.

See Also   **COleControl::GetText**, **COleControl::SetText**

COleControl::InvalidateControl

void InvalidateControl(LPCRECT *lpRect* **= NULL);**

Parameters

lpRect   A pointer to the region of the control to be invalidated.

Remarks

Call this function to force the control to redraw itself. If *lpRect* has a **NULL** value, the entire control will be redrawn. If *lpRect* is not **NULL**, this indicates the portion of the control's rectangle that is to be invalidated. In cases where the control has no window, or is currently not active, the rectangle is ignored, and a call is made to the client site's **IAdviseSink::OnViewChange** member function. Use this function instead of **CWnd::InvalidateRect** or **::InvalidateRect**.

See Also   **COleControl::Refresh**

COleControl::IsConvertingVBX

BOOL IsConvertingVBX( );

Return Value

Nonzero if the control is being converted; otherwise 0.

Remarks

When converting a form that uses VBX controls to one that uses OLE controls, special loading code for the OLE controls may be required. For example, if you are loading an instance of your OLE control, you might have a call to **PX_Font** in your **DoPropExchange**:

```
PX_Font(pPx, "Font", m_MyFont, pDefaultFont);
```

However, VBX controls did not have a Font object; each font property was saved individually. In this case, you would use **IsConvertingVBX** to distinguish between these two cases:

```
if (IsConvertingVBX()==FALSE)
    PX_Font(pPX, "Font", m_MyFont, pDefaultFont);
else
{
    PX_String(pPX, "FontName", tempString, DefaultName);
    m_MyFont->put_Name(tempString);
    PX_Bool(pPX, "FontUnderline", tempBool, DefaultValue);
    m_MyFont->put_Underline(tempBool);
...
}
```

Another case would be if your VBX control saved proprietary binary data (in its **VBM_SAVEPROPERTY** message handler), and your OLE control saves its binary data in a different format. If you want your OLE control to be backward-compatible with the VBX control, you could read both the old and new formats using the **IsConvertingVBX** function by distinguishing whether the VBX control or the OLE control was being loaded.

In your control's **DoPropExchange** function, you can check for this condition and if true, execute load code specific to this conversion (such as the previous examples). If the control is not being converted, you can execute normal load code. This ability is only applicable to controls being converted from VBX counterparts.

See Also   COleControl::DoPropExchange

COleControl::IsModified

BOOL IsModified( );

Return Value

Nonzero if the control's state has been modified since it was last saved; otherwise 0.

Remarks

Call this function to determine if the control's state has been modified. The state of a control is modified when a property changes value.

See Also   COleControl::SetModifiedFlag

COleControl::IsSubclassedControl

virtual BOOL IsSubclassedControl( );

Return Value

Nonzero if the control is subclassed; otherwise 0.

Remarks

Called by the framework to determine if the control subclasses a Windows control. You must override this function and return **TRUE** if your OLE control subclasses a Windows control.

COleControl::LockInPlaceActive

BOOL LockInPlaceActive(BOOL *bLock* **);**

Return Value

Nonzero if the lock was successful; otherwise 0.

Parameters

bLock   **TRUE** if the in-place active state of the control is to be locked; **FALSE** if it is to be unlocked.

Remarks

Call this function to prevent the container from deactivating your control. Note that every locking of the control must be paired with an unlocking of the control when finished. You should only lock your control for short periods, such as while firing an event.

COleControl::OnAmbientPropertyChange

virtual void OnAmbientPropertyChange(DISPID *dispID* **);**

Parameters

dispID   The dispatch ID of the ambient property that changed, or **DISPID_UNKNOWN** if multiple properties have changed.

Remarks

Called by the framework when an ambient property of the container has changed value.

See Also   **COleControl::GetAmbientProperty**

COleControl::OnBackColorChanged

virtual void OnBackColorChanged( );

Remarks

Called by the framework when the stock BackColor property value has changed.

Override this function if you want notification after this property changes. The default implementation calls **InvalidateControl**.

See Also   **COleControl::GetBackColor**, **COleControl::InvalidateControl**

COleControl::OnBorderStyleChanged

virtual void OnBorderStyleChanged( );

Remarks

Called by the framework when the stock BorderStyle property value has changed.
The default implementation calls **InvalidateControl**.

Override this function if you want notification after this property changes.

See Also **COleControl::SetBorderStyle**, **COleControl::InvalidateControl**

COleControl::OnClick

virtual void OnClick(USHORT *iButton* **);**

Parameters

iButton Index of a mouse button. Can have one of the following values:

- **LEFT_BUTTON** The left mouse button was clicked.

- **MIDDLE_BUTTON** The middle mouse button was clicked.

- **RIGHT_BUTTON** The right mouse button was clicked.

Remarks

Called by the framework when a mouse button has been clicked or the DoClick stock
method has been invoked. The default implementation calls
COleControl::FireClick.

Override this member function to modify or extend the default handling.

See Also **COleControl::DoClick**, **COleControl::FireClick**

COleControl::OnDoVerb

virtual BOOL OnDoVerb(LONG *iVerb*, **LPMSG** *lpMsg*, **HWND** *hWndParent*, **LPCRECT** *lpRect* **);**

Return Value

Nonzero if call was successful; otherwise 0.

Parameters

iVerb The index of the control verb to be invoked.

lpMsg A pointer to the Windows message that caused the verb to be invoked.

hWndParent The handle to the parent window of the control. If the execution of the
verb creates a window (or windows), *hWndParent* should be used as the parent.

lpRect A pointer to a **RECT** structure into which the coordinates of the control,
relative to the container, will be copied.

Remarks

Called by the framework when the container calls the **IOleObject::DoVerb** member function. The default implementation uses the **ON_OLEVERB** and **ON_STDOLEVERB** message map entries to determine the proper function to invoke.

Override this function to change the default handling of verb.

See Also **ON_OLEVERB**, **ON_STDOLEVERB**, **COleControl::OnEnumVerbs**

COleControl::OnDraw

virtual void OnDraw(CDC* *pDC*, **const CRect&** *rcBounds*, **const CRect&** *rcInvalid* **);**

Parameters

pDC   The device context in which the drawing occurs.

rcBounds   The rectangular area of the control, including the border.

rcInvalid   The rectangular area of the control that is invalid.

Remarks

Called by the framework to draw the OLE control in the specified bounding rectangle using the specified device context.

OnDraw is typically called for screen display, passing a screen device context as *pDC*. The *rcBounds* parameter identifies the rectangle in the target device context (relative to its current mapping mode). The *rcInvalid* parameter is the actual rectangle that is invalid. In some cases this will be a smaller area than *rcBounds*.

See Also **COleControl::OnDrawMetafile**, **COleControl::DrawContent**, **COleControl::DrawMetafile**

COleControl::OnDrawMetafile

virtual void OnDrawMetafile(CDC* *pDC*, **const CRect&** *rcBounds* **);**

Parameters

pDC   The device context in which the drawing occurs.

rcBounds   The rectangular area of the control, including the border.

Remarks

Called by the framework to draw the OLE control in the specified bounding rectangle using the specified metafile device context. The default implementation calls the OnDraw function.

See Also **COleControl::OnDraw**, **COleControl::DrawContent**, **COleControl::DrawMetafile**

COleControl::OnEdit

virtual BOOL OnEdit(LPMSG *lpMsg*, **HWND** *hWndParent*, **LPCRECT** *lpRect*);

Return Value

An OLE result code where the value is nonzero if the call is not successful; otherwise 0.

Parameters

lpMsg   A pointer to the Windows message that invoked the verb.

hWndParent   A handle to the parent window of the control.

lpRect   A pointer to the rectangle used by the control in the container.

Remarks

Call this function to cause the control to be UI activated. This has the same effect as invoking the control's **OLEIVERB_UIACTIVATE** verb.

This function is typically used as the handler function for an **ON_OLEVERB** message map entry. This makes an "Edit" verb available on the control's "Object" menu. For example:

```
ON_OLEVERB(AFX_IDS_VERB_EDIT, OnEdit)
```

COleControl::OnEnabledChanged

virtual void OnEnabledChanged( );

Remarks

Called by the framework when the stock Enabled property value has changed.

Override this function if you want notification after this property changes. The default implementation calls **InvalidateControl**.

See Also   **COleControl::SetEnabled**, **COleControl::GetEnabled**

COleControl::OnEnumVerbs

virtual BOOL OnEnumVerbs(LPENUMOLEVERB FAR* *ppenumOleVerb*);

Return Value

Nonzero if verbs are available; otherwise 0.

Parameters

ppenumOleVerb   A pointer to the **IEnumOLEVERB** object that enumerates the control's verbs.

Remarks

Called by the framework when the container calls the **IOleObject::EnumVerbs** member function. The default implementation enumerates the **ON_OLEVERB** entries in the message map.

Override this function to change the default way of enumerating verbs.

See Also   ON_OLEVERB, ON_STDOLEVERB

COleControl::OnEventAdvise

virtual void OnEventAdvise(BOOL *bAdvise* **);**

Parameters

bAdvise   **TRUE** indicates that an event handler has been connected to the control. **FALSE** indicates that an event handler has been disconnected from the control.

Remarks

Called by the framework when an event handler is connected to or disconnected from an OLE control.

COleControl::OnFontChanged

virtual void OnFontChanged( );

Remarks

Called by the framework when the stock Font property value has changed. The default implementation calls **COleControl::InvalidateControl**. If the control is subclassing a Windows control, the default implementation also sends a **WM_SETFONT** message to the control's window.

Override this function if you want notification after this property changes.

See Also   COleControl::GetFont, COleControl::InternalGetFont, COleControl::InvalidateControl

COleControl::OnForeColorChanged

virtual void OnForeColorChanged( );

Remarks

Called by the framework when the stock ForeColor property value has changed. The default implementation calls **InvalidateControl**.

Override this function if you want notification after this property changes.

See Also   COleControl::SetForeColor, COleControl::InvalidateControl

COleControl::OnFreezeEvents

virtual void OnFreezeEvents(BOOL *bFreeze* **);**

Parameters

bFreeze   **TRUE** if the control's event handling is frozen; otherwise **FALSE**.

Remarks

Called by the framework after the container calls **IOleControl::FreezeEvents**. The default implementation does nothing.

Override this function if you want additional behavior when event handling is frozen or unfrozen.

COleControl::OnGetColorSet

virtual BOOL OnGetColorSet(DVTARGETDEVICE FAR* *ptd*, **HDC** *hicTargetDev*,
LPLOGPALETTE FAR* *ppColorSet* **);**

Return Value

Nonzero if a valid color set is returned; otherwise 0.

Parameters

ptd   Points to the target device for which the picture should be rendered. If this value is **NULL**, the picture should be rendered for a default target device, usually a display device.

hicTargetDev   Specifies the information context on the target device indicated by *ptd*. This parameter can be a device context, but is not one necessarily. If *ptd* is **NULL**, *hicTargetDev* should also be **NULL**.

ppColorSet   A pointer to the location into which the set of colors that would be used should be copied. If the function does not return the color set, **NULL** is returned.

Remarks

Called by the framework when the container calls the **IOleObject::GetColorSet** member function. The container calls this function to obtain all the colors needed to draw the OLE control. The container can use the color sets obtained in conjunction with the colors it needs to set the overall color palette. The default implementation returns **FALSE**.

Override this function to do any special processing of this request.

COleControl::OnGetControlInfo

virtual void OnGetControlInfo(LPCONTROLINFO *pControlInfo* **);**

Parameters

pControlInfo   Pointer to a **CONTROLINFO** structure to be filled in. For more information on this structure, see "Keyboard Interface" in Appendix A of *Programming with MFC*.

Remarks

Called by the framework when the control's container has requested information about the control. This information consists primarily of a description of the control's mnemonic keys. The default implementation fills *pControlInfo* with default information.

Override this function if your control needs to process mnemonic keys.

COleControl::OnGetDisplayString

virtual BOOL OnGetDisplayString(DISPID *dispid*, **CString&** *strValue* **);**

Return Value

Nonzero if a string has been returned in *strValue;* otherwise 0.

Parameters

dispid   The dispatch ID of a property of the control.

strValue   A reference to a **CString** object through which a string will be returned.

Remarks

Called by the framework to obtain a string that represents the current value of the property identified by *dispid*.

Override this function if your control has a property whose value cannot be directly converted to a string and you want the property's value to be displayed in a container-supplied property browser.

See Also   **COleControl::OnMapPropertyToPage**

COleControl::OnGetInPlaceMenu

virtual HMENU OnGetInPlaceMenu( );

Return Value

The handle of the control's menu, or **NULL** if the control has none. The default implementation returns **NULL**.

Remarks

Called by the framework when the control is UI activated to obtain the menu to be merged into the container's existing menu.

For more information on merging OLE resources, see the article "Menus and Resources" in *Programming with MFC*.

COleControl::OnGetPredefinedStrings

virtual BOOL OnGetPredefinedStrings(DISPID *dispid***, CStringArray*** *pStringArray***, CDWordArray*** *pCookieArray* **);**

Return Value

Nonzero if elements have been added to *pStringArray* and *pCookieArray*.

Parameters

dispid   The dispatch ID of a property of the control.

pStringArray   A string array to be filled in with return values.

pCookieArray   A **DWORD** array to be filled in with return values.

Remarks

Called by the framework to obtain a set of predefined strings representing the possible values for a property.

Override this function if your control has a property with a set of possible values that can be represented by strings. For each element added to *pStringArray*, you should add a corresponding "cookie" element to *pCookieArray*. These "cookie" values may later be passed by the framework to the **COleControl::OnGetPredefinedValue** function.

See Also   **COleControl::OnGetPredefinedValue, COleControl::OnGetDisplayString**

COleControl::OnGetPredefinedValue

virtual BOOL OnGetPredefinedValue(DISPID *dispid***, DWORD** *dwCookie***, VARIANT FAR*** *lpvarOut* **);**

Return Value

Nonzero if a value has been returned in *lpvarOut*; otherwise 0.

Parameters

dispid   The dispatch ID of a property of the control.

dwCookie   A cookie value previously returned by an override of **COleControl::OnGetPredefinedStrings**.

lpvarOut   Pointer to a **VARIANT** structure through which a property value will be returned.

Remarks

Called by the framework to obtain the value corresponding to one of the predefined strings previously returned by an override of **COleControl::OnGetPredefinedStrings**.

See Also   **COleControl::OnGetPredefinedStrings**, **COleControl::OnGetDisplayString**

COleControl::OnHideToolBars

virtual void OnHideToolBars( );

Remarks

Called by the framework when the control is UI deactivated. The implementation should hide all toolbars displayed by **OnShowToolbars**.

See Also   **COleControl::OnShowToolbars**

COleControl::OnKeyDownEvent

virtual void OnKeyDownEvent(USHORT *nChar*, **USHORT** *nShiftState* **);**

Parameters

nChar   The virtual-key code value of the pressed key.

nShiftState   Contains a combination of the following flags:

- **SHIFT_MASK**   The SHIFT key was pressed during the action.
- **CTRL_MASK**   The CTRL key was pressed during the action.
- **ALT_MASK**   The ALT key was pressed during the action.

Remarks

Called by the framework after a stock KeyDown event has been processed.

Override this function if your control needs access to the key information after the event has been fired.

See Also   **COleControl::OnKeyUpEvent, COleControl::OnKeyPressEvent**

COleControl::OnKeyPressEvent

virtual void OnKeyPressEvent(USHORT *nChar* **);**

Parameters

nChar   Contains the virtual-key code value of the key pressed.

Remarks

Called by the framework after the stock KeyPress event has been fired. Note that the *nChar* value may have been modified by the container.

Override this function if you want notification after this event occurs.

See Also   **COleControl::FireKeyPress**

COleControl::OnKeyUpEvent

virtual void OnKeyUpEvent(USHORT *nChar*, **USHORT** *nShiftState* **);**

Parameters

nChar   The virtual-key code value of the pressed key.

nShiftState   Contains a combination of the following flags:

- **SHIFT_MASK**   The SHIFT key was pressed during the action.
- **CTRL_MASK**   The CTRL key was pressed during the action.
- **ALT_MASK**   The ALT key was pressed during the action.

Remarks

Called by the framework after a stock KeyDown event has been processed.

Override this function if your control needs access to the key information after the event has been fired.

See Also   **COleControl::OnKeyDownEvent**, **COleControl::OnKeyPressEvent**

COleControl::OnMapPropertyToPage

virtual BOOL OnMapPropertyToPage(DISPID *dispid*, **LPCLSID** *lpclsid*,
   BOOL* *pbPageOptional* **);**

Return Value

Nonzero if a class ID has been returned in *lpclsid*; otherwise 0.

Parameters

dispid   The dispatch ID of a property of the control.

lpclsid   Pointer to a **CLSID** structure through which a class ID will be returned.

pbPageOptional Returns an indicator of whether use of the specified property page is optional.

Remarks

Called by the framework to obtain the class ID of a property page that implements editing of the specified property.

Override this function to provide a way to invoke your control's property pages from the container's property browser.

See Also **COleControl::OnGetDisplayString**

COleControl::OnMnemonic

virtual void OnMnemonic(LPMSG *pMsg* **);**

Parameters

pMsg Pointer to the Windows message generated by a mnemonic key press.

Remarks

Called by the framework when the container has detected that a mnemonic key of the OLE control has been pressed.

COleControl::OnProperties

virtual BOOL OnProperties(LPMSG *lpMsg*, **HWND** *hWndParent*, **LPCRECT** *lpRect* **);**

Return Value

An OLE result code. Therefore nonzero if the call is not successful; otherwise 0.

Parameters

lpMsg A pointer to the Windows message that invoked the verb.

hWndParent A handle to the parent window of the control.

lpRect A pointer to the rectangle used by the control in the container.

Remarks

Called by the framework when the control's properties verb has been invoked by the container. The default implementation displays a modal property dialog box.

COleControl::OnRenderData

virtual BOOL OnRenderData(LPFORMATETC *lpFormatEtc*, **LPSTGMEDIUM** *lpStgMedium* **);**

Return Value

Nonzero if successful; otherwise 0.

Parameters

lpFormatEtc Points to the **FORMATETC** structure specifying the format in which
information is requested.

lpStgMedium Points to a **STGMEDIUM** structure in which the data is to be
returned.

Remarks

Called by the framework to retrieve data in the specified format. The specified format
is one previously placed in the control object using the **DelayRenderData** or
DelayRenderFileData member functions for delayed rendering. The default
implementation of this function calls **OnRenderFileData** or **OnRenderGlobalData**,
respectively, if the supplied storage medium is either a file or memory. If the
requested format is **CF_METAFILEPICT** or the persistent property set format, the
default implementation renders the appropriate data and returns nonzero. Otherwise,
it returns 0 and does nothing.

If *lpStgMedium->tymed* is **TYMED_NULL**, the **STGMEDIUM** should be allocated
and filled as specified by *lpFormatEtc->tymed*. If not **TYMED_NULL**, the
STGMEDIUM should be filled in place with the data.

Override this function to provide your data in the requested format and medium.
Depending on your data, you may want to override one of the other versions of this
function instead. If your data is small and fixed in size, override
OnRenderGlobalData. If your data is in a file, or is of variable size, override
OnRenderFileData.

For more information, see the **FORMATETC** and **STGMEDIUM** structures in the
OLE documentation.

See Also **COleControl::OnRenderFileData**,
COleControl::OnRenderGlobalData

COleControl::OnRenderFileData

virtual BOOL OnRenderFileData(LPFORMATETC *lpFormatEtc*, **CFile*** *pFile* **);**

Return Value

Nonzero if successful; otherwise 0.

Parameters

lpFormatEtc Points to the **FORMATETC** structure specifying the format in which
information is requested.

pFile Points to a **CFile** object in which the data is to be rendered.

Remarks

Called by the framework to retrieve data in the specified format when the storage
medium is a file. The specified format is one previously placed in the control object

using the **DelayRenderData** member function for delayed rendering. The default implementation of this function simply returns **FALSE**.

Override this function to provide your data in the requested format and medium. Depending on your data, you might want to override one of the other versions of this function instead. If you want to handle multiple storage mediums, override **OnRenderData**. If your data is in a file, or is of variable size, override **OnRenderFileData**.

For more information, see the **FORMATETC** structure in the OLE documentation.

See Also   **COleControl::OnRenderData**, **COleControl::OnRenderGlobalData**

COleControl::OnRenderGlobalData

virtual BOOL OnRenderGlobalData(LPFORMATETC *lpFormatEtc***, HGLOBAL*** *phGlobal* **);**

Return Value
Nonzero if successful; otherwise 0.

Parameters
lpFormatEtc   Points to the **FORMATETC** structure specifying the format in which information is requested.

phGlobal   Points to a handle to global memory in which the data is to be returned. If no memory has been allocated, this parameter can be **NULL**.

Remarks
Called by the framework to retrieve data in the specified format when the specified storage medium is global memory. The specified format is one previously placed in the control object using the **DelayRenderData** member function for delayed rendering. The default implementation of this function simply returns **FALSE**.

If *phGlobal* is **NULL**, then a new **HGLOBAL** should be allocated and returned in *phGlobal*. Otherwise, the **HGLOBAL** specified by *phGlobal* should be filled with the data. The amount of data placed in the **HGLOBAL** must not exceed the current size of the memory block. Also, the block cannot be reallocated to a larger size.

Override this function to provide your data in the requested format and medium. Depending on your data, you may want to override one of the other versions of this function instead. If you want to handle multiple storage mediums, override **OnRenderData**. If your data is in a file, or is of variable size, override **OnRenderFileData**.

For more information, see the **FORMATETC** structure in the OLE documentation.

See Also **COleControl::OnRenderFileData**, **COleControl::OnRenderData**

COleControl::OnResetState

virtual void OnResetState( );

Remarks

Called by the framework when the control's properties should be set to their default values. The default implementation calls **DoPropExchange**, passing a **CPropExchange** object that causes properties to be set to their default values.

The control writer can insert initialization code for the OLE control in this overridable. This function is called when **IPersistStream::Load** or **IPersistStorage::Load** fails, or **IPersistStreamInit::InitNew** or **IPersistStorage::InitNew** is called, without first calling either **IPersistStream::Load** or **IPersistStorage::Load**.

See Also **COleControl::OnSetClientSite**

COleControl::OnSetClientSite

virtual void OnSetClientSite( );

Remarks

Called by the framework when the container has called the control's **IOleControl::SetClientSite** function.

Override this function to do any special processing of this function.

COleControl::OnSetData

virtual BOOL OnSetData(LPFORMATETC *lpFormatEtc*,
  LPSTGMEDIUM *lpStgMedium*, **BOOL** *bRelease*);

Return Value

Nonzero if successful; otherwise 0.

Parameters

lpFormatEtc   Pointer to a **FORMATETC** structure specifying the format of the data.

lpStgMedium   Pointer to a **STGMEDIUM** structure in which the data resides.

bRelease   **TRUE** if the control should free the storage medium; **FALSE** if if the control should not free the storage medium.

Remarks

Called by the framework to replace the control's data with the specified data. If the data is in the persistent property set format, the default implementation modifies the control's state accordingly. Otherwise, the default implementation does nothing. If *bRelease* is **TRUE**, then a call to **ReleaseStgMedium** is made; otherwise not.

Override this function to replace the control's data with the specified data.

For more information, see the **FORMATETC** and **STGMEDIUM** structures in the OLE documentation.

See Also **COleControl::DoPropExchange**

COleControl::OnSetExtent

virtual BOOL OnSetExtent(LPSIZEL *lpSizeL* **);**

Return Value

Nonzero if the size change was accepted; otherwise 0.

Parameters

lpSizeL A pointer to the **SIZEL** structure that uses long integers to represent the width and height of the control, expressed in **HIMETRIC** units.

Remarks

Called by the framework when the control's extent needs to be changed, as a result of a call to **IOleObject::SetExtent**. The default implementation handles the resizing of the control's extent. If the control is in-place active, a call to the container's **OnPosRectChanged** is then made.

Override this function to alter the default resizing of your control.

COleControl::OnSetObjectRects

virtual BOOL OnSetObjectRects(LPCRECT *lpRectPos*, **LPCRECT** *lpRectClip* **);**

Return Value

Nonzero if the repositioning was accepted; otherwise 0.

Parameters

lpRectPos A pointer to a **RECT** structure indicating the control's new position and size relative to the container.

lpRectClip A pointer to a **RECT** structure indicating a rectangular area to which the control is to be clipped.

Remarks

Called by the framework to implement a call to
IOleInPlaceObject::SetObjectRects. The default implementation automatically
handles the repositioning and resizing of the control window and returns **TRUE**.

Override this function to alter the default behavior of this function.

COleControl::OnShowToolBars

virtual void OnShowToolBars( );

Remarks

Called by the framework when the control has been UI activated. The default
implementation does nothing.

See Also   **COleControl::OnHideToolbars**

COleControl::OnTextChanged

virtual void OnTextChanged( );

Remarks

Called by the framework when the stock Caption or Text property value has changed.
The default implementation calls **InvalidateControl**.

Override this function if you want notification after this property changes.

See Also   **COleControl::SetText**, **COleControl::InternalGetText**,
COleControl::InvalidateControl

COleControl::PreModalDialog

void PreModalDialog( );

Remarks

Call this function prior to displaying any modal dialog box. You must call this
function so that the container can disable all its top-level windows. After the modal
dialog box has been displayed, you must then call **PostModalDialog**.

See Also   **COleControl::PostModalDialog**

COleControl::PostModalDialog

void PostModalDialog( );

Remarks

Call this function after displaying any modal dialog box. You must call this function so that the container can enable any top-level windows disabled by **PreModalDialog**. This function should be paired with a call to **PreModalDialog**.

See Also   **COleControl::PreModalDialog**

COleControl::RecreateControlWindow

void RecreateControlWindow( );

Remarks

Call this function to destroy and re-create the control's window. This may be necessary if you need to change the window's style bits.

COleControl::Refresh

void Refresh( );

Remarks

Call this function to force a repaint of the OLE control.

This function is supported by the **COleControl** base class as a stock method, called Refresh. This allows users of your OLE control to repaint the control at a specific time. For more information on this method, see the article "Methods" in *Programming with MFC*.

See Also   **COleControl::InvalidateControl**

COleControl::SelectFontObject

CFont* SelectFontObject(CDC* *pDC*, **CFontHolder&** *fontHolder* **);**

Return Value

A pointer to the previously selected font. When the caller has finished all drawing operations that use *fontHolder,* it should reselect the previously selected font by passing it as a parameter to **CDC::SelectObject**.

Parameters

pDC   Pointer to a device context object.

fontHolder   Reference to the **CFontHolder** object representing the font to be selected.

Remarks

Call this function to select a font into a device context.

COleControl::SelectStockFont

CFont* SelectStockFont(CDC* *pDC* **);**

Return Value

A pointer to the previously selected **CFont** object. You should use
CDC::SelectObject to select this font back into the device context when you are
finished.

Parameters

pDC   The device context into which the font will be selected.

Remarks

Call this function to select the stock Font property into a device context.

See Also   **COleControl::GetFont, COleControl::SetFont**

COleControl::SetBackColor

void SetBackColor(OLE_COLOR *dwBackColor* **);**

Parameters

dwBackColor   An **OLE_COLOR** value to be used for background drawing of your
control.

Remarks

Call this function to set the stock BackColor property value of your control. For more
information on using this property and other related properties, see Chapter 22,
"Adding a Custom Notification Property," in the Circle Sample Tutorial in *Tutorials*
and the article "Properties" in *Programming with MFC*.

See Also   **COleControl::SetForeColor, COleControl::GetBackColor,**
COleControl::OnBackColorChanged

COleControl::SetBorderStyle

void SetBorderStyle(short *sBorderStyle* **);**

Parameters

sBorderStyle   The new border style for the control; 0 indicates no border and 1
indicates a normal border.

Remarks

Call this function to set the stock BorderStyle property value of your control. The control window will then be re-created and **OnBorderStyleChanged** called.

See Also   **COleControl::GetBorderStyle, COleControl::OnBorderStyleChanged**

COleControl::SetControlSize

BOOL SetControlSize(int *cx,* **int** *cy* **);**

Return Value

Nonzero if the call was successful; otherwise 0.

Parameters

cx   Specifies the new width of the control in pixels.

cy   Specifies the new height of the control in pixels.

Remarks

Call this function to set the size of the OLE control window and notify the container that the control site is changing. This function should not be used in your control's constructor.

Note that all coordinates for control windows are relative to the upper-left corner of the control.

See Also   **COleControl::GetControlSize, COleControl::GetRectInContainer**

COleControl::SetEnabled

void SetEnabled(BOOL *bEnabled* **);**

Parameters

bEnabled   **TRUE** if the control is to be enabled; otherwise **FALSE**.

Remarks

Call this function to set the stock Enabled property value of your control. After setting this property, **OnEnabledChange** is called.

See Also   **COleControl::GetEnabled, COleControl::OnEnabledChanged**

COleControl::SetFont

void SetFont(LPFONTDISP *pFontDisp* **);**

Parameters

pFontDisp   A pointer to a Font dispatch interface.

Remarks

Call this function to set the stock Font property of your control.

See Also   **COleControl::GetFont**, **COleControl::InternalGetText**,
COleControl::OnFontChanged

COleControl::SetForeColor

void SetForeColor(OLE_COLOR *dwForeColor* **);**

Parameters

dwForeColor   A **OLE_COLOR** value to be used for foreground drawing of your
control.

Remarks

Call this function to set the stock ForeColor property value of your control. For more
information on using this property and other related properties, see Chapter 22,
"Adding a Custom Notification Property," in the Circle Sample Tutorial in *Tutorials*
and the article "Properties" in *Programming with MFC*.

See Also   **COleControl::SetBackColor**, **COleControl::GetForeColor**,
COleControl::OnForeColorChanged

COleControl::SetInitialDataFormats

virtual void SetInitialDataFormats( );

Remarks

Called by the framework to initialize the list of data formats supported by the control.

The default implementation specifies two formats: **CF_METAFILEPICT** and the
persistent property set.

COleControl::SetInitialSize

void SetInitialSize(int *cx*, **int** *cy* **);**

Parameters

cx   The initial width of the OLE control in pixels.

cy   The initial height of the OLE control in pixels.

Remarks

Call this function in your constructor to set the initial size of your control. The initial
size is measured in device units, or pixels. It is recommended that this call be made
in your control's constructor.

COleControl::SetModifiedFlag

void SetModifiedFlag(BOOL *bModified* **= TRUE);**

Parameters

bModified   The new value for the control's modified flag. **TRUE** indicates that the control's state has been modified; **FALSE** indicates that the control's state has just been saved.

Remarks

Call this function whenever a change occurs that would affect your control's persistent state. For example, if the value of a persistent property changes, call this function with *bModified* **TRUE**.

See Also   **COleControl::IsModified**

COleControl::SetNotPermitted

void SetNotPermitted( );

Remarks

Call this function when **BoundPropertyRequestEdit** fails. This function throws an exception of type **COleDispScodeException** to indicate that the set operation was not permitted.

See Also   **COleControl::BoundPropertyRequestEdit**

COleControl::SetNotSupported

void SetNotSupported( );

Remarks

Call this function in place of the Set function of any property where modification of the property value by the control's user is not supported. One example would be a property that is read-only.

See Also   **COleControl::GetNotSupported**

COleControl::SetRectInContainer

BOOL SetRectInContainer(LPRECT *lpRect* **);**

Return Value

Nonzero if the call was successful; otherwise 0.

Parameters

lpRect   A pointer to a rectangle containing the control's new coordinates relative to the container.

Remarks

Call this function to set the coordinates of the control's rectangle relative to the container, expressed in device units. If the control is open, it is resized; otherwise the container's **OnPosRectChanged** function is called.

See Also   **COleControl::GetRectInContainer**, **COleControl::GetControlSize**

COleControl::SetText

void SetText(LPCTSTR *pszText* **);**

Parameters

pszText   A pointer to a character string.

Remarks

Call this function to set the value of your control's stock Caption or Text property.

Note that the stock Caption and Text properties are both mapped to the same value. This means that any changes made to either property will automatically change both properties. In general, a control should support either the stock Caption or Text property, but not both.

See Also   **COleControl::GetText**, **COleControl::InternalGetText**, **COleControl::OnTextChanged**

COleControl::ThrowError

void ThrowError(SCODE *sc*, **UINT** *nDescriptionID*, **UINT** *nHelpID* = -1 **);**
void ThrowError(SCODE *sc*, **LPCTSTR** *pszDescription* = **NULL**, **UINT** *nHelpID* = 0 **);**

Parameters

sc   The status code value to be reported. For a complete list of possible codes, see the article "OLE Controls: Advanced Topics" in *Programming with MFC*.

nDescriptionID   The string resource ID of the exception to be reported.

nHelpID   The help ID of the topic to be reported on.

pszDescription   A string containing an explanation of the exception to be reported.

Remarks

Call this function to signal the occurrence of an error in your control. This function should only be called from within a Get or Set function for an OLE property, or the implementation of an OLE automation method. If you need to signal errors that occur at other times, you should fire the stock Error event.

See Also   **COleControl::FireError**, **COleControl::DisplayError**

COleControl::TransformCoords

void TransformCoords(POINTL FAR* *lpptlHimetric***, POINTF FAR*** *lpptfContainer***, DWORD** *flags* **);**

Parameters

lpptlHimetric   Pointer to a **POINTL** structure containing coordinates in **HIMETRIC** units.

lpptfContainer   Pointer to a **POINTF** structure containing coordinates in the container's unit size.

flags   A combination of the following values:

- **XFORMCOORDS_POSITION**   A position in the container.

- **XFORMCOORDS_SIZE**   A size in the container.

- **XFORMCOORDS_HIMETERICTOCONTAINER**   Transform **HIMETRIC** units to the container's units.

- **XFORMCOORDS_CONTAINERTOHIMETERIC**   Transform the container's units to **HIMETRIC** units.

Remarks

Call this function to transform coordinate values between **HIMETRIC** units and the container's native units.

The first two flags, **XFORMCOORDS_POSITION** and **XFORMCOORDS_SIZE**, indicate whether the coordinates should be treated as a position or a size. The remaining two flags indicate the direction of transformation.

See Also   **COleControl::AmbientScaleUnits**

COleControl::TranslateColor

COLORREF TranslateColor(OLE_COLOR *clrColor***, HPALETTE** *hpal* **= NULL);**

Return Value

An RGB (red, green, blue) 32-bit color value that defines the solid color closest to the *clrColor* value that the device can represent.

Parameters

clrColor   A **OLE_COLOR** data type. For more information on the **OLE_COLOR** data type, see "Standard Color Type," in Appendix A of *Programming with MFC*.

hpal   A handle to an optional palette; can be **NULL**.

Remarks

Call this function to convert a color value from the **OLE_COLOR** data type to the **COLORREF** data type. This function is useful to translate the stock ForeColor and BackColor properties to **COLORREF** types used by **CDC** member functions.

See Also   **COleControl::GetForeColor**, **COleControl::GetBackColor**

COleControl::WillAmbientsBeValidDuringLoad

BOOL WillAmbientsBeValidDuringLoad( );

Return Value

Nonzero indicates that ambient properties will be valid; otherwise ambient properties will not be valid.

Remarks

Call this function to determine whether your control should use the values of ambient properties as default values, when it is subsequently loaded from its persistent state.

In some containers, your control may not have access to its ambient properties during the initial call to the override of **COleControl::DoPropExchange**. This is the case if the container calls **IPersistStreamInit::Load** or **IPersistStorage::Load** prior to calling **IOleObject::SetClientSite** (that is, if it does not honor the **OLEMISC_SETCLIENTSITEFIRST** status bit).

See Also   **COleControl::DoPropExchange**, **COleControl::GetAmbientProperty**

COleControlModule

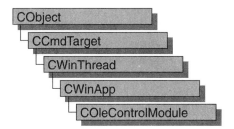

The **COleControlModule** class is the base class from which you derive an OLE control module object. This class provides member functions for initializing your control module. Each OLE control module that uses the Microsoft Foundation classes can only contain one object derived from **COleControlModule**. This object is constructed when other C++ global objects are constructed. Declare your derived **COleControlModule** object at the global level.

For more information on using the **COleControlModule** class, see the **CWinApp** class in this book and the article "OLE Controls" in *Programming with MFC*.

#include <afxctl.h>

See Also   CWinApp

COleConvertDialog

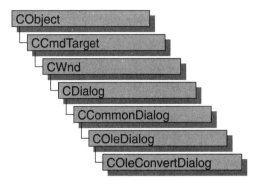

The **COleConvertDialog** class is used for the OLE Convert dialog box. Create an object of class **COleConvertDialog** when you want to call this dialog box. After a **COleConvertDialog** object has been constructed, you can use the **m_cv** structure to initialize the values or states of controls in the dialog box. The **m_cv** structure is of type **OLEUICONVERT**. For more information about using this dialog class, see the **DoModal** member function.

Note AppWizard-generated container code uses this class.

For more information, see the **OLEUICONVERT** structure in the OLE documentation.

For more information about OLE-specific dialog boxes, see the article "Dialog Boxes in OLE" in *Programming with MFC*.

#include <afxodlgs.h>

See Also **COleDialog**

Data Members

m_cv	A structure that controls the behavior of the dialog box.

Construction

COleConvertDialog	Constructs a **COleConvertDialog** object.

Operations and Attributes

DoModal	Displays the OLE Change Item dialog box.
DoConvert	Performs the conversion specified in the dialog box.
GetSelectionType	Gets the type of selection chosen.
GetClassID	Gets the **CLSID** associated with the chosen item.

| **GetDrawAspect** | Specifies whether to draw item as an icon. |
| **GetIconicMetafile** | Gets a handle to the metafile associated with the iconic form of this item. |

Member Functions

COleConvertDialog::COleConvertDialog

COleConvertDialog (COleClientItem* *pItem*, **DWORD** *dwFlags* **= CF_SELECTCONVERTTO, CLSID FAR*** *pClassID* **= NULL, CWnd*** *pParentWnd* **= NULL);**

Parameters

pItem   Points to the item to be converted or activated.

dwFlags   Creation flag, which contains any number of the following values combined using the bitwise-or operator:

- **CF_SELECTCONVERTTO**   Specifies that the Convert To radio button will be selected initially when the dialog box is called. This is the default.

- **CF_SELECTACTIVATEAS**   Specifies that the Activate As radio button will be selected initially when the dialog box is called.

- **CF_SETCONVERTDEFAULT**   Specifies that the class whose **CLSID** is specified by the **clsidConvertDefault** member of the **m_cv** structure will be used as the default selection in the class list box when the Convert To radio button is selected.

- **CF_SETACTIVATEDEFAULT**   Specifies that the class whose **CLSID** is specified by the **clsidActivateDefault** member of the **m_cv** structure will be used as the default selection in the class list box when the Activate As radio button is selected.

- **CF_SHOWHELPBUTTON**   Specifies that the Help button will be displayed when the dialog box is called.

pClassID   Points to the CLSID of the item to be converted or activated. If **NULL**, the **CLSID** associated with *pItem* will be used.

pParentWnd   Points to the parent or owner window object (of type **CWnd**) to which the dialog object belongs. If it is **NULL**, the parent window of the dialog box is set to the main application window.

Remarks

Constructs only a **COleConvertDialog** object. To display the dialog box, call the **DoModal** function.

For more information, see the **CLSID** and **OLEUICONVERT** structures and "Object Class Conversion and Emulation Functions" in the OLE documentation.

See Also   **COleConvertDialog::DoModal**, **COleConvertDialog::m_cv**

COleConvertDialog::DoConvert

BOOL DoConvert(COleClientItem* *pItem* **);**

Return Value

Nonzero if successful; otherwise 0.

Parameters

pItem   Points to the item to be converted or activated. Cannot be **NULL**.

Remarks

Call this function, after returning successfully from **DoModal**, either to convert or to activate an object of type **COleClientItem**. The item is converted or activated according to the information selected by the user in the Convert dialog box.

See Also   **COleClientItem**, **COleConvertDialog::DoModal**, **COleConvertDialog::GetSelectionType**, **COleClientItem::ConvertTo**, **COleClientItem::ActivateAs**

COleConvertDialog::DoModal

virtual int DoModal( );

Return Value

Completion status for the dialog box. One of the following values:

- **IDOK** if the dialog box was successfully displayed.
- **IDCANCEL** if the user canceled the dialog box.
- **IDABORT** if an error occurred. If **IDABORT** is returned, call the **COleDialog::GetLastError** member function to get more information about the type of error that occurred. For a listing of possible errors, see the **OleUIConvert** function in the OLE documentation.

Remarks

Call this function to display the OLE Convert dialog box.

If you want to initialize the various dialog box controls by setting members of the **m_cv** structure, you should do this before calling **DoModal**, but after the dialog object is constructed.

If **DoModal** returns **IDOK**, you can call other member functions to retrieve the settings or information that was input by the user into the dialog box.

See Also   **COleDialog::GetLastError**, **CDialog::DoModal**, **COleConvertDialog::m_cv**, **COleConvertDialog::DoConvert**, **COleConvertDialog::GetSelectionType**, **COleConvertDialog::GetClassID**, **COleConvertDialog::GetDrawAspect**, **COleConvertDialog::GetIconicMetafile**

COleConvertDialog::GetClassID

const CLSID& GetClassID( ) const;

Return Value

The **CLSID** associated with the item that was selected in the Convert dialog box.

Remarks

Call this function to get the **CLSID** associated with the item the user selected in the Convert dialog box. Call this function only after **DoModal** returns **IDOK**.

For more information, see **CLSID** in the OLE documentation.

See Also   **COleConvertDialog::DoModal**

COleConvertDialog::GetDrawAspect

DVASPECT GetDrawAspect( ) const;

Return Value

The method needed to render the object.

- **DVASPECT_CONTENT**   Returned if the Display As Icon check box was not checked.
- **DVASPECT_ICON**   Returned if the Display As Icon check box was checked.

Remarks

Call this function to determine whether the user chose to display the selected item as an icon. Call this function only after **DoModal** returns **IDOK**.

For more information on drawing aspect, see the **FORMATETC** data structure in the OLE documentation.

See Also   **COleConvertDialog::DoModal**, **COleConvertDialog::COleConvertDialog**

COleConvertDialog::GetIconicMetafile

HGLOBAL GetIconPicture( ) const;

Return Value

The handle to the metafile containing the iconic aspect of the selected item, if the Display As Icon check box was checked when the dialog was dismissed by choosing **OK**; otherwise **NULL**.

Remarks

Call this function to get a handle to the metafile that contains the iconic aspect of the selected item.

See Also   COleConvertDialog::DoModal, **COleConvertDialog::COleConvertDialog**, **COleConvertDialog::GetDrawAspect**

COleConvertDialog::GetSelectionType

UINT GetSelectionType( ) const;

Return Value

Type of selection made.

Remarks

Call this function to determine the type of conversion selected in the Convert dialog box.

The return type values are specified by the **Selection** enumeration type declared in the **COleConvertDialog** class.

```
enum Selection
{
   noConversion,
   convertItem,
   activateAs
};
```

Brief desccriptions of these values follow:

- **COleConvertDialog::noConversion**   Returned if either the dialog box was canceled or the user selected no conversion. If **COleConvertDialog::DoModal** returned **IDOK**, it is possible that the user selected a different icon than the one previously selected.

- **COleConvertDialog::convertItem**   Returned if the Convert To radio button was checked, the user selected a different item to convert to, and **DoModal** returned **IDOK**.

- **COleConvertDialog::activateAs**   Returned if the Activate As radio button was checked, the user selected a different item to activate, and **DoModal** returned **IDOK**.

See Also   **COleConvertDialog::DoModal**, **COleConvertDialog::COleConvertDialog**

Data Members

COleConvertDialog::m_cv

Remarks

Structure of type **OLEUICONVERT** used to control the behavior of the Convert dialog box. Members of this structure can be modified either directly or through member functions.

For more information, see the **OLEUICONVERT** structure in the OLE documentation.

See Also   **COleConvertDialog::COleConvertDialog**, **COleConvertDialog::DoModal**

COleCurrency

A **COleCurrency** object encapsulates the **CURRENCY** data type of OLE automation. **CURRENCY** is implemented as an 8-byte, two's-complement integer value scaled by 10,000. This gives a fixed-point number with 15 digits to the left of the decimal point and 4 digits to the right. The **CURRENCY** data type is extremely useful for calculations involving money, or for any fixed-point calculation where accuracy is important. It is one of the possible types for the **VARIANT** data type of OLE automation.

COleCurrency also implements some basic arithmetic operations for this fixed-point type. The supported operations have been selected to control the rounding errors which occur during fixed-point calculations.

For more information, see the **CURRENCY** and **VARIANT** entries in Chapter 5 of the *OLE 2 Programmer's Reference, Volume 2*.

#include <afxdisp.h>

See Also   **COleVariant**

Construction

COleCurrency	Constructs a **COleCurrency** object.

Attributes

GetStatus	Gets the status (validity) of this **COleCurrency** object.
SetStatus	Sets the status (validity) for this **COleCurrency** object.

Operations

SetCurrency	Sets the value of this **COleCurrency** object.
Format	Generates a formatted string representation of a **COleCurrency** object.
ParseCurrency	Reads a **CURRENCY** value from a string and sets the value of **COleCurrency**.

Operators

operator CURRENCY	Converts a **COleCurrency** value into a **CURRENCY**.
operator =	Copies a **COleCurrency** value.
operator +, -	Add, subtract, and change sign of **COleCurrency** values.
operator +=, -=	Adds and subtracts a **COleCurrency** value from this **COleCurrency** object.

operator *, /	Scales a **COleCurrency** value by an integer value.
operator *=, /=	Scales this **COleCurrency** value by an integer value.
operator ==, <, <=, etc.	Compares two **COleCurrency** values.

Data Members

| m_cur | Contains the underlying **CURRENCY** for this **COleCurrency** object. |
| m_status | Contains the status of this **COleCurrency** object. |

Archive/Dump

| operator << | Outputs a **COleCurrency** value to **CArchive** or **CDumpContext**. |
| operator >> | Inputs a **COleCurrency** object from **CArchive**. |

Member Functions

COleCurrency::COleCurrency

COleCurrency( );
COleCurrency(CURRENCY *cySrc* **);**
COleCurrency(const COleCurrency& *curSrc* **);**
COleCurrency(const VARIANT& *varSrc* **);**
COleCurrency(long *nUnits*, **long** *nFractionalUnits* **);**

Parameters

cySrc   A **CURRENCY** value to be copied into the new **COleCurrency** object.

curSrc   An existing **COleCurrency** object to be copied into the new **COleCurrency** object.

varSrc   An existing **VARIANT** data structure (possibly a **COleVariant** object) to be converted to a currency value (**VT_CY**) and copied into the new **COleCurrency** object.

nUnits, *nFractionalUnits*   Indicate the units and fractional part (in 1/10,000's) of the value to be copied into the new **COleCurrency** object.

Remarks

All of these constructors create new **COleCurrency** objects initialized to the specified value. A brief description of each of these constructors follows. Unless otherwise noted, the status of the new **COleCurrency** item is set to valid.

- **COleCurrency( )**   Constructs a **COleCurrency** object initialized to 0 (zero).

- **COleCurrency(** *cySrc* **)**   Constructs a **COleCurrency** object from a **CURRENCY** value.

- **COleCurrency**(*curSrc*) Constructs a **COleCurrency** object from an existing **COleCurrency** object. The new object has the same status as the source object.

- **COleCurrency**(*varSrc*) Constructs a **COleCurrency** object. Attempts to convert a **VARIANT** structure or **COleVariant** object to a currency (**VT_CY**) value. If this conversion is successful, the converted value is copied into the new **COleCurrency** object. If it is not, the value of the **COleCurrency** object is set to zero (0) and its status to invalid.

- **COleCurrency**(*nUnits*, *nFractionalUnits*) Constructs a **COleCurrency** object from the specified numerical components. If the absolute value of the fractional part is greater than 10,000, the appropriate adjustment is made to the units. Note that the units and fractional part are specified by signed long values.

For more information, see the **CURRENCY** and **VARIANT** entries in Chapter 5 of the *OLE 2 Programmer's Reference, Volume 2*.

Example

The following examples show the effects of the zero-parameter and two-parameter constructors:

```
COleCurrency curZero;          // value: 0.0000
COleCurrency curA(4, 500);     // value: 4.0500
COleCurrency curB(2, 11000);   // value: 3.1000
COleCurrency curC(2, -50);     // value: 1.9950
```

See Also   COleCurrency::SetCurrency, COleCurrency::operator =, COleCurrency::GetStatus, COleCurrency::m_cur, COleCurrency::m_status

COleCurrency::Format

CString Format(DWORD *dwFlags* = 0, **LCID** *lcid* = LANG_USER_DEFAULT);

Return Value

A **CString** that contains the formatted currency value.

Parameters

dwFlags   Indicates flags for locale settings, possibly the following flag:

- **LOCALE_NOUSEROVERRIDE**   Use the system default locale settings, rather than custom user settings.

lcid   Indicates locale ID to use for the conversion.

Remarks

Call this member function to create a formatted representation of the currency value. It formats the value using the national language specifications (locale IDs) for currency. If the status of this **COleCurrency** object is null, the return value is an empty string. If the status is invalid, the return string is specified by the string resource **IDS_INVALID_CURRENCY**.

Note For a discussion of locale ID values, see the section "Supporting Multiple National Languages" in the *OLE 2 Programmer's Reference, Volume 2*.

See Also **COleCurrency::ParseCurrency**, **COleCurrency::GetStatus**

COleCurrency::GetStatus

CurrencyStatus GetStatus( ) const;

Return Value

Returns the status of this **COleCurrency** value.

Remarks

Call this member function to get the status (validity) of a given **COleCurrency** object.

The return value is defined by the **CurrencyStatus** enumerated type which is defined within the **COleCurrency** class.

```
enum CurrencyStatus{
    valid = 0,
    invalid = 1,
    null = 2,
};
```

For a brief description of these status values, see the following list:

- **COleCurrency::valid**   Indicates that this **COleCurrency** object is valid.

- **COleCurrency::invalid**   Indicates that this **COleCurrency** object is invalid; that is, its value may be incorrect.

- **COleCurrency::null**   Indicates that this **COleCurrency** object is null, that is, that no value has been supplied for this object. (This is "null" in the database sense of "having no value," as opposed to the C++ **NULL**.)

The status of a **COleCurrency** object is invalid in the following cases:

- If its value is set from a **VARIANT** or **COleVariant** value that could not be converted to a currency value.

- If this object has experienced an overflow or underflow during an arithmetic assignment operation, for example += or *=.

- If an invalid value was assigned to this object.

- If the status of this object was explicitly set to invalid using **SetStatus**.

For more information on operations that may set the status to invalid, see the following member functions:

- **COleCurrency**

- **operator =**

- **operator +, -**
- **operator +=, -=**
- **operator *, /**
- **operator *=, /=**

See Also   **COleCurrency::SetStatus**, **COleCurrency::m_status**

COleCurrency::ParseCurrency

BOOL ParseCurrency(LPCTSTR *lpszCurrency*,
   DWORD *dwFlags* **= 0, LCID** *lcid* **= LANG_USER_DEFAULT);**
   throw(CMemoryException);
   throw(COleException);

Return Value

Nonzero if the string was successfully converted to a currency value, otherwise 0.

Parameters

lpszCurrency   A pointer to the null-terminated string which is to be parsed.

dwFlags   Indicates flags for locale settings, possibly the following flag:

- **LOCALE_NOUSEROVERRIDE**   Use the system default locale settings, rather than custom user settings.

lcid   Indicates locale ID to use for the conversion.

Remarks

Call this member function to parse a string to read a currency value. It uses national language specifications (locale IDs) for the meaning of nonnumeric characters in the source string.

For a discussion of locale ID values, see the section "Supporting Multiple National Languages" in the *OLE 2 Programmer's Reference, Volume 2*.

If the string was successfully converted to a currency value, the value of this **COleCurrency** object is set to that value and its status to valid.

If the string could not be converted to a currency value or if there was a numerical overflow, the status of this **COleCurrency** object is invalid.

If the string conversion failed due to memory allocation errors, this function throws a **CMemoryException**. In any other error state, this function throws a **COleException**.

See Also   **COleCurrency::Format**, **COleCurrency::GetStatus**

COleCurrency::SetCurrency

void SetCurrency(long *nUnits***, long** *nFractionalUnits* **);**

Parameters

nUnits, *nFractionalUnits*   Indicate the units and fractional part (in 1/10,000's) of the value to be copied into this **COleCurrency** object.

Remarks

Call this member function to set the units and fractional part of this **COleCurrency** object.

If the absolute value of the fractional part is greater than 10,000, the appropriate adjustment is made to the units, as shown in the third of the following examples.

Note that the units and fractional part are specified by signed long values. The fourth of the following examples shows what happens when the parameters have different signs.

Example

```
COleCurrency curA;            // value: 0.0000
curA.SetCurrency(4, 500);     // value: 4.0500
curA.SetCurrency(2, 11000);   // value: 3.1000
curA.SetCurrency(2, -50);     // value: 1.9950
```

See Also   **COleCurrency::COleCurrency**, **COleCurrency::operator =**, **COleCurrency::m_cur**

COleCurrency::SetStatus

void SetStatus(CurrencyStatus *nStatus* **);**

Parameters

nStatus   The new status for this **COleCurrency** object.

Remarks

Call this member function to set the status (validity) of this **COleCurrency** object. The *nStatus* parameter value is defined by the **CurrencyStatus** enumerated type, which is defined within the **COleCurrency** class.

```
enum CurrencyStatus{
   valid = 0,
   invalid = 1,
   null = 2,
};
```

For a brief description of these status values, see the following list:

- **COleCurrency::valid** Indicates that this **COleCurrency** object is valid.

- **COleCurrency::invalid** Indicates that this **COleCurrency** object is invalid; that is, its value may be incorrect.

- **COleCurrency::null** Indicates that this **COleCurrency** object is null, that is, that no value has been supplied for this object. (This is "null" in the database sense of "having no value," as opposed to the C++ **NULL**.)

Caution This function is for advanced programming situations. This function does not alter the data in this object. It will most often be used to set the status to null or invalid. Note that the assignment operator (**operator =**) and **SetCurrency** do set the status to of the object based on the source value(s).

See Also COleCurrency::GetStatus, COleCurrency::operator =, COleCurrency::SetCurrency, COleCurrency::m_status

---

Operators

COleCurrency::operator =

const **COleCurrency& operator =**(**CURRENCY** *cySrc*);
const **COleCurrency& operator =**(const **COleCurrency&** *curSrc*);
const **COleCurrency& operator =**(const **VARIANT&** *varSrc*);

Remarks

These overloaded assignment operators copy the source currency value into this **COleCurrency** object. A brief description of each operator follows:

- **operator =**(*cySrc*) The **CURRENCY** value is copied into the **COleCurrency** object and its status is set to valid.

- **operator =**(*curSrc*) The value and status of the operand, an existing **COleCurrency** object are copied into this **COleCurrency** object.

- **operator =**(*varSrc*) If the conversion of the **VARIANT** value (or **COleVariant** object) to a currency (**VT_CY**) is successful, the converted value is copied into this **COleCurrency** object and its status is set to valid. If the conversion is not successful, the value of the **COleCurrency** object is set to 0 and its status to invalid.

For more information, see the **CURRENCY** and **VARIANT** entries in Chapter 5 of the *OLE 2 Programmer's Reference, Volume 2*.

See Also COleCurrency::COleCurrency, COleCurrency::SetCurrency, COleCurrency::GetStatus

COleCurrency::operator +, -

COleCurrency operator +(const COleCurrency& *cur* **) const;**
COleCurrency operator -(const COleCurrency& *cur* **) const;**
COleCurrency operator -( ) const;

Remarks

These operators allow you to add and subtract two **COleCurrency** values to and from each other and to change the sign of a **COleCurrency** value.

If either of the operands is null, the status of the resulting **COleCurrency** value is null.

If the arithmetic operation overflows, the resulting **COleCurrency** value is invalid.

If the operands is invalid and the other is not null, the status of the resulting **COleCurrency** value is invalid.

For more information on the valid, invalid, and null status values, see the **m_status** member variable.

See Also   **COleCurrency::operator +=, -=, COleCurrency::GetStatus**

COleCurrency::operator +=, -=

const COleCurrency& operator +=(const COleCurrency& *cur* **);**
const COleCurrency& operator -=(const COleCurrency& *cur* **);**

Remarks

These operators allow you to add and subtract a **COleCurrency** value to and from this **COleCurrency** object.

If either of the operands is null, the status of this **COleCurrency** object is set to null.

If the arithmetic operation overflows, the status of this **COleCurrency** object is set to invalid.

If either of the operands is invalid and the other is not null, the status of this **COleCurrency** object is set to invalid.

For more information on the valid, invalid, and null status values, see the **m_status** member variable.

See Also   **COleCurrency::operator +, -, COleCurrency::GetStatus**

COleCurrency::operator *, /

COleCurrency operator *(long *nOperand* **) const;**
COleCurrency operator /(long *nOperand* **) const;**

Remarks

These operators allow you to scale a **COleCurrency** value by an integral value.

If the **COleCurrency** operand is null, the status of the resulting **COleCurrency** value is null.

If the arithmetic operation overflows or underflows, the status of the resulting **COleCurrency** value is invalid.

If the **COleCurrency** operand is invalid, the status of the resulting **COleCurrency** value is invalid.

For more information on the valid, invalid, and null status values, see the **m_status** member variable.

See Also **COleCurrency::operator *=, /=, COleCurrency::GetStatus**

COleCurrency::operator *=, /=

const COleCurrency& operator *=(long *nOperand* **);**
const COleCurrency& operator /=(long *nOperand* **);**

Remarks

These operators allow you to scale this **COleCurrency** value by an integral value.

If the **COleCurrency** operand is null, the status of this **COleCurrency** object is set to null.

If the arithmetic operation overflows, the status of this **COleCurrency** object is set to invalid.

If the **COleCurrency** operand is invalid, the status of this **COleCurrency** object is set to invalid.

For more information on the valid, invalid, and null status values, see the **m_status** member variable.

See Also **COleCurrency::operator *, /, COleCurrency::GetStatus**

COleCurrency::operator CURRENCY

operator CURRENCY( ) const;

Remarks

This operator returns a **CURRENCY** structure whose value is copied from this **COleCurrency** object.

For more information, see the **CURRENCY** entry in Chapter 5 of the *OLE 2 Programmer's Reference, Volume 2*.

See Also   **COleCurrency::m_cur**, **COleCurrency::SetCurrency**

COleCurrency Relational Operators

BOOL operator ==(const COleCurrency& *cur* **) const;**
BOOL operator !=(const COleCurrency& *cur* **) const;**
BOOL operator <(const COleCurrency& *cur* **) const;**
BOOL operator >(const COleCurrency& *cur* **) const;**
BOOL operator <=(const COleCurrency& *cur* **) const;**
BOOL operator >=(const COleCurrency& *cur* **) const;**

Remarks

These operators compare two currency values and return nonzero if the condition is true; otherwise 0.

Note   The return value of the ordering operations (<, <=, >, >=) is undefined if the status of either operand is null or invalid. The equality operators (==, !=) consider the status of the operands.

Example

```
COleCurrency curOne(3, 5000);          // 3.5
COleCurrency curTwo(curOne);           // 3.5
BOOL b;
b = curOne == curTwo;                  // TRUE

curTwo.SetStatus(COleCurrency::Invalid);
b = curOne == curTwo;                  // FALSE, different status
b = curOne != curTwo;                  // TRUE, different status
b = curOne < curTwo;                   // FALSE, same value
b = curOne > curTwo;                   // FALSE, same value
b = curOne <= curTwo;                  // TRUE, same value
b = curOne >= curTwo;                  // TRUE, same value
```

Note   The last four lines of the preceding example will **ASSERT** in debug mode.

See Also   **COleCurrency::GetStatus**

COleCurrency::operator <<, >>

friend CDumpContext& operator <<(CDumpContext& *dc***, COleCurrency** *curSrc* **);**
friend CArchive& operator <<(CArchive& *ar***, COleCurrency** *curSrc* **);**
friend CArchive& operator >>(CArchive& *ar***, COleCurrency&** *curSrc* **);**

Remarks

The **COleCurrency** insertion (<<) operator supports diagnostic dumping and storing
to an archive. The extraction (>>) operator supports loading from an archive.

See Also **CDumpContext**, **CArchive**

Data Members

COleCurrency::m_cur

Remarks

The underlying **CURRENCY** structure for this **COleCurrency** object.

Caution Changing the value in the **CURRENCY** structure accessed by the pointer returned
by this function will change the value of this **COleCurrency** object. It does not change the
status of this **COleCurrency** object.

For more information, see the **CURRENCY** entry in Chapter 5 of the *OLE 2*
Programmer's Reference, Volume 2.

See Also **COleCurrency::COleCurrency**, **COleCurrency::operator**,
CURRENCY, **COleCurrency::SetCurrency**

COleCurrency::m_status

Remarks

The type of this data member is the enumerated type **CurrencyStatus**, which is
defined within the **COleCurrency** class.

```
enum CurrencyStatus{
   valid = 0,
   invalid = 1,
   null = 2,
};
```

For a brief description of these status values, see the following list:

- **COleCurrency::valid** Indicates that this **COleCurrency** object is valid.

- **COleCurrency::invalid** Indicates that this **COleCurrency** object is invalid; that
  is, its value may be incorrect.

- **COleCurrency::null**   Indicates that this **COleCurrency** object is null, that is, that no value has been supplied for this object. (This is "null" in the database sense of "having no value," as opposed to the C++ **NULL**.)

The status of a **COleCurrency** object is invalid in the following cases:

- If its value is set from a **VARIANT** or **COleVariant** value that could not be converted to a currency value.

- If this object has experienced an overflow or underflow during an arithmetic assignment operation, for example **+=** or ***=**.

- If an invalid value was assigned to this object.

- If the status of this object was explicitly set to invalid using **SetStatus**.

For more information on operations that may set the status to invalid, see the following member functions:

- **COleCurrency**
- **operator =**
- **operator +, -**
- **operator +=, -=**
- **operator *, /**
- **operator *=, /=**

Caution   This data member is for advanced programming situations. You should use the inline member functions **GetStatus** and **SetStatus**. See **SetStatus** for further cautions regarding explicitly setting this data member.

See Also   COleCurrency::GetStatus, COleCurrency::SetStatus

COleDataObject

The **COleDataObject** class is used in data transfers for retrieving data in various formats from the Clipboard, through drag and drop, or from an embedded OLE item. These kinds of data transfers include a source and a destination. The data source is implemented as an object of the **COleDataSource** class. Whenever a destination application has data dropped in it or is asked to perform a paste operation from the Clipboard, an object of the **COleDataObject** class must be created.

This class enables you to determine whether the data exists in a specified format. You can also enumerate the available data formats or check whether a given format is available and then retrieve the data in the preferred format. Object retrieval can be accomplished in several different ways, including the use of a **CFile**, an **HGLOBAL**, or an **STGMEDIUM** structure.

For more information, see the **STGMEDIUM** structure in the *OLE 2 Programmer's Reference, Volume 1*.

For more information about using data objects in your application, see the article "Data Objects and Data Sources" in *Programming with MFC*.

#include <afxole.h>

See Also   **COleDataSource**, **COleClientItem**, **COleServerItem**, **COleDataSource::DoDragDrop**, **CView::OnDrop**

Construction

COleDataObject	Constructs a **COleDataObject** object.

Operations

AttachClipboard	Attaches the data object that is on the Clipboard.
IsDataAvailable	Checks whether data is available in a specified format.
GetData	Copies data from the attached OLE data object in a specified format.
GetFileData	Copies data from the attached OLE data object into a **CFile** pointer in the specified format.
GetGlobalData	Copies data from the attached OLE data object into an **HGLOBAL** in the specified format.
BeginEnumFormats	Prepares for one or more subsequent **GetNextFormat** calls.
GetNextFormat	Returns the next data format available.

Attach	Attaches the specified OLE data object to the COleDataObject.
Release	Detaches and releases the associated **IDataObject** object.
Detach	Detaches the associated **IDataObject** object.

Member Functions

COleDataObject::Attach

void Attach(LPDATAOBJECT *lpDataObject*, **BOOL** *bAutoRelease* = **TRUE**);

Parameters

lpDataObject   Points to an OLE data object.

bAutoRelease   **TRUE** if the OLE data object should be released when the **COleDataObject** object is destroyed; otherwise **FALSE**.

Remarks

Call this function to associate the **COleDataObject** object with an OLE data object.

For more information, see **IDataObject** in the *OLE 2 Programmer's Reference, Volume 1*.

See Also   **COleDataObject::AttachClipboard**, **COleDataObject::Detach**, **COleDataObject::Release**

COleDataObject::AttachClipboard

BOOL AttachClipboard( );

Return Value

Nonzero if successful; otherwise 0.

Remarks

Call this function to attach the data object that is currently on the Clipboard to the **COleDataObject** object.

Note   Calling this function locks the Clipboard until this data object is released. The data object is released in the destructor for the **COleDataObject**. For more information, see **OpenClipboard** and **CloseClipboard** in the Win32 documentation.

See Also   **COleDataObject::Attach**, **COleDataObject::Detach**, **COleDataObject::Release**

COleDataObject::BeginEnumFormats

void BeginEnumFormats( );

Remarks

Call this function to prepare for subsequent calls to **GetNextFormat** for retrieving a list of data formats from the item.

After a call to **BeginEnumFormats**, the position of the first format supported by this data object is stored. Successive calls to **GetNextFormat** will enumerate the list of available formats in the data object.

To check on the availability of data in a given format, use **COleDataObject::IsDataAvailable**.

For more information, see **IDataObject::EnumFormatEtc** in the *OLE 2 Programmer's Reference, Volume 1*.

See Also **COleDataObject::GetNextFormat**, **COleDataObject::IsDataAvailable**

COleDataObject::COleDataObject

COleDataObject( );

Remarks

Constructs a **COleDataObject** object. A call to **COleDataObject::Attach** or **COleDataObject::AttachClipboard** must be made before calling other **COleDataObject** functions.

Note Since one of the parameters to the drag-and-drop handlers is a pointer to a **COleDataObject**, there is no need to call this constructor to support drag and drop.

See Also **COleDataObject::Attach**, **COleDataObject::AttachClipboard**, **COleDataObject::Release**

COleDataObject::Detach

LPDATAOBJECT Detach( );

Return Value

A pointer to the OLE data object that was detached.

Remarks

Call this function to detach the **COleDataObject** object from its associated OLE data object without releasing the data object.

See Also **COleDataObject::Attach**, **COleDataObject::Release**

COleDataObject::GetData

BOOL GetData(CLIPFORMAT *cfFormat*, **LPSTGMEDIUM** *lpStgMedium*,
LPFORMATETC *lpFormatEtc* = **NULL**);

Return Value

Nonzero if successful; otherwise 0.

Parameters

cfFormat   The format in which data is to be returned. This parameter can be one of
the predefined Clipboard formats or the value returned by the native Windows
RegisterClipboardFormat function.

lpStgMedium   Points to a **STGMEDIUM** structure that will receive data.

lpFormatEtc   Points to a **FORMATETC** structure describing the format in which
data is to be returned. Provide a value for this parameter if you want to specify
additional format information beyond the Clipboard format specified by *cfFormat*.
If it is **NULL**, the default values are used for the other fields in the
FORMATETC structure.

Remarks

Call this function to retrieve data from the item in the specified format.

For more information, see **IDataObject::GetData**, **STGMEDIUM**, and
FORMATETC in the *OLE 2 Programmer's Reference*, *Volume 1*.

For more information, see **RegisterClipboardFormat** in the Win32 documentation.

See Also   **COleDataObject::GetFileData**, **COleDataObject::GetGlobalData**,
COleDataObject::IsDataAvailable

COleDataObject::GetFileData

CFile* GetFileData(CLIPFORMAT *cfFormat*, **LPFORMATETC** *lpFormatEtc* = **NULL**);

Return Value

Pointer to the new **CFile** or **CFile**-derived object containing the data if successful;
otherwise **NULL**.

Parameters

cfFormat   The format in which data is to be returned. This parameter can be one of
the predefined Clipboard formats or the value returned by the native Windows
RegisterClipboardFormat function.

lpFormatEtc   Points to a **FORMATETC** structure describing the format in which
data is to be returned. Provide a value for this parameter if you want to specify
additional format information beyond the Clipboard format specified by *cfFormat*.
If it is **NULL**, the default values are used for the other fields in the
FORMATETC structure.

Remarks

Call this function to create a **CFile** or **CFile**-derived object and to retrieve data in the specified format into a **CFile** pointer. Depending on the medium the data is stored in, the actual type pointed to by the return value may be **CFile**, **CSharedFile**, or **COleStreamFile**.

Note The **CFile** object accessed by the return value of this function is owned by the caller. It is the responsibility of the caller to **delete** the **CFile** object, thereby closing the file.

For more information, see **FORMATETC** in the *OLE 2 Programmer's Reference, Volume 1*.

For more information, see **RegisterClipboardFormat** in the Win32 documentation.

See Also **COleDataObject::GetData**, **COleDataObject::GetGlobalData**, **COleDataObject::IsDataAvailable**

COleDataObject::GetGlobalData

HGLOBAL GetGlobalData(CLIPFORMAT *cfFormat*, **LPFORMATETC** *lpFormatEtc* **= NULL);**

Return Value

The handle of the global memory block containing the data if successful; otherwise **NULL**.

Parameters

cfFormat   The format in which data is to be returned. This parameter can be one of the predefined Clipboard formats or the value returned by the native Windows **RegisterClipboardFormat** function.

lpFormatEtc   Points to a **FORMATETC** structure describing the format in which data is to be returned. Provide a value for this parameter if you want to specify additional format information beyond the Clipboard format specified by *cfFormat*. If it is **NULL**, the default values are used for the other fields in the **FORMATETC** structure.

Remarks

Call this function to allocate a global memory block and to retrieve data in the specified format into an **HGLOBAL**.

For more information, see **FORMATETC** in the *OLE 2 Programmer's Reference, Volume 1*.

For more information, see **RegisterClipboardFormat** in the Win32 documentation.

See Also **COleDataObject::GetData**, **COleDataObject::GetFileData**, **COleDataObject::IsDataAvailable**

COleDataObject::GetNextFormat

BOOL GetNextFormat(LPFORMATETC *lpFormatEtc* **);**

Return Value

Nonzero if another format is available; otherwise 0.

Parameters

lpFormatEtc   Points to the **FORMATETC** structure that receives the format information when the function call returns.

Remarks

Call this function repeatedly to obtain all the formats available for retrieving data from the item.

After a call to **COleDataObject::BeginEnumFormats**, the position of the first format supported by this data object is stored. Successive calls to **GetNextFormat** will enumerate the list of available formats in the data object. Use these functions to list the available formats.

To check for the availability of a given format, call **COleDataObject::IsDataAvailable**.

For more information, see **IEnumX::Next** in the *OLE 2 Programmer's Reference, Volume 1*.

See Also   **COleDataObject::BeginEnumFormats**, **COleDataObject::GetData**, **COleDataObject::GetFileData**, **COleDataObject::GetGlobalData**

COleDataObject::IsDataAvailable

BOOL IsDataAvailable(CLIPFORMAT *cfFormat*, **LPFORMATETC** *lpFormatEtc* = **NULL**);**

Return Value

Nonzero if data is available in the specified format; otherwise 0.

Parameters

cfFormat   The Clipboard data format to be used in the structure pointed to by *lpFormatEtc*. This parameter can be one of the predefined Clipboard formats or the value returned by the native Windows **RegisterClipboardFormat** function.

lpFormatEtc   Points to a **FORMATETC** structure describing the format desired. Provide a value for this parameter only if you want to specify additional format information beyond the Clipboard format specified by *cfFormat*. If it is **NULL**, the default values are used for the other fields in the **FORMATETC** structure.

Remarks

Call this function to determine if a particular format is available for retrieving data from the OLE item. This function is useful before calling **GetData**, **GetFileData**, or **GetGlobalData**.

For more information, see **IDataObject::QueryGetData** and **FORMATETC** in the *OLE 2 Programmer's Reference, Volume 1*.

For more information, see **RegisterClipboardFormat** in the Win32 documentation.

See Also **COleDataObject::BeginEnumFormats**, **COleDataObject::GetData**, **COleDataObject::GetFileData**, **COleDataObject::GetGlobalData**, **COleDataObject::GetNextFormat**

COleDataObject::Release

void Release( );

Remarks

Call this function to release ownership of the **IDataObject** object that was previously associated with the **COleDataObject** object. The **IDataObject** was associated with the **COleDataObject** by calling **Attach** or **AttachClipboard** explicitly or by the framework. If the *bAutoRelease* parameter of **Attach** is **FALSE**, the **IDataObject** object will not be released. In this case, the caller is responsible for releasing the **IDataObject** by calling **IUnknown::Release**.

See Also **COleDataObject::Attach**, **COleDataObject::COleDataObject**, **COleDataObject::Detach**

COleDataSource

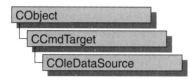

The **COleDataSource** class acts as a cache into which an application places the data that it will offer during data transfer operations, such as Clipboard or drag-and-drop operations.

You can create OLE data sources directly. Alternately, the **COleClientItem** and **COleServerItem** classes create OLE data sources in response to their **CopyToClipboard** and **DoDragDrop** member functions. See **COleServerItem::CopyToClipboard** for a brief description. Override the **OnGetClipboardData** member function of your client item or server item class to add additional Clipboard formats to the data in the OLE data source created for the **CopyToClipboard** or **DoDragDrop** member function.

Whenever you want to prepare data for a transfer, you should create an object of this class and fill it with your data using the most appropriate method for your data. The way it is inserted into a data source is directly affected by whether the data is supplied immediately (immediate rendering) or on demand (delayed rendering). For every Clipboard format in which you are providing data by passing the Clipboard format to be used (and an optional **FORMATETC** structure), call **DelayRenderData**.

For more information about data sources and data transfer, see the article "Data Objects and Data Sources (OLE)." In addition, the article "Clipboard" describes the OLE Clipboard mechanism. Both articles are in *Programming with MFC*.

#include <afxole.h>

See Also   **COleClientItem**, **COleDataObject**, **COleServerItem**

Construction

COleDataSource	Constructs a **COleDataSource** object.

Operations

CacheData	Offers data in a specified format using a **STGMEDIUM** structure.
CacheGlobalData	Offers data in a specified format using an **HGLOBAL**.
DoDragDrop	Performs drag-and-drop operations with a data source.
SetClipboard	Places a **COleDataSource** object on the Clipboard.
Empty	Empties the **COleDataSource** object of data.

FlushClipboard	Renders all data to the Clipboard.
GetClipboardOwner	Verifies that the data placed on the Clipboard is still there.
OnRenderData	Retrieves data as part of delayed rendering.
OnRenderFileData	Retrieves data into a **CFile** as part of delayed rendering.
OnRenderGlobalData	Retrieves data into an **HGLOBAL** as part of delayed rendering.
OnSetData	Called to replace the data in the **COleDataSource** object.
DelayRenderData	Offers data in a specified format using delayed rendering.
DelayRenderFileData	Offers data in a specified format in a **CFile** pointer.
DelaySetData	Called for every format that is supported in **OnSetData**.

Member Functions

COleDataSource::CacheData

> void **CacheData**(CLIPFORMAT *cfFormat*, **LPSTGMEDIUM** *lpStgMedium*,
> **LPFORMATETC** *lpFormatEtc* = **NULL**);

Parameters

cfFormat   The Clipboard format in which the data is to be offered. This parameter can be one of the predefined Clipboard formats or the value returned by the native Windows **RegisterClipboardFormat** function.

lpStgMedium   Points to a **STGMEDIUM** structure containing the data in the format specified.

lpFormatEtc   Points to a **FORMATETC** structure describing the format in which the data is to be offered. Provide a value for this parameter if you want to specify additional format information beyond the Clipboard format specified by *cfFormat*. If it is **NULL**, default values are used for the other fields in the **FORMATETC** structure.

Remarks

Call this function to specify a format in which data is offered during data transfer operations. You must supply the data, because this function provides it by using immediate rendering. The data is cached until needed.

Supply the data using a **STGMEDIUM** structure. You can also use the **CacheGlobalData** member function if the amount of data you are supplying is small enough to be transferred efficiently using an **HGLOBAL**.

After the call to **CacheData** the **ptd** member of *lpFormatEtc* and the contents of *lpStgMedium* are owned by the data object, not by the caller.

To use delayed rendering, call the **DelayRenderData** or **DelayRenderFileData** member function. For more information on delayed rendering as handled by MFC, see the article "Data Objects and Data Sources (OLE)" in *Programming with MFC*.

For more information, see the **STGMEDIUM** and **FORMATETC** structures in the *OLE 2 Programmer's Reference, Volume 1*.

For more information, see **RegisterClipboardFormat** in the Win32 documentation.

See Also   **COleDataSource::CacheGlobalData,
COleDataSource::DelayRenderData, COleDataSource::DelayRenderFileData,
COleDataSource::SetClipboard, COleDataSource::DoDragDrop**

COleDataSource::CacheGlobalData

void CacheGlobalData(CLIPFORMAT *cfFormat*, **HGLOBAL** *hGlobal*,
LPFORMATETC *lpFormatEtc* = **NULL**);

Parameters

cfFormat   The Clipboard format in which the data is to be offered. This parameter can be one of the predefined Clipboard formats or the value returned by the native Windows **RegisterClipboardFormat** function.

hGlobal   Handle to the global memory block containing the data in the format specified.

lpFormatEtc   Points to a **FORMATETC** structure describing the format in which the data is to be offered. Provide a value for this parameter if you want to specify additional format information beyond the Clipboard format specified by *cfFormat*. If it is **NULL**, default values are used for the other fields in the **FORMATETC** structure.

Remarks

Call this function to specify a format in which data is offered during data transfer operations. This function provides the data using immediate rendering, so you must supply the data when calling the function; the data is cached until needed. Use the **CacheData** member function if you are supplying a large amount of data or if you require a structured storage medium.

To use delayed rendering, call the **DelayRenderData** or **DelayRenderFileData** member function. For more information on delayed rendering as handled by MFC, see the article "Data Objects and Data Sources (OLE)" in *Programming with MFC*.

For more information, see the **FORMATETC** structure in the *OLE 2 Programmer's Reference, Volume 1*.

For more information, see **RegisterClipboardFormat** in the Win32 documentation.

See Also   **COleDataSource::CacheData, COleDataSource::DelayRenderData,
COleDataSource::DelayRenderFileData**

COleDataSource::COleDataSource

COleDataSource( );

Remarks

Constructs a **COleDataSource** object.

COleDataSource::DelayRenderData

void DelayRenderData(CLIPFORMAT *cfFormat*, **LPFORMATETC** *lpFormatEtc* = **NULL**);

Parameters

cfFormat   The Clipboard format in which the data is to be offered. This parameter
can be one of the predefined Clipboard formats or the value returned by the native
Windows **RegisterClipboardFormat** function.

lpFormatEtc   Points to a **FORMATETC** structure describing the format in which
the data is to be offered. Provide a value for this parameter if you want to specify
additional format information beyond the Clipboard format specified by *cfFormat*.
If it is **NULL**, default values are used for the other fields in the **FORMATETC**
structure.

Remarks

Call this function to specify a format in which data is offered during data transfer
operations. This function provides the data using delayed rendering, so the data is not
supplied immediately. The **OnRenderData** or **OnRenderGlobalData** member
function is called to request the data.

Use this function if you are not going to supply your data through a **CFile** object. If
you are going to supply the data through a **CFile** object, call the
DelayRenderFileData member function. For more information on delayed rendering
as handled by MFC, see the article "Data Objects and Data Sources (OLE)" in
Programming with MFC.

To use immediate rendering, call the **CacheData** or **CacheGlobalData** member
function.

For more information, see the **FORMATETC** structure in the *OLE 2 Programmer's
Reference, Volume 1*.

For more information, see **RegisterClipboardFormat** in the Win32 documentation.

See Also   **COleDataSource::CacheData, COleDataSource::CacheGlobalData,
COleDataSource::DelayRenderFileData, COleDataSource::OnRenderData,
COleDataSource::OnRenderGlobalData**

COleDataSource::DelayRenderFileData

void DelayRenderFileData(CLIPFORMAT *cfFormat*, **LPFORMATETC** *lpFormatEtc* = NULL);

Parameters

cfFormat   The Clipboard format in which the data is to be offered. This parameter can be one of the predefined Clipboard formats or the value returned by the native Windows **RegisterClipboardFormat** function.

lpFormatEtc   Points to a **FORMATETC** structure describing the format in which the data is to be offered. Provide a value for this parameter if you want to specify additional format information beyond the Clipboard format specified by *cfFormat*. If it is **NULL**, default values are used for the other fields in the **FORMATETC** structure.

Remarks

Call this function to specify a format in which data is offered during data transfer operations. This function provides the data using delayed rendering, so the data is not supplied immediately. The **OnRenderFileData** member function is called to request the data.

Use this function if you are going to use a **CFile** object to supply the data. If you are not going to use a **CFile** object, call the **DelayRenderData** member function. For more information on delayed rendering as handled by MFC, see the article "Data Objects and Data Sources (OLE)" in *Programming with MFC*.

To use immediate rendering, call the **CacheData** or **CacheGlobalData** member function.

For more information, see the **FORMATETC** structure in the *OLE 2 Programmer's Reference, Volume 1*.

For more information, see **RegisterClipboardFormat** in the Win32 documentation.

See Also   **COleDataSource::CacheData, COleDataSource::CacheGlobalData, COleDataSource::DelayRenderData, COleDataSource::OnRenderFileData**

COleDataSource::DelaySetData

void DelaySetData(CLIPFORMAT *cfFormat*, **LPFORMATETC** *lpFormatEtc* = NULL) **const;**

Parameters

cfFormat   The Clipboard format in which the data is to be placed. This parameter can be one of the predefined Clipboard formats or the value returned by the native Windows **RegisterClipboardFormat** function.

lpFormatEtc   Points to a **FORMATETC** structure describing the format in which the data is to be replaced. Provide a value for this parameter if you want to specify additional format information beyond the Clipboard format specified by *cfFormat*. If it is **NULL**, default values are used for the other fields in the **FORMATETC** structure.

Remarks

Call this function to support changing the contents of the data source. **OnSetData** will be called by the framework when this happens. This is only used when the framework returns the data source from **COleServerItem::GetDataSource**. If **DelaySetData** is not called, your **OnSetData** function will never be called. **DelaySetData** should be called for each Clipboard or **FORMATETC** format you support.

For more information, see the **FORMATETC** structure in the *OLE 2 Programmer's Reference, Volume 1*.

For more information, see **RegisterClipboardFormat** in the Win32 documentation.

See Also   **COleServerItem::GetDataSource**, **COleDataSource::OnSetData**

COleDataSource::DoDragDrop

DROPEFFECT DoDragDrop(DWORD *dwEffects* =
**DROPEFFECT_COPY|DROPEFFECT_MOVE|DROPEFFECT_LINK,
LPCRECT** *lpRectStartDrag* = **NULL, COleDropSource*** *pDropSource* = **NULL);**

Return Value

Drop effect generated by the drag-and-drop operation; otherwise **DROPEFFECT_NONE** if the operation never begins because the user released the mouse button before leaving the supplied rectangle.

Parameters

dwEffects   Drag-and-drop operations that are allowed on this data source. Can be one or more of the following:

- **DROPEFFECT_COPY**   A copy operation could be performed.
- **DROPEFFECT_MOVE**   A move operation could be performed.
- **DROPEFFECT_LINK**   A link from the dropped data to the original data could be established.
- **DROPEFFECT_SCROLL**   Indicates that a drag scroll operation could occur.

lpRectStartDrag   Pointer to the rectangle that defines where the drag actually starts. For more information, see the following "Remarks" section.

pDropSource   Points to a drop source. If **NULL** then a default implementation of **COleDropSource** will be used.

Remarks

Call the **DoDragDrop** member function to perform a drag-and-drop operation for this data source, typically in an **CWnd::OnLButtonDown** handler.

The drag-and-drop operation does not start immediately. It waits until the mouse cursor leaves the rectangle specified by *lpRectStartDrag* or until a specified number of milliseconds have passed. If *lpRectStartDrag* is **NULL**, the size of the rectangle is one pixel. The delay time is specified by the **DragDelay** value in the [Windows] section of WIN.INI. If this value is not in WIN.INI, the default value of 200 milliseconds is used.

For more information, see the article "Drag and Drop; Implementing a Drop Source" in *Programming with MFC*.

See Also   **COleDropSource::OnBeginDrag**, **COleDropSource**

COleDataSource::Empty

void Empty( );

Remarks

Call this function to empty the **COleDataSource** object of data. Both cached and delay render formats are emptied so they can be reused.

For more information, see **ReleaseStgMedium** in the *OLE 2 Programmer's Reference, Volume 1*.

COleDataSource::FlushClipboard

static void FlushClipboard( );

Remarks

Removes data from the Clipboard that was placed there by a previous call to **SetClipboard**. This function also causes any data still on the Clipboard to be immediately rendered. Call this function when it is necessary to delete the data object last placed on the Clipboard from memory. Calling this function ensures that OLE will not require the original data source to perform Clipboard rendering.

See Also   **COleDataSource::GetClipboardOwner**, **COleDataSource::SetClipboard**

COleDataSource::GetClipboardOwner

static COleDataSource* GetClipboardOwner( );

Return Value

The data source currently on the Clipboard, or **NULL** if there is nothing on the Clipboard or if the Clipboard is not owned by the calling application.

Remarks

Determines whether the data on the Clipboard has changed since **SetClipboard** was last called and, if so, identifies the current owner.

See Also **COleDataSource::FlushClipboard**, **COleDataSource::SetClipboard**

COleDataSource::OnRenderData

virtual BOOL OnRenderData(LPFORMATETC *lpFormatEtc***, LPSTGMEDIUM** *lpStgMedium* **);**

Return Value

Nonzero if successful; otherwise 0.

Parameters

lpFormatEtc Points to the **FORMATETC** structure specifying the format in which information is requested.

lpStgMedium Points to a **STGMEDIUM** structure in which the data is to be returned.

Remarks

Called by the framework to retrieve data in the specified format. The specified format is one previously placed in the **COleDataSource** object using the **DelayRenderData** or **DelayRenderFileData** member function for delayed rendering. The default implementation of this function will call **OnRenderFileData** or **OnRenderGlobalData** if the supplied storage medium is either a file or memory, respectively. If neither of these formats are supplied, then the default implementation will return 0 and do nothing. For more information on delayed rendering as handled by MFC, see the article "Data Objects and Data Sources (OLE)" in *Programming with MFC*.

If *lpStgMedium->tymed* is **TYMED_NULL**, the **STGMEDIUM** should be allocated and filled as specified by *lpFormatEtc->tymed*. If it is not **TYMED_NULL**, the **STGMEDIUM** should be filled in place with the data.

This is an advanced overridable. Override this function to supply your data in the requested format and medium. Depending on your data, you may want to override one of the other versions of this function instead. If your data is small and fixed in size, override **OnRenderGlobalData**. If your data is in a file, or is of variable size, override **OnRenderFileData**.

For more information, see the **STGMEDIUM** and **FORMATETC** structures, the **TYMED** enumeration type, and **IDataObject::GetData** in the *OLE 2 Programmer's Reference, Volume 1*.

See Also   **COleDataSource::DelayRenderData**, **COleDataSource::DelayRenderFileData**, **COleDataSource::OnRenderFileData**, **COleDataSource::OnRenderGlobalData**, **COleDataSource::OnSetData**

COleDataSource::OnRenderFileData

virtual BOOL OnRenderFileData(LPFORMATETC *lpFormatEtc***, CFile*** *pFile* **);**

Return Value
Nonzero if successful; otherwise 0.

Parameters
lpFormatEtc   Points to the **FORMATETC** structure specifying the format in which information is requested.

pFile   Points to a **CFile** object in which the data is to be rendered.

Remarks
Called by the framework to retrieve data in the specified format when the specified storage medium is a file. The specified format is one previously placed in the **COleDataSource** object using the **DelayRenderData** member function for delayed rendering. The default implementation of this function simply returns **FALSE**.

This is an advanced overridable. Override this function to supply your data in the requested format and medium. Depending on your data, you might want to override one of the other versions of this function instead. If you want to handle multiple storage media, override **OnRenderData**. If your data is in a file, or is of variable size, override **OnRenderFileData**. For more information on delayed rendering as handled by MFC, see the article "Data Objects and Data Sources (OLE)" in *Programming with MFC*.

For more information, see the **FORMATETC** structure and **IDataObject::GetData** in the *OLE 2 Programmer's Reference, Volume 1*.

See Also   **COleDataSource::DelayRenderData**, **COleDataSource::DelayRenderFileData**, **COleDataSource::OnRenderData**, **COleDataSource::OnRenderGlobalData**, **COleDataSource::OnSetData**, **CFile**

COleDataSource::OnRenderGlobalData

virtual BOOL OnRenderGlobalData(LPFORMATETC *lpFormatEtc*, **HGLOBAL*** *phGlobal* **);**

Return Value

Nonzero if successful; otherwise 0.

Parameters

lpFormatEtc   Points to the **FORMATETC** structure specifying the format in which information is requested.

phGlobal   Points to a handle to global memory in which the data is to be returned. If one has not yet been allocated, this parameter can be **NULL**.

Remarks

Called by the framework to retrieve data in the specified format when the specified storage medium is global memory. The specified format is one previously placed in the **COleDataSource** object using the **DelayRenderData** member function for delayed rendering. The default implementation of this function simply returns **FALSE**.

If *phGlobal* is **NULL**, then a new **HGLOBAL** should be allocated and returned in *phGlobal*. Otherwise, the **HGLOBAL** specified by *phGlobal* should be filled with the data. The amount of data placed in the **HGLOBAL** must not exceed the current size of the memory block. Also, the block cannot be reallocated to a larger size.

This is an advanced overridable. Override this function to supply your data in the requested format and medium. Depending on your data, you may want to override one of the other versions of this function instead. If you want to handle multiple storage media, override **OnRenderData**. If your data is in a file, or is of variable size, override **OnRenderFileData**. For more information on delayed rendering as handled by MFC, see the article "Data Objects and Data Sources (OLE)" in *Programming with MFC*.

For more information, see the **FORMATETC** structure and **IDataObject::GetData** in the *OLE 2 Programmer's Reference, Volume 1*.

See Also   **COleDataSource::DelayRenderData, COleDataSource::DelayRenderFileData, COleDataSource::OnRenderData, COleDataSource::OnRenderFileData, COleDataSource::OnSetData**

COleDataSource::OnSetData

virtual BOOL OnSetData(LPFORMATETC *lpFormatEtc*, **LPSTGMEDIUM** *lpStgMedium*, **BOOL** *bRelease* **);**

Return Value

Nonzero if successful; otherwise 0.

Parameters

lpFormatEtc   Points to the **FORMATETC** structure specifying the format in which data is being replaced.

lpStgMedium   Points to the **STGMEDIUM** structure containing the data that will replace the current contents of the **COleDataSource** object.

bRelease   Indicates who has ownership of the storage medium after completing the function call. The caller decides who is responsible for releasing the resources allocated on behalf of the storage medium. The caller does this by setting *bRelease*. If *bRelease* is nonzero, the data source takes ownership, freeing the medium when it has finished using it. When *bRelease* is 0, the caller retains ownership and the data source can use the storage medium only for the duration of the call.

Remarks

Called by the framework to set or replace the data in the **COleDataSource** object in the specified format. The data source does not take ownership of the data until it has successfully obtained it. That is, it does not take ownership if **OnSetData** returns 0. If the data source takes ownership, it frees the storage medium by calling the **ReleaseStgMedium** function.

The default implementation does nothing. Override this function to replace the data in the specified format. This is an advanced overridable.

For more information, see the **STGMEDIUM** and **FORMATETC** structures and the **ReleaseStgMedium** and **IDataObject::GetData** functions in the *OLE 2 Programmer's Reference, Volume 1*.

See Also   **COleDataSource::DelaySetData**, **COleDataSource::OnRenderData**, **COleDataSource::OnRenderFileData**, **COleDataSource::OnRenderGlobalData**, **COleServerItem::OnSetData**

COleDataSource::SetClipboard

void SetClipboard( );

Remarks

Puts the data contained in the **COleDataSource** object on the Clipboard after calling one of the following functions: **CacheData**, **CacheGlobalData**, **DelayRenderData**, or **DelayRenderFileData**.

See Also   **COleDataSource::GetClipboardOwner**, **COleDataSource::FlushClipboard**

COleDateTime

A **COleDateTime** object encapsulates the **DATE** data type used in OLE automation. It is one of the possible types for the **VARIANT** data type of OLE automation. A **COleDateTime** value represents an absolute date and time value.

The **DATE** type is implemented as a floating-point value, measuring days from midnight, 30 December 1899. So, midnight, 31 December 1899 is represented by 1.0. Similarly, 6 AM, 1 January 1900 is represented by 2.25, and midnight, 29 December 1899 is –1.0. However, 6 AM, 29 December 1899 is –1.25.

Note To interpret the time portion, take the absolute value of the fractional part of the number.

The **COleDateTime** class handles dates from 1 January 100–31 December 9999.

This type is also used to represent date-only or time-only values. By convention, the date 0 (30 December 1899) is used for time-only values. Similarly, the time 0:00 (midnight) is used for date-only values.

Basic arithmetic operations for the **COleDateTime** values use the companion class **COleDateTimeSpan**. **COleDateTimeSpan** values represent relative time, an interval. The relation between these classes is analogous to the one between **CTime** and **CTimeSpan**.

For more information on the **COleDateTime** and **COleDateTimeSpan** classes, see the article "Date and Time: OLE Automation Support" in *Programming in MFC*.

#include <afxdisp.h>

See Also **VARIANT**, **COleVariant**, **COleDateTimeSpan**, **CTime**

Construction

COleDateTime	Constructs a **COleDateTime** object.
GetCurrentTime	Creates a **COleDateTime** object that represents the current time (static member function).

Attributes

GetStatus	Gets the status (validity) of this **COleDateTime** object.
SetStatus	Sets the status (validity) of this **COleDateTime** object.
GetYear	Returns the year this **COleDateTime** object represents.
GetMonth	Returns the month this **COleDateTime** object represents (1–12).
GetDay	Returns the day this **COleDateTime** object represents (1–31).
GetHour	Returns the hour this **COleDateTime** object represents (0–23).

GetMinute	Returns the minute this **COleDateTime** object represents (0–59).
GetSecond	Returns the second this **COleDateTime** object represents (0–59).
GetDayOfWeek	Returns the day of the week this **COleDateTime** object represents (Sunday = 0).
GetDayOfYear	Returns the day of the year this **COleDateTime** object represents (Jan 1 = 1).

Operations

SetDateTime	Sets the value of this **COleDateTime** object to the specified date/time value.
SetDate	Sets the value of this **COleDateTime** object to the specified date-only value.
SetTime	Sets the value of this **COleDateTime** object to the specified time-only value.
Format	Generates a formatted string representation of a **COleDateTime** object.
ParseDateTime	Reads a date/time value from a string and sets the value of **COleDateTime**.

Operators

operator DATE	Converts a **COleDateTime** value into a **DATE**.
operator DATE*	Converts a **COleDateTime** value into a **DATE***.
operator =	Copies a **COleDateTime** value.
operator +, -	Add and subtract **COleDateTime** values.
operator +=, -=	Add and subtract a **COleDateTime** value from this **COleDateTime** object.
operator ==, <, <=, etc.	Compare two **COleDateTime** values.

Data Members

m_dt	Contains the underlying **DATE** for this **COleDateTime** object.
m_status	Contains the status of this **COleDateTime** object.

Archive/Dump

operator <<	Outputs a **COleDateTime** value to **CArchive** or **CDumpContext**.
operator >>	Inputs a **COleDateTime** object from **CArchive**.

Member Functions

COleDateTime::COleDateTime

COleDateTime( );
COleDateTime(const COleDateTime& *dateSrc* **);**
COleDateTime(const VARIANT& *varSrc* **);**
COleDateTime(DATE *dtSrc* **);**
COleDateTime(time_t *timeSrc* **);**
COleDateTime(const SYSTEMTIME& *systimeSrc* **);**
COleDateTime(const FILETIME& *filetimeSrc* **);**
COleDateTime(int *nYear*, **int** *nMonth*, **int** *nDay*, **int** *nHour*, **int** *nMin*, **int** *nSec* **);**
COleDateTime(WORD *wDosDate*, **WORD** *wDosTime* **);**

Parameters

dateSrc An existing **COleDateTime** object to be copied into the new **COleDateTime** object.

varSrc An existing **VARIANT** data structure (possibly a **COleVariant** object) to be converted to a date/time value (**VT_DATE**) and copied into the new **COleDateTime** object.

dtSrc A date/time (**DATE**) value to be copied into the new **COleDateTime** object.

timeSrc A **time_t** value to be converted to a date/time value and copied into the new **COleDateTime** object.

systimeSrc A **SYSTEMTIME** structure to be converted to a date/time value and copied into the new **COleDateTime** object.

filetimeSrc A **FILETIME** structure to be converted to a date/time value and copied into the new **COleDateTime** object.

nYear, nMonth, nDay, nHour, nMin, nSec Indicate the date and time values to be copied into the new **COleDateTime** object.

wDosDate, wDosTime MS-DOS date and time values to be converted to a date/time value and copied into the new **COleDateTime** object.

Remarks

All of these constructors create new **COleDateTime** objects initialized to the specified value. A brief description of each of these constructors follows:

- **COleDateTime( )** Constructs a **COleDateTime** object initialized to 0 (midnight, 30 December 1899).

- **COleDateTime(** *dateSrc* **)** Constructs a **COleDateTime** object from an existing **COleDateTime** object.

- **COleDateTime**(*varSrc*)   Constructs a **COleDateTime** object. Attempts to convert a **VARIANT** structure or **COleVariant** object to a date/time (**VT_DATE**) value. If this conversion is successful, the converted value is copied into the new **COleDateTime** object. If it is not, the value of the **COleDateTime** object is set to 0 (midnight, 30 December 1899) and its status to invalid.

- **COleDateTime**(*dtSrc*)   Constructs a **COleDateTime** object from a **DATE** value.

- **COleDateTime**(*timeSrc*)   Constructs a **COleDateTime** object from a **time_t** value.

- **COleDateTime**(*systimeSrc*)   Constructs a **COleDateTime** object from a **SYSTEMTIME** value.

- **COleDateTime**(*filetimeSrc*)   Constructs a **COleDateTime** object from a **FILETIME** value.

- **COleDateTime**(*nYear*, *nMonth*, *nDay*, *nHour*, *nMin*, *nSec*)   Constructs a **COleDateTime** object from the specified numerical values.

- **COleDateTime**(*wDosDate*, *wDosTime*)   Constructs a **COleDateTime** object from the specified MS-DOS date and time values.

For more information, see the **VARIANT** entry in Chapter 5 of the *OLE 2 Programmer's Reference, Volume 2*.

For more information on the **time_t** data type, see the **time** function in the *Run-Time Library Reference*.

For more information, see the **SYSTEMTIME** and **FILETIME** structures in the Win32 SDK documentation.

For more information on MS-DOS date and time values, see **DosDateTimeToVariantTime** in the Win32 SDK documentation.

For more information about the bounds for **COleDateTime** values, see the article "Date and Time: OLE Automation Support" in *Programming with MFC*.

See Also   **COleDateTime::SetDateTime**, **COleDateTime::operator =**, **COleDateTime::GetStatus**, **COleDateTime::m_dt**, **COleDateTime::m_status**

COleDateTime::Format

CString Format(DWORD *dwFlags* = 0, LCID *lcid* = LANG_USER_DEFAULT);
CString Format(LPCTSTR *lpszFormat*) **const**;
CString Format(UINT *nFormatID*) **const**;

Return Value

A **CString** that contains the formatted date/time value.

Parameters

dwFlags   Indicates flags for locale settings, possibly the following flag:

- **LOCALE_NOUSEROVERRIDE**   Use the system default locale settings, rather than custom user settings.

- **VAR_TIMEVALUEONLY**   Ignore the date portion during parsing.

- **VAR_DATEVALUEONLY**   Ignore the time portion during parsing.

lcid   Indicates locale ID to use for the conversion.

lpszFormat   The format-control string.

nFormatID   The resource ID for the format-control string.

Remarks

Call this member function to create a formatted representation of the date/time value. If the status of this **COleDateTime** object is null, the return value is an empty string. If the status is invalid, the return string is specified by the string resource **IDS_INVALID_DATETIME**.

A brief description of the three forms for this function follows:

Format(*dwFlags*, *lcid* **)**   This form formats the value using the national language specifications (locale IDs) for date/time. Using the default parameters, this form will print a time only if the date portion of the date/time value is date 0 (30 December 1899). Similarly, with the default parameters, this form will print a date only if the time portion of the date/time value is time 0 (midnight). If the date/time value is 0 (30 December 1899, midnight), this form with the default parameters will print midnight.

Format(*lpszFormat* **)**   This form formats the value using the format string which contains special formatting codes that are preceded by a percent sign (%), as in **printf**. The formatting string is passed as a parameter to the function. For more information about the formatting codes, see the entry **strftime, wcsftime** in the *Run-Time Library Reference*.

Format(*nFormatID* **)**   This form formats the value using the format string which contains special formatting codes that are preceded by a percent sign (%), as in **printf**. The formatting string is a resource. The ID of this string resource is passed as the parameter. For more information about the formatting codes, see the entry **strftime, wcsftime** in the *Run-Time Library Reference*.

For a listing of locale ID values, see the section "Supporting Multiple National Languages" in the *OLE 2 Programmer's Reference, Volume 2*.

See Also   **COleDateTime::ParseDateTime, COleDateTime::GetStatus**

COleDateTime::GetCurrentTime

static COleDateTime PASCAL GetCurrentTime( );

Remarks

Call this static member function to return the current date/time value.

Example

```
COleDateTime dateTest;
   // dateTest value = midnight 30 December 1899

dateTest = COleDateTime::GetCurrentTime();
   // dateTest value = current date and time
```

COleDateTime::GetDay

int GetDay( ) const;

Return Value

The day of the month represented by the value of this **COleDateTime** object.

Remarks

Call this member function to get the day of the month represented by this date/time value.

Valid return values range between 1 and 31. If the status of this **COleDateTime** object is not valid, the return value is **AFX_DATETIME_ERROR**.

For information on other member functions that query the value of this **COleDateTime** object, see the following member functions:

- **GetMonth**
- **GetYear**
- **GetHour**
- **GetMinute**
- **GetSecond**
- **GetDayOfWeek**
- **GetDayOfYear**

See Also   **COleDateTime::COleDateTime**, **COleDateTime::SetDateTime**, **COleDateTime::operator =**, **COleDateTime::GetStatus**

COleDateTime::GetDayOfWeek

int GetDayOfWeek( ) const;

Return Value

The day of the week represented by the value of this **COleDateTime** object.

Remarks

Call this member function to get the day of the month represented by this date/time value.

Valid return values range between 0 and 6, where Sunday = 0. If the status of this **COleDateTime** object is not valid, the return value is **AFX_DATETIME_ERROR**.

For information on other member functions that query the value of this **COleDateTime** object, see the following member functions:

- **GetDay**
- **GetMonth**
- **GetYear**
- **GetHour**
- **GetMinute**
- **GetSecond**
- **GetDayOfYear**

See Also   **COleDateTime::COleDateTime, COleDateTime::SetDateTime, COleDateTime::operator =, COleDateTime::GetStatus**

COleDateTime::GetDayOfYear

int GetDayOfYear( ) const;

Return Value

The day of the year represented by the value of this **COleDateTime** object.

Remarks

Call this member function to get the day of the year represented by this date/time value.

Valid return values range between 1 and 366, where January 1 = 1. If the status of this **COleDateTime** object is not valid, the return value is **AFX_DATETIME_ERROR**.

For information on other member functions that query the value of this **COleDateTime** object, see the following member functions:

- **GetDay**
- **GetMonth**
- **GetYear**
- **GetHour**
- **GetMinute**
- **GetSecond**
- **GetDayOfWeek**

See Also **COleDateTime::COleDateTime**, **COleDateTime::SetDateTime**, **COleDateTime::operator =**, **COleDateTime::GetStatus**

COleDateTime::GetHour

int GetHour( ) const;

Return Value

The hour represented by the value of this **COleDateTime** object.

Remarks

Call this member function to get the hour represented by this date/time value.

Valid return values range between 0 and 23. If the status of this **COleDateTime** object is not valid, the return value is **AFX_DATETIME_ERROR**.

For information on other member functions that query the value of this **COleDateTime** object, see the following member functions:

- **GetDay**
- **GetMonth**
- **GetYear**
- **GetMinute**
- **GetSecond**
- **GetDayOfWeek**
- **GetDayOfYear**

See Also **COleDateTime::COleDateTime**, **COleDateTime::SetDateTime**, **COleDateTime::operator =**, **COleDateTime::GetStatus**

COleDateTime::GetMinute

int GetMinute( ) const;

Return Value

The minute represented by the value of this **COleDateTime** object.

Remarks

Call this member function to get the minute represented by this date/time value.

Valid return values range between 0 and 59. If the status of this **COleDateTime** object is not valid, the return value is **AFX_DATETIME_ERROR**.

For information on other member functions that query the value of this **COleDateTime** object, see the following member functions:

- **GetDay**
- **GetMonth**
- **GetYear**
- **GetHour**
- **GetSecond**
- **GetDayOfWeek**
- **GetDayOfYear**

See Also   **COleDateTime::COleDateTime**, **COleDateTime::SetDateTime**, **COleDateTime::operator =**, **COleDateTime::GetStatus**

COleDateTime::GetMonth

int GetMonth( ) const;

Return Value

The month represented by the value of this **COleDateTime** object.

Remarks

Call this member function to get the month represented by this date/time value.

Valid return values range between 1 and 12. If the status of this **COleDateTime** object is not valid, the return value is **AFX_DATETIME_ERROR**.

For information on other member functions that query the value of this **COleDateTime** object, see the following member functions:

- **GetDay**
- **GetYear**
- **GetHour**

- **GetMinute**
- **GetSecond**
- **GetDayOfWeek**
- **GetDayOfYear**

See Also   **COleDateTime::COleDateTime**, **COleDateTime::SetDateTime**, **COleDateTime::operator =**, **COleDateTime::GetStatus**

COleDateTime::GetSecond

int GetSecond( ) const;

Return Value

The second represented by the value of this **COleDateTime** object.

Remarks

Call this member function to get the second represented by this date/time value.

Valid return values range between 0 and 59. If the status of this **COleDateTime** object is not valid, the return value is **AFX_DATETIME_ERROR**.

Note   The **COleDateTime** class does not support leap seconds.

For more information about the implementation for **COleDateTime**, see the article "Date and Time: OLE Automation Support" in *Programming with MFC*.

For information on other member functions that query the value of this **COleDateTime** object, see the following member functions:

- **GetDay**
- **GetMonth**
- **GetYear**
- **GetHour**
- **GetMinute**
- **GetDayOfWeek**
- **GetDayOfYear**

See Also   **COleDateTime::COleDateTime**, **COleDateTime::SetDateTime**, **COleDateTime::operator =**, **COleDateTime::GetStatus**

COleDateTime::GetStatus

DateTimeStatus GetStatus( ) const;

Return Value

Returns the status of this **COleDateTime** value.

Remarks

Call this member function to get the status (validity) of a given **COleDateTime** object.

The return value is defined by the **DateTimeStatus** enumerated type, which is defined within the **COleDateTime** class.

```
enum DateTimeStatus{
    valid = 0,
    invalid = 1,
    null = 2,
};
```

For a brief description of these status values, see the following list:

- **COleDateTime::valid**   Indicates that this **COleDateTime** object is valid.

- **COleDateTime::invalid**   Indicates that this **COleDateTime** object is invalid; that is, its value may be incorrect.

- **COleDateTime::null**   Indicates that this **COleDateTime** object is null, that is, that no value has been supplied for this object. (This is "null" in the database sense of "having no value," as opposed to the C++ **NULL**.)

The status of a **COleDateTime** object is invalid in the following cases:

- If its value is set from a **VARIANT** or **COleVariant** value that could not be converted to a date/time value.

- If its value is set from a **time_t**, **SYSTEMTIME**, or **FILETIME** value that could not be converted to a valid date/time value.

- If its value is set by **SetDateTime** with invalid parameter values.

- If this object has experienced an overflow or underflow during an arithmetic assignment operation, namely, **+=** or **-=**.

- If an invalid value was assigned to this object.

- If the status of this object was explicitly set to invalid using **SetStatus**.

For more information about the operations that may set the status to invalid, see the following member functions:

- **COleDateTime**

- **SetDateTime**

- **operator +, -**

- **operator +=, -=**

For more information about the bounds for **COleDateTime** values, see the article "Date and Time: OLE Automation Support" in *Programming with MFC*.

See Also   **COleDateTime::SetStatus, COleDateTime::m_status**

COleDateTime::GetYear

int GetYear( ) const;

Return Value

The year represented by the value of this **COleDateTime** object.

Remarks

Call this member function to get the year represented by this date/time value.

Valid return values range between 100 and 9999, which includes the century. If the status of this **COleDateTime** object is not valid, the return value is **AFX_DATETIME_ERROR**.

For information on other member functions that query the value of this **COleDateTime** object, see the following member functions:

- **GetDay**

- **GetMonth**

- **GetHour**

- **GetMinute**

- **GetSecond**

- **GetDayOfWeek**

- **GetDayOfYear**

For more information about the bounds for **COleDateTime** values, see the article "Date and Time: OLE Automation Support" in *Programming with MFC*.

See Also   **COleDateTime::COleDateTime, COleDateTime::SetDateTime, COleDateTime::operator =, COleDateTime::GetStatus**

COleDateTime::ParseDateTime

BOOL ParseDateTime(LPCTSTR *lpszDate***, DWORD** *dwFlags* **= 0,**
    LCID *lcid* **= LANG_USER_DEFAULT);**
    throw(CMemoryException);
    throw(COleException);

Return Value

Nonzero if the string was successfully converted to a date/time value, otherwise 0.

Parameters

lpszDate   A pointer to the null-terminated string which is to be parsed.

dwFlags   Indicates flags for locale settings and parsing. One or more of the following flags:

- **LOCALE_NOUSEROVERRIDE**   Use the system default locale settings, rather than custom user settings.

- **VAR_TIMEVALUEONLY**   Ignore the date portion during parsing.

- **VAR_DATEVALUEONLY**   Ignore the time portion during parsing.

lcid   Indicates locale ID to use for the conversion.

Remarks

Call this member function to parse a string to read a date/time value. If the string was successfully converted to a date/time value, the value of this **COleDateTime** object is set to that value and its status to valid.

Note   Year values less than 100 are interpreted as 20th-century values.

In the case of **VAR_DATEVALUEONLY**, the time value is set to time 0, midnight. In the case of **VAR_TIMEVALUEONLY**, the date value is set to date 0, 30 December 1899.

If the string could not be converted to a date/time value or if there was a numerical overflow, the status of this **COleDateTime** object is invalid.

If the string conversion failed due to memory allocation errors, this function throws a **CMemoryException**. In any other error state, this function throws a **COleException**.

For a listing of locale ID values, see the section "Supporting Multiple National Languages" in the *OLE 2 Programmer's Reference, Volume 2*.

For more information about the bounds and implementation for **COleDateTime** values, see the article "Date and Time: OLE Automation Support" in *Programming with MFC*.

See Also   **COleDateTime::Format**, **COleDateTime::GetStatus**

COleDateTime::SetDate

BOOL SetDate(int *nYear*, **int** *nMonth*, **int** *nDay* **)**;

Return Value

Nonzero if the value of this **COleDateTime** object was set, otherwise 0.

Parameters

nYear, nMonth, nDay   Indicate the date components to be copied into this
COleDateTime object.

Remarks

Call this member function to set the date and time of this **COleDateTime** object. The
date is set to the specified values. The time is set to time 0, midnight.

See the following table for bounds for the parameter values:

Parameter	Bounds
nYear	0–999
nMonth	1–12
nDay	1–31

Note   Year values less than 100 are interpreted as 20th-century values.

The actual upper bound for *nDay* values varies based on the month and year. For
months 1, 3, 5, 7, 8, 10, and 12, the upper bound is 31. For months 4, 6, 9, and 11, it
is 30. For month 2, it is 28, or 29 in a leap year.

If the date value specified by the parameters is not valid, the status of this object is set
to invalid and the value of this object is not changed.

Here are some examples of date values:

nYear	nMonth	nDay	Value
95	4	15	15 April 1995
1976	8	15	15 August 1976
1789	7	14	17 July 1789
25	2	30	Invalid
10000	1	1	Invalid

To set both date and time, see **COleDateTime::SetDateTime**.

For information on member functions that query the value of this **COleDateTime**
object, see the following member functions:

- **GetDay**
- **GetMonth**
- **GetYear**
- **GetHour**

- **GetMinute**
- **GetSecond**
- **GetDayOfWeek**
- **GetDayOfYear**

For more information about the bounds for **COleDateTime** values, see the article "Date and Time: OLE Automation Support" in *Programming with MFC*.

See Also   **COleDateTime::COleDateTime**, **COleDateTime::SetDateTime**, **COleDateTime::operator =**, **COleDateTime::GetStatus**, **COleDateTime::m_dt**

COleDateTime::SetDateTime

BOOL SetDateTime(int *nYear*, **int** *nMonth*, **int** *nDay*, **int** *nHour*, **int** *nMin*, **int** *nSec* **);**

Return Value

Nonzero if the value of this **COleDateTime** object was set, otherwise 0.

Parameters

nYear, nMonth, nDay, nHour, nMin, nSec   Indicate the date and time components to be copied into this **COleDateTime** object.

Remarks

Call this member function to set the date and time of this **COleDateTime** object.

See the following table for bounds for the parameter values:

Parameter	Bounds
nYear	0–9999
nMonth	1–12
nDay	1–31
nHour	0–23
nMin	0–59
nSec	0–59

Note   Year values less than 100 are interpreted as 20th-century values.

The actual upper bound for *nDay* values varies based on the month and year. For months 1, 3, 5, 7, 8, 10, and 12, the upper bound is 31. For months 4, 6, 9, and 11, it is 30. For month 2, it is 28, or 29 in a leap year.

If the date or time value specified by the parameters is not valid, the status of this object is set to invalid and the value of this object is not changed.

Here are some examples of time values:

nHour	nMin	nSec	Value
1	3	3	01:03:03
23	45	0	23:45:00
25	30	0	Invalid
9	60	0	Invalid

Here are some examples of date values:

nYear	nMonth	nDay	Value
95	4	15	15 April 1995
1976	8	15	15 August 1976
1789	7	14	17 July 1789
25	2	30	Invalid
10000	1	1	Invalid

To set the date only, see **COleDateTime::SetDate**. To set the time only, see **COleDateTime::SetTime**.

For information on member functions that query the value of this **COleDateTime** object, see the following member functions:

- **GetDay**
- **GetMonth**
- **GetYear**
- **GetHour**
- **GetMinute**
- **GetSecond**
- **GetDayOfWeek**
- **GetDayOfYear**

For more information about the bounds for **COleDateTime** values, see the article "Date and Time: OLE Automation Support" in *Programming with MFC*.

See Also   **COleDateTime::COleDateTime, COleDateTime::SetDate, COleDateTime::SetTime, COleDateTime::operator =, COleDateTime::GetStatus, COleDateTime::m_dt**

COleDateTime::SetStatus

void SetStatus(DateTimeStatus *nStatus* **);**

Parameters

nStatus   The new status value for this **COleDateTime** object.

Remarks

Call this member function to set the status of this **COleDateTime** object. The *nStatus* parameter value is defined by the **DateTimeStatus** enumerated type, which is defined within the **COleDateTime** class.

```
enum DateTimeStatus{
    valid = 0,
    invalid = 1,
    null = 2,
};
```

For a brief description of these status values, see the following list:

- **COleDateTime::valid**   Indicates that this **COleDateTime** object is valid.

- **COleDateTime::invalid**   Indicates that this **COleDateTime** object is invalid; that is, its value may be incorrect.

- **COleDateTime::null**   Indicates that this **COleDateTime** object is null, that is, that no value has been supplied for this object. (This is "null" in the database sense of "having no value," as opposed to the C++ **NULL**.)

Caution   This function is for advanced programming situations. This function does not alter the data in this object. It will most often be used to set the status to **null** or **invalid**. Note that the assignment operator (**operator =**) and **SetDateTime** do set the status of the object based on the source value(s).

See Also   **COleDateTime::GetStatus, COleDateTime::operator =, COleDateTime::SetDateTime, COleDateTime::m_dt**

COleDateTime::SetTime

BOOL SetTime(int *nHour*, **int** *nMin*, **int** *nSec* **);**

Return Value

Nonzero if the value of this **COleDateTime** object was set, otherwise 0.

Parameters

nHour, nMin, nSec   Indicate the time components to be copied into this **COleDateTime** object.

Remarks

Call this member function to set the date and time of this **COleDateTime** object. The time is set to the specified values. The date is set to date 0, 30 December 1899.

See the following table for bounds for the parameter values:

Parameter	Bounds
nHour	0–23
nMin	0–59
nSec	0–59

If the time value specified by the parameters is not valid, the status of this object is set to invalid and the value of this object is not changed.

Here are some examples of time values:

nHour	*nMin*	*nSec*	Value
1	3	3	01:03:03
23	45	0	23:45:00
25	30	0	Invalid
9	60	0	Invalid

To set both date and time, see **COleDateTime::SetDateTime**.

For information on member functions that query the value of this **COleDateTime** object, see the following member functions:

- **GetDay**
- **GetMonth**
- **GetYear**
- **GetHour**
- **GetMinute**
- **GetSecond**
- **GetDayOfWeek**
- **GetDayOfYear**

For more information about the bounds for **COleDateTime** values, see the article "Date and Time: OLE Automation Support" in *Programming with MFC*.

See Also   **COleDateTime::COleDateTime, COleDateTime::SetDateTime, COleDateTime::operator =, COleDateTime::GetStatus, COleDateTime::m_dt**

Operators

COleDateTime::operator =

const COleDateTime& operator =(const COleDateTime& *dateSrc* **);**
const COleDateTime& operator =(const VARIANT& *varSrc* **);**
const COleDateTime& operator =(DATE *dtSrc* **);**
const COleDateTime& operator =(const time_t& *timeSrc* **);**
const COleDateTime& operator =(const SYSTEMTIME& *systimeSrc* **);**
const COleDateTime& operator =(const FILETIME& *filetimeSrc* **);**

Remarks

These overloaded assignment operators copy the source date/time value into this **COleDateTime** object. A brief description of each these overloaded assignment operators follows:

- **operator =(** *dateSrc* **)**   The value and status of the operand are copied into this **COleDateTime** object.

- **operator =(** *varSrc* **)**   If the conversion of the **VARIANT** value (or **COleVariant** object) to a date/time (**VT_DATE**) is successful, the converted value is copied into this **COleDateTime** object and its status is set to valid. If the conversion is not successful, the value of this object is set to zero (30 December 1899, midnight) and its status to invalid.

- **operator =(** *dtSrc* **)**   The **DATE** value is copied into this **COleDateTime** object and its status is set to valid.

- **operator =(** *timeSrc* **)**   The **time_t** value is converted and copied into this **COleDateTime** object. If the conversion is successful, the status of this object is set to valid; if unsuccessful, it is set to invalid.

- **operator =(** *systimeSrc* **)**   The **SYSTEMTIME** value is converted and copied into this **COleDateTime** object. If the conversion is successful, the status of this object is set to valid; if unsuccessful, it is set to invalid.

- **operator =(** *filetimeSrc* **)**   The **FILETIME** value is converted and copied into this **COleDateTime** object. If the conversion is successful, the status of this object is set to valid; if unsuccessful, it is set to invalid.

For more information, see the **VARIANT** entry in Chapter 5 of the *OLE 2 Programmer's Reference, Volume 2.*

For more information on the **time_t** data type, see the **time** function in the *Run-Time Library Reference.*

For more information, see the **SYSTEMTIME** and **FILETIME** structures in the Win32 SDK documentation.

For more information about the bounds for **COleDateTime** values, see the article "Date and Time: OLE Automation Support" in *Programming with MFC*.

See Also   **COleDateTime::COleDateTime, COleDateTime::SetDateTime, COleDateTime::GetStatus**

COleDateTime::operator +, -

COleDateTime operator +(const COleDateTimeSpan& *dateSpan* **) const;**
COleDateTime operator -(const COleDateTimeSpan& *dateSpan* **) const;**
COleDateTimeSpan operator -(const COleDateTime& *date* **) const;**

Remarks

COleDateTime objects represent absolute times. **COleDateTimeSpan** objects represent relative times. The first two operators allow you to add and subtract a **COleDateTimeSpan** value from a **COleDateTime** value. The third operator allows you to subtract one **COleDateTime** value from another to yield a **COleDateTimeSpan** value.

If either of the operands is null, the status of the resulting **COleDateTime** value is null.

If the resulting **COleDateTime** value falls outside the bounds of acceptable values, the status of that **COleDateTime** value is invalid.

If either of the operands is invalid and the other is not null, the status of the resulting **COleDateTime** value is invalid.

For more information on the valid, invalid, and null status values, see the **m_status** member variable.

For more information about the bounds for **COleDateTime** values, see the article "Date and Time: OLE Automation Support" in *Programming with MFC*.

See Also   **COleDateTime::operator +=, -=, COleDateTime::GetStatus, COleDateTimeSpan**

COleDateTime::operator +=, -=

const COleDateTime& operator +=(const COleDateTimeSpan *dateSpan* **);**
const COleDateTime& operator -=(const COleDateTimeSpan *dateSpan* **);**

Remarks

These operators allow you to add and subtract a **COleDateTimeSpan** value to and from this **COleDateTime**.

If either of the operands is null, the status of the resulting **COleDateTime** value is null.

If the resulting **COleDateTime** value falls outside the bounds of acceptable values, the status of this **COleDateTime** value is set to invalid.

If either of the operands is invalid and other is not null, the status of the resulting **COleDateTime** value is invalid.

For more information on the valid, invalid, and null status values, see the **m_status** member variable.

For more information about the bounds for **COleDateTime** values, see the article "Date and Time: OLE Automation Support" in *Programming with MFC*.

See Also   **COleDateTime::operator +, -**, **COleDateTime::GetStatus**

COleDateTime::operator DATE

operator DATE( ) const;

Remarks

This operator returns a **DATE** object whose value is copied from this **COleDateTime** object.

For more information about the implementation of the **DATE** object, see the article "Date and Time: OLE Automation Support" in *Programming with MFC*.

See Also   **COleDateTime::m_dt**

COleDateTime Relational Operators

BOOL operator ==(const COleDateTime& *date* **) const;**
BOOL operator !=(const COleDateTime& *date* **) const;**
BOOL operator <(const COleDateTime& *date* **) const;**
BOOL operator >(const COleDateTime& *date* **) const;**
BOOL operator <=(const COleDateTime& *date* **) const;**
BOOL operator >=(const COleDateTime& *date* **) const;**

Remarks

These operators compare two date/time values and return nonzero if the condition is true; otherwise 0.

Note   The return value of the ordering operations (<, <=, >, >=) is undefined if the status of either operand is null or invalid. The equality operators (==, !=) consider the status of the operands.

Example

```
COleDateTime dateOne(95, 3, 15, 12, 0, 0); // 15 March 1995 12 noon
COleDateTime dateTwo(dateOne);              // 15 March 1995 12 noon
BOOL b;
b = dateOne == dateTwo;                     // TRUE

dateTwo.SetStatus(COleDateTime::invalid);
b = dateOne == dateTwo;                     // FALSE, different status
b = dateOne != dateTwo;                     // TRUE, different status
b = dateOne < dateTwo;                      // FALSE, same value
b = dateOne > dateTwo;                      // FALSE, same value
b = dateOne <= dateTwo;                     // TRUE, same value
b = dateOne >= dateTwo;                     // TRUE, same value
```

Note The last four lines of the preceding example will **ASSERT** in debug mode.

See Also   **COleDateTime::GetStatus**

COleDateTime::operator <<, >>

friend CDumpContext& AFXAPI operator <<(CDumpContext& *dc*, **COleDateTime** *timeSrc* **);**
friend CArchive& AFXAPI operator <<(CArchive& *ar*, **COleDateTime** *dateSrc* **);**
friend CArchive& AFXAPI operator >>(CArchive& *ar*, **COleDateTime&** *dateSrc* **);**

Remarks

The **COleDateTime** insertion (<<) operator supports diagnostic dumping and storing to an archive. The extraction (>>) operator supports loading from an archive.

See Also   **CDumpContext, CArchive**

Data Members

COleDateTime::m_dt

Remarks

The underlying **DATE** structure for this **COleDateTime** object.

Caution Changing the value in the **DATE** object accessed by the pointer returned by this function will change the value of this **COleDateTime** object. It does not change the status of this **COleDateTime** object.

For more information about the implementation of the **DATE** object, see the article "Date and Time: OLE Automation Support" in *Programming with MFC*.

See Also   **COleDateTime::COleDateTime, COleDateTime::SetDateTime, COleDateTime::SetDate, COleDateTime::SetTime, COleDateTime::operator, DATE**

COleDateTime::m_status

Remarks

The type of this data member is the enumerated type **DateTimeStatus**, which is defined within the **COleDateTime** class.

```
enum DateTimeStatus{
    valid = 0,
    invalid = 1,
    null = 2,
};
```

For a brief description of these status values, see the following list:

- **COleDateTime::valid**   Indicates that this **COleDateTime** object is valid.

- **COleDateTime::invalid**   Indicates that this **COleDateTime** object is invalid; that is, its value may be incorrect.

- **COleDateTime::null**   Indicates that this **COleDateTime** object is null, that is, that no value has been supplied for this object. (This is "null" in the database sense of "having no value," as opposed to the C++ **NULL**.)

The status of a **COleDateTime** object is invalid in the following cases:

- If its value is set from a **VARIANT** or **COleVariant** value that could not be converted to a date/time value.

- If its value is set from a **time_t**, **SYSTEMTIME**, or **FILETIME** value that could not be converted to a valid date/time value.

- If its value is set by **SetDateTime** with invalid parameter values.

- If this object has experienced an overflow or underflow during an arithmetic assignment operation, namely, **+=** or **-=**.

- If an invalid value was assigned to this object.

- If the status of this object was explicitly set to invalid using **SetStatus**.

For more information about the operations that may set the status to invalid, see the following member functions:

- **COleDateTime**
- **SetDateTime**
- **operator +, -**
- **operator +=, -=**

Caution This data member is for advanced programming situations. You should use the inline member functions **GetStatus** and **SetStatus**. See **SetStatus** for further cautions regarding explicitly setting this data member.

For more information about the bounds for **COleDateTime** values, see the article "Date and Time: OLE Automation Support" in *Programming with MFC*.

See Also **COleDateTime::GetStatus**, **COleDateTime::SetStatus**

COleDateTimeSpan

A **COleDateTimeSpan** object represents a relative time, a time span. A **COleDateTimeSpan** keeps time in days.

COleDateTimeSpan is used with its companion class **COleDateTime**. **COleDateTime** encapsulates the **DATE** data type of OLE automation. **COleDateTime** represents absolute time values. All **COleDateTime** calculations involve **COleDateTimeSpan** values. The relation between these classes is analogous to the one between **CTime** and **CTimeSpan**.

For more information on the **COleDateTime** and **COleDateTimeSpan** classes, see the article "Date and Time: OLE Automation Support" in *Programming with MFC*.

#include <afxdisp.h>

See Also   **CTimeSpan**, **COleDateTime**

Constructor

COleDateTimeSpan	Constructs a **COleDateTimeSpan** object.

Attributes

GetStatus	Gets the status (validity) of this **COleDateTimeSpan** object.
SetStatus	Sets the status (validity) of this **COleDateTimeSpan** object.
GetDays	Returns the day portion of the span this **COleDateTimeSpan** object represents.
GetHours	Returns the hour portion of the span this **COleDateTimeSpan** object represents.
GetMinutes	Returns the minute portion of the span this **COleDateTimeSpan** object represents.
GetSeconds	Returns the second portion of the span this **COleDateTimeSpan** object represents.
GetTotalDays	Returns the number of days this **COleDateTimeSpan** object represents.
GetTotalHours	Returns the number of hours this **COleDateTimeSpan** object represents.
GetTotalMinutes	Returns the number of minutes this **COleDateTimeSpan** object represents.
GetTotalSeconds	Returns the number of seconds this **COleDateTimeSpan** object represents.

Operations

SetDateTimeSpan	Sets the value of this **COleDateTimeSpan** object.
Format	Generates a formatted string representation of a **COleDateTimeSpan** object.

Operators

operator double	Converts this **COleDateTimeSpan** value to a **double**.
operator =	Copies a **COleDateTimeSpan** value.
operator +, -	Add, subtract, and change sign for **COleDateTimeSpan** values.
operator +=, -=	Add and subtract a **COleDateTimeSpan** value from this **COleDateTimeSpan** value.
operator ==, <, <=	Compare two **COleDateTimeSpan** values.

Data Members

m_span	Contains the underlying **double** for this **COleDateTimeSpan** object.
m_status	Contains the status of this **COleDateTimeSpan** object.

Dump/Archive

operator <<	Outputs a **COleDateTimeSpan** value to **CArchive** or **CDumpContext**.
operator >>	Inputs a **COleDateTimeSpan** object from **CArchive**.

Member Functions

COleDateTimeSpan::COleDateTimeSpan

COleDateTimeSpan( );
COleDateTimeSpan(const COleDateTimeSpan& *dateSpanSrc* **);**
COleDateTimeSpan(double *dblSpanSrc* **);**
COleDateTimeSpan(long *lDays***, int** *nHours***, int** *nMins***, int** *nSecs* **);**

Parameters

dateSpanSrc   An existing **COleDateTimeSpan** object to be copied into the new **COleDateTimeSpan** object.

dblSpanSrc   The number of days to be copied into the new **COleDateTimeSpan** object.

lDays, nHours, nMins, nSecs   Indicate the day and time values to be copied into the new **COleDateTimeSpan** object.

Remarks

All of these constructors create new **COleDateTimeSpan** objects initialized to the specified value. A brief description of each of these constructors follows:

- **COleDateTimeSpan( )** Constructs a **COleDateTimeSpan** object initialized to 0.

- **COleDateTimeSpan(** *dateSpanSrc* **)** Constructs a **COleDateTimeSpan** object from an existing **COleDateTimeSpan** object.

- **COleDateTimeSpan(** *dblSpanSrc* **)** Constructs a **COleDateTimeSpan** object from a floating-point value.

- **COleDateTimeSpan(** *lDays***,** *nHours***,** *nMins***,** *nSecs* **)** Constructs a **COleDateTimeSpan** object initialized to the specified numerical values.

The status of the new **COleDateTimeSpan** object is set to valid.

For more information about the bounds for **COleDateTimeSpan** values, see the article "Date and Time: OLE Automation Support" in *Programming with MFC*.

Example

```
COleDateTimeSpan spanOne( 2.75 );          // 2 days and 18 hours
COleDateTimeSpan spanTwo( 2, 18, 0, 0 );   // 2 days and 18 hours
COleDateTimeSpan spanThree( 3, -6, 0, 0 ); // 2 days and 18 hours
```

See Also   **COleDateTimeSpan::operator =, COleDateTimeSpan::GetStatus, COleDateTimeSpan::m_span, COleDateTimeSpan::m_status**

COleDateTimeSpan::Format

CString Format(LPCTSTR *pFormat* **) const;**
CString Format(UINT *nID* **) const;**

Return Value

A **CString** that contains the formatted date/time-span value.

Parameters

pFormat   The format-control string.

nID   The resource ID for the format-control string.

Remarks

Call these functions to create a formatted representation of the time-span value. If the status of this **COleDateTimeSpan** object is null, the return value is an empty string. If the status is invalid, the return string is specified by the string resource **IDS_INVALID_DATETIMESPAN**.

A brief description of the forms for this function follows:

Format(*pFormat* **)**   This form formats the value using the format string which contains special formatting codes that are preceded by a percent sign (%), as in **printf**. The formatting string is passed as a parameter to the function.

Format(*nID* **)** This form formats the value using the format string which contains special formatting codes that are preceded by a percent sign (%), as in **printf**. The formatting string is a resource. The ID of this string resource is passed as the parameter.

For more information about the formatting codes used in this function, see the entry **strftime, wcsftime** in the *Run-Time Library Reference*. For a listing of locale ID values, see the section "Supporting Multiple National Languages" in the *OLE 2 Programmer's Reference, Volume 2*.

See Also   **COleDateTimeSpan::GetStatus**

COleDateTimeSpan::GetDays

long GetDays( ) const;

Return Value

The day portion of this date/time-span value.

Remarks

Call this member function to retrieve the day portion of this date/time-span value.

The return values from this function range between approximately −3,615,000 and 3,615,000.

For other functions that query the value of a **COleDateTimeSpan** object, see the following member functions:

- **GetHours**
- **GetMinutes**
- **GetSeconds**
- **GetTotalDays**
- **GetTotalHours**
- **GetTotalMinutes**
- **GetTotalSeconds**

See Also   **COleDateTimeSpan::SetDateTimeSpan**

COleDateTimeSpan::GetHours

long GetHours( ) const;

Return Value

The hours portion of this date/time-span value.

Remarks

Call this member function to retrieve the hour portion of this date/time-span value.

The return values from this function range between −23 and 23.

For other functions that query the value of a **COleDateTimeSpan** object, see the following member functions:

- **GetDays**
- **GetMinutes**
- **GetSeconds**
- **GetTotalDays**
- **GetTotalHours**
- **GetTotalMinutes**
- **GetTotalSeconds**

See Also **COleDateTimeSpan::SetDateTimeSpan**

COleDateTimeSpan::GetMinutes

long GetMinutes( ) const;

Return Value

The minutes portion of this date/time-span value.

Remarks

Call this member function to retrieve the minute portion of this date/time-span value.

The return values from this function range between −59 and 59.

For other functions that query the value of a **COleDateTimeSpan** object, see the following member functions:

- **GetDays**
- **GetHours**
- **GetSeconds**
- **GetTotalDays**
- **GetTotalHours**
- **GetTotalMinutes**
- **GetTotalSeconds**

See Also **COleDateTimeSpan::SetDateTimeSpan**

COleDateTimeSpan::GetSeconds

long GetSeconds( ) const;

Return Value

The seconds portion of this date/time-span value.

Remarks

Call this member function to retrieve the second portion of this date/time-span value.

The return values from this function range between −59 and 59.

For other functions that query the value of a **COleDateTimeSpan** object, see the following member functions:

- **GetDays**
- **GetHours**
- **GetMinutes**
- **GetTotalDays**
- **GetTotalHours**
- **GetTotalMinutes**
- **GetTotalSeconds**

See Also   COleDateTimeSpan::SetDateTimeSpan

COleDateTimeSpan::GetStatus

DateTimeSpanStatus GetStatus( ) const;

Return Value

The status of this **COleDateTimeSpan** value.

Remarks

Call this member function to get the status (validity) of this **COleDateTimeSpan** object.

The return value is defined by the **DateTimeSpanStatus** enumerated type, which is defined within the **COleDateTimeSpan** class.

```
enum DateTimeSpanStatus{
    valid = 0,
    invalid = 1,
    null = 2,
};
```

For a brief description of these status values, see the following list:

- **COleDateTimeSpan::valid**   Indicates that this **COleDateTimeSpan** object is valid.

- **COleDateTimeSpan::invalid** Indicates that this **COleDateTimeSpan** object is invalid; that is, its value may be incorrect.

- **COleDateTimeSpan::null** Indicates that this **COleDateTimeSpan** object is null, that is, that no value has been supplied for this object. (This is "null" in the database sense of "having no value," as opposed to the C++ **NULL**.)

The status of a **COleDateTimeSpan** object is invalid in the following cases:

- If this object has experienced an overflow or underflow during an arithmetic assignment operation, namely, **+=** or **-=**.

- If an invalid value was assigned to this object.

- If the status of this object was explicitly set to invalid using **SetStatus**.

For more information about the operations that may set the status to invalid, see **COleDateTimeSpan::operator +, -** and **COleDateTimeSpan::operator +=, -=**.

For more information about the bounds for **COleDateTimeSpan** values, see the article "Date and Time: OLE Automation Support" in *Programming with MFC*.

See Also COleDateTimeSpan::SetStatus, COleDateTimeSpan::m_status

COleDateTimeSpan::GetTotalDays

double GetTotalDays( ) const;

Return Value

This date/time-span value expressed in days.

Remarks

Call this member function to retrieve this date/time-span value expressed in days.

The return values from this function range between approximately $-3.65e6$ and $3.65e6$.

For other functions that query the value of a **COleDateTimeSpan** object, see the following member functions:

- **GetDays**
- **GetHours**
- **GetMinutes**
- **GetSeconds**
- **GetTotalHours**, **GetTotalMinutes**
- **GetTotalSeconds**

See Also COleDateTimeSpan::SetDateTimeSpan, COleDateTimeSpan::operator double

COleDateTimeSpan::GetTotalHours

double GetTotalHours( ) const;

Return Value

This date/time-span value expressed in hours.

Remarks

Call this member function to retrieve this date/time-span value expressed in hours.

The return values from this function range between approximately −8.77e7 and 8.77e7.

For other functions that query the value of a **COleDateTimeSpan** object, see the following member functions:

- **GetDays**
- **GetHours**
- **GetMinutes**
- **GetSeconds**
- **GetTotalDays**
- **GetTotalMinutes**
- **GetTotalSeconds**

See Also   **COleDateTimeSpan::SetDateTimeSpan**

COleDateTimeSpan::GetTotalMinutes

double GetTotalMinutes( ) const;

Return Value

This date/time-span value expressed in minutes.

Remarks

Call this member function to retrieve this date/time-span value expressed in minutes.

The return values from this function range between approximately −5.26e9 and 5.26e9.

For other functions that query the value of a **COleDateTimeSpan** object, see the following member functions:

- **GetDays**
- **GetHours**
- **GetMinutes**
- **GetSeconds**

- **GetTotalDays**
- **GetTotalHours**
- **GetTotalSeconds**

See Also   **COleDateTimeSpan::SetDateTimeSpan**

COleDateTimeSpan::GetTotalSeconds

double GetTotalSeconds( ) const;

Return Value

This date/time-span value expressed in seconds.

Remarks

Call this member function to retrieve this date/time-span value expressed in seconds.

The return values from this function range between approximately $-3.16\mathrm{e}11$ to $3.16\mathrm{e}11$.

For other functions that query the value of a **COleDateTimeSpan** object, see the following member functions:

- **GetDays**
- **GetHours**
- **GetMinutes**
- **GetSeconds**
- **GetTotalDays**
- **GetTotalHours**
- **GetTotalMinutes**

See Also   **COleDateTimeSpan::SetDateTimeSpan**

COleDateTimeSpan::SetDateTimeSpan

void SetDateTimeSpan(long *lDays*, int *nHours*, int *nMins*, int *nSecs*);

Parameters

lDays, *nHours*, *nMins*, *nSecs*   Indicate the date-span and time-span values to be copied into this **COleDateTimeSpan** object.

Remarks

Call this member function to set the value of this date/time-span value.

For functions that query the value of a **COleDateTimeSpan** object, see the following member functions:

- **GetDays**
- **GetHours**
- **GetMinutes**
- **GetSeconds**
- **GetTotalDays**
- **GetTotalHours**
- **GetTotalMinutes**
- **GetTotalSeconds**

Example

```
COleDateTimeSpan spanOne;
COleDateTimeSpan spanTwo;
spanOne.SetDateTimeSpan(0, 2, 45, 0);  // 2 hours and 45 seconds
spanTwo.SetDateTimeSpan(0, 3, -15, 0); // 2 hours and 45 seconds
```

See Also   **COleDateTimeSpan::GetStatus**, **COleDateTimeSpan::m_span**

COleDateTimeSpan::SetStatus

void SetStatus(DateTimeSpanStatus *nStatus* **);**

Parameters

nStatus   The new status value for this **COleDateTimeSpan** object.

Remarks

Call this member function to set the status (validity) of this **COleDateTimeSpan** object. The *nStatus* parameter value is defined by the **DateTimeSpanStatus** enumerated type, which is defined within the **COleDateTimeSpan** class.

```
enum DateTimeSpanStatus{
    valid = 0,
    invalid = 1,
    null = 2,
};
```

For a brief description of these status values, see the following list:

- **COleDateTimeSpan::valid**   Indicates that this **COleDateTimeSpan** object is valid.
- **COleDateTimeSpan::invalid**   Indicates that this **COleDateTimeSpan** object is invalid; that is, its value may be incorrect.

- **COleDateTimeSpan::null**   Indicates that this **COleDateTimeSpan** object is null, that is, that no value has been supplied for this object. (This is "null" in the database sense of "having no value," as opposed to the C++ **NULL**.)

Caution   This function is for advanced programming situations. This function does not alter the data in this object. It will most often be used to set the status to **null** or **invalid**. Note that the assignment operator (**operator =**) and **SetDateTimeSpan** do set the status of the object based on the source value(s).

See Also   COleDateTimeSpan::GetStatus, COleDateTimeSpan::m_status

Operators

COleDateTimeSpan::operator =

const **COleDateTimeSpan& operator=(double** *dblSpanSrc* **);**
const **COleDateTimeSpan& operator=(const COleDateTimeSpan&** *dateSpanSrc* **);**

Remarks

These overloaded assignment operators copy the source date/time-span value into this **COleDateTimeSpan** object.

See Also   COleDateTimeSpan::COleDateTimeSpan

COleDateTimeSpan::operator +, -

COleDateTimeSpan operator+(const COleDateTimeSpan& *dateSpan* **) const;**
COleDateTimeSpan operator-(const COleDateTimeSpan& *dateSpan* **) const;**
COleDateTimeSpan operator-( ) const;

Remarks

The first two operators let you add and subtract date/time-span values. The third lets you change the sign of a date/time-span value.

If either of the operands is null, the status of the resulting **COleDateTimeSpan** value is null.

If either of the operands is invalid and the other is not null, the status of the resulting **COleDateTimeSpan** value is invalid.

For more information on the valid, invalid, and null status values, see the **m_status** member variable.

See Also   COleDateTimeSpan::operator +=, -=

COleDateTimeSpan::operator +=, -=

const COleDateTimeSpan& operator+=(const COleDateTimeSpan *dateSpan* **);**
const COleDateTimeSpan& operator-=(const COleDateTimeSpan *dateSpan* **);**

Remarks

These operators let you add and subtract date/time-span values from this
COleDateTimeSpan object.

If either of the operands is null, the status of the resulting **COleDateTimeSpan** value
is null.

If either of the operands is invalid and the other is not null, the status of the resulting
COleDateTimeSpan value is invalid.

For more information on the valid, invalid, and null status values, see the **m_status**
member variable.

See Also   **COleDateTimeSpan::operator +, -**

COleDateTimeSpan::operator double

operator double( ) const;

Remarks

This operator returns the value of this **COleDateTimeSpan** value as a floating-point
number of days.

See Also   **COleDateTimeSpan::GetTotalDays**,
COleDateTimeSpan::SetDateTimeSpan, COleDateTimeSpan::m_span

COleDateTimeSpan Relational Operators

BOOL operator==(const COleDateTimeSpan& *dateSpan* **) const;**
BOOL operator!=(const COleDateTimeSpan& *dateSpan* **) const;**
BOOL operator<(const COleDateTimeSpan& *dateSpan* **) const;**
BOOL operator>(const COleDateTimeSpan& *dateSpan* **) const;**
BOOL operator<=(const COleDateTimeSpan& *dateSpan* **) const;**
BOOL operator>=(const COleDateTimeSpan& *dateSpan* **) const;**

Remarks

These operators compare two date/time-span values and return nonzero if the
condition is true; otherwise 0.

Note   The return value of the ordering operations (<, <=, >, >=) is undefined if the status of
either operand is null or invalid. The equality operators (==, !=) consider the status of the
operands.

Example

```
COleDateTimeSpan spanOne(3, 12, 0, 0); // 3 days and 12 hours
COleDateTimeSpan spanTwo(spanOne);      // 3 days and 12 hours
BOOL b;
b = spanOne == spanTwo;                        // TRUE

spanTwo.SetStatus(COleDateTimeSpan::invalid);
b = spanOne == spanTwo;                 // FALSE, different status
b = spanOne != spanTwo;                 // TRUE, different status
b = spanOne < spanTwo;                  // FALSE, same value
b = spanOne > spanTwo;                  // FALSE, same value
b = spanOne <= spanTwo;                 // TRUE, same value
b = spanOne >= spanTwo;                 // TRUE, same value
```

Note The last four lines of the preceding example will **ASSERT** in debug mode.

COleDateTimeSpan::operator <<, >>

friend CDumpContext& AFXAPI operator<<(CDumpContext& *dc*,
   COleDateTimeSpan *dateSpan* **);**
friend CArchive& AFXAPI operator<<(CArchive& *ar*, **COleDateTimeSpan** *dateSpan* **);**
friend CArchive& AFXAPI operator>>(CArchive& *ar*, **COleDateTimeSpan&** *dateSpan* **);**

Remarks

The **COleDateTimeSpan** insertion (<<) operator supports diagnostic dumping and storing to an archive. The extraction (>>) operator supports loading from an archive.

See Also **CDumpContext**, **CArchive**

Data Members

COleDateTimeSpan::m_span

Remarks

The underlying **double** value for this **COleDateTime** object. This value expresses the date/time span in days.

Caution Changing the value in the **double** data member will change the value of this **COleDateTimeSpan** object. It does not change the status of this **COleDateTimeSpan** object.

See Also **COleDateTimeSpan::COleDateTimeSpan**,
COleDateTimeSpan::SetDateTimeSpan, **COleDateTimeSpan::operator double**

COleDateTimeSpan::m_status

Remarks

The type for this data member is the enumerated type **DateTimeSpanStatus**, which is defined within the **COleDateTimeSpan** class.

```
enum DateTimeSpanStatus{
    valid = 0,
    invalid = 1,
    null = 2,
};
```

For a brief description of these status values, see the following list:

- **COleDateTimeSpan::valid** Indicates that this **COleDateTimeSpan** object is valid.

- **COleDateTimeSpan::invalid** Indicates that this **COleDateTimeSpan** object is invalid; that is, its value may be incorrect.

- **COleDateTimeSpan::null** Indicates that this **COleDateTimeSpan** object is null, that is, that no value has been supplied for this object. (This is "null" in the database sense of "having no value," as opposed to the C++ **NULL**.)

The status of a **COleDateTimeSpan** object is invalid in the following cases:

- If this object has experienced an overflow or underflow during an arithmetic assignment operation, namely, **+=** or **-=**.

- If an invalid value was assigned to this object.

- If the status of this object was explicitly set to invalid using **SetStatus**.

For more information about the operations that may set the status to invalid, see **COleDateTimeSpan::operator +, -** and **COleDateTimeSpan::operator +=, -=**.

Caution This data member is for advanced programming situations. You should use the inline member functions **GetStatus** and **SetStatus**. See **SetStatus** for further cautions regarding explicitly setting this data member.

For more information about the bounds for **COleDateTimeSpan** values, see the article "Date and Time: OLE Automation Support" in *Programming with MFC*.

See Also   **COleDateTimeSpan::GetStatus**, **COleDateTimeSpan::SetStatus**

COleDialog

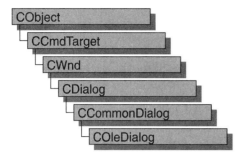

The **COleDialog** class provides functionality common to dialog boxes for OLE. The Microsoft Foundation Class Library provides several classes derived from **COleDialog**.

These are:

- **COleInsertDialog**
- **COleConvertDialog**
- **COleChangeIconDialog**
- **COleLinksDialog**
- **COleBusyDialog**
- **COleUpdateDialog**
- **COlePasteSpecialDialog**
- **COlePropertiesDialog**
- **COleChangeSourceDialog**

For more information about OLE-specific dialog boxes, see the article "Dialog Boxes in OLE" in *Programming with MFC*.

#include <afxodlgs.h>

See Also   **COleBusyDialog, COleChangeIconDialog, COleChangeSourceDialog, COleConvertDialog, COlePropertiesDialog, COleInsertDialog, COleLinksDialog, COlePasteSpecialDialog, COlePropertiesDialog, COleUpdateDialog**

Operations

GetLastError	Gets the error code returned by the dialog box.

Member Functions

COleDialog::GetLastError

UINT GetLastError( ) const;

Return Value

The error codes returned by **GetLastError** depend on the specific dialog box displayed.

Remarks

Call the **GetLastError** member function to get additional error information when **DoModal** returns **IDABORT**. See the **DoModal** member function in the derived classes for information about specific error messages.

See Also **COleBusyDialog::DoModal**, **COleChangeIconDialog::DoModal**, **COleChangeSourceDialog::DoModal**, **COleConvertDialog::DoModal**, **COleInsertDialog::DoModal**, **COleLinksDialog::DoModal**, **COlePasteSpecialDialog::DoModal**, **COlePropertiesDialog::DoModal**, **COleUpdateDialog::DoModal**

COleDispatchDriver

The **COleDispatchDriver** class implements the client side of OLE automation. OLE dispatch interfaces provide access to an object's methods and properties. Member functions of **COleDispatchDriver** attach, detach, create, and release a dispatch connection of type **IDispatch**. Other member functions use variable argument lists to simplify calling **IDispatch::Invoke**.

For more information, see **IDispatch** and **IDispatch::Invoke** in the *OLE 2 Programmer's Reference, Volume 2*.

This class can be used directly, but it is generally used only by classes created by ClassWizard. When you create new C++ classes by importing a type library, ClassWizard derives the new classes from **COleDispatchDriver**.

For more information on using **COleDispatchDriver**, see the following articles in *Programming with MFC*:

- "Automation Clients"
- "Automation Servers"
- "ClassWizard: OLE Automation Support"
- "AppWizard: OLE Support"

#include <afxdisp.h>

See Also   **CCmdTarget**

Data Members

m_bAutoRelease	Specifies whether to release the **IDispatch** during **ReleaseDispatch** or object destruction.
m_lpDispatch	Indicates the pointer to the **IDispatch** interface attached to this **COleDispatchDriver**.

Construction

COleDispatchDriver	Constructs a **COleDispatchDriver** object.

Operations

CreateDispatch	Creates an **IDispatch** connection and attaches it to the **COleDispatchDriver** object.
AttachDispatch	Attaches an **IDispatch** connection to the **COleDispatchDriver** object.
DetachDispatch	Detaches an **IDispatch** connection, without releasing it.
ReleaseDispatch	Releases an **IDispatch** connection.
InvokeHelper	Helper for calling automation methods.

| SetProperty | Sets an automation property. |
| GetProperty | Gets an automation property. |

Member Functions

COleDispatchDriver::AttachDispatch

void AttachDispatch(LPDISPATCH *lpDispatch*, **BOOL** *bAutoRelease* = **TRUE**);

Parameters

lpDispatch   Pointer to an OLE **IDispatch** object to be attached to the
COleDispatchDriver object.

bAutoRelease   Specifies whether the dispatch is to be released when this object goes
out of scope.

Remarks

Call the **AttachDispatch** member function to attach an **IDispatch** pointer to the
COleDispatchDriver object. This function releases any **IDispatch** pointer that is
already attached to the **COleDispatchDriver** object.

See Also   **COleDispatchDriver::DetachDispatch**,
COleDispatchDriver::ReleaseDispatch, **COleDispatchDriver::CreateDispatch**,
COleDispatchDriver::m_lpDispatch, **COleDispatchDriver::m_bAutoRelease**

COleDispatchDriver::COleDispatchDriver

COleDispatchDriver( );

Remarks

Constructs a **COleDispatchDriver** object. Before using this object, you should
connect an **IDispatch** to it using either **COleDispatchDriver::CreateDispatch** or
COleDispatchDriver::AttachDispatch.

See Also   **COleDispatchDriver::AttachDispatch**,
COleDispatchDriver::CreateDispatch

COleDispatchDriver::CreateDispatch

BOOL CreateDispatch(REFCLSID *clsid*, **COleException*** *pError* = **NULL**);
BOOL CreateDispatch(LPCTSTR *lpszProgID*, **COleException*** *pError* = **NULL**);

Return Value

Nonzero on success; otherwise 0.

Parameters

clsid   Class ID of the **IDispatch** connection object to be created.

pError   Pointer to an OLE exception object, which will hold the status code resulting from the creation.

lpszProgID   Pointer to the programmatic identifier, such as "Excel.Document.5", of the automation object for which the dispatch object is to be created.

Remarks

Creates an **IDispatch** object and attaches it to the **COleDispatchDriver** object.

See Also   **COleDispatchDriver::DetachDispatch, COleDispatchDriver::ReleaseDispatch, COleDispatchDriver::AttachDispatch, COleException, COleDispatchDriver::m_lpDispatch**

COleDispatchDriver::DetachDispatch

LPDISPATCH DetachDispatch( );

Return Value

A pointer to the previously attached OLE **IDispatch** object.

Remarks

Detaches the current **IDispatch** connection from this object. The **IDispatch** is not released.

For more information about the **LPDISPATCH** type, see **IDispatch** in the *OLE 2 Programmer's Reference, Volume 2*.

See Also   **COleDispatchDriver::ReleaseDispatch, COleDispatchDriver::CreateDispatch, COleDispatchDriver::AttachDispatch, COleDispatchDriver::m_lpDispatch**

COleDispatchDriver::GetProperty

void GetProperty(DISPID *dwDispID*, **VARTYPE** *vtProp*, **void*** *pvProp*) **const;**

Parameters

dwDispID   Identifies the property to be retrieved. This value is usually supplied by ClassWizard.

vtProp   Specifies the property to be retrieved. For possible values, see the "Remarks" section for **COleDispatchDriver::InvokeHelper**.

pvProp   Address of the variable that will receive the property value. It must match the type specified by *vtProp*.

Remarks

Gets the object property specified by *dwDispID*.

See Also   **COleDispatchDriver::InvokeHelper**, **COleDispatchDriver::SetProperty**

COleDispatchDriver::InvokeHelper

void InvokeHelper(DISPID *dwDispID***, WORD** *wFlags***, VARTYPE** *vtRet***,**
   void* *pvRet***, const BYTE FAR*** *pbParamInfo***, ...);**
   throw(COleException);
   throw(COleDispatchException);

Parameters

dwDispID   Identifies the method or property to be invoked. This value is usually supplied by ClassWizard.

wFlags   Flags describing the context of the call to **IDispatch::Invoke**. For possible values, see the *OLE 2 Programmer's Reference, Volume 1*.

vtRet   Specifies the type of the return value. For possible values, see the "Remarks" section.

pvRet   Address of the variable that will receive the property value or return value. It must match the type specified by *vtRet*.

pbParamInfo   Pointer to a null-terminated string of bytes specifying the types of the parameters following *pbParamInfo*.

...   Variable list of parameters, of types specified in *pbParamInfo*.

Remarks

Calls the object method or property specified by *dwDispID*, in the context specified by *wFlags*. The *pbParamInfo* parameter specifies the types of the parameters passed to the method or property. The variable list of arguments is represented by **...** in the syntax declaration.

Possible values for the *vtRet* argument are taken from the **VARENUM** enumeration. Possible values are as follows:

Symbol	Return Type
VT_EMPTY	void
VT_I2	short
VT_I4	long
VT_R4	float
VT_R8	double

Symbol	Return Type
VT_CY	**CY**
VT_DATE	**DATE**
VT_BSTR	**BSTR**
VT_DISPATCH	**LPDISPATCH**
VT_ERROR	**SCODE**
VT_BOOL	**BOOL**
VT_VARIANT	**VARIANT**
VT_UNKNOWN	**LPUNKNOWN**

The *pbParamInfo* argument is a space-separated list of **VTS_**. One or more of these values, separated by spaces (not commas), specifies the function's parameter list. Possible values are as follows:

Symbol	Parameter Type
VTS_I2	**short**
VTS_I4	**long**
VTS_R4	**float**
VTS_R8	**double**
VTS_CY	**const CY***
VTS_DATE	**DATE**
VTS_BSTR	**const char***
VTS_DISPATCH	**LPDISPATCH**
VTS_SCODE	**SCODE**
VTS_BOOL	**BOOL**
VTS_VARIANT	**const VARIANT***
VTS_UNKNOWN	**LPUNKNOWN**
VTS_PI2	**short***
VTS_PI4	**long***
VTS_PR4	**float***
VTS_PR8	**double***
VTS_PCY	**CY***
VTS_PDATE	**DATE**
VTS_PBSTR	**BSTR***
VTS_PDISPATCH	**LPDISPATCH***
VTS_PSCODE	**SCODE***

Symbol	Parameter Type
VTS_PBOOL	BOOL*
VTS_PVARIANT	VARIANT*
VTS_PUNKNOWN	LPUNKNOWN*

This function converts the parameters to **VARIANTARG** values, then invokes the **IDispatch::Invoke** method. If the call to **Invoke** fails, this function will throw an exception. If the **SCODE** (status code) returned by **IDispatch::Invoke** is **DISP_E_EXCEPTION**, this function throws a **COleException** object; otherwise it throws a **COleDispatchException**.

For more information, see **VARIANTARG**, **IDispatch**, **IDispatch::Invoke**, and "Structure of OLE Error Codes" in the *OLE 2 Programmer's Reference, Volume 2*.

See Also   **COleException**, **COleDispatchException**

COleDispatchDriver::ReleaseDispatch

void ReleaseDispatch( );

Remarks

Releases the **IDispatch** connection. If auto release has been set for this connection, this function calls **IDispatch::Release** before releasing the interface.

See Also   **COleDispatchDriver::DetachDispatch**, **COleDispatchDriver::CreateDispatch**, **COleDispatchDriver::AttachDispatch**, **COleDispatchDriver::m_lpDispatch**, **COleDispatchDriver::m_bAutoRelease**

COleDispatchDriver::SetProperty

void SetProperty(DISPID *dwDispID*, **VARTYPE** *vtProp*, **...);**

Parameters

dwDispID   Identifies the property to be set. This value is usually supplied by ClassWizard.

vtProp   Specifies the type of the property to be set. For possible values, see the "Remarks" section for **COleDispatchDriver::InvokeHelper**.

... A single parameter of the type specified by *vtProp*.

Remarks

Sets the OLE object property specified by *dwDispID*.

See Also   **COleDispatchDriver::InvokeHelper**, **COleDispatchDriver::GetProperty**

Data Members

COleDispatchDriver::m_bAutoRelease

Remarks

Specifies whether the COM object accessed by **m_lpDispatch** should be automatically released when **ReleaseDispatch** is called or when this **COleDispatchDriver** object is destroyed.

For more information on releasing COM objects, see "Implementing Reference Counting" and **IUnknown::Release** in the *OLE 2 Programmer's Reference, Volume 1*.

See Also   **COleDispatchDriver::AttachDispatch, COleDispatchDriver::ReleaseDispatch, COleDispatchDriver::m_lpDispatch**

COleDispatchDriver::m_lpDispatch

Remarks

The pointer to the **IDispatch** interface attached to this **COleDispatchDriver**. The **m_lpDispatch** data member is a public variable of type **LPDISPATCH**.

For more information, see **IDispatch** in the *OLE 2 Programmer's Reference, Volume 2*.

See Also   **COleDispatchDriver::AttachDispatch, COleDispatchDriver::ReleaseDispatch, COleDispatchDriver::CreateDispatch, COleDispatchDriver::DetachDispatch**

Index

A

ABC structure 2210
ABCFLOAT structure 2211
Ability to transact, Recordset 1383
Ability to update records, Recordset 1384
Abort member function, CFile class 657
AbortDoc member function, CDC class 425
Aborting database transactions 403
AbortPath member function, CDC class 426
Accept member function, CAsyncSocket class 70
Action queries
    defined 225
    described 251
    executing 225
Activate member function
    COleClientItem class 986
    CToolTipCtrl class 1720
ActivateAs member function, COleClientItem
    class 987
ActivateFrame member function, CFrameWnd
    class 721
ActivateInPlace member function, COleServerDoc
    class 1242
ActivateNext member function, CSplitterWnd
    class 1572
Activation 1242
Add member function
    CArray class 60
    CImageList class 756
    CObArray class 935
AddBitmap member function, CToolBarCtrl
    class 1699
AddButtons member function, CToolBarCtrl
    class 1699
AddDocTemplate member function, CWinApp
    class 1798
AddDocument member function, CDocTemplate
    class 568
AddFormat member function, COlePasteSpecialDialog
    class 1219

AddHead member function
    CList class 770
    CObList class 954
Adding new records 1381
AddItem member function, COleDocument class 1167
AddMetaFileComment member function, CDC
    class 427
AddNew member function
    CDaoRecordset class 277
    CRecordset class 1381
AddOtherClipboardData member function,
    COleServerItem class 1258
AddPage member function, CPropertySheet class 1359
AddStandardFormats member function,
    COlePasteSpecialDialog class 1220
AddString member function
    CComboBox class 168
    CListBox class 784
    CToolBarCtrl class 1701
AddTail member function
    CList class 771
    CObList class 954
AddTool member function, CToolTipCtrl class 1720
AddToParameterList, Record field exchange (DFX)
    described 247
    PARAMETERS clause, SQL 247
AddToRecentFileList member function, CWinApp
    class 1798
AddToSelectList, Record field exchange (DFX)
    described 247
    SELECT clause, SQL 247
AddView member function, CDocument class 581
AdjustDialogPosition member function,
    CRichEditView class 1495
AdjustRect member function
    CRectTracker class 1436
    CTabCtrl class 1648
AFX_DAO_ALL_INFO
    for database objects 380
    querydefs 229
    tabledefs 233
    workspaces 385

AFX_DAO_ERROR_DFX_BIND, error code 242
AFX_DAO_ERROR_ENGINE_INITIALIZATION,
  error code 242
AFX_DAO_ERROR_OBJECT_NOT_OPEN error
  code 242
AFX_DAO_PRIMARY_INFO
  for database objects 380
  querydefs 229
  relations 231
  tabledefs 233
  workspaces 385
AFX_DAO_SECONDARY_INFO
  for database objects 380
  querydefs 229
  relations 231
  tabledefs 233
  workspaces 385
AFX_DATA, ClassWizard comment 2203
AFX_DATA_INIT, ClassWizard comment 2203
AFX_DATA_MAP, ClassWizard comment 2203
AFX_DISP, ClassWizard comment 2204
AFX_DISP_MAP, ClassWizard comment 2204
AFX_EVENT, ClassWizard comment 2204
AFX_EVENT_MAP, ClassWizard comment 2205
AFX_FIELD, ClassWizard comment 2205
AFX_FIELD_INIT, ClassWizard comment 2205
AFX_FIELD_MAP, ClassWizard comment 2206
AFX_MANAGE_STATE, global function/macro 2082
AFX_MSG, ClassWizard comment 2206
AFX_MSG_MAP, ClassWizard comment 2206
AFX_SQL_ASYNC global function/macro 2061, 2095
AFX_SQL_ERROR codes 413
AFX_SQL_SYNC global function/macro 2061, 2096
AFX_VIRTUAL, ClassWizard comment 2207
AfxAbort global function/macro 2070
AfxBeginThread global function/macro 2071
AfxCheckMemory global function/macro 2072
AfxConnectionAdvise global function/macro 2073
AfxConnectionUnadvise global function/macro 2074
AfxDoForAllClasses global function/macro 2074
AfxDoForAllObjects global function/macro 2075
afxDump global function/macro 2075–2076
AfxEnableControlContainer global
  function/macro 2076
AfxEnableMemoryTracking global
  function/macro 2077
AfxEndThread global function/macro 2077
AfxFormatString1 global function/macro 2077
AfxFormatString2 global function/macro 2078

AfxGetApp global function/macro 2078
AfxGetAppName global function/macro 2079
AfxGetInstanceHandle global function/macro 2079
AfxGetMainWnd global function/macro 2079
AfxGetResourceHandle global function/macro 2080
AfxGetThread global function/macro 2080
AfxIsMemoryBlock global function/macro 2080
AfxIsValidAddress global function/macro 2081
AfxIsValidString global function/macro 2081
afxMemDF global function/macro 2082
AfxMessageBox global function/macro 2083
AfxOleCanExitApp global function/macro 2084
AfxOleGetMessageFilter global function/macro 2084
AfxOleGetUserCtrl global function/macro 2085
AfxOleInit global function/macro 2085
AfxOleLockApp global function/macro 2085
AfxOleRegisterControlClass global
  function/macro 2086
AfxOleRegisterPropertyPageClass global
  function/macro 2087
AfxOleRegisterServerClass global
  function/macro 2088
AfxOleRegisterTypeLib global function/macro 2089
AfxOleSetEditMenu global function/macro 2090
AfxOleSetUserCtrl global function/macro 2091
AfxOleTypeMatchGuid global function/macro 2091–
  2092
AfxOleUnlockApp global function/macro 2092
AfxOleUnregisterTypeLib global function/macro 2092
AfxRegisterClass global function/macro 2093
AfxRegisterWndClass global function/macro 2093
AfxSetAllocHook global function/macro 2094
AfxSetResourceHandle global function/macro 2094
AfxSocketInit global function/macro 2095
AfxThrowArchiveException global
  function/macro 2097
AfxThrowDaoException global function/macro 239,
  2097
AfxThrowDBException global function/macro 2098
AfxThrowFileException global function/macro 2098
AfxThrowMemoryException global
  function/macro 2099
AfxThrowNotSupportedException global
  function/macro 2099
AfxThrowOleDispatchException global
  function/macro 2099
AfxThrowOleException global function/macro 2100
AfxThrowResourceException global
  function/macro 2100

AfxThrowUserException global function/macro 2100
afxTraceEnabled global function/macro 2101
afxTraceFlags global function/macro 2101
AfxVerifyLicFile global function/macro 2102
Aggregate data
    collection classes 136, 609, 849, 851, 853, 861,
        863, 865, 867, 934
    template-based classes 58, 769, 842, 1754, 1757,
        1763
Alloc member function, CmemFile class 883
AllocCache, Record field exchange (DFX) 247
AllocSysString member function, CString class 1617
AmbientBackColor member function, COleControl
    class 1031
AmbientDisplayName member function, COleControl
    class 1032
AmbientFont member function, COleControl
    class 1032
AmbientForeColor member function, COleControl
    class 1032
AmbientLocaleID member function, COleControl
    class 1033
AmbientScaleUnits member function, COleControl
    class 1033
AmbientShowGrabHandles member function,
    COleControl class 1033
AmbientShowHatching member function, COleControl
    class 1034
AmbientTextAlign member function, COleControl
    class 1034
AmbientUIDead member function, COleControl
    class 1034
AmbientUserMode member function, COleControl
    class 1035
AND_CATCH global function/macro 2103
AND_CATCH_ALL global function/macro 2103
AngleArc member function, CDC class 427
AnimatePalette member function, CPalette class 1304
Animation control 33
AnsiToOem member function, CString class 1617
Append member function
    CArray class 60
    CDaoQueryDef class 253
    CDaoTableDef class 348
    CDaoWorkspace class 374
Append query 251
Appendability, determining recordset 1382

Appending
    querydefs 253
    workspaces 374
AppendMenu member function, CMenu class 895
Application architecture classes, listed 4
Application control functions, OLE 2062
Application framework, Microsoft Foundation Class
    Library 3
Application information, management 2056
Applications, management information 2056
ApplyPrintDevice member function, COleDocument
    class 1168
Arc member function, CDC class 428
Archive operators
    COleCurrency 1096
    COleDateTime 1137
    COleDateTimeSpan 1152
    COleVariant 1291
ArcTo member function, CDC class 429
argv, MFC encapsulation 189
Arrange member function, CListCtrl class 810
ArrangeIconicWindows member function, CWnd
    class 1865
Arrays, collection classes
    CArray 58
    CByteArray 136
    CDWordArray 609
    CObArray 934
    CTypedPtrArray 1754
ASSERT global function/macro 2104
ASSERT_VALID global function/macro 2105
AssertValid member function, CObject class 945
Assignment operator, COleVariant 1289
Asynchronous access
    canceling 1383
    default mode 403
    disabling 403
    enabling 403
    mode, setting 403
Asynchronous operations, canceling 395
AsyncSelect member function, CAsyncSocket class 71
Attach member function
    CAsyncSocket class 72
    CDC class 430
    CGdiObject class 737
    CImageList class 757
    CMemFile class 883
    CMenu class 897
    COleDataObject class 1099

Attach member function *(continued)*
  COleStreamFile class 1278
  CSocket class 1555
  CWnd class 1866
AttachClipboard member function, COleDataObject
  class 1099
AttachDataObject member function, COleClientItem
  class 988
AttachDispatch member function, COleDispatchDriver
  class 1157
Attaching data objects to Clipboard 1099
AutoLoad member function, CBitmapButton class 114
AutoSize member function, CToolBarCtrl class 1702

B

BASED_CODE global function/macro 2105
BEGIN_CONNECTION_MAP global
  function/macro 2106
BEGIN_CONNECTION_PART global
  function/macro 2106
BEGIN_DISPATCH_MAP global
  function/macro 2106
BEGIN_EVENT_MAP global function/macro 2107
BEGIN_EVENTSINK_MAP global
  function/macro 2107
BEGIN_MESSAGE_MAP global function/macro 2108
BEGIN_OLEFACTORY global function/macro 2109
BEGIN_PROPPAGEIDS global function/macro 2109
BeginBusyState member function, COleMessageFilter
  class 1205
BeginDrag member function
  CDragListBox class 601
  CImageList class 757
BeginEnumFormats member function, COleDataObject
  class 1100
BeginModalState member function, CFrameWnd
  class 721
BeginPaint member function, CWnd class 1866
BeginPath member function, CDC class 431
BeginTrans member function
  CDaoWorkspace class 374
  CDatabase class 394
BeginWaitCursor member function, CCmdTarget
  class 146
Binary Large Object, CLongBinary class 840
Bind member function, CAsyncSocket class 73
BindField, Record field exchange (DFX) 247
BindParam, Record field exchange (DFX) 247

BitBlt member function, CDC class 431
BITMAP structure 2211
BITMAP TOOLTIPTEXT 1693
BITMAPINFO structure 2212
Bitmaps as data, CLongBinary class 840
BLOB, CLongBinary class 840
BOOL, DDX field exchange 2134
Boolean
  DFX field exchange 2148
  RFX field exchange 2190
BottomRight member function, CRect class 1420
Bound fields, Recordset 1408
BoundPropertyChanged member function, COleControl
  class 1035
BoundPropertyRequestEdit member function,
  COleControl class 1035
BringWindowToTop member function, CWnd
  class 1867
Bulk query 251
Button styles 2270
BYTE
  DDX field exchange 2134
  DFX field exchange 2149
  Float field exchange 2134
  RFX field exchange 2190
Byte array
  DFX field exchange 2147
  RFX field exchange 2189

C

C language API, relationship of Microsoft Foundation
  Class Library to 3
CacheData member function, COleDataSource
  class 1106
CacheGlobalData member function, COleDataSource
  class 1107
CalcDynamicLayout member function, CControlBar
  class 202
CalcFixedLayout member function, CControlBar
  class 203
CalcWindowRect member function, CWnd class 1867
Callback functions for MFC member functions
  CDC 2208–2209
  described 2208
CanActivate member function, COleClientItem
  class 988
CanActivateNext member function, CSplitterWnd
  class 1572

CanAppend member function
   CDaoRecordset class 278
   CRecordset class 1382
CanBookmark member function, CDaoRecordset
  class 279
Cancel member function
   CDatabase class 395
   CRecordset class 1383
CancelBlockingCall member function, CSocket
  class 1556
CancelDrag member function, CDragListBox
  class 601
Canceling
   Asynchronous access 1383
   long recordset operations 1400
   operations 401
CancelToClose member function, CPropertyPage
  class 1351
CancelToolTips member function, CWnd class 1868
CancelUpdate member function, CDaoRecordseat
  class 279
CanCloseFrame member function, CDocument
  class 583
CanCreateFromData member function, COleClientItem
  class 988
CanCreateLinkFromData member function,
  COleClientItem class 989
CAnimateCtrl class
  described 33
  member functions
    CAnimateCtrl 34
    Close 34
    Create 35
    Open 36
    Play 36
    Seek 37
    Stop 37
CAnimateCtrl constructor 34
CAnimateCtrl member function, CAnimateCtrl
  class 34
CanPaste member function
   COleClientItem class 989
   CRichEditView class 1496
CanPasteLink member function, COleClientItem
  class 990
CanRestart member function
   CDaoRecordset class 280
   CRecordset class 1383

CanScroll member function
   CDaoRecordset class 280
   CRecordset class 1383
CanTransact member function
   CDaoDatabase class 219
   CDaoRecordset class 281
   CDatabase class 395
   CRecordset class 1383
CanUndo member function
   CEdit class 614
   CRichEditCtrl class 1464
CanUpdate member function
   CDaoDatabase class 219
   CDaoQueryDef class 254
   CDaoRecordset class 281
   CDaoTableDef class 348
   CDatabase class 396
   CRecordset class 1384
CArchive class
  data members, m_pDocument 55
  described 38
  member functions
    CArchive 39
    Close 41
    Flush 41
    GetFile 41
    GetObjectSchema 42
    IsBufferEmpty 43
    IsLoading 43
    IsStoring 44
    MapObject 44
    operator << 53
    operator >> 54
    Read 46
    ReadClass 46
    ReadObject 47
    ReadString 48
    SerializeClass 48
    SetLoadParams 49
    SetObjectSchema 50
    SetStoreParams 50
    Write 51
    WriteClass 52
    WriteObject 52
    WriteString 53
CArchive member function, CArchive class 39

CArchiveException class
    data members, m_cause 57
    described 56
    member functions, CArchiveException 56
CArchiveException constructor 56
CArchiveException member function,
  CArchiveException class 56
CArray class
    described 58
    member functions
        Add 60
        Append 60
        CArray 61
        Copy 61
        ElementAt 61
        FreeExtra 62
        GetAt 62
        GetData 62
        GetSize 63
        GetUpperBound 63
        InsertAt 63
        operator [ ] 67
        RemoveAll 64
        RemoveAt 64
        SetAt 65
        SetAtGrow 65
        SetSize 66
CArray member function, CArray class 61
Cascades, database relation 224
CAsyncSocket class
    data members
        described 101
        m_hSocket 101
    described 68
    member functions 70
        Accept 70
        AsyncSelect 71
        Attach 72
        Bind 73
        CAsyncSocket 74
        Close 74
        Connect 74
        Create 76
        Detach 77
        FromHandle 78
        GetLastError 78
        GetPeerName 78
        GetSockName 79
        GetSockOpt 80

CAsyncSocket class (continued)
    member functions 70 (continued)
        IOCtl 82
        Listen 84
        OnAccept 85
        OnClose 85
        OnConnect 86
        OnOutOfBandData 87
        OnReceive 88
        OnSend 88
        Receive 89
        ReceiveFrom 90
        Send 93
        SendTo 94
        SetSockOpt 97
        ShutDown 100
    members 68
CAsyncSocket member function, CAsyncSocket
  class 70, 74
CATCH global function/macro 2109
CATCH macro, use in DAO 239
CATCH_ALL global function/macro 2110
Categories, macros and globals 2046
CBitmap class
    described 102
    member functions
        CBitmap 103
        CreateBitmap 103
        CreateBitmapIndirect 104
        CreateCompatibleBitmap 105
        CreateDiscardableBitmap 106
        FromHandle 106
        GetBitmap 107
        GetBitmapBits 107
        GetBitmapDimension 108
        LoadBitmap 108
        LoadMappedBitmap 109
        LoadOEMBitmap 109
        operator HBITMAP 110
        SetBitmapBits 111
        SetBitmapDimension 111
CBitmap member function, CBitmap class 103
CBitmapButton class
    described 112
    member functions
        AutoLoad 114
        CBitmapButton 114
        LoadBitmaps 115
        SizeToContent 116

CBitmapButton member function, CBitmapButton class 114
CBrush class
    described 117
    member functions
        CBrush 118
        CreateBrushIndirect 119
        CreateDIBPatternBrush 119
        CreateHatchBrush 121
        CreatePatternBrush 122
        CreateSolidBrush 122
        CreateSysColorBrush 123
        FromHandle 124
        GetLogBrush 124–125
CBrush member function, CBrush class 118
CButton class
    described 126
    member functions
        CButton 128
        Create 128
        DrawItem 129
        GetBitmap 129
        GetButtonStyle 130
        GetCheck 130
        GetCursor 130
        GetIcon 131
        GetState 131
        SetBitmap 132
        SetButtonStyle 132
        SetCheck 133
        SetCursor 133
        SetIcon 134
        SetState 135
CButton member function, CButton class 128
CByteArray class 136
CCheckListBox class
    described 138
    member functions
        CCheckListBox 139
        Create 139
        Enable 140
        GetCheck 140
        GetCheckStyle 141
        IsEnabled 141
        OnGetCheckPosition 141
        SetCheck 142
        SetCheckStyle 142
CCheckListBox constructor 139

CCheckListBox member function, CCheckListBox class 139
CClientDC class
    data members, m_hWnd 144
    described 143
    member functions, CClientDC 143
CClientDC member function, CClientDC class 143
CCmdTarget class
    described 145
    member functions
        BeginWaitCursor 146
        EnableAutomation 148
        EndWaitCursor 148
        FromIDispatch 149
        GetIDispatch 150
        IsResultExpected 150
        OnCmdMsg 151
        OnFinalRelease 152
        RestoreWaitCursor 153
CCmdUI class
    described 155
    member functions
        ContinueRouting 156
        Enable 156
        SetCheck 157
        SetRadio 157
        SetText 157
CColorDialog class
    data members, m_cc 162
    described 158
    member functions
        CColorDialog 159
        DoModal 160
        GetColor 160
        GetSavedCustomColors 160
        OnColorOK 161
        SetCurrentColor 161
CColorDialog member function, CColorDialog class 159
CComboBox class
    described 163
    member functions
        AddString 168
        CComboBox 168
        Clear 168
        CompareItem 169
        Copy 169
        Create 169
        Cut 171

CComboBox class *(continued)*
  member functions *(continued)*
    DeleteItem 171
    DeleteString 171
    Dir 172
    DrawItem 172
    FindString 173
    FindStringExact 173
    GetCount 174
    GetCurSel 174
    GetDroppedControlRect 175
    GetDroppedState 175
    GetDroppedWidth 175
    GetEditSel 176
    GetExtendedUI 176
    GetHorizontalExtent 176
    GetItemData 177
    GetItemDataPtr 177
    GetItemHeight 178
    GetLBText 178
    GetLBTextLen 179
    GetLocale 179
    GetTopIndex 179
    InitStorage 180
    InsertString 180
    LimitText 181
    MeasureItem 181
    Paste 182
    ResetContent 182
    SelectString 182
    SetCurSel 183
    SetDroppedWidth 184
    SetEditSel 184
    SetExtendedUI 185
    SetHorizontalExtent 185
    SetItemData 186
    SetItemDataPtr 186
    SetItemHeight 187
    SetLocale 187
    SetTopIndex 188
    ShowDropDown 188
CComboBox member function, CComboBox class 168
CCommandLineInfo class
  data members
    described 191
    m_bRunAutomated 191
    m_bRunEmbedded 192
    m_bShowSplash 192
    m_nShellCommand 192

CCommandLineInfo class *(continued)*
  data members *(continued)*
    m_strDriverName 193
    m_strFileName 193
    m_strPortName 194
    m_strPrinterName 194
  member functions
    CCommandLineInfo 190
    described 190
    ParseParam 190
CCommandLineInfo constructor 190
CCommandLineInfo member function,
  CCommandLineInfo class 190
CCommonDialog class
  described 195
  member functions, CCommonDialog 195
CCommonDialog constructor 195
CCommonDialog member function, CCommonDialog
  class 195
CConnectionPoint class
  described 197
  member functions
    GetConnection 199
    GetContainer 199
    GetIID 199
    GetMaxConnections 200
    OnAdvise 200
CControlBar class
  data members, m_bAutoDelete 207
  described 201
  member functions
    CalcDynamicLayout 202
    CalcFixedLayout 203
    EnableDocking 204
    GetBarStyle 205
    GetCount 205
    GetDockingFrame 205
    IsFloating 206
    OnUpdateCmdUI 206
    SetBarStyle 206
CCreateContext structure 209
CCriticalSection class
  described 211
  member functions
    CCriticalSection 212
    Lock 212
    Unlock 213
CCriticalSection constructor 212

CCriticalSection member function, CCriticalSection
   class 212
CCtrlView class
   data members
      m_dwDefaultStyle 215
      m_strClass 215
   described 214
   member functions, CCtrlView 214
CCtrlView constructor 214
CCtrlView member function, CCtrlView class 214
CDaoDatabase class
   data members
      m_pDAODatabase 237
      m_pWorkspace 238
   described 216
   member functions
      CanTransact 219
      CanUpdate 219
      CDaoDatabase 219
      Close 220
      Create 221
      CreateRelation 223
      DeleteQueryDef 224
      DeleteRelation 225
      DeleteTableDef 225
      Execute 225
      GetConnect 227
      GetName 227
      GetQueryDefCount 228
      GetQueryDefInfo 229
      GetQueryTimeout 230
      GetRecordsAffected 230
      GetRelationCount 231
      GetRelationInfo 231
      GetTableDefCount 232
      GetTableDefInfo 233
      GetVersion 234
      IsOpen 234
      Open 235
      SetQueryTimeout 237
CDaoDatabase constructor 219
CDaoDatabase member function, CDaoDatabase
   class 219
CDaoDatabaseInfo structure 380, 2214
CDaoErrorInfo structure
   overview of structure members 243
   use of 243, 2217

CDaoException class
   data members
      m_nAfxDaoError 242
      m_pErrorInfo 243
      m_scode 244
   described 239
   member functions
      CDaoException 240
      GetErrorCount 241
      GetErrorInfo 241
CDaoException constructor 240
CDaoException member function, CDaoException
   class 240
CDaoFieldExchange
   FieldType values
      outputColumn 245
      param 245
   operations 245
   purpose of 245
CDaoFieldExchange class
   data members
      m_nOperation 247
      m_prs 249
   described 245
   member functions
      IsValidOperation 246
      SetFieldType 247
CDaoFieldInfo structure 2218
CDaoIndexFieldInfo structure 2225
CDaoIndexInfo structure 2222
CDaoParameterInfo structure 2226
CDaoQueryDef class
   data members
      m_pDAOQueryDef 270
      m_pDatabase 269
   described 250
   member functions
      Append 253
      CanUpdate 254
      CDaoQueryDef 254
      Close 255
      Create 255
      Execute 256
      GetConnect 257
      GetDateCreated 258
      GetDateLastUpdated 258
      GetFieldCount 259
      GetFieldInfo 259
      GetName 260

CDaoQueryDef class *(continued)*
member functions *(continued)*
GetODBCTimeout 260
GetParameterCount 261
GetParameterInfo 261
GetParamValue 262
GetRecordsAffected 263
GetReturnsRecords 263
GetSQL 263
GetType 264
IsOpen 265
Open 265
SetConnect 266
SetName 266
SetODBCTimeout 267
SetParamValue 267
SetReturnsRecords 268
SetSQL 269
CDaoQueryDef constructor 254
CDaoQueryDef member function, CDaoQueryDef
class 254
CDaoQueryDefInfo structure 229, 2227
CDaoRecordset class
data members
described 336
m_bCheckCacheForDirtyFields 336
m_nParams 336
m_pDAORecordset 337
m_pDatabase 337
m_strFilter 337
m_strSort 338
deriving classes 272
described 271
member functions
AddNew 277
CanAppend 278
CanBookmark 279
CancelUpdate 279
CanRestart 280
CanScroll 280
CanTransact 281
CanUpdate 281
CDaoRecordset 282
Close 282
Delete 283
DoFieldExchange 284
Edit 285
FillCache 286
Find 288

CDaoRecordset class *(continued)*
member functions *(continued)*
FindFirst 288
FindLast 290
FindNext 291
FindPrev 292
GetAbsolutePosition 294
GetBookmark 294
GetCacheSize 295
GetCacheStart 296
GetCurrentIndex 296
GetDateCreated 297
GetDateLastUpdated 297
GetDefaultDBName 297
GetDefaultSQL 298
GetEditMode 299
GetFieldCount 299
GetFieldInfo 300
GetFieldValue 301
GetIndexCount 301
GetIndexInfo 302
GetLastModifiedBookmark 303
GetLockingMode 303
GetName 304
GetParamValue 304
GetPercentPosition 305
GetRecordCount 306
GetSQL 307
GetType 307
GetValidationRule 308
GetValidationText 308
IsBOF 309
IsDeleted 310
IsEOF 311
IsFieldDirty 312
IsFieldNull 313
IsFieldNullable 314
IsOpen 315
Move 315
MoveFirst 316
MoveLast 317
MoveNext 318
MovePrev 319
Open 320
Requery 323
Seek 324
SetAbsolutePosition 325
SetBookmark 326
SetCacheSize 327–328

CDaoRecordset class *(continued)*
  member functions *(continued)*
    SetCurrentIndex 328
    SetFieldDirty 329
    SetFieldNull 330
    SetFieldValue 331
    SetFieldValueNull 332
    SetLockingMode 332
    SetParamValue 333
    SetParamValueNull 334
    SetPercentPosition 334
    Update 335
  using CDaoRecordset without deriving 272
CDaoRecordset member function, CDaoRecordset
  class 277, 282
CDaoRecordView
  described 339
  member functions, CDaoRecordView 341
CDaoRecordView class, member functions
  IsOnFirstRecord 342
  IsOnLastRecord 342
  OnGetRecordset 343
  OnMove 343
CDaoRecordView member function, CDaoRecordView
  class 341
CDaoRelationFieldInfo structure 2232
CDaoRelationInfo structure 231, 2230
CDaoTableDef
  described 345
  member functions, Append 348
CDaoTableDef class
  data members
    described 368
    m_DAOTableDef 369
    m_pDatabase 368
  member functions
    CanUpdate 348
    CDaoTableDef 349
    Close 349
    Create 350
    CreateField 351
    CreateIndex 352
    DeleteField 353
    DeleteIndex 354
    GetAttibutes 354
    GetConnect 355
    GetDateCreated 357
    GetDateLastUpdated 357
    GetFieldCount 358

CDaoTableDef class *(continued)*
  member functions *(continued)*
    GetFieldInfo 358
    GetIndexCount 359
    GetIndexInfo 359
    GetName 360
    GetRecordCount 361
    GetSourceTableName 361
    GetValidationRule 362
    GetValidationText 362
    IsOpen 363
    Open 363
    RefreshLink 364
    SetAttributes 364
    SetConnect 365
    SetName 366
    SetSourceTableName 367
    SetValidationRule 367
    SetValidationText 368
CDaoTableDef member functions
  Append 348
  CDaoTableDef class 349
CDaoTableDefInfo structure 233, 2233
CDaoWorkspace class
  See also Workspace
  data members, m_pDAOWorkspace 393
  described 370
  member functions
    Append 374
    BeginTrans 374
    CDaoWorkspace 375
    Close 375
    CommitTrans 376
    Create 377
    GetDatabaseCount 380
    GetDatabaseInfo 380
    GetIniPath 381
    GetIsolateODBCTrans 382
    GetLoginTimeout 382
    GetName 383
    GetUserName 383
    GetVersion 384
    GetWorkspaceCount 384
    GetWorkspaceInfo 385
    Idle 386
    IsOpen 386
    Open 387
    Rollback 388
    SetDefaultPassword 389

CDaoWorkspace class *(continued)*
    member functions *(continued)*
        SetDefaultUser 390
        SetIniPath 391
        SetIsolateODBCTrans 391
        SetLoginTimeout 392
CDaoWorkspace constructor 375
CDaoWorkspace member function, CDaoWorkspace class 375
CDaoWorkspaceInfo structure 385, 2235
CDatabase class
    data members, m_hdbc 405
    member functions
        BeginTrans 394
        Cancel 395
        CanTransact 395
        CanUpdate 396
        CDatabase 396
        Close 397
        CommitTrans 397
        ExecuteSQL 398
        GetConnect 399
        GetDatabaseName 399
        InWaitForDataSource 399
        IsOpen 400
        OnSetOptions 400
        OnWaitForDataSource 401
        Open 401
        Rollback 403
        SetLoginTimeout 404
        SetQueryTimeout 404
        SetSynchronousMode 403
CDatabase constructor 396
CDatabase member function, CDatabase class 396
CDatabase object
    closing 397
    creating 396
CDataExchange class
    described 408
    Dialog data exchange (DDX) 408
    member functions
        described 411
        Fail 408
        m_bSaveAndValidate 410
        PrepareCtrl 409
        PrepareEditCtrl 410
    members 408

CDBException class
    data members
        m_nRetCode 413
        m_strError 415
        m_strStateNativeOrigin 415
    described 412
CDC class
    data members
        m_hAttribDC 548
        m_hDC 548
    described 416
    member functions
        AbortDoc 425
        AbortPath 426
        AddMetaFileComment 427
        AngleArc 427
        Arc 428
        ArcTo 429
        Attach 430
        BeginPath 431
        BitBlt 431
        CDC 434
        Chord 434
        CloseFigure 435
        CreateCompatibleDC 435
        CreateDC 436
        CreateIC 437
        DeleteDC 438
        DeleteTempMap 438
        Detach 439
        DPtoHIMETRIC 439
        DPtoLP 439
        Draw3dRect 440
        DrawDragRect 441
        DrawEdge 441
        DrawEscape 443
        DrawFocusRect 444
        DrawFrameControl 444
        DrawIcon 446
        DrawState 446
        DrawText 448
        Ellipse 450
        EndDoc 451
        EndPage 452
        EndPath 452
        EnumObjects 452
        Escape 454
        ExcludeClipRect 455
        ExcludeUpdateRgn 456

CDC class *(continued)*
  member functions *(continued)*
    ExtFloodFill 456
    ExtTextOut 457
    FillPath 458
    FillRect 459
    FillRgn 459
    FillSolidRect 460
    FlattenPath 460
    FloodFill 461
    FrameRect 461
    FrameRgn 462
    FromHandle 462
    GetArcDirection 463
    GetAspectRatioFilter 463
    GetBkColor 463
    GetBkMode 464
    GetBoundsRect 464
    GetBrushOrg 465
    GetCharABCWidths 465
    GetCharWidth 466
    GetClipBox 467
    GetColorAdjustment 468
    GetCurrentBitmap 468
    GetCurrentBrush 468
    GetCurrentFont 468
    GetCurrentPalette 469
    GetCurrentPen 469
    GetCurrentPosition 469
    GetDeviceCaps 470
    GetFontData 474
    GetGlyphOutline 475
    GetHalftoneBrush 477
    GetKerningPairs 477
    GetMapMode 478
    GetMiterLimit 478
    GetNearestColor 478
    GetOutlineTextMetrics 479
    GetOutputCharWidth 479
    GetOutputTabbedTextExtent 480
    GetOutputTextExtent 481
    GetOutputTextMetrics 482
    GetPath 482
    GetPixel 483
    GetPolyFillMode 484
    GetROP2 484
    GetSafeHdc 484
    GetStretchBltMode 485
    GetTabbedTextExtent 485

CDC class *(continued)*
  member functions *(continued)*
    GetTextAlign 486
    GetTextCharacterExtra 487
    GetTextColor 487
    GetTextExtent 488
    GetTextFace 488
    GetTextMetrics 489
    GetViewportExt 489
    GetViewportOrg 490
    GetWindow 490
    GetWindowExt 490
    GetWindowOrg 490
    GrayString 491
    HIMETRICtoDP 492
    HIMETRICtoLP 493
    IntersectClipRect 493
    InvertRect 494
    InvertRgn 494
    IsPrinting 495
    LineTo 495
    LPtoDP 495
    LPtoHIMETRIC 496
    MaskBlt 496
    MoveTo 498
    OffsetClipRgn 498
    OffsetViewportOrg 499
    OffsetWindowOrg 499
    PaintRgn 500
    PatBlt 500
    Pie 501
    PlayMetaFile 502
    PlgBlt 503
    PolyBezier 505
    PolyBezierTo 506
    PolyDraw 506
    Polygon 507
    Polyline 508
    PolylineTo 508
    PolyPolygon 509
    PolyPolyline 510
    PtVisible 510
    QueryAbort 511
    RealizePalette 511
    Rectangle 512
    RectVisible 512
    ReleaseAttribDC 513
    ReleaseOutputDC 513
    ResetDC 513

CDC class *(continued)*
  member functions *(continued)*
    RestoreDC 514
    RoundRect 514
    SaveDC 515
    ScaleViewportExt 516
    ScaleWindowExt 516
    ScrollDC 517
    SelectClipPath 518
    SelectClipRgn 519
    SelectObject 520
    SelectPalette 521
    SelectStockObject 522
    SetAbortProc 523
    SetArcDirection 524
    SetAttribDC 525
    SetBkColor 525
    SetBkMode 526
    SetBoundsRect 526
    SetBrushOrg 527
    SetColorAdjustment 528
    SetMapMode 528
    SetMapperFlags 530
    SetMiterLimit 530
    SetOutputDC 530
    SetPixel 531
    SetPixelV 531
    SetPolyFillMode 532
    SetROP2 533
    SetStretchBltMode 534
    SetTextAlign 535
    SetTextCharacterExtra 536
    SetTextColor 537
    SetTextJustification 537
    SetViewportExt 538
    SetViewportOrg 539
    SetWindowExt 540
    SetWindowOrg 541
    StartDoc 541
    StartPage 542
    StretchBlt 542
    StrokeAndFillPath 544
    StrokePath 545
    TabbedTextOut 545
    TextOut 546
    UpdateColors 547
    WidenPath 547
CDC class, callback functions for *See* Callback
  functions for MFC member functions

CDC member function, CDC class 434
CDialog class
  described 549
  member functions
    CDialog 552
    Create 552
    CreateIndirect 553
    DoModal 554
    EndDialog 555
    GetDefID 555
    GotoDlgCtrl 556
    InitModalIndirect 556
    MapDialogRect 557
    NextDlgCtrl 557
    OnCancel 558
    OnInitDialog 558
    OnOK 559
    OnSetFont 559
    PrevDlgCtrl 559
    SetDefID 560
    SetHelpID 560
CDialog member function, CDialog class 552
CDialogBar class
  described 561
  member functions
    CDialogBar 562
    Create 562
CDialogBar member function, CDialogBar class 562
CDocItem class
  described 564
  member functions
    GetDocument 565
    IsBlank 564
CDocTemplate class
  described 566
  member functions
    AddDocument 568
    CDocTemplate 568
    CloseAllDocuments 569
    CreateNewDocument 570
    CreateNewFrame 570
    CreateOleFrame 571
    GetDocString 571
    GetFirstDocPosition 572
    GetNextDoc 573
    InitialUpdateFrame 573
    LoadTemplate 574
    MatchDocType 574
    OpenDocumentFile 575

CDocTemplate class *(continued)*
 member functions *(continued)*
  RemoveDocument 576
  SaveAllModified 576
  SetContainerInfo 576
  SetDefaultTitle 577
  SetServerInfo 577
CDocTemplate member function, CDocTemplate
 class 568
CDocument class
 described 579
 member functions
  AddView 581
  CanCloseFrame 583
  CDocument 584
  DeleteContents 584
  GetDocTemplate 585
  GetFile 585
  GetFirstViewPosition 586
  GetNextView 586
  GetPathName 587
  GetTitle 587
  IsModified 588
  OnChangedViewList 588
  OnCloseDocument 588
  OnFileSendMail 589
  OnNewDocument 589
  OnOpenDocument 591
  OnSaveDocument 593
  OnUpdateFileSendMail 593
  PreCloseFrame 594
  ReleaseFile 594
  RemoveView 594
  ReportSaveLoadException 596
  SaveModified 597
  SetModifiedFlag 597
  SetPathName 598
  SetTitle 598
  UpdateAllViews 598
CDocument member function, CDocument class 584
CDragListBox class
 described 600
 member functions
  BeginDrag 601
  CancelDrag 601
  CDragListBox 602
  Dragging 602
  DrawInsert 602

CDragListBox class *(continued)*
 member functions *(continued)*
  Dropped 603
  ItemFromPt 603
CDragListBox member function, CDragListBox
 class 602
CDumpContext class
 described 604
 member functions
  CDumpContext 605
  Flush 605
  GetDepth 606
  HexDump 606
  operator << 607
  SetDepth 607
CDumpContext member function, CDumpContext
 class 605
CDWordArray class 609
CEdit class
 member functions
  CanUndo 614
  CEdit 615
  CharFromPos 615
  Clear 615
  Copy 616
  Create 616
  Cut 617
  EmptyUndoBuffer 617
  FmtLines 618
  GetFirstVisibleLine 618
  GetHandle 619
  GetLimitText 619
  GetLine 620
  GetLineCount 620
  GetMargins 621
  GetModify 621
  GetPasswordChar 621
  GetRect 622
  GetSel 622
  LimitText 623
  LineFromChar 623
  LineIndex 624
  LineLength 624
  LineScroll 625
  Paste 625
  PosFromChar 626
  ReplaceSel 626
  SetHandle 627
  SetLimitText 627

CEdit class *(continued)*
  member functions *(continued)*
    SetMargins 628
    SetModify 628
    SetPasswordChar 629
    SetReadOnly 629
    SetRect 630
    SetRectNP 630
    3SetSel 631
    SetTabStops 631
    Undo 632
  overview 611
CEdit member function, CEdit class 615
CEditView class
  described 633
  member functions
    CEditView 635
    dwStyleDefault 642
    FindText 635
    GetBufferLength 636
    GetEditCtrl 636
    GetPrinterFont 636
    GetSelectedText 637
    LockBuffer 637
    OnFindNext 637
    OnReplaceAll 638
    OnReplaceSel 639
    OnTextNotFound 639
    PrintInsideRect 640
    SerializeRaw 640
    SetPrinterFont 641
    SetTabStops 641
    UnlockBuffer 641
CEditView member function, CEditView class 635
CenterWindow member function, CWnd class 1868
CEvent class
  described 643
  member functions
    CEvent 644
    PulseEvent 645
    ResetEvent 645
    SetEvent 645
    Unlock 646
CEvent constructor 644
CEvent member function, CEvent class 644
CException class
  described 647
  member functions, GetErrorMessage 648

CFieldExchange class
  described 652
  member functions
    IsFieldType 653
    SetFieldType 653
CFile class
  data members, m_hFile 672
  described 655
  member functions
    Abort 657
    CFile 657
    Close 659
    Duplicate 660
    Flush 660
    GetFileName 660
    GetFilePath 660
    GetFileTitle 661
    GetLength 661
    GetPosition 661
    GetStatus 662
    LockRange 663
    Open 664
    Read 665
    ReadHuge 666
    Remove 666
    Rename 667
    Seek 667
    SeekToBegin 668
    SeekToEnd 668
    SetFilePath 669
    SetLength 669
    SetStatus 670
    UnlockRange 670
    Write 671
    WriteHuge 671
CFile member function, CFile class 657
CFileDialog class
  data members, m_ofn 681
  described 673
  member functions
    CFileDialog 675
    DoModal 676
    GetFileExt 676
    GetFileName 677
    GetFileTitle 677
    GetNextPathName 678
    GetPathName 678
    GetReadOnlyPref 679
    GetStartPosition 679

CFileDialog class *(continued)*
   member functions *(continued)*
      OnFileNameOK 679
      OnLBSelChangedNotify 680
      OnShareViolation 680
CFileDialog member function, CFileDialog class 675
CFileException class
   data members
      m_cause 685
      m_lOsError 686
   described 682
   member functions
      CFileException 683
      ErrnoToException 683
      OsErrorToException 684
      ThrowErrno 684
      ThrowOsError 684
CFileException member function, CFileException class 683
CFindReplaceDialog class
   data members, m_fr 693
   described 687
   member functions
      CFindReplaceDialog 689
      Create 689
      FindNext 690
      GetFindString 690
      GetNotifier 691
      GetReplaceString 691
      IsTerminating 691
      MatchCase 692
      MatchWholeWord 692
      ReplaceAll 692
      ReplaceCurrent 693
      SearchDown 693
CFindReplaceDialog member function, CFindReplaceDialog class 689
CFont class
   described 694
   member functions
      CFont 695
      CreateFont 695
      CreateFontIndirect 699
      CreatePointFont 700–701
      FromHandle 701
      GetLogFont 702
      operator HFONT 702
CFont member function, CFont class 695

CFontDialog class
   data members, m_cf 708
   described 703
   member functions
      CFontDialog 704
      DoModal 705
      GetColor 705
      GetCurrentFont 706
      GetFaceName 706
      GetSize 706
      GetStyleName 707
      GetWeight 707
      IsBold 707
      IsItalic 707
      IsStrikeOut 708
      IsUnderline 708
CFontDialog member function, CFontDialog class 704
CFontHolder class
   data members, m_pFont 712
   described 709
   member functions
      CFontHolder 709
      GetDisplayString 710
      GetFontDispatch 710
      GetFontHandle 710
      InitializeFont 711
      ReleaseFont 711
      Select 712
      SetFont 712
CFontHolder member function, CFontHolder class 709
CFormView class
   described 713
   member functions, CFormView 716
CFormView member function, CFormView class 716
CFrameWnd class
   data members, m_bAutoMenuEnable 735
   described 717
   member functions
      ActivateFrame 721
      BeginModalState 721
      CFrameWnd 721
      CreateView 723
      DockControlBar 723
      EnableDocking 724
      EndModalState 724
      FloatControlBar 724
      GetActiveDocument 725
      GetActiveFrame 726
      GetActiveView 726

CFrameWnd class *(continued)*
  member functions *(continued)*
    GetControlBar 726
    GetDockState 727
    GetMessageBar 727
    GetMessageString 727
    InitialUpdateFrame 727
    InModalState 728
    IsTracking 728
    LoadAccelTable 728
    LoadBarState 729
    LoadFrame 729
    NegotiateBorderSpace 730
    OnContextHelp 731
    OnCreateClient 731
    OnSetPreviewMode 732
    RecalcLayout 732
    rectDefault 735
    SaveBarState 733
    SetActiveView 733
    SetDockState 733
    SetMessageText 734
    ShowControlBar 734
    ShowOwnedWindows 734
CFrameWnd member function, CFrameWnd class 721
CGdiObject class
  data members, m_hObject 743
  described 736
  member functions
    Attach 737
    CGdiObject 737
    CreateStockObject 737
    DeleteObject 739
    DeleteTempMap 739
    Detach 739
    FromHandle 740
    GetObject 740
    GetObjectType 741
    GetSafeHandle 742
    UnrealizeObject 742
CGdiObject member function, CGdiObject class 737
Change notifications, in-place editing 1247
ChangeClipboardChain member function, CWnd
  class 1868
ChangeType member function, ColeVariant class 1288
CharFromPos member function, CEdit class 615
CharToItem member function, CListBox class 784

CHeaderCtrl class
  described 744
  member functions
    CHeaderCtrl 745
    Create 745
    DeleteItem 747
    DrawItem 747
    GetItem 747
    GetItemCount 749
    InsertItem 749
    Layout 749
    SetItem 750
CHeaderCtrl constructor 745
CHeaderCtrl member function, CHeaderCtrl class 745
CheckButton member function, CToolBarCtrl
  class 1702
CheckDlgButton member function, CWnd class 1869
CheckMenuItem member function, CMenu class 898
CheckMenuRadioItem member function, CMenu
  class 898
Checkpoint member function, CMemoryState
  class 890
CheckRadioButton member function, CWnd
  class 1869
ChildWindowFromPoint member function, CWnd
  class 1870
Chord member function, CDC class 434
CHotKeyCtrl class
  described 751
  member functions
    CHotKeyCtrl 752
    Create 752
    GetHotKey 753
    SetHotKey 753
    SetRules 754
CHotKeyCtrl constructor 752
CHotKeyCtrl member function, CHotKeyCtrl
  class 752
CImageList class
  data members, m_hImageList 768
  described 755
  member functions
    Add 756
    Attach 757
    BeginDrag 757
    CImageList 758
    Create 758
    DeleteObject 759
    Detach 759

CImageList class *(continued)*
  member functions *(continued)*
    DragEnter 759
    DragLeave 760
    DragMove 760
    DragShowNolock 761
    Draw 761
    EndDrag 762
    ExtractIcon 762
    GetBkColor 763
    GetDragImage 763
    GetImageCount 763
    GetImageInfo 764
    GetSafeHandle 764
    Read 765
    Remove 765
    Replace 765
    SetBkColor 766
    SetDragCursorImage 766
    SetOverlayImage 767
    Write 767
CImageList constructor 758
CImageList member function, CImageList class 758
Class design philosophy 2
Class factories and licensing 2069
Class Library Reference, overview xi
Class Overview class 1
Classes
  See also specific class
  document/view, listed 7
  hierarchy charts xi
ClassWizard comment
  AFX_DATA_INIT 2203
  AFX_DATA_MAP 2203
  AFX_DATA 2203
  AFX_DISP_MAP 2204
  AFX_DISP 2204
  AFX_EVENT_MAP 2205
  AFX_EVENT 2204
  AFX_FIELD_INIT 2205
  AFX_FIELD_MAP 2206
  AFX_FIELD 2205
  AFX_MSG_MAP 2206
  AFX_MSG 2206
  AFX_VIRTUAL 2207
ClassWizard comment delimiters 2202
Clear member function
  CComboBox class 168
  CEdit class 615

Clear member function *(continued)*
  COleVariant 1289
  CRichEditCtrl class 1464
ClearSel member function, CSliderCtrl class 1543
ClearTics member function, CSliderCtrl class 1544
ClientToScreen member function, CWnd class 1870
Clipboard
  determining owner 1112
  emptying 1111
  formats 1258
  providing data 1115
CList class
  described 769
  member functions
    AddHead 770
    AddTail 771
    Find 771
    FindIndex 772
    GetAt 772
    GetCount 773
    GetHead 773
    GetHeadPosition 773
    GetNext 774
    GetPrev 774
    GetTail 775
    GetTailPosition 776
    InsertAfter 776
    InsertBefore 776
    IsEmpty 777
    RemoveAll 777
    RemoveAt 777
    RemoveHead 778
    RemoveTail 778
    SetAt 778
CListBox class
  described 780
  member functions
    AddString 784
    CharToItem 784
    CListBox 785
    CompareItem 785
    Create 786
    DeleteItem 787
    DeleteString 787
    Dir 788
    DrawItem 788
    FindString 789
    FindStringExact 789
    GetAnchorIndex 790

CListBox class *(continued)*
  member functions *(continued)*
    GetCaretIndex 790
    GetCount 791
    GetCurSel 791
    GetHorizontalExtent 791
    GetItemData 792
    GetItemDataPtr 792
    GetItemHeight 792
    GetItemRect 793
    GetLocale 793
    GetSel 794
    GetSelCount 794
    GetSelItems 794
    GetText 795
    GetTextLen 795
    GetTopIndex 796
    InitStorage 796
    InsertString 797
    ItemFromPoint 797
    MeasureItem 797
    ResetContent 798
    SelectString 798
    SelItemRange 799
    SetAnchorIndex 799
    SetCaretIndex 800
    SetColumnWidth 800
    SetCurSel 800
    SetHorizontalExtent 801
    SetItemData 801
    SetItemDataPtr 802
    SetItemHeight 802
    SetLocale 803
    SetSel 803
    SetTabStops 803
    SetTopIndex 804
    VKeyToItem 805
CListBox member function, CListBox class 785
CListCtrl class
  described 806
  member functions
    Arrange 810
    CListCtrl 811
    Create 811
    CreateDragImage 813
    DeleteAllItems 813
    DeleteColumn 813
    DeleteItem 814
    DrawItem 814

CListCtrl class *(continued)*
  member functions *(continued)*
    EditLabel 815
    EnsureVisible 815
    FindItem 815
    GetBkColor 816
    GetCallbackMask 817
    GetColumn 817
    GetColumnWidth 818
    GetCountPerPage 819
    GetEditControl 819
    GetImageList 819
    GetItem 820
    GetItemCount 821
    GetItemData 821
    GetItemPosition 822
    GetItemRect 822
    GetItemState 823
    GetItemText 823
    GetNextItem 824
    GetOrigin 825
    GetSelectedCount 825
    GetStringWidth 825
    GetTextBkColor 826
    GetTextColor 826
    GetTopIndex 826
    GetViewRect 826
    HitTest 827
    InsertColumn 828
    InsertItem 829
    RedrawItems 830
    Scroll 830
    SetBkColor 830
    SetCallbackMask 831
    SetColumn 831
    SetColumnWidth 832
    SetImageList 832
    SetItem 832
    SetItemCount 833
    SetItemData 834
    SetItemPosition 834
    SetItemState 835
    SetItemText 835
    SetTextBkColor 836
    SetTextColor 836
    SortItems 836
    Update 837
CListCtrl constructor 811
CListCtrl member function, CListCtrl class 811

CListView class
    described 838
    member functions
        CListView 838
        GetListCtrl 839
CListView constructor 838
CListView member function, CListView class 838
CLongBinary class
    Binary Large Object 840
    BLOB 840
    data handle 841
    data length 841
    data members
        m_dwDataLength 841
        m_hData 841
    described 840
    DFX field exchange 2154
    Large data objects 840
    member functions, CLongBinary 841
    RFX field exchange 2194
CLongBinary constructor 841
CLongBinary member function, CLongBinary
    class 841
Close member function
    CAnimateCtrl class 34
    CArchive class 41
    CAsyncSocket class 74
    CDaoDatabase class 220
    CDaoQueryDef class 255
    CDaoRecordset class 282
    CDaoTableDef class 349
    CDaoWorkspace class 375
    CDatabase class 397
    CFile class 659
    CMetaFileDC class 918
    COleClientItem class 990
    CRecordset class 1384
CloseAllDocuments member function
    CDocTemplate class 569
    CWinApp class 1799
CloseEnhanced member function, CMetaFileDC
    class 919
CloseFigure member function, CDC class 435
Closing
    CDatabase objects 397
    database objects 220
    Recordset 1384
    workspaces, DAO 375

CMap class
    described 842
    member functions
        CMap 843
        GetCount 843
        GetHashTableSize 844
        GetNextAssoc 844
        GetStartPosition 845
        InitHashTable 845
        IsEmpty 845
        Lookup 846
        operator [ ] 847
        RemoveAll 846
        RemoveKey 846
        SetAt 847
CMap member function, CMap class 843
CMapPtrToPtr class 849
CMapPtrToWord class 851
CMapStringToOb class
    described 853
    member functions
        CMapStringToOb 854
        GetCount 854
        GetNextAssoc 855
        GetStartPosition 856
        IsEmpty 856
        Lookup 857
        operator [ ] 860
        RemoveAll 857
        RemoveKey 858
        SetAt 859
CMapStringToOb member function, CMapStringToOb
    class 854
CMapStringToPtr class 861
CMapStringToString class 863
CMapWordToOb class 865
CMapWordToPtr class 867
CMDIChildWnd class
    described 869
    member functions
        CMDIChildWnd 871
        Create 871
        GetMDIFrame 872
        MDIActivate 872
        MDIDestroy 873
        MDIMaximize 873
        MDIRestore 873
CMDIChildWnd member function, CMDIChildWnd
    class 871

CMDIFrameWnd class
  described 874
  member functions
    CMDIFrameWnd 876
    CreateClient 876
    GetWindowMenuPopup 877
    MDIActivate 877
    MDICascade 878
    MDIGetActive 878
    MDIIconArrange 879
    MDIMaximize 879
    MDINext 879
    MDIRestore 880
    MDISetMenu 880
    MDITile 881
CMDIFrameWnd member function, CMDIFrameWnd
  class 876
CMemFile class
  described 882
  member functions
    Alloc 883
    Attach 883
    CMemFile 884
    Detach 885
    Free 885
    GrowFile 885
    Memcpy 886
    Realloc 886
CMemFile member function, CMemFile class 884
CMemoryException class
  described 888
  member functions, CMemoryException 888
CMemoryException member function,
  CMemoryException class 888
CMemoryState class
  described 889–890
  member functions
    Checkpoint 890
    CMemoryState 890
    Difference 891
    DumpAllObjectsSince 891
    DumpStatistics 892
CMemoryState member function, CMemoryState
  class 890
CMenu class
  data members, m_hMenu 916
  described 893

CMenu class *(continued)*
  member functions
    AppendMenu 895
    Attach 897
    CheckMenuItem 898
    CheckMenuRadioItem 898
    CMenu 899
    CreateMenu 899
    CreatePopupMenu 900
    DeleteMenu 900
    DeleteTempMap 901
    DestroyMenu 901
    Detach 902
    DrawItem 902
    EnableMenuItem 902
    FromHandle 903
    GetMenuContextHelpId 904
    GetMenuItemCount 904
    GetMenuItemID 904
    GetMenuState 905
    GetMenuString 906
    GetSafeHmenu 907
    GetSubMenu 907
    InsertMenu 907
    LoadMenu 909
    LoadMenuIndirect 910
    MeasureItem 911
    ModifyMenu 911
    RemoveMenu 912
    SetMenuContextHelpId 913
    SetMenuItemBitmaps 913
    TrackPopupMenu 914
CMenu member function, CMenu class 899
CMetaFileDC class
  described 917
  member functions
    Close 918
    CloseEnhanced 919
    CMetaFileDC 919
    Create 920
    CreateEnhanced 920
CMetaFileDC member function, CMetaFileDC
  class 919
CMiniFrameWnd class
  described 922
  member functions
    CMiniFrameWnd 922
    Create 923
CMiniFrameWnd constructor 922

CMiniFrameWnd member function, CMiniFrameWnd class 922
CMultiDocTemplate class
 described 924
 member functions, CMultiDocTemplate 925
CMultiDocTemplate member function, CMultiDocTemplate class 925
CMultiLock class
 described 927
 member functions
  CMultiLock 928
  IsLocked 928
  Lock 928
  Unlock 929
CMultiLock constructor 928
CMultiLock member function, CMultiLock class 928
CMutex class
 described 931
 member functions, CMutex 932
CMutex constructor 932
CMutex member function, CMutex class 932
CNotSupportedException class
 described 933
 member functions 933
CNotSupportedException member function, CNotSupportedException class 933
CObArray class
 described 934
 member functions
  Add 935
  CObArray 936
  ElementAt 936
  FreeExtra 937
  GetAt 937
  GetSize 938
  GetUpperBound 938
  InsertAt 938
  operator [ ] 943
  RemoveAll 939
  RemoveAt 940
  SetAt 941
  SetAtGrow 942
  SetSize 942
CObArray member function, CObArray class 936
CObject class
 described 944
 member functions
  AssertValid 945
  CObject 946

CObject class (continued)
 member functions (continued)
  Dump 946
  GetRuntimeClass 947
  IsKindOf 948
  IsSerializable 948
  operator = 950
  operator delete 950
  operator new 950
  Serialize 949
CObject member function, CObject class 946
CObList class
 described 952
 member functions
  AddHead 954
  AddTail 954
  CObList 955
  Find 956
  FindIndex 957
  GetAt 957
  GetCount 958
  GetHead 958
  GetHeadPosition 959
  GetNext 960
  GetPrev 961
  GetTail 962
  GetTailPosition 962
  InsertAfter 963
  InsertBefore 964
  IsEmpty 964
  RemoveAll 965
  RemoveAt 965
  RemoveHead 966
  RemoveTail 967
  SetAt 967
CObList member function, CObList class 955
COleBusyDialog class
 data members, m_bz 972
 described 969–970
 member functions
  COleBusyDialog 970
  DoModal 970
  GetSelectionType 971
COleBusyDialog constructor 970
COleBusyDialog member function, COleBusyDialog class 970
COleChangeIconDialog class
 data members, m_ci 976
 described 973

COleChangeIconDialog class *(continued)*
  member functions
    COleChangeIconDialog 974
    DoChangeIcon 974
    DoModal 975
    GetIconicMetafile 975
COleChangeIconDialog constructor 974
COleChangeIconDialog member function, COleChangeIconDialog class 974
COleChangeSourceDialog class
  data members
    described 981
    m_cs 981
  described 977
  member functions
    COleChangeSourceDialog 978
    described 978
    DoModal 978
    GetDisplayName 979
    GetFileName 979
    GetFromPrefix 979
    GetItemName 980
    GetToPrefix 980
    IsValidSource 981
COleChangeSourceDialog constructor 978
COleChangeSourceDialog member function, COleChangeSourceDialog class 978
COleClientItem class 1239
  described 982
  member functions
    Activate 986
    ActivateAs 987
    AttachDataObject 988
    CanActivate 988
    CanCreateFromData 988
    CanCreateLinkFromData 989
    CanPaste 989
    CanPasteLink 990
    Close 990
    COleClientItem 991
    ConvertTo 991
    CopyToClipboard 992
    CreateCloneFrom 992
    CreateFromClipboard 992
    CreateFromData 993
    CreateFromFile 994
    CreateLinkFromClipboard 995
    CreateLinkFromData 995
    CreateLinkFromFile 996

COleClientItem class 1239 *(continued)*
  member functions *(continued)*
    CreateNewItem 997
    CreateStaticFromClipboard 998
    CreateStaticFromData 998
    Deactivate 999
    DeactivateUI 1000
    Delete 1000
    DoDragDrop 1000
    DoVerb 1001
    Draw 1002
    GetActiveView 1003
    GetCachedExtent 1003
    GetClassID 1004
    GetClipboardData 1004
    GetDocument 1005
    GetDrawAspect 1005
    GetExtent 1005
    GetIconicMetafile 1006
    GetInPlaceWindow 1006
    GetItemState 1007
    GetLastStatus 1007
    GetLinkUpdateOptions 1007
    GetType 1008
    GetUserType 1008
    IsInPlaceActive 1009
    IsLinkUpToDate 1009
    IsModified 1010
    IsOpen 1010
    IsRunning 1010
    OnActivate 1011
    OnActivateUI 1011
    OnChange 1011
    OnChangeItemPosition 1012
    OnDeactivate 1013
    OnDeactivateAndUndo 1013
    OnDeactivateUI 1014
    OnDiscardUndoState 1014
    OnGetClipboardData 1014
    OnGetClipRect 1015
    OnGetItemPosition 1015
    OnGetWindowContext 1016
    OnInsertMenus 1016
    OnRemoveMenus 1017
    OnScrollBy 1018
    OnSetMenu 1018
    OnShowControlBars 1019
    OnShowItem 1019
    OnUpdateFrameTitle 1020

COleClientItem class 1239 *(continued)*
   member functions *(continued)*
      ReactivateAndUndo 1020
      Release 1020
      Reload 1021
      Run 1021
      SetDrawAspect 1021
      SetExtent 1022
      SetHostNames 1022
      SetIconicMetafile 1023
      SetItemRects 1023
      SetLinkUpdateOptions 1024
      SetPrintDevice 1024
      UpdateLink 1025
COleClientItem constructor 991
COleClientItem member function, COleClientItem
  class 991
COleControl class
   described 1026
   member functions
      AmbientBackColor 1031
      AmbientDisplayName 1032
      AmbientFont 1032
      AmbientForeColor 1032
      AmbientLocaleID 1033
      AmbientScaleUnits 1033
      AmbientShowGrabHandles 1033
      AmbientShowHatching 1034
      AmbientTextAlign 1034
      AmbientUIDead 1034
      AmbientUserMode 1035
      BoundPropertyChanged 1035
      BoundPropertyRequestEdit 1035
      COleControl 1036
      ControlInfoChanged 1036
      DisplayError 1036
      DoClick 1037
      DoPropExchange 1037
      DoSuperClassPaint 1038
      DrawContent 1038
      DrawMetaFile 1038
      EnableSimpleFrame 1039
      ExchangeExtent 1039
      ExchangeStockProps 1039
      ExchangeVersion 1040
      FireClick 1040
      FireDblClick 1041
      FireError 1041
      FireEvent 1041

COleControl class *(continued)*
   member functions *(continued)*
      FireKeyDown 1042
      FireKeyPress 1043
      FireKeyUp 1043
      FireMouseDown 1044
      FireMouseMove 1045
      FireMouseUp 1045
      GetAmbientProperty 1046
      GetBackColor 1047
      GetBorderStyle 1047
      GetClassID 1048
      GetControlSize 1048
      GetEnabled 1048
      GetExtendedControl 1049
      GetFont 1049
      GetFontTextMetrics 1049
      GetForeColor 1050
      GetHwnd 1050
      GetMessageString 1050
      GetNotSupported 1051
      GetRectInContainer 1051
      GetStockTextMetrics 1051
      GetText 1052
      InitializeIIDs 1052
      InternalGetFont 1052
      InternalGetText 1053
      InvalidateControl 1053
      IsConvertingVBX 1053
      IsModified 1054
      IsSubclassedControl 1054
      LockInPlaceActive 1055
      OnAmbientPropertyChange 1055
      OnBackColorChanged 1055
      OnBorderStyleChanged 1056
      OnClick 1056
      OnDoVerb 1056
      OnDraw 1057
      OnDrawMetafile 1057
      OnEdit 1058
      OnEnabledChanged 1058
      OnEnumVerbs 1058
      OnEventAdvise 1059
      OnFontChanged 1059
      OnForeColorChanged 1059
      OnFreezeEvents 1060
      OnGetColorSet 1060
      OnGetControlInfo 1061
      OnGetDisplayString 1061

COleControl class *(continued)*
member functions *(continued)*
OnGetInPlaceMenu 1061
OnGetPredefinedStrings 1062
OnGetPredefinedValue 1062
OnHideToolbars 1063
OnKeyDownEvent 1063
OnKeyPressEvent 1064
OnKeyUpEvent 1064
OnMapPropertyToPage 1064
OnMnemonic 1065
OnProperties 1065
OnRenderData 1065
OnRenderFileData 1066
OnRenderGlobalData 1067
OnResetState 1068
OnSetClientSite 1068
OnSetData 1068
OnSetExtent 1069
OnSetObjectRects 1069
OnShowToolbars 1070
OnTextChanged 1070
PostModalDialog 1071
PreModalDialog 1070
RecreateControlWindow 1071
Refresh 1071
SelectFontObject 1071
SelectStockFont 1072
SetBackColor 1072
SetBorderStyle 1072
SetControlSize 1073
SetEnabled 1073
SetFont 1073
SetForeColor 1074
SetInitialDataFormats 1074
SetInitialSize 1074
SetModifiedFlag 1075
SetNotPermitted 1075
SetNotSupported 1075
SetRectInContainer 1075
SetText 1076
ThrowError 1076
TransformCoords 1077
TranslateColor 1077
WillAmbientsBeValidDuringLoad 1078
COleControl member function, COleControl
class 1036
COleControlModule class 1079

COleConvertDialog class
data members, m_cv 1085
described 1080
member functions
COleConvertDialog 1081
DoConvert 1082
DoModal 1082
GetClassID 1083
GetDrawAspect 1083
GetIconicMetafile 1084
GetSelectionType 1084
COleConvertDialog constructor 1081
COleConvertDialog member function,
COleConvertDialog class 1081
COleCurrency
data members
described 1096
m_cur 1096
m_status 1096
member functions
COleCurrency 1087
Constructor 1087
described 1087
Format 1088
GetStatus 1089
operator + 1093
operator - 1093
ParseCurrency 1090
SetCurrency 1091
SetStatus 1091
operators
Archive 1096
described 1092
Dump 1096
operator != 1095
operator *= 1094
operator * 1094
operator += 1093
operator /= 1094
operator / 1094
operator << 1096
operator <= 1095
operator < 1095
operator == 1095
operator = 1092–1093
operator >= 1095
operator >> 1096
operator > 1095

COleCurrency *(continued)*
   operators *(continued)*
      operator CURRENCY 1095
      Relational 1095
COleCurrency class 1086
COleCurrency data, DFX field exchange 2150
COleCurrency member function, COleCurrency
  class 1087
COleDataObject class
  described 1098
  member functions
     Attach 1099
     AttachClipboard 1099
     BeginEnumFormats 1100
     COleDataObject 1100
     Detach 1100
     GetData 1101
     GetFileData 1101
     GetGlobalData 1102
     GetNextFormat 1103
     IsDataAvailable 1103
     Release 1104
COleDataObject constructor 1100
COleDataObject member function, COleDataObject
  class 1100
COleDataSource class
  described 1105, 1258
  member functions
     CacheData 1106
     CacheGlobalData 1107
     COleDataSource 1108
     DelayRenderData 1108
     DelayRenderFileData 1109
     DelaySetData 1109
     DoDragDrop 1110
     Empty 1111
     FlushClipboard 1111
     GetClipboardOwner 1112
     OnRenderData 1112
     OnRenderFileData 1113
     OnRenderGlobalData 1114
     OnSetData 1114
     SetClipboard 1115
COleDataSource constructor 1108
COleDataSource member function, COleDataSource
  class 1108

COleDateTime class
  data members
     m_dt 1137
     m_status 1138
  described 1116
  member functions
     COleDateTime 1118
     Constructor 1118
     described 1118
     Format 1119
     GetCurrentTime 1121
     GetDay 1121
     GetDayOfWeek 1122
     GetDayOfYear 1122
     GetHour 1123
     GetMinute 1124
     GetMonth 1124
     GetSecond 1125
     GetStatus 1126
     GetYear 1127
     ParseDateTime 1127
     SetDate 1128
     SetDateTime 1130
     SetStatus 1132
     SetTime 1132
  operators
     Archive 1137
     Dump 1137
     operator != 1136
     operator += 1135
     operator + 1135
     operator - 1135
     operator << 1137
     operator <= 1136
     operator < 1136
     operator == 1136
     operator = 1134–1135
     operator >= 1136
     operator >> 1137
     operator > 1136
     operator DATE 1136
     relational 1136
COleDateTime data, DFX field exchange 2151
COleDateTime member function, COleDateTime
  class 1118
COleDateTimeSpan
  data members
     m_span 1152
     m_status 1153

COleDateTimeSpan *(continued)*
  member functions
    COleDateTimeSpan 1141
    Constructor 1141
    described 1141
    Format 1142
    GetDays 1143
    GetHours 1143
    GetMinutes 1144
    GetSeconds 1145
    GetStatus 1145
    GetTotalDays 1146
    GetTotalHours 1147
    GetTotalMinutes 1147
    GetTotalSeconds 1148
    SetDateTimeSpan 1148
    SetStatus 1149
  operators
    Archive 1152
    Dump 1152
    operator != 1151
    operator += 1151
    operator + 1150
    operator - 1150
    operator << 1152
    operator <= 1151
    operator < 1151
    operator == 1151
    operator = 1150–1151
    operator >= 1151
    operator >> 1152
    operator > 1151
    operator double 1151
    relational 1151
COleDateTimeSpan class 1140
COleDateTimeSpan member function, COleDateTimeSpan class 1141
COleDialog class
  described 1154
  member functions, GetLastError 1155
COleDispatchDriver class
  data members
    m_bAutoRelease 1162
    m_lpDispatch 1162
  described 1156
  member functions
    AttachDispatch 1157
    COleDispatchDriver 1157
    CreateDispatch 1157

COleDispatchDriver class *(continued)*
  member functions *(continued)*
    DetachDispatch 1158
    GetProperty 1158
    InvokeHelper 1159
    ReleaseDispatch 1161
    SetProperty 1161
COleDispatchDriver constructor 1157
COleDispatchDriver member function, COleDispatchDriver class 1157
COleDispatchException class
  data members
    m_dwHelpContext 1164
    m_strDescription 1164
    m_strHelpFile 1164
    m_strSource 1164
    m_wCode 1165
  described 1163
COleDocument class
  described 1166
  member functions
    AddItem 1167
    ApplyPrintDevice 1168
    COleDocument 1169
    EnableCompoundFile 1169
    GetInPlaceActiveItem 1169
    GetNextClientItem 1170
    GetNextItem 1170
    GetNextServerItem 1171
    GetPrimarySelectedItem 1172
    GetStartPosition 1172
    HasBlankItems 1172
    OnFileSendMail 1173
    OnShowViews 1173
    RemoveItem 1173
    UpdateModifiedFlag 1174
COleDocument constructor 1169
COleDocument member function, COleDocument class 1169
COleDropSource class
  described 1175
  member functions
    COleDropSource 1176
    GiveFeedback 1176
    OnBeginDrag 1177
    QueryContinueDrag 1177
COleDropSource constructor 1176
COleDropSource member function, COleDropSource class 1176

COleDropTarget class
  described 1179
  member functions
    COleDropTarget 1180
    OnDragEnter 1180
    OnDragLeave 1181
    OnDragOver 1181
    OnDragScroll 1182
    OnDrop 1183
    OnDropEx 1184
    Register 1185
    Revoke 1185
COleDropTarget constructor 1180
COleDropTarget member function, COleDropTarget
  class 1180
COleException class
  data members, m_sc 1187
  described 1186
  member functions, process 1186
COleInsertDialog class
  data members, m_io 1193
  described 1188
  member functions
    COleInsertDialog 1189
    CreateItem 1190
    DoModal 1190
    GetClassID 1191
    GetDrawAspect 1191
    GetIconicMetafile 1192
    GetPathName 1192
    GetSelectionType 1192
COleInsertDialog constructor 1189
COleInsertDialog member function, COleInsertDialog
  class 1189
COleIPFrameWnd class
  described 1194
  member functions
    COleIPFrameWnd 1194
    OnCreateControlBars 1195
    RepositionFrame 1195
COleIPFrameWnd constructor 1194
COleIPFrameWnd member function,
  COleIPFrameWnd class 1194
COleLinkingDoc class
  described 1197
  member functions
    COleLinkingDoc 1198
    OnFindEmbeddedItem 1199
    OnGetLinkedItem 1199

COleLinkingDoc class (continued)
  member functions (continued)
    Register 1200
    Revoke 1200
COleLinkingDoc constructor 1198
COleLinkingDoc member function, COleLinkingDoc
  class 1198
COleLinksDialog class
  data members, m_el 1203
  described 1201
  member functions
    COleLinksDialog 1202
    DoModal 1202
COleLinksDialog constructor 1202
COleLinksDialog member function, COleLinksDialog
  class 1202
COleMessageFilter class
  described 1204
  member functions
    BeginBusyState 1205
    COleMessageFilter 1206
    EnableBusyDialog 1206
    EnableNotRespondingDialog 1206
    EndBusyState 1207
    OnMessagePending 1207
    Register 1208
    Revoke 1208
    SetBusyReply 1208
    SetMessagePendingDelay 1209
    SetRetryReply 1209
COleMessageFilter constructor 1206
COleMessageFilter member function,
  COleMessageFilter class 1206
COleObjectFactory class
  described 1211
  member functions
    COleObjectFactory 1212
    GetClassID 1213
    IsRegistered 1213
    OnCreateObject 1214
    Register 1214
    RegisterAll 1214
    Revoke 1215
    RevokeAll 1215
    UpdateRegistry 1215
    UpdateRegistryAll 1216
    VerifyUserLicense 1217
COleObjectFactory constructor 1212

COleObjectFactory member function,
    ColeObjectFactory class 1212
COleObjectFactoryEx class
    member functions
        GetLicenseKey 1213
        VerifyLicenseKey 1216
COlePasteSpecialDialog class
    data members, m_ps 1224
    described 1218
    member functions
        AddFormat 1219
        AddStandardFormats 1220
        COlePasteSpecialDialog 1220
        CreateItem 1221
        DoModal 1222
        GetDrawAspect 1222
        GetIconicMetafile 1223
        GetPasteIndex 1223
        GetSelectionType 1223
COlePasteSpecialDialog constructor 1220
COlePasteSpecialDialog member function,
    COlePasteSpecialDialog class 1220
COlePropertiesDialog class
    data members
        m_gp 1228
        m_lp 1228
        m_op 1229
        m_psh 1229
        m_vp 1229
    described 1225
    member functions
        COlePropertiesDialog 1226
        DoModal 1227
        OnApplyScale 1227
COlePropertiesDialog member function,
    COlePropertiesDialog class 1226
COlePropertyPage class
    described 1230
    member functions
        COlePropertyPage 1231
        GetControlStatus 1231
        GetObjectArray 1232
        GetPageSite 1232
        IgnoreApply 1233
        IsModified 1233
        OnEditProperty 1233
        OnHelp 1234
        OnInitDialog 1234
        OnObjectsChanged 1234

COlePropertyPage class *(continued)*
    member functions *(continued)*
        OnSetPageSite 1235
        SetControlStatus 1235
        SetDialogResource 1235
        SetHelpInfo 1236
        SetModifiedFlag 1236
        SetPageName 1236
COlePropertyPage member function,
    COlePropertyPage class 1231
COleResizeBar class
    described 1237
    member functions
        COleResizeBar 1238
        Create 1237
COleResizeBar constructor 1238
COleResizeBar member function, COleResizeBar
    class 1238
COleServerDoc class
    described 1239
    member functions
        ActivateInPlace 1242
        COleServerDoc 1242
        CreateInPlaceFrame 1243
        DeactivateAndUndo 1242
        DestroyInPlaceFrame 1243
        DiscardUndoState 1244
        GetEmbeddedItem 1244
        GetItemClipRect 1244
        GetItemPosition 1245
        GetZoomFactor 1245
        IsEmbedded 1246
        IsInPlaceActive 1246
        NotifyChanged 1247
        NotifyClosed 1247
        NotifyRename 1247
        NotifySaved 1248
        OnClose 1248
        OnDeactivate 1249
        OnDeactivateUI 1249
        OnDocWindowActivate 1249
        OnFrameWindowActivate 1250
        OnGetEmbeddedItem 1250
        OnReactivateAndUndo 1250
        OnResizeBorder 1251
        OnSetHostNames 1251
        OnSetItemRects 1252
        OnShowControlBars 1252
        OnShowDocument 1253

COleServerDoc class *(continued)*
    member functions *(continued)*
        OnUpdateDocument 1253
        RequestPositionChange 1254
        SaveEmbedding 1254
        ScrollContainerBy 1254
        UpdateAllItems 1255
COleServerDoc constructor 1242
COleServerDoc member function, COleServerDoc
  class 1242
COleServerItem class 1239
  data members, m_sizeExtent 1276
  described 1256
  member functions
    AddOtherClipboardData 1258
    COleServerItem 1258
    CopyToClipboard 1259
    DoDragDrop 1259
    GetClipboardData 1260
    GetDataSource 1261
    GetDocument 1261
    GetEmbedSourceData 1261
    GetItemName 1262
    GetLinkSourceData 1262
    GetObjectDescriptorData 1263
    IsConnected 1263
    IsLinkedItem 1264
    NotifyChanged 1264
    OnDoVerb 1265
    OnDraw 1265
    OnDrawEx 1266
    OnGetClipboardData 1267
    OnGetExtent 1267
    OnHide 1268
    OnInitFromData 1268
    OnOpen 1269
    OnQueryUpdateItems 1269
    OnRenderData 1270
    OnRenderFileData 1271
    OnRenderGlobalData 1271
    OnSetColorScheme 1272
    OnSetData 1273
    OnSetExtent 1273
    OnShow 1274
    OnUpdate 1274
    OnUpdateItems 1275
    SetItemName 1275
COleServerItem constructor 1258

COleServerItem member function, COleServerItem
  class 1258
COleStreamFile class
  described 1277
  member functions
    Attach 1278
    COleStreamFile 1278
    CreateMemoryStream 1278
    CreateStream 1279
    Detach 1279
    OpenStream 1280
COleStreamFile constructor 1278
COleStreamFile member function, COleStreamFile
  class 1278
COleTemplateServer class
  described 1281
  member functions
    COleTemplateServer 1282
    ConnectTemplate 1282
    UpdateRegistry 1282
COleTemplateServer constructor 1282
COleTemplateServer member function,
  COleTemplateServer class 1282
COleUpdateDialog class
  described 1284
  member functions
    COleUpdateDialog 1284
    DoModal 1285
COleUpdateDialog constructor 1284
COleUpdateDialog member function,
  COleUpdateDialog class 1284
COleVariant class
  described 1286
  member functions
    ChangeType 1288
    Clear 1289
    COleVariant 1287
    Constructor 1287
    described 1287
    Detach 1289
  operators
    Archive 1291
    Assignment 1289
    described 1289
    Dump 1291
    operator << 1291
    operator == 1290
    operator = 1289
    operator >> 1291

COleVariant class *(continued)*
 operators *(continued)*
  operator LPCVARIANT 1291
  operator LPVARIANT 1291
COleVariant member function, COleVariant 1287
Collate member function, CString class 1617
Collating order, specifying 221
Collection class helpers 2058
Collection classes
 arrays
  CByteArray 136
  CDWordArray 609
  CObArray 934
 CByteArray 136
 CDWordArray 609
 CMap 842
 CMapPtrToPtr 849
 CMapPtrToWord 851
 CMapStringToOb 853
 CMapStringToPtr 861
 CMapStringToString 863
 CMapWordToOb 865
 CMapWordToPtr 867
 CObArray 934
 listed 19
 maps
  CCMapStringToPtr 861
  CMapPtrToPtr 849
  CMapPtrToWord 851
  CMapStringToOb 853
  CMapStringToString 863
  CMapWordToOb 865
  CMapWordToPtr 867
 storing aggregate data 136, 609, 849, 851, 853,
  861, 863, 865, 867, 934
 template-based
  CArray 58
  CList 769
  CTypedPtrArray 1754
  CTypedPtrList 1757
  CTypedPtrMap 1763
Collections (DAO)
 QueryDefs 217
 Recordsets 217
 Relations 217
 TableDefs 217
 where stored in MFC 217
COLORADJUSTMENT structure 2236
CombineRgn member function, CRgn class 1446

Combo box
 DDX field exchange 2111, 2126, 2128
Combo-Box styles 2271
Command IDs 2057
Command-related classes, listed 6
CommandToIndex member function
 CStatusBar class 1596
 CToolBar class 1682
 CToolBarCtrl class 1703
Committing
 database transactions 397
 transactions (DAO) 376
CommitTrans member function
 CDaoWorkspace class 376
 CDatabase class 397
Common controls
 Rich Edit, MFC Encapsulation 1461
 Windows
  CAnimateCtrl 33
  CHeaderCtrl 744
  CHotKeyCtrl 751
  CImageList 755
  CListCtrl 806
  CProgressCtrl 1346
  CRichEditCtrl 1461
  CSliderCtrl 1542
  CSpinButtonCtrl 1562
  CStatusBarCtrl 1602
  CTabCtrl 1647
  CToolBarCtrl 1691
  CToolTipCtrl 1719
  CTreeCtrl 1727
Compacting databases 377
Compare member function, CString class 1618
CompareElements global function/macro 2111
CompareItem member function
 CComboBox class 169
 CListBox class 785
COMPAREITEMSTRUCT structure 2238
CompareNoCase member function, CString class 1618
Comparison operators member function
 CString class 1639
 CTime class 1670
Comparison operators member function, CTimeSpan
 class 1677
Completing add, Recordsets 1407
Completing edit, Recordsets 1407
Concurrency, supprt for cursor 1399
Connect member function, CAsyncSocket class 74

Connect strings
  defined 227
  for ISAM databases 227
  for ODBC databases 227
  not used for Jet databases 227
  queryDef 257
Connecting to databases 401
Connection handle 405
Connection maps 2067
Connection strings
  database
    described 401
    getting 399
  default
    getting 1389
    Recordset 1389
CONNECTION_IID global function/macro 2112
CONNECTION_PART global function/macro 2112
ConnectTemplate member function,
  COleTemplateServer class 1282
Consistent updates, defined 225
Construct member function
  CPropertyPage class 1352
  CPropertySheet class 1360
ConstructElements global function/macro 2111
Constructing
  CDaoDatabase objects 219
  Data Objects 1100
  Recordsets 1385
Constructors
  CAnimateCtrl 34
  CArchiveException 56
  CCheckListBox 139
  CCommandLineInfo 190
  CCommonDialog 195
  CCriticalSection 212
  CCtrlView 214
  CDaoDatabase 219
  CDaoException 240
  CDaoQueryDef 254
  CDaoWorkspace 375
  CDatabase 396
  CEvent 644
  CHeaderCtrl 745
  CHotKeyCtrl 752
  CImageList 758
  CListCtrl 811
  CListView 838
  CLongBinary 841

Constructors (continued)
  CMiniFrameWnd 922
  CMultiLock 928
  CMutex 932
  COleBusyDialog 970
  COleChangeIconDialog 974
  COleChangeSourceDialog 978
  COleClientItem 991
  COleConvertDialog 1081
  COleDataObject 1100
  COleDataSource 1108
  COleDispatchDriver 1157
  COleDocument 1169
  COleDropSource 1176
  COleDropTarget 1180
  COleInsertDialog 1189
  COleIPFrameWnd 1194
  COleLinkingDoc 1198
  COleLinksDialog 1202
  COleMessageFilter 1206
  COleObjectFactory 1212
  COlePasteSpecialDialog 1220
  COleResizeBar 1238
  COleServerDoc 1242
  COleServerItem 1258
  COleStreamFile 1278
  COleTemplateServer 1282
  COleUpdateDialog 1284
  CProgressCtrl 1347
  CPropertyPage 1352
  CPropertySheet 1360
  CRecordset 1385
  CRecordView 1414
  CRectTracker 1436
  CRichEditCntrItem 1460
  CRichEditCtrl 1466
  CRichEditView 1496
  CSemaphore 1531
  CSingleLock 1536
  CSliderCtrl 1545
  CSpinButtonCtrl 1564
  CStatusBarCtrl 1604
  CSyncObject 1645
  CTabCtrl 1650
  CToolBarCtrl 1705
  CToolTipCtrl 1721
  CTreeCtrl 1730
  CTreeView 1752
  CWinThread 1841

ContinueModal member function, Cwnd class 1871
ContinueRouting member function, CCmdUI class 156
Control classes, listed 14
ControlInfoChanged member function, COleControl
　class 1036
Controls
　Edit 611
　multi-line edit 611
ConvertTo member function, COleClientItem
　class 991
Copy member function
　CArray class 61
　CComboBox class 169
　CEdit class 616
　CRichEditCtrl class 1465
CopyRect member function, CRect class 1420
CopyRgn member function, CRgn class 1447
CopyToClipboard member function
　COleClientItem class 992
　COleServerItem class 1259
Counting errors in DAO Errors collection 241
Counting fields in a querydef 259
Counting querydefs 228
Counting relations 231
Counting tabledefs 232
Counting workspaces 384
CPageSetupDialog class
　data members, m_psd 1300
　described 1292
　member functions
　　CPageSetupDialog 1293
　　CreatePrinterDC 1295
　　DoModal 1295
　　GetDeviceName 1296
　　GetDevMode 1296
　　GetDriverMode 1296
　　GetMargins 1297
　　GetPaperSize 1297
　　GetPortName 1297
　　OnDrawPage 1298
　　PreDrawPage 1299
CPageSetupDialog member function,
　CPageSetupdialog class 1293
CPaintDC class
　data members
　　m_hWnd 1302
　　m_ps 1302
　described 1301
　member functions, CPaintDC 1301

CPaintDC member function, CPaintDC class 1301
CPalette class
　described 1303
　member functions
　　AnimatePalette 1304
　　CPalette 1305
　　CreateHalftonePalette 1305
　　CreatePalette 1305
　　FromHandle 1306
　　GetEntryCount 1306
　　GetNearestPaletteIndex 1307
　　GetPaletteEntries 1307
　　operator HPALETTE 1307
　　ResizePalette 1308
　　SetPaletteEntries 1308
CPalette member function, CPalette class 1305
CPen class
　described 1310
　member functions
　　CPen 1310
　　CreatePen 1313
　　CreatePenIndirect 1314
　　FromHandle 1315
　　GetExtLogPen 1315
　　GetLogPen 1316
　　operator HPEN 1317
CPen member function, CPen class 1310
CPictureHolder class
　data members, m_pPict 1323
　described 1318
　member functions
　　CPictureHolder 1318–1319
　　CreateEmpty 1319
　　CreateFromBitmap 1319
　　CreateFromIcon 1320
　　CreateFromMetafile 1320
　　GetDisplayString 1321
　　GetPictureDispatch 1321
　　GetType 1322
　　Render 1322
　　SetPictureDispatch 1322
CPictureHolder member function, CPictureHolder
　class 1318–1319
CPoint class
　described 1324
　member functions
　　CPoint 1325
　　Offset 1325
　　operator– 1328

CPoint class *(continued)*
  member functions *(continued)*
    operator −= 1327
    operator != 1326
    operator += 1326
    operator + 1327
    operator == 1326
CPoint member function, CPoint class 1325
CPrintDialog class
  data members, m_pd 1338
  described 1330
  member functions
    CPrintDialog 1332
    CreatePrinterDC 1333
    DoModal 1333
    GetCopies 1334
    GetDefaults 1334
    GetDeviceName 1334
    GetDevMode 1335
    GetDriverName 1335
    GetFromPage 1335
    GetPortName 1336
    GetPrinterDC 1336
    GetToPage 1336
    PrintAll 1337
    PrintCollate 1337
    PrintRange 1337
    PrintSelection 1337
CPrintDialog member function, CPrintDialog
  class 1332
CPrintInfo class
  data members
    m_bContinuePrinting 1342
    m_bDirect 1343
    m_bPreview 1343
    m_lpUserData 1343
    m_nCurPage 1343
    m_nNumPreviewPages 1344
    m_pPD 1344
    m_rectDraw 1344
    m_strPageDesc 1345
  described 1339
  member functions
    GetFromPage 1340
    GetMaxPage 1340
    GetMinPage 1341
    GetToPage 1341
    SetMaxPage 1341
    SetMinPage 1342

CProgressCtrl class
  described 1346
  member functions
    CProgressCtrl 1347
    Create 1347
    OffsetPos 1348
    SetPos 1348
    SetRange 1348
    SetStep 1349
    StepIt 1349
CProgressCtrl constructor 1347
CProgressCtrl member function, CProgressCtrl
  class 1347
CPropertyPage class
  data members, m_psp 1357
  described 1350
  member functions
    CancelToClose 1351
    CPropertyPage 1352
    OnApply 1353
    OnCancel 1353
    OnKillActive 1354
    OnOK 1354
    OnQueryCancel 1354
    OnReset 1355
    OnSetActive 1355
    OnWizardBack 1355
    OnWizardFinish 1356
    OnWizardNext 1356
    QuerySiblings 1356
    SetModified 1357
CPropertyPage constructor 1352
CPropertyPage member function, CpropertyPage
  class 1352
CPropertySheet class
  data meember, m_psh 1368
  described 1358
  member functions
    AddPage 1359
    Construct 1360
    CPropertySheet 1361
    Create 1361
    DoModal 1362
    EndDialog 1363
    GetActiveIndex 1363
    GetActivePage 1363
    GetPage 1364
    GetPageCount 1364
    GetPageIndex 1364

CPropertySheet class *(continued)*
  member functions *(continued)*
    GetTabControl 1365
    PressButton 1365
    RemovePage 1366
    SetActivePage 1366
    SetFinishText 1366
    SetTitle 1367
    SetWizardButtons 1367
    SetWizardMode 1368
CPropertySheet constructor 1360
CPropertySheet member function, CPropertySheet
  class 1361
CPropExchange class
  described 1369
  member functions
    ExchangeBlobProp 1370
    ExchangeFontProp 1370
    ExchangePersistentProp 1371
    ExchangeProp 1372
    ExchangeVersion 1373
    GetVersion 1373
    IsLoading 1373
CPtrArray class 1374
CPtrList class 1376
Create member function
  CAnimateCtrl class 35
  CAsyncSocket 76
  CButton class 128
  CCheckListBox class 139
  CComboBox class 169
  CDaoDatabase class 221
  CDaoQueryDef class 255
  CDaoTableDef class 350
  CDaoWorkspace class 377
  CDialog class 552
  CDialogBar class 562
  CEdit class 616
  CFindReplaceDialog class 689
  CHeaderCtrl class 745
  CHotKeyCtrl class 752
  CImageList class 758
  CListBox class 786
  CListCtrl class 811
  CMDIChildWnd class 871
  CMetaFileDC class 920
  CMiniFrameWnd class 923
  COleResizeBar class 1237
  CProgressCtrl class 1347

Create member function *(continued)*
  CPropertySheet class 1361
  CRichEditCtrl class 1465
  CScrollBar class 1516
  CSliderCtrl class 1544
  CSocket class 1556
  CSpinButtonCtrl class 1563
  CSplitterWnd class 1572
  CStatic class 1588
  CStatusBar class 1596
  CStatusBarCtrl class 1603
  CTabCtrl class 1649
  CToolBar class 1682
  CToolBarCtrl class 1703
  CToolTipCtrl class 1721
  CTreeCtrl class 1729
  CWnd class 1871
CreateBitmap member function, CBitmap class 103
CreateBitmapIndirect member function, CBitmap
  class 104
CreateBrushIndirect member function, CBrush
  class 119
CreateCaret member function, CWnd class 1872
CreateClient member function, CMDIFrameWnd
  class 876
CreateClientItem member function, CRichEditDoc
  class 1491
CreateCloneFrom member function, COleClientItem
  class 992
CreateCompatibleBitmap member function, CBitmap
  class 105
CreateCompatibleDC member function, CDC
  class 435
CreateControl member function, Cwnd class 1872
CreateDC member function, CDC class 436
CreateDIBPatternBrush member function, CBrush
  class 119
CreateDiscardableBitmap member function, CBitmap
  class 106
CreateDispatch member function, COleDispatchDriver
  class 1157
CreateDragImage member function
  CListCtrl class 813
  CTreeCtrl class 1730
CreateEllipticRgn member function, CRgn class 1448
CreateEllipticRgnIndirect member function, CRgn
  class 1448
CreateEmpty member function, CPictureHolder
  class 1319

CreateEnhanced member function, CMetaFileDC class 920

CreateEx member function, CWnd class 1874

CreateField member function, CDaoTableDef class 351

CreateFont member function, CFont class 695

CreateFontIndirect member function, CFont class 699

CreateFromBitmap member function, CPictureHolder class 1319

CreateFromClipboard member function, COleClientItem class 992

CreateFromData member function, COleClientItem class 993

CreateFromData member function, CRgn class 1449

CreateFromFile member function, COleClientItem class 994

CreateFromIcon member function, CPictureHolder class 1320

CreateFromMetafile member function, CPictureHolder class 1320

CreateFromPath member function, CRgn class 1449

CreateGrayCaret member function, CWnd class 1875

CreateHalftonePalette member function, CPalette clss 1305

CreateHatchBrush member function, CBrush class 121

CreateIC member function, CDC class 437

CreateIndex member function, CDaoTableDef class 352

CreateIndirect member function, CDialog class 553

CreateInPlaceFrame member function, COleServerDoc class 1243

CreateItem member function
    COleInsertDialog class 1190
    COlePasteSpecialDialog class 1221

CreateLinkFromClipboard member function, COleClientItem class 995

CreateLinkFromData member function, COleClientItem class 995

CreateLinkFromFile member function, COleClientItem class 996

CreateMemoryStream member function, COleStreamFile class 1278

CreateMenu member function, CMenu class 899

CreateNewDocument member function, CDocTemplate class 570

CreateNewFrame member function, CDocTemplate class 570

CreateNewItem member function, COleClientItem class 997

CreateOleFrame member function, CDocTemplate class 571

CreatePalette member function, CPalette class 1305

CreatePatternBrush member function, CBrush class 122

CreatePen member function, CPen class 1313

CreatePenIndirect member function, CPen class 1314

CreatePointFont member function, CFont class 700–701

CreatePolygonRgn member function, CRgn class 1450

CreatePolyPolygonRgn member function, CRgn class 1451

CreatePopupMenu member function, CMenu class 900

CreatePrinterDC member function
    CPageSetupDialog class 1295
    CPrintDialog class 1333
    CWinApp class 1799

CreateRectRgn member function, CRgn class 1452

CreateRectRgnIndirect member function, CRgn class 1452

CreateRelation member function, CDaoDatabase class 223

CreateRoundRectRgn member function, CRgn class 1453

CreateScrollBarCtrl member function, CSplitterWnd class 1574

CreateSolidBrush member function, CBrush class 122

CreateSolidCaret member function, Cwnd class 1876

CreateStatic member function, CSplitterWnd class 1574

CreateStaticFromClipboard member function, COleClientItem class 998

CreateStaticFromData member function, COleClientItem class 998

CreateStockObject member function, CGdiObject class 737

CreateStream member function, COleStreamFile class 1279

CREATESTRUCT structure 2239

CreateSysColorBrush member function, CBrush class 123

CreateThread member function, CWinThread class 1841

CreateView member function
    CFrameWnd class 723
    CSplitterWnd class 1575

Creating
    CDatabase objects 396
    CStreamFile objects 1279

Creating *(continued)*
    database objects 221
    Recordset 1385
    relations between tables 223
    workspaces 379
CRecordset class
    data members
        m_hstmt 1407
        m_nFields 1408
        m_nParams 1408
        m_pDatabase 1409
        m_strFilter 1409
        m_strSort 1410
    described 1378
    member functions
        AddNew 1381
        CanAppend 1382
        Cancel 1383
        CanRestart 1383
        CanScroll 1383
        CanTransact 1383
        CanUpdate 1384
        Close 1384
        CRecordset 1385
        Delete 1385
        DoFieldExchange 1386
        Edit 1387
        GetDefaultConnect 1389
        GetDefaultSQL 1389
        GetRecordCount 1390
        GetSQL 1391
        GetStatus 1390
        GetTableName 1392
        IsBOF 1392
        IsDeleted 1393
        IsEOF 1393
        IsFieldDirty 1394
        IsFieldNull 1394
        IsFieldNullable 1395
        IsOpen 1396
        Move 1396
        MoveFirst 1397
        MoveLast 1398
        MoveNext 1398
        MovePrev 1399
        OnSetOptions 1399
        OnWaitForDataSource 1400
        Open 1400
        Requery 1403

CRecordset class *(continued)*
    member functions *(continued)*
        SetFieldDirty 1404
        SetFieldNull 1405
        SetLockingMode 1406
        Update 1407
CRecordset constructor 1385
CRecordset member function, CRecordset class 1385
CRecordView class
    associated recordset, getting with
      ClassWizard 1416
    described 1412
    dialog template resource 1414
    forms, database 1412
    member functions
        CRecordView 1414
        IsOnFirstRecord 1415
        IsOnLastRecord 1415
        OnGetRecordset 1416
        OnMove 1416
    moving through records 1416
    navigating 1416
    record views 1412
    scrolling 1416
    whether on first record 1415
    whether on last record 1415
CRecordView constructor 1414
CRecordView member function, CRecordView
  class 1414
CRect class
    described 1418
    member functions
        BottomRight 1420
        CopyRect 1420
        CRect 1420
        EqualRect 1422
        Height 1422
        InflateRect 1423
        IntersectRect 1423
        IsRectEmpty 1424
        IsRectNull 1424
        NormalizeRect 1425
        OffsetRect 1425
        operator– 1433
        operator != 1430
        operator &= 1431
        operator & 1433
        operator += 1430
        operator + 1432

CRect class *(continued)*
  member functions *(continued)*
    operator == 1430
    operator = 1429, 1431
    operator != 1432
    operator | 1434
    operator LPCRECT 1429
    operator LPRECT 1429
    PtInRect 1425
    SetRect 1426
    SetRectEmpty 1426
    Size 1426
    SubtractRect 1427
    TopLeft 1428
    UnionRect 1428
    Width 1428
CRect member function, CRect class 1420
CRectTracker class
  data members
    m_nHandleSize 1442
    m_nStyle 1443
    m_rect 1443
    m_sizeMin 1443
  described 1435
  member functions
    AdjustRect 1436
    CRectTracker 1436
    Draw 1437
    DrawTrackerRect 1437
    GetHandleMask 1438
    GetTrueRect 1439
    HitTest 1439
    NormalizeHit 1440
    OnChangedRect 1440
    SetCursor 1441
    Track 1441
    TrackRubberBand 1442
  usage 1435
CRectTracker constructor 1436
CRectTracker member function, CRectTracker
  class 1436
CResourceException class
  described 1444
  member functions, CResourceException 1444
CResourceException member function,
  CResourceException class 1444

CRgn class
  described 1445
  member functions
    CombineRgn 1446
    CopyRgn 1447
    CreateEllipticRgn 1448
    CreateEllipticRgnIndirect 1448
    CreateFromData 1449
    CreateFromPath 1449
    CreatePolygonRgn 1450
    CreatePolyPolygonRgn 1451
    CreateRectRgn 1452
    CreateRectRgnIndirect 1452
    CreateRoundRectRgn 1453
    CRgn 1454
    EqualRgn 1454
    FromHandle 1454
    GetRegionData 1455
    GetRgnBox 1455
    OffsetRgn 1456
    operator HRGN 1458
    PtInRegion 1457
    RectInRegion 1457
    SetRectRgn 1458
CRgn member function, CRgn class 1454
CRichEditCntrItem class
  described 1459
  member functions
    CRichEditCntrItem 1460
    described 1460
    SyncToRichEditObject 1460
CRichEditCntrItem constructor 1460
CRichEditCntrItem member function,
  CRichEditCntrlItem class 1460
CRichEditCtrl class
  described 1461
  member functions 1464
    CanUndo 1464
    Clear 1464
    Copy 1465
    Create 1465
    CRichEditCtrl 1466
    Cut 1466
    DisplayBand 1467
    EmptyUndoBuffer 1467
    FindText 1467
    FormatRange 1468
    GetCharPos 1468
    GetDefaultCharFormat 1469

CRichEditCtrl class *(continued)*
  member functions 1464 *(continued)*
    GetEventMask 1469
    GetFirstVisibleLine 1470
    GetIRichEditOle 1470
    GetLimitText 1470
    GetLine 1471
    GetLineCount 1471
    GetModify 1472
    GetParaFormat 1472
    GetRect 1473
    GetSel 1473
    GetSelectionCharFormat 1474
    GetSelectionType 1474
    GetSelText 1475
    GetTextLength 1475
    HideSelection 1476
    LimitText 1476
    LineFromChar 1477
    LineIndex 1477
    LineLength 1478
    LineScroll 1478
    Paste 1479
    PasteSpecial 1479
    ReplaceSel 1479
    RequestResize 1480
    SetBackgroundColor 1480
    SetDefaultCharFormat 1481
    SetEventMask 1481
    SetModify 1481
    SetOLECallback 1482
    SetOptions 1482
    SetParaFormat 1483
    SetReadOnly 1484
    SetRect 1484
    SetSel 1485
    SetSelectionCharFormat 1485
    SetTargetDevice 1486
    SetWordCharFormat 1486
    StreamIn 1487
    StreamOut 1487
    Undo 1488
CRichEditCtrl constructor 1466
CRichEditCtrl member function, CRichEditCtrl
  class 1466
CRichEditDoc class
  data members
    described 1492
    m_bRTF 1492

CRichEditDoc class *(continued)*
  described 1490
  member functions 1491
    CreateClientItem 1491
    GetStreamFormat 1491
    GetView 1492
CRichEditView class
  data members
    described 1513
    m_nBulletIndent 1513
    m_nWordWrap 1513
  described 1493
  member functions
    AdjustDialogPosition 1495
    CanPaste 1496
    CRichEditView 1496
    described 1495
    DoPaste 1496
    FindText 1497
    FindTextSimple 1497
    GetCharFormatSelection 1498
    GetClipboardData 1498
    GetContextMenu 1499
    GetDocument 1500
    GetInPlaceActiveItem 1500
    GetMargins 1500
    GetPageRect 1501
    GetPaperSize 1501
    GetParaFormatSelection 1501
    GetPrintRect 1502
    GetPrintWidth 1502
    GetRichEditCtrl 1502
    GetSelectedItem 1503
    GetTextLength 1503
    InsertFileAsObject 1503
    InsertItem 1504
    IsRichEditFormat 1504
    IsSelected 1504
    OnCharEffect 1505
    OnFindNext 1505
    OnInitialUpdate 1506
    OnParaAlign 1506
    OnPasteNativeObject 1506
    OnPrinterChanged 1507
    OnReplaceAll 1507
    OnReplaceSel 1508
    OnTextNotFound 1508
    OnUpdateCharEffect 1508
    OnUpdateParaAlign 1509

CRichEditView class *(continued)*
  member functions *(continued)*
    PrintInsideRect 1509
    PrintPage 1510
    QueryAcceptData 1510
    SetCharFormat 1511
    SetMargins 1511
    SetPaperSize 1512
    SetParaFormat 1512
    WrapChanged 1512
CRichEditView constructor 1496
CRichEditView member function, CRichEditView
  class 1496
Cross-tab queries 251
CRuntimeClass class 1514
CScrollBar class
  described 1515
  member functions
    Create 1516
    CScrollBar 1517
    EnableScrollBar 1517
    GetScrollInfo 1517
    GetScrollLimit 1518
    GetScrollPos 1519
    GetScrollRange 1519
    SetScrollInfo 1519
    SetScrollPos 1520
    SetScrollRange 1520
    ShowScrollBar 1521
CScrollBar member function, CScrollBar class 1517
CScrollView class
  described 1522
  member functions
    CScrollView 1524
    FillOutsideRect 1524
    GetDeviceScrollPosition 1525
    GetDeviceScrollSizes 1525
    GetScrollPosition 1526
    GetTotalSize 1526
    ResizeParentToFit 1526
    ScrollToPosition 1527
    SetScaleToFitSize 1527
    SetScrollSizes 1528
CScrollView member function, CScrollView
  class 1524
CSemaphore class
  described 1530
  member functions, CSemaphore 1531
CSemaphore constructor 1531

CSemaphore member function, CSemaphore
  class 1531
CSingleDocTemplate class
  described 1532
  member functions, CSingleDocTemplate 1533
CSingleDocTemplate member function,
  CSingleDocTemplate class 1533
CSingleLock class
  described 1535
  member functions
    CSingleLock 1536
    IsLocked 1536
    Lock 1536
    Unlock 1537
CSingleLock constructor 1536
CSingleLock member function, CSingleLock
  class 1536
CSize class
  described 1538
  member functions
    CSize 1538
    operator− 1540
    operator −= 1540
    operator != 1539
    operator += 1539
    operator + 1540
    operator == 1539
CSize member function, CSize class 1538
CSliderCtrl class
  described 1542
  member functions
    ClearSel 1543
    ClearTics 1544
    Create 1544
    CSliderCtrl 1545
    GetChannelRect 1545
    GetLineSize 1546
    GetNumTics 1546
    GetPageSize 1546
    GetPos 1547
    GetRange 1547
    GetRangeMax 1547
    GetRangeMin 1547
    GetSelection 1548
    GetThumbRect 1548
    GetTic 1548
    GetTicArray 1549
    GetTicPos 1549
    SetLineSize 1549

CSliderCtrl class *(continued)*
  member functions *(continued)*
    SetPageSize 1550
    SetPos 1550
    SetRange 1550
    SetRangeMax 1551
    SetRangeMin 1551
    SetSelection 1551
    SetTic 1552
    SetTicFreq 1552
    VerifyPos 1553
CSliderCtrl constructor 1545
CSliderCtrl member function, CSliderCtrl class 1545
CSocket class
  described 1554
  member functions
    Attach 1555
    CancelBlockingCall 1556
    Create 1556
    CSocket 1557
    FromHandle 1557
    IsBlocking 1558
    OnMessagePending 1558
  members 1554
CSocket member function, CSocket class 1555, 1557
CSocketFile class
  described 1560
  member functions
    CSocketFile 1561
    described 1561
  members 1560
CSocketFile member function, CSocketFile class 1561
CSpinButtonCtrl class
  described 1562
  member functions
    Create 1563
    CSpinButtonCtrl 1564
    GetAccel 1564
    GetBase 1565
    GetBuddy 1565
    GetPos 1565
    GetRange 1566
    SetAccel 1566
    SetBase 1567
    SetBuddy 1567
    SetPos 1567
    SetRange 1568
CSpinButtonCtrl constructor 1564

CSpinButtonCtrl member function, CSpinButtonCtrl class 1564
CSplitterWnd class
  describled 1569
  member functions
    ActivateNext 1572
    CanActivateNext 1572
    Create 1572
    CreateScrollBarCtrl 1574
    CreateStatic 1574
    CreateView 1575
    CSplitterWnd 1576
    DeleteColumn 1576
    DeleteRow 1576
    DeleteView 1577
    DoKeyboardSplit 1577
    DoScroll 1578
    DoScrollBy 1578
    GetActivePane 1579
    GetColumnCount 1579
    GetColumnInfo 1580
    GetPane 1580
    GetRowCount 1580
    GetRowInfo 1580
    GetScrollStyle 1581
    IdFromRowCol 1581
    IsChildPane 1582
    OnDrawSplitter 1582
    OnInvertTracker 1583
    RecalcLayout 1583
    SetActivePane 1584
    SetColumnInfo 1584
    SetRowInfo 1584
    SetScrollStyle 1585
    SplitColumn 1585
    SplitRow 1586
CSplitterWnd member function, CSplitterWnd class 1576
CStatic class
  described 1587
  member functions
    Create 1588
    CStatic 1589
    GetBitmap 1589
    GetCursor 1589
    GetEnhMetaFile 1590
    GetIcon 1590
    SetBitmap 1590
    SetCursor 1591

CStatic class *(continued)*
 member functions *(continued)*
  SetEnhMetaFile 1592
  SetIcon 1592
CStatic member function, CStatic class 1589
CStatusBar class
 described 1594
 member functions
  CommandToIndex 1596
  Create 1596
  CStatusBar 1597
  GetItemID 1597
  GetItemRect 1597
  GetPaneInfo 1598
  GetPaneStyle 1598
  GetPaneText 1598
  GetStatusBarCtrl 1599
  ReportError 650
  SetIndicators 1599
  SetPaneInfo 1600
  SetPaneStyle 1600
  SetPaneText 1601
CStatusBar member function, CStatusBar class 1597
CStatusBarCtrl class
 described 1602
 member functions
  Create 1603
  CStatusBarCtrl 1604
  DrawItem 1604
  GetBorders 1605
  GetParts 1605
  GetRect 1606
  GetText 1606
  GetTextLength 1607
  SetMinHeight 1607
  SetParts 1608
  SetSimple 1608
  SetText 1609
CStatusBarCtrl constructor 1604
CStatusBarCtrl member function, CStatusBarCtrl
 class 1604
CStdioFile class
 data members, m_pStream 1613
 described 1610
 member functions
  CStdioFile 1611
  ReadString 1612
  WriteString 1613
CStdioFile member function, CStdioFile class 1611

CStreamFile objects
 attaching to LPSTREAM objects 1278
 creating 1279
 detaching from LPSTREAM objects 1279
 memory, opening 1278
 opening 1280
CString
 DDX field exchange 2134
 DFX field exchange 2157
 RFX field exchange 2195
CString class
 described 1614
 member functions
  AllocSysString 1617
  AnsiToOem 1617
  Collate 1617
  Compare 1618
  CompareNoCase 1618
  comparions operators 1639
  CString 1619
  Empty 1620
  Find 1621
  FindOneOf 1621
  Format 1622
  FormatMessage 1623
  FreeExtra 1623
  GetAt 1623
  GetBuffer 1624
  GetBufferSetLength 1625
  GetLength 1626
  IsEmpty 1626
  Left 1627
  LoadString 1627
  LockBuffer 1628
  MakeLower 1629
  MakeReverse 1629
  MakeUpper 1629
  Mid 1630
  OemToAnsi 1630
  operator += 1638
  operator + 1637
  operator <<, >> 1637
  operator = 1636
  operator [ ] 1640
  operator LPCTSTR ( ) 1636
  ReleaseBuffer 1631
  ReverseFind 1631
  Right 1632
  SetAt 1632

CString class *(continued)*
    member functions *(continued)*
        SetSysString 1633
        SpanExcluding 1633
        SpanIncluding 1634
        TrimLeft 1635
        TrimRight 1635
        UnlockBuffer 1635
    usage 1614
CString member function, CString class 1619
CString objects, formatting message-box display 2053
CStringArray class 1641
CStringList class 1643
CSyncObject class
    described 1645
    member functions
        CSyncObject 1645
        Lock 1646
        Unlock 1646
CSyncObject constructor 1645
CSyncObject member function, CSyncObject
  class 1645
CTabCtrl class
    described 1647
    member functions
        AdjustRect 1648
        Create 1649
        CTabCtrl 1650
        DeleteAllItems 1650
        DeleteItem 1651
        DrawItem 1651
        GetBkColor 1651
        GetCurFocus 1652
        GetCurSel 1652
        GetImageList 1652
        GetItem 1653
        GetItemCount 1654
        GetItemRect 1654
        GetRowCount 1655
        GetTooltips 1655
        HitTest 1655
        InsertItem 1656
        RemoveImage 1656
        SetBkColor 1657
        SetCurSel 1657
        SetImageList 1657
        SetItem 1658
        SetItemExtra 1658
        SetItemSize 1659

CTabCtrl class *(continued)*
    member functions *(continued)*
        SetPadding 1659
        SetTooltips 1659
CTabCtrl constructor 1650
CTabCtrl member function, CTabCtrl class 1650
CTime class
    described 1660
    member functions
        comparison operators 1670
        CTime 1661
        Format 1663
        FormatGmt 1664
        GetCurrentTime 1664
        GetDay 1665
        GetDayOfWeek 1665
        GetGmtTm 1665
        GetHour 1666
        GetLocalTm 1666
        GetMinute 1667
        GetMonth 1667
        GetSecond 1668
        GetTime 1668
        GetYear 1668
        operator +,− 1669
        operator +=, −= 1669
        operator = 1668
        operators <<, >> 1670
CTime member function, CTime class 1661
CTime, RFX field exchange 2191
CTimeSpan class
    described 1671
    member functions
        comparison operators 1677
        CTimeSpan 1672
        Format 1673
        GetDays 1674
        GetHours 1674
        GetMinutes 1674
        GetSeconds 1675
        GetTotalHours 1675
        GetTotalMinutes 1675
        GetTotalSeconds 1675
        operator +,− 1676
        operator +=, −= 1676
        operator = 1676
        operators <<, >> 1677
CTimeSpan member function, CTimeSpan class 1672

CToolBar class
  described 1679
  member functions
    CommandToIndex 1682
    Create 1682
    CToolBar 1683
    GetButtonInfo 1683
    GetButtonStyle 1684
    GetButtonText 1684
    GetItemID 1684
    GetItemRect 1685
    GetToolBarCtrl 1685
    LoadBitmap 1686
    LoadToolBar 1686
    SetBitmap 1687
    SetButtonInfo 1687
    SetButtons 1688
    SetButtonStyle 1688
    SetButtonText 1689
    SetHeight 1689
    SetSizes 1690
CToolBar member function, CToolBar class 1683
CToolBarCtrl class
  described 1691
  member functions
    AddBitmap 1699
    AddButtons 1699
    AddString 1701
    AddStrings 1701
    AutoSize 1702
    CheckButton 1702
    CommandToIndex 1703
    Create 1703
    CToolBarCtrl 1705
    Customize 1705
    DeleteButton 1705
    EnableButton 1706
    GetBitmapFlags 1706
    GetButton 1706
    GetButtonCount 1707
    GetItemRect 1707
    GetRows 1708
    GetState 1708
    GetToolTips 1709
    HideButton 1709
    Indeterminate 1709
    InsertButton 1710
    IsButtonChecked 1710
    IsButtonEnabled 1711

CToolBarCtrl class *(continued)*
  member functions *(continued)*
    IsButtonHidden 1711
    IsButtonIndeterminate 1712
    IsButtonPressed 1712
    PressButton 1712
    RestoreState 1713
    SaveState 1714
    SetBitmapSize 1714
    SetButtonSize 1715
    SetButtonStructSize 1715
    SetCmdID 1715
    SetOwner 1716
    SetRows 1716
    SetState 1717
    SetToolTips 1718
CToolBarCtrl constructor 1705
CToolBarCtrl member function, CToolBarCtrl
  class 1705
CToolTipCtrl class
  described 1719
  member functions
    Activate 1720
    AddTool 1720
    Create 1721
    CToolTipCtrl 1721
    DelTool 1721
    GetText 1722
    GetToolCount 1722
    GetToolInfo 1722
    HitTest 1724
    RelayEvent 1724
    SetDelayTime 1725
    SetToolInfo 1725
    SetToolRect 1725
    UpdateTipText 1726
CToolTipCtrl constructor 1721
CToolTipCtrl member function, CToolTipCtrl
  class 1721
CTreeCtrl class
  described 1727
  member functions
    Create 1729
    CreateDragImage 1730
    CTreeCtrl 1730
    DeleteAllItems 1730
    DeleteItem 1731
    EditLabel 1731
    EnsureVisible 1731

CTreeCtrl class *(continued)*
  member functions *(continued)*
    Expand 1732
    GetChildItem 1732
    GetCount 1733
    GetDropHilightItem 1733
    GetEditControl 1733
    GetFirstVisibleItem 1733
    GetImageList 1734
    GetIndent 1734
    GetItem 1735
    GetItemData 1737
    GetItemImage 1737
    GetItemRect 1738
    GetItemState 1738
    GetItemText 1739
    GetNextItem 1739
    GetNextSiblingItem 1740
    GetNextVisibleItem 1740
    GetParentItem 1740
    GetPrevSiblingItem 1741
    GetPrevVisibleItem 1741
    GetRootItem 1741
    GetSelectedItem 1742
    GetVisibleCount 1742
    HitTest 1742
    InsertItem 1744
    ItemHasChildren 1745
    Select 1745
    SelectDropTarget 1746
    SelectItem 1746
    SetImageList 1747
    SetIndent 1747
    SetItem 1748
    SetItemData 1748
    SetItemImage 1749
    SetItemState 1749
    SetItemText 1750
    SortChildren 1750
    SortChildrenCB 1750
CTreeCtrl constructor 1730
CTreeCtrl member function, CTreeCtrl class 1730
CTreeView class
  described 1752
  member functions
    CTreeView 1752
    GetTreeCtrl 1753
CTreeView constructor 1752
CTreeView member function, CTreeView class 1752

CTypedPtrArray class
  described 1754
  member functions
    ElementAt 1755
    GetAt 1755
    operator [ ] 1756
CTypedPtrList class
  described 1757
  member functions
    GetAt 1758
    GetHead 1759
    GetNext 1759
    GetPrev 1760
    GetTail 1761
    RemoveHead 1761
    RemoveTail 1762
CTypedPtrMap class
  described 1763
  member functions
    GetNextAssoc 1764
    Lookup 1764
    operator [ ] 1765
CUIntArray class 1766
Currency
  DDX field exchange 2134
  DFX field exchange 2150
Cursor concurrency, Recordset 1399
Cursor, support for scrollable 1399
CUserException class
  described 1768
Custom DDX routines, CDataExchange 409–410
Customize member function, CToolBarCtrl class 1705
Customizing SQL, Recordset 1400
Cut member function
  CComboBox class 171
  CEdit class 617
  CRichEditCtrl class 1466
CView class
  described 1770
  member functions
    CView 1773
    DoPreparePrinting 1773
    GetDocument 1774
    IsSelected 1774
    OnActivateFrame 1774
    OnActivateView 1775
    OnBeginPrinting 1776
    OnDragEnter 1776
    OnDragLeave 1777

CView class *(continued)*
    member functions *(continued)*
        OnDragOver 1778
        OnDragScroll 1779
        OnDraw 1780
        OnDrop 1780
        OnDropEx 1781
        OnEndPrinting 1782
        OnEndPrintPreview 1783
        OnInitialUpdate 1783
        OnPrepareDC 1784
        OnPreparePrinting 1785
        OnPrint 1786
        OnScroll 1787
        OnScrollBy 1788
        OnUpdate 1788
CView member function, CView class 1773
CWaitCursor class
    described 1790
    member functions
        CWaitCursor 1791
        Restore 1792
CWaitCursor member function, CWaitCursor
  class 1791
CWinApp class
    data members
        m_bHelpMode 1832
        m_hInstance 1832
        m_hPrevInstance 1833
        m_lpCmdLine 1833
        m_nCmdShow 1834
        m_pActiveWnd 1835
        m_pszAppName 1835
        m_pszExeName 1835
        m_pszHelpFilePath 1836
        m_pszProfileName 1836
        m_pszRegistryKey 1836
    described 1794
    member functions
        AddDocTemplate 1798
        AddToRecentFileList 1798
        CloseAllDocuments 1799
        CreatePrinterDC 1799
        CWinApp 1799
        DoMessageBox 1800
        DoWaitCursor 1800
        Enable3dControls 1801
        Enable3dControlsStatic 1801
        EnableShellOpen 1802

CWinApp class *(continued)*
    member functions *(continued)*
        ExitInstance 1803
        GetFirstDocTemplatePosition 1803
        GetNextDocTemplate 1804
        GetPrinterDeviceDefaults 1804
        GetProfileInt 1805
        GetProfileString 1805
        HideApplication 1806
        InitApplication 1806
        InitInstance 1807
        LoadCursor 1808
        LoadIcon 1809
        LoadOEMCursor 1810
        LoadOEMIcon 1810
        LoadStandardCursor 1811
        LoadStandardIcon 1812
        LoadStdProfileSettings 1812
        OnContextHelp 1813
        OnDDECommand 1813
        OnFileNew 1814
        OnFileOpen 1815
        OnFilePrintSetup 1816
        OnHelp 1817
        OnHelpFinder 1818
        OnHelpIndex 1818
        OnHelpUsing 1818
        OnIdle 1819
        OpenDocumentFile 1821
        ParseCommandLine 1822
        PreTranslateMessage 1823
        ProcessMessageFilter 1823
        ProcessShellCommand 1824
        ProcessWndProcException 1825
        RegisterShellFileTypes 1825
        Run 1826
        RunAutomated 1826
        RunEmbedded 1827
        SaveAllModified 1827
        SelectPrinter 1827
        SetDialogBkColor 1828
        SetRegistryKey 1828
        WinHelp 1829
        WriteProfileInt 1830
        WriteProfileString 1831
CWinApp member function, CWinApp class 1799

CWindowDC class
  data members, m_hWnd 1838
  described 1837
  member functions, CWindowDC 1837
CWindowDC member function, CWindowDC
  class 1837
CWinThread class
  data members
    m_bAutoDelete 1848
    m_hThread 1849
    m_nThreadID 1849
    m_pActiveWnd 1849
    m_pMainWnd 1849
  described 1839
  member functions
    CreateThread 1841
    CWinThread 1841
    ExitInstance 1842
    GetMainWnd 1842
    GetThreadPriority 1843
    InitInstance 1843
    IsIdleMessage 1844
    OnIdle 1844
    PreTranslateMessage 1845
    ProcessMessageFilter 1845
    ProcessWndProcException 1846
    ResumeThread 1847
    Run 1847
    SetThreadPriority 1847
    SuspendThread 1848
CWinThread constructor 1841
CWinThread member function, CWinThread
  class 1841
CWnd class
  data members, m_hWnd 2043
  described 1850
  member functions
    ArrangeIconicWindows 1865
    Attach 1866
    BeginPaint 1866
    BringWindowToTop 1867
    CalcWindowRect 1867
    CancelToolTips 1868
    CenterWindow 1868
    ChangeClipboardChain 1868
    CheckDlgButton 1869
    CheckRadioButton 1869
    ChildWindowFromPoint 1870
    ClientToScreen 1870

CWnd class *(continued)*
  member functions *(continued)*
    ContinueModal 1871
    Create 1871
    CreateCaret 1872
    CreateControl 1872
    CreateEx 1874
    CreateGrayCaret 1875
    CreateSolidCaret 1876
    CWnd 1877
    Default 1877
    DefWindowProc 1877
    DeleteTempMap 1878
    DestroyWindow 1878
    Detach 1878
    DlgDirList 1879
    DlgDirListComboBox 1880
    DlgDirSelect 1882
    DlgDirSelectComboBox 1882
    DoDataExchange 1883
    DragAcceptFiles 1884
    DrawMenuBar 1884
    EnableScrollBar 1885
    EnableScrollBarCtrl 1885
    EnableToolTips 1886
    EnableWindow 1886
    EndModalLoop 1887
    EndPaint 1887
    ExecuteDlgInit 1888
    FilterToolTipMessage 1888
    FindWindow 1889
    FlashWindow 1889
    FromHandle 1890
    FromHandlePermanent 1890
    GetActiveWindow 1891
    GetCapture 1891
    GetCaretPos 1891
    GetCheckedRadioButton 1892
    GetClientRect 1892
    GetClipboardOwner 1892
    GetClipboardViewer 1893
    GetControlUnknown 1893
    GetCurrentMessage 1893
    GetDC 1894
    GetDCEx 1894
    GetDescendantWindow 1896
    GetDesktopWindow 1896
    GetDlgCtrlID 1896
    GetDlgItem 1897

CWnd class *(continued)*

   member functions *(continued)*

      GetDlgItemInt 1897
      GetDlgItemText 1898
      GetExStyle 1898
      GetFocus 1899
      GetFont 1899
      GetForegroundWindow 1899
      GetIcon 1900
      GetLastActivePopup 1900
      GetMenu 1900
      GetNextDlgGroupItem 1901
      GetNextDlgTabItem 1901
      GetNextWindow 1902
      GetOpenClipboardWindow 1902
      GetOwner 1903
      GetParent 1903
      GetParentFrame 1903
      GetParentOwner 1904
      GetProperty 1904
      GetSafeHwnd 1905
      GetSafeOwner 1905
      GetScrollBarCtrl 1905
      GetScrollInfo 1906
      GetScrollLimit 1907
      GetScrollPos 1907
      GetScrollRange 1908
      GetStyle 1908
      GetSuperWndProcAddr 1909
      GetSystemMenu 1909
      GetTopLevelFrame 1910
      GetTopLevelOwner 1910
      GetTopLevelParent 1910
      GetTopWindow 1911
      GetUpdateRect 1911
      GetUpdateRgn 1912
      GetWindow 1913
      GetWindowContextHelpId 1913
      GetWindowDC 1914
      GetWindowPlacement 1914
      GetWindowRect 1915
      GetWindowText 1915
      GetWindowTextLength 1916
      HideCaret 1916
      HiliteMenuItem 1917
      Invalidate 1917
      InvalidateRect 1918
      InvalidateRgn 1919
      InvokeHelper 1919

CWnd class *(continued)*

   member functions *(continued)*

      IsChild 1920
      IsDialogMessage 1921
      IsDlgButtonChecked 1922
      IsIconic 1922
      IsWindowEnabled 1922
      IsWindowVisible 1923
      IsZoomed 1923
      KillTimer 1923
      LockWindowUpdate 1924
      MapWindowPoints 1924
      MessageBox 1925
      ModifyStyle 1926
      ModifyStyleEx 1927
      MoveWindow 1927
      OnActivate 1928
      OnActivateApp 1929
      OnAmbientProperty 1930
      OnAskCbFormatName 1930
      OnCancelMode 1931
      OnCaptureChanged 1931
      OnChangeCbChain 1932
      OnChar 1932
      OnCharToItem 1933
      OnChildActivate 1934
      OnChildNotify 1934
      OnClose 1935
      OnCommand 1935
      OnCompacting 1936
      OnCompareItem 1937
      OnContextMenu 1938
      OnCreate 1938
      OnCtlColor 1939
      OnDeadChar 1940
      OnDeleteItem 1941
      OnDestroy 1942
      OnDestroyClipboard 1942
      OnDeviceChange 1943
      OnDevModeChange 1944
      OnDrawClipboard 1944
      OnDrawItem 1945
      OnDropFiles 1945
      OnEnable 1946
      OnEndSession 1946
      OnEnterIdle 1947
      OnEnterMenuLoop 1948
      OnEraseBkgnd 1948
      OnExitMenuLoop 1949

CWnd class *(continued)*

 member functions *(continued)*

  OnFontChange 1950
  OnGetDlgCode 1950
  OnGetMinMaxInfo 1951
  OnHelpInfo 1951
  OnHScroll 1952
  OnHScrollClipboard 1953
  OnIconEraseBkgnd 1954
  OnInitMenu 1954
  OnInitMenuPopup 1955
  OnKeyDown 1956
  OnKeyUp 1957
  OnKillFocus 1958
  OnLButtonDblClk 1958
  OnLButtonDown 1959
  OnLButtonUp 1960
  OnMButtonDblClk 1961
  OnMButtonDown 1962
  OnMButtonUp 1962
  OnMDIActivate 1963
  OnMeasureItem 1964
  OnMenuChar 1965
  OnMenuSelect 1966
  OnMouseActivate 1967
  OnMouseMove 1968
  OnMove 1968
  OnMoving 1969
  OnNcActivate 1969
  OnNcCalcSize 1970
  OnNcCreate 1971
  OnNcDestroy 1971
  OnNcHitTest 1972
  OnNcLButtonDblClk 1973
  OnNcLButtonDown 1974
  OnNcLButtonUp 1974
  OnNcMButtonDblClk 1975
  OnNcMButtonDown 1975
  OnNcMButtonUp 1976
  OnNcMouseMove 1976
  OnNcPaint 1977
  OnNcRButtonDblClk 1977
  OnNcRButtonDown 1978
  OnNcRButtonUp 1978
  OnPaint 1979
  OnPaintClipboard 1980
  OnPaletteChanged 1982
  OnPaletteIsChanging 1981
  OnParentNotify 1982

CWnd class *(continued)*

 member functions *(continued)*

  OnQueryDragIcon 1983
  OnQueryEndSession 1984
  OnQueryNewPalette 1984
  OnQueryOpen 1984
  OnRButtonDblClk 1985
  OnRButtonDown 1986
  OnRButtonUp 1986
  OnRenderAllFormats 1987
  OnRenderFormat 1987
  OnSetCursor 1988
  OnSetFocus 1989
  OnShowWindow 1989
  OnSize 1990
  OnSizeClipboard 1991
  OnSizing 1991
  OnSpoolerStatus 1992
  OnStyleChanged 1992
  OnStyleChanging 1993
  OnSysChar 1993
  OnSysColorChange 1995
  OnSysCommand 1995
  OnSysDeadChar 1997
  OnSysKeyDown 1997
  OnSysKeyUp 1999
  OnTCard 2000
  OnTimeChange 2001
  OnTimer 2001
  OnToolHitTest 2002
  OnVKeyToItem 2003
  OnVScroll 2003
  OnVScrollClipboard 2004
  OnWindowPosChanged 2005
  OnWindowPosChanging 2006
  OnWinIniChange 2007
  OnWndMsg 2007
  OpenClipboard 2008
  PostMessage 2008
  PostNcDestroy 2009
  PreCreateWindow 2009
  PreSubclassWindow 2010
  PreTranslateMessage 2010
  Print 2010
  PrintClient 2011
  RedrawWindow 2012
  ReflectChildNotify 2014
  ReflectLastMsg 2014
  ReleaseDC 2015

CWnd class *(continued)*
member functions *(continued)*
RepositionBars 2015
RunModalLoop 2016
ScreenToClient 2016
ScrollWindow 2017
ScrollWindowEx 2018
SendChildNotifyLastMsg 2019
SendDlgItemMessage 2020
SendMessage 2020
SendMessageToDescendants 2021
SendNotifyMessage 2022
SetActiveWindow 2022
SetCapture 2023
SetCaretPos 2023
SetClipboardViewer 2023
SetDlgCtrlID 2024
SetDlgItemInt 2024
SetDlgItemText 2025
SetFocus 2026
SetFont 2026
SetForegroundWindow 2025
SetIcon 2026
SetMenu 2027
SetOwner 2027
SetParent 2028
SetProperty 2028
SetRedraw 2029
SetScrollInfo 2029
SetScrollPos 2030
SetScrollRange 2031
SetTimer 2032
SetWindowContextHelpId 2032
SetWindowPlacement 2033
SetWindowPos 2033
SetWindowText 2036
ShowCaret 2036
ShowOwnedPopups 2037
ShowScrollBar 2037
ShowWindow 2037
SubclassDlgItem 2038
SubclassWindow 2039
UnSubclassWindow 2039
UpdateData 2040
UpdateDialogControls 2040
UpdateWindow 2041
ValidateRect 2041
ValidateRgn 2042

CWnd class *(continued)*
member functions *(continued)*
WindowFromPoint 2042
WindowProc 2043
CWnd member function, CWnd class 1877
CWordArray class 2044

D

DAO
accessing database's workspace 238
accessing underlying DAO object workspace 393
appending a querydef 253
CDaoFieldExchange
IsValidOperation function 246
purpose of 245
closing database objects, effect on updates 220
compacting databases 377
constructing CDaoDatabase objects 219
counting errors in DAO Errors collection 241
counting open databases 380
counting parameters in a querydef 261
counting querydef fields 259
counting querydefs 228
counting relations in a database 231
counting tabledefs 232
counting workspaces 384
creating database objects 221
creating relations between tables 223
DAO Errors collection, and ODBC 239
database formats supported 228
database objects 216
Databases collection 216
dbFreeLocks option 386
DDX_Field functions 2060
deleting querydefs 224
deleting relations 225
deleting tabledefs 225
determining causes of exceptions 239
determining if DFX operations are valid 246
determining whether databases open 234
determining whether transactions allowed 219
determining whether updates allowed 219
DFX and RFX compared 245
DFX field types, setting 247
Dialog data exchange (DDX) 2060
direct access to DAO database object 237

DAO *(continued)*
  error codes
    described 239
    MFC error codes 242
  error handling 239
  exception handling
    CATCH expression 239
    CDaoErrorInfo structure 243
    DAO Errors collection 239
    DAO OLE error codes 244
    DAOERR.H file 239
    described 239
    explicit CDaoException construction 240
    m_pErrorInfo data member 243
    MFC error codes 242
    number of errors in Errors collection 241
    SCODE values 244
    used for all errors 239
  Execute member function, records affected by 230
  executing action queries 225
  executing SQL pass-through queries 225
  executing SQL statements 225
  getting connect string 227
  getting database engine version 234
  getting querydef parameters 262
  isolating ODBC transactions 382, 391
  Login timeout property
    described 382
    setting 392
  name, user-defined
    database 227
    workspace 383
  obtaining information about DAO errors 241
  obtaining information about open databases 380
  obtaining information about parameters in
    querydefs 261
  obtaining information about querydef fields 259
  obtaining information about querydefs 229
  obtaining information about relations 231
  obtaining information about tabledefs 233
  obtaining information about workspaces 385
  open status, obtaining workspace 386
  opening databases 235
  opening default workspace 387
  opening workspaces 387
  query timeout 230
  querydefs *See* Querydefs
  read locks 386

DAO *(continued)*
  Record field exchange (DFX)
    class CDaoFieldExchange 245
    described 2058
    DFX vs. RFX 245
    IsValidOperation function 246
  registry key settings 391
  repairing databases 388
  rolling back transactions 388
  setting default passwords 389
  setting default user names 390
  setting query timeouts 237
  setting querydef parameters 267
  setting SQL statement of querydefs 269
  setting workspace passwords 379
  transactions
    described 371
    role of database objects 217
  user names, getting 383
  using database objects 216
  version, getting database engine 384
  workspaces
    appending to collections 374
    beginning transactions 374
    closing workspaces 375
    constructing C++ objects 375
    creating 379
DAO classes
  DDL support 370
  exceptions, throwing 2097
  vs. ODBC classes 370
DAO database
  Login timeout property 382
  security support 371
  workspace 370
DAO Errors collection 239
DAO vs. ODBC
  described 216, 239, 245, 250
  role of DAO database objects 217
DAOERR.H file 239
Data definition (DDL) query 251
Data members
  CArchive class 55
  CArchiveException class 57
  CAsyncSocket class 101
  CClientDC class 144
  CColorDialog class 162
  CCommandLineInfo class 191
  CControlBar class 207

Data members *(continued)*
 CCtrlView class 215
 CDaoDatabase class 237
 CDaoException class 242
 CDaoFieldExchange class 247
 CDaoQueryDef class 269
 CDaoWorkspace class 393
 CDatabase class 405
 CDBException class 413
 CDC class 548
 CFile class 672
 CFileDialog class 681
 CFileException class 685
 CFindReplaceDialog class 693
 CFontDialog class 708
 CFontHolder class 712
 CFrameWnd class 735
 CGdiObject class 743
 CImageList class 768
 CLongBinary class 841
 CMenu class 916
 COleBusyDialog class 972
 COleChangeIconDialog class 976
 COleChangeSourceDialog class 981
 COleConvertDialog class 1085
 COleCurrency 1096
 COleDispatchDriver class 1162
 COleDispatchException class 1164
 COleException class 1187
 COleInsertDialog class 1193
 COleLinksDialog class 1203
 COlePasteSpecialDialog class 1224
 COlePropertiesDialog class 1228
 COleServerItem class 1276
 CPageSetupDialog class 1300
 CPaintDC class 1302
 CPictureHolder class 1323
 CPrintDialog class 1338
 CPrintInfo class 1342
 CPropertyPage class 1357
 CRecordset class 1407
 CRectTracker class 1442
 CRichEditDoc class 1492
 CRichEditView class 1513
 CStdioFile class 1613
 CWinApp class 1832
 CWindowDC class 1838
 CWinThread class 1848
 CWnd class 2043

Data Objects
 attaching to Clipboard 1099
 attaching to OLE DataObjects 1099
 constructing 1100
 determining available formats 1100, 1103
 determining whether data available 1103
 enumerating available formats 1103
 releasing 1100, 1104
 retrieving data 1101–1102
Data sources
 determining if connected 400
 determining if open 400
 emptying 1111
 modifying data when needed 1114
 modifying data 1109
 providing data when needed
  file 1113
  memory 1114
  undetermined format 1112
 providing data, delayed
  file 1109
  undetermined format 1108
 providing data, immediate
  memory 1107
  undetermined format 1106
Data source connection
 opening 401
 setting options 400
Data structures
 arrays
  CByteArray 136
  CDWordArray 609
  CObArray 934
 maps
  CMapPtrToPtr 849
  CMapPtrToWord 851
  CMapStringToOb 853
  CMapStringToPtr 861
  CMapStringToString 863
  CMapWordToOb 865
  CMapWordToPtr 867
Data transfer
 OLE 1098, 1105
 providing data 1105
Data types 2047
Data, deleting 1385
Database
 See also DAO
 accessing database's workspace 238

Database *(continued)*
 CDaoDatabase class 216
 CDaoFieldExchange, purpose of 245
 closing database objects 220
 collections in DAO databases 217
 connecting to 401
 constructing CDaoDatabase objects 219
 copying database files 377
 counting querydefs 228
 counting relations in databases 231
 counting tabledefs 232
 creating database objects 221
 creating relations between tables 223
 decryption 377
 deleting relations 225
 deleting tabledefs 225
 determining if DFX operation is valid 246
 determining whether open 234
 determining whether updates allowed 219
 DFX and RFX compared 245
 DFX field types, setting 247
 Dialog data exchange (DDX) 2060
 direct access to DAO object 237
 encryption 377
 exception handling 239
 Execute member function, records affected by 230
 executing action queries 225
 executing SQL pass-through queries 225
 executing SQL statements 225
 formats 228
 Getting connect string 227
 getting database engine version 234
 HDBC handle 405
 implicit construction of database object 220
 isolating ODBC transactions 391
 Login timeout property 382
 name, user-defined 227
 obtaining information about open 380
 obtaining information about querydefs 229
 obtaining information about relations 231
 obtaining information about tabledefs 233
 opening 235, 401
 query timeout 230
 Record field exchange (RFX and DFX)
  class CDaoFieldExchange 245
  described 2058
  DFX vs. RFX 245
 record field exchange (RFX), IsValidOperation
  function 246

Database *(continued)*
 repairing 388
 setting default password 389
 setting default user name 390
 setting query timeout 237
 specifying database format 221
 specifying encryption 221
 storing database object in document 220
 transactions, overview 217
 usage tips 216
Database classes
 BOOL, exchanging data (DDX) 2134
 Boolean
  exchanging field data (DFX) 2148
  exchanging field data (RFX) 2190
 Byte
  exchanging data (DDX) 2134
  exchanging field data (DFX) 2149
  exchanging field data (RFX) 2190
 Byte array
  exchanging field data (DFX) 2147
  exchanging field data (RFX) 2189
 calling ODBC functions 2095–2096
 CLongBinary
  exchanging field data (DFX) 2154
  exchanging field data (RFX) 2194
 COleCurrency data, exchanging field data
  (DFX) 2150
 COleDateTime data, exchanging field data
  (DFX) 2151
 Combo box, exchanging data (DDX) 2111, 2126,
  2128
 CString
  exchanging field data (DDX) 2134
  exchanging field data (DFX) 2157
  exchanging field data (RFX) 2195
 CTime, exchanging field data (RFX) 2191
 Currency
  exchanging data (DDX) 2134
  exchanging field data (DFX) 2150
 data exchange
  with BOOL 2134
  with BYTE 2134
  with Combo box 2111, 2126, 2128
  with CString 2134
  with Currency 2134
  with date/time 2134
  with DWORD 2134
  with Float 2134

Database classes *(continued)*
  data exchange *(continued)*
    with Integer 2134
    with List box 2129–2131
    with Long integer 2134
    with Radio button 2132
    with scroll-bar conrol 2133
    with UINT 2134
  Date/time
    exchanging field data (DDX) 2134
    exchanging field data (DFX) 2151
  Double
    exchanging field data (DFX) 2152
    exchanging field data (RFX) 2192
  DWORD, exchanging field data (DDX) 2134
  exceptions, throwing 2097–2098
  field data exchange
    for COleCurrency data 2150
    for COleDateTime data 2151
    for currency data 2150
    for date/time data 2151
    with Boolean 2148, 2190
    with Byte array 2147, 2189
    with Byte 2149, 2190
    with CLongBinary 2154, 2194
    with CString 2157, 2195
    with CTime 2191
    with Double 2152, 2192
    with Long integer 2153, 2193
    with Short integer 2155, 2192
    with Single precision float 2156, 2194
  Float, exchanging data (DDX) 2134
  Integer, exchanging field data (DDX) 2134
  List box, exchanging data (DDX) 2129–2131
  listed 23
  Long integer
    exchanging data (DDX) 2134
    exchanging field data (DFX) 2153
    exchanging field data (RFX) 2193
  Radio button, exchanging data (DDX) 2132
  Scroll-bar control, exchanging data (DDX) 2133
  Short integer
    exchanging field data (DFX) 2155
    exchanging field data (RFX) 2192
  Single precision float
    exchanging field data (DFX) 2156
    exchanging field data (RFX) 2194
  UINT, exchanging data (DDX) 2134

Database engine
  and MFC DLL 371
  initialization settings 381
  initializing 371
  registry key settings 381
  uninitializing 371
  version, getting 234, 384
Database format, specifying 221
Database forms, class CRecordView 1412
Database macros 2061
Database names, getting 399
Database object (DAO)
  defined 216
  obtaining information about 2214
Database operations, canceling 401
Databases collection
  DAO 216
  workspace 370
DataMembers, CPropertySheet class 1368
Date/time
  DDX field exchange 2134
  DFX field exchange 2151
DDP_CBIndex global function/macro 2113
DDP_CBString global function/macro 2113
DDP_CBStringExact global function/macro 2114
DDP_Check global function/macro 2114
DDP_LBIndex global function/macro 2115
DDP_LBString global function/macro 2116
DDP_LBStringExact global function/macro 2116
DDP_PostProcessing global function/macro 2117
DDP_Radio global function/macro 2117
DDP_Text global function/macro 2118
DDV, dialog data validation 409
DDV_MaxChars global function/macro 2119
DDV_MinMaxByte global function/macro 2119
DDV_MinMaxDouble global function/macro 2120
DDV_MinMaxDWord global function/macro 2120
DDV_MinMaxFloat global function/macro 2121
DDV_MinMaxInt global function/macro 2121
DDV_MinMaxLong global function/macro 2122
DDV_MinMaxUnsigned global function/macro 2122
DDX
  See also Dialog data exchange
  direction of exchange, CDataExchange 410
DDX field exchange
  BOOL 2134
  Combo box 2111, 2126, 2128
  CString 2134
  Currency 2134

DDX field exchange *(continued)*
  Date/time 2134
  DWORD 2134
  Float 2134
  Integer 2134
  List box 2129–2131
  Long integer 2134
  Radio button 2132
  Scroll-bar control 2133
  UINT 2134
DDX, dialog data exchange 409
DDX_CBIndex global function/macro 2123
DDX_CBString global function/macro 2123
DDX_CBStringExact global function/macro 2124
DDX_Check global function/macro 2125
  global function/macro 2125
DDX_Field functions, DAO and ODBC 2060
DDX_FieldCBIndex global function/macro 2126
DDX_FieldCBString global function/macro 2127
DDX_FieldCBStringExact global function/macro 2128
DDX_FieldCheck global function/macro 2129
DDX_FieldLBIndex global function/macro 2129
DDX_FieldLBString global function/macro 2130
DDX_FieldLBStringExact global function/macro 2131
DDX_FieldRadio global function/macro 2132
DDX_FieldScroll global function/macro 2133
DDX_FieldText global function/macro 2134
DDX_LBIndex global function/macro 2136
DDX_LBString global function/macro 2137
DDX_LBStringExact global function/macro 2137
DDX_Radio global function/macro 2138
DDX_Scroll global function/macro 2138
DDX_Text global function/macro 2139
Deactivate member function, COleClientItem
  class 999
DeactivateAndUndo member function, COleServerDoc
  class 1242
DeactivateUI member function,, COleClientItem
  class 1000
DEBUG_NEW
  global function/macro 2140
  macro, memory leaks 889
DECLARE_CONNECTION_MAP global
  function/macro 2140
DECLARE_DISPATCH_MAP global
  function/macro 2141
DECLARE_DYNAMIC global function/macro 2141
DECLARE_DYNCREATE global
  function/macro 2142

DECLARE_EVENT_MAP global
  function/macro 2142
DECLARE_EVENTSINK_MAP global
  function/macro 2143
DECLARE_MESSAGE_MAP global
  function/macro 2143
DECLARE_OLECREATE global function/macro 2144
DECLARE_OLECREATE_EX global
  function/macro 2144
DECLARE_OLETYPELIB global
  function/macro 2145
DECLARE_PROPPAGEIDS global
  function/macro 2145
DECLARE_SERIAL global function/macro 2145
Default member function, CWnd class 1877
Default password (DAO), setting 389
Default workspace, using implicitly 371
DeflateRect member function, CRect class 1421
DefWindowProc member function, CWnd class 1877
DelayRenderData member function, COleDataSource
  class 1108
DelayRenderFileData member function,
  COleDataSource class 1109
DelaySetData member function, COleDataSource
  class 1109
Delete member function
  CDaoRecordset class 283
  COleClientItem class 1000
  CRecordset class 1385
Delete operator, memory leaks 889
Delete query 251
DeleteAllItems member function
  CListCtrl class 813
  CTabCtrl class 1650
  CTreeCtrl class 1730
DeleteButton member function, CToolBarCtrl
  class 1705
DeleteColumn member function
  CListCtrl class 813
  CSplitterWnd class 1576
DeleteContents member function, CDocument
  class 584
Deleted, determining whether recordsets 1393
DeleteDC member function, CDC class 438
DeleteField member function, CDaoTableDef
  class 353
DeleteIndex member function, CDaoTableDef
  class 354

DeleteItem member function
    CComboBox class 171
    CHeaderCtrl class 747
    CListBox class 787
    CListCtrl class 814
    CTabCtrl class 1651
    CTreeCtrl class 1731
DELETEITEMSTRUCT structure 2240
DeleteMenu member function, CMenu class 900
DeleteObject member function
    CGdiObject class 739
    CImageList class 759
DeleteQueryDef member function, CDaoDatabase
    class 224
DeleteRelation member function, CDaoDatabase
    class 225
DeleteRow member function, CSplitterWnd
    class 1576
DeleteString member function
    CComboBox class 171
    CListBox class 787
DeleteTableDef member function, CDaoDatabase
    class 225
DeleteTempMap member function
    CDC class 438
    CGdiObject class 739
    CMenu class 901
    CWnd class 1878
DeleteView member function, CSplitterWnd
    class 1577
Deleting
    data 1385
    querydefs 224
    records 1385
    Recordset records 1385
    relations, database 225
    tabledefs 225
DelTool member function, CToolTipCtrl class 1721
DestroyInPlaceFrame member function,
    COleServerDoc class 1243
DestroyMenu member function, CMenu class 901
DestroyWindow member function, CWnd class 1878
DestructElements, global function/macro 2146
Detach member function
    CAsyncSocket 77
    CDC class 439
    CGdiObject class 739
    CImageList class 759
    CMemFile class 885

Detach member function *(continued)*
    CMenu class 902
    COleDataObject class 1100
    COleStreamFile class 1279
    COleVariant 1289
    CWnd class 1878
DetachDispatch member function, COleDispatchDriver
    class 1158
Determining
    abillity to scroll Recordsets 1383
    appendability of Recordsets 1382
    availability of Data Objects data 1103
    availability of transactions, database 1383
    availability of updates, database 1384
    available formats, Data Objects 1100, 1103
    causes of excemptions (DAO) 239
    Clipboard owner 1112
    if data sources connected 400
    if data sources open 400
    if DFX operations are valid 246
    status, waiting for data sources 399
    whether database open 234
    whether Recordset deleted 1393
    whether Recordset fields can be set to Null 1395
    whether Recordset fields dirty 1394
    whether Recordset fields Null 1394
    whether Recordset open 1396
    whether transactions allowed 219
    whether updates allowed 219
Device context classes, listed 17
DEVMODE structure 2241
DEVNAMES structure 2246
DFX
    See also Record Field Exchange
    field types, setting 247
    operations, validity of 246
DFX field exchange
    Boolean 2148
    Byte array 2147
    Byte 2149
    CLongBinary 2154
    COleCurrency data 2150
    COleDateTime data 2151
    CString 2157
    Currency data 2150
    Date/time data 2151
    Double 2152
    Long integer 2153

DFX field exchange *(continued)*
   Short integer 2155
   Single precision float 2156
DFX vs. RFX 245
DFX_Binary, global function/macro 2147
DFX_Bool, global function/macro 2148
DFX_Byte, global function/macro 2149
DFX_Currency, global function/macro 2150
DFX_DateTime, global function/macro 2151
DFX_Double, global function/macro 2152
DFX_Long, global function/macro 2153
DFX_LongBinary, global function/macro 2154
DFX_Short, global function/macro 2155
DFX_Single, global function/macro 2156
DFX_Text, global function/macro 2157
Diagnostic classes, listed 30
Diagnostic services 2050
Dialog box, OLE Change Source 977
Dialog classes, listed 12
Dialog data exchange (DDX)
   CDataExchange class 408
   CDataExchange 410
   Custom DDX routines
      CDataExchange class 408
      preparing controls 409
      preparing edit controls 410
   Data exchange object
      getting dialog object 411
      m_pDlgWnd member 411
   functions 2060
Dialog data validation (DDV)
   custom DDV routines
      CDataExchange class 408
      CDataExchange 408
      preparing edit controls 410
   dialog data exchange (DDX) 408
   validation failure 408
Dialog template resource, class CRecordView 1414
Difference member function, CMemoryState class 891
Dir member function
   CComboBox class 172
   CListBox class 788
Direct access to DAO database object 237
Directly executing SQL statements 398
Disabling
   asynchronous access 403
   synchronous access 403
   user commands, database 399

DiscardUndoState member function, COleServerDoc
   class 1244
DISP_DEFVALUE, global function/macro 2158
DISP_FUNCTION, global function/macro 2158
DISP_PROPERTY, global function/macro 2160
DISP_PROPERTY_EX, global function/macro 2161
Dispatch maps 2062
DisplayBand member function, RichEditCtrl
   class 1467
DisplayError member function, COleControl
   class 1036
DlgDirList member function, CWnd class 1879
DlgDirListComboBox member function, CWnd
   class 1880
DlgDirSelect member function, CWnd class 1882
DlgDirSelectComboBox member function, CWnd
   class 1882
DoChangeIcon member function,
   COleChangeIconDialog class 974
DOCINFO structure 2247
DockControlBar member function, CFrameWnd
   class 723
DoClick member function, COleControl class 1037
DoConvert member function, COleConvertDialog
   class 1082
Document/View, Rich edit 1490, 1493
Documents, mailing *See* MAPI
Documents, storing database objects in 220
DoDataExchange member function, Cwnd class 1883
DoDragDrop member function
   COleClientItem class 1000
   COleDataSource class 1110
   COleServerItem class 1259
DoFieldExchange function, and SetFieldType
   function 653
DoFieldExchange member function
   CDaoRecordset class 284
   CRecordset class 1386
DoKeyboardSplit member function, CSplitterWnd
   class 1577
DoMessageBox member function, CWinApp
   class 1800
DoModal member function
   CColorDialog class 160
   CDialog class 554
   CFileDialog class 676
   CFontDialog class 705
   COleBusyDialog class 970
   COleChangeIconDialog class 975

DoModal member function *(continued)*
   COleChangeSourceDialog class 978
   COleConvertDialog class 1082
   COleInsertDialog class 1190
   COleLinksDialog class 1202
   COlePasteSpecialDialog class 1222
   COlePropertiesDialog class 1227
   COleUpdateDialog class 1285
   CPageSetupDialog class 1295
   CPrintDialog class 1333
   CPropertySheet class 1362
DoPaste member function, CRichEditView class 1496
DoPreparePrinting member function, CView
  class 1773
DoPropExchange member function, COleControl
  class 1037
DoScroll member function, CSplitterWnd class 1578
DoScrollBy member function, CSplitterWnd
  class 1578
DoSuperClassPaint member function, COleControl
  class 1038
Double
   DFX field exchange 2152
   RFX field exchange 2192
DoVerb member function, COleClientItem class 1001
DoWaitCursor member function, CWinApp class 1800
DPtoHIMETRIC member function, CDC class 439
DPtoLP member function, CDC class 439
Drag and Drop
   crossing target window 1181
   determining when to start 1177
   determining whether to continue 1177
   dropping 1183–1184
   entering target window 1180
   initiating 1110
   leaving target window 1181
   modifying cursors 1176
   registering target windows 1185
   revoking target windows 1185
   scrolling target window 1182
   User Interface Issues 1176
DragAcceptFiles member function, CWnd class 1884
DragEnter member function, CImageList class 759
Dragging member function, CDragListBox class 602
DragLeave member function, CImageList class 760
DragMove member function, CImageList class 760
DragShowNolock member function, CImageList
  class 761

Draw member function
   CImageList class 761
   COleClientItem class 1002
   CRectTracker class 1437
Draw3dRect member function, CDC class 440
DrawContent member function, COleControl
  class 1038
DrawDragRect member function, CDC class 441
DrawEdge member function, CDC class 441
DrawEscape member function, CDC class 443
DrawFocusRect member function, CDC class 444
DrawFrameControl member function, CDC class 444
DrawIcon member function, CDC class 446
Drawing object classes, listed 18
DrawInsert member function, CDragListBox class 602
DrawItem member function
   CButton class 129
   CComboBox class 172
   CHeaderCtrl class 747
   CListBox class 788
   CListCtrl class 814
   CMenu class 902
   CStatusBarCtrl class 1604
   CTabCtrl class 1651
DRAWITEMSTRUCT structure 2247
DrawMenuBar member function, CWnd class 1884
DrawMetaFile member function, COleControl
  class 1038
DrawState member function, CDC class 446
DrawText member function, CDC class 448
DrawTrackerRect member function, CRectTracker
  class 1437
Dropped member function, CDragListBox class 603
Dump member function, CObject class 946
Dump operator
   COleCurrency 1096
   COleDateTime 1137
   COleDateTimeSpan 1152
   COleVariant 1291
DumpAllObjectsSince member function,
  CMemoryState class 891
DumpElements global function/macro 2162
DumpField, Record field exchange (DFX) 247
DumpStatistics member function, CMemoryState
  class 892
Duplicate member function, CFile class 660
DWORD, DDX field exchange 2134

dwstyle parameter, styles specified with 2270
dwStyleDefault member function, CEditView
class 642

E

Edit Control 611
Edit member function
    CDaoRecordset class 285
    CRecordset class 1387
Edit styles 2272
Editing
    records in Recordsets 1387
    records 1387
EditLabel member function
    CListCtrl class 815
    CTreeCtrl class 1731
ElementAt member function
    CArray class 61
    CObArray class 936
    CTypedPtrArray class 1755
Ellipse member function, CDC class 450
Empty member function
    COleDataSource class 1111
    CString class 1620
Emptying
    Clipboard 1111
    Data Source 1111
EmptyUndoBuffer member function
    CEdit class 617
    CRichEditCtrl class 1467
Enable member function
    CCheckListBox class 140
    CCmdUI class 156
Enable3dControls member function, CWinApp
    class 1801
Enable3dControlsStatic member function, CWinApp
    class 1801
EnableAutomation member function, CCmdTarget
    class 148
EnableBusyDialog member function,
    COleMEssageFilter class 1206
EnableButton member function, CToolBarCtrol
    class 1706
EnableCompoundFile member function,
    COleDocument class 1169
EnableDocking member function
    CControlBar class 204
    CFrameWnd class 724

EnableMenuItem member function, CMenu class 902
EnableNotRespondingDialog member function,
    COleMessageFilter class 1206
EnableScrollBar member function
    CScrollBar class 1517
    CWnd class 1885
EnableScrollBarCtrl member function, CWnd
    class 1885
EnableShellOpen member function, CWinApp
    class 1802
EnableSimpleFrame member function, COleControl
    class 1039
EnableToolTips member function, CWnd class 1886
EnableWindow member function, CWnd class 1886
Enabling
    asynchronous access 403
    synchronous access 403
Encryption
    database 377
    specifying 221
END_CATCH, global function/macro 2163
END_CATCH_ALL, global function/macro 2163
END_CONNECTION_MAP, global
    function/macro 2163
END_CONNECTION_PART, global
    function/macro 2163
END_DISPATCH_MAP, global function/macro 2164
END_EVENT_MAP, global function/macro 2164
END_EVENTSINK_MAP, global
    function/macro 2164
END_MESSAGE_MAP, global function/macro 2164
END_OLEFACTORY, global function/macro 2165
END_PROPPAGEIDS, global function/macro 2165
EndBusyState member function, COleMessageFilter
    class 1207
EndDialog member function
    CDialog class 555
    CPropertySheet class 1363
EndDoc member function, CDC class 451
EndDrag member function, CImageList class 762
EndModalLoop member function, CWnd class 1887
EndModalState member function, CFrameWnd
    class 724
EndPage member function, CDC class 452
EndPaint member function, CWnd class 1887
EndPath member function, CDC class 452
EndWaitCursor member function, CCmdTarget
    class 148
Engine, database *See* Database engine

EnsureVisible member function
    CListCtrl class 815
    CTreeCtrl class 1731
Enumerating available formats, Data objects 1103
EnumObjects member function, CDC class 452
EnumObjects, callback function for *See* Callback
    functions for MFC member functions
EqualRect member function, CRect class 1422
EqualRgn member function, CRgn class 1454
ErrnoToException member function, CFileException
    class 683
Error codes
    DAO 239
    human readable 415
    ODBC
        described 413
        values 413
    text message 415
Error object (DAO), obtaining information about 2217
Error strings
    human readable 415
    native
        ODBC 415
        SQLError function 415
        SQLSTATE 415
    ODBC 415
Errors collection, DAO 239
Escape member function, CDC class 454
Event Maps 2066
Event sink maps 2067
EVENT_CUSTOM, global function/macro 2165
EVENT_CUSTOM_ID, global function/macro 2166
Exception classes, listed 30
Exception handling, DAO
    DAOERR.H file 239
    described 239
    obtaining information about 2217
Exception processing 2052
Exceptions, throwing
    DAO classes 2097
    Database classes 2097–2098
ExchangeBlobProp member function, CPropExchange
    class 1370
ExchangeExtent member function, COleControl
    class 1039
ExchangeFontProp member function, CPropExchange
    class 1370
ExchangePersistentProp member function,
    CPropExchange class 1371

ExchangeProp member function, CPropExchange
    class 1372
ExchangeStockProps member function, COleControl
    class 1039
ExchangeVersion member function
    COleControl class 1040
    CPropExchange class 1373
Exchanging data
    with data source, Recordset 1386
    with recordset fields in DAO classes 245
ExcludeClipRect member function, CDC class 455
ExcludeUpdateRgn member function, CDC class 456
Execute member function
    CDaoDatabase class 225
    CDaoQueryDef class 256
    records affected by 230
ExecuteDlgInit member function, CWnd class 1888
ExecuteSQL member function, CDatabase class 398
ExitInstance member function
    CWinApp class 1803
    CWinThread class 1842
Expand member function, CTreeCtrl class 1732
Extended window styles 2279
ExtFloodFill member function, CDC class 456
ExtractIcon member function, CImageList class 762
ExtTextOut member function, CDC class 457

F

Fail member function, CDataExchange class 408
Failure, validation 408
Field exchange, records in DAO classes 245
Field object (DAO)
    in indexes, obtaining information about 2225
    in relations, obtaining information about 2232
    obtaining information about 2218
Fields, recordset
    determining whether dirty 1394
    determining whether Null 1394
    number of bound 1408
    setting dirty 1404
    setting null 1405
FieldType enum
    described 652
    values 652
FieldType values, CDaoFieldExchange
    outputColumn 245
    param 245
FILETIME structure 2249

FillCache member function, CDaoRecordset class 286

FillOutsideRect member function, CScrollView class 1524

FillPath member function, CDC class 458

FillRect member function, CDC class 459

FillRgn member function, CDC class 459

FillSolidRect member function, CDC class 460

Filter strings, Recordset 1409

FilterToolTipMessage member function, CWnd class 1888

Find member function
    CDaoRecordset class 288
    CList class 771
    CObList class 956
    CString class 1621

FindFirst member function, CDaoRecordset class 288

FindIndex member function
    CList class 772
    CObList class 957

FindItem member function, CListCtrl class 815

FindLast member function, CDaoRecordset class 290

FindNext member function
    CDaoRecordset class 291
    CFindReplaceDialog class 690

FindOneOf member function, CString class 1621

FindPrev member function, CDaoRecordset class 292

FindString member function
    CComboBox class 173
    CListBox class 789

FindStringExact member function
    CComboBox class 173
    CListBox class 789

FindText member function
    CEditView class 635
    CRichEditCtrl class 1467
    CRichEditView class 1497

FindTextSimple member function, CRichEditView class 1497

FindWindow member function, Cwnd class 1889

FireClick member function, COleControl class 1040

FireDblClick member function, COleControl class 1041

FireError member function, COleControl class 1041

FireEvent member function, COleControl class 1041

FireKeyDown member function, COleControl class 1042

FireKeyPressmember function, COleControl class 1043

FireKeyUp member function, COleControl class 1043

FireMouseDown member function, COleControl class 1044

FireMouseMove member function, COleControl class 1045

FireMouseUp member function, COlecontrol class 1045

Fixup, Record field exchange (DFX) 247

FlashWindow member function, CWnd class 1889

FlattenPath member function, CDC class 460

Float, DDX field exchange 2134

FloatControlBar member function, CFrameWnd class 724

FloodFill member function, CDC class 461

Flush member function
    CArchive class 41
    CDumpContext class 605
    CFile class 660

FlushClipboard member function, COleDataSource class 1111

FmtLines member function, CEdit class 618

Format member function
    COleCurrency 1088
    COleDateTime 1119
    COleDateTimeSpan 1142
    CString class 1622
    CTime class 1663
    CTimeSpan class 1673

FormatGmt member function, CTime class 1664

FormatMessage member function, CString class 1623

FormatRange member function, CRichEdit Ctrl class 1468

Formats, database, supported by DAO
    Btrieve 228
    dBASE 228
    Microsoft Excel 228
    Microsoft FoxPro 228
    Microsoft Jet (Access) 228
    ODBC 228
    Oracle (ODBC) 228
    Paradox 228
    SQL Server (ODBC) 228
    Text format 228

Forms, class CRecordView database 1412

Foundation Class Library *See* Microsoft Foundation Class Library

FrameRect member function, CDC class 461

FrameRgn member function, CDC class 462

Free member function, CMemFile class 885

FreeCache, Record field exchange (DFX) 247

FreeExtra member function
    CArray class 62
    CObArray class 937
    CString class 1623
FromHandle member function
    CAsyncSocket class 78
    CBitmap class 106
    CBrush class 124
    CDC class 462
    CFont class 701
    CGdiObject class 740
    CMenu class 903
    CPalette class 1306
    CPen class 1315
    CRgn class 1454
    CSocket class 1557
    CWnd class 1890
FromHandlePermanent member function, CWnd
    class 1890
FromIDispatch member function, CCmdTarget
    class 149
Functions, callback *See* Callback functions for MFC
    member functions

G

GDI classes (list) 18
GetAbsolutePosition member function, CDaoRecordset
    class 294
GetAccel member function, CSpinButtonCtrl
    class 1564
GetActiveDocument member function, CFrameWnd
    class 725
GetActiveFrame member function, CFrameWnd
    class 726
GetActiveIndex member function, CPropertySheet
    class 1363
GetActivePage member function, CPropertySheet
    class 1363
GetActivePane member function, CSplitterWnd
    class 1579
GetActiveView member function
    CFrameWnd class 726
    COleClientItem class 1003
GetActiveWindow member function, CWnd class 1891
GetAmbientProperty member function, COleControl
    class 1046
GetAnchorIndex member function, CListBox class 790
GetArcDirection member function, CDC class 463

GetAspectRatioFilter member function, CDC
    class 463
GetAt member function
    CArray class 62
    CList class 772
    CObArray class 937
    CObList class 957
    CString class 1623
    CTypedPtrArray class 1755
    CTypedPtrList class 1758
GetAttributes member function, CDaoTableDef
    class 354
GetBackColor member function, COleControl
    class 1047
GetBarStyle member function, CControlBar class 205
GetBase member function, CSpinButtonCtrl
    class 1565
GetBitmap member function
    CBitmap class 107
    CButton class 129
    CStatic class 1589
GetBitmapBits member function, CBitmap class 107
GetBitmapDimension member function, CBitmap
    class 108
GetBitmapFlags member function, CToolBarCtrl
    class 1706
GetBkColor member function
    CDC class 463
    CImageList class 763
    CListCtrl class 816
    CTabCtrl class 1651
GetBkMode member function, CDC class 464
GetBookmark member function, CDaoRecordset
    class 294
GetBorders member function, CStatusBarCtrl
    class 1605
GetBorderStyle member function, COleControl
    class 1047
GetBoundsRect member function, CDC class 464
GetBrushOrg member function, CDC class 465
GetBuddy member function, CSpinButtonCtrl
    class 1565
GetBuffer member function, CString class 1624
GetBufferLength member function, CEditView
    class 636
GetBufferSetLength member function, CString
    class 1625
GetButton member function, CToolBarCtrl class 1706

GetButtonCount member function, CToolBarCtrl
    class 1707
GetButtonInfo member function, CToolBar class 1683
GetButtonStyle member function
    CButton class 130
    CToolBar class 1684
GetButtonText member function, CToolBar class 1684
GetCachedExtent member function, COleClientItem
    class 1003
GetCacheSize member function, CDaoRecordset
    class 295–296
GetCallbackMask member function, CListCtrl
    class 817
GetCapture member function, CWnd class 1891
GetCaretIndex member function, CListBox class 790
GetCaretPos member function, CWnd class 1891
GetChannelRect member function, CSliderCtrl
    class 1545
GetCharABCWidths member function, CDC class 465
GetCharFormatSelection member function,
    CRichEditView class 1498
GetCharPos member function, CRichEditCtrl
    class 1468
GetCharWidth member function,, CDC class 466
GetCheck member function
    CButton class 130
    CCheckListBox class 140
GetCheckedRadioButton member function, CWnd
    class 1892
GetCheckStyle member function, CCheckListBox
    class 141
GetChildItem member function, CTreeCtrl class 1732
GetClassID member function
    COleClientItem class 1004
    COleControl class 1048
    COleConvertDialog class 1083
    COleInsertDialog class 1191
    COleObjectFactory class 1213
GetClientRect member function, CWnd class 1892
GetClipboardData member function
    COleClientItem class 1004
    COleServerItem class 1260
    CRichEditView class 1498
GetClipboardOwner member function
    COleDataSource class 1112
    CWnd class 1892
GetClipboardViewer member function, Cwnd
    class 1893
GetClipBox member function, CDC class 467

GetColor member function
    CColorDialog class 160
    CFontDialog class 705
GetColorAdjustment member function, CDC class 468
GetColumn member function, CListCtrl class 817
GetColumnCount member function, CSplitterWnd
    class 1579
GetColumnInfo member function, CSplitterWnd
    class 1580
GetColumnWidth member function, CListCtrl
    class 818
GetConnect member function
    CDaoDatabase class 227
    CDaoQueryDef class 257
    CDaoTableDef class 355
    CDatabase class 399
GetConnection member function, CConnectionPoint
    class 199
GetContainer member function, CConnectionPoint
    class 199
GetContextMenu member function, CRichEditView
    class 1499
GetControlBar member function, CFrameWnd
    class 726
GetControlSize member function, COleControl
    class 1048
GetControlStatus member function, COlePropertyPage
    class 1231
GetControlUnknown member function, CWnd
    class 1893
GetCopies member function, CPrintDialog class 1334
GetCount member function
    CComboBox class 174
    CControlBar class 205
    CList class 773
    CListBox class 791
    CMap class 843
    CMapStringToOb class 854
    CObList class 958
    CTreeCtrl class 1733
GetCountPerPage member function, CListCtrl
    class 819
GetCurFocus member function, CTabCtrl class 1652
GetCurrentBitmap member function, CDC class 468
GetCurrentBrush member function, CDC class 468
GetCurrentFont member function
    CDC class 468
    CFontDialog class 706

GetCurrentIndex member function, CDaoRecordset
    class 296
GetCurrentMessage member function, CWnd
    class 1893
GetCurrentPalette member function, CDC class 469
GetCurrentPen member function, CDC class 469
GetCurrentPosition member function, CDC class 469
GetCurrentTime member function
    COleDateTime 1121
    CTime class 1664
GetCurSel member function
    CComboBox class 174
    CListBox class 791
    CTabCtrl class 1652
GetCursor member function
    CButton class 130
    CStatic class 1589
GetData member function
    CArray class 62
    COleDataObject class 1101
GetDatabaseCount member function, CDaoWorkspace
    class 380
GetDatabaseInfo member function, CDaoWorkspace
    class 380
GetDatabaseName member function, CDatabase
    class 399
GetDataSource member function, COleServerItem
    class 1261
GetDateCreated member function
    CDaoQueryDef class 258
    CDaoRecordset class 297
GetDateCreated member functions
    CDaoTableDef class 357
GetDateLastUpdated member function
    CDaoQueryDef class 258
    CDaoRecordset class 297
    CDaoTableDef class 357
GetDay member function
    COleDateTime class 1121
    CTime class 1665
GetDayOfWeek member function
    COleDateTime 1122
    CTime class 1665
GetDayOfYear member function, COleDateTime
    class 1122
GetDays member function
    COleDateTimeSpan class 1143
    CTimeSpan class 1674
GetDC member function, CWnd class 1894

GetDCEx member function, Cwnd class 1894
GetDefaultCharFormat member function,
    CRichEditCtrl class 1469
GetDefaultConnect member function, CRecordset
    class 1389
GetDefaultDBName member function, CDaoRecordset
    class 297
GetDefaults member function, CPrintDialog
    class 1334
GetDefaultSQL member function
    CDaoRecordset class 298
    CRecordset class 1389
GetDefID member function, CDialog class 555
GetDepth member function, CDumpContext class 606
GetDescendantWindow member function, Cwnd
    class 1896
GetDesktopWindow member function, CWnd
    class 1896
GetDeviceCaps member function, CDC class 470
GetDeviceName member function
    CPageSetupDialog class 1296
    CPrintDialog class 1334
GetDeviceScrollPosition member function,
    CScrollView class 1525
GetDeviceScrollSizes member function, CScrollView
    class 1525
GetDevMode member function
    CPageSetupDialog class 1296
    CPrintDialog class 1335
GetDisplayName member function,
    COleChangeSourceDialog class 979
GetDisplayString member function
    CFontHolder class 710
    CPictureHolder class 1321
GetDlgCtrlID member function, CWnd class 1896
GetDlgItem member function, CWnd class 1897
GetDlgItemInt member function, CWnd class 1897
GetDlgItemText member function, CWnd class 1898
GetDockingFrame member function, CControlBar
    class 205
GetDockState member function, CFrameWnd
    class 727
GetDocString member function, CDocTemplate
    class 571
GetDocTemplate member function, CDocument
    class 585
GetDocument member function
    CDocItem class 565
    COleClientItem class 1005

GetDocument member function *(continued)*
  COleServerItem class 1261
  CRichEditView class 1500
  CView class 1774
GetDragImage member function, CImageList class 763
GetDrawAspect member function
  COleClientItem class 1005
  COleConvertDialog class 1083
  COleInsertDialog class 1191
  COlePasteSpecialDialog class 1222
GetDriverMode member function, CPageSetupDialog class 1296
GetDriverName member function, CPrintDialog class 1335
GetDropHilightItem member function, CTreeCtrl class 1733
GetDroppedControlRect member function, CComboBox class 175
GetDroppedState member function, CComboBox class 175
GetDroppedWidth member function, CComboBox class 175
GetEditControl member function
  CListCtrl class 819
  CTreeCtrl class 1733
GetEditCtrl member function, CEditView class 636
GetEditMode member function, CDaoRecordset class 299
GetEditSel member function, CComboBox class 176
GetEmbeddedItem member function, COleServerDoc class 1244
GetEmbedSourceData member function, COleServerItem class 1261
GetEnabled member function, COleControl class 1048
GetEnhMetaFile member function, CStatic class 1590
GetEntryCount member function, CPalette class 1306
GetErrorCount member function, CDaoException class 241
GetErrorInfo member function, CDaoException class 241
GetErrorMessage member function, CException class 648
GetEventMask member function, CRichEditCtrol class 1469
GetExStyle member function, CWnd class 1898
GetExtendedControl member function, COleControl class 1049
GetExtendedUI member function, CComboBox class 176

GetExtent member function, COleClientItem class 1005
GetExtLogPen member function, CPen Class 1315
GetFaceName member function, CFontDialog class 706
GetFieldCount member function
  CDaoQueryDef class 259
  CDaoRecordset class 299
  CDaoTableDef class 358
GetFieldIndex, Record field exchange (DFX) 247
GetFieldInfo member function
  CDaoQueryDef class 259
  CDaoRecordset class 300
  CDaoTableDef class 358
GetFieldValue member function, CDaoRecordset class 301
GetFile member function
  CArchive class 41
  CDocument class 585
GetFileData member function, COleDataObject class 1101
GetFileExt member function, CFileDialog class 676
GetFileName member function
  CFile class 660
  CFileDialog class 677
  COleChangeSourceDialog class 979
GetFilePath member function, CFile class 660
GetFileTitle member function
  CFile class 661
  CFileDialog class 677
GetFindString member function, CFindReplaceDialog class 690
GetFirstDocPosition member function, CDocTemplate class 572
GetFirstDocTemplatePosition member function, CWinApp class 1803
GetFirstViewPosition member function, CDocument class 586
GetFirstVisibleItem member function, CTreeCtrl class 1733
GetFirstVisibleLine member function
  CEdit class 618
  CRichEditCtrl class 1470
GetFocus member function, Cwnd class 1899
GetFont member function
  COleControl class 1049
  CWnd class 1899
GetFontData member function, CDC class 474

GetFontDispatch member function, CFontHolder
  class 710
GetFontHandle member function, CFontHolder
  class 710
GetFontTextMetrics member function, COleControl
  class 1049
GetForeColor member function, COleControl
  class 1050
GetForegroundWindow member function, CWnd
  class 1899
GetFromPage member function
  CPrintDialog class 1335
  CPrintInfo class 1340
GetFromPrefix member function,
  COleChangeSourceDialog class 979
GetGlobalData member function, COleDataObject
  class 1102
GetGlyphOutline member function, CDC class 475
GetGmtTm member function, CTime class 1665
GetHalftoneBrush member function, CDC class 477
GetHandle member function, CEdit class 619
GetHandleMask member function, CRectTracker
  class 1438
GetHashTableSize member function, CMap class 844
GetHead member function
  CList class 773
  CObList class 958
  CTypedPtrList class 1759
GetHeadPosition member function
  CList class 773
  CObList class 959
GetHorizontalExtent member function, CComboBox
  class 176
GetHorizontalExtent member function, CListBox
  class 791
GetHotKey member function, CHotKeyCtrl class 753
GetHour member function
  COleDateTime 1123
  CTime class 1666
GetHours member function
  COleDateTimeSpan 1143
  CTimeSpan class 1674
GetHwnd member function, COleControl class 1050
GetIcon member function
  CButton class 131
  CStatic class 1590
  CWnd class 1900

GetIconicMetafile member function
  COleChangeIconDialog class 975
  COleClientItem class 1006
  COleConvertDialog class 1084
  COleInsertDialog class 1192
  COlePasteSpecialDialog class 1223
GetIDispatch member function, CCmdTarget class 150
GetIID member function, CConnectionPoint class 199
GetImageCount member function, CImageList
  class 763
GetImageInfo member function, CImageList class 764
GetImageList member function
  CListCtrl class 819
  CTabCtrl class 1652
  CTreeCtrl class 1734
GetIndent member function, CTreeCtrl class 1734
GetIndexCount member function
  CDaoRecordset class 301
  CDaoTableDef class 359
GetIndexInfo member function
  CDaoRecordset class 302
  CDaoTableDef class 359
GetIniPath member function, CDaoWorkspace
  class 381
GetInPlaceActiveItem member function
  COleDocument class 1169
  CRichEditView class 1500
GetInPlaceWindow member function, COleClientItem
  class 1006
GetIRichEditOle member function, CRichEditCtrl
  class 1470
GetIsolateODBCTrans member function,
  CDaoWorkspace class 382
GetItem member function
  CHeaderCtrl class 747
  CListCtrl class 820
  CTabCtrl class 1653
  CTreeCtrl class 1735
GetItemClipRect member function, COleServerDoc
  class 1244
GetItemCount member function
  CHeaderCtrl class 749
  CListCtrl class 821
  CTabCtrl class 1654
GetItemData member function
  CComboBox class 177
  CListBox class 792
  CListCtrl class 821
  CTreeCtrl class 1737

GetItemDataPtr member function
    CComboBox class 177
    CListBox class 792
GetItemHeight member function
    CComboBox class 178
    CListBox class 792
GetItemID member function
    CStatusBar class 1597
    CToolBar class 1684
GetItemImage member function, CTreeCtrl class 1737
GetItemName member function
    COleChangeSourceDialog class 980
    COleServerItem class 1262
GetItemPosition member function
    CListCtrl class 822
    COleServerDoc class 1245
GetItemRect member function
    CListBox class 793
    CListCtrl class 822
    CStatusBar class 1597
    CTabCtrl class 1654
    CToolBar class 1685
    CToolBarCtrl class 1707
    CTreeCtrl class 1738
GetItemState member function
    CListCtrl class 823
    COleClientItem class 1007
    CTreeCtrl class 1738
GetItemText member function
    CListCtrl class 823
    CTreeCtrl class 1739
GetKerningPairs member function, CDC class 477
GetLastActivePopup member function, Cwnd
    class 1900
GetLastError member function
    CAsyncSocket class 78
    COleDialog class 1155
GetLastModifiedBookmark member function,
    CDaoRecordset class 303
GetLastStatus member function, COleClientItem
    class 1007
GetLBText member function, CComboBox class 178
GetLBTextLen member function, CComboBox
    class 179
GetLength member function
    CFile class 661
    CString class 1626
GetLicenseKey member function,
    COleObjectFactoryEx class 1213

GetLimitText member function
    CEdit class 619
    CRichEditCtrl class 1470
GetLine member function
    CEdit class 620
    CRichEditCtrl class 1471
GetLineCount member function
    CEdit class 620
    CRichEditCtrl class 1471
GetLineSize member function, CSliderCtrl class 1546
GetLinkSourceData member function, COleServerItem
    class 1262
GetLinkUpdateOptions member function,
    COleClientItem class 1007
GetListCtrl member function, CListView class 839
GetLocale member function
    CComboBox class 179
    CListBox class 793
GetLocalTm member function, CTime class 1666
GetLockingMode member function, CDaoRecordset
    class 303
GetLogBrush member function, CBrush class 124–125
GetLogFont member function, CFont class 702
GetLoginTimeout member function, CDaoWorkspace
    class 382
GetLogPen member function, CPen class 1316
GetMainWnd member function, CWinThread
    class 1842
GetMapMode member function, CDC class 478
GetMargins member function
    CEdit class 621
    CPageSetupDialog class 1297
    CRichEditView class 1500
GetMaxConnections member function,
    CConnectionPoint class 200
GetMaxPage member function, CPrintInfo class 1340
GetMDIFrame member function, CMDIChildWnd
    class 872
GetMenu member function, CWnd class 1900
GetMenuContextHelpId member function, CMenu
    class 904
GetMenuItemCount member function, CMenu
    class 904
GetMenuItemID member function, CMenu class 904
GetMenuState member function, CMenu class 905
GetMenuString member function, CMenu class 906
GetMessageBar member function, CFrameWnd
    class 727

GetMessageString member function
    CFrameWnd class 727
    COleControl class 1050
GetMinPage member function, CPrintInfo class 1341
GetMinute member function
    COleDateTime 1124
    CTime class 1667
GetMinutes member function
    COleDateTimeSpan 1144
    CTimeSpan class 1674
GetMiterLimit member function, CDC class 478
GetModify member function
    CEdit class 621
    CRichEditCtrl class 1472
GetMonth member function
    COleDateTime 1124
    CTime class 1667
GetName member function
    CDaoDatabase class 227
    CDaoQueryDef class 260
    CDaoRecordset class 304
    CDaoTableDef class 360
    CDaoWorkspace class 383
GetNearestColor member function, CDC class 478
GetNearestPaletteIndex member function, CPalette
    class 1307
GetNext member function
    CList class 774
    CObList class 960
    CTypedPtrList class 1759
GetNextAssoc member function
    CMap class 844
    CMapStringToOb class 855
    CTypedPtrMap class 1764
GetNextClientItem member function, COleDocument
    class 1170
GetNextDlgGroupItem member function, CWnd
    class 1901
GetNextDlgTabItem member function, CWnd
    class 1901
GetNextDoc member function, CDocTemplate
    class 573
GetNextDocTemplate member function, CWinApp
    class 1804
GetNextFormat member function, COleDataObject
    class 1103

GetNextItem member function
    CListCtrl class 824
    COleDocument class 1170
    CTreeCtrl class 1739
GetNextPathName member function, CFileDialog
    class 678
GetNextServerItem member function, COleDocument
    class 1171
GetNextSiblingItem member function, CTreeCtrl
    class 1740
GetNextView member function, CDocument class 586
GetNextVisibleItem member function, CTreeCtrl
    class 1740
GetNextWindow member function, Cwnd class 1902
GetNotifier member function, CFindReplaceDialog
    class 691
GetNotSupported member function, COleControl
    class 1051
GetNumTics member function, CSliderCtrl class 1546
GetObject member function, CGdiObject class 740
GetObjectArray member function, COlePropertyPage
    class 1232
GetObjectDescriptorData member function,
    COleServerItem class 1263
GetObjectSchema member function, CArchive
    class 42
GetObjectType member function, CGdiObject
    class 741
GetODBCTimeout member function, CDaoQueryDef
    class 260
GetOpenClipboardWindow member function, CWnd
    class 1902
GetOrigin member function, CListCtrl class 825
GetOutlineTextMetrics member function, CDC
    class 479
GetOutputCharWidth member function, CDC
    class 479
GetOutputTabbedTextExtent member function, CDC
    class 480
GetOutputTextExtent member function, CDC
    class 481
GetOutputTextMetrics member function, CDC
    class 482
GetOwner member function, CWnd class 1903
GetPage member function, CPropertySheet class 1364
GetPageCount member function, CPropertySheet
    class 1364
GetPageIndex member function, CPropertySheet
    class 1364

GetPageRect member function, CRichEditView class 1501

GetPageSite member function, COlePropertyPage class 1232

GetPageSize member function, CSliderCtrl class 1546

GetPaletteEntries member function, CPalette class 1307

GetPane member function, CSplitterWnd class 1580

GetPaneInfo member function, CStatusBar class 1598

GetPaneStyle member function, CStatusBar class 1598

GetPaneText member function, CStatusBar class 1598

GetPaperSize member function
    CPageSetupDialog class 1297
    CRichEditView class 1501

GetParaFormat member function, CRichEditCtrl class 1472

GetParaFormatSelection member function, CRichEditView class 1501

GetParameterCount member function, CDaoQueryDef class 261

GetParameterInfo member function, CDaoQueryDef class 261

GetParamValue member function
    CDaoQueryDef class 262
    CDaoRecordset class 304

GetParent member function, CWnd class 1903

GetParentFrame member function, CWnd class 1903

GetParentItem member function, CTreeCtrl class 1740

GetParentOwner member function, CWnd class 1904

GetParts member function, CStatusBarCtrl class 1605

GetPasswordChar member function, CEdit class 621

GetPasteIndex member function, COlePasteSpecialDialog class 1223

GetPath member function, CDC class 482

GetPathName member function
    CDocument class 587
    CFileDialog class 678
    COleInsertDialog class 1192

GetPeerName member function, CAsyncSocket class 78

GetPercentPosition member function, CDaoRecordset class 305

GetPictureDispatch member function, CPictureHolder class 1321

GetPixel member function, CDC class 483

GetPolyFillMode member function, CDC class 484

GetPortName member function
    CPageSetupDialog class 1297
    CPrintDialog class 1336

GetPos member function
    CSliderCtrl class 1547
    CSpinButtonCtrl class 1565

GetPosition member function, CFile class 661

GetPrev member function
    CList class 774
    CObList class 961
    CTypedPtrList class 1760

GetPrevSiblingItem member function, CTreeCtrl class 1741

GetPrevVisibleItem member function, CTreeCtrl class 1741

GetPrimarySelectedItem member function, COleDocument class 1172

GetPrinterDC member function, CPrintDialog class 1336

GetPrinterDeviceDefaults member function, CWinApp class 1804

GetPrinterFont member function, CEditView class 636

GetPrintRect member function, CRichEditView class 1502

GetPrintWidth member function, CRichEditView class 1502

GetProfileInt member function, CWinApp class 1805

GetProfileString member function, CWinApp class 1805

GetProperty member function
    COleDispatchDriver class 1158
    CWnd class 1904

GetQueryDefCount member function, CDaoDatabase class 228

GetQueryDefInfo member function, CDaoDatabase class 229

GetQueryTimeout member function, CDaoDatabase class 230

GetRange member function
    CSliderCtrl class 1547
    CSpinButtonCtrl class 1566

GetRangeMax member function, CSliderCtrl class 1547

GetRangeMin member function, CSliderCtrl class 1547

GetReadOnlyPref member function, CFileDialog class 679

GetRecordCount member function
    CDaoRecordset class 306
    CDaoTableDef class 361
    CRecordset class 1390

GetRecordsAffected member function
  CDaoDatabase class 230
  CDaoQueryDef class 263
GetRect member function
  CEdit class 622
  CRichEditCtrl class 1473
  CStatusBarCtrl class 1606
GetRectInContainer member function, COleControl
  class 1051
GetRegionData member function, CRgn class 1455
GetRelationCount member function, CDaoDatabase
  class 231
GetRelationInfo member function, CDaoDatabase
  class 231
GetReplaceString member function,
  CFindReplaceDialog class 691
GetReturnsRecords member function, CDaoQueryDef
  class 263
GetRgnBox member function, CRgn class 1455
GetRichEditCtrl member function, CRichEditView
  class 1502
GetRootItem member function, CTreeCtrl class 1741
GetROP2 member function, CDC class 484
GetRowCount member function
  CSplitterWnd class 1580
  CTabCtrl class 1655
GetRowInfo member function, CSplitterWnd
  class 1580
GetRows member function, CToolBarCtrl class 1708
GetRuntimeClass member function
  CObject class 947
GetSafeHandle member function
  CGdiObject class 742
  CImageList class 764
GetSafeHdc member function, CDC class 484
GetSafeHmenu member function, CMenu class 907
GetSafeHwnd member function, CWnd class 1905
GetSafeOwner member function, CWnd class 1905
GetSavedCustomColors member function,
  CColorDialog class 160
GetScrollBarCtrl member function, CWnd class 1905
GetScrollInfo member function
  CScrollBar class 1517
  CWnd class 1906
GetScrollLimit member function
  CScrollBar class 1518
  CWnd class 1907

GetScrollPos member function
  CScrollBar class 1519
  CWnd class 1907
GetScrollPosition member function, CScrollView
  class 1526
GetScrollRange member function, CScrollBar
  class 1519
GetScrollRange member function, CWnd class 1908
GetScrollStyle member function, CSplitterWnd
  class 1581
GetSecond member function
  COleDateTime 1125
  CTime class 1668
GetSeconds member function
  COleDateTimeSpan 1145
  CTimeSpan class 1675
GetSel member function
  CEdit class 622
  CListBox class 794
  CRichEditCtrl class 1473
GetSelCount member function, CListBox class 794
GetSelectedCount member function, CListCtrl
  class 825
GetSelectedItem member function
  CRichEditView class 1503
  CTreeCtrl class 1742
GetSelectedText member function, CEditView
  class 637
GetSelection member function, CSliderCtrl class 1548
GetSelectionCharFormat member function,
  CRichEditCtrl class 1474
GetSelectionType member function
  COleBusyDialog class 971
  COleConvertDialog class 1084
  COleInsertDialog class 1192
  COlePasteSpecialDialog class 1223
  CRichEditCtrl class 1474
GetSelItems member function, CListBox class 794
GetSelText member function, CRichEditCtrl
  class 1475
GetSize member function
  CArray class 63
  CFontDialog class 706
  CObArray class 938
GetSockName member function, CAsyncSocket
  class 79
GetSockOpt member function, CAsyncSocket class 80
GetSourceTableName member function,
  CDaoTableDef class 361

GetSQL member function
  CDaoQueryDef class 263
  CDaoRecordset class 307
  CRecordset class 1391
GetStartPosition member function
  CFileDialog class 679
  CMap class 845
  CMapStringToOb class 856
  COleDocument class 1172
GetState member function
  CButton class 131
  CToolBarCtrl class 1708
GetStatus member function
  CFile class 662
  COleCurrency 1089
  COleDateTime 1126
  COleDateTimeSpan 1145
  CRecordset class 1390
GetStatusBarCtrl member function, CStatusBar
  class 1599
GetStockTextMetrics member function, COleControl
  class 1051
GetStreamFormat member function, CRichEditDoc
  class 1491
GetStretchBltMode member function, CDC class 485
GetStringWidth member function, CListCtrl class 825
GetStyle member function, CWnd class 1908
GetStyleName member function, CFontDialog
  class 707
GetSubMenu member function, CMenu class 907
GetSuperWndProcAddr member function, CWnd
  class 1909
GetSystemMenu member function, CWnd class 1909
GetTabbedTextExtent member function, CDC
  class 485
GetTabControl member function, CPropertySheet
  class 1365
GetTableDefCount member function, CDaoDatabase
  class 232
GetTableDefInfo member function, CDaoDatabase
  class 233
GetTableName member function, CRecordset
  class 1392
GetTail member function
  CList class 775
  CObList class 962
  CTypedPtrList class 1761

GetTailPosition member function
  CList class 776
  CObList class 962
GetText member function
  CListBox class 795
  COleControl class 1052
  CStatusBarCtrl class 1606
  CToolTipCtrl class 1722
GetTextAlign member function, CDC class 486
GetTextBkColor member function, CListCtrl class 826
GetTextCharacterExtra member function, CDC
  class 487
GetTextColor member function
  CDC class 487
  CListCtrl class 826
GetTextExtent member function, CDC class 488
GetTextFace member function, CDC class 488
GetTextLen member function, CListBox class 795
GetTextLength member function
  CRichEditCtrl class 1475
  CRichEditView class 1503
  CStatusBarCtrl class 1607
GetTextMetrics member function, CDC class 489
GetThreadPriority member function, CWinThread
  class 1843
GetThumbRect member function, CSliderCtrl
  class 1548
GetTic member function, CSliderCtrl class 1548
GetTicArray member function, CSliderCtrl class 1549
GetTicPos member function, CSliderCtrl class 1549
GetTime member function, CTime class 1668
Getting connect strings 227
GetTitle member function, CDocument class 587
GetToolBarCtrl member function, CToolBar
  class 1685
GetToolCount member function, CToolTipCtrl
  class 1722
GetToolInfo member function, CToolTipCtrl
  class 1722
GetTooltips member function, CTabCtrl class 1655
GetToolTips member function, CToolBarCtrl
  class 1709
GetToPage member function
  CPrintDialog class 1336
  CPrintInfo class 1341
GetTopIndex member function
  CComboBox class 179
  CListBox class 796
  CListCtrl class 826

GetTopLevelFrame member function, CWnd class 1910

GetTopLevelOwner member function, CWnd class 1910

GetTopLevelParent member function, CWnd class 1910

GetToPrefix member function, COleChangeSourceDialog class 980

GetTopWindow member function, CWnd class 1911

GetTotalDays member function, COleDateTimeSpan class 1146

GetTotalHours member function, COleDateTimeSpan class 1147

GetTotalHours member function, CTimeSpan class 1675

GetTotalMinutes member function
   COleDateTimeSpan 1147
   CTimeSpan class 1675

GetTotalSeconds member function
   COleDateTimeSpan 1148
   CTimeSpan class 1675

GetTotalSize member function, CScrollView class 1526

GetTreeCtrl member function, CTreeView class 1753

GetTrueRect member function, CRectTracker class 1439

GetType member function
   CDaoQueryDef class 264
   CDaoRecordset class 307
   COleClientItem class 1008
   CPictureHolder class 1322

GetUpdateRect member function, CWnd class 1911

GetUpdateRgn member function, CWnd class 1912

GetUpperBound member function
   CArray class 63
   CObArray class 938

GetUserName member function, CDaoWorkspace class 383

GetUserType member function, COleClientItem class 1008

GetValidationRule member function
   CDaoRecordset class 308
   CDaoTableDef class 362

GetValidationText member function
   CDaoRecordset class 308
   CDaoTableDef class 362

GetVersion member function
   CDaoDatabase class 234
   CDaoWorkspace class 384
   CPropExchange class 1373

GetView member function, CRichEditDoc class 1492

GetViewportExt member function, CDC class 489

GetViewportOrg member function, CDC class 490

GetViewRect member function, CListCtrl class 826

GetVisibleCount member function, CTreeCtrl class 1742

GetWeight member function, CFontDialog class 707

GetWindow member function
   CDC class 490
   CWnd class 1913

GetWindowContextHelpId member function, CWnd class 1913

GetWindowDC member function, CWnd class 1914

GetWindowExt member function, CDC class 490

GetWindowMenuPopup member function, CMDIFrameWnd class 877

GetWindowOrg member function, CDC class 490

GetWindowPlacement member function, CWnd class 1914

GetWindowRect member function, CWnd class 1915

GetWindowText member function, CWnd class 1915

GetWindowTextLength member function, CWnd class 1916

GetWorkspaceCount member function, CDaoWorkspace class 384

GetWorkspaceInfo member function, CDaoWorkspace class 385

GetYear member function
   COleDateTime 1127
   CTime class 1668

GetZoomFactor member function, COleServerDoc class 1245

GiveFeedback member function, COleDropSource class 1176

Global function/macro
   AFX_MANAGE_STATE 2082
   AFX_SQL_ASYNC 2095
   AFX_SQL_SYNC 2096
   AfxAbort 2070
   AfxBeginThread 2071
   AfxCheckMemory 2072
   AfxConnectionAdvise 2073
   AfxConnectionUnadvise 2074
   AfxDoForAllClasses 2074
   AfxDoForAllObjects 2075

Global function/macro *(continued)*

afxDump 2075–2076
AfxEnableControlContainer 2076
AfxEnableMemoryTracking 2077
AfxEndThread 2077
AfxFormatString1 2077
AfxFormatString2 2078
AfxGetApp 2078
AfxGetAppName 2079
AfxGetInstanceHandle 2079
AfxGetMainWnd 2079
AfxGetResourceHandle 2080
AfxGetThread 2080
AfxIsMemoryBlock 2080
AfxIsValidAddress 2081
AfxIsValidString 2081
afxMemDF 2082
AfxMessageBox 2083
AfxOleCanExitApp 2084
AfxOleGetMessageFilter 2084
AfxOleGetUserCtrl 2085
AfxOleInit 2085
AfxOleLockApp 2085
AfxOleRegisterControlClass 2086
AfxOleRegisterPropertyPageClass 2087
AfxOleRegisterServerClass 2088
AfxOleRegisterTypeLib 2089
AfxOleSetEditMenu 2090
AfxOleSetUserCtrl 2091
AfxOleTypeMatchGuid 2091–2092
AfxOleUnlockApp 2092
AfxOleUnregisterTypeLib 2092
AfxRegisterClass 2093
AfxRegisterWndClass 2093
AfxSetAllocHook 2094
AfxSetResourceHandle 2094
AfxSocketInit 2095
AfxThrowArchiveException 2097
AfxThrowDaoException 2097
AfxThrowDBException 2098
AfxThrowFileException 2098
AfxThrowMemoryException 2099
AfxThrowNotSupportedException 2099
AfxThrowOleDispatchException 2099
AfxThrowOleException 2100
AfxThrowResourceException 2100
AfxThrowUserException 2100
afxTraceEnabled 2101
afxTraceFlags 2101

Global function/macro *(continued)*

AfxVerifyLicFile 2102
AND_CATCH_ALL 2103
AND_CATCH 2103
ASSERT_VALID 2105
ASSERT 2104
BASED_CODE 2105
BEGIN_CONNECTION_MAP 2106
BEGIN_CONNECTION_PART 2106
BEGIN_DISPATCH_MAP 2106
BEGIN_EVENT_MAP 2107
BEGIN_EVENTSINK_MAP 2107
BEGIN_MESSAGE_MAP 2108
BEGIN_OLEFACTORY 2109
BEGIN_PROPPAGEIDS 2109
CATCH_ALL 2110
CATCH 2109
CompareElements 2111
CONNECTION_IID 2112
CONNECTION_PART 2112
ConstructElements 2111
DDP_CBIndex 2113
DDP_CBString 2113
DDP_CBStringExact 2114
DDP_Check 2114
DDP_LBIndex 2115
DDP_LBString 2116
DDP_LBStringExact 2116
DDP_PostProcessing 2117
DDP_Radio 2117
DDP_Text 2118
DDV_MaxChars 2119
DDV_MinMaxByte 2119
DDV_MinMaxDouble 2120
DDV_MinMaxDWord 2120
DDV_MinMaxFloat 2121
DDV_MinMaxInt 2121
DDV_MinMaxLong 2122
DDV_MinMaxUnsigned 2122
DDX_CBIndex 2123
DDX_CBString 2123
DDX_CBStringExact 2124
DDX_Check 2125
DDX_FieldCBIndex 2126
DDX_FieldCBString 2127
DDX_FieldCBStringExact 2128
DDX_FieldCheck 2129
DDX_FieldLBIndex 2129
DDX_FieldLBString 2130

Global function/macro *(continued)*
DDX_FieldLBStringExact 2131
DDX_FieldRadio 2132
DDX_FieldScroll 2133
DDX_FieldText 2134
DDX_LBIndex 2136
DDX_LBString 2137
DDX_LBStringExact 2137
DDX_Radio 2138
DDX_Scroll 2138
DDX_Text 2139
DEBUG_NEW 2140
DECLARE_CONNECTION_MAP 2140
DECLARE_DISPATCH_MAP 2141
DECLARE_DYNAMIC 2141
DECLARE_DYNCREATE 2142
DECLARE_EVENT_MAP 2142
DECLARE_EVENTSINK_MAP 2143
DECLARE_MESSAGE_MAP 2143
DECLARE_OLECREATE_EX 2144
DECLARE_OLECREATE 2144
DECLARE_OLETYPELIB 2145
DECLARE_PROPPAGEIDS 2145
DECLARE_SERIAL 2145
DestructElements 2146
DFX_Binary 2147
DFX_Bool 2148
DFX_Byte 2149
DFX_Currency 2150
DFX_DateTime 2151
DFX_Double 2152
DFX_Long 2153
DFX_LongBinary 2154
DFX_Short 2155
DFX_Single 2156
DFX_Text 2157
DISP_DEFVALUE 2158
DISP_FUNCTION 2158
DISP_PROPERTY_EX 2161
DISP_PROPERTY 2160
DumpElements 2162
END_CATCH_ALL 2163
END_CATCH 2163
END_CONNECTION_MAP 2163
END_CONNECTION_PART 2163
END_DISPATCH_MAP 2164
END_EVENT_MAP 2164
END_EVENTSINK_MAP 2164
END_MESSAGE_MAP 2164

Global function/macro *(continued)*
END_OLEFACTORY 2165
END_PROPPAGEIDS 2165
EVENT_CUSTOM 2165
EVENT_CUSTOM_ID 2166
IMPLEMENT_DYNAMIC 2167
IMPLEMENT_DYNCREATE 2168
IMPLEMENT_OLECREATE_EX 2169
IMPLEMENT_OLECREATE 2168
IMPLEMENT_OLETYPELIB 2170
IMPLEMENT_SERIAL 2170
ON_COMMAND_RANGE 2171
ON_COMMAND 2170
ON_CONTROL_RANGE 2172
ON_CONTROL 2172
ON_EVENT_RANGE 2174
ON_EVENT 2173
ON_MESSAGE 2174
ON_OLEVERB 2175
ON_PROPNOTIFY_RANGE 2176
ON_PROPNOTIFY 2176
ON_REGISTERED_MESSAGE 2177
ON_STDOLEVERB 2178
ON_UPDATE_COMMAND_UI_RANGE 2179
ON_UPDATE_COMMAND_UI 2178
PROPPAGEID 2179
PX_Blob 2179
PX_Bool 2180
PX_Color 2181
PX_Currency 2181
PX_Double 2182
PX_Float 2183
PX_Font 2183
PX_IUnknown 2184
PX_Long 2185
PX_Picture 2185
PX_Short 2186
PX_String 2186
PX_ULong 2187
PX_UShort 2188
PX_VBXFontConvert 2188
RFX_Binary 2189
RFX_Bool 2190
RFX_Byte 2190
RFX_Date 2191
RFX_Double 2192
RFX_Int 2192
RFX_Long 2193
RFX_LongBinary 2194

Global function/macro *(continued)*
  RFX_Single 2194
  RFX_Text 2195
  RUNTIME_CLASS 2196
  SerializeElements 2197
  THIS_FILE 2197
  THROW_LAST 2198
  THROW 2197
  TRACE 2198
  TRACE0 2199
  TRACE1 2199
  TRACE2 2200
  TRACE3 2200
  TRY 2201
  VERIFY 2201
GlobalAlloc, memory leaks 889
GlobalFree, memory leaks 889
Globals categories (list) 2046
GotoDlgCtrl member function, CDialog class 556
GrayString member function, CDC class 491
GrayString, callback function for *See* Callback
  functions for MFC member functions
GrowFile member function, CMemFile class 885

H

HasBlankItems member function, COleDocument
  class 1172
HD_ITEM structure 747
HD_LAYOUT structure 749
HDBC handle
  Database 405
  ODBC 405
Header control 744
Height member function, CRect class 1422
HexDump member function, CDumpContext class 606
HideApplication member function, CWinApp
  class 1806
HideButton member function, CToolBarCtrl
  class 1709
HideCaret member function, CWnd class 1916
HideSelection member function, CRichEditCtrl
  class 1476
Hierarchy charts for classes xi
HiliteMenuItem member function, CWnd class 1917
HIMETRICtoDP member function, CDC class 492
HIMETRICtoLP member function, CDC class 493

HitTest member function
  CListCtrl class 827
  CRectTracker class 1439
  CTabCtrl class 1655
  CToolTipCtrl class 1724
  CTreeCtrl class 1742
Hot key control 751
HSTMT handle
  ODBC 1407
  Recordset 1407

I

ID, standard command and window 2057
IDataObject, MFC encapsulation 1098, 1105
IdFromRowCol member function, CSplitterWnd
  class 1581
Idle member function, CDaoWorkspace class 386
Idle processing, DAO 386
IgnoreApply member function, COlePropertyPage
  class 1233
Image Lists 755
IMAGEINFO structure 764
IMPLEMENT_DYNAMIC global
  function/macro 2167
IMPLEMENT_DYNCREATE global
  function/macro 2168
IMPLEMENT_OLECREATE global
  function/macro 2168
IMPLEMENT_OLECREATE_EX global
  function/macro 2169
IMPLEMENT_OLETYPELIB global
  function/macro 2170
IMPLEMENT_SERIAL global function/macro 2170
Implicit construction of database object 220
In-place editing
  activation status 1246
  change notifications 1247
  clipping rectangle 1244
  COleServerDoc class 1243
  embedded status 1246
  item coordinates 1245
  item zoom factor 1245
Inconsistent updates, defined 225
Indeterminate member function, CToolBarCtrl
  class 1709
Index field object (DAO), obtaining information
  about 2225
Index object (DAO), obtaining information about 2222

InflateRect member function, CRect class 1423

InitApplication member function, CWinApp
    class 1806

InitHashTable member function, CMap class 845

Initialization settings
    database engine 381
    workspace 391

Initialization, OLE system DLLs 2061

InitializeFont member function, CFontHolder
    class 711

InitializeIIDs member function, COleControl
    class 1052

InitialUpdateFrame member function
    CDocTemplate class 573
    CFrameWnd class 727

Initiating drag and drop 1110

InitInstance member function
    CWinApp class 1807
    CWinThread class 1843

InitModalIndirect member function, CDialog class 556

InitStorage member function
    CComboBox class 180
    CListBox class 796

InModalState member function, CFrameWnd
    class 728

InsertAfter member function
    CList class 776
    CObList class 963

InsertAt member function
    CArray class 63
    CObArray class 938

InsertBefore member function
    CList class 776
    CObList class 964

InsertButton member function, CToolBarCtrl
    class 1710

InsertColumn member function, CListCtrl class 828

InsertFileAsObject member function, CRichEditView
    class 1503

InsertItem member function
    CHeaderCtrl class 749
    CListCtrl class 829
    CRichEditView class 1504
    CTabCtrl class 1656
    CTreeCtrl class 1744

InsertMenu member function, CMenu class 907

InsertString member function
    CComboBox class 180
    CListBox class 797

Integer, DDX field exchange 2134

InternalGetFont member function, COleControl
    class 1052

InternalGetText member function, COleControl
    class 1053

IntersectClipRect member function, CDC class 493

IntersectRect member function, CRect class 1423

Invalidate member function, CWnd class 1917

InvalidateControl member function, COleControl
    class 1053

InvalidateRect member function, CWnd class 1918

InvalidateRgn member function, CWnd class 1919

InvertRect member function, CDC class 494

InvertRgn member function, CDC class 494

InvokeHelper member function
    COleDispatchDriver class 1159
    CWnd class 1919

InWaitForDataSource member function, CDatabase
    class 399

IOCtl member function, CAsyncSocket class 82

IsBlank member function, CDocItem class 564

IsBlocking member function, CSocket class 1558

IsBOF member function
    CDaoRecordset class 309
    CRecordset class 1392

IsBold member function, CFontDialog class 707

IsBufferEmpty member function, CArchive class 43

IsButtonChecked member function, CToolBarCtrl
    class 1710

IsButtonEnabled member function, CToolBarCtrl
    class 1711

IsButtonHidden member function, CToolBarCtrl
    class 1711

IsButtonIndeterminate member function, CToolBarCtrl
    class 1712

IsButtonPressed member function, CToolBarCtrl
    class 1712

IsChild member function, CWnd class 1920

IsChildPane member function, CSplitterWnd
    class 1582

IsConnected member function, COleServerItem
    class 1263

IsConvertingVBX member function, COleControl
    class 1053

IsDataAvailable member function, COleDataObject
    class 1103

IsDeleted member function
    CDaoRecordset class 310
    CRecordset class 1393

IsDialogMessage member function, CWnd class 1921
IsDlgButtonChecked member function, CWnd class 1922
IsEmbedded member function, COleServerDoc class 1246
IsEmpty member function
    CList class 777
    CMap class 845
    CMapStringToOb class 856
    CObList class 964
    CString class 1626
IsEnabled member function, CCheckListBox class 141
IsEOF member function
    CDaoRecordset class 311
    CRecordset class 1393
IsFieldDirty member function
    CDaoRecordset class 312
    CRecordset class 1394
IsFieldNull member function
    CDaoRecordset class 313
    CRecordset class 1394
IsFieldNullable member function
    CDaoRecordset class 314
    CRecordset class 1395
IsFieldType member function, CFieldExchange class 653
IsFloating member function, CControlBar class 206
IsIconic member function, CWnd class 1922
IsIdleMessage member function, CWinThread class 1844
IsInPlaceActive member function
    COleClientItem class 1009
    COleServerDoc class 1246
IsItalic member function, CFontDialog class 707
IsKindOf member function, CObject class 948
IsLinkedItem member function, COleServerItem class 1264
IsLinkUpToDate member function, COleClientItem class 1009
IsLoading member function
    CArchive class 43
    CPropExchange class 1373
IsLocked member function
    CMultiLock class 928
    CSingleLock class 1536
IsModified member function
    CDocument class 588
    COleClientItem class 1010

IsModified member function *(continued)*
    COleControl class 1054
    COlePropertyPage class 1233
Isolating ODBC transactions 391
IsOnFirstRecord member function
    CDaoRecordView class 342
    CRecordView class 1415
IsOnLastRecord member function
    CDaoRecordView class 342
    CRecordView class 1415
IsOpen member function
    CDaoDatabase class 234
    CDaoQueryDef class 265
    CDaoRecordset class 315
    CDaoTableDef class 363
    CDaoWorkspace class 386
    CDatabase class 400
    COleClientItem class 1010
    CRecordset class 1396
IsPrinting member function, CDC class 495
IsRectEmpty member function, CRect class 1424
IsRectNull member function, CRect class 1424
IsRegistered member function, COleObjectFactory class 1213
IsResultExpected member function, CCmdTarget class 150
IsRichEditFormat member function, CRichEditView class 1504
IsRunning member function, COleClientItem class 1010
IsSelected member function
    CRichEditView class 1504
    CView class 1774
IsSerializable member function, CObject class 948
IsStoring member function, CArchive class 44
IsStrikeOut member function, CFontDialog class 708
IsSubclassedControl member function, COleControl class 1054
IsTerminating member function, CFindReplaceDialog class 691
IsTracking member function, CFrameWnd 728
IsUnderline member function, CFontDialog class 708
IsValidOperation member function, CDaoFieldExchange class 246
IsValidSource member function, COleChangeSourceDialog class 981
IsWindowEnabled member function, CWnd class 1922
IsWindowVisible member function, CWnd class 1923
IsZoomed member function, CWnd class 1923

ItemFromPoint member function, CListBox class 797
ItemHasChildren member function, CTreeCtrl class 1745

J

Jet database engine *See* Database engine

K

KillTimer member function, CWnd class 1923

L

Large data objects, CLongBinary class 840
Layout member function, CHeaderCtrl class 749
Left member function, CString class 1627
LimitText member function
    CComboBox class 181
    CEdit class 623
    CRichEditCtrl class 1476
LineFromChar member function
    CEdit class 623
    CRichEditCtrl class 1477
LineIndex member function
    CEdit class 624
    CRichEditCtrl class 1477
LineLength member function
    CEdit class 624
    CRichEditCtrl class 1478
LineScroll member function
    CEdit class 625
    CRichEditCtrl class 1478
LineTo member function, CDC class 495
LINGER structure 2250
Linked items (OLE) 1239
List box, DDX field exchange 2129–2131
List view control 806
List-Box styles 2273
Listen member function, CAsyncSocket class 84
Lists, collection classes
    CList 769
    CTypedPtrList 1757
LoadAccelTable member function, CFrameWnd class 728
LoadBarState member function, CFrameWnd class 729
LoadBitmap member function
    CBitmap class 108
    CToolBar class 1686

LoadBitmaps member function, CBitmapButton class 115
LoadCursor member function, CWinApp class 1808
LoadField, Record field exchange (DFX) 247
LoadFrame member function, CFrameWnd class 729
LoadIcon member function, CWinApp class 1809
LoadMappedBitmap member function, CBitmap class 109
LoadMenu member function, CMenu class 909
LoadMenuIndirect member function, CMenu class 910
LoadOEMBitmap member function, CBitmap class 109
LoadOEMCursor member function, CWinApp class 1810
LoadOEMIcon member function, CWinApp class 1810
LoadStandardCursor member function, CWinApp class 1811
LoadStandardIcon member function, CWinApp class 1812
LoadStdProfileSettings member function, CWinApp class 1812
LoadString member function, CString class 1627
LoadTemplate member function, CDocTemplate class 574
LoadToolBar member function, CToolBar class 1686
LocalAlloc, memory leaks 889
LocalFree, memory leaks 889
Lock member function
    CCriticalSection class 212
    CMultiLock class 928
    CSingleLock class 1536
    CSyncObject class 1646
LockBuffer member function
    CEditView class 637
    CString class 1628
Locking modes, recordset
    described 1406
    setting 1406
LockInPlaceActive member function, COleControl class 1055
LockRange member function, CFile class 663
LockWindowUpdate member function, CWnd class 1924
LOGBRUSH structure 2250
LOGFONT structure 2251
Login timeout property, setting 392, 404
Login timeout *See* Workspace
LOGPEN structure 2255

Long integer
    DDX field exchange 2134
    DFX field exchange 2153
    RFX field exchange 2193
Lookup member function
    CMap class 846
    CMapStringToOb class 857
    CTypedPtrMap class 1764
LPtoDP member function, CDC class 495
LPtoHIMETRIC member function, CDC class 496
LV_COLUMN structure 817
LV_FINDINFO structure 815
LV_HITTESTINFO structure 827
LV_ITEM structure 820

M

m_bAutoDelete data member
    CControlBar class 207
    CWinThread class 1848
m_bAutoMenuEnable data member, CFrameWnd
    class 735
m_bAutoRelease data member, COleDisplatchDriver
    class 1162
m_bCheckCacheForDirtyFields data member,
    CDaoRecordset class 336
m_bContinuePrinting data member, CPrintInfo
    class 1342
m_bDirect data member, CPrintInfo class 1343
m_bHelpMode data member, CWinApp class 1832
m_bPreview data member, CPrintInfo class 1343
m_bRTF data member, CRichEditDoc class 1492
m_bRunAutomated data member, CCommandLineInfo
    class 191
m_bRunEmbedded data member, CCommandLineInfo
    class 192
m_bSaveAndValidate member function,
    CDataExchange class 410
m_bShowSplash data member, CCommandLineInfo
    class 192
m_bz data member, COleBusyDialog class 972
m_cause data member
    CArchiveException class 57
    CFileException class 685
m_cc data member, CColorDialog class 162
m_cf data member, CFontDialog class 708
m_ci data member, COleChangeIconDialog class 976
m_cs data member, COleChangeSourceDialog
    class 981

m_cur data member, COleCurrency class 1096
m_cv data member, COleConvertDialog class 1085
m_DAOTableDef data member, CDaoTableDef
    class 369
m_dt data member, COleDateTime class 1137
m_dwDataLength data member, CLongBinary
    class 841
m_dwDefaultStyle data member, CCtrlView class 215
m_dwHelpContext data member,
    COleDisplatchException class 1164
m_el data member, COleLinksDialog class 1203
m_fr data member, CFindReplaceDialog class 693
m_gp data member, COlePropertiesDialog class 1228
m_hAttribDC data member, CDC class 548
m_hData data member, CLongBinary class 841
m_hdbc data member, CDatabase class 405
m_hDC data member, CDC class 548
m_hFile data member, CFile class 672
m_hImageList data member, CImageList class 768
m_hInstance data member, CWinApp class 1832
m_hMenu data member, CMenu class 916
m_hObject data member, CGdiObject class 743
m_hPrevInstance data member, CWinApp class 1833
m_hSocket data member, CAsyncSocket class 101
m_hstmt data member, CRecordset class 1407
m_hThread data member, CWinThread class 1849
m_hWnd data member
    CClientDC class 144
    CPaintDC class 1302
    CWindowDC class 1838
    CWnd class 2043
m_io data member, COleInsertDialog class 1193
m_lOsError data member, CFileException class 686
m_lp data member, COlePropertiesDialog class 1228
m_lpCmdLine data member, CWinApp class 1833
m_lpDispatch data member, COleDispatchDriver
    class 1162
m_lpUserData data member, CPrintInfo class 1343
m_nAfxDaoError data member, CDaoException
    class 242
m_nBulletIndent data member, CRichEditView
    class 1513
m_nCmdShow data member, CWinApp class 1834
m_nCurPage data member, CPrintInfo class 1343
m_nFields data member, CRecordset class 1408
m_nHandleSize data member, CRectTracker
    class 1442
m_nNumPreviewPages data member, CPrintInfo
    class 1344

m_nOperation data member, CDaoFieldExchange
   class 247
m_nParams data member
   CDaoRecordset class 336
   CRecordset class 1408
m_nRetCode data member, CDBException class 413
m_nShellCommand data member, CCommandLineInfo
   class 192
m_nStyle data member, CRectTracker class 1443
m_nThreadID data member, CWinThread class 1849
m_nWordWrap data member, CRichEditView
   class 1513
m_ofn data member, CFileDialog class 681
m_op data member, COlePropertiesDialog class 1229
m_pActiveWnd data member
   CWinApp class 1835
   CWinThread class 1849
m_pd data member, CPrintDialog class 1338
m_pDAODatabase data member, CDaoDatabase
   class 237
m_pDAOQueryDef data member, CDaoQueryDef
   class 270
m_pDAORecordset data member, CDaoRecordset
   class 337
m_pDAOWorkspace data member, CDaoWorkspace
   class 393
m_pDatabase data member
   CDaoQueryDef class 269
   CDaoRecordset class 337
   CDaoTableDef class 368
   CRecordset class 1409
m_pDlgWnd member function, CDataExchange
   class 411
m_pDocument data member, CArchive class 55
m_pErrorInfo data member, CDaoException class 243
m_pFont data member, CFontHolder class 712
m_pMainWnd data member, CWinThread class 1849
m_pPD data member, CPrintInfo class 1344
m_pPict data member, CPictureHolder class 1323
m_prs data member, CDaoFieldExchange class 249
m_ps data member
   COlePasteSpecialDialog class 1224
   CPaintDC class 1302
m_psd data member, CPageSetupDialog class 1300
m_psh data member
   COlePropertiesDialog class 1229
   CPropertySheet class 1368
m_psp data member, CPropertyPage class 1357
m_pStream data member, CStdioFile class 1613

m_pszAppName data member, CWinApp class 1835
m_pszExeName data member, CWinApp class 1835
m_pszHelpFilePath data member, CWinApp
   class 1836
m_pszProfileName data member, CWinApp
   class 1836
m_pszRegistryKey data member, CWinApp class 1836
m_pWorkspace data member, CDaoDatabase
   class 238
m_rect data member, CRectTracker class 1443
m_rectDraw data member, CPrintInfo class 1344
m_sc data member, COleException class 1187
m_scode data member, CDaoException class 244
m_sizeExtent data member, CRectTracker class 1276
m_sizeMin data member, CRectTracker class 1443
m_span data member, COleDataTimeSpan class 1152
m_status data member
   COleCurrency class 1096
   COleDateTime class 1138
   COleDateTimeSpan class 1153
m_strClass data member, CCtrlView class 215
m_strDescription data member,
   COleDispatchException class 1164
m_strDriverName data member, CCommandLineInfo
   class 193
m_strError
   and m_strStateNativeOrigin 415
   example 415
m_strError data member, CDBException class 415
m_strFileName data member, CCommandLineInfo
   class 193
m_strFilter data member
   CDaoRecordset class 337
   CRecordset class 1409
m_strHelpFile data member, COleDispatchException
   class 1164
m_strPageDesc data member, CPrintInfo class 1345
m_strPortName data member, CCommandLineInfo
   class 194
m_strPrinterName data member, CCommandLineInfo
   class 194
m_strSort data member
   CDaoRecordset class 338
   CRecordset class 1410
m_strSource data member, COleDispatchException
   class 1164
m_strStateNativeOrigin
   and m_strError 415
   example 415

m_strStateNativeOrigin data member, CDBException class 415

m_vp data member, COlePropertiesDialog class 1229

m_wCode data member, COleDispatchException class 1165

Macro categories (list) 2046

Mail API *See* MAPI

Mailing documents *See* MAPI

Make-table query 251

MakeLower member function, CString class 1629

MakeReverse member function, CString class 1629

MakeUpper member function, CString class 1629

MapDialogRect member function, CDialog class 557

MAPI
   described 589, 593, 1173
   MFC support for 589, 593, 1173

MapObject member function, CArchive class 44

Maps
   CMapPtrToPtr 849
   CMapPtrToWord 851
   CMapStringToOb 853
   CMapStringToPtr 861
   CMapStringToString 863
   CMapWordToOb 865
   CMapWordToPtr 867
   CTypedPtrMap 1763

Maps, collection classes, CMap 842

MapWindowPoints member function, CWnd class 1924

MarkForAddNew, Record field exchange (DFX) 247

MarkForEdit, Record field exchange (DFX) 247

MaskBlt member function, CDC class 496

MatchCase member function, CFindReplaceDialog class 692

MatchDocType member function, CDocTemplate class 574

MatchWholeWord member function, CFindReplaceDialog class 692

MaxDFXOperation, Record field exchange (DFX) 247

MDIActivate member function
   CMDIChildWnd class 872
   CMDIFrameWnd class 877

MDICascade member function, CMDIFrameWnd class 878

MDIDestroy member function, CMDIChildWnd class 873

MDIGetActive member function, CMDIFrameWnd class 878

MDIIconArrange member function, CMDIFrameWnd class 879

MDIMaximize member function
   CMDIChildWnd class 873
   CMDIFrameWnd class 879

MDINext member function, CMDIFrameWnd class 879

MDIRestore member function
   CMDIChildWnd class 873
   CMDIFrameWnd class 880

MDISetMenu member function, CMDIFrameWnd class 880

MDITile member function, CMDIFrameWnd class 881

MeasureItem member function
   CComboBox class 181
   CListBox class 797
   CMenu class 911

MEASUREITEMSTRUCT structure 2256

Member functions
   CAnimateCtrl class 34
   CArchive class 39
   CArchiveException class 56
   CArray class 60
   CAsyncSocket class 70
   CBitmap class 103
   CBitmapButton class 114
   CBrush class 118
   CButton class 128
   CCheckListBox class 139
   CClientDC class 143
   CCmdTarget class 146
   CCmdUI class 156
   CColorDialog class 159
   CComboBox class 168
   CCommandLineInfo class 190
   CCommonDialog class 195
   CConnectionPoint 199
   CControlBar class 202
   CCriticalSection class 212
   CCtrlView class 214
   CDaoDatabase class 219
   CDaoException class 240
   CDaoFieldExchange class 246
   CDaoQueryDef class 253
   CDaoRecordset class 277
   CDaoRecordView class 341
   CDaoTableDef class 348
   CDaoWorkspace class 374

Member functions *(continued)*

    CDatabase class 394

    CDataExchange class 408

    CDC class 425, 427, 464, 496, 530

    CDialog class 552

    CDialogBar class 562

    CDocItem class 564

    CDocTemplate class 568

    CDocument class 581

    CDragListBox class 601–603

    CDumpContext class 605

    CEdit class 614

    CEditView class 635

    CEvent class 644

    CException class 648

    CFieldExchange class 653

    CFile class 657

    CFileDialog class 675

    CFileException class 683

    CFindReplaceDialog class 689

    CFont class 695

    CFontDialog class 704

    CFontHolder class 709

    CFormView class 716

    CFrameWnd class 721, 735

    CGdiObject class 737

    CHeaderCtrl class 745

    CHotKeyCtrl class 752

    CImageList class 756

    CList class 770

    CListBox class 784

    CListCtrl class 810

    CListView class 838

    CLongBinary class 841

    CMap class 843

    CMapStringToOb class 854

    CMDIChildWnd class 871

    CMDIFrameWnd class 876

    CMemFile class 883

    CMemoryException class 888

    CMemoryState class 890

    CMenu class 895

    CMetaFileDC class 918

    CMiniFrameWnd class 922

    CMultiDocTemplate class 925

    CMultiLock class 928

    CMutex class 932

    CNotSupportedException class 933

    CObArray class 935

Member functions *(continued)*

    CObject class 945

    CObList class 954

    COleBusyDialog class 970

    COleChangeIconDialog class 974

    COleChangeSourceDialog class 978

    COleClientItem class 986

    COleControl class 1031

    COleConvertDialog class 1081

    COleCurrency 1087

    COleDataObject class 1099

    COleDataSource class 1106

    COleDateTime 1118

    COleDateTimeSpan 1141

    COleDialog class 1155

    COleDispatchDriver class 1157

    COleDocument class 1167

    COleDropSource class 1176

    COleDropTarget class 1180

    COleInsertDialog class 1189

    COleIPFrameWnd class 1194

    COleLinkingDoc class 1198

    COleLinksDialog class 1202

    COleMessageFilter class 1205

    COleObjectFactory class 1212

    COlePasteSpecialDialog class 1219

    COlePropertiesDialog class 1226

    COlePropertyPage class 1231

    COleResizeBar class 1237

    COleServerDoc class 1242

    COleServerItem class 1258

    COleStreamFile class 1278

    COleTemplateServer class 1282

    COleUpdateDialog class 1284

    COleVariant 1287

    CPageSetupDialog class 1293

    CPaintDC class 1301

    CPalette class 1304

    CPen class 1310

    CPictureHolder class 1318

    CPoint class 1325

    CPrintDialog class 1332

    CPrintInfo class 1340

    CProgressCtrl class 1347

    CPropertyPage class 1351

    CPropertySheet class 1359

    CPropExchange class 1370

    CRecordset class 1381

    CRecordView class 1414

Member functions *(continued)*
    CRect class 1420
    CRectTracker class 1436
    CResourceException class 1444
    CRgn class 1446
    CRichEditCntrItem class 1460
    CRichEditCtrl 1464
    CRichEditDoc class 1491
    CRichEditView class 1495
    CScrollBar class 1516
    CScrollView class 1524
    CSemaphore class 1531
    CSingleDocTemplate class 1533
    CSingleLock class 1536
    CSize class 1538
    CSliderCtrl class 1543
    CSpinButtonCtrl class 1563
    CSplitterWnd class 1572
    CStatic class 1588
    CStatusBar class 1596
    CStatusBarCtrl class 1603
    CStdioFile class 1611
    CString class 1617
    CSyncObject class 1645
    CTabCtrl class 1648
    CTime class 1661
    CTimeSpan class 1672
    CToolBar class 1682
    CToolBarCtrl class 1699
    CToolTipCtrl class 1720
    CTreeCtrl class 1729
    CTreeView class 1752
    CTypedPtrArray class 1755
    CTypedPtrList class 1758
    CTypedPtrMap class 1764
    CView class 1773
    CWaitCursor class 1791
    CWinApp class 1798
    CWindowDC class 1837
    CWinThread class 1841
    CWnd class 1865–1866, 1889, 1909, 1934, 1959,
        1982, 2008, 2041
Memcpy member function, CMemFile class 886
Memory leaks
    and GlobalAlloc and GlobalFree 889
    and LocalAlloc and LocalFree 889
    and malloc and free 889
    DEBUG_NEW macro 889

Memory leaks *(continued)*
    detecting 889
    new operator 889
Menu classes (list) 10
Message maps 2054
Message-box display, CString object formatting 2053
Message-box styles 2274
MessageBox member function, Cwnd class 1925
Messaging API *See* MAPI
Microsoft Foundation Class Library
    application framework 3
    introduction, overview xi
    overview 1
    relationship to Windows API 2–3
Microsoft Jet database engine *See* Database engine
Mid member function, CString class 1630
MINMAXINFO structure 2257
Modifying data source data 1109
Modifying drag and drop cursors 1176
ModifyMenu member function, CMenu class 911
ModifyStyle member function, Cwnd class 1926
ModifyStyleEx member function, CWnd class 1927
Move member function
    CDaoRecordset class 315
    CRecordset class 1396
MoveFirst member function
    CDaoRecordset class 316
    CRecordset class 1397
MoveLast member function
    CDaoRecordset class 317
    CRecordset class 1398
MoveNext member function
    CDaoRecordset class 318
    CRecordset class 1398
MovePrev member function
    CDaoRecordset class 319
    CRecordset class 1399
MoveTo member function, CDC class 498
MoveWindow member function, CWnd class 1927
Moving
    through records, CRecordView class 1416
    to first Recordset record 1397
    to last Recordset record 1398
    to new Recordset records 1396
    to next Recordset record 1398
    to previous Recordset record 1399

N

Names
    user (default), setting 390
    user-defined workspace 383
Native ODBC error strings 415
Navigating
    class CRecordView 1416
    Recordsets 1396–1399
NCCALCSIZE_PARAMS structure 2258
NegotiateBorderSpace member function, CFrameWnd
    class 730
New operator, memory leaks 889
NextDlgCtrl member function, CDialog class 557
NMHDR structure 1695
NO_AFX_DAO_ERROR error code 242
NormalizeHit member function, CRectTracker
    class 1440
NormalizeRect member function, CRect class 1425
NotifyChanged member function
    COleServerDoc class 1247
    COleServerItem class 1264
NotifyClosed member function, COleServerDoc
    class 1247
NotifyRename member function, COleServerDoc
    class 1247
NotifySaved member function, COleServerDoc
    class 1248
Null, determining whether recordset fields 1394
Nullable, determining whether recordset fields 1395

O

Obtaining information
    about DAO errors 241
    about database relations 231
    about tabledefs 233
    about workspaces 385
ODBC
    Dialog data exchange (DDX) 2060
    error codes 413
    error string 415
    HDBC handle 405
    HSTMT handle 1407
    MFC database macros 2061
    Record field exchange (RFX) 2058
    timeout value, in DAO 260
ODBC functions, calling database class 2095–2096

ODBC transactions
    isolating 391
    isolating with DAO 382
ODBC vs. DAO
    described 216, 239, 250
    role of DAO database objects 217
ODBC with DAO
    islolating ODBC transactions 382
    isolating ODBC transactions 391
    Login timeout property 392
OemToAnsi member function, CString class 1630
Offset member function, CPoint class 1325
OffsetClipRgn member function, CDC class 498
OffsetPos member function, CProgressCtrl class 1348
OffsetRect member function, CRect class 1425
OffsetRgn member function, CRgn class 1456
OffsetViewportOrg member function, CDC class 499
OffsetWindowOrg member function, CDC class 499
OLE
    Activation 1242
    application control functions 2062
    base classes (list) 24
    client items, COleClientItem class 982
    compound documents 982
    data transfer classes (list) 27
    Data transfer 1098, 1105
    dialog box classes (list) 27
    embedded items 1244
    In-place editing
        activation 986–987, 1249
        deactivation 1249–1250
        resizing 1251
    initialization 2061
    linked items 1239
    miscellaneous classes (list) 29
    server documents
        closure notifications 1247
        notifications 1248
    server items
        creation 1250
        described 1256
    Uniform data transfer 1098, 1105
    verbs 986
    visual editing
        container classes listed 25
        server classes described 26

OLE Automation
    dispatch maps described 2062
    Event sink maps described 2067
    Parameter Type, MFC encapsulation 1286
OLE Change Source dialog box 977
OLE classes, overview 24
OLE container
    described 1026
    Rich edit as 1459
    Rich edit 1490, 1493
OLE controls extended features of 1026
OleUIChangeSource function, MFC encapsulation 977
OLEUICHANGESOURCE structure, MFC
    encapsulation 977
ON_COMMAND global function/macro 2170
ON_COMMAND_RANGE global
    function/macro 2171
ON_CONTROL global function/macro 2172
ON_CONTROL_RANGE global function/macro 2172
ON_EVENT global function/macro 2173
ON_EVENT_RANGE global function/macro 2174
ON_MESSAGE global function/macro 2174
ON_OLEVERB global function/macro 2175
ON_PROPNOTIFY global function/macro 2176
ON_PROPNOTIFY_RANGE global
    function/macro 2176
ON_REGISTERED_MESSAGE global
    function/macro 2177
ON_STDOLEVERB global function/macro 2178
ON_UPDATE_COMMAND_UI global
    function/macro 2178
ON_UPDATE_COMMAND_UI_RANGE global
    function/macro 2179
OnAccept member functionCAsyncSocket class 85
OnActivate member function
    COleClientItem class 1011
    CWnd class 1928
OnActivateApp member function, CWnd class 1929
OnActivateFrame member function, CView class 1774
OnActivateUI member function, COleClientItem
    class 1011
OnActivateView member function, CView class 1775
OnAdvise member function, CConnectionPoint
    class 200
OnAmbientProperty member function, CWnd
    class 1930
OnAmbientPropertyChange member function,
    COleControl class 1055–1056
OnApply member function, CPropertyPage class 1353

OnApplyScale member function, COlePropetiesDialog
    class 1227
OnAskCbFormatName member function, CWnd
    class 1930
OnBackColorChanged member function, COleControl
    class 1055
OnBeginDrag member function, COleDropSource
    class 1177
OnBeginPrinting member function, CView class 1776
OnCancel member function
    CDialog class 558
    CPropertyPage class 1353
OnCancelMode member function, Cwnd class 1931
OnCaptureChanged member function, CWnd
    class 1931
OnChange member function, COleClientItem
    class 1011
OnChangeCbChain member function, CWnd
    class 1932
OnChangedRect member function, CRectTracker
    class 1440
OnChangedViewList member function, CDocument
    class 588
OnChangeItemPosition member function,
    COleClientItem class 1012
OnChar member function, CWnd class 1932
OnCharEffect member function, CRichEditView
    class 1505
OnCharToItem member function, Cwnd class 1933
OnChildActivate member function, CWnd class 1934
OnChildNotify member function, CWnd class 1934
OnClick member function, COleControl class 1056
OnClose member function
    CAsyncSocket class 85
    COleServerDoc class 1248
    CWnd class 1935
OnCloseDocument member function, CDocument
    class 588
OnCmdMsg member function, CCmdTarget class 151
OnColorOK member function, CColorDialog class 161
OnCommand member function, CWnd class 1935
OnCompacting member function, CWnd class 1936
OnCompareItem member function, CWnd class 1937
OnConnect member function, CAsyncSocket class 86
OnContextHelp member function
    CFrameWnd class 731
    CWinApp class 1813
OnContextMenut member function, CWnd class 1938
OnCreate member function, CWnd class 1938

OnCreateClient member function, CFrameWnd class 731

OnCreateControlBars member function, COleIPFrameWnd class 1195

OnCreateObject member function, COleObjectFactory class 1214

OnCtlColor member function, CWnd class 1939

OnDDECommand member function, CWinApp class 1813

OnDeactivate member function
COleClientItem class 1013
COleServerDoc class 1249

OnDeactivateAndUndo member function, COleClientItem class 1013

OnDeactivateUI member function
COleClientItem class 1014
COleServerDoc class 1249

OnDeadChar member function, CWnd class 1940

OnDeleteItem member function, CWnd class 1941

OnDestroy member function, CWnd class 1942

OnDestroyClipboard member function, CWnd class 1942

OnDeviceChange member function, CWnd class 1943

OnDevModeChange member function, CWnd class 1944

OnDiscardUndoState member function, COleClientItem class 1014

OnDocWindowActivate member function, COleServerDoc class 1249

OnDoVerb member function
COleControl class 1056
COleServerItem class 1265

OnDragEnter member function
COleDropTarget class 1180
CView class 1776

OnDragLeave member function
COleDropTarget class 1181
CView class 1777

OnDragOver member function
COleDropTarget class 1181
CView class 1778

OnDragScroll member function
COleDropTarget class 1182
CView class 1779

OnDraw member function
COleControl class 1057
COleServerItem class 1265
CView class 1780

OnDrawClipboard member function, CWnd class 1944

OnDrawEx member function, COleServerItem class 1266

OnDrawItem member function, CWnd class 1945

OnDrawMetafile member function, COleControl class 1057

OnDrawPage member function, CPageSetupDialog class 1298

OnDrawSplitter member function, CSplitterWnd class 1582

OnDrop member function
COleDropTarget class 1183
CView class 1780

OnDropEx member function
COleDropTarget class 1184
CView class 1781

OnDropFiles member function, CWnd class 1945

OnEdit member function, COleControl class 1058

OnEditProperty member function, COlePropertyPage class 1233

OnEnable member function, CWnd class 1946

OnEnabledChanged member function, COleControl class 1058

OnEndPrinting member function, CView class 1782

OnEndPrintPreview member function, CView class 1783

OnEndSession member function, CWnd class 1946

OnEnterIdle member function, CWnd class 1947

OnEnterMenuLoop member function, CWnd class 1948

OnEnumVerbs member function, COleControl class 1058

OnEraseBkgnd member function, CWnd class 1948

OnEventAdvise member function, COleControl class 1059

OnExitMenuLoop member function, CWnd class 1949

OnFileNameOK member function, CFileDialog class 679

OnFileNew member function, CWinApp class 1814

OnFileOpen member function, CWinApp class 1815

OnFilePrintSetup member function, CWinApp class 1816

OnFileSendMail member function
CDocument class 589
COleDocument class 1173

OnFinalRelease member function, CCmdTarget class 152

OnFindEmbeddedItem member function, COleLinkingDoc class 1199

OnFindNext member function
CEditView class 637
CRichEditView class 1505
OnFontChange member function, CWnd class 1950
OnFontChanged member function, COleControl
class 1059
OnForeColorChanged member function, COleControl
class 1059
OnFrameWindowActivate member function,
COleServerDoc class 1250
OnFreezeEvents member function, COleControl
class 1060
OnGetCheckPosition member function,
CCheckListBox class 141
OnGetClipboardData member function
COleClientItem class 1014
COleServerItem class 1267
OnGetClipRect member function, COleClientItem
class 1015
OnGetColorSet member function, COleControl
class 1060
OnGetControlInfo member function, COleControl
class 1061
OnGetDisplayString member function, COleControl
class 1061
OnGetDlgCode member function, CWnd class 1950
OnGetEmbeddedItem member function,
COleServerDoc class 1250
OnGetExtent member function, COleServerItem
class 1267
OnGetInPlaceMenu member function, COleControl
class 1061
OnGetItemPosition member function, COleClientItem
class 1015
OnGetLinkedItem member function, COleLinkingDoc
class 1199
OnGetMinMaxInfo member function, CWnd
class 1951
OnGetPredefinedStrings member function,
COleControl class 1062
OnGetPredefinedValue member function, COleControl
class 1062
OnGetRecordset member function
CDaoRecordView class 343
CRecordView class 1416
OnGetWindowContext member function,
COleClientItem class 1016

OnHelp member function
COlePropertyPage class 1234
CWinApp class 1817
OnHelpFinder member function, CWinApp class 1818
OnHelpIndex member function, CWinApp class 1818
OnHelpInfo member function, CWnd class 1951
OnHelpUsing member function, CWinApp class 1818
OnHide member function, COleServerItem class 1268
OnHideToolbars member function, COleControl
class 1063
OnHScroll member function, CWnd class 1952
OnHScrollClipboard member function, CWnd
class 1953
OnIconEraseBkgnd member function, CWnd
class 1954
OnIdle member function
CWinApp class 1819
CWinThread class 1844
OnInitDialog member function
CDialog class 558
COlePropertyPage class 1234
OnInitFromData member function, COleServerItem
class 1268
OnInitialUpdate member function
CRichEditView class 1506
CView class 1783
OnInitMenu member function, CWnd class 1954
OnInitMenuPopup member function, CWnd class 1955
OnInsertMenus member function, COleClientItem
class 1016
OnInvertTracker member function, CSplitterWnd
class 1583
OnKeyDown member function, CWnd class 1956
OnKeyDownEvent member function, COleControl
class 1063
OnKeyPressEvent member function, COleControl
class 1064
OnKeyUp member function, CWnd class 1957
OnKeyUpEvent member function, COleControl
class 1064
OnKillActive member function, CPropertuPage
class 1354
OnKillFocus member function, CWnd class 1958
OnLBSelChangedNotify member function, CFileDialog
class 680
OnLButtonDblClk member function, CWnd class 1958
OnLButtonDown member function, CWnd class 1959
OnLButtonUp member function, CWnd class 1960

OnMapPropertyToPage member function, COleControl
  class 1064
OnMButtonDblClk member function, CWnd
  class 1961
OnMButtonDown member function, CWnd class 1962
OnMButtonUp member function, CWnd class 1962
OnMDIActivate member function, CWnd class 1963
OnMeasureItem member function, CWnd class 1964
OnMenuChar member function, CWnd class 1965
OnMenuSelect member function, CWnd class 1966
OnMessagePending member function
  COleMessageFilter class 1207
  CSocket class 1558
OnMnemonic member function, COleControl
  class 1065
OnMouseActivate member function, CWnd class 1967
OnMouseMove member function, CWnd class 1968
OnMove member function
  CDaoRecordView class 343
  CRecordView class 1416
  CWnd class 1968
OnMoving member function, CWnd class 1969
OnNcActivate member function, CWnd class 1969
OnNcCalcSize member function, CWnd class 1970
OnNcCreate member function, CWnd class 1971
OnNcDestroy member function, CWnd class 1971
OnNcHitTest member function, CWnd class 1972
OnNcLButtonDblClk member function, CWnd
  class 1973
OnNcLButtonDown member function, CWnd
  class 1974
OnNcLButtonUp member function, CWnd class 1974
OnNcMButtonDblClk member function, CWnd
  class 1975
OnNcMButtonDown member function, CWnd
  class 1975
OnNcMButtonUp member function, CWnd class 1976
OnNcMouseMove member function, CWnd class 1976
OnNcPaint member function, CWnd class 1977
OnNcRButtonDblClk member function, CWnd
  class 1977
OnNcRButtonDown member function, CWnd
  class 1978
OnNcRButtonUp member function, CWnd class 1978
OnNewDocument member function, CDocument
  class 589
OnObjectsChanged member function,
  COlePropertyPage class 1234

OnOK member function
  CDialog class 559
  CPropertyPage class 1354
OnOpen member function, COleServerItem class 1269
OnOpenDocument member function, CDocument
  class 591
OnOutOfBandData member function, CAsyncSocket
  class 87
OnPaint member function, CWnd class 1979
OnPaintClipboard member function, CWnd class 1980
OnPaletteChanged member function, CWnd
  class 1982
OnPaletteIsChanging member function, CWnd
  class 1981
OnParaAlign member function, CRichEditView
  class 1506
OnParentNotify member function, CWnd class 1982
OnPasteNativeObject member function,
  CRichEditView class 1506
OnPrepareDC member function, CView class 1784
OnPreparePrinting member function, CView
  class 1785
OnPrint member function, CView class 1786
OnPrinterChanged member function, CrichEditView
  class 1507
OnProperties member function, COleControl
  class 1065
OnQueryCancel member function, CPropertyPage
  class 1354
OnQueryDragIcon member function, CWnd class 1983
OnQueryEndSession member function, CWnd
  class 1984
OnQueryNewPalette member function, CWnd
  class 1984
OnQueryOpen member function, CWnd class 1984
OnQueryUpdateItems member function,
  COleServerItem class 1269
OnRButtonDblClk member function, CWnd
  class 1985
OnRButtonDown member function, CWnd class 1986
OnRButtonUp member function, CWnd class 1986
OnReactivateAndUndo member function,
  COleServerDoc class 1250
OnReceive member function, CAsyncSocket class 88
OnRemoveMenus member function, COleClientItem
  class 1017
OnRenderAllFormats member function, CWnd
  class 1987

OnRenderData member function
   COleControl class 1065
   COleDataSource class 1112
   COleServerItem class 1270
OnRenderFileData member function
   COleControl class 1066
   COleDataSource class 1113
   COleServerItem class 1271
OnRenderFormat member function, CWnd class 1987
OnRenderGlobalData member function
   COleControl class 1067
   COleDataSource class 1114
   COleServerItem class 1271
OnReplaceAll member function
   CEditView class 638
   CRichEditView class 1507
OnReplaceSel member function
   CEditView class 639
   CRichEditView class 1508
OnReset member function, CPropertyPage class 1355
OnResetState member function, COleControl
   class 1068
OnResizeBorder member function, COleServerDoc
   class 1251
OnSaveDocument member function, CDocument
   class 593
OnScroll member function, CView class 1787
OnScrollBy member function
   COleClientItem class 1018
   CView class 1788
OnSend member function, CAsyncSocket class 88
OnSetActive member function, CPropertyPage
   class 1355
OnSetClientSite member function, COleControl
   class 1068
OnSetColorScheme member function, COleServerItem
   class 1272
OnSetCursor member function, CWnd class 1988
OnSetData member function
   COleControl class 1068
   COleDataSource class 1114
   COleServerItem class 1273
OnSetExtent member function, COleServerItem
   class 1273
OnSetExtentmember function, COleControl class 1069
OnSetFocus member function, CWnd class 1989
OnSetFont member function, CDialog class 559
OnSetHostNames member function, COleServerDoc
   class 1251

OnSetItemRects member function, COleServerDoc
   class 1252
OnSetMenu member function, COleClientItem
   class 1018
OnSetObjectRects member function, COleControl
   class 1069
OnSetOptions member function
   CDatabase class 400
   CRecordset class 1399
OnSetPageSite member function, COlePropertyPage
   class 1235
OnSetPreviewMode member function, CFrameWnd
   class 732
OnShareViolation member function, CFileDialog
   class 680
OnShow member function, COleServerItem class 1274
OnShowControlBars member function
   COleClientItem class 1019
   COleServerDoc class 1252
OnShowDocument member function, COleServerDoc
   class 1253
OnShowItem member function, COleClientItem
   class 1019
OnShowToolbarsmember function, COleControl
   class 1070
OnShowViews member function, COleDocument
   class 1173
OnShowWindow member function, CWnd class 1989
OnSize member function, CWnd class 1990
OnSizeClipboard member function, CWnd class 1991
OnSizing member function, CWnd class 1991
OnSpoolerStatus member function, CWnd class 1992
OnStyleChanged member function, CWnd class 1992
OnStyleChanging member function, CWnd class 1993
OnSysChar member function, CWnd class 1993
OnSysColorChange member function, CWnd
   class 1995
OnSysCommand member function, CWnd class 1995
OnSysDeadChar member function, CWnd class 1997
OnSysKeyDown member function, CWnd class 1997
OnSysKeyUp member function, CWnd class 1999
OnTCard member function, CWnd class 2000
OnTextChanged member function, COleControl
   class 1070
OnTextNotFound member function
   CEditView class 639
   CRichEditView class 1508
OnTimeChange member function, CWnd class 2001
OnTimer member function, CWnd class 2001

OnToolHitTest member function, CWnd class 2002
OnUpdate member function
    COleServerItem class 1274
    CView class 1788
OnUpdateCharEffect member function,
    CRichEditView class 1508
OnUpdateCmdUI member function, CControlBar
    class 206
OnUpdateDocument member function, COleServerDoc
    class 1253
OnUpdateFileSendMail member function, CDocument
    class 593
OnUpdateFrameTitle member function,
    COleClientItem class 1020
OnUpdateItems member function, COleServerItem
    class 1275
OnUpdateParaAlign member function, CRichEditView
    class 1509
OnVKeyToItem member function, CWnd class 2003
OnVScroll member function, CWnd class 2003
OnVScrollClipboard member function, CWnd
    class 2004
OnWaitForDataSource member function
    CDatabase class 401
    CRecordset class 1400
OnWindowPosChanged member function, CWnd
    class 2005
OnWindowPosChanging member function, CWnd
    class 2006
OnWinIniChange member function, CWnd class 2007
OnWizardBack member function, CPropertyPage
    class 1355
OnWizardFinish member function, CPropertyPage
    class 1356
OnWizardNext member function, CPropertyPage
    class 1356
OnWndMsg member function, CWnd class 2007
Open databases (DAO)
    counting 380
    obtaining information about 380
Open member function
    CAnimateCtrl class 36
    CDaoDatabase class 235
    CDaoQueryDef class 265
    CDaoRecordset class 320
    CDaoTableDef class 363
    CDaoWorkspace class 387
    CDatabase class 401

Open member function (continued)
    CFile class 664
    CRecordset class 1400
Open status, obtaining workspace 386
OpenClipboard member function, CWnd class 2008
OpenDocumentFile member function
    CDocTemplate class 575
    CWinApp class 1821
Opening
    CStreamFile objects 1280
    data source connections 401
    databases
        described 235, 401
        Jet vs. ODBC 235
    recordsets 1400
    workspaces 387
OpenStream member function, COleStreamFile
    class 1280
Operations, validity of DFX 246
operator − member function
    CPoint class 1328
    CRect class 1433
    CSize class 1540
operator !=
    COleCurrency 1095
    COleDateTime 1136
    COleDateTimeSpan 1151
operator != member function
    CPoint class 1326
    CRect class 1430
    CSize class 1539
operator & member function, CRect class 1433
operator &= member function, CRect class 1431
operator *, COleCurrency class 1094
operator *=, COleCurrency class 1094
operator + member function
    COleCurrency 1093
    CReect class 1432
    CSize class 1540
    CString class 1637
operator + member function, CPoint class 1327
operator +,− member function
    CTime class 1669
    CTimeSpan class 1676
operator +=
    COleCurrency 1093
    COleDateTime 1135
    COleDateTimeSpan 1151

operator += member function
    CPoint class 1326
    CRect class 1430
    CSize class 1539
    CString class 1638
operator +=, −= member function
    CTime class 1669
    CTimeSpan class 1676
operator -
    COleDateTime class 1135
    COleDateTimeSpan class 1150
operator - member function
    COleCurrency 1093
operator /, COleCurrency class 1094
operator /=, COleCurrency class 1094
operator <, COleCurrency class 1095
operator <, COleDateTime class 1136
operator <, COleDateTimeSpan class 1151
operator <<
    COleCurrency 1096
    COleDateTime 1137
    COleDateTimeSpan 1152
    COleVariant 1291
operator << member function
    CArchive class 53
    CDumpContext class 607
operator <<, >> member function, CString class 1637
operator <=
    COleCurrency 1095
    COleDateTime 1136
    COleDateTimeSpan 1151
operator =
    COleCurrency 1092
    COleDateTime 1134
    COleDateTimeSpan 1150
    COleVariant class 1289
operator = member function
    CObject class 950
    CPoint class 1327
    CRect class 1429, 1431
    CSize class 1540
    CString class 1636
    CTime class 1668
    CTimeSpan class 1676
operator ==
    COleCurrency 1095
    COleDateTime 1136
    COleDateTimeSpan 1151
    COleVariant class 1290

operator == member function
    CPoint class 1326
    CRect class 1430
    CSize class 1539
operator >
    COleCurrency 1095
    COleDateTime 1136
    COleDateTimeSpan 1151
operator >=
    COleCurrency 1095
    COleDateTime 1136
    COleDateTimeSpan 1151
operator >>
    COleCurrency 1096
    COleDateTime 1137
    COleDateTimeSpan 1152
    COleVariant 1291
operator >> member function, CArchive class 54
operator [ ] member function
    CArray class 67
    CMap class 847
    CMapStringToOb class 860
    CObArray class 943
    CString class 1640
    CTypedPtrArray class 1756
    CTypedPtrMap class 1765
operator | member function, CRect class 1434
operator |= member function, CRect class 1432
operator CURRENCY, COleCurrency class 1095
operator DATE, COleDateTime class 1136
operator delete member function, CObject class 950
operator double, COleDateTimeSpan class 1151
operator HBITMAP member function, CBitmap
    class 110
operator HFONT member function, CFont class 702
operator HPALETTE member function, CPalette
    class 1307
operator HPEN member function, CPen class 1317
operator HRGN member function, CRgn class 1458
operator LPCRECT member function, CRect
    class 1429
operator LPCTSTR ( ) member function, CString
    class 1636
operator LPCVARIANTmember function, COleVariant
    class 1291
operator LPRECT member function, CRect class 1429
operator LPVARIANT member function, COleVariant
    class 1291
operator new member function, CObject class 950

operator+
  COleDateTime 1135
  COleDateTimeSpan 1150
operator-=
  COleCurrency 1093
  COleDateTime 1135
  COleDateTimeSpan 1151
Operators
  COleCurrency 1092
  COleVariant class 1289
operators <<, >> member function
  CTime class 1670
  CTimeSpan class 1677
Options, setting
  data source connections 400
  recordsets 1399
OsErrorToException member function, CFileException class 684
OutputColumn, CDaoFieldExchange class 245

P

PaintRgn member function, CDC class 500
PAINTSTRUCT structure 2259
param, CDaoField Exchange class 245
Parameter object (DAO), obtaining information about 2226
Parameters, getting querydef 262, 267
ParseCommandLine member function, CWinApp class 1822
ParseCurrency member function, COleCurrency class 1090
ParseDateTime member function, COleDateTime class 1127
ParseParam member function, CCommandLineInfo class 190
Pass-through queries
  defined 225
  executing 225
  SAL 251
  SQL 251
Passwords
  setting default 389
  setting for DAO workspace 379
Paste member function
  CComboBox class 182
  CEdit class 625
  CRichEditCtrl class 1479

PasteSpecial member function, CRichEditCtrl class 1479
PatBlt member function, CDC class 500
Persistence of OLE controls 2070
Pie member function, CDC class 501
Play member function, CAnimateCtrl class 36
PlayMetaFile member function, CDC class 502
PlgBlt member function, CDC class 503
POINT structure 2259
PolyBezier member function, CDC class 505
PolyBezierTo member function, CDC class 506
PolyDraw member function, CDC class 506
Polygon member function, CDC class 507
Polyline member function, CDC class 508
PolylineTo member function, CDC class 508
PolyPolygon member function, CDC class 509
PolyPolyline member function, CDC class 510
PosFromChar member function, CEdit class 626
PostMessage member function, CWnd class 2008
PostModalDialog member function, COleControl class 1071
PostNcDestroy member function, CWnd class 2009
PreCloseFrame member function, CDocument class 594
PreCreateWindow member function, CWnd class 2009
PreDrawPage member function, CPageSetupDialog class 1299
PreModalDialog member function, COleControl class 1070
PrepareCtrl member function, CDataExchange class 409
PrepareEditCtrl member function, CDataExchange class 410
PressButton member function
  CPropertySheet class 1365
  CToolBarCtrl class 1712
PreSubclassWindow member function, CWnd class 2010
PreTranslateMessage member function
  CWinApp class 1823
  CWinThread class 1845
  CWnd class 2010
PrevDlgCtrl member function, CDialog class 559
Print member function, CWnd class 2010
PrintAll member function, CPrintDialog class 1337
PrintClient member function, CWnd class 2011
PrintCollate member function, CPrintDialog class 1337

PrintInsideRect member function
   CEditView class 640
   CRichEditView class 1509
PrintPage member function, CRichEditView
   class 1510
PrintRange member function, CPrintDialog class 1337
PrintSelection member function, CPrintDialog
   class 1337
Process member function, COleException class 1186
ProcessMessageFilter member function
   CWinApp class 1823
   CWinThread class 1845
ProcessShellCommand member function, CWinApp
   class 1824
ProcessWndProcException member function
   CWinApp class 1825
   CWinThread class 1846
Progress bar control 1346
Property Pages 2064
Property sheet classes (list) 12
PROPPAGEID global function/macro 2179
Providing data
   Clipboard 1115
   data transfer 1105
PtInRect member function, CRect class 1425
PtInRegion member function, CRgn class 1457
PtVisible member function, CDC class 510
PulseEvent member function, CEvent class 645
PX_Blob global function/macro 2179
PX_Bool global function/macro 2180
PX_Color global function/macro 2181
PX_Currency global function/macro 2181
PX_Double global function/macro 2182
PX_Float global function/macro 2183
PX_Font global function/macro 2183
PX_IUnknown global function/macro 2184
PX_Long global function/macro 2185
PX_Picture global function/macro 2185
PX_Short global function/macro 2186
PX_String global function/macro 2186
PX_ULong global function/macro 2187
PX_UShort global function/macro 2188
PX_VBXFontConvert global function/macro 2188

Q

Query timeouts
   DAO 230
   setting 237
   values, setting 404
Query, database See QueryDef; Recordsets
QueryAbort member function, CDC class 511
QueryAcceptData member function, CRichEditView
   class 1510
QueryContinueDrag member function,
   COleDropSource class 1177
Querydef object (DAO), obtainaing information
   about 2227
QueryDefs
   action queries 251
   and recordsets 251
   and SQL
      described 251, 255
      getting SQL statement 263
      setting SQL statement 269
   automatic rollback on error 256
   closing 255
   connect string (ODBC) 257, 266
   consistent updates 256
   constructing 254
   counting fields in 259
   counting parameters in 261
   counting 228
   creating with MS Access 250
   creating 255
   creation date 258
   database owned by 269
   date created 258
   date last updated 258
   defined 250
   deleting 224
   Execute member function 256
   executing SQL directly 256
   fields in 259
   for ODBC 251
   Inconsistent updates 256
   m_pDAOQueryDef pointer 270
   m_pDatabase pointer 269
   name of 260, 266
   obtaining information about 229
   ODBC timeout property 260, 267
   on external data sources 251
   open status of 265

QueryDefs *(continued)*
  opening 265
  options
    dbConsistent 256
    dbDenyWrite 256
    dbFailOnError 256
    dbInconsistent 256
    dbSeeChanges 256
    dbSQLPassThrough 256
  parameters
    described 261
    getting value 262
    value, setting 267
  pass-through query, SQL 251
  pointer to parent database 269
  pointer to underlying DAO object 270
  purposes 251
  query type
    action 251, 264
    append 251, 264
    bulk 251, 264
    cross-tab 251, 264
    data definition (DDL) 251, 264
    delete 251, 264
    make-table 251, 264
    pass-through, SQL 251, 264
    select 251, 264
    SQL pass-through 251, 264
    union 251, 264
    update 251, 264
  records affected by Execute 263
  referential integrity 256
  ReturnsRecords property 263, 268
  saved/stored queries 254
  setting attributes of 254
  SQL pass-through query 251, 256
  SQL, executing directly 256
  temporary 250, 254–255
  timeout, ODBC 260, 267
  type of query 264
  underlying DAO object, pointer to 270
  usage 250
  write permission 256
QuerySiblings member function, CPropertyPage
  class 1356

R

Radio button, DDX field exchange 2132
ReactivateAndUndo member function, COleClientItem
  class 1020
Read locks, DAO 386
Read member function
  CArchive class 46
  CFile class 665
  CImageList class 765
ReadClass member function, CArchive class 46
ReadHuge member function, CFile class 666
ReadObject member function, CArchieve class 47
ReadString member function
  CArchive class 48
  CStdioFile class 1612
RealizePalette member function, CDC class 511
Realloc member function, CMemFile class 886
Rebuilding recordsets 1403
RecalcLayout member function
  CFrameWnd class 732
  CSplitterWnd class 1583
Receive member function, CAsyncSocket class 89
ReceiveFrom member function, CAsyncSocket
  class 90
Record field exchange (DFX)
  class CDaoFieldExchange 245
  DoFieldExchange mechanism 1386
  field exchange operations listed 247
  field types, setting 247
  functions 2058
  IsFieldType function 653
  m_prs data member 249
  operations, validity of 246
  PSEUDO_NULL values 247
  recordset, pointer to 249
  Recordset 1386
  SetFieldType function 653
Record views, CRecordView class 1412
Records
  adding new 1381
  deleting 1385
  editing 1387
  updating 1387
Records affected by Execute 230
Recordsets
  ability to transact 1383
  ability to update records 1384
  and querydefs 251

Recordsets *(continued)*
   asynchronous operation, canceling 1383
   beginning of, detecting 1392
   bound fields 1408
   canceling long operations 1400
   closing 1384
   columns selected, number 1408
   completing add 1407
   completing edit 1407
   constructing 1385
   creating 1385
   cursor concurrency, support for 1399
   customizing SQL 1400
   default connection string 1389
   deleting records 1385
   determining ability to scroll 1383
   determining appendability 1382
   determining whether dirty 1394
   determining whether field can be set Null 1395
   determining whether Null 1394
   determining whether open 1396
   editing records 1387
   end of, detecting 1393
   exchanging data with data source 1386
   fields
      setting dirty 1404
      setting null 1405
   filter string 1409
   HSTMT handle 1407
   locking mode, setting 1406
   moving to a new record 1396
   moving to first record 1397
   moving to last record 1398
   moving to next record 1398
   moving to previous record 1399
   navigating 1396–1399
   opening 1400
   operations
      binding dynamically 272
      differences between recordset types 272
      using DoFieldExchange 272
   options, setting 1399
   rebuilding 1403
   record field exchange 1386
   refreshing 1403
   requerying 1403
   RFX 1386
   scrollable cursors, support for 1399
   setting null 1405

Recordsets *(continued)*
   similarities between ODBC and DAO 271
   sort string 1410
   SQL statement, getting 1391
   status, getting 1390
   table name, getting 1389, 1392
   updating 1387, 1407
   waiting for data source 1400
   whether deleted, determining 1393
   yielding processing time 1400
RecreateControlWindow member function,
   COleControl class 1071
RECT structure 2260
Rectangle member function, CDC class 512
RectDefault member function, CFrameWnd class 735
RectInRegion member function, CRgn class 1457
RectVisible member function, CDC class 512
RedrawItems member function, CListCtrl class 830
RedrawWindow member function, CWnd class 2012
Referential integrity
   described 256
   enforcing database relations 223
ReflectChildNotify member function, CWnd
   class 2014
ReflectLastMsg member function, CWnd class 2014
Refresh member function, COleControl class 1071
Refreshing recordsets 1403
RefreshLink member function, CDaoTableDef
   class 364
Register member function
   COleDropTarget class 1185
   COleLinkingDoc class 1200
   COleMessageFilter class 1208
   COleObjectFactory class 1214
RegisterAll member function, COleObjectFactory
   class 1214
Registering OLE controls 2068
RegisterShellFileTypes member function, CWinApp
   class 1825
Registry key settings
   database engine 381
   setting 391
Relation field object (DAO), obtaining information
   about 2232
Relation object (DAO), obtaining information
   about 2230

Relational operators
  COleCurrency 1095
  COleDateTime 1136
  COleDateTimeSpan 1151
Relations (database)
  cascades 224
  counting 231
  creating 223
  deleting 225
  obtaining information about 231
  referential integrity, enforcing 223
RelayEvent member function, CToolTipCtrl
  class 1724
Release member function
  COleClientItem class 1020
  COleDataObject class 1104
ReleaseAttribDC member function, CDC class 513
ReleaseBuffer member function, CString class 1631
ReleaseDC member function, CWnd class 2015
ReleaseDispatch member function,
  COleDispatchDriver class 1161
ReleaseFile member function, CDocument class 594
ReleaseFont member function, CFontHolder class 711
ReleaseOutputDC member function, CDC class 513
Releasing data objects 1100, 1104
Reload member function, COleClientItem class 1021
Remove member function
  CFile class 666
  CImageList class 765
RemoveAll member function
  CArray class 64
  CList class 777
  CMap class 846
  CMapStringToOb class 857
  CObArray class 939
  CObList class 965
RemoveAt member function
  CArray class 64
  CList class 777
  CObArray class 940
  CObList class 965
RemoveDocument member function, CDocTemplate
  class 576
RemoveHead member function
  CList class 778
  CObList class 966
  CTypedPtrList class 1761
RemoveImage member function, CTabCtrl class 1656

RemoveItem member function, COleDocument
  class 1173
RemoveKey member function
  CMap class 846
  CMapStringToOb class 858
RemoveMenu member function, CMenu class 912
RemovePage member function, CPropertySheet
  class 1366
RemoveTail member function
  CList class 778
  CObList class 967
  CTypedPtrList class 1762
RemoveView member function, CDocument class 594
Rename member function, CFile class 667
Render member function, CPictureHolder class 1322
Repairing databases 388
Replace member function, CImageList class 765
ReplaceAll member function, CFindReplacedialog
  class 692
ReplaceCurrent member function, CFindReplaceDialog
  class 693
ReplaceSel member function
  CEdit class 626
  CRichEditCtrl class 1479
ReportError member function, CException class 650
ReportSaveLoadException member function,
  CDocument class 596
RepositionBars member function, CWnd class 2015
RepositionFrame member function, COleIPFrameWnd
  class 1195
Requery member function
  CDaoRecordset class 323
  CRecordset class 1403
Requerying recordsets 1403
RequestPositionChange member function,
  COleServerDoc class 1254
RequestResize member function, CRichEditCtrl
  class 1480
ResetContent member function
  CComboBox class 182
  CListBox class 798
ResetDC member function, CDC class 513
ResetEvent member function, CEvent class 645
ResizePalette member function, CPalette class 1308
ResizeParentToFit member function, CScrollView
  class 1526
Restore member function, CWaitCursor class 1792
RestoreDC member function, CDC class 514

RestoreState member function, CToolBarCtrl class 1713

RestoreWaitCursor member function, CCmdTarget clzass 153

ResumeThread member function, CWinThread class 1847

RETCODE
defined 413
values 413

Retrieving data from data objects 1101–1102

Return codes, values for ODBC 413

ReverseFind member function, CString class 1631

Revoke member function
COleDropTarget class 1185
COleLinkingDoc class 1200
COleMessageFilter class 1208
COleObjectFactory class 1215

RevokeAll member function, COleObjectFactory class 1215

RFX
See also Record Field Exchange
IsFieldType function 653
Recordset 1386
SetFieldType function 653
vs. DFX 245

RFX field exchange
Boolean 2190
Byte array 2189
Byte 2190
CLongBinary 2194
CString 2195
CTime 2191
Double 2192
Long integer 2193
Short integer 2192
Single precision float 2194

RFX_Binary global function/macro 2189
RFX_Bool global function/macro 2190
RFX_Byte global function/macro 2190
RFX_Date global function/macro 2191
RFX_Double global function/macro 2192
RFX_Int global function/macro 2192
RFX_Long global function/macro 2193
RFX_LongBinary global function/macro 2194
RFX_Single global function/macro 2194
RFX_Text global function/macro 2195

RGNDATA structure 2260

Rich Edit
as OLE container 1459–1490, 1493
Document/View version 1490, 1493

Rich Edit Control, MFC encapsulation 1461

RichEdit window class, MFC encapsulation 1461

Right member function, CString class 1632

Rollback member function
CDaoWorkspace class 388
CDatabase class 403

Rolling back database transactions 388, 403

Root classes (list) 4

RoundRect member function, CDC class 514

RTF controls, MFC encapsulation 1461

Run member function
COleClientItem class 1021
CWinApp class 1826
CWinThread class 1847

Run-time object model services 2048

RunAutomated member function, CWinApp class 1826

RunEmbedded member function, CWinApp class 1827

RunModalLoop member function, CWnd class 2016

RUNTIME_CLASS global function/macro 2196

S

SaveAllModified member function
CDocTemplate class 576
CWinApp class 1827

SaveBarState member function, CFrameWnd class 733

SaveDC member function, CDC class 515

SaveEmbedding member function, COleServerDoc class 1254

SaveModified member function, CDocument class 597

SaveState member function, CToolbarCtrl class 1714

ScaleViewportExt member function, CDC class 516

ScaleWindowExt member function, CDC class 516

SCODE, information about 244

ScreenToClient member function, CWnd class 2016

Scroll Bar styles 2275

Scroll member function, CListCtrl class 830

Scroll-bar control, DDX field exchange 2133

Scrollable cursors, recordset 1399

ScrollContainerBy member function, COleServerDoc class 1254

ScrollDC member function, CDC class 517

Scrolling
class CRecordView 1416
determining ability to scroll 1383

ScrollToPosition member function, CScrollView class 1527

ScrollWindow member function, CWnd class 2017

ScrollWindowEx member function, CWnd class 2018

SearchDown member function, CFindReplaceDialog class 693

Security support, DAO database 371

Seek member function
CAnimateCtrl class 37
CDaoRecordset class 324
CFile class 667

SeekToBegin member function, CFile class 668

SeekToEnd member function, CFile class 668

Select member function
CFontHolder class 712
CTreeCtrl class 1745

Select query 251

SelectClipPath member function, CDC class 518

SelectClipRgn member function, CDC class 519

SelectDropTarget member function, CTreeCtrl class 1746

SelectFontObject member function, COleControl class 1071

SelectItem member function, CTreeCtrl class 1746

SelectObject member function, CDC class 520

SelectPalette member function, CDC class 521

SelectPrinter member function, CWinApp class 1827

SelectStockFont member function, COleControl class 1072

SelectStockObject member function, CDC class 522

SelectString member function
CComboBox class 182
CListBox class 798

SelItemRange member function, CListBox class 799

Send member function, CAsyncSocket class 93

SendChildNotifyLastMsg member function, CWnd class 2019

SendDlgItemMessage member function, CWnd class 2020

SendMessage member function, CWnd class 2020

SendMessageToDescendants member function, CWnd class 2021

SendNotifyMessage member function, CWnd class 2022

SendTo member function, CAsyncSocket class 94

Serialize member function, CObject class 949

SerializeClass member function, CArchive class 48

SerializeElements global function/macro 2197

SerializeRaw member function, CEditView class 640

Server documents, COleServerDoc class 1239

SetAbortProc member function, CDC class 523

SetAbortProc, callback function for *See* Callback functions for MFC member functions

SetAbsolutePosition member function, CDaoRecordset class 325

SetAccel member function, CSpinButtonCtrl class 1566

SetActivePage member function, CPropertySheet class 1366

SetActivePane member function, CSplitterwnd class 1584

SetActiveView member function, CFrameWnd class 733

SetActiveWindow member function, CWnd class 2022

SetAnchorIndex member function, CListBox class 799

SetArcDirection member function, CDC class 524

SetAt member function
CArray class 65
CList class 778
CMap class 847
CMapStringToOb class 859
CObArray class 941
CObList class 967
CString class 1632

SetAtGrow member function
CArray class 65
CObArray class 942

SetAttribDC member function, CDC class 525

SetAttributes member function, CDaoTableDef class 364

SetBackColor member function, COleControl class 1072

SetBackgroundColor member function, CRichEditCtrl class 1480

SetBarStyle member function, CControlBar class 206

SetBase member function, CSpinButtonCtrl class 1567

SetBitmap member function
CButton class 132
CStatic class 1590
CToolBar class 1687

SetBitmapBits member function, CBitmap class 111

SetBitmapDimension member function, CBitmap class 111

SetBitmapSize member function, CToolBarCtrl class 1714

SetBkColor member function
CDC class 525
CImageList class 766

SetBkColor member function *(continued)*
  CListCtrl class 830
  CTabCtrl class 1657
SetBkMode member function, CDC class 526
SetBookmark member function, CDaoRecordset
  class 326
SetBorderStyle member function, COleControl
  class 1072
SetBoundsRect member function, CDC class 526
SetBrushOrg member function, CDC class 527
SetBuddy member function, CSpinButtonCtrl
  class 1567
SetBusyReply member function, COleMessageFilter
  class 1208
SetButtonInfo member function, CToolBar class 1687
SetButtons member function, CToolBar class 1688
SetButtonSize member function, CToolBarCtrl
  class 1715
SetButtonStructSize member function, CToolBarCtrl
  class 1715
SetButtonStyle member function
  CButton class 132
  CToolBar class 1688
SetButtonText member function, CToolBar class 1689
SetCacheSize member function, CDaoRecordset
  class 327–328
SetCallbackMask member function, CListCtrl
  class 831
SetCapture member function, CWnd class 2023
SetCaretIndex member function, CListBox class 800
SetCaretPos member function, CWnd class 2023
SetCharFormat member function, CRichEditView
  class 1511
SetCheck member function
  CButton class 133
  CCheckListBox class 142
  CCmdUI class 157
SetCheckStyle member function, CCheckListBox
  class 142
SetClipboard member function, COleDataSource
  class 1115
SetClipboardViewer member function, CWnd
  class 2023
SetCmdID member function, CToolBarCtrl class 1715
SetColorAdjustment member function, CDC class 528
SetColumn member function, CListCtrl class 831
SetColumnInfo member function, CSplitterWnd
  class 1584

SetColumnWidth member function
  CListBox class 800
  CListCtrl class 832
SetConnect member function
  CDaoQueryDef class 266
  CDaoTableDef class 365
SetContainerInfo member function, CDocTemplate
  class 576
SetControlSize member function, COleControl
  class 1073
SetControlStatus member function, COlePropertyPage
  class 1235
SetCurrency member function, COleCurrency 1091
SetCurrentColor member function, CColorDialog
  class 161
SetCurrentIndex member function, CDaoRecordset
  class 328
SetCurSel member function
  CComboBox class 183
  CListBox class 800
  CTabCtrl class 1657
SetCursor member function
  CButton class 133
  CRectTracker class 1441
  CStatic class 1591
SetDate member function, COleDateTime class 1128
SetDateTime member function, COleDateTime
  class 1130
SetDateTimeSpan member function,
  COleDateTimeSpan class 1148
SetDefaultCharFormat member function,
  CRichEditCtrl class 1481
SetDefaultPassword member function,
  CDaoWorkspace class 389
SetDefaultTitle member function, CDocTemplate
  class 577
SetDefaultUser member function, CDaoWorkspace
  class 390
SetDefID member function, CDialog class 560
SetDelayTime member function, CToolTipCtrl
  class 1725
SetDepth member function, CDumpContext class 607
SetDialogBkColor member function, CWinApp
  class 1828
SetDialogResource member function,
  COlePropertyPage class 1235
SetDirtyField, Record field exchange (DFX) 247
SetDlgCtrlID member function, CWnd class 2024
SetDlgItemInt member function, CWnd class 2024

SetDlgItemText member function, CWnd class 2025

SetDockState member function, CFrameWnd class 733

SetDragCursorImage member function, CImageList class 766

SetDrawAspect member function, COleClientItem class 1021

SetDroppedWidth member function CComboBox class 184

SetEditSel member function, CComboBox class 184

SetEnabled member function, COleControl class 1073

SetEnhMetaFile member function, CStatic class 1592

SetEvent member function, CEvent class 645

SetEventMask member function, CRichEditCtrl class 1481

SetExtendedUI member function, CComboBox class 185

SetExtent member function, ColeClientItem class 1022

SetFieldDirty member function
CDaoRecordset class 329
CRecordset class 1404

SetFieldNull member function
CDaoRecordset class 330
CRecordset class 1405
Record field exchange (DFX) 247

SetFieldType function
example 653
Record Field Exchange 653

SetFieldType member function
CDaoFieldExchange class 247
CFieldExchange class 653

SetFieldValue member function, CDaoRecordset class 331

SetFieldValueNull member function, CDaoRecordset class 332

SetFilePath member function, CFile class 669

SetFinishText member function, CPropertySheet class 1366

SetFocus member function, CWnd class 2026

SetFont member function
CFontHolder class 712
COleControl class 1073
CWnd class 2026

SetForeColor member function, COleControl class 1074

SetForegroundWindow member function, CWnd class 2025

SetHandle member function, CEdit class 627

SetHeight member function, CToolBar class 1689

SetHelpID member function, CDialog class 560

SetHelpInfo member function, COlePropertyPage class 1236

SetHorizontalExtent member function
CComboBox class 185
CListBox class 801

SetHostNames member function, COleClientItem class 1022

SetHotKey member function, CHotKeyCtrl class 753

SetIcon member function
CButton class 134
CStatic class 1592
CWnd class 2026

SetIconicMetafile member function, COleClientItem class 1023

SetImageList member function
CListCtrl class 832
CTabCtrl class 1657
CTreeCtrl class 1747

SetIndent member function, CTreeCtrl class 1747

SetIndicators member function, CStatusBar class 1599

SetIniPath member function, CDaoWorkspace class 391

SetInitialDataFormats member function, COlecontrol class 1074

SetInitialSize member function, COleControl class 1074

SetIsolateODBCTrans member function, CDaoWorkspace class 391

SetItem member function
CHeaderCtrl class 750
CListCtrl class 832
CTabCtrl class 1658
CTreeCtrl class 1748

SetItemCount member function, CListCtrl class 833

SetItemData member function
CComboBox class 186
CListBox class 801
CListCtrl class 834
CTreeCtrl class 1748

SetItemDataPtr member function
CComboBox class 186
CListBox class 802

SetItemExtra member function, CTabCtrl class 1658

SetItemHeight member function
CComboBox class 187
CListBox class 802

SetItemImage member function, CTreeCtrl class 1749

SetItemName member function, COleServerItem class 1275

SetItemPosition member function, CListCtrl class 834

SetItemRects member function, COleClientItem class 1023

SetItemSize member function, CTabCtrl class 1659

SetItemState member function
  CListCtrl class 835
  CTreeCtrl class 1749

SetItemText member function
  CListCtrl class 835
  CTreeCtrl class 1750

SetLength member function, CFile class 669

SetLimitText member function, CEdit class 627

SetLineSize member function, CSliderCtrl class 1549

SetLinkUpdateOptions member function, COleClientItem class 1024

SetLoadParams member function, CArchive class 49

SetLocale member function
  CComboBox class 187
  CListBox class 803

SetLockingMode member function
  CDaoRecordset class 332
  CRecordset class 1406

SetLoginTimeout member function
  CDaoWorkspace class 392
  CDatabase class 404

SetMapMode member function, CDC class 528

SetMapperFlags member function, CDC class 530

SetMargins member function
  CEdit class 628
  CRichEditView class 1511

SetMaxPage member function, CPrintInfo class 1341

SetMenu member function, CWnd class 2027

SetMenuContextHelpId member function, CMenu class 913

SetMenuItemBitmaps member function, CMenu class 913

SetMessagePendingDelay member function, COleMEssageFilter class 1209

SetMessageText member function, CFrameWnd class 734

SetMinHeight member function, CStatusBarCtrl class 1607

SetMinPage member function, CPrintInfo class 1342

SetMiterLimit member function, CDC class 530

SetModified member function, CPropertyPage class 1357

SetModifiedFlag member function
  CDocument class 597
  COleControl class 1075
  COlePropertyPage class 1236

SetModify member function
  CEdit class 628
  CRichEditCtrl class 1481

SetName member function
  CDaoQueryDef class 266
  CDaoTableDef class 366

SetNotPermitted member function, COleControl class 1075

SetNotSupported member function, COlecontrol class 1075

SetObjectSchema member function, CArchive class 50

SetODBCTimeout member function, CDaoQueryDef class 267

SetOLECallback member function, CRichEditCtrl class 1482

SetOptions member function, CRichEditCtrl class 1482

SetOutputDC member function, CDC class 530

SetOverlayImage member function, CImageList class 767

SetOwner member function
  CToolBarCtrl class 1716
  CWnd class 2027

SetPadding member function, CTabCtrl class 1659

SetPageName member function, COlePropertyPage class 1236

SetPageSize member function, CSliderCtrl class 1550

SetPaletteEntries member function, CPalette class 1308

SetPaneInfo member function, CStatusBar class 1600

SetPaneStyle member function, CStatusBar class 1600

SetPaneText member function, CStatusBar class 1601

SetPaperSize member function, CRichEditView class 1512

SetParaFormat member function
  CRichEditCtrl class 1483
  CRichEditView class 1512

SetParamValue member function
  CDaoQueryDef class 267
  CDaoRecordset class 333

SetParamValueNull member function, CDaoRecordset class 334

SetParent member function, CWnd class 2028

SetParts member function, CStatusBarCtrl class 1608

SetPasswordChar member function, CEdit class 629

SetPathName member function, CDocument class 598

SetPercentPosition member function, CDaoRecordset class 334

SetPictureDispatch member function, CPictureHolder class 1322

SetPixel member function, CDC class 531

SetPixelV member function, CDC class 531

SetPolyFillMode member function, CDC class 532

SetPos member function
CProgressCtrl class 1348
CSliderCtrl class 1550
CSpinButtonCtrl class 1567

SetPrintDevice member function, COleClientItem class 1024

SetPrinterFont member function, CEditView class 641

SetProperty member function
COleDispatchDriver class 1161
CWnd class 2028

SetQueryTimeout member function
CDaoDatabase class 237
CDatabase class 404

SetRadio member function, CCmdUI class 157

SetRange member function
CProgressCtrl class 1348
CSliderCtrl class 1550
CSpinButtonCtrl class 1568

SetRangeMax member function, CSliderCtrl class 1551

SetRangeMin member function, CSliderCtrl class 1551

SetReadOnly member function
CEdit class 629
CRichEditCtrl class 1484

SetRect member function
CEdit class 630
CRect class 1426
CRichEditCtrl class 1484

SetRectEmpty member function, CRect class 1426

SetRectInContainer member function, COleControl class 1075

SetRectNP member function, CEdit class 630

SetRectRgn member function, CRgn class 1458

SetRedraw member function, CWnd class 2029

SetRegistryKey member function, CWinApp class 1828

SetRetryReply member function, COleMessageFilter class 1209

SetReturnsRecords member function, CDaoQueryDef class 268

SetROP2 member function, CDC class 533

SetRowInfo member function, CSplitterWnd class 1584

SetRows member function, CToolBarCtrl class 1716

SetRules member function, CHotKeyCtrl class 754

SetScaleToFitSize member function, CScrollView class 1527

SetScrollInfo member function
CScrollBar class 1519
CWnd class 2029

SetScrollPos member function
CScrollBar class 1520
CWnd class 2030

SetScrollRange member function
CScrollBar class 1520
CWnd class 2031

SetScrollSizes member function, CScrollView class 1528

SetScrollStyle member function, CSplitterWnd class 1585

SetSel member function
CEdit class 631
CListBox class 803
CRichEditCtrl class 1485

SetSelection member function, CSliderCtrl class 1551

SetSelectionCharFormat member function, CRichEditCtrl class 1485

SetServerInfo member function, CDocTemplate class 577

SetSimple member function, CStatusBarCtrl class 1608

SetSize member function
CArray class 66
CObArray class 942

SetSizes member function, CToolBar class 1690

SetSockOpt member function, CAsyncSocket class 97

SetSourceTableName member function, CDaoTableDef class 367

SetSQL member function, CDaoQueryDef class 269

SetState member function
CButton class 135
CToolBarCtrl class 1717

SetStatus member function
CFile class 670
COleCurrency 1091
COleDateTime 1132
COleDateTimeSpan 1149

SetStep member function, CProgressCtrl class 1349

SetStoreParams member function, CArchive class 50

SetStretchBltMode member function, CDC class 534
SetSynchronousMode member function, CDatabase class 403
SetSysString member function, CString class 1633
SetTabStops member function
    CEdit class 631
    CEditView class 641
    CListBox class 803
SetTargetDevice member function, CRichEditCtrl class 1486
SetText member function
    CCmdUI class 157
    COleControl class 1076
    CStatusBarCtrl class 1609
SetTextAlign member function, CDC class 535
SetTextBkColor member function, CListCtrl class 836
SetTextCharacterExtra member function, CDC class 536
SetTextColor member function
    CDC class 537
    CListCtrl class 836
SetTextJustification member function, CDC class 537
SetThreadPriority member function, CWinThread class 1847
SetTic member function, CSliderCtrl class 1552
SetTicFreq member function, CSliderCtrl class 1552
SetTime member function, COleDateTime 1132
SetTimer member function, CWnd class 2032
Setting
    default passwords (DAO) 389
    default user names 390
    DFX field types 247
    login timeout values 404
    null, recordset 1405
    query timeout values 237, 404
    workspace passwords (DAO) 379
    worspace user names (DAO) 379
SetTitle member function
    CDocument class 598
    CPropertySheet class 1367
SetToolInfo member function, CToolTipCtrl class 1725
SetToolRect member function, CToolTipCtrl class 1725
SetTooltips member function, CTabCtrl class 1659
SetToolTips member function, CToolBarCtrl class 1718

SetTopIndex member function
    CComboBox class 188
    CListBox class 804
SetValidationRule member function, CDaoTableDef class 367–368
SetViewportExt member function, CDC class 538
SetViewportOrg member function, CDC class 539
SetWindowContextHelpId member function, CWnd class 2032
SetWindowExt member function, CDC class 540
SetWindowOrg member function, CDC class 541
SetWindowPlacement member function, CWnd class 2033
SetWindowPos member function, CWnd class 2033
SetWindowText member function, CWnd class 2036
SetWizardButtons member function, CPropertySheet class 1367
SetWizardMode member function, CPropertySheet class 1368
SetWordCharFormat member function, CRichEditCtrl class 1486
Short integer
    DFX field exchange 2155
    RFX field exchange 2192
ShowCaret member function, CWnd class 2036
ShowControlBar member function, CFrameWnd class 734
ShowDropDown member function, CComboBox class 188
ShowOwnedPopups member function, CWnd class 2037
ShowOwnedWindows member function, CFrameWnd class 734
ShowScrollBar member function
    CScrollBar class 1521
    CWnd class 2037
ShowWindow member function, CWnd class 2037
ShutDown member function, CAsyncSocket class 100
Single precision float
    DFX field exchange 2156
    RFX field exchange 2194
Size member function, CRect class 1426
SIZE structure 2261
SizeToContent member function, CBitmapButton class 116
Slider control 1542
SOCKADDR structure 2261
SOCKADDR_IN structure 2262
Sort strings, recordset 1410

SortChildren member function, CTreeCtrl class 1750
SortChildrenCB member function, CTreeCtrl
  class 1750
SortItems member function, CListCtrl class 836
SpanExcluding member function, CString class 1633
SpanIncluding member function, CString class 1634
Spin button control 1562
SplitColumn member function, CSplitterWnd
  class 1585
SplitRow member function, CSplitterWnd class 1586
SQL
    executing SQL statements directly (DAO) 225
    pass-through queries 251
        defined 225
        executing 225
    setting SQL statement of querydef 269
    statements
        customizing 1400
        described 251
        directly executing 398
        getting default 1389
        getting recordset 1391
        querydef, getting 263
        recordset, getting 1391
SQL_ERROR codes 413
SQLError function, native error strings 415
SQLSTATE, native error strings 415
Standard cvommand, window IDs 2057
Standard OLE container 1026
StartDoc member function, CDC class 541
StartPage member function, CDC class 542
Static control styles 2276
Status bar control 1602
Status, getting recordset 1390
StepIt member function, CProgressCtrl class 1349
Stop member function, CAnimateCtrl class 37
StoreField, Record field exchange (DFX) 247
StreamIn member function, CRichEditCtrl class 1487
StreamOut member function, CRichEditCtrl
  class 1487
StretchBlt member function, CDC class 542
StrokeAndFillPath member function, CDC class 544
StrokePath member function, CDC class 545
Structured storage, CFile implementation 1277
Structures, called from MFC function descriptions
    ABC structure 2210
    ABCFLOAT structure 2211
    BITMAP structure 2211
    BITMAPINFO structure 2212

Structures, called from MFC function descriptions
  (continued)
    CDaoDatabaseInfo structure 2214
    CDaoErrorInfo structure 2217
    CDaoFieldInfo structure 2218
    CDaoIndexFieldInfo structure 2225
    CDaoIndexInfo structure 2222
    CDaoParameterInfo structure 2226
    CDaoQueryDefInfo structure 2227
    CDaoRelationFieldInfo structure 2232
    CDaoRelationInfo structure 2230
    CDaoTableDefInfo structure 2233
    CDaoWorkspaceInfo structure 2235
    COLORADJUSTMENT structure 2236
    COMPAREITEMSTRUCT structure 2238
    CREATESTRUCT structure 2239
    DELETEITEMSTRUCT structure 2240
    described 2210
    DEVMODE structure 2241
    DEVNAMES structure 2246
    DOCINFO structure 2247
    DRAWITEMSTRUCT structure 2247
    FILETIME structure 2249
    HD_ITEM structure 747
    HD_LAYOUT structure 749
    IMAGEINFO structure 764
    LINGER structure 2250
    LOGBRUSH structure 2250
    LOGFONT structure 2251
    LOGPEN structure 2255
    LV_COLUMN structure 817
    LV_FINDINFO structure 815
    LV_HITTESTINFO structure 827
    LV_ITEM structure 820
    MEASUREITEMSTRUCT structure 2256
    MINMAXINFO structure 2257
    NCCALCSIZE_PARAMS structure 2258
    NMHDR structure 1695
    PAINSTSTRUCT structure 2259
    POINT structure 2259
    RECT structure 2260
    RGNDATA structure 2260
    SIZE structure 2261
    SOCKADDR structure 2261
    SOCKADDR_IN structure 2262
    SYSTEMTIME structure 2263
    TBBUTTON structure 1699
    TBNOTIFY structure 1695
    TC_HITTESTINFO structure 1655

Structures, called from MFC function descriptions
(*continued*)
TC_ITEM structure 1653
TC_ITEMHEADER structure 1653
TEXTMETRIC structure 2263
TOOLINFO structure 1722
TOOLTIPTEXT structure 1693
TTHITTESTINFO structure 1724
TV_HITTESTINFO structure 1742
TV_INSERTSTRUCT structure 1744
TV_ITEM structure 1735
TV_SORTCB structure 1750
WINDOWPLACEMENT structure 2264
WINDOWPOS structure 2266
WSADATA structure 2267
XFORM structure 2268
Styles
button 2270
combo-box 2271
edit 2272
list-box 2273
message-box 2274
scroll-bar 2275
specified with dwstyle parameter 2270
static control 2276
window
described 2270, 2277
extended 2279
SubclassDlgItem member function, CWnd class 2038
SubclassWindow member function, CWnd class 2039
SubtractRect member function, CRect class 1427
Support classes, miscellaneous (list) 18
SuspendThread member function, CWinThread
class 1848
Synchronous access
disabling 403
enabling 403
mode, setting 403
SyncToRichEditObject member function,
CRichEditCntrlItem class 1460
SYSTEMTIME structure 2263

T

Tab control 1647
TabbedTextOut member function, CDC class 545
Table names
getting Recordset 1392
getting 1389

Tabledef object (DAO), obtaining information
about 2233
TableDefs
counting 232
deleting 225
TBBUTTON structure 1699
TBNOTIFY structure 1695
TC_HITTESTINFO structure 1655
TC_ITEM structure 1653
TC_ITEMHEADER structure 1653
Template collection classes (list) 20
Templates, collection classes
CArray 58
CList 769
CMap 842
CTypedPtrArray 1754
CTypedPtrList 1757
CTypedPtrMap 1763
TEXTMETRIC structure 2263
TextOut member function, CDC class 546
THIS_FILE global function/macro 2197
Threading base class, listed 5
THROW global function/macro 2197
THROW_LAST global function/macro 2198
ThrowError member function
CFileException class 684
COleControl class 1076
ThrowOsError member function, CFileException
class 684
Timeouts
ODBC 260
query
described 230
setting 237
Tool tip control 1719
Toolbar control 1691
TOOLINFO structure 1722
TopLeft member function, CRect class 1428
TRACE global function/macro 2198
TRACE0 global function/macro 2199
TRACE1 global function/macro 2199
TRACE2 global function/macro 2200
TRACE3 global function/macro 2200
Track member function, CRectTracker class 1441
TrackPopupMenu member function, CMenu class 914
TrackRubberBand member function, CRectTracker
class 1442
Transaction log file 388

Transactions
  beginning 374
  CanTransact member function (DAO) 219
  committing 376
  DAO support 371
  determining whether allowed 219
  isolating ODBC 382, 391
  role of DAO database objects 217
  rolling back 388
  separate 371
Transactions, database
  beginning, described 394
  committing 397
  determining whether allowed 395
  determining whether available 1383
  rolling back 403
TransformCoords member function, COleControl
  class 1077
TranslateColor member function, COleControl
  class 1077
Tree view control 1727
TrimLeft member function, CString class 1635
TrimRight member function, CString class 1635
TRY global function/macro 2201
TTHITTESTINFO structure 1724
TV_HITTESTINFO structure 1742
TV_INSERTSTRUCT structure 1744
TV_ITEM structure 1735
TV_SORTCB structure 1750
Type library access 2064

U

UINT, DDX field exchange 2134
Undo member function
  CEdit class 632
  CRichEditCtrl class 1488
Undo support, COleServerDoc class 1242
Uniform data transfer, OLE 1098, 1105
Union queries 251
UnionRect member function, CRect class 1428
Unlock member function
  CCriticalSection class 213
  CEvent class 646
  CMultiLock class 929
  CSingleLock class 1537
  CSyncObject class 1646

UnlockBuffer member function
  CEditView class 641
  CString class 1635
UnlockRange member function, CFile class 670
UnrealizeObject member function, CGdiObject
  class 742
UnSubclassWindow member function, CWnd
  class 2039
Update member function
  CDaoRecordset class 335
  CListCtrl class 837
  CRecordset class 1407
Update queries 251
UpdateAllItems member function, COleServerDoc
  class 1255
UpdateAllViews member function, CDocument
  class 598
UpdateColors member function, CDC class 547
UpdateData member function, CWnd class 2040
UpdateDialogControls member function, CWnd
  class 2040
UpdateLink member function, COleClientItem
  class 1025
UpdateModifiedFlag member function, COleDocument
  class 1174
UpdateRegistry member function
  COleObjectFactory class 1215
  COleTemplateServer class 1282
UpdateRegistryAll member function,
  COleObjectFactory class 1216
Updates, database
  determining whether allowed 219, 396
  determining whether available 1384
UpdateTipText member function, CToolTipCtrl
  class 1726
UpdateWindow member function, CWnd class 2041
Updating
  records 1387
  Recordsets 1387, 1407
User commands, disabling database 399
User Interface Issues, Drag and Drop 1176
User names
  setting default (DAO) 390
  setting for DAO workspaces 379
  workspace 383
Using database objects 216

V

ValidateRect member function, CWnd class 2041
ValidateRgn member function, CWnd class 2042
Validation failures, dealing with 408
Variant parameter type constants 2063
VARIANT, MFC encapsulation 1286
VERIFY global function/macro 2201
VerifyLicenseKeymember function,
    COleObjectFactoryEx class 1216
VerifyPos member function, CSliderCtrl class 1553
VerifyUserLicense member function,
    COleObjectFactory class 1217
Version, getting database engine 234, 384
View classes (list) 11
VKeyToItem member function, CListBox class 805

W

Waiting for data sources
    described 401
    determining status 399
    Recordset 1400
WidenPath member function, CDC class 547
Width member function, CRect class 1428
WillAmbientsBeValidDuringLoad member function,
    COleControl class 1078
Window application classes (list) 5
Window classes, RichEdit, MFC encapsulation 1461
Window IDs described 2057
Window styles
    described 2277
    extended 2279
WindowFromPoint member function, CWnd
    class 2042
WINDOWPLACEMENT structure 2264
WINDOWPOS structure 2266
WindowProc member function, CWnd class 2043
Windows Common controls
    CAnimateCtrl 33
    CHeaderCtrl 744
    CHotKeyCtrl 751
    CImageList 755
    CListCtrl 806
    CProgressCtrl 1346
    CRichEditCtrl 1461
    CSliderCtrl 1542
    CSpinButtonCtrl 1562
    CStatusBarCtrl 1602

Windows Common controls (continued)
    CTabCtrl 1647
    CToolBarCtrl 1691
    CToolTipCtrl 1719
    CTreeCtrl 1727
Windows, yielding time to other other
    applications 401
WinHelp member function, CWinApp class 1829
Workspace
    accessing database workspaces 238
    accessing underlying DAO objects 393
    callable functions before Open 387
    capabilities of
        access to Databases collection 370
        access to default workspace 370
        access to Workspaces collection 370
        database engine properties 370
        transaction management 370
    closing, consequences of 375
    compacting databases 377
        database engine version options 377
        dbLangGeneral option 377
        language options 377
    constructing C++ object 375
    creating 371, 379
    DAO database 370
    database engine properties 387
    database sessions 370
    Databases collection 370
    database engine version, getting 384
    defined 370
    getting number of databases open 380
    initialization settings 391
    isolating ODBC transactions 382, 391
    Login timeout property, setting 392
    multiple, need for 370
    name, user-defined 383
    obtaining information about open databases 380
    obtaining information about workspaces 385
    open databases, counting 380
    open status, obtaining 386
    opening 387
    password, setting 379
    persistence 371, 375
    registry key settings 391
    repairing a database 388
    rolling back transactions 388
    setting default password 389
    setting default user name 390

Workspace *(continued)*
    setting user name 379
    static member functions 387
    transaction log file 388
    transaction manager 370
    transaction space 370
    usage tips
        creating new workspaces 371
        explicitly opening default workspace 371
        opening existing workspaces 371
    user name 383
    Workspaces collection
        appending to 374
        workspaces in 384
Workspace count, getting 384
Workspace object (DAO), obtaining information
  about 2235
Workspace, using default implicitly 371
WrapChanged member function, CRichEditView
  class 1512
Write member function
    CArchive class 51
    CFile class 671
    CImageList class 767
WriteClass member function, CArchive class 52
WriteHuge member function, CFile class 671
WriteObject member function, CArchive class 52
WriteProfileInt member function, CWinApp
  class 1830
WriteProfileString member function, CWinApp
  class 1831
WriteString member function
    CArchive class 53
    CStdioFile class 1613
WSADATA structure 2267

X

XFORM structure 2268

Y

Yielding processing time
    described 401
    Recordset 1400
*Insert existing text here and delete this text. Do not
  remove the following paragraph.

Register Today!

Return this
Microsoft® Foundation Class Library Reference
registration card for:

✔ a Microsoft Press® catalog

✔ special offers on
Microsoft Press books

U.S. and Canada addresses only. Fill in information below and mail postage-free. Please mail only the bottom half of this page.

1-55615-922-6A   *Microsoft Foundation Class Library Reference*   *Owner Registration Card*

_____

NAME

_____

INSTITUTION OR COMPANY NAME

_____

ADDRESS

_____

CITY   STATE   ZIP

Microsoft®*Press*
Quality Computer Books

For a free catalog of
Microsoft Press® products, call
1-800-MSPRESS